ACCOUNTING RESEARCH DIRECTORY

ACCOUNTING RESEARCH DIRECTORY

The Database of Accounting Literature

SECOND EDITION

Lawrence D. Brown
State University of New York at Buffalo

John C. Gardner
State University of New York at Buffalo

Miklos A. Vasarhelyi
AT&T Bell Laboratories

Markus Wiener Publishing, Inc.
New York

Cover design by Cheryl Mirkin

For information write to:
Markus Wiener Publishing Inc.
225 Lafayette, Suite 911
New York, NY 10012

Library of Congress Card Cataloging-in-Publication Data

Brown, Lawrence D. (lawrence David), 1946-
  Accounting research directory : the database of accounting
literature / by Lawrence D. Brown, John C. Gardner, Miklos A.
Vasarhelyi. -- 2nd updated and enl. ed.
    p.   cm.
  Includes index.
  ISBN 1-558-76003-2
  1. Accounting--Bibliography.   I. Gardner, John Consaul.
II. Vasarhelyi, Miklos A. III. Title.
Z7164.C81B884 1988
[HF5635]
O16.657--dc19

Printed in the United States of America

1. INTRODUCTION

The first edition of the Accounting Research Directory became possible in 1985 when the authors merged their two databases, the Brown/Gardner citation index and the Vasarhelyi/Berk attribute index. Both databases were originally developed by the authors to facilitate their own research. The result of their merger was a database comprehensive enough to be published as a book and useful to a wide range of accountants involved in various aspects of research. The first edition was published in America by Wiener Publishing, and was co-published in England by Manchester University Press and by Yushodo Company in Japan. The reviews on all three continents were very positive. Some contained useful suggestions, which have been incorporated into this new edition. This edition evaluates all articles published in the leading accounting journals in the 26-year period, 1963-1988.

Excerpts of some reviews for the first edition follow:

> "Graduate students, professors and anyone else concerned with reviewing the latest periodical literature on a subject will want to examine this book, which hopefully will be updated frequently."
> Journal of Accountancy
> November 1985

> "A major research tool, this directory lists all major articles published in the last 22 years by leading journals."
> Business Horizons
> January-February, 1986

> "This arrangement is unique and not the usual subject approach found in Accountants' Index Supplement (American Institute of Certified Public Accountants, 1920-) or Accounting Articles (Commerce Clearing House, 1970-).... Useful for academic researchers, professors assigning articles to students, accounting students identifying core articles, or practitioners locating articles that assist in preparing a response to the Financial Accounting Standards Board FASB Discussion Memoranda."
> American Reference Books Annual
> 1986

> "This pioneering effort would be useful primarily to accounting researchers and teachers in the selection of articles for reading lists and/or bibliographies."
> The Accounting Review
> October 1986

Introduction   ACCOUNTING RESEARCH DIRECTORY

The second edition of the Accounting Research Directory [ARD] has improved upon the first edition in four primary ways. First, the bibliographic listing of the revised ARD (Part I) includes major articles published between 1963 and 1988, four more years of accounting literature than the first edition. Second, the first edition of the ARD had no cross-reference between the bibliographic information of Part I and the taxonomies of Part II. Part I of the revised ARD includes the taxonomy classifications of each article in Part II, allowing for easy reference between Parts I and II. Third, the taxonomies of the first edition classified articles listed in Part I that were cited at least once by "contemporary accounting research". The taxonomies of the revised ARD (Part II) contain all articles listed in Part I, regardless of whether or not they have been cited. Fourth, the first edition of the ARD had no citation information in Part I. Part I of the revised ARD includes the citation information of each article in Part II, allowing for easier reference between Parts I and II.

Part I of the ARD is a complete listing of all major articles published during the 26-year period 1963-1988 in six accounting journals:

- The Accounting Review (TAR)

- Accounting, Organizations and Society (AOS)

- Auditing: A Journal of Theory and Practice (AUD)

- Journal of Accounting and Economics (JAE)

- Journal of Accounting Research (JAR)

- Journal of Accounting, Auditing & Finance (JAA).

It is organized alphabetically **by author**; each article is listed as many times as there are coauthors. Thus, an article by R. Ball and P. Brown **will appear** twice in the first part of the ARD.

Each entry in Part I consists of three (or four if more than 3 authors) lines:

1. Author's surname and initials; other coauthors' surnames and initials; and the order in which the other coauthors' names appear in the article. Citation index (discussed below).

2. Complete title of the paper, abbreviated only when necessitated by space constraints.

3. Journal, issue, year, volume, pages. :: Part II cross-reference (discussed below).

For example, the Autumn (AU) 1968 JAR paper by R. Ball and P. Brown is listed in Part I under P. Brown as:

> **BROWN, P ; FIRS: BALL, R CIT: 7.00**
> **AN EMPIRICAL EVALUATION OF ACCOUNTING INCOME NUMBERS**
> **JAR AU 68 VOL: 6 PG:159 - 178 :: NON-PAR. :PRIM. :EMH :FIN.METH.**

Part II of the ARD organizes all articles contained in Part I according to four taxonomies:

1. Mode of Reasoning (key method of analysis)

2. Research Method

3. School of Thought

4. Treatment (subject area).

The Table of Contents lists the groupings within the taxonomies along with their abbreviations, and the Glossary defines the terms.

The Autumn 1968 JAR article by Ball and Brown appears in Part II four times, corresponding to its grouping within each of the above four taxonomies:

1. Mode of Reasoning: NON-PAR.

2. Research Method: PRIM.

3. School of Thought: EMH

4. Treatment: FIN. METH.

Note that the terms,NON-PAR.,PRIM., EMH, and FIN. METH. for the four taxonomies are the same as those listed on the third line of the bibliographic reference in Part I. Each listing in Part II contains a citation index, which indicates the number of times per year that the paper has been cited since its year of publication (or 1976, whichever is later) by "contemporary accounting research," where the latter is defined as all major articles published in four accounting journals during the thirteen-year period, 1976 through 1988: TAR, AOS, JAE, and JAR. As two examples of how the citation index is determined, the Autumn 1968 JAR article by Ball and Brown has been cited 91 times, giving it a citation index of 91/(1989-1976), or 7.00; the Spring 1985 JAR article by R. Atiase has been cited 10 times, giving it a citation index of 10/(1989-1985), or 2.50. Within each taxonomy grouping, all articles are listed in decreasing order of citation index.

Each listing in Part II has nine columns:

- CITE INDEX (citation index)

- FIRST AUTHOR (surname, initials of first author)

- ISSUE (e.g., month of publication)

- YEAR (year of publication)

- JOURNAL (TAR, AOS, AUD, JAE, JAR, or JAA)

- SECOND AUTHOR (surname, initials of second author)

- THIRD AUTHOR (surname, initials of third author)

- PAGE BEG (beginning page number)

- PAGE END (ending page number).

For example, the AU 1968 JAR paper by R. Ball and P. Brown appears in Part II of the ARD in Sections PRIM., NON -PAR., EMH, and FIN. METH. as:

| 7.00 | BALL, R | AU | 68 | JAR | BROWN, P | 159 | 178 |

The citation index is also included in the first line of each article in Part1, abbreviated as CIT. This directory has been helping researchers to locate articles in specific areas quickly and efficiently, and to move ahead with their research. The authors expect that the use of this guide will result in further publications, which will be listed in future editions of this book.

Lawrence D. Brown
SUNY-Buffalo

John C. Gardner
SUNY-Buffalo

Miklos A. Vasarhelyi
Bell Laboratories
February 1989

TABLE OF CONTENTS

PART 1

COMPLETE LISTING OF ALL MAJOR ARTICLES PUBLISHED IN SIX ACCOUNTING JOURNALS

ABDEL-KHALIK,AR CIT: 0.00
CONTROLLERSHIP IN EGYPT
JAR SP 66 VOL: 4 PG:37 - 46 :: QUAL. :INT. LOG. :INSTIT. :PROF.RESP.

ABDEL-KHALIK,AR CIT: 0.31
USER PREFERENCE ORDERING VALUE
TAR JL 71 VOL: 46 PG:457 - 471 :: ANAL. :INT. LOG. :N/A :FIN.METH.

ABDEL-KHALIK,AR CIT: 0.85
THE EFFECT OF AGGREGATING ACCOUNTING REPORTS ON THE QUALITY OF THE LENDING
    DECISION: AN EMPIRICAL INVESTIGATION
JAR ST 73 VOL: 11 PG:104 - 138 :: ANOVA :LAB. :OTH. :PROF.RESP.

ABDEL-KHALIK,AR CIT: 0.31
THE ENTROPY LAW, ACCOUNTING DATA, AND RELEVANCE TO DECISION-MAKING
TAR AP 74 VOL: 49 PG:271 - 283 :: CORR. :FIELD :INF.ECO./AG. :FIN.ST.TIM.

ABDEL-KHALIK,AR ; SEC: LUSK ,EJ CIT: 0.77
TRANSFER PRICING - A SYNTHESIS
TAR JA 74 VOL: 49 PG:8 - 23 :: QUAL. :SEC. :N/A :TRANS.PRIC.

ABDEL-KHALIK,AR CIT: 1.31
ON THE EFFICIENCY OF SUBJECT SURROGATION IN ACCOUNTING RESEARCH
TAR OC 74 VOL: 49 PG:743 - 750 :: NON-PAR. :LAB. :N/A :METHOD.

ABDEL-KHALIK,AR CIT: 0.15
ADVERTISING EFFECTIVENESS AND ACCOUNTING POLICY
TAR OC 75 VOL: 50 PG:657 - 670 :: REGRESS. :PRIM. :TIME SER. :OTH. NON-C/A

ABDEL-KHALIK,AR ; SEC: MCKEOWN,JC CIT: 1.09
UNDERSTANDING ACCOUNTING CHANGES IN AN EFFICIENT MARKET: EVIDENCE OF
    DIFFERENTIAL REACTION
TAR OC 78 VOL: 53 PG:851 - 868 :: ANOVA :PRIM. :EMH :INV.

ABDEL-KHALIK,AR ; SEC: ESPEJO,J CIT: 0.36
EXPECTATIONS DATA AND THE PREDICTIVE VALUE OF INTERIM REPORTING
JAR SP 78 VOL: 16 PG:1 - 13 :: REGRESS. :LAB. :TIME SER. :FOREC.

ABDEL-KHALIK,AR ; SEC: MCKEOWN,JC CIT: 0.36
DISCLOSURE OF ESTIMATES OF HOLDING GAINS AND THE ASSESSMENT OF SYSTEMATIC RISK
JAR ST 78 VOL: 16 PG:46 - 77 :: ANOVA :PRIM. :EMH :VALUAT.(INFL.)

ABDEL-KHALIK,AR ; SEC: EL-SHESHAI,KM CIT: 0.89
INFORMATION CHOICE AND UTILIZATION IN AN EXPERIMENT ON DEFAULT PREDICTION
JAR AU 80 VOL: 18 PG:325 - 342 :: DES.STAT. :LAB. :HIPS :BUS.FAIL.

ABDEL-KHALIK,AR ; SEC: AJINKYA,BB CIT: 0.14
RETURNS TO INFORMATIONAL ADVANTAGES: THE CASE OF ANALYSTS' FORECAST REVISIONS
TAR OC 82 VOL: 57 PG:661 - 680 :: REGRESS. :PRIM. :EMH :FOREC.

ABDEL-KHALIK,AR ; SEC: SNOWBALL,D ; THIR: WRAGGE,JH CIT: 0.00
THE EFFECTS OF CERTAIN INTERNAL AUDIT VARIABLES ON THE PLANNING OF EXTERNAL
    AUDIT PROGRAMS
TAR AP 83 VOL: 58 PG:215 - 227 :: ANOVA :LAB. :OTH.BEH. :INT.AUD.

ABDEL-KHALIK,AR CIT: 0.00
OVERFITTING BIAS IN THE MODELS ASSESSING THE PREDICTIVE POWER OF QUARTERLY
    REPORTS
JAR SP 83 VOL: 21 PG:293 - 296 :: MIXED :PRIM. :TIME SER. :METHOD.

ABDEL-KHALIK,AR CIT: 1.00
THE EFFECT OF LIFO-SWITCHING AND FIRM OWNERSHIP ON EXECUTIVES' PAY
JAR AU 85 VOL: 23 PG:427 - 447 :: REGRESS. :PRIM. :OTH.STAT. :INV.

ABDEL-KHALIK,AR ; SEC: GRAUL ,PR ; THIR: NEWTON,JD CIT: 0.00
REPORTING UNCERTAINTY AND ASSESSMENT OF RISK: REPLICATION AND EXTENSION IN A
    CANADIAN SETTING
JAR AU 86 VOL: 24 PG:372 - 382 :: REGRESS. :LAB. :HIPS :OPIN.

ABDEL-MAGID,MF CIT: 0.00
TOWARD A BETTER UNDERSTANDING OF THE ROLE OF MEASUREMENT IN ACCOUNTING
TAR AP 79 VOL: 54 PG:346 - 357 :: QUAL. :INT. LOG. :OTH.STAT. :FIN.METH.

ABDOLMOHAMMADI,MJ CIT: 0.00
EFFICIENCY OF THE BAYESIAN APPROACH IN COMPLIANCE TESTING: SOME EMPIRICAL
    EVIDENCE
AUD SP 86 VOL: 5 PG:1 - 16 :: REGRESS. :LAB. :OTH.BEH. :SAMP.

ABDOLMOHAMMADI,MJ ; SEC: WRIGHT,A CIT: 0.00
AN EXAMINATION OF THE EFFECTS OF EXPERIENCE AND TASK COMPLEXITY ON AUDIT
    JUDGEMENTS
TAR JA 87 VOL: 62 PG:1 - 13 :: REGRESS. :LAB. :OTH.BEH. :JUDG.

ABDULKADER,AA ; FIRS: LOREK ,KS ; SEC: ICERMAN,JD CIT: 0.00
FURTHER DESCRIPTIVE AND PREDICTIVE EVIDENCE ON ALTERNATIVE TIME-SERIES MODELS
    FOR QUARTERLY EARNINGS
JAR SP 83 VOL: 21 PG:317 - 328 :: REGRESS. :PRIM. :TIME SER. :INT.REP.

ABEL ,R CIT: 0.08
A COMPARATIVE SIMULATION OF GERMAN AND U.S. ACCOUNTING PRINCIPLES
JAR SP 69 VOL: 7 PG:1 - 11 :: QUAL. :SIM. :OTH. :INT.DIFF.

ABRANOVIC,WA CIT: 0.00
PROBABILITY PLOTTING FOR ESTIMATING TIME-TO-PAYMENT CHARACTERISTICS FOR
    COLLECTIONS ON ACCOUNTS RECEIVABLE
TAR OC 76 VOL: 51 PG:863 - 874 :: ANAL. :INT. LOG. :OTH.STAT. :OTH.C/A

ACLAND,D CIT: 0.15
THE EFFECTS OF BEHAVIORAL INDICATORS ON INVESTOR DECISIONS: AN EXPLORATORY
    STUDY
AOS 23 76 VOL: 1 PG:133 - 142 :: NON-PAR. :LAB. :OTH.BEH. :HRA

ADAMS ,KD CIT: 0.00
HEDGE ACCOUNTING FOR ANTICIPATORY HEDGES OF SHORT-TERM LIABILITIES
JAA WI 84 VOL: 7 PG:151 - 163 :: QUAL. :INT. LOG. :THEORY :FIN.METH.

ADAMS ,SJ ; FIRS: LIGHTNER,SM ; THIR: LIGHTNER,KM CIT: 0.00
THE INFLUENCE OF SITUATIONAL, ETHICAL, AND EXPECTANCY THEORY VARIABLES ON
    ACCOUNTANTS' UNDERREPORTING BEHAVIOR
AUD AU 82 VOL: 2 PG:1 - 12 :: DES.STAT. :SURV. :OTH.STAT. :ORG.

ADAMS ,SJ ; FIRS: WHITTINGTON,OR CIT: 0.00
TEMPORARY BREAKDOWNS OF INTERNAL CONTROL: IMPLICATIONS FOR EXTERNAL AND
    INTERNAL AUDITORS
JAA SU 82 VOL: 5 PG:310 - 319 :: QUAL. :INT. LOG. :OTH. :N/A

ADAR ,Z ; SEC: BARNEA,A ; THIR: LEV ,B CIT: 0.08
A COMPREHENSIVE COST-VOLUME-PROFIT ANALYSIS UNDER UNCERTAINTY
TAR JA 77 VOL: 52 PG:137 - 149 :: QUAL. :INT. LOG. :THEORY :TAXES

ADELBERG,AH CIT: 0.30
A METHODOLOGY FOR MEASURING THE UNDERSTANDABILITY OF FINANCIAL REPORT MESSAGES
JAR AU 79 VOL: 17 PG:565 - 592 :: ANOVA :PRIM. :OTH.BEH. :FIN.METH.

AGGARWAL,R CIT: 0.00
FASB NO.8 AND REPORTED RESULTS OF MULTINATIONAL OPERATIONS: HAZARD FOR
   MANAGERS AND INVESTORS
JAA SP 78 VOL: 1 PG:197 - 216 :: MIXED :INT. LOG. :THEORY :FOR.CUR.

AGRAWAL,SP CIT: 0.00
ACCOUNTING FOR THE IMPACT OF INFLATION ON A BUSINESS ENTERPRISE
TAR OC 77 VOL: 52 PG:789 - 809 :: ANAL. :INT. LOG. :THEORY :VALUAT.(INFL.)

AGRAWAL,SP ; SEC: HALLBAUER,RC ; THIR: PERRITT,GW CIT: 0.00
MEASUREMENT OF THE CURRENT COST OF EQUIVALENT PRODUCTIVE CAPACITY
JAA WI 80 VOL: 3 PG:163 - 173 :: ANAL. :INT. LOG. :OTH.STAT. :VALUAT.(INFL.)

AHARONI,Y ; SEC: OPHIR ,T CIT: 0.00
ACCOUNTING FOR LINKED LOANS
JAR SP 67 VOL: 5 PG:1 - 26 :: QUAL. :INT. LOG. :THEORY :FIN.METH.

AHARONI,Y ; FIRS: BEJA ,A CIT: 0.00
SOME ASPECTS OF CONVENTIONAL ACCOUNTING PROFITS IN AN INFLATIONARY ENVIRONMENT
JAR AU 77 VOL: 15 PG:169 - 178 :: ANAL. :INT. LOG. :THEORY :VALUAT.(INFL.)

AIKEN ,M ; FIRS: COVALESKI,M CIT: 0.33
ACCOUNTING AND THEORIES OF ORGANIZATIONS: SOME PRELIMINARY CONSIDERATIONS
AOS 45 86 VOL: 11 PG:297 - 320 :: ANOVA :INT. LOG. :THEORY :ORG.& ENVIR.

AIKEN ,ME ; SEC: BLACKETT,LA ; THIR: ISAACS,G CIT: 0.08
MODELING BEHAVIOURAL INTERDEPENDENCIES FOR STEWARDSHIP REPORTING
TAR JL 75 VOL: 50 PG:544 - 562 :: ANAL. :INT. LOG. :THEORY :OTH.MANAG.

AJINKYA,BB CIT: 0.00
AN EMPIRICAL EVALUATION OF LINE-OF-BUSINESS REPORTING
JAR AU 80 VOL: 18 PG:343 - 361 :: ANOVA :PRIM. :EMH :SEG.REP.

AJINKYA,BB ; FIRS: ABDEL-KHALIK,AR CIT: 0.14
RETURNS TO INFORMATIONAL ADVANTAGES: THE CASE OF ANALYSTS' FORECAST REVISIONS
TAR OC 82 VOL: 57 PG:661 - 680 :: REGRESS. :PRIM. :EMH :FOREC.

AJINKYA,BB ; SEC: GIFT ,MJ CIT: 0.60
CORPORATE MANAGERS' EARNINGS FORECASTS AND SYMMETRICAL ADJUSTMENTS OF MARKET
   EXPECTATIONS
JAR AU 84 VOL: 22 PG:425 - 444 :: ANOVA :PRIM. :EMH :FOREC.

ALBRECHT,WS CIT: 0.08
ESTIMATION ERROR IN INCOME DETERMINATION
TAR OC 76 VOL: 51 PG:824 - 837 :: MIXED :CASE :OTH.STAT. :PROB.ELIC.

ALBRECHT,WS ; SEC: LOOKABILL,LL ; THIR: MCKEOWN,JC CIT: 2.00
THE TIME-SERIES PROPERTIES OF ANNUAL EARNINGS
JAR AU 77 VOL: 15 PG:226 - 244 :: MIXED :PRIM. :TIME SER. :FOREC.

ALDERMAN,CW ; FIRS: DEITRICK,JW CIT: 0.00
INTERIM REPORTING DEVELOPMENTS: A STEP TOWARD THE AUDITOR-OF-RECORD CONCEPT
JAA SU 79 VOL: 2 PG:316 - 328 :: QUAL. :INT. LOG. :INSTIT. :AUD.

ALDERMAN,CW ; FIRS: ROBERTSON,JC CIT: 0.00
COMPARATIVE AUDITING STANDARDS
JAA WI 81 VOL: 4 PG:144 - 161 :: QUAL. :INT. LOG. :THEORY :ORG.

ALDERMAN,CW ; SEC: DEITRICK,JW CIT: 0.00
AUDITORS' PERCEPTIONS OF TIME BUDGET PRESSURES AND PREMATURE SIGN-OFFS: A
  REPLICATION AND EXTENSION
AUD WI 82 VOL: 1 PG:54 - 68 :: DES.STAT. :SURV. :OTH.BEH. :ERRORS

ALFORD,MR ; SEC: EDMONDS,TP CIT: 0.13
A REPLICATION: DOES AUDIT INVOLVEMENT AFFECT THE QUALITY OF INTERIM REPORT
  NUMBERS?
JAA SP 81 VOL: 4 PG:255 - 264 :: DES.STAT. :SEC. :THEORY :INT.REP.

ALFRED,AM CIT: 0.00
INVESTMENT IN THE DEVELOPMENT DISTRICTS OF THE UNITED KINGDOM: TAX AND
  DISCOUNTED CASH FLOW
JAR AU 64 VOL: 2 PG:172 - 182 :: QUAL. :INT. LOG. :THEORY :TAXES

ALIBER,RZ ; SEC: STICKNEY,CP CIT: 0.15
ACCOUNTING MEASURES OF FOREIGN EXCHANGE EXPOSURE: THE LONG AND SHORT OF IT
TAR JA 75 VOL: 50 PG:44 - 57 :: QUAL. :INT. LOG. :INSTIT. :FOR.CUR.

ALLEN ,G ; FIRS: GARSOMBKE,HP CIT: 0.00
DID SFAS NO.19 LEAD TO OIL AND GAS COMPANY MERGERS?
JAA SU 83 VOL: 6 PG:285 - 298 :: NON-PAR. :PRIM. :THEORY :OIL & GAS

ALLYN ,RG CIT: 0.00
PLANNING FOR THE CPA EXAMINATION IN THE UNITED STATES
TAR JA 64 VOL: 39 PG:121 - 127 :: QUAL. :INT. LOG. :INSTIT. :OTH.MANAG.

ALLYN ,RG CIT: 0.00
ACCREDITATION OF ACCOUNTING CURRICULUMS
TAR AP 66 VOL: 41 PG:303 - 311 :: QUAL. :INT. LOG. :INSTIT. :OTH.MANAG.

ALTMAN,EI CIT: 0.14
ACCOUNTING IMPLICATIONS OF FAILURE PREDICTION MODELS
JAA AU 82 VOL: 6 PG:4 - 19 :: OTH.QUANT. :PRIM. :OTH.STAT. :FIN.METH.

ALVEY ,KL CIT: 0.00
ALTERNATIVE DERIVATION OF FORMULAS FOR THE INCOME TAX PROBLEM
TAR JA 63 VOL: 38 PG:124 - 125 :: ANAL. :INT. LOG. :THEORY :TAXES

ALY ,HF ; SEC: DUBOFF,JI CIT: 0.08
STATISTICAL VS. JUDGMENT SAMPLING: AN EMPIRICAL STUDY OF AUDITING THE
  ACCOUNTS RECEIVABLE OF A SMALL RETAIL STORE
TAR JA 71 VOL: 46 PG:119 - 128 :: ANOVA :CASE :OTH.STAT. :SAMP.

AMATO ,HN ; SEC: ANDERSON,EE ; THIR: HARVEY,DW CIT: 0.08
A GENERAL MODEL OF FUTURE PERIOD WARRANTY COSTS
TAR OC 76 VOL: 51 PG:854 - 862 :: ANAL. :INT. LOG. :OTH. :SPEC.ITEMS

AMERNIC,J ; FIRS: ARANYA,N ; SEC: POLLOCK,J CIT: 0.00
AN EXAMINATION OF PROFESSIONAL COMMITMENT IN PUBLIC ACCOUNTING
AOS 04 81 VOL: 6 PG:271 - 280 :: MIXED :LAB. :OTH.BEH. :PROF.RESP.

AMERNIC,J ; FIRS: ARANYA,N ; SEC: LACHMAN,R CIT: 0.00
ACCOUNTANTS' JOB SATISFACTION: A PATH ANALYSIS
AOS 03 82 VOL: 7 PG:201 - 216 :: CORR. :SURV. :OTH.BEH. :N/A

AMERSHI,AH ; SEC: SUNDER,S CIT: 0.00
FAILURE OF STOCK PRICES TO DISCIPLINE MANAGERS IN A RATIONAL EXPECTATIONS
  ECONOMY
JAR AU 87 VOL: 25 PG:177 - 195 :: DES.STAT. :INT. LOG. :INF.ECO./AG. :INV.

AMEY ,LR CIT: 0.10
TOWARDS A NEW PERSPECTIVE ON ACCOUNTING CONTROL
AOS 04 79 VOL: 4 PG:247 - 258 :: QUAL. :INT. LOG. :OTH. :MANAG.

AMIT ,R ; SEC: LIVNAT,J CIT: 0.00
DIVERSIFICATION, CAPITAL STRUCTURE, AND SYSTEMATIC RISK: AN EMPIRICAL
    INVESTIGATION
JAA WI 88 VOL: 03 PG:19 - 43 :: REGRESS. :PRIM. :EMH :OTH.FIN.ACC.

ANDERSON JR,KE CIT: 0.00
A HORIZONTAL EQUITY ANALYSIS OF THE MINIMUM TAX PROVISIONS: AN EMPIRICAL STUDY
TAR JL 85 VOL: 60 PG:357 - 371 :: REGRESS. :PRIM. :THEORY :TAXES

ANDERSON JR,TN ; SEC: KIDA ,TE CIT: 0.00
THE CROSS-LAGGED RESEARCH APPROACH: DESCRIPTION AND ILLUSTRATION
JAR AU 82 VOL: 20 PG:403 - 414 :: CORR. :LAB. :OTH.BEH. :MAN.DEC.CHAR.

ANDERSON,EE ; FIRS: AMATO ,HN ; THIR: HARVEY,DW CIT: 0.08
A GENERAL MODEL OF FUTURE PERIOD WARRANTY COSTS
TAR OC 76 VOL: 51 PG:854 - 862 :: ANAL. :INT. LOG. :OTH. :SPEC.ITEMS

ANDERSON,HM ; SEC: GRIFFIN,FB CIT: 0.00
THE ACCOUNTING CURRICULUM AND POSTGRADUATE ACHIEVEMENT
TAR OC 63 VOL: 38 PG:813 - 818 :: QUAL. :INT. LOG. :THEORY :EDUC.

ANDERSON,HM ; SEC: GIESE ,J ; THIR: BOOKER,J CIT: 0.15
SOME PROPOSITIONS ABOUT AUDITING
TAR JL 70 VOL: 45 PG:524 - 531 :: QUAL. :INT. LOG. :INSTIT. :AUD.

ANDERSON,JA CIT: 0.00
INFORMATION INTERACTIONS AND ACCOUNTING INFORMATION USER REACTIONS
TAR JL 75 VOL: 50 PG:509 - 511 :: ANAL. :INT. LOG. :N/A :FIN.METH.

ANDERSON,JA CIT: 0.17
THE POTENTIAL IMPACT OF KNOWLEDGE OF MARKET EFFICIENCY ON THE LEGAL LIABILITY
    OF AUDITORS
TAR AP 77 VOL: 52 PG:417 - 426 :: QUAL. :INT. LOG. :EMH :LIAB.

ANDERSON,JA ; FIRS: ST.PIERRE,K CIT: 0.00
AN ANALYSIS OF AUDIT FAILURES BASED ON DOCUMENTED LEGAL CASES
JAA SP 82 VOL: 5 PG:229 - 247 :: DES.STAT. :PRIM. :OTH. :ERRORS

ANDERSON,JA ; FIRS: ST.PIERRE,K CIT: 0.40
AN ANALYSIS OF THE FACTORS ASSOCIATED WITH LAWSUITS AGAINST PUBLIC ACCOUNTANTS
TAR AP 84 VOL: 59 PG:242 - 263 :: DES.STAT. :PRIM. :INSTIT. :LIAB.

ANDERSON,JC ; SEC: FRANKLE,AW CIT: 0.33
VOLUNTARY SOCIAL REPORTING: AN ISO-BETA PORTFOLIO ANALYSIS
TAR JL 80 VOL: 55 PG:467 - 479 :: REGRESS. :PRIM. :EMH :HRA

ANDERSON,JC ; SEC: KRAUSHAAR,JM CIT: 0.00
MEASUREMENT ERROR AND STATISTICAL SAMPLING IN AUDITING: THE POTENTIAL
    EFFECTS
TAR JL 86 VOL: 61 PG:379 - 399 :: DES.STAT. :SIM. :OTH.STAT. :SAMP.

ANDERSON,JJ CIT: 0.00
INTEGRATED INSTRUCTION IN COMPUTERS AND ACCOUNTING
TAR JL 67 VOL: 42 PG:583 - 588 :: QUAL. :INT. LOG. :N/A :OTH.MANAG.

ANDERSON,JM CIT: 0.00
DILEMMAS IN MODERN ACCOUNTING RESEARCH
JAR AU 64 VOL: 2 PG:236 - 238 :: QUAL. :INT. LOG. :THEORY :N/A

ANDERSON,MJ CIT: 0.25
SOME EVIDENCE ON THE EFFECT OF VERBALIZATION ON PROCESS: A METHODOLOGICAL NOTE
JAR AU 85 VOL: 23 PG:843 - 852 :: REGRESS. :LAB. :HIPS :METHOD.

ANDERSON,MJ CIT: 0.00
A COMPARATIVE ANALYSIS OF INFORMATION SEARCH AND EVALUATION BEHAVIOR OF
   PROFESSIONAL AND NON-PROFESSIONAL FINANCIAL ANALYSTS
AOS 05 88 VOL: 13 PG:431 - 446 :: REGRESS. :LAB. :HIPS :MAN.DEC.CHAR.

ANDERSON,PF ; FIRS: MARTIN,JD ; THIR: KEOWN ,AJ CIT: 0.00
LEASE CAPITALIZATION AND STOCK PRICE STABILITY: IMPLICATIONS FOR ACCOUNTING
JAA WI 79 VOL: 2 PG:151 - 164 :: REGRESS. :PRIM. :EMH :LEASES

ANDERSON,U ; SEC: YOUNG ,RA CIT: 0.00
INTERNAL AUDIT PLANNING IN AN INTERACTIVE ENVIRONMENT
AUD AU 88 VOL: 08 PG:23 - 42 :: DES.STAT. :INT. LOG. :OTH.BEH. :TIM.

ANDREWS,RW ; FIRS: GODFREY,JT CIT: 0.29
A FINITE POPULATION BAYESIAN MODEL FOR COMPLIANCE TESTING
JAR AU 82 VOL: 20 PG:304 - 315 :: ANAL. :INT. LOG. :OTH.STAT. :SAMP.

ANDREWS,VL ; FIRS: MEHTA ,DR CIT: 0.00
A NOTE ON INSTALLMENT REPORTING OF INCOME, PROFITABILITY, AND FUND FLOWS
JAR SP 68 VOL: 6 PG:50 - 57 :: DES.STAT. :SIM. :OTH.STAT. :TAXES

ANDREWS,WT ; FIRS: ROSE ,PS ; THIR: GIROUX,GA CIT: 0.00
PREDICTING BUSINESS FAILURE: A MACROECONOMIC PERSPECTIVE
JAA AU 82 VOL: 6 PG:20 - 31 :: REGRESS. :PRIM. :TIME SER. :BUS.FAIL.

ANELL ,B CIT: 0.25
EXERCISES IN ARBITRARINESS AND AMBIGUITY - A STUDY OF TWELVE COST BENEFIT
   ANALYSES OF INDUSTRIAL DISINVESTMENT DECISIONS
AOS 04 85 VOL: 10 PG:479 - 492 :: REGRESS. :PRIM. :THEORY :BUS.FAIL.

ANSARI,SL CIT: 0.46
BEHAVIOURAL FACTORS IN VARIANCE CONTROL: REPORT ON A LABORATORY EXPERIMENT
JAR AU 76 VOL: 14 PG:189 - 211 :: ANOVA :LAB. :OTH.BEH. :VAR.

ANSARI,SL CIT: 1.00
AN INTEGRATED APPROACH TO CONTROL SYSTEM DESIGN
AOS 02 77 VOL: 2 PG:101 - 112 :: QUAL. :INT. LOG. :OTH. :N/A

ANSARI,SL CIT: 0.70
TOWARDS AN OPEN SYSTEMS APPROACH TO BUDGETING
AOS 03 79 VOL: 4 PG:149 - 162 :: QUAL. :INT. LOG. :OTH.BEH. :BUDG.& PLAN.

ANSARI,SL ; SEC: MCDONOUGH,JJ CIT: 0.11
INTERSUBJECTIVITY - THE CHALLENGE AND OPPORTUNITY FOR ACCOUNTING
AOS 01 80 VOL: 5 PG:129 - 142 :: QUAL. :INT. LOG. :THEORY :N/A

ANSARI,SL ; SEC: EUSKE ,KJ CIT: 0.00
RATIONAL, RATIONALIZING, AND REIFYING USES OF ACCOUNTING DATA IN ORGANIZATIONS
AOS 06 87 VOL: 12 PG:549 - 570 :: REGRESS. :SURV. :OTH.BEH. :COST.ALLOC.

ANTAL ,AB ; FIRS: DIERKES,M CIT: 0.00
THE USEFULNESS AND USE OF SOCIAL REPORTING INFORMATION
AOS 01 85 VOL: 10 PG:29 - 34 :: DES.STAT. :INT. LOG. :OTH.BEH. :HRA

ANTLE ,R CIT: 1.14
THE AUDITOR AS AN ECONOMIC AGENT
JAR AU 82 VOL: 20 PG:504 - 527 :: ANAL. :INT. LOG. :INF.ECO./AG. :AUD.BEH.

ANTLE ,R CIT: 0.40
AUDITOR INDEPENDENCE
JAR SP 84 VOL: 22 PG:1 - 20 :: ANAL. :INT. LOG. :INF.ECO./AG. :INDEP.

ANTLE ,R ; SEC: SMITH ,A CIT: 0.75
MEASURING EXECUTIVE COMPENSATION: METHODS AND AN APPLICATION
JAR SP 85 VOL: 23 PG:296 - 325 :: REGRESS. :PRIM. :OTH.STAT. :EXEC.COMP.

ANTLE ,R ; SEC: SMITH ,A CIT: 0.67
AN EMPIRICAL INVESTIGATION OF THE RELATIVE PERFORMANCE EVALUATION OF
    CORPORATE EXECUTIVES
JAR SP 86 VOL: 24 PG:1 - 39 :: REGRESS. :PRIM. :OTH.STAT. :EXEC.COMP.

ANTON ,HR CIT: 0.23
SOME ASPECTS OF MEASUREMENT AND ACCOUNTING
JAR SP 64 VOL: 2 PG:1 - 9 :: QUAL. :INT. LOG. :THEORY :N/A

APOSTOLOU,NG ; SEC: GIROUX,GA ; THIR: WELKER,RB CIT: 0.00
THE INFORMATION CONTENT OF MUNICIPAL SPENDING RATE DATA
JAR AU 85 VOL: 23 PG:853 - 858 :: REGRESS. :PRIM. :INSTIT. :LTD

APOSTOLOU,NG ; FIRS: ROBBINS,WA ; THIR: STRAWSER,RH CIT: 0.00
MUNICIPAL ANNUAL REPORTS AND THE INFORMATION NEEDS OF INVESTORS
JAA SU 85 VOL: 8 PG:279 - 292 :: REGRESS. :PRIM. :THEORY :FIN.METH.

ARANYA,N ; SEC: POLLOCK,J ; THIR: AMERNIC,J CIT: 0.00
AN EXAMINATION OF PROFESSIONAL COMMITMENT IN PUBLIC ACCOUNTING
AOS 04 81 VOL: 6 PG:271 - 280 :: MIXED :LAB. :OTH.BEH. :PROF.RESP.

ARANYA,N ; SEC: LACHMAN,R ; THIR: AMERNIC,J CIT: 0.00
ACCOUNTANTS' JOB SATISFACTION: A PATH ANALYSIS
AOS 03 82 VOL: 7 PG:201 - 216 :: CORR. :SURV. :OTH.BEH. :N/A

ARANYA,N ; SEC: FERRIS,KR CIT: 0.20
A REEXAMINATION OF ACCOUNTANTS' ORGANIZATIONAL-PROFESSIONAL CONFLICT
TAR JA 84 VOL: 59 PG:1 - 15 :: ANOVA :SURV. :OTH.BEH. :PROF.RESP.

ARCHIBALD,TR ; FIRS: SORTER,GH ; SEC: BECKER,S ; FOUR: BEAVER,WH CIT: 0.46
CORPORATE PERSONALITY AS REFLECTED IN ACCOUNTING DECISIONS: SOME PRELIMINARY
    FINDINGS
JAR AU 64 VOL: 2 PG:183 - 196 :: ANOVA :SURV. :THEORY :ORG.FORM

ARCHIBALD,TR CIT: 0.69
THE RETURN TO STRAIGHT-LINE DEPRECIATION: AN ANALYSIS OF A CHANGE IN
    ACCOUNTING METHOD
JAR ST 67 VOL: 5 PG:164 - 186 :: DES.STAT. :PRIM. :THEORY :ACC.CHNG.

ARCHIBALD,TR CIT: 1.15
STOCK MARKET REACTION TO THE DEPRECIATION SWITCH-BACK
TAR JA 72 VOL: 47 PG:22 - 30 :: REGRESS. :PRIM. :EMH :ACC.CHNG.

ARGYRIS,C CIT: 0.83
ORGANIZATIONAL LEARNING AND MANAGEMENT INFORMATION SYSTEMS
AOS 02 77 VOL: 2 PG:113 - 124 :: QUAL. :INT. LOG. :OTH.BEH. :N/A

ARMSTRONG,P CIT: 2.00
CHANGING MANAGEMENT CONTROL STRATEGIES: THE ROLE OF COMPETITION BETWEEN
    ACCOUNTANCY AND OTHER ORGANIZATIONAL PROFESSIONS
AOS 02 85 VOL: 10 PG:129 - 148 :: REGRESS. :INT. LOG. :INSTIT. :ORG.& ENVIR.

ARMSTRONG,P CIT: 2.00
THE RISE OF ACCOUNTING CONTROLS IN BRITISH CAPITALIST ENTERPRISES
AOS 05 87 VOL: 12 PG:415 - 436 :: REGRESS. :INT. LOG. :HIST. :FIN.METH.

ARNETT,HE CIT: 0.00
RECOGNITION AS A FUNCTION OF MEASUREMENT IN THE REALIZATION CONCEPT
TAR OC 63 VOL: 38 PG:733 - 741 :: QUAL. :INT. LOG. :THEORY :VALUAT.(INFL.)

ARNETT,HE CIT: 0.00
APPLICATION OF THE CAPITAL GAINS AND LOSSES CONCEPT IN PRACTICE
TAR JA 65 VOL: 40 PG:54 - 64 :: DES.STAT. :PRIM. :THEORY :INFO.STRUC.

ARNETT,HE CIT: 0.08
THE CONCEPT OF FAIRNESS
TAR AP 67 VOL: 42 PG:291 - 297 :: QUAL. :INT. LOG. :THEORY :OTH.FIN.ACC.

ARNETT,HE CIT: 0.00
TAXABLE INCOME VS. FINANCIAL INCOME: HOW MUCH UNIFORMITY CAN WE STAND?
TAR JL 69 VOL: 44 PG:482 - 494 :: QUAL. :INT. LOG. :INSTIT. :FIN.METH.

ARNOLD,DF ; SEC: HUMANN,TE CIT: 0.08
EARNINGS PER SHARE: AN EMPIRICAL TEST OF THE MARKET PARITY AND THE INVESTMENT
    VALUE METHODS
TAR JA 73 VOL: 48 PG:23 - 33 :: NON-PAR. :PRIM. :OTH.STAT. :LTD

ARNOLD,DF ; SEC: HUEFNER,RJ CIT: 0.08
MEASURING AND EVALUATING REPLACEMENT COSTS: AN APPLICATION
JAR AU 77 VOL: 15 PG:245 - 252 :: QUAL. :FIELD :THEORY :VALUAT.(INFL.)

ARRINGTON,CE ; SEC: HILLISON,WA ; THIR: JENSEN,RE CIT: 0.00
AN APPLICATION OF ANALYTICAL HIERARCHY PROCESS TO MODEL EXPERT JUDGMENTS ON
    ANALYTICAL REVIEW PROCEDURES
JAR SP 84 VOL: 22 PG:298 - 312 :: OTH.QUANT. :LAB. :HIPS :ANAL.REV.

ARRINGTON,CE ; SEC: BAILEY,CD ; THIR: HOPWOOD,WS CIT: 0.00
AN ATTRIBUTION ANALYSIS OF RESPONSIBILITY ASSESSMENT FOR AUDIT PERFORMANCE
JAR SP 85 VOL: 23 PG:1 - 20 :: REGRESS. :LAB. :OTH.BEH. :AUD.

ARTMAN,JT ; FIRS: LIBBY ,R ; THIR: WILLINGHAM,JJ CIT: 0.50
PROCESS SUSCEPTIBILITY, CONTROL RISK, AND AUDIT PLANNING
TAR AP 85 VOL: 60 PG:212 - 230 :: REGRESS. :LAB. :HIPS :INT.CONT.

ASHTON,AH CIT: 0.29
THE DESCRIPTIVE VALIDITY OF NORMATIVE DECISION THEORY IN AUDITING CONTEXTS
JAR AU 82 VOL: 20 PG:415 - 428 :: ANOVA :LAB. :OTH.BEH. :METHOD.

ASHTON,AH CIT: 0.00
A FIELD TEST OF IMPLICATIONS OF LABORATORY STUDIES OF DECISION MAKING
TAR JL 84 VOL: 59 PG:361 - 375 :: REGRESS. :FIELD :HIPS :BUDG.& PLAN.

ASHTON,AH CIT: 0.50
DOES CONSENSUS IMPLY ACCURACY IN ACCOUNTING DECISION MAKING?
TAR AP 85 VOL: 60 PG:173 - 185 :: REGRESS. :LAB. :HIPS :FOREC.

ASHTON,AH ; SEC: ASHTON,RH CIT: 0.00
SEQUENTIAL BELIEF REVISION IN AUDITING
TAR OC 88 VOL: 63 PG:623 - 641 :: REGRESS. :LAB. :HIPS :JUDG.

ASHTON,RH CIT: 1.15
THE PREDICTIVE-ABILITY CRITERION AND USER PREDICTION MODELS
TAR OC 74 VOL: 49 PG:719 - 732 :: QUAL. :INT. LOG. :HIPS :FIN.METH.

ASHTON,RH CIT: 2.62
AN EXPERIMENTAL STUDY OF INTERNAL CONTROL JUDGMENTS
JAR SP 74 VOL: 12 PG:143 - 157 :: MIXED :LAB. :HIPS :INT.CONT.

ASHTON,RH CIT: 0.62
USER PREDICTION MODELS IN ACCOUNTING: AN ALTERNATIVE USE
TAR OC 75 VOL: 50 PG:710 - 722 :: QUAL. :SEC. :HIPS :BUDG.& PLAN.

ASHTON,RH CIT: 1.15
COGNITIVE CHANGES INDUCED BY ACCOUNTING CHANGES: EXPERIMENTAL EVIDENCE ON THE
   FUNCTIONAL FIXATION HYPOTHESIS
JAR ST 76 VOL: 14 PG:1 - 17 :: NON-PAR. :LAB. :HIPS :MANAG.

ASHTON,RH CIT: 0.38
DEVIATION-AMPLIFYING FEEDBACK AND UNINTENDED CONSEQUENCES OF MANAGEMENT
   ACCOUNTING SYSTEMS
AOS 04 76 VOL: 1 PG:289 - 300 :: QUAL. :INT. LOG. :OTH.BEH. :N/A

ASHTON,RH CIT: 0.33
OBJECTIVITY OF ACCOUNTING MEASURES: A MULTIRULE-MULTIMEASURER APPROACH
TAR JL 77 VOL: 52 PG:567 - 575 :: QUAL. :INT. LOG. :HIPS :OTH.FIN.ACC.

ASHTON,RH ; SEC: KRAMER,SS CIT: 1.78
STUDENTS AS SURROGATES IN BEHAVIOURAL ACCOUNTING RESEARCH: SOME EVIDENCE
JAR SP 80 VOL: 18 PG:1 - 15 :: NON-PAR. :LAB. :HIPS :METHOD.

ASHTON,RH ; SEC: BROWN ,PR CIT: 0.11
DESCRIPTIVE MODELING OF AUDITORS' INTERNAL CONTROL JUDGMENTS: REPLICATION AND
   EXTENSION
JAR SP 80 VOL: 18 PG:269 - 277 :: NON-PAR. :LAB. :HIPS :INT.CONT.

ASHTON,RH CIT: 0.63
A DESCRIPTIVE STUDY OF INFORMATION EVALUATION
JAR SP 81 VOL: 19 PG:42 - 61 :: REGRESS. :LAB. :HIPS :MANAG.

ASHTON,RH ; FIRS: KESSLER,L CIT: 0.38
FEEDBACK AND PREDICTION ACHIEVEMENT IN FINANCIAL ANALYSIS
JAR SP 81 VOL: 19 PG:146 - 162 :: ANOVA :LAB. :HIPS :BUDG.& PLAN.

ASHTON,RH ; SEC: HYLAS ,RE CIT: 0.00
INCREASING CONFIRMATION RESPONSE RATES
AUD SU 81 VOL: 1 PG:12 - 22 :: ANOVA :FIELD :OTH. :CONF.

ASHTON,RH ; SEC: HYLAS ,RE CIT: 0.00
A STUDY OF THE RESPONSE TO BALANCE AND INVOICE CONFIRMATION REQUESTS
JAA SU 81 VOL: 4 PG:325 - 332 :: DES.STAT. :FIELD :OTH. :OPER.AUD.

ASHTON,RH ; FIRS: HYLAS ,RE CIT: 0.86
AUDIT DETECTION OF FINANCIAL STATEMENT ERRORS
TAR OC 82 VOL: 57 PG:751 - 765 :: DES.STAT. :FIELD :N/A :ERRORS

ASHTON,RH ; SEC: WILLINGHAM,JJ ; THIR: ELLIOTT,RK CIT: 0.00
AN EMPIRICAL ANALYSIS OF AUDIT DELAY
JAR AU 87 VOL: 25 PG:275 - 292 :: REGRESS. :SURV. :INSTIT. :TIM.

ASHTON,RH ; FIRS: ASHTON,AH CIT: 0.00
SEQUENTIAL BELIEF REVISION IN AUDITING
TAR OC 88 VOL: 63 PG:623 - 641 :: REGRESS. :LAB. :HIPS :JUDG.

ASKARI,H ; SEC: CAIN ,P ; THIR: SHAW ,R CIT: 0.00
A GOVERNMENT TAX SUBSIDY
TAR AP 76 VOL: 51 PG:331 - 334 :: DES.STAT. :PRIM. :N/A :TAX PLNG.

ATIASE,RK CIT: 2.50
PREDISCLOSURE INFORMATION, FIRM CAPITALIZATION, AND SECURITY PRICE BEHAVIOR
   AROUND EARNINGS ANNOUNCEMENTS
JAR SP 85 VOL: 23 PG:21 - 36 :: REGRESS. :PRIM. :EMH :FIN.METH.

ATIASE,RK CIT: 0.00
MARKET IMPLICATIONS OF PREDISCLOSURE INFORMATION: SIZE AND EXCHANGE EFFECTS
JAR SP 87 VOL: 25 PG:168 - 176 :: REGRESS. :PRIM. :EMH :INFO.STRUC.

ATKINSON,AA CIT: 0.60
INFORMATION INCENTIVES IN A STANDARD-SETTING MODEL OF CONTROL
JAR SP 79 VOL: 17 PG:1 - 22 :: ANAL. :INT. LOG. :INF.ECO./AG. :MANAG.

AUSTIN,KR ; FIRS: ROBBINS,WA CIT: 0.00
DISCLOSURE QUALITY IN GOVERNMENT FINANCIAL REPORTS: AN ASSESSMENT OF THE
   APPROPRIATENESS OF A COMPOUND MEASURE
JAR AU 86 VOL: 24 PG:412 - 421 :: REGRESS. :SURV. :THEORY :METHOD.

AYRES ,FL CIT: 0.67
CHARACTERISTICS OF FIRMS ELECTING EARLY ADOPTION OF SFAS 52
JAE JN 86 VOL: 8 PG:143 - 158 :: REGRESS. :PRIM. :OTH.STAT. :FOR.CUR.

AYRES ,FL CIT: 0.00
A COMMENT ON CORPORATE PREFERENCES FOR FOREIGN CURRENCY ACCOUNTING STANDARDS
JAR SP 86 VOL: 24 PG:166 - 169 :: REGRESS. :PRIM. :THEORY :FOR.CUR.

BABER ,WR CIT: 0.50
TOWARD UNDERSTANDING THE ROLE OF AUDITING IN THE PUBLIC SECTOR
JAE DE 83 VOL: 5 PG:213 - 227 :: REGRESS. :INT. LOG. :OTH.STAT. :AUD.

BABER ,WR CIT: 0.00
BUDGET-BASED COMPENSATION AND DISCRETIONARY SPENDING
TAR JA 85 VOL: 60 PG:1 - 9 :: DES.STAT. :INT. LOG. :INF.ECO./AG. :BUDG.& PLAN.

BABER ,WR CIT: 0.00
A FRAMEWORK FOR MAKING A CLASS OF INTERNAL ACCOUNTING CONTROL DECISIONS
JAR SP 85 VOL: 23 PG:360 - 369 :: REGRESS. :INT. LOG. :OTH.STAT. :INT.CONT.

BABER ,WR ; SEC: BROOKS,EH ; THIR: RICKS ,WE CIT: 0.00
AN EMPIRICAL INVESTIGATION OF THE MARKET FOR AUDIT SERVICES IN THE PUBLIC
   SECTOR
JAR AU 87 VOL: 25 PG:293 - 305 :: REGRESS. :PRIM. :OTH.STAT. :ORG.

BACKER,M CIT: 0.00
COMMENTS ON "THE VALUE OF THE SEC'S ACCOUNTING DISCLOSURE REQUIREMENTS"
TAR JL 69 VOL: 44 PG:533 - 538 :: QUAL. :INT. LOG. :INSTIT. :INFO.STRUC.

BAGGETT,WD CIT: 0.00
INTERNAL CONTROL: INSIGHT FROM A GENERAL SYSTEMS THEORY PERSPECTIVE
JAA SP 83 VOL: 6 PG:227 - 233 :: QUAL. :INT. LOG. :OTH. :N/A

BAGINSKI,SP CIT: 0.00
INTRAINDUSTRY INFORMATION TRANSFERS ASSOCIATED WITH MANAGEMENT FORECASTS OF
EARNINGS
JAR AU 87 VOL: 25 PG:196 - 216 :: REGRESS. :PRIM. :OTH.STAT. :INV.

BAILEY JR,AD ; SEC: GRAY J CIT: 0.00
A STUDY OF THE IMPORTANCE OF THE PLANNING HORIZON ON REPORTS UTILIZING
DISCOUNTED FUTURE CASH FLOWS
JAR SP 68 VOL: 6 PG:98 - 105 :: DES.STAT. :SIM. :N/A :CAP.BUDG.

BAILEY JR,AD CIT: 0.08
A DYNAMIC PROGRAMMING APPROACH TO THE ANALYSIS OF DIFFERENT COSTING METHODS
IN ACCOUNTING FOR INVENTORIES
TAR JL 73 VOL: 48 PG:560 - 574 :: ANAL. :INT. LOG. :MATH.PROG. :INV.

BAILEY JR,AD ; SEC: BOE ,WJ CIT: 0.15
GOAL AND RESOURCE TRANSFERS IN THE MULTIGOAL ORGANIZATION
TAR JL 76 VOL: 51 PG:559 - 573 :: QUAL. :INT. LOG. :MATH.PROG. :TRANS.PRIC.

BAILEY JR,AD ; FIRS: CASH JR,JI ; THIR: WHINSTON,AB CIT: 0.08
A SURVEY OF TECHNIQUES FOR AUDITING EDP-BASED ACCOUNTING INFORMATION SYSTEMS
TAR OC 77 VOL: 52 PG:813 - 832 :: QUAL. :SEC. :N/A :ANAL.REV.

BAILEY JR,AD ; FIRS: VASARHELYI,MA ; THIR: CAMARDESSE JR,JE ; FOUR: GROOMER, SM
; FIFT: LAMPE ,JC CIT: 0.00
THE USAGE OF COMPUTERS IN AUDITING TEACHING AND RESEARCH
AUD SP 84 VOL: 3 PG:98 - 103 :: QUAL. :SIM. :OTH. :EDP AUD.

BAILEY JR,AD ; SEC: DUKE ,GL ; THIR: GERLACH,JH ; FOUR: KO   ,CE ; FIFT:
MESERVY,RD ; SIX: WHINSTON,AB CIT: 0.00
TICOM AND THE ANALYSIS OF INTERNAL CONTROLS
TAR AP 85 VOL: 60 PG:186 - 201 :: CORR. :INT. LOG. :OTH. :INT.CONT.

BAILEY JR,AD ; FIRS: MESERVY,RD ; THIR: JOHNSON,PE CIT: 0.00
INTERNAL CONTROL EVALUATION: A COMPUTATIONAL MODEL OF THE REVIEW PROCESS
AUD AU 86 VOL: 6 PG:44 - 74 :: DES.STAT. :LAB. :EXP.SYST. :INT.CONT.

BAILEY JR,AD ; FIRS: DANOS ,P ; SEC: HOLT ,DL CIT: 0.00
THE INTERACTION OF SCIENCE AND ATTESTATION STANDARD FORMATION
AUD SP 87 VOL: 6 PG:134 - 149 :: DES.STAT. :INT. LOG. :THEORY :OPIN.

BAILEY JR,AD ; FIRS: KO   ,CE ; SEC: NACHTSHEIM,CJ ; THIR: DUKE ,GL CIT: 0.00
ON THE ROBUSTNESS OF MODEL-BASED SAMPLING IN AUDITING
AUD SP 88 VOL: 07 PG:119 - 136 :: DES.STAT. :SIM. :OTH.STAT. :SAMP.

BAILEY,AP ; SEC: MCAFEE,RP ; THIR: WHINSTON,AB CIT: 0.13
AN APPLICATION OF COMPLEXITY THEORY TO THE ANALYSIS OF INTERNAL CONTROL
SYSTEMS
AUD SU 81 VOL: 1 PG:38 - 52 :: ANAL. :INT. LOG. :OTH.STAT. :INT.CONT.

BAILEY,CD ; FIRS: ARRINGTON,CE ; THIR: HOPWOOD,WS CIT: 0.00
AN ATTRIBUTION ANALYSIS OF RESPONSIBILITY ASSESSMENT FOR AUDIT PERFORMANCE
JAR SP 85 VOL: 23 PG:1 - 20 :: REGRESS. :LAB. :OTH.BEH. :AUD.

BAILEY,CD ; SEC: BALLARD,G CIT: 0.00
IMPROVING RESPONSE RATES TO ACCOUNTS RECEIVABLE CONFIRMATIONS: AN EXPERIMENT
USING FOUR TECHNIQUES
AUD SP 86 VOL: 5 PG:77 - 85 :: REGRESS. :LAB. :OTH.BEH. :CONF.

BAILEY,KE ; SEC: BYLINSKI,JH ; THIR: SHIELDS,MD CIT: 0.00
EFFECTS OF AUDIT REPORT WORDING CHANGES ON THE PERCEIVED MESSAGE
JAR AU 83 VOL: 21 PG:355 - 370 :: OTH.QUANT. :LAB. :OTH.BEH. :OPIN.

BAILEY,WT CIT: 0.00
THE EFFECTS OF AUDIT REPORTS ON CHARTERED FINANCIAL ANALYSTS' PERCEPTIONS OF
THE SOURCES OF FINANCIAL STATEMENT AND AUDIT-REPORT MESSAGES
TAR OC 81 VOL: 56 PG:882 - 896 :: MIXED :LAB. :OTH.BEH. :OPIN.

BAIMAN,S CIT: 0.62
THE EVALUATION AND CHOICE OF INTERNAL INFORMATION SYSTEMS WITHIN A
MULTIPERSON WORLD
JAR SP 75 VOL: 13 PG:1 - 15 :: ANAL. :INT. LOG. :INF.ECO./AG. :INFO.STRUC.

BAIMAN,S ; SEC: DEMSKI,JS CIT: 1.44
ECONOMICALLY OPTIMAL PERFORMANCE EVALUATION AND CONTROL SYSTEMS
JAR ST 80 VOL: 18 PG:184 - 220 :: ANAL. :INT. LOG. :OTH. :MANAG.

BAIMAN,S ; SEC: EVANS III,JH CIT: 1.67
PRE-DECISION INFORMATION AND PARTICIPATIVE MANAGEMENT CONTROL SYSTEMS
JAR AU 83 VOL: 21 PG:371 - 395 :: ANAL. :INT. LOG. :INF.ECO./AG. :MANAG.

BAIMAN,S ; SEC: NOEL J CIT: 0.50
NONCONTROLLABLE COSTS AND RESPONSIBILITY ACCOUNTING
JAR AU 85 VOL: 23 PG:486 - 501 :: ANAL. :INT. LOG. :INF.ECO./AG. :RESP.ACC.

BAIMAN,S ; SEC: EVANS III,JH ; THIR: NOEL J CIT: 0.00
OPTIMAL CONTRACTS WITH A UTILITY-MAXIMIZING AUDITOR
JAR AU 87 VOL: 25 PG:217 - 244 :: ANAL. :INT. LOG. :INF.ECO./AG. :AUD.BEH.

BAINBRIDGE,DR CIT: 0.00
IS DOLLAR-VALUE LIFO CONSISTENT WITH AUTHORITATIVE GAAP?
JAA SU 84 VOL: 7 PG:334 - 346 :: ANAL. :INT. LOG. :THEORY :INV.

BAKER ,CR CIT: 0.42
MANAGEMENT STRATEGY IN A LARGE ACCOUNTING FIRM
TAR JL 77 VOL: 52 PG:576 - 586 :: QUAL. :CASE :OTH.BEH. :AUD.BEH.

BAKER ,CR CIT: 0.11
LEASING AND THE SETTING OF ACCOUNTING STANDARDS: MAPPING THE LABYRINTH
JAA SP 80 VOL: 3 PG:197 - 206 :: QUAL. :INT. LOG. :INSTIT. :LEASES

BAKER ,RE CIT: 0.00
THE PENSION COST PROBLEM
TAR JA 64 VOL: 39 PG:52 - 61 :: QUAL. :INT. LOG. :THEORY :PENS.

BAKER ,RE CIT: 0.00
INCOME OF LIFE INSURANCE COMPANIES
TAR JA 66 VOL: 41 PG:98 - 105 :: QUAL. :INT. LOG. :N/A :REV.REC.

BALACHANDRAN,BV ; SEC: RAMAKRISHNAN,RT CIT: 0.22
INTERNAL CONTROL AND EXTERNAL AUDITING FOR INCENTIVE COMPENSATION SCHEDULES
JAR ST 80 VOL: 18 PG:140 - 171 :: ANAL. :INT. LOG. :INF.ECO./AG. :AUD.

BALACHANDRAN,BV ; SEC: RAMAKRISHNAN,RT CIT: 0.00
JOINT COST ALLOCATION: A UNIFIED APPROACH
TAR JA 81 VOL: 56 PG:85 - 96 :: ANAL. :INT. LOG. :MATH.PROG. :COST.ALLOC.

BALACHANDRAN,BV ; SEC: ZOLTNERS,AA CIT: 0.00
AN INTERACTIVE AUDIT-STAFF SCHEDULING DECISION SUPPORT SYSTEM
TAR OC 81 VOL: 56 PG:801 - 812 :: ANAL. :INT. LOG. :OTH.STAT. :AUD.BEH.

BALACHANDRAN,BV ; SEC: RAMAKRISHNAN,RT CIT: 0.00
A THEORY OF AUDIT PARTNERSHIPS: AUDIT FIRM SIZE AND FEES
JAR SP 87 VOL: 25 PG:111 - 126 :: DES.STAT. :INT. LOG. :INF.ECO./AG. :ORG.

BALACHANDRAN,BV ; SEC: RAMANAN,R CIT: 0.00
OPTIMAL INTERNAL CONTROL STRATEGY UNDER DYNAMIC CONDITIONS
JAA WI 88 VOL: 03 PG:1 - 13 :: DES.STAT. :INT. LOG. :INF.ECO./AG. :INT.CONT.

BALACHANDRAN,KR ; SEC: LIVINGSTONE,JL CIT: 0.00
COST AND EFFECTIVENESS OF PHYSICIAN PEER REVIEW IN REDUCING MEDICARE
    OVERUTILIZATION
AOS 02 77 VOL: 2 PG:153 - 164 :: DES.STAT. :PRIM. :OTH.STAT. :MANAG.

BALACHANDRAN,KR ; SEC: MASCHMEYER,R ; THIR: LIVINGSTONE,JL CIT: 0.13
PRODUCT WARRANTY PERIOD: A MARKOVIAN APPROACH TO ESTIMATION AND ANALYSIS OF
    REPAIR AND REPLACEMENT COSTS
TAR JA 81 VOL: 56 PG:115 - 124 :: MARKOV :INT. LOG. :OTH.STAT. :SPEC.ITEMS

BALACHANDRAN,KR ; SEC: STEUER,RE CIT: 0.14
AN INTERACTIVE MODEL FOR THE CPA FIRM AUDIT STAFF PLANNING PROBLEM WITH
    MULTIPLE OBJECTIVES
TAR JA 82 VOL: 57 PG:125 - 140 :: ANAL. :INT. LOG. :N/A :AUD.

BALACHANDRAN,KR ; SEC: SRINIDHI,BN CIT: 0.00
A RATIONALE FOR FIXED CHARGE APPLICATION
JAA SP 87 VOL: 2 PG:151 - 169 :: DES.STAT. :INT. LOG. :MATH.PROG. :COST.ALLOC.

BALACHANDRAN,KR ; FIRS: RONEN ,J CIT: 0.00
AN APPROACH TO TRANSFER PRICING UNDER UNCERTAINTY
JAR AU 88 VOL: 26 PG:300 - 314 :: ANAL. :INT. LOG. :INF.ECO./AG. :TRANS.PRIC.

BALADOUNI,V CIT: 0.08
THE ACCOUNTING PERSPECTIVE RE-EXAMINED
TAR AP 66 VOL: 41 PG:215 - 225 :: QUAL. :INT. LOG. :INSTIT. :OTH.MANAG.

BALDWIN,BA CIT: 0.40
SEGMENT EARNINGS DISCLOSURE AND THE ABILITY OF SECURITY ANALYSTS TO FORECAST
    EARNINGS PER SHARE
TAR JL 84 VOL: 59 PG:376 - 389 :: OTH.QUANT. :PRIM. :OTH.STAT. :SEG.REP.

BALL ,R ; FIRS: BROWN ,P CIT: 1.15
SOME PRELIMINARY FINDINGS ON THE ASSOCIATION BETWEEN THE EARNINGS OF A FIRM,
    ITS INDUSTRY, AND THE ECONOMY
JAR ST 67 VOL: 5 PG:55 - 77 :: CORR. :PRIM. :EMH :REV.REC.

BALL ,R ; SEC: BROWN ,P CIT: 7.00
AN EMPIRICAL EVALUATION OF ACCOUNTING INCOME NUMBERS
JAR AU 68 VOL: 6 PG:159 - 178 :: NON-PAR. :PRIM. :EMH :FIN.METH.

BALL ,R CIT: 0.15
INDEX OF EMPIRICAL RESEARCH IN ACCOUNTING
JAR SP 71 VOL: 9 PG:1 - 31 :: QUAL. :SEC. :OTH. :METHOD.

BALL ,R CIT: 2.54
CHANGES IN ACCOUNTING TECHNIQUES AND STOCK PRICES
JAR ST 72 VOL: 10 PG:1 - 38 :: REGRESS. :PRIM. :EMH :ACC.CHNG.

BALL ,R ; SEC: LEV ,B ; THIR: WATTS ,RL CIT: 0.23
INCOME VARIATION AND BALANCE SHEET COMPOSITIONS
JAR SP 76 VOL: 14 PG:1 - 9 :: REGRESS. :PRIM. :OTH.STAT. :REV.REC.

BALL ,R ; SEC: FOSTER,G CIT: 2.43
CORPORATE FINANCIAL REPORTING: A METHODOLOGICAL REVIEW OF EMPIRICAL RESEARCH
JAR ST 82 VOL: 20 PG:161 - 234 :: MIXED :SEC. :OTH. :FIN.METH.

BALLARD,G ; FIRS: BAILEY,CD CIT: 0.00
IMPROVING RESPONSE RATES TO ACCOUNTS RECEIVABLE CONFIRMATIONS: AN EXPERIMENT
    USING FOUR TECHNIQUES
AUD SP 86 VOL: 5 PG:77 - 85 :: REGRESS. :LAB. :OTH.BEH. :CONF.

BALLEW,V CIT: 0.00
TECHNOLOGICAL ROUTINENESS AND INTRA-UNIT STRUCTURE IN CPA FIRMS
TAR JA 82 VOL: 57 PG:88 - 104 :: REGRESS. :LAB. :OTH.STAT. :ORG.

BALLEW,V ; FIRS: SPICER,BH CIT: 1.00
MANAGEMENT ACCOUNTING SYSTEMS AND THE ECONOMICS OF INTERNAL ORGANIZATION
AOS 01 83 VOL: 8 PG:73 - 98 :: QUAL. :INT. LOG. :THEORY :MANAG.

BALOFF,N ; SEC: KENNELLY,JW CIT: 0.23
ACCOUNTING IMPLICATIONS OF PRODUCT AND PROCESS START-UPS
JAR AU 67 VOL: 5 PG:131 - 143 :: REGRESS. :CASE :TIME SER. :COST.ALLOC.

BALVERS,RJ ; SEC: MCDONALD,B ; THIR: MILLER,RE CIT: 0.00
UNDERPRICING OF NEW ISSUES AND THE CHOICE OF AUDITOR AS A SIGNAL OF
    INVESTMENT BANKER REPUTATION
TAR OC 88 VOL: 63 PG:605 - 622 :: REGRESS. :PRIM. :MATH.PROG. :AUD.THEOR.

BAMBER,EM CIT: 0.00
EXPERT JUDGMENT IN THE AUDIT TEAM: A SOURCE RELIABILITY APPROACH
JAR AU 83 VOL: 21 PG:396 - 412 :: ANOVA :LAB. :HIPS :JUDG.

BAMBER,EM ; SEC: SNOWBALL,D CIT: 0.00
AN EXPERIMENTAL STUDY OF THE EFFECTS OF AUDIT STRUCTURE IN UNCERTAIN TASK
    ENVIRONMENTS
AUD JL 88 VOL: 63 PG:490 - 504 :: REGRESS. :LAB. :OTH.BEH. :JUDG.

BAMBER,EM ; SEC: BAMBER,LS ; THIR: BYLINSKI,JH CIT: 0.00
A DESCRIPTIVE STUDY OF AUDIT MANAGERS' WORKING PAPER REVIEW
AUD SP 88 VOL: 07 PG:137 - 149 :: REGRESS. :LAB. :HIPS :AUD.BEH.

BAMBER,LS CIT: 1.33
THE INFORMATION CONTENT OF ANNUAL EARNINGS RELEASES: A TRADING VOLUME
    APPROACH
JAR SP 86 VOL: 24 PG:40 - 56 :: REGRESS. :PRIM. :EMH :FIN.METH.

BAMBER,LS CIT: 0.00
UNEXPECTED EARNINGS, FIRM SIZE, AND TRADING VOLUME AROUND QUARTERLY EARNINGS
    ANNOUNCEMENTS
TAR JL 87 VOL: 62 PG:510 - 532 :: REGRESS. :PRIM. :EMH :FIN.METH.

BAMBER,LS ; FIRS: BAMBER,EM ; THIR: BYLINSKI,JH CIT: 0.00
A DESCRIPTIVE STUDY OF AUDIT MANAGERS' WORKING PAPER REVIEW
AUD SP 88 VOL: 07 PG:137 - 149 :: REGRESS. :LAB. :HIPS :AUD.BEH.

BANBURY,J ; SEC: NAHAPIET,JE CIT: 1.00
TOWARDS A FRAMEWORK FOR THE STUDY OF THE ANTECEDENTS AND CONSEQUENCES OF
    INFORMATION SYSTEMS IN ORGANIZATIONS
AOS 03 79 VOL: 4 PG:163 - 178 :: QUAL. :INT. LOG. :OTH. :N/A

BANKER,RD ; SEC: DATAR ,SM ; THIR: RAJAN ,MV CIT: 0.00
MEASUREMENT OF PRODUCTIVITY IMPROVEMENTS: AN EMPIRICAL ANALYSIS
JAA AU 87 VOL: 2 PG:319 - 347 :: DES.STAT. :FIELD :OTH.STAT. :MANAG.

BANKER,RD ; SEC: DATAR ,SM ; THIR: KEKRE ,S CIT: 0.00
RELEVANT COSTS, CONGESTION AND STOCHASTICITY IN PRODUCTION ENVIRONMENTS
JAE JL 88 VOL: 10 PG:171 - 197 :: DES.STAT. :INT. LOG. :OTH.STAT. :REL.COSTS

BANKS ,DW ; SEC: KINNEY JR,WR CIT: 0.57
LOSS CONTINGENCY REPORTS AND STOCK PRICES: AN EMPIRICAL STUDY
JAR SP 82 VOL: 20 PG:240 - 254 :: REGRESS. :PRIM. :EMH :SPEC.ITEMS

BAO ,BH ; SEC: BAO ,DH ; THIR: VASARHELYI,MA CIT: 0.00
A STOCHASTIC MODEL OF PROFESSIONAL ACCOUNTANT TURNOVER
AOS 03 86 VOL: 11 PG:289 - 296 :: DES.STAT. :PRIM. :OTH.BEH. :ORG.

BAO ,DH ; FIRS: BAO ,BH ; THIR: VASARHELYI,MA CIT: 0.00
A STOCHASTIC MODEL OF PROFESSIONAL ACCOUNTANT TURNOVER
AOS 03 86 VOL: 11 PG:289 - 296 :: DES.STAT. :PRIM. :OTH.BEH. :ORG.

BARAN ,A ; SEC: LAKONISHOK,J ; THIR: OFER ,AR CIT: 0.11
THE INFORMATION CONTENT OF GENERAL PRICE LEVEL ADJUSTED EARNINGS: SOME
    EMPIRICAL EVIDENCE
TAR JA 80 VOL: 55 PG:22 - 35 :: REGRESS. :PRIM. :HIPS :VALUAT.(INFL.)

BAREFIELD,RM CIT: 0.08
A MODEL OF FORECAST BIASING BEHAVIOR
TAR JL 70 VOL: 45 PG:490 - 501 :: ANAL. :INT. LOG. :MATH.PROG. :FOREC.

BAREFIELD,RM ; SEC: COMISKEY,EE CIT: 0.23
DEPRECIATION POLICY AND THE BEHAVIOR OF CORPORATE PROFITS
JAR AU 71 VOL: 9 PG:351 - 358 :: NON-PAR. :PRIM. :TIME SER. :FIN.METH.

BAREFIELD,RM ; SEC: COMISKEY,EE CIT: 0.23
THE SMOOTHING HYPOTHESIS: AN ALTERNATIVE TEST
TAR AP 72 VOL: 47 PG:291 - 298 :: NON-PAR. :PRIM. :TIME SER. :FIN.METH.

BAREFIELD,RM CIT: 0.85
THE EFFECT OF AGGREGATION ON DECISION MAKING SUCCESS: A LABORATORY STUDY
JAR AU 72 VOL: 10 PG:229 - 242 :: ANOVA :LAB. :HIPS :INFO.STRUC.

BARENBAUM,L ; FIRS: MONAHAN,TF CIT: 0.00
THE USE OF CONSTANT DOLLAR INFORMATION TO PREDICT BOND RATING CHANGES
JAA SU 83 VOL: 6 PG:325 - 340 :: OTH.QUANT. :PRIM. :OTH.STAT. :VALUAT.(INFL.)

BARIFF,ML ; SEC: GALBRAITH,JR CIT: 0.73
INTRAORGANIZATIONAL POWER CONSIDERATIONS FOR DESIGNING INFORMATION SYSTEMS
AOS 01 78 VOL: 3 PG:15 - 28 :: QUAL. :INT. LOG. :OTH.BEH. :ORG.FORM

BARKMAN,A CIT: 0.00
WITHIN-ITEM VARIATION: A STOCHASTIC APPROACH TO AUDIT UNCERTAINTY
TAR JA 77 VOL: 52 PG:450 - 464 :: DES.STAT. :SIM. :OTH.STAT. :RISK

BARLEV,B ; FIRS: GOLDMAN,A CIT: 0.23
THE AUDITOR-FIRM CONFLICT OF INTERESTS: ITS IMPLICATIONS FOR INDEPENDENCE
TAR OC 74 VOL: 49 PG:707 - 718 :: QUAL. :INT. LOG. :INSTIT. :INDEP.

BARLEV,B ; SEC: LEVY ,H CIT: 0.00
ON THE VARIABILITY OF ACCOUNTING INCOME NUMBERS
JAR AU 79 VOL: 17 PG:305 - 315 :: DES.STAT. :PRIM. :TIME SER. :FIN.METH.

BARLEV,B CIT: 0.00
CONTINGENT EQUITY AND THE DILUTIVE EFFECT ON EPS
TAR AP 83 VOL: 58 PG:385 - 393 :: ANAL. :INT. LOG. :OTH. :FIN.METH.

BARNEA,A ; SEC: RONEN ,J ; THIR: SADAN ,S CIT: 0.31
THE IMPLEMENTATION OF ACCOUNTING OBJECTIVES: AN APPLICATION TO EXTRAORDINARY
    ITEMS
TAR JA 75 VOL: 50 PG:58 - 68 :: ANAL. :INT. LOG. :THEORY :SPEC.ITEMS

BARNEA,A ; SEC: RONEN ,J ; THIR: SADAN ,S CIT: 0.23
CLASSIFICATORY SMOOTHING OF INCOME WITH EXTRAORDINARY ITEMS
TAR JA 76 VOL: 51 PG:110 - 122 :: REGRESS. :PRIM. :TIME SER. :INFO.STRUC.

BARNEA,A ; FIRS: ADAR ,Z ; THIR: LEV ,B CIT: 0.08
A COMPREHENSIVE COST-VOLUME-PROFIT ANALYSIS UNDER UNCERTAINTY
TAR JA 77 VOL: 52 PG:137 - 149 :: QUAL. :INT. LOG. :THEORY :TAXES

BARNES,P ; SEC: WEBB ,J CIT: 0.67
MANAGEMENT INFORMATION CHANGES AND FUNCTIONAL FIXATION: SOME EXPERIMENTAL
    EVIDENCE FROM THE PUBLIC SECTOR
AOS 01 86 VOL: 11 PG:1 - 18 :: REGRESS. :LAB. :HIPS :COST.ALLOC.

BARNISEL,TS ; FIRS: SPENCER,CH CIT: 0.00
A DECADE OF PRICE-LEVEL CHANGES - THE EFFECT ON THE FINANCIAL STATEMENTS OF
    CUMMINS ENGINE COMPANY
TAR JA 65 VOL: 40 PG:144 - 153 :: DES.STAT. :CASE :THEORY :VALUAT.(INFL.)

BARON ,CD ; FIRS: KING ,RR CIT: 0.00
AN INTEGRATED ACCOUNT STRUCTURE FOR GOVERNMENTAL ACCOUNTING AND FINANCIAL
    REPORTING
TAR JA 74 VOL: 49 PG:76 - 87 :: QUAL. :INT. LOG. :THEORY :FIN.METH.

BARRETT,ME CIT: 0.38
ACCOUNTING FOR INTERCORPORATE INVESTMENTS: A BEHAVIOR FIELD STUDY
JAR ST 71 VOL: 9 PG:50 - 65 :: NON-PAR. :LAB. :OTH.BEH. :N/A

BARRETT,ME CIT: 0.31
FINANCIAL REPORTING PRACTICES: DISCLOSURE AND COMPREHENSIVENESS IN AN
    INTERNATIONAL SETTING
JAR SP 76 VOL: 14 PG:10 - 26 :: DES.STAT. :PRIM. :THEORY :INT.DIFF.

BARRETT,WB CIT: 0.00
A FUNCTIONAL APPROACH TO ACCOUNTING
TAR JA 68 VOL: 43 PG:105 - 112 :: QUAL. :INT. LOG. :THEORY :FIN.METH.

BARRON,FH ; FIRS: MORIARITY,S CIT: 0.92
MODELING THE MATERIALITY JUDGMENTS OF AUDIT PARTNERS
JAR AU 76 VOL: 14 PG:320 - 341 :: MIXED :LAB. :OTH.BEH. :MAT.

BARRON,FH ; FIRS: MORIARITY,S CIT: 0.70
A JUDGMENT-BASED DEFINITION OF MATERIALITY
JAR ST 79 VOL: 17 PG:114 - 135 :: OTH.QUANT. :LAB. :OTH.STAT. :MAT.

BARRON,FH ; FIRS: EMERY ,DR ; THIR: MESSIER JR,WF CIT: 0.14
CONJOINT MEASUREMENT AND THE ANALYSIS OF NOISY DATA: A COMMENT
JAR AU 82 VOL: 20 PG:450 - 458 :: NON-PAR. :SIM. :HIPS :METHOD.

BARTCZAK,N ; FIRS: CASEY JR,CJ CIT: 0.00
USING OPERATING CASH FLOW DATA TO PREDICT FINANCIAL DISTRESS: SOME EXTENSIONS
JAR SP 85 VOL: 23 PG:384 - 401 :: REGRESS. :PRIM. :MATH.PROG. :BUS.FAIL.

BARTLETT,RW ; FIRS: SEILER,RE CIT: 0.14
PERSONALITY VARIABLES AS PREDICTORS OF BUDGET SYSTEM CHARACTERISTICS
AOS 04 82 VOL: 7 PG:381 - 404 :: OTH.QUANT. :SURV. :OTH.BEH. :BUDG.& PLAN.

BARTON,AD CIT: 0.31
EXPECTATIONS AND ACHIEVEMENTS IN INCOME THEORY
TAR OC 74 VOL: 49 PG:664 - 681 :: QUAL. :INT. LOG. :THEORY :VALUAT.(INFL.)

BARTON,RF CIT: 0.00
AN EXPERIMENTAL STUDY ON THE IMPACT OF COMPETITIVE PRESSURES ON OVERHEAD
    ALLOCATION BIDS
JAR SP 69 VOL: 7 PG:116 - 122 :: DES.STAT. :LAB. :OTH.BEH. :OVER.ALLOC.

BASI ,BA ; SEC: CAREY ,KJ ; THIR: TWARK ,RD CIT: 1.00
A COMPARISON OF THE ACCURACY OF CORPORATE AND SECURITY ANALYSTS' FORECASTS
    OF EARNINGS
TAR AP 76 VOL: 51 PG:244 - 254 :: ANOVA :PRIM. :TIME SER. :FOREC.

BASKIN,EF CIT: 0.54
THE COMMUNICATIVE EFFECTIVENESS OF CONSISTENCY EXCEPTIONS
TAR JA 72 VOL: 47 PG:38 - 51 :: MIXED :PRIM. :EMH :ACC.CHNG.

BASKIN,EF ; FIRS: DAVIS ,DW ; SEC: BOATSMAN,JR CIT: 0.09
ON GENERALIZING STOCK MARKET RESEARCH TO A BROADER CLASS OF MARKETS
TAR JA 78 VOL: 53 PG:1 - 10 :: MIXED :PRIM. :EMH :FIN.METH.

BASKIN,EF ; FIRS: BOATSMAN,JR CIT: 0.13
ASSET VALUATION WITH INCOMPLETE MARKETS
TAR JA 81 VOL: 56 PG:38 - 53 :: ANAL. :INT. LOG. :EMH :FIN.METH.

BASTABLE,CW ; SEC: BEAMS ,FA CIT: 0.00
CASH FLOWS AND CASH COWS
JAA SP 81 VOL: 4 PG:248 - 254 :: ANAL. :INT. LOG. :OTH. :DEC.AIDS

BASU ,S CIT: 0.27
THE EFFECT OF EARNINGS YIELD ON ASSESSMENTS OF THE ASSOCIATION BETWEEN ANNUAL
    ACCOUNTING INCOME NUMBERS AND SECURITY PRICES
TAR JL 78 VOL: 53 PG:599 - 625 :: ANOVA :PRIM. :EMH :FIN.METH.

BATHKE,AW ; SEC: LOREK ,KS CIT: 0.00
THE RELATIONSHIP BETWEEN TIME-SERIES MODELS AND THE SECURITY MARKET'S
    EXPECTATION OF QUARTERLY EARNINGS
TAR AP 84 VOL: 59 PG:163 - 176 :: REGRESS. :PRIM. :TIME SER. :FOREC.

BATHKE,AW ; FIRS: LOREK ,KS CIT: 0.00
A TIME-SERIES ANALYSIS OF NONSEASONAL QUARTERLY EARNINGS DATA
JAR SP 84 VOL: 22 PG:369 - 379 :: CORR. :PRIM. :TIME SER. :INT.REP.

BAUMLER,JV ; FIRS: WATSON,DJ CIT: 0.69
TRANSFER PRICING: A BEHAVIOURAL CONTEXT
TAR JL 75 VOL: 50 PG:466 - 474 :: QUAL. :INT. LOG. :OTH.BEH. :TRANS.PRIC.

BAUMLER,JV ; FIRS: JIAMBALVO,J ; SEC: WATSON,DJ CIT: 0.17
AN EXAMINATION OF PERFORMANCE EVALUATION DECISIONS IN CPA FIRM SUBUNITS
AOS 01 83 VOL: 8 PG:13 - 30 :: REGRESS. :LAB. :OTH.BEH. :ORG.

BAVISHI,VB ; FIRS: HUSSEIN,ME ; THIR: GANGOLLY,JS CIT: 0.00
INTERNATIONAL SIMILARITIES AND DIFFERENCES IN THE AUDITOR'S REPORT
AUD AU 86 VOL: 6 PG:124 - 133 :: DES.STAT. :PRIM. :INSTIT. :INT.DIFF.

BAXTER,WT ; SEC: CARRIER,NH CIT: 0.08
DEPRECIATION, REPLACEMENT PRICE, AND COST OF CAPITAL
JAR AU 71 VOL: 9 PG:189 - 214 :: ANAL. :INT. LOG. :THEORY :VALUAT.(INFL.)

BEAMS ,FA CIT: 0.00
INDICATIONS OF PRAGMATISM AND EMPIRICISM IN ACCOUNTING THOUGHT
TAR AP 69 VOL: 44 PG:382 - 388 :: QUAL. :INT. LOG. :THEORY :FIN.METH.

BEAMS ,FA ; FIRS: BASTABLE,CW CIT: 0.00
CASH FLOWS AND CASH COWS
JAA SP 81 VOL: 4 PG:248 - 254 :: ANAL. :INT. LOG. :OTH. :DEC.AIDS

BEATTY,RP ; SEC: JOHNSON,SB CIT: 0.00
A MARKET-BASED METHOD OF CLASSIFYING CONVERTIBLE SECURITIES
JAA WI 85 VOL: 8 PG:112 - 124 :: REGRESS. :PRIM. :EMH :LTD

BEAVER,WH ; FIRS: SORTER,GH ; SEC: BECKER,S ; THIR: ARCHIBALD,TR CIT: 0.46
CORPORATE PERSONALITY AS REFLECTED IN ACCOUNTING DECISIONS: SOME PRELIMINARY
    FINDINGS
JAR AU 64 VOL: 2 PG:183 - 196 :: ANOVA :SURV. :THEORY :ORG.FORM

BEAVER,WH CIT: 1.38
FINANCIAL RATIOS AS PREDICTORS OF FAILURE
JAR ST 66 VOL: 4 PG:71 - 111 :: DES.STAT. :PRIM. :OTH.STAT. :BUS.FAIL.

BEAVER,WH CIT: 0.46
MARKET PRICES, FINANCIAL RATIOS, AND THE PREDICTION OF FAILURE
JAR AU 68 VOL: 6 PG:179 - 192 :: DES.STAT. :PRIM. :TIME SER. :BUS.FAIL.

BEAVER,WH CIT: 0.62
ALTERNATIVE ACCOUNTING MEASURES AS PREDICTORS OF FAILURE
TAR JA 68 VOL: 43 PG:113 - 122 :: DES.STAT. :PRIM. :N/A :BUS.FAIL.

BEAVER,WH ; SEC: KENNELLY,JW ; THIR: VOSS ,WM CIT: 0.92
PREDICTIVE ABILITY AS A CRITERION FOR THE EVALUATION OF ACCOUNTING DATA
TAR OC 68 VOL: 43 PG:675 - 683 :: QUAL. :INT. LOG. :THEORY :FIN.METH.

BEAVER,WH CIT: 4.85
THE INFORMATION CONTENT OF ANNUAL EARNINGS ANNOUNCEMENTS
JAR ST 68 VOL: 6 PG:67 - 92 :: REGRESS. :PRIM. :EMH :FIN.METH.

BEAVER,WH ; SEC: KETTLER,P ; THIR: SCHOLES,M CIT: 2.08
THE ASSOCIATION BETWEEN MARKET DETERMINED AND ACCOUNTING DETERMINED RISK MEA
TAR OC 70 VOL: 45 PG:654 - 682 :: REGRESS. :PRIM. :TIME SER. :FIN.METH.

BEAVER,WH CIT: 1.38
THE TIME SERIES BEHAVIOR OF EARNINGS
JAR ST 70 VOL: 8 PG:62 - 99 :: MIXED :PRIM. :TIME SER. :FIN.METH.

BEAVER,WH ; FIRS: ROSE ,R ; THIR: BECKER,S ; FOUR: SORTER,GH CIT: 0.77
TOWARD AN EMPIRICAL MEASURE OF MATERIALITY
JAR ST 70 VOL: 8 PG:138 - 148 :: DES.STAT. :LAB. :OTH.BEH. :MAT.

BEAVER,WH ; SEC: DUKES ,RE CIT: 1.62
INTERPERIOD TAX ALLOCATION, EARNINGS EXPECTATIONS, AND THE BEHAVIOR OF
    SECURITY PRICES
TAR AP 72 VOL: 47 PG:320 - 332 :: REGRESS. :PRIM. :EMH :PP&E / DEPR

BEAVER,WH ; SEC: DUKES ,RE CIT: 0.69
INTERPERIOD TAX ALLOCATION AND DELTA-DEPRECIATION METHODS: SOME EMPIRICAL
  RESULTS
TAR JL 73 VOL: 48 PG:549 - 559 :: REGRESS. :PRIM. :EMH :PP&E / DEPR

BEAVER,WH ; SEC: DUKES ,RE CIT: 0.08
DELTA-DEPRECIATION METHODS: SOME ANALYTICAL RESULTS
JAR AU 74 VOL: 12 PG:205 - 215 :: ANAL. :INT. LOG. :OTH.STAT. :PP&E / DEPR

BEAVER,WH ; SEC: DEMSKI,JS CIT: 0.85
THE NATURE OF FINANCIAL ACCOUNTING OBJECTIVES: A SUMMARY AND SYNTHESIS
JAR ST 74 VOL: 12 PG:170 - 187 :: ANAL. :SEC. :THEORY :FIN.METH.

BEAVER,WH ; SEC: CLARKE,R ; THIR: WRIGHT,WF CIT: 4.20
THE ASSOCIATION BETWEEN UNSYSTEMATIC SECURITY RETURNS AND THE MAGNITUDE OF
  EARNINGS FORECAST ERRORS
JAR AU 79 VOL: 17 PG:316 - 340 :: NON-PAR. :PRIM. :EMH :FOREC.

BEAVER,WH ; SEC: DEMSKI,JS CIT: 1.30
THE NATURE OF INCOME MEASUREMENT
TAR JA 79 VOL: 54 PG:38 - 46 :: QUAL. :INT. LOG. :INF.ECO./AG. :OTH.FIN.ACC.

BEAVER,WH ; SEC: CHRISTIE,AA ; THIR: GRIFFIN,PA CIT: 2.00
THE INFORMATION CONTENT OF SEC ACCOUNTING SERIES RELEASE NO.190
JAE AG 80 VOL: 2 PG:127 - 157 :: REGRESS. :PRIM. :EMH :VALUAT.(INFL.)

BEAVER,WH ; SEC: LAMBERT,RA ; THIR: MORSE ,D CIT: 2.44
THE INFORMATION CONTENT OF SECURITY PRICES
JAE MR 80 VOL: 2 PG:3 - 28 :: REGRESS. :PRIM. :EMH :FIN.METH.

BEAVER,WH ; SEC: LANDSMAN,WR CIT: 0.00
NOTE ON THE BEHAVIOR OF RESIDUAL SECURITY RETURNS FOR WINNER AND LOSER
  PORTFOLIOS
JAE DE 81 VOL: 3 PG:233 - 241 :: DES.STAT. :PRIM. :EMH :N/A

BEAVER,WH CIT: 0.25
MARKET EFFICIENCY
TAR JA 81 VOL: 56 PG:23 - 37 :: ANAL. :INT. LOG. :EMH :FIN.METH.

BEAVER,WH CIT: 1.38
ECONOMETRIC PROPERTIES OF ALTERNATIVE SECURITY RETURN METHODS
JAR SP 81 VOL: 19 PG:163 - 184 :: ANAL. :INT. LOG. :EMH :METHOD.

BEAVER,WH ; SEC: WOLFSON,MA CIT: 0.00
FOREIGN CURRENCY TRANSLATION AND CHANGING PRICES IN PERFECT AND COMPLETE
  MARKETS
JAR AU 82 VOL: 20 PG:528 - 550 :: ANAL. :INT. LOG. :OTH.STAT. :VALUAT.(INFL.)

BEAVER,WH ; SEC: GRIFFIN,PA ; THIR: LANDSMAN,WR CIT: 2.43
THE INCREMENTAL INFORMATION CONTENT OF REPLACEMENT COST EARNINGS
JAE JL 82 VOL: 4 PG:15 - 39 :: MIXED :PRIM. :EMH :VALUAT.(INFL.)

BEAVER,WH ; SEC: GRIFFIN,PA ; THIR: LANDSMAN,WR CIT: 0.00
TESTING FOR INCREMENTAL INFORMATION CONTENT IN THE PRESENCE OF COLLINEARITY:
  A COMMENT
JAE DE 84 VOL: 6 PG:219 - 223 :: QUAL. :INT. LOG. :OTH.STAT. :METHOD.

BEAVER,WH CIT: 0.50
THE PROPERTIES OF SEQUENTIAL REGRESSIONS WITH MULTIPLE EXPLANATORY VARIABLES
TAR JA 87 VOL: 62 PG:137 - 144 :: DES.STAT. :INT. LOG. :EMH :METHOD.

BEAVER,WH ; SEC: LAMBERT,RA ; THIR: RYAN ,SG CIT: 1.00
THE INFORMATION CONTENT OF SECURITY PRICES: A SECOND LOOK
JAE JL 87 VOL: 9 PG:139 - 157 :: REGRESS. :PRIM. :EMH :FIN.METH.

BECK ,PJ CIT: 0.22
A CRITICAL ANALYSIS OF THE REGRESSION ESTIMATOR IN AUDIT SAMPLING
JAR SP 80 VOL: 18 PG:16 - 37 :: MIXED :SIM. :OTH.STAT. :METHOD.

BECK ,PJ ; SEC: SOLOMON,I CIT: 0.00
EX POST SAMPLING RISKS AND DECISION RULE CHOICE IN SUBSTANTIVE TESTING
AUD SP 85 VOL: 4 PG:1 - 10 :: DES.STAT. :INT. LOG. :OTH.STAT. :SAMP.

BECK ,PJ ; SEC: SOLOMON,I ; THIR: TOMASSINI,LA CIT: 0.25
SUBJECTIVE PRIOR PROBABILITY DISTRIBUTIONS AND AUDIT RISK
JAR SP 85 VOL: 23 PG:37 - 56 :: REGRESS. :INT. LOG. :OTH.BEH. :RISK

BECKER,S ; FIRS: SORTER,GH ; THIR: ARCHIBALD,TR ; FOUR: BEAVER,WH CIT: 0.46
CORPORATE PERSONALITY AS REFLECTED IN ACCOUNTING DECISIONS: SOME PRELIMINARY
   FINDINGS
JAR AU 64 VOL: 2 PG:183 - 196 :: ANOVA :SURV. :THEORY :ORG.FORM

BECKER,S ; FIRS: ROSE ,R ; SEC: BEAVER,WH ; FOUR: SORTER,GH CIT: 0.77
TOWARD AN EMPIRICAL MEASURE OF MATERIALITY
JAR ST 70 VOL: 8 PG:138 - 148 :: DES.STAT. :LAB. :OTH.BEH. :MAT.

BECKER,S ; SEC: RONEN ,J ; THIR: SORTER,GH CIT: 0.38
OPPORTUNITY COSTS - AN EXPERIMENTAL APPROACH
JAR AU 74 VOL: 12 PG:317 - 329 :: ANOVA :LAB. :OTH.BEH. :REL.COSTS

BEDFORD,NM CIT: 0.00
THE NATURE OF FUTURE ACCOUNTING THEORY
TAR JA 67 VOL: 42 PG:82 - 85 :: QUAL. :INT. LOG. :THEORY :FIN.METH.

BEDFORD,NM ; SEC: IINO ,T CIT: 0.08
CONSISTENCY REEXAMINED
TAR JL 68 VOL: 43 PG:453 - 458 :: QUAL. :INT. LOG. :THEORY :OTH.FIN.ACC.

BEDFORD,NM ; FIRS: LEE ,LC CIT: 0.00
AN INFORMATION THEORY ANALYSIS OF THE ACCOUNTING PROCESS
TAR AP 69 VOL: 44 PG:256 - 275 :: ANAL. :INT. LOG. :INF.ECO./AG. :OTH.MANAG.

BEDFORD,NM ; SEC: MCKEOWN,JC CIT: 0.00
COMPARATIVE ANALYSIS OF NET REALIZABLE VALUE AND REPLACEMENT COSTING
TAR AP 72 VOL: 47 PG:333 - 338 :: QUAL. :INT. LOG. :THEORY :VALUAT.(INFL.)

BEDFORD,NM ; SEC: ZIEGLER,RE CIT: 0.08
THE CONTRIBUTIONS OF A.C. LITTLETON TO ACCOUNTING THOUGHT AND PRACTICE
TAR JL 75 VOL: 50 PG:435 - 443 :: QUAL. :SEC. :THEORY :FIN.METH.

BEECHY,TH CIT: 0.00
QUASI-DEBT ANALYSIS OF FINANCIAL LEASES
TAR AP 69 VOL: 44 PG:375 - 381 :: QUAL. :INT. LOG. :N/A :LEASES

BEEDLES,W ; FIRS: SMITH ,DB ; SEC: STETTLER,HF CIT: 0.00
AN INVESTIGATION OF THE INFORMATION CONTENT OF FOREIGN SENSITIVE PAYMENT
   DISCLOSURES
JAE AG 84 VOL: 6 PG:153 - 162 :: REGRESS. :PRIM. :EMH :N/A

BEIDLEMAN,CR CIT: 0.62
INCOME SMOOTHING: THE ROLE OF MANAGEMENT
TAR OC 73 VOL: 48 PG:653 - 667 :: REGRESS. :PRIM. :TIME SER. :FIN.METH.

BEJA ,A ; SEC: AHARONI,Y CIT: 0.00
SOME ASPECTS OF CONVENTIONAL ACCOUNTING PROFITS IN AN INFLATIONARY ENVIRONMENT
JAR AU 77 VOL: 15 PG:169 - 178 :: ANAL. :INT. LOG. :THEORY :VALUAT.(INFL.)

BELKAOUI,A CIT: 0.55
LINGUISTIC RELATIVITY IN ACCOUNTING
AOS 02 78 VOL: 3 PG:97 - 104 :: QUAL. :INT. LOG. :OTH. :N/A

BELKAOUI,A CIT: 0.33
THE INTERPROFESSIONAL LINGUISTIC COMMUNICATION OF ACCOUNTING CONCEPTS: AN
   EXPERIMENT IN SOCIOLINGUISTICS
JAR AU 80 VOL: 18 PG:362 - 374 :: REGRESS. :SURV. :OTH.BEH. :FIN.METH.

BELKAOUI,A CIT: 0.33
THE IMPACT OF SOCIO-ECONOMIC ACCOUNTING STATEMENTS ON THE INVESTMENT
   DECISION: AN EMPIRICAL STUDY
AOS 03 80 VOL: 5 PG:263 - 284 :: ANOVA :LAB. :OTH.BEH. :HRA

BELKAOUI,A CIT: 0.00
THE RELATIONSHIP BETWEEN SELF-DISCLOSURE STYLE AND ATTITUDES TO
   RESPONSIBILITY ACCOUNTING
AOS 04 81 VOL: 6 PG:281 - 290 :: OTH.QUANT. :SURV. :OTH.BEH. :RESP.ACC.

BELL ,J ; FIRS: LEWIS ,BL CIT: 0.00
DECISIONS INVOLVING SEQUENTIAL EVENTS: REPLICATIONS AND EXTENSIONS
JAR SP 85 VOL: 23 PG:228 - 239 :: REGRESS. :LAB. :HIPS :INFO.STRUC.

BELL ,TB CIT: 1.00
MARKET REACTION TO RESERVE RECOGNITION ACCOUNTING
JAR SP 83 VOL: 21 PG:1 - 17 :: REGRESS. :PRIM. :EMH :OIL & GAS

BELL ,TB ; FIRS: MCKEE ,AJ ; THIR: BOATSMAN,JR CIT: 0.40
MANAGEMENT PREFERENCES OVER ACCOUNTING STANDARDS: A REPLICATION AND
   ADDITIONAL TESTS
TAR OC 84 VOL: 59 PG:647 - 659 :: OTH.QUANT. :PRIM. :INSTIT. :FASB SUBM.

BENBASAT,I ; SEC: DEXTER,AS CIT: 0.90
VALUE AND EVENTS APPROACHES TO ACCOUNTING: AN EXPERIMENTAL EVALUATION
TAR OC 79 VOL: 54 PG:735 - 749 :: ANOVA :LAB. :HIPS :INFO.STRUC.

BENBASAT,I ; SEC: DEXTER,AS CIT: 0.29
INDIVIDUAL DIFFERENCES IN THE USE OF DECISION SUPPORT AIDS
JAR SP 82 VOL: 20 PG:1 - 11 :: ANOVA :LAB. :HIPS :DEC.AIDS

BENISHAY,H CIT: 0.15
MANAGERIAL CONTROLS OF ACCOUNTS RECEIVABLE: A DETERMINISTIC APPROACH
JAR SP 65 VOL: 3 PG:114 - 132 :: ANAL. :INT. LOG. :THEORY :OTH.C/A

BENISHAY,H CIT: 0.00
A FORTH-DEGREE POLYNOMIAL UTILITY FUNCTION AND ITS IMPLICATIONS FOR INVESTOR'
   RESPONSES TOWARD FOUR MOMENTS OF THE WEALTH DISTRIBUTION
JAA SU 87 VOL: 2 PG:203 - 238 :: DES.STAT. :INT. LOG. :INF.ECO./AG. :METHOD.

BENJAMIN,JJ ; SEC: GROSSMAN,SD ; THIR: WIGGIN,CE CIT: 0.00
THE IMPACT OF FOREIGN CURRENCY TRANSLATION ON REPORTING DURING THE PHASE-IN
   OF SFAS NO.52
JAA SU 86 VOL: 1 PG:177 - 184 :: REGRESS. :PRIM. :THEORY :FOR.CUR.

BENKE ,RL ; SEC: RHODE ,JG CIT: 0.22
THE JOB SATISFACTION OF HIGHER LEVEL EMPLOYEES IN LARGE CERTIFIED PUBLIC
   ACCOUNTING FIRMS
AOS 02 80 VOL: 5 PG:187 - 202 :: OTH.QUANT. :SURV. :OTH.BEH. :ORG.

BENNINGER,LJ CIT: 0.00
ACCOUNTING THEORY AND COST ACCOUNTING
TAR JL 65 VOL: 40 PG:547 - 557 :: QUAL. :INT. LOG. :THEORY :MANAG.

BENSTON,GJ CIT: 0.54
THE ROLE OF THE FIRM'S ACCOUNTING SYSTEM FOR MOTIVATION
TAR AP 63 VOL: 38 PG:347 - 354 :: QUAL. :INT. LOG. :OTH.BEH. :BUDG.& PLAN.

BENSTON,GJ CIT: 0.23
MULTIPLE REGRESSION ANALYSIS OF COST BEHAVIOR
TAR OC 66 VOL: 41 PG:657 - 672 :: REGRESS. :INT. LOG. :TIME SER. :BUDG.& PLAN.

BENSTON,GJ CIT: 0.38
PUBLISHED CORPORATE ACCOUNTING DATA AND STOCK PRICES
JAR ST 67 VOL: 5 PG:1 - 54 :: REGRESS. :PRIM. :EMH :FIN.METH.

BENSTON,GJ CIT: 0.62
THE VALUE OF THE SEC'S ACCOUNTING DISCLOSURE REQUIREMENTS
TAR JL 69 VOL: 44 PG:515 - 532 :: ANAL. :PRIM. :INSTIT. :INFO.STRUC.

BENSTON,GJ CIT: 0.00
PUBLIC (U.S.) COMPARED TO PRIVATE (U.K.) REGULATION OF CORPORATE FINANCIAL
   DISCLOSURE
TAR JL 76 VOL: 51 PG:483 - 498 :: QUAL. :INT. LOG. :INSTIT. :DEC.AIDS

BENSTON,GJ ; SEC: KRASNEY,MA CIT: 0.45
DAAM: THE DEMAND FOR ALTERNATIVE ACCOUNTING MEASUREMENTS
JAR ST 78 VOL: 16 PG:1 - 30 :: REGRESS. :SURV. :OTH.STAT. :VALUAT.(INFL.)

BENSTON,GJ CIT: 0.14
ACCOUNTING AND CORPORATE ACCOUNTABILITY
AOS 02 82 VOL: 7 PG:87 - 106 :: QUAL. :SURV. :THEORY :HRA

BENSTON,GJ CIT: 0.75
THE SELF-SERVING MANAGEMENT HYPOTHESIS: SOME EVIDENCE
JAE AP 85 VOL: 7 PG:67 - 84 :: DES.STAT. :PRIM. :THEORY :EXEC.COMP.

BERANEK,W CIT: 0.00
A NOTE ON THE EQUIVALENCE OF CERTAIN CAPITAL BUDGETING CRITERIA
TAR OC 64 VOL: 39 PG:914 - 916 :: ANAL. :INT. LOG. :N/A :CAP.BUDG.

BERG ,KB ; SEC: MUELLER,FJ CIT: 0.00
ACCOUNTING FOR INVESTMENT CREDITS
TAR JL 63 VOL: 38 PG:554 - 561 :: QUAL. :INT. LOG. :THEORY :TAXES

BERKOW,WF CIT: 0.00
NEED FOR ENGINEERING INFLUENCE UPON ACCOUNTING PROCEDURE
TAR AP 64 VOL: 39 PG:377 - 386 :: QUAL. :INT. LOG. :N/A :REL.COSTS

BERKOWITZ,B ; FIRS: BRANCH,B CIT: 0.00
THE PREDICTIVE ACCURACY OF THE BUSINESS WEEK EARNINGS FORECASTS
JAA SP 81 VOL: 4 PG:215 - 219 :: REGRESS. :SEC. :OTH.STAT. :FOREC.

BERNARD,VL CIT: 0.00
THE USE OF MARKET DATA AND ACCOUNTING DATA IN HEDGING AGAINST CONSUMER PRICE
   INFLATION
JAR AU 84 VOL: 22 PG:445 - 466 :: REGRESS. :PRIM. :HIPS :VALUAT.(INFL.)

BERNARD,VL ; SEC: RULAND,RG CIT: 0.00
THE INCREMENTAL INFORMATION CONTENT OF HISTORICAL COST AND CURRENT COST
   INCOME NUMBERS: TIME-SERIES ANALYSES FOR 1962-1980
TAR OC 87 VOL: 62 PG:707 - 722 :: REGRESS. :PRIM. :EMH :VALUAT.(INFL.)

BERNARD,VL CIT: 2.50
CROSS-SECTIONAL DEPENDENCE AND PROBLEMS IN INFERENCE IN MARKET-BASED
   ACCOUNTING RESEARCH
JAR SP 87 VOL: 25 PG:1 - 48 :: REGRESS. :PRIM. :EMH :METHOD.

BERNHARDT,I ; SEC: COPELAND,RM CIT: 0.15
SOME PROBLEMS IN APPLYING AN INFORMATION THEORY APPROACH TO ACCOUNTING
   AGGREGATION
JAR SP 70 VOL: 8 PG:95 - 98 :: QUAL. :INT. LOG. :INF.ECO./AG. :INFO.STRUC.

BERNSTEIN,LA CIT: 0.38
THE CONCEPT OF MATERIALITY
TAR JA 67 VOL: 42 PG:86 - 95 :: DES.STAT. :INT. LOG. :THEORY :MAT.

BERRY ,AJ ; FIRS: OTLEY ,DT CIT: 1.22
CONTROL, ORGANIZATION AND ACCOUNTING
AOS 02 80 VOL: 5 PG:231 - 246 :: QUAL. :INT. LOG. :OTH.BEH. :N/A

BERRY ,AJ ; SEC: CAPPS ,T ; THIR: COOPER,D ; FOUR: FERGUSON,P ; FIFT: HOPPER,T
; SIX: LOWE ,EA CIT: 3.50
MANAGEMENT CONTROL IN AN AREA OF THE NCB: RATIONALES OF ACCOUNTING PRACTICES
   IN A PUBLIC ENTERPRISE
AOS 01 85 VOL: 10 PG:3 - 28 :: REGRESS. :FIELD :OTH.BEH. :MANAG.

BERRY ,LE ; SEC: HARWOOD,GB ; THIR: KATZ ,JL CIT: 0.00
PERFORMANCE OF AUDITING PROCEDURES BY GOVERNMENTAL AUDITORS: SOME PRELIMINARY
   EVIDENCE
TAR JA 87 VOL: 62 PG:14 - 28 :: DES.STAT. :SURV. :OTH.STAT. :AUD.

BERRYMAN,RG ; FIRS: COGLITORE,F CIT: 0.00
ANALYTICAL PROCEDURES: A DEFENSIVE NECESSITY
AUD SP 88 VOL: 07 PG:150 - 163 :: REGRESS. :SIM. :THEORY :ANAL.REV.

BHAGAT,S ; FIRS: BRICKLEY,JA ; THIR: LEASE ,RC CIT: 0.75
THE IMPACT OF LONG-RANGE MANAGERIAL COMPENSATION PLANS ON SHAREHOLDER WEALTH
JAE AP 85 VOL: 7 PG:115 - 130 :: REGRESS. :PRIM. :EMH :EXEC.COMP.

BIDDLE,GC CIT: 1.56
ACCOUNTING METHODS AND MANAGEMENT DECISIONS: THE CASE OF INVENTORY COSTING
   AND INVENTORY POLICY
JAR ST 80 VOL: 18 PG:235 - 280 :: NON-PAR. :PRIM. :OTH. :INV.

BIDDLE,GC ; FIRS: JOYCE ,EJ CIT: 1.13
ARE AUDITORS' JUDGMENTS SUFFICIENTLY REGRESSIVE?
JAR AU 81 VOL: 19 PG:323 - 349 :: ANOVA :LAB. :HIPS :PLAN.

BIDDLE,GC ; FIRS: JOYCE ,EJ CIT: 1.63
ANCHORING AND ADJUSTMENT IN PROBABILISTIC INFERENCE IN AUDITING
JAR SP 81 VOL: 19 PG:120 - 145 :: ANOVA :LAB. :OTH.BEH. :DEC.AIDS

BIDDLE,GC ; SEC: LINDAHL,FW CIT: 2.43
STOCK PRICE REACTIONS TO LIFO ADOPTIONS: THE ASSOCIATION BETWEEN EXCESS
    RETURNS AND LIFO TAX SAVINGS
JAR AU 82 VOL: 20 PG:551 - 588 :: MIXED :PRIM. :EMH :INV.

BIDDLE,GC ; SEC: MARTIN,RK CIT: 0.25
INFLATION, TAXES, AND OPTIMAL INVENTORY POLICIES
JAR SP 85 VOL: 23 PG:57 - 83 :: REGRESS. :SIM. :OTH.STAT. :INV.

BIDDLE,GC ; SEC: RICKS ,WE CIT: 1.00
ANALYST FORECAST ERRORS AND STOCK PRICE BEHAVIOR NEAR THE EARNINGS
    ANNOUNCEMENT DATES OF LIFO ADOPTERS
JAR AU 88 VOL: 26 PG:169 - 194 :: REGRESS. :PRIM. :EMH :INV.

BIDWELL III,CM ; SEC: RIDDLE JR,JR CIT: 0.00
MARKET INEFFICIENCIES - OPPORTUNITIES FOR PROFITS
JAA SP 81 VOL: 4 PG:198 - 214 :: REGRESS. :PRIM. :EMH :INFO.STRUC.

BIERMAN JR,H CIT: 0.00
A PROBLEM IN EXPENSE RECOGNITION
TAR JA 63 VOL: 38 PG:61 - 63 :: QUAL. :INT. LOG. :THEORY :N/A

BIERMAN JR,H CIT: 0.15
MEASUREMENT AND ACCOUNTING
TAR JL 63 VOL: 38 PG:501 - 507 :: QUAL. :INT. LOG. :THEORY :FIN.METH.

BIERMAN JR,H CIT: 0.00
RECORDING OBSOLESCENCE
JAR AU 64 VOL: 2 PG:229 - 235 :: MIXED :INT. LOG. :THEORY :AMOR./DEPL.

BIERMAN JR,H CIT: 0.00
MYTHS AND ACCOUNTANTS
TAR JL 65 VOL: 40 PG:541 - 546 :: QUAL. :INT. LOG. :THEORY :FIN.METH.

BIERMAN JR,H CIT: 0.08
A FURTHER STUDY OF DEPRECIATION
TAR AP 66 VOL: 41 PG:271 - 274 :: ANAL. :INT. LOG. :THEORY :PP&E / DEPR

BIERMAN JR,H ; SEC: SMIDT ,S CIT: 0.00
ACCOUNTING FOR DEBT AND COSTS OF LIQUIDITY UNDER CONDITIONS OF UNCERTAINTY
JAR AU 67 VOL: 5 PG:144 - 153 :: ANAL. :INT. LOG. :THEORY :LTD

BIERMAN JR,H CIT: 0.00
INVENTORY VALUATION: THE USE OF MARKET PRICES
TAR OC 67 VOL: 42 PG:731 - 737 :: ANAL. :INT. LOG. :THEORY :INV.

BIERMAN JR,H ; SEC: LIU ,E CIT: 0.00
THE COMPUTATION OF EARNINGS PER SHARE
TAR JA 68 VOL: 43 PG:62 - 67 :: QUAL. :INT. LOG. :THEORY :PENS.

BIERMAN JR,H CIT: 0.00
THE TERM STRUCTURE OF INTEREST RATES AND ACCOUNTING FOR DEBT
TAR OC 68 VOL: 43 PG:657 - 661 :: ANAL. :INT. LOG. :THEORY :LTD

BIERMAN JR,H ; SEC: DAVIDSON,S CIT: 0.00
THE INCOME CONCEPT-VALUE-INCREMENT OR EARNINGS PREDICTOR
TAR AP 69 VOL: 44 PG:239 - 246 :: QUAL. :INT. LOG. :THEORY :FIN.METH.

BIERMAN JR,H CIT: 0.00
ACCELERATED DEPRECIATION AND RATE REGULATION
TAR JA 69 VOL: 44 PG:65 - 78 :: QUAL. :INT. LOG. :N/A :PP&E / DEPR

BIERMAN JR,H CIT: 0.00
INVESTMENT DECISIONS AND TAXES
TAR OC 70 VOL: 45 PG:690 - 697 :: ANAL. :INT. LOG. :N/A :TAX PLNG.

BIERMAN JR,H CIT: 0.00
DISCOUNTED CASH FLOWS, PRICE LEVEL ADJUSTMENTS AND EXPECTATIONS
TAR OC 71 VOL: 46 PG:693 - 700 :: ANAL. :INT. LOG. :THEORY :VALUAT.(INFL.)

BIERMAN JR,H CIT: 0.08
REGULATION, IMPLIED REVENUE REQUIREMENTS, AND METHOD DEPRECIATION
TAR JL 74 VOL: 49 PG:448 - 454 :: ANAL. :INT. LOG. :N/A :PP&E / DEPR

BIERMAN JR,H CIT: 0.00
COMMON STOCK EQUIVALENTS, EARNINGS PER SHARE AND STOCK VALUATION
JAA WI 86 VOL: 1 PG:62 - 70 :: DES.STAT. :INT. LOG. :THEORY :LTD

BIERMAN,H CIT: 0.00
DEPRECIATION AND INCOME TAX ALLOCATION
JAA SP 85 VOL: 8 PG:184 - 194 :: DES.STAT. :INT. LOG. :THEORY :TAXES

BIGGS ,SF ; SEC: MOCK ,TJ CIT: 0.83
AN INVESTIGATION OF AUDITOR DECISION PROCESSES IN THE EVALUATION OF INTERNAL
   CONTROLS AND AUDIT SCOPE DECISIONS
JAR SP 83 VOL: 21 PG:234 - 255 :: DES.STAT. :LAB. :HIPS :INT.CONT.

BIGGS ,SF ; SEC: WILD ,JJ CIT: 0.40
A NOTE ON THE PRACTICE OF ANALYTICAL REVIEW
AUD SP 84 VOL: 3 PG:68 - 79 :: CORR. :SURV. :OTH.STAT. :ANAL.REV.

BIGGS ,SF CIT: 0.40
FINANCIAL ANALYSTS' INFORMATION SEARCH IN THE ASSESSMENT OF CORPORATE EARNING
   POWER
AOS 34 84 VOL: 9 PG:313 - 323 :: DES.STAT. :LAB. :HIPS :N/A

BIGGS ,SF ; SEC: WILD ,JJ CIT: 0.25
AN INVESTIGATION OF AUDITOR JUDGMENT IN ANALYTICAL REVIEW
TAR OC 85 VOL: 60 PG:607 - 633 :: REGRESS. :LAB. :HIPS :ANAL.REV.

BIGGS ,SF ; SEC: MESSIER JR,WF ; THIR: HANSEN,JV CIT: 0.00
A DESCRIPTIVE ANALYSIS OF COMPUTER AUDIT SPECIALISTS' DECISION MAKING   G
   BEHAVIOR IN ADVANCED COMPUTER ENVIRONMENTS
AUD SP 87 VOL: 6 PG:1 - 21 :: REGRESS. :LAB. :HIPS :EDP AUD.

BIGGS ,SF ; SEC: MOCK ,TJ ; THIR: WATKINS,PR CIT: 0.00
AUDITOR'S USE OF ANALYTICAL REVIEW IN AUDIT PROGRAM DESIGN
TAR JA 88 VOL: 63 PG:148 - 162 :: REGRESS. :LAB. :OTH.BEH. :ANAL.REV.

BILDERSEE,JS CIT: 0.38
THE ASSOCIATION BETWEEN A MARKET-DETERMINED MEASURE OF RISK AND ALTERNATIVE
   MEASURES OF RISK
TAR JA 75 VOL: 50 PG:81 - 98 :: REGRESS. :PRIM. :EMH :FIN.METH.

BILDERSEE,JS ; SEC: KAHN ,N CIT: 0.00
A PRELIMINARY TEST OF THE PRESENCE OF WINDOW DRESSING: EVIDENCE FROM
   INSTITUTIONAL STOCK TRADING
JAA SU 87 VOL: 2 PG:239 - 256 :: REGRESS. :PRIM. :OTH.STAT. :INFO.STRUC.

BILLERA,LJ ; SEC: HEATH ,DC ; THIR: VERRECCHIA,RE CIT: 0.25
A UNIQUE PROCEDURE FOR ALLOCATING COMMON COSTS FROM A PRODUCTION PROCESS
JAR SP 81 VOL: 19 PG:185 - 196 :: ANAL. :INT. LOG. :INF.ECO./AG. :N/A

BINDER,JJ CIT: 0.00
ON THE USE OF THE MULTIVARIATE REGRESSION MODEL IN EVENT STUDIES
JAR SP 85 VOL: 23 PG:370 - 383 :: REGRESS. :PRIM. :EMH :METHOD.

BIRD ,FA ; SEC: DAVIDSON,LF ; THIR: SMITH ,CH CIT: 0.15
PERCEPTIONS OF EXTERNAL ACCOUNTING TRANSFERS UNDER ENTITY AND PROPRIETARY
  THEORY
TAR AP 74 VOL: 49 PG:233 - 244 :: QUAL. :INT. LOG. :THEORY :FIN.METH.

BIRD ,PA CIT: 0.00
TAX INCENTIVES TO CAPITAL INVESTMENT
JAR SP 65 VOL: 3 PG:1 - 11 :: QUAL. :INT. LOG. :THEORY :INT.DIFF.

BIRNBERG,JG CIT: 0.00
AN INFORMATION ORIENTED APPROACH TO THE PRESENTATION OF COMMON SHAREHOLDERS'
  EQUITY
TAR OC 64 VOL: 39 PG:963 - 971 :: QUAL. :INT. LOG. :N/A :OTH.FIN.ACC.

BIRNBERG,JG CIT: 0.08
THE REPORTING OF EXECUTORY CONTRACTS
TAR OC 65 VOL: 40 PG:814 - 820 :: QUAL. :INT. LOG. :THEORY :INFO.STRUC.

BIRNBERG,JG ; SEC: NATH ,R CIT: 0.23
IMPLICATIONS OF BEHAVIOURAL SCIENCE FOR MANAGERIAL ACCOUNTING
TAR JL 67 VOL: 42 PG:468 - 479 :: QUAL. :SEC. :OTH.BEH. :MANAG.

BIRNBERG,JG ; FIRS: DOPUCH,N ; THIR: DEMSKI,JS CIT: 0.15
AN EXTENSION OF STANDARD COST VARIANCE ANALYSIS
TAR JL 67 VOL: 42 PG:526 - 536 :: ANAL. :INT. LOG. :OTH.STAT. :VAR.

BIRNBERG,JG ; SEC: NATH ,R CIT: 0.54
LABORATORY EXPERIMENTATION IN ACCOUNTING RESEARCH
TAR JA 68 VOL: 43 PG:38 - 45 :: QUAL. :INT. LOG. :N/A :METHOD.

BIRNBERG,JG ; SEC: GANDHI,NM CIT: 0.08
TOWARD DEFINING THE ACCOUNTANT'S ROLE IN THE EVALUATION OF SOCIAL PROGRAMS
AOS 01 76 VOL: 1 PG:5 - 10 :: QUAL. :INT. LOG. :THEORY :HRA

BIRNBERG,JG ; SEC: FRIEZE,IH ; THIR: SHIELDS,MD CIT: 0.33
THE ROLE OF ATTRIBUTION THEORY IN CONTROL SYSTEMS
AOS 03 77 VOL: 2 PG:189 - 200 :: QUAL. :INT. LOG. :OTH.BEH. :MANAG.

BIRNBERG,JG ; FIRS: MCGHEE,W ; SEC: SHIELDS,MD CIT: 1.00
THE EFFECTS OF PERSONALITY ON A SUBJECT'S INFORMATION PROCESSING
TAR JL 78 VOL: 53 PG:681 - 697 :: ANOVA :LAB. :HIPS :OTH.MANAG.

BIRNBERG,JG CIT: 0.00
THE ROLE OF ACCOUNTING IN FINANCIAL DISCLOSURE
AOS 01 80 VOL: 5 PG:71 - 80 :: QUAL. :INT. LOG. :HIPS :N/A

BIRNBERG,JG ; FIRS: SHIELDS,MD ; THIR: FRIEZE,IH CIT: 0.50
ATTRIBUTIONS, COGNITIVE PROCESSES AND CONTROL SYSTEMS
AOS 01 81 VOL: 6 PG:69 - 96 :: ANOVA :LAB. :OTH.BEH. :BUDG.& PLAN.

BIRNBERG,JG ; SEC: TUROPOLEC,L ; THIR: YOUNG ,SM CIT: 1.83
THE ORGANIZATIONAL CONTEXT OF ACCOUNTING
AOS 23 83 VOL: 8 PG:111 - 130 :: QUAL. :SEC. :OTH.BEH. :REL.COSTS

BIRNBERG,JG ; SEC: SHIELDS,MD CIT: 0.20
THE ROLE OF ATTENTION AND MEMORY IN ACCOUNTING DECISIONS
AOS 34 84 VOL: 9 PG:365 - 382 :: QUAL. :INT. LOG. :HIPS :N/A

BIRNBERG,JG ; FIRS: WILNER,N CIT: 0.67
METHODOLOGICAL PROBLEMS IN FUNCTIONAL FIXATION RESEARCH: CRITICISM AND
    SUGGESTIONS
AOS 01 86 VOL: 11 PG:71 - 82 :: REGRESS. :INT. LOG. :HIPS :METHOD.

BIRNBERG,JG ; SEC: SNODGRASS,C CIT: 0.00
CULTURE AND CONTROL: A FIELD STUDY
AOS 05 88 VOL: 13 PG:447 - 464 :: REGRESS. :SURV. :OTH.BEH. :INT.DIFF.

BJORN-ANDERSEN,N ; SEC: PEDERSEN,PH CIT: 0.00
COMPUTER FACILITATED CHANGES IN THE MANAGEMENT POWER STRUCTURE
AOS 02 80 VOL: 5 PG:203 - 216 :: QUAL. :CASE :OTH.BEH. :N/A

BLACKBURN,JO ; FIRS: DICKENS,RL CIT: 0.08
HOLDING GAINS ON FIXED ASSETS: AN ELEMENT OF BUSINESS INCOME?
TAR AP 64 VOL: 39 PG:312 - 329 :: ANAL. :INT. LOG. :THEORY :VALUAT.(INFL.)

BLACKETT,LA ; FIRS: AIKEN ,ME ; THIR: ISAACS,G CIT: 0.08
MODELING BEHAVIOURAL INTERDEPENDENCIES FOR STEWARDSHIP REPORTING
TAR JL 75 VOL: 50 PG:544 - 562 :: ANAL. :INT. LOG. :THEORY :OTH.MANAG.

BLAKELY,EJ ; SEC: KNUTSON,PH CIT: 0.00
LIFO OR LOFI - WHICH?
TAR JA 63 VOL: 38 PG:75 - 86 :: QUAL. :INT. LOG. :THEORY :N/A

BLANCHARD,GA ; SEC: CHOW ,CW ; THIR: NOREEN,EW CIT: 0.00
INFORMATION ASYMMETRY, INCENTIVE SCHEMES, AND INFORMATION BIASING: THE CASE
    OF HOSPITAL BUDGETING UNDER RATE REGULATION
TAR JA 86 VOL: 61 PG:1 - 15 :: REGRESS. :PRIM. :N/A :BUDG.& PLAN.

BLOCHER,E CIT: 0.30
PERFORMANCE EFFECTS OF DIFFERENT AUDIT STAFF ASSIGNMENT STRATEGIES
TAR JL 79 VOL: 54 PG:563 - 573 :: DES.STAT. :CASE :OTH.BEH. :ORG.

BLOCHER,E ; SEC: ESPOSITO,RS ; THIR: WILLINGHAM,JJ CIT: 0.17
AUDITOR'S ANALYTICAL REVIEW JUDGMENTS FOR PAYROLL EXPENSE
AUD AU 83 VOL: 3 PG:75 - 91 :: DES.STAT. :LAB. :OTH.BEH. :ANAL.REV.

BLOCHER,E ; SEC: BYLINSKI,JH CIT: 0.00
THE INFLUENCE OF SAMPLE CHARACTERISTICS IN SAMPLE EVALUATION
AUD AU 85 VOL: 5 PG:79 - 90 :: REGRESS. :LAB. :OTH.BEH. :SAMP.

BLOCHER,E ; SEC: MOFFIE,RP ; THIR: ZMUD ,RW CIT: 0.00
REPORT FORMAT AND TASK COMPLEXITY: INTERACTION IN RISK JUDGMENTS
AOS 06 86 VOL: 11 PG:457 - 470 :: REGRESS. :LAB. :HIPS :INFO.STRUC.

BLOCHER,E ; SEC: COOPER,JC CIT: 0.00
A STUDY OF AUDITORS' ANALYTICAL REVIEW PERFORMANCE
AUD SP 88 VOL: 07 PG:1 - 28 :: REGRESS. :LAB. :OTH.BEH. :ANAL.REV.

BLOOM ,R ; SEC: ELGERS,PT ; THIR: MURRAY,D CIT: 0.20
FUNCTIONAL FIXATION IN PRODUCT PRICING: A COMPARISON OF INDIVIDUALS AND GROUPS
AOS 01 84 VOL: 9 PG:1 - 11 :: MIXED :LAB. :HIPS :PP&E / DEPR

BLUM ,M CIT: 0.38
FAILING COMPANY DISCRIMINANT ANALYSIS
JAR SP 74 VOL: 12 PG:1 - 25 :: OTH.QUANT. :PRIM. :OTH.STAT. :BUS.COMB.

BOATSMAN,JR ; FIRS: PATZ ,DH CIT: 0.15
ACCOUNTING PRINCIPLE FORMULATION IN AN EFFICIENT MARKETS ENVIRONMENT
JAR AU 72 VOL: 10 PG:392 - 403 :: ANOVA :PRIM. :EMH :OIL & GAS

BOATSMAN,JR ; SEC: ROBERTSON,JC CIT: 1.15
POLICY-CAPTURING ON SELECTED MATERIALITY JUDGMENTS
TAR AP 74 VOL: 49 PG:342 - 352 :: OTH.QUANT. :LAB. :OTH.STAT. :OTH.FIN.ACC.

BOATSMAN,JR ; FIRS: DAVIS ,DW ; THIR: BASKIN,EF CIT: 0.09
ON GENERALIZING STOCK MARKET RESEARCH TO A BROADER CLASS OF MARKETS
TAR JA 78 VOL: 53 PG:1 - 10 :: MIXED :PRIM. :EMH :FIN.METH.

BOATSMAN,JR ; FIRS: GHEYARA,K CIT: 1.67
MARKET REACTION TO THE 1976 REPLACEMENT COST DISCLOSURES
JAE AG 80 VOL: 2 PG:107 - 125 :: MIXED :PRIM. :EMH :VALUAT.(INFL.)

BOATSMAN,JR ; SEC: BASKIN,EF CIT: 0.13
ASSET VALUATION WITH INCOMPLETE MARKETS
TAR JA 81 VOL: 56 PG:38 - 53 :: ANAL. :INT. LOG. :EMH :FIN.METH.

BOATSMAN,JR ; SEC: DOWELL,CD ; THIR: KIMBRELL,JI CIT: 0.00
VALUING STOCK USED FOR A BUSINESS COMBINATION
JAA AU 84 VOL: 8 PG:35 - 43 :: ANAL. :INT. LOG. :OTH.STAT. :BUS.COMB.

BOATSMAN,JR ; FIRS: MCKEE ,AJ ; SEC: BELL ,TB CIT: 0.40
MANAGEMENT PREFERENCES OVER ACCOUNTING STANDARDS: A REPLICATION AND
    ADDITIONAL TESTS
TAR OC 84 VOL: 59 PG:647 - 659 :: OTH.QUANT. :PRIM. :INSTIT. :FASB SUBM.

BODNAR,G CIT: 0.38
RELIABILITY MODELING OF INTERNAL CONTROL SYSTEMS
TAR OC 75 VOL: 50 PG:747 - 757 :: ANAL. :INT. LOG. :OTH.STAT. :INT.CONT.

BODNAR,G ; SEC: LUSK ,EJ CIT: 0.00
MOTIVATIONAL CONSIDERATIONS IN COST ALLOCATION SYSTEMS: A CONDITIONING THEORY
    APPROACH
TAR OC 77 VOL: 52 PG:857 - 868 :: ANAL. :INT. LOG. :OTH.BEH. :OVER.ALLOC.

BOE ,WJ ; FIRS: BAILEY JR,AD CIT: 0.15
GOAL AND RESOURCE TRANSFERS IN THE MULTIGOAL ORGANIZATION
TAR JL 76 VOL: 51 PG:559 - 573 :: QUAL. :INT. LOG. :MATH.PROG. :TRANS.PRIC.

BOER ,G CIT: 0.00
REPLACEMENT COST: A HISTORICAL LOOK
TAR JA 66 VOL: 41 PG:92 - 97 :: QUAL. :INT. LOG. :HIST. :VALUAT.(INFL.)

BOGART,FO CIT: 0.00
TAX CONSIDERATIONS IN PARTNERSHIP AGREEMENTS
TAR OC 65 VOL: 40 PG:834 - 838 :: QUAL. :INT. LOG. :N/A :TAXES

BOLAND,RJ CIT: 1.20
CONTROL, CAUSALITY AND INFORMATION SYSTEM REQUIREMENTS
AOS 04 79 VOL: 4 PG:259 - 272 :: QUAL. :INT. LOG. :OTH. :MANAG.

BOLAND,RJ CIT: 0.25
A STUDY IN SYSTEM DESIGN: C. WEST CHURCHMAN AND CHRIS ARGYRIS
AOS 02 81 VOL: 6 PG:109 - 118 :: QUAL. :INT. LOG. :OTH. :N/A

BOLAND,RJ ; SEC: PONDY ,LR CIT: 2.33
ACCOUNTING IN ORGANIZATIONS: A UNION OF NATURAL AND RATIONAL PERSPECTIVES
AOS 23 83 VOL: 8 PG:223 - 234 :: QUAL. :CASE :OTH. :OTH.MANAG.

BOLAND,RJ ; SEC: PONDY ,LR CIT: 0.67
THE MICRO DYNAMICS OF A BUDGET-CUTTING PROCESS: MODES, MODELS AND STRUCTURE
AOS 45 86 VOL: 11 PG:403 - 422 :: REGRESS. :FIELD :HIPS :BUDG.& PLAN.

BOLCE ,WJ ; FIRS: HEARD ,JE CIT: 0.00
THE POLITICAL SIGNIFICANCE OF CORPORATE SOCIAL REPORTING IN THE U.S.A.
AOS 03 81 VOL: 6 PG:247 - 254 :: QUAL. :INT. LOG. :OTH. :HRA

BOLLOM,WJ ; SEC: WEYGANDT,JJ CIT: 0.08
AN EXAMINATION OF SOME INTERIM REPORTING THEORIES FOR A SEASONAL BUSINESS
TAR JA 72 VOL: 47 PG:75 - 84 :: QUAL. :SEC. :THEORY :INT.REP.

BOLLOM,WJ CIT: 0.08
TOWARDS A THEORY OF INTERIM REPORTING FOR A SEASONAL BUSINESS: A BEHAVIOURAL
   APPROACH
TAR JA 73 VOL: 48 PG:12 - 22 :: ANOVA :LAB. :THEORY :INT.REP.

BOOCKHOLDT,JL ; FIRS: FINLEY,DR CIT: 0.00
A CONTINUOUS CONSTRAINED OPTIMIZATION MODEL FOR AUDIT SAMPLING
AUD SP 87 VOL: 6 PG:22 - 39 :: DES.STAT. :SIM. :OTH.STAT. :SAMP.

BOOKER,J ; FIRS: ANDERSON,HM ; SEC: GIESE ,J CIT: 0.15
SOME PROPOSITIONS ABOUT AUDITING
TAR JL 70 VOL: 45 PG:524 - 531 :: QUAL. :INT. LOG. :INSTIT. :AUD.

BORITZ,JE ; SEC: BROCA ,DS CIT: 0.00
SCHEDULING INTERNAL AUDIT ACTIVITIES
AUD AU 86 VOL: 6 PG:1 - 19 :: DES.STAT. :SIM. :OTH.STAT. :INT.AUD.

BORITZ,JE CIT: 0.00
THE EFFECT OF RESEARCH METHOD ON AUDIT PLANNING AND REVIEW JUDGMENTS
JAR AU 86 VOL: 24 PG:335 - 348 :: REGRESS. :LAB. :HIPS :PLAN.

BOTTS ,RR CIT: 0.00
INTEREST AND THE TRUTH-IN-LENDING BILL
TAR OC 63 VOL: 38 PG:789 - 795 :: QUAL. :INT. LOG. :THEORY :N/A

BOUGEN,P ; FIRS: OGDEN ,S CIT: 0.25
A RADICAL PERSPECTIVE ON THE DISCLOSURE OF ACCOUNTING INFORMATION TO TRADE
   UNIONS
AOS 02 85 VOL: 10 PG:211 - 226 :: DES.STAT. :INT. LOG. :INSTIT. :METHOD.

BOURN ,AM CIT: 0.00
TRAINING FOR THE ACCOUNTANCY PROFESSION IN ENGLAND AND WALES
JAR AU 66 VOL: 4 PG:213 - 223 :: QUAL. :INT. LOG. :OTH. :EDUC.

BOUTELL,WS CIT: 0.00
BUSINESS-ORIENTED COMPUTERS: A FRAME OF REFERENCE
TAR AP 64 VOL: 39 PG:305 - 311 :: QUAL. :INT. LOG. :N/A :OTH.MANAG.

BOUWMAN,MJ ; FIRS: FRISHKOFF,P ; SEC: FRISHKOFF,PA CIT: 0.00
USE OF ACCOUNTING DATA IN SCREENING BY FINANCIAL ANALYSTS
JAA AU 84 VOL: 8 PG:44 - 53 :: DES.STAT. :LAB. :HIPS :INFO.STRUC.

BOUWMAN,MJ CIT: 0.60
EXPERT VS. NOVICE DECISION MAKING IN ACCOUNTING: A SUMMARY
AOS 34 84 VOL: 9 PG:325 - 327 :: MIXED :LAB. :HIPS :N/A

BOUWMAN,MJ ; SEC: FRISHKOFF,PA ; THIR: FRISHKOFF,P CIT: 0.00
HOW DO THE FIN. ANALYSTS MAKE DECISIONS? A PROCESS MODEL OF THE INVESTMENT
   SCREENING DECISION
AOS 01 87 VOL: 12 PG:1 - 30 :: REGRESS. :LAB. :HIPS :OTH.FIN.ACC.

BOWEN ,EK CIT: 0.00
MATHEMATICS IN THE UNDERGRADUATE BUSINESS CURRICULUM
TAR OC 67 VOL: 42 PG:782 - 787 :: QUAL. :INT. LOG. :N/A :OTH.MANAG.

BOWEN ,RM ; SEC: NOREEN,EW ; THIR: LACEY ,JM CIT: 3.63
DETERMINANTS OF THE CORPORATE DECISION TO CAPITALIZE INTEREST
JAE AG 81 VOL: 3 PG:151 - 179 :: DES.STAT. :INT. LOG. :INF.ECO./AG. :SPEC.ITEMS

BOWEN ,RM CIT: 0.75
VALUATION OF EARNINGS COMPONENTS IN THE ELECTRIC UTILITY INDUSTRY
TAR JA 81 VOL: 56 PG:1 - 22 :: REGRESS. :PRIM. :EMH :FIN.METH.

BOWEN ,RM ; SEC: SUNDEM,GL CIT: 0.00
EDITORIAL AND PUBLICATION LAGS IN THE ACCOUNTING AND FINANCE LITERATURE
TAR OC 82 VOL: 57 PG:778 - 784 :: DES.STAT. :PRIM. :OTH. :N/A

BOWEN ,RM ; SEC: BURGSTAHLER,D ; THIR: DALEY ,LA CIT: 0.67
EVIDENCE ON THE RELATIONSHIPS BETWEEN VARIOUS EARNINGS MEASURES OF CASH FLOW
TAR OC 86 VOL: 61 PG:713 - 725 :: REGRESS. :PRIM. :OTH.STAT. :REV.REC.

BOWEN ,RM ; SEC: BURGSTAHLER,D ; THIR: DALEY ,LA CIT: 0.00
THE INCREMENTAL INFORMATION CONTENT OF ACCRUAL VERSUS CASH FLOWS
TAR OC 87 VOL: 62 PG:723 - 747 :: REGRESS. :PRIM. :EMH :SPEC.ITEMS

BOWER ,JB ; SEC: SCHLOSSER,RE CIT: 0.00
INTERNAL CONTROL - ITS TRUE NATURE
TAR AP 65 VOL: 40 PG:338 - 344 :: QUAL. :INT. LOG. :INSTIT. :INT.CONT.

BOWER ,RS ; SEC: HERRINGER,F ; THIR: WILLIAMSON,JP CIT: 0.00
LEASE EVALUATION
TAR AP 66 VOL: 41 PG:257 - 265 :: ANAL. :INT. LOG. :OTH.STAT. :REL.COSTS

BOWMAN,EH ; SEC: HAIRE ,M CIT: 0.23
SOCIAL IMPACT DISCLOSURE AND CORPORATE ANNUAL REPORTS
AOS 01 76 VOL: 1 PG:11 - 22 :: DES.STAT. :PRIM. :THEORY :HRA

BOWMAN,RG CIT: 0.22
THE DEBT EQUIVALENCE OF LEASES: AN EMPIRICAL INVESTIGATION
TAR AP 80 VOL: 55 PG:237 - 253 :: REGRESS. :PRIM. :EMH :LEASES

BOWMAN,RG CIT: 0.44
THE IMPORTANCE OF A MARKET-VALUE MEASUREMENT OF DEBT IN ASSESSING LEVERAGE
JAR SP 80 VOL: 18 PG:242 - 254 :: ANOVA :PRIM. :EMH :LTD

BOWSHER,CA CIT: 0.00
REDUCING THE FEDERAL DEFICIT: A CRITICAL CHALLENGE
JAA WI 86 VOL: 1 PG:7 - 16 :: DES.STAT. :INT. LOG. :OTH. :ORG.& ENVIR.

BRADBURY,ME ; SEC: CALDERWOOD,SC CIT: 0.00
EQUITY ACCOUNTING FOR RECIPROCAL STOCKHOLDINGS
TAR AP 88 VOL: 63 PG:330 - 347 :: DES.STAT. :INT. LOG. :THEORY :BUS.COMB.

BRADFORD,WD CIT: 0.08
PRICE-LEVEL RESTATED ACCOUNTING AND THE MEASUREMENT OF INFLATION GAINS AND
    LOSSES
TAR AP 74 VOL: 49 PG:296 - 305 :: ANAL. :INT. LOG. :THEORY :VALUAT.(INFL.)

BRADISH,RD CIT: 0.08
CORPORATE REPORTING AND THE FINANCIAL ANALYST
TAR OC 65 VOL: 40 PG:757 - 766 :: QUAL. :SURV. :INSTIT. :FIN.METH.

BRADLEY,G ; FIRS: TROTMAN,KT CIT: 0.38
ASSOCIATIONS BETWEEN SOCIAL RESPONSIBILITY DISCLOSURE AND CHARACTERISTICS OF
    COMPANIES
AOS 04 81 VOL: 6 PG:355 - 362 :: NON-PAR. :PRIM. :OTH. :HRA

BRANCH,B ; SEC: BERKOWITZ,B CIT: 0.00
THE PREDICTIVE ACCURACY OF THE BUSINESS WEEK EARNINGS FORECASTS
JAA SP 81 VOL: 4 PG:215 - 219 :: REGRESS. :SEC. :OTH.STAT. :FOREC.

BRANDI,JT ; FIRS: BROWN ,BC CIT: 0.00
SECURITY PRICE REACTIONS TO CHANGES IN FOREIGN CURRENCY TRANSLATION
    STANDARDS
JAA SU 86 VOL: 1 PG:185 - 205 :: REGRESS. :PRIM. :EMH :FOR.CUR.

BRAVENEC,LL ; SEC: EPSTEIN,MJ ; THIR: CRUMBLEY,DL CIT: 0.00
TAX IMPACT IN CORPORATE SOCIAL RESPONSIBILITY DECISIONS AND REPORTING
AOS 02 77 VOL: 2 PG:131 - 140 :: QUAL. :INT. LOG. :THEORY :HRA

BREMSER,WG CIT: 0.23
THE EARNINGS CHARACTERISTICS OF FIRMS REPORTING DISCRETIONARY ACCOUNTING
    CHANGES
TAR JL 75 VOL: 50 PG:563 - 573 :: ANOVA :PRIM. :N/A :ACC.CHNG.

BREMSER,WG ; FIRS: HECK ,JL CIT: 0.00
SIX DECADES OF THE ACCOUNTING REVIEW: A SUMMARY OF AUTHOR AND INSTITUTIONAL
    CONTRIBUTORS
TAR OC 86 VOL: 61 PG:735 - 744 :: REGRESS. :SEC. :HIST. :METHOD.

BRENNER,VC CIT: 0.31
FINANCIAL STATEMENT USERS' VIEWS OF THE DESIRABILITY OF REPORTING CURRENT
    COST INFORMATION
JAR AU 70 VOL: 8 PG:159 - 166 :: NON-PAR. :SURV. :OTH. :VALUAT.(INFL.)

BRENNER,VC ; SEC: CARMACK,CW ; THIR: WEINSTEIN,MG CIT: 0.00
AN EMPIRICAL TEST OF THE MOTIVATION-HYGIENE THEORY
JAR AU 71 VOL: 9 PG:359 - 366 :: CORR. :SURV. :OTH.BEH. :AUD.BEH.

BRICKLEY,JA ; SEC: BHAGAT,S ; THIR: LEASE ,RC CIT: 0.75
THE IMPACT OF LONG-RANGE MANAGERIAL COMPENSATION PLANS ON SHAREHOLDER WEALTH
JAE AP 85 VOL: 7 PG:115 - 130 :: REGRESS. :PRIM. :EMH :EXEC.COMP.

BRIDEN,GE ; FIRS: REBELE,JE ; SEC: HEINTZ,JA CIT: 0.00
INDEPENDENT AUDITOR SENSITIVITY TO EVIDENCE RELIABILITY
AUD AU 88 VOL: 08 PG:43 - 52 :: REGRESS. :LAB. :OTH.BEH. :JUDG.

BRIEF ,AP ; FIRS: UECKER,WC ; THIR: KINNEY JR,WR CIT: 0.25
PERCEPTION OF THE INTERNAL AND EXTERNAL AUDITOR AS A DETERRENT TO CORPORATE
    IRREGULARITIES
TAR JL 81 VOL: 56 PG:465 - 478 :: ANOVA :LAB. :OTH.BEH. :AUD.BEH.

BRIEF ,RP CIT: 0.15
NINETEENTH CENTURY ACCOUNTING ERROR
JAR SP 65 VOL: 3 PG:12 - 31 :: QUAL. :INT. LOG. :HIST. :N/A

BRIEF ,RP CIT: 0.08
A LATE NINETEENTH CENTURY CONTRIBUTION TO THE THEORY OF DEPRECIATION
JAR SP 67 VOL: 5 PG:27 - 38 :: QUAL. :SEC. :HIST. :PP&E / DEPR

BRIEF ,RP ; SEC: OWEN ,J CIT: 0.00
DEPRECIATION AND CAPITAL GAINS: A "NEW" APPROACH
TAR AP 68 VOL: 43 PG:367 - 372 :: ANAL. :INT. LOG. :THEORY :PP&E / DEPR

BRIEF ,RP ; SEC: OWEN ,J CIT: 0.00
A LEAST SQUARES ALLOCATION MODEL
JAR AU 68 VOL: 6 PG:193 - 199 :: ANAL. :INT. LOG. :MATH.PROG. :COST.ALLOC.

BRIEF ,RP CIT: 0.00
AN ECONOMETRIC ANALYSIS OF GOODWILL: SOME FINDINGS IN A SEARCH FOR VALUATION
    RULES
TAR JA 69 VOL: 44 PG:20 - 26 :: REGRESS. :PRIM. :TIME SER. :OTH. NON-C/A

BRIEF ,RP ; SEC: OWEN ,J CIT: 0.00
ON THE BIAS IN ACCOUNTING ALLOCATIONS UNDER UNCERTAINTY
JAR SP 69 VOL: 7 PG:12 - 16 :: ANAL. :INT. LOG. :OTH.STAT. :COST.ALLOC.

BRIEF ,RP ; SEC: OWEN ,J CIT: 0.15
THE ESTIMATION PROBLEM IN FINANCIAL ACCOUNTING
JAR AU 70 VOL: 8 PG:167 - 177 :: ANAL. :INT. LOG. :OTH.STAT. :PP&E / DEPR

BRIEF ,RP ; SEC: OWEN ,J CIT: 0.08
PRESENT VALUE MODELS AND THE MULTI-ASSET PROBLEM
TAR OC 73 VOL: 48 PG:690 - 695 :: QUAL. :INT. LOG. :THEORY :PP&E / DEPR

BRIEF ,RP ; SEC: OWEN ,J CIT: 0.08
A REFORMULATION OF THE ESTIMATION PROBLEM
JAR SP 73 VOL: 11 PG:1 - 15 :: ANAL. :INT. LOG. :OTH.STAT. :PP&E / DEPR

BRIEF ,RP CIT: 0.15
THE ACCOUNTANT'S RESPONSIBILITY IN HISTORICAL PERSPECTIVE
TAR AP 75 VOL: 50 PG:285 - 297 :: QUAL. :INT. LOG. :THEORY :N/A

BRIEF ,RP CIT: 0.00
A NOTE ON "REDISCOVERY" AND THE RULE OF 69
TAR OC 77 VOL: 52 PG:810 - 812 :: QUAL. :SEC. :HIST. :PP&E / DEPR

BRIGHAM,EF CIT: 0.00
THE EFFECTS OF ALTERNATIVE DEPRECIATION POLICIES ON REPORTED PROFITS
TAR JA 68 VOL: 43 PG:46 - 61 :: ANAL. :SIM. :OTH.STAT. :PP&E / DEPR

BRIGHAM,EF ; SEC: NANTELL,TJ CIT: 0.00
NORMALIZATION VERSUS FLOW THROUGH FOR UTILITY COMPANIES USING LIBERALIZED TAX
    DEPRECIATION
TAR JL 74 VOL: 49 PG:436 - 447 :: ANAL. :SIM. :OTH.STAT. :TAXES

BRIGHTON,GD ; FIRS: BRUGEMAN,DC CIT: 0.00
INSTITUTIONAL ACCOUNTING - HOW IT DIFFERS FROM COMMERCIAL ACCOUNTING
TAR OC 63 VOL: 38 PG:764 - 770 :: QUAL. :INT. LOG. :THEORY :N/A

BRIGHTON,GD CIT: 0.00
ACCRUED EXPENSE TAX REFORM - NOT READY IN 1954 - READY IN 1969?
TAR JA 69 VOL: 44 PG:137 - 144 :: QUAL. :SEC. :HIST. :SPEC.ITEMS

BRILOFF,AJ CIT: 0.00
NEEDED: A REVOLUTION IN THE DETERMINATION AND APPLICATION OF ACCOUNTING
    PRINCIPLES
TAR JA 64 VOL: 39 PG:12 - 15 :: QUAL. :INT. LOG. :THEORY :FIN.METH.

BRILOFF,AJ CIT: 0.15
OLD MYTHS AND NEW REALITIES IN ACCOUNTANCY
TAR JL 66 VOL: 41 PG:484 - 495 :: DES.STAT. :SURV. :INSTIT. :AUD.

BRILOFF,AJ CIT: 0.00
DIRTY POOLING
TAR JL 67 VOL: 42 PG:489 - 496 :: QUAL. :INT. LOG. :THEORY :BUS.COMB.

BROCA ,DS ; FIRS: BORITZ,JE CIT: 0.00
SCHEDULING INTERNAL AUDIT ACTIVITIES
AUD AU 86 VOL: 6 PG:1 - 19 :: DES.STAT. :SIM. :OTH.STAT. :INT.AUD.

BROCKETT,P ; SEC: CHARNES,A ; THIR: COOPER,WW ; FOUR: SHIN ,HC CIT: 0.00
A CHANCE-CONSTRAINED PROGRAMMING APPROACH TO COST-VOLUME-PROFIT ANALYSIS
TAR JL 84 VOL: 59 PG:474 - 487 :: ANAL. :INT. LOG. :MATH.PROG. :C-V-P-A

BROCKHOFF,K CIT: 0.20
A NOTE ON EXTERNAL SOCIAL REPORTING BY GERMAN COMPANIES: A SURVEY OF 1973
    COMPANY REPORTS
AOS 12 79 VOL: 4 PG:77 - 86 :: DES.STAT. :PRIM. :THEORY :HRA

BROMWICH,M CIT: 0.17
THE USE OF PRESENT VALUE VALUATION MODELS IN PUBLISHED ACCOUNTING REPORTS
TAR JL 77 VOL: 52 PG:587 - 596 :: QUAL. :INT. LOG. :THEORY :VALUAT.(INFL.)

BROMWICH,M CIT: 0.22
THE POSSIBILITY OF PARTIAL ACCOUNTING STANDARDS
TAR AP 80 VOL: 55 PG:288 - 300 :: ANAL. :INT. LOG. :INSTIT. :FASB SUBM.

BROOKS,EH ; FIRS: BABER ,WR ; THIR: RICKS ,WE CIT: 0.00
AN EMPIRICAL INVESTIGATION OF THE MARKET FOR AUDIT SERVICES IN THE PUBLIC
    SECTOR
JAR AU 87 VOL: 25 PG:293 - 305 :: REGRESS. :PRIM. :OTH.STAT. :ORG.

BROWN ,BC ; SEC: BRANDI,JT CIT: 0.00
SECURITY PRICE REACTIONS TO CHANGES IN FOREIGN CURRENCY TRANSLATION
    STANDARDS
JAA SU 86 VOL: 1 PG:185 - 205 :: REGRESS. :PRIM. :EMH :FOR.CUR.

BROWN ,C CIT: 0.38
HUMAN INFORMATION PROCESSING FOR DECISIONS TO INVESTIGATE COST VARIANCES
JAR SP 81 VOL: 19 PG:62 - 85 :: ANOVA :LAB. :HIPS :VAR.

BROWN ,C CIT: 0.17
EFFECTS OF DYNAMIC TASK ENVIRONMENT ON THE LEARNING OF STANDARD COST VARIANCE
    SIGNIFICANCE
JAR AU 83 VOL: 21 PG:413 - 431 :: ANOVA :LAB. :HIPS :ORG.& ENVIR.

BROWN ,C CIT: 0.00
CASUAL REASONING IN PERFORMANCE ASSESSMENT: EFFECTS OF CAUSE AND EFFECT
    TEMPORAL ORDER AND COVARIATION
AOS 03 85 VOL: 10 PG:255 - 266 :: REGRESS. :LAB. :OTH.BEH. :VAR.

BROWN ,C ; SEC: SOLOMON,I CIT: 0.00
EFFECTS OF OUTCOME INFORMATION ON EVALUATIONS OF MANAGERIAL DECISIONS
TAR JL 87 VOL: 62 PG:564 - 577 :: REGRESS. :LAB. :OTH.BEH. :BUDG.& PLAN.

BROWN ,LD ; SEC: ROZEFF,MS CIT: 0.50
ADAPTIVE EXPECTATIONS, TIME-SERIES MODELS, AND ANALYST FORECAST REVISION
JAR AU 79 VOL: 17 PG:341 - 351 :: REGRESS. :PRIM. :TIME SER. :FOREC.

BROWN ,LD ; SEC: ROZEFF,MS CIT: 0.20
THE PREDICTIVE VALUE OF INTERIM REPORTS FOR IMPROVING FORECASTS OF FUTURE
    QUARTERLY EARNINGS
TAR JL 79 VOL: 54 PG:585 - 591 :: NON-PAR. :INT. LOG. :TIME SER. :FOREC.

BROWN ,LD ; SEC: ROZEFF,MS CIT: 2.20
UNIVARIATE TIME-SERIES MODELS OF QUARTERLY ACCOUNTING EARNINGS PER SHARE: A
    PROPOSED MODEL
JAR SP 79 VOL: 17 PG:179 - 189 :: MIXED :PRIM. :TIME SER. :AUD.TRAIN.

BROWN ,LD ; SEC: HUGHES,JS ; THIR: ROZEFF,MS ; FOUR: VANDERWEIDE,JH CIT: 0.00
EXPECTATIONS DATA AND THE PREDICTIVE VALUE OF INTERIM REPORTING: A COMMENT
JAR SP 80 VOL: 18 PG:278 - 288 :: REGRESS. :PRIM. :TIME SER. :FOREC.

BROWN ,LD CIT: 0.17
ACCOUNTING CHANGES AND THE ACCURACY OF ANALYSTS' EARNINGS FORECASTS
JAR AU 83 VOL: 21 PG:432 - 443 :: NON-PAR. :PRIM. :OTH.STAT. :ACC.CHNG.

BROWN ,LD ; SEC: GARDNER,JC CIT: 0.75
APPLYING CITATION ANALYSIS TO EVALUATE THE RESEARCH CONTRIBUTIONS OF
    ACCOUNTING FACULTY AND DOCTORAL PROGRAMS
TAR AP 85 VOL: 60 PG:262 - 277 :: REGRESS. :SEC. :OTH.STAT. :METHOD.

BROWN ,LD ; SEC: GARDNER,JC CIT: 0.50
USING CITATION ANALYSIS TO ASSESS THE IMPACT OF JOURNALS AND ARTICLES ON
    CONTEMPORARY ACCOUNTING RESEARCH (CAR)
JAR SP 85 VOL: 23 PG:84 - 109 :: REGRESS. :SEC. :HIST. :METHOD.

BROWN ,LD ; SEC: GRIFFIN,PA ; THIR: HAGERMAN,RL ; FOUR: ZMIJEWSKI,ME CIT: 2.50
SECURITY ANALYST SUPERIORITY RELATIVE TO UNIVARIATE TIME-SERIES MODELS IN
    FORECASTING QUARTERLY EARNINGS
JAE AP 87 VOL: 9 PG:61 - 87 :: REGRESS. :PRIM. :TIME SER. :FOREC.

BROWN ,LD ; SEC: GRIFFIN,PA ; THIR: HAGERMAN,RL ; FOUR: ZMIJEWSKI,ME CIT: 2.00
AN EVALUATION OF ALTERNATIVE PROXIES FOR THE MARKET'S ASSESSMENT OF
    UNEXPECTED EARNINGS
JAE JL 87 VOL: 9 PG:159 - 193 :: REGRESS. :PRIM. :TIME SER. :METHOD.

BROWN ,LD ; SEC: RICHARDSON,GD ; THIR: SCHWAGER,SJ CIT: 1.00
AN INFORMATION INTERPRETATION OF FINANCIAL ANALYST SUPERIORITY IN FORECASTING
    EARNINGS
JAR SP 87 VOL: 25 PG:49 - 67 :: REGRESS. :PRIM. :TIME SER. :FOREC.

BROWN ,LD ; SEC: GARDNER,JC ; THIR: VASARHELYI,MA CIT: 0.00
AN ANALYSIS OF THE RESEARCH CONTRIBUTIONS OF ACCOUNTING, ORGANIZATIONS AND
    SOCIETY, 1976-1984
AOS 02 87 VOL: 12 PG:193 - 204 :: REGRESS. :SEC. :HIST. :METHOD.

BROWN ,P ; SEC: BALL ,R CIT: 1.15
SOME PRELIMINARY FINDINGS ON THE ASSOCIATION BETWEEN THE EARNINGS OF A FIRM,
    ITS INDUSTRY, AND THE ECONOMY
JAR ST 67 VOL: 5 PG:55 - 77 :: CORR. :PRIM. :EMH :REV.REC.

BROWN ,P ; FIRS: BALL ,R CIT: 7.00
AN EMPIRICAL EVALUATION OF ACCOUNTING INCOME NUMBERS
JAR AU 68 VOL: 6 PG:159 - 178 :: NON-PAR. :PRIM. :EMH :FIN.METH.

BROWN ,PR ; FIRS: ASHTON,RH CIT: 0.11
DESCRIPTIVE MODELING OF AUDITORS' INTERNAL CONTROL JUDGMENTS: REPLICATION AND
   EXTENSION
JAR SP 80 VOL: 18 PG:269 - 277 :: NON-PAR. :LAB. :HIPS :INT.CONT.

BROWN ,PR CIT: 0.88
A DESCRIPTIVE ANALYSIS OF SELECT INPUT BASES OF THE FINANCIAL ACCOUNTING
   STANDARDS BOARD
JAR SP 81 VOL: 19 PG:232 - 246 :: OTH.QUANT. :PRIM. :INSTIT. :FASB SUBM.

BROWN ,PR CIT: 0.00
FASB RESPONSIVENESS TO CORPORATE INPUT
JAA SU 82 VOL: 5 PG:282 - 290 :: DES.STAT. :PRIM. :INSTIT. :FASB SUBM.

BROWN ,PR CIT: 0.00
INDEPENDENT AUDITOR JUDGMENT IN THE EVALUATION OF INTERNAL AUDIT FUNCTIONS
JAR AU 83 VOL: 21 PG:444 - 455 :: NON-PAR. :LAB. :HIPS :INT.AUD.

BROWN ,PR ; SEC: KARAN ,V CIT: 0.00
ONE APPROACH FOR ASSESSING THE OPERATIONAL NATURE OF AUDITING STANDARDS: AN
   ANALYSIS OF SAS NO. 9
AUD AU 86 VOL: 6 PG:134 - 147 :: ANOVA :LAB. :INSTIT. :INT.AUD.

BROWN ,RM CIT: 1.11
SHORT-RANGE MARKET REACTION TO CHANGES TO LIFO ACCOUNTING USING PRELIMINARY
   EARNINGS ANNOUNCEMENT DATES
JAR SP 80 VOL: 18 PG:38 - 63 :: REGRESS. :PRIM. :EMH :INV.

BROWN ,SH ; FIRS: COPELAND,RM ; SEC: TAYLOR,RL CIT: 0.13
OBSERVATION ERROR AND BIAS IN ACCOUNTING RESEARCH
JAR SP 81 VOL: 19 PG:197 - 207 :: ANOVA :LAB. :OTH.BEH. :METHOD.

BROWNELL,P CIT: 1.38
PARTICIPATION IN BUDGETING, LOCUS OF CONTROL AND ORGANIZATIONAL EFFECTIVENESS
TAR OC 81 VOL: 56 PG:844 - 860 :: REGRESS. :LAB. :OTH.BEH. :BUDG.& PLAN.

BROWNELL,P CIT: 0.00
A FIELD STUDY EXAMINATION OF BUDGETARY PARTICIPATION AND LOCUS OF CONTROL
TAR OC 82 VOL: 57 PG:766 - 777 :: MIXED :FIELD :OTH.BEH. :BUDG.& PLAN.

BROWNELL,P CIT: 1.57
THE ROLE OF ACCOUNTING DATA IN PERFORMANCE EVALUATION, BUDGETARY
   PARTICIPATION, AND ORGANIZATIONAL EFFECTIVENESS
JAR SP 82 VOL: 20 PG:12 - 27 :: REGRESS. :LAB. :OTH.BEH. :BUDG.& PLAN.

BROWNELL,P CIT: 0.33
THE MOTIVATIONAL IMPACT OF MANAGEMENT-BY-EXCEPTION IN A BUDGETARY CONTEXT
JAR AU 83 VOL: 21 PG:456 - 472 :: REGRESS. :SURV. :OTH.BEH. :BUDG.& PLAN.

BROWNELL,P CIT: 0.17
LEADERSHIP STYLE, BUDGETARY PARTICIPATION AND MANAGERIAL BEHAVIOR
AOS 04 83 VOL: 8 PG:307 - 322 :: ANOVA :SURV. :OTH.BEH. :BUDG.& PLAN.

BROWNELL,P CIT: 0.25
BUDGETARY SYSTEMS AND THE CONTROL OF FUNCTIONALLY DIFFERENTIATED
   ORGANIZATIONAL ACTIVITIES
JAR AU 85 VOL: 23 PG:502 - 512 :: REGRESS. :SURV. :OTH.BEH. :BUDG.& PLAN.

BROWNELL,P ; SEC: HIRST ,MK CIT: 0.00
RELIANCE ON ACCT. INFO., BUDGETARY PARTICIPATION, AND TASK UNCERTAINTY: TESTS
  OF A THREE-WAY INTERACTION
JAR AU 86 VOL: 24 PG:241 - 249 :: REGRESS. :SURV. :OTH.BEH. :BUDG.& PLAN.

BROWNELL,P ; SEC: MCINNES, M CIT: 0.67
BUDGETARY PARTICIPATION, MOTIVATION, AND MANAGERIAL PERFORMANCE
TAR OC 86 VOL: 61 PG:587 - 600 :: REGRESS. :SURV. :OTH.BEH. :BUDG.& PLAN.

BROWNELL,P ; FIRS: CHENHALL,RH CIT: 0.00
THE EFFECT OF PARTICIPATIVE BUDGETING ON JOB SATISFACTION AND PERFORMANCE:
  ROLE AMBIGUITY AS AN INTERVENING VARIABLE
AOS 03 88 VOL: 13 PG:225 - 233 :: ANOVA :SURV. :EMH :BUDG.& PLAN.

BRUGEMAN,DC ; SEC: BRIGHTON,GD CIT: 0.00
INSTITUTIONAL ACCOUNTING - HOW IT DIFFERS FROM COMMERCIAL ACCOUNTING
TAR OC 63 VOL: 38 PG:764 - 770 :: QUAL. :INT. LOG. :THEORY :N/A

BRUGGE,WG CIT: 0.00
THE ACCOUNTANCY PROFESSION IN GREECE
TAR JL 63 VOL: 38 PG:596 - 600 :: QUAL. :INT. LOG. :THEORY :FIN.METH.

BRUMMET,RL ; SEC: FLAMHOLTZ,EG ; THIR: PYLE ,WC CIT: 0.54
HUMAN RESOURCE MEASUREMENT - A CHALLENGE FOR ACCOUNTANTS
TAR AP 68 VOL: 43 PG:217 - 224 :: QUAL. :INT. LOG. :OTH.BEH. :HRA

BRUNDAGE,MV ; SEC: LIVINGSTONE,JL CIT: 0.00
SIMULATION ON A TIME-SHARING COMPUTER UTILITY SYSTEM
TAR JL 69 VOL: 44 PG:539 - 545 :: ANAL. :SIM. :N/A :OTH.MANAG.

BRUNS JR,WJ CIT: 0.23
INVENTORY VALUATION AND MANAGEMENT DECISIONS
TAR AP 65 VOL: 40 PG:345 - 357 :: NON-PAR. :LAB. :N/A :INV.

BRUNS JR,WJ CIT: 0.08
THE ACCOUNTING PERIOD CONCEPT AND ITS EFFECT ON MANAGEMENT DECISIONS
JAR ST 66 VOL: 4 PG:1 - 14 :: DES.STAT. :LAB. :OTH.BEH. :INT.REP.

BRUNS JR,WJ CIT: 0.38
ACCOUNTING INFORMATION AND DECISION-MAKING: SOME BEHAVIOURAL HYPOTHESES
TAR JL 68 VOL: 43 PG:469 - 480 :: QUAL. :INT. LOG. :OTH.BEH. :MANAG.

BRUNS JR,WJ ; SEC: WATERHOUSE,JH CIT: 3.62
BUDGETARY CONTROL AND ORGANIZATION STRUCTURE
JAR AU 75 VOL: 13 PG:177 - 203 :: OTH.QUANT. :FIELD :OTH.BEH. :ORG.FORM

BUBLITZ,B ; FIRS: STONE ,M CIT: 0.20
AN ANALYSIS OF THE RELIABILITY OF THE FASB DATA BANK OF CHANGING PRICE AND
  PENSION INFORMATION
TAR JL 84 VOL: 59 PG:469 - 473 :: DES.STAT. :PRIM. :OTH. :METHOD.

BUBLITZ,B ; SEC: KEE ,R CIT: 0.00
DO WE NEED SUNSET REQUIREMENTS FOR FASB PRONOUNCEMENTS?
JAA WI 84 VOL: 7 PG:123 - 137 :: QUAL. :INT. LOG. :INSTIT. :FASB SUBM.

BUBLITZ,B ; SEC: FRECKA,TJ ; THIR: MCKEOWN,JC CIT: 1.50
MARKET ASSOCIATION TESTS AND FASB STATEMENT NO. 33 DISCLOSURES: A
  REEXAMINATION
JAR ST 85 VOL: 23 PG:1 - 23 :: REGRESS. :PRIM. :EMH :VALUAT.(INFL.)

BUCHMAN,TA CIT: 0.00
THE RELIABILITY OF INTERNAL AUDITORS' WORKING PAPERS
AUD AU 83 VOL: 3 PG:92 - 103 :: NON-PAR. :SURV. :OTH.BEH. :INT.AUD.

BUCHMAN,TA CIT: 0.00
AN EFFECT OF HINDSIGHT ON PREDICTING BANKRUPTCY WITH ACCOUNTING INFORMATION
AOS 03 85 VOL: 10 PG:267 - 286 :: REGRESS. :LAB. :OTH.BEH. :BUS.FAIL.

BUCKLEY,JW CIT: 0.00
MEDICARE AND ACCOUNTING
TAR JA 66 VOL: 41 PG:75 - 82 :: QUAL. :SEC. :N/A :FIN.METH.

BUCKLEY,JW CIT: 0.00
PROGRAMMED INSTRUCTION: WITH EMPHASIS ON ACCOUNTING
TAR JL 67 VOL: 42 PG:572 - 582 :: QUAL. :INT. LOG. :N/A :OTH.MANAG.

BUCKLEY,JW ; SEC: KIRCHER,P ; THIR: MATHEWS,RL CIT: 0.08
METHODOLOGY IN ACCOUNTING THEORY
TAR AP 68 VOL: 43 PG:274 - 283 :: QUAL. :INT. LOG. :THEORY :FIN.METH.

BUCKLEY,JW CIT: 0.00
POLICY MODELS IN ACCOUNTING: A CRITICAL COMMENTARY
AOS 01 80 VOL: 5 PG:49 - 64 :: QUAL. :SEC. :THEORY :N/A

BUCKMAN,AG ; FIRS: OHLSON,JA CIT: 0.38
TOWARD A THEORY OF FINANCIAL ACCOUNTING: WELFARE AND PUBLIC INFORMATION
JAR AU 81 VOL: 19 PG:399 - 433 :: ANAL. :INT. LOG. :THEORY :N/A

BUCKMAN,AG ; SEC: MILLER,BL CIT: 0.00
OPTIMAL INVESTIGATION OF A MULTIPLE COST PROCESSES SYSTEM
JAR SP 82 VOL: 20 PG:28 - 41 :: ANAL. :INT. LOG. :OTH.STAT. :N/A

BULLEN,ML ; SEC: FLAMHOLTZ,EG CIT: 0.00
A THEORETICAL AND EMPIRICAL INVESTIGATION OF JOB SATISFACTION AND INTENDED
  TURNOVER IN THE LARGE CPA FIRM
AOS 03 85 VOL: 10 PG:287 - 302 :: REGRESS. :SURV. :OTH.BEH. :ORG.

BULLOCH,J ; FIRS: DUVALL,RM CIT: 0.00
ADJUSTING RATE OF RETURN AND PRESENT VALUE FOR PRICE-LEVEL CHANGES
TAR JL 65 VOL: 40 PG:569 - 573 :: ANAL. :INT. LOG. :OTH.STAT. :OTH.MANAG.

BULLOCK,CL CIT: 0.08
RECONCILING ECONOMIC DEPRECIATION WITH TAX ALLOCATION
TAR JA 74 VOL: 49 PG:98 - 103 :: ANAL. :INT. LOG. :THEORY :PP&E / DEPR

BURCHELL,S ; SEC: CLUBB ,C ; THIR: HOPWOOD,AG ; FOUR: HUGHES,JS ; FIFT:
NAHAPIET,JE CIT: 3.89
THE ROLES OF ACCOUNTING IN ORGANIZATIONS AND SOCIETY
AOS 01 80 VOL: 5 PG:5 - 27 :: QUAL. :INT. LOG. :THEORY :N/A

BURCHELL,S ; SEC: CLUBB ,C ; THIR: HOPWOOD,AG CIT: 3.75
ACCOUNTING IN ITS SOCIAL CONTEXT: TOWARDS A HISTORY OF VALUE ADDED IN THE
  UNITED KINGDOM
AOS 04 85 VOL: 10 PG:381 - 414 :: DES.STAT. :INT. LOG. :THEORY :HRA

BURGHER,PH CIT: 0.00
PERT AND THE AUDITOR
TAR JA 64 VOL: 39 PG:103 - 120 :: ANAL. :INT. LOG. :OTH.STAT. :INT.AUD.

BURGSTAHLER,D ; SEC: JIAMBALVO,J CIT: 0.00
SAMPLE ERROR CHARACTERISTICS AND PROJECTION OF ERROR TO AUDIT POPULATIONS
TAR AP 86 VOL: 61 PG:233 - 248 :: REGRESS. :LAB. :HIPS :ERRORS

BURGSTAHLER,D ; FIRS: BOWEN ,RM ; THIR: DALEY ,LA CIT: 0.67
EVIDENCE ON THE RELATIONSHIPS BETWEEN VARIOUS EARNINGS MEASURES OF CASH FLOW
TAR OC 86 VOL: 61 PG:713 - 725 :: REGRESS. :PRIM. :OTH.STAT. :REV.REC.

BURGSTAHLER,D ; SEC: NOREEN,EW CIT: 0.00
DETECTING CONTEMPORANEOUS SECURITY MARKET REACTIONS TO A SEQUENCE OF
   RELATED EVENTS
JAR SP 86 VOL: 24 PG:170 - 186 :: REGRESS. :PRIM. :EMH :METHOD.

BURGSTAHLER,D ; FIRS: BOWEN ,RM ; THIR: DALEY ,LA CIT: 0.00
THE INCREMENTAL INFORMATION CONTENT OF ACCRUAL VERSUS CASH FLOWS
TAR OC 87 VOL: 62 PG:723 - 747 :: REGRESS. :PRIM. :EMH :SPEC.ITEMS

BURKE ,EJ CIT: 0.08
OBJECTIVITY AND ACCOUNTING
TAR OC 64 VOL: 39 PG:837 - 849 :: QUAL. :INT. LOG. :THEORY :OTH.FIN.ACC.

BURKE ,WL CIT: 0.00
COST ALLOCATION AND DISTRIBUTION - MERCHANDISE ACCOUNTING
TAR OC 63 VOL: 38 PG:802 - 812 :: QUAL. :INT. LOG. :THEORY :N/A

BURNS ,JS ; SEC: JAEDICKE,RK ; THIR: SANGSTER,JM CIT: 0.00
FINANCIAL REPORTING OF PURCHASE CONTRACTS USED TO GUARANTEE LARGE INVESTMENTS
TAR JA 63 VOL: 38 PG:1 - 13 :: QUAL. :INT. LOG. :THEORY :SPEC.ITEMS

BURRELL,G CIT: 0.00
NO ACCOUNTING FOR SEXUALITY
AOS 01 87 VOL: 12 PG:89 - 102 :: DES.STAT. :INT. LOG. :INSTIT. :ORG.& ENVIR.

BURT ,OR CIT: 0.00
A UNIFIED THEORY OF DEPRECIATION
JAR SP 72 VOL: 10 PG:28 - 57 :: ANAL. :INT. LOG. :THEORY :PP&E / DEPR

BURTON,JC ; SEC: FAIRFIELD,P CIT: 0.00
AUDITING EVOLUTION IN A CHANGING ENVIRONMENT
AUD WI 82 VOL: 1 PG:1 - 22 :: DES.STAT. :INT. LOG. :INSTIT. :ORG.

BUTLER,SA CIT: 0.00
APPLICATION OF A DECISION AID IN THE JUDGMENTAL EVALUATION OF SUBSTANTIVE
   TEST OF DETAILS SAMPLES
JAR AU 85 VOL: 23 PG:513 - 526 :: REGRESS. :LAB. :HIPS :DEC.AIDS

BUTLER,SA CIT: 0.00
ANCHORING IN THE JUDGMENTAL EVALUATION OF AUDIT SAMPLES
TAR JA 86 VOL: 61 PG:101 - 111 :: REGRESS. :LAB. :HIPS :RISK

BUTT ,JL CIT: 0.00
FREQUENCY JUDGMENTS IN AN AUDITING-RELATED TASK
JAR AU 88 VOL: 26 PG:315 - 330 :: REGRESS. :LAB. :OTH.BEH. :JUDG.

BUTTERWORTH,JE ; SEC: SIGLOCH,BA CIT: 0.08
A GENERALIZED MULTI-STAGE INPUT-OUTPUT MODEL AND SOME DERIVED EQUIVALENT
   SYSTEMS
TAR OC 71 VOL: 46 PG:701 - 716 :: ANAL. :INT. LOG. :MATH.PROG. :MANAG.

BUTTERWORTH,JE CIT: 0.46
THE ACCOUNTING SYSTEM AS AN INFORMATION FUNCTION
JAR SP 72 VOL: 10 PG:1 - 27 :: ANAL. :INT. LOG. :INF.ECO./AG. :INFO.STRUC.

BUZBY ,SL ; FIRS: MORRISON,TA CIT: 0.00
EFFECT OF THE INVESTMENT TAX CREDIT ON THE CAPITALIZE-EXPENSE DECISION
TAR JL 68 VOL: 43 PG:517 - 521 :: ANAL. :INT. LOG. :N/A :TAX PLNG.

BUZBY ,SL CIT: 0.38
EXTENDING THE APPLICABILITY OF PROBABILISTIC MANAGEMENT PLANNING AND CONTROL
    MODELS
TAR JA 74 VOL: 49 PG:42 - 49 :: ANAL. :INT. LOG. :OTH.STAT. :C-V-P-A

BUZBY ,SL CIT: 0.77
SELECTED ITEMS OF INFORMATION AND THEIR DISCLOSURE IN ANNUAL REPORTS
TAR JL 74 VOL: 49 PG:423 - 435 :: DES.STAT. :SURV. :N/A :INFO.STRUC.

BUZBY ,SL CIT: 0.08
COMPANY SIZE, LISTED VERSUS UNLISTED STOCKS, AND THE EXTENT OF FINANCIAL
    DISCLOSURE
JAR SP 75 VOL: 13 PG:16 - 37 :: NON-PAR. :SURV. :THEORY :N/A

BUZBY ,SL ; SEC: FALK ,H CIT: 0.27
A SURVEY OF THE INTEREST IN SOCIAL RESPONSIBILITY INFORMATION BY MUTUAL FUNDS
AOS 34 78 VOL: 3 PG:191 - 202 :: DES.STAT. :SURV. :OTH.BEH. :METHOD.

BUZBY ,SL ; SEC: FALK ,H CIT: 0.40
DEMAND FOR SOCIAL RESPONSIBILITY INFORMATION BY UNIVERSITY INVESTORS
TAR JA 79 VOL: 54 PG:23 - 37 :: DES.STAT. :SURV. :INSTIT. :HRA

BYLINSKI,JH ; FIRS: BAILEY,KE ; THIR: SHIELDS,MD CIT: 0.00
EFFECTS OF AUDIT REPORT WORDING CHANGES ON THE PERCEIVED MESSAGE
JAR AU 83 VOL: 21 PG:355 - 370 :: OTH.QUANT. :LAB. :OTH.BEH. :OPIN.

BYLINSKI,JH ; FIRS: BLOCHER,E CIT: 0.00
THE INFLUENCE OF SAMPLE CHARACTERISTICS IN SAMPLE EVALUATION
AUD AU 85 VOL: 5 PG:79 - 90 :: REGRESS. :LAB. :OTH.BEH. :SAMP.

BYLINSKI,JH ; FIRS: BAMBER,EM ; SEC: BAMBER,LS CIT: 0.00
A DESCRIPTIVE STUDY OF AUDIT MANAGERS' WORKING PAPER REVIEW
AUD SP 88 VOL: 07 PG:137 - 149 :: REGRESS. :LAB. :HIPS :AUD.BEH.

BYRNE ,R ; SEC: CHARNES,A ; THIR: COOPER,WW ; FOUR: KORTANEK,KO CIT: 0.00
SOME NEW APPROACHES TO RISK
TAR JA 68 VOL: 43 PG:18 - 37 :: ANAL. :INT. LOG. :MATH.PROG. :BUDG.& PLAN.

BYUN ,YH ; FIRS: LEVY ,H CIT: 0.00
AN EMPIRICAL TEST OF THE BLACK-SCHOLES OPTION PRICING MODEL AND THE IMPLIED
    VARIANCE: A CONFIDENCE INTERVAL APPROACH
JAA AU 87 VOL: 2 PG:355 - 369 :: DES.STAT. :PRIM. :OTH. :OTH.MANAG.

CAIN ,P ; FIRS: ASKARI,H ; THIR: SHAW ,R CIT: 0.00
A GOVERNMENT TAX SUBSIDY
TAR AP 76 VOL: 51 PG:331 - 334 :: DES.STAT. :PRIM. :N/A :TAX PLNG.

CALDERWOOD,SC ; FIRS: BRADBURY,ME CIT: 0.00
EQUITY ACCOUNTING FOR RECIPROCAL STOCKHOLDINGS
TAR AP 88 VOL: 63 PG:330 - 347 :: DES.STAT. :INT. LOG. :THEORY :BUS.COMB.

CALL ,DV CIT: 0.00
SOME SALIENT FACTORS OFTEN OVERLOOKED IN STOCK OPTIONS
TAR OC 69 VOL: 44 PG:711 - 719 :: ANAL. :INT. LOG. :N/A :OTH.MANAG.

CALLAHAN,C ; FIRS: ELGERS,P ; THIR: STROCK,E CIT: 0.00
THE EFFECT OF EARNINGS YIELDS UPON THE ASSOCIATION BETWEEN UNEXPECTED
   EARNINGS AND SECURITY RETURNS; A RE-EXAMINATION
TAR OC 87 VOL: 62 PG:763 - 773 :: REGRESS. :PRIM. :EMH :METHOD.

CALLEN,JL CIT: 0.27
FINANCIAL COST ALLOCATIONS: A GAME THEORETIC APPROACH
TAR AP 78 VOL: 53 PG:303 - 308 :: ANAL. :INT. LOG. :OTH.STAT. :COST.ALLOC.

CALLEN,JL CIT: 0.00
AN INDEX NUMBER THEORY OF ACCOUNTING COST VARIANCES
JAA SP 88 VOL: 03 PG:87 - 108 :: DES.STAT. :INT. LOG. :OTH.STAT. :VAR.

CAMARDESSE JR,JE ; FIRS: VASARHELYI,MA ; SEC: BAILEY JR,AD ; FOUR: GROOMER, SM
; FIFT: LAMPE ,JC CIT: 0.00
THE USAGE OF COMPUTERS IN AUDITING TEACHING AND RESEARCH
AUD SP 84 VOL: 3 PG:98 - 103 :: QUAL. :SIM. :OTH. :EDP AUD.

CAMMANN,C CIT: 0.38
EFFECTS OF THE USE OF CONTROL SYSTEMS
AOS 04 76 VOL: 1 PG:301 - 314 :: REGRESS. :CASE :OTH.BEH. :BUDG.& PLAN.

CAMPBELL,DR CIT: 0.00
AN ANALYSIS OF THE GROWTH IN PUBLIC ACCOUNTING: IMPLICATIONS FOR FUTURE
   PLANNING STRATEGIES
JAA SP 83 VOL: 6 PG:196 - 211 :: DES.STAT. :PRIM. :OTH. :PROF.RESP.

CAMPBELL,JE CIT: 0.00
AN APPLICATION OF PROTOCOL ANALYSIS TO THE "LITTLE GAAP" CONTROVERSY
AOS 34 84 VOL: 9 PG:329 - 342 :: DES.STAT. :LAB. :HIPS :MAN.DEC.CHAR.

CAMPFIELD,WL CIT: 0.00
CRITICAL PATHS FOR PROFESSIONAL ACCOUNTANTS DURING THE NEW MANAGEMENT
   REVOLUTION
TAR JL 63 VOL: 38 PG:521 - 527 :: QUAL. :INT. LOG. :INSTIT. :PROF.RESP.

CAMPFIELD,WL CIT: 0.00
PROFESSIONAL STATUS FOR INTERNAL AUDITORS
TAR JL 65 VOL: 40 PG:594 - 598 :: QUAL. :INT. LOG. :INSTIT. :OTH.MANAG.

CAMPFIELD,WL CIT: 0.00
TOWARD MAKING ACCOUNTING EDUCATION ADAPTIVE AND NORMATIVE
TAR OC 70 VOL: 45 PG:683 - 689 :: QUAL. :INT. LOG. :N/A :OTH.MANAG.

CAPLAN,EM CIT: 0.85
BEHAVIOURAL ASSUMPTIONS OF MANAGEMENT ACCOUNTING
TAR JL 66 VOL: 41 PG:496 - 509 :: QUAL. :INT. LOG. :OTH.BEH. :MANAG.

CAPLAN,EM CIT: 0.23
BEHAVIOURAL ASSUMPTIONS OF MANAGEMENT ACCOUNTING - REPORT OF A FIELD STUDY
TAR AP 68 VOL: 43 PG:342 - 362 :: DES.STAT. :SURV. :OTH.BEH. :MANAG.

CAPPS ,T ; FIRS: BERRY ,AJ ; THIR: COOPER,D ; FOUR: FERGUSON,P ; FIFT: HOPPER,T
; SIX: LOWE ,EA CIT: 3.50
MANAGEMENT CONTROL IN AN AREA OF THE NCB: RATIONALES OF ACCOUNTING PRACTICES
   IN A PUBLIC ENTERPRISE
AOS 01 85 VOL: 10 PG:3 - 28 :: REGRESS. :FIELD :OTH.BEH. :MANAG.

CAREY ,JL CIT: 0.00
WHAT IS THE PROFESSIONAL PRACTICE OF ACCOUNTING?
TAR JA 68 VOL: 43 PG:1 - 9 :: QUAL. :INT. LOG. :INSTIT. :AUD.

CAREY ,JL CIT: 0.00
TEACHERS AND PRACTITIONERS
TAR JA 69 VOL: 44 PG:79 - 85 :: QUAL. :INT. LOG. :INSTIT. :OTH.MANAG.

CAREY ,KJ ; FIRS: BASI ,BA ; THIR: TWARK ,RD CIT: 1.00
A COMPARISON OF THE ACCURACY OF CORPORATE AND SECURITY ANALYSTS' FORECASTS
   OF EARNINGS
TAR AP 76 VOL: 51 PG:244 - 254 :: ANOVA :PRIM. :TIME SER. :FOREC.

CARLISLE,HM CIT: 0.00
COST ACCOUNTING FOR ADVANCED TECHNOLOGY PROGRAMS
TAR JA 66 VOL: 41 PG:115 - 120 :: QUAL. :INT. LOG. :N/A :MANAG.

CARLSON,ML ; SEC: LAMB ,JW CIT: 0.00
CONSTRUCTING A THEORY OF ACCOUNTING - AN AXIOMATIC APPROACH
TAR JL 81 VOL: 56 PG:554 - 573 :: ANAL. :INT. LOG. :THEORY :N/A

CARLSSON,J ; SEC: EHN ,P ; THIR: ERLANDER,B ; FOUR: PERBY ,M ; FIFT:
SANDBERG,A CIT: 0.09
PLANNING AND CONTROL FROM THE PERSPECTIVE OF LABOR: A SHORT REPRESENTATION OF
   THE DEMOS PROJECT
AOS 34 78 VOL: 3 PG:249 - 260 :: QUAL. :FIELD :OTH. :BUDG.& PLAN.

CARMACK,CW ; FIRS: BRENNER,VC ; THIR: WEINSTEIN,MG CIT: 0.00
AN EMPIRICAL TEST OF THE MOTIVATION-HYGIENE THEORY
JAR AU 71 VOL: 9 PG:359 - 366 :: CORR. :SURV. :OTH.BEH. :AUD.BEH.

CARMICHAEL,DR ; SEC: SWIERINGA,RJ CIT: 0.00
THE COMPATIBILITY OF AUDITING INDEPENDENCE AND MANAGEMENT SERVICES: AN
   IDENTIFICATION OF ISSUES
TAR OC 68 VOL: 43 PG:697 - 705 :: QUAL. :INT. LOG. :INSTIT. :INDEP.

CARMICHAEL,DR CIT: 0.38
BEHAVIOURAL HYPOTHESES OF INTERNAL CONTROL
TAR AP 70 VOL: 45 PG:235 - 245 :: QUAL. :INT. LOG. :OTH.BEH. :INT.CONT.

CARMICHAEL,DR CIT: 0.00
THE COHEN COMMISSION IN PERSPECTIVE: ACTIONS AND REACTIONS
JAA SU 79 VOL: 2 PG:294 - 306 :: QUAL. :INT. LOG. :INSTIT. :AUD.

CARMICHAEL,DR ; SEC: WHITTINGTON,OR CIT: 0.00
THE AUDITOR'S CHANGING ROLE IN FINANCIAL REPORTING
JAA SU 84 VOL: 7 PG:347 - 361 :: QUAL. :INT. LOG. :OTH. :PROF.RESP.

CARPENTER,CG ; SEC: STRAWSER,RH CIT: 0.00
A STUDY OF THE JOB SATISFACTION OF ACADEMIC ACCOUNTANTS
TAR JL 71 VOL: 46 PG:509 - 518 :: NON-PAR. :SURV. :INSTIT. :OTH.MANAG.

CARPER,WB ; SEC: POSEY ,JM CIT: 0.08
THE VALIDITY OF SELECTED SURROGATE MEASURES OF HUMAN RESOURCE VALUE: A FIELD
    STUDY
AOS 23 76 VOL: 1 PG:143 - 152 :: NON-PAR. :SURV. :OTH.BEH. :HRA

CARRIER,NH ; FIRS: BAXTER,WT CIT: 0.08
DEPRECIATION, REPLACEMENT PRICE, AND COST OF CAPITAL
JAR AU 71 VOL: 9 PG:189 - 214 :: ANAL. :INT. LOG. :THEORY :VALUAT.(INFL.)

CARROLL,R ; FIRS: HOLT ,RN CIT: 0.44
CLASSIFICATION OF COMMERCIAL BANK LOANS THROUGH POLICY CAPTURING
AOS 03 80 VOL: 5 PG:285 - 296 :: OTH.QUANT. :LAB. :HIPS :BUS.FAIL.

CARSBERG,BV CIT: 0.08
THE CONTRIBUTION OF P.D. LEAKE TO THE THEORY OF GOODWILL VALUATION
JAR SP 66 VOL: 4 PG:1 - 15 :: QUAL. :INT. LOG. :HIST. :OTH. NON-C/A

CARSBERG,BV CIT: 0.00
ON THE LINEAR PROGRAMMING APPROACH TO ASSET VALUATION
JAR AU 69 VOL: 7 PG:165 - 182 :: ANAL. :INT. LOG. :MATH.PROG. :PP&E / DEPR

CARSLAW,C CIT: 0.00
ANOMALIES IN INCOME NUMBERS: EVIDENCE OF GOAL ORIENTED BEHAVIOR
TAR AP 88 VOL: 63 PG:321 - 327 :: REGRESS. :PRIM. :OTH. :METHOD.

CARSON,AB CIT: 0.00
CASH MOVEMENT: THE HEART OF INCOME MEASUREMENT
TAR AP 65 VOL: 40 PG:334 - 337 :: QUAL. :INT. LOG. :THEORY :FIN.METH.

CARTER,WK CIT: 0.00
A BENEFITS APPROACH TO CERTAIN ACCOUNTING POLICY CHOICES
TAR JA 81 VOL: 56 PG:108 - 114 :: QUAL. :INT. LOG. :THEORY :FIN.METH.

CASEY JR,CJ CIT: 1.00
VARIATION IN ACCOUNTING INFORMATION LOAD: THE EFFECT ON LOAN OFFICERS'
    PREDICTIONS OF BANKRUPTCY
TAR JA 80 VOL: 55 PG:36 - 49 :: ANOVA :LAB. :HIPS :BUS.FAIL.

CASEY JR,CJ CIT: 0.17
PRIOR PROBABILITY DISCLOSURE AND LOAN OFFICERS' JUDGMENTS: SOME EVIDENCE OF
    THE IMPACT
JAR SP 83 VOL: 21 PG:300 - 307 :: OTH.QUANT. :PRIM. :OTH.BEH. :N/A

CASEY JR,CJ ; SEC: BARTCZAK,N CIT: 0.00
USING OPERATING CASH FLOW DATA TO PREDICT FINANCIAL DISTRESS: SOME EXTENSIONS
JAR SP 85 VOL: 23 PG:384 - 401 :: REGRESS. :PRIM. :MATH.PROG. :BUS.FAIL.

CASEY JR,CJ ; SEC: MCGEE ,VE ; THIR: STICKNEY,CP CIT: 0.33
DISCRIMINATING BETWEEN REORGANIZED AND LIQUIDATED FIRMS IN BANKRUPTCY
TAR AP 86 VOL: 61 PG:249 - 262 :: REGRESS. :PRIM. :OTH.STAT. :BUS.FAIL.

CASEY JR,CJ ; SEC: SELLING,T CIT: 0.00
THE EFFECT OF TASK PREDICTABILITY AND PRIOR PROBABILITY DISCLOSURE ON
    JUDGMENT QUALITY AND CONFIDENCE
TAR AP 86 VOL: 61 PG:302 - 317 :: REGRESS. :LAB. :HIPS :BUS.FAIL.

CASH JR,JI ; SEC: BAILEY JR,AD ; THIR: WHINSTON,AB CIT: 0.08
A SURVEY OF TECHNIQUES FOR AUDITING EDP-BASED ACCOUNTING INFORMATION SYSTEMS
TAR OC 77 VOL: 52 PG:813 - 832 :: QUAL. :SEC. :N/A :ANAL.REV.

CASLER,DJ ; FIRS: HALL ,TW CIT: 0.00
USING INDEXING TO ESTIMATE CURRENT COSTS - COMPOSITE OR MULTIPLE INDEXES?
JAA SP 85 VOL: 8 PG:210 - 224 :: REGRESS. :PRIM. :THEORY :VALUAT.(INFL.)

CASLER,DJ ; SEC: HALL ,TW CIT: 0.50
FIRM-SPECIFIC ASSET VALUATION ACCURACY USING A COMPOSITE PRICE INDEX
JAR SP 85 VOL: 23 PG:110 - 122 :: REGRESS. :SIM. :OTH.STAT. :VALUAT.(INFL.)

CASPARI,JA CIT: 0.00
WHEREFORE ACCOUNTING DATA-EXPLANATION, PREDICTION AND DECISIONS
TAR OC 76 VOL: 51 PG:739 - 746 :: ANAL. :INT. LOG. :THEORY :OTH.MANAG.

CASSIDY,DB CIT: 0.00
INVESTOR EVALUATION OF ACCOUNTING INFORMATION: SOME ADDITIONAL EMPIRICAL
   EVIDENCE
JAR AU 76 VOL: 14 PG:212 - 229 :: REGRESS. :PRIM. :EMH :N/A

CAUSEY JR,DY CIT: 0.00
FORESEEABILITY AS A DETERMINANT OF AUDIT RESPONSIBILITY
TAR AP 73 VOL: 48 PG:258 - 267 :: QUAL. :INT. LOG. :OTH. :N/A

CAUSEY JR,DY CIT: 0.15
NEWLY EMERGING STANDARDS OF AUDITOR RESPONSIBILITY
TAR JA 76 VOL: 51 PG:19 - 30 :: QUAL. :SEC. :INSTIT. :LIAB.

CERF ,AR CIT: 0.00
ACCOUNTING FOR RETAIL LAND SALES
TAR JL 75 VOL: 50 PG:451 - 465 :: ANAL. :INT. LOG. :THEORY :REV.REC.

CHALOS,P CIT: 0.00
FINANCIAL DISTRESS: A COMPARATIVE STUDY OF INDIVIDUAL, MODEL, AND COMMITTEE
   ASSESSMENTS
JAR AU 85 VOL: 23 PG:527 - 543 :: REGRESS. :LAB. :OTH.BEH. :BUS.FAIL.

CHAMBERS,AE ; SEC: PENMAN,SH CIT: 2.40
TIMELINESS OF REPORTING AND THE STOCK PRICE REACTION TO EARNINGS ANNOUNCEMENTS
JAR SP 84 VOL: 22 PG:21 - 47 :: REGRESS. :PRIM. :EMH :FIN.ST.TIM.

CHAMBERS,RJ CIT: 0.15
WHY BOTHER WITH POSTULATES?
JAR SP 63 VOL: 1 PG:3 - 15 :: QUAL. :INT. LOG. :THEORY :N/A

CHAMBERS,RJ CIT: 0.23
MEASUREMENT AND OBJECTIVITY IN ACCOUNTING
TAR AP 64 VOL: 39 PG:264 - 274 :: QUAL. :INT. LOG. :THEORY :OTH.FIN.ACC.

CHAMBERS,RJ CIT: 0.15
THE PRICE LEVEL PROBLEM AND SOME INTELLECTUAL GROOVES
JAR AU 65 VOL: 3 PG:242 - 252 :: ANAL. :INT. LOG. :THEORY :VALUAT.(INFL.)

CHAMBERS,RJ CIT: 0.23
EDWARDS AND BELL ON BUSINESS INCOME
TAR OC 65 VOL: 40 PG:731 - 741 :: QUAL. :INT. LOG. :THEORY :VALUAT.(INFL.)

CHAMBERS,RJ CIT: 0.15
MEASUREMENT IN ACCOUNTING
JAR SP 65 VOL: 3 PG:32 - 62 :: QUAL. :INT. LOG. :THEORY :VALUAT.(INFL.)

CHAMBERS,RJ CIT: 0.15
A MATTER OF PRINCIPLE
TAR JL 66 VOL: 41 PG:443 - 457 :: QUAL. :INT. LOG. :THEORY :FIN.METH.

CHAMBERS,RJ CIT: 0.00
PROSPECTIVE ADVENTURES IN ACCOUNTING IDEAS
TAR AP 67 VOL: 42 PG:241 - 253 :: QUAL. :INT. LOG. :THEORY :FIN.METH.

CHAMBERS,RJ CIT: 0.15
CONTINUOUSLY CONTEMPORARY ACCOUNTING - ADDITIVITY AND ACTION
TAR OC 67 VOL: 42 PG:751 - 757 :: QUAL. :INT. LOG. :THEORY :VALUAT.(INFL.)

CHAMBERS,RJ CIT: 0.00
MEASURES AND VALUES
TAR AP 68 VOL: 43 PG:239 - 247 :: QUAL. :INT. LOG. :THEORY :VALUAT.(INFL.)

CHAMBERS,RJ CIT: 0.00
MEASUREMENT IN CURRENT ACCOUNTING PRACTICES: A CRITIQUE
TAR JL 72 VOL: 47 PG:488 - 509 :: ANAL. :INT. LOG. :THEORY :OTH.FIN.ACC.

CHAMBERS,RJ CIT: 0.00
CANNING'S THE ECONOMICS OF ACCOUNTANCY - AFTER 50 YEARS
TAR OC 79 VOL: 54 PG:764 - 775 :: QUAL. :INT. LOG. :HIST. :N/A

CHAMBERS,RJ CIT: 0.00
THE MYTHS AND SCIENCE OF ACCOUNTING
AOS 01 80 VOL: 5 PG:167 - 180 :: QUAL. :INT. LOG. :THEORY :N/A

CHAN ,JL CIT: 0.00
ORGANIZATIONAL CONSENSUS REGARDING THE RELATIVE IMPORTANCE OF RESEARCH OUTPUT
    INDICATORS
TAR AP 78 VOL: 53 PG:309 - 323 :: NON-PAR. :CASE :HIPS :MANAG.

CHAN ,JL CIT: 0.10
CORPORATE DISCLOSURE IN OCCUPATIONAL SAFETY AND HEALTH: SOME EMPIRICAL
    EVIDENCE
AOS 04 79 VOL: 4 PG:273 - 282 :: DES.STAT. :PRIM. :THEORY :HRA

CHAN ,KH ; SEC: CHENG ,TT CIT: 0.00
THE RECOVERY OF NUCLEAR POWER PLANT DECOMMISSIONING COSTS
JAA WI 84 VOL: 7 PG:164 - 177 :: QUAL. :INT. LOG. :THEORY :COST.ALLOC.

CHAN ,KH ; SEC: DODIN ,B CIT: 0.00
A DECISION SUPPORT SYSTEM FOR AUDIT-STAFF SCHEDULING WITH PRECEDENCE
    CONSTRAINTS
TAR OC 86 VOL: 61 PG:726 - 734 :: DES.STAT. :INT. LOG. :MATH.PROG. :ORG.

CHANDLER,AD ; SEC: DAEMS ,H CIT: 0.70
ADMINISTRATIVE COORDINATION, ALLOCATION AND MONITORING: A COMPARATIVE
    ANALYSIS OF EMERGENCE OF ACCOUNTING AND ORGANIZATIONS IN USA AND EUROPE
AOS 12 79 VOL: 4 PG:3 - 20 :: QUAL. :INT. LOG. :HIST. :N/A

CHANDRA,G CIT: 0.31
A STUDY OF THE CONSENSUS ON DISCLOSURE AMONG PUBLIC ACCOUNTANTS AND SECURITY
    ANALYSTS
TAR OC 74 VOL: 49 PG:733 - 742 :: DES.STAT. :LAB. :N/A :INFO.STRUC.

CHAPMAN,G ; FIRS: KROSS ,W ; THIR: STRAND,KH CIT: 0.00
FULLY DILUTED EARNINGS PER SHARE AND SECURITY RETURNS: SOME ADDITIONAL
    EVIDENCE
JAA AU 80 VOL: 4 PG:36 - 46 :: CORR. :SEC. :EMH :CASH DIV.

CHARNES,A ; SEC: COOPER,WW ; THIR: IJIRI ,Y CIT: 0.08
BREAKEVEN BUDGETING AND PROGRAMMING TO GOALS
JAR SP 63 VOL: 1 PG:16 - 43 :: ANAL. :INT. LOG. :MATH.PROG. :C-V-P-A

CHARNES,A ; SEC: DAVIDSON,HJ ; THIR: KORTANEK,KO CIT: 0.00
ON A MIXED-SEQUENTIAL ESTIMATING PROCEDURE WITH APPLICATION TO AUDIT TESTS IN
    ACCOUNTING
TAR AP 64 VOL: 39 PG:241 - 250 :: ANAL. :INT. LOG. :OTH.STAT. :SAMP.

CHARNES,A ; SEC: COOPER,WW CIT: 0.08
SOME NETWORK CHARACTERIZATIONS FOR MATHEMATICAL PROGRAMMING AND ACCOUNTINC
    APPROACHES TO PLANNING AND CONTROL
TAR JA 67 VOL: 42 PG:24 - 52 :: ANAL. :INT. LOG. :MATH.PROG. :MANAG.

CHARNES,A ; FIRS: BYRNE ,R ; THIR: COOPER,WW ; FOUR: KORTANEK,KO CIT: 0.00
SOME NEW APPROACHES TO RISK
TAR JA 68 VOL: 43 PG:18 - 37 :: ANAL. :INT. LOG. :MATH.PROG. :BUDG.& PLAN.

CHARNES,A ; SEC: COLANTONI,CS ; THIR: COOPER,WW ; FOUR: KORTANEK,KO CIT: 0.08
ECONOMIC SOCIAL AND ENTERPRISE ACCOUNTING AND MATHEMATICAL MODES
TAR JA 72 VOL: 47 PG:85 - 108 :: ANAL. :INT. LOG. :MATH.PROG. :FIN.METH.

CHARNES,A ; SEC: COLANTONI,CS ; THIR: COOPER,WW CIT: 0.00
A FUTUROLOGICAL JUSTIFICATION FOR HISTORICAL COST AND MULTI-DIMENSIONAL
    ACCOUNTING
AOS 04 76 VOL: 1 PG:315 - 338 :: ANAL. :INT. LOG. :MATH.PROG. :HRA

CHARNES,A ; SEC: COOPER,WW CIT: 0.00
AUDITING AND ACCOUNTING FOR PROBLEM EFFICIENCY AND MANAGEMENT EFFICIENCY IN
    NOT-FOR PROFIT ENTITIES
AOS 01 80 VOL: 5 PG:87 - 107 :: MIXED :PRIM. :OTH.STAT. :AUD.

CHARNES,A ; FIRS: BROCKETT,P ; THIR: COOPER,WW ; FOUR: SHIN ,HC CIT: 0.00
A CHANCE-CONSTRAINED PROGRAMMING APPROACH TO COST-VOLUME-PROFIT ANALYSIS
TAR JL 84 VOL: 59 PG:474 - 487 :: ANAL. :INT. LOG. :MATH.PROG. :C-V-P-A

CHASTEEN,LG CIT: 0.23
AN EMPIRICAL STUDY OF DIFFERENCES IN ECONOMIC CIRCUMSTANCES AS A
    JUSTIFICATION FOR ALTERNATIVE INVENTORY PRICING METHODS
TAR JL 71 VOL: 46 PG:504 - 508 :: ANOVA :PRIM. :N/A :INV.

CHASTEEN,LG CIT: 0.00
IMPLICIT FACTORS IN THE EVALUATION OF LEASE VS. BUY ALTERNATIVES
TAR OC 73 VOL: 48 PG:764 - 767 :: ANAL. :INT. LOG. :N/A :LEASES

CHATFIELD,M CIT: 0.00
THE ACCOUNTING REVIEW'S FIRST FIFTY YEARS
TAR JA 75 VOL: 50 PG:1 - 6 :: QUAL. :SEC. :HIST. :N/A

CHEN ,JT CIT: 0.00
COST ALLOCATION AND EXTERNAL ACQUISITION OF SERVICES WHEN SELF-SERVICES EXIST
TAR JL 83 VOL: 58 PG:600 - 605 :: ANAL. :INT. LOG. :OTH.STAT. :COST.ALLOC.

CHEN ,K ; SEC: SUMMERS,EL CIT: 0.25
A STUDY OF REPORTING PROBABILISTIC ACCOUNTING FIGURES
AOS 01 81 VOL: 6 PG:1 - 16 :: ANOVA :LAB. :HIPS :MANAG.

CHEN ,RS CIT: 0.31
SOCIAL AND FINANCIAL STEWARDSHIP
TAR JL 75 VOL: 50 PG:533 - 543 :: QUAL. :INT. LOG. :THEORY :OTH.MANAG.

CHENG ,TT ; FIRS: CHAN ,KH CIT: 0.00
THE RECOVERY OF NUCLEAR POWER PLANT DECOMMISSIONING COSTS
JAA WI 84 VOL: 7 PG:164 - 177 :: QUAL. :INT. LOG. :THEORY :COST.ALLOC.

CHENHALL,RH CIT: 0.00
AUTHORITARIANISM AND PARTICIPATIVE BUDGETING - A DYADIC ANALYSIS
TAR AP 86 VOL: 61 PG:263 - 272 :: REGRESS. :SURV. :OTH.BEH. :BUDG.& PLAN.

CHENHALL,RH ; SEC: MORRIS,D CIT: 1.00
THE IMPACT OF STRUCTURE, ENVIRONMENT, AND INTERDEPENDENCE ON THE PERCEIVED
   USEFULNESS OF MANAGEMENT ACCOUNTING SYSTEMS
TAR JA 86 VOL: 61 PG:16 - 35 :: REGRESS. :SURV. :OTH.STAT. :ORG.& ENVIR.

CHENHALL,RH ; SEC: BROWNELL,P CIT: 0.00
THE EFFECT OF PARTICIPATIVE BUDGETING ON JOB SATISFACTION AND PERFORMANCE:
   ROLE AMBIGUITY AS AN INTERVENING VARIABLE
AOS 03 88 VOL: 13 PG:225 - 233 :: ANOVA :SURV. :EMH :BUDG.& PLAN.

CHERNS,AB CIT: 0.36
ALIENATION AND ACCOUNTANCY
AOS 02 78 VOL: 3 PG:105 - 114 :: QUAL. :INT. LOG. :OTH. :N/A

CHERRINGTON,DJ ; SEC: CHERRINGTON,JO CIT: 0.85
APPROPRIATE REINFORCEMENT CONTINGENCIES IN THE BUDGETING PROCESS
JAR ST 73 VOL: 11 PG:225 - 253 :: ANOVA :LAB. :OTH.BEH. :BUDG.& PLAN.

CHERRINGTON,JO ; FIRS: CHERRINGTON,DJ CIT: 0.85
APPROPRIATE REINFORCEMENT CONTINGENCIES IN THE BUDGETING PROCESS
JAR ST 73 VOL: 11 PG:225 - 253 :: ANOVA :LAB. :OTH.BEH. :BUDG.& PLAN.

CHESLEY,GR CIT: 1.00
ELICITATION OF SUBJECTIVE PROBABILITIES: A REVIEW
TAR AP 75 VOL: 50 PG:325 - 337 :: QUAL. :SEC. :OTH.BEH. :PROB.ELIC.

CHESLEY,GR CIT: 0.54
THE ELICITATION OF SUBJECTIVE PROBABILITIES: A LABORATORY STUDY IN AN
   ACCOUNTING CONTEXT
JAR SP 76 VOL: 14 PG:27 - 48 :: ANOVA :LAB. :HIPS :PROB.ELIC.

CHESLEY,GR ; FIRS: HEIMANN,SR CIT: 0.17
AUDIT SAMPLE SIZES FOR AGGREGATED STATEMENT ACCOUNTS
JAR AU 77 VOL: 15 PG:193 - 206 :: ANAL. :INT. LOG. :MATH.PROG. :SAMP.

CHESLEY,GR CIT: 0.58
SUBJECTIVE PROBABILITY ELICITATION: THE EFFECT OF CONGRUITY OF DATUM AND
   RESPONSE MODE ON PERFORMANCE
JAR SP 77 VOL: 15 PG:1 - 11 :: NON-PAR. :LAB. :HIPS :PROB.ELIC.

CHESLEY,GR CIT: 0.27
SUBJECTIVE PROBABILITY ELICITATION TECHNIQUES: A PERFORMANCE COMPARISON
JAR AU 78 VOL: 16 PG:225 - 241 :: ANOVA :LAB. :HIPS :PROB.ELIC.

CHEUNG,JK ; FIRS: WHALEY,RE CIT: 0.14
ANTICIPATION OF QUARTERLY EARNINGS ANNOUNCEMENTS: A TEST OF OPTION MARKET
   EFFICIENCY
JAE OC 82 VOL: 4 PG:57 - 83 :: REGRESS. :SEC. :EMH :INT.REP.

CHEWNING,EG ; FIRS: INGRAM,RW CIT: 0.00
THE EFFECT OF FINANCIAL DISCLOSURE REGULATION ON SECURITY MARKET BEHAVIOR
TAR JL 83 VOL: 58 PG:562 - 580 :: REGRESS. :PRIM. :EMH :FIN.METH.

CHEWNING,EG ; FIRS: HARRELL,AM ; THIR: TAYLOR,M CIT: 0.00
ORGANIZATIONAL-PROFESSIONAL CONFLICT AND THE JOB SATISFACTION AND TURNOVER
  INTENTIONS OF INTERNAL AUDITORS
AUD SP 86 VOL: 5 PG:111 - 121 :: REGRESS. :SURV. :OTH.BEH. :AUD.TRAIL

CHIU ,JS ; SEC: DECOSTER,DT CIT: 0.00
MULTIPLE PRODUCT COSTING BY MULTIPLE CORRELATION ANALYSIS
TAR OC 66 VOL: 41 PG:673 - 680 :: REGRESS. :INT. LOG. :TIME SER. :COST.ALLOC.

CHOI ,FD CIT: 0.23
FINANCIAL DISCLOSURE AND ENTRY TO THE EUROPEAN CAPITAL MARKET
JAR AU 73 VOL: 11 PG:159 - 175 :: NON-PAR. :PRIM. :INSTIT. :INFO.STRUC.

CHOO ,F CIT: 0.00
JOB STRESS, JOB PERFORMANCE, AND AUDITOR PERSONALITY CHARACTERISTICS
AUD SP 86 VOL: 5 PG:17 - 34 :: REGRESS. :SURV. :HIPS :AUD.BEH.

CHOTTINER,S ; SEC: YOUNG ,AE CIT: 0.08
A TEST OF THE AICPA DIFFERENTIATION BETWEEN STOCK DIVIDENDS AND STOCK SPLITS
JAR AU 71 VOL: 9 PG:367 - 374 :: DES.STAT. :PRIM. :OTH. :STK.DIV.

CHOUDHURY,N CIT: 0.00
THE SEEKING OF ACCOUNTING WHERE IT IS NOT: TOWARDS A THEORY OF NON-ACCOUNTING
  IN ORGANIZATIONAL SETTINGS
AOS 06 88 VOL: 13 PG:549 - 557 :: DES.STAT. :INT. LOG. :THEORY :ORG.& ENVIR.

CHOW ,CW CIT: 1.14
THE DEMAND FOR EXTERNAL AUDITING: SIZE, DEBT AND OWNERSHIP INFLUENCES
TAR AP 82 VOL: 57 PG:272 - 291 :: DES.STAT. :PRIM. :INF.ECO./AG. :AUD.

CHOW ,CW ; SEC: RICE ,SJ CIT: 0.71
QUALIFIED AUDIT OPINIONS AND AUDITOR SWITCHING
TAR AP 82 VOL: 57 PG:326 - 335 :: DES.STAT. :PRIM. :OTH. :OPIN.

CHOW ,CW ; SEC: RICE ,SJ CIT: 0.43
QUALIFIED AUDIT OPINIONS AND SHARE PRICES - AN INVESTIGATION
AUD WI 82 VOL: 1 PG:35 - 53 :: MIXED :PRIM. :EMH :OPIN.

CHOW ,CW CIT: 0.33
THE IMPACTS OF ACCOUNTING REGULATION ON BONDHOLDER AND SHAREHOLDER WEALTH:
  THE CASE OF THE SECURITIES ACTS
TAR JL 83 VOL: 58 PG:485 - 520 :: REGRESS. :PRIM. :EMH :FIN.METH.

CHOW ,CW CIT: 0.67
THE EFFECTS OF JOB STANDARD TIGHTNESS AND COMPENSATION SCHEME ON PERFORMANCE:
  AN EXPLORATION OF LINKAGES
TAR OC 83 VOL: 58 PG:667 - 685 :: ANOVA :LAB. :OTH.STAT. :BUDG.& PLAN.

CHOW ,CW ; FIRS: WALLER,WS CIT: 0.50
THE SELF-SELECTION AND EFFORT EFFECTS OF STANDARD-BASED EMPLOYEE CONTRACTS: A
  FRAMEWORK AND SOME EMPIRICAL EVIDENCE
TAR JL 85 VOL: 60 PG:458 - 476 :: REGRESS. :LAB. :OTH.BEH. :EXEC.COMP.

CHOW ,CW ; FIRS: BLANCHARD,GA ; THIR: NOREEN,EW CIT: 0.00
INFORMATION ASYMMETRY, INCENTIVE SCHEMES, AND INFORMATION BIASING: THE CASE
  OF HOSPITAL BUDGETING UNDER RATE REGULATION
TAR JA 86 VOL: 61 PG:1 - 15 :: REGRESS. :PRIM. :N/A :BUDG.& PLAN.

CHOW ,CW ; SEC: WONG-BOREN,A CIT: 0.00
VOLUNTARY FINANCIAL DISCLOSURE BY MEXICAN CORPORATIONS
TAR JL 87 VOL: 62 PG:533 - 541 :: REGRESS. :PRIM. :OTH.STAT. :FIN.METH.

CHOW ,CW ; SEC: MCNAMEE,AH ; THIR: PLUMLEE,RD CIT: 0.00
PRACTITIONERS' PERCEPTIONS OF AUDIT STEP DIFFICULTY AND CRITICALNESS
    IMPLICATIONS FOR AUDIT RESEARCH
AUD SP 87 VOL: 6 PG:123 - 133 :: REGRESS. :SURV. :OTH.STAT. :AUD.THEOR.

CHOW ,CW ; SEC: COOPER,JC ; THIR: WALLER,WS CIT: 0.00
PARTICIPATIVE BUDGETING: EFFECTS OF A TRUTH-INDUCING PAY SCHEME AND
    INFORMATION ASYMMETRY ON SLACK AND PERFORMANCE
TAR JA 88 VOL: 63 PG:111 - 122 :: REGRESS. :LAB. :OTH.BEH. :BUDG.& PLAN.

CHRISTENSEN,J CIT: 1.00
THE DETERMINATION OF PERFORMANCE STANDARDS AND PARTICIPATION
JAR AU 82 VOL: 20 PG:589 - 603 :: ANAL. :INT. LOG. :INF.ECO./AG. :BUDG.& PLAN.

CHRISTENSON,C CIT: 1.50
THE METHODOLOGY OF POSITIVE ACCOUNTING
TAR JA 83 VOL: 58 PG:1 - 22 :: QUAL. :SEC. :OTH. :METHOD.

CHRISTIE,AA ; FIRS: BEAVER,WH ; THIR: GRIFFIN,PA CIT: 2.00
THE INFORMATION CONTENT OF SEC ACCOUNTING SERIES RELEASE NO.190
JAE AG 80 VOL: 2 PG:127 - 157 :: REGRESS. :PRIM. :EMH :VALUAT.(INFL.)

CHRISTIE,AA ; SEC: KENNELLEY,MD ; THIR: KING ,JW ; FOUR: SCHAEFER,TF CIT: 1.20
TESTING FOR INCREMENTAL INFORMATION CONTENT IN THE PRESENCE OF COLLINEARITY
JAE DE 84 VOL: 6 PG:205 - 217 :: ANAL. :INT. LOG. :OTH.STAT. :METHOD.

CHRISTIE,AA CIT: 1.00
ON CROSS-SECTIONAL ANALYSIS IN ACCOUNTING RESEARCH
JAE DE 87 VOL: 9 PG:231 - 258 :: DES.STAT. :INT. LOG. :EMH :METHOD.

CHUA ,WF CIT: 0.67
RADICAL DEVELOPMENTS IN ACCOUNTING THOUGHT
TAR OC 86 VOL: 61 PG:601 - 632 :: DES.STAT. :INT. LOG. :THEORY :METHOD.

CHUA ,WF CIT: 0.00
THEORETICAL CONSTRUCTIONS OF AND BY THE REAL
AOS 06 86 VOL: 11 PG:583 - 598 :: DES.STAT. :INT. LOG. :THEORY :FASB SUBM.

CHUMACHENKO,NG CIT: 0.00
ONCE AGAIN: THE VOLUME-MIX-PRICE/COST BUDGET VARIANCE ANALYSIS
TAR OC 68 VOL: 43 PG:753 - 762 :: ANAL. :INT. LOG. :N/A :VAR.

CHURCHILL,NC CIT: 0.08
LINEAR ALGEBRA AND COST ALLOCATIONS: SOME EXAMPLES
TAR OC 64 VOL: 39 PG:894 - 904 :: ANAL. :INT. LOG. :MATH.PROG. :COST.ALLOC.

CHURCHILL,NC ; SEC: COOPER,WW CIT: 0.15
A FIELD STUDY OF INTERNAL AUDITING
TAR OC 65 VOL: 40 PG:767 - 781 :: DES.STAT. :FIELD :OTH.BEH. :AUD.

CHURCHILL,NC CIT: 0.08
AUDIT RECOMMENDATIONS AND MANAGEMENT AUDITING: A CASE STUDY AND SOME REMARKS
JAR ST 66 VOL: 4 PG:128 - 156 :: QUAL. :CASE :THEORY :AUD.

CHURCHILL,NC ; SEC: SHANK ,JK CIT: 0.15
ACCOUNTING FOR AFFIRMATIVE ACTION PROGRAMS: A STOCHASTIC FLOW APPROACH
TAR OC 75 VOL: 50 PG:643 - 656 :: ANOVA :FIELD :OTH.STAT. :HRA

CHURCHILL,NC ; SEC: COOPER,WW ; THIR: GOVINDARAJAN,V CIT: 0.00
EFFECTS OF AUDITS ON THE BEHAVIOR OF MEDICAL PROFESSIONALS UNDER THE BENNETT
AMENDMENT
AUD WI 82 VOL: 1 PG:69 - 91 :: ANOVA :PRIM. :OTH.STAT. :OPER.AUD.

CHURCHMAN,CW CIT: 0.00
ON THE FACILITY, FELICITY, AND MORALITY OF MEASURING SOCIAL CHANGE
TAR JA 71 VOL: 46 PG:30 - 35 :: QUAL. :INT. LOG. :INSTIT. :HRA

CIANCIOLO,ST ; FIRS: NURNBERG,H CIT: 0.00
THE MEASUREMENT VALUATION ALLOWANCE: HELP FOR DEFERRED TAXES
JAA AU 85 VOL: 9 PG:50 - 59 :: DES.STAT. :INT. LOG. :THEORY :TAXES

CLANCY,DK ; SEC: COLLINS,F CIT: 0.30
INFORMAL ACCOUNTING INFORMATION SYSTEMS: SOME TENTATIVE FINDINGS
AOS 12 79 VOL: 4 PG:21 - 30 :: OTH.QUANT. :SURV. :THEORY :N/A

CLARK ,JJ ; SEC: ELGERS,PT CIT: 0.00
FORECASTED INCOME STATEMENTS: AN INVESTOR PERSPECTIVE
TAR OC 73 VOL: 48 PG:668 - 678 :: CORR. :CASE :OTH.STAT. :BUDG.& PLAN.

CLARK ,TN CIT: 0.00
FISCAL MANAGEMENT OF AMERICAN CITIES: FUNDS FLOW INDICATORS
JAR ST 77 VOL: 15 PG:54 - 94 :: REGRESS. :PRIM. :OTH.STAT. :OTH.MANAG.

CLARKE,CK ; FIRS: PESANDO,JE CIT: 0.00
ECONOMIC MODELS OF THE LABOR MARKET AND PENSION ACCOUNTING: AN EXPLORATORY
ANALYSIS
TAR OC 83 VOL: 58 PG:733 - 748 :: ANAL. :INT. LOG. :OTH.STAT. :PENS.

CLARKE,R ; FIRS: BEAVER,WH ; THIR: WRIGHT,WF CIT: 4.20
THE ASSOCIATION BETWEEN UNSYSTEMATIC SECURITY RETURNS AND THE MAGNITUDE OF
EARNINGS FORECAST ERRORS
JAR AU 79 VOL: 17 PG:316 - 340 :: NON-PAR. :PRIM. :EMH :FOREC.

CLARKE,RW CIT: 0.08
EXTENSION OF THE CPA'S ATTEST FUNCTION IN CORPORATE ANNUAL REPORTS
TAR OC 68 VOL: 43 PG:769 - 776 :: QUAL. :INT. LOG. :INSTIT. :OPIN.

CLARKE,RW ; FIRS: ROBERTSON,JC CIT: 0.15
VERIFICATION OF MANAGEMENT REPRESENTATIONS: A FIRST STEP TOWARD INDEPENDENT
AUDITS OF MANAGEMENT
TAR JL 71 VOL: 46 PG:562 - 571 :: DES.STAT. :PRIM. :N/A :AUD.

CLAY JR,RJ ; FIRS: SUMNERS,GE ; SEC: WHITE ,RA CIT: 0.00
THE USE OF ENGAGEMENT LETTERS IN AUDIT, REVIEW, AND COMPILATION ENGAGEMENTS:
AN EMPIRICAL STUDY
AUD SP 87 VOL: 6 PG:116 - 122 :: REGRESS. :SURV. :OTH.BEH. :ORG.

CLINCH,GJ ; SEC: SINCLAIR,NA CIT: 0.00
INTRA-INDUSTRY INFORMATION RELEASES: A RECURSIVE SYSTEMS APPROACH
JAE AP 87 VOL: 9 PG:89 - 106 :: REGRESS. :PRIM. :EMH :FIN.METH.

CLOUSE,ML ; FIRS: SELTO ,FH CIT: 0.00
AN INVESTIGATION OF MANAGERS' ADAPTATIONS TO SFAS NO. 2: ACCOUNTING FOR
RESEARCH AND DEVELOPMENT COSTS
JAR AU 85 VOL: 23 PG:700 - 717 :: REGRESS. :PRIM. :EMH :R & D

CLUBB ,C ; FIRS: BURCHELL,S ; THIR: HOPWOOD,AG ; FOUR: HUGHES,JS ; FIFT:
NAHAPIET,JE CIT: 3.89
THE ROLES OF ACCOUNTING IN ORGANIZATIONS AND SOCIETY
AOS 01 80 VOL: 5 PG:5 - 27 :: QUAL. :INT. LOG. :THEORY :N/A

CLUBB ,C ; FIRS: BURCHELL,S ; THIR: HOPWOOD,AG CIT: 3.75
ACCOUNTING IN ITS SOCIAL CONTEXT: TOWARDS A HISTORY OF VALUE ADDED IN THE
    UNITED KINGDOM
AOS 04 85 VOL: 10 PG:381 - 414 :: DES.STAT. :INT. LOG. :THEORY :HRA

COATES,R CIT: 0.38
THE PREDICTIVE CONTENT OF INTERIM REPORTS - A TIME SERIES ANALYSIS
JAR ST 72 VOL: 10 PG:132 - 144 :: MIXED :PRIM. :TIME SER. :INT.REP.

COE ,TL CIT: 0.00
AN ANALYSIS OF THE SEC MONITORING OF PROSPECT USES
JAA SP 79 VOL: 2 PG:244 - 253 :: DES.STAT. :PRIM. :INSTIT. :OTH.MANAG.

COGGER,KO CIT: 0.25
A TIME-SERIES ANALYTIC APPROACH TO AGGREGATION ISSUES IN ACCOUNTING DATA
JAR AU 81 VOL: 19 PG:285 - 298 :: ANAL. :INT. LOG. :TIME SER. :INFO.STRUC.

COGGER,KO ; FIRS: EMERY ,GW CIT: 0.14
THE MEASUREMENT OF LIQUIDITY
JAR AU 82 VOL: 20 PG:290 - 303 :: ANAL. :PRIM. :OTH.STAT. :BUS.FAIL.

COGGER,KO ; SEC: RULAND,W CIT: 0.00
A NOTE ON ALTERNATIVE TESTS FOR INDEPENDENCE OF FINANCIAL TIME SERIES
JAR AU 82 VOL: 20 PG:733 - 737 :: CORR. :PRIM. :TIME SER. :METHOD.

COGLITORE,F ; SEC: BERRYMAN,RG CIT: 0.00
ANALYTICAL PROCEDURES: A DEFENSIVE NECESSITY
AUD SP 88 VOL: 07 PG:150 - 163 :: REGRESS. :SIM. :THEORY :ANAL.REV.

COHEN ,MA ; SEC: HALPERIN,R CIT: 0.33
OPTIMAL INVENTORY ORDER POLICY FOR A FIRM USING THE LIFO INVENTORY COSTING
    METHOD
JAR AU 80 VOL: 18 PG:375 - 389 :: ANAL. :SIM. :MATH.PROG. :INV.

COHEN ,MF CIT: 0.00
CURRENT DEVELOPMENTS AT THE SEC
TAR JA 65 VOL: 40 PG:1 - 8 :: QUAL. :SEC. :INSTIT. :AUD.

COHEN ,SI ; SEC: LOEB ,M CIT: 0.00
PUBLIC GOODS, COMMON INPUTS, AND THE EFFICIENCY OF FULL COST ALLOCATIONS
TAR AP 82 VOL: 57 PG:336 - 347 :: ANAL. :INT. LOG. :OTH.STAT. :COST.ALLOC.

COLANTONI,CS ; SEC: MANES ,RP ; THIR: WHINSTON,AB CIT: 0.08
PROGRAMMING, PROFIT RATES AND PRICING DECISIONS
TAR JL 69 VOL: 44 PG:467 - 481 :: ANAL. :INT. LOG. :MATH.PROG. :REL.COSTS

COLANTONI,CS ; SEC: MANES ,RP ; THIR: WHINSTON,AB CIT: 0.46
A UNIFIED APPROACH TO THE THEORY OF ACCOUNTING AND INFORMATION SYSTEMS
TAR JA 71 VOL: 46 PG:90 - 102 :: QUAL. :INT. LOG. :N/A :MANAG.

COLANTONI,CS ; FIRS: CHARNES,A ; THIR: COOPER,WW ; FOUR: KORTANEK,KO CIT: 0.08
ECONOMIC SOCIAL AND ENTERPRISE ACCOUNTING AND MATHEMATICAL MODES
TAR JA 72 VOL: 47 PG:85 - 108 :: ANAL. :INT. LOG. :MATH.PROG. :FIN.METH.

COLANTONI,CS ; FIRS: CHARNES,A ; THIR: COOPER,WW CIT: 0.00
A FUTUROLOGICAL JUSTIFICATION FOR HISTORICAL COST AND MULTI-DIMENSIONAL
    ACCOUNTING
AOS 04 76 VOL: 1 PG:315 - 338 :: ANAL. :INT. LOG. :MATH.PROG. :HRA

COLBERT,JL CIT: 0.00
INHERENT RISK: AN INVESTIGATION OF AUDITORS' JUDGMENTS
AOS 02 88 VOL: 13 PG:111 - 121 :: REGRESS. :LAB. :HIPS :JUDG.

COLDWELL,S ; FIRS: HORVITZ,JS CIT: 0.00
ANALYSIS OF THE ARTHUR YOUNG DECISION AND ITS POTENTIAL IMPACT ON PUBLIC
    ACCOUNTING
JAA WI 85 VOL: 8 PG:86 - 99 :: REGRESS. :CASE :THEORY :LITIG.

COLIGNON,R ; SEC: COVALESKI,M CIT: 0.00
AN EXAMINATION OF MANAGERIAL ACCOUNTING PRACTICES AS A PROCESS OF MUTUAL
    ADJUSTMENT
AOS 06 88 VOL: 13 PG:559 - 579 :: REGRESS. :CASE :THEORY :BUDG.& PLAN.

COLLINS,DW ; SEC: SIMONDS,RR CIT: 0.20
SEC LINE-OF-BUSINESS DISCLOSURE AND MARKET RISK ADJUSTMENTS
JAR AU 79 VOL: 17 PG:352 - 383 :: MIXED :PRIM. :EMH :SEG.REP.

COLLINS,DW ; SEC: DENT ,WT CIT: 3.00
THE PROPOSED ELIMINATION OF FULL COST ACCOUNTING IN THE EXTRACTIVE PETROLEUM
    INDUSTRY: AN EMPIRICAL ASSESSMENT OF MARKET CONSEQUENCES
JAE MR 79 VOL: 1 PG:3 - 44 :: NON-PAR. :PRIM. :EMH :OIL & GAS

COLLINS,DW ; SEC: ROZEFF,MS ; THIR: DHALIWAL,DS CIT: 3.88
THE ECONOMIC DETERMINANTS OF THE MARKET REACTION TO PROPOSED MANDATORY
    ACCOUNTING CHANGES IN THE OIL AND GAS INDUSTRY: A CROSS-SECTIONAL ANALYSIS
JAE MR 81 VOL: 3 PG:37 - 71 :: REGRESS. :PRIM. :EMH :OIL & GAS

COLLINS,DW ; SEC: ROZEFF,MS ; THIR: SALATKA,WK CIT: 1.00
THE SEC'S REJECTION OF SFAS NO.19: TESTS OF MARKET PRICE REVERSAL
TAR JA 82 VOL: 57 PG:1 - 17 :: CORR. :PRIM. :EMH :OIL & GAS

COLLINS,DW ; SEC: DENT ,WT CIT: 1.40
A COMPARISON OF ALTERNATIVE TESTING METHODOLOGIES USED IN CAPITAL MARKET
    RESEARCH
JAR SP 84 VOL: 22 PG:48 - 84 :: MIXED :SIM. :EMH :METHOD.

COLLINS,DW ; SEC: KOTHARI,SP ; THIR: RAYBURN,JD CIT: 1.00
FIRM SIZE AND THE INFORMATION CONTENT OF PRICES WITH RESPECT TO EARNINGS
JAE JL 87 VOL: 9 PG:111 - 138 :: REGRESS. :PRIM. :EMH :ORG.& ENVIR.

COLLINS,DW ; FIRS: DORAN ,BM ; THIR: DHALIWAL,DS CIT: 0.00
THE INFORMATION OF HISTORICAL COST EARNINGS RELATIVE TO SUPPLEMENTAL
    RESERVE-BASED ACCOUNTING DATA IN THE EXTRACTIVE PETROLEUM INDUSTRY
TAR JL 88 VOL: 63 PG:389 - 413 :: REGRESS. :PRIM. :EMH :OIL & GAS

COLLINS,F CIT: 1.09
THE INTERACTION OF BUDGET CHARACTERISTICS AND PERSONALITY VARIABLES WITH
    BUDGETARY RESPONSE ATTITUDES
TAR AP 78 VOL: 53 PG:324 - 335 :: REGRESS. :FIELD :OTH.BEH. :BUDG.& PLAN.

COLLINS,F ; FIRS: CLANCY,DK CIT: 0.30
INFORMAL ACCOUNTING INFORMATION SYSTEMS: SOME TENTATIVE FINDINGS
AOS 12 79 VOL: 4 PG:21 - 30 :: OTH.QUANT. :SURV. :THEORY :N/A

COLLINS,F CIT: 0.57
MANAGERIAL ACCOUNTING SYSTEMS AND ORGANIZATIONAL CONTROL: A ROLE PERSPECTIVE
AOS 02 82 VOL: 7 PG:107 - 122 :: QUAL. :SURV. :OTH.BEH. :N/A

COLLINS,F ; SEC: MUNTER,P ; THIR: FINN ,DW CIT: 0.00
THE BUDGETING GAMES PEOPLE PLAY
TAR JA 87 VOL: 62 PG:29 - 49 :: REGRESS. :SURV. :OTH.BEH. :BUDG.& PLAN.

COLLINS,WA ; SEC: HOPWOOD,WS CIT: 1.22
A MULTIVARIATE ANALYSIS OF ANNUAL EARNINGS FORECASTS GENERATED FROM QUARTERLY
    FORECASTS OF FINANCIAL ANALYSTS AND UNIVARIATE TIME-SERIES MODELS
JAR AU 80 VOL: 18 PG:390 - 406 :: ANOVA :PRIM. :TIME SER. :FOREC.

COLLINS,WA ; SEC: HOPWOOD,WS ; THIR: MCKEOWN,JC CIT: 0.20
THE PREDICTABILITY OF INTERIM EARNINGS OVER ALTERNATIVE QUARTERS
JAR AU 84 VOL: 22 PG:467 - 479 :: NON-PAR. :PRIM. :TIME SER. :INT.REP.

COLLINSON,D ; FIRS: KNIGHTS,D CIT: 0.00
DISCIPLINING THE SHOPFLOOR: A COMPARISON OF THE DISCIPLINARY EFFECTS
    OF MANAGERIAL PSYCHOLOGY AND FINANCIAL ACCOUNTING
AOS 05 87 VOL: 12 PG:457 - 477 :: DES.STAT. :INT. LOG. :THEORY :HRA

COLVILLE,I CIT: 1.38
RECONSTRUCTING "BEHAVIOURAL ACCOUNTING"
AOS 02 81 VOL: 6 PG:119 - 132 :: QUAL. :INT. LOG. :OTH.BEH. :N/A

COMISKEY,EE CIT: 0.08
COST CONTROL BY REGRESSION ANALYSIS
TAR AP 66 VOL: 41 PG:235 - 238 :: REGRESS. :INT. LOG. :OTH.STAT. :VAR.

COMISKEY,EE ; SEC: MLYNARCZYK,FA CIT: 0.00
RECOGNITION OF INCOME BY FINANCE COMPANIES
TAR AP 68 VOL: 43 PG:248 - 256 :: ANAL. :SIM. :THEORY :REV.REC.

COMISKEY,EE CIT: 0.38
MARKET RESPONSE TO CHANGES IN DEPRECIATION ACCOUNTING
TAR AP 71 VOL: 46 PG:279 - 285 :: ANOVA :PRIM. :N/A :PP&E / DEPR

COMISKEY,EE ; FIRS: BAREFIELD,RM CIT: 0.23
DEPRECIATION POLICY AND THE BEHAVIOR OF CORPORATE PROFITS
JAR AU 71 VOL: 9 PG:351 - 358 :: NON-PAR. :PRIM. :TIME SER. :FIN.METH.

COMISKEY,EE ; FIRS: BAREFIELD,RM CIT: 0.23
THE SMOOTHING HYPOTHESIS: AN ALTERNATIVE TEST
TAR AP 72 VOL: 47 PG:291 - 298 :: NON-PAR. :PRIM. :TIME SER. :FIN.METH.

COMISKEY,EE ; FIRS: MULFORD,CW CIT: 0.00
INVESTMENT DECISIONS AND THE EQUITY ACCOUNTING STANDARD
TAR JL 86 VOL: 61 PG:519 - 525 :: REGRESS. :PRIM. :OTH.STAT. :BUS.COMB.

CONROY, RM ; SEC: HUGHES,JS CIT: 0.50
DELEGATING INFORMATION GATHERING DECISIONS
TAR JA 87 VOL: 62 PG:50 - 66 :: DES.STAT. :INT. LOG. :INF.ECO./AG. :MANAG.

COOK ,DM CIT: 0.46
THE EFFECT OF FREQUENCY OF FEEDBACK ON ATTITUDES AND PERFORMANCE
JAR ST 67 VOL: 5 PG:213 - 224 :: ANOVA :LAB. :OTH.BEH. :BUDG.& PLAN.

COOK ,E ; FIRS: FLAMHOLTZ,EG CIT: 0.55
CONNOTATIVE MEANING AND ITS ROLE IN ACCOUNTING CHANGE: A FIELD STUDY
AOS 02 78 VOL: 3 PG:115 - 140 :: OTH.QUANT. :FIELD :OTH.BEH. :METHOD.

COOK ,FX ; FIRS: MAXIM ,LD ; SEC: CULLEN,PE CIT: 0.00
OPTIMAL ACCEPTANCE SAMPLING PLANS FOR AUDITING "BATCHED" STOP AND GO VS.
CONVENTIONAL SINGLE-STAGE ATTRIBUTES
TAR JA 76 VOL: 51 PG:97 - 109 :: ANAL. :INT. LOG. :OTH.STAT. :SAMP.

COOK ,JS ; SEC: HOLZMANN,OJ CIT: 0.08
CURRENT COST AND PRESENT VALUE IN INCOME THEORY
TAR OC 76 VOL: 51 PG:778 - 787 :: ANAL. :INT. LOG. :THEORY :VALUAT.(INFL.)

COOPER,D ; FIRS: BERRY ,AJ ; SEC: CAPPS ,T ; FOUR: FERGUSON,P ; FIFT: HOPPER,T
; SIX: LOWE ,EA CIT: 3.50
MANAGEMENT CONTROL IN AN AREA OF THE NCB: RATIONALES OF ACCOUNTING PRACTICES
IN A PUBLIC ENTERPRISE
AOS 01 85 VOL: 10 PG:3 - 28 :: REGRESS. :FIELD :OTH.BEH. :MANAG.

COOPER,DJ ; SEC: ESSEX ,S CIT: 0.42
ACCOUNTING INFORMATION AND EMPLOYEE DECISION MAKING
AOS 03 77 VOL: 2 PG:201 - 218 :: DES.STAT. :SURV. :OTH.BEH. :HRA

COOPER,DJ ; SEC: HAYES ,DC ; THIR: WOLF ,FM CIT: 0.75
ACCOUNTING IN ORGANIZED ANARCHIES: UNDERSTANDING AND DESIGNING ACCOUNTING
SYSTEMS IN AMBIGUOUS SITUATIONS
AOS 03 81 VOL: 6 PG:175 - 192 :: QUAL. :INT. LOG. :THEORY :N/A

COOPER,DJ CIT: 1.83
TIDINESS, MUDDLE AND THINGS: COMMONALITIES AND DIVERGENCIES IN TWO APPROACHES
TO MANAGEMENT ACCOUNTING RESEARCH
AOS 23 83 VOL: 8 PG:269 - 286 :: QUAL. :SEC. :OTH. :MANAG.

COOPER,DJ ; SEC: SHERER,MJ CIT: 2.60
THE VALUE OF CORPORATE ACCOUNTING REPORTS: ARGUMENTS FOR A POLITICAL ECONOMY
OF ACCOUNTING
AOS 34 84 VOL: 9 PG:207 - 232 :: QUAL. :SURV. :THEORY :N/A

COOPER,DJ ; FIRS: PUXTY ,AG ; SEC: WILLMOTT,HC ; FOUR: LOWE ,T CIT: 0.50
MODES OF REGULATION IN ADVANCED CAPITALISM: LOCATING ACCOUNTANCY IN
FOUR COUNTRIES
AOS 03 87 VOL: 12 PG:273 - 291 :: DES.STAT. :INT. LOG. :THEORY :ORG.& ENVIR.

COOPER,DJ ; SEC: HOPPER,TM CIT: 0.00
CRITICAL STUDIES IN ACCOUNTING
AOS 05 87 VOL: 12 PG:407 - 414 :: DES.STAT. :INT. LOG. :THEORY :FIN.METH.

COOPER,JC ; FIRS: CHOW ,CW ; THIR: WALLER,WS CIT: 0.00
PARTICIPATIVE BUDGETING: EFFECTS OF A TRUTH-INDUCING PAY SCHEME AND
INFORMATION ASYMMETRY ON SLACK AND PERFORMANCE
TAR JA 88 VOL: 63 PG:111 - 122 :: REGRESS. :LAB. :OTH.BEH. :BUDG.& PLAN.

COOPER,JC ; FIRS: BLOCHER,E CIT: 0.00
A STUDY OF AUDITORS' ANALYTICAL REVIEW PERFORMANCE
AUD SP 88 VOL: 07 PG:1 - 28 :: REGRESS. :LAB. :OTH.BEH. :ANAL.REV.

COOPER,T CIT: 0.00
REPLACEMENT COST AND BETA: A FINANCIAL MODEL
JAA WI 80 VOL: 3 PG:138 - 146 :: MIXED :SEC. :EMH :VALUAT.(INFL.)

COOPER,WW ; FIRS: CHARNES,A ; THIR: IJIRI ,Y CIT: 0.08
BREAKEVEN BUDGETING AND PROGRAMMING TO GOALS
JAR SP 63 VOL: 1 PG:16 - 43 :: ANAL. :INT. LOG. :MATH.PROG. :C-V-P-A

COOPER,WW ; FIRS: CHURCHILL,NC CIT: 0.15
A FIELD STUDY OF INTERNAL AUDITING
TAR OC 65 VOL: 40 PG:767 - 781 :: DES.STAT. :FIELD :OTH.BEH. :AUD.

COOPER,WW ; FIRS: CHARNES,A CIT: 0.08
SOME NETWORK CHARACTERIZATIONS FOR MATHEMATICAL PROGRAMMING AND ACCOUNTING
   APPROACHES TO PLANNING AND CONTROL
TAR JA 67 VOL: 42 PG:24 - 52 :: ANAL. :INT. LOG. :MATH.PROG. :MANAG.

COOPER,WW ; FIRS: BYRNE ,R ; SEC: CHARNES,A ; FOUR: KORTANEK,KO CIT: 0.00
SOME NEW APPROACHES TO RISK
TAR JA 68 VOL: 43 PG:18 - 37 :: ANAL. :INT. LOG. :MATH.PROG. :BUDG.& PLAN.

COOPER,WW ; SEC: DOPUCH,N ; THIR: KELLER,TF CIT: 0.08
BUDGETARY DISCLOSURE AND OTHER SUGGESTIONS FOR IMPROVING ACCOUNTING REPORTS
TAR OC 68 VOL: 43 PG:640 - 648 :: QUAL. :INT. LOG. :THEORY :FIN.METH.

COOPER,WW ; FIRS: CHARNES,A ; SEC: COLANTONI,CS ; FOUR: KORTANEK,KO CIT: 0.08
ECONOMIC SOCIAL AND ENTERPRISE ACCOUNTING AND MATHEMATICAL MODES
TAR JA 72 VOL: 47 PG:85 - 108 :: ANAL. :INT. LOG. :MATH.PROG. :FIN.METH.

COOPER,WW ; FIRS: CHARNES,A ; SEC: COLANTONI,CS CIT: 0.00
A FUTUROLOGICAL JUSTIFICATION FOR HISTORICAL COST AND MULTI-DIMENSIONAL
   ACCOUNTING
AOS 04 76 VOL: 1 PG:315 - 338 :: ANAL. :INT. LOG. :MATH.PROG. :HRA

COOPER,WW ; FIRS: CHARNES,A CIT: 0.00
AUDITING AND ACCOUNTING FOR PROBLEM EFFICIENCY AND MANAGEMENT EFFICIENCY IN
   NOT-FOR PROFIT ENTITIES
AOS 01 80 VOL: 5 PG:87 - 107 :: MIXED :PRIM. :OTH.STAT. :AUD.

COOPER,WW ; FIRS: CHURCHILL,NC ; THIR: GOVINDARAJAN,V CIT: 0.00
EFFECTS OF AUDITS ON THE BEHAVIOR OF MEDICAL PROFESSIONALS UNDER THE BENNETT
   AMENDMENT
AUD WI 82 VOL: 1 PG:69 - 91 :: ANOVA :PRIM. :OTH.STAT. :OPER.AUD.

COOPER,WW ; FIRS: BROCKETT,P ; SEC: CHARNES,A ; FOUR: SHIN ,HC CIT: 0.00
A CHANCE-CONSTRAINED PROGRAMMING APPROACH TO COST-VOLUME-PROFIT ANALYSIS
TAR JL 84 VOL: 59 PG:474 - 487 :: ANAL. :INT. LOG. :MATH.PROG. :C-V-P-A

COOPER,WW ; SEC: HO   ,JL ; THIR: HUNTER,JE ; FOUR: RODGERS,RC CIT: 0.00
THE IMPACT OF THE FOREIGN CORRUPT PRACTICES ACT ON INTERNAL CONTROL PRACTICES
JAA AU 85 VOL: 9 PG:22 - 39 :: REGRESS. :SEC. :THEORY :CAP.BUDG.

COPELAND,RM ; SEC: LICASTRO,RD CIT: 0.23
A NOTE ON INCOME SMOOTHING
TAR JL 68 VOL: 43 PG:540 - 545 :: ANOVA :PRIM. :TIME SER. :CASH DIV.

COPELAND,RM ; SEC: FREDERICKS,W CIT: 0.15
EXTENT OF DISCLOSURE
JAR SP 68 VOL: 6 PG:106 - 113 :: NON-PAR. :PRIM. :THEORY :INFO.STRUC.

COPELAND,RM CIT: 0.77
INCOME SMOOTHING
JAR ST 68 VOL: 6 PG:101 - 116 :: NON-PAR. :PRIM. :N/A :FIN.ST.TIM.

COPELAND,RM ; SEC: WOJDAK,JF CIT: 0.08
INCOME MANIPULATION AND THE PURCHASE-POOLING CHOICE
JAR AU 69 VOL: 7 PG:188 - 195 :: DES.STAT. :PRIM. :OTH. :BUS.COMB.

COPELAND,RM ; FIRS: BERNHARDT,I CIT: 0.15
SOME PROBLEMS IN APPLYING AN INFORMATION THEORY APPROACH TO ACCOUNTING
AGGREGATION
JAR SP 70 VOL: 8 PG:95 - 98 :: QUAL. :INT. LOG. :INF.ECO./AG. :INFO.STRUC.

COPELAND,RM ; FIRS: DASCHER,PE CIT: 0.23
SOME FURTHER EVIDENCE ON "CRITERIA FOR JUDGING DISCLOSURE IMPROVEMENT"
JAR SP 71 VOL: 9 PG:32 - 39 :: ANOVA :LAB. :OTH.BEH. :SEG.REP.

COPELAND,RM ; SEC: SHANK ,JK CIT: 0.38
LIFO AND THE DIFFUSION OF INNOVATION
JAR ST 71 VOL: 9 PG:196 - 224 :: DES.STAT. :PRIM. :THEORY :INV.

COPELAND,RM ; SEC: FRANCIA,AJ ; THIR: STRAWSER,RH CIT: 0.69
STUDENTS AS SUBJECTS IN BEHAVIOURAL BUSINESS RESEARCH
TAR AP 73 VOL: 48 PG:365 - 374 :: QUAL. :SURV. :OTH.BEH. :METHOD.

COPELAND,RM ; FIRS: SHANK ,JK CIT: 0.31
CORPORATE PERSONALITY THEORY AND CHANGES IN ACCOUNTING METHODS: AN EMPIRICAL
TEST
TAR JL 73 VOL: 48 PG:494 - 501 :: NON-PAR. :PRIM. :OTH.STAT. :ORG.FORM

COPELAND,RM ; FIRS: INGRAM,RW CIT: 0.25
MUNICIPAL ACCOUNTING INFORMATION AND VOTING BEHAVIOR
TAR OC 81 VOL: 56 PG:830 - 843 :: OTH.QUANT. :PRIM. :INSTIT. :N/A

COPELAND,RM ; SEC: TAYLOR,RL ; THIR: BROWN ,SH CIT: 0.13
OBSERVATION ERROR AND BIAS IN ACCOUNTING RESEARCH
JAR SP 81 VOL: 19 PG:197 - 207 :: ANOVA :LAB. :OTH.BEH. :METHOD.

COPELAND,RM ; SEC: INGRAM,RW CIT: 0.43
THE ASSOCIATION BETWEEN MUNICIPAL ACCOUNTING INFORMATION AND BOND RATING
CHANGES
JAR AU 82 VOL: 20 PG:275 - 289 :: OTH.QUANT. :PRIM. :OTH.STAT. :FIN.METH.

COPELAND,RM ; FIRS: INGRAM,RW CIT: 0.14
MUNICIPAL MARKET MEASURES AND REPORTING PRACTICES: AN EXTENSION
JAR AU 82 VOL: 20 PG:766 - 772 :: REGRESS. :PRIM. :OTH.STAT. :FIN.METH.

COPELAND,TE CIT: 0.00
EFFICIENT CAPITAL MARKETS: EVIDENCE AND IMPLICATIONS FOR FINANCIAL REPORTING
JAA AU 78 VOL: 2 PG:33 - 48 :: QUAL. :SEC. :EMH :FIN.METH.

COPPOCK,R CIT: 0.17
LIFE AMONG THE ENVIRONMENTALISTS: AN ELABORATION ON WILDAVSKY'S "ECONOMICS
AND ENVIRONMENT/RATIONALITY AND RITUAL"
AOS 02 77 VOL: 2 PG:125 - 130 :: QUAL. :INT. LOG. :OTH. :N/A

CORBIN,DA CIT: 0.00
COMMENTS ON "THE ACCRETION CONCEPT OF INCOME"
TAR OC 63 VOL: 38 PG:742 - 744 :: QUAL. :INT. LOG. :THEORY :VALUAT.(INFL.)

CORBIN,DA CIT: 0.00
ON THE FEASIBILITY OF DEVELOPING CURRENT COST INFORMATION
TAR OC 67 VOL: 42 PG:635 - 641 :: QUAL. :INT. LOG. :THEORY :VALUAT.(INFL.)

CORCORAN,AW ; SEC: KWANG ,CW CIT: 0.00
A SET THEORY APPROACH TO FUNDS-FLOW ANALYSIS
JAR AU 65 VOL: 3 PG:206 - 217 :: ANAL. :INT. LOG. :THEORY :PP&E / DEPR

CORCORAN,AW CIT: 0.00
COMPUTERS VERSUS MATHEMATICS
TAR AP 69 VOL: 44 PG:359 - 374 :: ANAL. :INT. LOG. :N/A :OTH.MANAG.

CORCORAN,AW ; SEC: LEININGER,WE CIT: 0.08
STOCHASTIC PROCESS COSTING MODELS
TAR JA 73 VOL: 48 PG:105 - 114 :: ANAL. :INT. LOG. :MATH.PROG. :COST.ALLOC.

CORLESS,JC CIT: 1.31
ASSESSING PRIOR DISTRIBUTIONS FOR APPLYING BAYESIAN STATISTICS IN AUDITING
TAR JL 72 VOL: 47 PG:556 - 566 :: DES.STAT. :LAB. :OTH.STAT. :SAMP.

COTTELL JR,PG CIT: 0.00
LIFO LAYER LIQUIDATIONS: SOME EMPIRICAL EVIDENCE
JAA WI 86 VOL: 1 PG:30 - 45 :: REGRESS. :SURV. :THEORY :INV.

COTTON,W ; FIRS: WELLS ,MC CIT: 0.00
HOLDING GAINS ON FIXED ASSETS
TAR OC 65 VOL: 40 PG:829 - 833 :: QUAL. :INT. LOG. :THEORY :VALUAT.(INFL.)

COUGHLAN,AT ; SEC: SCHMIDT,RM CIT: 1.50
EXECUTIVE COMPENSATION, MANAGEMENT TURNOVER, AND FIRM PERFORMANCE: AN
    EMPIRICAL INVESTIGATION
JAE AP 85 VOL: 7 PG:43 - 66 :: REGRESS. :PRIM. :OTH.STAT. :EXEC.COMP.

COVALESKI,M ; SEC: AIKEN ,M CIT: 0.33
ACCOUNTING AND THEORIES OF ORGANIZATIONS: SOME PRELIMINARY CONSIDERATIONS
AOS 45 86 VOL: 11 PG:297 - 320 :: ANOVA :INT. LOG. :THEORY :ORG.& ENVIR.

COVALESKI,M ; FIRS: COLIGNON,R CIT: 0.00
AN EXAMINATION OF MANAGERIAL ACCOUNTING PRACTICES AS A PROCESS OF MUTUAL
    ADJUSTMENT
AOS 06 88 VOL: 13 PG:559 - 579 :: REGRESS. :CASE :THEORY :BUDG.& PLAN.

COVALESKI,MA ; SEC: DIRSMITH,MW CIT: 0.50
BUDGETING AS A MEANS FOR CONTROL AND LOOSE COUPLING
AOS 04 83 VOL: 8 PG:323 - 340 :: CORR. :SURV. :OTH.BEH. :BUDG.& PLAN.

COVALESKI,MA ; FIRS: DIRSMITH,MW CIT: 0.00
PRACTICE MANAGEMENT ISSUES IN PUBLIC ACCOUNTING FIRMS
JAA AU 85 VOL: 9 PG:5 - 21 :: REGRESS. :SURV. :OTH. :ORG.

COVALESKI,MA ; FIRS: DIRSMITH,MW CIT: 0.00
INFORMAL COMMUNICATIONS, NONFORMAL COMMUNICATIONS AND MENTORING IN PUBLIC
    ACCOUNTING FIRMS
AOS 02 85 VOL: 10 PG:149 - 170 :: REGRESS. :INT. LOG. :INSTIT. :ORG.

COVALESKI,MA ; SEC: DIRSMITH,MW CIT: 0.33
THE BUDGETARY PROCESS OF POWER AND POLITICS
AOS 03 86 VOL: 11 PG:193 - 214 :: REGRESS. :SURV. :OTH.BEH. :BUDG.& PLAN.

COVALESKI,MA ; SEC: DIRSMITH,MW CIT: 0.00
THE USE OF BUDGETARY SYMBOLS IN THE POLITICAL ARENA: AN HISTORICALLY INFORMED
    FIELD STUDY
AOS 01 88 VOL: 13 PG:1 - 24 :: REGRESS. :CASE :THEORY :BUDG.& PLAN.

COWAN ,TK CIT: 0.00
A RESOURCES THEORY OF ACCOUNTING
TAR JA 65 VOL: 40 PG:9 - 20 :: QUAL. :INT. LOG. :THEORY :FIN.METH.

COWAN ,TK CIT: 0.08
ARE TRUTH AND FAIRNESS GENERALLY ACCEPTABLE?
TAR OC 65 VOL: 40 PG:788 - 794 :: QUAL. :INT. LOG. :INSTIT. :FIN.METH.

COWAN ,TK CIT: 0.00
A PRAGMATIC APPROACH TO ACCOUNTING THEORY
TAR JA 68 VOL: 43 PG:94 - 100 :: QUAL. :INT. LOG. :THEORY :FIN.METH.

COWEN ,SS ; SEC: FERRERI,LB ; THIR: PARKER,LD CIT: 0.00
THE IMPACT OF CORPORATE CHARACTERISTICS ON SOCIAL RESPONSIBILITY DIS
    CLOSURE: A TYPOLOGY AND FREQUENCY-BASED ANALYSIS
AOS 02 87 VOL: 12 PG:111 - 122 :: REGRESS. :PRIM. :THEORY :HRA

COWIE ,JB ; SEC: FREMGEN,JM CIT: 0.00
COMPUTERS VERSUS MATHEMATICS: ROUND 2
TAR JA 70 VOL: 45 PG:27 - 37 :: QUAL. :INT. LOG. :N/A :OTH.MANAG.

COX   ,CT CIT: 0.00
FURTHER EVIDENCE ON THE REPRESENTATIVENESS OF MANAGEMENT EARNINGS FORECASTS
TAR OC 85 VOL: 60 PG:692 - 701 :: REGRESS. :PRIM. :EMH :FOREC.

CRAIG ,PW ; FIRS: GROBSTEIN,M CIT: 0.00
A RISK ANALYSIS APPROACH TO AUDITING
AUD SP 84 VOL: 3 PG:1 - 16 :: QUAL. :INT. LOG. :OTH. :RISK

CRAMER JR,JJ CIT: 0.00
A NOTE ON PENSION TRUST ACCOUNTINGS
TAR OC 64 VOL: 39 PG:869 - 875 :: QUAL. :INT. LOG. :N/A :FIN.METH.

CRAMER JR,JJ CIT: 0.00
LEGAL INFLUENCES ON PENSION TRUST ACCOUNTING
TAR JL 65 VOL: 40 PG:606 - 616 :: QUAL. :INT. LOG. :INSTIT. :FIN.METH.

CRAMER JR,JJ ; SEC: SCHRADER,WJ CIT: 0.00
DEPRECIATION ACCOUNTING AND THE ANOMALOUS SELF-INSURANCE COST
TAR OC 70 VOL: 45 PG:698 - 703 :: QUAL. :INT. LOG. :THEORY :SPEC.ITEMS

CRAMER JR,JJ ; SEC: NEYHART,CA CIT: 0.00
A COMPREHENSIVE ACCOUNTING FRAMEWORK FOR EVALUATING EXECUTORY CONTRACTS
JAA WI 79 VOL: 2 PG:135 - 150 :: QUAL. :INT. LOG. :THEORY :N/A

CRANDALL,RH CIT: 0.00
INFORMATION ECONOMICS AND ITS IMPLICATIONS FOR THE FURTHER DEVELOPMENT OF
    ACCOUNTING THEORY
TAR JL 69 VOL: 44 PG:457 - 466 :: QUAL. :INT. LOG. :INF.ECO./AG. :OTH.MANAG.

CREADY,WM ; SEC: SHANK ,JK CIT: 0.00
UNDERSTANDING ACCOUNTING CHANGES IN EFFICIENT MARKET: A COMMENT,
    REPLICATION, AND RE-INTERPRETATION
TAR JL 87 VOL: 62 PG:589 - 596 :: REGRESS. :PRIM. :EMH :ACC.CHNG.

CREADY,WM CIT: 0.00
INFORMATION VALUE AND INVESTOR WEALTH: THE CASE OF EARNINGS ANNOUNCEMENTS
JAR SP 88 VOL: 26 PG:1 - 27 :: REGRESS. :PRIM. :EMH :INT.REP.

CRICHFIELD,T ; SEC: DYCKMAN,TR ; THIR: LAKONISHOK,J CIT: 1.09
AN EVALUATION OF SECURITY ANALYSTS' FORECASTS
TAR JL 78 VOL: 53 PG:651 - 668 :: ANOVA :PRIM. :TIME SER. :FOREC.

CROSBY,MA CIT: 0.33
IMPLICATIONS OF PRIOR PROBABILITY ELICITATION ON AUDITOR SAMPLE SIZE DECISIONS
JAR AU 80 VOL: 18 PG:585 - 593 :: ANAL. :INT. LOG. :OTH.BEH. :PROB.ELIC.

CROSBY,MA CIT: 0.63
BAYESIAN STATISTICS IN AUDITING: A COMPARISON OF PROBABILITY ELICITATION
   TECHNIQUES
TAR AP 81 VOL: 56 PG:355 - 365 :: DES.STAT. :LAB. :OTH.BEH. :PROB.ELIC.

CROSBY,MA CIT: 0.00
THE DEVELOPMENT OF BAYESIAN DECISION THEORETIC CONCEPTS IN ATTRIBUTE SAMPLING
AUD SP 85 VOL: 4 PG:118 - 132 :: REGRESS. :SEC. :OTH.STAT. :SAMP.

CRUMBLEY,DL CIT: 0.00
NARROWING THE TAXABLE AND ACCOUNTING INCOME GAP FOR CONSOLIDATIONS
TAR JL 68 VOL: 43 PG:554 - 564 :: QUAL. :INT. LOG. :N/A :BUS.COMB.

CRUMBLEY,DL CIT: 0.31
BEHAVIOURAL IMPLICATIONS OF TAXATION
TAR OC 73 VOL: 48 PG:759 - 763 :: QUAL. :INT. LOG. :INSTIT. :TAXES

CRUMBLEY,DL ; SEC: SAVICH,RS CIT: 0.00
USE OF HUMAN RESOURCE ACCOUNTING IN TAXATION
TAR JA 75 VOL: 50 PG:112 - 117 :: QUAL. :INT. LOG. :THEORY :HRA

CRUMBLEY,DL ; FIRS: BRAVENEC,LL ; SEC: EPSTEIN,MJ CIT: 0.00
TAX IMPACT IN CORPORATE SOCIAL RESPONSIBILITY DECISIONS AND REPORTING
AOS 02 77 VOL: 2 PG:131 - 140 :: QUAL. :INT. LOG. :THEORY :HRA

CRUSE ,RB ; SEC: SUMMERS,EL CIT: 0.00
ECONOMICS, ACCOUNTING PRACTICE AND ACCOUNTING RESEARCH STUDY NO.3
TAR JA 65 VOL: 40 PG:82 - 88 :: QUAL. :INT. LOG. :THEORY :FIN.METH.

CULLEN,PE ; FIRS: MAXIM ,LD ; THIR: COOK ,FX CIT: 0.00
OPTIMAL ACCEPTANCE SAMPLING PLANS FOR AUDITING "BATCHED" STOP AND GO VS.
   CONVENTIONAL SINGLE-STAGE ATTRIBUTES
TAR JA 76 VOL: 51 PG:97 - 109 :: ANAL. :INT. LOG. :OTH.STAT. :SAMP.

CULPEPPER,RC CIT: 0.08
A STUDY OF SOME RELATIONSHIPS BETWEEN ACCOUNTING AND DECISION-MAKING PROCESSES
TAR AP 70 VOL: 45 PG:322 - 332 :: ANOVA :PRIM. :INSTIT. :FIN.METH.

CUMMING,J CIT: 0.08
AN EMPIRICAL EVALUATION OF POSSIBLE EXPLANATIONS FOR THE DIFFERING TREATMENT
   OF APPARENTLY SIMILAR UNUSUAL EVENTS
JAR ST 73 VOL: 11 PG:60 - 95 :: NON-PAR. :SURV. :OTH.BEH. :SPEC.ITEMS

CURLEY,AJ CIT: 0.00
CONGLOMERATE EARNINGS PER SHARE: REAL AND TRANSITORY GROWTH
TAR JL 71 VOL: 46 PG:519 - 528 :: ANAL. :INT. LOG. :N/A :BUS.COMB.

CURRY ,DW CIT: 0.08
OPINION 15 VS. A COMPREHENSIVE FINANCIAL REPORTING METHOD FOR CONVERTIBLE DEBT
TAR JL 71 VOL: 46 PG:490 - 503 :: QUAL. :INT. LOG. :THEORY :LTD

CUSHING,BE CIT: 0.00
SOME OBSERVATIONS ON DEMSKI'S EX POST ACCOUNTING SYSTEM
TAR OC 68 VOL: 43 PG:668 - 671 :: QUAL. :INT. LOG. :INF.ECO./AG. :VAR.

CUSHING,BE CIT: 0.92
AN EMPIRICAL STUDY OF CHANGES IN ACCOUNTING POLICY
JAR AU 69 VOL: 7 PG:196 - 203 :: DES.STAT. :PRIM. :OTH. :ACC.CHNG.

CUSHING,BE CIT: 0.62
A MATHEMATICAL APPROACH TO THE ANALYSIS AND DESIGN OF INTERNAL CONTROL SYSTEMS
TAR JA 74 VOL: 49 PG:24 - 41 :: ANAL. :INT. LOG. :OTH.STAT. :INT.CONT.

CUSHING,BE CIT: 0.50
ON THE POSSIBILITY OF OPTIMAL ACCOUNTING PRINCIPLES
TAR AP 77 VOL: 52 PG:308 - 321 :: ANAL. :INT. LOG. :INSTIT. :FIN.METH.

CUSHING,BE ; SEC: SEARFOSS,DG ; THIR: RANDALL,RH CIT: 0.20
MATERIALITY ALLOCATION IN AUDIT PLANNING: A FEASIBILITY STUDY
JAR ST 79 VOL: 17 PG:172 - 216 :: DES.STAT. :FIELD :OTH.STAT. :PLAN.

CUSHING,BE ; SEC: LOEBBECKE,JK CIT: 0.67
ANALYTICAL APPROACHES TO AUDIT RISK: A SURVEY AND ANALYSIS
AUD AU 83 VOL: 3 PG:23 - 41 :: ANAL. :SEC. :OTH.STAT. :RISK

CYERT ,RM ; SEC: IJIRI ,Y CIT: 0.15
PROBLEMS OF IMPLEMENTING THE TRUEBLOOD OBJECTIVES REPORT
JAR ST 74 VOL: 12 PG:29 - 42 :: QUAL. :INT. LOG. :THEORY :FIN.METH.

CZARNIAWSKA-,B CIT: 0.00
DYNAMICS OF ORGANIZATIONAL CONTROL: THE CASE OF BEROL KEMI AB
AOS 04 88 VOL: 13 PG:415 - 430 :: REGRESS. :CASE :HIST. :MANAG.

DAEMS ,H ; FIRS: CHANDLER,AD CIT: 0.70
ADMINISTRATIVE COORDINATION, ALLOCATION AND MONITORING: A COMPARATIVE
    ANALYSIS OF EMERGENCE OF ACCOUNTING AND ORGANIZATIONS IN USA AND EUROPE
AOS 12 79 VOL: 4 PG:3 - 20 :: QUAL. :INT. LOG. :HIST. :N/A

DAFT ,RL ; FIRS: GIROUX,GA ; SEC: MAYPER,AG CIT: 0.00
ORGANIZATION SIZE, BUDGET CYCLE, AND BUDGET RELATED INFLUENCE IN CITY
    GOVERNMENTS: AN EMPIRICAL STUDY
AOS 06 86 VOL: 11 PG:499 - 520 :: REGRESS. :SURV. :OTH.STAT. :BUDG.& PLAN.

DAFT ,RL ; FIRS: MACINTOSH,NB CIT: 0.50
MANAGEMENT CONTROL SYSTEMS AND DEPARTMENTAL INTERDEPENDENCIES: AN EMPIRICAL
    STUDY
AOS 01 87 VOL: 12 PG:49 - 61 :: REGRESS. :SURV. :OTH.BEH. :ORG.& ENVIR.

DAILY ,RA CIT: 0.62
THE FEASIBILITY OF REPORTING FORECASTED INFORMATION
TAR OC 71 VOL: 46 PG:686 - 692 :: CORR. :PRIM. :N/A :FOREC.

DALEY ,LA ; SEC: VIGELAND,RL CIT: 0.83
THE EFFECTS OF DEBT COVENANTS AND POLITICAL COSTS ON THE CHOICE OF ACCOUNTING
    METHODS: THE CASE OF ACCOUNTING FOR R & D COSTS
JAE DE 83 VOL: 5 PG:195 - 211 :: OTH.QUANT. :PRIM. :OTH.STAT. :R & D

DALEY ,LA CIT: 0.60
THE VALUATION OF REPORTED PENSION MEASURES FOR FIRMS SPONSORING DEFINED
    BENEFIT PLANS
TAR AP 84 VOL: 59 PG:177 - 198 :: REGRESS. :PRIM. :OTH.STAT. :PENS.

DALEY ,LA ; FIRS: BOWEN ,RM ; SEC: BURGSTAHLER,D CIT: 0.67
EVIDENCE ON THE RELATIONSHIPS BETWEEN VARIOUS EARNINGS MEASURES OF CASH FLOW
TAR OC 86 VOL: 61 PG:713 - 725 :: REGRESS. :PRIM. :OTH.STAT. :REV.REC.

DALEY ,LA ; FIRS: BOWEN ,RM ; SEC: BURGSTAHLER,D CIT: 0.00
THE INCREMENTAL INFORMATION CONTENT OF ACCRUAL VERSUS CASH FLOWS
TAR OC 87 VOL: 62 PG:723 - 747 :: REGRESS. :PRIM. :EMH :SPEC.ITEMS

DALEY ,LA ; SEC: SENKOW,DW ; THIR: VIGELAND,RL CIT: 0.00
ANALYSTS' FORECASTS, EARNINGS VARIABILITY, AND OPTION PRICING: EMPIRICAL
    EVIDENCE
TAR OC 88 VOL: 63 PG:563 - 585 :: REGRESS. :PRIM. :TIME SER. :FOREC.

DALTON,FE ; SEC: MINER ,JB CIT: 0.08
THE ROLE OF ACCOUNTING TRAINING IN TOP MANAGEMENT DECISION MAKING
TAR JA 70 VOL: 45 PG:134 - 139 :: ANOVA :LAB. :N/A :AUD.TRAIN.

DANIEL,SJ CIT: 0.00
SOME EMPIRICAL EVIDENCE ABOUT THE ASSESSMENT OF AUDIT RISK IN PRACTICE
AUD SP 88 VOL: 07 PG:174 - 181 :: REGRESS. :LAB. :OTH. :RISK

DANOS ,P ; FIRS: EICHENSEHER,JW CIT: 0.88
THE ANALYSIS OF INDUSTRY-SPECIFIC AUDITOR CONCENTRATION: TOWARDS AN
    EXPLANATORY MODEL
TAR JL 81 VOL: 56 PG:479 - 492 :: MIXED :PRIM. :OTH.STAT. :ORG.

DANOS ,P ; SEC: EICHENSEHER,JW CIT: 0.43
AUDIT INDUSTRY DYNAMICS: FACTORS AFFECTING CHANGES IN CLIENT-INDUSTRY MARKET
    SHARES
JAR AU 82 VOL: 20 PG:604 - 616 :: ANOVA :PRIM. :OTH.STAT. :ORG.

DANOS ,P ; SEC: IMHOFF JR,EA CIT: 0.57
AUDITOR REVIEW OF FINANCIAL FORECASTS: AN ANALYSIS OF FACTORS AFFECTING
    REASONABLENESS JUDGMENTS
TAR JA 82 VOL: 57 PG:39 - 54 :: ANOVA :LAB. :OTH.BEH. :AUD.

DANOS ,P ; SEC: IMHOFF JR,EA CIT: 0.43
FORECAST SYSTEMS, CONSTRUCTION AND ATTESTATION
AUD WI 82 VOL: 1 PG:23 - 34 :: DES.STAT. :LAB. :OTH.BEH. :FOREC.

DANOS ,P ; SEC: IMHOFF JR,EA CIT: 0.17
FACTORS AFFECTING AUDITORS' EVALUATIONS OF FORECASTS
JAR AU 83 VOL: 21 PG:473 - 494 :: ANOVA :LAB. :OTH.BEH. :JUDG.

DANOS ,P ; SEC: HOLT ,DL ; THIR: IMHOFF JR,EA CIT: 0.40
BOND RATERS' USE OF MANAGEMENT FINANCIAL FORECASTS: EXPERIMENT IN EXPERT
    JUDGEMENT
TAR OC 84 VOL: 59 PG:547 - 573 :: ANOVA :LAB. :OTH.BEH. :FOREC.

DANOS ,P ; SEC: EICHENSEHER,JW CIT: 0.33
LONG-TERM TRENDS TOWARD SELLER CONCENTRATION IN THE US AUDIT MARKET
TAR OC 86 VOL: 61 PG:633 - 650 :: REGRESS. :PRIM. :OTH.STAT. :ORG.& ENVIR.

DANOS ,P ; SEC: HOLT ,DL ; THIR: BAILEY JR,AD CIT: 0.00
THE INTERACTION OF SCIENCE AND ATTESTATION STANDARD FORMATION
AUD SP 87 VOL: 6 PG:134 - 149 :: DES.STAT. :INT. LOG. :THEORY :OPIN.

DAROCA,FP CIT: 0.20
INFORMATIONAL INFLUENCES ON GROUP DECISION MAKING IN A PARTICIPATIVE
    BUDGETING CONTEXT
AOS 01 84 VOL: 9 PG:13 - 32 :: ANOVA :LAB. :OTH.BEH. :BUDG.& PLAN.

DAROCA,FP ; SEC: HOLDER,WW CIT: 0.00
THE USE OF ANALYTICAL PROCEDURES IN REVIEW AND AUDIT ENGAGEMENTS
AUD SP 85 VOL: 4 PG:80 - 92 :: REGRESS. :SURV. :INSTIT. :ANAL.REV.

DAS ,H CIT: 0.00
ORGANIZATIONAL AND DECISION CHARACTERISTICS AND PERSONALITY AS DETERMINANTS
OF CONTROL ACTIONS: A LABORATORY EXPERIMENT
AOS 03 86 VOL: 11 PG:215 - 232 :: REGRESS. :LAB. :OTH.BEH. :INT.CONT.

DAS ,TK ; FIRS: FLAMHOLTZ,EG ; THIR: TSUI ,AS CIT: 0.25
TOWARD AN INTEGRATIVE FRAMEWORK OF ORGANIZATIONAL CONTROL
AOS 01 85 VOL: 10 PG:35 - 50 :: DES.STAT. :INT. LOG. :OTH.BEH. :HRA

DASCHER,PE ; SEC: MALCOM,RE CIT: 0.31
A NOTE ON INCOME SMOOTHING IN THE CHEMICAL INDUSTRY
JAR AU 70 VOL: 8 PG:253 - 259 :: DES.STAT. :PRIM. :TIME SER. :FIN.METH.

DASCHER,PE ; SEC: COPELAND,RM CIT: 0.23
SOME FURTHER EVIDENCE ON "CRITERIA FOR JUDGING DISCLOSURE IMPROVEMENT"
JAR SP 71 VOL: 9 PG:32 - 39 :: ANOVA :LAB. :OTH.BEH. :SEG.REP.

DATAR ,SM ; FIRS: BANKER,RD ; THIR: RAJAN ,MV CIT: 0.00
MEASUREMENT OF PRODUCTIVITY IMPROVEMENTS: AN EMPIRICAL ANALYSIS
JAA AU 87 VOL: 2 PG:319 - 347 :: DES.STAT. :FIELD :OTH.STAT. :MANAG.

DATAR ,SM ; FIRS: BANKER,RD ; THIR: KEKRE ,S CIT: 0.00
RELEVANT COSTS, CONGESTION AND STOCHASTICITY IN PRODUCTION ENVIRONMENTS
JAE JL 88 VOL: 10 PG:171 - 197 :: DES.STAT. :INT. LOG. :OTH.STAT. :REL.COSTS

DAVIDSON,HJ ; FIRS: CHARNES,A ; THIR: KORTANEK,KO CIT: 0.00
ON A MIXED-SEQUENTIAL ESTIMATING PROCEDURE WITH APPLICATION TO AUDIT TESTS IN
ACCOUNTING
TAR AP 64 VOL: 39 PG:241 - 250 :: ANAL. :INT. LOG. :OTH.STAT. :SAMP.

DAVIDSON,HJ ; SEC: NETER ,J ; THIR: PETRAN,AS CIT: 0.15
ESTIMATING THE LIABILITY FOR UNREDEEMED STAMPS
JAR AU 67 VOL: 5 PG:186 - 207 :: ANAL. :INT. LOG. :OTH.STAT. :SPEC.ITEMS

DAVIDSON,LF ; FIRS: BIRD ,FA ; THIR: SMITH ,CH CIT: 0.15
PERCEPTIONS OF EXTERNAL ACCOUNTING TRANSFERS UNDER ENTITY AND PROPRIETARY
THEORY
TAR AP 74 VOL: 49 PG:233 - 244 :: QUAL. :INT. LOG. :THEORY :FIN.METH.

DAVIDSON,LF ; FIRS: KELLER,SB CIT: 0.33
AN ASSESSMENT OF INDIVIDUAL INVESTOR REACTION TO CERTAIN QUALIFIED AUDIT
OPINIONS
AUD AU 83 VOL: 3 PG:1 - 22 :: ANOVA :PRIM. :EMH :OPIN.

DAVIDSON,S CIT: 0.00
OLD WINE INTO NEW BOTTLES
TAR AP 63 VOL: 38 PG:278 - 284 :: QUAL. :SEC. :HIST. :OVER.ALLOC.

DAVIDSON,S CIT: 0.08
THE DAY OF RECKONING: ACCOUNTING THEORY AND MANAGEMENT ANALYSIS
JAR AU 63 VOL: 1 PG:117 - 126 :: QUAL. :INT. LOG. :THEORY :N/A

DAVIDSON,S ; SEC: KOHLMEIER,JM CIT: 0.08
A MEASURE OF THE IMPACT OF SOME FOREIGN ACCOUNTING PRINCIPLES
JAR AU 66 VOL: 4 PG:183 - 212 :: DES.STAT. :SIM. :OTH.STAT. :INT.DIFF.

DAVIDSON,S ; FIRS: BIERMAN JR,H CIT: 0.00
THE INCOME CONCEPT-VALUE-INCREMENT OR EARNINGS PREDICTOR
TAR AP 69 VOL: 44 PG:239 - 246 :: QUAL. :INT. LOG. :THEORY :FIN.METH.

DAVIDSON,S ; SEC: WEIL ,RL CIT: 0.09
INCOME TAX IMPLICATIONS OF VARIOUS METHODS OF ACCOUNTING FOR CHANGING PRICE
JAR ST 78 VOL: 16 PG:154 - 233 :: DES.STAT. :PRIM. :OTH.STAT. :VALUAT.(INFL.)

DAVIS ,DW ; SEC: BOATSMAN,JR ; THIR: BASKIN,EF CIT: 0.09
ON GENERALIZING STOCK MARKET RESEARCH TO A BROADER CLASS OF MARKETS
TAR JA 78 VOL: 53 PG:1 - 10 :: MIXED :PRIM. :EMH :FIN.METH.

DAVIS ,GB CIT: 0.00
THE APPLICATION OF NETWORK TECHNIQUES (PERT/CPM) TO THE PLANNING AND CONTROL
   OF AN AUDIT
JAR SP 63 VOL: 1 PG:96 - 101 :: ANAL. :INT. LOG. :MATH.PROG. :AUD.

DAVIS ,GB ; SEC: WEBER ,R CIT: 0.00
THE IMPACT OF ADVANCED COMPUTER SYSTEMS ON CONTROLS AND AUDIT PROCEDURES: A
   THEORY AND AN EMPIRICAL TEST
AUD SP 86 VOL: 5 PG:35 - 49 :: REGRESS. :LAB. :OTH.STAT. :EDP AUD.

DAVIS ,HZ ; SEC: KAHN ,N CIT: 0.00
SOME ADDITIONAL EVIDENCE ON THE LIFO-FIFO CHOICE USING REPLACEMENT COST DATA
JAR AU 82 VOL: 20 PG:738 - 744 :: NON-PAR. :PRIM. :OTH.STAT. :INV.

DAVIS ,HZ ; SEC: KAHN ,N ; THIR: ROZEN ,E CIT: 0.00
LIFO INVENTORY LIQUIDATIONS: AN EMPIRICAL STUDY
JAR AU 84 VOL: 22 PG:480 - 490 :: NON-PAR. :PRIM. :OTH.STAT. :INV.

DAVIS ,ML ; SEC: LARGAY III,JA CIT: 0.00
REPORTING CONSOLIDATED GAINS AND LOSSES ON SUBSIDIARY STOCK ISSUANCES
TAR AP 88 VOL: 63 PG:348 - 363 :: REGRESS. :PRIM. :THEORY :BUS.COMB.

DAVIS ,PM CIT: 0.00
MARGINAL ANALYSIS OF CREDIT SALES
TAR JA 66 VOL: 41 PG:121 - 126 :: ANAL. :INT. LOG. :N/A :MANAG.

DAVIS ,RR CIT: 0.29
AN EMPIRICAL EVALUATION OF AUDITORS' 'SUBJECT-TO' OPINIONS
AUD AU 82 VOL: 2 PG:13 - 32 :: REGRESS. :PRIM. :EMH :OPIN.

DAVIS ,SW ; SEC: MENON ,K ; THIR: MORGAN,G CIT: 0.43
THE IMAGES THAT HAVE SHAPED ACCOUNTING THEORY
AOS 04 82 VOL: 7 PG:307 - 318 :: QUAL. :INT. LOG. :THEORY :N/A

DAVISON,AG ; SEC: STENING,BW ; THIR: WAI ,WT CIT: 0.00
AUDITOR CONCENTRATION AND THE IMPACT OF INTERLOCKING DIRECTORATES
JAR SP 84 VOL: 22 PG:313 - 317 :: CORR. :PRIM. :OTH. :ORG.& ENVIR.

DAY ,P ; FIRS: ROSENBERG,D ; SEC: TOMKINS,L CIT: 0.00
A WORK ROLE PERSPECTIVE OF ACCOUNTANTS IN LOCAL GOVERNMENT SERVICE DEPARTMENTS
AOS 02 82 VOL: 7 PG:123 - 138 :: QUAL. :SURV. :OTH.BEH. :N/A

DEAKIN,EB CIT: 1.15
A DISCRIMINANT ANALYSIS OF PREDICTORS OF BUSINESS FAILURE
JAR SP 72 VOL: 10 PG:167 - 179 :: OTH.QUANT. :PRIM. :EMH :BUS.FAIL.

DEAKIN,EB ; SEC: GRANOF,MH CIT: 0.46
REGRESSION ANALYSIS AS A MEANS OF DETERMINING AUDIT SAMPLE SIZE
TAR OC 74 VOL: 49 PG:764 - 771 :: REGRESS. :INT. LOG. :OTH.STAT. :SAMP.

DEAKIN,EB CIT: 0.31
DISTRIBUTIONS OF FINANCIAL ACCOUNTING RATIOS: SOME EMPIRICAL EVIDENCE
TAR JA 76 VOL: 51 PG:90 - 96 :: ANOVA :PRIM. :OTH.STAT. :FIN.METH.

DEAKIN,EB CIT: 0.23
ACCOUNTING REPORTS, POLICY INTERVENTIONS AND THE BEHAVIOR OF SECURITIES
RETURNS
TAR JL 76 VOL: 51 PG:590 - 603 :: REGRESS. :PRIM. :EMH :FIN.METH.

DEAKIN,EB CIT: 1.00
AN ANALYSIS OF DIFFERENCES BETWEEN NON-MAJOR OIL FIRMS USING SUCCESSFUL
EFFORTS AND FULL COST METHODS
TAR OC 79 VOL: 54 PG:722 - 734 :: OTH.QUANT. :PRIM. :OTH.STAT. :OIL & GAS

DEAN ,J ; SEC: HARRISS,CL CIT: 0.00
RAILROAD ACCOUNTING UNDER THE NEW DEPRECIATION GUIDELINES AND INVESTMENT TAX
CREDIT
TAR AP 63 VOL: 38 PG:229 - 242 :: QUAL. :INT. LOG. :THEORY :TAXES

DEAN ,RA ; SEC: FERRIS,KR ; THIR: KONSTANS,C CIT: 0.00
OCCUPATIONAL REALITY SHOCK AND ORGANIZATIONAL COMMITMENT: EVIDENCE FROM THE
ACCOUNTING PROFESSION
AOS 03 88 VOL: 13 PG:235 - 250 :: REGRESS. :SURV. :OTH.BEH. :AUD.BEH.

DEANGELO,LE CIT: 1.25
AUDITOR INDEPENDENCE, 'LOW BALLING', AND DISCLOSURE REGULATION
JAE AG 81 VOL: 3 PG:113 - 127 :: ANAL. :INT. LOG. :TIME SER. :INDEP.

DEANGELO,LE CIT: 1.38
AUDITOR SIZE AND AUDIT QUALITY
JAE DE 81 VOL: 3 PG:183 - 199 :: QUAL. :INT. LOG. :THEORY :JUDG.

DEANGELO,LE CIT: 0.71
MANDATED SUCCESSFUL EFFORTS AND AUDITOR CHOICE
JAE DE 82 VOL: 4 PG:171 - 203 :: DES.STAT. :SEC. :THEORY :ACC.CHNG.

DEANGELO,LE CIT: 0.67
ACCOUNTING NUMBERS AS MARKET VALUATION SUBSTITUTES: A STUDY OF MANAGEMENT
BUYOUTS OF PUBLIC STOCKHOLDERS
TAR JL 86 VOL: 61 PG:400 - 420 :: REGRESS. :PRIM. :THEORY :INFO.STRUC.

DEANGELO,LE CIT: 0.00
MANAGERIAL COMPETITION, INFORMATION COSTS, AND CORPORATE GOVERNANCE: THE USE
OF ACCOUNTING PERFORMANCE MEASURES IN PROXY CONTESTS
JAE JA 88 VOL: 10 PG:3 - 36 :: REGRESS. :PRIM. :EMH :BUS.COMB.

DECOSTER,DT CIT: 0.00
MEASUREMENT OF THE IDLE-CAPACITY VARIANCE
TAR AP 66 VOL: 41 PG:297 - 302 :: QUAL. :INT. LOG. :N/A :VAR.

DECOSTER,DT ; FIRS: CHIU ,JS CIT: 0.00
MULTIPLE PRODUCT COSTING BY MULTIPLE CORRELATION ANALYSIS
TAR OC 66 VOL: 41 PG:673 - 680 :: REGRESS. :INT. LOG. :TIME SER. :COST.ALLOC.

DECOSTER,DT ; SEC: FERTAKIS,JP CIT: 1.46
BUDGET-INDUCED PRESSURE AND ITS RELATIONSHIP TO SUPERVISORY BEHAVIOR
JAR AU 68 VOL: 6 PG:237 - 246 :: DES.STAT. :SURV. :OTH.BEH. :BUDG.& PLAN.

DECOSTER,DT ; FIRS: ROSEN ,LS CIT: 0.00
"FUNDS" STATEMENTS: A HISTORICAL PERSPECTIVE
TAR JA 69 VOL: 44 PG:124 - 136 :: QUAL. :SEC. :HIST. :FIN.METH.

DECOSTER,DT ; SEC: RHODE ,JG CIT: 0.15
THE ACCOUNTANT'S STEREOTYPE: REAL OR IMAGINED, DESERVED OR UNWARRANTED
TAR OC 71 VOL: 46 PG:651 - 664 :: ANOVA :SURV. :OTH.BEH. :AUD.

DECOSTER,DT ; FIRS: FORAN ,MF CIT: 0.85
AN EXPER. STUDY OF THE EFFECTS OF PARTICIP., AUTHORITARIANISM, AND FEEDBACK
   ON COGNITIVE DISSONANCE IN A STANDARD SETTING SITUATION.
TAR OC 74 VOL: 49 PG:751 - 763 :: ANOVA :LAB. :OTH.BEH. :BUDG.& PLAN.

DEFEO ,VJ CIT: 0.00
AN EMPIRICAL INVESTIGATION OF THE SPEED OF THE MARKET REACTION TO EARNINGS A
   ANNOUNCEMENTS
JAR AU 86 VOL: 24 PG:349 - 363 :: ANOVA :PRIM. :EMH :REV.REC.

DEFLIESE,PL CIT: 0.00
A PRACTITIONER'S VIEW OF THE REALIZATION CONCEPT
TAR JL 65 VOL: 40 PG:517 - 521 :: QUAL. :INT. LOG. :THEORY :VALUAT.(INFL.)

DEINZER,HT CIT: 0.00
EXPLANATION STRAINS IN FINANCIAL ACCOUNTING
TAR JA 66 VOL: 41 PG:21 - 31 :: QUAL. :INT. LOG. :THEORY :OTH.MANAG.

DEITRICK,JW ; SEC: ALDERMAN,CW CIT: 0.00
INTERIM REPORTING DEVELOPMENTS: A STEP TOWARD THE AUDITOR-OF-RECORD CONCEPT
JAA SU 79 VOL: 2 PG:316 - 328 :: QUAL. :INT. LOG. :INSTIT. :AUD.

DEITRICK,JW ; FIRS: ALDERMAN,CW CIT: 0.00
AUDITORS' PERCEPTIONS OF TIME BUDGET PRESSURES AND PREMATURE SIGN-OFFS: A
   REPLICATION AND EXTENSION
AUD WI 82 VOL: 1 PG:54 - 68 :: DES.STAT. :SURV. :OTH.BEH. :ERRORS

DEJONG,DV ; SEC: SMITH ,JH CIT: 0.00
THE DETERMINATION OF AUDIT RESPONSIBILITIES: AN APPLICATION OF AGENCY THEORY
AUD AU 84 VOL: 4 PG:20 - 34 :: QUAL. :INT. LOG. :INF.ECO./AG. :LIAB.

DEJONG,DV ; SEC: FORSYTHE,R ; THIR: UECKER,WC CIT: 0.25
THE METHODOLOGY OF LABORATORY MARKETS AND ITS IMPLICATIONS FOR AGENCY
   RESEARCH IN ACCOUNTING AND AUDITING
JAR AU 85 VOL: 23 PG:753 - 793 :: REGRESS. :LAB. :INF.ECO./AG. :METHOD.

DEJONG,DV ; SEC: FORSYTHE,R ; THIR: LUNDHOLM,RJ ; FOUR: UECKER,WC CIT: 0.00
A LABORATORY INVESTIGATION OF THE MORAL HAZARD PROBLEM IN AN AGENCY
   RELATIONSHIP
JAR ST 85 VOL: 23 PG:81 - 120 :: REGRESS. :LAB. :INF.ECO./AG. :MAN.DEC.CHAR.

DEMARIS,EJ CIT: 0.00
"SUCCESS INDICATOR" FUNCTION OF INCOME CONCEPT ARGUES ITS FURTHER DEVELOPMENT
TAR JA 63 VOL: 38 PG:37 - 45 :: QUAL. :INT. LOG. :THEORY :REV.REC.

DEMING,WE CIT: 0.00
ON A PROBLEM IN STANDARDS OF AUDITING FROM THE VIEWPOINT OF STATISTICAL
   PRACTICE
JAA SP 79 VOL: 2 PG:197 - 208 :: ANAL. :INT. LOG. :OTH.STAT. :SAMP.

DEMSKI,JS ; FIRS: DOPUCH,N ; SEC: BIRNBERG,JG CIT: 0.15
AN EXTENSION OF STANDARD COST VARIANCE ANALYSIS
TAR JL 67 VOL: 42 PG:526 - 536 :: ANAL. :INT. LOG. :OTH.STAT. :VAR.

DEMSKI,JS CIT: 0.38
AN ACCOUNTING SYSTEM STRUCTURED ON A LINEAR PROGRAMMING MODEL
TAR OC 67 VOL: 42 PG:701 - 712 :: ANAL. :INT. LOG. :INF.ECO./AG. :MANAG.

DEMSKI,JS CIT: 0.15
DECISION-PERFORMANCE CONTROL
TAR OC 69 VOL: 44 PG:669 - 679 :: ANAL. :INT. LOG. :INF.ECO./AG. :MANAG.

DEMSKI,JS CIT: 0.00
PREDICTIVE ABILITY OF ALTERNATIVE PERFORMANCE MEASUREMENT MODELS
JAR SP 69 VOL: 7 PG:96 - 115 :: REGRESS. :SIM. :OTH.STAT. :VAR.

DEMSKI,JS CIT: 0.23
SOME DECOMPOSITION RESULTS FOR INFORMATION EVALUATION
JAR AU 70 VOL: 8 PG:178 - 198 :: ANAL. :INT. LOG. :INF.ECO./AG. :MANAG.

DEMSKI,JS CIT: 0.23
THE DECISION IMPLEMENTATION INTERFACE: EFFECTS OF ALTERNATIVE PERFORMANCE
   MEASUREMENT MODELS
TAR JA 70 VOL: 45 PG:76 - 87 :: ANAL. :SIM. :OTH.STAT. :VAR.

DEMSKI,JS ; FIRS: FELTHAM,GA CIT: 1.00
THE USE OF MODELS IN INFORMATION EVALUATION
TAR OC 70 VOL: 45 PG:623 - 640 :: ANAL. :INT. LOG. :INF.ECO./AG. :MANAG.

DEMSKI,JS CIT: 0.15
IMPLEMENTATION EFFECTS OF ALTERNATIVE PERFORMANCE MEASUREMENT MODELS IN A
   MULTIVARIABLE CONTEXT
TAR AP 71 VOL: 46 PG:268 - 278 :: ANAL. :SIM. :INF.ECO./AG. :BUDG.& PLAN.

DEMSKI,JS CIT: 0.69
OPTIMAL PERFORMANCE MEASUREMENT
JAR AU 72 VOL: 10 PG:243 - 258 :: ANAL. :INT. LOG. :INF.ECO./AG. :MANAG.

DEMSKI,JS ; SEC: FELTHAM,GA CIT: 0.54
FORECAST EVALUATION
TAR JL 72 VOL: 47 PG:533 - 548 :: MIXED :SIM. :INF.ECO./AG. :BUDG.& PLAN.

DEMSKI,JS CIT: 0.46
INFORMATION IMPROVEMENT BOUNDS
JAR SP 72 VOL: 10 PG:58 - 76 :: ANAL. :INT. LOG. :INF.ECO./AG. :INFO.STRUC.

DEMSKI,JS CIT: 0.15
RATIONAL CHOICE OF ACCOUNTING METHOD FOR A CLASS OF PARTNERSHIPS
JAR AU 73 VOL: 11 PG:176 - 190 :: ANAL. :INT. LOG. :OTH.STAT. :FIN.METH.

DEMSKI,JS CIT: 1.23
THE GENERAL IMPOSSIBILITY OF NORMATIVE ACCOUNTING STANDARDS
TAR OC 73 VOL: 48 PG:718 - 723 :: QUAL. :INT. LOG. :THEORY :FIN.METH.

DEMSKI,JS CIT: 1.00
CHOICE AMONG FINANCIAL REPORTING ALTERNATIVES
TAR AP 74 VOL: 49 PG:221 - 232 :: ANAL. :INT. LOG. :INF.ECO./AG. :FIN.METH.

DEMSKI,JS ; SEC: SWIERINGA,RJ CIT: 0.62
A COOPERATIVE FORMULATION OF THE AUDIT CHOICE PROBLEM
TAR JL 74 VOL: 49 PG:506 - 513 :: ANAL. :INT. LOG. :OTH.STAT. :AUD.

DEMSKI,JS ; FIRS: BEAVER,WH CIT: 0.85
THE NATURE OF FINANCIAL ACCOUNTING OBJECTIVES: A SUMMARY AND SYNTHESIS
JAR ST 74 VOL: 12 PG:170 - 187 :: ANAL. :SEC. :THEORY :FIN.METH.

DEMSKI,JS CIT: 0.77
UNCERTAINTY AND EVALUATION BASED ON CONTROLLABLE PERFORMANCE
JAR AU 76 VOL: 14 PG:230 - 245 :: ANAL. :INT. LOG. :INF.ECO./AG. :MANAG.

DEMSKI,JS ; SEC: FELTHAM,GA CIT: 3.18
ECONOMIC INCENTIVES IN BUDGETARY CONTROL SYSTEMS
TAR AP 78 VOL: 53 PG:336 - 359 :: ANAL. :INT. LOG. :INF.ECO./AG. :BUDG.& PLAN.

DEMSKI,JS ; FIRS: BEAVER,WH CIT: 1.30
THE NATURE OF INCOME MEASUREMENT
TAR JA 79 VOL: 54 PG:38 - 46 :: QUAL. :INT. LOG. :INF.ECO./AG. :OTH.FIN.ACC.

DEMSKI,JS ; FIRS: BAIMAN,S CIT: 1.44
ECONOMICALLY OPTIMAL PERFORMANCE EVALUATION AND CONTROL SYSTEMS
JAR ST 80 VOL: 18 PG:184 - 220 :: ANAL. :INT. LOG. :OTH. :MANAG.

DEMSKI,JS ; SEC: KREPS ,DM CIT: 1.00
MODELS IN MANAGERIAL ACCOUNTING
JAR ST 82 VOL: 20 PG:117 - 148 :: QUAL. :SEC. :OTH.STAT. :METHOD.

DEMSKI,JS ; SEC: PATELL,JM ; THIR: WOLFSON,MA CIT: 1.60
DECENTRALIZED CHOICE OF MONITORING SYSTEMS
TAR JA 84 VOL: 59 PG:16 - 34 :: ANAL. :INT. LOG. :INF.ECO./AG. :MANAG.

DEMSKI,JS ; SEC: SAPPINGTON,DEM CIT: 1.33
LINE-ITEM REPORTING, FACTOR ACQUISITION, AND SUBCONTRACTING
JAR AU 86 VOL: 24 PG:250 - 269 :: ANAL. :INT. LOG. :INF.ECO./AG. :INFO.STRUC.

DEMSKI,JS ; SEC: SAPPINGTON,DEM CIT: 1.50
DELEGATED EXPERTISE
JAR SP 87 VOL: 25 PG:68 - 89 :: DES.STAT. :INT. LOG. :INF.ECO./AG. :MANAG.

DENT ,WT ; FIRS: COLLINS,DW CIT: 3.00
THE PROPOSED ELIMINATION OF FULL COST ACCOUNTING IN THE EXTRACTIVE PETROLEUM
    INDUSTRY: AN EMPIRICAL ASSESSMENT OF MARKET CONSEQUENCES
JAE MR 79 VOL: 1 PG:3 - 44 :: NON-PAR. :PRIM. :EMH :OIL & GAS

DENT ,WT ; FIRS: COLLINS,DW CIT: 1.40
A COMPARISON OF ALTERNATIVE TESTING METHODOLOGIES USED IN CAPITAL MARKET
    RESEARCH
JAR SP 84 VOL: 22 PG:48 - 84 :: MIXED :SIM. :EMH :METHOD.

DERMER,JD CIT: 1.46
COGNITIVE CHARACTERISTICS AND THE PERCEIVED IMPORTANCE OF INFORMATION
TAR JL 73 VOL: 48 PG:511 - 519 :: CORR. :LAB. :OTH.BEH. :MAN.DEC.CHAR.

DERMER,JD ; SEC: SIEGEL,JP CIT: 0.15
THE ROLE OF BEHAVIOURAL MEASURES IN ACCOUNTING FOR HUMAN RESOURCES
TAR JA 74 VOL: 49 PG:88 - 97 :: CORR. :LAB. :OTH.BEH. :HRA

DERMER,JD ; SEC: LUCAS ,RG CIT: 0.00
THE ILLUSION OF MANAGERIAL CONTROL
AOS 06 86 VOL: 11 PG:471 - 482 :: DES.STAT. :INT. LOG. :THEORY :INT.CONT.

DERMER,JD CIT: 0.00
CONTROL AND ORGANIZATIONAL ORDER
AOS 01 88 VOL: 13 PG:25 - 36 :: DES.STAT. :INT. LOG. :INSTIT. :ORG.FORM

DERSTINE,RP ; SEC: HUEFNER,RJ CIT: 0.54
LIFO-FIFO, ACCOUNTING RATIOS AND MARKET RISK
JAR AU 74 VOL: 12 PG:216 - 234 :: NON-PAR. :PRIM. :OTH. :INV.

DERY ,D CIT: 0.00
ERRING AND LEARNING: AN ORGANIZATIONAL ANALYSIS
AOS 03 82 VOL: 7 PG:217 - 224 :: QUAL. :INT. LOG. :OTH. :N/A

DESAI ,HB ; FIRS: SINGHVI,SS CIT: 0.46
AN EMPIRICAL ANALYSIS OF THE QUALITY OF CORPORATE FINANCIAL DISCLOSURE
TAR JA 71 VOL: 46 PG:129 - 138 :: DES.STAT. :PRIM. :N/A :INFO.STRUC.

DESKINS,JW CIT: 0.00
ON THE NATURE OF THE PUBLIC INTEREST
TAR JA 65 VOL: 40 PG:76 - 81 :: ANAL. :INT. LOG. :INSTIT. :N/A

DESKINS,JW ; FIRS: SUMMERS,EL CIT: 0.00
A CLASSIFICATION SCHEMA OF METHODS FOR REPORTING EFFECTS OF RESOURCE PRICE
    CHANGES
JAR SP 70 VOL: 8 PG:113 - 117 :: QUAL. :INT. LOG. :THEORY :VALUAT.(INFL.)

DEVINE,CT CIT: 0.08
THE RULE OF CONSERVATISM REEXAMINED
JAR AU 63 VOL: 1 PG:127 - 138 :: QUAL. :INT. LOG. :THEORY :N/A

DEVINE,CT CIT: 0.00
PROFESSIONAL RESPONSIBILITIES - AN EMPIRICAL SUGGESTION
JAR ST 66 VOL: 4 PG:160 - 176 :: DES.STAT. :SURV. :OTH. :PROF.RESP.

DEWHIRST,JF CIT: 0.00
A CONCEPTUAL APPROACH TO PENSION ACCOUNTING
TAR AP 71 VOL: 46 PG:365 - 373 :: QUAL. :INT. LOG. :THEORY :SPEC.ITEMS

DEXTER,AS ; FIRS: BENBASAT,I CIT: 0.90
VALUE AND EVENTS APPROACHES TO ACCOUNTING: AN EXPERIMENTAL EVALUATION
TAR OC 79 VOL: 54 PG:735 - 749 :: ANOVA :LAB. :HIPS :INFO.STRUC.

DEXTER,AS ; FIRS: BENBASAT,I CIT: 0.29
INDIVIDUAL DIFFERENCES IN THE USE OF DECISION SUPPORT AIDS
JAR SP 82 VOL: 20 PG:1 - 11 :: ANOVA :LAB. :HIPS :DEC.AIDS

DHALIWAL,DS ; FIRS: COLLINS,DW ; SEC: ROZEFF,MS CIT: 3.88
THE ECONOMIC DETERMINANTS OF THE MARKET REACTION TO PROPOSED MANDATORY
    ACCOUNTING CHANGES IN THE OIL AND GAS INDUSTRY: A CROSS-SECTIONAL ANALYSIS
JAE MR 81 VOL: 3 PG:37 - 71 :: REGRESS. :PRIM. :EMH :OIL & GAS

DHALIWAL,DS ; SEC: SALAMON,GL ; THIR: SMITH ,ED CIT: 1.86
THE EFFECT OF OWNER VERSUS MANAGEMENT CONTROL ON THE CHOICE OF ACCOUNTING
    METHODS
JAE JL 82 VOL: 4 PG:41 - 53 :: NON-PAR. :SEC. :TIME SER. :AMOR./DEPL.

DHALIWAL,DS CIT: 0.00
MEASUREMENT OF FIN. LEVERAGE IN THE PRESENCE OF UNFUNDED PENSION OBLIGATIONS
TAR OC 86 VOL: 61 PG:651 - 661 :: REGRESS. :PRIM. :EMH :PENS.

DHALIWAL,DS ; FIRS: JOHNSON,WB CIT: 0.00
LIFO ABANDONMENT
JAR AU 88 VOL: 26 PG:236 - 272 :: REGRESS. :PRIM. :EMH :INV.

DHALIWAL,DS ; FIRS: DORAN ,BM ; SEC: COLLINS,DW CIT: 0.00
THE INFORMATION OF HISTORICAL COST EARNINGS RELATIVE TO SUPPLEMENTAL
   RESERVE-BASED ACCOUNTING DATA IN THE EXTRACTIVE PETROLEUM INDUSTRY
TAR JL 88 VOL: 63 PG:389 - 413 :: REGRESS. :PRIM. :EMH :OIL & GAS

DHARAN,BG CIT: 0.33
IDENTIFICATION AND ESTIMATION ISSUES FOR A CAUSAL EARNINGS MODEL
JAR SP 83 VOL: 21 PG:18 - 41 :: ANAL. :SIM. :TIME SER. :N/A

DHARAN,BG CIT: 0.00
EMPIRICAL IDENTIFICATION PROCEDURES FOR EARNINGS MODELS
JAR SP 83 VOL: 21 PG:256 - 270 :: NON-PAR. :PRIM. :TIME SER. :METHOD.

DHARAN,BG CIT: 0.40
EXPECTATION MODELS AND POTENTIAL INFORMATION CONTENT OF OIL AND GAS RESERVE
   VALUE DISCLOSURES
TAR AP 84 VOL: 59 PG:199 - 217 :: NON-PAR. :PRIM. :OTH.STAT. :OIL & GAS

DIAS ,FJB ; FIRS: OTLEY ,DT CIT: 0.14
ACCOUNTING AGGREGATION AND DECISION-MAKING PERFORMANCE: AN EXPERIMENTAL
   INVESTIGATION
JAR SP 82 VOL: 20 PG:171 - 188 :: ANOVA :LAB. :HIPS :INFO.STRUC.

DICKENS,RL ; SEC: BLACKBURN,JO CIT: 0.08
HOLDING GAINS ON FIXED ASSETS: AN ELEMENT OF BUSINESS INCOME?
TAR AP 64 VOL: 39 PG:312 - 329 :: ANAL. :INT. LOG. :THEORY :VALUAT.(INFL.)

DICKHAUT,JW CIT: 0.92
ALTERNATIVE INFORMATION STRUCTURES AND PROBABILITY REVISIONS
TAR JA 73 VOL: 48 PG:61 - 79 :: ANOVA :LAB. :HIPS :INFO.STRUC.

DICKHAUT,JW ; SEC: EGGLETON,IRC CIT: 0.54
AN EXAMINATION OF THE PROCESSES UNDERLYING COMPARATIVE JUDGMENTS OF NUMERICAL
   STIMULI
JAR SP 75 VOL: 13 PG:38 - 72 :: DES.STAT. :LAB. :HIPS :N/A

DICKHAUT,JW ; FIRS: MAGEE ,RP CIT: 0.55
EFFECTS OF COMPENSATION PLANS ON HEURISTICS IN COST VARIANCE INVESTIGATIONS
JAR AU 78 VOL: 16 PG:294 - 314 :: ANOVA :LAB. :HIPS :VAR.

DICKHAUT,JW ; FIRS: EGER ,C CIT: 0.14
AN EXAMINATION OF THE CONSERVATIVE INFORMATION PROCESSING BIAS IN AN
   ACCOUNTING FRAMEWORK
JAR AU 82 VOL: 20 PG:711 - 723 :: REGRESS. :LAB. :HIPS :MAN.DEC.CHAR.

DICKHAUT,JW ; SEC: LERE ,JC CIT: 0.17
COMPARISON OF ACCOUNTING SYSTEMS AND HEURISTICS IN SELECTING ECONOMIC OPTIMA
JAR AU 83 VOL: 21 PG:495 - 513 :: ANAL. :INT. LOG. :INF.ECO./AG. :INFO.STRUC.

DIERKES,M ; SEC: PRESTON,LE CIT: 0.42
CORPORATE SOCIAL ACCOUNTING REPORTING FOR THE PHYSICAL ENVIRONMENT: A
   CRITICAL REVIEW AND IMPLEMENTATION PROPOSAL
AOS 01 77 VOL: 2 PG:3 - 22 :: QUAL. :INT. LOG. :THEORY :HRA

DIERKES,M CIT: 0.20
CORPORATE SOCIAL REPORTING IN GERMANY: CONCEPTUAL DEVELOPMENTS AND PRACTICAL
   EXPERIENCE
AOS 12 79 VOL: 4 PG:87 - 108 :: DES.STAT. :PRIM. :THEORY :HRA

DIERKES,M ; SEC: ANTAL ,AB CIT: 0.00
THE USEFULNESS AND USE OF SOCIAL REPORTING INFORMATION
AOS 01 85 VOL: 10 PG:29 - 34 :: DES.STAT. :INT. LOG. :OTH.BEH. :HRA

DIETRICH,JR ; SEC: KAPLAN,RS CIT: 0.43
EMPIRICAL ANALYSIS OF THE COMMERCIAL LOAN CLASSIFICATION DECISION
TAR JA 82 VOL: 57 PG:18 - 38 :: REGRESS. :PRIM. :OTH.STAT. :N/A

DIETRICH,JR ; FIRS: HARRISON JR,WT ; SEC: TOMASSINI,LA CIT: 0.17
THE USE OF CONTROL GROUPS IN CAPITAL MARKET RESEARCH
JAR SP 83 VOL: 21 PG:65 - 77 :: NON-PAR. :PRIM. :EMH :METHOD.

DIETRICH,JR CIT: 0.00
EFFECTS OF EARLY BOND REFUNDINGS: AN EMPIRICAL INVESTIGATION OF SECURITY
   RETURNS
JAE AP 84 VOL: 6 PG:67 - 96 :: REGRESS. :PRIM. :EMH :LTD

DIETRICH,JR ; FIRS: OLSEN ,C CIT: 0.50
VERTICAL INFORMATION TRANSFERS: THE ASSOCIATION BETWEEN RETAILERS' SALES
   ANNOUNCEMENTS AND SUPPLIERS' SECURITY RETURNS
JAR ST 85 VOL: 23 PG:144 - 166 :: REGRESS. :PRIM. :EMH :FIN.METH.

DIETRICH,JR ; FIRS: THOMPSON II,RB ; SEC: OLSEN ,C CIT: 0.00
ATTRIBUTES OF NEWS ABOUT FIRMS: AN ANALYSIS OF FIRM-SPECIFIC NEWS REPORTED IN
   THE WALL STREET JOURNAL INDEX
JAR AU 87 VOL: 25 PG:245 - 274 :: REGRESS. :PRIM. :INSTIT. :INFO.STRUC.

DIETRICH,JR ; FIRS: THOMPSON,RB ; SEC: OLSEN ,C CIT: 0.00
THE INFLUENCE OF ESTIMATION PERIOD NEWS EVENTS ON STANDARDIZED MARKET MODEL
   PREDICTION ERRORS
TAR JL 88 VOL: 63 PG:448 - 471 :: REGRESS. :PRIM. :EMH :METHOD.

DILLARD,JF ; SEC: FERRIS,KR CIT: 0.50
SOURCES OF PROFESSIONAL STAFF TURNOVER IN PUBLIC ACCOUNTING FIRMS: SOME
   FURTHER EVIDENCE
AOS 03 79 VOL: 4 PG:179 - 186 :: OTH.QUANT. :SURV. :OTH.BEH. :AUD.BEH.

DILLARD,JF CIT: 0.20
VALENCE-INSTRUMENTALITY-EXPECTANCY MODEL VALIDATION USING SELECTED ACCOUNTING
   GROUPS
AOS 12 79 VOL: 4 PG:31 - 38 :: OTH.QUANT. :SURV. :OTH.BEH. :AUD.BEH.

DILLARD,JF ; FIRS: FERRIS,KR ; THIR: NETHERCOTT,L CIT: 0.11
A COMPARISON OF V-I-E MODEL PREDICTIONS: A CROSS-NATIONAL STUDY IN
   PROFESSIONAL ACCOUNTING FIRMS
AOS 04 80 VOL: 5 PG:361 - 368 :: DES.STAT. :LAB. :OTH.BEH. :INT.DIFF.

DILLARD,JF CIT: 0.13
A LONGITUDINAL EVALUATION OF AN OCCUPATIONAL GOAL-EXPECTANCY MODEL IN
   PROFESSIONAL ACCOUNTING ORGANIZATIONS
AOS 01 81 VOL: 6 PG:17 - 26 :: MIXED :SURV. :OTH.BEH. :ORG.

DILLARD,JF CIT: 0.00
COGNITIVE SCIENCE AND DECISION MAKING RESEARCH IN ACCOUNTING
AOS 34 84 VOL: 9 PG:343 - 354 :: QUAL. :INT. LOG. :HIPS :N/A

DILLON,RD ; SEC: NASH ,JF CIT: 0.18
THE TRUE RELEVANCE OF RELEVANT COSTS
TAR JA 78 VOL: 53 PG:11 - 17 :: QUAL. :INT. LOG. :THEORY :REL.COSTS

DIRSMITH,MW ; SEC: JABLONSKY,SF CIT: 0.36
THE PATTERN OF PPB REJECTION: SOMETHING ABOUT ORGANIZATIONS, SOMETHING ABOUT
  PPB
AOS 34 78 VOL: 3 PG:215 - 226 :: QUAL. :INT. LOG. :THEORY :BUDG.& PLAN.

DIRSMITH,MW ; SEC: JABLONSKY,SF CIT: 0.40
MBO, POLITICAL RATIONALITY AND INFORMATION INDUCTANCE
AOS 12 79 VOL: 4 PG:39 - 52 :: QUAL. :INT. LOG. :OTH. :N/A

DIRSMITH,MW ; SEC: MCALLISTER,JP CIT: 0.00
THE ORGANIC VS. THE MECHANISTIC AUDIT: PROBLEMS AND PITFALLS (PART II)
JAA AU 82 VOL: 6 PG:60 - 74 :: QUAL. :INT. LOG. :OTH. :AUD.

DIRSMITH,MW ; SEC: MCALLISTER,JP CIT: 0.00
THE ORGANIC VS. THE MECHANISTIC AUDIT
JAA SP 82 VOL: 5 PG:214 - 228 :: QUAL. :INT. LOG. :OTH. :AUD.

DIRSMITH,MW ; SEC: LEWIS ,BL CIT: 0.00
THE EFFECT OF EXTERNAL REPORTING ON MANAGERIAL DECISION-MAKING: SOME
  ANTECEDENT CONDITIONS
AOS 04 82 VOL: 7 PG:319 - 336 :: NON-PAR. :SURV. :HIPS :FIN.METH.

DIRSMITH,MW ; FIRS: COVALESKI,MA CIT: 0.50
BUDGETING AS A MEANS FOR CONTROL AND LOOSE COUPLING
AOS 04 83 VOL: 8 PG:323 - 340 :: CORR. :SURV. :OTH.BEH. :BUDG.& PLAN.

DIRSMITH,MW ; SEC: COVALESKI,MA CIT: 0.00
PRACTICE MANAGEMENT ISSUES IN PUBLIC ACCOUNTING FIRMS
JAA AU 85 VOL: 9 PG:5 - 21 :: REGRESS. :SURV. :OTH. :ORG.

DIRSMITH,MW ; SEC: COVALESKI,MA CIT: 0.00
INFORMAL COMMUNICATIONS, NONFORMAL COMMUNICATIONS AND MENTORING IN PUBLIC
  ACCOUNTING FIRMS
AOS 02 85 VOL: 10 PG:149 - 170 :: REGRESS. :INT. LOG. :INSTIT. :ORG.

DIRSMITH,MW ; FIRS: COVALESKI,MA CIT: 0.33
THE BUDGETARY PROCESS OF POWER AND POLITICS
AOS 03 86 VOL: 11 PG:193 - 214 :: REGRESS. :SURV. :OTH.BEH. :BUDG.& PLAN.

DIRSMITH,MW ; FIRS: COVALESKI,MA CIT: 0.00
THE USE OF BUDGETARY SYMBOLS IN THE POLITICAL ARENA: AN HISTORICALLY INFORMED
  FIELD STUDY
AOS 01 88 VOL: 13 PG:1 - 24 :: REGRESS. :CASE :THEORY :BUDG.& PLAN.

DIRSMITH,MW ; FIRS: WILLIAMS,DD CIT: 0.00
THE EFFECTS OF AUDIT TECHNOLOGY ON AUDITOR EFFICIENCY: AUDITING AND THE
  TIMELINESS OF CLIENT EARNINGS ANNOUNCEMENTS
AOS 05 88 VOL: 13 PG:487 - 508 :: REGRESS. :PRIM. :INSTIT. :OPER.AUD.

DITTMAN,DA ; SEC: JURIS ,HA ; THIR: REVSINE,L CIT: 0.38
ON THE EXISTENCE OF UNRECORDED HUMAN ASSETS: AN ECONOMIC PERSPECTIVE
JAR SP 76 VOL: 14 PG:49 - 65 :: ANAL. :INT. LOG. :OTH.BEH. :HRA

DITTMAN,DA ; SEC: PRAKASH,P CIT: 0.36
COST VARIANCE INVESTIGATION: MARKOVIAN CONTROL OF MARKOV PROCESSES
JAR SP 78 VOL: 16 PG:14 - 25 :: ANAL. :INT. LOG. :OTH.STAT. :VAR.

DITTMAN,DA ; SEC: PRAKASH,P CIT: 0.40
COST VARIANCE INVESTIGATION: MARKOVIAN CONTROL VERSUS OPTIMAL CONTROL
TAR AP 79 VOL: 54 PG:358 - 373 :: DES.STAT. :SIM. :OTH.STAT. :VAR.

DOCKWEILER,RC CIT: 0.15
THE PRACTICABILITY OF DEVELOPING MULTIPLE FINANCIAL STATEMENTS: A CASE STUDY
TAR OC 69 VOL: 44 PG:729 - 742 :: QUAL. :CASE :THEORY :VALUAT.(INFL.)

DODD ,P ; SEC: DOPUCH,N ; THIR: HOLTHAUSEN,RW ; FOUR: LEFTWICH,R CIT: 1.60
QUALIFIED AUDIT OPINIONS AND STOCK PRICES: INFORMATION CONTENT, ANNOUNCEMENT
    DATES, AND CONCURRENT DISCLOSURES
JAE AP 84 VOL: 6 PG:3 - 38 :: REGRESS. :PRIM. :EMH :OPIN.

DODIN ,B ; FIRS: CHAN ,KH CIT: 0.00
A DECISION SUPPORT SYSTEM FOR AUDIT-STAFF SCHEDULING WITH PRECEDENCE
    CONSTRAINTS
TAR OC 86 VOL: 61 PG:726 - 734 :: DES.STAT. :INT. LOG. :MATH.PROG. :ORG.

DOLPHIN,R ; FIRS: SOPER ,FJ CIT: 0.08
READABILITY AND CORPORATE ANNUAL REPORTS
TAR AP 64 VOL: 39 PG:358 - 362 :: DES.STAT. :PRIM. :N/A :OTH.MANAG.

DONEY ,LD ; FIRS: WILKINSON,JR CIT: 0.08
EXTENDING AUDIT AND REPORTING BOUNDARIES
TAR OC 65 VOL: 40 PG:753 - 756 :: QUAL. :INT. LOG. :INSTIT. :AUD.

DOPUCH,N CIT: 0.00
MATHEMATICAL PROGRAMMING AND ACCOUNTING APPROACHES TO INCREMENTAL COST
    ANALYSIS
TAR OC 63 VOL: 38 PG:745 - 753 :: ANAL. :INT. LOG. :MATH.PROG. :N/A

DOPUCH,N ; SEC: DRAKE ,DF CIT: 0.08
ACCOUNTING IMPLICATIONS OF A MATHEMATICAL PROGRAMMING APPROACH TO THE
    TRANSFER PRICE PROBLEM
JAR SP 64 VOL: 2 PG:10 - 24 :: ANAL. :INT. LOG. :MATH.PROG. :TRANS.PRIC.

DOPUCH,N ; FIRS: DRAKE ,DF CIT: 0.62
ON THE CASE FOR DICHOTOMIZING INCOME
JAR AU 65 VOL: 3 PG:192 - 205 :: QUAL. :INT. LOG. :THEORY :REV.REC.

DOPUCH,N ; SEC: DRAKE ,DF CIT: 0.15
THE EFFECT OF ALTERNATIVE ACCOUNTING RULES FOR NONSUBSIDIARY INVESTMENTS
JAR ST 66 VOL: 4 PG:192 - 219 :: DES.STAT. :PRIM. :THEORY :FIN.METH.

DOPUCH,N ; SEC: BIRNBERG,JG ; THIR: DEMSKI,JS CIT: 0.15
AN EXTENSION OF STANDARD COST VARIANCE ANALYSIS
TAR JL 67 VOL: 42 PG:526 - 536 :: ANAL. :INT. LOG. :OTH.STAT. :VAR.

DOPUCH,N ; FIRS: COOPER,WW ; THIR: KELLER,TF CIT: 0.08
BUDGETARY DISCLOSURE AND OTHER SUGGESTIONS FOR IMPROVING ACCOUNTING REPORTS
TAR OC 68 VOL: 43 PG:640 - 648 :: QUAL. :INT. LOG. :THEORY :FIN.METH.

DOPUCH,N ; SEC: WATTS ,RL CIT: 1.08
USING TIME-SERIES MODELS TO ASSESS THE SIGNIFICANCE OF ACCOUNTING CHANGES
JAR SP 72 VOL: 10 PG:180 - 194 :: MIXED :PRIM. :TIME SER. :ACC.CHNG.

DOPUCH,N ; SEC: RONEN ,J CIT: 0.54
THE EFFECTS OF ALTERNATIVE INVENTORY VALUATION METHODS - AN EXPERIMENTAL STUDY
JAR AU 73 VOL: 11 PG:191 - 211 :: DES.STAT. :LAB. :THEORY :INV.

DOPUCH,N ; FIRS: GONEDES,NJ CIT: 5.15
CAPITAL MARKET EQUILIBRIUM, INFORMATION PRODUCTION, AND SELECTING ACCOUNTING
    TECHNIQUES: THEORETICAL FRAMEWORK AND REVIEW OF EMPIRICAL WORK
JAR ST 74 VOL: 12 PG:48 - 129 :: ANAL. :SEC. :EMH :FIN.METH.

DOPUCH,N ; FIRS: GONEDES,NJ ; THIR: PENMAN,SH CIT: 3.00
DISCLOSURE RULES, INFORMATION-PRODUCTION, AND CAPITAL MARKET EQUILIBRIUM: THE
   CASE OF FORECAST DISCLOSURE RULES
JAR SP 76 VOL: 14 PG:89 - 137 :: NON-PAR. :PRIM. :EMH :FOREC.

DOPUCH,N ; FIRS: GONEDES,NJ CIT: 0.70
ECONOMIC ANALYSES AND ACCOUNTING TECHNIQUES: PERSPECTIVES AND PROPOSALS
JAR AU 79 VOL: 17 PG:384 - 410 :: QUAL. :INT. LOG. :THEORY :METHOD.

DOPUCH,N ; SEC: SUNDER,S CIT: 0.44
FASB'S STATEMENTS ON OBJECTIVES AND ELEMENTS OF FINANCIAL ACCOUNTING: A REVIEW
TAR JA 80 VOL: 55 PG:1 - 21 :: QUAL. :INT. LOG. :INSTIT. :FASB SUBM.

DOPUCH,N ; FIRS: DODD ,P ; THIR: HOLTHAUSEN,RW ; FOUR: LEFTWICH,R CIT: 1.60
QUALIFIED AUDIT OPINIONS AND STOCK PRICES: INFORMATION CONTENT, ANNOUNCEMENT
   DATES, AND CONCURRENT DISCLOSURES
JAE AP 84 VOL: 6 PG:3 - 38 :: REGRESS. :PRIM. :EMH :OPIN.

DOPUCH,N ; SEC: HOLTHAUSEN,RW ; THIR: LEFTWICH,RW CIT: 0.33
ABNORMAL STOCK RETURNS ASSOCIATED WITH MEDIA DISCLOSURES OF 'SUBJECT TO'
   QUALIFIED AUDIT OPINIONS
JAE JN 86 VOL: 8 PG:93 - 118 :: REGRESS. :PRIM. :EMH :OPIN.

DOPUCH,N ; SEC: HOLTHAUSEN,RW ; THIR: LEFTWICH,RW CIT: 0.50
PREDICTING AUDIT QUALIFICATIONS WITH FINANCIAL AND MARKET VARIABLES
TAR JL 87 VOL: 62 PG:431 - 454 :: REGRESS. :PRIM. :EMH :OPIN.

DOPUCH,N ; SEC: PINCUS,M CIT: 0.00
EVIDENCE ON THE CHOICE OF INVENTORY ACCOUNTING METHODS: LIFO VERSUS FIFO
JAR SP 88 VOL: 26 PG:28 - 59 :: REGRESS. :PRIM. :OTH.STAT. :INV.

DOPUCH,N CIT: 0.00
IMPLICATIONS OF TORTS RULES OF THE ACCOUNTANT'S LIABILITY FOR THE ACCOUNTING
   MODEL
JAA SU 88 VOL: 03 PG:245 - 250 :: DES.STAT. :INT. LOG. :INSTIT. :LIAB.

DORAN ,BM ; SEC: COLLINS,DW ; THIR: DHALIWAL,DS CIT: 0.00
THE INFORMATION OF HISTORICAL COST EARNINGS RELATIVE TO SUPPLEMENTAL
   RESERVE-BASED ACCOUNTING DATA IN THE EXTRACTIVE PETROLEUM INDUSTRY
TAR JL 88 VOL: 63 PG:389 - 413 :: REGRESS. :PRIM. :EMH :OIL & GAS

DORAN ,DT ; SEC: NACHTMANN,R CIT: 0.00
THE ASSOCIATION OF STOCK DISTRIBUTION ANNOUNCEMENTS AND EARNINGS PERFORMANCE
JAA SP 88 VOL: 03 PG:113 - 132 :: REGRESS. :PRIM. :EMH :STK.DIV.

DOWELL,CD ; SEC: HALL ,JA CIT: 0.00
EDP CONTROLS WITH AUDIT COST IMPLICATIONS
JAA AU 81 VOL: 5 PG:30 - 40 :: QUAL. :SURV. :THEORY :EDP AUD.

DOWELL,CD ; FIRS: BOATSMAN,JR ; THIR: KIMBRELL,JI CIT: 0.00
VALUING STOCK USED FOR A BUSINESS COMBINATION
JAA AU 84 VOL: 8 PG:35 - 43 :: ANAL. :INT. LOG. :OTH.STAT. :BUS.COMB.

DOWNES,D ; SEC: DYCKMAN,TR CIT: 0.38
A CRITICAL LOOK AT THE EFFICIENT MARKET EMPIRICAL RESEARCH LITERATURE AS IT
   RELATES TO ACCOUNTING INFORMATION
TAR AP 73 VOL: 48 PG:300 - 317 :: MIXED :SEC. :EMH :FIN.METH.

DRAKE ,DF ; FIRS: DOPUCH,N CIT: 0.08
ACCOUNTING IMPLICATIONS OF A MATHEMATICAL PROGRAMMING APPROACH TO THE
   TRANSFER PRICE PROBLEM
JAR SP 64 VOL: 2 PG:10 - 24 :: ANAL. :INT. LOG. :MATH.PROG. :TRANS.PRIC.

DRAKE ,DF ; SEC: DOPUCH,N CIT: 0.62
ON THE CASE FOR DICHOTOMIZING INCOME
JAR AU 65 VOL: 3 PG:192 - 205 :: QUAL. :INT. LOG. :THEORY :REV.REC.

DRAKE ,DF ; FIRS: DOPUCH,N CIT: 0.15
THE EFFECT OF ALTERNATIVE ACCOUNTING RULES FOR NONSUBSIDIARY INVESTMENTS
JAR ST 66 VOL: 4 PG:192 - 219 :: DES.STAT. :PRIM. :THEORY :FIN.METH.

DREBIN,AR CIT: 0.00
RECOGNIZING IMPLICIT INTEREST IN NON-FUNDED PENSION PLANS
TAR JL 63 VOL: 38 PG:579 - 583 :: QUAL. :INT. LOG. :THEORY :SPEC.ITEMS

DREBIN,AR CIT: 0.00
"CASH-FLOWITIS": MALADY OR SYNDROME?
JAR SP 64 VOL: 2 PG:25 - 34 :: QUAL. :INT. LOG. :THEORY :N/A

DREBIN,AR CIT: 0.08
PRICE LEVEL ADJUSTMENTS AND INVENTORY FLOW ASSUMPTIONS
TAR JA 65 VOL: 40 PG:154 - 162 :: ANAL. :INT. LOG. :THEORY :INV.

DREBIN,AR CIT: 0.00
ACCOUNTING FOR PROPRIETARY RESEARCH
TAR JL 66 VOL: 41 PG:413 - 425 :: ANAL. :INT. LOG. :THEORY :OTH. NON-C/A

DREBIN,AR CIT: 0.00
THE INVENTORY CALCULUS
JAR SP 66 VOL: 4 PG:68 - 86 :: ANAL. :INT. LOG. :OTH.STAT. :INV.

DREBIN,AR CIT: 0.00
A FALLACY OF DEPRECIATION TRANSLATION
JAR AU 69 VOL: 7 PG:204 - 214 :: ANAL. :INT. LOG. :OTH. :VALUAT.(INFL.)

DRINKWATER,D ; SEC: EDWARDS,JD CIT: 0.00
THE NATURE OF TAXES AND THE MATCHING PRINCIPLE
TAR JL 65 VOL: 40 PG:579 - 582 :: QUAL. :INT. LOG. :THEORY :TAXES

DRIVER,MJ ; SEC: MOCK ,TJ CIT: 2.00
HUMAN INFORMATION PROCESSING, DECISION STYLE THEORY, AND ACCOUNTING
   INFORMATION SYSTEMS
TAR JL 75 VOL: 50 PG:490 - 508 :: MIXED :LAB. :HIPS :INFO.STRUC.

DRTINA,RE ; FIRS: THODE ,SF ; THIR: LARGAY III,JA CIT: 0.00
OPERATING CASH FLOWS: A GROWING NEED FOR SEPARATE REPORTING
JAA WI 86 VOL: 1 PG:46 - 61 :: REGRESS. :PRIM. :EMH :OTH.FIN.ACC.

DUBOFF,JI ; FIRS: ALY ,HF CIT: 0.08
STATISTICAL VS. JUDGMENT SAMPLING: AN EMPIRICAL STUDY OF AUDITING THE
   ACCOUNTS RECEIVABLE OF A SMALL RETAIL STORE
TAR JA 71 VOL: 46 PG:119 - 128 :: ANOVA :CASE :OTH.STAT. :SAMP.

DUGAN ,MT ; SEC: GENTRY,JA ; THIR: SHRIVER,KA CIT: 0.00
THE X-11 MODEL: A NEW ANALYTICAL REVIEW TECHNIQUE FOR THE AUDITOR
AUD SP 85 VOL: 4 PG:11 - 22 :: DES.STAT. :INT. LOG. :TIME SER. :ANAL.REV.

DUKE ,GL ; SEC: NETER ,J ; THIR: LEITCH,RA CIT: 1.14
POWER CHARACTERISTICS OF TEST STATISTICS IN THE AUDITING ENVIRONMENT: AN
    EMPIRICAL STUDY
JAR SP 82 VOL: 20 PG:42 - 67 :: MIXED :PRIM. :OTH.STAT. :ERRORS

DUKE ,GL ; FIRS: BAILEY JR,AD ; THIR: GERLACH,JH ; FOUR: KO   ,CE ; FIFT:
MESERVY,RD ; SIX: WHINSTON,AB CIT: 0.00
TICOM AND THE ANALYSIS OF INTERNAL CONTROLS
TAR AP 85 VOL: 60 PG:186 - 201 :: CORR. :INT. LOG. :OTH. :INT.CONT.

DUKE ,GL ; FIRS: KO   ,CE ; SEC: NACHTSHEIM,CJ ; FOUR: BAILEY JR,AD CIT: 0.00
ON THE ROBUSTNESS OF MODEL-BASED SAMPLING IN AUDITING
AUD SP 88 VOL: 07 PG:119 - 136 :: DES.STAT. :SIM. :OTH.STAT. :SAMP.

DUKES ,RE ; FIRS: BEAVER,WH CIT: 1.62
INTERPERIOD TAX ALLOCATION, EARNINGS EXPECTATIONS, AND THE BEHAVIOR OF
    SECURITY PRICES
TAR AP 72 VOL: 47 PG:320 - 332 :: REGRESS. :PRIM. :EMH :PP&E / DEPR

DUKES ,RE ; FIRS: BEAVER,WH CIT: 0.69
INTERPERIOD TAX ALLOCATION AND DELTA-DEPRECIATION METHODS: SOME EMPIRICAL
    RESULTS
TAR JL 73 VOL: 48 PG:549 - 559 :: REGRESS. :PRIM. :EMH :PP&E / DEPR

DUKES ,RE ; FIRS: BEAVER,WH CIT: 0.08
DELTA-DEPRECIATION METHODS: SOME ANALYTICAL RESULTS
JAR AU 74 VOL: 12 PG:205 - 215 :: ANAL. :INT. LOG. :OTH.STAT. :PP&E / DEPR

DUKES ,RE ; SEC: DYCKMAN,TR ; THIR: ELLIOTT,JA CIT: 1.44
ACCOUNTING FOR RESEARCH AND DEVELOPMENT COSTS: THE IMPACT ON RESEARCH AND
    DEVELOPMENT EXPENDITURES
JAR ST 80 VOL: 18 PG:1 - 26 :: NON-PAR. :PRIM. :THEORY :R & D

DUKES ,RE ; FIRS: ELLIOTT,JA ; SEC: RICHARDSON,G ; THIR: DYCKMAN,TR CIT: 1.00
THE IMPACT OF SFAS NO.2 ON FIRM EXPENDITURES ON RESEARCH AND DEVELOPMENT:
    REPLICATIONS AND EXTENSIONS
JAR SP 84 VOL: 22 PG:85 - 102 :: NON-PAR. :PRIM. :EMH :R & D

DUVALL,RM ; SEC: BULLOCH,J CIT: 0.00
ADJUSTING RATE OF RETURN AND PRESENT VALUE FOR PRICE-LEVEL CHANGES
TAR JL 65 VOL: 40 PG:569 - 573 :: ANAL. :INT. LOG. :OTH.STAT. :OTH.MANAG.

DWORIN,L ; SEC: GRIMLUND,RA CIT: 0.60
DOLLAR UNIT SAMPLING FOR ACCOUNTS RECEIVABLE AND INVENTORY
TAR AP 84 VOL: 59 PG:218 - 241 :: MIXED :SIM. :OTH.STAT. :SAMP.

DWORIN,L ; SEC: GRIMLUND,RA CIT: 0.33
DOLLAR-UNIT SAMPLING: A COMPARISON OF THE QUASI-BAYESIAN AND MOMENT BOUNDS
TAR JA 86 VOL: 61 PG:36 - 57 :: DES.STAT. :SIM. :OTH.STAT. :SAMP.

DYCKMAN,TR CIT: 0.23
ON THE INVESTMENT DECISION
TAR AP 64 VOL: 39 PG:285 - 295 :: NON-PAR. :LAB. :N/A :INV.

DYCKMAN,TR CIT: 0.46
THE EFFECTS OF ALTERNATIVE ACCOUNTING TECHNIQUES ON CERTAIN MANAGEMENT
    DECISIONS
JAR SP 64 VOL: 2 PG:91 - 107 :: NON-PAR. :LAB. :OTH.BEH. :INV.

DYCKMAN,TR CIT: 0.69
THE INVESTIGATION OF COST VARIANCES
JAR AU 69 VOL: 7 PG:215 - 244 :: ANAL. :INT. LOG. :MATH.PROG. :VAR.

DYCKMAN,TR ; FIRS: OZAN ,T CIT: 0.31
A NORMATIVE MODEL FOR INVESTIGATION DECISIONS INVOLVING MULTIORIGIN COST
    VARIANCES
JAR SP 71 VOL: 9 PG:88 - 115 :: ANAL. :INT. LOG. :MATH.PROG. :VAR.

DYCKMAN,TR ; FIRS: DOWNES,D CIT: 0.38
A CRITICAL LOOK AT THE EFFICIENT MARKET EMPIRICAL RESEARCH LITERATURE AS IT
    RELATES TO ACCOUNTING INFORMATION
TAR AP 73 VOL: 48 PG:300 - 317 :: MIXED :SEC. :EMH :FIN.METH.

DYCKMAN,TR ; FIRS: CRICHFIELD,T ; THIR: LAKONISHOK,J CIT: 1.09
AN EVALUATION OF SECURITY ANALYSTS' FORECASTS
TAR JL 78 VOL: 53 PG:651 - 668 :: ANOVA :PRIM. :TIME SER. :FOREC.

DYCKMAN,TR ; SEC: SMITH ,AJ CIT: 2.40
FINANCIAL ACCOUNTING AND REPORTING BY OIL AND GAS PRODUCING COMPANIES: A
    STUDY OF INFORMATION EFFECTS
JAE MR 79 VOL: 1 PG:45 - 75 :: NON-PAR. :PRIM. :EMH :OIL & GAS

DYCKMAN,TR ; FIRS: DUKES ,RE ; THIR: ELLIOTT,JA CIT: 1.44
ACCOUNTING FOR RESEARCH AND DEVELOPMENT COSTS: THE IMPACT ON RESEARCH AND
    DEVELOPMENT EXPENDITURES
JAR ST 80 VOL: 18 PG:1 - 26 :: NON-PAR. :PRIM. :THEORY :R & D

DYCKMAN,TR CIT: 0.25
THE INTELLIGENCE OF AMBIGUITY
AOS 04 81 VOL: 6 PG:291 - 300 :: QUAL. :INT. LOG. :THEORY :N/A

DYCKMAN,TR ; SEC: HOSKIN,RE ; THIR: SWIERINGA,RJ CIT: 0.57
AN ACCOUNTING CHANGE AND INFORMATION PROCESSING CHANGES
AOS 01 82 VOL: 7 PG:1 - 12 :: REGRESS. :LAB. :HIPS :ACC.CHNG.

DYCKMAN,TR ; FIRS: ELLIOTT,JA ; SEC: RICHARDSON,G ; FOUR: DUKES ,RE CIT: 1.00
THE IMPACT OF SFAS NO.2 ON FIRM EXPENDITURES ON RESEARCH AND DEVELOPMENT:
    REPLICATIONS AND EXTENSIONS
JAR SP 84 VOL: 22 PG:85 - 102 :: NON-PAR. :PRIM. :EMH :R & D

DYCKMAN,TR ; SEC: ZEFF ,SA CIT: 1.20
TWO DECADES OF THE JOURNAL OF ACCOUNTING RESEARCH
JAR SP 84 VOL: 22 PG:225 - 297 :: DES.STAT. :SEC. :INSTIT. :METHOD.

DYCKMAN,TR ; SEC: PHILBRICK,D ; THIR: STEPHAN,J CIT: 0.60
A COMPARISON OF EVENT STUDY METHODOLOGIES USING DAILY STOCK RETURNS: A
    SIMULATION APPROACH
JAR ST 84 VOL: 22 PG:1 - 30 :: REGRESS. :SIM. :OTH.BEH. :METHOD.

DYE ,RA CIT: 1.50
COMMUNICATION AND POST-DECISION INFORMATION
JAR AU 83 VOL: 21 PG:514 - 533 :: ANAL. :INT. LOG. :INF.ECO./AG. :MAN.DEC.CHAR.

DYE ,RA CIT: 0.25
STRATEGIC ACCOUNTING CHOICE AND THE EFFECTS OF ALTERNATIVE FINANCIAL
    REPORTING REQUIREMENTS
JAR AU 85 VOL: 23 PG:544 - 574 :: REGRESS. :INT. LOG. :THEORY :INFO.STRUC.

DYE ,RA CIT: 1.00
DISCLOSURE OF NONPROPRIETARY INFORMATION
JAR SP 85 VOL: 23 PG:123 - 145 :: REGRESS. :INT. LOG. :INF.ECO./AG. :FIN.METH.

DYE ,RA CIT: 0.00
EARNINGS MANAGEMENT IN AN OVERLAPPING GENERATIONS MODEL
JAR AU 88 VOL: 26 PG:195 - 235 :: DES.STAT. :INT. LOG. :INF.ECO./AG. :REV.REC.

DYER ,JC ; SEC: MCHUGH,AJ CIT: 0.46
THE TIMELINESS OF THE AUSTRALIAN ANNUAL REPORT
JAR AU 75 VOL: 13 PG:204 - 219 :: NON-PAR. :PRIM. :OTH.STAT. :TIM.

DYKXHOORN,HJ ; SEC: SINNING,KE CIT: 0.00
WIRTSCHAFTSPRUFER PERCEPTION OF AUDITOR INDEPENDENCE
TAR JA 81 VOL: 56 PG:97 - 107 :: NON-PAR. :SURV. :OTH.BEH. :INDEP.

DYKXHOORN,HJ ; SEC: SINNING,KE CIT: 0.00
PERCEPTIONS OF AUDITOR INDEPENDENCE: ITS PERCEIVED EFFECT ON THE LOAN AND
    INVESTMENT DECISIONS OF GERMAN FINANCIAL STATEMENT USERS
AOS 04 82 VOL: 7 PG:337 - 348 :: ANOVA :LAB. :HIPS :INDEP.

DYL ,EA ; SEC: LILLY ,MS CIT: 0.00
A NOTE ON INSTITUTIONAL CONTRIBUTIONS TO THE ACCOUNTING LITERATURE
AOS 02 85 VOL: 10 PG:171 - 176 :: REGRESS. :SEC. :INSTIT. :METHOD.

EASTON,PD CIT: 0.25
ACCOUNTING EARNINGS AND SECURITY VALUATION: EMPIRICAL EVIDENCE OF THE
    FUNDAMENTAL LINKS
JAR ST 85 VOL: 23 PG:54 - 77 :: REGRESS. :PRIM. :EMH :CASH DIV.

EAVES ,BC CIT: 0.15
OPERATIONAL AXIOMATIC ACCOUNTING MECHANICS
TAR JL 66 VOL: 41 PG:426 - 442 :: ANAL. :INT. LOG. :THEORY :FIN.METH.

ECKEL ,LG CIT: 0.08
ARBITRARY AND INCORRIGIBLE ALLOCATIONS
TAR OC 76 VOL: 51 PG:764 - 777 :: QUAL. :INT. LOG. :THEORY :COST.ALLOC.

EDEY ,HC CIT: 0.00
COMPANY ACCOUNTS IN BRITAIN: THE JENKINS REPORT
TAR AP 63 VOL: 38 PG:262 - 265 :: QUAL. :INT. LOG. :INSTIT. :FIN.METH.

EDGAR ,SM ; FIRS: PEAVY ,JW CIT: 0.00
RATING ELECTRIC UTILITY COMMERCIAL PAPER
JAA WI 85 VOL: 8 PG:125 - 135 :: REGRESS. :PRIM. :OTH.STAT. :LTD

EDMONDS,TP ; FIRS: ALFORD,MR CIT: 0.13
A REPLICATION: DOES AUDIT INVOLVEMENT AFFECT THE QUALITY OF INTERIM REPORT
    NUMBERS?
JAA SP 81 VOL: 4 PG:255 - 264 :: DES.STAT. :SEC. :THEORY :INT.REP.

EDWARDS,EO CIT: 0.15
THE STATE OF CURRENT VALUE ACCOUNTING
TAR AP 75 VOL: 50 PG:235 - 245 :: QUAL. :INT. LOG. :THEORY :VALUAT.(INFL.)

EDWARDS,JD ; FIRS: DRINKWATER,D CIT: 0.00
THE NATURE OF TAXES AND THE MATCHING PRINCIPLE
TAR JL 65 VOL: 40 PG:579 - 582 :: QUAL. :INT. LOG. :THEORY :TAXES

EGER ,C ; SEC: DICKHAUT,JW CIT: 0.14
AN EXAMINATION OF THE CONSERVATIVE INFORMATION PROCESSING BIAS IN AN
  ACCOUNTING FRAMEWORK
JAR AU 82 VOL: 20 PG:711 - 723 :: REGRESS. :LAB. :HIPS :MAN.DEC.CHAR.

EGGLETON,IRC ; FIRS: DICKHAUT,JW CIT: 0.54
AN EXAMINATION OF THE PROCESSES UNDERLYING COMPARATIVE JUDGMENTS OF NUMERICAL
  STIMULI
JAR SP 75 VOL: 13 PG:38 - 72 :: DES.STAT. :LAB. :HIPS :N/A

EGGLETON,IRC ; SEC: PENMAN,SH ; THIR: TWOMBLY,JR CIT: 0.92
ACCOUNTING CHANGES AND STOCK PRICES: AN EXAMINATION OF SELECTED UNCONTROLLED
  VARIABLES
JAR SP 76 VOL: 14 PG:66 - 88 :: NON-PAR. :PRIM. :EMH :ACC.CHNG.

EGGLETON,IRC CIT: 0.38
PATTERNS, PROTOTYPES, AND PREDICTIONS: AN EXPLORATORY STUDY
JAR ST 76 VOL: 14 PG:68 - 131 :: ANOVA :LAB. :HIPS :N/A

EGGLETON,IRC CIT: 0.14
INTUITIVE TIME-SERIES EXTRAPOLATION
JAR SP 82 VOL: 20 PG:68 - 102 :: DES.STAT. :LAB. :HIPS :BUDG.& PLAN.

EHN ,P ; FIRS: CARLSSON,J ; THIR: ERLANDER,B ; FOUR: PERBY ,M ; FIFT:
SANDBERG,A CIT: 0.09
PLANNING AND CONTROL FROM THE PERSPECTIVE OF LABOR: A SHORT REPRESENTATION OF
  THE DEMOS PROJECT
AOS 34 78 VOL: 3 PG:249 - 260 :: QUAL. :FIELD :OTH. :BUDG.& PLAN.

EHRENREICH,K ; FIRS: GROVE ,HD ; SEC: MOCK ,TJ CIT: 0.08
A REVIEW OF HUMAN RESOURCE ACCOUNTING MEASUREMENT SYSTEMS FROM A MEASUREMENT
  THEORY PERSPECTIVE
AOS 03 77 VOL: 2 PG:219 - 236 :: QUAL. :SEC. :OTH.BEH. :HRA

EICHENSEHER,JW ; SEC: DANOS ,P CIT: 0.88
THE ANALYSIS OF INDUSTRY-SPECIFIC AUDITOR CONCENTRATION: TOWARDS AN
  EXPLANATORY MODEL
TAR JL 81 VOL: 56 PG:479 - 492 :: MIXED :PRIM. :OTH.STAT. :ORG.

EICHENSEHER,JW ; FIRS: DANOS ,P CIT: 0.43
AUDIT INDUSTRY DYNAMICS: FACTORS AFFECTING CHANGES IN CLIENT-INDUSTRY MARKET
  SHARES
JAR AU 82 VOL: 20 PG:604 - 616 :: ANOVA :PRIM. :OTH.STAT. :ORG.

EICHENSEHER,JW ; SEC: SHIELDS,D CIT: 0.33
THE CORRELATES OF CPA-FIRM CHANGE FOR PUBLICLY-HELD CORPORATIONS
AUD SP 83 VOL: 2 PG:23 - 37 :: NON-PAR. :SURV. :OTH.BEH. :ORG.

EICHENSEHER,JW CIT: 0.00
THE EFFECTS OF FOREIGN OPERATIONS ON DOMESTIC AUDITOR SELECTION
JAA SP 85 VOL: 8 PG:195 - 209 :: REGRESS. :PRIM. :OTH. :SEG.REP.

EICHENSEHER,JW ; FIRS: DANOS ,P CIT: 0.33
LONG-TERM TRENDS TOWARD SELLER CONCENTRATION IN THE US AUDIT MARKET
TAR OC 86 VOL: 61 PG:633 - 650 :: REGRESS. :PRIM. :OTH.STAT. :ORG.& ENVIR.

EICKHOFF,R ; FIRS: HARRELL,AM CIT: 0.00
AUDITORS' INFLUENCE ORIENTATION AND THEIR AFFECTIVE RESPONSES TO THE BIG
  EIGHT WORK ENVIRONMENT
AUD SP 88 VOL: 07 PG:105 - 118 :: REGRESS. :SURV. :OTH.BEH. :AUD.BEH.

EIGEN ,MM CIT: 0.00
IS POOLING REALLY NECESSARY?
TAR JL 65 VOL: 40 PG:536 - 540 :: QUAL. :INT. LOG. :THEORY :BUS.COMB.

EINHORN,HJ CIT: 1.00
A SYNTHESIS: ACCOUNTING AND BEHAVIOURAL SCIENCE
JAR ST 76 VOL: 14 PG:196 - 206 :: QUAL. :INT. LOG. :HIPS :METHOD.

EINHORN,HJ ; SEC: HOGARTH,RM CIT: 1.38
BEHAVIOURAL DECISION THEORY: PROCESSES OF JUDGMENT AND CHOICE
JAR SP 81 VOL: 19 PG:1 - 31 :: QUAL. :SEC. :HIPS :N/A

EL-GAZZAR,S ; SEC: LILIEN,S ; THIR: PASTENA,V CIT: 0.33
ACCOUNTING FOR LEASES BY LESSEES
JAE OC 86 VOL: 8 PG:217 - 238 :: REGRESS. :PRIM. :OTH.STAT. :LEASES

EL-SHESHAI,KM ; FIRS: ABDEL-KHALIK,AR CIT: 0.89
INFORMATION CHOICE AND UTILIZATION IN AN EXPERIMENT ON DEFAULT PREDICTION
JAR AU 80 VOL: 18 PG:325 - 342 :: DES.STAT. :LAB. :HIPS :BUS.FAIL.

ELAM ,R CIT: 0.46
THE EFFECT OF LEASE DATA ON THE PREDICTIVE ABILITY OF FINANCIAL RATIOS
TAR JA 75 VOL: 50 PG:25 - 43 :: NON-PAR. :PRIM. :OTH. :BUS.FAIL.

ELAM ,R ; FIRS: NIKOLAI,LA CIT: 0.00
THE POLLUTION CONTROL TAX INCENTIVE: A NON-INCENTIVE
TAR JA 79 VOL: 54 PG:119 - 131 :: ANAL. :SIM. :OTH.STAT. :TAXES

ELGERS,P ; SEC: CALLAHAN,C ; THIR: STROCK,E CIT: 0.00
THE EFFECT OF EARNINGS YIELDS UPON THE ASSOCIATION BETWEEN UNEXPECTED
   EARNINGS AND SECURITY RETURNS; A RE-EXAMINATION
TAR OC 87 VOL: 62 PG:763 - 773 :: REGRESS. :PRIM. :EMH :METHOD.

ELGERS,PT ; FIRS: CLARK ,JJ CIT: 0.00
FORECASTED INCOME STATEMENTS: AN INVESTOR PERSPECTIVE
TAR OC 73 VOL: 48 PG:668 - 678 :: CORR. :CASE :OTH.STAT. :BUDG.& PLAN.

ELGERS,PT CIT: 0.00
ACCOUNTING-BASED RISK PREDICTIONS: A RE-EXAMINATION
TAR JL 80 VOL: 55 PG:389 - 408 :: REGRESS. :PRIM. :EMH :N/A

ELGERS,PT ; SEC: MURRAY,D CIT: 0.00
THE IMPACT OF THE CHOICE OF MARKET INDEX ON THE EMPIRICAL EVALUATION OF
   ACCOUNTING DETERMINED RISK MEASURES
TAR AP 82 VOL: 57 PG:358 - 375 :: REGRESS. :PRIM. :EMH :N/A

ELGERS,PT ; FIRS: BLOOM ,R ; THIR: MURRAY,D CIT: 0.20
FUNCTIONAL FIXATION IN PRODUCT PRICING: A COMPARISON OF INDIVIDUALS AND GROUPS
AOS 01 84 VOL: 9 PG:1 - 11 :: MIXED :LAB. :HIPS :PP&E / DEPR

ELIAS ,N CIT: 1.08
THE EFFECTS OF HUMAN ASSET STATEMENTS ON THE INVESTMENT DECISION: AN
   EXPERIMENT
JAR ST 72 VOL: 10 PG:215 - 233 :: ANOVA :LAB. :OTH.BEH. :HRA

ELLIOTT,EL ; SEC: LARREA,J ; THIR: RIVERA,JM CIT: 0.00
ACCOUNTING AID TO DEVELOPING COUNTRIES: SOME ADDITIONAL CONSIDERATIONS
TAR OC 68 VOL: 43 PG:763 - 768 :: QUAL. :INT. LOG. :INSTIT. :OTH.MANAG.

ELLIOTT,JA ; FIRS: DUKES ,RE ; SEC: DYCKMAN,TR CIT: 1.44
ACCOUNTING FOR RESEARCH AND DEVELOPMENT COSTS: THE IMPACT ON RESEARCH AND
  DEVELOPMENT EXPENDITURES
JAR ST 80 VOL: 18 PG:1 - 26 :: NON-PAR. :PRIM. :THEORY :R & D

ELLIOTT,JA CIT: 1.00
"SUBJECT TO" AUDIT OPINIONS AND ABNORMAL SECURITY RETURNS: OUTCOMES AND
  AMBIGUITIES
JAR AU 82 VOL: 20 PG:617 - 638 :: REGRESS. :PRIM. :EMH :OPIN.

ELLIOTT,JA ; SEC: RICHARDSON,G ; THIR: DYCKMAN,TR ; FOUR: DUKES ,RE CIT: 1.00
THE IMPACT OF SFAS NO.2 ON FIRM EXPENDITURES ON RESEARCH AND DEVELOPMENT:
  REPLICATIONS AND EXTENSIONS
JAR SP 84 VOL: 22 PG:85 - 102 :: NON-PAR. :PRIM. :EMH :R & D

ELLIOTT,JW ; SEC: UPHOFF,HL CIT: 0.15
PREDICTING THE NEAR TERM PROFIT AND LOSS STATEMENT WITH AN ECONOMETRIC MODEL:
  A FEASIBILITY STUDY
JAR AU 72 VOL: 10 PG:259 - 274 :: MIXED :PRIM. :TIME SER. :BUDG.& PLAN.

ELLIOTT,RK CIT: 0.33
UNIQUE AUDIT METHODS: PEAT MARWICK INTERNATIONAL
AUD SP 83 VOL: 2 PG:1 - 12 :: QUAL. :INT. LOG. :OTH. :AUD.THEOR.

ELLIOTT,RK ; FIRS: ASHTON,RH ; SEC: WILLINGHAM,JJ CIT: 0.00
AN EMPIRICAL ANALYSIS OF AUDIT DELAY
JAR AU 87 VOL: 25 PG:275 - 292 :: REGRESS. :SURV. :INSTIT. :TIM.

ELNICKI,RA CIT: 0.00
HOSPITAL WORKING CAPITAL: AN EMPIRICAL STUDY
JAR ST 77 VOL: 15 PG:209 - 218 :: REGRESS. :PRIM. :TIME SER. :OTH.MANAG.

EMERY ,DR ; SEC: BARRON,FH ; THIR: MESSIER JR,WF CIT: 0.14
CONJOINT MEASUREMENT AND THE ANALYSIS OF NOISY DATA: A COMMENT
JAR AU 82 VOL: 20 PG:450 - 458 :: NON-PAR. :SIM. :HIPS :METHOD.

EMERY ,GW ; SEC: COGGER,KO CIT: 0.14
THE MEASUREMENT OF LIQUIDITY
JAR AU 82 VOL: 20 PG:290 - 303 :: ANAL. :PRIM. :OTH.STAT. :BUS.FAIL.

ENG ,R ; FIRS: WIESEN,JL CIT: 0.00
CORPORATE PERKS: DISCLOSURE AND TAX CONSIDERATIONS
JAA WI 79 VOL: 2 PG:101 - 121 :: QUAL. :INT. LOG. :THEORY :TAXES

ENGLEBRECHT,TD ; SEC: JAMISON,RW CIT: 0.10
AN EMPIRICAL INQUIRY INTO THE ROLE OF THE TAX COURT IN THE VALUATION OF
  PROPERTY FOR CHARITABLE CONTRIBUTION PURPOSES
TAR JL 79 VOL: 54 PG:554 - 562 :: REGRESS. :PRIM. :OTH.STAT. :TAXES

ENGSTROM,JH CIT: 0.00
PENSION REPORTING BY MUNICIPALITIES
JAA SP 84 VOL: 7 PG:197 - 211 :: DES.STAT. :INT. LOG. :THEORY :PENS.

ENGSTROM,JH CIT: 0.00
THE GOVERNMENTAL REPORTING ENTITY
JAA SU 85 VOL: 8 PG:305 - 318 :: REGRESS. :SURV. :THEORY :FIN.METH.

ENIS ,CR CIT: 0.00
THE IMPACT OF CURRENT-VALUED DATA ON THE PREDICTIVE JUDGMENTS OF INVESTORS
AOS 02 88 VOL: 13 PG:123 - 145 :: REGRESS. :LAB. :HIPS :VALUAT.(INFL.)

EPSTEIN,MJ ; SEC: FLAMHOLTZ,EG ; THIR: MCDONOUGH,JJ CIT: 0.54
CORPORATE SOCIAL ACCOUNTING IN THE U.S.A.: STATE OF THE ART AND FUTURE
    PROSPECTS
AOS 01 76 VOL: 1 PG:23 - 42 :: QUAL. :SEC. :THEORY :HRA

EPSTEIN,MJ ; FIRS: BRAVENEC,LL ; THIR: CRUMBLEY,DL CIT: 0.00
TAX IMPACT IN CORPORATE SOCIAL RESPONSIBILITY DECISIONS AND REPORTING
AOS 02 77 VOL: 2 PG:131 - 140 :: QUAL. :INT. LOG. :THEORY :HRA

ERLANDER,B ; FIRS: CARLSSON,J ; SEC: EHN   ,P ; FOUR: PERBY ,M ; FIFT:
SANDBERG,A CIT: 0.09
PLANNING AND CONTROL FROM THE PERSPECTIVE OF LABOR: A SHORT REPRESENTATION OF
    THE DEMOS PROJECT
AOS 34 78 VOL: 3 PG:249 - 260 :: QUAL. :FIELD :OTH. :BUDG.& PLAN.

ESKEW ,RK CIT: 0.23
AN EXAMINATION OF THE ASSOCIATION BETWEEN ACCOUNTING AND SHARE PRICE DATA IN
    THE EXTRACTIVE PETROLEUM INDUSTRY
TAR AP 75 VOL: 50 PG:316 - 324 :: REGRESS. :PRIM. :EMH :FIN.METH.

ESKEW ,RK CIT: 0.20
THE FORECASTING ABILITY OF ACCOUNTING RISK MEASURES: SOME ADDITIONAL EVIDENCE
TAR JA 79 VOL: 54 PG:107 - 118 :: ANOVA :PRIM. :OTH.STAT. :FIN.METH.

ESPEJO,J ; FIRS: ABDEL-KHALIK,AR CIT: 0.36
EXPECTATIONS DATA AND THE PREDICTIVE VALUE OF INTERIM REPORTING
JAR SP 78 VOL: 16 PG:1 - 13 :: REGRESS. :LAB. :TIME SER. :FOREC.

ESPOSITO,RS ; FIRS: BLOCHER,E ; THIR: WILLINGHAM,JJ CIT: 0.17
AUDITOR'S ANALYTICAL REVIEW JUDGMENTS FOR PAYROLL EXPENSE
AUD AU 83 VOL: 3 PG:75 - 91 :: DES.STAT. :LAB. :OTH.BEH. :ANAL.REV.

ESSEX ,S ; FIRS: COOPER,DJ CIT: 0.42
ACCOUNTING INFORMATION AND EMPLOYEE DECISION MAKING
AOS 03 77 VOL: 2 PG:201 - 218 :: DES.STAT. :SURV. :OTH.BEH. :HRA

ESTES ,RW CIT: 0.08
AN ASSESSMENT OF THE USEFULNESS OF CURRENT COST AND PRICE-LEVEL INFORMATION
    BY FINANCIAL STATEMENT USERS
JAR AU 68 VOL: 6 PG:200 - 207 :: NON-PAR. :SURV. :N/A :VALUAT.(INFL.)

ESTES ,RW CIT: 0.54
SOCIO-ECONOMIC ACCOUNTING AND EXTERNAL DISECONOMIES
TAR AP 72 VOL: 47 PG:284 - 290 :: QUAL. :INT. LOG. :INSTIT. :HRA

ESTRIN,TL ; FIRS: MOCK   ,TJ ; THIR: VASARHELYI,MA CIT: 0.77
LEARNING PATTERNS, DECISION APPROACH, AND VALUE OF INFORMATION
JAR SP 72 VOL: 10 PG:129 - 153 :: ANOVA :LAB. :HIPS :INFO.STRUC.

ETTENSON,RT ; FIRS: KROGSTAD,JL ; THIR: SHANTEAU,J CIT: 0.40
CONTEXT AND EXPERIENCE IN AUDITORS' MATERIALITY JUDGMENTS
AUD AU 84 VOL: 4 PG:54 - 74 :: ANOVA :LAB. :OTH.BEH. :MAT.

ETTREDGE,M ; SEC: SHANE ,PB ; THIR: SMITH ,D CIT: 0.00
AUDIT FIRM SIZE AND THE ASSOCIATION BETWEEN REPORTED EARNINGS AND SECURITY
    RETURNS
AUD SP 88 VOL: 07 PG:29 - 42 :: REGRESS. :PRIM. :EMH :AUD.THEOR.

EUDY ,KH ; FIRS: HOLDER,WW CIT: 0.00
A FRAMEWORK FOR BUILDING AN ACCOUNTING CONSTITUTION
JAA WI 82 VOL: 5 PG:110 - 125 :: QUAL. :INT. LOG. :THEORY :FASB SUBM.

EUSKE ,KJ ; FIRS: ANSARI,SL CIT: 0.00
RATIONAL, RATIONALIZING, AND REIFYING USES OF ACCOUNTING DATA IN ORGANIZATIONS
AOS 06 87 VOL: 12 PG:549 - 570 :: REGRESS. :SURV. :OTH.BEH. :COST.ALLOC.

EVANS III,JH CIT: 0.33
OPTIMAL CONTRACTS WITH COSTLY CONDITIONAL AUDITING
JAR ST 80 VOL: 18 PG:108 - 128 :: ANAL. :INT. LOG. :INF.ECO./AG. :AUD.

EVANS III,JH CIT: 0.33
OPTIMAL CONTRACTS WITH COSTLY CONDITIONAL AUDITING
JAR ST 80 VOL: 18 PG:108 - 128 :: ANAL. :INT. LOG. :INF.ECO./AG. :AUD.

EVANS III,JH ; SEC: PATTON,JM CIT: 1.00
AN ECONOMIC ANALYSIS OF PARTICIPATION IN THE MUNICIPAL FINANCE OFFICERS
   ASSOCIATION CERTIFICATE OF CONFORMANCE PROGRAM
JAE AG 83 VOL: 5 PG:151 - 175 :: OTH.QUANT. :PRIM. :INSTIT. :FIN.METH.

EVANS III,JH ; FIRS: BAIMAN,S CIT: 1.67
PRE-DECISION INFORMATION AND PARTICIPATIVE MANAGEMENT CONTROL SYSTEMS
JAR AU 83 VOL: 21 PG:371 - 395 :: ANAL. :INT. LOG. :INF.ECO./AG. :MANAG.

EVANS III,JH ; SEC: LEWIS ,BL ; THIR: PATTON,JM CIT: 0.00
AN ECONOMIC MODELING APPROACH TO CONTINGENCY THEORY AND MANAGEMENT CONTROL
AOS 06 86 VOL: 11 PG:483 - 498 :: DES.STAT. :INT. LOG. :INF.ECO./AG. :INT.CONT.

EVANS III,JH ; FIRS: BAIMAN,S ; THIR: NOEL J CIT: 0.00
OPTIMAL CONTRACTS WITH A UTILITY-MAXIMIZING AUDITOR
JAR AU 87 VOL: 25 PG:217 - 244 :: ANAL. :INT. LOG. :INF.ECO./AG. :AUD.BEH.

EVANS III,JH ; SEC: PATTON,JM CIT: 0.00
SIGNALING AND MONITORING IN PUBLIC-SECTOR ACCOUNTING
JAR ST 87 VOL: 25 PG:130 - 164 :: MIXED :SURV. :INF.ECO./AG. :FIN.METH.

EVEREST,GL ; SEC: WEBER ,R CIT: 0.25
A RELATIONAL APPROACH TO ACCOUNTING MODELS
TAR AP 77 VOL: 52 PG:340 - 359 :: ANAL. :INT. LOG. :OTH.STAT. :N/A

EVERETT,JO ; SEC: PORTER,GA CIT: 0.00
SAFE-HARBOR LEASING - UNRAVELING THE TAX IMPLICATIONS
JAA SP 84 VOL: 7 PG:241 - 256 :: MIXED :INT. LOG. :THEORY :LEASES

EWUSI-MENSAH,K CIT: 0.38
THE EXTERNAL ORGANIZATIONAL ENVIRONMENT AND ITS IMPACT ON MANAGEMENT
   INFORMATION SYSTEMS
AOS 04 81 VOL: 6 PG:301 - 316 :: QUAL. :INT. LOG. :OTH. :N/A

FAGERBERG,P CIT: 0.00
CONCERNING THREE MISCHIEVOUS ACCOUNTS
TAR JL 72 VOL: 47 PG:454 - 457 :: QUAL. :INT. LOG. :N/A :FIN.METH.

FAIRCLOTH,AW ; SEC: RICCHIUTE,DN CIT: 0.00
AMBIGUITY INTOLERANCE AND FINANCIAL REPORTING ALTERNATIVES
AOS 01 81 VOL: 6 PG:53 - 68 :: DES.STAT. :SURV. :HIPS :FIN.METH.

FAIRFIELD,P ; FIRS: BURTON,JC CIT: 0.00
AUDITING EVOLUTION IN A CHANGING ENVIRONMENT
AUD WI 82 VOL: 1 PG:1 - 22 :: DES.STAT. :INT. LOG. :INSTIT. :ORG.

FALK ,G ; FIRS: RONEN ,J CIT: 0.15
ACCOUNTING AGGREGATION AND THE ENTROPY MEASURE: AN EXPERIMENTAL APPROACH
TAR OC 73 VOL: 48 PG:696 - 717 :: NON-PAR. :LAB. :INF.ECO./AG. :INFO.STRUC.

FALK ,H CIT: 0.00
ASSESSING THE EFFECTIVENESS OF ACCOUNTING COURSES THROUGH FACET ANALYSIS
JAR AU 72 VOL: 10 PG:359 - 375 :: MIXED :FIELD :OTH.STAT. :EDUC.

FALK ,H ; SEC: OPHIR ,T CIT: 0.15
THE EFFECT OF RISK ON USE OF FINANCIAL STATEMENTS BY INVESTMENT
   DECISION-MAKERS: A CASE STUDY
TAR AP 73 VOL: 48 PG:323 - 338 :: NON-PAR. :CASE :THEORY :N/A

FALK ,H ; SEC: OPHIR ,T CIT: 0.23
THE INFLUENCE OF DIFFERENCES IN ACCOUNTING POLICIES ON INVESTMENT DECISIONS
JAR SP 73 VOL: 11 PG:108 - 116 :: DES.STAT. :LAB. :OTH.BEH. :FIN.METH.

FALK ,H ; SEC: HEINTZ,JA CIT: 0.00
ASSESSING INDUSTRY RISK BY RATIO ANALYSIS
TAR OC 75 VOL: 50 PG:758 - 779 :: NON-PAR. :PRIM. :N/A :FIN.METH.

FALK ,H ; SEC: MILLER,JC CIT: 0.08
AMORTIZATION OF ADVERTISING EXPENDITURES
JAR SP 77 VOL: 15 PG:12 - 22 :: REGRESS. :PRIM. :OTH.STAT. :AMOR./DEPL.

FALK ,H ; FIRS: BUZBY ,SL CIT: 0.27
A SURVEY OF THE INTEREST IN SOCIAL RESPONSIBILITY INFORMATION BY MUTUAL FUNDS
AOS 34 78 VOL: 3 PG:191 - 202 :: DES.STAT. :SURV. :OTH.BEH. :METHOD.

FALK ,H ; FIRS: BUZBY ,SL CIT: 0.40
DEMAND FOR SOCIAL RESPONSIBILITY INFORMATION BY UNIVERSITY INVESTORS
TAR JA 79 VOL: 54 PG:23 - 37 :: DES.STAT. :SURV. :INSTIT. :HRA

FARAG ,SM CIT: 0.00
A PLANNING MODEL FOR THE DIVISIONALIZED ENTERPRISE
TAR AP 68 VOL: 43 PG:312 - 320 :: ANAL. :INT. LOG. :MATH.PROG. :BUDG.& PLAN.

FARBER,A ; FIRS: GOMBERG,M CIT: 0.00
THE BALANCE SHEET OF THE FUTURE
TAR JL 64 VOL: 39 PG:615 - 617 :: QUAL. :INT. LOG. :THEORY :FIN.METH.

FARMAN,WL ; SEC: HOU   ,C CIT: 0.00
THE BALANCE OF PAYMENTS: AN ACCOUNTING ANALYSIS
TAR JA 63 VOL: 38 PG:133 - 141 :: QUAL. :INT. LOG. :THEORY :INT.DIFF.

FARMAN,WL CIT: 0.00
NATIONAL FLOW-OF-FUNDS: AN ACCOUNTING ANALYSIS
TAR AP 64 VOL: 39 PG:392 - 404 :: QUAL. :INT. LOG. :INSTIT. :HRA

FARMER,TA ; SEC: RITTENBERG,LE ; THIR: TROMPETER,GM CIT: 0.00
AN INVESTIGATION OF THE IMPACT OF ECONOMIC AND ORGANIZATIONAL FACTORS
   ON AUDITOR INDEPENDENCE
AUD AU 87 VOL: 7 PG:1 - 14 :: REGRESS. :LAB. :OTH.BEH. :INDEP.

FARRELY,GE ; SEC: FERRIS,KR ; THIR: REICHENSTEIN,WR CIT: 0.00
PERCEIVED RISK, MARKET RISK, AND ACCOUNTING-DETERMINED RISK MEASURES
TAR AP 85 VOL: 60 PG:278 - 288 :: REGRESS. :SURV. :OTH.STAT. :FOREC.

FEINSCHREIBER,R CIT: 0.00
ACCELERATED DEPRECIATION: A PROPOSED NEW METHOD
JAR SP 69 VOL: 7 PG:17 - 21 :: DES.STAT. :SIM. :INSTIT. :PP&E / DEPR

FEKRAT,MA CIT: 0.08
THE CONCEPTUAL FOUNDATIONS OF ABSORPTION COSTING
TAR AP 72 VOL: 47 PG:351 - 355 :: QUAL. :INT. LOG. :THEORY :OVER.ALLOC.

FELIX JR,WL CIT: 0.00
ESTIMATING THE RELATIONSHIP BETWEEN TECHNICAL CHANGE AND REPORTED PERFORMANCE
TAR JA 72 VOL: 47 PG:52 - 63 :: REGRESS. :PRIM. :TIME SER. :AUD.BEH.

FELIX JR,WL CIT: 1.00
EVIDENCE ON ALTERNATIVE MEANS OF ASSESSING PRIOR PROBABILITY DISTRIBUTIONS
    FOR AUDIT DECISION MAKING
TAR OC 76 VOL: 51 PG:800 - 807 :: DES.STAT. :LAB. :OTH.STAT. :PROB.ELIC.

FELIX JR,WL ; SEC: GRIMLUND,RA CIT: 1.17
A SAMPLING MODEL FOR AUDIT TESTS OF COMPOSITE ACCOUNTS
JAR SP 77 VOL: 15 PG:23 - 41 :: ANAL. :INT. LOG. :OTH.STAT. :SAMP.

FELIX JR,WL ; SEC: KINNEY JR,WR CIT: 0.86
RESEARCH IN THE AUDITOR'S OPINION FORMULATION PROCESS: STATE OF THE ART
TAR AP 82 VOL: 57 PG:245 - 271 :: QUAL. :SEC. :OTH. :N/A

FELIX JR,WL ; FIRS: WALLER,WS CIT: 0.40
THE EFFECTS OF INCOMPLETE OUTCOME FEEDBACK ON AUDITORS' SELF-PERCEPTIONS OF
    JUDGEMENT ABILITY
TAR OC 84 VOL: 59 PG:637 - 646 :: ANOVA :LAB. :HIPS :JUDG.

FELIX JR,WL ; FIRS: WALLER,WS CIT: 1.40
THE AUDITOR AND LEARNING FROM EXPERIENCE: SOME CONJECTURES
AOS 34 84 VOL: 9 PG:383 - 406 :: QUAL. :INT. LOG. :HIPS :N/A

FELIX JR,WL ; FIRS: WALLER,WS CIT: 0.00
AUDITORS' COVARIATION JUDGMENTS
TAR AP 87 VOL: 62 PG:275 - 292 :: REGRESS. :LAB. :HIPS :JUDG.

FELIX JR,WL ; FIRS: GRIMLUND,RA CIT: 0.00
SIMULATION EVIDENCE AND ANALYSIS OF ALTERNATIVE METHODS OF EVALUATING
    DOLLAR-UNIT SAMPLES
TAR JL 87 VOL: 62 PG:455 - 479 :: DES.STAT. :SIM. :OTH.STAT. :SAMP.

FELIX JR,WL ; SEC: NILES ,MS CIT: 0.00
RESEARCH IN INTERNAL CONTROL EVALUATION
AUD SP 88 VOL: 07 PG:43 - 60 :: DES.STAT. :SEC. :THEORY :INT.CONT.

FELLINGHAM,JC ; SEC: WOLFSON,MA CIT: 0.00
TAXES AND RISK SHARING
TAR JA 85 VOL: 60 PG:10 - 17 :: DES.STAT. :INT. LOG. :INF.ECO./AG. :TAXES

FELLINGHAM,JC ; SEC: NEWMAN,DP CIT: 0.00
STRATEGIC CONSIDERATIONS IN AUDITING
TAR OC 85 VOL: 60 PG:634 - 650 :: REGRESS. :INT. LOG. :OTH.STAT. :PLAN.

FELTHAM,GA CIT: 0.54
THE VALUE OF INFORMATION
TAR OC 68 VOL: 43 PG:684 - 696 :: ANAL. :INT. LOG. :THEORY :INFO.STRUC.

FELTHAM,GA CIT: 0.08
SOME QUANTITATIVE APPROACHES TO PLANNING FOR MULTIPRODUCT PRODUCTION SYSTEMS
TAR JA 70 VOL: 45 PG:11 - 26 :: ANAL. :INT. LOG. :MATH.PROG. :BUDG.& PLAN.

FELTHAM,GA ; SEC: DEMSKI,JS CIT: 1.00
THE USE OF MODELS IN INFORMATION EVALUATION
TAR OC 70 VOL: 45 PG:623 - 640 :: ANAL. :INT. LOG. :INF.ECO./AG. :MANAG.

FELTHAM,GA ; FIRS: DEMSKI,JS CIT: 0.54
FORECAST EVALUATION
TAR JL 72 VOL: 47 PG:533 - 548 :: MIXED :SIM. :INF.ECO./AG. :BUDG.& PLAN.

FELTHAM,GA CIT: 0.42
COST AGGREGATION: AN INFORMATION ECONOMIC ANALYSIS
JAR SP 77 VOL: 15 PG:42 - 70 :: MIXED :SIM. :INF.ECO./AG. :INFO.STRUC.

FELTHAM,GA ; FIRS: DEMSKI,JS CIT: 3.18
ECONOMIC INCENTIVES IN BUDGETARY CONTROL SYSTEMS
TAR AP 78 VOL: 53 PG:336 - 359 :: ANAL. :INT. LOG. :INF.ECO./AG. :BUDG.& PLAN.

FERGUSON,P ; FIRS: BERRY ,AJ ; SEC: CAPPS ,T ; THIR: COOPER,D ; FIFT: HOPPER,T
; SIX: LOWE ,EA CIT: 3.50
MANAGEMENT CONTROL IN AN AREA OF THE NCB: RATIONALES OF ACCOUNTING PRACTICES
    IN A PUBLIC ENTERPRISE
AOS 01 85 VOL: 10 PG:3 - 28 :: REGRESS. :FIELD :OTH.BEH. :MANAG.

FERRARA,WL CIT: 0.00
RELEVANT COSTING - TWO POINTS OF VIEW
TAR OC 63 VOL: 38 PG:719 - 722 :: QUAL. :INT. LOG. :THEORY :REL.COSTS

FERRARA,WL CIT: 0.00
SHOULD INVESTMENT AND FINANCING DECISIONS BE SEPARATED?
TAR JA 66 VOL: 41 PG:106 - 114 :: ANAL. :INT. LOG. :N/A :BUDG.& PLAN.

FERRARA,WL ; SEC: HAYYA ,JC ; THIR: NACHMAN,DA CIT: 0.31
NORMALCY OF PROFIT IN THE JAEDICKE-ROBICHEK MODEL
TAR AP 72 VOL: 47 PG:299 - 307 :: ANAL. :SIM. :OTH.STAT. :C-V-P-A

FERRARA,WL CIT: 0.00
PROBABILISTIC APPROACHES TO RETURN ON INVESTMENT AND RESIDUAL INCOME
TAR JL 77 VOL: 52 PG:597 - 604 :: ANAL. :SIM. :OTH.STAT. :RESP.ACC.

FERRERI,LB ; FIRS: COWEN ,SS ; THIR: PARKER,LD CIT: 0.00
THE IMPACT OF CORPORATE CHARACTERISTICS ON SOCIAL RESPONSIBILITY DIS
    CLOSURE: A TYPOLOGY AND FREQUENCY-BASED ANALYSIS
AOS 02 87 VOL: 12 PG:111 - 122 :: REGRESS. :PRIM. :THEORY :HRA

FERRIS,KR CIT: 1.25
A TEST OF THE EXPECTANCY THEORY OF MOTIVATION IN AN ACCOUNTING ENVIRONMENT
TAR JL 77 VOL: 52 PG:605 - 615 :: REGRESS. :FIELD :OTH.BEH. :AUD.BEH.

FERRIS,KR CIT: 0.08
PERCEIVED UNCERTAINTY AND JOB SATISFACTION IN THE ACCOUNTING ENVIRONMENT
AOS 01 77 VOL: 2 PG:23 - 28 :: CORR. :SURV. :OTH.BEH. :OTH.MANAG.

FERRIS,KR ; FIRS: DILLARD,JF CIT: 0.50
SOURCES OF PROFESSIONAL STAFF TURNOVER IN PUBLIC ACCOUNTING FIRMS: SOME
    FURTHER EVIDENCE
AOS 03 79 VOL: 4 PG:179 - 186 :: OTH.QUANT. :SURV. :OTH.BEH. :AUD.BEH.

FERRIS,KR ; SEC: DILLARD,JF ; THIR: NETHERCOTT,L CIT: 0.11
A COMPARISON OF V-I-E MODEL PREDICTIONS: A CROSS-NATIONAL STUDY IN
    PROFESSIONAL ACCOUNTING FIRMS
AOS 04 80 VOL: 5 PG:361 - 368 :: DES.STAT. :LAB. :OTH.BEH. :INT.DIFF.

FERRIS,KR CIT: 0.13
ORGANIZATIONAL COMMITMENT AND PERFORMANCE IN A PROFESSIONAL ACCOUNTING FIRM
AOS 04 81 VOL: 6 PG:317 - 326 :: CORR. :SURV. :OTH.BEH. :AUD.BEH.

FERRIS,KR CIT: 0.00
PERCEIVED ENVIRONMENTAL UNCERTAINTY, ORGANIZATIONAL ADAPTATION AND EMPLOYEE
  PERFORMANCE: A LONGITUDINAL STUDY IN PROFESSIONAL ACCOUNTING FIRMS
AOS 01 82 VOL: 7 PG:13 - 26 :: ANOVA :SURV. :OTH.BEH. :ORG.

FERRIS,KR CIT: 0.00
EDUCATIONAL PREDICTORS OF PROFESSIONAL PAY AND PERFORMANCE
AOS 03 82 VOL: 7 PG:225 - 230 :: REGRESS. :SURV. :OTH.BEH. :EDUC.

FERRIS,KR ; SEC: LARCKER,DF CIT: 0.17
EXPLANATORY VARIABLES OF AUDITOR PERFORMANCE IN A LARGE PUBLIC ACCOUNTING FIRM
AOS 01 83 VOL: 8 PG:1 - 12 :: CORR. :SURV. :OTH.BEH. :ORG.

FERRIS,KR ; FIRS: ARANYA,N CIT: 0.20
A REEXAMINATION OF ACCOUNTANTS' ORGANIZATIONAL-PROFESSIONAL CONFLICT
TAR JA 84 VOL: 59 PG:1 - 15 :: ANOVA :SURV. :OTH.BEH. :PROF.RESP.

FERRIS,KR ; SEC: TENNANT,KL CIT: 0.20
AN INVESTIGATION OF THE IMPACT OF THE QUALITATIVE NATURE OF COMPLIANCE ERRORS
  ON INTERNAL CONTROL ASSESSMENTS
AUD SP 84 VOL: 3 PG:31 - 43 :: NON-PAR. :LAB. :OTH.STAT. :INT.CONT.

FERRIS,KR ; FIRS: FARRELY,GE ; THIR: REICHENSTEIN,WR CIT: 0.00
PERCEIVED RISK, MARKET RISK, AND ACCOUNTING-DETERMINED RISK MEASURES
TAR AP 85 VOL: 60 PG:278 - 288 :: REGRESS. :SURV. :OTH.STAT. :FOREC.

FERRIS,KR ; FIRS: DEAN ,RA ; THIR: KONSTANS,C CIT: 0.00
OCCUPATIONAL REALITY SHOCK AND ORGANIZATIONAL COMMITMENT: EVIDENCE FROM THE
  ACCOUNTING PROFESSION
AOS 03 88 VOL: 13 PG:235 - 250 :: REGRESS. :SURV. :OTH.BEH. :AUD.BEH.

FERTAKIS,JP ; FIRS: DECOSTER,DT CIT: 1.46
BUDGET-INDUCED PRESSURE AND ITS RELATIONSHIP TO SUPERVISORY BEHAVIOR
JAR AU 68 VOL: 6 PG:237 - 246 :: DES.STAT. :SURV. :OTH.BEH. :BUDG.& PLAN.

FERTAKIS,JP CIT: 0.23
ON COMMUNICATION, UNDERSTANDING, AND RELEVANCE IN ACCOUNTING REPORTING
TAR OC 69 VOL: 44 PG:680 - 691 :: QUAL. :INT. LOG. :OTH.BEH. :INFO.STRUC.

FERTAKIS,JP CIT: 0.00
EMPIRICAL EVIDENCE - A REPLY
TAR JL 70 VOL: 45 PG:509 - 512 :: QUAL. :INT. LOG. :OTH.BEH. :INFO.STRUC.

FESS ,PE CIT: 0.00
THE RELEVANT COSTING CONCEPT FOR INCOME MEASUREMENT - CAN IT BE DEFENDED?
TAR OC 63 VOL: 38 PG:723 - 732 :: QUAL. :INT. LOG. :THEORY :REL.COSTS

FESS ,PE CIT: 0.00
THE WORKING CAPITAL CONCEPT
TAR AP 66 VOL: 41 PG:266 - 270 :: QUAL. :INT. LOG. :THEORY :INFO.STRUC.

FIELD ,JE CIT: 0.08
TOWARD A MULTI-LEVEL, MULTI-GOAL INFORMATION SYSTEM
TAR JL 69 VOL: 44 PG:593 - 599 :: QUAL. :INT. LOG. :OTH.BEH. :MANAG.

FIENBERG,SE ; FIRS: NETER ,J ; SEC: LEITCH,RA CIT: 0.82
DOLLAR UNIT SAMPLING: MULTINOMIAL BOUNDS FOR TOTAL OVERSTATEMENT AND
    UNDERSTATEMENT ERRORS
TAR JA 78 VOL: 53 PG:77 - 93 :: NON-PAR. :SIM. :MATH.PROG. :SAMP.

FINLEY,DR CIT: 0.00
NORMAL FORM DECISION THEORY DEVELOPMENT OF THE AUDIT SAMPLING MODEL
AUD AU 83 VOL: 3 PG:104 - 116 :: MIXED :INT. LOG. :OTH.STAT. :SAMP.

FINLEY,DR ; SEC: BOOCKHOLDT,JL CIT: 0.00
A CONTINUOUS CONSTRAINED OPTIMIZATION MODEL FOR AUDIT SAMPLING
AUD SP 87 VOL: 6 PG:22 - 39 :: DES.STAT. :SIM. :OTH.STAT. :SAMP.

FINN ,DW ; FIRS: COLLINS,F ; SEC: MUNTER,P CIT: 0.00
THE BUDGETING GAMES PEOPLE PLAY
TAR JA 87 VOL: 62 PG:29 - 49 :: REGRESS. :SURV. :OTH.BEH. :BUDG.& PLAN.

FIRMIN,PA CIT: 0.00
DOLLAR-VALUE LIFO: LEGITIMATE OR NOT?
TAR AP 63 VOL: 38 PG:270 - 277 :: QUAL. :INT. LOG. :THEORY :INV.

FIRMIN,PA ; SEC: LINN ,JJ CIT: 0.08
INFORMATION SYSTEMS AND MANAGERIAL ACCOUNTING
TAR JA 68 VOL: 43 PG:75 - 82 :: QUAL. :INT. LOG. :N/A :OTH.MANAG.

FIRMIN,PA ; SEC: GOODMAN,SS ; THIR: HENDRICKS,TE ; FOUR: LINN ,JJ CIT: 0.00
UNIVERSITY COST STRUCTURE AND BEHAVIOR: AN EMPIRICAL STUDY
JAR ST 68 VOL: 6 PG:122 - 155 :: DES.STAT. :SIM. :OTH.STAT. :MANAG.

FIRTH ,MA CIT: 0.00
AN EMPIRICAL EXAMINATION OF THE APPLICABILITY OF ADOPTING THE AICPA AND NYSE
    REGULATIONS ON FREE SHARE DISTRIBUTIONS IN THE U.K.
JAR SP 73 VOL: 11 PG:16 - 24 :: OTH.QUANT. :PRIM. :OTH. :STK.DIV.

FIRTH ,MA CIT: 0.55
QUALIFIED AUDIT REPORTS: THEIR IMPACT ON INVESTMENT DECISIONS
TAR JL 78 VOL: 53 PG:642 - 650 :: ANOVA :PRIM. :EMH :OPIN.

FIRTH ,MA CIT: 0.30
CONSENSUS VIEWS AND JUDGMENT MODELS IN MATERIALITY DECISIONS
AOS 04 79 VOL: 4 PG:283 - 296 :: ANOVA :LAB. :HIPS :MAT.

FIRTH ,MA CIT: 0.11
PERCEPTIONS OF AUDITOR INDEPENDENCE AND OFFICIAL ETHICAL GUIDELINES
TAR JL 80 VOL: 55 PG:451 - 466 :: ANOVA :SURV. :OTH. :INDEP.

FIRTH ,MA CIT: 0.00
THE RELATIVE INFORMATION CONTENT OF THE RELEASE OF FINANCIAL RESULTS DATA
JAR AU 81 VOL: 19 PG:521 - 529 :: REGRESS. :PRIM. :EMH :N/A

FIRTH ,MA CIT: 0.00
AN ANALYSIS OF AUDIT FEES AND THEIR DETERMINATION IN NEW ZEALAND
AUD SP 85 VOL: 4 PG:23 - 37 :: REGRESS. :PRIM. :OTH.STAT. :ORG.

FIRTH ,MA ; FIRS: MEAR ,R CIT: 0.00
CUE USAGE AND SELF-INSIGHT OF FINANCIAL ANALYSTS
TAR JA 87 VOL: 62 PG:176 - 182 :: REGRESS. :LAB. :HIPS :MAN.DEC.CHAR.

FIRTH ,MA ; FIRS: MEAR ,R CIT: 0.00
ASSESSING THE ACCURACY OF FINANCIAL ANALYST SECURITY RETURN PREDICTIONS
AOS 04 87 VOL: 12 PG:331 - 340 :: REGRESS. :PRIM. :HIPS :FOREC.

FISHBURN,PC ; FIRS: LIBBY ,R CIT: 0.83
BEHAVIOURAL MODELS OF RISK TAKING IN BUSINESS DECISIONS: A SURVEY AND
EVALUATION
JAR AU 77 VOL: 15 PG:272 - 292 :: QUAL. :SEC. :OTH.BEH. :OTH.MANAG.

FISHER,M CIT: 0.00
INTERNAL CONTROLS: GUIDELINES FOR MANAGEMENT ACTION
JAA SU 78 VOL: 1 PG:349 - 360 :: QUAL. :INT. LOG. :INSTIT. :INT.CONT.

FITZGERALD,RD ; SEC: KELLEY,EM CIT: 0.00
INTERNATIONAL DISCLOSURE STANDARDS - THE UNITED NATIONS POSITION
JAA AU 79 VOL: 3 PG:5 - 20 :: QUAL. :INT. LOG. :INSTIT. :INT.DIFF.

FLAHERTY,RE ; FIRS: STERLING,RR CIT: 0.00
THE ROLE OF LIQUIDITY IN EXCHANGE VALUATION
TAR JL 71 VOL: 46 PG:441 - 456 :: ANAL. :INT. LOG. :THEORY :VALUAT.(INFL.)

FLAHERTY,RE ; FIRS: STERLING,RR ; SEC: TOLLEFSON,SO CIT: 0.00
EXCHANGE VALUATION: AN EMPIRICAL TEST
TAR OC 72 VOL: 47 PG:709 - 721 :: DES.STAT. :LAB. :THEORY :VALUAT.(INFL.)

FLAHERTY,RE ; SEC: SCHWARTZ,BN CIT: 0.11
EARNINGS PER SHARE: COMPLIANCE AND UNDERSTANDABILITY
JAA AU 80 VOL: 4 PG:47 - 56 :: DES.STAT. :SEC. :THEORY :INFO.STRUC.

FLAMHOLTZ,EG ; FIRS: BRUMMET,RL ; THIR: PYLE ,WC CIT: 0.54
HUMAN RESOURCE MEASUREMENT - A CHALLENGE FOR ACCOUNTANTS
TAR AP 68 VOL: 43 PG:217 - 224 :: QUAL. :INT. LOG. :OTH.BEH. :HRA

FLAMHOLTZ,EG CIT: 0.77
A MODEL FOR HUMAN RESOURCE VALUATION: A STOCHASTIC PROCESS WITH SERVICE
REWARDS
TAR AP 71 VOL: 46 PG:253 - 267 :: QUAL. :INT. LOG. :OTH.BEH. :HRA

FLAMHOLTZ,EG CIT: 0.46
TOWARD A THEORY OF HUMAN RESOURCE VALUE IN FORMAL ORGANIZATIONS
TAR OC 72 VOL: 47 PG:666 - 678 :: QUAL. :INT. LOG. :OTH.BEH. :HRA

FLAMHOLTZ,EG CIT: 0.31
ASSESSING THE VALIDITY OF A THEORY OF HUMAN RESOURCE VALUE: A FIELD STUDY
JAR ST 72 VOL: 10 PG:241 - 266 :: NON-PAR. :FIELD :OTH.BEH. :HRA

FLAMHOLTZ,EG ; FIRS: EPSTEIN,MJ ; THIR: MCDONOUGH,JJ CIT: 0.54
CORPORATE SOCIAL ACCOUNTING IN THE U.S.A.: STATE OF THE ART AND FUTURE
PROSPECTS
AOS 01 76 VOL: 1 PG:23 - 42 :: QUAL. :SEC. :THEORY :HRA

FLAMHOLTZ,EG CIT: 0.54
THE IMPACT OF HUMAN RESOURCE VALUATION ON MANAGEMENT DECISIONS: A LABORATORY
EXPERIMENT
AOS 23 76 VOL: 1 PG:153 - 166 :: NON-PAR. :LAB. :OTH.BEH. :HRA

FLAMHOLTZ,EG ; SEC: COOK ,E CIT: 0.55
CONNOTATIVE MEANING AND ITS ROLE IN ACCOUNTING CHANGE: A FIELD STUDY
AOS 02 78 VOL: 3 PG:115 - 140 :: OTH.QUANT. :FIELD :OTH.BEH. :METHOD.

FLAMHOLTZ,EG CIT: 0.11
THE PROCESS OF MEASUREMENT IN MANAGERIAL ACCOUNTING: A PSYCHO-TECHNICAL
SYSTEMS PERSPECTIVE
AOS 01 80 VOL: 5 PG:31 - 42 :: QUAL. :INT. LOG. :THEORY :MANAG.

FLAMHOLTZ,EG CIT: 1.00
ACCOUNTING, BUDGETING AND CONTROL SYSTEMS IN THEIR ORGANIZATIONAL CONTEXT:
  THEORETICAL AND EMPIRICAL PERSPECTIVES
AOS 23 83 VOL: 8 PG:153 - 170 :: QUAL. :FIELD :OTH.BEH. :BUDG.& PLAN.

FLAMHOLTZ,EG ; SEC: DAS   ,TK ; THIR: TSUI ,AS CIT: 0.25
TOWARD AN INTEGRATIVE FRAMEWORK OF ORGANIZATIONAL CONTROL
AOS 01 85 VOL: 10 PG:35 - 50 :: DES.STAT. :INT. LOG. :OTH.BEH. :HRA

FLAMHOLTZ,EG ; FIRS: BULLEN,ML CIT: 0.00
A THEORETICAL AND EMPIRICAL INVESTIGATION OF JOB SATISFACTION AND INTENDED
  TURNOVER IN THE LARGE CPA FIRM
AOS 03 85 VOL: 10 PG:287 - 302 :: REGRESS. :SURV. :OTH.BEH. :ORG.

FLAMHOLTZ,EG CIT: 0.00
VALUATION OF HUMAN ASSETS IN A SECURITIES BROKERAGE FIRM: AN EMPIRICAL STUDY
AOS 04 87 VOL: 12 PG:309 - 318 :: DES.STAT. :FIELD :OTH.BEH. :HRA

FLESHER,DL ; SEC: FLESHER,TK CIT: 0.00
MANAGERIAL ACCOUNTING IN AN EARLY 19TH CENTURY GERMAN-AMERICAN RELIGIOUS
  COMMUNE
AOS 04 79 VOL: 4 PG:297 - 304 :: QUAL. :INT. LOG. :HIST. :N/A

FLESHER,DL ; FIRS: MOODY ,SM CIT: 0.00
ANALYSIS OF FASB VOTING PATTERNS: STATEMENT NOS. 1-86
JAA AU 86 VOL: 1 PG:319 - 330 :: REGRESS. :PRIM. :INSTIT. :FASB SUBM.

FLESHER,DL ; SEC: FLESHER,TK CIT: 0.00
IVER KREUGER'S CONTRIBUTION TO U.S. FINANCIAL REPORTING
TAR JL 86 VOL: 61 PG:421 - 434 :: REGRESS. :SEC. :HIST. :BUS.FAIL.

FLESHER,TK ; FIRS: FLESHER,DL CIT: 0.00
MANAGERIAL ACCOUNTING IN AN EARLY 19TH CENTURY GERMAN-AMERICAN RELIGIOUS
  COMMUNE
AOS 04 79 VOL: 4 PG:297 - 304 :: QUAL. :INT. LOG. :HIST. :N/A

FLESHER,TK ; FIRS: FLESHER,DL CIT: 0.00
IVER KREUGER'S CONTRIBUTION TO U.S. FINANCIAL REPORTING
TAR JL 86 VOL: 61 PG:421 - 434 :: REGRESS. :SEC. :HIST. :BUS.FAIL.

FLOWER,JF CIT: 0.08
THE CASE OF THE PROFITABLE BLOODHOUND
JAR SP 66 VOL: 4 PG:16 - 36 :: QUAL. :CASE :INSTIT. :MANAG.

FOGELBERG,G CIT: 0.08
INTERIM INCOME DETERMINATION: AN EXAMINATION OF THE EFFECTS OF ALTERNATIVE
  MEASUREMENT TECHNIQUES
JAR AU 71 VOL: 9 PG:215 - 235 :: DES.STAT. :CASE :THEORY :INT.REP.

FOGLER,HR CIT: 0.00
RANKING TECHNIQUES AND CAPITAL BUDGETING
TAR JA 72 VOL: 47 PG:134 - 143 :: ANAL. :INT. LOG. :MATH.PROG. :CAP.BUDG.

FORAN ,MF ; SEC: DECOSTER,DT CIT: 0.85
AN EXPER. STUDY OF THE EFFECTS OF PARTICIP., AUTHORITARIANISM, AND FEEDBACK
  ON COGNITIVE DISSONANCE IN A STANDARD SETTING SITUATION.
TAR OC 74 VOL: 49 PG:751 - 763 :: ANOVA :LAB. :OTH.BEH. :BUDG.& PLAN.

FORD ,A CIT: 0.00
SHOULD COST BE ASSIGNED TO CONVERSION VALUE?
TAR OC 69 VOL: 44 PG:818 - 822 :: QUAL. :INT. LOG. :THEORY :LTD

FORD ,A CIT: 0.00
TRAVEL EXPENSES FOR A VISITING PROFESSOR
TAR AP 75 VOL: 50 PG:338 - 344 :: QUAL. :INT. LOG. :OTH. :N/A

FORSYTHE,R ; FIRS: DEJONG,DV ; THIR: UECKER,WC CIT: 0.25
THE METHODOLOGY OF LABORATORY MARKETS AND ITS IMPLICATIONS FOR AGENCY
    RESEARCH IN ACCOUNTING AND AUDITING
JAR AU 85 VOL: 23 PG:753 - 793 :: REGRESS. :LAB. :INF.ECO./AG. :METHOD.

FORSYTHE,R ; FIRS: DEJONG,DV ; THIR: LUNDHOLM,RJ ; FOUR: UECKER,WC CIT: 0.00
A LABORATORY INVESTIGATION OF THE MORAL HAZARD PROBLEM IN AN AGENCY
    RELATIONSHIP
JAR ST 85 VOL: 23 PG:81 - 120 :: REGRESS. :LAB. :INF.ECO./AG. :MAN.DEC.CHAR.

FOSSUM,RL ; FIRS: ZEFF ,SA CIT: 0.31
AN ANALYSIS OF LARGE AUDIT CLIENTS
TAR AP 67 VOL: 42 PG:298 - 320 :: DES.STAT. :PRIM. :INSTIT. :AUD.

FOSTER III,TW ; SEC: VICKREY,DW CIT: 0.00
THE INFORMATION CONTENT OF STOCK DIVIDEND ANNOUNCEMENTS
TAR AP 78 VOL: 53 PG:360 - 370 :: REGRESS. :PRIM. :EMH :STK.DIV.

FOSTER III,TW ; SEC: VICKREY,DW CIT: 0.36
THE INCREMENTAL INFORMATION CONTENT OF THE 10-K
TAR OC 78 VOL: 53 PG:921 - 934 :: ANOVA :PRIM. :EMH :FIN.METH.

FOSTER,G CIT: 1.31
STOCK MARKET REACTION TO ESTIMATES OF EARNINGS PER SHARE BY COMPANY OFFICIALS
JAR SP 73 VOL: 11 PG:25 - 37 :: REGRESS. :PRIM. :EMH :FOREC.

FOSTER,G CIT: 0.38
SECURITY PRICE REVALUATION IMPLICATIONS OF SUB-EARNINGS DISCLOSURE
JAR AU 75 VOL: 13 PG:283 - 292 :: REGRESS. :PRIM. :EMH :SEG.REP.

FOSTER,G CIT: 0.54
ACCOUNTING EARNINGS AND STOCK PRICES OF INSURANCE COMPANIES
TAR OC 75 VOL: 50 PG:686 - 698 :: MIXED :PRIM. :EMH :FIN.METH.

FOSTER,G CIT: 4.25
QUARTERLY ACCOUNTING DATA: TIME-SERIES PROPERTIES AND PREDICTIVE-ABILITY
    RESULTS
TAR JA 77 VOL: 52 PG:1 - 21 :: MIXED :PRIM. :TIME SER. :FOREC.

FOSTER,G CIT: 3.67
ACCOUNTING POLICY DECISIONS AND CAPITAL MARKET RESEARCH
JAE MR 80 VOL: 2 PG:29 - 62 :: ANAL. :SEC. :EMH :OIL & GAS

FOSTER,G CIT: 1.75
INTRA-INDUSTRY INFORMATION TRANSFERS ASSOCIATED WITH EARNINGS RELEASES
JAE DE 81 VOL: 3 PG:201 - 232 :: CORR. :PRIM. :EMH :FIN.METH.

FOSTER,G ; FIRS: BALL ,R CIT: 2.43
CORPORATE FINANCIAL REPORTING: A METHODOLOGICAL REVIEW OF EMPIRICAL RESEARCH
JAR ST 82 VOL: 20 PG:161 - 234 :: MIXED :SEC. :OTH. :FIN.METH.

FOSTER,G ; SEC: OLSEN ,C ; THIR: SHEVLIN,T CIT: 1.40
EARNINGS RELEASES, ANOMALIES, AND THE BEHAVIOR OF SECURITY RETURNS
TAR OC 84 VOL: 59 PG:574 - 603 :: REGRESS. :PRIM. :EMH :N/A

FRANCIA,AJ ; FIRS: COPELAND,RM ; THIR: STRAWSER,RH CIT: 0.69
STUDENTS AS SUBJECTS IN BEHAVIOURAL BUSINESS RESEARCH
TAR AP 73 VOL: 48 PG:365 - 374 :: QUAL. :SURV. :OTH.BEH. :METHOD.

FRANCIS,JR CIT: 0.60
THE EFFECT OF AUDIT FIRM SIZE ON AUDIT PRICES: A STUDY OF THE AUSTRALIAN
    MARKET
JAE AG 84 VOL: 6 PG:133 - 151 :: REGRESS. :PRIM. :OTH.STAT. :ORG.

FRANCIS,JR ; SEC: STOKES,DJ CIT: 0.67
AUDIT PRICES, PRODUCT DIFFERENTIATION, AND SCALE ECONOMIES: FURTHER
    EVIDENCE FROM THE AUSTRALIAN MARKET
JAR AU 86 VOL: 24 PG:383 - 393 :: REGRESS. :PRIM. :OTH.STAT. :OPER.AUD.

FRANCIS,JR ; SEC: REITER,SA CIT: 0.50
DETERMINANTS OF CORPORATE PENSION FUNDING STRATEGY
JAE AP 87 VOL: 9 PG:35 - 59 :: REGRESS. :PRIM. :OTH.STAT. :PENS.

FRANCIS,JR ; SEC: SIMON ,DT CIT: 0.50
A TEST OF AUDIT PRICING IN THE SMALL-CLIENT SEGMENT OF THE U.S. AUDIT MARKET
TAR JA 87 VOL: 62 PG:145 - 157 :: REGRESS. :SURV. :OTH.STAT. :ORG.

FRANCIS,JR ; FIRS: SIMON ,DT CIT: 0.00
THE EFFECTS OF AUDITOR CHANGE ON AUDIT FEES: TESTS OF PRICE CUTTING AND PRICE
    RECOVERY
TAR AP 88 VOL: 63 PG:255 - 269 :: REGRESS. :PRIM. :OTH.STAT. :ORG.

FRANCIS,JR ; SEC: WILSON,ER CIT: 0.00
AUDITOR CHANGES: A JOINT TEST OF THEORIES RELATING TO AGENCY COSTS AND
    AUDITOR DIFFERENTIATION
TAR OC 88 VOL: 63 PG:663 - 682 :: REGRESS. :PRIM. :OTH.STAT. :ORG.

FRANCIS,ME CIT: 0.08
ACCOUNTING AND THE EVALUATION OF SOCIAL PROGRAMS: A CRITICAL COMMENT
TAR AP 73 VOL: 48 PG:245 - 257 :: QUAL. :INT. LOG. :THEORY :HRA

FRANK ,WG CIT: 0.00
A COMPUTER APPLICATION IN PROCESS COST ACCOUNTING
TAR OC 65 VOL: 40 PG:854 - 862 :: QUAL. :INT. LOG. :N/A :OTH.MANAG.

FRANK ,WG ; SEC: MANES ,RP CIT: 0.08
A STANDARD COST APPLICATION OF MATRIX ALGEBRA
TAR JL 67 VOL: 42 PG:516 - 525 :: ANAL. :INT. LOG. :MATH.PROG. :VAR.

FRANK ,WG CIT: 0.23
A STUDY OF THE PREDICTIVE SIGNIFICANCE OF TWO INCOME MEASURES
JAR SP 69 VOL: 7 PG:123 - 136 :: NON-PAR. :PRIM. :OTH. :VALUAT.(INFL.)

FRANK ,WG ; SEC: WEYGANDT,JJ CIT: 0.15
CONVERTIBLE DEBT AND EARNINGS PER SHARE: PRAGMATISM VS. GOOD THEORY
TAR AP 70 VOL: 45 PG:280 - 289 :: DES.STAT. :PRIM. :N/A :PENS.

FRANK ,WG ; SEC: WEYGANDT,JJ CIT: 0.08
A PREDICTION MODEL FOR CONVERTIBLE DEBENTURES
JAR SP 71 VOL: 9 PG:116 - 126 :: OTH.QUANT. :PRIM. :OTH. :LTD

FRANK ,WG CIT: 0.20
AN EMPIRICAL ANALYSIS OF INTERNATIONAL ACCOUNTING PRINCIPLES
JAR AU 79 VOL: 17 PG:593 - 605 :: OTH.QUANT. :PRIM. :INSTIT. :FIN.METH.

FRANK ,WG ; FIRS: NAIR ,RD CIT: 0.33
THE IMPACT OF DISCLOSURE AND MEASUREMENT PRACTICES ON INTERNATIONAL
  ACCOUNTING CLASSIFICATIONS
TAR JL 80 VOL: 55 PG:426 - 450 :: OTH.QUANT. :PRIM. :OTH.STAT. :INT.DIFF.

FRANKFURTER,GM ; SEC: HORWITZ,BN CIT: 0.08
THE EFFECTS OF ACCOUNTING PRINCIPLES BOARD OPINION NO.15 ON EARNINGS PER
  SHARE: A SIMULATION STUDY
TAR AP 72 VOL: 47 PG:245 - 259 :: DES.STAT. :SIM. :THEORY :FIN.METH.

FRANKFURTER,GM ; SEC: YOUNG ,AE CIT: 0.00
FINANCIAL THEORY: ITS MESSAGE TO THE ACCOUNTANT
JAA SU 83 VOL: 6 PG:314 - 324 :: QUAL. :INT. LOG. :OTH. :N/A

FRANKLE,AW ; FIRS: ANDERSON,JC CIT: 0.33
VOLUNTARY SOCIAL REPORTING: AN ISO-BETA PORTFOLIO ANALYSIS
TAR JL 80 VOL: 55 PG:467 - 479 :: REGRESS. :PRIM. :EMH :HRA

FRANKS,DD ; FIRS: SORENSEN,JE CIT: 0.15
THE RELATIVE CONTRIBUTION OF ABILITY, SELF-ESTEEM AND EVALUATIVE FEEDBACK TO
  PERFORMANCE: IMPLICATIONS FOR ACCOUNTING SYSTEMS
TAR OC 72 VOL: 47 PG:735 - 746 :: ANOVA :FIELD :OTH.BEH. :OTH.MANAG.

FRAZIER,KB ; SEC: INGRAM,RW ; THIR: TENNYSON,BM CIT: 0.20
A METHODOLOGY FOR THE ANALYSIS OF NARRATIVE ACCOUNTING DISCLOSURES
JAR SP 84 VOL: 22 PG:318 - 331 :: OTH.QUANT. :PRIM. :OTH.STAT. :FOREC.

FRAZIER,KB ; FIRS: MURRAY,D CIT: 0.00
A WITHIN-SUBJECTS TEST OF EXPECTANCY THEORY IN A PUBLIC ACCOUNTING ENVIRONMENT
JAR AU 86 VOL: 24 PG:400 - 404 :: REGRESS. :LAB. :OTH.BEH. :INFO.STRUC.

FRECKA,TJ ; SEC: HOPWOOD,WS CIT: 0.33
THE EFFECTS OF OUTLIERS ON THE CROSS-SECTIONAL DISTRIBUTIONAL PROPERTIES OF
  FINANCIAL RATIOS
TAR JA 83 VOL: 58 PG:115 - 128 :: DES.STAT. :LAB. :OTH.STAT. :METHOD.

FRECKA,TJ ; SEC: LEE ,CF CIT: 0.00
GENERALIZED FINANCIAL RATIO ADJUSTMENT PROCESSES AND THEIR IMPLICATIONS
JAR SP 83 VOL: 21 PG:308 - 316 :: REGRESS. :PRIM. :EMH :N/A

FRECKA,TJ ; FIRS: BUBLITZ,B ; THIR: MCKEOWN,JC CIT: 1.50
MARKET ASSOCIATION TESTS AND FASB STATEMENT NO. 33 DISCLOSURES: A
  REEXAMINATION
JAR ST 85 VOL: 23 PG:1 - 23 :: REGRESS. :PRIM. :EMH :VALUAT.(INFL.)

FREDERICK,DM ; SEC: LIBBY ,R CIT: 0.33
EXPERTISE AND AUDITORS' JUDGMENTS OF CONJUNCTIVE EVENTS
JAR AU 86 VOL: 24 PG:270 - 290 :: REGRESS. :LAB. :HIPS :JUDG.

FREDERICKS,W ; FIRS: COPELAND,RM CIT: 0.15
EXTENT OF DISCLOSURE
JAR SP 68 VOL: 6 PG:106 - 113 :: NON-PAR. :PRIM. :THEORY :INFO.STRUC.

FREDRIKSON,EB CIT: 0.00
ON THE MEASUREMENT OF FOREIGN INCOME
JAR AU 68 VOL: 6 PG:208 - 221 :: DES.STAT. :SIM. :THEORY :CASH

FREEMAN,RN   CIT: 0.00
ON THE ASSOCIATION BETWEEN NET MONETARY POSITION AND EQUITY SECURITY PRICES
JAR ST 78 VOL: 16 PG:111 - 145 :: REGRESS. :PRIM. :EMH :CASH

FREEMAN,RN ; SEC: OHLSON,JA ; THIR: PENMAN,SH   CIT: 0.86
BOOK RATE-OF-RETURN AND PREDICTION OF EARNINGS CHANGES: AN EMPIRICAL
    INVESTIGATION
JAR AU 82 VOL: 20 PG:639 - 653 :: REGRESS. :PRIM. :EMH :REV.REC.

FREEMAN,RN   CIT: 0.83
ALTERNATIVE MEASURES OF PROFIT MARGIN: AN EMPIRICAL STUDY OF THE POTENTIAL
    INFORMATION CONTENT OF CURRENT COST ACCOUNTING
JAR SP 83 VOL: 21 PG:42 - 64 :: REGRESS. :PRIM. :EMH :VALUAT.(INFL.)

FREEMAN,RN   CIT: 1.00
THE ASSOCIATION BETWEEN ACCOUNTING EARNINGS AND SECURITY RETURNS FOR LARGE
    AND SMALL FIRMS
JAE JL 87 VOL: 9 PG:195 - 228 :: REGRESS. :PRIM. :EMH :FIN.METH.

FREMGEN,JM   CIT: 0.00
THE DIRECT COSTING CONTROVERSY - AN IDENTIFICATION OF ISSUES
TAR JA 64 VOL: 39 PG:43 - 51 :: QUAL. :INT. LOG. :THEORY :COST.ALLOC.

FREMGEN,JM   CIT: 0.00
UTILITY AND ACCOUNTING PRINCIPLES
TAR JL 67 VOL: 42 PG:457 - 467 :: QUAL. :INT. LOG. :THEORY :FIN.METH.

FREMGEN,JM   CIT: 0.08
THE GOING CONCERN ASSUMPTION: A CRITICAL APPRAISAL
TAR OC 68 VOL: 43 PG:649 - 656 :: QUAL. :INT. LOG. :THEORY :OTH.FIN.ACC.

FREMGEN,JM ; FIRS: COWIE ,JB   CIT: 0.00
COMPUTERS VERSUS MATHEMATICS: ROUND 2
TAR JA 70 VOL: 45 PG:27 - 37 :: QUAL. :INT. LOG. :N/A :OTH.MANAG.

FRIBERG,RA   CIT: 0.23
PROBABILISTIC DEPRECIATION WITH A VARYING SALVAGE VALUE
TAR JA 73 VOL: 48 PG:50 - 60 :: ANAL. :INT. LOG. :OTH.STAT. :PP&E / DEPR

FRIED ,D ; SEC: SCHIFF,A   CIT: 0.38
CPA SWITCHES AND ASSOCIATED MARKET REACTIONS
TAR AP 81 VOL: 56 PG:326 - 341 :: NON-PAR. :PRIM. :EMH :OTH.MANAG.

FRIED ,D ; SEC: LIVNAT,J   CIT: 0.13
INTERIM STATEMENTS: AN ANALYTICAL EXAMINATION OF ALTERNATIVE ACCOUNTING
    TECHNIQUES
TAR JL 81 VOL: 56 PG:493 - 509 :: ANAL. :INT. LOG. :TIME SER. :N/A

FRIED ,D   CIT: 0.00
COMPENSATING FOR INFLATION: SHORTER LIFE VS. ACCELERATED DEPRECIATION METHODS
JAA SU 81 VOL: 4 PG:295 - 308 :: ANAL. :INT. LOG. :OTH.STAT. :PP&E / DEPR

FRIED ,D ; SEC: GIVOLY,D   CIT: 2.14
FINANCIAL ANALYSTS' FORECASTS OF EARNINGS: A BETTER SURROGATE FOR MARKET
    EXPECTATIONS
JAE OC 82 VOL: 4 PG:85 - 107 :: OTH.QUANT. :SEC. :TIME SER. :FOREC.

FRIED ,D ; SEC: HOSLER,C   CIT: 0.00
S&LS, REPORTING CHANGES AND THE IMPACT ON THE GNMA MARKET
JAA WI 87 VOL: 2 PG:5 - 23 :: REGRESS. :PRIM. :THEORY :LTD

FRIEDLOB,GT CIT: 0.00
HOW ECONOMIC STATISTICIANS VIEW ACCOUNTING PROFITS
JAA WI 83 VOL: 6 PG:100 - 107 :: DES.STAT. :PRIM. :THEORY :REV.REC.

FRIEDMAN,A ; SEC: LEV ,B CIT: 0.31
A SURROGATE MEASURE FOR THE FIRM'S INVESTMENT IN HUMAN RESOURCES
JAR AU 74 VOL: 12 PG:235 - 250 :: ANAL. :INT. LOG. :OTH.BEH. :HRA

FRIEDMAN,L ; FIRS: HAKA ,S ; THIR: JONES ,V CIT: 0.00
FUNCTIONAL FIXATION AND INTERFERENCE THEORY: A THEORETICAL AND EMPIRICAL
INVESTIGATION
TAR JL 86 VOL: 61 PG:455 - 474 :: REGRESS. :LAB. :HIPS :REL.COSTS

FRIEDMAN,LA ; FIRS: NEUMANN,BR CIT: 0.45
OPPORTUNITY COSTS: FURTHER EVIDENCE THROUGH AN EXPERIMENTAL REPLICATION
JAR AU 78 VOL: 16 PG:400 - 410 :: ANOVA :LAB. :OTH.BEH. :REL.COSTS

FRIEDMAN,LA CIT: 0.00
AN EXIT-PRICE INCOME STATEMENT
TAR JA 78 VOL: 53 PG:18 - 30 :: QUAL. :INT. LOG. :THEORY :VALUAT.(INFL.)

FRIEDMAN,LA CIT: 0.00
EXIT-PRICE LIABILITIES: AN ANALYSIS OF THE ALTERNATIVES
TAR OC 78 VOL: 53 PG:895 - 909 :: QUAL. :INT. LOG. :THEORY :VALUAT.(INFL.)

FRIEDMAN,LA ; SEC: NEUMANN,BR CIT: 0.33
EFFECTS OF OPPORTUNITY COSTS ON PROJECT INVESTMENT DECISIONS: A REPLICATION
AND EXTENSION
JAR AU 80 VOL: 18 PG:407 - 419 :: ANOVA :LAB. :OTH.BEH. :MANAG.

FRIEZE,IH ; FIRS: BIRNBERG,JG ; THIR: SHIELDS,MD CIT: 0.33
THE ROLE OF ATTRIBUTION THEORY IN CONTROL SYSTEMS
AOS 03 77 VOL: 2 PG:189 - 200 :: QUAL. :INT. LOG. :OTH.BEH. :MANAG.

FRIEZE,IH ; FIRS: SHIELDS,MD ; SEC: BIRNBERG,JG CIT: 0.50
ATTRIBUTIONS, COGNITIVE PROCESSES AND CONTROL SYSTEMS
AOS 01 81 VOL: 6 PG:69 - 96 :: ANOVA :LAB. :OTH.BEH. :BUDG.& PLAN.

FRISHKOFF,P CIT: 0.62
AN EMPIRICAL INVESTIGATION OF THE CONCEPT OF MATERIALITY IN ACCOUNTING
JAR ST 70 VOL: 8 PG:116 - 129 :: OTH.QUANT. :PRIM. :THEORY :MAT.

FRISHKOFF,P ; SEC: FRISHKOFF,PA ; THIR: BOUWMAN,MJ CIT: 0.00
USE OF ACCOUNTING DATA IN SCREENING BY FINANCIAL ANALYSTS
JAA AU 84 VOL: 8 PG:44 - 53 :: DES.STAT. :LAB. :HIPS :INFO.STRUC.

FRISHKOFF,P ; FIRS: BOUWMAN,MJ ; SEC: FRISHKOFF,PA CIT: 0.00
HOW DO THE FIN. ANALYSTS MAKE DECISIONS? A PROCESS MODEL OF THE INVESTMENT
SCREENING DECISION
AOS 01 87 VOL: 12 PG:1 - 30 :: REGRESS. :LAB. :HIPS :OTH.FIN.ACC.

FRISHKOFF,PA ; FIRS: FRISHKOFF,P ; THIR: BOUWMAN,MJ CIT: 0.00
USE OF ACCOUNTING DATA IN SCREENING BY FINANCIAL ANALYSTS
JAA AU 84 VOL: 8 PG:44 - 53 :: DES.STAT. :LAB. :HIPS :INFO.STRUC.

FRISHKOFF,PA ; FIRS: BOUWMAN,MJ ; THIR: FRISHKOFF,P CIT: 0.00
HOW DO THE FIN. ANALYSTS MAKE DECISIONS? A PROCESS MODEL OF THE INVESTMENT
SCREENING DECISION
AOS 01 87 VOL: 12 PG:1 - 30 :: REGRESS. :LAB. :HIPS :OTH.FIN.ACC.

FROST ,PA ; SEC: TAMURA,H CIT: 0.57
JACKKNIFED RATIO ESTIMATION IN STATISTICAL AUDITING
JAR SP 82 VOL: 20 PG:103 - 120 :: DES.STAT. :SIM. :OTH.STAT. :SAMP.

FROST ,PA ; FIRS: TAMURA,H CIT: 0.33
TIGHTENING CAV (DUS) BOUNDS BY USING A PARAMETRIC MODEL
JAR AU 86 VOL: 24 PG:364 - 371 :: DES.STAT. :SIM. :OTH.STAT. :SAMP.

FROST ,PA ; SEC: TAMURA,H CIT: 0.00
ACCURACY OF AUXILIARY INFORMATION INTERVAL ESTIMATION IN STATISTICAL
    AUDITING
JAR SP 86 VOL: 24 PG:57 - 75 :: DES.STAT. :SIM. :OTH.STAT. :SAMP.

FU   ,P CIT: 0.00
GOVERNMENTAL ACCOUNTING IN CHINA DURING THE CHOU DYNASTY (1122 B.C.-256 B.C.)
JAR SP 71 VOL: 9 PG:40 - 51 :: QUAL. :PRIM. :HIST. :OTH.MANAG.

FULMER,JG ; SEC: MOON ,JE CIT: 0.00
TESTS FOR COMMON STOCK EQUIVALENCY
JAA AU 84 VOL: 8 PG:5 - 14 :: NON-PAR. :PRIM. :OTH.STAT. :FIN.METH.

FURLONG,WL CIT: 0.00
MINIMIZING FOREIGN EXCHANGE LOSSES
TAR AP 66 VOL: 41 PG:244 - 252 :: QUAL. :INT. LOG. :N/A :SPEC.ITEMS

GAA   ,JC CIT: 0.67
USER PRIMACY IN FINANCIAL REPORTING: A SOCIAL CONTRACT APPROACH
TAR JL 86 VOL: 61 PG:435 - 454 :: DES.STAT. :INT. LOG. :THEORY :ORG.& ENVIR.

GAGNON,JM CIT: 0.69
PURCHASE VERSUS POOLING OF INTERESTS: THE SEARCH FOR A PREDICTOR
JAR ST 67 VOL: 5 PG:187 - 204 :: DES.STAT. :PRIM. :THEORY :BUS.COMB.

GAGNON,JM CIT: 0.23
THE PURCHASE-POOLING CHOICE: SOME EMPIRICAL EVIDENCE
JAR SP 71 VOL: 9 PG:52 - 72 :: NON-PAR. :PRIM. :OTH. :BUS.COMB.

GALBRAITH,JR ; FIRS: BARIFF,ML CIT: 0.73
INTRAORGANIZATIONAL POWER CONSIDERATIONS FOR DESIGNING INFORMATION SYSTEMS
AOS 01 78 VOL: 3 PG:15 - 28 :: QUAL. :INT. LOG. :OTH.BEH. :ORG.FORM

GAMBLE,GO CIT: 0.00
CONCEPTS OF CAPITAL MAINTENANCE
JAA SP 81 VOL: 4 PG:220 - 237 :: QUAL. :INT. LOG. :THEORY :METHOD.

GAMBLE,GO CIT: 0.00
AN APPLICATION OF CURRENT VALUE THEORY TO ACCOUNTING FOR INVESTMENTS IN BONDS
JAA SU 82 VOL: 5 PG:320 - 326 :: QUAL. :INT. LOG. :THEORY :VALUAT.(INFL.)

GAMBLE,GO CIT: 0.00
PROPERTY RIGHTS THEORY AND THE FORMULATION OF FINANCIAL STATEMENTS
JAA SP 86 VOL: 1 PG:102 - 117 :: DES.STAT. :INT. LOG. :INSTIT. :FASB SUBM.

GAMBLING,T CIT: 0.00
THE ACCOUNTANT'S GUIDE TO THE GALAXY, INCLUDING THE PROFESSION AT THE END OF
    THE UNIVERSE
AOS 04 85 VOL: 10 PG:415 - 426 :: DES.STAT. :INT. LOG. :THEORY :HRA

GAMBLING,T CIT: 0.00
ACCOUNTING FOR RITUALS
AOS 04 87 VOL: 12 PG:319 - 329 :: DES.STAT. :INT. LOG. :THEORY :ORG.& ENVIR.

GAMBLING,TE ; SEC: NOUR ,A CIT: 0.00
A NOTE ON INPUT-OUTPUT ANALYSIS: ITS USES IN MACRO-ECONOMICS AND
   MICRO-ECONOMICS
TAR JA 70 VOL: 45 PG:98 - 102 :: ANAL. :INT. LOG. :OTH.STAT. :BUDG.& PLAN.

GAMBLING,TE CIT: 0.08
SYSTEMS DYNAMICS AND HUMAN RESOURCE ACCOUNTING
AOS 23 76 VOL: 1 PG:167 - 174 :: QUAL. :INT. LOG. :OTH.BEH. :HRA

GAMBLING,TE CIT: 1.00
MAGIC, ACCOUNTING AND MORALE
AOS 02 77 VOL: 2 PG:141 - 152 :: QUAL. :INT. LOG. :THEORY :N/A

GANDHI,NM ; FIRS: BIRNBERG,JG CIT: 0.08
TOWARD DEFINING THE ACCOUNTANT'S ROLE IN THE EVALUATION OF SOCIAL PROGRAMS
AOS 01 76 VOL: 1 PG:5 - 10 :: QUAL. :INT. LOG. :THEORY :HRA

GANGOLLY,JS CIT: 0.13
ON JOINT COST ALLOCATION: INDEPENDENT COST PROPORTIONAL SCHEME (ICPS) AND ITS
   PROPERTIES
JAR AU 81 VOL: 19 PG:299 - 312 :: ANAL. :INT. LOG. :OTH.STAT. :COST.ALLOC.

GANGOLLY,JS ; FIRS: HUSSEIN,ME ; SEC: BAVISHI,VB CIT: 0.00
INTERNATIONAL SIMILARITIES AND DIFFERENCES IN THE AUDITOR'S REPORT
AUD AU 86 VOL: 6 PG:124 - 133 :: DES.STAT. :PRIM. :INSTIT. :INT.DIFF.

GANS ,MS ; FIRS: SORTER,GH CIT: 0.00
OPPORTUNITIES AND IMPLICATIONS OF THE REPORT ON OBJECTIVES OF FINANCIAL
   STATEMENTS
JAR ST 74 VOL: 12 PG:1 - 12 :: QUAL. :INT. LOG. :THEORY :FIN.METH.

GARDNER,JC ; FIRS: BROWN ,LD CIT: 0.75
APPLYING CITATION ANALYSIS TO EVALUATE THE RESEARCH CONTRIBUTIONS OF
   ACCOUNTING FACULTY AND DOCTORAL PROGRAMS
TAR AP 85 VOL: 60 PG:262 - 277 :: REGRESS. :SEC. :OTH.STAT. :METHOD.

GARDNER,JC ; FIRS: BROWN ,LD CIT: 0.50
USING CITATION ANALYSIS TO ASSESS THE IMPACT OF JOURNALS AND ARTICLES ON
   CONTEMPORARY ACCOUNTING RESEARCH (CAR)
JAR SP 85 VOL: 23 PG:84 - 109 :: REGRESS. :SEC. :HIST. :METHOD.

GARDNER,JC ; FIRS: BROWN ,LD ; THIR: VASARHELYI,MA CIT: 0.00
AN ANALYSIS OF THE RESEARCH CONTRIBUTIONS OF ACCOUNTING, ORGANIZATIONS AND
   SOCIETY, 1976-1984
AOS 02 87 VOL: 12 PG:193 - 204 :: REGRESS. :SEC. :HIST. :METHOD.

GARDNER,JC ; FIRS: SWANSON,GA CIT: 0.00
NOT-FOR-PROFIT ACCOUNTING AND AUDITING IN THE EARLY EIGHTEENTH CENTURY: SOME
   ARCHIVAL EVIDENCE
TAR JL 88 VOL: 63 PG:436 - 447 :: REGRESS. :INT. LOG. :HIST. :AUD.

GARMAN,MB ; SEC: OHLSON,JA CIT: 0.44
INFORMATION AND THE SEQUENTIAL VALUATION OF ASSETS IN ARBITRAGE-FREE ECONOMIES
JAR AU 80 VOL: 18 PG:420 - 440 :: ANAL. :INT. LOG. :OTH. :OTH.MANAG.

GARSOMBKE,HP ; SEC: ALLEN ,G CIT: 0.00
DID SFAS NO.19 LEAD TO OIL AND GAS COMPANY MERGERS?
JAA SU 83 VOL: 6 PG:285 - 298 :: NON-PAR. :PRIM. :THEORY :OIL & GAS

GARSTKA,SJ CIT: 0.25
MODELS FOR COMPUTING UPPER ERROR LIMITS IN DOLLAR-UNIT SAMPLING
JAR AU 77 VOL: 15 PG:179 - 192 :: DES.STAT. :SIM. :OTH.STAT. :SAMP.

GARSTKA,SJ ; SEC: OHLSON,PA CIT: 0.70
RATIO ESTIMATION IN ACCOUNTING POPULATIONS WITH PROBABILITIES OF SAMPLE
    SELECTION PROPORTIONAL TO SIZE OF BOOK VALUES
JAR SP 79 VOL: 17 PG:23 - 59 :: DES.STAT. :SIM. :OTH.STAT. :SAMP.

GAUMNITZ,BR ; SEC: NUNAMAKER,TR ; THIR: SURDICK,JJ ; FOUR: THOMAS,MF CIT: 0.14
AUDITOR CONSENSUS IN INTERNAL CONTROL EVALUATION AND AUDIT PROGRAM PLANNING
JAR AU 82 VOL: 20 PG:745 - 755 :: CORR. :LAB. :HIPS :INT.CONT.

GELFAND,J ; FIRS: PETRI ,E CIT: 0.00
THE PRODUCTION FUNCTION: A NEW PERSPECTIVE IN CAPITAL MAINTENANCE
TAR AP 79 VOL: 54 PG:330 - 345 :: ANAL. :INT. LOG. :OTH. :OTH.MANAG.

GENTRY,JA ; FIRS: DUGAN ,MT ; THIR: SHRIVER,KA CIT: 0.00
THE X-11 MODEL: A NEW ANALYTICAL REVIEW TECHNIQUE FOR THE AUDITOR
AUD SP 85 VOL: 4 PG:11 - 22 :: DES.STAT. :INT. LOG. :TIME SER. :ANAL.REV.

GENTRY,JA ; SEC: NEWBOLD,P ; THIR: WHITFORD,DT CIT: 0.50
CLASSIFYING BANKRUPT FIRMS WITH FUNDS FLOW COMPONENTS
JAR SP 85 VOL: 23 PG:146 - 160 :: REGRESS. :PRIM. :OTH.STAT. :BUS.FAIL.

GERBOTH,DL CIT: 0.23
RESEARCH, INTUITION, AND POLITICS IN ACCOUNTING INQUIRY
TAR JL 73 VOL: 48 PG:475 - 482 :: QUAL. :INT. LOG. :INSTIT. :METHOD.

GERLACH,JH ; FIRS: BAILEY JR,AD ; SEC: DUKE ,GL ; FOUR: KO ,CE ; FIFT:
MESERVY,RD ; SIX: WHINSTON,AB CIT: 0.00
TICOM AND THE ANALYSIS OF INTERNAL CONTROLS
TAR AP 85 VOL: 60 PG:186 - 201 :: CORR. :INT. LOG. :OTH. :INT.CONT.

GERLACH,JH CIT: 0.00
A MODEL FOR TESTING THE RELIABILITY OF COMPUTER PROGRAMS AND EDP MANAGEMENT
    :INTERNAL CONTROL IMPLICATIONS
AUD SP 88 VOL: 07 PG:61 - 76 :: DES.STAT. :SIM. :OTH.STAT. :INT.CONT.

GHEYARA,K ; SEC: BOATSMAN,JR CIT: 1.67
MARKET REACTION TO THE 1976 REPLACEMENT COST DISCLOSURES
JAE AG 80 VOL: 2 PG:107 - 125 :: MIXED :PRIM. :EMH :VALUAT.(INFL.)

GIBBINS,M ; FIRS: SWIERINGA,RJ ; THIR: LARSSON,L ; FOUR: SWEENEY,JL CIT: 1.85
EXPERIMENTS IN THE HEURISTICS OF HUMAN INFORMATION PROCESSING
JAR ST 76 VOL: 14 PG:159 - 187 :: MIXED :LAB. :HIPS :MANAG.

GIBBINS,M ; SEC: WOLF ,FM CIT: 0.57
AUDITORS' SUBJECTIVE DECISION ENVIRONMENT - THE CASE OF A NORMAL EXTERNAL
    AUDIT
TAR JA 82 VOL: 57 PG:105 - 124 :: DES.STAT. :SURV. :OTH.BEH. :AUD.

GIBBINS,M CIT: 0.14
REGRESSION AND OTHER STATISTICAL IMPLICATIONS FOR RESEARCH ON JUDGMENT USING
    INTERCORRELATED DATA SOURCES
JAR SP 82 VOL: 20 PG:121 - 138 :: ANAL. :INT. LOG. :HIPS :METHOD.

GIBBINS,M CIT: 1.60
PROPOSITIONS ABOUT THE PSYCHOLOGY OF PROFESSIONAL JUDGMENT IN PUBLIC
   ACCOUNTING
JAR SP 84 VOL: 22 PG:103 - 125 :: QUAL. :INT. LOG. :HIPS :JUDG.

GIBBS ,G CIT: 0.00
PROFESSORS' TAXABLE INCOME AND DEDUCTIONS
TAR OC 64 VOL: 39 PG:004 - 007 :: QUAL. :SEC. :N/A :OTH.MANAG.

GIBSON,JL CIT: 0.00
ACCOUNTING IN THE DECISION-MAKING PROCESS: SOME EMPIRICAL EVIDENCE
TAR JL 63 VOL: 38 PG:492 - 500 :: QUAL. :CASE :THEORY :MANAG.

GIBSON,RW CIT: 0.00
COMPARATIVE PROFESSIONAL ACCOUNTANCY - AUSTRALIA
TAR JA 65 VOL: 40 PG:196 - 203 :: QUAL. :INT. LOG. :INSTIT. :AUD.

GIESE ,J ; FIRS: ANDERSON,HM ; THIR: BOOKER,J CIT: 0.15
SOME PROPOSITIONS ABOUT AUDITING
TAR JL 70 VOL: 45 PG:524 - 531 :: QUAL. :INT. LOG. :INSTIT. :AUD.

GIFT ,MJ ; FIRS: AJINKYA,BB CIT: 0.60
CORPORATE MANAGERS' EARNINGS FORECASTS AND SYMMETRICAL ADJUSTMENTS OF MARKET
   EXPECTATIONS
JAR AU 84 VOL: 22 PG:425 - 444 :: ANOVA :PRIM. :EMH :FOREC.

GILLES JR,LH CIT: 0.00
STATUTORY DEPLETION - SUBSIDY IN DISGUISE?
TAR OC 63 VOL: 38 PG:776 - 784 :: QUAL. :INT. LOG. :THEORY :AMOR./DEPL.

GINZBERG,MJ CIT: 0.56
AN ORGANIZATIONAL CONTINGENCIES VIEW OF ACCOUNTING AND INFORMATION SYSTEMS
   IMPLEMENTATION
AOS 04 80 VOL: 5 PG:369 - 382 :: QUAL. :INT. LOG. :OTH. :AUD.BEH.

GIRARD,D ; FIRS: HAWKINS,CA CIT: 0.00
REPLACEMENT DECISIONS UNDER THE ACCELERATED COST RECOVERY SYSTEM
JAA SP 84 VOL: 7 PG:225 - 240 :: MIXED :INT. LOG. :THEORY :PP&E / DEPR

GIROUX,GA ; FIRS: ROSE ,PS ; SEC: ANDREWS,WT CIT: 0.00
PREDICTING BUSINESS FAILURE: A MACROECONOMIC PERSPECTIVE
JAA AU 82 VOL: 6 PG:20 - 31 :: REGRESS. :PRIM. :TIME SER. :BUS.FAIL.

GIROUX,GA ; FIRS: APOSTOLOU,NG ; THIR: WELKER,RB CIT: 0.00
THE INFORMATION CONTENT OF MUNICIPAL SPENDING RATE DATA
JAR AU 85 VOL: 23 PG:853 - 858 :: REGRESS. :PRIM. :INSTIT. :LTD

GIROUX,GA ; SEC: MAYPER,AG ; THIR: DAFT ,RL CIT: 0.00
ORGANIZATION SIZE, BUDGET CYCLE, AND BUDGET RELATED INFLUENCE IN CITY
   GOVERNMENTS: AN EMPIRICAL STUDY
AOS 06 86 VOL: 11 PG:499 - 520 :: REGRESS. :SURV. :OTH.STAT. :BUDG.& PLAN.

GIVENS,HR CIT: 0.00
BASIC ACCOUNTING POSTULATES
TAR JL 66 VOL: 41 PG:458 - 463 :: QUAL. :INT. LOG. :THEORY :FIN.METH.

GIVOLY,D ; SEC: RONEN ,J ; THIR: SCHIFF,A CIT: 0.09
DOES AUDIT INVOLVEMENT AFFECT THE QUALITY OF INTERIM REPORT NUMBERS?
JAA SU 78 VOL: 1 PG:361 - 372 :: ANOVA :PRIM. :INSTIT. :AUD.

GIVOLY,D ; SEC: LAKONISHOK,J CIT: 1.00
THE INFORMATION CONTENT OF FINANCIAL ANALYSTS' FORECASTS OF EARNINGS: SOME
  EVIDENCE ON SEMI-STRONG INEFFICIENCY
JAE DE 79 VOL: 1 PG:165 - 185 :: DES.STAT. :PRIM. :EMH :FOREC.

GIVOLY,D ; SEC: PALMON,D CIT: 0.00
CLASSIFICATION OF CONVERTIBLE DEBT AS COMMON STOCK EQUIVALENTS: SOME
  EMPIRICAL EVIDENCE ON THE EFFECTS OF APB OPINION 15
JAR AU 81 VOL: 19 PG:530 - 543 :: CORR. :PRIM. :EMH :LTD

GIVOLY,D ; SEC: PALMON,D CIT: 1.86
TIMELINESS OF ANNUAL EARNINGS ANNOUNCEMENTS: SOME EMPIRICAL EVIDENCE
TAR JL 82 VOL: 57 PG:486 - 508 :: REGRESS. :PRIM. :EMH :FIN.ST.TIM.

GIVOLY,D ; FIRS: FRIED ,D CIT: 2.14
FINANCIAL ANALYSTS' FORECASTS OF EARNINGS: A BETTER SURROGATE FOR MARKET
  EXPECTATIONS
JAE OC 82 VOL: 4 PG:85 - 107 :: OTH.QUANT. :SEC. :TIME SER. :FOREC.

GIVOLY,D CIT: 0.00
THE FORMATION OF EARNINGS EXPECTATIONS
TAR JL 85 VOL: 60 PG:372 - 386 :: REGRESS. :PRIM. :N/A :FOREC.

GIVOLY,D ; SEC: LAKONISHOK,J CIT: 0.00
AGGREGATE EARNINGS EXPECTATIONS AND STOCK MARKET BEHAVIOR
JAA SP 87 VOL: 2 PG:117 - 137 :: REGRESS. :PRIM. :EMH :FOREC.

GJESDAL,F CIT: 1.25
ACCOUNTING FOR STEWARDSHIP
JAR SP 81 VOL: 19 PG:208 - 231 :: ANAL. :INT. LOG. :INF.ECO./AG. :INFO.STRUC.

GLATZER,W CIT: 0.00
AN OVERVIEW OF THE INTERNATIONAL DEVELOPMENT IN MACRO SOCIAL INDICATORS
AOS 03 81 VOL: 6 PG:219 - 234 :: QUAL. :INT. LOG. :OTH. :HRA

GLEZEN,GW ; SEC: MILLAR,JA CIT: 0.00
AN EMPIRICAL INVESTIGATION OF STOCKHOLDER REACTION TO DISCLOSURES REQUIRED
  BY ASR NO. 250
JAR AU 85 VOL: 23 PG:859 - 870 :: REGRESS. :PRIM. :INSTIT. :ORG.

GLOVER,F CIT: 0.00
MANAGEMENT DECISION AND INTEGER PROGRAMMING
TAR AP 69 VOL: 44 PG:300 - 303 :: ANAL. :INT. LOG. :MATH.PROG. :LTD

GODFREY,JT CIT: 0.00
SHORT-RUN PLANNING IN A DECENTRALIZED FIRM
TAR AP 71 VOL: 46 PG:286 - 297 :: ANAL. :INT. LOG. :MATH.PROG. :BUDG.& PLAN.

GODFREY,JT ; SEC: PRINCE,TR CIT: 0.15
THE ACCOUNTING MODEL FROM AN INFORMATION SYSTEMS PERSPECTIVE
TAR JA 71 VOL: 46 PG:75 - 89 :: QUAL. :INT. LOG. :INF.ECO./AG. :MANAG.

GODFREY,JT ; SEC: ANDREWS,RW CIT: 0.29
A FINITE POPULATION BAYESIAN MODEL FOR COMPLIANCE TESTING
JAR AU 82 VOL: 20 PG:304 - 315 :: ANAL. :INT. LOG. :OTH.STAT. :SAMP.

GODFREY,JT ; SEC: NETER ,J CIT: 0.40
BAYESIAN BOUNDS FOR MONETARY UNIT SAMPLING IN ACCOUNTING AND AUDITING
JAR AU 84 VOL: 22 PG:497 - 525 :: ANAL. :SIM. :OTH.STAT. :SAMP.

GODFREY,JT ; FIRS: ROSHWALB,A ; SEC: WRIGHT,RL CIT: 0.00
A NEW APPROACH FOR STRATIFIED SAMPLING IN INVENTORY COST ESTIMATION
AUD AU 87 VOL: 7 PG:54 - 70 :: DES.STAT. :SIM. :OTH.STAT. :SAMP.

GODFREY,JT ; FIRS: KIM ,HS ; SEC: NETER ,J CIT: 0.00
BEHAVIOR OF STATISTICAL ESTIMATORS IN MULTILOCATION AUDIT SAMPLING
AUD SP 87 VOL: 6 PG:40 - 58 :: DES.STAT. :SIM. :OTH.STAT. :SAMP.

GOETZ ,BE CIT: 0.15
PROFESSORIAL OBSOLESCENCE
TAR JA 67 VOL: 42 PG:53 - 61 :: QUAL. :INT. LOG. :INSTIT. :OTH.MANAG.

GOETZ ,BE CIT: 0.00
TRANSFER PRICES: AN EXERCISE IN RELEVANCY AND GOAL CONGRUENCE
TAR JL 67 VOL: 42 PG:435 - 440 :: QUAL. :INT. LOG. :N/A :TRANS.PRIC.

GOGGANS,TP CIT: 0.00
THE ACCOUNTANT'S ROLE IN WAGE NEGOTIATIONS
TAR JL 64 VOL: 39 PG:627 - 630 :: QUAL. :INT. LOG. :INSTIT. :OTH.MANAG.

GOLDBERG,L CIT: 0.00
THE PRESENT STATE OF ACCOUNTING THEORY
TAR JL 63 VOL: 38 PG:457 - 469 :: QUAL. :INT. LOG. :THEORY :OTH.MANAG.

GOLDIN,HJ CIT: 0.00
CHANGES IN MUNICIPAL ACCOUNTING: THE NEW YORK CITY COMPTROLLER'S OVERVIEW
JAA SU 85 VOL: 8 PG:269 - 278 :: DES.STAT. :INT. LOG. :THEORY :FIN.METH.

GOLDMAN,A ; SEC: BARLEV,B CIT: 0.23
THE AUDITOR-FIRM CONFLICT OF INTERESTS: ITS IMPLICATIONS FOR INDEPENDENCE
TAR OC 74 VOL: 49 PG:707 - 718 :: QUAL. :INT. LOG. :INSTIT. :INDEP.

GOLDSCHMIDT,Y ; SEC: SMIDT ,S CIT: 0.00
VALUING THE FIRM'S DURABLE ASSETS FOR MANAGERIAL INFORMATION
TAR AP 69 VOL: 44 PG:317 - 329 :: QUAL. :INT. LOG. :THEORY :VALUAT.(INFL.)

GOLDSCHMIDT,Y ; SEC: SHASHUA,L CIT: 0.00
DISTORTION OF INCOME BY SFAS NO.33
JAA AU 84 VOL: 8 PG:54 - 67 :: QUAL. :INT. LOG. :THEORY :VALUAT.(INFL.)

GOLDWASSER,DL CIT: 0.00
POLICY CONSIDERATIONS IN ACCOUNTANTS' LIABILITY TO THIRD PARTIES FOR
    NEGLIGENCE
JAA SU 88 VOL: 03 PG:217 - 232 :: DES.STAT. :INT. LOG. :INSTIT. :LIAB.

GOLEMBIEWSKI,RT CIT: 0.38
ACCOUNTANCY AS A FUNCTION OF ORGANIZATION THEORY
TAR AP 64 VOL: 39 PG:333 - 341 :: QUAL. :INT. LOG. :OTH.BEH. :OTH.MANAG.

GOMBERG,M ; SEC: FARBER,A CIT: 0.00
THE BALANCE SHEET OF THE FUTURE
TAR JL 64 VOL: 39 PG:615 - 617 :: QUAL. :INT. LOG. :THEORY :FIN.METH.

GOMBOLA,MJ ; SEC: KETZ ,JE CIT: 0.00
A NOTE ON CASH FLOW AND CLASSIFICATION PATTERNS OF FINANCIAL RATIOS
TAR JA 83 VOL: 58 PG:105 - 114 :: OTH.QUANT. :LAB. :OTH.STAT. :SPEC.ITEMS

GONEDES,NJ ; FIRS: LARSON,KD CIT: 0.00
BUSINESS COMBINATIONS: AN EXCHANGE RATIO DETERMINATION MODEL
TAR OC 69 VOL: 44 PG:720 - 728 :: ANAL. :INT. LOG. :N/A :OTH.MANAG.

GONEDES,NJ CIT: 0.00
THE SIGNIFICANCE OF SELECTED ACCOUNTING PROCEDURES: A STATISTICAL TEST
JAR ST 69 VOL: 7 PG:90 - 113 :: REGRESS. :PRIM. :EMH :FIN.METH.

GONEDES,NJ CIT: 0.08
ACCOUNTING FOR MANAGERIAL CONTROL: AN APPLICATION OF CHANCE-CONSTRAINED
   PROGRAMMING
JAR SP 70 VOL: 8 PG:1 - 20 :: ANAL. :INT. LOG. :MATH.PROG. :MANAG.

GONEDES,NJ CIT: 0.00
SOME EVIDENCE ON INVESTOR ACTIONS AND ACCOUNTING MESSAGES - PART I
TAR AP 71 VOL: 46 PG:320 - 328 :: ANAL. :INT. LOG. :TIME SER. :FIN.METH.

GONEDES,NJ CIT: 0.08
OPTIMAL TIMING OF CONTROL MESSAGES FOR A TWO-STATE MARKOV PROCESS
JAR AU 71 VOL: 9 PG:236 - 252 :: MARKOV :INT. LOG. :OTH.STAT. :MANAG.

GONEDES,NJ CIT: 0.00
SOME EVIDENCE ON INVESTOR ACTIONS AND ACCOUNTING MESSAGES - PART II
TAR JL 71 VOL: 46 PG:535 - 551 :: REGRESS. :PRIM. :EMH :FIN.METH.

GONEDES,NJ CIT: 0.46
EFFICIENT CAPITAL MARKETS AND EXTERNAL ACCOUNTING
TAR JA 72 VOL: 47 PG:11 - 21 :: QUAL. :INT. LOG. :EMH :FIN.METH.

GONEDES,NJ CIT: 1.15
PROPERTIES OF ACCOUNTING NUMBERS: MODELS AND TESTS
JAR AU 73 VOL: 11 PG:212 - 237 :: REGRESS. :PRIM. :TIME SER. :FIN.METH.

GONEDES,NJ ; SEC: IJIRI ,Y CIT: 0.46
IMPROVING SUBJECTIVE PROBABILITY ASSESSMENT FOR PLANNING AND CONTROL IN
   TEAM-LIKE ORGANIZATIONS
JAR AU 74 VOL: 12 PG:251 - 269 :: ANAL. :INT. LOG. :INF.ECO./AG. :PROB.ELIC.

GONEDES,NJ CIT: 1.00
CAPITAL MARKET EQUILIBRIUM AND ANNUAL ACCOUNTING NUMBERS: EMPIRICAL EVIDENCE
JAR SP 74 VOL: 12 PG:26 - 62 :: REGRESS. :PRIM. :EMH :FIN.METH.

GONEDES,NJ ; SEC: DOPUCH,N CIT: 5.15
CAPITAL MARKET EQUILIBRIUM, INFORMATION PRODUCTION, AND SELECTING ACCOUNTING
   TECHNIQUES: THEORETICAL FRAMEWORK AND REVIEW OF EMPIRICAL WORK
JAR ST 74 VOL: 12 PG:48 - 129 :: ANAL. :SEC. :EMH :FIN.METH.

GONEDES,NJ CIT: 2.23
RISK, INFORMATION, AND THE EFFECTS OF SPECIAL ACCOUNTING ITEMS ON CAPITAL
   MARKET EQUILIBRIUM
JAR AU 75 VOL: 13 PG:220 - 256 :: REGRESS. :PRIM. :EMH :SPEC.ITEMS

GONEDES,NJ ; SEC: DOPUCH,N ; THIR: PENMAN,SH CIT: 3.00
DISCLOSURE RULES, INFORMATION-PRODUCTION, AND CAPITAL MARKET EQUILIBRIUM: THE
   CASE OF FORECAST DISCLOSURE RULES
JAR SP 76 VOL: 14 PG:89 - 137 :: NON-PAR. :PRIM. :EMH :FOREC.

GONEDES,NJ CIT: 1.82
CORPORATE SIGNALING, EXTERNAL ACCOUNTING, AND CAPITAL MARKET EQUILIBRIUM:
   EVIDENCE ON DIVIDENDS INCOME, AND EXTRAORDINARY ITEMS
JAR SP 78 VOL: 16 PG:26 - 79 :: MIXED :PRIM. :EMH :CASH DIV.

GONEDES,NJ ; SEC: DOPUCH,N CIT: 0.70
ECONOMIC ANALYSES AND ACCOUNTING TECHNIQUES: PERSPECTIVES AND PROPOSALS
JAR AU 79 VOL: 17 PG:384 - 410 :: QUAL. :INT. LOG. :THEORY :METHOD.

GONEDES,NJ CIT: 0.44
PUBLIC DISCLOSURE RULES, PRIVATE INFORMATION-PRODUCTION DECISIONS AND CAPITAL
    MARKET EQUILIBRIUM
JAR AU 80 VOL: 18 PG:441 - 476 :: ANAL. :INT. LOG. :INF.ECO./AG. :INFO.STRUC.

GOODMAN,SS ; FIRS: FIRMIN,PA ; THIR: HENDRICKS,TE ; FOUR: LINN ,JJ CIT: 0.00
UNIVERSITY COST STRUCTURE AND BEHAVIOR: AN EMPIRICAL STUDY
JAR ST 68 VOL: 6 PG:122 - 155 :: DES.STAT. :SIM. :OTH.STAT. :MANAG.

GORDON,FE ; SEC: RHODE ,JG ; THIR: MERCHANT,KA CIT: 0.25
THE EFFECTS OF SALARY AND HUMAN RESOURCE ACCOUNTING DISCLOSURES ON SMALL
    GROUP RELATIONS AND PERFORMANCE
AOS 04 77 VOL: 2 PG:295 - 306 :: ANOVA :LAB. :OTH.BEH. :HRA

GORDON,LA ; SEC: MILLER,D CIT: 1.69
A CONTINGENCY FRAMEWORK FOR THE DESIGN OF ACCOUNTING INFORMATION SYSTEMS
AOS 01 76 VOL: 1 PG:59 - 70 :: QUAL. :INT. LOG. :OTH.BEH. :INFO.STRUC.

GORDON,LA ; SEC: LARCKER,DF ; THIR: TUGGLE,FD CIT: 0.82
STRATEGIC DECISION PROCESSES AND THE DESIGN OF ACCOUNTING INFORMATION
    SYSTEMS: CONCEPTUAL LINKAGES
AOS 34 78 VOL: 3 PG:203 - 214 :: QUAL. :INT. LOG. :OTH. :INFO.STRUC.

GORDON,LA ; SEC: NARAYANAN,VK CIT: 0.60
MANAGEMENT ACCOUNTING SYSTEMS, PERCEIVED ENVIRONMENTAL UNCERTAINTY AND
    ORGANIZATION STRUCTURE: AN EMPIRICAL INVESTIGATION
AOS 01 84 VOL: 9 PG:33 - 47 :: CORR. :SURV. :OTH. :ORG.FORM

GORDON,LA ; SEC: HAKA ,S ; THIR: SCHICK,AG CIT: 0.00
STRATEGIES FOR INFORMATION SYSTEMS IMPLEMENTATION: THE CASE OF ZERO BASE
    BUDGETING
AOS 02 84 VOL: 9 PG:111 - 123 :: NON-PAR. :PRIM. :OTH. :BUDG.& PLAN.

GORDON,LA ; FIRS: HAKA ,SF ; THIR: PINCHES,GE CIT: 0.50
SOPHISTICATED CAPITAL BUDGETING SELECTION TECHNIQUES AND FIRM PERFORMANCE
TAR OC 85 VOL: 60 PG:651 - 669 :: REGRESS. :PRIM. :EMH :CAP.BUDG.

GORDON,LA ; SEC: HAMER ,MH CIT: 0.00
RATES OF RETURN AND CASH FLOW PROFILES: AN EXTENSION
AUD JL 88 VOL: 63 PG:514 - 521 :: DES.STAT. :INT. LOG. :THEORY :FIN.METH.

GORDON,MJ CIT: 0.85
POSTULATES, PRINCIPLES AND RESEARCH IN ACCOUNTING
TAR AP 64 VOL: 39 PG:251 - 263 :: QUAL. :INT. LOG. :THEORY :OTH.FIN.ACC.

GORDON,MJ CIT: 0.15
A METHOD OF PRICING FOR A SOCIALIST ECONOMY
TAR JL 70 VOL: 45 PG:427 - 443 :: ANAL. :INT. LOG. :N/A :TRANS.PRIC.

GORMLEY,RJ CIT: 0.00
PROFESSIONAL RISKS IN PURCHASE AUDITS AND REVIEWS
JAA SU 80 VOL: 3 PG:293 - 312 :: QUAL. :INT. LOG. :THEORY :RISK

GORMLEY,RJ CIT: 0.00
RICO AND THE PROFESSIONAL ACCOUNTANT
JAA AU 82 VOL: 6 PG:51 - 59 :: QUAL. :INT. LOG. :OTH. :PROF.RESP.

GORMLEY,RJ CIT: 0.00
DEVELOPMENTS IN ACCOUNTANTS' LIABILITY TO NONCLIENTS FOR NEGLIGENCE
JAA SU 88 VOL: 03 PG:185 - 212 :: REGRESS. :PRIM. :INSTIT. :LIAB.

GOSMAN,ML CIT: 0.92
CHARACTERISTICS OF FIRMS MAKING ACCOUNTING CHANGES
TAR JA 73 VOL: 48 PG:1 - 11 :: DES.STAT. :PRIM. :OTH.BEH. :AUD.BEH.

GOVINDARAJAN,V ; FIRS: SAN MIGUEL,JG ; SEC: SHANK ,JK CIT: 0.08
EXTENDING CORPORATE ACCOUNTABILITY: A SURVEY AND FRAMEWORK FOR ANALYSIS
AOS 04 77 VOL: 2 PG:333 - 348 :: DES.STAT. :PRIM. :OTH. :AUD.

GOVINDARAJAN,V CIT: 0.00
OBJECTIVES OF FINANCIAL REPORTING BY BUSINESS ENTERPRISES: SOME EVIDENCE OF
    USER PREFERENCE
JAA SU 79 VOL: 2 PG:339 - 343 :: DES.STAT. :PRIM. :THEORY :FIN.METH.

GOVINDARAJAN,V CIT: 0.00
THE OBJECTIVES OF FINANCIAL STATEMENTS: AN EMPIRICAL STUDY OF THE USE OF CASH
    FLOW AND EARNINGS BY SECURITY ANALYSTS
AOS 04 80 VOL: 5 PG:383 - 392 :: DES.STAT. :PRIM. :THEORY :CASH

GOVINDARAJAN,V ; FIRS: CHURCHILL,NC ; SEC: COOPER,WW CIT: 0.00
EFFECTS OF AUDITS ON THE BEHAVIOR OF MEDICAL PROFESSIONALS UNDER THE BENNETT
    AMENDMENT
AUD WI 82 VOL: 1 PG:69 - 91 :: ANOVA :PRIM. :OTH.STAT. :OPER.AUD.

GOVINDARAJAN,V CIT: 1.80
APPROPRIATENESS OF ACCOUNTING DATA IN PERFORMANCE EVALUATION: AN EMPIRICAL
    EXAMINATION OF ENVIRONMENTAL UNCERTAINTY AS AN INTERVAL VARIABLE
AOS 02 84 VOL: 9 PG:125 - 135 :: DES.STAT. :SURV. :OTH.BEH. :ORG.& ENVIR.

GOVINDARAJAN,V ; FIRS: SAN MIGUEL,JG CIT: 0.00
THE CONTINGENT RELATIONSHIP BETWEEN THE CONTROLLER AND INTERNAL AUDIT
    FUNCTIONS IN LARGE ORGANIZATIONS
AOS 02 84 VOL: 9 PG:179 - 188 :: NON-PAR. :SURV. :OTH.BEH. :INT.AUD.

GOVINDARAJAN,V ; SEC: GUPTA ,AK CIT: 1.25
LINKING CONTROL SYSTEMS TO BUSINESS UNIT STRATEGY: IMPACT ON PERFORMANCE
AOS 01 85 VOL: 10 PG:51 - 66 :: REGRESS. :SURV. :OTH.BEH. :MANAG.

GRADY ,P CIT: 0.00
INVENTORY OF GENERALLY ACCEPTED ACCOUNTING PRINCIPLES IN THE U.S.A.
TAR JA 65 VOL: 40 PG:21 - 30 :: QUAL. :SEC. :THEORY :FIN.METH.

GRAESE,CE CIT: 0.00
RESPONSIBILITY REPORTING TO MANAGEMENT
TAR AP 64 VOL: 39 PG:387 - 391 :: QUAL. :INT. LOG. :N/A :RESP.ACC.

GRAHAM,LE ; FIRS: NETER ,J ; SEC: KIM ,HS CIT: 0.20
ON COMBINING STRINGER BOUNDS FOR INDEPENDENT MONETARY UNIT SAMPLES FROM
    SEVERAL POPULATIONS
AUD AU 84 VOL: 4 PG:75 - 88 :: ANAL. :INT. LOG. :OTH.STAT. :SAMP.

GRAHAM,LE ; FIRS: SHPILBERG,D CIT: 0.00
DEVELOPING EXPERTAX: AN EXPERT SYSTEM FOR CORPORATE TAX ACCRUAL
    ND PLANNING
AUD AU 86 VOL: 6 PG:75 - 94 :: QUAL. :LAB. :EXP.SYST. :TAXES

GRANOF,MH ; FIRS: DEAKIN,EB CIT: 0.46
REGRESSION ANALYSIS AS A MEANS OF DETERMINING AUDIT SAMPLE SIZE
TAR OC 74 VOL: 49 PG:764 - 771 :: REGRESS. :INT. LOG. :OTH.STAT. :SAMP.

GRANOF,MH ; SEC: SHORT ,DG CIT: 0.00
WHY DO COMPANIES REJECT LIFO?
JAA SU 84 VOL: 7 PG:323 - 333 :: DES.STAT. :SURV. :THEORY :INV.

GRANT ,EB CIT: 1.44
MARKET IMPLICATIONS OF DIFFERENTIAL AMOUNTS OF INTERIM INFORMATION
JAR SP 80 VOL: 18 PG:255 - 268 :: REGRESS. :PRIM. :EMH :INT.REP.

GRAUL ,PR ; FIRS: ABDEL-KHALIK,AR ; THIR: NEWTON,JD CIT: 0.00
REPORTING UNCERTAINTY AND ASSESSMENT OF RISK: REPLICATION AND EXTENSION IN A
  CANADIAN SETTING
JAR AU 86 VOL: 24 PG:372 - 382 :: REGRESS. :LAB. :HIPS :OPIN.

GRAWOIG,DE ; FIRS: NICHOLS,AC CIT: 0.00
ACCOUNTING REPORTS WITH TIME AS A VARIABLE
TAR OC 68 VOL: 43 PG:631 - 639 :: QUAL. :INT. LOG. :THEORY :OTH.MANAG.

GRAY ,D CIT: 0.00
CORPORATE PREFERENCES FOR FOREIGN CURRENCY ACCOUNTING STANDARDS
JAR AU 84 VOL: 22 PG:760 - 764 :: DES.STAT. :PRIM. :THEORY :FOR.CUR.

GRAY ,J ; SEC: WILLINGHAM,JJ ; THIR: JOHNSTON,K CIT: 0.00
A BUSINESS GAME FOR THE INTRODUCTORY COURSE IN ACCOUNTING
TAR AP 63 VOL: 38 PG:336 - 346 :: QUAL. :INT. LOG. :OTH. :EDUC.

GRAY ,J ; FIRS: BAILEY JR,AD CIT: 0.00
A STUDY OF THE IMPORTANCE OF THE PLANNING HORIZON ON REPORTS UTILIZING
  DISCOUNTED FUTURE CASH FLOWS
JAR SP 68 VOL: 6 PG:98 - 105 :: DES.STAT. :SIM. :N/A :CAP.BUDG.

GRAY ,J ; FIRS: SIMMONS,JK CIT: 0.46
AN INVESTIGATION OF THE EFFECT OF DIFFERING ACCOUNTING FRAMEWORKS ON THE
  PREDICTION OF NET INCOME
TAR OC 69 VOL: 44 PG:757 - 776 :: ANAL. :SIM. :THEORY :VALUAT.(INFL.)

GRAY ,J ; FIRS: PURDY ,CR ; SEC: SMITH JR,JM CIT: 0.00
THE VISIBILITY OF THE AUDITOR'S DISCLOSURE OF DEVIANCE FROM APB OPINION: AN
  EMPIRICAL TEST
JAR ST 69 VOL: 7 PG:1 - 18 :: ANOVA :LAB. :OTH.BEH. :INFO.STRUC.

GRAY ,SJ CIT: 0.09
SEGMENT REPORTING AND THE EEC MULTINATIONALS
JAR AU 78 VOL: 16 PG:242 - 253 :: DES.STAT. :PRIM. :THEORY :INT.DIFF.

GRAY ,SJ CIT: 0.22
THE IMPACT OF INTERNATIONAL ACCOUNTING DIFFERENCES FROM A SECURITY-ANALYSIS
  PERSPECTIVE: SOME EUROPEAN EVIDENCE
JAR SP 80 VOL: 18 PG:64 - 76 :: ANOVA :PRIM. :OTH. :INT.DIFF.

GRAY ,SJ ; SEC: RADEBAUGH,LH CIT: 0.00
INTERNATIONAL SEGMENT DISCLOSURES BY U.S. AND U.K. MULTINATIONAL ENTERPRISES:
  A DESCRIPTIVE STUDY
JAR SP 84 VOL: 22 PG:351 - 360 :: DES.STAT. :PRIM. :THEORY :INT.DIFF.

GREEN ,D CIT: 0.08
TOWARDS A THEORY OF INTERIM REPORTS
JAR SP 64 VOL: 2 PG:35 - 49 :: QUAL. :INT. LOG. :THEORY :N/A

GREEN ,D CIT: 0.15
EVALUATING THE ACCOUNTING LITERATURE
TAR JA 66 VOL: 41 PG:52 - 64 :: QUAL. :INT. LOG. :N/A :OTH.MANAG.

GREEN ,D ; SEC: SEGALL,J CIT: 0.62
THE PREDICTIVE POWER OF FIRST-QUARTER EARNINGS REPORTS: A REPLICATION
JAR ST 66 VOL: 4 PG:21 - 36 :: DES.STAT. :PRIM. :OTH.STAT. :INT.REP.

GREEN ,SL ; FIRS: LEWIS ,BL ; SEC: PATTON,JM CIT: 0.00
THE EFFECTS OF INFORMATION CHOICE AND INFORMATION USE ON ANALYSTS'
  PREDICTIONS OF MUNICIPAL BOND RATING CHANGES
TAR AP 88 VOL: 63 PG:270 - 282 :: REGRESS. :LAB. :OTH.STAT. :FOREC.

GREENBALL,MN CIT: 0.15
THE ACCURACY OF DIFFERENT METHODS OF ACCOUNTING FOR EARNINGS - A SIMULATION
  APPROACH
JAR SP 68 VOL: 6 PG:114 - 129 :: DES.STAT. :SIM. :OTH.STAT. :VALUAT.(INFL.)

GREENBALL,MN CIT: 0.00
EVALUATION OF THE USEFULNESS TO INVESTORS OF DIFFERENT ACCOUNTING ESTIMATORS
  OF EARNINGS: A SIMULATION APPROACH
JAR ST 68 VOL: 6 PG:27 - 49 :: DES.STAT. :SIM. :THEORY :FIN.METH.

GREENBALL,MN CIT: 0.08
APPRAISING ALTERNATIVE METHODS OF ACCOUNTING FOR ACCELERATED TAX
  DEPRECIATION: A RELATIVE-ACCURACY APPROACH
JAR AU 69 VOL: 7 PG:262 - 289 :: ANAL. :INT. LOG. :OTH.STAT. :TAXES

GREENBALL,MN CIT: 0.15
A STATISTICAL MODEL OF EARNINGS ESTIMATION
JAR ST 71 VOL: 9 PG:172 - 190 :: MIXED :PRIM. :TIME SER. :N/A

GREENBERG,R CIT: 0.00
ADAPTIVE ESTIMATION: AN ALTERNATIVE TO THE TRADITIONAL STATIONARITY ASSUMPTION
JAR AU 84 VOL: 22 PG:719 - 730 :: NON-PAR. :PRIM. :TIME SER. :FOREC.

GREENBERG,RR ; SEC: JOHNSON,GL ; THIR: RAMESH,K CIT: 0.00
EARNINGS VERSUS CASH FLOW AS A PREDICTOR OF FUTURE CASH FLOW MEASURES
JAA AU 86 VOL: 1 PG:266 - 277 :: REGRESS. :PRIM. :THEORY :SPEC.ITEMS

GREENE,ED CIT: 0.08
CHANGING FROM DECLINING BALANCE TO STRAIGHT-LINE DEPRECIATION
TAR AP 63 VOL: 38 PG:355 - 362 :: QUAL. :INT. LOG. :INSTIT. :PP&E / DEPR

GREER ,HC CIT: 0.00
THE CORPORATION STOCKHOLDER - ACCOUNTING'S FORGOTTEN MAN
TAR JA 64 VOL: 39 PG:22 - 31 :: QUAL. :INT. LOG. :THEORY :FIN.METH.

GREER JR,WR CIT: 0.15
CAPITAL BUDGETING ANALYSIS WITH THE TIMING OF EVENTS UNCERTAIN
TAR JA 70 VOL: 45 PG:103 - 114 :: ANAL. :INT. LOG. :OTH.STAT. :CAP.BUDG.

GREER JR,WR CIT: 0.08
THEORY VERSUS PRACTICE IN RISK ANALYSIS: AN EMPIRICAL STUDY
TAR JL 74 VOL: 49 PG:496 - 505 :: NON-PAR. :LAB. :N/A :CAP.BUDG.

GREER JR,WR ; SEC: MORRISSEY,LE CIT: 0.00
ACCOUNTING RULE-MAKING IN A WORLD OF EFFICIENT MARKETS
JAA AU 78 VOL: 2 PG:49 - 57 :: QUAL. :INT. LOG. :INSTIT. :FIN.METH.

GRIFFIN,CH ; FIRS: WILLIAMS,TH CIT: 0.08
MATRIX THEORY AND COST ALLOCATION
TAR JL 64 VOL: 39 PG:671 - 678 :: ANAL. :INT. LOG. :MATH.PROG. :COST.ALLOC.

GRIFFIN,CH ; FIRS: WILLIAMS,TH CIT: 0.00
INCOME DEFINITION AND MEASUREMENT: A STRUCTURAL APPROACH
TAR OC 67 VOL: 42 PG:642 - 649 :: QUAL. :INT. LOG. :THEORY :OTH.MANAG.

GRIFFIN,FB ; FIRS: ANDERSON,HM CIT: 0.00
THE ACCOUNTING CURRICULUM AND POSTGRADUATE ACHIEVEMENT
TAR OC 63 VOL: 38 PG:813 - 818 :: QUAL. :INT. LOG. :THEORY :EDUC.

GRIFFIN,PA CIT: 0.15
THE ASSOCIATION BETWEEN RELATIVE RISK AND RISK ESTIMATES DERIVED FROM
QUARTERLY EARNINGS AND DIVIDENDS
TAR JL 76 VOL: 51 PG:499 - 515 :: REGRESS. :PRIM. :EMH :TAXES

GRIFFIN,PA CIT: 2.25
THE TIME-SERIES BEHAVIOR OF QUARTERLY EARNINGS: PRELIMINARY EVIDENCE
JAR SP 77 VOL: 15 PG:71 - 83 :: MIXED :PRIM. :TIME SER. :FOREC.

GRIFFIN,PA ; FIRS: BEAVER,WH ; SEC: CHRISTIE,AA CIT: 2.00
THE INFORMATION CONTENT OF SEC ACCOUNTING SERIES RELEASE NO.190
JAE AG 80 VOL: 2 PG:127 - 157 :: REGRESS. :PRIM. :EMH :VALUAT.(INFL.)

GRIFFIN,PA ; FIRS: BEAVER,WH ; THIR: LANDSMAN,WR CIT: 2.43
THE INCREMENTAL INFORMATION CONTENT OF REPLACEMENT COST EARNINGS
JAE JL 82 VOL: 4 PG:15 - 39 :: MIXED :PRIM. :EMH :VALUAT.(INFL.)

GRIFFIN,PA ; FIRS: BEAVER,WH ; THIR: LANDSMAN,WR CIT: 0.00
TESTING FOR INCREMENTAL INFORMATION CONTENT IN THE PRESENCE OF COLLINEARITY:
A COMMENT
JAE DE 84 VOL: 6 PG:219 - 223 :: QUAL. :INT. LOG. :OTH.STAT. :METHOD.

GRIFFIN,PA ; FIRS: BROWN ,LD ; THIR: HAGERMAN,RL ; FOUR: ZMIJEWSKI,ME CIT: 2.50
SECURITY ANALYST SUPERIORITY RELATIVE TO UNIVARIATE TIME-SERIES MODELS IN
FORECASTING QUARTERLY EARNINGS
JAE AP 87 VOL: 9 PG:61 - 87 :: REGRESS. :PRIM. :TIME SER. :FOREC.

GRIFFIN,PA ; FIRS: BROWN ,LD ; THIR: HAGERMAN,RL ; FOUR: ZMIJEWSKI,ME CIT: 2.00
AN EVALUATION OF ALTERNATIVE PROXIES FOR THE MARKET'S ASSESSMENT OF
UNEXPECTED EARNINGS
JAE JL 87 VOL: 9 PG:159 - 193 :: REGRESS. :PRIM. :TIME SER. :METHOD.

GRIMLUND,RA ; FIRS: FELIX JR,WL CIT: 1.17
A SAMPLING MODEL FOR AUDIT TESTS OF COMPOSITE ACCOUNTS
JAR SP 77 VOL: 15 PG:23 - 41 :: ANAL. :INT. LOG. :OTH.STAT. :SAMP.

GRIMLUND,RA CIT: 0.71
AN INTEGRATION OF INTERNAL CONTROL SYSTEM AND ACCOUNT BALANCE EVIDENCE
JAR AU 82 VOL: 20 PG:316 - 342 :: ANAL. :INT. LOG. :OTH.STAT. :SAMP.

GRIMLUND,RA ; FIRS: DWORIN,L CIT: 0.60
DOLLAR UNIT SAMPLING FOR ACCOUNTS RECEIVABLE AND INVENTORY
TAR AP 84 VOL: 59 PG:218 - 241 :: MIXED :SIM. :OTH.STAT. :SAMP.

GRIMLUND,RA CIT: 0.00
A PROPOSAL FOR IMPLEMENTING THE FASB'S "REASONABLY POSSIBLE" DISCLOSURE
  PROVISION FOR PRODUCT WARRANTY LIABILITIES
JAR AU 85 VOL: 23 PG:575 - 594 :: DES.STAT. :SIM. :OTH.STAT. :SPEC.ITEMS

GRIMLUND,RA ; FIRS: DWORIN,L CIT: 0.33
DOLLAR-UNIT SAMPLING: A COMPARISON OF THE QUASI-BAYESIAN AND MOMENT BOUNDS
TAR JA 86 VOL: 61 PG:36 - 57 :: DES.STAT. :SIM. :OTH.STAT. :SAMP.

GRIMLUND,RA ; SEC: FELIX JR,WL CIT: 0.00
SIMULATION EVIDENCE AND ANALYSIS OF ALTERNATIVE METHODS OF EVALUATING
  DOLLAR-UNIT SAMPLES
TAR JL 87 VOL: 62 PG:455 - 479 :: DES.STAT. :SIM. :OTH.STAT. :SAMP.

GRIMLUND,RA ; SEC: SCHROEDER,MS CIT: 0.00
ON THE CURRENT USE OF THE STRINGER METHOD OF MUS: SOME NEW DIRECTIONS
AUD AU 88 VOL: 08 PG:53 - 62 :: REGRESS. :SIM. :OTH.STAT. :SAMP.

GRIMLUND,RA CIT: 0.00
SAMPLE SIZE PLANNING FOR THE MOMENT METHOD OF MUS: INCORPORATING AUDIT
  JUDGMENTS
AUD SP 88 VOL: 07 PG:77 - 104 :: DES.STAT. :SIM. :OTH.STAT. :SAMP.

GROBSTEIN,M ; SEC: CRAIG ,PW CIT: 0.00
A RISK ANALYSIS APPROACH TO AUDITING
AUD SP 84 VOL: 3 PG:1 - 16 :: QUAL. :INT. LOG. :OTH. :RISK

GROFF ,JE ; FIRS: WRIGHT,CJ CIT: 0.33
USES OF INDEXES AND DATA BASES FOR INFORMATION RELEASE ANALYSIS
TAR JA 86 VOL: 61 PG:91 - 100 :: REGRESS. :PRIM. :EMH :METHOD.

GROJER,JE ; SEC: STARK ,A CIT: 0.33
SOCIAL ACCOUNTING: A SWEDISH ATTEMPT
AOS 04 77 VOL: 2 PG:349 - 385 :: QUAL. :CASE :THEORY :HRA

GRONLUND,A ; FIRS: JONSSON,S CIT: 0.00
LIFE WITH A SUB-CONTRACTOR: NEW TECHNOLOGY AND MANAGEMENT ACCOUNTING
AOS 05 88 VOL: 13 PG:513 - 532 :: DES.STAT. :CASE :THEORY :MANAG.

GROOMER, SM ; FIRS: VASARHELYI,MA ; SEC: BAILEY JR,AD ; THIR: CAMARDESSE JR,JE
 ; FIFT: LAMPE ,JC CIT: 0.00
THE USAGE OF COMPUTERS IN AUDITING TEACHING AND RESEARCH
AUD SP 84 VOL: 3 PG:98 - 103 :: QUAL. :SIM. :OTH. :EDP AUD.

GROSS ,H CIT: 0.00
MAKE OR BUY DECISIONS IN GROWING FIRMS
TAR OC 66 VOL: 41 PG:745 - 753 :: QUAL. :INT. LOG. :N/A :REL.COSTS

GROSSMAN,SD ; SEC: KRATCHMAN,SH ; THIR: WELKER,RB CIT: 0.00
COMMENT: THE EFFECT OF REPLACEMENT COST DISCLOSURES ON SECURITY PRICES
JAA WI 81 VOL: 4 PG:136 - 143 :: DES.STAT. :PRIM. :EMH :VALUAT.(INFL.)

GROSSMAN,SD ; FIRS: BENJAMIN,JJ ; THIR: WIGGIN,CE CIT: 0.00
THE IMPACT OF FOREIGN CURRENCY TRANSLATION ON REPORTING DURING THE PHASE-IN
  OF SFAS NO.52
JAA SU 86 VOL: 1 PG:177 - 184 :: REGRESS. :PRIM. :THEORY :FOR.CUR.

GROVE ,HD ; FIRS: SORENSEN,JE CIT: 0.08
COST-OUTCOME AND COST-EFFECTIVENESS ANALYSIS: EMERGING NONPROFIT PERFORMANCE
EVALUATION TECHNIQUES
TAR JL 77 VOL: 52 PG:658 - 675 :: ANAL. :SEC. :OTH.STAT. :REL.COSTS

GROVE ,HD ; SEC: MOCK ,TJ ; THIR: EHRENREICH,K CIT: 0.08
A REVIEW OF HUMAN RESOURCE ACCOUNTING MEASUREMENT SYSTEMS FROM A MEASUREMEN
THEORY PERSPECTIVE
AOS 03 77 VOL: 2 PG:219 - 236 :: QUAL. :SEC. :OTH.BEH. :HRA

GROVE ,HD ; SEC: SAVICH,RS CIT: 0.20
ATTITUDE RESEARCH IN ACCOUNTING: A MODEL FOR RELIABILITY AND VALIDITY
CONSIDERATIONS
TAR JL 79 VOL: 54 PG:522 - 537 :: QUAL. :SEC. :OTH.BEH. :METHOD.

GROVE ,HD ; FIRS: SELTO ,FH CIT: 0.14
VOTING POWER INDICES AND THE SETTING OF FINANCIAL ACCOUNTING STANDARDS:
EXTENSIONS
JAR AU 82 VOL: 20 PG:676 - 688 :: DES.STAT. :PRIM. :INSTIT. :FASB SUBM.

GROVE ,HD ; FIRS: SELTO ,FH CIT: 0.00
THE PREDICTIVE POWER OF VOTING POWER INDICES: FASB VOTING ON STATEMENTS OF
FINANCIAL ACCOUNTING STANDARDS NOS. 45-69
JAR AU 83 VOL: 21 PG:619 - 622 :: NON-PAR. :PRIM. :INSTIT. :FASB SUBM.

GROVES,R ; SEC: MANES ,RP ; THIR: SORENSEN,R CIT: 0.08
THE APPLICATION OF THE HIRSCH-DANTZIG "FIXED CHARGE" ALGORITHM TO PROFIT
PLANNING: A FORMAL STATEMENT OF PRODUCT PROFITABILITY ANALYSIS
TAR JL 70 VOL: 45 PG:481 - 489 :: ANAL. :INT. LOG. :MATH.PROG. :BUDG.& PLAN.

GROVES,R ; FIRS: TOMKINS,C CIT: 2.50
THE EVERYDAY ACCOUNTANT AND RESEARCHING HIS REALITY
AOS 04 83 VOL: 8 PG:361 - 374 :: QUAL. :INT. LOG. :THEORY :METHOD.

GUL ,FA CIT: 0.20
THE JOINT AND MODERATING ROLE OF PERSONALITY AND COGNITIVE STYLE ON DECISION
MAKING
TAR AP 84 VOL: 59 PG:264 - 277 :: ANOVA :LAB. :HIPS :N/A

GUL ,FA CIT: 0.00
AN EMPIRICAL STUDY OF THE USEFULNESS OF HUMAN RESOURCES TURNOVER COSTS IN
AUSTRALIAN ACCOUNTING FIRMS
AOS 34 84 VOL: 9 PG:233 - 239 :: NON-PAR. :LAB. :OTH.BEH. :HRA

GUNN ,S ; FIRS: JOHNSON,O CIT: 0.00
CONFLICT RESOLUTION: THE MARKET AND/OR ACCOUNTING?
TAR OC 74 VOL: 49 PG:649 - 663 :: QUAL. :INT. LOG. :INSTIT. :FIN.METH.

GUPTA ,AK ; FIRS: GOVINDARAJAN,V CIT: 1.25
LINKING CONTROL SYSTEMS TO BUSINESS UNIT STRATEGY: IMPACT ON PERFORMANCE
AOS 01 85 VOL: 10 PG:51 - 66 :: REGRESS. :SURV. :OTH.BEH. :MANAG.

GUPTA ,MC ; SEC: HUEFNER,RJ CIT: 0.23
A CLUSTER ANALYSIS STUDY OF FINANCIAL RATIOS AND INDUSTRY CHARACTERISTICS
JAR SP 72 VOL: 10 PG:77 - 95 :: OTH.QUANT. :PRIM. :OTH.STAT. :N/A

GUSTAVSON,SG ; FIRS: SCHULTZ JR,JJ CIT: 0.64
ACTUARIES' PERCEPTIONS OF VARIABLES AFFECTING THE INDEPENDENT AUDITOR'S LEGAL
LIABILITY
TAR JL 78 VOL: 53 PG:626 - 641 :: ANOVA :LAB. :HIPS :LIAB.

GUTBERLET,LG CIT: 0.00
COMPILATION AND REVIEW OF FINANCIAL STATEMENTS BY AN ACCOUNTANT
JAA SU 80 VOL: 3 PG:313 - 338 :: QUAL. :INT. LOG. :THEORY :PROF.RESP.

GUTBERLET,LG CIT: 0.00
AN OPPORTUNITY-DIFFERENTIAL STANDARDS
JAA AU 83 VOL: 7 PG:16 - 28 :: QUAL. :INT. LOG. :THEORY :FASB SUBM.

GYNTHER,MM CIT: 0.00
FUTURE GROWTH ASPECTS OF THE CASH FLOW COMPUTATION
TAR OC 68 VOL: 43 PG:706 - 718 :: ANAL. :SIM. :OTH.STAT. :PP&E / DEPR

GYNTHER,RS CIT: 0.31
ACCOUNTING CONCEPTS AND BEHAVIOURAL HYPOTHESES
TAR AP 67 VOL: 42 PG:274 - 290 :: QUAL. :INT. LOG. :OTH.BEH. :FIN.METH.

GYNTHER,RS CIT: 0.00
SOME "CONCEPTUALIZING" ON GOODWILL
TAR AP 69 VOL: 44 PG:247 - 255 :: QUAL. :INT. LOG. :THEORY :OTH. NON-C/A

GYNTHER,RS CIT: 0.15
CAPITAL MAINTENANCE, PRICE CHANGES, AND PROFIT DETERMINATION
TAR OC 70 VOL: 45 PG:712 - 730 :: QUAL. :INT. LOG. :THEORY :VALUAT.(INFL.)

HAFNER,GF CIT: 0.00
AUDITING EDP
TAR OC 64 VOL: 39 PG:979 - 982 :: QUAL. :INT. LOG. :N/A :AUD.

HAGERMAN,RL CIT: 0.31
A TEST OF GOVERNMENT REGULATION OF ACCOUNTING PRINCIPLES
TAR OC 75 VOL: 50 PG:699 - 709 :: MIXED :PRIM. :EMH :FIN.METH.

HAGERMAN,RL ; SEC: ZMIJEWSKI,ME CIT: 3.80
SOME ECONOMIC DETERMINANTS OF ACCOUNTING POLICY CHOICE
JAE AG 79 VOL: 1 PG:141 - 161 :: OTH.QUANT. :PRIM. :OTH.STAT. :ACC.CHNG.

HAGERMAN,RL ; FIRS: ZMIJEWSKI,ME CIT: 2.63
AN INCOME STRATEGY APPROACH TO THE POSITIVE THEORY OF ACCOUNTING STANDARD
    SETTING/CHOICE
JAE AG 81 VOL: 3 PG:129 - 149 :: OTH.QUANT. :SEC. :OTH.STAT. :METHOD.

HAGERMAN,RL ; SEC: ZMIJEWSKI,ME ; THIR: SHAH ,P CIT: 0.00
THE ASSOCIATION BETWEEN THE MAGNITUDE OF QUARTERLY EARNINGS FORECAST ERRORS
    AND RISK-ADJUSTED STOCK RETURNS
JAR AU 84 VOL: 22 PG:526 - 540 :: REGRESS. :PRIM. :EMH :FOREC.

HAGERMAN,RL ; FIRS: BROWN ,LD ; SEC: GRIFFIN,PA ; FOUR: ZMIJEWSKI,ME CIT: 2.50
SECURITY ANALYST SUPERIORITY RELATIVE TO UNIVARIATE TIME-SERIES MODELS IN
    FORECASTING QUARTERLY EARNINGS
JAE AP 87 VOL: 9 PG:61 - 87 :: REGRESS. :PRIM. :TIME SER. :FOREC.

HAGERMAN,RL ; FIRS: BROWN ,LD ; SEC: GRIFFIN,PA ; FOUR: ZMIJEWSKI,ME CIT: 2.00
AN EVALUATION OF ALTERNATIVE PROXIES FOR THE MARKET'S ASSESSMENT OF
    UNEXPECTED EARNINGS
JAE JL 87 VOL: 9 PG:159 - 193 :: REGRESS. :PRIM. :TIME SER. :METHOD.

HAGG J ; SEC: HEDLUND,G CIT: 0.50
"CASE STUDIES" IN ACCOUNTING RESEARCH
AOS 12 79 VOL: 4 PG:135 - 143 :: QUAL. :INT. LOG. :OTH. :METHOD.

HAIN ,HP CIT: 0.00
ACCOUNTING CONTROL IN THE ZENON PAPYRI
TAR OC 66 VOL: 41 PG:699 - 703 :: QUAL. :PRIM. :HIST. :FIN.METH.

HAIN ,HP CIT: 0.00
CASTING THE ACCOUNT
JAR AU 67 VOL: 5 PG:154 - 163 :: QUAL. :SEC. :HIST. :MAN.DEC.CHAR.

HAINKEL,M ; FIRS: HORVITZ,JS CIT: 0.00
THE IRS SUMMONS POWER AND ITS EFFECT ON THE INDEPENDENT AUDITOR
JAA WI 81 VOL: 4 PG:114 - 127 :: QUAL. :CASE :INSTIT. :PROF.RESP.

HAIRE ,M ; FIRS: BOWMAN,EH CIT: 0.23
SOCIAL IMPACT DISCLOSURE AND CORPORATE ANNUAL REPORTS
AOS 01 76 VOL: 1 PG:11 - 22 :: DES.STAT. :PRIM. :THEORY :HRA

HAKA ,S ; FIRS: GORDON,LA ; THIR: SCHICK,AG CIT: 0.00
STRATEGIES FOR INFORMATION SYSTEMS IMPLEMENTATION: THE CASE OF ZERO BASE
    BUDGETING
AOS 02 84 VOL: 9 PG:111 - 123 :: NON-PAR. :PRIM. :OTH. :BUDG.& PLAN.

HAKA ,S ; SEC: FRIEDMAN,L ; THIR: JONES ,V CIT: 0.00
FUNCTIONAL FIXATION AND INTERFERENCE THEORY: A THEORETICAL AND EMPIRICAL
    INVESTIGATION
TAR JL 86 VOL: 61 PG:455 - 474 :: REGRESS. :LAB. :HIPS :REL.COSTS

HAKA ,SF ; SEC: GORDON,LA ; THIR: PINCHES,GE CIT: 0.50
SOPHISTICATED CAPITAL BUDGETING SELECTION TECHNIQUES AND FIRM PERFORMANCE
TAR OC 85 VOL: 60 PG:651 - 669 :: REGRESS. :PRIM. :EMH :CAP.BUDG.

HAKA ,SF CIT: 0.00
CAPITAL BUDGETING TECHNIQUES AND FIRM SPECIFIC CONTINGENCIES: A CORRELATIONAL
    ANALYSIS
AOS 01 87 VOL: 12 PG:31 - 48 :: REGRESS. :SURV. :OTH.BEH. :BUDG.& PLAN.

HAKANSSON,NH CIT: 0.00
AN INDUCED THEORY OF ACCOUNTING UNDER RISK
TAR JL 69 VOL: 44 PG:495 - 514 :: ANAL. :INT. LOG. :INF.ECO./AG. :INFO.STRUC.

HAKANSSON,NH CIT: 0.00
ON THE RELEVANCE OF PRICE-LEVEL ACCOUNTING
JAR SP 69 VOL: 7 PG:11 - 31 :: ANAL. :INT. LOG. :OTH.STAT. :VALUAT.(INFL.)

HAKANSSON,NH CIT: 0.83
INTERIM DISCLOSURE AND PUBLIC FORECASTS: AN ECONOMIC ANALYSIS AND A FRAMEWORK
    FOR CHOICE
TAR AP 77 VOL: 52 PG:396 - 416 :: ANAL. :INT. LOG. :THEORY :INT.REP.

HAKANSSON,NH CIT: 0.00
WHERE WE ARE IN ACCOUNTING: A REVIEW OF "STATEMENT ON ACCOUNTING THEORY AND
    THEORY ACCEPTANCE"
TAR JL 78 VOL: 53 PG:717 - 725 :: QUAL. :INT. LOG. :THEORY :FIN.METH.

HAKANSSON,NH CIT: 0.63
ON THE POLICIES OF ACCOUNTING DISCLOSURE AND MEASUREMENT: AN ANALYSIS OF
    ECONOMIC INCENTIVES
JAR ST 81 VOL: 19 PG:1 - 35 :: ANAL. :INT. LOG. :INSTIT. :INFO.STRUC.

HALL ,JA ; FIRS: DOWELL,CD CIT: 0.00
EDP CONTROLS WITH AUDIT COST IMPLICATIONS
JAA AU 81 VOL: 5 PG:30 - 40 :: QUAL. :SURV. :THEORY :EDP AUD.

HALL ,TP ; FIRS: ROBINSON,LA CIT: 0.00
SYSTEMS EDUCATION AND THE ACCOUNTING CURRICULUM
TAR JA 64 VOL: 39 PG:62 - 69 :: QUAL. :INT. LOG. :N/A :OTH.MANAG.

HALL ,TW CIT: 0.43
AN EMPIRICAL TEST OF THE EFFECT OF ASSET AGGREGATION ON VALUATION ACCURACY
JAR SP 82 VOL: 20 PG:139 - 151 :: ANOVA :PRIM. :OTH.STAT. :PP&E / DEPR

HALL ,TW CIT: 0.00
INFLATION AND RATES OF EXCHANGE: SUPPORT FOR SFAS NO.52
JAA SU 83 VOL: 6 PG:299 - 313 :: REGRESS. :PRIM. :THEORY :FOR.CUR.

HALL ,TW ; SEC: CASLER,DJ CIT: 0.00
USING INDEXING TO ESTIMATE CURRENT COSTS - COMPOSITE OR MULTIPLE INDEXES?
JAA SP 85 VOL: 8 PG:210 - 224 :: REGRESS. :PRIM. :THEORY :VALUAT.(INFL.)

HALL ,TW ; FIRS: CASLER,DJ CIT: 0.50
FIRM-SPECIFIC ASSET VALUATION ACCURACY USING A COMPOSITE PRICE INDEX
JAR SP 85 VOL: 23 PG:110 - 122 :: REGRESS. :SIM. :OTH.STAT. :VALUAT.(INFL.)

HALLBAUER,RC ; FIRS: AGRAWAL,SP ; THIR: PERRITT,GW CIT: 0.00
MEASUREMENT OF THE CURRENT COST OF EQUIVALENT PRODUCTIVE CAPACITY
JAA WI 80 VOL: 3 PG:163 - 173 :: ANAL. :INT. LOG. :OTH.STAT. :VALUAT.(INFL.)

HALPERIN,R CIT: 0.30
THE EFFECTS OF LIFO INVENTORY COSTING ON RESOURCE ALLOCATION: A PUBLIC POLICY
    PERSPECTIVE
TAR JA 79 VOL: 54 PG:58 - 71 :: ANAL. :INT. LOG. :N/A :INV.

HALPERIN,R ; FIRS: COHEN ,MA CIT: 0.33
OPTIMAL INVENTORY ORDER POLICY FOR A FIRM USING THE LIFO INVENTORY COSTING
    METHOD
JAR AU 80 VOL: 18 PG:375 - 389 :: ANAL. :SIM. :MATH.PROG. :INV.

HALPERIN,R ; SEC: TZUR ,J CIT: 0.00
MONETARY COMPENSATION AND NONTAXABLE EMPLOYEE BENEFITS: AN ANALYTICAL
    PERSPECTIVE
TAR OC 85 VOL: 60 PG:670 - 680 :: REGRESS. :INT. LOG. :THEORY :EXEC.COMP.

HALPERIN,R ; SEC: LANEN ,WN CIT: 0.00
THE EFFECTS OF THE THOR POWER TOOL DECISION ON THE LIFO/FIFO CHOICE
TAR AP 87 VOL: 62 PG:378 - 384 :: REGRESS. :PRIM. :EMH :INV.

HALPERIN,R ; SEC: SRINIDHI,BN CIT: 0.00
THE EFFECTS OF THE U.S. INCOME TAX REGULATIONS' TRANSFER PRICING RULES
    ON ALLOCATIVE EFFICIENCY
TAR OC 87 VOL: 62 PG:686 - 706 :: REGRESS. :INT. LOG. :THEORY :TRANS.PRIC.

HAM   ,J ; SEC: LOSELL,D ; THIR: SMIELIAUSKAS,W CIT: 0.50
AN EMPIRICAL STUDY OF ERROR CHARACTERISTICS IN ACCOUNTING POPULATIONS
TAR JL 85 VOL: 60 PG:387 - 406 :: REGRESS. :PRIM. :OTH.STAT. :ERRORS

HAMER ,MH ; FIRS: GORDON,LA CIT: 0.00
RATES OF RETURN AND CASH FLOW PROFILES: AN EXTENSION
AUD JL 88 VOL: 63 PG:514 - 521 :: DES.STAT. :INT. LOG. :THEORY :FIN.METH.

HAMILTON,RE ; SEC: WRIGHT,WF CIT: 0.43
INTERNAL CONTROL JUDGMENTS AND EFFECTS OF EXPERIENCE: REPLICATIONS AND
EXTENSIONS
JAR AU 82 VOL: 20 PG:756 - 765 :: MIXED :LAB. :HIPS :INT.CONT.

HAMLEN,SS ; SEC: HAMLEN,WA ; THIR: TSCHIRHART,JT CIT: 0.58
THE USE OF CORE THEORY IN EVALUATING JOINT COST ALLOCATION SCHEMES
TAR JL 77 VOL: 52 PG:616 - 627 :: ANAL. :INT. LOG. :MATH.PROG. :OVER.ALLOC.

HAMLEN,SS ; SEC: HAMLEN,WA ; THIR: TSCHIRHART,JT CIT: 0.11
THE USE OF THE GENERALIZED SHAPLEY ALLOCATION IN JOINT COST ALLOCATION
TAR AP 80 VOL: 55 PG:269 - 287 :: ANAL. :INT. LOG. :OTH.STAT. :COST.ALLOC.

HAMLEN,SS CIT: 0.22
A CHANCE-CONSTRAINED MIXED INTEGER PROGRAMMING MODEL FOR INTERNAL CONTROL
DESIGN
TAR OC 80 VOL: 55 PG:578 - 593 :: ANAL. :INT. LOG. :MATH.PROG. :MANAG.

HAMLEN,WA ; FIRS: HAMLEN,SS ; THIR: TSCHIRHART,JT CIT: 0.58
THE USE OF CORE THEORY IN EVALUATING JOINT COST ALLOCATION SCHEMES
TAR JL 77 VOL: 52 PG:616 - 627 :: ANAL. :INT. LOG. :MATH.PROG. :OVER.ALLOC.

HAMLEN,WA ; FIRS: HAMLEN,SS ; THIR: TSCHIRHART,JT CIT: 0.11
THE USE OF THE GENERALIZED SHAPLEY ALLOCATION IN JOINT COST ALLOCATION
TAR AP 80 VOL: 55 PG:269 - 287 :: ANAL. :INT. LOG. :OTH.STAT. :COST.ALLOC.

HAMRE ,JC ; FIRS: O'CONNOR,MC CIT: 0.00
ALTERNATIVE METHODS OF ACCOUNTING FOR LONG-TERM NONSUBSIDIARY INTERCORPORAT
INVESTMENTS IN COMMON STOCK
TAR AP 72 VOL: 47 PG:308 - 319 :: QUAL. :INT. LOG. :THEORY :BUS.COMB.

HANNUM,WH ; SEC: WASSERMAN,W CIT: 0.00
GENERAL ADJUSTMENTS AND PRICE LEVEL MEASUREMENT
TAR AP 68 VOL: 43 PG:295 - 302 :: QUAL. :INT. LOG. :THEORY :VALUAT.(INFL.)

HANSEN,DR ; SEC: SHAFTEL,TL CIT: 0.00
SAMPLING FOR INTEGRATED AUDITING OBJECTIVES
TAR JA 77 VOL: 52 PG:109 - 123 :: ANAL. :INT. LOG. :MATH.PROG. :SAMP.

HANSEN,ES CIT: 0.00
MUNICIPAL FINANCES IN PERSPECTIVE: A LOOK AT INTERJURISDICTIONAL SPENDING AND
REVENUE PATTERNS
JAR ST 77 VOL: 15 PG:156 - 201 :: QUAL. :PRIM. :INSTIT. :OTH.MANAG.

HANSEN,JV ; SEC: MESSIER JR,WF CIT: 0.00
A PRELIMINARY INVESTIGATION OF EDP-XPERT
AUD AU 86 VOL: 6 PG:109 - 123 :: ANAL. :LAB. :EXP.SYST. :EDP AUD.

HANSEN,JV ; FIRS: MESSIER JR,WF CIT: 0.00
EXPERT SYSTEMS IN AUDITING: THE STATE OF THE ART
AUD AU 87 VOL: 7 PG:94 - 105 :: REGRESS. :SURV. :EXP.SYST. :JUDG.

HANSEN,JV ; FIRS: BIGGS ,SF ; SEC: MESSIER JR,WF CIT: 0.00
A DESCRIPTIVE ANALYSIS OF COMPUTER AUDIT SPECIALISTS' DECISION MAKING
BEHAVIOR IN ADVANCED COMPUTER ENVIRONMENTS
AUD SP 87 VOL: 6 PG:1 - 21 :: REGRESS. :LAB. :HIPS :EDP AUD.

HANSON,EI CIT: 0.15
THE BUDGETARY CONTROL FUNCTION
TAR AP 66 VOL: 41 PG:239 - 243 :: QUAL. :INT. LOG. :HIPS :BUDG.& PLAN.

HARIED,AA CIT: 0.77
THE SEMANTIC DIMENSIONS OF FINANCIAL STATEMENTS
JAR AU 72 VOL: 10 PG:376 - 391 :: CORR. :LAB. :OTH.STAT. :METHOD.

HARIED,AA CIT: 0.85
MEASUREMENT OF MEANING IN FINANCIAL REPORTS
JAR SP 73 VOL: 11 PG:117 - 145 :: DES.STAT. :SURV. :OTH.BEH. :FIN.METH.

HARMELINK,PJ CIT: 0.08
AN EMPIRICAL EXAMINATION OF THE PREDICTIVE ABILITY OF ALTERNATE SETS OF
   INSURANCE COMPANY ACCOUNTING DATA
JAR SP 73 VOL: 11 PG:146 - 158 :: OTH.QUANT. :PRIM. :OTH. :OTH.C/A

HARMON,WK CIT: 0.00
EARNINGS VS. FUNDS FLOWS: AN EMPIRICAL INVESTIGATION OF MARKET REACTION
JAA AU 84 VOL: 8 PG:24 - 34 :: REGRESS. :PRIM. :EMH :FIN.METH.

HARPER JR,RM ; SEC: MISTER,WG ; THIR: STRAWSER,JR CIT: 0.00
THE IMPACT OF NEW PENSION DISCLOSURE RULES ON PERCEPTIONS OF DEBT
JAR AU 87 VOL: 25 PG:327 - 330 :: REGRESS. :LAB. :OTH.STAT. :PENS.

HARRELL,AM CIT: 0.58
THE DECISION-MAKING BEHAVIOR OF AIR FORCE OFFICERS AND THE MANAGEMENT CONTROL
   PROCESS
TAR OC 77 VOL: 52 PG:833 - 841 :: ANOVA :LAB. :HIPS :RESP.ACC.

HARRELL,AM ; SEC: KLICK ,HD CIT: 0.22
COMPARING THE IMPACT OF MONETARY AND NONMONETARY HUMAN ASSET MEASURES ON
   EXECUTIVE DECISION MAKING
AOS 04 80 VOL: 5 PG:393 - 400 :: REGRESS. :LAB. :OTH.BEH. :HRA

HARRELL,AM ; SEC: STAHL ,MJ CIT: 0.00
MCCLELLAND'S TRICHOTOMY OF NEEDS THEORY AND THE JOB SATISFACTION AND WORK
   PERFORMANCE OF CPA FIRM PROFESSIONALS
AOS 34 84 VOL: 9 PG:241 - 252 :: CORR. :LAB. :OTH.BEH. :AUD.BEH.

HARRELL,AM ; SEC: CHEWNING,EG ; THIR: TAYLOR,M CIT: 0.00
ORGANIZATIONAL-PROFESSIONAL CONFLICT AND THE JOB SATISFACTION AND TURNOVER
   INTENTIONS OF INTERNAL AUDITORS
AUD SP 86 VOL: 5 PG:111 - 121 :: REGRESS. :SURV. :OTH.BEH. :AUD.TRAIL

HARRELL,AM ; SEC: EICKHOFF,R CIT: 0.00
AUDITORS' INFLUENCE ORIENTATION AND THEIR AFFECTIVE RESPONSES TO THE BIG
   EIGHT WORK ENVIRONMENT
AUD SP 88 VOL: 07 PG:105 - 118 :: REGRESS. :SURV. :OTH.BEH. :AUD.BEH.

HARRIS,RS ; FIRS: MARSTON,F CIT: 0.00
SUITABILITY OF LEASES AND DEBT IN CORPORATE CAPITAL STRUCTURES
JAA SP 88 VOL: 03 PG:147 - 164 :: REGRESS. :PRIM. :EMH :LEASES

HARRIS,TS ; SEC: OHLSON,JA CIT: 1.00
ACCOUNTING DISCLOSURES AND THE MARKET'S VALUATION OF OIL AND GAS PROPERTIES
TAR OC 87 VOL: 62 PG:651 - 670 :: REGRESS. :PRIM. :EMH :OIL & GAS

HARRISON JR,WT ; SEC: TOMASSINI,LA ; THIR: DIETRICH,JR CIT: 0.17
THE USE OF CONTROL GROUPS IN CAPITAL MARKET RESEARCH
JAR SP 83 VOL: 21 PG:65 - 77 :: NON-PAR. :PRIM. :EMH :METHOD.

HARRISON,GL ; SEC: MCKINNON,JL CIT: 0.00
CULTURE AND ACCOUNTING CHANGE: A NEW PROSPECTIVE ON CORPORATE REPORTING
   REGULATION AND ACCOUNTING POLICY FORMULATION
AOS 03 86 VOL: 11 PG:233 - 252 :: DES.STAT. :INT. LOG. :INSTIT. :FASB SUBM.

HARRISON,PD ; SEC: WEST ,SG ; THIR: RENEAU,JH CIT: 0.00
INITIAL ATTRIBUTIONS AND INFORMATION-SEEKING BY SUPERIORS AND SUBORDINATES IN
   PRODUCTION VARIANCE INVESTIGATIONS
TAR AP 88 VOL: 63 PG:307 - 320 :: REGRESS. :LAB. :OTH.BEH. :VAR.

HARRISON,T CIT: 1.33
DIFFERENT MARKET REACTIONS TO DISCRETIONARY AND NONDISCRETIONARY ACCOUNTING
   CHANGES
JAR SP 77 VOL: 15 PG:84 - 107 :: REGRESS. :PRIM. :EMH :ACC.CHNG.

HARRISS,CL ; FIRS: DEAN J CIT: 0.00
RAILROAD ACCOUNTING UNDER THE NEW DEPRECIATION GUIDELINES AND INVESTMENT TAX
   CREDIT
TAR AP 63 VOL: 38 PG:229 - 242 :: QUAL. :INT. LOG. :THEORY :TAXES

HARTE ,GF ; SEC: OWEN ,DL CIT: 0.00
FIGHTING DE-INDUSTRIALIZATION: THE ROLE OF LOCAL GOVERNMENT SOCIAL AUDITS
AOS 02 87 VOL: 12 PG:123 - 142 :: REGRESS. :INT. LOG. :THEORY :ORG.& ENVIR.

HARTLEY,RV CIT: 0.00
OPERATIONS RESEARCH AND ITS IMPLICATIONS FOR THE ACCOUNTING PROFESSION
TAR AP 68 VOL: 43 PG:321 - 332 :: QUAL. :INT. LOG. :MATH.PROG. :MANAG.

HARTLEY,RV CIT: 0.08
SOME EXTENSIONS OF SENSITIVITY ANALYSIS
TAR AP 70 VOL: 45 PG:223 - 234 :: ANAL. :INT. LOG. :MATH.PROG. :BUDG.& PLAN.

HARTLEY,RV CIT: 0.15
DECISION MAKING WHEN JOINT PRODUCTS ARE INVOLVED
TAR OC 71 VOL: 46 PG:746 - 755 :: ANAL. :INT. LOG. :MATH.PROG. :BUDG.& PLAN.

HARVEY,DW CIT: 0.08
FINANCIAL PLANNING INFORMATION FOR PRODUCTION START-UPS
TAR OC 76 VOL: 51 PG:838 - 845 :: ANAL. :INT. LOG. :OTH.STAT. :MANAG.

HARVEY,DW ; FIRS: AMATO ,HN ; SEC: ANDERSON,EE CIT: 0.08
A GENERAL MODEL OF FUTURE PERIOD WARRANTY COSTS
TAR OC 76 VOL: 51 PG:854 - 862 :: ANAL. :INT. LOG. :OTH. :SPEC.ITEMS

HARVEY,DW ; SEC: RHODE ,JG ; THIR: MERCHANT,KA CIT: 0.20
ACCOUNTING AGGREGATION: USER PREFERENCES AND DECISION MAKING
AOS 03 79 VOL: 4 PG:187 - 210 :: ANOVA :LAB. :OTH.BEH. :N/A

HARWOOD,GB ; FIRS: BERRY ,LE ; THIR: KATZ ,JL CIT: 0.00
PERFORMANCE OF AUDITING PROCEDURES BY GOVERNMENTAL AUDITORS: SOME PRELIMINARY
   EVIDENCE
TAR JA 87 VOL: 62 PG:14 - 28 :: DES.STAT. :SURV. :OTH.STAT. :AUD.

HASEMAN,WC CIT: 0.00
AN INTERPRETIVE FRAMEWORK FOR COST
TAR OC 68 VOL: 43 PG:738 - 752 :: QUAL. :INT. LOG. :THEORY :MANAG.

HASEMAN,WD ; SEC: WHINSTON,AB CIT: 0.46
DESIGN OF A MULTIDIMENSIONAL ACCOUNTING SYSTEM
TAR JA 76 VOL: 51 PG:65 - 79 :: ANAL. :INT. LOG. :N/A :MANAG.

HASKINS,M CIT: 0.00
CLIENT CONTROL ENVIRONMENTS: AN EXAMINATION OF AUDITORS' PERCEPTIONS
TAR JL 87 VOL: 62 PG:542 - 563 :: REGRESS. :SURV. :OTH.BEH. :INT.CONT.

HASSELBACK,JR CIT: 0.00
AN EMPIRICAL EXAMINATION OF ANNUAL REPORT PRESENTATION OF THE CORPORATE
    INCOME TAX EXPENSE
TAR AP 76 VOL: 51 PG:269 - 276 :: ANOVA :INT. LOG. :INSTIT. :TAXES

HASSELDINE,CR CIT: 0.08
MIX AND YIELD VARIANCES
TAR JL 67 VOL: 42 PG:497 - 515 :: ANAL. :INT. LOG. :OTH.STAT. :VAR.

HASSELL,JM ; SEC: JENNINGS,RH CIT: 0.33
RELATIVE FORECAST ACCURACY AND THE TIMING OF EARNINGS FORECAST ANNOUNCEMENTS
TAR JA 86 VOL: 61 PG:58 - 75 :: REGRESS. :PRIM. :TIME SER. :FOREC.

HATFIELD,HR CIT: 0.00
SOME VARIATIONS IN ACCOUNTING PRACTICE IN ENGLAND, FRANCE, GERMANY AND THE
    UNITED STATES
JAR AU 66 VOL: 4 PG:169 - 182 :: QUAL. :INT. LOG. :THEORY :INT.DIFF.

HAW ,IM ; SEC: PASTENA,V ; THIR: LILIEN,S CIT: 0.00
THE ASSOCIATION BETWEEN MARKET-BASED MERGER PREMIUMS AND FIRMS' FINANCIAL
    POSITION PRIOR TO MERGER
JAA WI 87 VOL: 2 PG:24 - 42 :: REGRESS. :PRIM. :EMH :BUS.COMB.

HAW ,IM ; SEC: LUSTGARTEN,S CIT: 0.00
EVIDENCE ON INCOME MEASUREMENT PROPERTIES OF ASR NO. 190 AND SFAS NO. 33 DATA
JAR AU 88 VOL: 26 PG:331 - 352 :: REGRESS. :PRIM. :EMH :VALUAT.(INFL.)

HAWKINS,CA ; SEC: GIRARD,D CIT: 0.00
REPLACEMENT DECISIONS UNDER THE ACCELERATED COST RECOVERY SYSTEM
JAA SP 84 VOL: 7 PG:225 - 240 :: MIXED :INT. LOG. :THEORY :PP&E / DEPR

HAYES ,DC CIT: 2.75
THE CONTINGENCY THEORY OF MANAGERIAL ACCOUNTING
TAR JA 77 VOL: 52 PG:22 - 39 :: OTH.QUANT. :FIELD :OTH.STAT. :RESP.ACC.

HAYES ,DC ; FIRS: COOPER,DJ ; THIR: WOLF ,FM CIT: 0.75
ACCOUNTING IN ORGANIZED ANARCHIES: UNDERSTANDING AND DESIGNING ACCOUNTING
    SYSTEMS IN AMBIGUOUS SITUATIONS
AOS 03 81 VOL: 6 PG:175 - 192 :: QUAL. :INT. LOG. :THEORY :N/A

HAYES ,DC CIT: 2.00
ACCOUNTING FOR ACCOUNTING: A STORY ABOUT MANAGERIAL ACCOUNTING
AOS 23 83 VOL: 8 PG:241 - 250 :: QUAL. :INT. LOG. :INF.ECO./AG. :MANAG.

HAYES ,SC ; FIRS: TAUSSIG,RA CIT: 0.00
CASH TAKE-OVERS AND ACCOUNTING VALUATIONS
TAR JA 68 VOL: 43 PG:68 - 74 :: ANOVA :PRIM. :N/A :INV.

HAYYA ,JC ; FIRS: FERRARA,WL ; THIR: NACHMAN,DA CIT: 0.31
NORMALCY OF PROFIT IN THE JAEDICKE-ROBICHEK MODEL
TAR AP 72 VOL: 47 PG:299 - 307 :: ANAL. :SIM. :OTH.STAT. :C-V-P-A

HEALY ,PM CIT: 3.50
THE EFFECT OF BONUS SCHEMES ON ACCOUNTING DECISIONS
JAE AP 85 VOL: 7 PG:85 - 108 :: REGRESS. :PRIM. :OTH.STAT. :EXEC.COMP.

HEALY ,PM ; SEC: KANG ,SH ; THIR: PALEPU,KG CIT: 1.00
THE EFFECT OF ACCOUNTING PROCEDURE CHANGES ON CEOS' CASH SALARY AND
   BONUS COMPENSATION
JAE AP 87 VOL: 9 PG:7 - 34 :: REGRESS. :PRIM. :OTH.STAT. :INV.

HEARD ,JE ; SEC: BOLCE ,WJ CIT: 0.00
THE POLITICAL SIGNIFICANCE OF CORPORATE SOCIAL REPORTING IN THE U.S.A.
AOS 03 81 VOL: 6 PG:247 - 254 :: QUAL. :INT. LOG. :OTH. :HRA

HEATH ,DC ; FIRS: BILLERA,LJ ; THIR: VERRECCHIA,RE CIT: 0.25
A UNIQUE PROCEDURE FOR ALLOCATING COMMON COSTS FROM A PRODUCTION PROCESS
JAR SP 81 VOL: 19 PG:185 - 196 :: ANAL. :INT. LOG. :INF.ECO./AG. :N/A

.HEATH ,LC CIT: 0.08
DISTINGUISHING BETWEEN MONETARY AND NONMONETARY ASSETS AND LIABILITIES IN
   GENERAL PRICE-LEVEL ACCOUNTING
TAR JL 72 VOL: 47 PG:458 - 468 :: QUAL. :INT. LOG. :THEORY :VALUAT.(INFL.)

HECK ,JL ; SEC: BREMSER,WG CIT: 0.00
SIX DECADES OF THE ACCOUNTING REVIEW: A SUMMARY OF AUTHOR AND INSTITUTIONAL
   CONTRIBUTORS
TAR OC 86 VOL: 61 PG:735 - 744 :: REGRESS. :SEC. :HIST. :METHOD.

HECK ,WR CIT: 0.08
ACCOUNTING FOR WARRANTY COSTS
TAR JL 63 VOL: 38 PG:577 - 578 :: QUAL. :INT. LOG. :THEORY :SPEC.ITEMS

HEDBERG,B ; SEC: JONSSON,S CIT: 2.18
DESIGNING SEMI-CONFUSING INFORMATION SYSTEMS FOR ORGANIZATIONS IN CHANGING
   ENVIRONMENTS
AOS 01 78 VOL: 3 PG:47 - 64 :: QUAL. :INT. LOG. :OTH. :N/A

HEDLUND,G ; FIRS: HAGG ,J CIT: 0.50
"CASE STUDIES" IN ACCOUNTING RESEARCH
AOS 12 79 VOL: 4 PG:135 - 143 :: QUAL. :INT. LOG. :OTH. :METHOD.

HEEBINK,DV CIT: 0.00
THE OPTIMUM CAPITAL BUDGET
TAR JA 64 VOL: 39 PG:90 - 93 :: ANAL. :INT. LOG. :N/A :CAP.BUDG.

HEIMANN,SR ; SEC: LUSK ,EJ CIT: 0.08
DECISION FLEXIBILITY: AN ALTERNATIVE EVALUATION CRITERION
TAR JA 76 VOL: 51 PG:51 - 64 :: ANAL. :INT. LOG. :OTH.STAT. :MANAG.

HEIMANN,SR ; SEC: CHESLEY,GR CIT: 0.17
AUDIT SAMPLE SIZES FOR AGGREGATED STATEMENT ACCOUNTS
JAR AU 77 VOL: 15 PG:193 - 206 :: ANAL. :INT. LOG. :MATH.PROG. :SAMP.

HEIN ,LW CIT: 0.00
NEW BRITISH ACCOUNTING RECOMMENDATIONS
TAR AP 63 VOL: 38 PG:252 - 261 :: QUAL. :INT. LOG. :INSTIT. :FIN.METH.

HEIN ,LW CIT: 0.00
THE AUDITOR AND THE BRITISH COMPANIES ACTS
TAR JL 63 VOL: 38 PG:508 - 520 :: QUAL. :INT. LOG. :HIST. :OTH.MANAG.

HEINS ,EB CIT: 0.00
A SURVEY OF ACCOUNTING IN JUNIOR COLLEGES
TAR AP 66 VOL: 41 PG:323 - 326 :: QUAL. :SURV. :N/A :OTH.MANAG.

HEINTZ,JA CIT: 0.23
PRICE-LEVEL RESTATED FINANCIAL STATEMENTS AND INVESTMENT DECISION MAKING
TAR OC 73 VOL: 48 PG:679 - 689 :: DES.STAT. :LAB. :THEORY :VALUAT.(INFL.)

HEINTZ,JA ; FIRS: FALK ,H CIT: 0.00
ASSESSING INDUSTRY RISK BY RATIO ANALYSIS
TAR OC 75 VOL: 50 PG:758 - 779 :: NON-PAR. :PRIM. :N/A :FIN.METH.

HEINTZ,JA ; FIRS: REBELE,JE ; THIR: BRIDEN,GE CIT: 0.00
INDEPENDENT AUDITOR SENSITIVITY TO EVIDENCE RELIABILITY
AUD AU 88 VOL: 08 PG:43 - 52 :: REGRESS. :LAB. :OTH.BEH. :JUDG.

HELMKAMP,JG CIT: 0.00
TECHNICAL INFORMATION CENTER MANAGEMENT: AN ACCOUNTING DEFICIENCY
TAR JL 69 VOL: 44 PG:605 - 610 :: QUAL. :INT. LOG. :N/A :MANAG.

HENDRICKS,JA CIT: 0.54
THE IMPACT OF HUMAN RESOURCE ACCOUNTING INFORMATION AND STOCK INVESTMENT
   DECISIONS: AN EMPIRICAL STUDY
TAR AP 76 VOL: 51 PG:292 - 305 :: CORR. :LAB. :THEORY :HRA

HENDRICKS,TE ; FIRS: FIRMIN,PA ; SEC: GOODMAN,SS ; FOUR: LINN ,JJ CIT: 0.00
UNIVERSITY COST STRUCTURE AND BEHAVIOR: AN EMPIRICAL STUDY
JAR ST 68 VOL: 6 PG:122 - 155 :: DES.STAT. :SIM. :OTH.STAT. :MANAG.

HENDRICKSON,HS CIT: 0.00
SOME COMMENTS ON "DIRTY POOLING"
TAR AP 68 VOL: 43 PG:363 - 366 :: QUAL. :INT. LOG. :THEORY :REV.REC.

HENDRIKSEN,ES CIT: 0.00
PURCHASING POWER AND REPLACEMENT COST CONCEPTS - ARE THEY RELATED?
TAR JL 63 VOL: 38 PG:483 - 491 :: QUAL. :INT. LOG. :THEORY :VALUAT.(INFL.)

HENNESSY,VC CIT: 0.00
ACCOUNTING FOR PENSION LIABILITIES CREATED BY ERISA
JAA SU 78 VOL: 1 PG:317 - 330 :: QUAL. :INT. LOG. :THEORY :SPEC.ITEMS

HERBERT,L CIT: 0.00
A PERSPECTIVE OF ACCOUNTING
TAR JL 71 VOL: 46 PG:433 - 440 :: QUAL. :INT. LOG. :HIST. :OTH.MANAG.

HERRINGER,F ; FIRS: BOWER ,RS ; THIR: WILLIAMSON,JP CIT: 0.00
LEASE EVALUATION
TAR AP 66 VOL: 41 PG:257 - 265 :: ANAL. :INT. LOG. :OTH.STAT. :REL.COSTS

HERTOG,JF CIT: 0.45
THE ROLE OF INFORMATION AND CONTROL SYSTEMS IN THE PROCESS OF ORGANIZATIONAL
   RENEWAL: ROADBLOCK OR ROAD BRIDGE?
AOS 01 78 VOL: 3 PG:29 - 46 :: QUAL. :INT. LOG. :OTH.BEH. :ORG.FORM

HICKS ,EL CIT: 0.08
MATERIALITY
JAR AU 64 VOL: 2 PG:158 - 171 :: QUAL. :INT. LOG. :THEORY :MAT.

HICKS ,SA CIT: 0.00
CHOOSING THE FORM FOR BUSINESS TAX INCENTIVES
TAR JL 78 VOL: 53 PG:708 - 716 :: QUAL. :INT. LOG. :N/A :TAXES

HICKS JR,JO CIT: 0.27
AN EXAMINATION OF ACCOUNTING INTEREST GROUPS' DIFFERENTIAL PERCEPTIONS OF
    INNOVATIONS
TAR AP 78 VOL: 53 PG:371 - 388 :: ANOVA :SURV. :INSTIT. :N/A

HILKE ,JC CIT: 0.00
REGULATORY COMPLIANCE COSTS AND LIFO: NO WONDER SMALL COMPANIES HAVEN'T
    SWITCHED
JAA WI 86 VOL: 1 PG:17 - 29 :: REGRESS. :SURV. :THEORY :INV.

HILL ,HP CIT: 0.00
RATIONAL EXPECTATIONS AND ACCOUNTING PRINCIPLES
JAA WI 82 VOL: 5 PG:99 - 109 :: QUAL. :INT. LOG. :THEORY :FASB SUBM.

HILLIARD,JE ; SEC: LEITCH,RA CIT: 0.38
COST-VOLUME-PROFIT ANALYSIS UNDER UNCERTAINTY: A LOG NORMAL APPROACH
TAR JA 75 VOL: 50 PG:69 - 80 :: ANAL. :INT. LOG. :OTH.STAT. :C-V-P-A

HILLISON,WA CIT: 0.10
EMPIRICAL INVESTIGATION OF GENERAL PURCHASING POWER ADJUSTMENTS ON EARNINGS
    PER SHARE AND THE MOVEMENT OF SECURITY PRICES
JAR SP 79 VOL: 17 PG:60 - 73 :: REGRESS. :PRIM. :EMH :VALUAT.(INFL.)

HILLISON,WA ; FIRS: ARRINGTON,CE ; THIR: JENSEN,RE CIT: 0.00
AN APPLICATION OF ANALYTICAL HIERARCHY PROCESS TO MODEL EXPERT JUDGMENTS ON
    ANALYTICAL REVIEW PROCEDURES
JAR SP 84 VOL: 22 PG:298 - 312 :: OTH.QUANT. :LAB. :HIPS :ANAL.REV.

HILLMAN,AP ; FIRS: WOLK ,HI CIT: 0.08
MATERIALS MIX AND YIELD VARIANCES: A SUGGESTED IMPROVEMENT
TAR JL 72 VOL: 47 PG:549 - 555 :: ANAL. :INT. LOG. :MATH.PROG. :VAR.

HILTON,RW CIT: 0.30
THE DETERMINANTS OF COST INFORMATION VALUE: AN ILLUSTRATIVE ANALYSIS
JAR AU 79 VOL: 17 PG:411 - 435 :: ANAL. :INT. LOG. :INF.ECO./AG. :C-V-P-A

HILTON,RW CIT: 1.00
INTEGRATING NORMATIVE AND DESCRIPTIVE THEORIES OF INFORMATION PROCESSING
JAR AU 80 VOL: 18 PG:477 - 505 :: ANAL. :INT. LOG. :HIPS :OTH.MANAG.

HILTON,RW ; SEC: SWIERINGA,RJ ; THIR: HOSKIN,RE CIT: 0.88
PERCEPTION OF ACCURACY AS A DETERMINANT OF INFORMATION VALUE
JAR SP 81 VOL: 19 PG:86 - 108 :: ANOVA :LAB. :OTH.BEH. :MANAG.

HILTON,RW ; SEC: SWIERINGA,RJ CIT: 0.50
PERCEPTION OF INITIAL UNCERTAINTY AS A DETERMINANT OF INFORMATION VALUE
JAR SP 81 VOL: 19 PG:109 - 119 :: ANOVA :LAB. :HIPS :OTH.MANAG.

HILTON,RW ; SEC: SWIERINGA,RJ ; THIR: TURNER,MJ CIT: 0.00
PRODUCT PRICING, ACCOUNTING COSTS AND USE OF PRODUCT-COSTING SYSTEMS
TAR AP 88 VOL: 63 PG:195 - 218 :: REGRESS. :LAB. :OTH.BEH. :REL.COSTS

HINES ,RD CIT: 0.00
POPPER'S METHODOLOGY OF FALSIFICATIONISM AND ACCOUNTING RESEARCH
TAR OC 88 VOL: 63 PG:642 - 656 :: DES.STAT. :INT. LOG. :THEORY :METHOD.

HINES ,RD CIT: 0.00
FINANCIAL ACCOUNTING: IN COMMUNICATING REALITY, WE CONSTRUCT REALITY
AOS 03 88 VOL: 13 PG:251 - 261 :: ANOVA :INT. LOG. :THEORY :FIN.METH.

HININGS,CR ; FIRS: WILLIAMS,JJ CIT: 0.00
A NOTE ON MATCHING CONTROL SYSTEM IMPLICATIONS WITH ORGANIZATIONAL
    CHARACTERISTICS: ZBB AND MBO REVISITED
AOS 02 88 VOL: 13 PG:191 - 198 :: REGRESS. :SURV. :OTH.BEH. :BUDG.& PLAN.

HINOMOTO,H CIT: 0.15
OPTIMUM STRATEGIES FOR MANAGEMENT INFORMATION PROCESSING AND CONTROL
JAR AU 71 VOL: 9 PG:253 - 267 :: ANAL. :INT. LOG. :MATH.PROG. :MANAG.

HIRSCH JR,ML CIT: 0.27
DISAGGREGATED PROBABILISTIC ACCOUNTING INFORMATION: THE EFFECT OF SEQUENTIAL
    EVENTS ON EXPECTED VALUE MAXIMIZATION DECISIONS
JAR AU 78 VOL: 16 PG:254 - 269 :: ANOVA :LAB. :OTH.STAT. :INFO.STRUC.

HIRSCH,AJ CIT: 0.00
ACCOUNTING FOR FIXED ASSETS: A NEW PERSPECTIVE
TAR OC 64 VOL: 39 PG:972 - 978 :: QUAL. :INT. LOG. :THEORY :PP&E / DEPR

HIRSCHEY,M ; SEC: WEYGANDT,JJ CIT: 0.00
AMORTIZATION POLICY FOR ADVERTISING AND RESEARCH AND DEVELOPMENT EXPENDITURES
JAR SP 85 VOL: 23 PG:326 - 335 :: REGRESS. :PRIM. :TIME SER. :R & D

HIRSCHMAN,RW CIT: 0.00
DIRECT COSTING AND THE LAW
TAR JA 65 VOL: 40 PG:176 - 183 :: QUAL. :INT. LOG. :THEORY :INV.

HIRST ,MK CIT: 0.75
ACCOUNTING INFORMATION AND THE EVALUATION OF SUBORDINATE PERFORMANCE: A
    SITUATIONAL APPROACH
TAR OC 81 VOL: 56 PG:771 - 784 :: QUAL. :INT. LOG. :OTH.BEH. :N/A

HIRST ,MK CIT: 0.00
RELIANCE ON ACCOUNTING PERFORMANCE MEASURES, TASK UNCERTAINTY, AND
    DISFUNCTIONAL BEHAVIOR: SOME EXTENSIONS
JAR AU 83 VOL: 21 PG:596 - 605 :: REGRESS. :SURV. :OTH.BEH. :ORG.& ENVIR.

HIRST ,MK ; FIRS: BROWNELL,P CIT: 0.00
RELIANCE ON ACCT. INFO., BUDGETARY PARTICIPATION, AND TASK UNCERTAINTY: TESTS
    OF A THREE-WAY INTERACTION
JAR AU 86 VOL: 24 PG:241 - 249 :: REGRESS. :SURV. :OTH.BEH. :BUDG.& PLAN.

HIRST ,MK CIT: 0.00
THE EFFECT OF SETTING BUDGET GOALS AND TASK UNCERTAINTY ON PERFORMANCE: A
    THEORETICAL ANALYSIS
TAR OC 87 VOL: 62 PG:774 - 784 :: DES.STAT. :INT. LOG. :OTH.BEH. :BUDG.& PLAN.

HITE ,GL ; SEC: LONG ,MS CIT: 0.71
TAXES AND EXECUTIVE STOCK OPTIONS
JAE JL 82 VOL: 4 PG:3 - 14 :: QUAL. :INT. LOG. :THEORY :TAXES

HO   ,JL ; FIRS: COOPER,WW ; THIR: HUNTER,JE ; FOUR: RODGERS,RC CIT: 0.00
THE IMPACT OF THE FOREIGN CORRUPT PRACTICES ACT ON INTERNAL CONTROL PRACTICES
JAA AU 85 VOL: 9 PG:22 - 39 :: REGRESS. :SEC. :THEORY :CAP.BUDG.

HOBBS ,JB CIT: 0.00
VOLUME-MIX-PRICE/COST BUDGET VARIANCE ANALYSIS: A PROPER APPROACH
TAR OC 64 VOL: 39 PG:905 - 913 :: ANAL. :INT. LOG. :OTH.STAT. :VAR.

HOFSTEDE,G CIT: 0.63
MANAGEMENT CONTROL OF PUBLIC AND NOT-FOR-PROFIT ACTIVITIES
AOS 03 81 VOL: 6 PG:193 - 216 :: QUAL. :INT. LOG. :OTH. :BUDG.& PLAN.

HOFSTEDT,TR ; SEC: KINARD,JC CIT: 0.46
A STRATEGY FOR BEHAVIOURAL ACCOUNTING RESEARCH
TAR JA 70 VOL: 45 PG:38 - 54 :: QUAL. :INT. LOG. :OTH.BEH. :OTH.MANAG.

HOFSTEDT,TR ; SEC: WEST ,RR CIT: 0.08
THE APB, YIELD INDICES, AND PREDICTIVE ABILITY
TAR AP 71 VOL: 46 PG:329 - 337 :: DES.STAT. :PRIM. :OTH.STAT. :PENS.

HOFSTEDT,TR CIT: 0.77
SOME BEHAVIOURAL PARAMETERS OF FINANCIAL ANALYSIS
TAR OC 72 VOL: 47 PG:679 - 692 :: ANOVA :LAB. :OTH.BEH. :INFO.STRUC.

HOFSTEDT,TR CIT: 0.31
BEHAVIOURAL ACCOUNTING RESEARCH: PATHOLOGIES, PARADIGMS AND PRESCRIPTIONS
AOS 01 76 VOL: 1 PG:43 - 58 :: DES.STAT. :SEC. :OTH.BEH. :MANAG.

HOFSTEDT,TR ; SEC: HUGHES,GD CIT: 0.92
AN EXPERIMENTAL STUDY OF THE JUDGMENT ELEMENT IN DISCLOSURE DECISIONS
TAR AP 77 VOL: 52 PG:379 - 395 :: MIXED :LAB. :HIPS :INFO.STRUC.

HOGARTH,RM ; FIRS: EINHORN,HJ CIT: 1.38
BEHAVIOURAL DECISION THEORY: PROCESSES OF JUDGMENT AND CHOICE
JAR SP 81 VOL: 19 PG:1 - 31 :: QUAL. :SEC. :HIPS :N/A

HOLDER,WW ; SEC: EUDY ,KH CIT: 0.00
A FRAMEWORK FOR BUILDING AN ACCOUNTING CONSTITUTION
JAA WI 82 VOL: 5 PG:110 - 125 :: QUAL. :INT. LOG. :THEORY :FASB SUBM.

HOLDER,WW CIT: 0.17
ANALYTICAL REVIEW PROCEDURES IN PLANNING THE AUDIT: AN APPLICATION STUDY
AUD SP 83 VOL: 2 PG:100 - 108 :: DES.STAT. :LAB. :OTH. :ANAL.REV.

HOLDER,WW ; FIRS: DAROCA,FP CIT: 0.00
THE USE OF ANALYTICAL PROCEDURES IN REVIEW AND AUDIT ENGAGEMENTS
AUD SP 85 VOL: 4 PG:80 - 92 :: REGRESS. :SURV. :INSTIT. :ANAL.REV.

HOLDREN,GC CIT: 0.00
LIFO AND RATIO ANALYSIS
TAR JA 64 VOL: 39 PG:70 - 85 :: DES.STAT. :PRIM. :N/A :INV.

HOLMES,W CIT: 0.00
GOVERNMENT ACCOUNTING IN COLONIAL MASSACHUSETTS
TAR JA 79 VOL: 54 PG:47 - 57 :: QUAL. :SEC. :HIST. :FIN.METH.

HOLSTRUM,GL CIT: 0.23
THE EFFECT OF BUDGET ADAPTIVENESS AND TIGHTNESS ON MANAGERIAL DECISION
   BEHAVIOR
JAR AU 71 VOL: 9 PG:268 - 277 :: ANOVA :LAB. :OTH.BEH. :BUDG.& PLAN.

HOLSTRUM,GL ; SEC: MESSIER JR,WF CIT: 0.00
A REVIEW AND INTEGRATION OF EMPIRICAL RESEARCH ON MATERIALITY
AUD AU 82 VOL: 2 PG:45 - 63 :: QUAL. :SEC. :OTH. :MAT.

HOLT ,DL ; FIRS: DANOS ,P ; THIR: IMHOFF JR,EA CIT: 0.40
BOND RATERS' USE OF MANAGEMENT FINANCIAL FORECASTS: EXPERIMENT IN EXPERT
   JUDGEMENT
TAR OC 84 VOL: 59 PG:547 - 573 :: ANOVA :LAB. :OTH.BEH. :FOREC.

HOLT ,DL ; FIRS: DANOS ,P ; THIR: BAILEY JR,AD CIT: 0.00
THE INTERACTION OF SCIENCE AND ATTESTATION STANDARD FORMATION
AUD SP 87 VOL: 6 PG:134 - 149 :: DES.STAT. :INT. LOG. :THEORY :OPIN.

HOLT ,DL CIT: 0.00
AUDITORS AND BASE RATES REVISITED
AOS 06 87 VOL: 12 PG:571 - 578 :: REGRESS. :LAB. :HIPS :JUDG.

HOLT ,RN ; SEC: CARROLL,R CIT: 0.44
CLASSIFICATION OF COMMERCIAL BANK LOANS THROUGH POLICY CAPTURING
AOS 03 80 VOL: 5 PG:285 - 296 :: OTH.QUANT. :LAB. :HIPS :BUS.FAIL.

HOLT ,RN ; FIRS: SHOCKLEY,RA CIT: 0.50
A BEHAVIOURAL INVESTIGATION OF SUPPLIER DIFFERENTIATION IN THE MARKET FOR
   AUDIT SERVICES
JAR AU 83 VOL: 21 PG:545 - 564 :: OTH.QUANT. :LAB. :INSTIT. :ORG.

HOLTHAUSEN,RW CIT: 3.50
EVIDENCE ON THE EFFECT OF BOND COVENANTS AND MANAGEMENT COMPENSATION

CONTRACTS ON THE CHOICE OF ACCOUNTING TECHNIQUES: CASE OF DEPRECIATION SWITCH-
JAE MR 81 VOL: 3 PG:73 - 109 :: REGRESS. :PRIM. :EMH :AMOR./DEPL.

HOLTHAUSEN,RW ; SEC: LEFTWICH,RW CIT: 4.83
THE ECONOMIC CONSEQUENCES OF ACCOUNTING CHOICES: IMPLICATIONS OF COSTLY
   CONTRACTING AND MONITORING
JAE AG 83 VOL: 5 PG:77 - 117 :: QUAL. :SEC. :EMH :METHOD.

HOLTHAUSEN,RW ; FIRS: DODD ,P ; SEC: DOPUCH,N ; FOUR: LEFTWICH,R CIT: 1.60
QUALIFIED AUDIT OPINIONS AND STOCK PRICES: INFORMATION CONTENT, ANNOUNCEMENT
   DATES, AND CONCURRENT DISCLOSURES
JAE AP 84 VOL: 6 PG:3 - 38 :: REGRESS. :PRIM. :EMH :OPIN.

HOLTHAUSEN,RW ; FIRS: DOPUCH,N ; THIR: LEFTWICH,RW CIT: 0.33
ABNORMAL STOCK RETURNS ASSOCIATED WITH MEDIA DISCLOSURES OF 'SUBJECT TO'
   QUALIFIED AUDIT OPINIONS
JAE JN 86 VOL: 8 PG:93 - 118 :: REGRESS. :PRIM. :EMH :OPIN.

HOLTHAUSEN,RW ; FIRS: DOPUCH,N ; THIR: LEFTWICH,RW CIT: 0.50
PREDICTING AUDIT QUALIFICATIONS WITH FINANCIAL AND MARKET VARIABLES
TAR JL 87 VOL: 62 PG:431 - 454 :: REGRESS. :PRIM. :EMH :OPIN.

HOLTHAUSEN,RW ; SEC: VERRECCHIA,RE CIT: 0.00
THE EFFECT OF SEQUENTIAL INFORMATION RELEASES ON THE VARIANCE OF PRICE
   CHANGES IN AN INTERTEMPORAL MULTI-ASSET MARKET
JAR SP 88 VOL: 26 PG:82 - 106 :: ANAL. :INT. LOG. :INF.ECO./AG. :INFO.STRUC.

HOLZER,HP ; SEC: SCHONFELD,HM CIT: 0.00
THE GERMAN SOLUTION OF THE POST-WAR PRICE LEVEL PROBLEM
TAR AP 63 VOL: 38 PG:377 - 381 :: QUAL. :INT. LOG. :HIST. :FIN.METH.

HOLZER,HP ; SEC: SCHONFELD,HM CIT: 0.00
THE FRENCH APPROACH TO THE POST-WAR PRICE LEVEL PROBLEM
TAR AP 63 VOL: 38 PG:382 - 388 :: QUAL. :INT. LOG. :HIST. :FIN.METH.

HOLZER,HP ; SEC: SCHONFELD,HM CIT: 0.00
THE "FUNKTIONALE KONTORECHNUNG" OF WALTER THOMS
TAR AP 64 VOL: 39 PG:405 - 413 :: QUAL. :INT. LOG. :THEORY :FIN.METH.

HOLZMANN,OJ ; FIRS: COOK ,JS CIT: 0.08
CURRENT COST AND PRESENT VALUE IN INCOME THEORY
TAR OC 76 VOL: 51 PG:778 - 787 :: ANAL. :INT. LOG. :THEORY :VALUAT.(INFL.)

HOLZMANN,OJ ; SEC: MEANS ,KM CIT: 0.00
ACCOUNTING FOR SAVINGS AND LOAN MERGERS: CONFLICT AND ACCOUNTING ERROR
JAA WI 84 VOL: 7 PG:138 - 150 :: QUAL. :INT. LOG. :THEORY :BUS.COMB.

HONG ,H ; SEC: KAPLAN,RS ; THIR: MANDELKER,G CIT: 1.18
POOLING VS. PURCHASE: THE EFFECTS OF ACCOUNTING FOR MERGERS ON STOCK PRICES
TAR JA 78 VOL: 53 PG:31 - 47 :: MIXED :PRIM. :EMH :BUS.COMB.

HONIG ,LE CIT: 0.00
THEORY VS. PRACTICE: PARSIMONY AS REFEREE
JAA SP 78 VOL: 1 PG:231 - 236 :: DES.STAT. :SURV. :OTH. :METHOD.

HOPPER,T ; FIRS: BERRY ,AJ ; SEC: CAPPS ,T ; THIR: COOPER,D ; FOUR: FERGUSON,P
; SIX: LOWE ,EA CIT: 3.50
MANAGEMENT CONTROL IN AN AREA OF THE NCB: RATIONALES OF ACCOUNTING PRACTICES
    IN A PUBLIC ENTERPRISE
AOS 01 85 VOL: 10 PG:3 - 28 :: REGRESS. :FIELD :OTH.BEH. :MANAG.

HOPPER,T ; SEC: STOREY,J ; THIR: WILLMOTT,H CIT: 0.00
ACCOUNTING FOR ACCOUNTING: TOWARDS THE DEVELOPMENT OF A DIALECTICAL VIEW
AOS 05 87 VOL: 12 PG:437 - 456 :: DES.STAT. :INT. LOG. :THEORY :MANAG.

HOPPER,TM CIT: 0.11
ROLE CONFLICTS OF MANAGEMENT ACCOUNTANTS AND THEIR POSITION WITHIN
    ORGANIZATION STRUCTURES
AOS 04 80 VOL: 5 PG:401 - 412 :: NON-PAR. :FIELD :OTH.BEH. :BUDG.& PLAN.

HOPPER,TM ; FIRS: COOPER,DJ CIT: 0.00
CRITICAL STUDIES IN ACCOUNTING
AOS 05 87 VOL: 12 PG:407 - 414 :: DES.STAT. :INT. LOG. :THEORY :FIN.METH.

HOPWOOD,AG CIT: 2.08
AN EMPIRICAL STUDY OF THE ROLE OF ACCOUNTING DATA IN PERFORMANCE EVALUATION
JAR ST 72 VOL: 10 PG:156 - 182 :: MIXED :FIELD :OTH.BEH. :MAN.DEC.CHAR.

HOPWOOD,AG CIT: 1.15
LEADERSHIP CLIMATE AND THE USE OF ACCOUNTING DATA IN PERFORMANCE EVALUATION
TAR JL 74 VOL: 49 PG:485 - 495 :: NON-PAR. :FIELD :OTH.BEH. :BUDG.& PLAN.

HOPWOOD,AG CIT: 2.18
TOWARDS AN ORGANIZATIONAL PERSPECTIVE FOR THE STUDY OF ACCOUNTING AND
    INFORMATION SYSTEMS
AOS 01 78 VOL: 3 PG:3 - 14 :: QUAL. :SEC. :OTH. :AUD.BEH.

HOPWOOD,AG ; FIRS: BURCHELL,S ; SEC: CLUBB ,C ; FOUR: HUGHES,JS ; FIFT:
NAHAPIET,JE CIT: 3.89
THE ROLES OF ACCOUNTING IN ORGANIZATIONS AND SOCIETY
AOS 01 80 VOL: 5 PG:5 - 27 :: QUAL. :INT. LOG. :THEORY :N/A

HOPWOOD,AG CIT: 2.67
ON TRYING TO STUDY ACCOUNTING IN THE CONTEXTS IN WHICH IT OPERATES
AOS 23 83 VOL: 8 PG:287 - 305 :: QUAL. :INT. LOG. :THEORY :ORG.& ENVIR.

HOPWOOD,AG CIT: 1.25
THE TALE OF A COMMITTEE THAT NEVER REPORTED: DISAGREEMENTS ON INTERWINNING
ACCOUNTING WITH THE SOCIAL
AOS 03 85 VOL: 10 PG:361 - 376 :: REGRESS. :INT. LOG. :INSTIT. :FASB SUBM.

HOPWOOD,AG ; FIRS: BURCHELL,S ; SEC: CLUBB ,C CIT: 3.75
ACCOUNTING IN ITS SOCIAL CONTEXT: TOWARDS A HISTORY OF VALUE ADDED IN THE
UNITED KINGDOM
AOS 04 85 VOL: 10 PG:381 - 414 :: DES.STAT. :INT. LOG. :THEORY :HRA

HOPWOOD,AG CIT: 0.00
ACCOUNTING AND GENDER: AN INTRODUCTION
AOS 01 87 VOL: 12 PG:65 - 70 :: DES.STAT. :INT. LOG. :INSTIT. :ORG.& ENVIR.

HOPWOOD,AG CIT: 4.50
THE ARCHEOLOGY OF ACCOUNTING SYSTEMS
AOS 03 87 VOL: 12 PG:207 - 234 :: DES.STAT. :INT. LOG. :HIST. :ORG.& ENVIR.

HOPWOOD,WS ; FIRS: COLLINS,WA CIT: 1.22
A MULTIVARIATE ANALYSIS OF ANNUAL EARNINGS FORECASTS GENERATED FROM QUARTERLY
FORECASTS OF FINANCIAL ANALYSTS AND UNIVARIATE TIME-SERIES MODELS
JAR AU 80 VOL: 18 PG:390 - 406 :: ANOVA :PRIM. :TIME SER. :FOREC.

HOPWOOD,WS CIT: 0.33
THE TRANSFER FUNCTION RELATIONSHIP BETWEEN EARNINGS AND MARKET-INDUSTRY
INDICES: AN EMPIRICAL STUDY
JAR SP 80 VOL: 18 PG:77 - 90 :: MIXED :PRIM. :TIME SER. :METHOD.

HOPWOOD,WS CIT: 0.00
ON THE AUTOMATION OF THE BOX-JENKINS MODELING PROCEDURES: AN ALGORITHM WITH
AN EMPIRICAL TEST
JAR SP 80 VOL: 18 PG:289 - 296 :: MIXED :PRIM. :TIME SER. :FOREC.

HOPWOOD,WS ; SEC: MCKEOWN,JC CIT: 0.38
AN EVALUATION OF UNIVARIATE TIME-SERIES EARNINGS MODELS AND THEIR
GENERALIZATION TO A SINGLE INPUT TRANSFER FUNCTION
JAR AU 81 VOL: 19 PG:313 - 322 :: CORR. :PRIM. :TIME SER. :FOREC.

HOPWOOD,WS ; SEC: MCKEOWN,JC ; THIR: NEWBOLD,P CIT: 0.71
THE ADDITIONAL INFORMATION CONTENT OF QUARTERLY EARNINGS REPORTS:
INTERTEMPORAL DISAGGREGATION
JAR AU 82 VOL: 20 PG:343 - 349 :: REGRESS. :PRIM. :TIME SER. :INT.REP.

HOPWOOD,WS ; SEC: NEWBOLD,P ; THIR: SILHAN,PA CIT: 0.29
THE POTENTIAL FOR GAINS IN PREDICTIVE ABILITY THROUGH DISAGGREGATION:
SEGMENTED ANNUAL EARNINGS
JAR AU 82 VOL: 20 PG:724 - 732 :: DES.STAT. :PRIM. :TIME SER. :SEG.REP.

HOPWOOD,WS ; FIRS: FRECKA,TJ CIT: 0.33
THE EFFECTS OF OUTLIERS ON THE CROSS-SECTIONAL DISTRIBUTIONAL PROPERTIES OF
FINANCIAL RATIOS
TAR JA 83 VOL: 58 PG:115 - 128 :: DES.STAT. :LAB. :OTH.STAT. :METHOD.

HOPWOOD,WS ; FIRS: COLLINS,WA ; THIR: MCKEOWN,JC CIT: 0.20
THE PREDICTABILITY OF INTERIM EARNINGS OVER ALTERNATIVE QUARTERS
JAR AU 84 VOL: 22 PG:467 - 479 :: NON-PAR. :PRIM. :TIME SER. :INT.REP.

HOPWOOD,WS ; FIRS: ARRINGTON,CE ; SEC: BAILEY,CD CIT: 0.00
AN ATTRIBUTION ANALYSIS OF RESPONSIBILITY ASSESSMENT FOR AUDIT PERFORMANCE
JAR SP 85 VOL: 23 PG:1 - 20 :: REGRESS. :LAB. :OTH.BEH. :AUD.

HOPWOOD,WS ; SEC: MCKEOWN,JC CIT: 0.00
THE INCREMENTAL INFORMATIONAL CONTENT OF INTERIM EXPENSES OVER INTERIM SALES
JAR SP 85 VOL: 23 PG:161 - 174 :: REGRESS. :PRIM. :EMH :TAXES

HORNE ,JC CIT: 0.00
A LOOK AT THE LOSS CARRY-FORWARD
TAR JA 63 VOL: 38 PG:56 - 60 :: QUAL. :INT. LOG. :THEORY :TAXES

HORNGREN,CT ; SEC: SORTER,GH CIT: 0.00
AN EVALUATION OF SOME CRITICISMS OF RELEVANT COSTING
TAR AP 64 VOL: 39 PG:417 - 420 :: QUAL. :INT. LOG. :N/A :COST.ALLOC.

HORNGREN,CT CIT: 0.08
HOW SHOULD WE INTERPRET THE REALIZATION CONCEPT?
TAR AP 65 VOL: 40 PG:323 - 333 :: QUAL. :INT. LOG. :THEORY :VALUAT.(INFL.)

HORNGREN,CT CIT: 0.00
A CONTRIBUTION MARGIN APPROACH TO THE ANALYSIS OF CAPACITY UTILIZATION
TAR AP 67 VOL: 42 PG:254 - 264 :: QUAL. :INT. LOG. :N/A :VAR.

HORNGREN,CT CIT: 0.00
CAPACITY UTILIZATION AND THE EFFICIENCY VARIANCE
TAR JA 69 VOL: 44 PG:86 - 89 :: QUAL. :INT. LOG. :N/A :VAR.

HORNGREN,CT CIT: 0.08
THE ACCOUNTING DISCIPLINE IN 1999
TAR JA 71 VOL: 46 PG:1 - 11 :: QUAL. :INT. LOG. :INSTIT. :OTH.MANAG.

HORRIGAN,JO CIT: 0.00
SOME EMPIRICAL BASES OF FINANCIAL RATIO ANALYSIS
TAR JL 65 VOL: 40 PG:558 - 568 :: DES.STAT. :PRIM. :N/A :OTH.MANAG.

HORRIGAN,JO CIT: 0.69
THE DETERMINATION OF LONG-TERM CREDIT STANDING WITH FINANCIAL RATIOS
JAR ST 66 VOL: 4 PG:44 - 62 :: CORR. :PRIM. :OTH.STAT. :LTD

HORRIGAN,JO CIT: 0.00
A SHORT HISTORY OF FINANCIAL RATIO ANALYSIS
TAR AP 68 VOL: 43 PG:284 - 294 :: QUAL. :SEC. :HIST. :FIN.METH.

HORVITZ,JS ; SEC: HAINKEL,M CIT: 0.00
THE IRS SUMMONS POWER AND ITS EFFECT ON THE INDEPENDENT AUDITOR
JAA WI 81 VOL: 4 PG:114 - 127 :: QUAL. :CASE :INSTIT. :PROF.RESP.

HORVITZ,JS ; SEC: COLDWELL,S CIT: 0.00
ANALYSIS OF THE ARTHUR YOUNG DECISION AND ITS POTENTIAL IMPACT ON PUBLIC
    ACCOUNTING
JAA WI 85 VOL: 8 PG:86 - 99 :: REGRESS. :CASE :THEORY :LITIG.

HORWITZ,B ; SEC: NORMOLLE,D CIT: 0.00
FEDERAL AGENCY R&D CONTRACT AWARDS AND THE FASB RULE FOR PRIVATELY-FUNDED R&
TAR JL 88 VOL: 63 PG:414 - 435 :: REGRESS. :PRIM. :OTH.STAT. :R & D

HORWITZ,BN CIT: 0.00
DEPRECIATION AND COST STABILITY IN SOVIET ACCOUNTING
TAR OC 63 VOL: 38 PG:819 - 826 :: QUAL. :INT. LOG. :THEORY :PP&E / DEPR

HORWITZ,BN ; SEC: SHABAHANG,R CIT: 0.23
PUBLISHED CORPORATE ACCOUNTING DATA AND GENERAL WAGE INCREASES OF THE FIRM
TAR AP 71 VOL: 46 PG:243 - 252 :: CORR. :PRIM. :N/A :FIN.METH.

HORWITZ,BN ; FIRS: FRANKFURTER,GM CIT: 0.08
THE EFFECTS OF ACCOUNTING PRINCIPLES BOARD OPINION NO.15 ON EARNINGS PER
   SHARE: A SIMULATION STUDY
TAR AP 72 VOL: 47 PG:245 - 259 :: DES.STAT. :SIM. :THEORY :FIN.METH.

HORWITZ,BN ; SEC: YOUNG ,AE CIT: 0.00
AN EMPIRICAL STUDY OF ACCOUNTING POLICY AND TENDER OFFERS
JAR SP 72 VOL: 10 PG:96 - 107 :: DES.STAT. :PRIM. :OTH.STAT. :BUS.COMB.

HORWITZ,BN ; SEC: KOLODNY,R CIT: 0.00
SEGMENT REPORTING: HINDSIGHT AFTER TEN YEARS
JAA AU 80 VOL: 4 PG:20 - 35 :: QUAL. :INT. LOG. :THEORY :SEG.REP.

HORWITZ,BN ; SEC: KOLODNY,R CIT: 0.67
THE ECONOMIC EFFECTS OF INVOLUNTARY UNIFORMITY IN THE FINANCIAL REPORTING OF
   R & D EXPENDITURES
JAR ST 80 VOL: 18 PG:38 - 74 :: NON-PAR. :PRIM. :OTH. :R & D

HORWITZ,BN ; SEC: KOLODNY,R CIT: 0.13
THE IMPACT OF RULE MAKING ON R & D INVESTMENTS OF SMALL HIGH-TECHNOLOGY FIRMS
JAA WI 81 VOL: 4 PG:102 - 113 :: NON-PAR. :SURV. :THEORY :ACC.CHNG.

HORWITZ,RM CIT: 0.00
THE INVESTMENT CREDIT, "DEFERRED INCOME TAXES" AND ACCOUNTING MEASUREMENT
TAR JL 64 VOL: 39 PG:618 - 621 :: QUAL. :INT. LOG. :THEORY :TAXES

HOSKIN,KW ; SEC: MACVE ,RH CIT: 1.33
ACCOUNTING AND THE EXAMINATION: A GENEALOGY OF DISCIPLINARY POWER
AOS 02 86 VOL: 11 PG:105 - 136 :: DES.STAT. :INT. LOG. :HIST. :FASB SUBM.

HOSKIN,KW ; SEC: MACVE ,RH CIT: 0.00
THE GENESIS OF ACCOUNTABILITY: THE WEST POINT CONNECTIONS
AOS 01 88 VOL: 13 PG:37 - 73 :: DES.STAT. :INT. LOG. :THEORY :OTH.MANAG.

HOSKIN,RE ; FIRS: HILTON,RW ; SEC: SWIERINGA,RJ CIT: 0.88
PERCEPTION OF ACCURACY AS A DETERMINANT OF INFORMATION VALUE
JAR SP 81 VOL: 19 PG:86 - 108 :: ANOVA :LAB. :OTH.BEH. :MANAG.

HOSKIN,RE ; FIRS: DYCKMAN,TR ; THIR: SWIERINGA,RJ CIT: 0.57
AN ACCOUNTING CHANGE AND INFORMATION PROCESSING CHANGES
AOS 01 82 VOL: 7 PG:1 - 12 :: REGRESS. :LAB. :HIPS :ACC.CHNG.

HOSKIN,RE CIT: 0.17
OPPORTUNITY COST AND BEHAVIOR
JAR SP 83 VOL: 21 PG:78 - 95 :: ANOVA :LAB. :OTH.BEH. :REL.COSTS

HOSKIN,RE ; SEC: HUGHES,JS ; THIR: RICKS ,WE CIT: 0.67
EVIDENCE ON THE INCREMENTAL INFORMATION CONTENT OF ADDITIONAL FIRM
   DISCLOSURES MADE CONCURRENTLY WITH EARNINGS
JAR ST 86 VOL: 24 PG:1 - 36 :: REGRESS. :PRIM. :EMH :SPEC.ITEMS

HOSLER,C ; FIRS: FRIED ,D CIT: 0.00
S&LS, REPORTING CHANGES AND THE IMPACT ON THE GNMA MARKET
JAA WI 87 VOL: 2 PG:5 - 23 :: REGRESS. :PRIM. :THEORY :LTD

HOU ,C ; FIRS: FARMAN,WL CIT: 0.00
THE BALANCE OF PAYMENTS: AN ACCOUNTING ANALYSIS
TAR JA 63 VOL: 38 PG:133 - 141 :: QUAL. :INT. LOG. :THEORY :INT.DIFF.

HOUGHTON,KA ; SEC: SENGUPTA,R CIT: 0.00
THE EFFECT OF PRIOR PROBABILITY DISCLOSURE AND INFORMATION SET CONSTRUCTION
   ON BANKERS' ABILITY TO PREDICT FAILURE
JAR AU 84 VOL: 22 PG:768 - 775 :: DES.STAT. :LAB. :HIPS :BUS.FAIL.

HOUGHTON,KA CIT: 0.00
ACCOUNTING DATA AND THE PREDICTION OF BUSINESS FAILURE: THE SETTING OF PRIORS
   AND THE AGE OF DATA
JAR SP 84 VOL: 22 PG:361 - 368 :: DES.STAT. :PRIM. :OTH.BEH. :BUS.FAIL.

HOUGHTON,KA CIT: 0.00
TRUE AND FAIR VIEW: AN EMPIRICAL STUDY OF CONNOTATIVE MEANING
AOS 02 87 VOL: 12 PG:143 - 152 :: REGRESS. :LAB. :OTH.BEH. :MAN.DEC.CHAR.

HOUGHTON,KA CIT: 0.00
THE MEASUREMENT OF MEANING IN ACCOUNTING: A CRITICAL ANALYSIS OF THE
   PRINCIPAL EVIDENCE
AOS 03 88 VOL: 13 PG:263 - 280 :: REGRESS. :LAB. :OTH.BEH. :METHOD.

HOWARD,TP ; SEC: NIKOLAI,LA CIT: 0.50
ATTITUDE MEASUREMENT AND PERCEPTIONS OF ACCOUNTING FACULTY PUBLICATION OUTLET
TAR OC 83 VOL: 58 PG:765 - 776 :: DES.STAT. :SURV. :OTH. :METHOD.

HOWARD,TP ; FIRS: WILSON,ER CIT: 0.00
THE ASSOCIATION BETWEEN MUNICIPAL MARKET MEASURES AND SELECTED FINANCIAL
   REPORTING PRACTICES: ADDITIONAL EVIDENCE
JAR SP 84 VOL: 22 PG:207 - 224 :: REGRESS. :PRIM. :OTH.STAT. :N/A

HSIEH ,DA ; FIRS: LEE ,CJ CIT: 0.50
CHOICE OF INVENTORY ACCOUNTING METHODS: COMPARATIVE ANALYSES OF ALTERNATIVE
   HYPOTHESES
JAR AU 85 VOL: 23 PG:468 - 485 :: REGRESS. :PRIM. : :INV.

HUDSON,J ; FIRS: MCROBERTS,HA CIT: 0.00
AUDITING PROGRAM EVALUATIONS: THE CANADIAN CASE
AOS 04 85 VOL: 10 PG:493 - 502 :: REGRESS. :FIELD :INSTIT. :OPER.AUD.

HUDSON,RR CIT: 0.00
ACCOUNTING FOR UNEARNED DISCOUNT OF FINANCE COMPANIES
TAR OC 63 VOL: 38 PG:796 - 801 :: QUAL. :INT. LOG. :THEORY :REV.REC.

HUEFNER,RJ ; FIRS: JEN ,FC CIT: 0.15
DEPRECIATION BY PROBABILITY-LIFE
TAR AP 70 VOL: 45 PG:290 - 298 :: ANAL. :INT. LOG. :OTH.STAT. :PP&E / DEPR

HUEFNER,RJ CIT: 0.08
ANALYZING AND REPORTING SENSITIVITY DATA
TAR OC 71 VOL: 46 PG:717 - 732 :: ANAL. :INT. LOG. :OTH.STAT. :OTH.MANAG.

HUEFNER,RJ ; FIRS: GUPTA ,MC CIT: 0.23
A CLUSTER ANALYSIS STUDY OF FINANCIAL RATIOS AND INDUSTRY CHARACTERISTICS
JAR SP 72 VOL: 10 PG:77 - 95 :: OTH.QUANT. :PRIM. :OTH.STAT. :N/A

HUEFNER,RJ ; FIRS: DERSTINE,RP CIT: 0.54
LIFO-FIFO, ACCOUNTING RATIOS AND MARKET RISK
JAR AU 74 VOL: 12 PG:216 - 234 :: NON-PAR. :PRIM. :OTH. :INV.

HUEFNER,RJ ; FIRS: ARNOLD,DF CIT: 0.08
MEASURING AND EVALUATING REPLACEMENT COSTS: AN APPLICATION
JAR AU 77 VOL: 15 PG:245 - 252 :: QUAL. :FIELD :THEORY :VALUAT.(INFL.)

HUGHES,GD ; FIRS: HOFSTEDT,TR CIT: 0.92
AN EXPERIMENTAL STUDY OF THE JUDGMENT ELEMENT IN DISCLOSURE DECISIONS
TAR AP 77 VOL: 52 PG:379 - 395 :: MIXED :LAB. :HIPS :INFO.STRUC.

HUGHES,JS CIT: 0.17
OPTIMAL INTERNAL AUDIT TIMING
TAR JA 77 VOL: 52 PG:56 - 68 :: ANAL. :INT. LOG. :OTH.STAT. :TIM.

HUGHES,JS CIT: 0.18
TOWARD A CONTRACT BASIS OF VALUATION IN ACCOUNTING
TAR OC 78 VOL: 53 PG:882 - 894 :: ANAL. :INT. LOG. :THEORY :SPEC.ITEMS

HUGHES,JS ; FIRS: BROWN ,LD ; THIR: ROZEFF,MS ; FOUR: VANDERWEIDE,JH CIT: 0.00
EXPECTATIONS DATA AND THE PREDICTIVE VALUE OF INTERIM REPORTING: A COMMENT
JAR SP 80 VOL: 18 PG:278 - 288 :: REGRESS. :PRIM. :TIME SER. :FOREC.

HUGHES,JS ; FIRS: BURCHELL,S ; SEC: CLUBB ,C ; THIR: HOPWOOD,AG ; FIFT:
NAHAPIET,JE CIT: 3.89
THE ROLES OF ACCOUNTING IN ORGANIZATIONS AND SOCIETY
AOS 01 80 VOL: 5 PG:5 - 27 :: QUAL. :INT. LOG. :THEORY :N/A

HUGHES,JS ; SEC: RICKS ,WE CIT: 1.00
ACCOUNTING FOR RETAIL LAND SALES: ANALYSIS OF A MANDATED CHANGE
JAE AG 84 VOL: 6 PG:101 - 132 :: REGRESS. :PRIM. :EMH :ACC.CHNG.

HUGHES,JS ; FIRS: RICKS ,WE CIT: 0.00
MARKET REACTIONS TO A NON-DISCRETIONARY ACCOUNTING CHANGE: THE CASE OF
   LONG-TERM INVESTMENTS
TAR JA 85 VOL: 60 PG:33 - 52 :: ANOVA :PRIM. :EMH :ACC.CHNG.

HUGHES,JS ; FIRS: HOSKIN,RE ; THIR: RICKS ,WE CIT: 0.67
EVIDENCE ON THE INCREMENTAL INFORMATION CONTENT OF ADDITIONAL FIRM
   DISCLOSURES MADE CONCURRENTLY WITH EARNINGS
JAR ST 86 VOL: 24 PG:1 - 36 :: REGRESS. :PRIM. :EMH :SPEC.ITEMS

HUGHES,JS ; FIRS: CONROY, RM CIT: 0.50
DELEGATING INFORMATION GATHERING DECISIONS
TAR JA 87 VOL: 62 PG:50 - 66 :: DES.STAT. :INT. LOG. :INF.ECO./AG. :MANAG.

HUGHES,JS ; SEC: RICKS ,WE CIT: 2.00
ASSOCIATIONS BETWEEN FORECAST ERRORS AND EXCESS RETURNS NEAR TO EARNINGS
   ANNOUNCEMENTS
TAR JA 87 VOL: 62 PG:158 - 175 :: REGRESS. :PRIM. :EMH :FOREC.

HUGHES,PJ CIT: 1.33
SIGNALLING BY DIRECT DISCLOSURE UNDER ASYMMETRIC INFORMATION
JAE JN 86 VOL: 8 PG:119 - 142 :: DES.STAT. :INT. LOG. :INF.ECO./AG. :
INFO.STRUC.

HUMANN,TE ; FIRS: ARNOLD,DF CIT: 0.08
EARNINGS PER SHARE: AN EMPIRICAL TEST OF THE MARKET PARITY AND THE INVESTMENT
   VALUE METHODS
TAR JA 73 VOL: 48 PG:23 - 33 :: NON-PAR. :PRIM. :OTH.STAT. :LTD

HUME ,LJ CIT: 0.08
THE DEVELOPMENT OF INDUSTRIAL ACCOUNTING: THE BENTHAMS' CONTRIBUTION
JAR SP 70 VOL: 8 PG:21 - 33 :: QUAL. :PRIM. :HIST. :OTH.MANAG.

HUNT III,HG CIT: 0.50
POTENTIAL DETERMINANTS OF CORPORATE INVENTORY ACCOUNTING DECISIONS
JAR AU 85 VOL: 23 PG:448 - 467 :: REGRESS. :PRIM. :EMH :INV.

HUNTER,JE ; FIRS: COOPER,WW ; SEC: HO   ,JL ; FOUR: RODGERS,RC CIT: 0.00
THE IMPACT OF THE FOREIGN CORRUPT PRACTICES ACT ON INTERNAL CONTROL PRACTICES
JAA AU 85 VOL: 9 PG:22 - 39 :: REGRESS. :SEC. :THEORY :CAP.BUDG.

HUSS ,HF CIT: 0.00
A CONTINGENCY APPROACH TO ACCOUNTING FOR INCOME TAXES
JAA AU 85 VOL: 9 PG:60 - 66 :: DES.STAT. :INT. LOG. :THEORY :TAXES

HUSS ,HF ; SEC: TRADER,RL CIT: 0.00
A NOTE ON OPT. SAM. SIZE IN COMPLIANCE TESTS USING A FORMAL BAYESIAN
   DECISION-THEORETIC APPROACH FOR FINITE AND INFINITE POPULATIONS
JAR AU 86 VOL: 24 PG:394 - 399 :: DES.STAT. :SIM. :OTH.STAT. :SAMP.

HUSSEIN,ME ; SEC: KETZ ,JE CIT: 0.22
RULING ELITES OF THE FASB: A STUDY OF THE BIG EIGHT
JAA SU 80 VOL: 3 PG:354 - 367 :: DES.STAT. :SEC. :OTH.STAT. :FASB SUBM.

HUSSEIN,ME CIT: 0.25
THE INNOVATIVE PROCESS IN FINANCIAL ACCOUNTING STANDARDS SETTING
AOS 01 81 VOL: 6 PG:27 - 38 :: MIXED :SURV. :INSTIT. :FASB SUBM.

HUSSEIN,ME ; SEC: BAVISHI,VB ; THIR: GANGOLLY,JS CIT: 0.00
INTERNATIONAL SIMILARITIES AND DIFFERENCES IN THE AUDITOR'S REPORT
AUD AU 86 VOL: 6 PG:124 - 133 :: DES.STAT. :PRIM. :INSTIT. :INT.DIFF.

HYLAS ,RE ; FIRS: ASHTON,RH CIT: 0.00
INCREASING CONFIRMATION RESPONSE RATES
AUD SU 81 VOL: 1 PG:12 - 22 :: ANOVA :FIELD :OTH. :CONF.

HYLAS ,RE ; FIRS: ASHTON,RH CIT: 0.00
A STUDY OF THE RESPONSE TO BALANCE AND INVOICE CONFIRMATION REQUESTS
JAA SU 81 VOL: 4 PG:325 - 332 :: DES.STAT. :FIELD :OTH. :OPER.AUD.

HYLAS ,RE ; SEC: ASHTON,RH CIT: 0.86
AUDIT DETECTION OF FINANCIAL STATEMENT ERRORS
TAR OC 82 VOL: 57 PG:751 - 765 :: DES.STAT. :FIELD :N/A :ERRORS

HYLTON,DP CIT: 0.00
ARE CONSULTING AND AUDITING COMPATIBLE? - A CONTRARY VIEW
TAR JL 64 VOL: 39 PG:667 - 670 :: QUAL. :INT. LOG. :N/A :OTH.MANAG.

HYLTON,DP CIT: 0.00
ON MATCHING REVENUE WITH EXPENSE
TAR OC 65 VOL: 40 PG:824 - 828 :: QUAL. :INT. LOG. :THEORY :REV.REC.

ICERMAN,JD ; FIRS: LOREK ,KS ; THIR: ABDULKADER,AA CIT: 0.00
FURTHER DESCRIPTIVE AND PREDICTIVE EVIDENCE ON ALTERNATIVE TIME-SERIES MODELS
   FOR QUARTERLY EARNINGS
JAR SP 83 VOL: 21 PG:317 - 328 :: REGRESS. :PRIM. :TIME SER. :INT.REP.

IINO ,T ; FIRS: BEDFORD,NM CIT: 0.08
CONSISTENCY REEXAMINED
TAR JL 68 VOL: 43 PG:453 - 458 :: QUAL. :INT. LOG. :THEORY :OTH.FIN.ACC.

IJIRI ,Y ; SEC: LEVY ,FK ; THIR: LYON ,RC CIT: 0.15
A LINEAR PROGRAMMING MODEL FOR BUDGETING AND FINANCIAL PLANNING
JAR AU 63 VOL: 1 PG:198 - 212 :: ANAL. :INT. LOG. :MATH.PROG. :BUDG.& PLAN.

IJIRI ,Y ; FIRS: CHARNES,A ; SEC: COOPER,WW CIT: 0.08
BREAKEVEN BUDGETING AND PROGRAMMING TO GOALS
JAR SP 63 VOL: 1 PG:16 - 43 :: ANAL. :INT. LOG. :MATH.PROG. :C-V-P-A

IJIRI ,Y CIT: 0.00
AXIOMS AND STRUCTURES OF CONVENTIONAL ACCOUNTING MEASUREMENT
TAR JA 65 VOL: 40 PG:36 - 53 :: ANAL. :INT. LOG. :THEORY :FIN.METH.

IJIRI ,Y ; SEC: JAEDICKE,RK ; THIR: LIVINGSTONE,JL CIT: 0.08
THE EFFECT OF INVENTORY COSTING METHODS ON FULL AND DIRECT COSTING
JAR SP 65 VOL: 3 PG:63 - 74 :: ANAL. :INT. LOG. :THEORY :MANAG.

IJIRI ,Y ; SEC: JAEDICKE,RK CIT: 0.77
RELIABILITY AND OBJECTIVITY OF ACCOUNTING MEASUREMENTS
TAR JL 66 VOL: 41 PG:474 - 483 :: ANAL. :INT. LOG. :OTH.STAT. :OTH.FIN.ACC.

IJIRI ,Y CIT: 0.00
ON BUDGETING PRINCIPLES AND BUDGET-AUDITING STANDARDS
TAR OC 68 VOL: 43 PG:662 - 667 :: QUAL. :INT. LOG. :THEORY :AUD.

IJIRI ,Y ; SEC: KINARD,JC ; THIR: PUTNEY,FB CIT: 0.38
AN INTEGRATED EVALUATION SYSTEM FOR BUDGET FORECASTING AND OPERATING
    PERFORMANCE WITH A CLASSIFIED BUDGETING BIBLIOGRAPHY
JAR SP 68 VOL: 6 PG:1 - 28 :: QUAL. :SEC. :OTH.BEH. :BUDG.& PLAN.

IJIRI ,Y ; SEC: KAPLAN,RS CIT: 0.31
PROBABILISTIC DEPRECIATION AND ITS IMPLICATIONS FOR GROUP DEPRECIATION
TAR OC 69 VOL: 44 PG:743 - 756 :: ANAL. :INT. LOG. :OTH.STAT. :PP&E / DEPR

IJIRI ,Y ; SEC: THOMPSON,GL CIT: 0.00
APPLICATIONS OF MATHEMATICAL CONTROL THEORY TO ACCOUNTING AND BUDGETING (THE
    CONTINUOUS WHEAT TRADING MODEL)
TAR AP 70 VOL: 45 PG:246 - 258 :: ANAL. :INT. LOG. :OTH.STAT. :BUDG.& PLAN.

IJIRI ,Y ; SEC: KAPLAN,RS CIT: 0.08
SEQUENTIAL MODELS IN PROBABILISTIC DEPRECIATION
JAR SP 70 VOL: 8 PG:34 - 46 :: ANAL. :INT. LOG. :OTH.STAT. :PP&E / DEPR

IJIRI ,Y ; SEC: KAPLAN,RS CIT: 0.38
A MODEL FOR INTEGRATING SAMPLING OBJECTIVES IN AUDITING
JAR SP 71 VOL: 9 PG:73 - 87 :: CORR. :INT. LOG. :OTH. :SAMP.

IJIRI ,Y CIT: 0.00
MEASUREMENT IN CURRENT ACCOUNTING PRACTICES: A REPLY
TAR JL 72 VOL: 47 PG:510 - 526 :: QUAL. :INT. LOG. :THEORY :OTH.FIN.ACC.

IJIRI ,Y ; SEC: ITAMI ,H CIT: 0.23
QUADRATIC COST-VOLUME RELATIONSHIP AND TIMING OF DEMAND INFORMATION
TAR OC 73 VOL: 48 PG:724 - 737 :: ANAL. :INT. LOG. :OTH.STAT. :C-V-P-A

IJIRI ,Y ; FIRS: GONEDES,NJ CIT: 0.46
IMPROVING SUBJECTIVE PROBABILITY ASSESSMENT FOR PLANNING AND CONTROL IN
    TEAM-LIKE ORGANIZATIONS
JAR AU 74 VOL: 12 PG:251 - 269 :: ANAL. :INT. LOG. :INF.ECO./AG. :PROB.ELIC.

IJIRI ,Y ; FIRS: CYERT ,RM CIT: 0.15
PROBLEMS OF IMPLEMENTING THE TRUEBLOOD OBJECTIVES REPORT
JAR ST 74 VOL: 12 PG:29 - 42 :: QUAL. :INT. LOG. :THEORY :FIN.METH.

IJIRI ,Y CIT: 0.15
THE PRICE-LEVEL RESTATEMENT AND ITS DUAL INTERPRETATION
TAR AP 76 VOL: 51 PG:227 - 243 :: ANAL. :INT. LOG. :THEORY :VALUAT.(INFL.)

IJIRI ,Y CIT: 0.18
CASH-FLOW ACCOUNTING AND ITS STRUCTURE
JAA SU 78 VOL: 1 PG:331 - 348 :: QUAL. :INT. LOG. :THEORY :FIN.METH.

IJIRI ,Y ; SEC: LEITCH,RA CIT: 0.22
STEIN'S PARADOX AND AUDIT SAMPLING
JAR SP 80 VOL: 18 PG:91 - 108 :: MIXED :INT. LOG. :OTH.STAT. :N/A

IJIRI ,Y ; SEC: KELLY ,EC CIT: 0.00
MULTIDIMENSIONAL ACCOUNTING AND DISTRIBUTED DATABASES: THEIR IMPLICATIONS FOR
    ORGANIZATIONS AND SOCIETY
AOS 01 80 VOL: 5 PG:115 - 123 :: QUAL. :INT. LOG. :THEORY :INFO.STRUC.

IJIRI ,Y ; SEC: NOEL ,J CIT: 0.00
A RELIABILITY COMPARISON OF THE MEASUREMENT OF WEALTH, INCOME AND FORCE
TAR JA 84 VOL: 59 PG:52 - 63 :: ANAL. :INT. LOG. :THEORY :REV.REC.

IJIRI ,Y CIT: 0.00
A FRAMEWORK FOR TRIPLE-ENTRY BOOKKEEPING
TAR OC 86 VOL: 61 PG:745 - 760 :: DES.STAT. :INT. LOG. :THEORY :INFO.STRUC.

IMDIEKE,LF ; SEC: WEYGANDT,JJ CIT: 0.00
CLASSIFICATION OF CONVERTIBLE DEBT
TAR OC 69 VOL: 44 PG:798 - 805 :: QUAL. :INT. LOG. :THEORY :LTD

IMDIEKE,LF ; FIRS: SCHROEDER,RG CIT: 0.08
LOCAL-COSMOPOLITAN AND BUREAUCRATIC PERCEPTIONS IN PUBLIC ACCOUNTING FIRMS
AOS 01 77 VOL: 2 PG:39 - 46 :: DES.STAT. :INT. LOG. :OTH.STAT. :ORG.

IMHOFF JR,EA CIT: 0.55
THE REPRESENTATIVENESS OF MANAGEMENT EARNINGS FORECASTS
TAR OC 78 VOL: 53 PG:836 - 850 :: NON-PAR. :PRIM. :OTH. :FOREC.

IMHOFF JR,EA CIT: 0.00
EMPLOYMENT EFFECTS ON AUDITOR INDEPENDENCE
TAR OC 78 VOL: 53 PG:869 - 881 :: NON-PAR. :SURV. :INSTIT. :INDEP.

IMHOFF JR,EA CIT: 0.00
ANALYTICAL REVIEW OF INCOME ELEMENTS
JAA SU 81 VOL: 4 PG:333 - 351 :: REGRESS. :PRIM. :OTH.STAT. :ANAL.REV.

IMHOFF JR,EA ; SEC: PARE ,PV CIT: 1.00
ANALYSIS AND COMPARISON OF EARNINGS FORECAST AGENTS
JAR AU 82 VOL: 20 PG:429 - 439 :: DES.STAT. :PRIM. :TIME SER. :METHOD.

IMHOFF JR,EA ; FIRS: DANOS ,P CIT: 0.57
AUDITOR REVIEW OF FINANCIAL FORECASTS: AN ANALYSIS OF FACTORS AFFECTING
    REASONABLENESS JUDGMENTS
TAR JA 82 VOL: 57 PG:39 - 54 :: ANOVA :LAB. :OTH.BEH. :AUD.

IMHOFF JR,EA ; FIRS: DANOS ,P CIT: 0.43
FORECAST SYSTEMS, CONSTRUCTION AND ATTESTATION
AUD WI 82 VOL: 1 PG:23 - 34 :: DES.STAT. :LAB. :OTH.BEH. :FOREC.

IMHOFF JR,EA ; FIRS: DANOS ,P CIT: 0.17
FACTORS AFFECTING AUDITORS' EVALUATIONS OF FORECASTS
JAR AU 83 VOL: 21 PG:473 - 494 :: ANOVA :LAB. :OTH.BEH. :JUDG.

IMHOFF JR,EA ; SEC: LOBO ,GJ CIT: 0.40
INFORMATION CONTENT OF ANALYSTS' COMPOSITE FORECAST REVISIONS
JAR AU 84 VOL: 22 PG:541 - 554 :: REGRESS. :PRIM. :EMH :FOREC.

IMHOFF JR,EA ; FIRS: DANOS ,P ; SEC: HOLT ,DL CIT: 0.40
BOND RATERS' USE OF MANAGEMENT FINANCIAL FORECASTS: EXPERIMENT IN EXPERT
    JUDGEMENT
TAR OC 84 VOL: 59 PG:547 - 573 :: ANOVA :LAB. :OTH.BEH. :FOREC.

IMHOFF JR,EA CIT: 0.00
A COMPARISON OF ANALYSTS' ACCOUNTING QUALITY JUDGMENTS AMONG CPA FIRMS'
    CLIENTS
AUD SP 88 VOL: 07 PG:182 - 191 :: REGRESS. :SURV. :INSTIT. :ORG.

IMKE ,FJ CIT: 0.00
RELATIONSHIPS IN ACCOUNTING THEORY
TAR AP 66 VOL: 41 PG:318 - 322 :: QUAL. :INT. LOG. :THEORY :OTH.MANAG.

INGBERMAN,M ; SEC: SORTER,GH CIT: 0.00
THE ROLE OF FINANCIAL STATEMENTS IN AN EFFICIENT MARKET
JAA AU 78 VOL: 2 PG:58 - 62 :: QUAL. :INT. LOG. :INSTIT. :FIN.METH.

INGBERMAN,M CIT: 0.00
THE EVOLUTION OF REPLACEMENT COST ACCOUNTING
JAA WI 80 VOL: 3 PG:101 - 112 :: QUAL. :INT. LOG. :HIST. :VALUAT.(INFL.)

INGBERMAN,M ; FIRS: SORTER,GH CIT: 0.00
THE IMPLICIT CRITERIA FOR THE RECOGNITION, QUANTIFICATION , AND REPORTING OF
    ACCOUNTING EVENTS
JAA SP 87 VOL: 2 PG:99 - 116 :: DES.STAT. :INT. LOG. :THEORY :REV.REC.

INGRAM,RW CIT: 0.36
AN INVESTIGATION OF THE INFORMATION CONTENT OF (CERTAIN) SOCIAL
    RESPONSIBILITY DISCLOSURES
JAR AU 78 VOL: 16 PG:270 - 285 :: ANOVA :PRIM. :OTH.STAT. :HRA

INGRAM,RW ; SEC: COPELAND,RM CIT: 0.25
MUNICIPAL ACCOUNTING INFORMATION AND VOTING BEHAVIOR
TAR OC 81 VOL: 56 PG:830 - 843 :: OTH.QUANT. :PRIM. :INSTIT. :N/A

INGRAM,RW ; FIRS: COPELAND,RM CIT: 0.43
THE ASSOCIATION BETWEEN MUNICIPAL ACCOUNTING INFORMATION AND BOND RATING
    CHANGES
JAR AU 82 VOL: 20 PG:275 - 289 :: OTH.QUANT. :PRIM. :OTH.STAT. :FIN.METH.

INGRAM,RW ; SEC: COPELAND,RM CIT: 0.14
MUNICIPAL MARKET MEASURES AND REPORTING PRACTICES: AN EXTENSION
JAR AU 82 VOL: 20 PG:766 - 772 :: REGRESS. :PRIM. :OTH.STAT. :FIN.METH.

INGRAM,RW ; SEC: CHEWNING,EG CIT: 0.00
THE EFFECT OF FINANCIAL DISCLOSURE REGULATION ON SECURITY MARKET BEHAVIOR
TAR JL 83 VOL: 58 PG:562 - 580 :: REGRESS. :PRIM. :EMH :FIN.METH.

INGRAM,RW CIT: 0.60
ECONOMIC INCENTIVES AND THE CHOICE OF STATE GOVERNMENT ACCOUNTING PRACTICES
JAR SP 84 VOL: 22 PG:126 - 144 :: MIXED :PRIM. :INSTIT. :ORG.& ENVIR.

INGRAM,RW ; FIRS: FRAZIER,KB ; THIR: TENNYSON,BM CIT: 0.20
A METHODOLOGY FOR THE ANALYSIS OF NARRATIVE ACCOUNTING DISCLOSURES
JAR SP 84 VOL: 22 PG:318 - 331 :: OTH.QUANT. :PRIM. :OTH.STAT. :FOREC.

INGRAM,RW CIT: 0.25
A DESCRIPTIVE ANALYSIS OF MUNICIPAL BOND PRICE DATA FOR USE IN ACCOUNTING RESEARCH
JAR AU 85 VOL: 23 PG:595 - 618 :: REGRESS. :PRIM. :EMH :LTD

ISAACS,G ; FIRS: AIKEN ,ME ; SEC: BLACKETT,LA CIT: 0.08
MODELING BEHAVIOURAL INTERDEPENDENCIES FOR STEWARDSHIP REPORTING
TAR JL 75 VOL: 50 PG:544 - 562 :: ANAL. :INT. LOG. :THEORY :OTH.MANAG.

ISELIN,ER CIT: 0.08
CHAMBERS ON ACCOUNTING THEORY
TAR AP 68 VOL: 43 PG:231 - 238 :: QUAL. :INT. LOG. :THEORY :VALUAT.(INFL.)

ISELIN,ER CIT: 0.00
THE EFFECTS OF INFORMATION LOAD AND INFORMATION DIVERSITY ON DECISION QUALITY IN A STRUCTURED DECISION TASK
AOS 02 88 VOL: 13 PG:147 - 164 :: REGRESS. :LAB. :HIPS :INFO.STRUC.

ITAMI ,H ; FIRS: IJIRI ,Y CIT: 0.23
QUADRATIC COST-VOLUME RELATIONSHIP AND TIMING OF DEMAND INFORMATION
TAR OC 73 VOL: 48 PG:724 - 737 :: ANAL. :INT. LOG. :OTH.STAT. :C-V-P-A

ITAMI ,H CIT: 0.77
EVALUATION MEASURES AND GOAL CONGRUENCE UNDER UNCERTAINTY
JAR SP 75 VOL: 13 PG:73 - 96 :: ANAL. :INT. LOG. :INF.ECO./AG. :MANAG.

IVES ,M CIT: 0.00
THE GASB: A FRESH LOOK AT GOVERNMENTAL ACCOUNTING AND FINANCIAL REPORTING
JAA SU 85 VOL: 8 PG:253 - 268 :: DES.STAT. :INT. LOG. :THEORY :FIN.METH.

JABLONSKY,SF ; FIRS: DIRSMITH,MW CIT: 0.36
THE PATTERN OF PPB REJECTION: SOMETHING ABOUT ORGANIZATIONS, SOMETHING ABOUT PPB
AOS 34 78 VOL: 3 PG:215 - 226 :: QUAL. :INT. LOG. :THEORY :BUDG.& PLAN.

JABLONSKY,SF ; FIRS: DIRSMITH,MW CIT: 0.40
MBO, POLITICAL RATIONALITY AND INFORMATION INDUCTANCE
AOS 12 79 VOL: 4 PG:39 - 52 :: QUAL. :INT. LOG. :OTH. :N/A

JACKSON-COX,J ; SEC: THIRKELL,JE ; THIR: MCQUEENEY,J CIT: 0.00
THE DISCLOSURE OF COMPANY INFORMATION TO TRADE UNIONS: THE RELEVANCE OF THE ACAS CODE OF PRACTICE ON DISCLOSURE
AOS 34 84 VOL: 9 PG:253 - 273 :: QUAL. :SURV. :INSTIT. :N/A

JACOBS,FH CIT: 0.09
AN EVALUATION OF THE EFFECTIVENESS OF SOME COST VARIANCE INVESTIGATION MODELS
JAR SP 78 VOL: 16 PG:190 - 203 :: DES.STAT. :FIELD :OTH.STAT. :VAR.

JACOBS,FH ; SEC: MARSHALL,RM CIT: 0.00
A RECIPROCAL SERVICE COST APPROXIMATION
TAR JA 87 VOL: 62 PG:67 - 78 :: DES.STAT. :INT. LOG. :THEORY :COST.ALLOC.

JACOBSEN,LE CIT: 0.00
THE RISE OF THE PROFIT DEFERRAL NOTION - THE CONCEPT AND PRACTICE OF OPTIMEASUREMENT
TAR AP 63 VOL: 38 PG:285 - 292 :: QUAL. :INT. LOG. :THEORY :REV.REC.

JACOBSEN,LE CIT: 0.00
THE ANCIENT INCA EMPIRE OF PERU AND THE DOUBLE ENTRY ACCOUNTING CONCEPT
JAR AU 64 VOL: 2 PG:221 - 228 :: QUAL. :INT. LOG. :HIST. :N/A

JAEDICKE,RK ; FIRS: BURNS ,JS ; THIR: SANGSTER,JM CIT: 0.00
FINANCIAL REPORTING OF PURCHASE CONTRACTS USED TO GUARANTEE LARGE INVESTMENTS
TAR JA 63 VOL: 38 PG:1 - 13 :: QUAL. :INT. LOG. :THEORY :SPEC.ITEMS

JAEDICKE,RK ; SEC: ROBICHEK,AA CIT: 0.54
COST-VOLUME-PROFIT ANALYSIS UNDER CONDITIONS OF UNCERTAINTY
TAR OC 64 VOL: 39 PG:917 - 926 :: ANAL. :INT. LOG. :OTH.STAT. :C-V-P-A

JAEDICKE,RK ; FIRS: IJIRI ,Y ; THIR: LIVINGSTONE,JL CIT: 0.08
THE EFFECT OF INVENTORY COSTING METHODS ON FULL AND DIRECT COSTING
JAR SP 65 VOL: 3 PG:63 - 74 :: ANAL. :INT. LOG. :THEORY :MANAG.

JAEDICKE,RK ; FIRS: IJIRI ,Y CIT: 0.77
RELIABILITY AND OBJECTIVITY OF ACCOUNTING MEASUREMENTS
TAR JL 66 VOL: 41 PG:474 - 483 :: ANAL. :INT. LOG. :OTH.STAT. :OTH.FIN.ACC.

JAENICKE,HR CIT: 0.08
ACCOUNTING FOR RESTRICTED STOCK PLANS AND DEFERRED STOCK PLANS
TAR JA 70 VOL: 45 PG:115 - 128 :: QUAL. :INT. LOG. :N/A :STK.DIV.

JAGGI ,B ; SEC: LAU ,HS CIT: 0.38
TOWARD A MODEL FOR HUMAN RESOURCE VALUATION
TAR AP 74 VOL: 49 PG:321 - 329 :: MARKOV :INT. LOG. :OTH.STAT. :HRA

JAGGI ,B CIT: 0.36
A NOTE ON THE INFORMATION CONTENT OF CORPORATE ANNUAL EARNINGS FORECASTS
TAR OC 78 VOL: 53 PG:961 - 967 :: REGRESS. :PRIM. :EMH :FOREC.

JAIN ,PC CIT: 1.00
CROSS-SECTIONAL ASSOCIATION BETWEEN ABNORMAL RETURNS AND FIRM SPECIFIC
    VARIABLES
JAE DE 82 VOL: 4 PG:205 - 228 :: REGRESS. :PRIM. :EMH :SPEC.ITEMS

JAIN ,PC CIT: 0.00
THE IMPACT OF ACCOUNTING REGULATION ON THE STOCK MARKET: THE CASE OF OIL AND
    GAS COMPANIES - SOME ADDITIONAL RESULTS
TAR JL 83 VOL: 58 PG:633 - 638 :: REGRESS. :PRIM. :EMH :OIL & GAS

JAIN ,PC CIT: 0.00
ANALYSES OF THE DISTRIBUTION OF SECURITY MARKET MODEL PREDICTION ERRORS FOR
    DAILY RETURNS DATA
JAR SP 86 VOL: 24 PG:76 - 96 :: REGRESS. :PRIM. :EMH :METHOD.

JAIN ,PC CIT: 0.00
RELATION BETWEEN MARKET MODEL PREDICTION ERRORS AND OMITTED VARIABLES:
    A METHODOLOGICAL NOTE
JAR SP 86 VOL: 24 PG:187 - 193 :: REGRESS. :INT. LOG. :EMH :METHOD.

JAIN ,TN CIT: 0.38
ALTERNATIVE METHODS OF ACCOUNTING AND DECISION MAKING: A PSYCHO-LINGUISTICAL
    ANALYSIS
TAR JA 73 VOL: 48 PG:95 - 104 :: QUAL. :INT. LOG. :HIPS :FIN.METH.

JAMISON,RW ; FIRS: ENGLEBRECHT,TD CIT: 0.10
AN EMPIRICAL INQUIRY INTO THE ROLE OF THE TAX COURT IN THE VALUATION OF
    PROPERTY FOR CHARITABLE CONTRIBUTION PURPOSES
TAR JL 79 VOL: 54 PG:554 - 562 :: REGRESS. :PRIM. :OTH.STAT. :TAXES

JANSON,EC ; FIRS: WYER ,JC ; SEC: WHITE ,GT CIT: 0.00
AUDITS OF PUBLIC COMPANIES BY SMALLER CPA FIRMS: CLIENTS, REPORTS, AND QUALITY
AUD SP 88 VOL: 07 PG:164 - 173 :: REGRESS. :PRIM. :INSTIT. :ORG.

JARRELL,GA CIT: 0.50
PRO-PRODUCER REGULATION AND ACCOUNTING FOR ASSETS: THE CASE OF ELECTRIC
UTILITIES
JAE AG 79 VOL: 1 PG:93 - 116 :: REGRESS. :SEC. :INF.ECO./AG. :PP&E / DEPR

JARRETT,JE CIT: 0.00
NOTES ON THE ESTIMATION PROBLEM IN FINANCIAL ACCOUNTING
JAR SP 72 VOL: 10 PG:108 - 112 :: ANAL. :INT. LOG. :OTH.STAT. :N/A

JARRETT,JE CIT: 0.00
BIAS IN ADJUSTING ASSET VALUES FOR CHANGES IN THE PRICE LEVEL: AN APPLICATION
OF ESTIMATION THEORY
JAR SP 74 VOL: 12 PG:63 - 66 :: ANAL. :INT. LOG. :THEORY :VALUAT.(INFL.)

JEN ,FC ; SEC: HUEFNER,RJ CIT: 0.15
DEPRECIATION BY PROBABILITY-LIFE
TAR AP 70 VOL: 45 PG:290 - 298 :: ANAL. :INT. LOG. :OTH.STAT. :PP&E / DEPR

JENKINS,DO CIT: 0.00
ACCOUNTING FOR FUNDED INDUSTRIAL PENSION PLANS
TAR JL 64 VOL: 39 PG:648 - 653 :: QUAL. :INT. LOG. :THEORY :PENS.

JENNINGS,M ; SEC: KNEER ,DC ; THIR: RECKERS,PMJ CIT: 0.00
A REEXAMINATION OF THE CONCEPT OF MATERIALITY: VIEWS OF AUDITORS, USERS AND
OFFICERS OF THE COURT
AUD SP 87 VOL: 6 PG:104 - 115 :: REGRESS. :LAB. :OTH.BEH. :MAT.

JENNINGS,R ; SEC: STARKS,L CIT: 0.25
INFORMATION CONTENT AND THE SPEED OF STOCK PRICE ADJUSTMENT
JAR SP 85 VOL: 23 PG:336 - 350 :: REGRESS. :PRIM. :EMH :N/A

JENNINGS,R CIT: 0.00
UNSYSTEMATIC SECURITY PRICE MOVEMENTS, MANAGEMENT EARNINGS FORECASTS, AND
REVISIONS IN CONSENSUS ANALYST EARNINGS FORECASTS
JAR SP 87 VOL: 25 PG:90 - 110 :: REGRESS. :PRIM. :EMH :FOREC.

JENNINGS,RH ; FIRS: HASSELL,JM CIT: 0.33
RELATIVE FORECAST ACCURACY AND THE TIMING OF EARNINGS FORECAST ANNOUNCEMENTS
TAR JA 86 VOL: 61 PG:58 - 75 :: REGRESS. :PRIM. :TIME SER. :FOREC.

JENSEN,DL CIT: 0.08
THE ROLE OF COST IN PRICING JOINT PRODUCTS: A CASE OF PRODUCTION IN FIXED
PROPORTIONS
TAR JL 74 VOL: 49 PG:465 - 476 :: ANAL. :INT. LOG. :N/A :REL.COSTS

JENSEN,DL CIT: 0.58
A CLASS OF MUTUALLY SATISFACTORY ALLOCATIONS
TAR OC 77 VOL: 52 PG:842 - 856 :: ANAL. :INT. LOG. :MATH.PROG. :OVER.ALLOC.

JENSEN,HL ; SEC: WYNDELTS,RW CIT: 0.00
THROUGH THE LOOKING GLASS: AN EMPIRICAL LOOK AT DISCRIMINATION IN THE FEDERAL
INCOME TAX RATE STRUCTURE
TAR OC 76 VOL: 51 PG:846 - 853 :: ANAL. :SIM. :INSTIT. :OTH.MANAG.

JENSEN,MC ; SEC: ZIMMERMAN,JL CIT: 0.00
MANAGEMENT COMPENSATION AND THE MANAGERIAL LABOR MARKET
JAE AP 85 VOL: 7 PG:3 - 10 :: REGRESS. :INT. LOG. :THEORY :EXEC.COMP.

JENSEN,RE CIT: 0.46
AN EXPERIMENTAL DESIGN FOR STUDY OF EFFECTS OF ACCOUNTING VARIATIONS IN
DECISION MAKING
JAR AU 66 VOL: 4 PG:224 - 238 :: ANOVA :LAB. :HIPS :INFO.STRUC.

JENSEN,RE CIT: 0.08
A MULTIPLE REGRESSION MODEL FOR COST CONTROL - ASSUMPTIONS AND LIMITATIONS
TAR AP 67 VOL: 42 PG:265 - 273 :: REGRESS. :INT. LOG. :TIME SER. :BUDG.& PLAN.

JENSEN,RE ; SEC: THOMSEN,CT CIT: 0.00
STATISTICAL ANALYSIS IN COST MEASUREMENT AND CONTROL
TAR JA 68 VOL: 43 PG:83 - 93 :: ANAL. :INT. LOG. :OTH.STAT. :VAR.

JENSEN,RE CIT: 0.00
SENSITIVITY ANALYSIS AND INTEGER LINEAR PROGRAMMING
TAR JL 68 VOL: 43 PG:425 - 446 :: ANAL. :INT. LOG. :MATH.PROG. :BUDG.& PLAN.

JENSEN,RE CIT: 0.00
EMPIRICAL EVIDENCE FROM THE BEHAVIOURAL SCIENCES: FISH OUT OF WATER
TAR JL 70 VOL: 45 PG:502 - 508 :: QUAL. :INT. LOG. :OTH.BEH. :INFO.STRUC.

JENSEN,RE CIT: 0.08
A CLUSTER ANALYSIS STUDY OF FINANCIAL PERFORMANCE OF SELECTED BUSINESS FIRMS
TAR JA 71 VOL: 46 PG:36 - 56 :: OTH.QUANT. :PRIM. :OTH.STAT. :AUD.BEH.

JENSEN,RE ; FIRS: MANES ,RP ; SEC: PARK ,SH CIT: 0.00
RELEVANT COSTS OF INTERMEDIATE GOODS AND SERVICES
TAR JL 82 VOL: 57 PG:594 - 606 :: ANAL. :INT. LOG. :MATH.PROG. :N/A

JENSEN,RE ; FIRS: ARRINGTON,CE ; SEC: HILLISON,WA CIT: 0.00
AN APPLICATION OF ANALYTICAL HIERARCHY PROCESS TO MODEL EXPERT JUDGMENTS ON
ANALYTICAL REVIEW PROCEDURES
JAR SP 84 VOL: 22 PG:298 - 312 :: OTH.QUANT. :LAB. :HIPS :ANAL.REV.

JENTZ ,GA CIT: 0.00
THE CASE AGAINST THE PRESENT CPA COMMERCIAL LAW EXAMINATION
TAR JL 66 VOL: 41 PG:535 - 541 :: QUAL. :INT. LOG. :INSTIT. :OTH.MANAG.

JENTZ ,GA CIT: 0.00
TEN-YEAR REVIEW OF THE CPA LAW EXAMINATION
TAR AP 67 VOL: 42 PG:362 - 365 :: QUAL. :SEC. :N/A :OTH.MANAG.

JERSTON,JE CIT: 0.00
ANALYST'S VIEW OF DEFERRED INCOME TAXES
TAR OC 65 VOL: 40 PG:812 - 813 :: QUAL. :INT. LOG. :THEORY :TAXES

JEYNES,PH CIT: 0.00
A DISCIPLINE FOR INVESTMENT DECISIONS
TAR JA 65 VOL: 40 PG:105 - 118 :: QUAL. :INT. LOG. :N/A :CAP.BUDG.

JIAMBALVO,J CIT: 1.30
PERFORMANCE EVALUATION AND DIRECTED JOB EFFORT: MODEL DEVELOPMENT AND
ANALYSIS IN A CPA FIRM SETTING
JAR AU 79 VOL: 17 PG:436 - 455 :: REGRESS. :LAB. :OTH.BEH. :AUD.BEH.

JIAMBALVO,J ; FIRS: PRATT ,J CIT: 0.38
RELATIONSHIPS BETWEEN LEADER BEHAVIORS AND AUDIT TEAM PERFORMANCE
AOS 02 81 VOL: 6 PG:133 - 142 :: CORR. :FIELD :OTH.BEH. :AUD.BEH.

JIAMBALVO,J ; SEC: PRATT ,J CIT: 0.14
TASK COMPLEXITY AND LEADERSHIP EFFECTIVENESS IN CPA FIRMS
TAR OC 82 VOL: 57 PG:734 - 750 :: ANOVA :LAB. :OTH.BEH. :ORG.

JIAMBALVO,J CIT: 0.14
MEASURES OF ACCURACY AND CONGRUENCE IN THE PERFORMANCE EVALUATION OF CPA
    PERSONNEL: REPLICATION AND EXTENSIONS
JAR SP 82 VOL: 20 PG:152 - 161 :: DES.STAT. :LAB. :OTH.BEH. :ERRORS

JIAMBALVO,J ; FIRS: PRATT ,J CIT: 0.00
DETERMINANTS OF LEADER BEHAVIOR IN AN AUDIT ENVIRONMENT
AOS 04 82 VOL: 7 PG:369 - 380 :: NON-PAR. :SURV. :HIPS :AUD.BEH.

JIAMBALVO,J ; SEC: WATSON,DJ ; THIR: BAUMLER,JV CIT: 0.17
AN EXAMINATION OF PERFORMANCE EVALUATION DECISIONS IN CPA FIRM SUBUNITS
AOS 01 83 VOL: 8 PG:13 - 30 :: REGRESS. :LAB. :OTH.BEH. :ORG.

JIAMBALVO,J ; SEC: WALLER,WS CIT: 0.00
DECOMPOSITION AND ASSESSMENTS OF AUDIT RISK
AUD SP 84 VOL: 3 PG:80 - 88 :: NON-PAR. :LAB. :OTH.STAT. :RISK

JIAMBALVO,J ; SEC: WILNER,N CIT: 0.00
AUDITOR EVALUATION OF CONTINGENT CLAIMS
AUD AU 85 VOL: 5 PG:1 - 11 :: REGRESS. :SURV. :OTH.STAT. :AUD.

JIAMBALVO,J ; FIRS: BURGSTAHLER,D CIT: 0.00
SAMPLE ERROR CHARACTERISTICS AND PROJECTION OF ERROR TO AUDIT POPULATIONS
TAR AP 86 VOL: 61 PG:233 - 248 :: REGRESS. :LAB. :HIPS :ERRORS

JOHNSON,DA ; SEC: PANY ,K ; THIR: WHITE ,RA CIT: 0.00
AUDIT REPORTS AND THE LOAN DECISION: ACTIONS AND PERCEPTIONS
AUD SP 83 VOL: 2 PG:38 - 51 :: ANOVA :LAB. :OTH.BEH. :OPIN.

JOHNSON,DA ; SEC: PANY ,K CIT: 0.00
FORECASTS, AUDITOR REVIEW, AND BANK LOAN DECISIONS
JAR AU 84 VOL: 22 PG:731 - 743 :: ANOVA :LAB. :OTH.BEH. :FOREC.

JOHNSON,GL CIT: 0.00
THE MONETARY AND NONMONETARY DISTINCTION
TAR OC 65 VOL: 40 PG:821 - 823 :: QUAL. :INT. LOG. :THEORY :FIN.METH.

JOHNSON,GL CIT: 0.00
FUNDS-FLOW EQUATIONS
TAR JL 66 VOL: 41 PG:510 - 517 :: ANAL. :INT. LOG. :OTH.STAT. :FIN.METH.

JOHNSON,GL ; SEC: NEWTON,SW CIT: 0.00
TAX CONSIDERATIONS IN EQUIPMENT REPLACEMENT DECISIONS
TAR OC 67 VOL: 42 PG:738 - 746 :: ANAL. :INT. LOG. :N/A :CAP.BUDG.

JOHNSON,GL ; SEC: SIMIK ,SS CIT: 0.15
MULTIPRODUCT C-V-P ANALYSIS UNDER UNCERTAINTY
JAR AU 71 VOL: 9 PG:278 - 286 :: ANAL. :INT. LOG. :OTH.STAT. :C-V-P-A

JOHNSON,GL ; SEC: SIMIK ,SS CIT: 0.15
THE USE OF PROBABILITY INEQUALITIES IN MULTIPRODUCT C-V-P ANALYSIS UNDER
    UNCERTAINTY
JAR SP 74 VOL: 12 PG:67 - 79 :: ANAL. :INT. LOG. :OTH.STAT. :C-V-P-A

JOHNSON,GL ; FIRS: GREENBERG,RR ; THIR: RAMESH,K CIT: 0.00
EARNINGS VERSUS CASH FLOW AS A PREDICTOR OF FUTURE CASH FLOW MEASURES
JAA AU 86 VOL: 1 PG:266 - 277 :: REGRESS. :PRIM. :THEORY :SPEC.ITEMS

JOHNSON,HT CIT: 0.31
THE ROLE OF ACCOUNTING HISTORY IN THE STUDY OF MODERN BUSINESS ENTERPRISE
TAR JL 75 VOL: 50 PG:444 - 450 :: QUAL. :INT. LOG. :HIST. :OTH.MANAG.

JOHNSON,HT CIT: 0.75
TOWARD A NEW UNDERSTANDING OF NINETEENTH-CENTURY COST ACCOUNTING
TAR JL 81 VOL: 56 PG:510 - 518 :: QUAL. :INT. LOG. :HIST. :N/A

JOHNSON,HT CIT: 1.33
THE SEARCH FOR GAIN IN MARKETS AND FIRMS: A REVIEW OF THE HISTORICAL
  EMERGENCE OF MANAGEMENT ACCOUNTING SYSTEMS
AOS 23 83 VOL: 8 PG:139 - 146 :: QUAL. :INT. LOG. :HIST. :MANAG.

JOHNSON,JR ; SEC: LEITCH,RA ; THIR: NETER ,J CIT: 1.75
CHARACTERISTICS OF ERRORS IN ACCOUNTS RECEIVABLE AND INVENTORY AUDITS
TAR AP 81 VOL: 56 PG:270 - 293 :: DES.STAT. :PRIM. :OTH. :ERRORS

JOHNSON,O CIT: 0.00
CORPORATE GIVING: A NOTE ON PROFIT MAXIMIZATION AND ACCOUNTING DISCLOSURE
JAR SP 65 VOL: 3 PG:75 - 85 :: QUAL. :INT. LOG. :THEORY :N/A

JOHNSON,O CIT: 0.15
A CONSEQUENTIAL APPROACH TO ACCOUNTING FOR R&D
JAR AU 67 VOL: 5 PG:164 - 172 :: CORR. :PRIM. :TIME SER. :R & D

JOHNSON,O CIT: 0.00
SOME RESERVATIONS ON THE SIGNIFICANCE OF PROSPECTIVE INCOME DATA
TAR JL 68 VOL: 43 PG:546 - 548 :: QUAL. :INT. LOG. :THEORY :PP&E / DEPR

JOHNSON,O CIT: 0.08
TWO GENERAL CONCEPTS OF DEPRECIATION
JAR SP 68 VOL: 6 PG:29 - 37 :: ANAL. :INT. LOG. :THEORY :PP&E / DEPR

JOHNSON,O CIT: 0.15
TOWARD AN "EVENTS" THEORY OF ACCOUNTING
TAR OC 70 VOL: 45 PG:641 - 653 :: ANAL. :INT. LOG. :THEORY :FIN.METH.

JOHNSON,O CIT: 0.08
ON TAXONOMY AND ACCOUNTING RESEARCH
TAR JA 72 VOL: 47 PG:64 - 74 :: QUAL. :INT. LOG. :N/A :METHOD.

JOHNSON,O ; SEC: GUNN ,S CIT: 0.00
CONFLICT RESOLUTION: THE MARKET AND/OR ACCOUNTING?
TAR OC 74 VOL: 49 PG:649 - 663 :: QUAL. :INT. LOG. :INSTIT. :FIN.METH.

JOHNSON,O CIT: 0.00
CONTRA-EQUITY ACCOUNTING FOR R&D
TAR OC 76 VOL: 51 PG:808 - 823 :: DES.STAT. :PRIM. :THEORY :OTH. NON-C/A

JOHNSON,O CIT: 0.00
SOME IMPLICATIONS OF THE UNITED STATES CONSTITUTION FOR ACCOUNTING
  INSTITUTION ALTERNATIVES
JAR ST 81 VOL: 19 PG:89 - 119 :: QUAL. :INT. LOG. :INSTIT. :N/A

JOHNSON,PE ; FIRS: MESERVY,RD ; SEC: BAILEY JR,AD CIT: 0.00
INTERNAL CONTROL EVALUATION: A COMPUTATIONAL MODEL OF THE REVIEW PROCESS
AUD AU 86 VOL: 6 PG:44 - 74 :: DES.STAT. :LAB. :EXP.SYST. :INT.CONT.

JOHNSON,R ; FIRS: MURRAY,D CIT: 0.00
DIFFERENTIAL GAAP AND THE FASB'S CONCEPTUAL FRAMEWORK
JAA AU 83 VOL: 7 PG:4 - 15 :: QUAL. :INT. LOG. :THEORY :FASB SUBM.

JOHNSON,SB ; SEC: MESSIER JR,WF CIT: 0.00
THE NATURE OF ACCOUNTING STANDARDS SETTING: AN ALTERNATIVE EXPLANATION
JAA SP 82 VOL: 5 PG:195 - 213 :: QUAL. :INT. LOG. :INSTIT. :FASB SUBM.

JOHNSON,SB ; FIRS: BEATTY,RP CIT: 0.00
A MARKET-BASED METHOD OF CLASSIFYING CONVERTIBLE SECURITIES
JAA WI 85 VOL: 8 PG:112 - 124 :: REGRESS. :PRIM. :EMH :LTD

JOHNSON,WB CIT: 0.00
THE IMPACT OF CONFIDENCE INTERVAL INFORMATION ON PROBABILITY JUDGMENTS
AOS 04 82 VOL: 7 PG:349 - 368 :: ANOVA :LAB. :OTH.BEH. :PROB.ELIC.

JOHNSON,WB CIT: 0.17
"REPRESENTATIVENESS" IN JUDGMENTAL PREDICTIONS OF CORPORATE BANKRUPTCY
TAR JA 83 VOL: 58 PG:78 - 97 :: ANOVA :LAB. :HIPS :BUS.FAIL.

JOHNSON,WB ; SEC: MAGEE ,RP ; THIR: NAGARAJAN,NJ ; FOUR: NEWMAN,HA CIT: 0.00
AN ANALYSIS OF THE STOCK PRICE REACTION TO SUDDEN EXECUTIVE DEATHS:
    IMPLICATIONS FOR THE MANAGEMENT LABOR MARKET
JAE AP 85 VOL: 7 PG:151 - 174 :: REGRESS. :PRIM. :EMH :OTH.MANAG.

JOHNSON,WB ; SEC: DHALIWAL,DS CIT: 0.00
LIFO ABANDONMENT
JAR AU 88 VOL: 26 PG:236 - 272 :: REGRESS. :PRIM. :EMH :INV.

JOHNSON,WB ; SEC: RAMANAN,R CIT: 0.00
DISCRETIONARY ACCOUNTING CHANGES FROM "SUCCESSFUL EFFORTS" TO "FULL COST"
    METHOD
TAR JA 88 VOL: 63 PG:96 - 110 :: REGRESS. :PRIM. :OTH.STAT. :OIL & GAS

JOHNSTON,DJ ; SEC: LEMON ,WM ; THIR: NEUMANN,FL CIT: 0.00
THE CANADIAN STUDY OF THE ROLE OF THE AUDITOR
JAA SP 80 VOL: 3 PG:251 - 263 :: QUAL. :INT. LOG. :THEORY :PROF.RESP.

JOHNSTON,K ; FIRS: GRAY ,J ; SEC: WILLINGHAM,JJ CIT: 0.00
A BUSINESS GAME FOR THE INTRODUCTORY COURSE IN ACCOUNTING
TAR AP 63 VOL: 38 PG:336 - 346 :: QUAL. :INT. LOG. :OTH. :EDUC.

JOLIVET,V CIT: 0.00
THE CURRENT FRENCH APPROACH TO INVENTORY PRICE LEVEL PROBLEMS
TAR JL 64 VOL: 39 PG:689 - 692 :: QUAL. :INT. LOG. :THEORY :VALUAT.(INFL.)

JONES ,CS CIT: 0.00
AN EMPIRICAL STUDY OF THE ROLE OF MANAGEMENT ACCOUNTING SYSTEMS FOLLOWING
    TAKEOVER OR MERGER
AOS 02 85 VOL: 10 PG:177 - 200 :: REGRESS. :SURV. :THEORY :BUS.COMB.

JONES ,CS CIT: 0.00
AN EMPIRICAL STUDY OF THE EVIDENCE FOR CONTINGENCY THEORIES OF MANAGEMENT
    ACCOUNTING SYSTEMS IN CONDITIONS OF RAPID CHANGE
AOS 03 85 VOL: 10 PG:303 - 328 :: REGRESS. :SURV. :THEORY :BUS.COMB.

JONES ,V ; FIRS: HAKA ,S ; SEC: FRIEDMAN,L CIT: 0.00
FUNCTIONAL FIXATION AND INTERFERENCE THEORY: A THEORETICAL AND EMPIRICAL
    INVESTIGATION
TAR JL 86 VOL: 61 PG:455 - 474 :: REGRESS. :LAB. :HIPS :REL.COSTS

JONSON,LC ; SEC: JONSSON,B ; THIR: SVENSSON,G CIT: 0.00
THE APPLICATION OF SOCIAL ACCOUNTING TO ABSENTEEISM AND PERSONNEL TURNOVER
AOS 34 78 VOL: 3 PG:261 - 268 :: DES.STAT. :CASE :OTH.BEH. :METHOD.

JONSSON,B ; FIRS: JONSON,LC ; THIR: SVENSSON,G CIT: 0.00
THE APPLICATION OF SOCIAL ACCOUNTING TO ABSENTEEISM AND PERSONNEL TURNOVER
AOS 34 78 VOL: 3 PG:261 - 268 :: DES.STAT. :CASE :OTH.BEH. :METHOD.

JONSSON,S ; FIRS: HEDBERG,B CIT: 2.18
DESIGNING SEMI-CONFUSING INFORMATION SYSTEMS FOR ORGANIZATIONS IN CHANGING
   ENVIRONMENTS
AOS 01 78 VOL: 3 PG:47 - 64 :: QUAL. :INT. LOG. :OTH. :N/A

JONSSON,S CIT: 0.43
BUDGETARY BEHAVIOR IN LOCAL GOVERNMENT - A CASE STUDY OVER 3 YEARS
AOS 03 82 VOL: 7 PG:287 - 304 :: QUAL. :CASE :OTH. :BUDG.& PLAN.

JONSSON,S ; SEC: GRONLUND,A CIT: 0.00
LIFE WITH A SUB-CONTRACTOR: NEW TECHNOLOGY AND MANAGEMENT ACCOUNTING
AOS 05 88 VOL: 13 PG:513 - 532 :: DES.STAT. :CASE :THEORY :MANAG.

JOY ,OM ; SEC: LITZENBERGER,RH ; THIR: MCENALLY,RW CIT: 0.83
THE ADJUSTMENT OF STOCK PRICES TO ANNOUNCEMENTS OF UNANTICIPATED CHANGES IN
   QUARTERLY EARNINGS
JAR AU 77 VOL: 15 PG:207 - 225 :: REGRESS. :PRIM. :EMH :INT.REP.

JOYCE ,EJ CIT: 2.38
EXPERT JUDGMENT IN AUDIT PROGRAM PLANNING
JAR ST 76 VOL: 14 PG:29 - 60 :: ANOVA :LAB. :HIPS :PLAN.

JOYCE ,EJ ; SEC: BIDDLE,GC CIT: 1.13
ARE AUDITORS' JUDGMENTS SUFFICIENTLY REGRESSIVE?
JAR AU 81 VOL: 19 PG:323 - 349 :: ANOVA :LAB. :HIPS :PLAN.

JOYCE ,EJ ; SEC: LIBBY ,R CIT: 0.50
SOME ACCOUNTING IMPLICATIONS OF "BEHAVIOURAL DECISION THEORY: PROCESSES OF
   JUDGMENT AND CHOICE"
JAR AU 81 VOL: 19 PG:544 - 550 :: QUAL. :INT. LOG. :HIPS :MANAG.

JOYCE ,EJ ; SEC: BIDDLE,GC CIT: 1.63
ANCHORING AND ADJUSTMENT IN PROBABILISTIC INFERENCE IN AUDITING
JAR SP 81 VOL: 19 PG:120 - 145 :: ANOVA :LAB. :OTH.BEH. :DEC.AIDS

JOYCE ,EJ ; SEC: LIBBY ,R ; THIR: SUNDER,S CIT: 0.00
USING THE FASB'S QUALITATIVE CHARACTERISTICS IN ACCOUNTING POLICY CHOICES
JAR AU 82 VOL: 20 PG:654 - 675 :: DES.STAT. :SURV. :INSTIT. :FASB SUBM.

JUNG ,WO ; SEC: KWON ,YK CIT: 0.00
DISCLOSURE WHEN THE MARKET IS UNSURE OF INFORMATION ENDOWMENT OF MANAGERS
JAR SP 88 VOL: 26 PG:146 - 153 :: DES.STAT. :INT. LOG. :INF.ECO./AG. :
INFO.STRUC.

JURIS ,HA ; FIRS: DITTMAN,DA ; THIR: REVSINE,L CIT: 0.38
ON THE EXISTENCE OF UNRECORDED HUMAN ASSETS: AN ECONOMIC PERSPECTIVE
JAR SP 76 VOL: 14 PG:49 - 65 :: ANAL. :INT. LOG. :OTH.BEH. :HRA

KABBES,SM CIT: 0.00
IS ACCOUNTING MEETING THE CHALLENGE IN EUROPE?
TAR AP 65 VOL: 40 PG:395 - 400 :: QUAL. :INT. LOG. :INSTIT. :FIN.METH.

KACZKA,E ; FIRS: MORRISON,TA CIT: 0.08
A NEW APPLICATION OF CALCULUS AND RISK ANALYSIS TO COST-VOLUME-PROFIT CHANGES
TAR AP 69 VOL: 44 PG:330 - 343 :: ANAL. :INT. LOG. :OTH.STAT. :C-V-P-A

KAHN ,N ; FIRS: DAVIS ,HZ CIT: 0.00
SOME ADDITIONAL EVIDENCE ON THE LIFO-FIFO CHOICE USING REPLACEMENT COST DATA
JAR AU 82 VOL: 20 PG:738 - 744 :: NON-PAR. :PRIM. :OTH.STAT. :INV.

KAHN ,N CIT: 0.00
CORPORATE MOTIVATION FOR CONVERTIBLE BOND DEBT EXCHANGES
JAA SU 82 VOL: 5 PG:327 - 337 :: DES.STAT. :PRIM. :OTH.STAT. :LTD

KAHN ,N ; FIRS: DAVIS ,HZ ; THIR: ROZEN ,E CIT: 0.00
LIFO INVENTORY LIQUIDATIONS: AN EMPIRICAL STUDY
JAR AU 84 VOL: 22 PG:480 - 490 :: NON-PAR. :PRIM. :OTH.STAT. :INV.

KAHN ,N ; SEC: SCHIFF,A CIT: 0.00
TANGIBLE EQUITY CHANGE AND THE EVOLUTION OF THE FASB'S DEFINITION OF INCOME
JAA AU 85 VOL: 9 PG:40 - 49 :: REGRESS. :INT. LOG. :THEORY :REV.REC.

KAHN ,N ; FIRS: BILDERSEE,JS CIT: 0.00
A PRELIMINARY TEST OF THE PRESENCE OF WINDOW DRESSING: EVIDENCE FROM
  INSTITUTIONAL STOCK TRADING
JAA SU 87 VOL: 2 PG:239 - 256 :: REGRESS. :PRIM. :OTH.STAT. :INFO.STRUC.

KALINSKI,BD CIT: 0.00
A CASE OF OVER-ACCOUNTING
TAR JL 63 VOL: 38 PG:591 - 595 :: QUAL. :INT. LOG. :INSTIT. :OTH.MANAG.

KAMIN ,JY ; SEC: RONEN ,J CIT: 0.18
THE SMOOTHING ON INCOME NUMBERS: SOME EMPIRICAL EVIDENCE OF SYSTEMATIC
  DIFFERENCES AMONG MANAGEMENT AND OWNER-CONTROLLED FIRMS
AOS 02 78 VOL: 3 PG:141 - 160 :: ANOVA :PRIM. :OTH.STAT. :N/A

KANG ,SH ; FIRS: HEALY ,PM ; THIR: PALEPU,KG CIT: 1.00
THE EFFECT OF ACCOUNTING PROCEDURE CHANGES ON CEOS' CASH SALARY AND
  BONUS COMPENSATION
JAE AP 87 VOL: 9 PG:7 - 34 :: REGRESS. :PRIM. :OTH.STAT. :INV.

KANODIA,CS CIT: 0.30
RISK SHARING AND TRANSFER PRICE SYSTEMS UNDER UNCERTAINTY
JAR SP 79 VOL: 17 PG:74 - 98 :: ANAL. :INT. LOG. :MATH.PROG. :BUDG.& PLAN.

KANODIA,CS CIT: 0.00
STOCHASTIC MONITORING AND MORAL HAZARD
JAR SP 85 VOL: 23 PG:175 - 193 :: ANAL. :INT. LOG. :INF.ECO./AG. :MANAG.

KAPLAN,HG ; SEC: SOLOMON,KI CIT: 0.00
REGULATION OF THE ACCOUNTING PROFESSION IN ISRAEL
TAR JA 64 VOL: 39 PG:145 - 149 :: QUAL. :INT. LOG. :INSTIT. :OTH.MANAG.

KAPLAN,RS ; FIRS: IJIRI ,Y CIT: 0.31
PROBABILISTIC DEPRECIATION AND ITS IMPLICATIONS FOR GROUP DEPRECIATION
TAR OC 69 VOL: 44 PG:743 - 756 :: ANAL. :INT. LOG. :OTH.STAT. :PP&E / DEPR

KAPLAN,RS CIT: 0.77
OPTIMAL INVESTIGATION STRATEGIES WITH IMPERFECT INFORMATION
JAR SP 69 VOL: 7 PG:32 - 43 :: ANAL. :INT. LOG. :MATH.PROG. :VAR.

KAPLAN,RS ; FIRS: IJIRI ,Y CIT: 0.08
SEQUENTIAL MODELS IN PROBABILISTIC DEPRECIATION
JAR SP 70 VOL: 8 PG:34 - 46 :: ANAL. :INT. LOG. :OTH.STAT. :PP&E / DEPR

KAPLAN,RS ; SEC: THOMPSON,GL CIT: 0.38
OVERHEAD ALLOCATION VIA MATHEMATICAL PROGRAMMING MODELS
TAR AP 71 VOL: 46 PG:352 - 364 :: ANAL. :INT. LOG. :MATH.PROG. :OVER.ALLOC.

KAPLAN,RS ; FIRS: IJIRI ,Y CIT: 0.38
A MODEL FOR INTEGRATING SAMPLING OBJECTIVES IN AUDITING
JAR SP 71 VOL: 9 PG:73 - 87 :: CORR. :INT. LOG. :OTH. :SAMP.

KAPLAN,RS CIT: 1.46
STATISTICAL SAMPLING IN AUDITING WITH AUXILIARY INFORMATION ESTIMATORS
JAR AU 73 VOL: 11 PG:238 - 258 :: NON-PAR. :SIM. :OTH.STAT. :SAMP.

KAPLAN,RS CIT: 0.15
VARIABLE AND SELF-SERVICE COSTS IN RECIPROCAL ALLOCATION MODELS
TAR OC 73 VOL: 48 PG:738 - 748 :: ANAL. :INT. LOG. :MATH.PROG. :COST.ALLOC.

KAPLAN,RS CIT: 0.85
A STOCHASTIC MODEL FOR AUDITING
JAR SP 73 VOL: 11 PG:38 - 46 :: ANAL. :INT. LOG. :OTH.STAT. :SAMP.

KAPLAN,RS ; SEC: WELAM ,VP CIT: 0.38
OVERHEAD ALLOCATION WITH IMPERFECT MARKETS AND NONLINEAR TECHNOLOGY
TAR JL 74 VOL: 49 PG:477 - 484 :: ANAL. :INT. LOG. :MATH.PROG. :OVER.ALLOC.

KAPLAN,RS CIT: 0.38
SAMPLE SIZE COMPUTATIONS FOR DOLLAR-UNIT SAMPLING
JAR ST 75 VOL: 13 PG:126 - 133 :: ANAL. :INT. LOG. :OTH.STAT. :SAMP.

KAPLAN,RS CIT: 0.33
PURCHASING POWER GAINS ON DEBT: THE EFFECT OF EXPECTED AND UNEXPECTED
    INFLATION
TAR AP 77 VOL: 52 PG:369 - 378 :: ANAL. :INT. LOG. :THEORY :VALUAT.(INFL.)

KAPLAN,RS ; FIRS: HONG ,H ; THIR: MANDELKER,G CIT: 1.18
POOLING VS. PURCHASE: THE EFFECTS OF ACCOUNTING FOR MERGERS ON STOCK PRICES
TAR JA 78 VOL: 53 PG:31 - 47 :: MIXED :PRIM. :EMH :BUS.COMB.

KAPLAN,RS ; FIRS: DIETRICH,JR CIT: 0.43
EMPIRICAL ANALYSIS OF THE COMMERCIAL LOAN CLASSIFICATION DECISION
TAR JA 82 VOL: 57 PG:18 - 38 :: REGRESS. :PRIM. :OTH.STAT. :N/A

KAPLAN,RS CIT: 1.83
MEASURING MANUFACTURING PERFORMANCE: A NEW CHALLENGE FOR MANAGERIAL
    ACCOUNTING RESEARCH
TAR OC 83 VOL: 58 PG:686 - 705 :: QUAL. :INT. LOG. :THEORY :METHOD.

KAPLAN,RS CIT: 0.00
A FINANCIAL PLANNING MODEL FOR AN ANALYTIC REVIEW: THE CASE OF A SAVINGS AND
AUD SP 83 VOL: 2 PG:52 - 65 :: REGRESS. :CASE :OTH.STAT. :ANAL.REV.

KAPLAN,RS CIT: 3.40
THE EVOLUTION OF MANAGEMENT ACCOUNTING
TAR JL 84 VOL: 59 PG:390 - 418 :: QUAL. :INT. LOG. :THEORY :MANAG.

KAPLAN,RS CIT: 1.00
THE ROLE FOR EMPIRICAL RESEARCH IN MANAGEMENT ACCOUNTING
AOS 45 86 VOL: 11 PG:429 - 452 :: REGRESS. :INT. LOG. :THEORY :METHOD.

KAPLAN,SE ; SEC: RECKERS,PMJ CIT: 0.00
AN EMPIRICAL EXAMINATION OF AUDITORS' INITIAL PLANNING PROCESSES
AUD AU 84 VOL: 4 PG:1 - 19 :: ANOVA :LAB. :OTH.BEH. :PLAN.

KAPLAN,SE CIT: 0.00
AN EXAMINATION OF THE EFFECTS OF ENVIRONMENT AND EXPLICIT INTERNAL CONTROL
EVALUATION ON PLANNED AUDIT HOURS
AUD AU 85 VOL: 5 PG:12 - 25 :: REGRESS. :LAB. :OTH.STAT. :PLAN.

KAPLAN,SE CIT: 0.00
THE EFFECT OF COMBINING COMPLIANCE AND SUBSTANTIVE TASKS ON AUDITOR C
JAR AU 85 VOL: 23 PG:871 - 877 :: REGRESS. :LAB. :HIPS :INT.CONT.

KAPLAN,SE ; SEC: RECKERS,PMJ ; THIR: ROARK ,SJ CIT: 0.00
AN ATTRIBUTION THEORY ANALYSIS OF TAX EVASION RELATED JUDGMENTS
AOS 04 88 VOL: 13 PG:371 - 379 :: REGRESS. :LAB. :OTH.BEH. :TAXES

KARAN ,V ; FIRS: BROWN ,PR CIT: 0.00
ONE APPROACH FOR ASSESSING THE OPERATIONAL NATURE OF AUDITING STANDARDS: AN
ANALYSIS OF SAS NO. 9
AUD AU 86 VOL: 6 PG:134 - 147 :: ANOVA :LAB. :INSTIT. :INT.AUD.

KARLINSKY,SS CIT: 0.00
NEW TAX LAWS IMPACT ON CORPORATE FINANCIAL REPORTING
JAA AU 83 VOL: 7 PG:65 - 76 :: QUAL. :INT. LOG. :THEORY :TAXES

KARLINSKY,SS CIT: 0.00
CAPITAL GAINS PROVISIONS: CHANGED BY THE TAX ACT OF 1981, BUT NO LESS COMPLEX
JAA WI 83 VOL: 6 PG:157 - 167 :: QUAL. :INT. LOG. :THEORY :TAXES

KATZ ,BG ; SEC: OWEN J · CIT: 0.00
INITIAL PUBLIC OFFERINGS: AN EQUILIBRIUM MODEL OF PRICE DETERMINATION
JAA SU 87 VOL: 2 PG:266 - 298 :: DES.STAT. :INT. LOG. :THEORY :SPEC.ITEMS

KATZ ,JL ; FIRS: BERRY ,LE ; SEC: HARWOOD,GB CIT: 0.00
PERFORMANCE OF AUDITING PROCEDURES BY GOVERNMENTAL AUDITORS: SOME PRELIMINAR
EVIDENCE
TAR JA 87 VOL: 62 PG:14 - 28 :: DES.STAT. :SURV. :OTH.STAT. :AUD.

KAUFMAN,F CIT: 0.00
PROFESSIONAL CONSULTING BY CPA'S
TAR OC 67 VOL: 42 PG:713 - 720 :: QUAL. :INT. LOG. :INSTIT. :OTH.MANAG.

KAY ,RS CIT: 0.00
THE COHEN COMMISSION REPORT: SOME COMPLIMENTS, SOME CRITICISMS
JAA SU 79 VOL: 2 PG:307 - 315 :: QUAL. :INT. LOG. :INSTIT. :AUD.

KEE ,R ; FIRS: BUBLITZ,B CIT: 0.00
DO WE NEED SUNSET REQUIREMENTS FOR FASB PRONOUNCEMENTS?
JAA WI 84 VOL: 7 PG:123 - 137 :: QUAL. :INT. LOG. :INSTIT. :FASB SUBM.

KEISTER JR,OR CIT: 0.00
COMMERCIAL RECORD-KEEPING IN ANCIENT MESOPOTAMIA
TAR AP 63 VOL: 38 PG:371 - 376 :: QUAL. :INT. LOG. :HIST. :OTH.MANAG.

KEISTER JR,OR CIT: 0.00
THE INCAN QUIPU
TAR AP 64 VOL: 39 PG:414 - 416 :: QUAL. :INT. LOG. :HIST. :FIN.METH.

KEKRE ,S ; FIRS: BANKER,RD ; SEC: DATAR ,SM CIT: 0.00
RELEVANT COSTS, CONGESTION AND STOCHASTICITY IN PRODUCTION ENVIRONMENTS
JAE JL 88 VOL: 10 PG:171 - 197 :: DES.STAT. :INT. LOG. :OTH.STAT. :REL.COSTS

KELL ,WG CIT: 0.00
PUBLIC ACCOUNTING'S IRRESISTIBLE FORCE AND IMMOVABLE OBJECT
TAR AP 68 VOL: 43 PG:266 - 273 :: QUAL. :INT. LOG. :INSTIT. :INDEP.

KELLER,SB ; SEC: DAVIDSON,LF CIT: 0.33
AN ASSESSMENT OF INDIVIDUAL INVESTOR REACTION TO CERTAIN QUALIFIED AUDIT
    OPINIONS
AUD AU 83 VOL: 3 PG:1 - 22 :: ANOVA :PRIM. :EMH :OPIN.

KELLER,TF CIT: 0.00
THE INVESTMENT TAX CREDIT AND THE ANNUAL TAX CHARGE
TAR JA 65 VOL: 40 PG:184 - 189 :: QUAL. :INT. LOG. :THEORY :TAXES

KELLER,TF ; FIRS: COOPER,WW ; SEC: DOPUCH,N CIT: 0.08
BUDGETARY DISCLOSURE AND OTHER SUGGESTIONS FOR IMPROVING ACCOUNTING REPORTS
TAR OC 68 VOL: 43 PG:640 - 648 :: QUAL. :INT. LOG. :THEORY :FIN.METH.

KELLEY,EM ; FIRS: FITZGERALD,RD CIT: 0.00
INTERNATIONAL DISCLOSURE STANDARDS - THE UNITED NATIONS POSITION
JAA AU 79 VOL: 3 PG:5 - 20 :: QUAL. :INT. LOG. :INSTIT. :INT.DIFF.

KELLOGG,RL CIT: 0.20
ACCOUNTING ACTIVITIES, SECURITY PRICES, AND CLASS ACTION LAWSUITS
JAE DE 84 VOL: 6 PG:185 - 204 :: REGRESS. :PRIM. :EMH :LITIG.

KELLY ,EC ; FIRS: IJIRI ,Y CIT: 0.00
MULTIDIMENSIONAL ACCOUNTING AND DISTRIBUTED DATABASES: THEIR IMPLICATIONS FOR
    ORGANIZATIONS AND SOCIETY
AOS 01 80 VOL: 5 PG:115 - 123 :: QUAL. :INT. LOG. :THEORY :INFO.STRUC.

KELLY ,LK CIT: 0.25
THE RISK FACTOR IN MATERIALITY DECISIONS
TAR JA 77 VOL: 52 PG:97 - 108 :: DES.STAT. :LAB. :THEORY :MAT.

KELLY ,LK CIT: 0.08
THE RISK FACTOR IN MATERIALITY DECISIONS
TAR JA 77 VOL: 52 PG:97 - 108 :: DES.STAT. :LAB. :THEORY :MAT.

KELLY ,LK CIT: 0.11
A SOCIOLOGICAL INVESTIGATION OF THE U.S.A. MANDATE FOR REPLACEMENT COST
    DISCLOSURES
AOS 03 80 VOL: 5 PG:311 - 322 :: OTH.QUANT. :PRIM. :OTH.STAT. :VALUAT.(INFL.)

KELLY ,R CIT: 0.25
CORPORATE MANAGEMENT LOBBYING ON FAS NO. 8: SOME FURTHER EVIDENCE
JAR AU 85 VOL: 23 PG:619 - 632 :: REGRESS. :PRIM. :THEORY :FASB SUBM.

KELSEY,RL ; FIRS: RHODE ,JG ; SEC: WHITSELL,GM CIT: 0.31
AN ANALYSIS OF CLIENT-INDUSTRY CONCENTRATIONS FOR LARGE PUBLIC ACCOUNTING
    FIRMS
TAR OC 74 VOL: 49 PG:772 - 787 :: DES.STAT. :PRIM. :INSTIT. :AUD.

KEMP ,PS CIT: 0.00
CONTROVERSIES ON THE CONSTRUCTION OF FINANCIAL STATEMENTS
TAR JA 63 VOL: 38 PG:126 - 132 :: QUAL. :INT. LOG. :THEORY :N/A

KEMP ,PS CIT: 0.08
THE AUTHORITY OF THE ACCOUNTING PRINCIPLES BOARD
TAR OC 65 VOL: 40 PG:782 - 787 :: QUAL. :INT. LOG. :INSTIT. :FIN.METH.

KEMPER,EL ; FIRS: THOMPSON,WW CIT: 0.00
PROBABILITY MEASURES FOR ESTIMATED DATA
TAR JL 65 VOL: 40 PG:574 - 578 :: ANAL. :INT. LOG. :N/A :PROB.ELIC.

KENIS ,I CIT: 1.70
EFFECTS OF BUDGETARY GOAL CHARACTERISTICS ON MANAGERIAL ATTITUDES AND
   PERFORMANCE
TAR OC 79 VOL: 54 PG:707 - 721 :: CORR. :SURV. :OTH.BEH. :BUDG.& PLAN.

KENNEDY,HA CIT: 0.77
A BEHAVIOURAL STUDY OF THE USEFULNESS OF FOUR FINANCIAL RATIOS
JAR SP 75 VOL: 13 PG:97 - 116 :: DES.STAT. :LAB. :HIPS :BUS.FAIL.

KENNELLEY,M ; FIRS: SCHAEFER,T CIT: 0.00
ALTERNATIVE CASH FLOW MEASURES AND RISK-ADJUSTED RETURNS
JAA AU 86 VOL: 1 PG:278 - 287 :: REGRESS. :PRIM. :EMH :SPEC.ITEMS

KENNELLEY,MD ; FIRS: CHRISTIE,AA ; THIR: KING ,JW ; FOUR: SCHAEFER,TF CIT: 1.20
TESTING FOR INCREMENTAL INFORMATION CONTENT IN THE PRESENCE OF COLLINEARITY
JAE DE 84 VOL: 6 PG:205 - 217 :: ANAL. :INT. LOG. :OTH.STAT. :METHOD.

KENNELLY,JW ; FIRS: BALOFF,N CIT: 0.23
ACCOUNTING IMPLICATIONS OF PRODUCT AND PROCESS START-UPS
JAR AU 67 VOL: 5 PG:131 - 143 :: REGRESS. :CASE :TIME SER. :COST.ALLOC.

KENNELLY,JW ; FIRS: BEAVER,WH ; THIR: VOSS ,WM CIT: 0.92
PREDICTIVE ABILITY AS A CRITERION FOR THE EVALUATION OF ACCOUNTING DATA
TAR OC 68 VOL: 43 PG:675 - 683 :: QUAL. :INT. LOG. :THEORY :FIN.METH.

KEOWN ,AJ ; FIRS: MARTIN,JD ; SEC: ANDERSON,PF CIT: 0.00
LEASE CAPITALIZATION AND STOCK PRICE STABILITY: IMPLICATIONS FOR ACCOUNTING
JAA WI 79 VOL: 2 PG:151 - 164 :: REGRESS. :PRIM. :EMH :LEASES

KESSLER,L ; SEC: ASHTON,RH CIT: 0.38
FEEDBACK AND PREDICTION ACHIEVEMENT IN FINANCIAL ANALYSIS
JAR SP 81 VOL: 19 PG:146 - 162 :: ANOVA :LAB. :HIPS :BUDG.& PLAN.

KETTLER,P ; FIRS: BEAVER,WH ; THIR: SCHOLES,M CIT: 2.08
THE ASSOCIATION BETWEEN MARKET DETERMINED AND ACCOUNTING DETERMINED RISK MEA
TAR OC 70 VOL: 45 PG:654 - 682 :: REGRESS. :PRIM. :TIME SER. :FIN.METH.

KETZ ,JE CIT: 0.36
THE VALIDATION OF SOME GENERAL PRICE LEVEL ESTIMATING MODELS
TAR OC 78 VOL: 53 PG:952 - 960 :: ANAL. :SEC. :OTH.STAT. :VALUAT.(INFL.)

KETZ ,JE CIT: 0.18
THE EFFECT OF GENERAL PRICE-LEVEL ADJUSTMENTS ON THE PREDICTIVE ABILITY OF
   FINANCIAL RATIOS
JAR ST 78 VOL: 16 PG:273 - 284 :: OTH.QUANT. :PRIM. :EMH :VALUAT.(INFL.)

KETZ ,JE ; FIRS: HUSSEIN,ME CIT: 0.22
RULING ELITES OF THE FASB: A STUDY OF THE BIG EIGHT
JAA SU 80 VOL: 3 PG:354 - 367 :: DES.STAT. :SEC. :OTH.STAT. :FASB SUBM.

KETZ ,JE ; SEC: WYATT ,AR CIT: 0.00
THE FASB IN A WORLD WITH PARTIALLY EFFICIENT MARKETS
JAA AU 83 VOL: 7 PG:29 - 43 :: QUAL. :INT. LOG. :EMH :OTH.MANAG.

KETZ ,JE ; FIRS: GOMBOLA,MJ CIT: 0.00
A NOTE ON CASH FLOW AND CLASSIFICATION PATTERNS OF FINANCIAL RATIOS
TAR JA 83 VOL: 58 PG:105 - 114 :: OTH.QUANT. :LAB. :OTH.STAT. :SPEC.ITEMS

KEYS ,DE CIT: 0.36
CONFIDENCE INTERVAL FINANCIAL STATEMENTS: AN EMPIRICAL INVESTIGATION
JAR AU 78 VOL: 16 PG:389 - 399 :: ANOVA :LAB. :OTH.STAT. :PROB.ELIC.

KHANDWALLA,PN CIT: 1.15
THE EFFECT OF DIFFERENT TYPES OF COMPETITION ON THE USE OF MANAGEMENT CONTROLS
JAR AU 72 VOL: 10 PG:275 - 285 :: CORR. :SURV. :OTH. :MANAG.

KHEMAKHEM,A CIT: 0.00
A SIMULATION OF MANAGEMENT-DECISION BEHAVIOR: "FUNDS" AND INCOME
TAR JL 68 VOL: 43 PG:522 - 534 :: ANOVA :LAB. :N/A :FIN.METH.

KIDA ,TE CIT: 0.33
AN INVESTIGATION INTO AUDITORS' CONTINUITY AND RELATED QUALIFICATION JUDGMENTS
JAR AU 80 VOL: 18 PG:506 - 523 :: NON-PAR. :LAB. :OTH.BEH. :OPIN.

KIDA ,TE ; FIRS: ANDERSON JR,TN CIT: 0.00
THE CROSS-LAGGED RESEARCH APPROACH: DESCRIPTION AND ILLUSTRATION
JAR AU 82 VOL: 20 PG:403 - 414 :: CORR. :LAB. :OTH.BEH. :MAN.DEC.CHAR.

KIDA ,TE CIT: 0.00
THE EFFECT OF CAUSALITY AND SPECIFICITY ON DATA USE
JAR SP 84 VOL: 22 PG:145 - 152 :: ANOVA :LAB. :HIPS :BUS.FAIL.

KIDA ,TE CIT: 0.00
THE IMPACT OF HYPOTHESIS-TESTING STRATEGIES ON AUDITORS' USE OF JUDGMENT DATA
JAR SP 84 VOL: 22 PG:332 - 340 :: ANOVA :LAB. :HIPS :JUDG.

KIDA ,TE CIT: 0.00
PERFORMANCE EVALUATION AND REVIEW MEETING CHARACTERISTICS IN PUBLIC
    ACCOUNTING FIRMS
AOS 02 84 VOL: 9 PG:137 - 147 :: NON-PAR. :SURV. :HIPS :AUD.BEH.

KIGER ,JE CIT: 0.38
AN EMPIRICAL INVESTIGATION OF NYSE VOLUME AND PRICE REACTIONS TO THE
    ANNOUNCEMENT OF QUARTERLY EARNINGS
JAR SP 72 VOL: 10 PG:113 - 128 :: NON-PAR. :PRIM. :EMH :INT.REP.

KIGER ,JE CIT: 0.15
VOLATILITY IN QUARTERLY ACCOUNTING DATA
TAR JA 74 VOL: 49 PG:1 - 7 :: DES.STAT. :PRIM. :TIME SER. :INT.REP.

KIGER ,JE ; FIRS: SCHEINER,JH CIT: 0.00
AN EMPIRICAL INVESTIGATION OF AUDITOR INVOLVEMENT IN NON-AUDIT SERVICES
JAR AU 82 VOL: 20 PG:482 - 496 :: DES.STAT. :PRIM. :HIPS :PROF.RESP.

KILLOUGH,LN ; SEC: SOUDERS,TL CIT: 0.31
A GOAL PROGRAMMING MODEL FOR PUBLIC ACCOUNTING FIRMS
TAR AP 73 VOL: 48 PG:268 - 279 :: ANAL. :INT. LOG. :MATH.PROG. :ORG.

KILMANN,RH CIT: 0.17
THE COSTS OF ORGANIZATION STRUCTURE: DISPELLING THE MYTHS OF INDEPENDENT
    DIVISIONS AND ORGANIZATION-WIDE DECISION MAKING
AOS 04 83 VOL: 8 PG:341 - 360 :: QUAL. :INT. LOG. :THEORY :ORG.FORM

KIM ,DH ; FIRS: ZIEBART,DA CIT: 0.00
AN EXAMINATION OF THE MARKET REACTIONS ASSOCIATED WITH SFAS NO. 8 AND SFAS NO. 52
TAR AP 87 VOL: 62 PG:343 - 357 :: REGRESS. :PRIM. :EMH :FOR.CUR.

KIM ,HS ; FIRS: NETER ,J ; THIR: GRAHAM,LE CIT: 0.20
ON COMBINING STRINGER BOUNDS FOR INDEPENDENT MONETARY UNIT SAMPLES FROM SEVERAL POPULATIONS
AUD AU 84 VOL: 4 PG:75 - 88 :: ANAL. :INT. LOG. :OTH.STAT. :SAMP.

KIM ,HS ; SEC: NETER ,J ; THIR: GODFREY,JT CIT: 0.00
BEHAVIOR OF STATISTICAL ESTIMATORS IN MULTILOCATION AUDIT SAMPLING
AUD SP 87 VOL: 6 PG:40 - 58 :: DES.STAT. :SIM. :OTH.STAT. :SAMP.

KIM ,KK CIT: 0.00
ORGANIZATIONAL COORDINATION AND PERFORMANCE IN HOSPITAL ACCOUNTING INFORMATION SYSTEMS: AN EMPIRICAL INVESTIGATION
TAR JL 88 VOL: 63 PG:472 - 489 :: REGRESS. :SURV. :OTH.BEH. :INFO.STRUC.

KIM ,M ; SEC: MOORE ,G CIT: 0.00
ECONOMIC VS. ACCOUNTING DEPRECIATION
JAE AP 88 VOL: 10 PG:111 - 125 :: REGRESS. :PRIM. :THEORY :PP&E / DEPR

KIMBRELL,JI ; FIRS: BOATSMAN,JR ; SEC: DOWELL,CD CIT: 0.00
VALUING STOCK USED FOR A BUSINESS COMBINATION
JAA AU 84 VOL: 8 PG:35 - 43 :: ANAL. :INT. LOG. :OTH.STAT. :BUS.COMB.

KINARD,JC ; FIRS: IJIRI ,Y ; THIR: PUTNEY,FB CIT: 0.38
AN INTEGRATED EVALUATION SYSTEM FOR BUDGET FORECASTING AND OPERATING PERFORMANCE WITH A CLASSIFIED BUDGETING BIBLIOGRAPHY
JAR SP 68 VOL: 6 PG:1 - 28 :: QUAL. :SEC. :OTH.BEH. :BUDG.& PLAN.

KINARD,JC ; FIRS: HOFSTEDT,TR CIT: 0.46
A STRATEGY FOR BEHAVIOURAL ACCOUNTING RESEARCH
TAR JA 70 VOL: 45 PG:38 - 54 :: QUAL. :INT. LOG. :OTH.BEH. :OTH.MANAG.

KING ,JW ; FIRS: CHRISTIE,AA ; SEC: KENNELLEY,MD ; FOUR: SCHAEFER,TF CIT: 1.20
TESTING FOR INCREMENTAL INFORMATION CONTENT IN THE PRESENCE OF COLLINEARITY
JAE DE 84 VOL: 6 PG:205 - 217 :: ANAL. :INT. LOG. :OTH.STAT. :METHOD.

KING ,RD CIT: 0.00
THE EFFECT OF CONVERTIBLE BOND EQUITY VALUES ON DILUTION AND LEVERAGE
TAR JL 84 VOL: 59 PG:419 - 431 :: DES.STAT. :PRIM. :OTH.STAT. :LTD

KING ,RD ; SEC: O'KEEFE,TB CIT: 0.00
LOBBYING ACTIVITIES AND INSIDER TRADING
TAR JA 86 VOL: 61 PG:76 - 90 :: REGRESS. :PRIM. :OTH.STAT. :OIL & GAS

KING ,RR ; SEC: BARON ,CD CIT: 0.00
AN INTEGRATED ACCOUNT STRUCTURE FOR GOVERNMENTAL ACCOUNTING AND FINANCIAL REPORTING
TAR JA 74 VOL: 49 PG:76 - 87 :: QUAL. :INT. LOG. :THEORY :FIN.METH.

KING ,TE CIT: 0.00
ACCOUNTING STANDARDS FOR REPORTING UNINCORPORATED PARTNERSHIPS IN CORPORATE FINANCIAL STATEMENTS
JAA SP 79 VOL: 2 PG:209 - 223 :: QUAL. :INT. LOG. :THEORY :BUS.COMB.

KING ,TE ; SEC: ORTEGREN,AK CIT: 0.00
ACCOUNTING FOR HYBRID SECURITIES: THE CASE OF ADJUSTABLE RATE CONVERTIBLE
  NOTES
AUD JL 88 VOL: 63 PG:522 - 535 :: DES.STAT. :INT. LOG. :THEORY :SPEC.ITEMS

KINNEY JR,WR CIT: 0.08
AN ENVIRONMENTAL MODEL FOR PERFORMANCE MEASUREMENT IN MULTI-OUTLET BUSINESSES
JAR SP 69 VOL: 7 PG:44 - 52 :: ANAL. :INT. LOG. :TIME SER. :OPIN.

KINNEY JR,WR CIT: 0.92
PREDICTING EARNINGS: ENTITY VERSUS SUBENTITY DATA
JAR SP 71 VOL: 9 PG:127 - 136 :: ANOVA :PRIM. :TIME SER. :SEG.REP.

KINNEY JR,WR CIT: 0.08
COVARIABILITY OF SEGMENT EARNINGS AND MULTISEGMENT COMPANY RETURNS
TAR AP 72 VOL: 47 PG:339 - 345 :: CORR. :PRIM. :EMH :SEG.REP.

KINNEY JR,WR CIT: 0.92
A DECISION THEORY APPROACH TO THE SAMPLING PROBLEM IN AUDITING
JAR SP 75 VOL: 13 PG:117 - 132 :: ANAL. :INT. LOG. :INF.ECO./AG. :SAMP.

KINNEY JR,WR CIT: 1.00
DECISION THEORY ASPECTS OF INTERNAL CONTROL SYSTEM DESIGN/COMPLIANCE AND
  SUBSTANTIVE TESTS
JAR ST 75 VOL: 13 PG:14 - 29 :: ANAL. :INT. LOG. :OTH.STAT. :SAMP.

KINNEY JR,WR ; FIRS: UECKER,WC CIT: 0.83
JUDGMENTAL EVALUATION OF SAMPLE RESULTS: A STUDY OF THE TYPE AND SEVERITY OF
  ERRORS MADE BY PRACTICING CPAS
AOS 03 77 VOL: 2 PG:269 - 275 :: DES.STAT. :LAB. :OTH.STAT. :SAMP.

KINNEY JR,WR CIT: 0.91
ARIMA AND REGRESSION IN ANALYTICAL REVIEW: AN EMPIRICAL TEST
TAR JA 78 VOL: 53 PG:48 - 60 :: REGRESS. :PRIM. :TIME SER. :ANAL.REV.

KINNEY JR,WR CIT: 0.40
INTEGRATING AUDIT TESTS: REGRESSION ANALYSIS AND PARTITIONED DOLLAR-UNIT
  SAMPLING
JAR AU 79 VOL: 17 PG:456 - 475 :: REGRESS. :SIM. :OTH.STAT. :SAMP.

KINNEY JR,WR CIT: 1.20
THE PREDICTIVE POWER OF LIMITED INFORMATION IN PRELIMINARY ANALYTICAL REVIEW:
  AN EMPIRICAL STUDY
JAR ST 79 VOL: 17 PG:148 - 165 :: DES.STAT. :PRIM. :OTH.STAT. :ANAL.REV.

KINNEY JR,WR CIT: 0.00
PREDICTING AUDITOR-INITIATED ADJUSTMENTS USING PAIRED BALANCE METHODS
JAA AU 81 VOL: 5 PG:5 - 17 :: MIXED :SEC. :OTH.STAT. :ANAL.REV.

KINNEY JR,WR ; FIRS: UECKER,WC ; SEC: BRIEF ,AP CIT: 0.25
PERCEPTION OF THE INTERNAL AND EXTERNAL AUDITOR AS A DETERRENT TO CORPORATE
  IRREGULARITIES
TAR JL 81 VOL: 56 PG:465 - 478 :: ANOVA :LAB. :OTH.BEH. :AUD.BEH.

KINNEY JR,WR ; FIRS: FELIX JR,WL CIT: 0.86
RESEARCH IN THE AUDITOR'S OPINION FORMULATION PROCESS: STATE OF THE ART
TAR AP 82 VOL: 57 PG:245 - 271 :: QUAL. :SEC. :OTH. :N/A

KINNEY JR,WR ; SEC: SALAMON,GL CIT: 0.14
REGRESSION ANALYSIS IN AUDITING: A COMPARISON OF ALTERNATIVE INVESTIGATION
  RULES
JAR AU 82 VOL: 20 PG:350 - 366 :: REGRESS. :SIM. :OTH.STAT. :ANAL.REV.

KINNEY JR,WR ; SEC: UECKER,WC CIT: 0.57
MITIGATING THE CONSEQUENCES OF ANCHORING IN AUDITOR JUDGMENTS
TAR JA 82 VOL: 57 PG:55 - 69 :: DES.STAT. :LAB. :HIPS :ANAL.REV.

KINNEY JR,WR ; FIRS: BANKS ,DW CIT: 0.57
LOSS CONTINGENCY REPORTS AND STOCK PRICES: AN EMPIRICAL STUDY
JAR SP 82 VOL: 20 PG:240 - 254 :: REGRESS. :PRIM. :EMH :SPEC.ITEMS

KINNEY JR,WR CIT: 0.67
A NOTE ON COMPOUNDING PROBABILITIES IN AUDITING
AUD SP 83 VOL: 2 PG:13 - 22 :: ANAL. :INT. LOG. :OTH.STAT. :RISK

KINNEY JR,WR CIT: 0.67
AUDIT TECHNOLOGY AND PREFERENCES FOR AUDITING STANDARDS
JAE MR 86 VOL: 8 PG:73 - 89 :: REGRESS. :PRIM. :INSTIT. :FASB SUBM.

KINNEY JR,WR CIT: 0.00
ATTENTION-DIRECTING ANALYTICAL REVIEW USING ACCOUNTING RATIOS: A CASE
  STUDY
AUD SP 87 VOL: 6 PG:59 - 73 :: DES.STAT. :CASE :OTH.STAT. :ANAL.REV.

KIRCHER,P CIT: 0.00
CODING ACCOUNTING PRINCIPLES
TAR OC 65 VOL: 40 PG:742 - 752 :: QUAL. :INT. LOG. :THEORY :OTH.MANAG.

KIRCHER,P CIT: 0.00
CLASSIFICATION AND CODING OF ACCOUNTING INFORMATION
TAR JL 67 VOL: 42 PG:537 - 543 :: QUAL. :INT. LOG. :THEORY :OTH.MANAG.

KIRCHER,P ; FIRS: BUCKLEY,JW ; THIR: MATHEWS,RL CIT: 0.08
METHODOLOGY IN ACCOUNTING THEORY
TAR AP 68 VOL: 43 PG:274 - 283 :: QUAL. :INT. LOG. :THEORY :FIN.METH.

KISSINGER,JN CIT: 0.08
A GENERAL THEORY OF EVIDENCE AS THE CONCEPTUAL FOUNDATION IN AUDITING THEORY:
  SOME COMMENTS AND EXTENSIONS
TAR AP 77 VOL: 52 PG:322 - 339 :: ANAL. :INT. LOG. :THEORY :OPIN.

KISSINGER,JN CIT: 0.00
AUDIT TIMING DECISIONS: A NORMATIVE MODEL, A PRACTICAL HEURISTIC, AND SOME
  EMPIRICAL EVIDENCE
AUD AU 83 VOL: 3 PG:42 - 54 :: MIXED :PRIM. :OTH. :TIM.

KISSINGER,JN CIT: 0.00
IN DEFENSE OF INTERPERIOD INCOME TAX ALLOCATION
JAA SP 86 VOL: 1 PG:90 - 101 :: REGRESS. :INT. LOG. :THEORY :TAX PLNG.

KISTLER,LH CIT: 0.00
STOCK OPTION DISCLOSURES ARE INADEQUATE
TAR OC 67 VOL: 42 PG:758 - 766 :: QUAL. :CASE :N/A :STK.DIV.

KISTNER,KP ; SEC: SALMI ,T CIT: 0.00
GENERAL PRICE LEVEL ACCOUNTING AND INVENTORY VALUATION: A COMMENT
JAR SP 80 VOL: 18 PG:297 - 311 :: ANAL. :INT. LOG. :THEORY :VALUAT.(INFL.)

KLAASSEN,J ; FIRS: SCHREUDER,H CIT: 0.20
CONFIDENTIAL REVENUE AND PROFIT FORECASTS BY MANAGEMENT AND FINANCIAL
    ANALYSTS: EVIDENCE FROM THE NETHERLANDS
TAR JA 84 VOL: 59 PG:64 - 77 :: NON-PAR. :PRIM. :OTH.STAT. :FOREC.

KLAMMER,T CIT: 0.31
THE ASSOCIATION OF CAPITAL BUDGETING TECHNIQUES WITH FIRM PERFORMANCE
TAR AP 73 VOL: 48 PG:353 - 364 :: REGRESS. :SURV. :EMH :CAP.BUDG.

KLEESPIE,DC ; FIRS: WINBORNE,MG CIT: 0.00
TAX ALLOCATION IN PERSPECTIVE
TAR OC 66 VOL: 41 PG:737 - 744 :: QUAL. :INT. LOG. :N/A :TAXES

KLICK ,HD ; FIRS: HARRELL,AM CIT: 0.22
COMPARING THE IMPACT OF MONETARY AND NONMONETARY HUMAN ASSET MEASURES ON
    EXECUTIVE DECISION MAKING
AOS 04 80 VOL: 5 PG:393 - 400 :: REGRESS. :LAB. :OTH.BEH. :HRA

KNAPP ,MC CIT: 0.00
AUDIT CO AN EMPIRICAL STUDY OF THE PERCEIVED ABILITY OF AUDITORS TO RESIST
    MANAGEMENT PRESSURE
TAR AP 85 VOL: 60 PG:202 - 211 :: REGRESS. :LAB. :OTH.BEH. :OPIN.

KNAPP ,MC CIT: 0.00
AN EMPIRICAL STUDY OF AUDIT COMMITTEE SUPPORT FOR AUDITORS INVOLVED IN
    TECHNICAL DISPUTES WITH CLIENT MANAGEMENT
TAR JL 87 VOL: 62 PG:578 - 588 :: REGRESS. :LAB. :OTH.BEH. :AUD.

KNAUF ,JB ; SEC: VASARHELYI,MA CIT: 0.00
EMPIRICAL CHARACTERISTICS OF DEBENTURE CONVERSIONS: THE ISSUE OF EQUIVALENCY
JAA WI 87 VOL: 2 PG:43 - 64 :: REGRESS. :PRIM. :THEORY :LTD

KNECHEL,WR CIT: 0.00
A SIMULATION MODEL FOR EVALUATING ACCOUNTING SYSTEM RELIABILITY
AUD SP 85 VOL: 4 PG:38 - 62 :: REGRESS. :SIM. :OTH.STAT. :INT.CONT.

KNECHEL,WR CIT: 0.00
AN ANALYSIS OF ALTERNATIVE ERROR ASSUMPTIONS IN MODELING THE RELIABILITY OF
    ACCOUNTING SYSTEMS
JAR SP 85 VOL: 23 PG:194 - 212 :: REGRESS. :SIM. :OTH.STAT. :ERRORS

KNECHEL,WR CIT: 0.00
THE EFFECTIVENESS OF NONSTATISTICAL ANALYTICAL REVIEW PROCEDURES USED AS
    SUBSTANTIVE AUDIT TESTS
AUD AU 88 VOL: 08 PG:87 - 107 :: DES.STAT. :SIM. :OTH.STAT. :ANAL.REV.

KNECHEL,WR CIT: 0.00
THE EFFECTIVENESS OF STATISTICAL ANALYTICAL REVIEW AS A SUBSTANTIVE AUDITING
    PROCEDURE: A SIMULATION ANALYSIS
TAR JA 88 VOL: 63 PG:74 - 95 :: DES.STAT. :SIM. :OTH.STAT. :ANAL.REV.

KNEER ,DC ; FIRS: JENNINGS,M ; THIR: RECKERS,PMJ CIT: 0.00
A REEXAMINATION OF THE CONCEPT OF MATERIALITY: VIEWS OF AUDITORS, USERS AND
    OFFICERS OF THE COURT
AUD SP 87 VOL: 6 PG:104 - 115 :: REGRESS. :LAB. :OTH.BEH. :MAT.

KNIGHTS,D ; SEC: COLLINSON,D CIT: 0.00
DISCIPLINING THE SHOPFLOOR: A COMPARISON OF THE DISCIPLINARY EFFECTS
    OF MANAGERIAL PSYCHOLOGY AND FINANCIAL ACCOUNTING
AOS 05 87 VOL: 12 PG:457 - 477 :: DES.STAT. :INT. LOG. :THEORY :HRA

KNOBLETT,JA ; FIRS: LEVITAN,AS CIT: 0.00
INDICATORS OF EXCEPTIONS TO THE GOING CONCERN ASSUMPTION
AUD AU 85 VOL: 5 PG:26 - 39 :: REGRESS. :PRIM. :OTH.STAT. :OPIN.

KNUTSON,PH ; FIRS: BLAKELY,EJ CIT: 0.00
LIFO OR LOFI - WHICH?
TAR JA 63 VOL: 38 PG:75 - 86 :: QUAL. :INT. LOG. :THEORY :N/A

KNUTSON,PH CIT: 0.15
INCOME DISTRIBUTION: THE KEY TO EARNINGS PER SHARE
TAR JA 70 VOL: 45 PG:55 - 68 :: QUAL. :INT. LOG. :THEORY :INFO.STRUC.

KNUTSON,PH CIT: 0.00
AN EMPIRICAL STUDY OF THE COSTS OF CONVERTIBLE SECURITIES
JAR ST 71 VOL: 9 PG:99 - 112 :: DES.STAT. :PRIM. :THEORY :LTD

KO   ,CE ; FIRS: BAILEY JR,AD ; SEC: DUKE ,GL ; THIR: GERLACH,JH ; FIFT:
MESERVY,RD ; SIX: WHINSTON,AB CIT: 0.00
TICOM AND THE ANALYSIS OF INTERNAL CONTROLS
TAR AP 85 VOL: 60 PG:186 - 201 :: CORR. :INT. LOG. :OTH. :INT.CONT.

KO   ,CE ; SEC: NACHTSHEIM,CJ ; THIR: DUKE ,GL ; FOUR: BAILEY JR,AD CIT: 0.00
ON THE ROBUSTNESS OF MODEL-BASED SAMPLING IN AUDITING
AUD SP 88 VOL: 07 PG:119 - 136 :: DES.STAT. :SIM. :OTH.STAT. :SAMP.

KOCH ,BS CIT: 0.13
INCOME SMOOTHING: AN EXPERIMENT
TAR JL 81 VOL: 56 PG:574 - 586 :: ANOVA :LAB. :THEORY :REV.REC.

KOCH ,BS ; FIRS: MERINO,BD ; THIR: MACRITCHIE,KL CIT: 0.00
HISTORICAL ANALYSIS- A DIAGNOSTIC TOOL FOR "EVENTS" STUDIES: THE IMPACT OF
    THE SECURITIES ACT OF 1933
TAR OC 87 VOL: 62 PG:748 - 762 :: REGRESS. :INT. LOG. :HIST. :FIN.METH.

KOCHANEK,RF CIT: 0.23
SEGMENTAL FINANCIAL DISCLOSURE BY DIVERSIFIED FIRMS AND SECURITY PRICES
TAR AP 74 VOL: 49 PG:245 - 258 :: MIXED :PRIM. :OTH.STAT. :SEG.REP.

KOHLER,EL CIT: 0.00
THE JENKINS REPORT
TAR AP 63 VOL: 38 PG:266 - 269 :: QUAL. :INT. LOG. :INSTIT. :FIN.METH.

KOHLMEIER,JM ; FIRS: DAVIDSON,S CIT: 0.08
A MEASURE OF THE IMPACT OF SOME FOREIGN ACCOUNTING PRINCIPLES
JAR AU 66 VOL: 4 PG:183 - 212 :: DES.STAT. :SIM. :OTH.STAT. :INT.DIFF.

KOLLARITSCH,FP CIT: 0.00
INTERNATIONAL ACCOUNTING PRACTICES
TAR AP 65 VOL: 40 PG:382 - 385 :: QUAL. :INT. LOG. :INSTIT. :FIN.METH.

KOLODNY,R ; FIRS: HORWITZ,BN CIT: 0.00
SEGMENT REPORTING: HINDSIGHT AFTER TEN YEARS
JAA AU 80 VOL: 4 PG:20 - 35 :: QUAL. :INT. LOG. :THEORY :SEG.REP.

KOLODNY,R ; FIRS: HORWITZ,BN CIT: 0.67
THE ECONOMIC EFFECTS OF INVOLUNTARY UNIFORMITY IN THE FINANCIAL REPORTING OF
    R & D EXPENDITURES
JAR ST 80 VOL: 18 PG:38 - 74 :: NON-PAR. :PRIM. :OTH. :R & D

KOLODNY,R ; FIRS: HORWITZ,BN CIT: 0.13
THE IMPACT OF RULE MAKING ON R & D INVESTMENTS OF SMALL HIGH-TECHNOLOGY FIRMS
JAA WI 81 VOL: 4 PG:102 - 113 :: NON-PAR. :SURV. :THEORY :ACC.CHNG.

KONSTANS,C ; FIRS: DEAN ,RA ; SEC: FERRIS,KR CIT: 0.00
OCCUPATIONAL REALITY SHOCK AND ORGANIZATIONAL COMMITMENT: EVIDENCE FROM THE
    ACCOUNTING PROFESSION
AOS 03 88 VOL: 13 PG:235 - 250 :: REGRESS. :SURV. :OTH.BEH. :AUD.BEH.

KORNBLUTH,JS CIT: 0.15
ACCOUNTING IN MULTIPLE OBJECTIVE LINEAR PROGRAMMING
TAR AP 74 VOL: 49 PG:284 - 295 :: ANAL. :INT. LOG. :MATH.PROG. :MANAG.

KORTANEK,KO ; FIRS: CHARNES,A ; SEC: DAVIDSON,HJ CIT: 0.00
ON A MIXED-SEQUENTIAL ESTIMATING PROCEDURE WITH APPLICATION TO AUDIT TESTS IN
    ACCOUNTING
TAR AP 64 VOL: 39 PG:241 - 250 :: ANAL. :INT. LOG. :OTH.STAT. :SAMP.

KORTANEK,KO ; FIRS: BYRNE ,R ; SEC: CHARNES,A ; THIR: COOPER,WW CIT: 0.00
SOME NEW APPROACHES TO RISK
TAR JA 68 VOL: 43 PG:18 - 37 :: ANAL. :INT. LOG. :MATH.PROG. :BUDG.& PLAN.

KORTANEK,KO ; FIRS: CHARNES,A ; SEC: COLANTONI,CS ; THIR: COOPER,WW CIT: 0.08
ECONOMIC SOCIAL AND ENTERPRISE ACCOUNTING AND MATHEMATICAL MODES
TAR JA 72 VOL: 47 PG:85 - 108 :: ANAL. :INT. LOG. :MATH.PROG. :FIN.METH.

KOSTOLANSKY,JW ; FIRS: WERNER,CA CIT: 0.00
ACCOUNTING LIABILITIES UNDER ERISA
JAA AU 83 VOL: 7 PG:54 - 64 :: QUAL. :INT. LOG. :THEORY :PENS.

KOSTOLANSKY,JW ; FIRS: WERNER,CA CIT: 0.00
ACCOUNTING LIABILITIES UNDER THE MULTIEMPLOYER PENSION PLAN AMENDMENTS ACT
JAA SP 84 VOL: 7 PG:212 - 224 :: QUAL. :INT. LOG. :THEORY :PENS.

KOTHARI,SP ; FIRS: COLLINS,DW ; THIR: RAYBURN,JD CIT: 1.00
FIRM SIZE AND THE INFORMATION CONTENT OF PRICES WITH RESPECT TO EARNINGS
JAE JL 87 VOL: 9 PG:111 - 138 :: REGRESS. :PRIM. :EMH :ORG.& ENVIR.

KOTTAS,JF ; SEC: LAU ,AH ; THIR: LAU ,HS CIT: 0.27
A GENERAL APPROACH TO STOCHASTIC MANAGEMENT PLANNING MODELS: AN OVERVIEW
TAR AP 78 VOL: 53 PG:389 - 401 :: ANAL. :INT. LOG. :MATH.PROG. :C-V-P-A

KOTTAS,JF ; SEC: LAU ,HS CIT: 0.09
DIRECT SIMULATION IN STOCHASTIC CVP ANALYSIS
TAR JL 78 VOL: 53 PG:698 - 707 :: QUAL. :INT. LOG. :OTH.STAT. :C-V-P-A

KRAMER,JL ; FIRS: NORDHAUSER,SL CIT: 0.00
REPEAL OF THE DEFERRAL PRIVILEGE FOR EARNINGS FROM DIRECT FOREIGN
    INVESTMENTS: AN ANALYSIS
TAR JA 81 VOL: 56 PG:54 - 69 :: ANAL. :INT. LOG. :OTH.STAT. :BUS.COMB.

KRAMER,SS ; FIRS: ASHTON,RH CIT: 1.78
STUDENTS AS SURROGATES IN BEHAVIOURAL ACCOUNTING RESEARCH: SOME EVIDENCE
JAR SP 80 VOL: 18 PG:1 - 15 :: NON-PAR. :LAB. :HIPS :METHOD.

KRAMER,SS CIT: 0.00
BLOCKAGE: VALUATION OF LARGE BLOCKS OF PUBLICLY TRADED STOCKS FOR TAX PURPOSES
TAR JA 82 VOL: 57 PG:70 - 87 :: REGRESS. :PRIM. :EMH :TAXES

KRASNEY,MA ; FIRS: BENSTON,GJ CIT: 0.45
DAAM: THE DEMAND FOR ALTERNATIVE ACCOUNTING MEASUREMENTS
JAR ST 78 VOL: 16 PG:1 - 30 :: REGRESS. :SURV. :OTH.STAT. :VALUAT.(INFL.)

KRATCHMAN,SH ; SEC: MALCOM,RE ; THIR: TWARK ,RD CIT: 0.08
AN INTRA-INDUSTRY COMPARISON OF ALTERNATIVE INCOME CONCEPTS AND RELATIVE
PERFORMANCE EVALUATIONS
TAR OC 74 VOL: 49 PG:682 - 689 :: NON-PAR. :PRIM. :N/A :VALUAT.(INFL.)

KRATCHMAN,SH ; FIRS: GROSSMAN,SD ; THIR: WELKER,RB CIT: 0.00
COMMENT: THE EFFECT OF REPLACEMENT COST DISCLOSURES ON SECURITY PRICES
JAA WI 81 VOL: 4 PG:136 - 143 :: DES.STAT. :PRIM. :EMH :VALUAT.(INFL.)

KRAUSHAAR,JM ; FIRS: ANDERSON,JC CIT: 0.00
MEASUREMENT ERROR AND STATISTICAL SAMPLING IN AUDITING: THE POTENTIAL
EFFECTS
TAR JL 86 VOL: 61 PG:379 - 399 :: DES.STAT. :SIM. :OTH.STAT. :SAMP.

KREISER,L CIT: 0.00
MAINTAINING AND IMPROVING THE AUDIT COMPETENCE OF CPAS: CPA AND SELECTED USER
REACTION
TAR AP 77 VOL: 52 PG:427 - 437 :: DES.STAT. :SURV. :N/A :AUD.TRAIN.

KREPS ,DM ; FIRS: DEMSKI,JS CIT: 1.00
MODELS IN MANAGERIAL ACCOUNTING
JAR ST 82 VOL: 20 PG:117 - 148 :: QUAL. :SEC. :OTH.STAT. :METHOD.

KREUTZFELDT,RW ; SEC: WALLACE,WA CIT: 0.00
ERROR CHARACTERISTICS IN AUDIT POPULATIONS: THEIR PROFILE AND RELATIONSHIP TO
ENVIRONMENTAL FACTORS
AUD AU 86 VOL: 6 PG:20 - 43 :: DES.STAT. :SURV. :OTH.STAT. :ERRORS

KRIEGER,AM ; FIRS: RAMAGE,JG ; THIR: SPERO ,LL CIT: 0.90
AN EMPIRICAL STUDY OF ERROR CHARACTERISTICS IN AUDIT POPULATIONS
JAR ST 79 VOL: 17 PG:72 - 102 :: DES.STAT. :PRIM. :OTH.STAT. :ERRORS

KRIPKE,H CIT: 0.00
WHERE ARE WE ON SECURITIES DISCLOSURE AFTER THE ADVISORY COMMITTEE REPORT?
JAA AU 78 VOL: 2 PG:4 - 32 :: QUAL. :INT. LOG. :INSTIT. :OTH.MANAG.

KROGSTAD,JL ; FIRS: SOLOMON,I ; THIR: ROMNEY,MB ; FOUR: TOMASSINI,LA CIT: 0.57
AUDITORS' PRIOR PROBABILITY DISTRIBUTIONS FOR ACCOUNT BALANCES
AOS 01 82 VOL: 7 PG:27 - 42 :: DES.STAT. :LAB. :HIPS :PROB.ELIC.

KROGSTAD,JL ; SEC: ETTENSON,RT ; THIR: SHANTEAU,J CIT: 0.40
CONTEXT AND EXPERIENCE IN AUDITORS' MATERIALITY JUDGMENTS
AUD AU 84 VOL: 4 PG:54 - 74 :: ANOVA :LAB. :OTH.BEH. :MAT.

KROGSTAD,JL ; FIRS: SMITH ,G CIT: 0.20
IMPACT OF SOURCES AND AUTHORS ON AUDITING: A JOURNAL OF PRACTICE & THEORY - A
CITATION ANALYSIS
AUD AU 84 VOL: 4 PG:107 - 117 :: DES.STAT. :SEC. :OTH.STAT. :METHOD.

KROSS ,W ; SEC: CHAPMAN,G ; THIR: STRAND,KH CIT: 0.00
FULLY DILUTED EARNINGS PER SHARE AND SECURITY RETURNS: SOME ADDITIONAL
EVIDENCE
JAA AU 80 VOL: 4 PG:36 - 46 :: CORR. :SEC. :EMH :CASH DIV.

KROSS ,W CIT: 0.00
STOCK RETURNS AND OIL AND GAS PRONOUNCEMENTS: REPLICATION AND EXTENSION
JAR AU 82 VOL: 20 PG:459 - 471 :: NON-PAR. :PRIM. :EMH :FIN.METH.

KROSS ,W ; SEC: SCHROEDER,DA CIT: 0.80
AN EMPIRICAL INVESTIGATION OF THE EFFECT OF QUARTERLY EARNINGS ANNOUNCEMENT
    TIMING ON STOCK RETURNS
JAR SP 84 VOL: 22 PG:153 - 176 :: REGRESS. :PRIM. :EMH :FIN.ST.TIM.

KUBLIN,M CIT: 0.00
ACCEPTABILITY OF A PROFESSIONAL SCHOOL OF ACCOUNTANCY
TAR JL 65 VOL: 40 PG:626 - 635 :: DES.STAT. :SURV. :INSTIT. :OTH.MANAG.

KUNITAKE,WK ; SEC: WHITE JR,CE CIT: 0.00
ETHICS FOR INDEPENDENT AUDITORS
JAA SU 86 VOL: 1 PG:222 - 231 :: DES.STAT. :INT. LOG. :INSTIT. :PROF.RESP.

KUNITZKY,S ; FIRS: LEV ,B CIT: 0.46
ON THE ASSOCIATION BETWEEN SMOOTHING MEASURES AND THE RISK OF COMMON STOCKS
TAR AP 74 VOL: 49 PG:259 - 270 :: CORR. :PRIM. :TIME SER. :FIN.METH.

KWANG ,CW ; FIRS: CORCORAN,AW CIT: 0.00
A SET THEORY APPROACH TO FUNDS-FLOW ANALYSIS
JAR AU 65 VOL: 3 PG:206 - 217 :: ANAL. :INT. LOG. :THEORY :PP&E / DEPR

KWATINETZ,M ; FIRS: PALMON,D CIT: 0.11
THE SIGNIFICANT ROLE INTERPRETATION PLAYS IN THE IMPLEMENTATION OF SFAS NO.13
JAA SP 80 VOL: 3 PG:207 - 226 :: QUAL. :INT. LOG. :THEORY :LEASES

KWON ,YK ; FIRS: JUNG ,WO CIT: 0.00
DISCLOSURE WHEN THE MARKET IS UNSURE OF INFORMATION ENDOWMENT OF MANAGERS
JAR SP 88 VOL: 26 PG:146 - 153 :: DES.STAT. :INT. LOG. :INF.ECO./AG. :
INFO.STRUC.

LACEY ,JM ; FIRS: BOWEN ,RM ; SEC: NOREEN,EW CIT: 3.63
DETERMINANTS OF THE CORPORATE DECISION TO CAPITALIZE INTEREST
JAE AG 81 VOL: 3 PG:151 - 179 :: DES.STAT. :INT. LOG. :INF.ECO./AG. :SPEC.ITEMS

LACHMAN,R ; FIRS: ARANYA,N ; THIR: AMERNIC,J CIT: 0.00
ACCOUNTANTS' JOB SATISFACTION: A PATH ANALYSIS
AOS 03 82 VOL: 7 PG:201 - 216 :: CORR. :SURV. :OTH.BEH. :N/A

LAIBSTAIN,S CIT: 0.00
A NEW LOOK AT ACCOUNTING FOR OPERATING LOSS CARRYFORWARDS
TAR AP 71 VOL: 46 PG:342 - 351 :: QUAL. :INT. LOG. :THEORY :TAXES

LAKONISHOK,J ; FIRS: CRICHFIELD,T ; SEC: DYCKMAN,TR CIT: 1.09
AN EVALUATION OF SECURITY ANALYSTS' FORECASTS
TAR JL 78 VOL: 53 PG:651 - 668 :: ANOVA :PRIM. :TIME SER. :FOREC.

LAKONISHOK,J ; FIRS: GIVOLY,D CIT: 1.00
THE INFORMATION CONTENT OF FINANCIAL ANALYSTS' FORECASTS OF EARNINGS: SOME
    EVIDENCE ON SEMI-STRONG INEFFICIENCY
JAE DE 79 VOL: 1 PG:165 - 185 :: DES.STAT. :PRIM. :EMH :FOREC.

LAKONISHOK,J ; FIRS: BARAN ,A ; THIR: OFER ,AR CIT: 0.11
THE INFORMATION CONTENT OF GENERAL PRICE LEVEL ADJUSTED EARNINGS: SOME
    EMPIRICAL EVIDENCE
TAR JA 80 VOL: 55 PG:22 - 35 :: REGRESS. :PRIM. :HIPS :VALUAT.(INFL.)

LAKONISHOK,J ; FIRS: GIVOLY,D CIT: 0.00
AGGREGATE EARNINGS EXPECTATIONS AND STOCK MARKET BEHAVIOR
JAA SP 87 VOL: 2 PG:117 - 137 :: REGRESS. :PRIM. :EMH :FOREC.

LAMB ,JW ; FIRS: CARLSON,ML CIT: 0.00
CONSTRUCTING A THEORY OF ACCOUNTING - AN AXIOMATIC APPROACH
TAR JL 81 VOL: 56 PG:554 - 573 :: ANAL. :INT. LOG. :THEORY :N/A

LAMBERT,RA ; FIRS: BEAVER,WH ; THIR: MORSE ,D CIT: 2.44
THE INFORMATION CONTENT OF SECURITY PRICES
JAE MR 80 VOL: 2 PG:3 - 28 :: REGRESS. :PRIM. :EMH :FIN.METH.

LAMBERT,RA CIT: 0.60
INCOME SMOOTHING AS RATIONAL EQUILIBRIUM BEHAVIOR
TAR OC 84 VOL: 59 PG:604 - 618 :: ANAL. :INT. LOG. :EMH :REV.REC.

LAMBERT,RA ; SEC: LARCKER,DF CIT: 0.25
GOLDEN PARACHUTES, EXECUTIVE DECISION-MAKING, AND SHAREHOLDER WEALTH
JAE AP 85 VOL: 7 PG:179 - 204 :: REGRESS. :PRIM. :EMH :EXEC.COMP.

LAMBERT,RA CIT: 0.00
VARIANCE INVESTIGATION IN AGENCY SETTINGS
JAR AU 85 VOL: 23 PG:633 - 647 :: REGRESS. :INT. LOG. :INF.ECO./AG. :VAR.

LAMBERT,RA ; FIRS: BEAVER,WH ; THIR: RYAN ,SG CIT: 1.00
THE INFORMATION CONTENT OF SECURITY PRICES: A SECOND LOOK
JAE JL 87 VOL: 9 PG:139 - 157 :: REGRESS. :PRIM. :EMH :FIN.METH.

LAMBERT,RA ; SEC: LARCKER,DF CIT: 0.00
AN ANALYSIS OF THE USE OF ACCOUNTING AND MARKET MEASURES OF PERFORMANCE IN
    EXECUTIVE COMPENSATION CONTRACTS
JAR ST 87 VOL: 25 PG:85 - 125 :: REGRESS. :PRIM. :EMH :EXEC.COMP.

LAMDEN,CW CIT: 0.00
THE FUNCTION OF THE STATE BOARD OF ACCOUNTANCY IN IMPROVING REPORTING
    STANDARDS IN CALIFORNIA
TAR JA 64 VOL: 39 PG:128 - 132 :: QUAL. :INT. LOG. :INSTIT. :OTH.MANAG.

LAMPE ,JC ; FIRS: VASARHELYI,MA ; SEC: BAILEY JR,AD ; THIR: CAMARDESSE JR,JE
; FOUR: GROOMER, SM CIT: 0.00
THE USAGE OF COMPUTERS IN AUDITING TEACHING AND RESEARCH
AUD SP 84 VOL: 3 PG:98 - 103 :: QUAL. :SIM. :OTH. :EDP AUD.

LANDSITTEL,DL ; SEC: SERLIN,JE CIT: 0.00
EVALUATING THE MATERIALITY OF ERRORS IN FINANCIAL STATEMENTS
JAA SU 82 VOL: 5 PG:291 - 300 :: QUAL. :INT. LOG. :OTH. :MAT.

LANDSMAN,WR ; FIRS: BEAVER,WH CIT: 0.00
NOTE ON THE BEHAVIOR OF RESIDUAL SECURITY RETURNS FOR WINNER AND LOSER
    PORTFOLIOS
JAE DE 81 VOL: 3 PG:233 - 241 :: DES.STAT. :PRIM. :EMH :N/A

LANDSMAN,WR ; FIRS: BEAVER,WH ; SEC: GRIFFIN,PA CIT: 2.43
THE INCREMENTAL INFORMATION CONTENT OF REPLACEMENT COST EARNINGS
JAE JL 82 VOL: 4 PG:15 - 39 :: MIXED :PRIM. :EMH :VALUAT.(INFL.)

LANDSMAN,WR ; FIRS: BEAVER,WH ; SEC: GRIFFIN,PA CIT: 0.00
TESTING FOR INCREMENTAL INFORMATION CONTENT IN THE PRESENCE OF COLLINEARITY:
    A COMMENT
JAE DE 84 VOL: 6 PG:219 - 223 :: QUAL. :INT. LOG. :OTH.STAT. :METHOD.

LANDSMAN,WR CIT: 0.00
AN EMPIRICAL INVESTIGATION OF PENSION AND PROPERTY RIGHTS
TAR OC 86 VOL: 61 PG:662 - 691 :: REGRESS. :PRIM. :EMH :PENS.

LANDSMAN,WR ; SEC: MAGLIOLO,J CIT: 0.00
CROSS-SECTIONAL CAPITAL MARKET RESEARCH AND MODEL SPECIFICATION
TAR OC 88 VOL: 63 PG:586 - 604 :: DES.STAT. :INT. LOG. :EMH :METHOD.

LANEN ,WN ; FIRS: HALPERIN,R CIT: 0.00
THE EFFECTS OF THE THOR POWER TOOL DECISION ON THE LIFO/FIFO CHOICE
TAR AP 87 VOL: 62 PG:378 - 384 :: REGRESS. :PRIM. :EMH :INV.

LANEN ,WN ; FIRS: VERRECCHIA,RE CIT: 0.00
OPERATING DECISIONS AND THE DISCLOSURE OF MANAGEMENT ACCOUNTING INFORMATION
JAR ST 87 VOL: 25 PG:165 - 189 :: ANAL. :INT. LOG. :THEORY :MANAG.

LANGENDERFER,HQ ; SEC: ROBERTSON,JC CIT: 0.08
A THEORETICAL STRUCTURE FOR INDEPENDENT AUDITS OF MANAGEMENT
TAR OC 69 VOL: 44 PG:777 - 787 :: QUAL. :INT. LOG. :INSTIT. :OTH.MANAG.

LANGHOLM,O CIT: 0.00
COST STRUCTURE AND COSTING METHOD: AN EMPIRICAL STUDY
JAR AU 65 VOL: 3 PG:218 - 227 :: ANAL. :INT. LOG. :THEORY :N/A

LANIER,RA ; FIRS: SMITH ,CH ; THIR: TAYLOR,ME CIT: 0.15
THE NEED FOR AND SCOPE OF THE AUDIT OF MANAGEMENT: A SURVEY OF ATTITUDES
TAR AP 72 VOL: 47 PG:270 - 283 :: DES.STAT. :SURV. :INSTIT. :AUD.

LARCKER,DF ; FIRS: GORDON,LA ; THIR: TUGGLE,FD CIT: 0.82
STRATEGIC DECISION PROCESSES AND THE DESIGN OF ACCOUNTING INFORMATION
  SYSTEMS: CONCEPTUAL LINKAGES
AOS 34 78 VOL: 3 PG:203 - 214 :: QUAL. :INT. LOG. :OTH. :INFO.STRUC.

LARCKER,DF CIT: 0.75
THE PERCEIVED IMPORTANCE OF SELECTED INFORMATION CHARACTERISTICS FOR
  STRATEGIC CAPITAL BUDGETING DECISIONS
TAR JL 81 VOL: 56 PG:519 - 538 :: ANOVA :LAB. :OTH.BEH. :CAP.BUDG.

LARCKER,DF CIT: 2.50
THE ASSOCIATION BETWEEN PERFORMANCE PLAN ADOPTION AND CORPORATE CAPITAL
  INVESTMENT
JAE AP 83 VOL: 5 PG:3 - 30 :: REGRESS. :PRIM. :EMH :EXEC.COMP.

LARCKER,DF ; SEC: LESSIG,VP CIT: 0.17
AN EXAMINATION OF THE LINEAR AND RETROSPECTIVE PROCESS TRACING APPROACHES TO
  JUDGMENT MODELING
TAR JA 83 VOL: 58 PG:58 - 77 :: OTH.QUANT. :LAB. :HIPS :METHOD.

LARCKER,DF ; SEC: REDER ,RE ; THIR: SIMON ,DT CIT: 0.33
TRADES BY INSIDERS AND MANDATED ACCOUNTING STANDARDS
TAR JL 83 VOL: 58 PG:606 - 620 :: NON-PAR. :INT. LOG. :EMH :OIL & GAS

LARCKER,DF ; SEC: REVSINE,L CIT: 0.67
THE OIL AND GAS ACCOUNTING CONTROVERSY: AN ANALYSIS OF ECONOMIC CONSEQUENCES
TAR OC 83 VOL: 58 PG:706 - 732 :: REGRESS. :PRIM. :EMH :OIL & GAS

LARCKER,DF ; FIRS: FERRIS,KR CIT: 0.17
EXPLANATORY VARIABLES OF AUDITOR PERFORMANCE IN A LARGE PUBLIC ACCOUNTING FIRM
AOS 01 83 VOL: 8 PG:1 - 12 :: CORR. :SURV. :OTH.BEH. :ORG.

LARCKER,DF ; FIRS: LAMBERT,RA CIT: 0.25
GOLDEN PARACHUTES, EXECUTIVE DECISION-MAKING, AND SHAREHOLDER WEALTH
JAE AP 85 VOL: 7 PG:179 - 204 :: REGRESS. :PRIM. :EMH :EXEC.COMP.

LARCKER,DF ; FIRS: LAMBERT,RA CIT: 0.00
AN ANALYSIS OF THE USE OF ACCOUNTING AND MARKET MEASURES OF PERFORMANCE IN
    EXECUTIVE COMPENSATION CONTRACTS
JAR ST 87 VOL: 25 PG:85 - 125 :: REGRESS. :PRIM. :EMH :EXEC.COMP.

LARGAY III,JA CIT: 0.00
MICROECONOMIC FOUNDATIONS OF VARIABLE COSTING
TAR JA 73 VOL: 48 PG:115 - 119 :: QUAL. :INT. LOG. :N/A :INV.

LARGAY III,JA CIT: 0.00
SFAS NO.52: EXPEDIENCY OR PRINCIPLE?
JAA AU 83 VOL: 7 PG:44 - 53 :: QUAL. :INT. LOG. :THEORY :FOR.CUR.

LARGAY III,JA ; FIRS: THODE ,SF ; SEC: DRTINA,RE CIT: 0.00
OPERATING CASH FLOWS: A GROWING NEED FOR SEPARATE REPORTING
JAA WI 86 VOL: 1 PG:46 - 61 :: REGRESS. :PRIM. :EMH :OTH.FIN.ACC.

LARGAY III,JA ; FIRS: DAVIS ,ML CIT: 0.00
REPORTING CONSOLIDATED GAINS AND LOSSES ON SUBSIDIARY STOCK ISSUANCES
TAR AP 88 VOL: 63 PG:348 - 363 :: REGRESS. :PRIM. :THEORY :BUS.COMB.

LARKIN,PD ; FIRS: NICHOLS,DR ; SEC: TSAY ,JJ CIT: 0.00
INVESTOR TRADING RESPONSES TO DIFFERING CHARACTERISTICS OF VOLUNTARILY
    DISCLOSED EARNINGS FORECASTS
TAR AP 79 VOL: 54 PG:376 - 382 :: NON-PAR. :PRIM. :EMH :FOREC.

LARREA,J ; FIRS: ELLIOTT,EL ; THIR: RIVERA,JM CIT: 0.00
ACCOUNTING AID TO DEVELOPING COUNTRIES: SOME ADDITIONAL CONSIDERATIONS
TAR OC 68 VOL: 43 PG:763 - 768 :: QUAL. :INT. LOG. :INSTIT. :OTH.MANAG.

LARSON,KD ; SEC: SCHATTKE,RW CIT: 0.00
CURRENT CASH EQUIVALENT, ADDITIVITY, AND FINANCIAL ACTION
TAR OC 66 VOL: 41 PG:634 - 641 :: QUAL. :INT. LOG. :THEORY :VALUAT.(INFL.)

LARSON,KD CIT: 0.08
DESCRIPTIVE VALIDITY OF ACCOUNTING CALCULATIONS
TAR JL 67 VOL: 42 PG:480 - 488 :: QUAL. :INT. LOG. :THEORY :OTH.FIN.ACC.

LARSON,KD CIT: 0.15
IMPLICATIONS OF MEASUREMENT THEORY ON ACCOUNTING CONCEPT FORMULATION
TAR JA 69 VOL: 44 PG:38 - 47 :: QUAL. :INT. LOG. :THEORY :OTH.FIN.ACC.

LARSON,KD ; SEC: GONEDES,NJ CIT: 0.00
BUSINESS COMBINATIONS: AN EXCHANGE RATIO DETERMINATION MODEL
TAR OC 69 VOL: 44 PG:720 - 728 :: ANAL. :INT. LOG. :N/A :OTH.MANAG.

LARSSON,L ; FIRS: SWIERINGA,RJ ; SEC: GIBBINS,M ; FOUR: SWEENEY,JL CIT: 1.85
EXPERIMENTS IN THE HEURISTICS OF HUMAN INFORMATION PROCESSING
JAR ST 76 VOL: 14 PG:159 - 187 :: MIXED :LAB. :HIPS :MANAG.

LAU ,AH ; FIRS: KOTTAS,JF ; THIR: LAU ,HS CIT: 0.27
A GENERAL APPROACH TO STOCHASTIC MANAGEMENT PLANNING MODELS: AN OVERVIEW
TAR AP 78 VOL: 53 PG:389 - 401 :: ANAL. :INT. LOG. :MATH.PROG. :C-V-P-A

LAU ,AH ; SEC: LAU ,HS CIT: 0.00
SOME PROPOSED APPROACHES FOR WRITING OFF CAPITALIZED HUMAN RESOURCE ASSETS
JAR SP 78 VOL: 16 PG:80 - 102 :: ANAL. :INT. LOG. :OTH.BEH. :HRA

LAU   ,AH CIT: 0.00
A FIVE-STATE FINANCIAL DISTRESS PREDICTION MODEL
JAR SP 87 VOL: 25 PG:127 - 138 :: REGRESS. :PRIM. :OTH.STAT. :BUS.FAIL.

LAU   ,HS ; FIRS: JAGGI ,B CIT: 0.38
TOWARD A MODEL FOR HUMAN RESOURCE VALUATION
TAR AP 74 VOL: 49 PG:321 - 329 :: MARKOV :INT. LOG. :OTH.STAT. :HRA

LAU   ,HS ; FIRS: KOTTAS,JF ; SEC: LAU   ,AH CIT: 0.27
A GENERAL APPROACH TO STOCHASTIC MANAGEMENT PLANNING MODELS: AN OVERVIEW
TAR AP 78 VOL: 53 PG:389 - 401 :: ANAL. :INT. LOG. :MATH.PROG. :C-V-P-A

LAU   ,HS ; FIRS: KOTTAS,JF CIT: 0.09
DIRECT SIMULATION IN STOCHASTIC CVP ANALYSIS
TAR JL 78 VOL: 53 PG:698 - 707 :: QUAL. :INT. LOG. :OTH.STAT. :C-V-P-A

LAU   ,HS ; FIRS: LAU   ,AH CIT: 0.00
SOME PROPOSED APPROACHES FOR WRITING OFF CAPITALIZED HUMAN RESOURCE ASSETS
JAR SP 78 VOL: 16 PG:80 - 102 :: ANAL. :INT. LOG. :OTH.BEH. :HRA

LAUGHLIN,RC CIT: 0.00
ACCOUNTING SYSTEMS IN ORGANIZATIONAL CONTEXTS: A CASE FOR CRITICAL THEORY
AOS 05 87 VOL: 12 PG:479 - 502 :: DES.STAT. :INT. LOG. :THEORY :OTH.MANAG.

LAUVER,RC CIT: 0.00
THE CASE FOR POOLINGS
TAR JA 66 VOL: 41 PG:65 - 74 :: QUAL. :INT. LOG. :THEORY :BUS.COMB.

LAVALLE,IH ; SEC: RAPPAPORT,A CIT: 0.00
ON THE ECONOMICS OF ACQUIRING INFORMATION OF IMPERFECT RELIABILITY
TAR AP 68 VOL: 43 PG:225 - 230 :: ANAL. :INT. LOG. :INF.ECO./AG. :REL.COSTS

LAVIN ,D CIT: 0.38
PERCEPTIONS OF THE INDEPENDENCE OF THE AUDITOR
TAR JA 76 VOL: 51 PG:41 - 50 :: ANOVA :SURV. :INSTIT. :INDEP.

LAVIN ,D CIT: 0.17
SOME EFFECTS OF THE PERCEIVED INDEPENDENCE OF THE AUDITOR
AOS 03 77 VOL: 2 PG:237 - 244 :: QUAL. :SEC. :OTH.BEH. :INDEP.

LAVOIE,D CIT: 0.00
THE ACCOUNTING OF INTERPRETATIONS AND THE INTERPRETATION OF ACCOUNTS:
   THE COMMUNICATIVE FUNCTION OF "THE LANGUAGE OF BUSINESS"
AOS 06 87 VOL: 12 PG:579 - 604 :: DES.STAT. :INT. LOG. :THEORY :FIN.METH.

LAWLER III,EE ; FIRS: RHODE ,JG ; SEC: SORENSEN,JE CIT: 0.67
SOURCES OF PROFESSIONAL STAFF TURNOVER IN PUBLIC ACCOUNTING FIRMS REVEALED BY
   THE EXIT INTERVIEW
AOS 02 77 VOL: 2 PG:165 - 176 :: NON-PAR. :SURV. :OTH. :ORG.

LAWLER III,EE ; FIRS: MIRVIS,PH CIT: 0.33
SYSTEMS ARE NOT SOLUTIONS: ISSUES IN CREATING INFORMATION SYSTEMS THAT
   ACCOUNT FOR THE HUMAN ORGANIZATION
AOS 23 83 VOL: 8 PG:175 - 190 :: QUAL. :FIELD :OTH.BEH. :ORG.& ENVIR.

LAWLER,J CIT: 0.00
THE QUEST FOR ACCOUNTING PHILOSOPHERS
JAR ST 67 VOL: 5 PG:86 - 92 :: QUAL. :SURV. :THEORY :N/A

LAWRENCE,EC CIT: 0.00
REPORTING DELAYS FOR FAILED FIRMS
JAR AU 83 VOL: 21 PG:606 - 610 :: DES.STAT. :PRIM. :EMH :FIN.ST.TIM.

LEA ,RB CIT: 0.00
A NOTE ON THE DEFINITION OF COST COEFFICIENTS IN A LINEAR PROGRAMMING MODEL
TAR AP 72 VOL: 47 PG:346 - 350 :: ANAL. :INT. LOG. :MATH.PROG. :MANAG.

LEA ,RB CIT: 0.00
RECOMMENDATIONS OF THE COMMISSION ON AUDITOR'S RESPONSIBILITIES - AN ANALYSIS
OF THE PROFESSION'S RESPONSES
AUD SU 81 VOL: 1 PG:53 - 94 :: QUAL. :INT. LOG. :INSTIT. :ORG.

LEASE ,RC ; FIRS: BRICKLEY,JA ; SEC: BHAGAT,S CIT: 0.75
THE IMPACT OF LONG-RANGE MANAGERIAL COMPENSATION PLANS ON SHAREHOLDER WEALTH
JAE AP 85 VOL: 7 PG:115 - 130 :: REGRESS. :PRIM. :EMH :EXEC.COMP.

LEE ,CF ; FIRS: FRECKA,TJ CIT: 0.00
GENERALIZED FINANCIAL RATIO ADJUSTMENT PROCESSES AND THEIR IMPLICATIONS
JAR SP 83 VOL: 21 PG:308 - 316 :: REGRESS. :PRIM. :EMH :N/A

LEE ,CF ; SEC: WU ,C CIT: 0.00
EXPECTATION FORMATION AND FINANCIAL RATIO ADJUSTMENT PROCESSES
TAR AP 88 VOL: 63 PG:292 - 306 :: DES.STAT. :PRIM. :OTH.STAT. :METHOD.

LEE ,CJ CIT: 0.00
THE SPEED OF ADJUSTMENT OF FINANCIAL RATIONS: AN ERROR-IN-VARIABLE PROBLEM
JAR AU 84 VOL: 22 PG:776 - 781 :: ANAL. :INT. LOG. :OTH. :METHOD.

LEE ,CJ ; SEC: HSIEH ,DA CIT: 0.50
CHOICE OF INVENTORY ACCOUNTING METHODS: COMPARATIVE ANALYSES OF ALTERNATIVE
HYPOTHESES
JAR AU 85 VOL: 23 PG:468 - 485 :: REGRESS. :PRIM. : :INV.

LEE ,CJ CIT: 0.00
STOCHASTIC PROPERTIES OF CROSS-SECTIONAL FINANCIAL DATA
JAR SP 85 VOL: 23 PG:213 - 227 :: REGRESS. :PRIM. :EMH :METHOD.

LEE ,GA CIT: 0.00
THE FLORENTINE BANK LEDGER FRAGMENTS OF 1211: SOME NEW INSIGHTS
JAR SP 73 VOL: 11 PG:47 - 61 :: QUAL. :INT. LOG. :HIST. :OTH.MANAG.

LEE ,GA CIT: 0.00
THE FRANCIS WILLUGHBY EXECUTORSHIP ACCOUNTS, 1672-1682: AN EARLY DOUBLE-ENTRY
SYSTEM IN ENGLAND
TAR JL 81 VOL: 56 PG:539 - 553 :: QUAL. :INT. LOG. :HIST. :N/A

LEE ,LC ; SEC: BEDFORD,NM CIT: 0.00
AN INFORMATION THEORY ANALYSIS OF THE ACCOUNTING PROCESS
TAR AP 69 VOL: 44 PG:256 - 275 :: ANAL. :INT. LOG. :INF.ECO./AG. :OTH.MANAG.

LEE ,SS CIT: 0.00
KOREAN ACCOUNTING REVALUATION LAWS
TAR JL 65 VOL: 40 PG:622 - 625 :: QUAL. :INT. LOG. :THEORY :VALUAT.(INFL.)

LEFTWICH,R ; FIRS: DODD ,P ; SEC: DOPUCH,N ; THIR: HOLTHAUSEN,RW CIT: 1.60
QUALIFIED AUDIT OPINIONS AND STOCK PRICES: INFORMATION CONTENT, ANNOUNCEMENT
DATES, AND CONCURRENT DISCLOSURES
JAE AP 84 VOL: 6 PG:3 - 38 :: REGRESS. :PRIM. :EMH :OPIN.

LEFTWICH,RW ; FIRS: WATTS ,RL CIT: 2.58
THE TIME SERIES OF ANNUAL ACCOUNTING EARNINGS
JAR AU 77 VOL: 15 PG:253 - 271 :: MIXED :PRIM. :TIME SER. :FOREC.

LEFTWICH,RW CIT: 0.56
MARKET FAILURE FALLACIES AND ACCOUNTING INFORMATION
JAE DE 80 VOL: 2 PG:193 - 211 :: QUAL. :INT. LOG. :INF.ECO./AG. :METHOD.

LEFTWICH,RW CIT: 3.63
EVIDENCE OF THE IMPACT OF MANDATORY CHANGES IN ACCOUNTING PRINCIPLES ON
    CORPORATE LOAN AGREEMENTS
JAE MR 81 VOL: 3 PG:3 - 36 :: MIXED :PRIM. :EMH :ACC.CHNG.

LEFTWICH,RW ; SEC: WATTS ,RL ; THIR: ZIMMERMAN,JL CIT: 0.75
VOLUNTARY CORPORATE DISCLOSURE: THE CASE OF INTERIM REPORTING
JAR ST 81 VOL: 19 PG:50 - 77 :: ANAL. :PRIM. :OTH.STAT. :FIN.METH.

LEFTWICH,RW ; FIRS: HOLTHAUSEN,RW CIT: 4.83
THE ECONOMIC CONSEQUENCES OF ACCOUNTING CHOICES: IMPLICATIONS OF COSTLY
    CONTRACTING AND MONITORING
JAE AG 83 VOL: 5 PG:77 - 117 :: QUAL. :SEC. :EMH :METHOD.

LEFTWICH,RW CIT: 2.17
ACCOUNTING INFORMATION IN PRIVATE MARKETS: EVIDENCE FROM PRIVATE LENDING
    AGREEMENTS
TAR JA 83 VOL: 58 PG:23 - 42 :: DES.STAT. :PRIM. :THEORY :FASB SUBM.

LEFTWICH,RW ; FIRS: DOPUCH,N ; SEC: HOLTHAUSEN,RW CIT: 0.33
ABNORMAL STOCK RETURNS ASSOCIATED WITH MEDIA DISCLOSURES OF 'SUBJECT TO'
    QUALIFIED AUDIT OPINIONS
JAE JN 86 VOL: 8 PG:93 - 118 :: REGRESS. :PRIM. :EMH :OPIN.

LEFTWICH,RW ; FIRS: DOPUCH,N ; SEC: HOLTHAUSEN,RW CIT: 0.50
PREDICTING AUDIT QUALIFICATIONS WITH FINANCIAL AND MARKET VARIABLES
TAR JL 87 VOL: 62 PG:431 - 454 :: REGRESS. :PRIM. :EMH :OPIN.

LEHMAN,C ; SEC: TINKER,T CIT: 0.00
THE "REAL" CULTURAL SIGNIFICANCE OF ACCOUNTS
AOS 05 87 VOL: 12 PG:503 - 522 :: DES.STAT. :SEC. :HIST. :OTH.MANAG.

LEININGER,WE ; FIRS: CORCORAN,AW CIT: 0.08
STOCHASTIC PROCESS COSTING MODELS
TAR JA 73 VOL: 48 PG:105 - 114 :: ANAL. :INT. LOG. :MATH.PROG. :COST.ALLOC.

LEITCH,RA ; FIRS: HILLIARD,JE CIT: 0.38
COST-VOLUME-PROFIT ANALYSIS UNDER UNCERTAINTY: A LOG NORMAL APPROACH
TAR JA 75 VOL: 50 PG:69 - 80 :: ANAL. :INT. LOG. :OTH.STAT. :C-V-P-A

LEITCH,RA ; FIRS: NETER ,J ; THIR: FIENBERG,SE CIT: 0.82
DOLLAR UNIT SAMPLING: MULTINOMIAL BOUNDS FOR TOTAL OVERSTATEMENT AND
    UNDERSTATEMENT ERRORS
TAR JA 78 VOL: 53 PG:77 - 93 :: NON-PAR. :SIM. :MATH.PROG. :SAMP.

LEITCH,RA ; FIRS: IJIRI ,Y CIT: 0.22
STEIN'S PARADOX AND AUDIT SAMPLING
JAR SP 80 VOL: 18 PG:91 - 108 :: MIXED :INT. LOG. :OTH.STAT. :N/A

LEITCH,RA ; FIRS: JOHNSON,JR ; THIR: NETER ,J CIT: 1.75
CHARACTERISTICS OF ERRORS IN ACCOUNTS RECEIVABLE AND INVENTORY AUDITS
TAR AP 81 VOL: 56 PG:270 - 293 :: DES.STAT. :PRIM. :OTH. :ERRORS

LEITCH,RA ; SEC: NETER ,J ; THIR: PLANTE,R ; FOUR: SINHA ,P CIT: 0.86
MODIFIED MULTINOMIAL BOUNDS FOR LARGER NUMBERS OF ERRORS IN AUDITS
TAR AP 82 VOL: 57 PG:384 - 400 :: DES.STAT. :SIM. :OTH.STAT. :SAMP.

LEITCH,RA ; FIRS: DUKE ,GL ; SEC: NETER ,J CIT: 1.14
POWER CHARACTERISTICS OF TEST STATISTICS IN THE AUDITING ENVIRONMENT: AN
    EMPIRICAL STUDY
JAR SP 82 VOL: 20 PG:42 - 67 :: MIXED :PRIM. :OTH.STAT. :ERRORS

LEITCH,RA ; FIRS: PLANTE,R ; SEC: NETER ,J CIT: 0.00
COMPARATIVE PERFORMANCE OF MULTINOMIAL, CELL, AND STRINGER BOUNDS
AUD AU 85 VOL: 5 PG:40 - 56 :: DES.STAT. :SIM. :OTH.STAT. :SAMP.

LEMBKE,VC CIT: 0.00
SOME CONSIDERATIONS IN ACCOUNTING FOR DIVISIVE REORGANIZATIONS
TAR JL 70 VOL: 45 PG:458 - 464 :: QUAL. :INT. LOG. :THEORY :FIN.METH.

LEMBKE,VC ; SEC: SMITH ,JH CIT: 0.00
REPLACEMENT COSTS: AN ANALYSIS OF FINANCIAL STATEMENT AND TAX POLICY EFFECTS
JAA WI 80 VOL: 3 PG:147 - 162 :: DES.STAT. :PRIM. :THEORY :VALUAT.(INFL.)

LEMBKE,VC ; SEC: TOOLE ,HR CIT: 0.00
DIFFERENCES IN DEPRECIATION METHODS AND THE ANALYSIS OF SUPPLEMENTAL
    CURRENT-COST AND REPLACEMENT COST DATA
JAA WI 81 VOL: 4 PG:128 - 135 :: ANAL. :INT. LOG. :THEORY :VALUAT.(INFL.)

LEMKE ,KW CIT: 0.15
ASSET VALUATION AND INCOME THEORY
TAR JA 66 VOL: 41 PG:32 - 41 :: QUAL. :INT. LOG. :THEORY :VALUAT.(INFL.)

LEMKE ,KW CIT: 0.08
THE EVALUATION OF LIQUIDITY: AN ANALYTICAL STUDY
JAR SP 70 VOL: 8 PG:47 - 77 :: ANAL. :INT. LOG. :OTH.STAT. :FIN.METH.

LEMON ,WM ; FIRS: JOHNSTON,DJ ; THIR: NEUMANN,FL CIT: 0.00
THE CANADIAN STUDY OF THE ROLE OF THE AUDITOR
JAA SP 80 VOL: 3 PG:251 - 263 :: QUAL. :INT. LOG. :THEORY :PROF.RESP.

LENGERMANN,JJ CIT: 0.15
SUPPOSED AND ACTUAL DIFFERENCES IN PROFESSIONAL AUTONOMY AMONG CPAS AS
    RELATED TO TYPE OF WORK ORGANIZATION AND SIZE OF FIRM
TAR OC 71 VOL: 46 PG:665 - 675 :: ANOVA :SURV. :OTH.BEH. :AUD.

LENTILHON,RW CIT: 0.00
DIRECT COSTING - EITHER ... OR?
TAR OC 64 VOL: 39 PG:880 - 883 :: QUAL. :INT. LOG. :THEORY :OVER.ALLOC.

LERE ,JC ; FIRS: DICKHAUT,JW CIT: 0.17
COMPARISON OF ACCOUNTING SYSTEMS AND HEURISTICS IN SELECTING ECONOMIC OPTIMA
JAR AU 83 VOL: 21 PG:495 - 513 :: ANAL. :INT. LOG. :INF.ECO./AG. :INFO.STRUC.

LERE ,JC CIT: 0.00
PRODUCT PRICING BASED ON ACCOUNTING COSTS
TAR AP 86 VOL: 61 PG:318 - 324 :: DES.STAT. :INT. LOG. :THEORY :COST.ALLOC.

LESSARD,DR ; SEC: LORANGE,P CIT: 0.00
CURRENCY CHANGES AND MANAGEMENT CONTROL: RESOLVING THE
    CENTRALIZATION/DECENTRALIZATION DILEMMA
TAR JL 77 VOL: 52 PG:628 - 637 :: QUAL. :INT. LOG. :THEORY :TRANS.PRIC.

LESSEM,R CIT: 0.17
CORPORATE SOCIAL REPORTING IN ACTION: AN EVALUATION OF BRITISH, EUROPEAN AND
    AMERICAN PRACTICE
AOS 04 77 VOL: 2 PG:279 - 294 :: QUAL. :PRIM. :THEORY :HRA

LESSIG,VP ; FIRS: LARCKER,DF CIT: 0.17
AN EXAMINATION OF THE LINEAR AND RETROSPECTIVE PROCESS TRACING APPROACHES TO
    JUDGMENT MODELING
TAR JA 83 VOL: 58 PG:58 - 77 :: OTH.QUANT. :LAB. :HIPS :METHOD.

LEV ,B CIT: 0.38
THE AGGREGATION PROBLEM IN FINANCIAL STATEMENTS: AN INFORMATIONAL APPROACH
JAR AU 68 VOL: 6 PG:247 - 261 :: ANAL. :INT. LOG. :INF.ECO./AG. :INFO.STRUC.

LEV ,B CIT: 0.31
INDUSTRY AVERAGES AS TARGETS FOR FINANCIAL RATIOS
JAR AU 69 VOL: 7 PG:290 - 299 :: REGRESS. :PRIM. :TIME SER. :LEASES

LEV ,B CIT: 0.00
AN INFORMATION THEORY ANALYSIS OF BUDGET VARIANCES
TAR OC 69 VOL: 44 PG:704 - 710 :: ANAL. :INT. LOG. :INF.ECO./AG. :VAR.

LEV ,B CIT: 0.00
TESTING A PREDICTION METHOD FOR MULTIVARIATE BUDGETS
JAR ST 69 VOL: 7 PG:182 - 197 :: DES.STAT. :PRIM. :OTH.STAT. :BUDG.& PLAN.

LEV ,B CIT: 0.00
A COMMENT ON "BUSINESS COMBINATIONS: AN EXCHANGE RATIO DETERMINATION MODEL"
TAR JL 70 VOL: 45 PG:532 - 534 :: ANAL. :INT. LOG. :N/A :BUS.COMB.

LEV ,B CIT: 0.15
THE INFORMATIONAL APPROACH TO AGGREGATION IN FINANCIAL STATEMENTS: EXTENSIONS
JAR SP 70 VOL: 8 PG:78 - 94 :: ANAL. :INT. LOG. :INF.ECO./AG. :INFO.STRUC.

LEV ,B ; SEC: SCHWARTZ,A CIT: 0.85
ON THE USE OF THE ECONOMIC CONCEPT OF HUMAN CAPITAL IN FINANCIAL STATEMENTS
TAR JA 71 VOL: 46 PG:103 - 112 :: ANAL. :INT. LOG. :THEORY :HRA

LEV ,B ; SEC: KUNITZKY,S CIT: 0.46
ON THE ASSOCIATION BETWEEN SMOOTHING MEASURES AND THE RISK OF COMMON STOCKS
TAR AP 74 VOL: 49 PG:259 - 270 :: CORR. :PRIM. :TIME SER. :FIN.METH.

LEV ,B ; FIRS: FRIEDMAN,A CIT: 0.31
A SURROGATE MEASURE FOR THE FIRM'S INVESTMENT IN HUMAN RESOURCES
JAR AU 74 VOL: 12 PG:235 - 250 :: ANAL. :INT. LOG. :OTH.BEH. :HRA

LEV ,B ; FIRS: BALL ,R ; THIR: WATTS ,RL CIT: 0.23
INCOME VARIATION AND BALANCE SHEET COMPOSITIONS
JAR SP 76 VOL: 14 PG:1 - 9 :: REGRESS. :PRIM. :OTH.STAT. :REV.REC.

LEV ,B ; FIRS: ADAR ,Z ; SEC: BARNEA,A CIT: 0.08
A COMPREHENSIVE COST-VOLUME-PROFIT ANALYSIS UNDER UNCERTAINTY
TAR JA 77 VOL: 52 PG:137 - 149 :: QUAL. :INT. LOG. :THEORY :TAXES

LEV ,B ; SEC: THEIL ,H CIT: 0.00
A MAXIMUM ENTROPY APPROACH TO THE CHOICE OF ASSET DEPRECIATION
JAR AU 78 VOL: 16 PG:286 - 293 :: ANAL. :INT. LOG. :THEORY :PP&E / DEPR

LEV ,B ; SEC: SUNDER,S CIT: 0.60
METHODOLOGICAL ISSUES IN THE USE OF FINANCIAL RATIOS
JAE DE 79 VOL: 1 PG:187 - 210 :: QUAL. :INT. LOG. :OTH.STAT. :METHOD.

LEV ,B CIT: 2.40
THE IMPACT OF ACCOUNTING REGULATION ON THE STOCK MARKET: THE CASE OF OIL AND
GAS COMPANIES
TAR JL 79 VOL: 54 PG:485 - 503 :: REGRESS. :PRIM. :EMH :OIL & GAS

LEV ,B ; SEC: TAYLOR,KW CIT: 0.00
ACCOUNTING RECOGNITION OF IMPUTED INTEREST ON EQUITY: AN EMPIRICAL
INVESTIGATION
JAA SP 79 VOL: 2 PG:232 - 243 :: REGRESS. :PRIM. :EMH :FIN.METH.

LEV ,B CIT: 0.44
ON THE USE OF INDEX MODELS IN ANALYTICAL REVIEWS BY AUDITORS
JAR AU 80 VOL: 18 PG:524 - 550 :: REGRESS. :PRIM. :TIME SER. :ANAL.REV.

LEV ,B ; SEC: OHLSON,JA CIT: 2.43
MARKET-BASED EMPIRICAL RESEARCH IN ACCOUNTING: A REVIEW, INTERPRETATION, AND
EXTENSION
JAR ST 82 VOL: 20 PG:249 - 322 :: QUAL. :SEC. :EMH :METHOD.

LEV ,B CIT: 0.00
SOME ECONOMIC DETERMINANTS OF TIME-SERIES PROPERTIES OF EARNINGS
JAE AP 83 VOL: 5 PG:31 - 48 :: CORR. :PRIM. :EMH :METHOD.

LEV ,B CIT: 0.00
TOWARD A THEORY OF EQUITABLE AND EFFICIENT ACCOUNTING POLICY
TAR JA 88 VOL: 63 PG:1 - 22 :: ANAL. :INT. LOG. :THEORY :FIN.METH.

LEVITAN,AS ; SEC: KNOBLETT,JA CIT: 0.00
INDICATORS OF EXCEPTIONS TO THE GOING CONCERN ASSUMPTION
AUD AU 85 VOL: 5 PG:26 - 39 :: REGRESS. :PRIM. :OTH.STAT. :OPIN.

LEVY ,FK ; FIRS: IJIRI ,Y ; THIR: LYON ,RC CIT: 0.15
A LINEAR PROGRAMMING MODEL FOR BUDGETING AND FINANCIAL PLANNING
JAR AU 63 VOL: 1 PG:198 - 212 :: ANAL. :INT. LOG. :MATH.PROG. :BUDG.& PLAN.

LEVY ,H ; FIRS: BARLEV,B CIT: 0.00
ON THE VARIABILITY OF ACCOUNTING INCOME NUMBERS
JAR AU 79 VOL: 17 PG:305 - 315 :: DES.STAT. :PRIM. :TIME SER. :FIN.METH.

LEVY ,H ; SEC: BYUN ,YH CIT: 0.00
AN EMPIRICAL TEST OF THE BLACK-SCHOLES OPTION PRICING MODEL AND THE IMPLIED
VARIANCE: A CONFIDENCE INTERVAL APPROACH
JAA AU 87 VOL: 2 PG:355 - 369 :: DES.STAT. :PRIM. :OTH. :OTH.MANAG.

LEWELLEN,W ; SEC: LODERER,C ; THIR: ROSENFELD,A CIT: 0.50
MERGER DECISIONS AND EXECUTIVE STOCK OWNERSHIP IN ACQUIRING FIRMS
JAE AP 85 VOL: 7 PG:209 - 232 :: REGRESS. :PRIM. :OTH.STAT. :BUS.COMB.

LEWELLEN,W ; SEC: LODERER,C ; THIR: MARTIN,K CIT: 0.00
EXECUTIVE COMPENSATION AND EXECUTIVE INCENTIVE PROBLEMS: AN EMPIRICAL
ANALYSIS
JAE DE 87 VOL: 9 PG:287 - 310 :: REGRESS. :PRIM. :OTH.STAT. :EXEC.COMP.

LEWIN ,AY ; FIRS: SCHIFF,M CIT: 1.23
THE IMPACT OF PEOPLE ON BUDGETS
TAR AP 70 VOL: 45 PG:259 - 268 :: QUAL. :INT. LOG. :OTH.BEH. :BUDG.& PLAN.

LEWIS ,BL ; FIRS: LIBBY ,R CIT: 2.92
HUMAN INFORMATION PROCESSING RESEARCH IN ACCOUNTING: THE STATE OF THE ART
AOS 03 77 VOL: 2 PG:245 - 268 :: QUAL. :SEC. :HIPS :MANAG.

LEWIS ,BL CIT: 0.78
EXPERT JUDGMENT IN AUDITING: AN EXPECTED UTILITY APPROACH
JAR AU 80 VOL: 18 PG:594 - 602 :: ANOVA :LAB. :HIPS :JUDG.

LEWIS ,BL ; FIRS: LIBBY ,R CIT: 2.71
HUMAN INFORMATION PROCESSING RESEARCH IN ACCOUNTING: THE STATE OF THE ART IN
   1982
AOS 03 82 VOL: 7 PG:231 - 286 :: QUAL. :SEC. :HIPS :MANAG.

LEWIS ,BL ; FIRS: DIRSMITH,MW CIT: 0.00
THE EFFECT OF EXTERNAL REPORTING ON MANAGERIAL DECISION-MAKING: SOME
   ANTECEDENT CONDITIONS
AOS 04 82 VOL: 7 PG:319 - 336 :: NON-PAR. :SURV. :HIPS :FIN.METH.

LEWIS ,BL ; SEC: SHIELDS,MD ; THIR: YOUNG ,SM CIT: 1.17
EVALUATING HUMAN JUDGMENTS AND DECISION AIDS
JAR SP 83 VOL: 21 PG:271 - 285 :: DES.STAT. :LAB. :HIPS :ORG.& ENVIR.

LEWIS ,BL ; SEC: BELL J CIT: 0.00
DECISIONS INVOLVING SEQUENTIAL EVENTS: REPLICATIONS AND EXTENSIONS
JAR SP 85 VOL: 23 PG:228 - 239 :: REGRESS. :LAB. :HIPS :INFO.STRUC.

LEWIS ,BL ; FIRS: EVANS III,JH ; THIR: PATTON,JM CIT: 0.00
AN ECONOMIC MODELING APPROACH TO CONTINGENCY THEORY AND MANAGEMENT CONTROL
AOS 06 86 VOL: 11 PG:483 - 498 :: DES.STAT. :INT. LOG. :INF.ECO./AG. :INT.CONT.

LEWIS ,BL ; SEC: PATTON,JM ; THIR: GREEN ,SL CIT: 0.00
THE EFFECTS OF INFORMATION CHOICE AND INFORMATION USE ON ANALYSTS'
   PREDICTIONS OF MUNICIPAL BOND RATING CHANGES
TAR AP 88 VOL: 63 PG:270 - 282 :: REGRESS. :LAB. :OTH.STAT. :FOREC.

LEWIS ,CD CIT: 0.00
TAX DEDUCTIBILITY OF EDUCATORS' TRAVEL EXPENSES
TAR JA 67 VOL: 42 PG:96 - 105 :: QUAL. :SEC. :N/A :TAXES

LEWIS ,NR ; SEC: PARKER,LD ; THIR: SUTCLIFFE,P CIT: 0.00
FINANCIAL REPORTING TO EMPLOYEES: THE PATTERN OF DEVELOPMENT 1919 TO 1979
AOS 34 84 VOL: 9 PG:275 - 289 :: DES.STAT. :SEC. :HIST. :HRA

LI   ,DH CIT: 0.00
ALTERNATIVE ACCOUNTING PROCEDURES AND THE ENTITY CONCEPT
TAR JA 63 VOL: 38 PG:52 - 55 :: QUAL. :INT. LOG. :THEORY :N/A

LI   ,DH CIT: 0.00
THE FUNDS STATEMENT UNDER THE ENTITY CONCEPT
TAR OC 63 VOL: 38 PG:771 - 775 :: QUAL. :INT. LOG. :THEORY :N/A

LI   ,DH CIT: 0.00
THE SEMANTIC ASPECT OF COMMUNICATION THEORY AND ACCOUNTANCY
JAR SP 63 VOL: 1 PG:102 - 107 :: QUAL. :INT. LOG. :THEORY :N/A

LI   ,DH CIT: 0.00
THE OBJECTIVES OF THE CORPORATION UNDER THE ENTITY CONCEPT
TAR OC 64 VOL: 39 PG:946 - 950 :: QUAL. :INT. LOG. :THEORY :OTH.MANAG.

LIAO ,M CIT: 0.38
MODEL SAMPLING: A STOCHASTIC COST-VOLUME-PROFIT ANALYSIS
TAR OC 75 VOL: 50 PG:780 - 790 :: ANAL. :INT. LOG. :OTH.STAT. :C-V-P-A

LIBBY ,R CIT: 1.69
THE USE OF SIMULATED DECISION MAKERS IN INFORMATION EVALUATION
TAR JL 75 VOL: 50 PG:475 - 489 :: ANOVA :LAB. :HIPS :OTH.MANAG.

LIBBY ,R CIT: 1.23
ACCOUNTING RATIOS AND THE PREDICTION OF FAILURE: SOME BEHAVIOURAL EVIDENCE
JAR SP 75 VOL: 13 PG:150 - 161 :: MIXED :LAB. :HIPS :BUS.FAIL.

LIBBY ,R ; SEC: FISHBURN,PC CIT: 0.83
BEHAVIOURAL MODELS OF RISK TAKING IN BUSINESS DECISIONS: A SURVEY AND
EVALUATION
JAR AU 77 VOL: 15 PG:272 - 292 :: QUAL. :SEC. :OTH.BEH. :OTH.MANAG.

LIBBY ,R ; SEC: LEWIS ,BL CIT: 2.92
HUMAN INFORMATION PROCESSING RESEARCH IN ACCOUNTING: THE STATE OF THE ART
AOS 03 77 VOL: 2 PG:245 - 268 :: QUAL. :SEC. :HIPS :MANAG.

LIBBY ,R CIT: 0.80
BANKERS' AND AUDITORS' PERCEPTIONS OF THE MESSAGE COMMUNICATED BY THE AUDIT
REPORT
JAR SP 79 VOL: 17 PG:99 - 122 :: OTH.QUANT. :LAB. :HIPS :OPIN.

LIBBY ,R CIT: 0.70
THE IMPACT OF UNCERTAINTY REPORTING ON THE LOAN DECISION
JAR ST 79 VOL: 17 PG:35 - 57 :: ANOVA :LAB. :HIPS :OPIN.

LIBBY ,R ; FIRS: JOYCE ,EJ CIT: 0.50
SOME ACCOUNTING IMPLICATIONS OF "BEHAVIOURAL DECISION THEORY: PROCESSES OF
JUDGMENT AND CHOICE"
JAR AU 81 VOL: 19 PG:544 - 550 :: QUAL. :INT. LOG. :HIPS :MANAG.

LIBBY ,R ; FIRS: JOYCE ,EJ ; THIR: SUNDER,S CIT: 0.00
USING THE FASB'S QUALITATIVE CHARACTERISTICS IN ACCOUNTING POLICY CHOICES
JAR AU 82 VOL: 20 PG:654 - 675 :: DES.STAT. :SURV. :INSTIT. :FASB SUBM.

LIBBY ,R ; SEC: LEWIS ,BL CIT: 2.71
HUMAN INFORMATION PROCESSING RESEARCH IN ACCOUNTING: THE STATE OF THE ART IN
1982
AOS 03 82 VOL: 7 PG:231 - 286 :: QUAL. :SEC. :HIPS :MANAG.

LIBBY ,R ; SEC: ARTMAN,JT ; THIR: WILLINGHAM,JJ CIT: 0.50
PROCESS SUSCEPTIBILITY, CONTROL RISK, AND AUDIT PLANNING
TAR AP 85 VOL: 60 PG:212 - 230 :: REGRESS. :LAB. :HIPS :INT.CONT.

LIBBY ,R CIT: 1.25
AVAILABILITY AND THE GENERATION OF HYPOTHESES IN ANALYTICAL REVIEW
JAR AU 85 VOL: 23 PG:648 - 667 :: REGRESS. :LAB. :HIPS :ANAL.REV.

LIBBY ,R ; FIRS: FREDERICK,DM CIT: 0.33
EXPERTISE AND AUDITORS' JUDGMENTS OF CONJUNCTIVE EVENTS
JAR AU 86 VOL: 24 PG:270 - 290 :: REGRESS. :LAB. :HIPS :JUDG.

LIBERTY, SE ; SEC: ZIMMERMAN,JL CIT: 1.00
LABOR UNION CONTRACT NEGOTIATIONS AND ACCOUNTING CHOICES
TAR OC 86 VOL: 61 PG:692 - 712 :: REGRESS. :PRIM. :OTH.STAT. :INFO.STRUC.

LICASTRO,RD ; FIRS: COPELAND,RM CIT: 0.23
A NOTE ON INCOME SMOOTHING
TAR JL 68 VOL: 43 PG:540 - 545 :: ANOVA :PRIM. :TIME SER. :CASH DIV.

LICATA,MP ; SEC: STRAWSER,RH ; THIR: WELKER,RB CIT: 0.00
A NOTE ON PARTICIPATION IN BUDGETING AND LOCUS OF CONTROL
TAR JA 86 VOL: 61 PG:112 - 117 :: REGRESS. :LAB. :OTH.BEH. :BUDG.& PLAN.

LIEBERMAN,AZ ; SEC: WHINSTON,AB CIT: 0.46
A STRUCTURING OF AN EVENTS-ACCOUNTING INFORMATION SYSTEM
TAR AP 75 VOL: 50 PG:246 - 258 :: QUAL. :INT. LOG. :OTH.STAT. :N/A

LIGHTNER,KM ; FIRS: LIGHTNER,SM ; SEC: ADAMS ,SJ CIT: 0.00
THE INFLUENCE OF SITUATIONAL, ETHICAL, AND EXPECTANCY THEORY VARIABLES ON
   ACCOUNTANTS' UNDERREPORTING BEHAVIOR
AUD AU 82 VOL: 2 PG:1 - 12 :: DES.STAT. :SURV. :OTH.STAT. :ORG.

LIGHTNER,SM ; SEC: ADAMS ,SJ ; THIR: LIGHTNER,KM CIT: 0.00
THE INFLUENCE OF SITUATIONAL, ETHICAL, AND EXPECTANCY THEORY VARIABLES ON
   ACCOUNTANTS' UNDERREPORTING BEHAVIOR
AUD AU 82 VOL: 2 PG:1 - 12 :: DES.STAT. :SURV. :OTH.STAT. :ORG.

LILIEN,S ; SEC: PASTENA,V CIT: 1.29
DETERMINANTS OF INTRAMETHOD CHOICE IN THE OIL AND GAS INDUSTRY
JAE DE 82 VOL: 4 PG:145 - 170 :: REGRESS. :PRIM. :OTH.STAT. :OIL & GAS

LILIEN,S ; FIRS: EL-GAZZAR,S ; THIR: PASTENA,V CIT: 0.33
ACCOUNTING FOR LEASES BY LESSEES
JAE OC 86 VOL: 8 PG:217 - 238 :: REGRESS. :PRIM. :OTH.STAT. :LEASES

LILIEN,S ; FIRS: HAW ,IM ; SEC: PASTENA,V CIT: 0.00
THE ASSOCIATION BETWEEN MARKET-BASED MERGER PREMIUMS AND FIRMS' FINANCIAL
   POSITION PRIOR TO MERGER
JAA WI 87 VOL: 2 PG:24 - 42 :: REGRESS. :PRIM. :EMH :BUS.COMB.

LILIEN,S ; SEC: MELLMAN,M ; THIR: PASTENA,V CIT: 0.00
ACCOUNTING CHANGES: SUCCESSFUL VERSUS UNSUCCESSFUL FIRMS
TAR OC 88 VOL: 63 PG:642 - 656 :: REGRESS. :PRIM. :THEORY :ACC.CHNG.

LILLESTOL,J CIT: 0.00
A NOTE ON COMPUTING UPPER ERROR LIMITS IN DOLLAR-UNIT SAMPLING
JAR SP 81 VOL: 19 PG:263 - 267 :: ANAL. :SIM. :OTH.STAT. :LIAB.

LILLIS,A ; FIRS: WILLIAMS,DJ CIT: 0.00
EDP AUDITS OF OPERATING SYSTEMS - AN EXPLORATORY STUDY OF THE DETERMINANTS OF
   THE PRIOR PROBABILITY RISK
AUD SP 85 VOL: 4 PG:110 - 117 :: REGRESS. :SURV. :OTH.STAT. :EDP AUD.

LILLY ,MS ; FIRS: DYL ,EA CIT: 0.00
A NOTE ON INSTITUTIONAL CONTRIBUTIONS TO THE ACCOUNTING LITERATURE
AOS 02 85 VOL: 10 PG:171 - 176 :: REGRESS. :SEC. :INSTIT. :METHOD.

LIM ,R CIT: 0.15
THE MATHEMATICAL PROPRIETY OF ACCOUNTING MEASUREMENTS AND CALCULATIONS
TAR OC 66 VOL: 41 PG:642 - 651 :: ANAL. :INT. LOG. :OTH.STAT. :OTH.FIN.ACC.

LIN ,WT CIT: 0.18
MULTIPLE OBJECTIVE BUDGETING MODELS: A SIMULATION
TAR JA 78 VOL: 53 PG:61 - 76 :: ANOVA :SIM. :MATH.PROG. :BUDG.& PLAN.

LIN ,WT ; SEC: MOCK ,TJ ; THIR: WRIGHT,A CIT: 0.00
THE USE OF ANALYTIC HIERARCHY PROCESS AS AN AID IN PLANNING THE NATURE AND
   EXTENT OF AUDIT PROCEDURES
AUD AU 84 VOL: 4 PG:89 - 99 :: ANAL. :INT. LOG. :OTH.STAT. :PLAN.

LINDAHL,FW ; FIRS: BIDDLE,GC CIT: 2.43
STOCK PRICE REACTIONS TO LIFO ADOPTIONS: THE ASSOCIATION BETWEEN EXCESS
RETURNS AND LIFO TAX SAVINGS
JAR AU 82 VOL: 20 PG:551 - 588 :: MIXED :PRIM. :EMH :INV.

LINDGREN,JH ; FIRS: PEARSON,MA ; THIR: MYERS ,BL CIT: 0.10
A PRELIMINARY ANALYSIS OF AUDSEC VOTING PATTERNS
JAA WI 79 VOL: 2 PG:122 - 134 :: OTH.QUANT. :PRIM. :INSTIT. :FASB SUBM.

LINDHE,R CIT: 0.15
ACCELERATED DEPRECIATION FOR INCOME TAX PURPOSES - A STUDY OF THE DECISION
AND SOME FIRMS WHO MADE IT
JAR AU 63 VOL: 1 PG:139 - 148 :: DES.STAT. :PRIM. :THEORY :PP&E / DEPR

LINN ,JJ ; FIRS: FIRMIN,PA CIT: 0.08
INFORMATION SYSTEMS AND MANAGERIAL ACCOUNTING
TAR JA 68 VOL: 43 PG:75 - 82 :: QUAL. :INT. LOG. :N/A :OTH.MANAG.

LINN ,JJ ; FIRS: FIRMIN,PA ; SEC: GOODMAN,SS ; THIR: HENDRICKS,TE CIT: 0.00
UNIVERSITY COST STRUCTURE AND BEHAVIOR: AN EMPIRICAL STUDY
JAR ST 68 VOL: 6 PG:122 - 155 :: DES.STAT. :SIM. :OTH.STAT. :MANAG.

LINOWES,DF CIT: 0.00
FUTURE OF THE ACCOUNTING PROFESSION
TAR JA 65 VOL: 40 PG:97 - 104 :: QUAL. :INT. LOG. :INSTIT. :OTH.MANAG.

LIPE ,RC CIT: 0.67
THE INFORMATION CONTAINED IN THE COMPONENTS OF EARNINGS
JAR ST 86 VOL: 24 PG:37 - 68 :: REGRESS. :PRIM. :EMH :FIN.METH.

LITTLETON,AC CIT: 0.00
FACTORS LIMITING ACCOUNTING
TAR JL 70 VOL: 45 PG:476 - 480 :: QUAL. :INT. LOG. :THEORY :REV.REC.

LITZENBERGER,RH ; FIRS: JOY ,OM ; THIR: MCENALLY,RW CIT: 0.83
THE ADJUSTMENT OF STOCK PRICES TO ANNOUNCEMENTS OF UNANTICIPATED CHANGES IN
QUARTERLY EARNINGS
JAR AU 77 VOL: 15 PG:207 - 225 :: REGRESS. :PRIM. :EMH :INT.REP.

LIU ,E ; FIRS: BIERMAN JR,H CIT: 0.00
THE COMPUTATION OF EARNINGS PER SHARE
TAR JA 68 VOL: 43 PG:62 - 67 :: QUAL. :INT. LOG. :THEORY :PENS.

LIVINGSTONE,JL ; FIRS: IJIRI ,Y ; SEC: JAEDICKE,RK CIT: 0.08
THE EFFECT OF INVENTORY COSTING METHODS ON FULL AND DIRECT COSTING
JAR SP 65 VOL: 3 PG:63 - 74 :: ANAL. :INT. LOG. :THEORY :MANAG.

LIVINGSTONE,JL CIT: 0.31
ELECTRIC UTILITY PLANT REPLACEMENT COSTS
TAR AP 67 VOL: 42 PG:233 - 240 :: DES.STAT. :PRIM. :THEORY :VALUAT.(INFL.)

LIVINGSTONE,JL CIT: 0.00
A BEHAVIOURAL STUDY OF TAX ALLOCATION IN ELECTRIC UTILITY REGULATION
TAR JL 67 VOL: 42 PG:544 - 552 :: ANOVA :PRIM. :N/A :TAXES

LIVINGSTONE,JL CIT: 0.00
ACCELERATED DEPRECIATION, CYCLICAL ASSET EXPENDITURES AND DEFERRED TAXES
JAR SP 67 VOL: 5 PG:77 - 94 :: DES.STAT. :PRIM. :TIME SER. :PP&E / DEPR

LIVINGSTONE,JL CIT: 0.00
ACCELERATED DEPRECIATION AND DEFERRED TAXES: AN EMPIRICAL STUDY OF
  FLUCTUATING ASSET EXPENDITURES
JAR ST 67 VOL: 5 PG:93 - 123 :: REGRESS. :PRIM. :OTH.STAT. :PP&E / DEPR

LIVINGSTONE,JL CIT: 0.08
MATRIX ALGEBRA AND COST ALLOCATION
TAR JL 68 VOL: 43 PG:503 - 508 :: ANAL. :INT. LOG. :MATH.PROG. :COST.ALLOC.

LIVINGSTONE,JL CIT: 0.08
ACCELERATED DEPRECIATION, TAX ALLOCATION, AND CYCLICAL ASSET EXPENDITURES OF
  LARGE MANUFACTURING COMPANIES
JAR AU 69 VOL: 7 PG:245 - 256 :: REGRESS. :SIM. :OTH.STAT. :TAXES

LIVINGSTONE,JL CIT: 0.00
INPUT-OUTPUT ANALYSIS FOR COST ACCOUNTING, PLANNING AND CONTROL
TAR JA 69 VOL: 44 PG:48 - 64 :: ANAL. :INT. LOG. :MATH.PROG. :COST.ALLOC.

LIVINGSTONE,JL ; FIRS: BRUNDAGE,MV CIT: 0.00
SIMULATION ON A TIME-SHARING COMPUTER UTILITY SYSTEM
TAR JL 69 VOL: 44 PG:539 - 545 :: ANAL. :SIM. :N/A :OTH.MANAG.

LIVINGSTONE,JL ; SEC: SALAMON,GL CIT: 0.15
RELATIONSHIP BETWEEN THE ACCOUNTING AND THE INTERNAL RATE OF RETURN MEASURES:
  A SYNTHESIS AND AN ANALYSIS
JAR AU 70 VOL: 8 PG:199 - 216 :: DES.STAT. :SIM. :OTH.STAT. :FIN.METH.

LIVINGSTONE,JL ; FIRS: RONEN ,J CIT: 1.77
AN EXPECTANCY THEORY APPROACH TO THE MOTIVATIONAL IMPACTS OF BUDGETS
TAR OC 75 VOL: 50 PG:671 - 685 :: QUAL. :INT. LOG. :OTH.BEH. :BUDG.& PLAN.

LIVINGSTONE,JL ; FIRS: BALACHANDRAN,KR CIT: 0.00
COST AND EFFECTIVENESS OF PHYSICIAN PEER REVIEW IN REDUCING MEDICARE
  OVERUTILIZATION
AOS 02 77 VOL: 2 PG:153 - 164 :: DES.STAT. :PRIM. :OTH.STAT. :MANAG.

LIVINGSTONE,JL ; FIRS: BALACHANDRAN,KR ; SEC: MASCHMEYER,R CIT: 0.13
PRODUCT WARRANTY PERIOD: A MARKOVIAN APPROACH TO ESTIMATION AND ANALYSIS OF
  REPAIR AND REPLACEMENT COSTS
TAR JA 81 VOL: 56 PG:115 - 124 :: MARKOV :INT. LOG. :OTH.STAT. :SPEC.ITEMS

LIVNAT,J CIT: 0.00
A GENERALIZATION OF THE API METHODOLOGY AS A WAY OF MEASURING THE ASSOCIATION
  BETWEEN INCOME AND STOCK PRICES
JAR AU 81 VOL: 19 PG:350 - 359 :: REGRESS. :PRIM. :EMH :METHOD.

LIVNAT,J ; FIRS: RONEN ,J CIT: 0.25
INCENTIVES FOR SEGMENT REPORTING
JAR AU 81 VOL: 19 PG:459 - 481 :: ANAL. :INT. LOG. :EMH :SEG.REP.

LIVNAT,J ; FIRS: FRIED ,D CIT: 0.13
INTERIM STATEMENTS: AN ANALYTICAL EXAMINATION OF ALTERNATIVE ACCOUNTING
  TECHNIQUES
TAR JL 81 VOL: 56 PG:493 - 509 :: ANAL. :INT. LOG. :TIME SER. :N/A

LIVNAT,J ; FIRS: AMIT ,R CIT: 0.00
DIVERSIFICATION, CAPITAL STRUCTURE, AND SYSTEMATIC RISK: AN EMPIRICAL
  INVESTIGATION
JAA WI 88 VOL: 03 PG:19 - 43 :: REGRESS. :PRIM. :EMH :OTH.FIN.ACC.

LIVOCK,DM CIT: 0.00
THE ACCOUNTS OF THE CORPORATION OF BRISTOL: 1532 TO 1835
JAR SP 65 VOL: 3 PG:86 - 102 :: QUAL. :INT. LOG. :HIST. :N/A

LLOYD ,AJ ; FIRS: OWEN ,DL CIT: 0.00
THE USE OF FINANCIAL INFORMATION BY TRADE UNION NEGOTIATORS IN PLANT LEVEL
   COLLECTIVE BARGAINING
AOS 03 85 VOL: 10 PG:329 - 352 :: DES.STAT. :INT. LOG. :THEORY :ORG.& ENVIR.

LLOYD ,BM ; SEC: WEYGANDT,JJ CIT: 0.00
MARKET VALUE INFORMATION FOR NONSUBSIDIARY INVESTMENTS
TAR OC 71 VOL: 46 PG:756 - 764 :: DES.STAT. :PRIM. :N/A :BUS.COMB.

LOBO ,GJ ; FIRS: IMHOFF JR,EA CIT: 0.40
INFORMATION CONTENT OF ANALYSTS' COMPOSITE FORECAST REVISIONS
JAR AU 84 VOL: 22 PG:541 - 554 :: REGRESS. :PRIM. :EMH :FOREC.

LODERER,C ; FIRS: LEWELLEN,W ; THIR: ROSENFELD,A CIT: 0.50
MERGER DECISIONS AND EXECUTIVE STOCK OWNERSHIP IN ACQUIRING FIRMS
JAE AP 85 VOL: 7 PG:209 - 232 :: REGRESS. :PRIM. :OTH.STAT. :BUS.COMB.

LODERER,C ; FIRS: LEWELLEN,W ; THIR: MARTIN,K CIT: 0.00
EXECUTIVE COMPENSATION AND EXECUTIVE INCENTIVE PROBLEMS: AN EMPIRICAL
   ANALYSIS
JAE DE 87 VOL: 9 PG:287 - 310 :: REGRESS. :PRIM. :OTH.STAT. :EXEC.COMP.

LOEB ,M ; SEC: MAGAT ,WA CIT: 0.27
SOVIET SUCCESS INDICATORS AND THE EVALUATION OF DIVISIONAL MANAGEMENT
JAR SP 78 VOL: 16 PG:103 - 121 :: ANAL. :INT. LOG. :INF.ECO./AG. :INT.DIFF.

LOEB ,M ; FIRS: COHEN ,SI CIT: 0.00
PUBLIC GOODS, COMMON INPUTS, AND THE EFFICIENCY OF FULL COST ALLOCATIONS
TAR AP 82 VOL: 57 PG:336 - 347 :: ANAL. :INT. LOG. :OTH.STAT. :COST.ALLOC.

LOEB ,SE CIT: 0.15
A SURVEY OF ETHICAL BEHAVIOR IN THE ACCOUNTING PROFESSION
JAR AU 71 VOL: 9 PG:287 - 306 :: MIXED :SURV. :OTH.BEH. :AUD.BEH.

LOEB ,SE CIT: 0.08
ENFORCEMENT OF THE CODE OF ETHICS: A SURVEY
TAR JA 72 VOL: 47 PG:1 - 10 :: DES.STAT. :PRIM. :INSTIT. :OTH.MANAG.

LOEBBECKE,JK ; SEC: NETER ,J CIT: 0.08
CONSIDERATIONS IN CHOOSING STATISTICAL SAMPLING PROCEDURES IN AUDITING
JAR ST 75 VOL: 13 PG:38 - 52 :: QUAL. :INT. LOG. :OTH.STAT. :SAMP.

LOEBBECKE,JK ; FIRS: CUSHING,BE CIT: 0.67
ANALYTICAL APPROACHES TO AUDIT RISK: A SURVEY AND ANALYSIS
AUD AU 83 VOL: 3 PG:23 - 41 :: ANAL. :SEC. :OTH.STAT. :RISK

LOEBBECKE,JK ; SEC: STEINBART,PJ CIT: 0.00
AN INVESTIGATION OF THE USE OF PRELIMINARY ANALYTICAL REVIEW TO PROVIDE
   SUBSTANTIVE AUDIT EVIDENCE
AUD SP 87 VOL: 6 PG:74 - 89 :: REGRESS. :SIM. :OTH.STAT. :ANAL.REV.

LOFT ,A CIT: 3.00
TOWARDS A CRITICAL UNDERSTANDING OF ACCOUNTING: THE CASE OF COST ACCOUNTING
   IN THE U.K., 1914-1925
AOS 02 86 VOL: 11 PG:137 - 170 :: DES.STAT. :INT. LOG. :HIST. :COST.ALLOC.

LONG ,MS ; FIRS: HITE ,GL CIT: 0.71
TAXES AND EXECUTIVE STOCK OPTIONS
JAE JL 82 VOL: 4 PG:3 - 14 :: QUAL. :INT. LOG. :THEORY :TAXES

LONGSTRETH,B CIT: 0.00
THE SEC'S ROLE IN FINANCIAL DISCLOSURE
JAA WI 84 VOL: 7 PG:110 - 122 :: QUAL. :INT. LOG. :INSTIT. :FIN.METH.

LOOKABILL,LL CIT: 0.46
SOME ADDITIONAL EVIDENCE ON THE TIME SERIES PROPERTIES OF ACCOUNTING EARNINGS
TAR OC 76 VOL: 51 PG:724 - 738 :: REGRESS. :PRIM. :TIME SER. :OTH.MANAG.

LOOKABILL,LL ; FIRS: ALBRECHT,WS ; THIR: MCKEOWN,JC CIT: 2.00
THE TIME-SERIES PROPERTIES OF ANNUAL EARNINGS
JAR AU 77 VOL: 15 PG:226 - 244 :: MIXED :PRIM. :TIME SER. :FOREC.

LORANGE,P ; FIRS: LESSARD,DR CIT: 0.00
CURRENCY CHANGES AND MANAGEMENT CONTROL: RESOLVING THE
    CENTRALIZATION/DECENTRALIZATION DILEMMA
TAR JL 77 VOL: 52 PG:628 - 637 :: QUAL. :INT. LOG. :THEORY :TRANS.PRIC.

LOREK ,KS ; SEC: MCDONALD,CL ; THIR: PATZ ,DH CIT: 0.77
A COMPARATIVE EXAMINATION OF MANAGEMENT FORECASTS AND BOX-JENKINS FORECASTS
    OF EARNINGS
TAR AP 76 VOL: 51 PG:321 - 330 :: REGRESS. :PRIM. :TIME SER. :METHOD.

LOREK ,KS CIT: 0.90
PREDICTING ANNUAL NET EARNINGS WITH QUARTERLY EARNINGS TIME SERIES MODELS
JAR SP 79 VOL: 17 PG:190 - 204 :: REGRESS. :PRIM. :TIME SER. :FOREC.

LOREK ,KS ; SEC: ICERMAN,JD ; THIR: ABDULKADER,AA CIT: 0.00
FURTHER DESCRIPTIVE AND PREDICTIVE EVIDENCE ON ALTERNATIVE TIME-SERIES MODELS
    FOR QUARTERLY EARNINGS
JAR SP 83 VOL: 21 PG:317 - 328 :: REGRESS. :PRIM. :TIME SER. :INT.REP.

LOREK ,KS ; FIRS: BATHKE,AW CIT: 0.00
THE RELATIONSHIP BETWEEN TIME-SERIES MODELS AND THE SECURITY MARKET'S
    EXPECTATION OF QUARTERLY EARNINGS
TAR AP 84 VOL: 59 PG:163 - 176 :: REGRESS. :PRIM. :TIME SER. :FOREC.

LOREK ,KS ; SEC: BATHKE,AW CIT: 0.00
A TIME-SERIES ANALYSIS OF NONSEASONAL QUARTERLY EARNINGS DATA
JAR SP 84 VOL: 22 PG:369 - 379 :: CORR. :PRIM. :TIME SER. :INT.REP.

LORIG ,AN CIT: 0.00
SUGGESTED IMPROVEMENTS IN GOVERNMENTAL ACCOUNTING
TAR OC 63 VOL: 38 PG:759 - 763 :: QUAL. :INT. LOG. :THEORY :N/A

LORIG ,AN CIT: 0.15
SOME BASIC CONCEPTS OF ACCOUNTING AND THEIR IMPLICATIONS
TAR JL 64 VOL: 39 PG:563 - 573 :: QUAL. :INT. LOG. :THEORY :FIN.METH.

LOSELL,D ; FIRS: HAM ,J ; THIR: SMIELIAUSKAS,W CIT: 0.50
AN EMPIRICAL STUDY OF ERROR CHARACTERISTICS IN ACCOUNTING POPULATIONS
TAR JL 85 VOL: 60 PG:387 - 406 :: REGRESS. :PRIM. :OTH.STAT. :ERRORS

LOUDERBACK,JG CIT: 0.00
PROJECTABILITY AS A CRITERION FOR INCOME DETERMINATION METHODS
TAR AP 71 VOL: 46 PG:298 - 305 :: QUAL. :INT. LOG. :THEORY :FIN.METH.

LOVATA,LM CIT: 0.00
THE UTILIZATION OF GENERALIZED AUDIT SOFTWARE
AUD AU 88 VOL: 08 PG:72 - 86 :: REGRESS. :SURV. :OTH. :EDP AUD.

LOWE ,EA ; FIRS: BERRY ,AJ ; SEC: CAPPS ,T ; THIR: COOPER,D ; FOUR: FERGUSON,P
FIFT: HOPPER,T CIT: 3.50
MANAGEMENT CONTROL IN AN AREA OF THE NCB: RATIONALES OF ACCOUNTING PRACTICES
IN A PUBLIC ENTERPRISE
AOS 01 85 VOL: 10 PG:3 - 28 :: REGRESS. :FIELD :OTH.BEH. :MANAG.

LOWE ,HD CIT: 0.00
THE ESSENTIALS OF A GENERAL THEORY OF DEPRECIATION
TAR AP 63 VOL: 38 PG:293 - 301 :: ANAL. :INT. LOG. :THEORY :PP&E / DEPR

LOWE ,HD CIT: 0.00
ACCOUNTING AID FOR DEVELOPING COUNTRIES
TAR AP 67 VOL: 42 PG:356 - 360 :: QUAL. :INT. LOG. :INSTIT. :OTH.MANAG.

LOWE ,RE CIT: 0.00
PUBLIC ACCOUNTING INTERNSHIPS
TAR OC 65 VOL: 40 PG:839 - 846 :: DES.STAT. :SURV. :INSTIT. :OTH.MANAG.

LOWE ,T ; FIRS: PUXTY ,AG ; SEC: WILLMOTT,HC ; THIR: COOPER,DJ CIT: 0.50
MODES OF REGULATION IN ADVANCED CAPITALISM: LOCATING ACCOUNTANCY IN
FOUR COUNTRIES
AOS 03 87 VOL: 12 PG:273 - 291 :: DES.STAT. :INT. LOG. :THEORY :ORG.& ENVIR.

LOY ,LD ; SEC: TOOLE ,HR CIT: 0.11
ACCOUNTING FOR DISCOUNTED CONVERTIBLE BOND EXCHANGES: A SURVEY OF RESULTS
JAA SP 80 VOL: 3 PG:227 - 243 :: DES.STAT. :PRIM. :OTH. :METHOD.

LUCAS ,HC CIT: 0.00
THE USE OF AN ACCOUNTING INFORMATION SYSTEM, ACTION AND ORGANIZATIONAL
PERFORMANCE
TAR OC 75 VOL: 50 PG:735 - 746 :: REGRESS. :FIELD :OTH.BEH. :OTH.MANAG.

LUCAS ,RG ; FIRS: DERMER,JD CIT: 0.00
THE ILLUSION OF MANAGERIAL CONTROL
AOS 06 86 VOL: 11 PG:471 - 482 :: DES.STAT. :INT. LOG. :THEORY :INT.CONT.

LUDMAN,EA CIT: 0.00
INSIDER TRADING: THE CASE FOR REGULATION
JAA SP 86 VOL: 1 PG:118 - 124 :: DES.STAT. :INT. LOG. :THEORY :LITIG.

LUH ,FS CIT: 0.15
CONTROLLED COST: AN OPERATIONAL CONCEPT AND STATISTICAL APPROACH TO STANDARD
COSTING
TAR JA 68 VOL: 43 PG:123 - 132 :: ANAL. :INT. LOG. :OTH.STAT. :VAR.

LUKKA ,K CIT: 0.00
BUDGETARY BIASING IN ORGANIZATIONS: THEORETICAL FRAMEWORK AND EMPIRICAL
EVIDENCE
AOS 03 88 VOL: 13 PG:281 - 301 :: REGRESS. :CASE :OTH.BEH. :BUDG.& PLAN.

LUNDHOLM,RJ ; FIRS: DEJONG,DV ; SEC: FORSYTHE,R ; FOUR: UECKER,WC CIT: 0.00
A LABORATORY INVESTIGATION OF THE MORAL HAZARD PROBLEM IN AN AGENCY
RELATIONSHIP
JAR ST 85 VOL: 23 PG:81 - 120 :: REGRESS. :LAB. :INF.ECO./AG. :MAN.DEC.CHAR.

LUNDHOLM,RJ CIT: 0.00
PRICE-SIGNAL RELATIONS IN THE PRESENCE OF CORRELATED PUBLIC AND PRIVATE
INFORMATION
JAR SP 88 VOL: 26 PG:107 - 118 :: ANAL. :INT. LOG. :INF.ECO./AG. :INFO.STRUC.

LUNESKI,C CIT: 0.00
SOME ASPECTS OF THE MEANING OF CONTROL
TAR JL 64 VOL: 39 PG:591 - 597 :: QUAL. :INT. LOG. :N/A :MANAG.

LUNESKI,C CIT: 0.00
CONTINUOUS VERSUS DISCRETE COMPOUNDING FOR CAPITAL BUDGETING DECISIONS
TAR OC 67 VOL: 42 PG:767 - 771 :: ANAL. :INT. LOG. :N/A :OTH.MANAG.

LUSK ,EJ CIT: 0.08
DISCRIMINANT ANALYSIS AS APPLIED TO THE RESOURCE ALLOCATION DECISION
TAR JL 72 VOL: 47 PG:567 - 575 :: OTH.QUANT. :INT. LOG. :OTH.STAT. :CAP.BUDG.

LUSK ,EJ CIT: 0.62
COGNITIVE ASPECTS OF ANNUAL REPORTS: FIELD INDEPENDENCE/DEPENDENCE
JAR ST 73 VOL: 11 PG:191 - 202 :: NON-PAR. :LAB. :HIPS :INFO.STRUC.

LUSK ,EJ ; FIRS: ABDEL-KHALIK,AR CIT: 0.77
TRANSFER PRICING - A SYNTHESIS
TAR JA 74 VOL: 49 PG:8 - 23 :: QUAL. :SEC. :N/A :TRANS.PRIC.

LUSK ,EJ ; FIRS: HEIMANN,SR CIT: 0.08
DECISION FLEXIBILITY: AN ALTERNATIVE EVALUATION CRITERION
TAR JA 76 VOL: 51 PG:51 - 64 :: ANAL. :INT. LOG. :OTH.STAT. :MANAG.

LUSK ,EJ ; FIRS: BODNAR,G CIT: 0.00
MOTIVATIONAL CONSIDERATIONS IN COST ALLOCATION SYSTEMS: A CONDITIONING THEORY
  APPROACH
TAR OC 77 VOL: 52 PG:857 - 868 :: ANAL. :INT. LOG. :OTH.BEH. :OVER.ALLOC.

LUSTGARTEN,S CIT: 0.43
THE IMPACT OF REPLACEMENT COST DISCLOSURE ON SECURITY PRICES: NEW EVIDENCE
JAE OC 82 VOL: 4 PG:121 - 141 :: REGRESS. :PRIM. :EMH :VALUAT.(INFL.)

LUSTGARTEN,S ; FIRS: HAW ,IM CIT: 0.00
EVIDENCE ON INCOME MEASUREMENT PROPERTIES OF ASR NO. 190 AND SFAS NO. 33 DATA
JAR AU 88 VOL: 26 PG:331 - 352 :: REGRESS. :PRIM. :EMH :VALUAT.(INFL.)

LYNN ,ES CIT: 0.00
EDUCATION FOR THE PROFESSION
TAR AP 64 VOL: 39 PG:371 - 376 :: QUAL. :INT. LOG. :INSTIT. :OTH.MANAG.

LYON ,RC ; FIRS: IJIRI ,Y ; SEC: LEVY ,FK CIT: 0.15
A LINEAR PROGRAMMING MODEL FOR BUDGETING AND FINANCIAL PLANNING
JAR AU 63 VOL: 1 PG:198 - 212 :: ANAL. :INT. LOG. :MATH.PROG. :BUDG.& PLAN.

LYS ,T CIT: 1.00
MANDATED ACCOUNTING CHANGES AND DEBT COVENANTS: THE CASE OF OIL AND GAS
  ACCOUNTING
JAE AP 84 VOL: 6 PG:39 - 65 :: REGRESS. :PRIM. :EMH :OIL & GAS

LYS ,T ; SEC: SIVARAMAKRISHNAN,K CIT: 0.00
EARNINGS EXPECTATIONS AND CAPITAL RESTRUCTURING: THE CASE OF EQUITY-FOR-DEBT
  SWAPS
JAR AU 88 VOL: 26 PG:273 - 299 :: REGRESS. :PRIM. :EMH :LTD

MABERT,VA ; SEC: RADCLIFFE,RC CIT: 0.08
A FORECASTING METHODOLOGY AS APPLIED TO FINANCIAL TIME SERIES
TAR JA 74 VOL: 49 PG:61 - 75 :: REGRESS. :INT. LOG. :TIME SER. :BUDG.& PLAN.

MACINTOSH,NB CIT: 0.50
A CONTEXTUAL MODEL OF INFORMATION SYSTEMS
AOS 01 81 VOL: 6 PG:39 - 52 :: QUAL. :INT. LOG. :OTH. :N/A

MACINTOSH,NB ; SEC: DAFT ,RL CIT: 0.50
MANAGEMENT CONTROL SYSTEMS AND DEPARTMENTAL INTERDEPENDENCIES: AN EMPIRICAL
    STUDY
AOS 01 87 VOL: 12 PG:49 - 61 :: REGRESS. :SURV. :OTH.BEH. :ORG.& ENVIR.

MACKENZIE,O CIT: 0.00
ACCREDITATION OF ACCOUNTING CURRICULA
TAR AP 64 VOL: 39 PG:363 - 370 :: QUAL. :INT. LOG. :INSTIT. :OTH.MANAG.

MACRITCHIE,KL ; FIRS: MERINO,BD ; SEC: KOCH ,BS CIT: 0.00
HISTORICAL ANALYSIS- A DIAGNOSTIC TOOL FOR "EVENTS" STUDIES: THE IMPACT OF
    THE SECURITIES ACT OF 1933
TAR OC 87 VOL: 62 PG:748 - 762 :: REGRESS. :INT. LOG. :HIST. :FIN.METH.

MACVE ,RH ; FIRS: HOSKIN,KW CIT: 1.33
ACCOUNTING AND THE EXAMINATION: A GENEALOGY OF DISCIPLINARY POWER
AOS 02 86 VOL: 11 PG:105 - 136 :: DES.STAT. :INT. LOG. :HIST. :FASB SUBM.

MACVE ,RH ; FIRS: HOSKIN,KW CIT: 0.00
THE GENESIS OF ACCOUNTABILITY: THE WEST POINT CONNECTIONS
AOS 01 88 VOL: 13 PG:37 - 73 :: DES.STAT. :INT. LOG. :THEORY :OTH.MANAG.

MACY ,BA ; SEC: MIRVIS,PH CIT: 0.23
ACCOUNTING FOR THE COSTS AND BENEFITS OF HUMAN RESOURCE DEVELOPMENT PROGRAM
    AN INTERDISCIPLINARY APPROACH
AOS 23 76 VOL: 1 PG:179 - 194 :: QUAL. :CASE :OTH.BEH. :HRA

MADEO ,SA CIT: 0.10
AN EMPIRICAL ANALYSIS OF TAX COURT DECISIONS IN ACCUMULATED EARNINGS CASES
TAR JL 79 VOL: 54 PG:538 - 553 :: OTH.QUANT. :PRIM. :OTH.STAT. :TAXES

MADEO ,SA ; SEC: PINCUS,M CIT: 0.25
STOCK MARKET BEHAVIOR AND TAX RULE CHANGES: THE CASE OF THE DISALLOWANCE OF
    CERTAIN INTEREST DEDUCTIONS CLAIMED BY BANKS
TAR JL 85 VOL: 60 PG:407 - 429 :: REGRESS. :LAB. :EMH :TAXES

MADEO ,SA ; SEC: SCHEPANSKI,A ; THIR: UECKER,WC CIT: 0.00
MODELING JUDGMENTS OF TAXPAYER COMPLIANCE
TAR AP 87 VOL: 62 PG:323 - 342 :: REGRESS. :LAB. :OTH.STAT. :TAXES

MAGAT ,WA ; FIRS: LOEB ,M CIT: 0.27
SOVIET SUCCESS INDICATORS AND THE EVALUATION OF DIVISIONAL MANAGEMENT
JAR SP 78 VOL: 16 PG:103 - 121 :: ANAL. :INT. LOG. :INF.ECO./AG. :INT.DIFF.

MAGEE ,RP CIT: 0.62
INDUSTRY-WIDE COMMONALITIES IN EARNINGS
JAR AU 74 VOL: 12 PG:270 - 287 :: ANOVA :PRIM. :EMH :FIN.METH.

MAGEE ,RP CIT: 0.08
COST-VOLUME-PROFIT ANALYSIS, UNCERTAINTY AND CAPITAL MARKET EQUILIBRIUM
JAR AU 75 VOL: 13 PG:257 - 266 :: ANAL. :INT. LOG. :EMH :C-V-P-A

MAGEE ,RP CIT: 0.85
A SIMULATION ANALYSIS OF ALTERNATIVE COST VARIANCE INVESTIGATION MODELS
TAR JL 76 VOL: 51 PG:529 - 544 :: ANAL. :SIM. :INF.ECO./AG. :VAR.

MAGEE ,RP CIT: 0.08
COST CONTROL WITH IMPERFECT PARAMETER KNOWLEDGE
TAR JA 77 VOL: 52 PG:190 - 199 :: DES.STAT. :SIM. :MATH.PROG. :COST.ALLOC.

MAGEE ,RP CIT: 0.17
THE USEFULNESS OF COMMONALITY INFORMATION IN COST CONTROL DECISIONS
TAR OC 77 VOL: 52 PG:869 - 880 :: ANAL. :SIM. :INF.ECO./AG. :COST.ALLOC.

MAGEE ,RP ; SEC: DICKHAUT,JW CIT: 0.55
EFFECTS OF COMPENSATION PLANS ON HEURISTICS IN COST VARIANCE INVESTIGATIONS
JAR AU 78 VOL: 16 PG:294 - 314 :: ANOVA :LAB. :HIPS :VAR.

MAGEE ,RP CIT: 0.56
EQUILIBRIA IN BUDGET PARTICIPATION
JAR AU 80 VOL: 18 PG:551 - 573 :: ANAL. :INT. LOG. :INF.ECO./AG. :BUDG.& PLAN.

MAGEE ,RP ; FIRS: JOHNSON,WB ; THIR: NAGARAJAN,NJ ; FOUR: NEWMAN,HA CIT: 0.00
AN ANALYSIS OF THE STOCK PRICE REACTION TO SUDDEN EXECUTIVE DEATHS:
    IMPLICATIONS FOR THE MANAGEMENT LABOR MARKET
JAE AP 85 VOL: 7 PG:151 - 174 :: REGRESS. :PRIM. :EMH :OTH.MANAG.

MAGEE ,RP CIT: 0.00
VARIABLE COST ALLOCATION IN A PRINCIPAL/AGENT SETTING
TAR JA 88 VOL: 63 PG:42 - 54 :: DES.STAT. :INT. LOG. :INF.ECO./AG. :COST.ALLOC.

MAGLIOLO,J CIT: 0.67
CAPITAL MARKET ANALYSIS OF RESERVE RECOGNITION ACCOUNTING
JAR ST 86 VOL: 24 PG:69 - 111 :: REGRESS. :PRIM. :EMH :OIL & GAS

MAGLIOLO,J ; FIRS: LANDSMAN,WR CIT: 0.00
CROSS-SECTIONAL CAPITAL MARKET RESEARCH AND MODEL SPECIFICATION
TAR OC 88 VOL: 63 PG:586 - 604 :: DES.STAT. :INT. LOG. :EMH :METHOD.

MAHER ,JJ CIT: 0.00
PENSION OBLIGATIONS AND THE BOND CREDIT MARKET: AN EMPIRICAL ANALYSIS OF
    ACCOUNTING NUMBERS
TAR OC 87 VOL: 62 PG:785 - 798 :: REGRESS. :PRIM. :OTH.STAT. :PENS.

MAHER ,MW ; SEC: RAMANATHAN,KV ; THIR: PETERSON,RB CIT: 0.40
PREFERENCE CONGRUENCE, INFORMATION ACCURACY, AND EMPLOYEE PERFORMANCE: A
    FIELD STUDY
JAR AU 79 VOL: 17 PG:476 - 503 :: ANOVA :FIELD :OTH.BEH. :AUD.BEH.

MAHER ,MW CIT: 0.13
THE IMPACT OF REGULATION ON CONTROLS: FIRMS' RESPONSE TO THE FOREIGN CORRUPT
    PRACTICES ACT
TAR OC 81 VOL: 56 PG:751 - 770 :: DES.STAT. :PRIM. :INSTIT. :N/A

MAHER ,MW ; SEC: NANTELL,TJ CIT: 0.00
THE TAX EFFECTS OF INFLATION: DEPRECIATION, DEBT, AND MILLER'S EQUILIBRIUM
    TAX RATES
JAR SP 83 VOL: 21 PG:329 - 340 :: ANAL. :INT. LOG. :THEORY :VALUAT.(INFL.)

MAITRE,P CIT: 0.00
THE MEASUREMENT OF THE CREATION AND DISTRIBUTION OF WEALTH IN A FIRM BY THE
METHOD OF SURPLUS ACCOUNTS
AOS 34 78 VOL: 3 PG:227 - 236 :: ANAL. :INT. LOG. :THEORY :FIN.METH.

MAKSY ,MM CIT: 0.00
ARTICULATION PROBLEMS BETWEEN BALANCE SHEET AND THE FUNDS STATEMENT
TAR OC 88 VOL: 63 PG:683 - 699 :: REGRESS. :INT. LOG. :THEORY :FIN.METH.

MALCOM,RE ; FIRS: DASCHER,PE CIT: 0.31
A NOTE ON INCOME SMOOTHING IN THE CHEMICAL INDUSTRY
JAR AU 70 VOL: 8 PG:253 - 259 :: DES.STAT. :PRIM. :TIME SER. :FIN.METH.

MALCOM,RE ; FIRS: KRATCHMAN,SH ; THIR: TWARK ,RD CIT: 0.08
AN INTRA-INDUSTRY COMPARISON OF ALTERNATIVE INCOME CONCEPTS AND RELATIVE
PERFORMANCE EVALUATIONS
TAR OC 74 VOL: 49 PG:682 - 689 :: NON-PAR. :PRIM. :N/A :VALUAT.(INFL.)

MANDELKER,G ; FIRS: HONG ,H ; SEC: KAPLAN,RS CIT: 1.18
POOLING VS. PURCHASE: THE EFFECTS OF ACCOUNTING FOR MERGERS ON STOCK PRICES
TAR JA 78 VOL: 53 PG:31 - 47 :: MIXED :PRIM. :EMH :BUS.COMB.

MANEGOLD,JG CIT: 0.13
TIME-SERIES PROPERTIES OF EARNINGS: A COMPARISON OF EXTRAPOLATIVE AND
COMPONENT MODELS
JAR AU 81 VOL: 19 PG:360 - 373 :: REGRESS. :PRIM. :TIME SER. :FOREC.

MANEGOLD,JG ; FIRS: MCNICHOLS,M CIT: 0.50
THE EFFECT OF THE INFORMATION ENVIRONMENT ON THE RELATIONSHIP BETWEEN
FINANCIAL DISCLOSURE AND SECURITY PRICE VARIABILITY
JAE AP 83 VOL: 5 PG:49 - 74 :: MIXED :PRIM. :EMH :INT.REP.

MANEGOLD,JG CIT: 0.00
SMALL-COMPANY INITIAL PUBLIC OFFERINGS: THE IMPACT OF SEC REGISTRATION FORM
S-18
JAA SU 86 VOL: 1 PG:206 - 221 :: REGRESS. :PRIM. :THEORY :SPEC.ITEMS

MANES ,RP CIT: 0.00
THE GRANT-IN-AID SYSTEM FOR INTERSTATE HIGHWAY CONSTRUCTION: AN ACCOUNTING OF
ECONOMIC PROBLEM?
TAR JL 64 VOL: 39 PG:631 - 638 :: QUAL. :SEC. :N/A :FIN.METH.

MANES ,RP ; SEC: SMITH ,VL CIT: 0.00
ECONOMIC JOINT COST THEORY AND ACCOUNTING PRACTICE
TAR JA 65 VOL: 40 PG:31 - 35 :: ANAL. :INT. LOG. :N/A :COST.ALLOC.

MANES ,RP CIT: 0.00
A NEW DIMENSION TO BREAKEVEN ANALYSIS
JAR SP 66 VOL: 4 PG:87 - 100 :: ANAL. :INT. LOG. :OTH.STAT. :C-V-P-A

MANES ,RP ; FIRS: FRANK ,WG CIT: 0.08
A STANDARD COST APPLICATION OF MATRIX ALGEBRA
TAR JL 67 VOL: 42 PG:516 - 525 :: ANAL. :INT. LOG. :MATH.PROG. :VAR.

MANES ,RP ; SEC: SAMUELS,JM ; THIR: SMYTH ,DJ CIT: 0.00
INVENTORIES AND SALES: A CROSS SECTION STUDY
JAR ST 67 VOL: 5 PG:139 - 156 :: REGRESS. :PRIM. :THEORY :INV.

MANES ,RP ; FIRS: COLANTONI,CS ; THIR: WHINSTON,AB CIT: 0.08
PROGRAMMING, PROFIT RATES AND PRICING DECISIONS
TAR JL 69 VOL: 44 PG:467 - 481 :: ANAL. :INT. LOG. :MATH.PROG. :REL.COSTS

MANES ,RP ; FIRS: GROVES,R ; THIR: SORENSEN,R CIT: 0.08
THE APPLICATION OF THE HIRSCH-DANTZIG "FIXED CHARGE" ALGORITHM TO PROFIT
PLANNING: A FORMAL STATEMENT OF PRODUCT PROFITABILITY ANALYSIS
TAR JL 70 VOL: 45 PG:481 - 489 :: ANAL. :INT. LOG. :MATH.PROG. :BUDG.& PLAN.

MANES ,RP ; FIRS: COLANTONI,CS ; THIR: WHINSTON,AB CIT: 0.46
A UNIFIED APPROACH TO THE THEORY OF ACCOUNTING AND INFORMATION SYSTEMS
TAR JA 71 VOL: 46 PG:90 - 102 :: QUAL. :INT. LOG. :N/A :MANAG.

MANES ,RP ; SEC: PARK ,SH ; THIR: JENSEN,RE CIT: 0.00
RELEVANT COSTS OF INTERMEDIATE GOODS AND SERVICES
TAR JL 82 VOL: 57 PG:594 - 606 :: ANAL. :INT. LOG. :MATH.PROG. :N/A

MARAIS,ML CIT: 0.80
AN APPLICATION OF THE BOOTSTRAP METHOD TO THE ANALYSIS OF SQUARED,
STANDARDIZED MARKET MODEL PREDICTION ERRORS
JAR ST 84 VOL: 22 PG:34 - 54 :: DES.STAT. :PRIM. :EMH :METHOD.

MARAIS,ML ; SEC: PATELL,JM ; THIR: WOLFSON,MA CIT: 0.20
THE EXPERIMENTAL DESIGN OF CLASSIFICATORY MODELS: AN APPLICATION OF RECURSIVE
PARTITIONING AND BOOTSTRAPPING COMMERCIAL BANK LOAN CLASSIFICATION
JAR ST 84 VOL: 22 PG:87 - 114 :: OTH.QUANT. :PRIM. :OTH.STAT. :BUS.FAIL.

MARCH ,JG CIT: 0.00
AMBIGUITY AND ACCOUNTING: THE ELUSIVE LINK BETWEEN INFORMATION AND DECISION
MAKING
AOS 02 87 VOL: 12 PG:153 - 168 :: DES.STAT. :INT. LOG. :THEORY :FIN.METH.

MARCINKO,D ; SEC: PETRI ,E CIT: 0.00
USE OF THE PRODUCTION FUNCTION IN CALCULATION OF STANDARD COST VARIANCES - AN
EXTENSION
TAR JL 84 VOL: 59 PG:488 - 495 :: ANAL. :INT. LOG. :OTH. :VAR.

MARGHEIM,LL ; SEC: PANY ,K CIT: 0.00
QUALITY CONTROL, PREMATURE SIGNOFF, AND UNDERREPORTING OF TIME: SOME
EMPIRICAL FINDINGS
AUD SP 86 VOL: 5 PG:50 - 63 :: REGRESS. :LAB. :OTH.BEH. :ORG.

MARGHEIM,LL CIT: 0.00
FURTHER EVIDENCE ON EXTERNAL AUDITORS' RELIANCE ON INTERNAL AUDITORS
JAR SP 86 VOL: 24 PG:194 - 205 :: REGRESS. :LAB. :OTH. :ORG.

MARKS ,BR ; SEC: RAMAN ,KK CIT: 0.00
THE IMPORTANCE OF PENSION DATA FOR MUNICIPAL & STATE CREDITOR DECISIONS:
REPLICATIONS & EXTENSIONS
JAR AU 85 VOL: 23 PG:878 - 886 :: REGRESS. :PRIM. :OTH.STAT. :PENS.

MARKS ,BR ; SEC: RAMAN ,KK CIT: 0.00
SOME ADDITIONAL EVIDENCE ON THE DETERMINANTS OF STATE AUDIT BUDGETS
AUD AU 87 VOL: 7 PG:106 - 117 :: REGRESS. :PRIM. :THEORY :AUD.

MARKUS,ML ; SEC: PFEFFER,J CIT: 0.50
POWER AND THE DESIGN AND IMPLEMENTATION OF ACCOUNTING AND CONTROL SYSTEMS
AOS 23 83 VOL: 8 PG:205 - 218 :: QUAL. :CASE :OTH. :MANAG.

MARPLE,RM CIT: 0.00
VALUE-ITIS
TAR JL 63 VOL: 38 PG:478 - 482 :: QUAL. :INT. LOG. :THEORY :FIN.METH.

MARQUES,E CIT: 0.08
HUMAN RESOURCE ACCOUNTING: SOME QUESTIONS AND REFLECTIONS
AOS 23 76 VOL: 1 PG:175 - 178 :: QUAL. :SURV. :THEORY :HRA

MARSHALL,RM CIT: 0.46
DETERMINING AN OPTIMAL ACCOUNTING INFORMATION SYSTEM FOR AN UNIDENTIFIED USER
JAR AU 72 VOL: 10 PG:286 - 307 :: ANAL. :INT. LOG. :INF.ECO./AG. :INFO.STRUC.

MARSHALL,RM CIT: 0.23
INTERPRETING THE API
TAR JA 75 VOL: 50 PG:99 - 111 :: ANAL. :INT. LOG. :EMH :METHOD.

MARSHALL,RM ; FIRS: JACOBS,FH CIT: 0.00
A RECIPROCAL SERVICE COST APPROXIMATION
TAR JA 87 VOL: 62 PG:67 - 78 :: DES.STAT. :INT. LOG. :THEORY :COST.ALLOC.

MARSTON,F ; SEC: HARRIS,RS CIT: 0.00
SUITABILITY OF LEASES AND DEBT IN CORPORATE CAPITAL STRUCTURES
JAA SP 88 VOL: 03 PG:147 - 164 :: REGRESS. :PRIM. :EMH :LEASES

MARTIN,A CIT: 0.00
AN EMPIRICAL TEST OF THE RELEVANCE OF ACCOUNTING INFORMATION FOR INVESTMENT
  DECISIONS
JAR ST 71 VOL: 9 PG:1 - 31 :: REGRESS. :PRIM. :HIPS :FIN.METH.

MARTIN,JD ; SEC: ANDERSON,PF ; THIR: KEOWN ,AJ CIT: 0.00
LEASE CAPITALIZATION AND STOCK PRICE STABILITY: IMPLICATIONS FOR ACCOUNTING
JAA WI 79 VOL: 2 PG:151 - 164 :: REGRESS. :PRIM. :EMH :LEASES

MARTIN,K ; FIRS: LEWELLEN,W ; SEC: LODERER,C CIT: 0.00
EXECUTIVE COMPENSATION AND EXECUTIVE INCENTIVE PROBLEMS: AN EMPIRICAL
  ANALYSIS
JAE DE 87 VOL: 9 PG:287 - 310 :: REGRESS. :PRIM. :OTH.STAT. :EXEC.COMP.

MARTIN,RK ; FIRS: BIDDLE,GC CIT: 0.25
INFLATION, TAXES, AND OPTIMAL INVENTORY POLICIES
JAR SP 85 VOL: 23 PG:57 - 83 :: REGRESS. :SIM. :OTH.STAT. :INV.

MASCHMEYER,R ; FIRS: BALACHANDRAN,KR ; THIR: LIVINGSTONE,JL CIT: 0.13
PRODUCT WARRANTY PERIOD: A MARKOVIAN APPROACH TO ESTIMATION AND ANALYSIS OF
  REPAIR AND REPLACEMENT COSTS
TAR JA 81 VOL: 56 PG:115 - 124 :: MARKOV :INT. LOG. :OTH.STAT. :SPEC.ITEMS

MASON ,RO ; FIRS: MITROFF,II CIT: 0.33
CAN WE DESIGN SYSTEMS FOR MANAGING MESSES? OR, WHY SO MANY MANAGEMENT
  INFORMATION SYSTEMS ARE UNINFORMATIVE
AOS 23 83 VOL: 8 PG:195 - 204 :: QUAL. :INT. LOG. :OTH. :MAN.DEC.CHAR.

MATEER,WH CIT: 0.00
TAX ALLOCATION: A MACRO APPROACH
TAR JL 65 VOL: 40 PG:583 - 586 :: QUAL. :INT. LOG. :THEORY :N/A

MATHEWS,RL ; FIRS: BUCKLEY,JW ; SEC: KIRCHER,P CIT: 0.08
METHODOLOGY IN ACCOUNTING THEORY
TAR AP 68 VOL: 43 PG:274 - 283 :: QUAL. :INT. LOG. :THEORY :FIN.METH.

MATHEWS,RL CIT: 0.08
INCOME, PRICE CHANGES AND THE VALUATION CONTROVERSY IN ACCOUNTING
TAR JL 68 VOL: 43 PG:509 - 516 :: QUAL. :INT. LOG. :THEORY :VALUAT.(INFL.)

MATOLCSY,ZP CIT: 0.60
EVIDENCE ON THE JOINT AND MARGINAL INFORMATION CONTENT OF INFLATION ADJUSTED
   ACCOUNTING INCOME NUMBERS
JAR AU 84 VOL: 22 PG:555 - 569 :: ANAL. :INT. LOG. :OTH.STAT. :LIAB.

MATSUMURA,EM ; SEC: TSUI ,KW CIT: 0.14
STEIN-TYPE POISSON ESTIMATORS IN AUDIT SAMPLING
JAR SP 82 VOL: 20 PG:162 - 170 :: CORR. :INT. LOG. :N/A :SAMP.

MATSUMURA,EM ; FIRS: TSUI ,KW ; THIR: TSUI ,KL CIT: 0.50
MULTINOMINAL-DIRICHLET BOUNDS FOR DOLLAR-UNIT SAMPLING IN AUDITING
TAR JA 85 VOL: 60 PG:76 - 96 :: DES.STAT. :SIM. :OTH.STAT. :SAMP.

MATTESSICH,R CIT: 0.15
METHODOLOGICAL PRECONDITIONS AND PROBLEMS OF A GENERAL THEORY OF ACCOUNTING
TAR JL 72 VOL: 47 PG:469 - 487 :: QUAL. :INT. LOG. :THEORY :FIN.METH.

MATTINGLY,LA CIT: 0.00
FORMATION AND DEVELOPMENT OF THE INSTITUTE OF CERTIFIED PUBLIC ACCOUNTANTS OF
   GREECE
TAR OC 64 VOL: 39 PG:996 - 003 :: QUAL. :INT. LOG. :INSTIT. :OTH.MANAG.

MAURIELLO,JA CIT: 0.00
REALIZATION AS THE BASIS FOR ASSET CLASSIFICATION AND MEASUREMENT
TAR JA 63 VOL: 38 PG:26 - 28 :: QUAL. :INT. LOG. :THEORY :REV.REC.

MAURIELLO,JA CIT: 0.00
THE ALL-INCLUSIVE STATEMENT OF FUNDS
TAR AP 64 VOL: 39 PG:347 - 357 :: QUAL. :INT. LOG. :THEORY :INFO.STRUC.

MAUTZ ,RD ; FIRS: TILLER,MG CIT: 0.00
THE IMPACT OF STATE-MANDATED ACCOUNTING AND AUDITING REQUIREMENTS ON
   MUNICIPAL BOND RATINGS
JAA SU 85 VOL: 8 PG:293 - 304 :: REGRESS. :PRIM. :OTH.STAT. :LTD

MAUTZ ,RK CIT: 0.15
ACCOUNTING AS A SOCIAL SCIENCE
TAR AP 63 VOL: 38 PG:317 - 325 :: QUAL. :INT. LOG. :THEORY :OTH.MANAG.

MAUTZ ,RK CIT: 0.00
CHALLENGES TO THE ACCOUNTING PROFESSION
TAR AP 65 VOL: 40 PG:299 - 311 :: QUAL. :INT. LOG. :INSTIT. :OTH.MANAG.

MAUTZ ,RK ; SEC: MINI ,DL CIT: 0.08
INTERNAL CONTROL EVALUATION AND AUDIT PROGRAM MODIFICATION
TAR AP 66 VOL: 41 PG:283 - 291 :: QUAL. :INT. LOG. :N/A :INT.CONT.

MAUTZ ,RK ; SEC: SKOUSEN,KF CIT: 0.00
SOME PROBLEMS IN EMPIRICAL RESEARCH IN ACCOUNTING
TAR JL 69 VOL: 44 PG:447 - 456 :: QUAL. :INT. LOG. :N/A :OTH.MANAG.

MAUTZ ,RK ; SEC: PREVITS,GJ CIT: 0.00
ERIC KOHLER: AN ACCOUNTING ORIGINAL
TAR AP 77 VOL: 52 PG:301 - 307 :: QUAL. :INT. LOG. :HIST. :N/A

MAXIM ,LD ; SEC: CULLEN,PE ; THIR: COOK ,FX CIT: 0.00
OPTIMAL ACCEPTANCE SAMPLING PLANS FOR AUDITING "BATCHED" STOP AND GO VS.
CONVENTIONAL SINGLE-STAGE ATTRIBUTES
TAR JA 76 VOL: 51 PG:97 - 109 :: ANAL. :INT. LOG. :OTH.STAT. :SAMP.

MAXWELL,WD ; FIRS: ZEFF ,SA CIT: 0.00
HOLDING GAINS ON FIXED ASSETS - A DEMURRER
TAR JA 65 VOL: 40 PG:65 - 75 :: QUAL. :INT. LOG. :THEORY :VALUAT.(INFL.)

MAY ,PT CIT: 0.00
SYSTEM CONTROL: COMPUTERS THE WEAK LINK?
TAR JL 69 VOL: 44 PG:583 - 592 :: QUAL. :INT. LOG. :N/A :OTH.MANAG.

MAY ,RG CIT: 1.92
THE INFLUENCE OF QUARTERLY EARNINGS ANNOUNCEMENTS ON INVESTOR DECISIONS AS
REFLECTED IN COMMON STOCK PRICE CHANGES
JAR ST 71 VOL: 9 PG:119 - 163 :: REGRESS. :PRIM. :EMH :INT.REP.

MAY ,RG ; SEC: SUNDEM,GL CIT: 0.38
COST OF INFORMATION AND SECURITY PRICES: MARKET ASSOCIATION TESTS FOR
ACCOUNTING POLICY DECISIONS
TAR JA 73 VOL: 48 PG:80 - 94 :: ANAL. :INT. LOG. :EMH :INFO.STRUC.

MAY ,RG ; SEC: SUNDEM,GL CIT: 0.69
RESEARCH FOR ACCOUNTING POLICY: AN OVERVIEW
TAR OC 76 VOL: 51 PG:747 - 763 :: QUAL. :INT. LOG. :THEORY :FIN.METH.

MAYER-SOMMER,AP CIT: 0.40
UNDERSTANDING AND ACCEPTANCE OF THE EFFICIENT MARKETS HYPOTHESIS AND ITS
ACCOUNTING IMPLICATIONS
TAR JA 79 VOL: 54 PG:88 - 106 :: DES.STAT. :SURV. :EMH :OTH.MANAG.

MAYNE ,LS ; FIRS: PHILIPS,GE CIT: 0.00
INCOME MEASURE AND BANK STOCK VALUES
JAR ST 70 VOL: 8 PG:178 - 188 :: REGRESS. :PRIM. :TIME SER. :VALUAT.(INFL.)

MAYPER,AG CIT: 0.00
CONSENSUS OF AUDITORS' MATERIALITY JUDGMENTS OF INTERNAL ACCOUNTING CONTROL
WEAKNESSES
JAR AU 82 VOL: 20 PG:773 - 783 :: NON-PAR. :LAB. :HIPS :MAT.

MAYPER,AG ; FIRS: GIROUX,GA ; THIR: DAFT ,RL CIT: 0.00
ORGANIZATION SIZE, BUDGET CYCLE, AND BUDGET RELATED INFLUENCE IN CITY
GOVERNMENTS: AN EMPIRICAL STUDY
AOS 06 86 VOL: 11 PG:499 - 520 :: REGRESS. :SURV. :OTH.STAT. :BUDG.& PLAN.

MCAFEE,RP ; FIRS: BAILEY,AP ; THIR: WHINSTON,AB CIT: 0.13
AN APPLICATION OF COMPLEXITY THEORY TO THE ANALYSIS OF INTERNAL CONTROL
SYSTEMS
AUD SU 81 VOL: 1 PG:38 - 52 :: ANAL. :INT. LOG. :OTH.STAT. :INT.CONT.

MCALLISTER,JP ; FIRS: DIRSMITH,MW CIT: 0.00
THE ORGANIC VS. THE MECHANISTIC AUDIT: PROBLEMS AND PITFALLS (PART II)
JAA AU 82 VOL: 6 PG:60 - 74 :: QUAL. :INT. LOG. :OTH. :AUD.

MCALLISTER,JP ; FIRS: DIRSMITH,MW CIT: 0.00
THE ORGANIC VS. THE MECHANISTIC AUDIT
JAA SP 82 VOL: 5 PG:214 - 228 :: QUAL. :INT. LOG. :OTH. :AUD.

MCBRIDE,HJ CIT: 0.00
ASSIGNING TAX LOADS TO PROSPECTIVE PROJECTS
TAR AP 63 VOL: 38 PG:363 - 370 :: ANAL. :INT. LOG. :OTH. :INT.CONT.

MCCARTHY,WE CIT: 0.40
AN ENTITY-RELATIONSHIP VIEW OF ACCOUNTING MODELS
TAR OC 79 VOL: 54 PG:667 - 686 :: QUAL. :INT. LOG. :OTH. :N/A

MCCARTHY,WE CIT: 0.14
THE REA ACCOUNTING MODEL: A GENERALIZED FRAMEWORK FOR ACCOUNTING SYSTEMS IN A
    SHARED DATA ENVIRONMENT
TAR JL 82 VOL: 57 PG:554 - 578 :: QUAL. :INT. LOG. :THEORY :N/A

MCCLENON,PR CIT: 0.00
COST FINDING THROUGH MULTIPLE CORRELATION ANALYSIS
TAR JL 63 VOL: 38 PG:540 - 547 :: CORR. :INT. LOG. :OTH.STAT. :COST.ALLOC.

MCCONNELL,DK CIT: 0.00
AUDITOR CHANGES AND RELATED DISAGREEMENTS
AUD SP 84 VOL: 3 PG:44 - 56 :: DES.STAT. :PRIM. :OTH.STAT. :AUD.

MCCONNELL,DK CIT: 0.40
ARE THE BIG 8 INCREASING THEIR SHARE OF THE NYSE, AMEX, AND OTC AUDIT MARKETS?
JAA WI 84 VOL: 7 PG:178 - 181 :: NON-PAR. :PRIM. :INSTIT. :AUD.

MCCOSH,AM CIT: 0.00
ACCOUNTING CONSISTENCY - KEY TO STOCKHOLDER INFORMATION
TAR OC 67 VOL: 42 PG:693 - 700 :: ANAL. :SIM. :THEORY :FIN.METH.

MCCOSH,AM ; SEC: RAHMAN,M CIT: 0.08
THE INFLUENCE OF ORGANIZATIONAL AND PERSONAL FACTORS ON THE USE OF ACCOUNTING
    INFORMATION: AN EMPIRICAL STUDY
AOS 04 76 VOL: 1 PG:339 - 356 :: DES.STAT. :LAB. :HIPS :MAN.DEC.CHAR.

MCCRAY,JH CIT: 0.60
A QUASI-BAYESIAN AUDIT RISK MODEL FOR DOLLAR UNIT SAMPLING
TAR JA 84 VOL: 59 PG:35 - 51 :: MIXED :SIM. :OTH.STAT. :SAMP.

MCDONALD,B ; SEC: MORRIS,MH CIT: 0.40
THE RELEVANCE OF SFAS 33 INFLATION ACCOUNTING DISCLOSURES IN THE ADJUSTMENT
    OF STOCK PRICES TO INFLATION
TAR JL 84 VOL: 59 PG:432 - 446 :: REGRESS. :PRIM. :EMH :VALUAT.(INFL.)

MCDONALD,B ; FIRS: BALVERS,RJ ; THIR: MILLER,RE CIT: 0.00
UNDERPRICING OF NEW ISSUES AND THE CHOICE OF AUDITOR AS A SIGNAL OF
    INVESTMENT BANKER REPUTATION
TAR OC 88 VOL: 63 PG:605 - 622 :: REGRESS. :PRIM. :MATH.PROG. :AUD.THEOR.

MCDONALD,CL CIT: 0.92
AN EMPIRICAL EXAMINATION OF THE RELIABILITY OF PUBLISHED PREDICTIONS OF
    FUTURE EARNINGS
TAR JL 73 VOL: 48 PG:502 - 510 :: DES.STAT. :PRIM. :OTH.STAT. :FOREC.

MCDONALD,CL ; FIRS: LOREK ,KS ; THIR: PATZ ,DH CIT: 0.77
A COMPARATIVE EXAMINATION OF MANAGEMENT FORECASTS AND BOX-JENKINS FORECASTS
    OF EARNINGS
TAR AP 76 VOL: 51 PG:321 - 330 :: REGRESS. :PRIM. :TIME SER. :METHOD.

MCDONALD,DL CIT: 0.08
FEASIBILITY CRITERIA FOR ACCOUNTING MEASURES
TAR OC 67 VOL: 42 PG:662 - 679 :: ANAL. :INT. LOG. :THEORY :OTH.FIN.ACC.

MCDONALD,DL CIT: 0.15
A TEST APPLICATION OF THE FEASIBILITY OF MARKET BASED MEASURES IN ACCOUNTING
JAR SP 68 VOL: 6 PG:38 - 49 :: NON-PAR. :LAB. :N/A :VALUAT.(INFL.)

MCDONALD,DL ; SEC: PUXTY ,AG CIT: 0.00
AN INDUCEMENT-CONTRIBUTION APPROACH TO CORPORATE FINANCIAL REPORTING
AOS 12 79 VOL: 4 PG:53 - 66 :: QUAL. :INT. LOG. :THEORY :N/A

MCDONOUGH,JJ CIT: 0.08
THE ACCOUNTANT, DATA COLLECTION AND SOCIAL EXCHANGE
TAR OC 71 VOL: 46 PG:676 - 685 :: QUAL. :INT. LOG. :OTH.BEH. :MANAG.

MCDONOUGH,JJ ; FIRS: EPSTEIN,MJ ; SEC: FLAMHOLTZ,EG CIT: 0.54
CORPORATE SOCIAL ACCOUNTING IN THE U.S.A.: STATE OF THE ART AND FUTURE
PROSPECTS
AOS 01 76 VOL: 1 PG:23 - 42 :: QUAL. :SEC. :THEORY :HRA

MCDONOUGH,JJ ; FIRS: ANSARI,SL CIT: 0.11
INTERSUBJECTIVITY - THE CHALLENGE AND OPPORTUNITY FOR ACCOUNTING
AOS 01 80 VOL: 5 PG:129 - 142 :: QUAL. :INT. LOG. :THEORY :N/A

MCENALLY,RW ; FIRS: JOY ,OM ; SEC: LITZENBERGER,RH CIT: 0.83
THE ADJUSTMENT OF STOCK PRICES TO ANNOUNCEMENTS OF UNANTICIPATED CHANGES IN
QUARTERLY EARNINGS
JAR AU 77 VOL: 15 PG:207 - 225 :: REGRESS. :PRIM. :EMH :INT.REP.

MCGAHRAN,KT CIT: 0.00
SEC DISCLOSURE REGULATION AND MANAGEMENT PERQUISITES
TAR JA 88 VOL: 63 PG:23 - 41 :: DES.STAT. :PRIM. :EMH :EXEC.COMP.

MCGEE ,VE ; FIRS: CASEY JR,CJ ; THIR: STICKNEY,CP CIT: 0.33
DISCRIMINATING BETWEEN REORGANIZED AND LIQUIDATED FIRMS IN BANKRUPTCY
TAR AP 86 VOL: 61 PG:249 - 262 :: REGRESS. :PRIM. :OTH.STAT. :BUS.FAIL.

MCGHEE,W ; SEC: SHIELDS,MD ; THIR: BIRNBERG,JG CIT: 1.00
THE EFFECTS OF PERSONALITY ON A SUBJECT'S INFORMATION PROCESSING
TAR JL 78 VOL: 53 PG:681 - 697 :: ANOVA :LAB. :HIPS :OTH.MANAG.

MCHUGH,AJ ; FIRS: DYER ,JC CIT: 0.46
THE TIMELINESS OF THE AUSTRALIAN ANNUAL REPORT
JAR AU 75 VOL: 13 PG:204 - 219 :: NON-PAR. :PRIM. :OTH.STAT. :TIM.

MCINNES, M ; FIRS: BROWNELL,P CIT: 0.67
BUDGETARY PARTICIPATION, MOTIVATION, AND MANAGERIAL PERFORMANCE
TAR OC 86 VOL: 61 PG:587 - 600 :: REGRESS. :SURV. :OTH.BEH. :BUDG.& PLAN.

MCINTYRE,EV CIT: 0.38
CURRENT-COST FINANCIAL STATEMENTS AND COMMON-STOCK INVESTMENTS DECISIONS
TAR JL 73 VOL: 48 PG:575 - 585 :: ANOVA :LAB. :THEORY :VALUAT.(INFL.)

MCINTYRE,EV CIT: 0.08
PRESENT VALUE DEPRECIATION AND THE DISAGGREGATION PROBLEM
TAR JA 77 VOL: 52 PG:162 - 171 :: ANAL. :INT. LOG. :THEORY :PP&E / DEPR

MCINTYRE,EV CIT: 0.00
INTERACTION EFFECTS OF INFLATION ACCOUNTING MODELS AND ACCOUNTING TECHNIQUES
TAR JL 82 VOL: 57 PG:607 - 618 :: ANAL. :INT. LOG. :THEORY :VALUAT.(INFL.)

MCKEE ,AJ ; SEC: BELL ,TB ; THIR: BOATSMAN,JR CIT: 0.40
MANAGEMENT PREFERENCES OVER ACCOUNTING STANDARDS: A REPLICATION AND
   ADDITIONAL TESTS
TAR OC 84 VOL: 59 PG:647 - 659 :: OTH.QUANT. :PRIM. :INSTIT. :FASB SUBM.

MCKENNA,EF CIT: 0.00
AN ANALYSIS OF LEADERSHIP PATTERNS IN THE FINANCE FUNCTION
AOS 03 80 VOL: 5 PG:297 - 310 :: CORR. :LAB. :OTH.STAT. :MANAG.

MCKEOWN,JC CIT: 0.23
AN EMPIRICAL TEST OF A MODEL PROPOSED BY CHAMBERS
TAR JA 71 VOL: 46 PG:12 - 29 :: ANAL. :CASE :THEORY :VALUAT.(INFL.)

MCKEOWN,JC ; FIRS: BEDFORD,NM CIT: 0.00
COMPARATIVE ANALYSIS OF NET REALIZABLE VALUE AND REPLACEMENT COSTING
TAR AP 72 VOL: 47 PG:333 - 338 :: QUAL. :INT. LOG. :THEORY :VALUAT.(INFL.)

MCKEOWN,JC CIT: 0.00
ADDITIVITY OF NET REALIZABLE VALUES
TAR JL 72 VOL: 47 PG:527 - 532 :: ANAL. :INT. LOG. :THEORY :VALUAT.(INFL.)

MCKEOWN,JC CIT: 0.08
COMPARATIVE APPLICATION OF MARKET AND COST BASED ACCOUNTING MODELS
JAR SP 73 VOL: 11 PG:62 - 99 :: REGRESS. :CASE :OTH. :VALUAT.(INFL.)

MCKEOWN,JC ; FIRS: ALBRECHT,WS ; SEC: LOOKABILL,LL CIT: 2.00
THE TIME-SERIES PROPERTIES OF ANNUAL EARNINGS
JAR AU 77 VOL: 15 PG:226 - 244 :: MIXED :PRIM. :TIME SER. :FOREC.

MCKEOWN,JC ; FIRS: ABDEL-KHALIK,AR CIT: 1.09
UNDERSTANDING ACCOUNTING CHANGES IN AN EFFICIENT MARKET: EVIDENCE OF
   DIFFERENTIAL REACTION
TAR OC 78 VOL: 53 PG:851 - 868 :: ANOVA :PRIM. :EMH :INV.

MCKEOWN,JC ; FIRS: ABDEL-KHALIK,AR CIT: 0.36
DISCLOSURE OF ESTIMATES OF HOLDING GAINS AND THE ASSESSMENT OF SYSTEMATIC RISK
JAR ST 78 VOL: 16 PG:46 - 77 :: ANOVA :PRIM. :EMH :VALUAT.(INFL.)

MCKEOWN,JC ; FIRS: HOPWOOD,WS CIT: 0.38
AN EVALUATION OF UNIVARIATE TIME-SERIES EARNINGS MODELS AND THEIR
   GENERALIZATION TO A SINGLE INPUT TRANSFER FUNCTION
JAR AU 81 VOL: 19 PG:313 - 322 :: CORR. :PRIM. :TIME SER. :FOREC.

MCKEOWN,JC ; FIRS: HOPWOOD,WS ; THIR: NEWBOLD,P CIT: 0.71
THE ADDITIONAL INFORMATION CONTENT OF QUARTERLY EARNINGS REPORTS:
   INTERTEMPORAL DISAGGREGATION
JAR AU 82 VOL: 20 PG:343 - 349 :: REGRESS. :PRIM. :TIME SER. :INT.REP.

MCKEOWN,JC ; FIRS: COLLINS,WA ; SEC: HOPWOOD,WS CIT: 0.20
THE PREDICTABILITY OF INTERIM EARNINGS OVER ALTERNATIVE QUARTERS
JAR AU 84 VOL: 22 PG:467 - 479 :: NON-PAR. :PRIM. :TIME SER. :INT.REP.

MCKEOWN,JC ; FIRS: HOPWOOD,WS CIT: 0.00
THE INCREMENTAL INFORMATIONAL CONTENT OF INTERIM EXPENSES OVER INTERIM SALES
JAR SP 85 VOL: 23 PG:161 - 174 :: REGRESS. :PRIM. :EMH :TAXES

MCKEOWN,JC ; FIRS: SILHAN,PA CIT: 0.00
FURTHER EVIDENCE ON THE USEFULNESS OF SIMULATED MERGERS
JAR SP 85 VOL: 23 PG:416 - 426 :: REGRESS. :PRIM. :TIME SER. :BUS.COMB.

MCKEOWN,JC ; FIRS: BUBLITZ,B ; SEC: FRECKA,TJ CIT: 1.50
MARKET ASSOCIATION TESTS AND FASB STATEMENT NO. 33 DISCLOSURES: A
REEXAMINATION
JAR ST 85 VOL: 23 PG:1 - 23 :: REGRESS. :PRIM. :EMH :VALUAT.(INFL.)

MCKINELY,S ; SEC: PANY ,K ; THIR: RECKERS,PMJ CIT: 0.00
AN EXAMINATION OF THE INFLUENCE OF CPA FIRM TYPE, SIZE, AND MAS PROVISION ON
LOAN OFFICER DECISIONS & PERCEPTIONS
JAR AU 85 VOL: 23 PG:887 - 896 :: REGRESS. :LAB. :OTH.BEH. :ORG.

MCKINNEY,G ; FIRS: RONEN ,J CIT: 0.38
TRANSFER PRICING FOR DIVISIONAL AUTONOMY
JAR SP 70 VOL: 8 PG:99 - 112 :: ANAL. :INT. LOG. :OTH. :TRANS.PRIC.

MCKINNON,JL ; FIRS: HARRISON,GL CIT: 0.00
CULTURE AND ACCOUNTING CHANGE: A NEW PROSPECTIVE ON CORPORATE REPORTING
REGULATION AND ACCOUNTING POLICY FORMULATION
AOS 03 86 VOL: 11 PG:233 - 252 :: DES.STAT. :INT. LOG. :INSTIT. :FASB SUBM.

MCLEAY,S CIT: 0.17
VALUE ADDED: A COMPARATIVE STUDY
AOS 01 83 VOL: 8 PG:31 - 56 :: DES.STAT. :PRIM. :OTH.STAT. :INT.DIFF.

MCNAMEE,AH ; FIRS: CHOW ,CW ; THIR: PLUMLEE,RD CIT: 0.00
PRACTITIONERS' PERCEPTIONS OF AUDIT STEP DIFFICULTY AND CRITICALNESS   :
IMPLICATIONS FOR AUDIT RESEARCH
AUD SP 87 VOL: 6 PG:123 - 133 :: REGRESS. :SURV. :OTH.STAT. :AUD.THEOR.

MCNICHOLS,M ; SEC: MANEGOLD,JG CIT: 0.50
THE EFFECT OF THE INFORMATION ENVIRONMENT ON THE RELATIONSHIP BETWEEN
FINANCIAL DISCLOSURE AND SECURITY PRICE VARIABILITY
JAE AP 83 VOL: 5 PG:49 - 74 :: MIXED :PRIM. :EMH :INT.REP.

MCNICHOLS,M CIT: 0.00
A COMPARISON OF THE SKEWNESS OF STOCK RETURN DISTRIBUTIONS AT EARNINGS AND
NON-EARNINGS ANNOUNCEMENT DATES
JAE JL 88 VOL: 10 PG:239 - 273 :: REGRESS. :SIM. :EMH :METHOD.

MCQUEENEY,J ; FIRS: JACKSON-COX,J ; SEC: THIRKELL,JE CIT: 0.00
THE DISCLOSURE OF COMPANY INFORMATION TO TRADE UNIONS: THE RELEVANCE OF THE
ACAS CODE OF PRACTICE ON DISCLOSURE
AOS 34 84 VOL: 9 PG:253 - 273 :: QUAL. :SURV. :INSTIT. :N/A

MCRAE ,TW CIT: 0.00
ACCOUNTANCY TRAINING IN SCOTLAND
JAR AU 65 VOL: 3 PG:255 - 260 :: QUAL. :INT. LOG. :OTH. :AUD.TRAIN.

MCRAE ,TW CIT: 0.08
OPPORTUNITY AND INCREMENTAL COST: AN ATTEMPT TO DEFINE IN SYSTEMS TERMS
TAR AP 70 VOL: 45 PG:315 - 321 :: QUAL. :SEC. :N/A :REL.COSTS

MCRAE ,TW CIT: 0.31
A CITATIONAL ANALYSIS OF THE ACCOUNTING INFORMATION NETWORK
JAR SP 74 VOL: 12 PG:80 - 92 :: DES.STAT. :SEC. :OTH. :METHOD.

MCROBERTS,HA ; SEC: HUDSON,J CIT: 0.00
AUDITING PROGRAM EVALUATIONS: THE CANADIAN CASE
AOS 04 85 VOL: 10 PG:493 - 502 :: REGRESS. :FIELD :INSTIT. :OPER.AUD.

MEANS ,KM ; FIRS: HOLZMANN,OJ CIT: 0.00
ACCOUNTING FOR SAVINGS AND LOAN MERGERS: CONFLICT AND ACCOUNTING ERROR
JAA WI 84 VOL: 7 PG:138 - 150 :: QUAL. :INT. LOG. :THEORY :BUS.COMB.

MEAR ,R ; SEC: FIRTH ,MA CIT: 0.00
CUE USAGE AND SELF-INSIGHT OF FINANCIAL ANALYSTS
TAR JA 87 VOL: 62 PG:176 - 182 :: REGRESS. :LAB. :HIPS :MAN.DEC.CHAR.

MEAR ,R ; SEC: FIRTH ,MA CIT: 0.00
ASSESSING THE ACCURACY OF FINANCIAL ANALYST SECURITY RETURN PREDICTIONS
AOS 04 87 VOL: 12 PG:331 - 340 :: REGRESS. :PRIM. :HIPS :FOREC.

MEEK ,GK CIT: 0.00
U.S. SECURITIES MARKET RESPONSES TO ALTERNATE EARNINGS DISCLOSURES OF
   NON-U.S. MULTINATIONAL CORPORATIONS
TAR AP 83 VOL: 58 PG:394 - 402 :: ANOVA :PRIM. :EMH :FIN.METH.

MEHTA ,DR ; SEC: ANDREWS,VL CIT: 0.00
A NOTE ON INSTALLMENT REPORTING OF INCOME, PROFITABILITY, AND FUND FLOWS
JAR SP 68 VOL: 6 PG:50 - 57 :: DES.STAT. :SIM. :OTH.STAT. :TAXES

MEIXNER,WF ; SEC: WELKER,RB CIT: 0.00
JUDGMENT CONSENSUS AND AUDITOR EXPERIENCE: AN EXAMINATION OF ORGANIZATIONAL
   RELATIONS
AUD JL 88 VOL: 63 PG:505 - 513 :: CORR. :LAB. :OTH.BEH. :JUDG.

MELBERG,WF CIT: 0.00
BENISHAYAN TIMES SERIES AS MODELS FOR DEBT PROCESSES OVER TIME
TAR JA 72 VOL: 47 PG:116 - 133 :: ANAL. :INT. LOG. :TIME SER. :OTH.MANAG.

MELLMAN,M CIT: 0.00
MARKETING COST ANALYSIS - DEVELOPMENT AND CURRENT PRACTICES
TAR JA 63 VOL: 38 PG:118 - 123 :: DES.STAT. :SURV. :OTH.STAT. :COST.ALLOC.

MELLMAN,M ; SEC: SEILER,ME CIT: 0.00
STRUCTURE NEEDED FOR IMPLEMENTING MANDATED ACCOUNTING CHANGES
JAA AU 86 VOL: 1 PG:305 - 318 :: REGRESS. :PRIM. :INSTIT. :FASB SUBM.

MELLMAN,M ; FIRS: LILIEN,S ; THIR: PASTENA,V CIT: 0.00
ACCOUNTING CHANGES: SUCCESSFUL VERSUS UNSUCCESSFUL FIRMS
TAR OC 88 VOL: 63 PG:642 - 656 :: REGRESS. :PRIM. :THEORY :ACC.CHNG.

MELUMAD,ND ; SEC: REICHELSTEIN,S CIT: 0.50
CENTRALIZATION VERSUS DELEGATION AND THE VALUE OF COMMUNICATION
JAR ST 87 VOL: 25 PG:1 - 18 :: DES.STAT. :INT. LOG. :INF.ECO./AG. :ORG.& ENVIR.

MENON ,K ; FIRS: DAVIS ,SW ; THIR: MORGAN,G CIT: 0.43
THE IMAGES THAT HAVE SHAPED ACCOUNTING THEORY
AOS 04 82 VOL: 7 PG:307 - 318 :: QUAL. :INT. LOG. :THEORY :N/A

MENON ,K ; FIRS: SCHWARTZ,KB CIT: 0.25
AUDITOR SWITCHES BY FAILING FIRMS
TAR AP 85 VOL: 60 PG:248 - 261 :: REGRESS. :PRIM. :N/A :BUS.FAIL.

MENSAH,YM CIT: 0.00
A DYNAMIC APPROACH TO THE EVALUATION OF INPUT-VARIABLE COST CENTER PERFORMANCE
TAR OC 82 VOL: 57 PG:681 - 700 :: ANAL. :INT. LOG. :N/A :N/A

MENSAH,YM CIT: 0.00
THE DIFFERENTIAL BANKRUPTCY PREDICTIVE ABILITY OF SPECIFIC PRICE LEVEL
ADJUSTMENTS: SOME EMPIRICAL EVIDENCE
TAR AP 83 VOL: 58 PG:228 - 246 :: OTH.QUANT. :PRIM. :OTH.STAT. :BUS.FAIL.

MENSAH,YM CIT: 0.00
THE USEFULNESS OF THE HOLDING GAINS AND LOSSES DISCLOSURE
JAA WI 83 VOL: 6 PG:130 - 141 :: OTH.QUANT. :PRIM. :THEORY :REV.REC.

MENSAH,YM CIT: 0.00
AN EXAMINATION OF THE STATIONARITY OF MULTIVARIATE BANKRUPTCY PREDICTION
MODELS: A METHODOLOGICAL STUDY
JAR SP 84 VOL: 22 PG:380 - 395 :: OTH.QUANT. :PRIM. :OTH.STAT. :BUS.FAIL.

MENZEFRICKE,U CIT: 0.33
ON SAMPLING PLAN SELECTION WITH DOLLAR-UNIT SAMPLING
JAR SP 83 VOL: 21 PG:96 - 105 :: ANAL. :INT. LOG. :OTH.STAT. :SAMP.

MENZEFRICKE,U CIT: 0.00
USING DECISION THEORY FOR PLANNING AUDIT SAMPLE SIZE WITH DOLLAR UNIT SAMPLING
JAR AU 84 VOL: 22 PG:570 - 587 :: DES.STAT. :SIM. :OTH.STAT. :LIAB.

MENZEFRICKE,U ; SEC: SMIELIAUSKAS,W CIT: 0.60
A SIMULATION STUDY OF THE PERFORMANCE OF PARAMETRIC DOLLAR UNIT SAMPLING
STATISTICAL PROCEDURES
JAR AU 84 VOL: 22 PG:588 - 604 :: DES.STAT. :SIM. :OTH.STAT. :LIAB.

MEPHAM,MJ CIT: 0.00
ROBERT HAMILTON'S CONTRIBUTION TO ACCOUNTING
TAR JA 83 VOL: 58 PG:43 - 57 :: QUAL. :INT. LOG. :HIST. :N/A

MERCHANT,KA ; FIRS: GORDON,FE ; SEC: RHODE ,JG CIT: 0.25
THE EFFECTS OF SALARY AND HUMAN RESOURCE ACCOUNTING DISCLOSURES ON SMALL
GROUP RELATIONS AND PERFORMANCE
AOS 04 77 VOL: 2 PG:295 - 306 :: ANOVA :LAB. :OTH.BEH. :HRA

MERCHANT,KA ; FIRS: HARVEY,DW ; SEC: RHODE ,JG CIT: 0.20
ACCOUNTING AGGREGATION: USER PREFERENCES AND DECISION MAKING
AOS 03 79 VOL: 4 PG:187 - 210 :: ANOVA :LAB. :OTH.BEH. :N/A

MERCHANT,KA CIT: 1.88
THE DESIGN OF THE CORPORATE BUDGETING SYSTEM: INFLUENCES ON MANAGERIAL
BEHAVIOR AND PERFORMANCE
TAR OC 81 VOL: 56 PG:813 - 829 :: CORR. :SURV. :OTH.BEH. :BUDG.& PLAN.

MERCHANT,KA CIT: 0.60
INFLUENCES ON DEPARTMENTAL BUDGETING: AN EMPIRICAL EXAMINATION OF A
CONTINGENCY MODEL
AOS 34 84 VOL: 9 PG:291 - 309 :: OTH.QUANT. :SURV. :OTH.BEH. :N/A

MERCHANT,KA CIT: 0.50
ORGANIZATIONAL CONTROLS AND DISCRETIONARY PROGRAM DECISION MAKING: A FIELD
STUDY
AOS 01 85 VOL: 10 PG:67 - 86 :: REGRESS. :FIELD :OTH.BEH. :MANAG.

MERCHANT,KA CIT: 0.75
BUDGETING AND THE PROPENSITY TO CREATE BUDGETARY SLACK
AOS 02 85 VOL: 10 PG:201 - 210 :: REGRESS. :FIELD :OTH.BEH. :BUDG.& PLAN.

MERINO,BD ; FIRS: TINKER,AM ; THIR: NEIMARK,M CIT: 1.57
THE NORMATIVE ORIGINS OF POSITIVE THEORIES: IDEOLOGY AND ACCOUNTING THOUGHT
AOS 02 82 VOL: 7 PG:167 - 200 :: QUAL. :INT. LOG. :THEORY :N/A

MERINO,BD ; SEC: KOCH ,BS ; THIR: MACRITCHIE,KL CIT: 0.00
HISTORICAL ANALYSIS- A DIAGNOSTIC TOOL FOR "EVENTS" STUDIES: THE IMPACT OF
    THE SECURITIES ACT OF 1933
TAR OC 87 VOL: 62 PG:748 - 762 :: REGRESS. :INT. LOG. :HIST. :FIN.METH.

MERVILLE,LJ ; SEC: PETTY ,JW CIT: 0.18
TRANSFER PRICING FOR THE MULTINATIONAL FIRM
TAR OC 78 VOL: 53 PG:935 - 951 :: ANAL. :INT. LOG. :MATH.PROG. :TRANS.PRIC.

MESERVY,RD ; FIRS: BAILEY JR,AD ; SEC: DUKE ,GL ; THIR: GERLACH,JH ; FOUR:
KO   ,CE ; SIX: WHINSTON,AB CIT: 0.00
TICOM AND THE ANALYSIS OF INTERNAL CONTROLS
TAR AP 85 VOL: 60 PG:186 - 201 :: CORR. :INT. LOG. :OTH. :INT.CONT.

MESERVY,RD ; SEC: BAILEY JR,AD ; THIR: JOHNSON,PE CIT: 0.00
INTERNAL CONTROL EVALUATION: A COMPUTATIONAL MODEL OF THE REVIEW PROCESS
AUD AU 86 VOL: 6 PG:44 - 74 :: DES.STAT. :LAB. :EXP.SYST. :INT.CONT.

MESSIER JR,WF ; FIRS: HOLSTRUM,GL CIT: 0.00
A REVIEW AND INTEGRATION OF EMPIRICAL RESEARCH ON MATERIALITY
AUD AU 82 VOL: 2 PG:45 - 63 :: QUAL. :SEC. :OTH. :MAT.

MESSIER JR,WF ; FIRS: EMERY ,DR ; SEC: BARRON,FH CIT: 0.14
CONJOINT MEASUREMENT AND THE ANALYSIS OF NOISY DATA: A COMMENT
JAR AU 82 VOL: 20 PG:450 - 458 :: NON-PAR. :SIM. :HIPS :METHOD.

MESSIER JR,WF ; FIRS: JOHNSON,SB CIT: 0.00
THE NATURE OF ACCOUNTING STANDARDS SETTING: AN ALTERNATIVE EXPLANATION
JAA SP 82 VOL: 5 PG:195 - 213 :: QUAL. :INT. LOG. :INSTIT. :FASB SUBM.

MESSIER JR,WF CIT: 0.67
THE EFFECT OF EXPERIENCE AND FIRM TYPE ON MATERIALITY/DISCLOSURE JUDGMENTS
JAR AU 83 VOL: 21 PG:611 - 618 :: ANOVA :SIM. :HIPS :MAT.

MESSIER JR,WF ; FIRS: HANSEN,JV CIT: 0.00
A PRELIMINARY INVESTIGATION OF EDP-XPERT
AUD AU 86 VOL: 6 PG:109 - 123 :: ANAL. :LAB. :EXP.SYST. :EDP AUD.

MESSIER JR,WF ; SEC: HANSEN,JV CIT: 0.00
EXPERT SYSTEMS IN AUDITING: THE STATE OF THE ART
AUD AU 87 VOL: 7 PG:94 - 105 :: REGRESS. :SURV. :EXP.SYST. :JUDG.

MESSIER JR,WF ; FIRS: BIGGS ,SF ; THIR: HANSEN,JV CIT: 0.00
A DESCRIPTIVE ANALYSIS OF COMPUTER AUDIT SPECIALISTS' DECISION MAKING
    BEHAVIOR IN ADVANCED COMPUTER ENVIRONMENTS
AUD SP 87 VOL: 6 PG:1 - 21 :: REGRESS. :LAB. :HIPS :EDP AUD.

METCALF,RW CIT: 0.00
THE "BASIC POSTULATES" IN PERSPECTIVE
TAR JA 64 VOL: 39 PG:16 - 21 :: QUAL. :INT. LOG. :THEORY :OTH.FIN.ACC.

MEYER ,JW CIT: 0.33
SOCIAL ENVIRONMENTS AND ORGANIZATIONAL ACCOUNTING
AOS 45 86 VOL: 11 PG:345 - 356 :: ANOVA :INT. LOG. :THEORY :OTH.MANAG.

MEYER ,PE CIT: 0.00
A FRAMEWORK FOR UNDERSTANDING "SUBSTANCE OVER FORM" IN ACCOUNTING
TAR JA 76 VOL: 51 PG:80 - 89 :: QUAL. :SEC. :THEORY :FIN.METH.

MEYERS,SL CIT: 0.15
THE STATIONARITY PROBLEM IN THE USE OF THE MARKET MODEL OF SECURITY PRICE
   BEHAVIOR
TAR AP 73 VOL: 48 PG:318 - 322 :: REGRESS. :PRIM. :EMH :METHOD.

MEYERS,SL CIT: 0.08
AN EXAMINATION OF THE RELATIONSHIP BETWEEN INTERPERIOD TAX ALLOCATION AND
   PRESENT-VALUE DEPRECIATION
TAR JA 73 VOL: 48 PG:44 - 49 :: QUAL. :INT. LOG. :THEORY :TAXES

MIA   ,L CIT: 0.00
MANAGERIAL ATTITUDE, MOTIVATION AND THE EFFECTIVENESS OF BUDGET PARTICIPATION
AOS 05 88 VOL: 13 PG:465 - 475 :: REGRESS. :LAB. :OTH.BEH. :BUDG.& PLAN.

MIELKE,DE ; SEC: SEIFERT,J CIT: 0.00
A SURVEY ON THE EFFECTS OF DEFEASING DEBT
JAA WI 87 VOL: 2 PG:65 - 78 :: REGRESS. :PRIM. :THEORY :LTD

MILANI,K CIT: 1.92
THE RELATIONSHIP OF PARTICIPATION IN BUDGET-SETTING TO INDUSTRIAL SUPERVISOR
   PERFORMANCE AND ATTITUDES: A FIELD STUDY
TAR AP 75 VOL: 50 PG:274 - 284 :: NON-PAR. :FIELD :OTH.BEH. :BUDG.& PLAN.

MILLAR,JA CIT: 0.00
SPLIT OR DIVIDEND: DO THE WORDS REALLY MATTER?
TAR JA 77 VOL: 52 PG:52 - 55 :: DES.STAT. :PRIM. :EMH :STK.DIV.

MILLAR,JA ; FIRS: GLEZEN,GW CIT: 0.00
AN EMPIRICAL INVESTIGATION OF STOCKHOLDER REACTION TO DISCLOSURES REQUIRED
   BY ASR NO. 250
JAR AU 85 VOL: 23 PG:859 - 870 :: REGRESS. :PRIM. :INSTIT. :ORG.

MILLER,BL ; FIRS: BUCKMAN,AG CIT: 0.00
OPTIMAL INVESTIGATION OF A MULTIPLE COST PROCESSES SYSTEM
JAR SP 82 VOL: 20 PG:28 - 41 :: ANAL. :INT. LOG. :OTH.STAT. :N/A

MILLER,D ; FIRS: GORDON,LA CIT: 1.69
A CONTINGENCY FRAMEWORK FOR THE DESIGN OF ACCOUNTING INFORMATION SYSTEMS
AOS 01 76 VOL: 1 PG:59 - 70 :: QUAL. :INT. LOG. :OTH.BEH. :INFO.STRUC.

MILLER,EM CIT: 0.00
WHY OVERSTATED EARNINGS AFFECT STOCK PRICES BUT NOT THE REVERSE - AN
   IMPORTANT ASYMMETRY
JAA AU 80 VOL: 4 PG:6 - 19 :: QUAL. :INT. LOG. :EMH :INFO.STRUC.

MILLER,H CIT: 0.46
ENVIRONMENTAL COMPLEXITY AND FINANCIAL REPORTS
TAR JA 72 VOL: 47 PG:31 - 37 :: QUAL. :INT. LOG. :HIPS :INFO.STRUC.

MILLER,HE CIT: 0.00
TEXTBOOKS OR RESEARCH
TAR JA 66 VOL: 41 PG:1 - 7 :: QUAL. :INT. LOG. :INSTIT. :OTH.MANAG.

MILLER,JC ; FIRS: FALK ,H CIT: 0.08
AMORTIZATION OF ADVERTISING EXPENDITURES
JAR SP 77 VOL: 15 PG:12 - 22 :: REGRESS. :PRIM. :OTH.STAT. :AMOR./DEPL.

MILLER,MC CIT: 0.00
GOODWILL - AN AGGREGATION ISSUE
TAR AP 73 VOL: 48 PG:280 - 291 :: QUAL. :INT. LOG. :THEORY :OTH. NON-C/A

MILLER,P ; SEC: O'LEARY,T CIT: 2.50
ACCOUNTING AND THE CONSTRUCTION OF THE GOVERNABLE PERSON
AOS 03 87 VOL: 12 PG:235 - 265 :: DES.STAT. :INT. LOG. :HIST. :MANAG.

MILLER,RE ; FIRS: BALVERS,RJ ; SEC: MCDONALD,B CIT: 0.00
UNDERPRICING OF NEW ISSUES AND THE CHOICE OF AUDITOR AS A SIGNAL OF
   INVESTMENT BANKER REPUTATION
TAR OC 88 VOL: 63 PG:605 - 622 :: REGRESS. :PRIM. :MATH.PROG. :AUD.THEOR.

MILLIRON,VC CIT: 0.25
A BEHAVIOURAL STUDY OF THE MEANING AND INFLUENCE OF TAX COMPLEXITY
JAR AU 85 VOL: 23 PG:794 - 816 :: REGRESS. :LAB. :HIPS :TAXES

MILLS ,RH CIT: 0.00
INVESTMENT LOSS RESERVES FOR CORPORATE BOND INVESTORS
TAR JA 67 VOL: 42 PG:74 - 81 :: DES.STAT. :PRIM. :N/A :OTH. NON-C/A

MINCH ,RA ; FIRS: PETRI ,E CIT: 0.15
THE TREASURY STOCK METHOD AND CONVENTIONAL METHOD IN RECIPROCAL STOCKHOLDINGS
   - AN AMALGAMATION
TAR AP 74 VOL: 49 PG:330 - 341 :: ANAL. :INT. LOG. :N/A :SPEC.ITEMS

MINCH ,RA ; FIRS: PETRI ,E CIT: 0.00
EVALUATION OF RESOURCE ACQUISITION DECISIONS BY THE PARTITIONING OF HOLDING
   ACTIVITY
TAR JL 74 VOL: 49 PG:455 - 464 :: ANAL. :INT. LOG. :N/A :INV.

MINCH ,RA ; FIRS: PETRI ,E CIT: 0.00
A DECISION MODEL FOR TAX PREFERENCE ITEMS
TAR AP 78 VOL: 53 PG:415 - 428 :: ANAL. :INT. LOG. :OTH.STAT. :OTH.MANAG.

MINER ,JB ; FIRS: DALTON,FE CIT: 0.08
THE ROLE OF ACCOUNTING TRAINING IN TOP MANAGEMENT DECISION MAKING
TAR JA 70 VOL: 45 PG:134 - 139 :: ANOVA :LAB. :N/A :AUD.TRAIN.

MINI ,DL ; FIRS: MAUTZ ,RK CIT: 0.08
INTERNAL CONTROL EVALUATION AND AUDIT PROGRAM MODIFICATION
TAR AP 66 VOL: 41 PG:283 - 291 :: QUAL. :INT. LOG. :N/A :INT.CONT.

MIRVIS,PH ; FIRS: MACY ,BA CIT: 0.23
ACCOUNTING FOR THE COSTS AND BENEFITS OF HUMAN RESOURCE DEVELOPMENT PROGRAMS:
   AN INTERDISCIPLINARY APPROACH
AOS 23 76 VOL: 1 PG:179 - 194 :: QUAL. :CASE :OTH.BEH. :HRA

MIRVIS,PH ; SEC: LAWLER III,EE CIT: 0.33
SYSTEMS ARE NOT SOLUTIONS: ISSUES IN CREATING INFORMATION SYSTEMS THAT
   ACCOUNT FOR THE HUMAN ORGANIZATION
AOS 23 83 VOL: 8 PG:175 - 190 :: QUAL. :FIELD :OTH.BEH. :ORG.& ENVIR.

MISTER,WG ; FIRS: HARPER JR,RM ; THIR: STRAWSER,JR CIT: 0.00
THE IMPACT OF NEW PENSION DISCLOSURE RULES ON PERCEPTIONS OF DEBT
JAR AU 87 VOL: 25 PG:327 - 330 :: REGRESS. :LAB. :OTH.STAT. :PENS.

MITCHELL,GB CIT: 0.00
AFTER-TAX COST OF LEASING
TAR AP 70 VOL: 45 PG:308 - 314 :: ANAL. :INT. LOG. :N/A :REL.COSTS

MITROFF,II ; SEC: MASON ,RO CIT: 0.33
CAN WE DESIGN SYSTEMS FOR MANAGING MESSES? OR, WHY SO MANY MANAGEMENT
  INFORMATION SYSTEMS ARE UNINFORMATIVE
AOS 23 83 VOL: 8 PG:195 - 204 :: QUAL. :INT. LOG. :OTH. :MAN.DEC.CHAR.

MLYNARCZYK,FA ; FIRS: COMISKEY,EE CIT: 0.00
RECOGNITION OF INCOME BY FINANCE COMPANIES
TAR AP 68 VOL: 43 PG:248 - 256 :: ANAL. :SIM. :THEORY :REV.REC.

MLYNARCZYK,FA CIT: 0.15
AN EMPIRICAL STUDY OF ACCOUNTING METHODS AND STOCK PRICES
JAR ST 69 VOL: 7 PG:63 - 81 :: REGRESS. :PRIM. :EMH :FIN.METH.

MOBLEY,SC CIT: 0.00
THE CONCEPT OF REALIZATION: A USEFUL DEVICE
TAR AP 66 VOL: 41 PG:292 - 296 :: QUAL. :INT. LOG. :THEORY :REV.REC.

MOBLEY,SC CIT: 0.00
REVENUE EXPERIENCE AS A GUIDE TO ASSET VALUATION
TAR JA 67 VOL: 42 PG:114 - 123 :: ANAL. :INT. LOG. :THEORY :PP&E / DEPR

MOBLEY,SC CIT: 0.00
MEASURES OF INCOME
TAR AP 68 VOL: 43 PG:333 - 341 :: QUAL. :INT. LOG. :THEORY :REV.REC.

MOBLEY,SC CIT: 0.23
THE CHALLENGES OF SOCIO-ECONOMIC ACCOUNTING
TAR OC 70 VOL: 45 PG:762 - 768 :: QUAL. :INT. LOG. :THEORY :HRA

MOCK ,TJ CIT: 0.38
COMPARATIVE VALUES OF INFORMATION STRUCTURES
JAR ST 69 VOL: 7 PG:124 - 159 :: ANOVA :LAB. :OTH.BEH. :INFO.STRUC.

MOCK ,TJ CIT: 0.23
CONCEPTS OF INFORMATION VALUE AND ACCOUNTING
TAR OC 71 VOL: 46 PG:765 - 777 :: ANAL. :INT. LOG. :INF.ECO./AG. :INFO.STRUC.

MOCK ,TJ ; SEC: ESTRIN,TL ; THIR: VASARHELYI,MA CIT: 0.77
LEARNING PATTERNS, DECISION APPROACH, AND VALUE OF INFORMATION
JAR SP 72 VOL: 10 PG:129 - 153 :: ANOVA :LAB. :HIPS :INFO.STRUC.

MOCK ,TJ CIT: 0.23
THE VALUE OF BUDGET INFORMATION
TAR JL 73 VOL: 48 PG:520 - 534 :: REGRESS. :LAB. :OTH.BEH. :INFO.STRUC.

MOCK ,TJ ; FIRS: DRIVER,MJ CIT: 2.00
HUMAN INFORMATION PROCESSING, DECISION STYLE THEORY, AND ACCOUNTING
  INFORMATION SYSTEMS
TAR JL 75 VOL: 50 PG:490 - 508 :: MIXED :LAB. :HIPS :INFO.STRUC.

MOCK ,TJ ; FIRS: GROVE ,HD ; THIR: EHRENREICH,K CIT: 0.08
A REVIEW OF HUMAN RESOURCE ACCOUNTING MEASUREMENT SYSTEMS FROM A MEASUREME
  THEORY PERSPECTIVE
AOS 03 77 VOL: 2 PG:219 - 236 :: QUAL. :SEC. :OTH.BEH. :HRA

MOCK ,TJ ; SEC: VASARHELYI,MA CIT: 0.00
A SYNTHESIS OF THE INFORMATION ECONOMICS AND LENS MODELS
JAR AU 78 VOL: 16 PG:414 - 423 :: ANAL. :INT. LOG. :HIPS :METHOD.

MOCK ,TJ ; SEC: WRIGHT,A CIT: 0.00
EVALUATING THE EFFECTIVENESS OF AUDIT PROCEDURES
AUD AU 82 VOL: 2 PG:33 - 44 :: QUAL. :INT. LOG. :THEORY :OPER.AUD.

MOCK ,TJ ; SEC: WILLINGHAM,JJ CIT: 0.00
AN IMPROVED METHOD OF DOCUMENTING AND EVALUATING A SYSTEM OF INTERNAL
ACCOUNTING CONTROLS
AUD SP 83 VOL: 2 PG:91 - 99 :: QUAL. :INT. LOG. :OTH. :INT.CONT.

MOCK ,TJ ; FIRS: BIGGS ,SF CIT: 0.83
AN INVESTIGATION OF AUDITOR DECISION PROCESSES IN THE EVALUATION OF INTERNAL
CONTROLS AND AUDIT SCOPE DECISIONS
JAR SP 83 VOL: 21 PG:234 - 255 :: DES.STAT. :LAB. :HIPS :INT.CONT.

MOCK ,TJ ; FIRS: LIN ,WT ; THIR: WRIGHT,A CIT: 0.00
THE USE OF ANALYTIC HIERARCHY PROCESS AS AN AID IN PLANNING THE NATURE AND
EXTENT OF AUDIT PROCEDURES
AUD AU 84 VOL: 4 PG:89 - 99 :: ANAL. :INT. LOG. :OTH.STAT. :PLAN.

MOCK ,TJ ; FIRS: BIGGS ,SF ; THIR: WATKINS,PR CIT: 0.00
AUDITOR'S USE OF ANALYTICAL REVIEW IN AUDIT PROGRAM DESIGN
TAR JA 88 VOL: 63 PG:148 - 162 :: REGRESS. :LAB. :OTH.BEH. :ANAL.REV.

MOFFIE,RP ; FIRS: BLOCHER,E ; THIR: ZMUD ,RW CIT: 0.00
REPORT FORMAT AND TASK COMPLEXITY: INTERACTION IN RISK JUDGMENTS
AOS 06 86 VOL: 11 PG:457 - 470 :: REGRESS. :LAB. :HIPS :INFO.STRUC.

MOIZER,P ; SEC: TURLEY,S CIT: 0.00
SURROGATES FOR AUDIT FEES IN CONCENTRATION STUDIES
AUD AU 87 VOL: 7 PG:118 - 123 :: REGRESS. :PRIM. :OTH.STAT. :ORG.

MONAHAN,TF ; SEC: BARENBAUM,L CIT: 0.00
THE USE OF CONSTANT DOLLAR INFORMATION TO PREDICT BOND RATING CHANGES
JAA SU 83 VOL: 6 PG:325 - 340 :: OTH.QUANT. :PRIM. :OTH.STAT. :VALUAT.(INFL.)

MONCUR,RH ; FIRS: SWIERINGA,RJ CIT: 0.46
THE RELATIONSHIP BETWEEN MANAGERS' BUDGET-ORIENTED BEHAVIOR AND SELECTED
ATTITUDE, POSITION, SIZE, AND PERFORMANCE MEASURES
JAR ST 72 VOL: 10 PG:194 - 209 :: OTH.QUANT. :FIELD :OTH.BEH. :BUDG.& PLAN.

MONSON,NP ; SEC: TRACY ,JA CIT: 0.00
STOCK RIGHTS AND ACCOUNTING WRONGS
TAR OC 64 VOL: 39 PG:890 - 893 :: ANAL. :INT. LOG. :THEORY :STK.DIV.

MOODY ,SM ; SEC: FLESHER,DL CIT: 0.00
ANALYSIS OF FASB VOTING PATTERNS: STATEMENT NOS. 1-86
JAA AU 86 VOL: 1 PG:319 - 330 :: REGRESS. :PRIM. :INSTIT. :FASB SUBM.

MOON ,JE ; FIRS: FULMER,JG CIT: 0.00
TESTS FOR COMMON STOCK EQUIVALENCY
JAA AU 84 VOL: 8 PG:5 - 14 :: NON-PAR. :PRIM. :OTH.STAT. :FIN.METH.

MOONITZ,M ; SEC: RUSS ,A CIT: 0.08
ACCRUAL ACCOUNTING FOR EMPLOYERS' PENSION COSTS
JAR AU 66 VOL: 4 PG:155 - 168 :: QUAL. :INT. LOG. :THEORY :PENS.

MOONITZ,M CIT: 0.00
SOME REFLECTIONS ON THE INVESTMENT CREDIT EXPERIENCE
JAR SP 66 VOL: 4 PG:47 - 61 :: QUAL. :INT. LOG. :INSTIT. :TAXES

MOONITZ,M CIT: 0.15
PRICE-LEVEL ACCOUNTING AND SCALES OF MEASUREMENT
TAR JL 70 VOL: 45 PG:465 - 475 :: QUAL. :INT. LOG. :THEORY :VALUAT.(INFL.)

MOORE ,CL CIT: 0.00
THE PRESENT-VALUE METHOD AND THE REPLACEMENT DECISION
TAR JA 64 VOL: 39 PG:94 - 102 :: ANAL. :INT. LOG. :N/A :CAP.BUDG.

MOORE ,G ; FIRS: KIM ,M CIT: 0.00
ECONOMIC VS. ACCOUNTING DEPRECIATION
JAE AP 88 VOL: 10 PG:111 - 125 :: REGRESS. :PRIM. :THEORY :PP&E / DEPR

MOORE ,ML CIT: 0.62
MANAGEMENT CHANGES AND DISCRETIONARY ACCOUNTING DECISIONS
JAR SP 73 VOL: 11 PG:100 - 107 :: NON-PAR. :PRIM. :OTH. :ACC.CHNG.

MOORE ,ML ; SEC: STEECE,BM ; THIR: SWENSON,CW CIT: 0.00
SOME EMPIRICAL EVIDENCE ON TAXPAYER RATIONALITY
TAR JA 85 VOL: 60 PG:18 - 32 :: REGRESS. :PRIM. :TIME SER. :TAXES

MOORE ,ML ; SEC: STEECE,BM ; THIR: SWENSON,CW CIT: 0.00
AN ANALYSIS OF THE IMPACT OF STATE INCOME TAX RATES AND BASES ON FOREIGN
   INVESTMENT
TAR OC 87 VOL: 62 PG:671 - 685 :: REGRESS. :PRIM.':TIME SER. :TAXES

MOORES,K ; SEC: STEADMAN,GT CIT: 0.00
THE COMPARATIVE VIEWPOINTS OF GROUPS OF ACCOUNTANTS: MORE ON THE
   ENTITY-PROPRIETARY DEBATE
AOS 01 86 VOL: 11 PG:19 - 34 :: REGRESS. :SURV. :INSTIT. :FASB SUBM.

MORENO,RG CIT: 0.00
THE UNIFICATION OF THE PROFESSIONAL TEACHING OF ACCOUNTING IN THE AMERICAS
TAR OC 64 VOL: 39 PG:990 - 995 :: QUAL. :INT. LOG. :INSTIT. :OTH.MANAG.

MOREY ,L CIT: 0.00
PROGRESS OF THE INDEPENDENT POST AUDIT PROGRAM IN ILLINOIS
TAR JA 63 VOL: 38 PG:102 - 108 :: QUAL. :INT. LOG. :N/A :AUD.

MORGAN,EA ; FIRS: WILLIAMS,JJ ; SEC: NEWTON,JD CIT: 0.00
THE INTEGRATION OF ZERO-BASE BUDGETING WITH MANAGEMENT-BY-OBJECTIVES: AN
   EMPIRICAL INQUIRY
AOS 04 85 VOL: 10 PG:457 - 478 :: REGRESS. :FIELD :OTH.BEH. :BUDG.& PLAN.

MORGAN,G ; FIRS: DAVIS ,SW ; SEC: MENON ,K CIT: 0.43
THE IMAGES THAT HAVE SHAPED ACCOUNTING THEORY
AOS 04 82 VOL: 7 PG:307 - 318 :: QUAL. :INT. LOG. :THEORY :N/A

MORGAN,G CIT: 0.00
ACCOUNTING AS REALITY CONTRUCTION: TOWARDS A NEW EPISTEMOLOGY FOR ACCOUNTING
   PRACTICE
AOS 05 88 VOL: 13 PG:477 - 485 :: DES.STAT. :INT. LOG. :THEORY :OTH.MANAG.

MORGENSON,DL ; FIRS: REILLY,FK ; THIR: WEST ,M CIT: 0.23
THE PREDICTIVE ABILITY OF ALTERNATIVE PARTS OF INTERIM FINANCIAL STATEMENTS
JAR ST 72 VOL: 10 PG:105 - 124 :: REGRESS. :PRIM. :EMH :INT.REP.

MORIARITY,S CIT: 0.38
ANOTHER APPROACH TO ALLOCATING JOINT COSTS
TAR OC 75 VOL: 50 PG:791 - 795 :: ANAL. :INT. LOG. :THEORY :COST.ALLOC.

MORIARITY,S ; SEC: BARRON,FH CIT: 0.92
MODELING THE MATERIALITY JUDGMENTS OF AUDIT PARTNERS
JAR AU 76 VOL: 14 PG:320 - 341 :: MIXED :LAB. :OTH.BEH. :MAT.

MORIARITY,S CIT: 0.60
COMMUNICATING FINANCIAL INFORMATION THROUGH MULTIDIMENSIONAL GRAPHICS
JAR SP 79 VOL: 17 PG:205 - 224 :: DES.STAT. :LAB. :OTH.BEH. :INFO.STRUC.

MORIARITY,S ; SEC: BARRON,FH CIT: 0.70
A JUDGMENT-BASED DEFINITION OF MATERIALITY
JAR ST 79 VOL: 17 PG:114 - 135 :: OTH.QUANT. :LAB. :OTH.STAT. :MAT.

MORRIS,D ; FIRS: CHENHALL,RH CIT: 1.00
THE IMPACT OF STRUCTURE, ENVIRONMENT, AND INTERDEPENDENCE ON THE PERCEIVED
USEFULNESS OF MANAGEMENT ACCOUNTING SYSTEMS
TAR JA 86 VOL: 61 PG:16 - 35 :: REGRESS. :SURV. :OTH.STAT. :ORG.& ENVIR.

MORRIS,MH ; FIRS: MCDONALD,B CIT: 0.40
THE RELEVANCE OF SFAS 33 INFLATION ACCOUNTING DISCLOSURES IN THE ADJUSTMENT
OF STOCK PRICES TO INFLATION
TAR JL 84 VOL: 59 PG:432 - 446 :: REGRESS. :PRIM. :EMH :VALUAT.(INFL.)

MORRIS,MH ; SEC: NICHOLS,WD CIT: 0.00
PENSION ACCOUNTING AND THE BALANCE SHEET: THE POTENTIAL EFFECT OF THE FASB'S
PRELIMINARY VIEWS
JAA SU 84 VOL: 7 PG:293 - 305 :: MIXED :PRIM. :OTH.STAT. :PENS.

MORRIS,MH ; SEC: NICHOLS,WD CIT: 0.00
CONSISTENCY EXCEPTIONS: MATERIALITY JUDGMENTS AND AUDIT FIRM STRUCTURE
TAR AP 88 VOL: 63 PG:237 - 254 :: REGRESS. :PRIM. :EMH :MAT.

MORRISON,TA CIT: 0.00
TAXATION OF INTERNATIONAL INVESTMENTS
TAR OC 66 VOL: 41 PG:704 - 713 :: QUAL. :INT. LOG. :N/A :TAX PLNG.

MORRISON,TA ; SEC: BUZBY ,SL CIT: 0.00
EFFECT OF THE INVESTMENT TAX CREDIT ON THE CAPITALIZE-EXPENSE DECISION
TAR JL 68 VOL: 43 PG:517 - 521 :: ANAL. :INT. LOG. :N/A :TAX PLNG.

MORRISON,TA ; SEC: KACZKA,E CIT: 0.08
A NEW APPLICATION OF CALCULUS AND RISK ANALYSIS TO COST-VOLUME-PROFIT CHANGES
TAR AP 69 VOL: 44 PG:330 - 343 :: ANAL. :INT. LOG. :OTH.STAT. :C-V-P-A

MORRISSEY,LE ; FIRS: GREER JR,WR CIT: 0.00
ACCOUNTING RULE-MAKING IN A WORLD OF EFFICIENT MARKETS
JAA AU 78 VOL: 2 PG:49 - 57 :: QUAL. :INT. LOG. :INSTIT. :FIN.METH.

MORSE ,D ; FIRS: BEAVER,WH ; SEC: LAMBERT,RA CIT: 2.44
THE INFORMATION CONTENT OF SECURITY PRICES
JAE MR 80 VOL: 2 PG:3 - 28 :: REGRESS. :PRIM. :EMH :FIN.METH.

MORSE ,D CIT: 1.13
PRICE AND TRADING VOLUME REACTION SURROUNDING EARNINGS ANNOUNCEMENTS: A
CLOSER EXAMINATION
JAR AU 81 VOL: 19 PG:374 - 383 :: REGRESS. :PRIM. :EMH :N/A

MORSE ,D ; SEC: USHMAN,N CIT: 0.17
THE EFFECT OF INFORMATION ANNOUNCEMENTS ON THE MARKET MICROSTRUCTURE
TAR AP 83 VOL: 58 PG:247 - 258 :: ANOVA :PRIM. :OTH. :FIN.METH.

MORSE ,D ; SEC: RICHARDSON,G CIT: 1.00
THE LIFO/FIFO DECISION
JAR SP 83 VOL: 21 PG:106 - 127 :: DES.STAT. :PRIM. :OTH.STAT. :INV.

MORSE ,D CIT: 0.20
AN ECONOMETRIC ANALYSIS OF THE CHOICE OF DAILY VERSUS MONTHLY RETURNS IN
    TESTS OF INFORMATION CONTENT
JAR AU 84 VOL: 22 PG:605 - 623 :: ANAL. :SEC. :EMH :METHOD.

MORSE ,WJ CIT: 0.08
REPORTING PRODUCTION COSTS THAT FOLLOW THE LEARNING CURVE PHENOMENON
TAR OC 72 VOL: 47 PG:761 - 773 :: ANAL. :INT. LOG. :OTH.STAT. :COST.ALLOC.

MORTON,JR CIT: 0.15
QUALITATIVE OBJECTIVES OF FINANCIAL ACCOUNTING: A COMMENT ON RELEVANCE AND
    UNDERSTANDABILITY
JAR AU 74 VOL: 12 PG:288 - 298 :: NON-PAR. :SURV. :OTH.BEH. :FIN.METH.

MOSES ,OD CIT: 0.00
INCOME SMOOTHING AND INCENTIVES: EMPIRICAL TESTS USING ACCOUNTING CHANGES
TAR AP 87 VOL: 62 PG:358 - 377 :: REGRESS. :PRIM. :EMH :ACC.CHNG.

MOST ,KS CIT: 0.00
THE VALUE OF INVENTORIES
JAR SP 67 VOL: 5 PG:39 - 50 :: QUAL. :SEC. :HIST. :INV.

MOST ,KS CIT: 0.00
TWO FORMS OF EXPERIMENTAL ACCOUNTS
TAR JA 69 VOL: 44 PG:145 - 152 :: QUAL. :INT. LOG. :THEORY :INFO.STRUC.

MOST ,KS CIT: 0.00
SOMBART'S PROPOSITIONS REVISITED
TAR OC 72 VOL: 47 PG:722 - 734 :: QUAL. :SEC. :HIST. :OTH.MANAG.

MOST ,KS CIT: 0.20
DEPRECIATION EXPENSE AND THE EFFECT OF INFLATION
JAR AU 84 VOL: 22 PG:782 - 788 :: DES.STAT. :SURV. :THEORY :PP&E / DEPR

MUELLER,FJ ; FIRS: BERG ,KB CIT: 0.00
ACCOUNTING FOR INVESTMENT CREDITS
TAR JL 63 VOL: 38 PG:554 - 561 :: QUAL. :INT. LOG. :THEORY :TAXES

MUELLER,GG CIT: 0.00
THE DIMENSIONS OF THE INTERNATIONAL ACCOUNTING PROBLEM
TAR JA 63 VOL: 38 PG:142 - 147 :: QUAL. :INT. LOG. :THEORY :INT.DIFF.

MUELLER,GG CIT: 0.00
VALUING INVENTORIES AT OTHER THAN HISTORICAL COSTS - SOME INTERNATIONAL
    DIFFERENCES
JAR AU 64 VOL: 2 PG:148 - 157 :: QUAL. :INT. LOG. :THEORY :INT.DIFF.

MUELLER,GG CIT: 0.00
WHYS AND HOWS OF INTERNATIONAL ACCOUNTING
TAR AP 65 VOL: 40 PG:386 - 394 :: QUAL. :INT. LOG. :INSTIT. :FIN.METH.

MULFORD,CW CIT: 0.25
THE IMPORTANCE OF A MARKET VALUE MEASUREMENT OF DEBT IN LEVERAGE
JAR AU 85 VOL: 23 PG:897 - 906 :: REGRESS. :PRIM. :EMH :LTD

MULFORD,CW ; SEC: COMISKEY,EE CIT: 0.00
INVESTMENT DECISIONS AND THE EQUITY ACCOUNTING STANDARD
TAR JL 86 VOL: 61 PG:519 - 525 :: REGRESS. :PRIM. :OTH.STAT. :BUS.COMB.

MUNTER,P ; SEC: RATCLIFFE,TA CIT: 0.00
AN ASSESSMENT OF USER REACTIONS TO LEASE ACCOUNTING DISCLOSURES
JAA WI 83 VOL: 6 PG:108 - 114 :: NON-PAR. :LAB. :THEORY :LEASES

MUNTER,P ; FIRS: COLLINS,F ; THIR: FINN ,DW CIT: 0.00
THE BUDGETING GAMES PEOPLE PLAY
TAR JA 87 VOL: 62 PG:29 - 49 :: REGRESS. :SURV. :OTH.BEH. :BUDG.& PLAN.

MURDOCH,B CIT: 0.33
THE INFORMATION CONTENT OF FAS 33 RETURNS ON EQUITY
TAR AP 86 VOL: 61 PG:273 - 287 :: REGRESS. :PRIM. :EMH :VALUAT.(INFL.)

MURDOCK,RJ ; FIRS: SHANK ,JK CIT: 0.36
COMPARABILITY IN THE APPLICATION OF REPORTING STANDARDS: SOME FURTHER EVIDENCE
TAR OC 78 VOL: 53 PG:824 - 835 :: DES.STAT. :PRIM. :EMH :OPIN.

MURPHY,GJ CIT: 0.08
A NUMERICAL REPRESENTATION OF SOME ACCOUNTING CONVENTIONS
TAR AP 76 VOL: 51 PG:277 - 286 :: QUAL. :INT. LOG. :OTH.STAT. :OTH.FIN.ACC.

MURPHY,KJ CIT: 1.75
CORPORATE PERFORMANCE AND MANAGERIAL REMUNERATION: AN EMPIRICAL ANALYSIS
JAE AP 85 VOL: 7 PG:11 - 42 :: REGRESS. :PRIM. :OTH.STAT. :EXEC.COMP.

MURRAY,D ; FIRS: ELGERS,PT CIT: 0.00
THE IMPACT OF THE CHOICE OF MARKET INDEX ON THE EMPIRICAL EVALUATION OF
   ACCOUNTING DETERMINED RISK MEASURES
TAR AP 82 VOL: 57 PG:358 - 375 :: REGRESS. :PRIM. :EMH :N/A

MURRAY,D CIT: 0.00
THE IRRELEVANCE OF LEASE CAPITALIZATION
JAA WI 82 VOL: 5 PG:154 - 159 :: REGRESS. :PRIM. :EMH :FIN.METH.

MURRAY,D ; SEC: JOHNSON,R CIT: 0.00
DIFFERENTIAL GAAP AND THE FASB'S CONCEPTUAL FRAMEWORK
JAA AU 83 VOL: 7 PG:4 - 15 :: QUAL. :INT. LOG. :THEORY :FASB SUBM.

MURRAY,D CIT: 0.17
THE EFFECT OF CERTAIN RESEARCH DESIGN CHOICES ON THE ASSESSMENT OF THE
   MARKET'S REACTION TO LIFO CHANGES: A METHODOLOGICAL STUDY
JAR SP 83 VOL: 21 PG:128 - 140 :: NON-PAR. :PRIM. :EMH :INV.

MURRAY,D ; FIRS: BLOOM ,R ; SEC: ELGERS,PT CIT: 0.20
FUNCTIONAL FIXATION IN PRODUCT PRICING: A COMPARISON OF INDIVIDUALS AND GROUPS
AOS 01 84 VOL: 9 PG:1 - 11 :: MIXED :LAB. :HIPS :PP&E / DEPR

MURRAY,D ; SEC: FRAZIER,KB CIT: 0.00
A WITHIN-SUBJECTS TEST OF EXPECTANCY THEORY IN A PUBLIC ACCOUNTING ENVIRONMENT
JAR AU 86 VOL: 24 PG:400 - 404 :: REGRESS. :LAB. :OTH.BEH. :INFO.STRUC.

MUTCHLER,JF CIT: 0.20
AUDITORS' PERCEPTIONS OF THE GOING-CONCERN OPINION DECISION
AUD SP 84 VOL: 3 PG:17 - 30 :: DES.STAT. :SURV. :OTH. :OPIN.

MUTCHLER,JF CIT: 0.75
A MULTIVARIATE ANALYSIS OF THE AUDITOR'S GOING-CONCERN OPINION DECISION
JAR AU 85 VOL: 23 PG:668 - 682 :: REGRESS. :PRIM. :OTH.STAT. :OPIN.

MUTCHLER,JF CIT: 0.00
EMPIRICAL EVIDENCE REGARDING THE AUDITOR'S GOING-CONCERN OPINION DECISION
AUD AU 86 VOL: 6 PG:148 - :: DES.STAT. :PRIM. :OTH.STAT. :OPIN.

MYERS ,BL ; FIRS: PEARSON,MA ; SEC: LINDGREN,JH CIT: 0.10
A PRELIMINARY ANALYSIS OF AUDSEC VOTING PATTERNS
JAA WI 79 VOL: 2 PG:122 - 134 :: OTH.QUANT. :PRIM. :INSTIT. :FASB SUBM.

NACHMAN,DA ; FIRS: FERRARA,WL ; SEC: HAYYA ,JC CIT: 0.31
NORMALCY OF PROFIT IN THE JAEDICKE-ROBICHEK MODEL
TAR AP 72 VOL: 47 PG:299 - 307 :: ANAL. :SIM. :OTH.STAT. :C-V-P-A

NACHTMANN,R ; FIRS: DORAN ,DT CIT: 0.00
THE ASSOCIATION OF STOCK DISTRIBUTION ANNOUNCEMENTS AND EARNINGS PERFORMANCE
JAA SP 88 VOL: 03 PG:113 - 132 :: REGRESS. :PRIM. :EMH :STK.DIV.

NACHTSHEIM,CJ ; FIRS: KO   ,CE ; THIR: DUKE ,GL ; FOUR: BAILEY JR,AD CIT: 0.00
ON THE ROBUSTNESS OF MODEL-BASED SAMPLING IN AUDITING
AUD SP 88 VOL: 07 PG:119 - 136 :: DES.STAT. :SIM. :OTH.STAT. :SAMP.

NAGARAJAN,NJ ; FIRS: JOHNSON,WB ; SEC: MAGEE ,RP ; FOUR: NEWMAN,HA CIT: 0.00
AN ANALYSIS OF THE STOCK PRICE REACTION TO SUDDEN EXECUTIVE DEATHS:
  IMPLICATIONS FOR THE MANAGEMENT LABOR MARKET
JAE AP 85 VOL: 7 PG:151 - 174 :: REGRESS. :PRIM. :EMH :OTH.MANAG.

NAHAPIET,JE ; FIRS: BANBURY,J CIT: 1.00
TOWARDS A FRAMEWORK FOR THE STUDY OF THE ANTECEDENTS AND CONSEQUENCES OF
  INFORMATION SYSTEMS IN ORGANIZATIONS
AOS 03 79 VOL: 4 PG:163 - 178 :: QUAL. :INT. LOG. :OTH. :N/A

NAHAPIET,JE ; FIRS: BURCHELL,S ; SEC: CLUBB ,C ; THIR: HOPWOOD,AG ; FOUR:
HUGHES,JS CIT: 3.89
THE ROLES OF ACCOUNTING IN ORGANIZATIONS AND SOCIETY
AOS 01 80 VOL: 5 PG:5 - 27 :: QUAL. :INT. LOG. :THEORY :N/A

NAHAPIET,JE CIT: 0.00
THE RHETORIC AND REALITY OF AN ACCOUNTING CHANGE: A STUDY OF RESOURCE
  ALLOCATION
AOS 04 88 VOL: 13 PG:333 - 358 :: REGRESS. :SURV. :INSTIT. :COST.ALLOC.

NAIR ,RD CIT: 0.30
ECONOMIC ANALYSES AND ACCOUNTING TECHNIQUES: AN EMPIRICAL STUDY
JAR SP 79 VOL: 17 PG:225 - 242 :: DES.STAT. :PRIM. :OTH.STAT. :METHOD.

NAIR ,RD ; SEC: FRANK ,WG CIT: 0.33
THE IMPACT OF DISCLOSURE AND MEASUREMENT PRACTICES ON INTERNATIONAL
  ACCOUNTING CLASSIFICATIONS
TAR JL 80 VOL: 55 PG:426 - 450 :: OTH.QUANT. :PRIM. :OTH.STAT. :INT.DIFF.

NAIR ,RD ; SEC: RITTENBERG,LE CIT: 0.00
ACCOUNTING COSTS OF PRIVATELY HELD BUSINESSES
JAA SP 83 VOL: 6 PG:234 - 243 :: DES.STAT. :SURV. :OTH.BEH. :N/A

NAIR ,RD ; SEC: RITTENBERG,LE CIT: 0.00
MESSAGES PERCEIVED FROM AUDIT, REVIEW, AND COMPILATION REPORTS: EXTENSION
  TO MORE DIVERSE GROUPS
AUD AU 87 VOL: 7 PG:15 - 38 :: REGRESS. :LAB. :HIPS :AUD.THEOR.

NAKANO,I CIT: 0.00
NOISE AND REDUNDANCY IN ACCOUNTING COMMUNICATIONS
TAR OC 72 VOL: 47 PG:693 - 708 :: ANAL. :INT. LOG. :INF.ECO./AG. :
VALUAT.(INFL.)

NANNI JR,AJ CIT: 0.20
AN EXPLORATION OF THE MEDIATING EFFECTS OF AUDITOR EXPERIENCE AND POSITION IN
    INTERNAL ACCOUNTING CONTROL EVALUATION
AOS 02 84 VOL: 9 PG:149 - 163 :: ANOVA :LAB. :OTH.BEH. :INT.CONT.

NANTELL,TJ ; FIRS: BRIGHAM,EF CIT: 0.00
NORMALIZATION VERSUS FLOW THROUGH FOR UTILITY COMPANIES USING LIBERALIZED TAX
    DEPRECIATION
TAR JL 74 VOL: 49 PG:436 - 447 :: ANAL. :SIM. :OTH.STAT. :TAXES

NANTELL,TJ ; FIRS: MAHER ,MW CIT: 0.00
THE TAX EFFECTS OF INFLATION: DEPRECIATION, DEBT, AND MILLER'S EQUILIBRIUM
    TAX RATES
JAR SP 83 VOL: 21 PG:329 - 340 :: ANAL. :INT. LOG. :THEORY :VALUAT.(INFL.)

NARAYANAN,VK ; FIRS: GORDON,LA CIT: 0.60
MANAGEMENT ACCOUNTING SYSTEMS, PERCEIVED ENVIRONMENTAL UNCERTAINTY AND
    ORGANIZATION STRUCTURE: AN EMPIRICAL INVESTIGATION
AOS 01 84 VOL: 9 PG:33 - 47 :: CORR. :SURV. :OTH. :ORG.FORM

NASH ,JF ; FIRS: DILLON,RD CIT: 0.18
THE TRUE RELEVANCE OF RELEVANT COSTS
TAR JA 78 VOL: 53 PG:11 - 17 :: QUAL. :INT. LOG. :THEORY :REL.COSTS

NATH ,R ; FIRS: BIRNBERG,JG CIT: 0.23
IMPLICATIONS OF BEHAVIOURAL SCIENCE FOR MANAGERIAL ACCOUNTING
TAR JL 67 VOL: 42 PG:468 - 479 :: QUAL. :SEC. :OTH.BEH. :MANAG.

NATH ,R ; FIRS: BIRNBERG,JG CIT: 0.54
LABORATORY EXPERIMENTATION IN ACCOUNTING RESEARCH
TAR JA 68 VOL: 43 PG:38 - 45 :: QUAL. :INT. LOG. :N/A :METHOD.

NEIMARK,M ; FIRS: TINKER,AM ; SEC: MERINO,BD CIT: 1.57
THE NORMATIVE ORIGINS OF POSITIVE THEORIES: IDEOLOGY AND ACCOUNTING THOUGHT
AOS 02 82 VOL: 7 PG:167 - 200 :: QUAL. :INT. LOG. :THEORY :N/A

NEIMARK,M ; SEC: TINKER,T CIT: 0.67
THE SOCIAL CONSTRUCTION OF MANAGEMENT CONTROL SYSTEM
AOS 45 86 VOL: 11 PG:369 - 396 :: REGRESS. :INT. LOG. :THEORY :INT.CONT.

NEIMARK,M ; FIRS: TINKER,T CIT: 0.00
THE ROLE OF ANNUAL REPORTS IN GENDER AND CLASS CONTRADICTIONS AT GENERAL
    MOTORS: 1917-1976
AOS 01 87 VOL: 12 PG:71 - 88 :: DES.STAT. :INT. LOG. :INSTIT. :ORG.& ENVIR.

NELSON,GK CIT: 0.00
CURRENT AND HISTORICAL COSTS IN FINANCIAL STATEMENTS
TAR JA 66 VOL: 41 PG:42 - 47 :: QUAL. :INT. LOG. :THEORY :VALUAT.(INFL.)

NELSON,J ; SEC: RONEN ,J ; THIR: WHITE ,L CIT: 0.00
LEGAL LIABILITIES AND THE MARKET FOR AUDITING SERVICES
JAA SU 88 VOL: 03 PG:255 - 296 :: DES.STAT. :INT. LOG. :INF.ECO./AG. :LIAB.

NETER ,J ; FIRS: DAVIDSON,HJ ; THIR: PETRAN,AS CIT: 0.15
ESTIMATING THE LIABILITY FOR UNREDEEMED STAMPS
JAR AU 67 VOL: 5 PG:186 - 207 :: ANAL. :INT. LOG. :OTH.STAT. :SPEC.ITEMS

NETER ,J ; FIRS: YU   ,S CIT: 0.62
A STOCHASTIC MODEL OF THE INTERNAL CONTROL SYSTEM
JAR AU 73 VOL: 11 PG:273 - 295 :: ANAL. :INT. LOG. :OTH.STAT. :INT.CONT.

NETER ,J ; FIRS: LOEBBECKE,JK CIT: 0.08
CONSIDERATIONS IN CHOOSING STATISTICAL SAMPLING PROCEDURES IN AUDITING
JAR ST 75 VOL: 13 PG:38 - 52 :: QUAL. :INT. LOG. :OTH.STAT. :SAMP.

NETER ,J ; SEC: LEITCH,RA ; THIR: FIENBERG,SE CIT: 0.82
DOLLAR UNIT SAMPLING: MULTINOMIAL BOUNDS FOR TOTAL OVERSTATEMENT AND
    UNDERSTATEMENT ERRORS
TAR JA 78 VOL: 53 PG:77 - 93 :: NON-PAR. :SIM. :MATH.PROG. :SAMP.

NETER ,J ; FIRS: JOHNSON,JR ; SEC: LEITCH,RA CIT: 1.75
CHARACTERISTICS OF ERRORS IN ACCOUNTS RECEIVABLE AND INVENTORY AUDITS
TAR AP 81 VOL: 56 PG:270 - 293 :: DES.STAT. :PRIM. :OTH. :ERRORS

NETER ,J ; FIRS: LEITCH,RA ; THIR: PLANTE,R ; FOUR: SINHA ,P CIT: 0.86
MODIFIED MULTINOMIAL BOUNDS FOR LARGER NUMBERS OF ERRORS IN AUDITS
TAR AP 82 VOL: 57 PG:384 - 400 :: DES.STAT. :SIM. :OTH.STAT. :SAMP.

NETER ,J ; FIRS: DUKE ,GL ; THIR: LEITCH,RA CIT: 1.14
POWER CHARACTERISTICS OF TEST STATISTICS IN THE AUDITING ENVIRONMENT: AN
    EMPIRICAL STUDY
JAR SP 82 VOL: 20 PG:42 - 67 :: MIXED :PRIM. :OTH.STAT. :ERRORS

NETER ,J ; SEC: KIM ,HS ; THIR: GRAHAM,LE CIT: 0.20
ON COMBINING STRINGER BOUNDS FOR INDEPENDENT MONETARY UNIT SAMPLES FROM
    SEVERAL POPULATIONS
AUD AU 84 VOL: 4 PG:75 - 88 :: ANAL. :INT. LOG. :OTH.STAT. :SAMP.

NETER ,J ; FIRS: GODFREY,JT CIT: 0.40
BAYESIAN BOUNDS FOR MONETARY UNIT SAMPLING IN ACCOUNTING AND AUDITING
JAR AU 84 VOL: 22 PG:497 - 525 :: ANAL. :SIM. :OTH.STAT. :SAMP.

NETER ,J ; FIRS: PLANTE,R ; THIR: LEITCH,RA CIT: 0.00
COMPARATIVE PERFORMANCE OF MULTINOMIAL, CELL, AND STRINGER BOUNDS
AUD AU 85 VOL: 5 PG:40 - 56 :: DES.STAT. :SIM. :OTH.STAT. :SAMP.

NETER ,J ; FIRS: KIM ,HS ; THIR: GODFREY,JT CIT: 0.00
BEHAVIOR OF STATISTICAL ESTIMATORS IN MULTILOCATION AUDIT SAMPLING
AUD SP 87 VOL: 6 PG:40 - 58 :: DES.STAT. :SIM. :OTH.STAT. :SAMP.

NETHERCOTT,L ; FIRS: FERRIS,KR ; SEC: DILLARD,JF CIT: 0.11
A COMPARISON OF V-I-E MODEL PREDICTIONS: A CROSS-NATIONAL STUDY IN
    PROFESSIONAL ACCOUNTING FIRMS
AOS 04 80 VOL: 5 PG:361 - 368 :: DES.STAT. :LAB. :OTH.BEH. :INT.DIFF.

NEUBIG,RD ; FIRS: RABY ,WL CIT: 0.00
INTER-PERIOD TAX ALLOCATION OR BASIS ADJUSTMENT?
TAR JL 63 VOL: 38 PG:568 - 576 :: QUAL. :INT. LOG. :THEORY :TAXES

NEUBIG,RD CIT: 0.00
SALES GROWTH - FACT OR FICTION?
TAR JA 64 VOL: 39 PG:86 - 89 :: QUAL. :INT. LOG. :N/A :FIN.METH.

NEUMANN,BR ; SEC: FRIEDMAN,LA CIT: 0.45
OPPORTUNITY COSTS: FURTHER EVIDENCE THROUGH AN EXPERIMENTAL REPLICATION
JAR AU 78 VOL: 16 PG:400 - 410 :: ANOVA :LAB. :OTH.BEH. :REL.COSTS

NEUMANN,BR CIT: 0.00
AN EMPIRICAL INVESTIGATION OF THE RELATIONSHIP BETWEEN AN AID HOSPITAL
    CLASSIFICATION MODEL AND ACCT. MEASURES OF PERFORMANCE
JAR SP 79 VOL: 17 PG:123 - 139 :: OTH.QUANT. :PRIM. :OTH.STAT. :MANAG.

NEUMANN,BR ; FIRS: FRIEDMAN,LA CIT: 0.33
EFFECTS OF OPPORTUNITY COSTS ON PROJECT INVESTMENT DECISIONS: A REPLICATION
    AND EXTENSION
JAR AU 80 VOL: 18 PG:407 - 419 :: ANOVA :LAB. :OTH.BEH. :MANAG.

NEUMANN,FL CIT: 0.46
THE AUDITING STANDARD OF CONSISTENCY
JAR ST 68 VOL: 6 PG:1 - 17 :: DES.STAT. :PRIM. :THEORY :MAT.

NEUMANN,FL CIT: 0.08
THE INCIDENCE AND NATURE OF CONSISTENCY EXCEPTIONS
TAR JL 69 VOL: 44 PG:546 - 554 :: DES.STAT. :PRIM. :THEORY :ACC.CHNG.

NEUMANN,FL ; FIRS: JOHNSTON,DJ ; SEC: LEMON ,WM CIT: 0.00
THE CANADIAN STUDY OF THE ROLE OF THE AUDITOR
JAA SP 80 VOL: 3 PG:251 - 263 :: QUAL. :INT. LOG. :THEORY :PROF.RESP.

NEWBOLD,P ; FIRS: HOPWOOD,WS ; SEC: MCKEOWN,JC CIT: 0.71
THE ADDITIONAL INFORMATION CONTENT OF QUARTERLY EARNINGS REPORTS:
    INTERTEMPORAL DISAGGREGATION
JAR AU 82 VOL: 20 PG:343 - 349 :: REGRESS. :PRIM. :TIME SER. :INT.REP.

NEWBOLD,P ; FIRS: HOPWOOD,WS ; THIR: SILHAN,PA CIT: 0.29
THE POTENTIAL FOR GAINS IN PREDICTIVE ABILITY THROUGH DISAGGREGATION:
    SEGMENTED ANNUAL EARNINGS
JAR AU 82 VOL: 20 PG:724 - 732 :: DES.STAT. :PRIM. :TIME SER. :SEG.REP.

NEWBOLD,P ; FIRS: GENTRY,JA ; THIR: WHITFORD,DT CIT: 0.50
CLASSIFYING BANKRUPT FIRMS WITH FUNDS FLOW COMPONENTS
JAR SP 85 VOL: 23 PG:146 - 160 :: REGRESS. :PRIM. :OTH.STAT. :BUS.FAIL.

NEWMAN,DP CIT: 0.33
PROSPECT THEORY: IMPLICATIONS FOR INFORMATION EVALUATION
AOS 02 80 VOL: 5 PG:217 - 230 :: ANAL. :INT. LOG. :HIPS :METHOD.

NEWMAN,DP CIT: 0.00
COALITION FORMATION IN THE APB AND THE FASB: SOME EVIDENCE ON THE SIZE
    PRINCIPLE
TAR OC 81 VOL: 56 PG:897 - 909 :: MIXED :PRIM. :INSTIT. :FASB SUBM.

NEWMAN,DP CIT: 0.50
AN INVESTIGATION OF THE DISTRIBUTION OF POWER IN THE APB AND FASB
JAR SP 81 VOL: 19 PG:247 - 262 :: MIXED :CASE :INSTIT. :FASB SUBM.

NEWMAN,DP CIT: 0.13
THE SEC'S INFLUENCE ON ACCOUNTING STANDARDS: THE POWER OF THE VETO
JAR ST 81 VOL: 19 PG:134 - 156 :: ANAL. :INT. LOG. :INSTIT. :FASB SUBM.

NEWMAN,DP ; FIRS: FELLINGHAM,JC CIT: 0.00
STRATEGIC CONSIDERATIONS IN AUDITING
TAR OC 85 VOL: 60 PG:634 - 650 :: REGRESS. :INT. LOG. :OTH.STAT. :PLAN.

NEWMAN,HA ; FIRS: JOHNSON,WB ; SEC: MAGEE ,RP ; THIR: NAGARAJAN,NJ CIT: 0.00
AN ANALYSIS OF THE STOCK PRICE REACTION TO SUDDEN EXECUTIVE DEATHS:
  IMPLICATIONS FOR THE MANAGEMENT LABOR MARKET
JAE AP 85 VOL: 7 PG:151 - 174 :: REGRESS. :PRIM. :EMH :OTH.MANAG.

NEWTON,JD ; FIRS: WILLIAMS,JJ ; THIR: MORGAN,EA CIT: 0.00
THE INTEGRATION OF ZERO-BASE BUDGETING WITH MANAGEMENT-BY-OBJECTIVES: AN
  EMPIRICAL INQUIRY
AOS 04 85 VOL: 10 PG:457 - 478 :: REGRESS. :FIELD :OTH.BEH. :BUDG.& PLAN.

NEWTON,JD ; FIRS: ABDEL-KHALIK,AR ; SEC: GRAUL ,PR CIT: 0.00
REPORTING UNCERTAINTY AND ASSESSMENT OF RISK: REPLICATION AND EXTENSION IN A
  CANADIAN SETTING
JAR AU 86 VOL: 24 PG:372 - 382 :: REGRESS. :LAB. :HIPS :OPIN.

NEWTON,SW ; FIRS: JOHNSON,GL CIT: 0.00
TAX CONSIDERATIONS IN EQUIPMENT REPLACEMENT DECISIONS
TAR OC 67 VOL: 42 PG:738 - 746 :: ANAL. :INT. LOG. :N/A :CAP.BUDG.

NEYHART,CA ; FIRS: CRAMER JR,JJ CIT: 0.00
A COMPREHENSIVE ACCOUNTING FRAMEWORK FOR EVALUATING EXECUTORY CONTRACTS
JAA WI 79 VOL: 2 PG:135 - 150 :: QUAL. :INT. LOG. :THEORY :N/A

NG   ,DS CIT: 0.64
AN INFORMATION ECONOMICS ANALYSIS OF FINANCIAL REPORTING AND EXTERNAL AUDITING
TAR OC 78 VOL: 53 PG:910 - 920 :: ANAL. :INT. LOG. :INF.ECO./AG. :AUD.

NG   ,DS ; SEC: STOECKENIUS,J CIT: 0.60
AUDITING: INCENTIVES AND TRUTHFUL REPORTING
JAR ST 79 VOL: 17 PG:1 - 24 :: ANAL. :INT. LOG. :INF.ECO./AG. :AUD.

NICHOLS,AC ; SEC: GRAWOIG,DE CIT: 0.00
ACCOUNTING REPORTS WITH TIME AS A VARIABLE
TAR OC 68 VOL: 43 PG:631 - 639 :: QUAL. :INT. LOG. :THEORY :OTH.MANAG.

NICHOLS,DR ; SEC: PRICE ,KH CIT: 0.23
THE AUDITOR-FIRM CONFLICT: AN ANALYSIS USING CONCEPTS OF EXCHANGE THEORY
TAR AP 76 VOL: 51 PG:335 - 346 :: QUAL. :INT. LOG. :OTH.BEH. :AUD.

NICHOLS,DR ; SEC: TSAY ,JJ ; THIR: LARKIN,PD CIT: 0.00
INVESTOR TRADING RESPONSES TO DIFFERING CHARACTERISTICS OF VOLUNTARILY
  DISCLOSED EARNINGS FORECASTS
TAR AP 79 VOL: 54 PG:376 - 382 :: NON-PAR. :PRIM. :EMH :FOREC.

NICHOLS,DR ; SEC: TSAY ,JJ CIT: 0.60
SECURITY PRICE REACTIONS TO LONG-RANGE EXECUTIVE EARNINGS FORECASTS
JAR SP 79 VOL: 17 PG:140 - 155 :: REGRESS. :PRIM. :EMH :FOREC.

NICHOLS,DR ; FIRS: SMITH ,DB CIT: 0.00
A MARKET TEST OF INVESTOR REACTION TO DISAGREEMENTS
JAE OC 82 VOL: 4 PG:109 - 120 :: DES.STAT. :SEC. :EMH :MAN.DEC.CHAR.

NICHOLS,DR ; SEC: SMITH ,DB CIT: 0.33
AUDITOR CREDIBILITY AND AUDITOR CHANGES
JAR AU 83 VOL: 21 PG:534 - 544 :: REGRESS. :PRIM. :EMH :AUD.

NICHOLS,DR CIT: 0.00
A MODEL OF AUDITORS' PRELIMINARY EVALUATIONS OF INTERNAL CONTROL FROM AUDIT
  DATA
TAR JA 87 VOL: 62 PG:183 - 190 :: REGRESS. :PRIM. :OTH.STAT. :INT.CONT.

NICHOLS,WD ; FIRS: MORRIS,MH CIT: 0.00
PENSION ACCOUNTING AND THE BALANCE SHEET: THE POTENTIAL EFFECT OF THE FASB'S
   PRELIMINARY VIEWS
JAA SU 84 VOL: 7 PG:293 - 305 :: MIXED :PRIM. :OTH.STAT. :PENS.

NICHOLS,WD ; FIRS: MORRIS,MH CIT: 0.00
CONSISTENCY EXCEPTIONS: MATERIALITY JUDGMENTS AND AUDIT FIRM STRUCTURE
TAR AP 88 VOL: 63 PG:237 - 254 :: REGRESS. :PRIM. :EMH :MAT.

NICOL ,RE ; FIRS: SCHWAB,B CIT: 0.08
FROM DOUBLE-DECLINING-BALANCE TO SUM-OF-THE-YEAR'S DIGITS DEPRECIATION: AN
   OPTIMUM SWITCHING RULE
TAR AP 69 VOL: 44 PG:292 - 296 :: ANAL. :SIM. :OTH.STAT. :PP&E / DEPR

NIEBUHR,RE ; FIRS: NORRIS,DR CIT: 0.00
PROFESSIONALISM, ORGANIZATIONAL COMMITMENT AND JOB SATISFACTION IN AN
   ACCOUNTING ORGANIZATION
AOS 01 84 VOL: 9 PG:49 - 59 :: CORR. :SURV. :OTH.BEH. :PROF.RESP.

NIELSEN,CC CIT: 0.00
REPORTING JOINT-VENTURE CORPORATIONS
TAR OC 65 VOL: 40 PG:795 - 804 :: DES.STAT. :PRIM. :THEORY :BUS.COMB.

NIKOLAI,LA ; SEC: ELAM ,R CIT: 0.00
THE POLLUTION CONTROL TAX INCENTIVE: A NON-INCENTIVE
TAR JA 79 VOL: 54 PG:119 - 131 :: ANAL. :SIM. :OTH.STAT. :TAXES

NIKOLAI,LA ; FIRS: HOWARD,TP CIT: 0.50
ATTITUDE MEASUREMENT AND PERCEPTIONS OF ACCOUNTING FACULTY PUBLICATION OUTLETS
TAR OC 83 VOL: 58 PG:765 - 776 :: DES.STAT. :SURV. :OTH. :METHOD.

NILES ,MS ; FIRS: FELIX JR,WL CIT: 0.00
RESEARCH IN INTERNAL CONTROL EVALUATION
AUD SP 88 VOL: 07 PG:43 - 60 :: DES.STAT. :SEC. :THEORY :INT.CONT.

NIX   ,HM ; SEC: WICHMANN JR,H CIT: 0.00
THE GOVERNMENTAL AUDIT REPORT
JAA SU 83 VOL: 6 PG:341 - 352 :: DES.STAT. :PRIM. :OTH. :OPIN.

NOBES ,CW CIT: 0.00
THE GALLERANI ACCOUNT BOOK OF 1305-1308
TAR AP 82 VOL: 57 PG:303 - 310 :: QUAL. :INT. LOG. :HIST. :N/A

NOEL ,J ; FIRS: IJIRI ,Y CIT: 0.00
A RELIABILITY COMPARISON OF THE MEASUREMENT OF WEALTH, INCOME AND FORCE
TAR JA 84 VOL: 59 PG:52 - 63 :: ANAL. :INT. LOG. :THEORY :REV.REC.

NOEL ,J ; FIRS: BAIMAN,S CIT: 0.50
NONCONTROLLABLE COSTS AND RESPONSIBILITY ACCOUNTING
JAR AU 85 VOL: 23 PG:486 - 501 :: ANAL. :INT. LOG. :INF.ECO./AG. :RESP.ACC.

NOEL ,J ; FIRS: BAIMAN,S ; SEC: EVANS III,JH CIT: 0.00
OPTIMAL CONTRACTS WITH A UTILITY-MAXIMIZING AUDITOR
JAR AU 87 VOL: 25 PG:217 - 244 :: ANAL. :INT. LOG. :INF.ECO./AG. :AUD.BEH.

NORDHAUSER,SL ; SEC: KRAMER,JL CIT: 0.00
REPEAL OF THE DEFERRAL PRIVILEGE FOR EARNINGS FROM DIRECT FOREIGN
   INVESTMENTS: AN ANALYSIS
TAR JA 81 VOL: 56 PG:54 - 69 :: ANAL. :INT. LOG. :OTH.STAT. :BUS.COMB.

NOREEN,EW ; FIRS: BOWEN ,RM ; THIR: LACEY ,JM CIT: 3.63
DETERMINANTS OF THE CORPORATE DECISION TO CAPITALIZE INTEREST
JAE AG 81 VOL: 3 PG:151 - 179 :: DES.STAT. :INT. LOG. :INF.ECO./AG. :SPEC.ITEMS

NOREEN,EW ; SEC: SEPE ,J CIT: 1.25
MARKET REACTIONS TO ACCOUNTING POLICY DELIBERATIONS: THE INFLATION ACCOUNTING
CASE
TAR AP 81 VOL: 56 PG:253 - 269 :: CORR. :PRIM. :EMH :VALUAT.(INFL.)

NOREEN,EW ; SEC: WOLFSON,MA CIT: 0.38
EQUILIBRIUM WARRANT PRICING MODELS AND ACCOUNTING FOR EXECUTIVE STOCK OPTIONS
JAR AU 81 VOL: 19 PG:384 - 398 :: CORR. :PRIM. :EMH :N/A

NOREEN,EW ; FIRS: BLANCHARD,GA ; SEC: CHOW ,CW CIT: 0.00
INFORMATION ASYMMETRY, INCENTIVE SCHEMES, AND INFORMATION BIASING: THE CASE
OF HOSPITAL BUDGETING UNDER RATE REGULATION
TAR JA 86 VOL: 61 PG:1 - 15 :: REGRESS. :PRIM. :N/A :BUDG.& PLAN.

NOREEN,EW ; FIRS: BURGSTAHLER,D CIT: 0.00
DETECTING CONTEMPORANEOUS SECURITY MARKET REACTIONS TO A SEQUENCE OF
RELATED EVENTS
JAR SP 86 VOL: 24 PG:170 - 186 :: REGRESS. :PRIM. :EMH :METHOD.

NOREEN,EW CIT: 0.00
AN EMPIRICAL COMPARISON OF PROBIT AND OLS REGRESSION HYPOTHESIS TESTS
JAR SP 88 VOL: 26 PG:119 - 133 :: REGRESS. :PRIM. :OTH.STAT. :METHOD.

NOREEN,EW CIT: 0.00
THE ECONOMICS OF ETHICS: A NEW PERSPECTIVE ON AGENCY THEORY
AOS 04 88 VOL: 13 PG:359 - 369 :: DES.STAT. :INT. LOG. :INF.ECO./AG. :
ORG.& ENVIR.

NORGAARD,CT CIT: 0.00
EXTENDING THE BOUNDARIES OF THE ATTEST FUNCTION
TAR JL 72 VOL: 47 PG:433 - 442 :: QUAL. :SEC. :INSTIT. :OPIN.

NORMOLLE,D ; FIRS: HORWITZ,B CIT: 0.00
FEDERAL AGENCY R&D CONTRACT AWARDS AND THE FASB RULE FOR PRIVATELY-FUNDED R&
TAR JL 88 VOL: 63 PG:414 - 435 :: REGRESS. :PRIM. :OTH.STAT. :R & D

NORRIS,DR ; SEC: NIEBUHR,RE CIT: 0.00
PROFESSIONALISM, ORGANIZATIONAL COMMITMENT AND JOB SATISFACTION IN AN
ACCOUNTING ORGANIZATION
AOS 01 84 VOL: 9 PG:49 - 59 :: CORR. :SURV. :OTH.BEH. :PROF.RESP.

NORTON,CL ; SEC: SMITH ,RE CIT: 0.30
A COMPARISON OF GENERAL PRICE LEVEL AND HISTORICAL COST FINANCIAL STATEMENTS
IN THE PREDICTION OF BANKRUPTCY
TAR JA 79 VOL: 54 PG:72 - 87 :: OTH.QUANT. :PRIM. :OTH.STAT. :VALUAT.(INFL.)

NOUR ,A ; FIRS: GAMBLING,TE CIT: 0.00
A NOTE ON INPUT-OUTPUT ANALYSIS: ITS USES IN MACRO-ECONOMICS AND
MICRO-ECONOMICS
TAR JA 70 VOL: 45 PG:98 - 102 :: ANAL. :INT. LOG. :OTH.STAT. :BUDG.& PLAN.

NUNAMAKER,TR ; FIRS: GAUMNITZ,BR ; THIR: SURDICK,JJ ; FOUR: THOMAS,MF CIT: 0.14
AUDITOR CONSENSUS IN INTERNAL CONTROL EVALUATION AND AUDIT PROGRAM PLANNING
JAR AU 82 VOL: 20 PG:745 - 755 :: CORR. :LAB. :HIPS :INT.CONT.

NURNBERG,H CIT: 0.08
PRESENT VALUE DEPRECIATION AND INCOME TAX ALLOCATION
TAR OC 68 VOL: 43 PG:719 - 729 :: QUAL. :INT. LOG. :THEORY :PP&E / DEPR

NURNBERG,H CIT: 0.00
A NOTE ON THE FINANCIAL REPORTING OF DEPRECIATION AND INCOME TAXES
JAR AU 69 VOL: 7 PG:257 - 261 :: REGRESS. :SIM. :OTH. :TAXES

NURNBERG,H CIT: 0.00
TAX ALLOCATION FOR DIFFERENCES IN ORIGINAL BASES
JAR AU 70 VOL: 8 PG:217 - 231 :: ANAL. :INT. LOG. :HIST. :TAXES

NURNBERG,H CIT: 0.00
DISCOUNTING DEFERRED TAX LIABILITIES
TAR OC 72 VOL: 47 PG:655 - 665 :: QUAL. :INT. LOG. :THEORY :TAXES

NURNBERG,H ; SEC: CIANCIOLO,ST CIT: 0.00
THE MEASUREMENT VALUATION ALLOWANCE: HELP FOR DEFERRED TAXES
JAA AU 85 VOL: 9 PG:50 - 59 :: DES.STAT. :INT. LOG. :THEORY :TAXES

NYSTROM,PC CIT: 0.08
MANAGERIAL RESISTANCE TO A MANAGEMENT SYSTEM
AOS 04 77 VOL: 2 PG:317 - 322 :: CORR. :SURV. :OTH.BEH. :N/A

O'BRIEN,PC CIT: 0.00
ANALYSTS' FORECASTS AS EARNINGS EXPECTATIONS
JAE JA 88 VOL: 10 PG:53 - 83 :: REGRESS. :PRIM. :TIME SER. :FOREC.

O'CONNOR,MC ; SEC: HAMRE ,JC CIT: 0.00
ALTERNATIVE METHODS OF ACCOUNTING FOR LONG-TERM NONSUBSIDIARY INTERCORPORATE
    INVESTMENTS IN COMMON STOCK
TAR AP 72 VOL: 47 PG:308 - 319 :: QUAL. :INT. LOG. :THEORY :BUS.COMB.

O'CONNOR,MC CIT: 0.15
ON THE USEFULNESS OF FINANCIAL RATIOS TO INVESTORS IN COMMON STOCK
TAR AP 73 VOL: 48 PG:339 - 352 :: REGRESS. :PRIM. :EMH :PENS.

O'DONNELL,JL CIT: 0.00
RELATIONSHIPS BETWEEN REPORTED EARNINGS AND STOCK PRICES IN THE ELECTRIC
    UTILITY INDUSTRY
TAR JA 65 VOL: 40 PG:135 - 143 :: DES.STAT. :PRIM. :TIME SER. :PP&E / DEPR

O'DONNELL,JL CIT: 0.00
FURTHER OBSERVATIONS ON REPORTED EARNINGS AND STOCK PRICES
TAR JL 68 VOL: 43 PG:549 - 553 :: DES.STAT. :PRIM. :N/A :TAXES

O'KEEFE,TB ; FIRS: KING ,RD CIT: 0.00
LOBBYING ACTIVITIES AND INSIDER TRADING
TAR JA 86 VOL: 61 PG:76 - 90 :: REGRESS. :PRIM. :OTH.STAT. :OIL & GAS

O'LEARY,T CIT: 0.50
OBSERVATIONS ON CORPORATE FINANCIAL REPORTING IN THE NAME OF POLITICS
AOS 01 85 VOL: 10 PG:87 - 104 :: REGRESS. :INT. LOG. :INSTIT. :FASB SUBM.

O'LEARY,T ; FIRS: MILLER,P CIT: 2.50
ACCOUNTING AND THE CONSTRUCTION OF THE GOVERNABLE PERSON
AOS 03 87 VOL: 12 PG:235 - 265 :: DES.STAT. :INT. LOG. :HIST. :MANAG.

OFER ,AR ; FIRS: BARAN ,A ; SEC: LAKONISHOK,J CIT: 0.11
THE INFORMATION CONTENT OF GENERAL PRICE LEVEL ADJUSTED EARNINGS: SOME
EMPIRICAL EVIDENCE
TAR JA 80 VOL: 55 PG:22 - 35 :: REGRESS. :PRIM. :HIPS :VALUAT.(INFL.)

OGAN ,P CIT: 0.23
A HUMAN RESOURCE VALUE MODEL FOR PROFESSIONAL SERVICE ORGANIZATIONS
TAR AP 76 VOL: 51 PG:306 - 320 :: QUAL. :INT. LOG. :N/A :HRA

OGAN ,P CIT: 0.08
APPLICATION OF A HUMAN RESOURCE VALUE MODEL: A FIELD STUDY
AOS 23 76 VOL: 1 PG:195 - 218 :: QUAL. :FIELD :OTH.BEH. :HRA

OGDEN ,S ; SEC: BOUGEN,P CIT: 0.25
A RADICAL PERSPECTIVE ON THE DISCLOSURE OF ACCOUNTING INFORMATION TO TRADE
UNIONS
AOS 02 85 VOL: 10 PG:211 - 226 :: DES.STAT. :INT. LOG. :INSTIT. :METHOD.

OHLSON,JA CIT: 0.00
ANALYSIS OF THE USEFULNESS OF ACCOUNTING DATA FOR THE PORTFOLIO DECISION: A
DECISION-THEORY APPROACH
JAR ST 72 VOL: 10 PG:45 - 84 :: REGRESS. :PRIM. :EMH :FIN.METH.

OHLSON,JA CIT: 0.23
THE COMPLETE ORDERING OF INFORMATION ALTERNATIVES FOR A CLASS OF PORTFOLIO
SELECTION MODELS
JAR AU 75 VOL: 13 PG:267 - 282 :: ANAL. :INT. LOG. :EMH :INFO.STRUC.

OHLSON,JA ; SEC: PATELL,JM CIT: 0.20
AN INTRODUCTION TO RESIDUAL (API) ANALYSIS AND THE PRIVATE VALUE OF
INFORMATION AND THE API AND DESIGN OF EXPERIMENTS
JAR AU 79 VOL: 17 PG:504 - 505 :: QUAL. :INT. LOG. :EMH :METHOD.

OHLSON,JA CIT: 0.10
RESIDUAL (API) ANALYSIS AND THE PRIVATE VALUE OF INFORMATION
JAR AU 79 VOL: 17 PG:506 - 527 :: ANAL. :INT. LOG. :EMH :METHOD.

OHLSON,JA CIT: 0.60
ON FINANCIAL DISCLOSURE AND THE BEHAVIOR OF SECURITY PRICES
JAE DE 79 VOL: 1 PG:211 - 232 :: ANAL. :INT. LOG. :EMH :INFO.STRUC.

OHLSON,JA ; FIRS: GARMAN,MB CIT: 0.44
INFORMATION AND THE SEQUENTIAL VALUATION OF ASSETS IN ARBITRAGE-FREE ECONOMIES
JAR AU 80 VOL: 18 PG:420 - 440 :: ANAL. :INT. LOG. :OTH. :OTH.MANAG.

OHLSON,JA CIT: 1.44
FINANCIAL RATIOS AND THE PROBABILISTIC PREDICTION OF BANKRUPTCY
JAR SP 80 VOL: 18 PG:109 - 131 :: MIXED :PRIM. :OTH.STAT. :BUS.FAIL.

OHLSON,JA ; SEC: BUCKMAN,AG CIT: 0.38
TOWARD A THEORY OF FINANCIAL ACCOUNTING: WELFARE AND PUBLIC INFORMATION
JAR AU 81 VOL: 19 PG:399 - 433 :: ANAL. :INT. LOG. :THEORY :N/A

OHLSON,JA ; FIRS: FREEMAN,RN ; THIR: PENMAN,SH CIT: 0.86
BOOK RATE-OF-RETURN AND PREDICTION OF EARNINGS CHANGES: AN EMPIRICAL
INVESTIGATION
JAR AU 82 VOL: 20 PG:639 - 653 :: REGRESS. :PRIM. :EMH :REV.REC.

OHLSON,JA ; FIRS: LEV ,B CIT: 2.43
MARKET-BASED EMPIRICAL RESEARCH IN ACCOUNTING: A REVIEW, INTERPRETATION, AND
EXTENSION
JAR ST 82 VOL: 20 PG:249 - 322 :: QUAL. :SEC. :EMH :METHOD.

OHLSON,JA CIT: 0.50
PRICE-EARNINGS RATIOS AND EARNINGS CAPITALIZATION UNDER UNCERTAINTY
JAR SP 83 VOL: 21 PG:141 - 154 :: ANAL. :INT. LOG. :EMH :N/A

OHLSON,JA ; FIRS: HARRIS,TS CIT: 1.00
ACCOUNTING DISCLOSURES AND THE MARKET'S VALUATION OF OIL AND GAS PROPERTIES
TAR OC 87 VOL: 62 PG:651 - 670 :: REGRESS. :PRIM. :EMH :OIL & GAS

OHLSON,PA ; FIRS: GARSTKA,SJ CIT: 0.70
RATIO ESTIMATION IN ACCOUNTING POPULATIONS WITH PROBABILITIES OF SAMPLE
SELECTION PROPORTIONAL TO SIZE OF BOOK VALUES
JAR SP 79 VOL: 17 PG:23 - 59 :: DES.STAT. :SIM. :OTH.STAT. :SAMP.

OLIPHANT,WJ CIT: 0.00
THE SEARCH FOR ACCOUNTING PRINCIPLES
JAR ST 71 VOL: 9 PG:93 - 98 :: QUAL. :INT. LOG. :THEORY :N/A

OLIVER,BL CIT: 0.54
A STUDY OF CONFIDENCE INTERVAL FINANCIAL STATEMENTS
JAR SP 72 VOL: 10 PG:154 - 166 :: NON-PAR. :LAB. :OTH.BEH. :FIN.METH.

OLIVER,BL CIT: 0.62
THE SEMANTIC DIFFERENTIAL: A DEVICE FOR MEASURING THE INTERPROFESSIONAL
COMMUNICATION OF SELECTED ACCOUNTING CONCEPTS
JAR AU 74 VOL: 12 PG:299 - 316 :: ANOVA :SURV. :OTH.BEH. :FIN.METH.

OLSEN ,C ; FIRS: FOSTER,G ; THIR: SHEVLIN,T CIT: 1.40
EARNINGS RELEASES, ANOMALIES, AND THE BEHAVIOR OF SECURITY RETURNS
TAR OC 84 VOL: 59 PG:574 - 603 :: REGRESS. :PRIM. :EMH :N/A

OLSEN ,C CIT: 0.75
VALUATION IMPLICATIONS OF SFAS NO. 33 DATA FOR ELECTRIC UTILITY INVESTORS
JAR ST 85 VOL: 23 PG:28 - 53 :: REGRESS. :SURV. :EMH :VALUAT.(INFL.)

OLSEN ,C ; SEC: DIETRICH,JR CIT: 0.50
VERTICAL INFORMATION TRANSFERS: THE ASSOCIATION BETWEEN RETAILERS' SALES
ANNOUNCEMENTS AND SUPPLIERS' SECURITY RETURNS
JAR ST 85 VOL: 23 PG:144 - 166 :: REGRESS. :PRIM. :EMH :FIN.METH.

OLSEN ,C ; FIRS: THOMPSON II,RB ; THIR: DIETRICH,JR CIT: 0.00
ATTRIBUTES OF NEWS ABOUT FIRMS: AN ANALYSIS OF FIRM-SPECIFIC NEWS REPORTED IN
THE WALL STREET JOURNAL INDEX
JAR AU 87 VOL: 25 PG:245 - 274 :: REGRESS. :PRIM. :INSTIT. :INFO.STRUC.

OLSEN ,C ; FIRS: THOMPSON,RB ; THIR: DIETRICH,JR CIT: 0.00
THE INFLUENCE OF ESTIMATION PERIOD NEWS EVENTS ON STANDARDIZED MARKET MODEL
PREDICTION ERRORS
TAR JL 88 VOL: 63 PG:448 - 471 :: REGRESS. :PRIM. :EMH :METHOD.

ONSI ,M CIT: 0.00
QUANTITATIVE MODELS FOR ACCOUNTING CONTROL
TAR AP 67 VOL: 42 PG:321 - 330 :: ANAL. :INT. LOG. :OTH.STAT. :VAR.

ONSI ,M CIT: 0.08
A TRANSFER PRICING SYSTEM BASED ON OPPORTUNITY COST
TAR JL 70 VOL: 45 PG:535 - 543 :: ANAL. :INT. LOG. :MATH.PROG. :TRANS.PRIC.

ONSI ,M CIT: 1.00
FACTOR ANALYSIS OF BEHAVIOURAL VARIABLES AFFECTING BUDGETARY STOCK
TAR JL 73 VOL: 48 PG:535 - 548 :: OTH.QUANT. :SURV. :OTH.BEH. :MAN.DEC.CHAR.

OPHIR ,T ; FIRS: AHARONI,Y CIT: 0.00
ACCOUNTING FOR LINKED LOANS
JAR SP 67 VOL: 5 PG:1 - 26 :: QUAL. :INT. LOG. :THEORY :FIN.METH.

OPHIR ,T ; FIRS: FALK ,H CIT: 0.15
THE EFFECT OF RISK ON USE OF FINANCIAL STATEMENTS BY INVESTMENT
DECISION-MAKERS: A CASE STUDY
TAR AP 73 VOL: 48 PG:323 - 338 :: NON-PAR. :CASE :THEORY :N/A

OPHIR ,T ; FIRS: FALK ,H CIT: 0.23
THE INFLUENCE OF DIFFERENCES IN ACCOUNTING POLICIES ON INVESTMENT DECISIONS
JAR SP 73 VOL: 11 PG:108 - 116 :: DES.STAT. :LAB. :OTH.BEH. :FIN.METH.

OPPONG,A CIT: 0.33
INFORMATION CONTENT OF ANNUAL EARNINGS ANNOUNCEMENTS REVISITED
JAR AU 80 VOL: 18 PG:574 - 584 :: REGRESS. :PRIM. :EMH :FIN.ST.TIM.

ORTEGREN,AK ; FIRS: KING ,TE CIT: 0.00
ACCOUNTING FOR HYBRID SECURITIES: THE CASE OF ADJUSTABLE RATE CONVERTIBLE
NOTES
AUD JL 88 VOL: 63 PG:522 - 535 :: DES.STAT. :INT. LOG. :THEORY :SPEC.ITEMS

ORTMAN,RF CIT: 0.23
THE EFFECTS ON INVESTMENT ANALYSIS OF ALTERNATIVE REPORTING PROCEDURES FOR
DIVERSIFIED FIRMS
TAR AP 75 VOL: 50 PG:298 - 304 :: DES.STAT. :FIELD :THEORY :SEG.REP.

OTLEY ,DT CIT: 2.00
BUDGET USE AND MANAGERIAL PERFORMANCE
JAR SP 78 VOL: 16 PG:122 - 149 :: CORR. :FIELD :OTH.BEH. :BUDG.& PLAN.

OTLEY ,DT ; SEC: BERRY ,AJ CIT: 1.22
CONTROL, ORGANIZATION AND ACCOUNTING
AOS 02 80 VOL: 5 PG:231 - 246 :: QUAL. :INT. LOG. :OTH.BEH. :N/A

OTLEY ,DT CIT: 2.67
THE CONTINGENCY THEORY OF MANAGEMENT ACCOUNTING: ACHIEVEMENT AND PROGNOSIS
AOS 04 80 VOL: 5 PG:413 - 428 :: QUAL. :INT. LOG. :OTH. :MANAG.

OTLEY ,DT ; SEC: DIAS ,FJB CIT: 0.14
ACCOUNTING AGGREGATION AND DECISION-MAKING PERFORMANCE: AN EXPERIMENTAL
INVESTIGATION
JAR SP 82 VOL: 20 PG:171 - 188 :: ANOVA :LAB. :HIPS :INFO.STRUC.

OUTSLAY,E ; SEC: WHEELER,JE CIT: 0.00
SEPARATING THE ANNUITY AND INCOME TRANSFER ELEMENTS OF SOCIAL SECURITY
TAR OC 82 VOL: 57 PG:716 - 733 :: DES.STAT. :PRIM. :OTH.STAT. :TAXES

OVADIA,A ; SEC: RONEN ,J CIT: 0.00
GENERAL PRICE-LEVEL ADJUSTMENT AND REPLACEMENT COST ACCOUNTING AS SPECIAL
CASES OF THE INDEX NUMBER PROBLEM
JAA WI 80 VOL: 3 PG:113 - 137 :: ANAL. :SEC. :TIME SER. :VALUAT.(INFL.)

OVADIA,A ; SEC: RONEN ,J CIT: 0.00
ON THE VALUE OF CURRENT-COST INFORMATION
JAA WI 83 VOL: 6 PG:115 - 129 :: ANAL. :INT. LOG. :THEORY :VALUAT.(INFL.)

OWEN ,DL ; SEC: LLOYD ,AJ CIT: 0.00
THE USE OF FINANCIAL INFORMATION BY TRADE UNION NEGOTIATORS IN PLANT LEVEL
   COLLECTIVE BARGAINING
AOS 03 85 VOL: 10 PG:329 - 352 :: DES.STAT. :INT. LOG. :THEORY :ORG.& ENVIR.

OWEN ,DL ; FIRS: HARTE ,GF CIT: 0.00
FIGHTING DE-INDUSTRIALIZATION: THE ROLE OF LOCAL GOVERNMENT SOCIAL AUDITS
AOS 02 87 VOL: 12 PG:123 - 142 :: REGRESS. :INT. LOG. :THEORY :ORG.& ENVIR.

OWEN ,J ; FIRS: BRIEF ,RP CIT: 0.00
DEPRECIATION AND CAPITAL GAINS: A "NEW" APPROACH
TAR AP 68 VOL: 43 PG:367 - 372 :: ANAL. :INT. LOG. :THEORY :PP&E / DEPR

OWEN ,J ; FIRS: BRIEF ,RP CIT: 0.00
A LEAST SQUARES ALLOCATION MODEL
JAR AU 68 VOL: 6 PG:193 - 199 :: ANAL. :INT. LOG. :MATH.PROG. :COST.ALLOC.

OWEN ,J ; FIRS: BRIEF ,RP CIT: 0.00
ON THE BIAS IN ACCOUNTING ALLOCATIONS UNDER UNCERTAINTY
JAR SP 69 VOL: 7 PG:12 - 16 :: ANAL. :INT. LOG. :OTH.STAT. :COST.ALLOC.

OWEN ,J ; FIRS: BRIEF ,RP CIT: 0.15
THE ESTIMATION PROBLEM IN FINANCIAL ACCOUNTING
JAR AU 70 VOL: 8 PG:167 - 177 :: ANAL. :INT. LOG. :OTH.STAT. :PP&E / DEPR

OWEN ,J ; FIRS: BRIEF ,RP CIT: 0.08
PRESENT VALUE MODELS AND THE MULTI-ASSET PROBLEM
TAR OC 73 VOL: 48 PG:690 - 695 :: QUAL. :INT. LOG. :THEORY :PP&E / DEPR

OWEN ,J ; FIRS: BRIEF ,RP CIT: 0.08
A REFORMULATION OF THE ESTIMATION PROBLEM
JAR SP 73 VOL: 11 PG:1 - 15 :: ANAL. :INT. LOG. :OTH.STAT. :PP&E / DEPR

OWEN ,J ; FIRS: KATZ ,BG CIT: 0.00
INITIAL PUBLIC OFFERINGS: AN EQUILIBRIUM MODEL OF PRICE DETERMINATION
JAA SU 87 VOL: 2 PG:266 - 298 :: DES.STAT. :INT. LOG. :THEORY :SPEC.ITEMS

OZAN ,T ; SEC: DYCKMAN,TR CIT: 0.31
A NORMATIVE MODEL FOR INVESTIGATION DECISIONS INVOLVING MULTIORIGIN COST
   VARIANCES
JAR SP 71 VOL: 9 PG:88 - 115 :: ANAL. :INT. LOG. :MATH.PROG. :VAR.

PAINE ,NR CIT: 0.00
UNCERTAINTY AND CAPITAL BUDGETING
TAR AP 64 VOL: 39 PG:330 - 332 :: ANAL. :INT. LOG. :N/A :LTD

PALEPU,KG CIT: 0.67
PREDICTING TAKEOVER TARGETS: A METHODOLOGICAL AND EMPIRICAL ANALYSIS
JAE MR 86 VOL: 8 PG:3 - 36 :: REGRESS. :PRIM. :OTH.STAT. :BUS.COMB.

PALEPU,KG ; FIRS: HEALY ,PM ; SEC: KANG ,SH CIT: 1.00
THE EFFECT OF ACCOUNTING PROCEDURE CHANGES ON CEOS' CASH SALARY AND
   BONUS COMPENSATION
JAE AP 87 VOL: 9 PG:7 - 34 :: REGRESS. :PRIM. :OTH.STAT. :INV.

PALMON,D ; SEC: KWATINETZ,M CIT: 0.11
THE SIGNIFICANT ROLE INTERPRETATION PLAYS IN THE IMPLEMENTATION OF SFAS NO.13
JAA SP 80 VOL: 3 PG:207 - 226 :: QUAL. :INT. LOG. :THEORY :LEASES

PALMON,D ; FIRS: GIVOLY,D CIT: 0.00
CLASSIFICATION OF CONVERTIBLE DEBT AS COMMON STOCK EQUIVALENTS: SOME
EMPIRICAL EVIDENCE ON THE EFFECTS OF APB OPINION 15
JAR AU 81 VOL: 19 PG:530 - 543 :: CORR. :PRIM. :EMH :LTD

PALMON,D ; FIRS: GIVOLY,D CIT: 1.86
TIMELINESS OF ANNUAL EARNINGS ANNOUNCEMENTS: SOME EMPIRICAL EVIDENCE
TAR JL 82 VOL: 57 PG:486 - 508 :: REGRESS. :PRIM. :EMH :FIN.ST.TIM.

PALMROSE,ZV CIT: 0.33
THE EFFECT OF NONAUDIT SERVICES ON THE PRICING OF AUDIT SERVICES: FURTHER
EVIDENCE
JAR AU 86 VOL: 24 PG:405 - 411 :: REGRESS. :PRIM. :OTH.STAT. :OPER.AUD.

PALMROSE,ZV CIT: 1.33
AUDIT FEES AND AUDITOR SIZE: FURTHER EVIDENCE
JAR SP 86 VOL: 24 PG:97 - 110 :: REGRESS. :PRIM. :OTH.STAT. :OPER.AUD.

PALMROSE,ZV CIT: 0.00
LITIGATION AND INDEPENDENT AUDITORS: THE ROLE OF BUSINESS FAILURES AND
MANAGEMENT FRAUD
AUD SP 87 VOL: 6 PG:90 - 103 :: DES.STAT. :SURV. :THEORY :LITIG.

PALMROSE,ZV CIT: 0.00
PUBLIC ACCOUNTING FIRMS AND THE ACQUISITION OF NONAUDIT SERVICES BY PUBLIC
AND CLOSELY-HELD COMPANIES
AUD AU 88 VOL: 08 PG:63 - 71 :: REGRESS. :SURV. :INSTIT. :ORG.

PALMROSE,ZV CIT: 0.00
AN ANALYSIS OF AUDITOR LITIGATION AND AUDIT SERVICE QUALITY
TAR JA 88 VOL: 63 PG:55 - 73 :: REGRESS. :PRIM. :THEORY :LITIG.

PANKOFF,LD ; SEC: VIRGIL JR,RL CIT: 0.15
ON THE USEFULNESS OF FINANCIAL STATEMENT INFORMATION: A SUGGESTED RESEARCH
APPROACH
TAR AP 70 VOL: 45 PG:269 - 279 :: DES.STAT. :LAB. :N/A :OTH.MANAG.

PANKOFF,LD ; SEC: VIRGIL JR,RL CIT: 0.62
SOME PRELIMINARY FINDINGS FROM A LABORATORY EXPERIMENT ON THE USEFULNESS OF
FINANCIAL ACCOUNTING INFORMATION TO SECURITY ANALYSTS
JAR ST 70 VOL: 8 PG:1 - 48 :: MIXED :LAB. :OTH.BEH. :FIN.METH.

PANY ,K ; SEC: RECKERS,PMJ CIT: 0.22
THE EFFECT OF GIFTS, DISCOUNTS, AND CLIENT SIZE ON PERCEIVED AUDITOR
INDEPENDENCE
TAR JA 80 VOL: 55 PG:50 - 61 :: ANOVA :LAB. :OTH.BEH. :INDEP.

PANY ,K ; SEC: SMITH ,CH CIT: 0.00
AUDITOR ASSOCIATION WITH QUARTERLY FINANCIAL INFORMATION: AN EMPIRICAL TEST
JAR AU 82 VOL: 20 PG:472 - 481 :: ANOVA :LAB. :OTH.BEH. :OPIN.

PANY ,K ; FIRS: JOHNSON,DA ; THIR: WHITE ,RA CIT: 0.00
AUDIT REPORTS AND THE LOAN DECISION: ACTIONS AND PERCEPTIONS
AUD SP 83 VOL: 2 PG:38 - 51 :: ANOVA :LAB. :OTH.BEH. :OPIN.

PANY ,K ; FIRS: JOHNSON,DA CIT: 0.00
FORECASTS, AUDITOR REVIEW, AND BANK LOAN DECISIONS
JAR AU 84 VOL: 22 PG:731 - 743 :: ANOVA :LAB. :OTH.BEH. :FOREC.

PANY ,K ; SEC: RECKERS,PMJ CIT: 0.00
NON-AUDIT SERVICES AND AUDITOR INDEPENDENCE - A CONTINUING PROBLEM
AUD SP 84 VOL: 3 PG:89 - 97 :: DES.STAT. :SURV. :OTH.STAT. :INDEP.

PANY ,K ; FIRS: MCKINELY,S ; THIR: RECKERS,PMJ CIT: 0.00
AN EXAMINATION OF THE INFLUENCE OF CPA FIRM TYPE, SIZE, AND MAS PROVISION ON
  LOAN OFFICER DECISIONS & PERCEPTIONS
JAR AU 85 VOL: 23 PG:887 - 896 :: REGRESS. :LAB. :OTH.BEH. :ORG.

PANY ,K ; FIRS: MARGHEIM,LL CIT: 0.00
QUALITY CONTROL, PREMATURE SIGNOFF, AND UNDERREPORTING OF TIME: SOME
  EMPIRICAL FINDINGS
AUD SP 86 VOL: 5 PG:50 - 63 :: REGRESS. :LAB. :OTH.BEH. :ORG.

PANY ,K ; SEC: RECKERS,PMJ CIT: 0.00
WITHIN- VS. BETWEEN-SUBJECTS EXPERIMENTAL DESIGNS: A STUDY OF DEMAND
  EFFECTS
AUD AU 87 VOL: 7 PG:39 - 53 :: REGRESS. :LAB. :OTH.BEH. :INDEP.

PARE ,PV ; FIRS: IMHOFF JR,EA CIT: 1.00
ANALYSIS AND COMPARISON OF EARNINGS FORECAST AGENTS
JAR AU 82 VOL: 20 PG:429 - 439 :: DES.STAT. :PRIM. :TIME SER. :METHOD.

PARK ,SH ; FIRS: MANES ,RP ; THIR: JENSEN,RE CIT: 0.00
RELEVANT COSTS OF INTERMEDIATE GOODS AND SERVICES
TAR JL 82 VOL: 57 PG:594 - 606 :: ANAL. :INT. LOG. :MATH.PROG. :N/A

PARKE ,R ; SEC: PETERSON,JL CIT: 0.00
INDICATORS OF SOCIAL CHANGE: DEVELOPMENTS IN THE U.S.A.
AOS 03 81 VOL: 6 PG:235 - 246 :: QUAL. :INT. LOG. :OTH. :HRA

PARKER,JE CIT: 0.08
TESTING COMPARABILITY AND OBJECTIVITY OF EXIT VALUE ACCOUNTING
TAR JL 75 VOL: 50 PG:512 - 524 :: ANOVA :SURV. :THEORY :OTH.FIN.ACC.

PARKER,JE CIT: 0.75
IMPACT OF PRICE-LEVEL ACCOUNTING
TAR JA 77 VOL: 52 PG:69 - 96 :: DES.STAT. :PRIM. :THEORY :VALUAT.(INFL.)

PARKER,LD ; FIRS: LEWIS ,NR ; THIR: SUTCLIFFE,P CIT: 0.00
FINANCIAL REPORTING TO EMPLOYEES: THE PATTERN OF DEVELOPMENT 1919 TO 1979
AOS 34 84 VOL: 9 PG:275 - 289 :: DES.STAT. :SEC. :HIST. :HRA

PARKER,LD ; FIRS: COWEN ,SS ; SEC: FERRERI,LB CIT: 0.00
THE IMPACT OF CORPORATE CHARACTERISTICS ON SOCIAL RESPONSIBILITY DIS
  CLOSURE: A TYPOLOGY AND FREQUENCY-BASED ANALYSIS
AOS 02 87 VOL: 12 PG:111 - 122 :: REGRESS. :PRIM. :THEORY :HRA

PARKER,RH CIT: 0.08
DISCOUNTED CASH FLOW IN HISTORICAL PERSPECTIVE
JAR SP 68 VOL: 6 PG:58 - 71 :: QUAL. :SEC. :HIST. :CAP.BUDG.

PARKER,WM CIT: 0.00
THE TREATMENT OF SHORT-TERM CREDIT IN THE FUNDS STATEMENT
TAR OC 63 VOL: 38 PG:785 - 788 :: QUAL. :INT. LOG. :THEORY :N/A

PARKER,WM CIT: 0.00
BUSINESS COMBINATIONS AND ACCOUNTING VALUATION
JAR AU 66 VOL: 4 PG:149 - 154 :: QUAL. :INT. LOG. :THEORY :BUS.COMB.

PASTENA,V ; SEC: RONEN ,J CIT: 0.50
SOME HYPOTHESES ON THE PATTERN OF MANAGEMENT'S INFORMAL DISCLOSURES
JAR AU 79 VOL: 17 PG:550 - 564 :: NON-PAR. :PRIM. :OTH. :OTH.MANAG.

PASTENA,V ; FIRS: LILIEN,S CIT: 1.29
DETERMINANTS OF INTRAMETHOD CHOICE IN THE OIL AND GAS INDUSTRY
JAE DE 82 VOL: 4 PG:145 - 170 :: REGRESS. :PRIM. :OTH.STAT. :OIL & GAS

PASTENA,V ; SEC: RULAND,W CIT: 0.33
THE MERGER/BANKRUPTCY ALTERNATIVE
TAR AP 86 VOL: 61 PG:288 - 301 :: REGRESS. :PRIM. :THEORY :BUS.COMB.

PASTENA,V ; FIRS: EL-GAZZAR,S ; SEC: LILIEN,S CIT: 0.33
ACCOUNTING FOR LEASES BY LESSEES
JAE OC 86 VOL: 8 PG:217 - 238 :: REGRESS. :PRIM. :OTH.STAT. :LEASES

PASTENA,V ; FIRS: HAW ,IM ; THIR: LILIEN,S CIT: 0.00
THE ASSOCIATION BETWEEN MARKET-BASED MERGER PREMIUMS AND FIRMS' FINANCIAL
POSITION PRIOR TO MERGER
JAA WI 87 VOL: 2 PG:24 - 42 :: REGRESS. :PRIM. :EMH :BUS.COMB.

PASTENA,V ; FIRS: LILIEN,S ; SEC: MELLMAN,M CIT: 0.00
ACCOUNTING CHANGES: SUCCESSFUL VERSUS UNSUCCESSFUL FIRMS
TAR OC 88 VOL: 63 PG:642 - 656 :: REGRESS. :PRIM. :THEORY :ACC.CHNG.

PATELL,JM CIT: 4.54
CORPORATE FORECASTS OF EARNINGS PER SHARE AND STOCK PRICE BEHAVIOR: EMPIRICAL
TESTS
JAR AU 76 VOL: 14 PG:246 - 276 :: REGRESS. :PRIM. :EMH :FOREC.

PATELL,JM ; SEC: WOLFSON,MA CIT: 1.30
ANTICIPATED INFORMATION RELEASES REFLECTED IN CALL OPTION PRICES
JAE AG 79 VOL: 1 PG:117 - 140 :: ANOVA :PRIM. :EMH :INFO.STRUC.

PATELL,JM ; FIRS: OHLSON,JA CIT: 0.20
AN INTRODUCTION TO RESIDUAL (API) ANALYSIS AND THE PRIVATE VALUE OF
INFORMATION AND THE API AND DESIGN OF EXPERIMENTS
JAR AU 79 VOL: 17 PG:504 - 505 :: QUAL. :INT. LOG. :EMH :METHOD.

PATELL,JM CIT: 0.60
THE API AND THE DESIGN OF EXPERIMENTS
JAR AU 79 VOL: 17 PG:528 - 549 :: ANAL. :INT. LOG. :EMH :METHOD.

PATELL,JM ; SEC: WOLFSON,MA CIT: 1.50
THE EX ANTE AND EX POST PRICE EFFECTS OF QUARTERLY EARNINGS ANNOUNCEMENTS
REFLECTED IN OPTION AND STOCK PRICES
JAR AU 81 VOL: 19 PG:434 - 458 :: REGRESS. :PRIM. :EMH :FIN.METH.

PATELL,JM ; SEC: WOLFSON,MA CIT: 1.71
GOOD NEWS, BAD NEWS, AND THE INTRADAY TIMING OF CORPORATE DISCLOSURES
TAR JL 82 VOL: 57 PG:509 - 527 :: REGRESS. :PRIM. :EMH :FIN.ST.TIM.

PATELL,JM ; FIRS: DEMSKI,JS ; THIR: WOLFSON,MA CIT: 1.60
DECENTRALIZED CHOICE OF MONITORING SYSTEMS
TAR JA 84 VOL: 59 PG:16 - 34 :: ANAL. :INT. LOG. :INF.ECO./AG. :MANAG.

PATELL,JM ; FIRS: MARAIS,ML ; THIR: WOLFSON,MA CIT: 0.20
THE EXPERIMENTAL DESIGN OF CLASSIFICATORY MODELS: AN APPLICATION OF RECURSIVE
    PARTITIONING AND BOOTSTRAPPING COMMERCIAL BANK LOAN CLASSIFICATION
JAR ST 84 VOL: 22 PG:87 - 114 :: OTH.QUANT. :PRIM. :OTH.STAT. :BUS.FAIL.

PATON ,WA CIT: 0.00
THE "CASH FLOW" ILLUSION
TAR AP 63 VOL: 38 PG:243 - 251 :: QUAL. :INT. LOG. :THEORY :FIN.METH.

PATON ,WA CIT: 0.00
ACCOUNTING AND UTILIZATION OF RESOURCES
JAR SP 63 VOL: 1 PG:44 - 72 :: QUAL. :INT. LOG. :THEORY :N/A

PATON ,WA CIT: 0.00
SOME REFLECTIONS ON EDUCATION AND PROFESSORING
TAR JA 67 VOL: 42 PG:7 - 23 :: QUAL. :INT. LOG. :INSTIT. :OTH.MANAG.

PATON ,WA CIT: 0.00
OBSERVATIONS ON INFLATION FROM AN ACCOUNTING STANCE
JAR SP 68 VOL: 6 PG:72 - 85 :: QUAL. :INT. LOG. :THEORY :VALUAT.(INFL.)

PATON ,WA CIT: 0.00
POSTSCRIPT ON "TREASURY" SHARES
TAR AP 69 VOL: 44 PG:276 - 283 :: QUAL. :INT. LOG. :THEORY :SPEC.ITEMS

PATRICK,AW ; SEC: QUITTMEYER,CL CIT: 0.00
THE CPA AND MANAGEMENT SERVICES
TAR JA 63 VOL: 38 PG:109 - 117 :: QUAL. :INT. LOG. :N/A :N/A

PATTEN,RJ CIT: 0.00
INTRAPERIOD INCOME TAX ALLOCATION - A PRACTICAL CONCEPT
TAR OC 64 VOL: 39 PG:876 - 879 :: DES.STAT. :PRIM. :THEORY :TAXES

PATTERSON,RG CIT: 0.00
MATERIALITY AND THE ECONOMIC ENVIRONMENT
TAR OC 67 VOL: 42 PG:772 - 774 :: QUAL. :INT. LOG. :THEORY :OTH.FIN.ACC.

PATTON,JM CIT: 0.18
AN EXPERIMENTAL INVESTIGATION OF SOME EFFECTS OF CONSOLIDATING MUNICIPAL
    FINANCIAL REPORTS
TAR AP 78 VOL: 53 PG:402 - 414 :: ANOVA :LAB. :HIPS :BUS.COMB.

PATTON,JM ; FIRS: EVANS III,JH CIT: 1.00
AN ECONOMIC ANALYSIS OF PARTICIPATION IN THE MUNICIPAL FINANCE OFFICERS
    ASSOCIATION CERTIFICATE OF CONFORMANCE PROGRAM
JAE AG 83 VOL: 5 PG:151 - 175 :: OTH.QUANT. :PRIM. :INSTIT. :FIN.METH.

PATTON,JM ; FIRS: EVANS III,JH ; SEC: LEWIS ,BL CIT: 0.00
AN ECONOMIC MODELING APPROACH TO CONTINGENCY THEORY AND MANAGEMENT CONTROL
AOS 06 86 VOL: 11 PG:483 - 498 :: DES.STAT. :INT. LOG. :INF.ECO./AG. :INT.CONT.

PATTON,JM ; FIRS: EVANS III,JH CIT: 0.00
SIGNALING AND MONITORING IN PUBLIC-SECTOR ACCOUNTING
JAR ST 87 VOL: 25 PG:130 - 164 :: MIXED :SURV. :INF.ECO./AG. :FIN.METH.

PATTON,JM ; FIRS: LEWIS ,BL ; THIR: GREEN ,SL CIT: 0.00
THE EFFECTS OF INFORMATION CHOICE AND INFORMATION USE ON ANALYSTS'
    PREDICTIONS OF MUNICIPAL BOND RATING CHANGES
TAR AP 88 VOL: 63 PG:270 - 282 :: REGRESS. :LAB. :OTH.STAT. :FOREC.

PATZ ,DH ; SEC: BOATSMAN,JR CIT: 0.15
ACCOUNTING PRINCIPLE FORMULATION IN AN EFFICIENT MARKETS ENVIRONMENT
JAR AU 72 VOL: 10 PG:392 - 403 :: ANOVA :PRIM. :EMH :OIL & GAS

PATZ ,DH ; FIRS: LOREK ,KS ; SEC: MCDONALD,CL CIT: 0.77
A COMPARATIVE EXAMINATION OF MANAGEMENT FORECASTS AND BOX-JENKINS FORECASTS
OF EARNINGS
TAR AP 76 VOL: 51 PG:321 - 330 :: REGRESS. :PRIM. :TIME SER. :METHOD.

PEARSON,MA ; SEC: LINDGREN,JH ; THIR: MYERS ,BL CIT: 0.10
A PRELIMINARY ANALYSIS OF AUDSEC VOTING PATTERNS
JAA WI 79 VOL: 2 PG:122 - 134 :: OTH.QUANT. :PRIM. :INSTIT. :FASB SUBM.

PEASNELL,KV CIT: 0.00
A NOTE ON THE DISCOUNTED PRESENT VALUE CONCEPT
TAR JA 77 VOL: 52 PG:186 - 189 :: QUAL. :INT. LOG. :THEORY :VALUAT.(INFL.)

PEASNELL,KV ; SEC: SKERRATT,CL CIT: 0.33
HOW WELL DOES A SINGLE INDEX REPRESENT THE NINETEEN SANDILANDS PLANT AND
MACHINERY INDICES?
JAR SP 77 VOL: 15 PG:108 - 119 :: CORR. :PRIM. :THEORY :VALUAT.(INFL.)

PEAVY ,JW ; SEC: EDGAR ,SM CIT: 0.00
RATING ELECTRIC UTILITY COMMERCIAL PAPER
JAA WI 85 VOL: 8 PG:125 - 135 :: REGRESS. :PRIM. :OTH.STAT. :LTD

PEDERSEN,PH ; FIRS: BJORN-ANDERSEN,N CIT: 0.00
COMPUTER FACILITATED CHANGES IN THE MANAGEMENT POWER STRUCTURE
AOS 02 80 VOL: 5 PG:203 - 216 :: QUAL. :CASE :OTH.BEH. :N/A

PEIRSON,CG ; FIRS: YOUNG ,TN CIT: 0.00
DEPRECIATION - FUTURE SERVICES BASIS
TAR AP 67 VOL: 42 PG:338 - 341 :: ANAL. :INT. LOG. :THEORY :PP&E / DEPR

PEIRSON,G CIT: 0.00
THREE KINDS OF ADJUSTMENTS FOR PRICE CHANGES
TAR OC 66 VOL: 41 PG:729 - 736 :: QUAL. :INT. LOG. :N/A :VALUAT.(INFL.)

PELES ,YC CIT: 0.15
AMORTIZATION OF ADVERTISING EXPENDITURES IN THE FINANCIAL STATEMENTS
JAR SP 70 VOL: 8 PG:128 - 137 :: REGRESS. :CASE :THEORY :OTH. NON-C/A

PELES ,YC CIT: 0.00
A NOTE ON YIELD VARIANCE AND MIX VARIANCE
TAR AP 86 VOL: 61 PG:325 - 329 :: DES.STAT. :INT. LOG. :THEORY :VAR.

PENMAN,SH CIT: 0.08
WHAT NET ASSET VALUE? - AN EXTENSION OF A FAMILIAR DEBATE
TAR AP 70 VOL: 45 PG:333 - 346 :: QUAL. :INT. LOG. :THEORY :VALUAT.(INFL.)

PENMAN,SH ; FIRS: EGGLETON,IRC ; THIR: TWOMBLY,JR CIT: 0.92
ACCOUNTING CHANGES AND STOCK PRICES: AN EXAMINATION OF SELECTED UNCONTROLLED
VARIABLES
JAR SP 76 VOL: 14 PG:66 - 88 :: NON-PAR. :PRIM. :EMH :ACC.CHNG.

PENMAN,SH ; FIRS: GONEDES,NJ ; SEC: DOPUCH,N CIT: 3.00
DISCLOSURE RULES, INFORMATION-PRODUCTION, AND CAPITAL MARKET EQUILIBRIUM: THE
CASE OF FORECAST DISCLOSURE RULES
JAR SP 76 VOL: 14 PG:89 - 137 :: NON-PAR. :PRIM. :EMH :FOREC.

PENMAN,SH CIT: 1.89
AN EMPIRICAL INVESTIGATION OF THE VOLUNTARY DISCLOSURE OF CORPORATE EARNINGS
   FORECASTS OF EARNINGS
JAR SP 80 VOL: 18 PG:132 - 160 :: REGRESS. :PRIM. :EMH :FOREC.

PENMAN,SH ; FIRS: FREEMAN,RN ; SEC: OHLSON,JA CIT: 0.86
BOOK RATE-OF-RETURN AND PREDICTION OF EARNINGS CHANGES: AN EMPIRICAL
   INVESTIGATION
JAR AU 82 VOL: 20 PG:639 - 653 :: REGRESS. :PRIM. :EMH :REV.REC.

PENMAN,SH CIT: 0.00
ABNORMAL RETURNS TO INVESTMENT STRATEGIES BASED ON THE TIMING OF EARNINGS
   REPORTS
JAE DE 84 VOL: 6 PG:165 - 183 :: REGRESS. :PRIM. :EMH :FIN.ST.TIM.

PENMAN,SH ; FIRS: CHAMBERS,AE CIT: 2.40
TIMELINESS OF REPORTING AND THE STOCK PRICE REACTION TO EARNINGS ANNOUNCEMENTS
JAR SP 84 VOL: 22 PG:21 - 47 :: REGRESS. :PRIM. :EMH :FIN.ST.TIM.

PENNO ,M CIT: 1.20
ASYMMETRY OF PRE-DECISION INFORMATION AND MANAGERIAL ACCOUNTING
JAR SP 84 VOL: 22 PG:177 - 191 :: ANAL. :INT. LOG. :INF.ECO./AG. :MANAG.

PENNO ,M CIT: 0.25
INFORMATIONAL ISSUES IN THE FINANCIAL REPORTING PROCESS
JAR SP 85 VOL: 23 PG:240 - 255 :: REGRESS. :INT. LOG. :INF.ECO./AG. :BUS.FAIL.

PERAGALLO,E CIT: 0.00
A COMMENT ON VIGANO'S HISTORICAL DEVELOPMENT OF LEDGER BALANCING PROCESS

ADJUSTMENTS AND FINANCIAL STATEMENTS DURING THE 15TH, 16TH AND 17TH CENTURIES
TAR JL 71 VOL: 46 PG:529 - 534 :: QUAL. :SEC. :HIST. :FIN.METH.

PERAGALLO,E CIT: 0.25
THE LEDGER OF JACHOMO BADOER: CONSTANTINOPLE SEPTEMBER 2, 1436 TO FEBRUARY 2
TAR OC 77 VOL: 52 PG:881 - 892 :: QUAL. :PRIM. :HIST. :FIN.METH.

PERAGALLO,E CIT: 0.13
CLOSING PROCEDURES IN THE 15TH CENTURY LEDGER OF JACHOMO BADOER, A VENETIAN
   MERCHANT
TAR JL 81 VOL: 56 PG:587 - 595 :: QUAL. :INT. LOG. :HIST. :N/A

PERAGALLO,E CIT: 0.00
DEVELOPMENT OF THE COMPOUND ENTRY IN 15TH CENTURY LEDGER OF JACHOMO BADOER, A
   VENETIAN MERCHANT
TAR JA 83 VOL: 58 PG:98 - 104 :: QUAL. :INT. LOG. :HIST. :N/A

PERBY ,M ; FIRS: CARLSSON,J ; SEC: EHN   ,P ; THIR: ERLANDER,B ; FIFT:
SANDBERG,A CIT: 0.09
PLANNING AND CONTROL FROM THE PERSPECTIVE OF LABOR: A SHORT REPRESENTATION OF
   THE DEMOS PROJECT
AOS 34 78 VOL: 3 PG:249 - 260 :: QUAL. :FIELD :OTH. :BUDG.& PLAN.

PERRITT,GW ; FIRS: AGRAWAL,SP ; SEC: HALLBAUER,RC CIT: 0.00
MEASUREMENT OF THE CURRENT COST OF EQUIVALENT PRODUCTIVE CAPACITY
JAA WI 80 VOL: 3 PG:163 - 173 :: ANAL. :INT. LOG. :OTH.STAT. :VALUAT.(INFL.)

PESANDO,JE ; SEC: CLARKE,CK CIT: 0.00
ECONOMIC MODELS OF THE LABOR MARKET AND PENSION ACCOUNTING: AN EXPLORATORY
ANALYSIS
TAR OC 83 VOL: 58 PG:733 - 748 :: ANAL. :INT. LOG. :OTH.STAT. :PENS.

PETERSEN,RJ CIT: 0.54
INTERINDUSTRY ESTIMATION OF GENERAL PRICE-LEVEL IMPACT ON FINANCIAL
INFORMATION
TAR JA 73 VOL: 48 PG:34 - 43 :: NON-PAR. :PRIM. :THEORY :VALUAT.(INFL.)

PETERSEN,RJ CIT: 0.00
A PORTFOLIO ANALYSIS OF GENERAL PRICE LEVEL RESTATEMENT
TAR JL 75 VOL: 50 PG:525 - 532 :: NON-PAR. :PRIM. :EMH :VALUAT.(INFL.)

PETERSON,JL ; FIRS: PARKE ,R CIT: 0.00
INDICATORS OF SOCIAL CHANGE: DEVELOPMENTS IN THE U.S.A.
AOS 03 81 VOL: 6 PG:235 - 246 :: QUAL. :INT. LOG. :OTH. :HRA

PETERSON,RB ; FIRS: MAHER ,MW ; SEC: RAMANATHAN,KV CIT: 0.40
PREFERENCE CONGRUENCE, INFORMATION ACCURACY, AND EMPLOYEE PERFORMANCE: A
FIELD STUDY
JAR AU 79 VOL: 17 PG:476 - 503 :: ANOVA :FIELD :OTH.BEH. :AUD.BEH.

PETERSON,WA CIT: 0.00
SIGNIFICANCE OF PROSPECTIVE INCOME DATA
TAR AP 66 VOL: 41 PG:275 - 282 :: QUAL. :INT. LOG. :THEORY :VALUAT.(INFL.)

PETRAN,AS ; FIRS: DAVIDSON,HJ ; SEC: NETER ,J CIT: 0.15
ESTIMATING THE LIABILITY FOR UNREDEEMED STAMPS
JAR AU 67 VOL: 5 PG:186 - 207 :: ANAL. :INT. LOG. :OTH.STAT. :SPEC.ITEMS

PETRI ,E CIT: 0.00
HOLDING GAINS AND LOSSES AS COST SAVINGS: A COMMENT ON SUPPLEMENTARY
STATEMENT NO.2 ON INVENTORY VALUATION
TAR JL 73 VOL: 48 PG:483 - 488 :: ANAL. :INT. LOG. :THEORY :INV.

PETRI ,E ; SEC: MINCH ,RA CIT: 0.15
THE TREASURY STOCK METHOD AND CONVENTIONAL METHOD IN RECIPROCAL STOCKHOLDIN
- AN AMALGAMATION
TAR AP 74 VOL: 49 PG:330 - 341 :: ANAL. :INT. LOG. :N/A :SPEC.ITEMS

PETRI ,E ; SEC: MINCH ,RA CIT: 0.00
EVALUATION OF RESOURCE ACQUISITION DECISIONS BY THE PARTITIONING OF HOLDING
ACTIVITY
TAR JL 74 VOL: 49 PG:455 - 464 :: ANAL. :INT. LOG. :N/A :INV.

PETRI ,E ; FIRS: SEAGLE,JP CIT: 0.00
GIFT VS. ESTATE TRANSFER: THE METHOD OF EQUATED RATES
TAR JA 77 VOL: 52 PG:124 - 136 :: ANAL. :INT. LOG. :THEORY :N/A

PETRI ,E ; SEC: MINCH ,RA CIT: 0.00
A DECISION MODEL FOR TAX PREFERENCE ITEMS
TAR AP 78 VOL: 53 PG:415 - 428 :: ANAL. :INT. LOG. :OTH.STAT. :OTH.MANAG.

PETRI ,E ; SEC: GELFAND,J CIT: 0.00
THE PRODUCTION FUNCTION: A NEW PERSPECTIVE IN CAPITAL MAINTENANCE
TAR AP 79 VOL: 54 PG:330 - 345 :: ANAL. :INT. LOG. :OTH. :OTH.MANAG.

PETRI ,E ; FIRS: MARCINKO,D CIT: 0.00
USE OF THE PRODUCTION FUNCTION IN CALCULATION OF STANDARD COST VARIANCES - AN
   EXTENSION
TAR JL 84 VOL: 59 PG:488 - 495 :: ANAL. :INT. LOG. :OTH. :VAR.

PETTY ,JW ; FIRS: MERVILLE,LJ CIT: 0.18
TRANSFER PRICING FOR THE MULTINATIONAL FIRM
TAR OC 78 VOL: 53 PG:935 - 951 :: ANAL. :INT. LOG. :MATH.PROG. :TRANS.PRIC.

PFEFFER,J ; FIRS: MARKUS,ML CIT: 0.50
POWER AND THE DESIGN AND IMPLEMENTATION OF ACCOUNTING AND CONTROL SYSTEMS
AOS 23 83 VOL: 8 PG:205 - 218 :: QUAL. :CASE :OTH. :MANAG.

PHILBRICK,D ; FIRS: DYCKMAN,TR ; THIR: STEPHAN,J CIT: 0.60
A COMPARISON OF EVENT STUDY METHODOLOGIES USING DAILY STOCK RETURNS: A
   SIMULATION APPROACH
JAR ST 84 VOL: 22 PG:1 - 30 :: REGRESS. :SIM. :OTH.BEH. :METHOD.

PHILIPS,GE CIT: 0.00
THE ACCRETION CONCEPT OF INCOME
TAR JA 63 VOL: 38 PG:14 - 25 :: QUAL. :INT. LOG. :THEORY :REV.REC.

PHILIPS,GE CIT: 0.00
THE REVOLUTION IN ACCOUNTING THEORY
TAR OC 63 VOL: 38 PG:696 - 708 :: QUAL. :INT. LOG. :THEORY :N/A

PHILIPS,GE CIT: 0.00
PENSION LIABILITIES AND ASSETS
TAR JA 68 VOL: 43 PG:10 - 17 :: QUAL. :INT. LOG. :THEORY :PENS.

PHILIPS,GE ; SEC: MAYNE ,LS CIT: 0.00
INCOME MEASURE AND BANK STOCK VALUES
JAR ST 70 VOL: 8 PG:178 - 188 :: REGRESS. :PRIM. :TIME SER. :VALUAT.(INFL.)

PHILLIPS,LC CIT: 0.00
ACCOUNTING FOR BUSINESS COMBINATIONS
TAR AP 65 VOL: 40 PG:377 - 381 :: QUAL. :INT. LOG. :THEORY :BUS.COMB.

PIERCE,LT ; FIRS: WALKER,NR CIT: 0.00
THE PRICE WATERHOUSE AUDIT: A STATE OF THE ART APPROACH
AUD AU 88 VOL: 08 PG:1 - 22 :: DES.STAT. :INT. LOG. :THEORY :AUD.THEOR.

PILLSBURY,CM CIT: 0.00
LIMITED ASSURANCE ENGAGEMENTS
AUD SP 85 VOL: 4 PG:63 - 79 :: REGRESS. :LAB. :OTH.STAT. :OPIN.

PINCHES,GE ; FIRS: HAKA ,SF ; SEC: GORDON,LA CIT: 0.50
SOPHISTICATED CAPITAL BUDGETING SELECTION TECHNIQUES AND FIRM PERFORMANCE
TAR OC 85 VOL: 60 PG:651 - 669 :: REGRESS. :PRIM. :EMH :CAP.BUDG.

PINCUS,M CIT: 0.83
INFORMATION CHARACTERISTICS OF EARNINGS ANNOUNCEMENTS AND STOCK MARKET
   BEHAVIOR
JAR SP 83 VOL: 21 PG:155 - 183 :: NON-PAR. :PRIM. :EMH :FOREC.

PINCUS,M ; FIRS: MADEO ,SA CIT: 0.25
STOCK MARKET BEHAVIOR AND TAX RULE CHANGES: THE CASE OF THE DISALLOWANCE OF
   CERTAIN INTEREST DEDUCTIONS CLAIMED BY BANKS
TAR JL 85 VOL: 60 PG:407 - 429 :: REGRESS. :LAB. :EMH :TAXES

PINCUS,M ; FIRS: DOPUCH,N CIT: 0.00
EVIDENCE ON THE CHOICE OF INVENTORY ACCOUNTING METHODS: LIFO VERSUS FIFO
JAR SP 88 VOL: 26 PG:28 - 59 :: REGRESS. :PRIM. :OTH.STAT. :INV.

PLANTE,R ; FIRS: LEITCH,RA ; SEC: NETER ,J ; FOUR: SINHA ,P CIT: 0.86
MODIFIED MULTINOMIAL BOUNDS FOR LARGER NUMBERS OF ERRORS IN AUDITS
TAR AP 82 VOL: 57 PG:384 - 400 :: DES.STAT. :SIM. :OTH.STAT. :SAMP.

PLANTE,R ; SEC: NETER ,J ; THIR: LEITCH,RA CIT: 0.00
COMPARATIVE PERFORMANCE OF MULTINOMIAL, CELL, AND STRINGER BOUNDS
AUD AU 85 VOL: 5 PG:40 - 56 :: DES.STAT. :SIM. :OTH.STAT. :SAMP.

PLUMLEE,RD CIT: 0.25
THE STANDARD OF OBJECTIVITY FOR INTERNAL AUDITORS: MEMORY AND BIAS EFFECT
JAR AU 85 VOL: 23 PG:683 - 699 :: REGRESS. :LAB. :HIPS :INT.AUD.

PLUMLEE,RD ; FIRS: CHOW ,CW ; SEC: MCNAMEE,AH CIT: 0.00
PRACTITIONERS' PERCEPTIONS OF AUDIT STEP DIFFICULTY AND CRITICALNESS
IMPLICATIONS FOR AUDIT RESEARCH
AUD SP 87 VOL: 6 PG:123 - 133 :: REGRESS. :SURV. :OTH.STAT. :AUD.THEOR.

POLLOCK,J ; FIRS: ARANYA,N ; THIR: AMERNIC,J CIT: 0.00
AN EXAMINATION OF PROFESSIONAL COMMITMENT IN PUBLIC ACCOUNTING
AOS 04 81 VOL: 6 PG:271 - 280 :: MIXED :LAB. :OTH.BEH. :PROF.RESP.

POMERANZ,F CIT: 0.00
HOW THE AUDIT COMMITTEE SHOULD WORK
JAA AU 77 VOL: 1 PG:45 - 52 :: QUAL. :INT. LOG. :INSTIT. :OTH.MANAG.

PONDY ,LR ; FIRS: BOLAND,RJ CIT: 2.33
ACCOUNTING IN ORGANIZATIONS: A UNION OF NATURAL AND RATIONAL PERSPECTIVES
AOS 23 83 VOL: 8 PG:223 - 234 :: QUAL. :CASE :OTH. :OTH.MANAG.

PONDY ,LR ; FIRS: BOLAND,RJ CIT: 0.67
THE MICRO DYNAMICS OF A BUDGET-CUTTING PROCESS: MODES, MODELS AND STRUCTURE
AOS 45 86 VOL: 11 PG:403 - 422 :: REGRESS. :FIELD :HIPS :BUDG.& PLAN.

PORCANO,TM CIT: 0.00
DISTRIBUTIVE JUSTICE AND TAX POLICY
TAR OC 84 VOL: 59 PG:619 - 636 :: REGRESS. :LAB. :OTH.BEH. :TAXES

PORTER,GA ; FIRS: EVERETT,JO CIT: 0.00
SAFE-HARBOR LEASING - UNRAVELING THE TAX IMPLICATIONS
JAA SP 84 VOL: 7 PG:241 - 256 :: MIXED :INT. LOG. :THEORY :LEASES

POSEY ,JM ; FIRS: CARPER,WB CIT: 0.08
THE VALIDITY OF SELECTED SURROGATE MEASURES OF HUMAN RESOURCE VALUE: A FIELD
STUDY
AOS 23 76 VOL: 1 PG:143 - 152 :: NON-PAR. :SURV. :OTH.BEH. :HRA

POWELL,RM CIT: 0.00
CAREER CHOICES AMONG BETA ALPHA PSI MEMBERS
TAR JL 66 VOL: 41 PG:525 - 534 :: DES.STAT. :SURV. :INSTIT. :OTH.MANAG.

POWNALL,G ; FIRS: WAYMIRE,G CIT: 0.00
SOME EVIDENCE ON POTENTIAL EFFECTS OF CONTEMPORANEOUS EARN. DISCLOSURES IN
TESTS OF CAPITAL MARKET EFFECTS ASSOC. WITH FASB EXPOSURE DRAFT NO.19
JAR AU 83 VOL: 21 PG:629 - 643 :: REGRESS. :PRIM. :EMH :OIL & GAS

POWNALL,G CIT: 0.00
AN EMPIRICAL ANALYSIS OF THE REGULATION OF THE DEFENSE CONTRACTING INDUSTRY:
THE COST ACCOUNTING STANDARDS BOARD
JAR AU 86 VOL: 24 PG:291 - 315 :: REGRESS. :PRIM. :INSTIT. :FASB SUBM.

PRAKASH,P ; SEC: RAPPAPORT,A CIT: 0.23
INFORMATIONAL INTERDEPENDENCIES: SYSTEM STRUCTURED INDUCED BY ACCOUNTING
INFORMATION
TAR OC 75 VOL: 50 PG:723 - 734 :: QUAL. :INT. LOG. :INSTIT. :OTH.MANAG.

PRAKASH,P ; SEC: RAPPAPORT,A CIT: 1.75
INFORMATION INDUCTANCE AND ITS SIGNIFICANCE FOR ACCOUNTING
AOS 01 77 VOL: 2 PG:29 - 38 :: QUAL. :INT. LOG. :HIPS :N/A

PRAKASH,P ; FIRS: DITTMAN,DA CIT: 0.36
COST VARIANCE INVESTIGATION: MARKOVIAN CONTROL OF MARKOV PROCESSES
JAR SP 78 VOL: 16 PG:14 - 25 :: ANAL. :INT. LOG. :OTH.STAT. :VAR.

PRAKASH,P ; FIRS: DITTMAN,DA CIT: 0.40
COST VARIANCE INVESTIGATION: MARKOVIAN CONTROL VERSUS OPTIMAL CONTROL
TAR AP 79 VOL: 54 PG:358 - 373 :: DES.STAT. :SIM. :OTH.STAT. :VAR.

PRAKASH,P ; SEC: SUNDER,S CIT: 0.40
THE CASE AGAINST SEPARATION OF CURRENT OPERATING PROFIT AND HOLDING GAIN
TAR JA 79 VOL: 54 PG:1 - 22 :: QUAL. :INT. LOG. :THEORY :VALUAT.(INFL.)

PRATER,GI CIT: 0.00
TIME-SHARING COMPUTERS IN ACCOUNTING EDUCATION
TAR OC 66 VOL: 41 PG:619 - 625 :: QUAL. :INT. LOG. :N/A :OTH.MANAG.

PRATT ,J ; SEC: JIAMBALVO,J CIT: 0.38
RELATIONSHIPS BETWEEN LEADER BEHAVIORS AND AUDIT TEAM PERFORMANCE
AOS 02 81 VOL: 6 PG:133 - 142 :: CORR. :FIELD :OTH.BEH. :AUD.BEH.

PRATT ,J ; FIRS: JIAMBALVO,J CIT: 0.14
TASK COMPLEXITY AND LEADERSHIP EFFECTIVENESS IN CPA FIRMS
TAR OC 82 VOL: 57 PG:734 - 750 :: ANOVA :LAB. :OTH.BEH. :ORG.

PRATT ,J CIT: 0.14
POST-COGNITIVE STRUCTURE: ITS DETERMINANTS AND RELATIONSHIP TO PERCEIVED
INFORMATION AND PREDICTIVE ACCURACY
JAR SP 82 VOL: 20 PG:189 - 209 :: CORR. :LAB. :HIPS :INFO.STRUC.

PRATT ,J ; SEC: JIAMBALVO,J CIT: 0.00
DETERMINANTS OF LEADER BEHAVIOR IN AN AUDIT ENVIRONMENT
AOS 04 82 VOL: 7 PG:369 - 380 :: NON-PAR. :SURV. :HIPS :AUD.BEH.

PRATT ,J CIT: 0.00
SFAS NO. 2: AUDITOR EVALUATIONS AND INPUT TO THE HOME OFFICE
AOS 04 85 VOL: 10 PG:427 - 442 :: REGRESS. :SURV. :OTH.BEH. :R & D

PRESTON,A CIT: 0.33
INTERACTIONS AND ARRANGEMENTS IN THE PROCESS OF INFORMING
AOS 06 86 VOL: 11 PG:521 - 540 :: REGRESS. :CASE :OTH.BEH. :MANAG.

PRESTON,LE ; FIRS: DIERKES,M CIT: 0.42
CORPORATE SOCIAL ACCOUNTING REPORTING FOR THE PHYSICAL ENVIRONMENT: A
CRITICAL REVIEW AND IMPLEMENTATION PROPOSAL
AOS 01 77 VOL: 2 PG:3 - 22 :: QUAL. :INT. LOG. :THEORY :HRA

PRESTON,LE CIT: 0.00
RESEARCH ON CORPORATE SOCIAL REPORTING: DIRECTIONS FOR DEVELOPMENT
AOS 03 81 VOL: 6 PG:255 - 262 :: QUAL. :INT. LOG. :OTH. :HRA

PREVITS,GJ ; FIRS: MAUTZ ,RK CIT: 0.00
ERIC KOHLER: AN ACCOUNTING ORIGINAL
TAR AP 77 VOL: 52 PG:301 - 307 :: QUAL. :INT. LOG. :HIST. :N/A

PRICE ,KH ; FIRS: NICHOLS,DR CIT: 0.23
THE AUDITOR-FIRM CONFLICT: AN ANALYSIS USING CONCEPTS OF EXCHANGE THEORY
TAR AP 76 VOL: 51 PG:335 - 346 :: QUAL. :INT. LOG. :OTH.BEH. :AUD.

PRINCE,TR CIT: 0.00
THE MOTIVATIONAL ASSUMPTION FOR ACCOUNTING THEORY
TAR JL 64 VOL: 39 PG:553 - 562 :: QUAL. :INT. LOG. :THEORY :FIN.METH.

PRINCE,TR ; FIRS: GODFREY,JT CIT: 0.15
THE ACCOUNTING MODEL FROM AN INFORMATION SYSTEMS PERSPECTIVE
TAR JA 71 VOL: 46 PG:75 - 89 :: QUAL. :INT. LOG. :INF.ECO./AG. :MANAG.

PROBST,FR CIT: 0.23
PROBABILISTIC COST CONTROLS: A BEHAVIOURAL DIMENSION
TAR JA 71 VOL: 46 PG:113 - 118 :: DES.STAT. :FIELD :OTH.STAT. :RESP.ACC.

PURDY ,CR CIT: 0.00
INDUSTRY PATTERNS OF CAPACITY OR VOLUME CHOICE: THEIR EXISTENCE AND RATIONALE
JAR AU 65 VOL: 3 PG:228 - 241 :: ANAL. :INT. LOG. :OTH. :N/A

PURDY ,CR ; SEC: SMITH JR,JM ; THIR: GRAY J CIT: 0.00
THE VISIBILITY OF THE AUDITOR'S DISCLOSURE OF DEVIANCE FROM APB OPINION: AN
EMPIRICAL TEST
JAR ST 69 VOL: 7 PG:1 - 18 :: ANOVA :LAB. :OTH.BEH. :INFO.STRUC.

PURDY ,D CIT: 0.00
THE PROVISION OF FINANCIAL INFORMATION TO EMPLOYEES: A STUDY OF THE REPORTING
PRACTICES OF SOME LARGE PUBLIC COMPANIES IN THE UK
AOS 04 81 VOL: 6 PG:327 - 338 :: DES.STAT. :SURV. :OTH. :MANAG.

PURO ,M CIT: 0.20
AUDIT FIRM LOBBYING BEFORE THE FINANCIAL ACCOUNTING STANDARDS BOARD: AN
EMPIRICAL STUDY
JAR AU 84 VOL: 22 PG:624 - 646 :: OTH.QUANT. :PRIM. :INSTIT. :FASB SUBM.

PURO ,M CIT: 0.00
DO LARGE ACCOUNTING FIRMS COLLUDE IN THE STANDARDS-SETTING PROCESS?
JAA SP 85 VOL: 8 PG:165 - 177 :: REGRESS. :PRIM. :INSTIT. :FASB SUBM.

PUTNAM,K ; SEC: THOMAS,LR CIT: 0.00
DOES PREDICTABILITY CHANGE WHEN GAAP CHANGE?
JAA AU 84 VOL: 8 PG:15 - 23 :: MIXED :PRIM. :TIME SER. :FOREC.

PUTNEY,FB ; FIRS: IJIRI ,Y ; SEC: KINARD,JC CIT: 0.38
AN INTEGRATED EVALUATION SYSTEM FOR BUDGET FORECASTING AND OPERATING
PERFORMANCE WITH A CLASSIFIED BUDGETING BIBLIOGRAPHY
JAR SP 68 VOL: 6 PG:1 - 28 :: QUAL. :SEC. :OTH.BEH. :BUDG.& PLAN.

PUXTY ,AG ; FIRS: MCDONALD,DL CIT: 0.00
AN INDUCEMENT-CONTRIBUTION APPROACH TO CORPORATE FINANCIAL REPORTING
AOS 12 79 VOL: 4 PG:53 - 66 :: QUAL. :INT. LOG. :THEORY :N/A

PUXTY ,AG ; SEC: WILLMOTT,HC ; THIR: COOPER,DJ ; FOUR: LOWE ,T CIT: 0.50
MODES OF REGULATION IN ADVANCED CAPITALISM: LOCATING ACCOUNTANCY IN
FOUR COUNTRIES
AOS 03 87 VOL: 12 PG:273 - 291 :: DES.STAT. :INT. LOG. :THEORY :ORG.& ENVIR.

PYLE ,WC ; FIRS: BRUMMET,RL ; SEC: FLAMHOLTZ,EG CIT: 0.54
HUMAN RESOURCE MEASUREMENT - A CHALLENGE FOR ACCOUNTANTS
TAR AP 68 VOL: 43 PG:217 - 224 :: QUAL. :INT. LOG. :OTH.BEH. :HRA

QUITTMEYER,CL ; FIRS: PATRICK,AW CIT: 0.00
THE CPA AND MANAGEMENT SERVICES
TAR JA 63 VOL: 38 PG:109 - 117 :: QUAL. :INT. LOG. :N/A :N/A

RABY ,WL ; SEC: NEUBIG,RD CIT: 0.00
INTER-PERIOD TAX ALLOCATION OR BASIS ADJUSTMENT?
TAR JL 63 VOL: 38 PG:568 - 576 :: QUAL. :INT. LOG. :THEORY :TAXES

RABY ,WL CIT: 0.00
ETHICS IN TAX PRACTICE
TAR OC 66 VOL: 41 PG:714 - 720 :: QUAL. :INT. LOG. :N/A :ORG.

RABY ,WL CIT: 0.00
TAX ALLOCATION AND NON-HISTORICAL FINANCIAL STATEMENTS
TAR JA 69 VOL: 44 PG:1 - 11 :: QUAL. :INT. LOG. :THEORY :VALUAT.(INFL.)

RADCLIFFE,RC ; FIRS: MABERT,VA CIT: 0.08
A FORECASTING METHODOLOGY AS APPLIED TO FINANCIAL TIME SERIES
TAR JA 74 VOL: 49 PG:61 - 75 :: REGRESS. :INT. LOG. :TIME SER. :BUDG.& PLAN.

RADEBAUGH,LH ; FIRS: GRAY ,SJ CIT: 0.00
INTERNATIONAL SEGMENT DISCLOSURES BY U.S. AND U.K. MULTINATIONAL ENTERPRISES:
A DESCRIPTIVE STUDY
JAR SP 84 VOL: 22 PG:351 - 360 :: DES.STAT. :PRIM. :THEORY :INT.DIFF.

RADOSEVICH,R ; FIRS: STERLING,RR CIT: 0.15
A VALUATION EXPERIMENT
JAR SP 69 VOL: 7 PG:90 - 95 :: DES.STAT. :LAB. :OTH. :AUD.

RAHMAN,M ; FIRS: MCCOSH,AM CIT: 0.08
THE INFLUENCE OF ORGANIZATIONAL AND PERSONAL FACTORS ON THE USE OF ACCOUNTING
INFORMATION: AN EMPIRICAL STUDY
AOS 04 76 VOL: 1 PG:339 - 356 :: DES.STAT. :LAB. :HIPS :MAN.DEC.CHAR.

RAJAN ,MV ; FIRS: BANKER,RD ; SEC: DATAR ,SM CIT: 0.00
MEASUREMENT OF PRODUCTIVITY IMPROVEMENTS: AN EMPIRICAL ANALYSIS
JAA AU 87 VOL: 2 PG:319 - 347 :: DES.STAT. :FIELD :OTH.STAT. :MANAG.

RAMAGE,JG ; SEC: KRIEGER,AM ; THIR: SPERO ,LL CIT: 0.90
AN EMPIRICAL STUDY OF ERROR CHARACTERISTICS IN AUDIT POPULATIONS
JAR ST 79 VOL: 17 PG:72 - 102 :: DES.STAT. :PRIM. :OTH.STAT. :ERRORS

RAMAKRISHNAN,RT ; FIRS: BALACHANDRAN,BV CIT: 0.22
INTERNAL CONTROL AND EXTERNAL AUDITING FOR INCENTIVE COMPENSATION SCHEDULES
JAR ST 80 VOL: 18 PG:140 - 171 :: ANAL. :INT. LOG. :INF.ECO./AG. :AUD.

RAMAKRISHNAN,RT ; FIRS: BALACHANDRAN,BV CIT: 0.00
JOINT COST ALLOCATION: A UNIFIED APPROACH
TAR JA 81 VOL: 56 PG:85 - 96 :: ANAL. :INT. LOG. :MATH.PROG. :COST.ALLOC.

RAMAKRISHNAN,RT ; FIRS: BALACHANDRAN,BV CIT: 0.00
A THEORY OF AUDIT PARTNERSHIPS: AUDIT FIRM SIZE AND FEES
JAR SP 87 VOL: 25 PG:111 - 126 :: DES.STAT. :INT. LOG. :INF.ECO./AG. :ORG.

RAMAN ,KK CIT: 0.10
THE TIEBOUT HYPOTHESIS: IMPLICATIONS FOR MUNICIPAL FINANCIAL REPORTING
JAA AU 79 VOL: 3 PG:31 - 41 :: QUAL. :INT. LOG. :INSTIT. :FIN.METH.

RAMAN ,KK CIT: 0.50
FINANCIAL REPORTING AND MUNICIPAL BOND RATING CHANGES
TAR OC 81 VOL: 56 PG:910 - 926 :: OTH.QUANT. :PRIM. :OTH.STAT. :FIN.METH.

RAMAN ,KK CIT: 0.00
MUNICIPAL FINANCIAL REPORTING: MONITORING "FULL" ACCOUNTABILITY
JAA SU 81 VOL: 4 PG:352 - 359 :: QUAL. :INT. LOG. :THEORY :AUD.

RAMAN ,KK CIT: 0.00
ALTERNATIVE ACCOUNTING MEASURES AS PREDICTORS OF MUNICIPAL FINANCIAL DISTRESS
JAA AU 82 VOL: 6 PG:44 - 50 :: OTH.QUANT. :PRIM. :THEORY :BUS.FAIL.

RAMAN ,KK CIT: 0.00
FINANCIAL REPORTING AND MUNICIPAL BOND RATINGS
JAA WI 82 VOL: 5 PG:144 - 153 :: OTH.QUANT. :PRIM. :THEORY :FIN.METH.

RAMAN ,KK ; FIRS: MARKS ,BR CIT: 0.00
THE IMPORTANCE OF PENSION DATA FOR MUNICIPAL & STATE CREDITOR DECISIONS:
REPLICATIONS & EXTENSIONS
JAR AU 85 VOL: 23 PG:878 - 886 :: REGRESS. :PRIM. :OTH.STAT. :PENS.

RAMAN ,KK ; FIRS: MARKS ,BR CIT: 0.00
SOME ADDITIONAL EVIDENCE ON THE DETERMINANTS OF STATE AUDIT BUDGETS
AUD AU 87 VOL: 7 PG:106 - 117 :: REGRESS. :PRIM. :THEORY :AUD.

RAMANAN,R ; FIRS: JOHNSON,WB CIT: 0.00
DISCRETIONARY ACCOUNTING CHANGES FROM "SUCCESSFUL EFFORTS" TO "FULL COST"
METHOD
TAR JA 88 VOL: 63 PG:96 - 110 :: REGRESS. :PRIM. :OTH.STAT. :OIL & GAS

RAMANAN,R ; FIRS: BALACHANDRAN,BV CIT: 0.00
OPTIMAL INTERNAL CONTROL STRATEGY UNDER DYNAMIC CONDITIONS
JAA WI 88 VOL: 03 PG:1 - 13 :: DES.STAT. :INT. LOG. :INF.ECO./AG. :INT.CONT.

RAMANATHAN,KV ; SEC: RAPPAPORT,A CIT: 0.00
SIZE, GROWTH RATES, AND MERGER VALUATION
TAR OC 71 VOL: 46 PG:733 - 745 :: ANAL. :SIM. :OTH.STAT. :BUS.COMB.

RAMANATHAN,KV CIT: 0.38
TOWARD A THEORY OF CORPORATE SOCIAL ACCOUNTING
TAR JL 76 VOL: 51 PG:516 - 528 :: QUAL. :INT. LOG. :INSTIT. :HRA

RAMANATHAN,KV ; FIRS: MAHER ,MW ; THIR: PETERSON,RB CIT: 0.40
PREFERENCE CONGRUENCE, INFORMATION ACCURACY, AND EMPLOYEE PERFORMANCE: A
FIELD STUDY
JAR AU 79 VOL: 17 PG:476 - 503 :: ANOVA :FIELD :OTH.BEH. :AUD.BEH.

RAMANATHAN,KV ; SEC: WEIS ,WL CIT: 0.13
SUPPLEMENTING COLLEGIATE FINANCIAL STATEMENTS WITH ACROSS-FUND AGGREGATIONS:
AN EXPERIMENTAL INQUIRY
AOS 02 81 VOL: 6 PG:143 - 152 :: ANOVA :LAB. :THEORY :INFO.STRUC.

RAMESH,K ; FIRS: GREENBERG,RR ; SEC: JOHNSON,GL CIT: 0.00
EARNINGS VERSUS CASH FLOW AS A PREDICTOR OF FUTURE CASH FLOW MEASURES
JAA AU 86 VOL: 1 PG:266 - 277 :: REGRESS. :PRIM. :THEORY :SPEC.ITEMS

RANDALL,RH ; FIRS: CUSHING,BE ; SEC: SEARFOSS,DG CIT: 0.20
MATERIALITY ALLOCATION IN AUDIT PLANNING: A FEASIBILITY STUDY
JAR ST 79 VOL: 17 PG:172 - 216 :: DES.STAT. :FIELD :OTH.STAT. :PLAN.

RANSOM,CR CIT: 0.00
THE EX ANTE INFORMATION CONTENT OF ACCOUNTING INFORMATION SYSTEMS
JAR ST 85 VOL: 23 PG:124 - 143 :: REGRESS. :PRIM. :EMH :FIN.METH.

RAPPAPORT,A CIT: 0.00
ESTABLISHING OBJECTIVES FOR PUBLISHED CORPORATE ACCOUNTING REPORTS
TAR OC 64 VOL: 39 PG:951 - 962 :: QUAL. :INT. LOG. :INSTIT. :OTH.MANAG.

RAPPAPORT,A CIT: 0.08
LEASE CAPITALIZATION AND THE TRANSACTION CONCEPT
TAR AP 65 VOL: 40 PG:373 - 376 :: QUAL. :INT. LOG. :THEORY :LEASES

RAPPAPORT,A CIT: 0.08
SENSITIVITY ANALYSIS IN DECISION MAKING
TAR JL 67 VOL: 42 PG:441 - 456 :: ANAL. :INT. LOG. :MATH.PROG. :BUDG.& PLAN.

RAPPAPORT,A ; FIRS: LAVALLE,IH CIT: 0.00
ON THE ECONOMICS OF ACQUIRING INFORMATION OF IMPERFECT RELIABILITY
TAR AP 68 VOL: 43 PG:225 - 230 :: ANAL. :INT. LOG. :INF.ECO./AG. :REL.COSTS

RAPPAPORT,A CIT: 0.00
INTEGER PROGRAMMING AND MANAGERIAL ANALYSIS
TAR AP 69 VOL: 44 PG:297 - 299 :: ANAL. :INT. LOG. :MATH.PROG. :LTD

RAPPAPORT,A ; FIRS: RAMANATHAN,KV CIT: 0.00
SIZE, GROWTH RATES, AND MERGER VALUATION
TAR OC 71 VOL: 46 PG:733 - 745 :: ANAL. :SIM. :OTH.STAT. :BUS.COMB.

RAPPAPORT,A ; FIRS: PRAKASH,P CIT: 0.23
INFORMATIONAL INTERDEPENDENCIES: SYSTEM STRUCTURED INDUCED BY ACCOUNTING
   INFORMATION
TAR OC 75 VOL: 50 PG:723 - 734 :: QUAL. :INT. LOG. :INSTIT. :OTH.MANAG.

RAPPAPORT,A ; FIRS: PRAKASH,P CIT: 1.75
INFORMATION INDUCTANCE AND ITS SIGNIFICANCE FOR ACCOUNTING
AOS 01 77 VOL: 2 PG:29 - 38 :: QUAL. :INT. LOG. :HIPS :N/A

RATCLIFFE,TA ; FIRS: MUNTER,P CIT: 0.00
AN ASSESSMENT OF USER REACTIONS TO LEASE ACCOUNTING DISCLOSURES
JAA WI 83 VOL: 6 PG:108 - 114 :: NON-PAR. :LAB. :THEORY :LEASES

RATSCH,H CIT: 0.00
THE NEW PROFESSIONAL CODE FOR CERTIFIED ACCOUNTANTS AND LICENSED ACCOUNTANTS
   IN THE FEDERAL REPUBLIC OF GERMANY
TAR JA 64 VOL: 39 PG:140 - 144 :: QUAL. :INT. LOG. :INSTIT. :OTH.MANAG.

RAUN ,DL CIT: 0.00
THE APPLICATION OF MONTE CARLO ANALYSIS TO AN INVENTORY PROBLEM
TAR OC 63 VOL: 38 PG:754 - 758 :: ANAL. :INT. LOG. :OTH.STAT. :INV.

RAUN ,DL CIT: 0.00
THE LIMITATIONS OF PROFIT GRAPHS, BREAKEVEN ANALYSIS, AND BUDGETS
TAR OC 64 VOL: 39 PG:927 - 945 :: REGRESS. :INT. LOG. :TIME SER. :C-V-P-A

RAVIV ,A CIT: 0.00
MANAGEMENT COMPENSATION AND THE MANAGERIAL LABOR MARKET: AN OVERVIEW
JAE AP 85 VOL: 7 PG:239 - 246 :: REGRESS. :INT. LOG. :THEORY :EXEC.COMP.

RAYBURN,J CIT: 2.00
THE ASSOCIATION OF OPERATING CASH FLOW AND ACCRUALS WITH SECURITY RETURNS
JAR ST 86 VOL: 24 PG:112 - 137 :: REGRESS. :PRIM. :EMH :SPEC.ITEMS

RAYBURN,JD ; FIRS: COLLINS,DW ; SEC: KOTHARI,SP CIT: 1.00
FIRM SIZE AND THE INFORMATION CONTENT OF PRICES WITH RESPECT TO EARNINGS
JAE JL 87 VOL: 9 PG:111 - 138 :: REGRESS. :PRIM. :EMH :ORG.& ENVIR.

RAYMAN,RA CIT: 0.00
AN EXTENSION OF THE SYSTEM OF ACCOUNTS: THE SEGREGATION OF FUNDS AND VALUE
JAR SP 69 VOL: 7 PG:53 - 89 :: QUAL. :INT. LOG. :THEORY :FIN.METH.

REBELE,JE ; SEC: HEINTZ,JA ; THIR: BRIDEN,GE CIT: 0.00
INDEPENDENT AUDITOR SENSITIVITY TO EVIDENCE RELIABILITY
AUD AU 88 VOL: 08 PG:43 - 52 :: REGRESS. :LAB. :OTH.BEH. :JUDG.

RECKERS,PMJ ; SEC: TAYLOR,ME CIT: 0.30
CONSISTENCY IN AUDITORS' EVALUATIONS OF INTERNAL ACCOUNTING CONTROLS
JAA AU 79 VOL: 3 PG:42 - 55 :: ANOVA :LAB. :OTH.BEH. :INT.CONT.

RECKERS,PMJ ; FIRS: PANY ,K CIT: 0.22
THE EFFECT OF GIFTS, DISCOUNTS, AND CLIENT SIZE ON PERCEIVED AUDITOR
    INDEPENDENCE
TAR JA 80 VOL: 55 PG:50 - 61 :: ANOVA :LAB. :OTH.BEH. :INDEP.

RECKERS,PMJ ; FIRS: SCHULTZ JR,JJ CIT: 0.75
THE IMPACT OF GROUP PROCESSING ON SELECTED AUDIT DISCLOSURE DECISIONS
JAR AU 81 VOL: 19 PG:482 - 501 :: ANOVA :PRIM. :OTH.BEH. :AUD.BEH.

RECKERS,PMJ ; SEC: STAGLIANO,AJ CIT: 0.13
NON-AUDIT SERVICES AND PERCEIVED INDEPENDENCE: SOME NEW EVIDENCE
AUD SU 81 VOL: 1 PG:23 - 37 :: ANOVA :LAB. :OTH.BEH. :INDEP.

RECKERS,PMJ ; SEC: SCHULTZ JR,JJ CIT: 0.00
INDIVIDUAL VERSUS GROUP ASSISTED AUDIT EVALUATIONS
AUD AU 82 VOL: 2 PG:64 - 74 :: ANOVA :LAB. :OTH.BEH. :JUDG.

RECKERS,PMJ ; FIRS: KAPLAN,SE CIT: 0.00
AN EMPIRICAL EXAMINATION OF AUDITORS' INITIAL PLANNING PROCESSES
AUD AU 84 VOL: 4 PG:1 - 19 :: ANOVA :LAB. :OTH.BEH. :PLAN.

RECKERS,PMJ ; FIRS: PANY ,K CIT: 0.00
NON-AUDIT SERVICES AND AUDITOR INDEPENDENCE - A CONTINUING PROBLEM
AUD SP 84 VOL: 3 PG:89 - 97 :: DES.STAT. :SURV. :OTH.STAT. :INDEP.

RECKERS,PMJ ; FIRS: MCKINELY,S ; SEC: PANY ,K CIT: 0.00
AN EXAMINATION OF THE INFLUENCE OF CPA FIRM TYPE, SIZE, AND MAS PROVISION ON
    LOAN OFFICER DECISIONS & PERCEPTIONS
JAR AU 85 VOL: 23 PG:887 - 896 :: REGRESS. :LAB. :OTH.BEH. :ORG.

RECKERS,PMJ ; FIRS: PANY ,K CIT: 0.00
WITHIN- VS. BETWEEN-SUBJECTS EXPERIMENTAL DESIGNS: A STUDY OF DEMAND
    EFFECTS
AUD AU 87 VOL: 7 PG:39 - 53 :: REGRESS. :LAB. :OTH.BEH. :INDEP.

RECKERS,PMJ ; FIRS: JENNINGS,M ; SEC: KNEER ,DC CIT: 0.00
A REEXAMINATION OF THE CONCEPT OF MATERIALITY: VIEWS OF AUDITORS, USERS AND
OFFICERS OF THE COURT
AUD SP 87 VOL: 6 PG:104 - 115 :: REGRESS. :LAB. :OTH.BEH. :MAT.

RECKERS,PMJ ; FIRS: KAPLAN,SE ; THIR: ROARK ,SJ CIT: 0.00
AN ATTRIBUTION THEORY ANALYSIS OF TAX EVASION RELATED JUDGMENTS
AOS 04 88 VOL: 13 PG:371 - 379 :: REGRESS. :LAB. :OTH.BEH. :TAXES

REDER ,RE ; FIRS: LARCKER,DF ; THIR: SIMON ,DT CIT: 0.33
TRADES BY INSIDERS AND MANDATED ACCOUNTING STANDARDS
TAR JL 83 VOL: 58 PG:606 - 620 :: NON-PAR. :INT. LOG. :EMH :OIL & GAS

REICHELSTEIN,S ; FIRS: MELUMAD,ND CIT: 0.50
CENTRALIZATION VERSUS DELEGATION AND THE VALUE OF COMMUNICATION
JAR ST 87 VOL: 25 PG:1 - 18 :: DES.STAT. :INT. LOG. :INF.ECO./AG. :ORG.& ENVIR.

REICHENSTEIN,WR ; FIRS: FARRELY,GE ; SEC: FERRIS,KR CIT: 0.00
PERCEIVED RISK, MARKET RISK, AND ACCOUNTING-DETERMINED RISK MEASURES
TAR AP 85 VOL: 60 PG:278 - 288 :: REGRESS. :SURV. :OTH.STAT. :FOREC.

REILLY,FK ; SEC: STETTLER,HF CIT: 0.00
FACTORS INFLUENCING SUCCESS ON THE CPA EXAMINATION
JAR AU 72 VOL: 10 PG:308 - 321 :: REGRESS. :PRIM. :OTH.STAT. :EDUC.

REILLY,FK ; SEC: MORGENSON,DL ; THIR: WEST ,M CIT: 0.23
THE PREDICTIVE ABILITY OF ALTERNATIVE PARTS OF INTERIM FINANCIAL STATEMENTS
JAR ST 72 VOL: 10 PG:105 - 124 :: REGRESS. :PRIM. :EMH :INT.REP.

REITER,SA ; FIRS: FRANCIS,JR CIT: 0.50
DETERMINANTS OF CORPORATE PENSION FUNDING STRATEGY
JAE AP 87 VOL: 9 PG:35 - 59 :: REGRESS. :PRIM. :OTH.STAT. :PENS.

RENEAU,JH CIT: 0.55
CAV BOUNDS IN DOLLAR UNIT SAMPLING: SOME SIMULATION RESULTS
TAR JL 78 VOL: 53 PG:669 - 680 :: ANAL. :SIM. :OTH.STAT. :SAMP.

RENEAU,JH ; FIRS: HARRISON,PD ; SEC: WEST ,SG CIT: 0.00
INITIAL ATTRIBUTIONS AND INFORMATION-SEEKING BY SUPERIORS AND SUBORDINATES IN
PRODUCTION VARIANCE INVESTIGATIONS
TAR AP 88 VOL: 63 PG:307 - 320 :: REGRESS. :LAB. :OTH.BEH. :VAR.

REVSINE,L CIT: 0.00
SOME CONTROVERSY CONCERNING "CONTROVERSIAL" ACCOUNTING CHANGES
TAR AP 69 VOL: 44 PG:354 - 358 :: QUAL. :INT. LOG. :THEORY :TAXES

REVSINE,L CIT: 0.46
ON THE CORRESPONDENCE BETWEEN REPLACEMENT COST INCOME AND ECONOMIC INCOME
TAR JL 70 VOL: 45 PG:513 - 523 :: ANAL. :INT. LOG. :THEORY :VALUAT.(INFL.)

REVSINE,L CIT: 0.69
DATA EXPANSION AND CONCEPTUAL STRUCTURE
TAR OC 70 VOL: 45 PG:704 - 711 :: QUAL. :INT. LOG. :OTH.BEH. :INFO.STRUC.

REVSINE,L CIT: 0.00
PREDICTIVE ABILITY, MARKET PRICES, AND OPERATING FLOWS
TAR JL 71 VOL: 46 PG:480 - 489 :: QUAL. :INT. LOG. :N/A :FIN.METH.

REVSINE,L ; SEC: THIES ,JB CIT: 0.15
PRODUCTIVITY CHANGES AND ALTERNATIVE INCOME SERIES: A SIMULATION
TAR AP 76 VOL: 51 PG:255 - 268 :: ANAL. :SIM. :OTH.STAT. :DEC.AIDS

REVSINE,L ; FIRS: DITTMAN,DA ; SEC: JURIS ,HA CIT: 0.38
ON THE EXISTENCE OF UNRECORDED HUMAN ASSETS: AN ECONOMIC PERSPECTIVE
JAR SP 76 VOL: 14 PG:49 - 65 :: ANAL. :INT. LOG. :OTH.BEH. :HRA

REVSINE,L CIT: 0.30
TECHNOLOGICAL CHANGES AND REPLACEMENT COSTS: A BEGINNING
TAR AP 79 VOL: 54 PG:306 - 322 :: QUAL. :INT. LOG. :THEORY :VALUAT.(INFL.)

REVSINE,L CIT: 0.00
THE THEORY AND MEASUREMENT OF BUSINESS INCOME: A REVIEW ARTICLE
TAR AP 81 VOL: 56 PG:342 - 354 :: QUAL. :SEC. :THEORY :VALUAT.(INFL.)

REVSINE,L ; FIRS: LARCKER,DF CIT: 0.67
THE OIL AND GAS ACCOUNTING CONTROVERSY: AN ANALYSIS OF ECONOMIC CONSEQUENCES
TAR OC 83 VOL: 58 PG:706 - 732 :: REGRESS. :PRIM. :EMH :OIL & GAS

REYNOLDS,IN CIT: 0.00
A VANISHING ACCOUNTING ITEM - REPLACEMENT ACCOUNTING?
TAR AP 64 VOL: 39 PG:342 - 346 :: QUAL. :INT. LOG. :THEORY :PP&E / DEPR

RHODE ,JG ; FIRS: DECOSTER,DT CIT: 0.15
THE ACCOUNTANT'S STEREOTYPE: REAL OR IMAGINED, DESERVED OR UNWARRANTED
TAR OC 71 VOL: 46 PG:651 - 664 :: ANOVA :SURV. :OTH.BEH. :AUD.

RHODE ,JG ; SEC: WHITSELL,GM ; THIR: KELSEY,RL CIT: 0.31
AN ANALYSIS OF CLIENT-INDUSTRY CONCENTRATIONS FOR LARGE PUBLIC ACCOUNTING
FIRMS
TAR OC 74 VOL: 49 PG:772 - 787 :: DES.STAT. :PRIM. :INSTIT. :AUD.

RHODE ,JG ; SEC: SORENSEN,JE ; THIR: LAWLER III,EE CIT: 0.67
SOURCES OF PROFESSIONAL STAFF TURNOVER IN PUBLIC ACCOUNTING FIRMS REVEALED BY
THE EXIT INTERVIEW
AOS 02 77 VOL: 2 PG:165 - 176 :: NON-PAR. :SURV. :OTH. :ORG.

RHODE ,JG ; FIRS: GORDON,FE ; THIR: MERCHANT,KA CIT: 0.25
THE EFFECTS OF SALARY AND HUMAN RESOURCE ACCOUNTING DISCLOSURES ON SMALL
GROUP RELATIONS AND PERFORMANCE
AOS 04 77 VOL: 2 PG:295 - 306 :: ANOVA :LAB. :OTH.BEH. :HRA

RHODE ,JG ; FIRS: HARVEY,DW ; THIR: MERCHANT,KA CIT: 0.20
ACCOUNTING AGGREGATION: USER PREFERENCES AND DECISION MAKING
AOS 03 79 VOL: 4 PG:187 - 210 :: ANOVA :LAB. :OTH.BEH. :N/A

RHODE ,JG ; FIRS: BENKE ,RL CIT: 0.22
THE JOB SATISFACTION OF HIGHER LEVEL EMPLOYEES IN LARGE CERTIFIED PUBLIC
ACCOUNTING FIRMS
AOS 02 80 VOL: 5 PG:187 - 202 :: OTH.QUANT. :SURV. :OTH.BEH. :ORG.

RICCHIUTE,DN CIT: 0.20
STANDARD SETTING AND THE ENTITY-PROPRIETARY DEBATE
AOS 12 79 VOL: 4 PG:67 - 76 :: DES.STAT. :LAB. :INSTIT. :AUD.BEH.

RICCHIUTE,DN ; FIRS: FAIRCLOTH,AW CIT: 0.00
AMBIGUITY INTOLERANCE AND FINANCIAL REPORTING ALTERNATIVES
AOS 01 81 VOL: 6 PG:53 - 68 :: DES.STAT. :SURV. :HIPS :FIN.METH.

RICCHIUTE,DN CIT: 0.20
AN EMPIRICAL ASSESSMENT OF THE IMPACT OF ALTERNATIVE TASK PRESENTATION MODES
ON DECISION-MAKING RESEARCH IN AUDITING
JAR SP 84 VOL: 22 PG:341 - 350 :: NON-PAR. :LAB. :HIPS :METHOD.

RICE ,SJ CIT: 0.36
THE INFORMATION CONTENT OF FULLY DILUTED EARNINGS PER SHARE
TAR AP 78 VOL: 53 PG:429 - 438 :: REGRESS. :PRIM. :EMH :FIN.METH.

RICE ,SJ ; FIRS: CHOW ,CW CIT: 0.71
QUALIFIED AUDIT OPINIONS AND AUDITOR SWITCHING
TAR AP 82 VOL: 57 PG:326 - 335 :: DES.STAT. :PRIM. :OTH. :OPIN.

RICE ,SJ ; FIRS: CHOW ,CW CIT: 0.43
QUALIFIED AUDIT OPINIONS AND SHARE PRICES - AN INVESTIGATION
AUD WI 82 VOL: 1 PG:35 - 53 :: MIXED :PRIM. :EMH :OPIN.

RICHARD,DL CIT: 0.00
DIFFICULTIES IN TAX ALLOCATION ON GENERAL PRICE-LEVEL INCREASES
TAR OC 68 VOL: 43 PG:730 - 737 :: QUAL. :INT. LOG. :THEORY :TAXES

RICHARDSON,AJ CIT: 0.00
ACCOUNTING AS A LEGITIMATING INSTITUTION
AOS 04 87 VOL: 12 PG:341 - 355 :: DES.STAT. :INT. LOG. :THEORY :FIN.METH.

RICHARDSON,AJ CIT: 0.00
ACCOUNTING KNOWLEDGE AND PROFESSIONAL PRIVILEGE
AOS 04 88 VOL: 13 PG:381 - 396 :: REGRESS. :PRIM. :INSTIT. :INT.DIFF.

RICHARDSON,G ; FIRS: MORSE ,D CIT: 1.00
THE LIFO/FIFO DECISION
JAR SP 83 VOL: 21 PG:106 - 127 :: DES.STAT. :PRIM. :OTH.STAT. :INV.

RICHARDSON,G ; FIRS: ELLIOTT,JA ; THIR: DYCKMAN,TR ; FOUR: DUKES ,RE CIT: 1.00
THE IMPACT OF SFAS NO.2 ON FIRM EXPENDITURES ON RESEARCH AND DEVELOPMENT:
    REPLICATIONS AND EXTENSIONS
JAR SP 84 VOL: 22 PG:85 - 102 :: NON-PAR. :PRIM. :EMH :R & D

RICHARDSON,GD ; FIRS: BROWN ,LD ; THIR: SCHWAGER,SJ CIT: 1.00
AN INFORMATION INTERPRETATION OF FINANCIAL ANALYST SUPERIORITY IN FORECASTING
    EARNINGS
JAR SP 87 VOL: 25 PG:49 - 67 :: REGRESS. :PRIM. :TIME SER. :FOREC.

RICKS ,RB CIT: 0.08
YEAR TO SWITCH TO STRAIGHT LINE DEPRECIATION
TAR JL 64 VOL: 39 PG:685 - 688 :: ANAL. :INT. LOG. :N/A :PP&E / DEPR

RICKS ,WE CIT: 2.29
THE MARKET'S RESPONSE TO THE 1974 LIFO ADOPTIONS
JAR AU 82 VOL: 20 PG:367 - 387 :: REGRESS. :PRIM. :EMH :INV.

RICKS ,WE ; FIRS: HUGHES,JS CIT: 1.00
ACCOUNTING FOR RETAIL LAND SALES: ANALYSIS OF A MANDATED CHANGE
JAE AG 84 VOL: 6 PG:101 - 132 :: REGRESS. :PRIM. :EMH :ACC.CHNG.

RICKS ,WE ; SEC: HUGHES,JS CIT: 0.00
MARKET REACTIONS TO A NON-DISCRETIONARY ACCOUNTING CHANGE: THE CASE OF
    LONG-TERM INVESTMENTS
TAR JA 85 VOL: 60 PG:33 - 52 :: ANOVA :PRIM. :EMH :ACC.CHNG.

RICKS ,WE CIT: 0.67
FIRM SIZE EFFECTS AND THE ASSOCIATION BETWEEN EXCESS RETURNS AND LIFO
    TAX SAVINGS
JAR SP 86 VOL: 24 PG:206 - 216 :: REGRESS. :PRIM. :EMH :INV.

RICKS ,WE ; FIRS: HOSKIN,RE ; SEC: HUGHES,JS CIT: 0.67
EVIDENCE ON THE INCREMENTAL INFORMATION CONTENT OF ADDITIONAL FIRM
DISCLOSURES MADE CONCURRENTLY WITH EARNINGS
JAR ST 86 VOL: 24 PG:1 - 36 :: REGRESS. :PRIM. :EMH :SPEC.ITEMS

RICKS ,WE ; FIRS: BABER ,WR ; SEC: BROOKS,EH CIT: 0.00
AN EMPIRICAL INVESTIGATION OF THE MARKET FOR AUDIT SERVICES IN THE PUBLIC
SECTOR
JAR AU 87 VOL: 25 PG:293 - 305 :: REGRESS. :PRIM. :OTH.STAT. :ORG.

RICKS ,WE ; FIRS: HUGHES,JS CIT: 2.00
ASSOCIATIONS BETWEEN FORECAST ERRORS AND EXCESS RETURNS NEAR TO EARNINGS
ANNOUNCEMENTS
TAR JA 87 VOL: 62 PG:158 - 175 :: REGRESS. :PRIM. :EMH :FOREC.

RICKS ,WE ; FIRS: BIDDLE,GC CIT: 1.00
ANALYST FORECAST ERRORS AND STOCK PRICE BEHAVIOR NEAR THE EARNINGS
ANNOUNCEMENT DATES OF LIFO ADOPTERS
JAR AU 88 VOL: 26 PG:169 - 194 :: REGRESS. :PRIM. :EMH :INV.

RIDDLE JR,JR ; FIRS: BIDWELL III,CM CIT: 0.00
MARKET INEFFICIENCIES - OPPORTUNITIES FOR PROFITS
JAA SP 81 VOL: 4 PG:198 - 214 :: REGRESS. :PRIM. :EMH :INFO.STRUC.

RITTENBERG,LE ; FIRS: NAIR ,RD CIT: 0.00
ACCOUNTING COSTS OF PRIVATELY HELD BUSINESSES
JAA SP 83 VOL: 6 PG:234 - 243 :: DES.STAT. :SURV. :OTH.BEH. :N/A

RITTENBERG,LE ; FIRS: FARMER,TA ; THIR: TROMPETER,GM CIT: 0.00
AN INVESTIGATION OF THE IMPACT OF ECONOMIC AND ORGANIZATIONAL FACTORS
ON AUDITOR INDEPENDENCE
AUD AU 87 VOL: 7 PG:1 - 14 :: REGRESS. :LAB. :OTH.BEH. :INDEP.

RITTENBERG,LE ; FIRS: NAIR ,RD CIT: 0.00
MESSAGES PERCEIVED FROM AUDIT, REVIEW, AND COMPILATION REPORTS: EXTENSION
TO MORE DIVERSE GROUPS
AUD AU 87 VOL: 7 PG:15 - 38 :: REGRESS. :LAB. :HIPS :AUD.THEOR.

RITTS ,BA CIT: 0.15
A STUDY OF THE IMPACT OF APB OPINIONS UPON PRACTICING CPAS
JAR SP 74 VOL: 12 PG:93 - 111 :: DES.STAT. :SURV. :THEORY :FASB SUBM.

RIVERA,JM ; FIRS: ELLIOTT,EL ; SEC: LARREA,J CIT: 0.00
ACCOUNTING AID TO DEVELOPING COUNTRIES: SOME ADDITIONAL CONSIDERATIONS
TAR OC 68 VOL: 43 PG:763 - 768 :: QUAL. :INT. LOG. :INSTIT. :OTH.MANAG.

RO ,BT CIT: 0.64
THE DISCLOSURES OF CAPITALIZED LEASE INFORMATION AND STOCK PRICES
JAR AU 78 VOL: 16 PG:315 - 340 :: REGRESS. :PRIM. :EMH :LEASES

RO ,BT CIT: 1.56
THE ADJUSTMENT OF SECURITY RETURNS TO THE DISCLOSURE OF REPLACEMENT COST
ACCOUNTING INFORMATION
JAE AG 80 VOL: 2 PG:159 - 189 :: REGRESS. :PRIM. :EMH :VALUAT.(INFL.)

RO ,BT CIT: 0.38
THE DISCLOSURE OF REPLACEMENT COST ACCOUNTING DATA AND ITS EFFECT ON
TRANSACTION VOLUMES
TAR JA 81 VOL: 56 PG:70 - 84 :: ANOVA :PRIM. :EMH :VALUAT.(INFL.)

ROARK ,SJ ; FIRS: KAPLAN,SE ; SEC: RECKERS,PMJ CIT: 0.00
AN ATTRIBUTION THEORY ANALYSIS OF TAX EVASION RELATED JUDGMENTS
AOS 04 88 VOL: 13 PG:371 - 379 :: REGRESS. :LAB. :OTH.BEH. :TAXES

ROBBINS,SM CIT: 0.00
RISK ANALYSIS IN CAPITAL BUDGETING
JAA AU 77 VOL: 1 PG:5 - 18 :: ANAL. :INT. LOG. :OTH. :CAP.BUDG.

ROBBINS,WA ; SEC: APOSTOLOU,NG ; THIR: STRAWSER,RH CIT: 0.00
MUNICIPAL ANNUAL REPORTS AND THE INFORMATION NEEDS OF INVESTORS
JAA SU 85 VOL: 8 PG:279 - 292 :: REGRESS. :PRIM. :THEORY :FIN.METH.

ROBBINS,WA ; SEC: AUSTIN,KR CIT: 0.00
DISCLOSURE QUALITY IN GOVERNMENT FINANCIAL REPORTS: AN ASSESSMENT OF THE
   APPROPRIATENESS OF A COMPOUND MEASURE
JAR AU 86 VOL: 24 PG:412 - 421 :: REGRESS. :SURV. :THEORY :METHOD.

ROBERTS,DM CIT: 0.00
CONTROLLING AUDIT RISK - A METHOD FOR OPTIMAL SAMPLE DESIGN
JAA AU 80 VOL: 4 PG:57 - 69 :: ANAL. :INT. LOG. :THEORY :SAMP.

ROBERTS,DM CIT: 0.33
STRATIFIED SAMPLING USING A STOCHASTIC MODEL
JAR SP 86 VOL: 24 PG:111 - 126 :: DES.STAT. :SIM. :OTH.STAT. :SAMP.

ROBERTS,J ; SEC: SCAPENS,RW CIT: 2.00
ACCOUNTING SYSTEMS AND SYSTEMS OF ACCOUNTABILITY - UNDERSTANDING ACCOUNTING
   PRACTICES IN THEIR ORGANIZATIONAL CONTEXTS
AOS 04 85 VOL: 10 PG:443 - 456 :: DES.STAT. :INT. LOG. :THEORY :FIN.METH.

ROBERTSON,JC ; FIRS: LANGENDERFER,HQ CIT: 0.08
A THEORETICAL STRUCTURE FOR INDEPENDENT AUDITS OF MANAGEMENT
TAR OC 69 VOL: 44 PG:777 - 787 :: QUAL. :INT. LOG. :INSTIT. :OTH.MANAG.

ROBERTSON,JC ; SEC: CLARKE,RW CIT: 0.15
VERIFICATION OF MANAGEMENT REPRESENTATIONS: A FIRST STEP TOWARD INDEPENDENT
   AUDITS OF MANAGEMENT
TAR JL 71 VOL: 46 PG:562 - 571 :: DES.STAT. :PRIM. :N/A :AUD.

ROBERTSON,JC ; FIRS: BOATSMAN,JR CIT: 1.15
POLICY-CAPTURING ON SELECTED MATERIALITY JUDGMENTS
TAR AP 74 VOL: 49 PG:342 - 352 :: OTH.QUANT. :LAB. :OTH.STAT. :OTH.FIN.ACC.

ROBERTSON,JC ; SEC: ALDERMAN,CW CIT: 0.00
COMPARATIVE AUDITING STANDARDS
JAA WI 81 VOL: 4 PG:144 - 161 :: QUAL. :INT. LOG. :THEORY :ORG.

ROBERTSON,JC CIT: 0.00
A DEFENSE OF EXTANT AUDITING THEORY
AUD SP 84 VOL: 3 PG:57 - 67 :: QUAL. :INT. LOG. :THEORY :AUD.THEOR.

ROBICHEK,AA ; FIRS: JAEDICKE,RK CIT: 0.54
COST-VOLUME-PROFIT ANALYSIS UNDER CONDITIONS OF UNCERTAINTY
TAR OC 64 VOL: 39 PG:917 - 926 :: ANAL. :INT. LOG. :OTH.STAT. :C-V-P-A

ROBINSON,CF ; FIRS: TEITLEBAUM,AD CIT: 0.15
THE REAL RISKS IN AUDIT SAMPLING
JAR ST 75 VOL: 13 PG:70 - 91 :: MIXED :INT. LOG. :OTH.STAT. :SAMP.

ROBINSON,LA ; SEC: HALL ,TP CIT: 0.00
SYSTEMS EDUCATION AND THE ACCOUNTING CURRICULUM
TAR JA 64 VOL: 39 PG:62 - 69 :: QUAL. :INT. LOG. :N/A :OTH.MANAG.

ROCKNESS,HO CIT: 0.67
EXPECTANCY THEORY IN A BUDGETARY SETTING: AN EXPERIMENTAL EXAMINATION
TAR OC 77 VOL: 52 PG:893 - 903 :: ANOVA :LAB. :OTH.BEH. :BUDG.& PLAN.

ROCKNESS,HO ; SEC: SHIELDS,MD CIT: 0.60
ORGANIZATIONAL CONTROL SYSTEMS IN RESEARCH AND DEVELOPMENT
AOS 02 84 VOL: 9 PG:165 - 177 :: CORR. :SURV. :OTH.BEH. :R & D

ROCKNESS,J ; SEC: WILLIAMS,PF CIT: 0.00
A DESCRIPTIVE STUDY OF SOCIAL RESPONSIBILITY MUTUAL FUNDS
AOS 04 88 VOL: 13 PG:397 - 411 :: REGRESS. :SURV. :INSTIT. :HRA

RODEN ,PF CIT: 0.00
THE FINANCIAL IMPLICATIONS OF IN-SUBSTANCE DEFEASANCE
JAA WI 87 VOL: 2 PG:79 - 89 :: DES.STAT. :INT. LOG. :THEORY :LTD

RODGERS,RC ; FIRS: COOPER,WW ; SEC: HO ,JL ; THIR: HUNTER,JE CIT: 0.00
THE IMPACT OF THE FOREIGN CORRUPT PRACTICES ACT ON INTERNAL CONTROL PRACTICES
JAA AU 85 VOL: 9 PG:22 - 39 :: REGRESS. :SEC. :THEORY :CAP.BUDG.

ROHRBACH.KJ CIT: 0.00
MONETARY UNIT ACCEPTANCE SAMPLING
JAR SP 86 VOL: 24 PG:127 - 150 :: DES.STAT. :SIM. :OTH.STAT. :SAMP.

ROLLER,J ; SEC: WILLIAMS,TH CIT: 0.00
PROFESSIONAL SCHOOLS OF ACCOUNTING
TAR AP 67 VOL: 42 PG:349 - 355 :: QUAL. :INT. LOG. :INSTIT. :OTH.MANAG.

ROMNEY,MB ; FIRS: SOLOMON,I ; SEC: KROGSTAD,JL ; FOUR: TOMASSINI,LA CIT: 0.57
AUDITORS' PRIOR PROBABILITY DISTRIBUTIONS FOR ACCOUNT BALANCES
AOS 01 82 VOL: 7 PG:27 - 42 :: DES.STAT. :LAB. :HIPS :PROB.ELIC.

RONEN ,J CIT: 0.00
CAPACITY AND OPERATING VARIANCES: AN EX POST APPROACH
JAR AU 70 VOL: 8 PG:232 - 252 :: ANAL. :INT. LOG. :OTH.STAT. :VAR.

RONEN ,J ; SEC: MCKINNEY,G CIT: 0.38
TRANSFER PRICING FOR DIVISIONAL AUTONOMY
JAR SP 70 VOL: 8 PG:99 - 112 :: ANAL. :INT. LOG. :OTH. :TRANS.PRIC.

RONEN ,J CIT: 0.62
SOME EFFECTS OF SEQUENTIAL AGGREGATION IN ACCOUNTING ON DECISION-MAKING
JAR AU 71 VOL: 9 PG:307 - 332 :: ANOVA :LAB. :OTH.BEH. :INFO.STRUC.

RONEN ,J ; FIRS: DOPUCH,N CIT: 0.54
THE EFFECTS OF ALTERNATIVE INVENTORY VALUATION METHODS - AN EXPERIMENTAL STUDY
JAR AU 73 VOL: 11 PG:191 - 211 :: DES.STAT. :LAB. :THEORY :INV.

RONEN ,J ; SEC: FALK ,G CIT: 0.15
ACCOUNTING AGGREGATION AND THE ENTROPY MEASURE: AN EXPERIMENTAL APPROACH
TAR OC 73 VOL: 48 PG:696 - 717 :: NON-PAR. :LAB. :INF.ECO./AG. :INFO.STRUC.

RONEN ,J ; FIRS: BECKER,S ; THIR: SORTER,GH CIT: 0.38
OPPORTUNITY COSTS - AN EXPERIMENTAL APPROACH
JAR AU 74 VOL: 12 PG:317 - 329 :: ANOVA :LAB. :OTH.BEH. :REL.COSTS

RONEN J CIT: 0.23
NONAGGREGATION VERSUS DISAGGREGATION OF VARIANCES
TAR JA 74 VOL: 49 PG:50 - 60 :: ANAL. :INT. LOG. :OTH.STAT. :VAR.

RONEN J ; FIRS: BARNEA,A ; THIR: SADAN ,S CIT: 0.31
THE IMPLEMENTATION OF ACCOUNTING OBJECTIVES: AN APPLICATION TO EXTRAORDINARY
    ITEMS
TAR JA 75 VOL: 50 PG:58 - 68 :: ANAL. :INT. LOG. :THEORY :SPEC.ITEMS

RONEN J ; SEC: LIVINGSTONE,JL CIT: 1.77
AN EXPECTANCY THEORY APPROACH TO THE MOTIVATIONAL IMPACTS OF BUDGETS
TAR OC 75 VOL: 50 PG:671 - 685 :: QUAL. :INT. LOG. :OTH.BEH. :BUDG.& PLAN.

RONEN J ; SEC: SADAN ,S CIT: 0.23
CLASSIFICATION SMOOTHING: ALTERNATIVE INCOME MODELS
JAR SP 75 VOL: 13 PG:133 - 149 :: CORR. :PRIM. :THEORY :REV.REC.

RONEN J ; FIRS: BARNEA,A ; THIR: SADAN ,S CIT: 0.23
CLASSIFICATORY SMOOTHING OF INCOME WITH EXTRAORDINARY ITEMS
TAR JA 76 VOL: 51 PG:110 - 122 :: REGRESS. :PRIM. :TIME SER. :INFO.STRUC.

RONEN J CIT: 0.17
THE EFFECT OF INSIDER TRADING RULES ON INFORMATION GENERATION AND DISCLOSURE
    BY CORPORATIONS
TAR AP 77 VOL: 52 PG:438 - 449 :: QUAL. :INT. LOG. :THEORY :INS.TRAD.

RONEN J ; FIRS: GIVOLY,D ; THIR: SCHIFF,A CIT: 0.09
DOES AUDIT INVOLVEMENT AFFECT THE QUALITY OF INTERIM REPORT NUMBERS?
JAA SU 78 VOL: 1 PG:361 - 372 :: ANOVA :PRIM. :INSTIT. :AUD.

RONEN J ; FIRS: KAMIN ,JY CIT: 0.18
THE SMOOTHING ON INCOME NUMBERS: SOME EMPIRICAL EVIDENCE OF SYSTEMATIC
    DIFFERENCES AMONG MANAGEMENT AND OWNER-CONTROLLED FIRMS
AOS 02 78 VOL: 3 PG:141 - 160 :: ANOVA :PRIM. :OTH.STAT. :N/A

RONEN J ; FIRS: PASTENA,V CIT: 0.50
SOME HYPOTHESES ON THE PATTERN OF MANAGEMENT'S INFORMAL DISCLOSURES
JAR AU 79 VOL: 17 PG:550 - 564 :: NON-PAR. :PRIM. :OTH. :OTH.MANAG.

RONEN J ; SEC: SADAN ,S CIT: 0.22
ACCOUNTING CLASSIFICATION AS A TOOL FOR INCOME PREDICTION
JAA SU 80 VOL: 3 PG:339 - 353 :: DES.STAT. :SEC. :TIME SER. :FOREC.

RONEN J ; FIRS: OVADIA,A CIT: 0.00
GENERAL PRICE-LEVEL ADJUSTMENT AND REPLACEMENT COST ACCOUNTING AS SPECIAL
    CASES OF THE INDEX NUMBER PROBLEM
JAA WI 80 VOL: 3 PG:113 - 137 :: ANAL. :SEC. :TIME SER. :VALUAT.(INFL.)

RONEN J ; SEC: LIVNAT,J CIT: 0.25
INCENTIVES FOR SEGMENT REPORTING
JAR AU 81 VOL: 19 PG:459 - 481 :: ANAL. :INT. LOG. :EMH :SEG.REP.

RONEN J ; FIRS: OVADIA,A CIT: 0.00
ON THE VALUE OF CURRENT-COST INFORMATION
JAA WI 83 VOL: 6 PG:115 - 129 :: ANAL. :INT. LOG. :THEORY :VALUAT.(INFL.)

RONEN J ; SEC: BALACHANDRAN,KR CIT: 0.00
AN APPROACH TO TRANSFER PRICING UNDER UNCERTAINTY
JAR AU 88 VOL: 26 PG:300 - 314 :: ANAL. :INT. LOG. :INF.ECO./AG. :TRANS.PRIC.

RONEN ,J ; FIRS: NELSON,J ; THIR: WHITE ,L CIT: 0.00
LEGAL LIABILITIES AND THE MARKET FOR AUDITING SERVICES
JAA SU 88 VOL: 03 PG:255 - 296 :: DES.STAT. :INT. LOG. :INF.ECO./AG. :LIAB.

RORKE ,CH CIT: 0.00
AN EARLY PRICING MODEL REGARDING THE VALUE OF A CAT: A HISTORICAL NOTE
AOS 03 82 VOL: 7 PG:305 - 306 :: QUAL. :INT. LOG. :THEORY :VALUAT.(INFL.)

ROSE ,H CIT: 0.00
SOURCES AND USES: A BRITISH VIEW
JAR AU 64 VOL: 2 PG:137 - 147 :: QUAL. :INT. LOG. :THEORY :INT.DIFF.

ROSE ,PS ; SEC: ANDREWS,WT ; THIR: GIROUX,GA CIT: 0.00
PREDICTING BUSINESS FAILURE: A MACROECONOMIC PERSPECTIVE
JAA AU 82 VOL: 6 PG:20 - 31 :: REGRESS. :PRIM. :TIME SER. :BUS.FAIL.

ROSE ,R ; SEC: BEAVER,WH ; THIR: BECKER,S ; FOUR: SORTER,GH CIT: 0.77
TOWARD AN EMPIRICAL MEASURE OF MATERIALITY
JAR ST 70 VOL: 8 PG:138 - 148 :: DES.STAT. :LAB. :OTH.BEH. :MAT.

ROSEN ,LS CIT: 0.00
REPLACEMENT-VALUE ACCOUNTING
TAR JA 67 VOL: 42 PG:106 - 113 :: QUAL. :INT. LOG. :THEORY :VALUAT.(INFL.)

ROSEN ,LS ; SEC: DECOSTER,DT CIT: 0.00
"FUNDS" STATEMENTS: A HISTORICAL PERSPECTIVE
TAR JA 69 VOL: 44 PG:124 - 136 :: QUAL. :SEC. :HIST. :FIN.METH.

ROSENBERG,D ; SEC: TOMKINS,L ; THIR: DAY ,P CIT: 0.00
A WORK ROLE PERSPECTIVE OF ACCOUNTANTS IN LOCAL GOVERNMENT SERVICE DEPARTMENT
AOS 02 82 VOL: 7 PG:123 - 138 :: QUAL. :SURV. :OTH.BEH. :N/A

ROSENFELD,A ; FIRS: LEWELLEN,W ; SEC: LODERER,C CIT: 0.50
MERGER DECISIONS AND EXECUTIVE STOCK OWNERSHIP IN ACQUIRING FIRMS
JAE AP 85 VOL: 7 PG:209 - 232 :: REGRESS. :PRIM. :OTH.STAT. :BUS.COMB.

ROSENFIELD,P ; SEC: STOREY,R CIT: 0.08
THE ACCOUNTING PRINCIPLES BOARD - A CORRECTION
TAR AP 66 VOL: 41 PG:327 - 330 :: QUAL. :INT. LOG. :INSTIT. :N/A

ROSENFIELD,P CIT: 0.00
REPORTING SUBJUNCTIVE GAINS AND LOSSES
TAR OC 69 VOL: 44 PG:788 - 797 :: QUAL. :INT. LOG. :THEORY :VALUAT.(INFL.)

ROSENZWEIG,K CIT: 0.13
AN EXPLORATORY FIELD STUDY OF THE RELATIONSHIPS BETWEEN CONTROLLER'S
    DEPARTMENT AND OVERALL ORGANIZATIONAL CHARACTERISTICS
AOS 04 81 VOL: 6 PG:339 - 354 :: CORR. :SURV. :OTH.BEH. :MANAG.

ROSHWALB,A ; SEC: WRIGHT,RL ; THIR: GODFREY,JT CIT: 0.00
A NEW APPROACH FOR STRATIFIED SAMPLING IN INVENTORY COST ESTIMATION
AUD AU 87 VOL: 7 PG:54 - 70 :: DES.STAT. :SIM. :OTH.STAT. :SAMP.

ROSS ,H CIT: 0.00
THE WONDERFUL WORLD OF ACCOUNTING
JAR ST 70 VOL: 8 PG:108 - 115 :: QUAL. :INT. LOG. :INSTIT. :FIN.METH.

ROSS ,WR CIT: 0.00
PERT/COST RESOURCE ALLOCATION PROCEDURE
TAR JL 66 VOL: 41 PG:464 - 473 :: ANAL. :INT. LOG. :OTH.STAT. :BUDG.& PLAN.

ROZEFF,MS ; FIRS: BROWN ,LD CIT: 0.50
ADAPTIVE EXPECTATIONS, TIME-SERIES MODELS, AND ANALYST FORECAST REVISION
JAR AU 79 VOL: 17 PG:341 - 351 :: REGRESS. :PRIM. :TIME SER. :FOREC.

ROZEFF,MS ; FIRS: BROWN ,LD CIT: 0.20
THE PREDICTIVE VALUE OF INTERIM REPORTS FOR IMPROVING FORECASTS OF FUTURE
   QUARTERLY EARNINGS
TAR JL 79 VOL: 54 PG:585 - 591 :: NON-PAR. :INT. LOG. :TIME SER. :FOREC.

ROZEFF,MS ; FIRS: BROWN ,LD CIT: 2.20
UNIVARIATE TIME-SERIES MODELS OF QUARTERLY ACCOUNTING EARNINGS PER SHARE: A
   PROPOSED MODEL
JAR SP 79 VOL: 17 PG:179 - 189 :: MIXED :PRIM. :TIME SER. :AUD.TRAIN.

ROZEFF,MS ; FIRS: BROWN ,LD ; SEC: HUGHES,JS ; FOUR: VANDERWEIDE,JH CIT: 0.00
EXPECTATIONS DATA AND THE PREDICTIVE VALUE OF INTERIM REPORTING: A COMMENT
JAR SP 80 VOL: 18 PG:278 - 288 :: REGRESS. :PRIM. :TIME SER. :FOREC.

ROZEFF,MS ; FIRS: COLLINS,DW ; THIR: DHALIWAL,DS CIT: 3.88
THE ECONOMIC DETERMINANTS OF THE MARKET REACTION TO PROPOSED MANDATORY
   ACCOUNTING CHANGES IN THE OIL AND GAS INDUSTRY: A CROSS-SECTIONAL ANALYSIS
JAE MR 81 VOL: 3 PG:37 - 71 :: REGRESS. :PRIM. :EMH :OIL & GAS

ROZEFF,MS ; FIRS: COLLINS,DW ; THIR: SALATKA,WK CIT: 1.00
THE SEC'S REJECTION OF SFAS NO.19: TESTS OF MARKET PRICE REVERSAL
TAR JA 82 VOL: 57 PG:1 - 17 :: CORR. :PRIM. :EMH :OIL & GAS

ROZEN ,E ; FIRS: DAVIS ,HZ ; SEC: KAHN ,N CIT: 0.00
LIFO INVENTORY LIQUIDATIONS: AN EMPIRICAL STUDY
JAR AU 84 VOL: 22 PG:480 - 490 :: NON-PAR. :PRIM. :OTH.STAT. :INV.

RUBIN ,MA CIT: 1.00
MUNICIPAL AUDIT FEE DETERMINANTS
TAR AP 88 VOL: 63 PG:219 - 236 :: REGRESS. :PRIM. :INSTIT. :ORG.

RUE   ,JC ; SEC: VOLKAN,AG CIT: 0.00
FINANCIAL AND ECONOMIC CONSEQUENCES OF THE NEW PENSION ACCOUNTING PROPOSALS:
   IS THE GLOOM JUSTIFIED?
JAA SU 84 VOL: 7 PG:306 - 322 :: DES.STAT. :PRIM. :THEORY :PENS.

RULAND,RG ; FIRS: BERNARD,VL CIT: 0.00
THE INCREMENTAL INFORMATION CONTENT OF HISTORICAL COST AND CURRENT COST
   INCOME NUMBERS: TIME-SERIES ANALYSES FOR 1962-1980
TAR OC 87 VOL: 62 PG:707 - 722 :: REGRESS. :PRIM. :EMH :VALUAT.(INFL.)

RULAND,W CIT: 0.55
THE ACCURACY OF FORECASTS BY MANAGEMENT AND BY FINANCIAL ANALYSTS
TAR AP 78 VOL: 53 PG:439 - 447 :: DES.STAT. :PRIM. :TIME SER. :FOREC.

RULAND,W ; FIRS: COGGER,KO CIT: 0.00
A NOTE ON ALTERNATIVE TESTS FOR INDEPENDENCE OF FINANCIAL TIME SERIES
JAR AU 82 VOL: 20 PG:733 - 737 :: CORR. :PRIM. :TIME SER. :METHOD.

RULAND,W ; FIRS: PASTENA,V CIT: 0.33
THE MERGER/BANKRUPTCY ALTERNATIVE
TAR AP 86 VOL: 61 PG:288 - 301 :: REGRESS. :PRIM. :THEORY :BUS.COMB.

RUNDFELT,R CIT: 0.00
INSIDER TRADING: REGULATION IN EUROPE
JAA SP 86 VOL: 1 PG:125 - 130 :: DES.STAT. :INT. LOG. :THEORY :LITIG.

RUSS ,A ; FIRS: MOONITZ,M CIT: 0.08
ACCRUAL ACCOUNTING FOR EMPLOYERS' PENSION COSTS
JAR AU 66 VOL: 4 PG:155 - 168 :: QUAL. :INT. LOG. :THEORY :PENS.

RYAN ,SG ; FIRS: BEAVER,WH ; SEC: LAMBERT,RA CIT: 1.00
THE INFORMATION CONTENT OF SECURITY PRICES: A SECOND LOOK
JAE JL 87 VOL: 9 PG:139 - 157 :: REGRESS. :PRIM. :EMH :FIN.METH.

SADAN ,S ; FIRS: BARNEA,A ; SEC: RONEN ,J CIT: 0.31
THE IMPLEMENTATION OF ACCOUNTING OBJECTIVES: AN APPLICATION TO EXTRAORDINARY
ITEMS
TAR JA 75 VOL: 50 PG:58 - 68 :: ANAL. :INT. LOG. :THEORY :SPEC.ITEMS

SADAN ,S ; FIRS: RONEN ,J CIT: 0.23
CLASSIFICATION SMOOTHING: ALTERNATIVE INCOME MODELS
JAR SP 75 VOL: 13 PG:133 - 149 :: CORR. :PRIM. :THEORY :REV.REC.

SADAN ,S ; FIRS: BARNEA,A ; SEC: RONEN ,J CIT: 0.23
CLASSIFICATORY SMOOTHING OF INCOME WITH EXTRAORDINARY ITEMS
TAR JA 76 VOL: 51 PG:110 - 122 :: REGRESS. :PRIM. :TIME SER. :INFO.STRUC.

SADAN ,S ; FIRS: RONEN ,J CIT: 0.22
ACCOUNTING CLASSIFICATION AS A TOOL FOR INCOME PREDICTION
JAA SU 80 VOL: 3 PG:339 - 353 :: DES.STAT. :SEC. :TIME SER. :FOREC.

SALAMON,GL ; FIRS: LIVINGSTONE,JL CIT: 0.15
RELATIONSHIP BETWEEN THE ACCOUNTING AND THE INTERNAL RATE OF RETURN MEASURES:
A SYNTHESIS AND AN ANALYSIS
JAR AU 70 VOL: 8 PG:199 - 216 :: DES.STAT. :SIM. :OTH.STAT. :FIN.METH.

SALAMON,GL CIT: 0.15
MODELS OF THE RELATIONSHIP BETWEEN THE ACCOUNTING AND INTERNAL RATE OF
RETURN: AN EXAMINATION OF THE METHODOLOGY
JAR AU 73 VOL: 11 PG:296 - 303 :: ANAL. :INT. LOG. :OTH.STAT. :FIN.METH.

SALAMON,GL CIT: 0.00
CASH RECOVERY RATES AND MEASURES OF FIRM PROFITABILITY
TAR AP 82 VOL: 57 PG:292 - 302 :: CORR. :INT. LOG. :OTH.STAT. :N/A

SALAMON,GL ; FIRS: KINNEY JR,WR CIT: 0.14
REGRESSION ANALYSIS IN AUDITING: A COMPARISON OF ALTERNATIVE INVESTIGATION
RULES
JAR AU 82 VOL: 20 PG:350 - 366 :: REGRESS. :SIM. :OTH.STAT. :ANAL.REV.

SALAMON,GL ; FIRS: DHALIWAL,DS ; THIR: SMITH ,ED CIT: 1.86
THE EFFECT OF OWNER VERSUS MANAGEMENT CONTROL ON THE CHOICE OF ACCOUNTING
METHODS
JAE JL 82 VOL: 4 PG:41 - 53 :: NON-PAR. :SEC. :TIME SER. :AMOR./DEPL.

SALATKA,WK ; FIRS: COLLINS,DW ; SEC: ROZEFF,MS CIT: 1.00
THE SEC'S REJECTION OF SFAS NO.19: TESTS OF MARKET PRICE REVERSAL
TAR JA 82 VOL: 57 PG:1 - 17 :: CORR. :PRIM. :EMH :OIL & GAS

SALE ,JT ; FIRS: SCAPENS,RW CIT: 0.00
AN INTERNATIONAL STUDY OF ACCOUNTING PRACTICES IN DIVISIONALIZED COMPANIES
AND THEIR ASSOCIATIONS WITH ORGANIZATIONAL VARIABLES
TAR AP 85 VOL: 60 PG:231 - 247 :: REGRESS. :SURV. :OTH.STAT. :ORG.& ENVIR.

SALGADO,AP CIT: 0.00
ACCOUNTING REPORTS IN CHILE
TAR AP 63 VOL: 38 PG:389 - 397 :: QUAL. :INT. LOG. :HIST. :FIN.METH.

SALMI ,T ; FIRS: KISTNER,KP CIT: 0.00
GENERAL PRICE LEVEL ACCOUNTING AND INVENTORY VALUATION: A COMMENT
JAR SP 80 VOL: 18 PG:297 - 311 :: ANAL. :INT. LOG. :THEORY :VALUAT.(INFL.)

SAMUELS,JM CIT: 0.15
OPPORTUNITY COSTING: AN APPLICATION OF MATHEMATICAL PROGRAMMING
JAR AU 65 VOL: 3 PG:182 - 191 :: ANAL. :INT. LOG. :MATH.PROG. :REL.COSTS

SAMUELS,JM ; FIRS: MANES ,RP ; THIR: SMYTH ,DJ CIT: 0.00
INVENTORIES AND SALES: A CROSS SECTION STUDY
JAR ST 67 VOL: 5 PG:139 - 156 :: REGRESS. :PRIM. :THEORY :INV.

SAMUELSON,LA CIT: 0.00
DISCREPANCIES BETWEEN THE ROLES OF BUDGETING
AOS 01 86 VOL: 11 PG:35 - 46 :: DES.STAT. :INT. LOG. :OTH.BEH. :BUDG.& PLAN.

SAMUELSON,RA CIT: 0.23
PREDICTION AND PRICE-LEVEL ADJUSTMENT
JAR AU 72 VOL: 10 PG:322 - 344 :: REGRESS. :PRIM. :TIME SER. :VALUAT.(INFL.)

SAMUELSON,RA CIT: 0.00
SHOULD REPLACEMENT-COST CHANGES BE INCLUDED IN INCOME?
TAR AP 80 VOL: 55 PG:254 - 268 :: ANAL. :INT. LOG. :THEORY :REV.REC.

SAN MIGUEL,JG CIT: 0.77
HUMAN INFORMATION PROCESSING AND ITS RELEVANCE TO ACCOUNTING: A LABORATORY
STUDY
AOS 04 76 VOL: 1 PG:357 - 374 :: OTH.QUANT. :LAB. :MATH.PROG. :MAN.DEC.CHAR.

SAN MIGUEL,JG CIT: 0.00
THE RELIABILITY OF R&D DATA IN COMPUSTAT AND 10-K REPORTS
TAR JL 77 VOL: 52 PG:638 - 641 :: DES.STAT. :PRIM. :N/A :N/A

SAN MIGUEL,JG CIT: 0.00
THE BEHAVIOURAL SCIENCES AND CONCEPTS AND STANDARDS FOR MANAGEMENT PLANNING
AND CONTROL
AOS 02 77 VOL: 2 PG:177 - 186 :: QUAL. :INT. LOG. :OTH.BEH. :N/A

SAN MIGUEL,JG ; SEC: SHANK ,JK ; THIR: GOVINDARAJAN,V CIT: 0.08
EXTENDING CORPORATE ACCOUNTABILITY: A SURVEY AND FRAMEWORK FOR ANALYSIS
AOS 04 77 VOL: 2 PG:333 - 348 :: DES.STAT. :PRIM. :OTH. :AUD.

SAN MIGUEL,JG ; SEC: GOVINDARAJAN,V CIT: 0.00
THE CONTINGENT RELATIONSHIP BETWEEN THE CONTROLLER AND INTERNAL AUDIT
FUNCTIONS IN LARGE ORGANIZATIONS
AOS 02 84 VOL: 9 PG:179 - 188 :: NON-PAR. :SURV. :OTH.BEH. :INT.AUD.

SANDBERG,A ; FIRS: CARLSSON,J ; SEC: EHN ,P ; THIR: ERLANDER,B ; FOUR:
PERBY ,M CIT: 0.09
PLANNING AND CONTROL FROM THE PERSPECTIVE OF LABOR: A SHORT REPRESENTATION OF
THE DEMOS PROJECT
AOS 34 78 VOL: 3 PG:249 - 260 :: QUAL. :FIELD :OTH. :BUDG.& PLAN.

SANGSTER,JM ; FIRS: BURNS ,JS ; SEC: JAEDICKE,RK CIT: 0.00
FINANCIAL REPORTING OF PURCHASE CONTRACTS USED TO GUARANTEE LARGE INVESTMENTS
TAR JA 63 VOL: 38 PG:1 - 13 :: QUAL. :INT. LOG. :THEORY :SPEC.ITEMS

SANNELLA,AJ CIT: 0.00
AN APPLICATION OF INCOME STRATEGY TO COST ALLOCATION AND SEGMENT REPORTING
JAA AU 86 VOL: 1 PG:288 - 304 :: REGRESS. :SURV. :THEORY :SEG.REP.

SAPIENZA,SR CIT: 0.00
BUSINESS COMBINATIONS - A CASE STUDY
TAR JA 63 VOL: 38 PG:91 - 101 :: QUAL. :CASE :THEORY :BUS.COMB.

SAPIENZA,SR CIT: 0.00
AN EXAMINATION OF AICPA RESEARCH STUDY NO.5 - STANDARDS FOR POOLING
TAR JL 64 VOL: 39 PG:582 - 590 :: QUAL. :INT. LOG. :THEORY :BUS.COMB.

SAPIENZA,SR CIT: 0.00
BUSINESS COMBINATIONS AND ENTERPRISE EVALUATION
JAR SP 64 VOL: 2 PG:50 - 66 :: QUAL. :INT. LOG. :THEORY :BUS.COMB.

SAPPINGTON,DEM ; FIRS: DEMSKI,JS CIT: 1.33
LINE-ITEM REPORTING, FACTOR ACQUISITION, AND SUBCONTRACTING
JAR AU 86 VOL: 24 PG:250 - 269 :: ANAL. :INT. LOG. :INF.ECO./AG. :INFO.STRUC.

SAPPINGTON,DEM ; FIRS: DEMSKI,JS CIT: 1.50
DELEGATED EXPERTISE
JAR SP 87 VOL: 25 PG:68 - 89 :: DES.STAT. :INT. LOG. :INF.ECO./AG. :MANAG.

SAULS ,EH CIT: 0.08
AN EXPERIMENT ON NONSAMPLING ERRORS
JAR ST 70 VOL: 8 PG:157 - 171 :: ANOVA :LAB. :OTH.BEH. :SAMP.

SAULS ,EH CIT: 0.08
NONSAMPLING ERRORS IN ACCOUNTS RECEIVABLE CONFIRMATION
TAR JA 72 VOL: 47 PG:109 - 115 :: DES.STAT. :FIELD :N/A :SAMP.

SAVICH,RS ; FIRS: CRUMBLEY,DL CIT: 0.00
USE OF HUMAN RESOURCE ACCOUNTING IN TAXATION
TAR JA 75 VOL: 50 PG:112 - 117 :: QUAL. :INT. LOG. :THEORY :HRA

SAVICH,RS CIT: 0.50
THE USE OF ACCOUNTING INFORMATION IN DECISION MAKING
TAR JL 77 VOL: 52 PG:642 - 652 :: REGRESS. :LAB. :HIPS :MAN.DEC.CHAR.

SAVICH,RS ; FIRS: GROVE ,HD CIT: 0.20
ATTITUDE RESEARCH IN ACCOUNTING: A MODEL FOR RELIABILITY AND VALIDITY
    CONSIDERATIONS
TAR JL 79 VOL: 54 PG:522 - 537 :: QUAL. :SEC. :OTH.BEH. :METHOD.

SAVOIE,LM CIT: 0.00
RAISING ACCOUNTING STANDARDS
JAR ST 69 VOL: 7 PG:55 - 62 :: QUAL. :INT. LOG. :THEORY :FASB SUBM.

SCAPENS,RW CIT: 0.09
A NEOCLASSICAL MEASURE OF PROFIT
TAR AP 78 VOL: 53 PG:448 - 469 :: ANAL. :INT. LOG. :THEORY :OTH. NON-C/A

SCAPENS,RW CIT: 0.09
A NEOCLASSICAL MEASURE OF PROFIT
TAR AP 78 VOL: 53 PG:448 - 469 :: ANAL. :INT. LOG. :THEORY :OTH. NON-C/A

SCAPENS,RW ; SEC: SALE ,JT CIT: 0.00
AN INTERNATIONAL STUDY OF ACCOUNTING PRACTICES IN DIVISIONALIZED COMPANIES
    AND THEIR ASSOCIATIONS WITH ORGANIZATIONAL VARIABLES
TAR AP 85 VOL: 60 PG:231 - 247 :: REGRESS. :SURV. :OTH.STAT. :ORG.& ENVIR.

SCAPENS,RW ; FIRS: ROBERTS,J CIT: 2.00
ACCOUNTING SYSTEMS AND SYSTEMS OF ACCOUNTABILITY - UNDERSTANDING ACCOUNTING
    PRACTICES IN THEIR ORGANIZATIONAL CONTEXTS
AOS 04 85 VOL: 10 PG:443 - 456 :: DES.STAT. :INT. LOG. :THEORY :FIN.METH.

SCHACHNER,L CIT: 0.00
ACCOUNTABILITY UNDER INDUSTRIAL DIVERSIFICATION
TAR AP 68 VOL: 43 PG:303 - 311 :: QUAL. :INT. LOG. :THEORY :AMOR./DEPL.

SCHACHTER,B CIT: 0.00
OPEN INTEREST AND CONSENSUS AMONG INVESTORS
JAR AU 85 VOL: 23 PG:907 - 910 :: DES.STAT. :INT. LOG. :OTH.STAT. :N/A

SCHACHTER,B CIT: 0.00
OPEN INTEREST IN STOCK OPTIONS AROUND QUARTERLY EARNINGS ANNOUNCEMENTS
JAR AU 88 VOL: 26 PG:353 - 372 :: REGRESS. :PRIM. :EMH :INT.REP.

SCHAEFER,T ; SEC: KENNELLEY,M CIT: 0.00
ALTERNATIVE CASH FLOW MEASURES AND RISK-ADJUSTED RETURNS
JAA AU 86 VOL: 1 PG:278 - 287 :: REGRESS. :PRIM. :EMH :SPEC.ITEMS

SCHAEFER,TF CIT: 0.80
THE INFORMATION CONTENT OF CURRENT COST INCOME RELATIVE TO DIVIDENDS AND
    HISTORICAL COST INCOME
JAR AU 84 VOL: 22 PG:647 - 656 :: REGRESS. :PRIM. :EMH :VALUAT.(INFL.)

SCHAEFER,TF ; FIRS: CHRISTIE,AA ; SEC: KENNELLEY,MD ; THIR: KING ,JW CIT: 1.20
TESTING FOR INCREMENTAL INFORMATION CONTENT IN THE PRESENCE OF COLLINEARITY
JAE DE 84 VOL: 6 PG:205 - 217 :: ANAL. :INT. LOG. :OTH.STAT. :METHOD.

SCHATTKE,RW CIT: 0.00
FINANCIAL REPORTING OF ANTITRUST ACTIONS
TAR OC 65 VOL: 40 PG:805 - 811 :: QUAL. :CASE :THEORY :FIN.METH.

SCHATTKE,RW ; FIRS: LARSON,KD CIT: 0.00
CURRENT CASH EQUIVALENT, ADDITIVITY, AND FINANCIAL ACTION
TAR OC 66 VOL: 41 PG:634 - 641 :: QUAL. :INT. LOG. :THEORY :VALUAT.(INFL.)

SCHATTKE,RW CIT: 0.00
AN ANALYSIS OF ACCOUNTING PRINCIPLES BOARD STATEMENT NO.4
TAR AP 72 VOL: 47 PG:233 - 244 :: QUAL. :INT. LOG. :THEORY :FIN.METH.

SCHATZBERG,J ; FIRS: SMITH ,VL ; THIR: WALLER,WS CIT: 0.00
EXPERIMENTAL ECONOMICS AND AUDITING
AUD AU 87 VOL: 7 PG:71 - 93 :: DES.STAT. :INT. LOG. :OTH. :METHOD.

SCHEINER,JH ; SEC: KIGER ,JE CIT: 0.00
AN EMPIRICAL INVESTIGATION OF AUDITOR INVOLVEMENT IN NON-AUDIT SERVICES
JAR AU 82 VOL: 20 PG:482 - 496 :: DES.STAT. :PRIM. :HIPS :PROF.RESP.

SCHEINER,JH CIT: 0.00
AN EMPIRICAL ASSESSMENT OF THE IMPACT OF SEC NONAUDIT SERVICE DISCLOSURE
    REQUIREMENTS ON INDEPENDENT AUDITORS AND THEIR CLIENTS
JAR AU 84 VOL: 22 PG:789 - 797 :: DES.STAT. :PRIM. :INSTIT. :FASB SUBM.

SCHEPANSKI,A ; SEC: UECKER,WC CIT: 0.17
TOWARD A POSITIVE THEORY OF INFORMATION EVALUATION
TAR AP 83 VOL: 58 PG:259 - 283 :: ANAL. :INT. LOG. :INF.ECO./AG. :OTH.MANAG.

SCHEPANSKI,A CIT: 0.33
TESTS OF THEORIES OF INFORMATION PROCESSING BEHAVIOR IN CREDIT JUDGMENT
TAR JL 83 VOL: 58 PG:581 - 599 :: CORR. :LAB. :HIPS :N/A

SCHEPANSKI,A ; FIRS: UECKER,WC ; THIR: SHIN ,J CIT: 0.00
TOWARD A POSITIVE THEORY OF INFORMATION EVALUATION: RELEVANT TESTS OF
COMPETING MODELS IN A PRINCIPAL-AGENCY SETTING
TAR JL 85 VOL: 60 PG:430 - 457 :: REGRESS. :LAB. :INF.ECO./AG. :MANAG.

SCHEPANSKI,A ; FIRS: MADEO ,SA ; THIR: UECKER,WC CIT: 0.00
MODELING JUDGMENTS OF TAXPAYER COMPLIANCE
TAR AP 87 VOL: 62 PG:323 - 342 :: REGRESS. :LAB. :OTH.STAT. :TAXES

SCHICK,AG ; FIRS: GORDON,LA ; SEC: HAKA ,S CIT: 0.00
STRATEGIES FOR INFORMATION SYSTEMS IMPLEMENTATION: THE CASE OF ZERO BASE
BUDGETING
AOS 02 84 VOL: 9 PG:111 - 123 :: NON-PAR. :PRIM. :OTH. :BUDG.& PLAN.

SCHIENEMAN,GS CIT: 0.00
INTERNATIONAL ACCOUNTING: ISSUES AND PERSPECTIVE
JAA AU 79 VOL: 3 PG:21 - 30 :: QUAL. :INT. LOG. :INSTIT. :INT.DIFF.

SCHIENEMAN,GS CIT: 0.00
THE ACCOUNTING PROFESSION FACING THE CHALLENGES OF A CHANGING WORLD
JAA SP 83 VOL: 6 PG:212 - 226 :: QUAL. :INT. LOG. :OTH. :PROF.RESP.

SCHIFF,A ; FIRS: GIVOLY,D ; SEC: RONEN ,J CIT: 0.09
DOES AUDIT INVOLVEMENT AFFECT THE QUALITY OF INTERIM REPORT NUMBERS?
JAA SU 78 VOL: 1 PG:361 - 372 :: ANOVA :PRIM. :INSTIT. :AUD.

SCHIFF,A ; FIRS: FRIED ,D CIT: 0.38
CPA SWITCHES AND ASSOCIATED MARKET REACTIONS
TAR AP 81 VOL: 56 PG:326 - 341 :: NON-PAR. :PRIM. :EMH :OTH.MANAG.

SCHIFF,A ; FIRS: KAHN ,N CIT: 0.00
TANGIBLE EQUITY CHANGE AND THE EVOLUTION OF THE FASB'S DEFINITION OF INCOME
JAA AU 85 VOL: 9 PG:40 - 49 :: REGRESS. :INT. LOG. :THEORY :REV.REC.

SCHIFF,M CIT: 0.15
ACCOUNTING TACTICS AND THE THEORY OF THE FIRM
JAR SP 66 VOL: 4 PG:62 - 67 :: QUAL. :CASE :THEORY :OTH. NON-C/A

SCHIFF,M ; SEC: LEWIN ,AY CIT: 1.23
THE IMPACT OF PEOPLE ON BUDGETS
TAR AP 70 VOL: 45 PG:259 - 268 :: QUAL. :INT. LOG. :OTH.BEH. :BUDG.& PLAN.

SCHIFF,M ; SEC: SORTER,GH ; THIR: WIESEN,JL CIT: 0.00
THE EVOLVING ROLE OF CORPORATE AUDIT COMMITTEES
JAA AU 77 VOL: 1 PG:19 - 44 :: QUAL. :INT. LOG. :INSTIT. :OTH.MANAG.

SCHIFF,M CIT: 0.00
A NOTE ON TRANSFER PRICING AND INDUSTRY SEGMENT REPORTING
JAA SP 79 VOL: 2 PG:224 - 231 :: DES.STAT. :PRIM. :OTH. :TRANS.PRIC.

SCHIPPER,K CIT: 0.17
FINANCIAL DISTRESS IN PRIVATE COLLEGES
JAR ST 77 VOL: 15 PG:1 - 40 :: ANOVA :PRIM. :OTH.STAT. :BUS.FAIL.

SCHIPPER,K ; SEC: THOMPSON,R CIT: 2.67
THE IMPACT OF MERGER-RELATED REGULATIONS ON THE SHAREHOLDERS OF ACQUIRING
    FIRMS
JAR SP 83 VOL: 21 PG:184 - 221 :: REGRESS. :PRIM. :EMH :BUS.COMB.

SCHIPPER,K ; SEC: THOMPSON,R CIT: 0.00
THE IMPACT OF MERGER-RELATED REGULATIONS USING EXACT DISTRIBUTIONS OF TEST
    STATISTICS
JAR SP 85 VOL: 23 PG:408 - 415 :: DES.STAT. :PRIM. :EMH :BUS.COMB.

SCHLOSSER,RE ; FIRS: BOWER ,JB CIT: 0.00
INTERNAL CONTROL - ITS TRUE NATURE
TAR AP 65 VOL: 40 PG:338 - 344 :: QUAL. :INT. LOG. :INSTIT. :INT.CONT.

SCHMIDT,RM ; FIRS: COUGHLAN,AT CIT: 1.50
EXECUTIVE COMPENSATION, MANAGEMENT TURNOVER, AND FIRM PERFORMANCE: AN
    EMPIRICAL INVESTIGATION
JAE AP 85 VOL: 7 PG:43 - 66 :: REGRESS. :PRIM. :OTH.STAT. :EXEC.COMP.

SCHNEE,EJ ; SEC: TAYLOR,ME CIT: 0.00
IRS ACCESS TO ACCOUNTANTS' WORK PAPERS - THE RULES MAY BE CHANGING
JAA AU 81 VOL: 5 PG:18 - 29 :: QUAL. :INT. LOG. :INSTIT. :PROF.RESP.

SCHNEIDER,A CIT: 0.00
MODELING EXTERNAL AUDITORS' EVALUATIONS OF INTERNAL AUDITING
JAR AU 84 VOL: 22 PG:657 - 678 :: NON-PAR. :LAB. :HIPS :INT.AUD.

SCHNEIDER,A CIT: 0.00
THE RELIANCE OF EXTERNAL AUDITORS ON THE INTERNAL AUDIT FUNCTION
JAR AU 85 VOL: 23 PG:911 - 919 :: REGRESS. :LAB. :OTH.BEH. :INT.AUD.

SCHNEIDER,AJ CIT: 0.00
FLOW-GRAPH NOTATION IN ACCOUNTING
TAR AP 67 VOL: 42 PG:342 - 348 :: QUAL. :INT. LOG. :N/A :OTH.MANAG.

SCHNEPPER,JA CIT: 0.00
THE ACCOUNTANT'S LIABILITY UNDER RULE 10B-5 AND SECTION 10(B) OF THE
    SECURITIES EXCHANGE ACT OF 1934: THE HOLE IN HOCHFELDER
TAR JL 77 VOL: 52 PG:653 - 657 :: QUAL. :SEC. :N/A :LIAB.

SCHOLES,M ; FIRS: BEAVER,WH ; SEC: KETTLER,P CIT: 2.08
THE ASSOCIATION BETWEEN MARKET DETERMINED AND ACCOUNTING DETERMINED RISK MEA
TAR OC 70 VOL: 45 PG:654 - 682 :: REGRESS. :PRIM. :TIME SER. :FIN.METH.

SCHONFELD,HM ; FIRS: HOLZER,HP CIT: 0.00
THE GERMAN SOLUTION OF THE POST-WAR PRICE LEVEL PROBLEM
TAR AP 63 VOL: 38 PG:377 - 381 :: QUAL. :INT. LOG. :HIST. :FIN.METH.

SCHONFELD,HM ; FIRS: HOLZER,HP CIT: 0.00
THE FRENCH APPROACH TO THE POST-WAR PRICE LEVEL PROBLEM
TAR AP 63 VOL: 38 PG:382 - 388 :: QUAL. :INT. LOG. :HIST. :FIN.METH.

SCHONFELD,HM ; FIRS: HOLZER,HP CIT: 0.00
THE "FUNKTIONALE KONTORECHNUNG" OF WALTER THOMS
TAR AP 64 VOL: 39 PG:405 - 413 :: QUAL. :INT. LOG. :THEORY :FIN.METH.

SCHRADER,WJ ; FIRS: CRAMER JR,JJ CIT: 0.00
DEPRECIATION ACCOUNTING AND THE ANOMALOUS SELF-INSURANCE COST
TAR OC 70 VOL: 45 PG:698 - 703 :: QUAL. :INT. LOG. :THEORY :SPEC.ITEMS

SCHREUDER,H CIT: 0.30
CORPORATE SOCIAL REPORTING IN THE FEDERAL REPUBLIC OF GERMANY: AN OVERVIEW
AOS 12 79 VOL: 4 PG:109 - 122 :: QUAL. :INT. LOG. :THEORY :HRA

SCHREUDER,H CIT: 0.13
EMPLOYEES AND THE CORPORATE SOCIAL REPORT: THE DUTCH CASE
TAR AP 81 VOL: 56 PG:294 - 308 :: NON-PAR. :SURV. :INSTIT. :HRA

SCHREUDER,H ; SEC: KLAASSEN,J CIT: 0.20
CONFIDENTIAL REVENUE AND PROFIT FORECASTS BY MANAGEMENT AND FINANCIAL
ANALYSTS: EVIDENCE FROM THE NETHERLANDS
TAR JA 84 VOL: 59 PG:64 - 77 :: NON-PAR. :PRIM. :OTH.STAT. :FOREC.

SCHREUDER,H ; FIRS: SOETERS,J CIT: 0.00
THE INTERACTION BETWEEN NATIONAL AND ORGANIZATIONAL CULTURES IN ACCOUNTING
FIRMS
AOS 01 88 VOL: 13 PG:75 - 85 :: REGRESS. :SURV. :OTH.BEH. :AUD.BEH.

SCHRODERHEIM,G CIT: 0.08
USING MATHEMATICAL PROBABILITY TO ESTIMATE THE ALLOWANCE FOR DOUBTFUL ACCOU
TAR JL 64 VOL: 39 PG:679 - 684 :: ANAL. :INT. LOG. :OTH.STAT. :OTH.C/A

SCHROEDER,DA ; FIRS: KROSS ,W CIT: 0.80
AN EMPIRICAL INVESTIGATION OF THE EFFECT OF QUARTERLY EARNINGS ANNOUNCEMENT
TIMING ON STOCK RETURNS
JAR SP 84 VOL: 22 PG:153 - 176 :: REGRESS. :PRIM. :EMH :FIN.ST.TIM.

SCHROEDER,MS ; SEC: SOLOMON,I ; THIR: VICKREY,DW CIT: 0.00
AUDIT QUALITY: THE PERCEPTIONS OF AUDIT-COMMITTEE CHAIRPERSONS AND AUDIT
PARTNERS
AUD SP 86 VOL: 5 PG:86 - 94 :: REGRESS. :SURV. :OTH.BEH. :OPER.AUD.

SCHROEDER,MS ; FIRS: GRIMLUND,RA CIT: 0.00
ON THE CURRENT USE OF THE STRINGER METHOD OF MUS: SOME NEW DIRECTIONS
AUD AU 88 VOL: 08 PG:53 - 62 :: REGRESS. :SIM. :OTH.STAT. :SAMP.

SCHROEDER,RG ; SEC: IMDIEKE,LF CIT: 0.08
LOCAL-COSMOPOLITAN AND BUREAUCRATIC PERCEPTIONS IN PUBLIC ACCOUNTING FIRMS
AOS 01 77 VOL: 2 PG:39 - 46 :: DES.STAT. :INT. LOG. :OTH.STAT. :ORG.

SCHULTE JR,AA CIT: 0.15
COMPATIBILITY OF MANAGEMENT CONSULTING AND AUDITING
TAR JL 65 VOL: 40 PG:587 - 593 :: ANOVA :SURV. :INSTIT. :INDEP.

SCHULTE JR,AA CIT: 0.00
MANAGEMENT SERVICES: A CHALLENGE TO AUDIT INDEPENDENCE?
TAR OC 66 VOL: 41 PG:721 - 728 :: QUAL. :INT. LOG. :N/A :INDEP.

SCHULTZ JR,JJ ; SEC: GUSTAVSON,SG CIT: 0.64
ACTUARIES' PERCEPTIONS OF VARIABLES AFFECTING THE INDEPENDENT AUDITOR'S LEGAL
LIABILITY
TAR JL 78 VOL: 53 PG:626 - 641 :: ANOVA :LAB. :HIPS :LIAB.

SCHULTZ JR,JJ ; SEC: RECKERS,PMJ CIT: 0.75
THE IMPACT OF GROUP PROCESSING ON SELECTED AUDIT DISCLOSURE DECISIONS
JAR AU 81 VOL: 19 PG:482 - 501 :: ANOVA :PRIM. :OTH.BEH. :AUD.BEH.

SCHULTZ JR,JJ ; FIRS: RECKERS,PMJ CIT: 0.00
INDIVIDUAL VERSUS GROUP ASSISTED AUDIT EVALUATIONS
AUD AU 82 VOL: 2 PG:64 - 74 :: ANOVA :LAB. :OTH.BEH. :JUDG.

SCHWAB,B ; SEC: NICOL ,RE CIT: 0.08
FROM DOUBLE-DECLINING-BALANCE TO SUM-OF-THE-YEAR'S DIGITS DEPRECIATION: AN
   OPTIMUM SWITCHING RULE
TAR AP 69 VOL: 44 PG:292 - 296 :: ANAL. :SIM. :OTH.STAT. :PP&E / DEPR

SCHWAGER,SJ ; FIRS: BROWN ,LD ; SEC: RICHARDSON,GD CIT: 1.00
AN INFORMATION INTERPRETATION OF FINANCIAL ANALYST SUPERIORITY IN FORECASTING
   EARNINGS
JAR SP 87 VOL: 25 PG:49 - 67 :: REGRESS. :PRIM. :TIME SER. :FOREC.

SCHWAN,ES CIT: 0.62
THE EFFECTS OF HUMAN RESOURCE ACCOUNTING DATA ON FINANCIAL DECISIONS: AN
   EMPIRICAL TEST
AOS 23 76 VOL: 1 PG:219 - 238 :: DES.STAT. :LAB. :OTH.BEH. :HRA

SCHWARTZ,A ; FIRS: LEV ,B CIT: 0.85
ON THE USE OF THE ECONOMIC CONCEPT OF HUMAN CAPITAL IN FINANCIAL STATEMENTS
TAR JA 71 VOL: 46 PG:103 - 112 :: ANAL. :INT. LOG. :THEORY :HRA

SCHWARTZ,BN ; FIRS: FLAHERTY,RE CIT: 0.11
EARNINGS PER SHARE: COMPLIANCE AND UNDERSTANDABILITY
JAA AU 80 VOL: 4 PG:47 - 56 :: DES.STAT. :SEC. :THEORY :INFO.STRUC.

SCHWARTZ,BN CIT: 0.00
INCOME TAX ALLOCATION: IT IS TIME FOR A CHANGE
JAA SP 81 VOL: 4 PG:238 - 247 :: QUAL. :INT. LOG. :THEORY :TAXES

SCHWARTZ,BN CIT: 0.00
DEFERRED TAXES: COMPLIANCE AND UNDERSTANDABILITY
JAA SP 83 VOL: 6 PG:244 - 253 :: DES.STAT. :PRIM. :THEORY :TAXES

SCHWARTZ,KB CIT: 0.14
ACCOUNTING CHANGES BY CORPORATIONS FACING POSSIBLE INSOLVENCY
JAA AU 82 VOL: 6 PG:32 - 43 :: DES.STAT. :PRIM. :OTH.STAT. :ACC.CHNG.

SCHWARTZ,KB ; SEC: MENON ,K CIT: 0.25
AUDITOR SWITCHES BY FAILING FIRMS
TAR AP 85 VOL: 60 PG:248 - 261 :: REGRESS. :PRIM. :N/A :BUS.FAIL.

SCHWEIKART,JA CIT: 0.00
THE RELEVANCE OF MANAGERIAL ACCOUNTING INFORMATION: A MULTINATIONAL
   ANALYSIS
AOS 06 86 VOL: 11 PG:541 - 554 :: REGRESS. :SURV. :THEORY :INT.DIFF.

SCOTT ,RA CIT: 0.00
OWNERS' EQUITY, THE ANACHRONISTIC ELEMENT
TAR OC 79 VOL: 54 PG:750 - 763 :: QUAL. :INT. LOG. :THEORY :OTH.FIN.ACC.

SCOTT ,WR CIT: 1.08
A BAYESIAN APPROACH TO ASSET VALUATION AND AUDIT SIZE
JAR AU 73 VOL: 11 PG:304 - 330 :: ANAL. :INT. LOG. :OTH.STAT. :SAMP.

SCOTT ,WR CIT: 0.69
AUDITOR'S LOSS FUNCTIONS IMPLICIT IN CONSUMPTION-INVESTMENT MODELS
JAR ST 75 VOL: 13 PG:98 - 117 :: ANAL. :SIM. :OTH.STAT. :SAMP.

SCOTT ,WR CIT: 0.25
GROUP PREFERENCE ORDERINGS FOR AUDIT AND VALUATION ALTERNATIVES: THE
   SINGLE-PEAKEDNESS CONDITION
JAR SP 77 VOL: 15 PG:120 - 137 :: ANAL. :INT. LOG. :OTH.STAT. :AUD.

SCOTT ,WR CIT: 0.00
SCORING RULES FOR PROBABILISTIC REPORTING
JAR SP 79 VOL: 17 PG:156 - 178 :: ANAL. :INT. LOG. :INF.ECO./AG. :PROB.ELIC.

SEAGLE,JP ; SEC: PETRI ,E CIT: 0.00
GIFT VS. ESTATE TRANSFER: THE METHOD OF EQUATED RATES
TAR JA 77 VOL: 52 PG:124 - 136 :: ANAL. :INT. LOG. :THEORY :N/A

SEAMAN,JL CIT: 0.00
LESSONS FROM THE INVESTMENT CREDIT
TAR JL 65 VOL: 40 PG:617 - 621 :: QUAL. :INT. LOG. :INSTIT. :TAXES

SEARFOSS,DG CIT: 0.23
SOME BEHAVIOURAL ASPECTS OF BUDGETING FOR CONTROL: AN EMPIRICAL STUDY
AOS 04 76 VOL: 1 PG:375 - 388 :: OTH.QUANT. :FIELD :OTH.BEH. :BUDG.& PLAN.

SEARFOSS,DG ; FIRS: CUSHING,BE ; THIR: RANDALL,RH CIT: 0.20
MATERIALITY ALLOCATION IN AUDIT PLANNING: A FEASIBILITY STUDY
JAR ST 79 VOL: 17 PG:172 - 216 :: DES.STAT. :FIELD :OTH.STAT. :PLAN.

SEELYE,AL CIT: 0.00
THE ROLE OF BUSINESS SCHOOLS IN A CHANGING ENVIRONMENT
TAR AP 63 VOL: 38 PG:302 - 309 :: QUAL. :INT. LOG. :INSTIT. :EDUC.

SEFCIK,SE ; SEC: THOMPSON,R CIT: 0.33
AN APPROACH TO STAT. INFERENCE IN CROSS-SECTIONAL MODELS WITH SECURITY
    ABNORMAL RETURNS AS DEPENDENT VARIABLE
JAR AU 86 VOL: 24 PG:316 - 334 :: DES.STAT. :INT. LOG. :OTH.STAT. :METHOD.

SEGALL,J ; FIRS: GREEN ,D CIT: 0.62
THE PREDICTIVE POWER OF FIRST-QUARTER EARNINGS REPORTS: A REPLICATION
JAR ST 66 VOL: 4 PG:21 - 36 :: DES.STAT. :PRIM. :OTH.STAT. :INT.REP.

SEIDLER,LJ CIT: 0.15
INTERNATIONAL ACCOUNTING - THE ULTIMATE THEORY COURSE
TAR OC 67 VOL: 42 PG:775 - 781 :: QUAL. :INT. LOG. :N/A :OTH.MANAG.

SEIDLER,LJ CIT: 0.00
THE COHEN COMMISSION AFTER ONE YEAR: A PERSONAL VIEW
JAA SU 79 VOL: 2 PG:285 - 293 :: QUAL. :INT. LOG. :INSTIT. :AUD.

SEIFERT,J ; FIRS: MIELKE,DE CIT: 0.00
A SURVEY ON THE EFFECTS OF DEFEASING DEBT
JAA WI 87 VOL: 2 PG:65 - 78 :: REGRESS. :PRIM. :THEORY :LTD

SEILER,ME ; FIRS: MELLMAN,M CIT: 0.00
STRUCTURE NEEDED FOR IMPLEMENTING MANDATED ACCOUNTING CHANGES
JAA AU 86 VOL: 1 PG:305 - 318 :: REGRESS. :PRIM. :INSTIT. :FASB SUBM.

SEILER,RE CIT: 0.00
ACCOUNTING, INFORMATION SYSTEMS, AND UNDERDEVELOPED NATIONS
TAR OC 66 VOL: 41 PG:652 - 656 :: QUAL. :INT. LOG. :INSTIT. :OTH.MANAG.

SEILER,RE ; SEC: BARTLETT,RW CIT: 0.14
PERSONALITY VARIABLES AS PREDICTORS OF BUDGET SYSTEM CHARACTERISTICS
AOS 04 82 VOL: 7 PG:381 - 404 :: OTH.QUANT. :SURV. :OTH.BEH. :BUDG.& PLAN.

SELLING,T ; FIRS: CASEY JR,CJ CIT: 0.00
THE EFFECT OF TASK PREDICTABILITY AND PRIOR PROBABILITY DISCLOSURE ON
    JUDGMENT QUALITY AND CONFIDENCE
TAR AP 86 VOL: 61 PG:302 - 317 :: REGRESS. :LAB. :HIPS :BUS.FAIL.

SELTO ,FH ; SEC: GROVE ,HD CIT: 0.14
VOTING POWER INDICES AND THE SETTING OF FINANCIAL ACCOUNTING STANDARDS:
  EXTENSIONS
JAR AU 82 VOL: 20 PG:676 - 688 :: DES.STAT. :PRIM. :INSTIT. :FASB SUBM.

SELTO ,FH CIT: 0.14
INTERNAL ADAPTATIONS TO EFFECTS OF CHANGES IN FINANCIAL ACCOUNTING STANDARDS
AOS 02 82 VOL: 7 PG:139 - 148 :: QUAL. :INT. LOG. :INSTIT. :N/A

SELTO ,FH ; SEC: GROVE ,HD CIT: 0.00
THE PREDICTIVE POWER OF VOTING POWER INDICES: FASB VOTING ON STATEMENTS OF
  FINANCIAL ACCOUNTING STANDARDS NOS. 45-69
JAR AU 83 VOL: 21 PG:619 - 622 :: NON-PAR. :PRIM. :INSTIT. :FASB SUBM.

SELTO ,FH ; SEC: CLOUSE,ML CIT: 0.00
AN INVESTIGATION OF MANAGERS' ADAPTATIONS TO SFAS NO. 2: ACCOUNTING FOR
  RESEARCH AND DEVELOPMENT COSTS
JAR AU 85 VOL: 23 PG:700 - 717 :: REGRESS. :PRIM. :EMH :R & D

SENATRA,PT CIT: 0.33
ROLE CONFLICT, ROLE AMBIGUITY, AND ORGANIZATIONAL CLIMATE IN A PUBLIC
  ACCOUNTING FIRM
TAR OC 80 VOL: 55 PG:594 - 603 :: REGRESS. :SURV. :OTH.BEH. :ORG.

SENGUPTA,R ; FIRS: HOUGHTON,KA CIT: 0.00
THE EFFECT OF PRIOR PROBABILITY DISCLOSURE AND INFORMATION SET CONSTRUCTION
  ON BANKERS' ABILITY TO PREDICT FAILURE
JAR AU 84 VOL: 22 PG:768 - 775 :: DES.STAT. :LAB. :HIPS :BUS.FAIL.

SENKOW,DW ; FIRS: DALEY ,LA ; THIR: VIGELAND,RL CIT: 0.00
ANALYSTS' FORECASTS, EARNINGS VARIABILITY, AND OPTION PRICING: EMPIRICAL
  EVIDENCE
TAR OC 88 VOL: 63 PG:563 - 585 :: REGRESS. :PRIM. :TIME SER. :FOREC.

SEPE ,J ; FIRS: NOREEN,EW CIT: 1.25
MARKET REACTIONS TO ACCOUNTING POLICY DELIBERATIONS: THE INFLATION ACCOUNTING
  CASE
TAR AP 81 VOL: 56 PG:253 - 269 :: CORR. :PRIM. :EMH :VALUAT.(INFL.)

SEPE ,J CIT: 0.14
THE IMPACT OF THE FASB'S 1974 GPL PROPOSAL ON THE SECURITY PRICE STRUCTURE
TAR JL 82 VOL: 57 PG:467 - 485 :: REGRESS. :PRIM. :EMH :VALUAT.(INFL.)

SERLIN,JE ; FIRS: LANDSITTEL,DL CIT: 0.00
EVALUATING THE MATERIALITY OF ERRORS IN FINANCIAL STATEMENTS
JAA SU 82 VOL: 5 PG:291 - 300 :: QUAL. :INT. LOG. :OTH. :MAT.

SHABAHANG,R ; FIRS: HORWITZ,BN CIT: 0.23
PUBLISHED CORPORATE ACCOUNTING DATA AND GENERAL WAGE INCREASES OF THE FIRM
TAR AP 71 VOL: 46 PG:243 - 252 :: CORR. :PRIM. :N/A :FIN.METH.

SHAFTEL,TL ; FIRS: HANSEN,DR CIT: 0.00
SAMPLING FOR INTEGRATED AUDITING OBJECTIVES
TAR JA 77 VOL: 52 PG:109 - 123 :: ANAL. :INT. LOG. :MATH.PROG. :SAMP.

SHAH ,P ; FIRS: HAGERMAN,RL ; SEC: ZMIJEWSKI,ME CIT: 0.00
THE ASSOCIATION BETWEEN THE MAGNITUDE OF QUARTERLY EARNINGS FORECAST ERRORS
  AND RISK-ADJUSTED STOCK RETURNS
JAR AU 84 VOL: 22 PG:526 - 540 :: REGRESS. :PRIM. :EMH :FOREC.

SHANE ,PB ; SEC: SPICER,BH CIT: 0.50
MARKET RESPONSE TO ENVIRONMENTAL INFORMATION PRODUCED OUTSIDE THE FIRM
TAR JL 83 VOL: 58 PG:521 - 538 :: DES.STAT. :PRIM. :EMH :ORG.& ENVIR.

SHANE ,PB ; FIRS: ETTREDGE,M ; THIR: SMITH ,D CIT: 0.00
AUDIT FIRM SIZE AND THE ASSOCIATION BETWEEN REPORTED EARNINGS AND SECURITY
   RETURNS
AUD SP 88 VOL: 07 PG:29 - 42 :: REGRESS. :PRIM. :EMH :AUD.THEOR.

SHANK ,JK CIT: 0.08
INCOME DETERMINATION UNDER UNCERTAINTY: AN APPLICATION OF MARKOV CHAINS
TAR JA 71 VOL: 46 PG:57 - 74 :: MARKOV :CASE :OTH.STAT. :REV.REC.

SHANK ,JK ; FIRS: COPELAND,RM CIT: 0.38
LIFO AND THE DIFFUSION OF INNOVATION
JAR ST 71 VOL: 9 PG:196 - 224 :: DES.STAT. :PRIM. :THEORY :INV.

SHANK ,JK ; SEC: COPELAND,RM CIT: 0.31
CORPORATE PERSONALITY THEORY AND CHANGES IN ACCOUNTING METHODS: AN EMPIRIC/
   TEST
TAR JL 73 VOL: 48 PG:494 - 501 :: NON-PAR. :PRIM. :OTH.STAT. :ORG.FORM

SHANK ,JK ; FIRS: CHURCHILL,NC CIT: 0.15
ACCOUNTING FOR AFFIRMATIVE ACTION PROGRAMS: A STOCHASTIC FLOW APPROACH
TAR OC 75 VOL: 50 PG:643 - 656 :: ANOVA :FIELD :OTH.STAT. :HRA

SHANK ,JK ; FIRS: SAN MIGUEL,JG ; THIR: GOVINDARAJAN,V CIT: 0.08
EXTENDING CORPORATE ACCOUNTABILITY: A SURVEY AND FRAMEWORK FOR ANALYSIS
AOS 04 77 VOL: 2 PG:333 - 348 :: DES.STAT. :PRIM. :OTH. :AUD.

SHANK ,JK ; SEC: MURDOCK,RJ CIT: 0.36
COMPARABILITY IN THE APPLICATION OF REPORTING STANDARDS: SOME FURTHER EVIDENC
TAR OC 78 VOL: 53 PG:824 - 835 :: DES.STAT. :PRIM. :EMH :OPIN.

SHANK ,JK ; FIRS: CREADY,WM CIT: 0.00
UNDERSTANDING ACCOUNTING CHANGES IN EFFICIENT MARKET: A COMMENT,
   REPLICATION, AND RE-INTERPRETATION
TAR JL 87 VOL: 62 PG:589 - 596 :: REGRESS. :PRIM. :EMH :ACC.CHNG.

SHANTEAU,J ; FIRS: KROGSTAD,JL ; SEC: ETTENSON,RT CIT: 0.40
CONTEXT AND EXPERIENCE IN AUDITORS' MATERIALITY JUDGMENTS
AUD AU 84 VOL: 4 PG:54 - 74 :: ANOVA :LAB. :OTH.BEH. :MAT.

SHARPE,IG ; SEC: WALKER,RG CIT: 0.08
ASSET REVALUATIONS AND STOCK MARKET PRICES
JAR AU 75 VOL: 13 PG:293 - 310 :: REGRESS. :PRIM. :EMH :VALUAT.(INFL.)

SHASHUA,L ; FIRS: GOLDSCHMIDT,Y CIT: 0.00
DISTORTION OF INCOME BY SFAS NO.33
JAA AU 84 VOL: 8 PG:54 - 67 :: QUAL. :INT. LOG. :THEORY :VALUAT.(INFL.)

SHAW ,R ; FIRS: ASKARI,H ; SEC: CAIN ,P CIT: 0.00
A GOVERNMENT TAX SUBSIDY
TAR AP 76 VOL: 51 PG:331 - 334 :: DES.STAT. :PRIM. :N/A :TAX PLNG.

SHAW ,WH CIT: 0.00
SAFE HARBOR OR MUDDY WATERS
TAR AP 87 VOL: 62 PG:385 - 400 :: REGRESS. :PRIM. :THEORY :LEASES

SHAW ,WH CIT: 0.00
MEASURING THE IMPACT OF THE SAFE HARBOR LEASE LAW ON SECURITY PRICES
JAR SP 88 VOL: 26 PG:60 - 81 :: REGRESS. :PRIM. :EMH :TAXES

SHEARON,WT ; FIRS: SWANSON,EP ; THIR: THOMAS,LR CIT: 0.00
PREDICTING CURRENT COST OPERATING PROFIT USING COMPONENT MODELS INCORPORATING
ANALYSTS' FORECASTS
TAR OC 85 VOL: 60 PG:681 - 691 :: REGRESS. :PRIM. :TIME SER. :VALUAT.(INFL.)

SHERER,MJ ; FIRS: COOPER,DJ CIT: 2.60
THE VALUE OF CORPORATE ACCOUNTING REPORTS: ARGUMENTS FOR A POLITICAL ECONOMY
OF ACCOUNTING
AOS 34 84 VOL: 9 PG:207 - 232 :: QUAL. :SURV. :THEORY :N/A

SHERMAN,HD CIT: 0.00
DATA ENVELOPMENT ANALYSIS AS A NEW MANAGERIAL AUDIT METHODOLOGY - TEST AND
EVALUATION
AUD AU 84 VOL: 4 PG:35 - 53 :: ANAL. :INT. LOG. :MATH.PROG. :OPER.AUD.

SHEVLIN,T ; FIRS: FOSTER,G ; SEC: OLSEN ,C CIT: 1.40
EARNINGS RELEASES, ANOMALIES, AND THE BEHAVIOR OF SECURITY RETURNS
TAR OC 84 VOL: 59 PG:574 - 603 :: REGRESS. :PRIM. :EMH :N/A

SHEVLIN,T CIT: 0.00
TAXES AND OFF-BALANCE-SHEET FINANCING: RESEARCH AND DEVELOPMENT LIMIT
ED PARTNERSHIPS
TAR JL 87 VOL: 62 PG:480 - 509 :: REGRESS. :PRIM. :OTH.STAT. :ORG.FORM

SHIELDS,D ; FIRS: EICHENSEHER,JW CIT: 0.33
THE CORRELATES OF CPA-FIRM CHANGE FOR PUBLICLY-HELD CORPORATIONS
AUD SP 83 VOL: 2 PG:23 - 37 :: NON-PAR. :SURV. :OTH.BEH. :ORG.

SHIELDS,D CIT: 0.00
SMALL CPA FIRM PRODUCT DIFFERENTIATION IN THE SMALL BUSINESS MARKET
AOS 01 84 VOL: 9 PG:61 - 80 :: CORR. :SURV. :HIPS :ORG.FORM

SHIELDS,MD ; FIRS: BIRNBERG,JG ; SEC: FRIEZE,IH CIT: 0.33
THE ROLE OF ATTRIBUTION THEORY IN CONTROL SYSTEMS
AOS 03 77 VOL: 2 PG:189 - 200 :: QUAL. :INT. LOG. :OTH.BEH. :MANAG.

SHIELDS,MD ; FIRS: MCGHEE,W ; THIR: BIRNBERG,JG CIT: 1.00
THE EFFECTS OF PERSONALITY ON A SUBJECT'S INFORMATION PROCESSING
TAR JL 78 VOL: 53 PG:681 - 697 :: ANOVA :LAB. :HIPS :OTH.MANAG.

SHIELDS,MD CIT: 1.11
SOME EFFECTS OF INFORMATION LOAD ON SEARCH PATTERNS USED TO ANALYZE
PERFORMANCE REPORTS
AOS 04 80 VOL: 5 PG:429 - 442 :: ANOVA :LAB. :HIPS :INFO.STRUC.

SHIELDS,MD ; SEC: BIRNBERG,JG ; THIR: FRIEZE,IH CIT: 0.50
ATTRIBUTIONS, COGNITIVE PROCESSES AND CONTROL SYSTEMS
AOS 01 81 VOL: 6 PG:69 - 96 :: ANOVA :LAB. :OTH.BEH. :BUDG.& PLAN.

SHIELDS,MD CIT: 1.17
EFFECTS OF INFORMATION SUPPLY AND DEMAND ON JUDGMENT ACCURACY: EVIDENCE FROM
CORPORATE MANAGERS
TAR AP 83 VOL: 58 PG:284 - 303 :: ANOVA :LAB. :HIPS :DEC.AIDS

SHIELDS,MD ; FIRS: BAILEY,KE ; SEC: BYLINSKI,JH CIT: 0.00
EFFECTS OF AUDIT REPORT WORDING CHANGES ON THE PERCEIVED MESSAGE
JAR AU 83 VOL: 21 PG:355 - 370 :: OTH.QUANT. :LAB. :OTH.BEH. :OPIN.

SHIELDS,MD ; FIRS: LEWIS ,BL ; THIR: YOUNG ,SM CIT: 1.17
EVALUATING HUMAN JUDGMENTS AND DECISION AIDS
JAR SP 83 VOL: 21 PG:271 - 285 :: DES.STAT. :LAB. :HIPS :ORG.& ENVIR.

SHIELDS,MD ; FIRS: ROCKNESS,HO CIT: 0.60
ORGANIZATIONAL CONTROL SYSTEMS IN RESEARCH AND DEVELOPMENT
AOS 02 84 VOL: 9 PG:165 - 177 :: CORR. :SURV. :OTH.BEH. :R & D

SHIELDS,MD CIT: 0.40
A PREDECISIONAL APPROACH TO THE MEASUREMENT OF THE DEMAND FOR INFORMATION IN
A PERFORMANCE REPORT
AOS 34 84 VOL: 9 PG:355 - 363 :: CORR. :LAB. :HIPS :MANAG.

SHIELDS,MD ; FIRS: BIRNBERG,JG CIT: 0.20
THE ROLE OF ATTENTION AND MEMORY IN ACCOUNTING DECISIONS
AOS 34 84 VOL: 9 PG:365 - 382 :: QUAL. :INT. LOG. :HIPS :N/A

SHIELDS,MD ; SEC: SOLOMON,I ; THIR: WALLER,WS CIT: 0.00
EFFECTS OF ALTERNATIVE SAMPLE SPACE REPRESENTATIONS ON THE ACCURACY OF
AUDITORS' UNCERTAINTY JUDGEMENTS
AOS 04 87 VOL: 12 PG:375 - 385 :: REGRESS. :LAB. :HIPS :MAN.DEC.CHAR.

SHIELDS,MD ; SEC: WALLER,WS CIT: 0.00
A BEHAVIORAL STUDY OF ACCOUNTING VARIABLES IN PERFORMANCE-INCENTIVE CONTRACTS
AOS 06 88 VOL: 13 PG:581 - 594 :: REGRESS. :LAB. :INF.ECO./AG. :EXEC.COMP.

SHIELDS,MD ; FIRS: YOUNG ,SM ; THIR: WOLF ,G CIT: 0.00
MANUFACTURING CONTROLS AND PERFORMANCE: AN EXPERIMENT
AOS 06 88 VOL: 13 PG:607 - 618 :: REGRESS. :LAB. :OTH.BEH. :EXEC.COMP.

SHIH ,W CIT: 0.10
A GENERAL DECISION MODEL FOR COST-VOLUME-PROFIT ANALYSIS UNDER UNCERTAINTY
TAR OC 79 VOL: 54 PG:687 - 706 :: ANAL. :INT. LOG. :OTH.STAT. :C-V-P-A

SHILLINGLAW,G CIT: 0.00
THE CONCEPT OF ATTRIBUTABLE COST
JAR SP 63 VOL: 1 PG:73 - 85 :: QUAL. :INT. LOG. :THEORY :N/A

SHIN ,HC ; FIRS: BROCKETT,P ; SEC: CHARNES,A ; THIR: COOPER,WW CIT: 0.00
A CHANCE-CONSTRAINED PROGRAMMING APPROACH TO COST-VOLUME-PROFIT ANALYSIS
TAR JL 84 VOL: 59 PG:474 - 487 :: ANAL. :INT. LOG. :MATH.PROG. :C-V-P-A

SHIN ,J ; FIRS: UECKER,WC ; SEC: SCHEPANSKI,A CIT: 0.00
TOWARD A POSITIVE THEORY OF INFORMATION EVALUATION: RELEVANT TESTS OF
COMPETING MODELS IN A PRINCIPAL-AGENCY SETTING
TAR JL 85 VOL: 60 PG:430 - 457 :: REGRESS. :LAB. :INF.ECO./AG. :MANAG.

SHOCKLEY,RA CIT: 0.38
PERCEPTIONS OF AUDITORS' INDEPENDENCE: AN EMPIRICAL ANALYSIS
TAR OC 81 VOL: 56 PG:785 - 800 :: ANOVA :SURV. :OTH.BEH. :INDEP.

SHOCKLEY,RA CIT: 0.14
PERCEPTIONS OF AUDIT INDEPENDENCE: A CONCEPTUAL MODEL
JAA WI 82 VOL: 5 PG:126 - 143 :: QUAL. :INT. LOG. :OTH. :INDEP.

SHOCKLEY,RA ; SEC: HOLT ,RN CIT: 0.50
A BEHAVIOURAL INVESTIGATION OF SUPPLIER DIFFERENTIATION IN THE MARKET FOR
   AUDIT SERVICES
JAR AU 83 VOL: 21 PG:545 - 564 :: OTH.QUANT. :LAB. :INSTIT. :ORG.

SHORT ,DG CIT: 0.18
THE IMPACT OF PRICE-LEVEL ADJUSTMENT IN THE CONTEXT OF RISK ASSESSMENT
JAR ST 78 VOL: 16 PG:259 - 272 :: OTH.QUANT. :PRIM. :EMH :VALUAT.(INFL.)

SHORT ,DG ; FIRS: GRANOF,MH CIT: 0.00
WHY DO COMPANIES REJECT LIFO?
JAA SU 84 VOL: 7 PG:323 - 333 :: DES.STAT. :SURV. :THEORY :INV.

SHPILBERG,D ; SEC: GRAHAM,LE CIT: 0.00
DEVELOPING EXPERTAX: AN EXPERT SYSTEM FOR CORPORATE TAX ACCRUAL
   ND PLANNING
AUD AU 86 VOL: 6 PG:75 - 94 :: QUAL. :LAB. :EXP.SYST. :TAXES

SHRIVER,KA ; FIRS: DUGAN ,MT ; SEC: GENTRY,JA CIT: 0.00
THE X-11 MODEL: A NEW ANALYTICAL REVIEW TECHNIQUE FOR THE AUDITOR
AUD SP 85 VOL: 4 PG:11 - 22 :: DES.STAT. :INT. LOG. :TIME SER. :ANAL.REV.

SHRIVER,KA CIT: 0.33
FURTHER EVIDENCE ON THE MARGINAL GAINS IN ACCURACY OF ALTERNATIVE LEV
   ELS OF SPECIFICITY OF THE PRODUCER PRICE INDEXES
JAR SP 86 VOL: 24 PG:151 - 165 :: REGRESS. :PRIM. :THEORY :VALUAT.(INFL.)

SHRIVER,KA CIT: 0.00
AN EMPIRICAL EXAMINATION OF THE EFFECTS OF ALTERNATIVE MEASUREMENT TECHNIQUES
   ON CURRENT COST DATA
TAR JA 87 VOL: 62 PG:79 - 96 :: REGRESS. :FIELD :THEORY :VALUAT.(INFL.)

SHWAYDER,KR CIT: 0.00
A NOTE ON A CONTRIBUTION MARGIN APPROACH TO THE ANALYSIS OF CAPACITY
   UTILIZATION
TAR JA 68 VOL: 43 PG:101 - 104 :: QUAL. :INT. LOG. :N/A :VAR.

SHWAYDER,KR CIT: 0.00
RELEVANCE
JAR SP 68 VOL: 6 PG:86 - 97 :: QUAL. :INT. LOG. :THEORY :FIN.METH.

SHWAYDER,KR CIT: 0.08
THE CAPITAL MAINTENANCE RULE AND THE NET ASSET VALUATION RULE
TAR AP 69 VOL: 44 PG:304 - 316 :: ANAL. :INT. LOG. :THEORY :VALUAT.(INFL.)

SHWAYDER,KR CIT: 0.00
A PROPOSED MODIFICATION TO RESIDUAL INCOME - INTEREST ADJUSTED INCOME
TAR AP 70 VOL: 45 PG:299 - 307 :: ANAL. :INT. LOG. :N/A :COST.ALLOC.

SHWAYDER,KR CIT: 0.08
EXPECTED AND UNEXPECTED PRICE LEVEL CHANGES
TAR AP 71 VOL: 46 PG:306 - 319 :: ANAL. :INT. LOG. :THEORY :VALUAT.(INFL.)

SHWAYDER,KR CIT: 0.00
ACCOUNTING FOR EXCHANGE RATE FLUCTUATIONS
TAR OC 72 VOL: 47 PG:747 - 760 :: ANAL. :INT. LOG. :THEORY :SPEC.ITEMS

SHWAYDER,KR CIT: 0.08
TWO "WRONGS" MAKING A "RIGHT"
JAR AU 73 VOL: 11 PG:259 - 272 :: ANAL. :SIM. :THEORY :PP&E / DEPR

SIEGEL,JP ; FIRS: DERMER,JD CIT: 0.15
THE ROLE OF BEHAVIOURAL MEASURES IN ACCOUNTING FOR HUMAN RESOURCES
TAR JA 74 VOL: 49 PG:88 - 97 :: CORR. :LAB. :OTH.BEH. :HRA

SIEGEL,S ; FIRS: SORTER,GH ; THIR: SLAIN ,J CIT: 0.00
ACCOUNTANTS' LEGAL LIABILITY: A DETERMINANT OF THE ACCOUNTING MODEL
JAA SU 88 VOL: 03 PG:233 - 244 :: DES.STAT. :INT. LOG. :THEORY :LIAB.

SIGLOCH,BA ; FIRS: BUTTERWORTH,JE CIT: 0.08
A GENERALIZED MULTI-STAGE INPUT-OUTPUT MODEL AND SOME DERIVED EQUIVALENT
SYSTEMS
TAR OC 71 VOL: 46 PG:701 - 716 :: ANAL. :INT. LOG. :MATH.PROG. :MANAG.

SILHAN,PA ; FIRS: HOPWOOD,WS ; SEC: NEWBOLD,P CIT: 0.29
THE POTENTIAL FOR GAINS IN PREDICTIVE ABILITY THROUGH DISAGGREGATION:
SEGMENTED ANNUAL EARNINGS
JAR AU 82 VOL: 20 PG:724 - 732 :: DES.STAT. :PRIM. :TIME SER. :SEG.REP.

SILHAN,PA CIT: 0.57
SIMULATED MERGERS OF EXISTENT AUTONOMOUS FIRMS, A NEW APPROACH TO
SEGMENTATION RESEARCH
JAR SP 82 VOL: 20 PG:255 - 262 :: DES.STAT. :SIM. :OTH.STAT. :BUS.COMB.

SILHAN,PA CIT: 0.00
THE EFFECTS OF SEGMENTING QUARTERLY SALES AND MARGINS ON EXTRAPOLATIVE
FORECASTS OF CONGLOMERATE EARNINGS: EXTENSION AND REPLICATION
JAR SP 83 VOL: 21 PG:341 - 347 :: NON-PAR. :PRIM. :EMH :FOREC.

SILHAN,PA ; SEC: MCKEOWN,JC CIT: 0.00
FURTHER EVIDENCE ON THE USEFULNESS OF SIMULATED MERGERS
JAR SP 85 VOL: 23 PG:416 - 426 :: REGRESS. :PRIM. :TIME SER. :BUS.COMB.

SIMIK ,SS ; FIRS: JOHNSON,GL CIT: 0.15
MULTIPRODUCT C-V-P ANALYSIS UNDER UNCERTAINTY
JAR AU 71 VOL: 9 PG:278 - 286 :: ANAL. :INT. LOG. :OTH.STAT. :C-V-P-A

SIMIK ,SS ; FIRS: JOHNSON,GL CIT: 0.15
THE USE OF PROBABILITY INEQUALITIES IN MULTIPRODUCT C-V-P ANALYSIS UNDER
UNCERTAINTY
JAR SP 74 VOL: 12 PG:67 - 79 :: ANAL. :INT. LOG. :OTH.STAT. :C-V-P-A

SIMMONS,JK CIT: 0.00
A CONCEPT OF COMPARABILITY IN FINANCIAL REPORTING
TAR OC 67 VOL: 42 PG:680 - 692 :: QUAL. :INT. LOG. :THEORY :FIN.METH.

SIMMONS,JK ; SEC: GRAY ,J CIT: 0.46
AN INVESTIGATION OF THE EFFECT OF DIFFERING ACCOUNTING FRAMEWORKS ON THE
PREDICTION OF NET INCOME
TAR OC 69 VOL: 44 PG:757 - 776 :: ANAL. :SIM. :THEORY :VALUAT.(INFL.)

SIMON ,DT ; FIRS: LARCKER,DF ; SEC: REDER ,RE CIT: 0.33
TRADES BY INSIDERS AND MANDATED ACCOUNTING STANDARDS
TAR JL 83 VOL: 58 PG:606 - 620 :: NON-PAR. :INT. LOG. :EMH :OIL & GAS

SIMON ,DT CIT: 0.00
THE AUDIT SERVICES MARKET: ADDITIONAL EMPIRICAL EVIDENCE
AUD AU 85 VOL: 5 PG:71 - 78 :: REGRESS. :PRIM. :OTH.STAT. :ORG.

SIMON ,DT ; FIRS: FRANCIS,JR CIT: 0.50
A TEST OF AUDIT PRICING IN THE SMALL-CLIENT SEGMENT OF THE U.S. AUDIT MARKET
TAR JA 87 VOL: 62 PG:145 - 157 :: REGRESS. :SURV. :OTH.STAT. :ORG.

SIMON ,DT ; SEC: FRANCIS,JR CIT: 0.00
THE EFFECTS OF AUDITOR CHANGE ON AUDIT FEES: TESTS OF PRICE CUTTING AND PRICE
    RECOVERY
TAR AP 88 VOL: 63 PG:255 - 269 :: REGRESS. :PRIM. :OTH.STAT. :ORG.

SIMON ,SI CIT: 0.00
COST ACCOUNTING AND THE LAW
TAR OC 64 VOL: 39 PG:884 - 889 :: QUAL. :SEC. :INSTIT. :MANAG.

SIMON ,SI CIT: 0.00
FRAUD IN THE BALANCE SHEET
TAR AP 65 VOL: 40 PG:401 - 406 :: QUAL. :SEC. :INSTIT. :FIN.METH.

SIMONDS,RR ; FIRS: COLLINS,DW CIT: 0.20
SEC LINE-OF-BUSINESS DISCLOSURE AND MARKET RISK ADJUSTMENTS
JAR AU 79 VOL: 17 PG:352 - 383 :: MIXED :PRIM. :EMH :SEG.REP.

SIMONS,R CIT: 0.00
ACCOUNTING CONTROL SYSTEMS AND BUSINESS STRATEGY: AN EMPIRICAL ANALYSIS
AOS 04 87 VOL: 12 PG:357 - 374 :: REGRESS. :SURV. :OTH.BEH. :BUDG.& PLAN.

SIMPSON,RH CIT: 0.08
AN EMPIRICAL STUDY OF POSSIBLE INCOME MANIPULATION
TAR OC 69 VOL: 44 PG:806 - 817 :: DES.STAT. :PRIM. :N/A :FIN.METH.

SIMUNIC,DA CIT: 2.00
THE PRICING OF AUDIT SERVICES: THEORY AND EVIDENCE
JAR SP 80 VOL: 18 PG:161 - 190 :: REGRESS. :FIELD :OTH.STAT. :AUD.BEH.

SIMUNIC,DA CIT: 0.20
AUDITING, CONSULTING, AND AUDITOR INDEPENDENCE
JAR AU 84 VOL: 22 PG:679 - 702 :: REGRESS. :PRIM. :OTH.STAT. :INDEP.

SINCLAIR,NA ; FIRS: CLINCH,GJ CIT: 0.00
INTRA-INDUSTRY INFORMATION RELEASES: A RECURSIVE SYSTEMS APPROACH
JAE AP 87 VOL: 9 PG:89 - 106 :: REGRESS. :PRIM. :EMH :FIN.METH.

SINGER,FA CIT: 0.00
PROGRESS IN PROGRAMMED INSTRUCTION
TAR OC 65 VOL: 40 PG:847 - 853 :: DES.STAT. :LAB. :N/A :OTH.MANAG.

SINGHVI,SS ; SEC: DESAI ,HB CIT: 0.46
AN EMPIRICAL ANALYSIS OF THE QUALITY OF CORPORATE FINANCIAL DISCLOSURE
TAR JA 71 VOL: 46 PG:129 - 138 :: DES.STAT. :PRIM. :N/A :INFO.STRUC.

SINHA ,P ; FIRS: LEITCH,RA ; SEC: NETER ,J ; THIR: PLANTE,R CIT: 0.86
MODIFIED MULTINOMIAL BOUNDS FOR LARGER NUMBERS OF ERRORS IN AUDITS
TAR AP 82 VOL: 57 PG:384 - 400 :: DES.STAT. :SIM. :OTH.STAT. :SAMP.

SINNING,KE ; FIRS: DYKXHOORN,HJ CIT: 0.00
WIRTSCHAFTSPRUFER PERCEPTION OF AUDITOR INDEPENDENCE
TAR JA 81 VOL: 56 PG:97 - 107 :: NON-PAR. :SURV. :OTH.BEH. :INDEP.

SINNING,KE ; FIRS: DYKXHOORN,HJ CIT: 0.00
PERCEPTIONS OF AUDITOR INDEPENDENCE: ITS PERCEIVED EFFECT ON THE LOAN AND
    INVESTMENT DECISIONS OF GERMAN FINANCIAL STATEMENT USERS
AOS 04 82 VOL: 7 PG:337 - 348 :: ANOVA :LAB. :HIPS :INDEP.

SIVARAMAKRISHNAN,K ; FIRS: LYS ,T CIT: 0.00
EARNINGS EXPECTATIONS AND CAPITAL RESTRUCTURING: THE CASE OF EQUITY-FOR-DEBT
   SWAPS
JAR AU 88 VOL: 26 PG:273 - 299 :: REGRESS. :PRIM. :EMH :LTD

SKERRATT,CL ; FIRS: PEASNELL,KV CIT: 0.33
HOW WELL DOES A SINGLE INDEX REPRESENT THE NINETEEN SANDILANDS PLANT AND
   MACHINERY INDICES?
JAR SP 77 VOL: 15 PG:108 - 119 :: CORR. :PRIM. :THEORY :VALUAT.(INFL.)

SKERRATT,LC CIT: 0.00
THE BIAS IN CURRENT COST INCOME: AN EXTENSION
JAA SU 84 VOL: 7 PG:362 - 368 :: ANAL. :INT. LOG. :THEORY :VALUAT.(INFL.)

SKINNER,RC CIT: 0.14
FIXED ASSET LIVES AND REPLACEMENT COST ACCOUNTING
JAR SP 82 VOL: 20 PG:210 - 226 :: DES.STAT. :PRIM. :THEORY :PP&E / DEPR

SKOUSEN,KF ; FIRS: MAUTZ ,RK CIT: 0.00
SOME PROBLEMS IN EMPIRICAL RESEARCH IN ACCOUNTING
TAR JL 69 VOL: 44 PG:447 - 456 :: QUAL. :INT. LOG. :N/A :OTH.MANAG.

SLAIN ,J ; FIRS: SORTER,GH ; SEC: SIEGEL,S CIT: 0.00
ACCOUNTANTS' LEGAL LIABILITY: A DETERMINANT OF THE ACCOUNTING MODEL
JAA SU 88 VOL: 03 PG:233 - 244 :: DES.STAT. :INT. LOG. :THEORY :LIAB.

SLAVIN,NS CIT: 0.00
THE ELIMINATION OF 'SCIENTER' IN DETERMINING THE AUDITOR'S STATUTORY LIABILITY
TAR AP 77 VOL: 52 PG:360 - 368 :: QUAL. :SEC. :THEORY :LIAB.

SMIDT ,S ; FIRS: BIERMAN JR,H CIT: 0.00
ACCOUNTING FOR DEBT AND COSTS OF LIQUIDITY UNDER CONDITIONS OF UNCERTAINTY
JAR AU 67 VOL: 5 PG:144 - 153 :: ANAL. :INT. LOG. :THEORY :LTD

SMIDT ,S ; FIRS: GOLDSCHMIDT,Y CIT: 0.00
VALUING THE FIRM'S DURABLE ASSETS FOR MANAGERIAL INFORMATION
TAR AP 69 VOL: 44 PG:317 - 329 :: QUAL. :INT. LOG. :THEORY :VALUAT.(INFL.)

SMIELIAUSKAS,W ; FIRS: MENZEFRICKE,U CIT: 0.60
A SIMULATION STUDY OF THE PERFORMANCE OF PARAMETRIC DOLLAR UNIT SAMPLING
   STATISTICAL PROCEDURES
JAR AU 84 VOL: 22 PG:588 - 604 :: DES.STAT. :SIM. :OTH.STAT. :LIAB.

SMIELIAUSKAS,W CIT: 0.00
SENSITIVITY ANALYSIS OF THE REALIZED RISKS OF AUDITING WITH UNCERTAINTY
   CONCERNING INTERNAL CONTROL EVALUATIONS
JAR AU 85 VOL: 23 PG:718 - 739 :: REGRESS. :SIM. :OTH.STAT. :RISK

SMIELIAUSKAS,W ; FIRS: HAM ,J ; SEC: LOSELL,D CIT: 0.50
AN EMPIRICAL STUDY OF ERROR CHARACTERISTICS IN ACCOUNTING POPULATIONS
TAR JL 85 VOL: 60 PG:387 - 406 :: REGRESS. :PRIM. :OTH.STAT. :ERRORS

SMIELIAUSKAS,W CIT: 0.00
A NOTE ON COMPARISON OF BAYESIAN WITH NON-BAYESIAN DOLLAR-UNIT SAMPLING
   BOUNDS FOR OVERSTATEMENT ERRORS IN AUDITS
TAR JA 86 VOL: 61 PG:118 - 128 :: DES.STAT. :INT. LOG. :OTH.STAT. :SAMP.

SMIELIAUSKAS,W CIT: 0.00
A SIMULATION ANALYSIS OF THE POWER CHARACTERISTICS OF SOME POPULAR ESTIMATORS
    UNDER DIFFERENT RISK AND MATERIALITY LEVELS
JAR SP 86 VOL: 24 PG:217 - 230 :: DES.STAT. :SIM. :OTH.STAT. :SAMP.

SMITH ,A ; FIRS: ANTLE ,R CIT: 0.75
MEASURING EXECUTIVE COMPENSATION: METHODS AND AN APPLICATION
JAR SP 85 VOL: 23 PG:296 - 325 :: REGRESS. :PRIM. :OTH.STAT. :EXEC.COMP.

SMITH ,A ; FIRS: ANTLE ,R CIT: 0.67
AN EMPIRICAL INVESTIGATION OF THE RELATIVE PERFORMANCE EVALUATION OF
    CORPORATE EXECUTIVES
JAR SP 86 VOL: 24 PG:1 - 39 :: REGRESS. :PRIM. :OTH.STAT. :EXEC.COMP.

SMITH ,AJ ; FIRS: DYCKMAN,TR CIT: 2.40
FINANCIAL ACCOUNTING AND REPORTING BY OIL AND GAS PRODUCING COMPANIES: A
    STUDY OF INFORMATION EFFECTS
JAE MR 79 VOL: 1 PG:45 - 75 :: NON-PAR. :PRIM. :EMH :OIL & GAS

SMITH ,AJ CIT: 0.88
THE SEC "REVERSAL" OF FASB STATEMENT NO.19: AN INVESTIGATION OF INFORMATION
    EFFECTS
JAR ST 81 VOL: 19 PG:174 - 211 :: CORR. :PRIM. :EMH :OIL & GAS

SMITH ,CH ; SEC: LANIER,RA ; THIR: TAYLOR,ME CIT: 0.15
THE NEED FOR AND SCOPE OF THE AUDIT OF MANAGEMENT: A SURVEY OF ATTITUDES
TAR AP 72 VOL: 47 PG:270 - 283 :: DES.STAT. :SURV. :INSTIT. :AUD.

SMITH ,CH ; FIRS: BIRD ,FA ; SEC: DAVIDSON,LF CIT: 0.15
PERCEPTIONS OF EXTERNAL ACCOUNTING TRANSFERS UNDER ENTITY AND PROPRIETARY
    THEORY
TAR AP 74 VOL: 49 PG:233 - 244 :: QUAL. :INT. LOG. :THEORY :FIN.METH.

SMITH ,CH ; FIRS: WILCOX,KA CIT: 0.00
ROLE DISCREPANCIES AND THE AUDITOR-CLIENT RELATIONSHIP
AOS 01 77 VOL: 2 PG:81 - 97 :: NON-PAR. :FIELD :OTH.STAT. :AUD.

SMITH ,CH ; FIRS: PANY ,K CIT: 0.00
AUDITOR ASSOCIATION WITH QUARTERLY FINANCIAL INFORMATION: AN EMPIRICAL TEST
JAR AU 82 VOL: 20 PG:472 - 481 :: ANOVA :LAB. :OTH.BEH. :OPIN.

SMITH ,D ; FIRS: ETTREDGE,M ; SEC: SHANE ,PB CIT: 0.00
AUDIT FIRM SIZE AND THE ASSOCIATION BETWEEN REPORTED EARNINGS AND SECURITY
    RETURNS
AUD SP 88 VOL: 07 PG:29 - 42 :: REGRESS. :PRIM. :EMH :AUD.THEOR.

SMITH ,DB ; SEC: NICHOLS,DR CIT: 0.00
A MARKET TEST OF INVESTOR REACTION TO DISAGREEMENTS
JAE OC 82 VOL: 4 PG:109 - 120 :: DES.STAT. :SEC. :EMH :MAN.DEC.CHAR.

SMITH ,DB ; FIRS: NICHOLS,DR CIT: 0.33
AUDITOR CREDIBILITY AND AUDITOR CHANGES
JAR AU 83 VOL: 21 PG:534 - 544 :: REGRESS. :PRIM. :EMH :AUD.

SMITH ,DB ; SEC: STETTLER,HF ; THIR: BEEDLES,W CIT: 0.00
AN INVESTIGATION OF THE INFORMATION CONTENT OF FOREIGN SENSITIVE PAYMENT
    DISCLOSURES
JAE AG 84 VOL: 6 PG:153 - 162 :: REGRESS. :PRIM. :EMH :N/A

SMITH ,DB CIT: 0.33
AUDITOR "SUBJECT TO" OPINIONS, DISCLAIMERS, AND AUDITOR CHANGES
AUD AU 86 VOL: 6 PG:95 - 108 :: DES.STAT. :PRIM. :OTH.STAT. :OPIN.

SMITH ,DB CIT: 0.00
AN INVESTIGATION OF SECURITIES AND EXCHANGE COMMISSION REGULATION OF AUDITOR
CHANGE DISCLOSURES: THE CASE OF ACCOUNTING SERIES RELEASE NO.165
JAR SP 88 VOL: 26 PG:134 - 145 :: REGRESS. :PRIM. :EMH :AUD.THEOR.

SMITH ,ED CIT: 0.77
THE EFFECT OF SEPARATION OF OWNERSHIP FROM CONTROL ON ACCOUNTING POLICY
DECISIONS
TAR OC 76 VOL: 51 PG:707 - 723 :: NON-PAR. :PRIM. :OTH. :FIN.METH.

SMITH ,ED ; FIRS: DHALIWAL,DS ; SEC: SALAMON,GL CIT: 1.86
THE EFFECT OF OWNER VERSUS MANAGEMENT CONTROL ON THE CHOICE OF ACCOUNTING
METHODS
JAE JL 82 VOL: 4 PG:41 - 53 :: NON-PAR. :SEC. :TIME SER. :AMOR./DEPL.

SMITH ,G ; SEC: KROGSTAD,JL CIT: 0.20
IMPACT OF SOURCES AND AUTHORS ON AUDITING: A JOURNAL OF PRACTICE & THEORY - A
CITATION ANALYSIS
AUD AU 84 VOL: 4 PG:107 - 117 :: DES.STAT. :SEC. :OTH.STAT. :METHOD.

SMITH ,G CIT: 0.00
A TAXONOMY OF CONTENT AND CITATIONS IN AUDITING: A JOURNAL OF PRACTICE AND
THEORY
AUD AU 88 VOL: 08 PG:108 - 117 :: REGRESS. :SEC. :THEORY :METHOD.

SMITH ,JE ; SEC: SMITH ,NP CIT: 0.31
READABILITY: A MEASURE OF THE PERFORMANCE OF THE COMMUNICATION FUNCTION OF
FINANCIAL REPORTING
TAR JL 71 VOL: 46 PG:552 - 561 :: NON-PAR. :PRIM. :N/A :OTH.MANAG.

SMITH ,JH ; FIRS: LEMBKE,VC CIT: 0.00
REPLACEMENT COSTS: AN ANALYSIS OF FINANCIAL STATEMENT AND TAX POLICY EFFECTS
JAA WI 80 VOL: 3 PG:147 - 162 :: DES.STAT. :PRIM. :THEORY :VALUAT.(INFL.)

SMITH ,JH ; FIRS: DEJONG,DV CIT: 0.00
THE DETERMINATION OF AUDIT RESPONSIBILITIES: AN APPLICATION OF AGENCY THEORY
AUD AU 84 VOL: 4 PG:20 - 34 :: QUAL. :INT. LOG. :INF.ECO./AG. :LIAB.

SMITH ,KA CIT: 0.15
THE RELATIONSHIP OF INTERNAL CONTROL EVALUATION AND AUDIT SAMPLE SIZE
TAR AP 72 VOL: 47 PG:260 - 269 :: ANAL. :INT. LOG. :OTH.STAT. :SAMP.

SMITH ,NP ; FIRS: SMITH ,JE CIT: 0.31
READABILITY: A MEASURE OF THE PERFORMANCE OF THE COMMUNICATION FUNCTION OF
FINANCIAL REPORTING
TAR JL 71 VOL: 46 PG:552 - 561 :: NON-PAR. :PRIM. :N/A :OTH.MANAG.

SMITH ,RE ; FIRS: NORTON,CL CIT: 0.30
A COMPARISON OF GENERAL PRICE LEVEL AND HISTORICAL COST FINANCIAL STATEMENTS
IN THE PREDICTION OF BANKRUPTCY
TAR JA 79 VOL: 54 PG:72 - 87 :: OTH.QUANT. :PRIM. :OTH.STAT. :VALUAT.(INFL.)

SMITH ,VL ; FIRS: MANES ,RP CIT: 0.00
ECONOMIC JOINT COST THEORY AND ACCOUNTING PRACTICE
TAR JA 65 VOL: 40 PG:31 - 35 :: ANAL. :INT. LOG. :N/A :COST.ALLOC.

SMITH ,VL ; SEC: SCHATZBERG,J ; THIR: WALLER,WS CIT: 0.00
EXPERIMENTAL ECONOMICS AND AUDITING
AUD AU 87 VOL: 7 PG:71 - 93 :: DES.STAT. :INT. LOG. :OTH. :METHOD.

SMITH JR,JM ; FIRS: PURDY ,CR ; THIR: GRAY J CIT: 0.00
THE VISIBILITY OF THE AUDITOR'S DISCLOSURE OF DEVIANCE FROM APB OPINION: AN
EMPIRICAL TEST
JAR ST 69 VOL: 7 PG:1 - 18 :: ANOVA :LAB. :OTH.BEH. :INFO.STRUC.

SMOLINSKI,EJ CIT: 0.00
THE ADJUNCT METHOD IN CONSOLIDATIONS
JAR AU 63 VOL: 1 PG:149 - 178 :: QUAL. :INT. LOG. :THEORY :BUS.COMB.

SMYTH ,DJ ; FIRS: MANES ,RP ; SEC: SAMUELS,JM CIT: 0.00
INVENTORIES AND SALES: A CROSS SECTION STUDY
JAR ST 67 VOL: 5 PG:139 - 156 :: REGRESS. :PRIM. :THEORY :INV.

SNAVELY,HJ CIT: 0.15
ACCOUNTING INFORMATION CRITERIA
TAR AP 67 VOL: 42 PG:223 - 232 :: QUAL. :INT. LOG. :THEORY :FIN.METH.

SNAVELY,HJ CIT: 0.08
CURRENT COST FOR LONG-LIVED ASSETS: A CRITICAL VIEW
TAR AP 69 VOL: 44 PG:344 - 353 :: QUAL. :INT. LOG. :THEORY :VALUAT.(INFL.)

SNODGRASS,C ; FIRS: BIRNBERG,JG CIT: 0.00
CULTURE AND CONTROL: A FIELD STUDY
AOS 05 88 VOL: 13 PG:447 - 464 :: REGRESS. :SURV. :OTH.BEH. :INT.DIFF.

SNOWBALL,D CIT: 0.56
SOME EFFECTS OF ACCOUNTING EXPERTISE AND INFORMATION LOAD: AN EMPIRICAL STUDY
AOS 03 80 VOL: 5 PG:323 - 340 :: ANOVA :LAB. :HIPS :AUD.BEH.

SNOWBALL,D ; FIRS: ABDEL-KHALIK,AR ; THIR: WRAGGE,JH CIT: 0.00
THE EFFECTS OF CERTAIN INTERNAL AUDIT VARIABLES ON THE PLANNING OF EXTERNAL
AUDIT PROGRAMS
TAR AP 83 VOL: 58 PG:215 - 227 :: ANOVA :LAB. :OTH.BEH. :INT.AUD.

SNOWBALL,D CIT: 0.00
ACCOUNTING LABORATORY EXPERIMENTS ON HUMAN JUDGMENT: SOME CHARACTERISTICS AND
INFLUENCES
AOS 01 86 VOL: 11 PG:47 - 70 :: REGRESS. :SEC. :HIPS :METHOD.

SNOWBALL,D ; FIRS: BAMBER,EM CIT: 0.00
AN EXPERIMENTAL STUDY OF THE EFFECTS OF AUDIT STRUCTURE IN UNCERTAIN TASK
ENVIRONMENTS
AUD JL 88 VOL: 63 PG:490 - 504 :: REGRESS. :LAB. :OTH.BEH. :JUDG.

SOETERS,J ; SEC: SCHREUDER,H CIT: 0.00
THE INTERACTION BETWEEN NATIONAL AND ORGANIZATIONAL CULTURES IN ACCOUNTING
FIRMS
AOS 01 88 VOL: 13 PG:75 - 85 :: REGRESS. :SURV. :OTH.BEH. :AUD.BEH.

SOLOMON,I CIT: 1.14
PROBABILITY ASSESSMENT BY INDIVIDUAL AUDITORS AND AUDIT TEAMS: AN EMPIRICAL
INVESTIGATION
JAR AU 82 VOL: 20 PG:689 - 710 :: DES.STAT. :LAB. :HIPS :AUD.BEH.

SOLOMON,I ; SEC: KROGSTAD,JL ; THIR: ROMNEY,MB ; FOUR: TOMASSINI,LA CIT: 0.57
AUDITORS' PRIOR PROBABILITY DISTRIBUTIONS FOR ACCOUNT BALANCES
AOS 01 82 VOL: 7 PG:27 - 42 :: DES.STAT. :LAB. :HIPS :PROB.ELIC.

SOLOMON,I ; FIRS: BECK ,PJ CIT: 0.00
EX POST SAMPLING RISKS AND DECISION RULE CHOICE IN SUBSTANTIVE TESTING
AUD SP 85 VOL: 4 PG:1 - 10 :: DES.STAT. :INT. LOG. :OTH.STAT. :SAMP.

SOLOMON,I ; FIRS: BECK ,PJ ; THIR: TOMASSINI,LA CIT: 0.25
SUBJECTIVE PRIOR PROBABILITY DISTRIBUTIONS AND AUDIT RISK
JAR SP 85 VOL: 23 PG:37 - 56 :: REGRESS. :INT. LOG. :OTH.BEH. :RISK

SOLOMON,I ; FIRS: SCHROEDER,MS ; THIR: VICKREY,DW CIT: 0.00
AUDIT QUALITY: THE PERCEPTIONS OF AUDIT-COMMITTEE CHAIRPERSONS AND AUDIT
  PARTNERS
AUD SP 86 VOL: 5 PG:86 - 94 :: REGRESS. :SURV. :OTH.BEH. :OPER.AUD.

SOLOMON,I ; FIRS: BROWN ,C CIT: 0.00
EFFECTS OF OUTCOME INFORMATION ON EVALUATIONS OF MANAGERIAL DECISIONS
TAR JL 87 VOL: 62 PG:564 - 577 :: REGRESS. :LAB. :OTH.BEH. :BUDG.& PLAN.

SOLOMON,I ; FIRS: SHIELDS,MD ; THIR: WALLER,WS CIT: 0.00
EFFECTS OF ALTERNATIVE SAMPLE SPACE REPRESENTATIONS ON THE ACCURACY OF
  AUDITORS' UNCERTAINTY JUDGEMENTS
AOS 04 87 VOL: 12 PG:375 - 385 :: REGRESS. :LAB. :HIPS :MAN.DEC.CHAR.

SOLOMON,KI ; FIRS: KAPLAN,HG CIT: 0.00
REGULATION OF THE ACCOUNTING PROFESSION IN ISRAEL
TAR JA 64 VOL: 39 PG:145 - 149 :: QUAL. :INT. LOG. :INSTIT. :OTH.MANAG.

SOLOMONS,D CIT: 0.00
BREAKEVEN ANALYSIS UNDER ABSORPTION COSTING
TAR JL 68 VOL: 43 PG:447 - 452 :: ANAL. :INT. LOG. :N/A :C-V-P-A

SOMEYA,K CIT: 0.00
THE USE OF FUNDS STATEMENTS IN JAPAN
TAR OC 64 VOL: 39 PG:983 - 989 :: DES.STAT. :SURV. :INSTIT. :MANAG.

SOMMERFELD,RM CIT: 0.00
TAX IMPLICATIONS FOR THE VISITING PROFESSOR
TAR OC 67 VOL: 42 PG:747 - 750 :: QUAL. :INT. LOG. :N/A :TAXES

SOPER ,FJ ; SEC: DOLPHIN,R CIT: 0.08
READABILITY AND CORPORATE ANNUAL REPORTS
TAR AP 64 VOL: 39 PG:358 - 362 :: DES.STAT. :PRIM. :N/A :OTH.MANAG.

SORENSEN,JE CIT: 0.69
PROFESSIONAL AND BUREAUCRATIC ORGANIZATION IN THE PUBLIC ACCOUNTING FIRM
TAR JL 67 VOL: 42 PG:553 - 565 :: ANOVA :SURV. :OTH.BEH. :AUD.BEH.

SORENSEN,JE CIT: 0.54
BAYESIAN ANALYSIS IN AUDITING
TAR JL 69 VOL: 44 PG:555 - 561 :: ANAL. :INT. LOG. :OTH.STAT. :SAMP.

SORENSEN,JE ; SEC: FRANKS,DD CIT: 0.15
THE RELATIVE CONTRIBUTION OF ABILITY, SELF-ESTEEM AND EVALUATIVE FEEDBACK TO
  PERFORMANCE: IMPLICATIONS FOR ACCOUNTING SYSTEMS
TAR OC 72 VOL: 47 PG:735 - 746 :: ANOVA :FIELD :OTH.BEH. :OTH.MANAG.

SORENSEN,JE ; SEC: GROVE ,HD CIT: 0.08
COST-OUTCOME AND COST-EFFECTIVENESS ANALYSIS: EMERGING NONPROFIT PERFORMANCE
EVALUATION TECHNIQUES
TAR JL 77 VOL: 52 PG:658 - 675 :: ANAL. :SEC. :OTH.STAT. :REL.COSTS

SORENSEN,JE ; FIRS: RHODE ,JG ; THIR: LAWLER III,EE CIT: 0.67
SOURCES OF PROFESSIONAL STAFF TURNOVER IN PUBLIC ACCOUNTING FIRMS REVEALED BY
THE EXIT INTERVIEW
AOS 02 77 VOL: 2 PG:165 - 176 :: NON-PAR. :SURV. :OTH. :ORG.

SORENSEN,R ; FIRS: GROVES,R ; SEC: MANES ,RP CIT: 0.08
THE APPLICATION OF THE HIRSCH-DANTZIG "FIXED CHARGE" ALGORITHM TO PROFIT
PLANNING: A FORMAL STATEMENT OF PRODUCT PROFITABILITY ANALYSIS
TAR JL 70 VOL: 45 PG:481 - 489 :: ANAL. :INT. LOG. :MATH.PROG. :BUDG.& PLAN.

SORTER,GH ; FIRS: HORNGREN,CT CIT: 0.00
AN EVALUATION OF SOME CRITICISMS OF RELEVANT COSTING
TAR AP 64 VOL: 39 PG:417 - 420 :: QUAL. :INT. LOG. :N/A :COST.ALLOC.

SORTER,GH ; SEC: BECKER,S ; THIR: ARCHIBALD,TR ; FOUR: BEAVER,WH CIT: 0.46
CORPORATE PERSONALITY AS REFLECTED IN ACCOUNTING DECISIONS: SOME PRELIMINARY
FINDINGS
JAR AU 64 VOL: 2 PG:183 - 196 :: ANOVA :SURV. :THEORY :ORG.FORM

SORTER,GH CIT: 1.00
AN "EVENTS" APPROACH TO BASIC ACCOUNTING THEORY
TAR JA 69 VOL: 44 PG:12 - 19 :: QUAL. :INT. LOG. :THEORY :INFO.STRUC.

SORTER,GH ; FIRS: ROSE ,R ; SEC: BEAVER,WH ; THIR: BECKER,S CIT: 0.77
TOWARD AN EMPIRICAL MEASURE OF MATERIALITY
JAR ST 70 VOL: 8 PG:138 - 148 :: DES.STAT. :LAB. :OTH.BEH. :MAT.

SORTER,GH ; FIRS: BECKER,S ; SEC: RONEN ,J CIT: 0.38
OPPORTUNITY COSTS - AN EXPERIMENTAL APPROACH
JAR AU 74 VOL: 12 PG:317 - 329 :: ANOVA :LAB. :OTH.BEH. :REL.COSTS

SORTER,GH ; SEC: GANS ,MS CIT: 0.00
OPPORTUNITIES AND IMPLICATIONS OF THE REPORT ON OBJECTIVES OF FINANCIAL
STATEMENTS
JAR ST 74 VOL: 12 PG:1 - 12 :: QUAL. :INT. LOG. :THEORY :FIN.METH.

SORTER,GH ; FIRS: SCHIFF,M ; THIR: WIESEN,JL CIT: 0.00
THE EVOLVING ROLE OF CORPORATE AUDIT COMMITTEES
JAA AU 77 VOL: 1 PG:19 - 44 :: QUAL. :INT. LOG. :INSTIT. :OTH.MANAG.

SORTER,GH ; FIRS: INGBERMAN,M CIT: 0.00
THE ROLE OF FINANCIAL STATEMENTS IN AN EFFICIENT MARKET
JAA AU 78 VOL: 2 PG:58 - 62 :: QUAL. :INT. LOG. :INSTIT. :FIN.METH.

SORTER,GH CIT: 0.00
THE EMPHASIS ON CASH AND ITS IMPACT ON THE FUNDS STATEMENT - SENSE AND NONSE
JAA SP 82 VOL: 5 PG:188 - 194 :: QUAL. :INT. LOG. :THEORY :CASH

SORTER,GH ; SEC: INGBERMAN,M CIT: 0.00
THE IMPLICIT CRITERIA FOR THE RECOGNITION, QUANTIFICATION , AND REPORTING OF
ACCOUNTING EVENTS
JAA SP 87 VOL: 2 PG:99 - 116 :: DES.STAT. :INT. LOG. :THEORY :REV.REC.

SORTER,GH ; SEC: SIEGEL,S ; THIR: SLAIN ,J CIT: 0.00
ACCOUNTANTS' LEGAL LIABILITY: A DETERMINANT OF THE ACCOUNTING MODEL
JAA SU 88 VOL: 03 PG:233 - 244 :: DES.STAT. :INT. LOG. :THEORY :LIAB.

SOTTO ,R CIT: 0.00
SCIENTIFIC UTOPIA AND ACCOUNTING
AOS 01 83 VOL: 8 PG:57 - 72 :: QUAL. :INT. LOG. :THEORY :N/A

SOUDERS,TL ; FIRS: KILLOUGH,LN CIT: 0.31
A GOAL PROGRAMMING MODEL FOR PUBLIC ACCOUNTING FIRMS
TAR AP 73 VOL: 48 PG:268 - 279 :: ANAL. :INT. LOG. :MATH.PROG. :ORG.

SPACEK,L CIT: 0.00
A SUGGESTED SOLUTION TO THE PRINCIPLES DILEMMA
TAR AP 64 VOL: 39 PG:275 - 284 :: QUAL. :INT. LOG. :THEORY :OTH.FIN.ACC.

SPENCER,CH ; SEC: BARNISEL,TS CIT: 0.00
A DECADE OF PRICE-LEVEL CHANGES - THE EFFECT ON THE FINANCIAL STATEMENTS OF
  CUMMINS ENGINE COMPANY
TAR JA 65 VOL: 40 PG:144 - 153 :: DES.STAT. :CASE :THEORY :VALUAT.(INFL.)

SPENCER,MH CIT: 0.00
AXIOMATIC METHOD AND ACCOUNTING SCIENCE
TAR AP 63 VOL: 38 PG:310 - 316 :: QUAL. :INT. LOG. :THEORY :OTH.MANAG.

SPERO ,LL ; FIRS: RAMAGE,JG ; SEC: KRIEGER,AM CIT: 0.90
AN EMPIRICAL STUDY OF ERROR CHARACTERISTICS IN AUDIT POPULATIONS
JAR ST 79 VOL: 17 PG:72 - 102 :: DES.STAT. :PRIM. :OTH.STAT. :ERRORS

SPICER,BH ; FIRS: SHANE ,PB CIT: 0.50
MARKET RESPONSE TO ENVIRONMENTAL INFORMATION PRODUCED OUTSIDE THE FIRM
TAR JL 83 VOL: 58 PG:521 - 538 :: DES.STAT. :PRIM. :EMH :ORG.& ENVIR.

SPICER,BH ; SEC: BALLEW,V CIT: 1.00
MANAGEMENT ACCOUNTING SYSTEMS AND THE ECONOMICS OF INTERNAL ORGANIZATION
AOS 01 83 VOL: 8 PG:73 - 98 :: QUAL. :INT. LOG. :THEORY :MANAG.

SPICER,BH CIT: 0.00
TOWARDS AN ORGANIZATIONAL THEORY OF THE TRANSFER PRICING PROCESS
AOS 03 88 VOL: 13 PG:303 - 322 :: DES.STAT. :INT. LOG. :THEORY :TRANS.PRIC.

SPICER,BM CIT: 0.73
INVESTORS, CORPORATE SOCIAL PERFORMANCE AND INFORMATION DISCLOSURE: AN
  EMPIRICAL STUDY
TAR JA 78 VOL: 53 PG:94 - 111 :: NON-PAR. :PRIM. :OTH.STAT. :HRA

SPILLER JR,EA CIT: 0.00
THEORY AND PRACTICE IN THE DEVELOPMENT OF ACCOUNTING
TAR OC 64 VOL: 39 PG:850 - 859 :: QUAL. :INT. LOG. :THEORY :FIN.METH.

SPILLER JR,EA ; SEC: VIRGIL JR,RL CIT: 0.08
EFFECTIVENESS OF APB OPINION NO.19 IN IMPROVING FUNDS REPORTING
JAR SP 74 VOL: 12 PG:112 - 142 :: DES.STAT. :LAB. :THEORY :INFO.STRUC.

SPROUSE,RT CIT: 0.00
HISTORICAL COSTS AND CURRENT ASSETS - TRADITIONAL AND TREACHEROUS
TAR OC 63 VOL: 38 PG:687 - 695 :: QUAL. :INT. LOG. :THEORY :VALUAT.(INFL.)

SPROUSE,RT CIT: 0.00
OBSERVATIONS CONCERNING THE REALIZATION CONCEPT
TAR JL 65 VOL: 40 PG:522 - 526 :: QUAL. :INT. LOG. :THEORY :VALUAT.(INFL.)

SRINIDHI,BN ; SEC: VASARHELYI,MA CIT: 0.00
AUDITOR JUDGMENT CONCERNING ESTABLISHMENT OF SUBSTANTIVE TESTS BASED ON
INTERNAL CONTROL RELIABILITY
AUD SP 86 VOL: 5 PG:64 - 76 :: REGRESS. :LAB. :OTH.STAT. :INT.CONT.

SRINIDHI,BN ; FIRS: HALPERIN,R CIT: 0.00
THE EFFECTS OF THE U.S. INCOME TAX REGULATIONS' TRANSFER PRICING RULES
ON ALLOCATIVE EFFICIENCY
TAR OC 87 VOL: 62 PG:686 - 706 :: REGRESS. :INT. LOG. :THEORY :TRANS.PRIC.

SRINIDHI,BN ; FIRS: BALACHANDRAN,KR CIT: 0.00
A RATIONALE FOR FIXED CHARGE APPLICATION
JAA SP 87 VOL: 2 PG:151 - 169 :: DES.STAT. :INT. LOG. :MATH.PROG. :COST.ALLOC.

SRIVASTAVA,RP CIT: 0.00
AUDITING FUNCTIONS FOR INTERNAL CONTROL SYSTEMS WITH INTERDEPENDENT
DOCUMENTS AND CHANNELS
JAR AU 86 VOL: 24 PG:422 - 427 :: DES.STAT. :INT. LOG. :OTH.STAT. :INT.CONT.

ST.PIERRE,K ; SEC: ANDERSON,JA CIT: 0.00
AN ANALYSIS OF AUDIT FAILURES BASED ON DOCUMENTED LEGAL CASES
JAA SP 82 VOL: 5 PG:229 - 247 :: DES.STAT. :PRIM. :OTH. :ERRORS

ST.PIERRE,K ; SEC: ANDERSON,JA CIT: 0.40
AN ANALYSIS OF THE FACTORS ASSOCIATED WITH LAWSUITS AGAINST PUBLIC ACCOUNTANTS
TAR AP 84 VOL: 59 PG:242 - 263 :: DES.STAT. :PRIM. :INSTIT. :LIAB.

ST.PIERRE,K CIT: 0.00
INDEPENDENCE AND AUDITOR SANCTIONS
JAA SP 84 VOL: 7 PG:257 - 263 :: QUAL. :INT. LOG. :OTH. :INDEP.

STAATS,EB CIT: 0.00
AUDITING AS WE ENTER THE 21ST CENTURY - WHAT NEW CHALLENGES WILL HAVE TO BE
MET
AUD SU 81 VOL: 1 PG:1 - 11 :: QUAL. :INT. LOG. :INSTIT. :AUD.

STAGLIANO,AJ ; FIRS: RECKERS,PMJ CIT: 0.13
NON-AUDIT SERVICES AND PERCEIVED INDEPENDENCE: SOME NEW EVIDENCE
AUD SU 81 VOL: 1 PG:23 - 37 :: ANOVA :LAB. :OTH.BEH. :INDEP.

STAHL ,MJ ; FIRS: HARRELL,AM CIT: 0.00
MCCLELLAND'S TRICHOTOMY OF NEEDS THEORY AND THE JOB SATISFACTION AND WORK
PERFORMANCE OF CPA FIRM PROFESSIONALS
AOS 34 84 VOL: 9 PG:241 - 252 :: CORR. :LAB. :OTH.BEH. :AUD.BEH.

STALLMAN,JC CIT: 0.38
TOWARD EXPERIMENTAL CRITERIA FOR JUDGING DISCLOSURE IMPROVEMENT
JAR ST 69 VOL: 7 PG:29 - 43 :: ANOVA :LAB. :OTH.STAT. :INFO.STRUC.

STALLMAN,JC CIT: 0.08
A FRAMEWORK FOR EVALUATING COST CONTROL PROCEDURES FOR A PROCESS
TAR OC 72 VOL: 47 PG:774 - 790 :: ANAL. :INT. LOG. :OTH.STAT. :MANAG.

STANDISH,PEM CIT: 0.00
AN APPRAISAL OF THE TEACHING AND STUDY OF AUDITING
TAR JL 64 VOL: 39 PG:654 - 666 :: QUAL. :INT. LOG. :INSTIT. :OTH.MANAG.

STANDISH,PEM ; SEC: UNG ,S CIT: 0.00
CORPORATE SIGNALING, ASSET REVALUATIONS, AND STOCK PRICES OF BRITISH COMPANIES
TAR OC 82 VOL: 57 PG:701 - 715 :: REGRESS. :PRIM. :EMH :VALUAT.(INFL.)

STANLEY,CH CIT: 0.00
COST-BASIS VALUATIONS IN TRANSACTIONS BETWEEN ENTITIES
TAR JL 64 VOL: 39 PG:639 - 647 :: QUAL. :INT. LOG. :THEORY :VALUAT.(INFL.)

STARK ,A ; FIRS: GROJER,JE CIT: 0.33
SOCIAL ACCOUNTING: A SWEDISH ATTEMPT
AOS 04 77 VOL: 2 PG:349 - 385 :: QUAL. :CASE :THEORY :HRA

STARKS,L ; FIRS: JENNINGS,R CIT: 0.25
INFORMATION CONTENT AND THE SPEED OF STOCK PRICE ADJUSTMENT
JAR SP 85 VOL: 23 PG:336 - 350 :: REGRESS. :PRIM. :EMH :N/A

STAUBUS,GJ CIT: 0.00
DIRECT, RELEVANT OR ABSORPTION COSTING?
TAR JA 63 VOL: 38 PG:64 - 74 :: QUAL. :INT. LOG. :THEORY :COST.ALLOC.

STAUBUS,GJ CIT: 0.15
THE ASSOCIATION OF FINANCIAL ACCOUNTING VARIABLES WITH COMMON STOCK VALUES
TAR JA 65 VOL: 40 PG:119 - 134 :: REGRESS. :PRIM. :TIME SER. :VALUAT.(INFL.)

STAUBUS,GJ CIT: 0.00
ALTERNATIVE ASSET FLOW CONCEPTS
TAR JL 66 VOL: 41 PG:397 - 412 :: QUAL. :INT. LOG. :N/A :INFO.STRUC.

STAUBUS,GJ CIT: 0.08
CURRENT CASH EQUIVALENT FOR ASSETS: A DISSENT
TAR OC 67 VOL: 42 PG:650 - 661 :: QUAL. :INT. LOG. :THEORY :VALUAT.(INFL.)

STAUBUS,GJ CIT: 0.00
TESTING INVENTORY ACCOUNTING
TAR JL 68 VOL: 43 PG:413 - 424 :: ANOVA :PRIM. :N/A :INV.

STAUBUS,GJ CIT: 0.08
THE EFFECTS OF PRICE-LEVEL RESTATEMENTS ON EARNINGS
TAR JL 76 VOL: 51 PG:574 - 589 :: QUAL. :INT. LOG. :THEORY :VALUAT.(INFL.)

STAUBUS,GJ CIT: 0.25
AN INDUCED THEORY OF ACCOUNTING MEASUREMENT
TAR JA 85 VOL: 60 PG:53 - 75 :: DES.STAT. :INT. LOG. :THEORY :INFO.STRUC.

STEADMAN,GT ; FIRS: MOORES,K CIT: 0.00
THE COMPARATIVE VIEWPOINTS OF GROUPS OF ACCOUNTANTS: MORE ON THE
    ENTITY-PROPRIETARY DEBATE
AOS 01 86 VOL: 11 PG:19 - 34 :: REGRESS. :SURV. :INSTIT. :FASB SUBM.

STEECE,BM ; FIRS: MOORE ,ML ; THIR: SWENSON,CW CIT: 0.00
SOME EMPIRICAL EVIDENCE ON TAXPAYER RATIONALITY
TAR JA 85 VOL: 60 PG:18 - 32 :: REGRESS. :PRIM. :TIME SER. :TAXES

STEECE,BM ; FIRS: MOORE ,ML ; THIR: SWENSON,CW CIT: 0.00
AN ANALYSIS OF THE IMPACT OF STATE INCOME TAX RATES AND BASES ON FOREIGN
    INVESTMENT
TAR OC 87 VOL: 62 PG:671 - 685 :: REGRESS. :PRIM. :TIME SER. :TAXES

STEINBART,PJ CIT: 0.00
MATERIALITY: A CASE STUDY USING EXPERT SYSTEMS
TAR JA 87 VOL: 62 PG:97 - 116 :: REGRESS. :INT. LOG. :EXP.SYST. :MAT.

STEINBART,PJ ; FIRS: LOEBBECKE,JK CIT: 0.00
AN INVESTIGATION OF THE USE OF PRELIMINARY ANALYTICAL REVIEW TO PROVIDE
  SUBSTANTIVE AUDIT EVIDENCE
AUD SP 87 VOL: 6 PG:74 - 89 :: REGRESS. :SIM. :OTH.STAT. :ANAL.REV.

STENING,BW ; FIRS: DAVISON,AG ; THIR: WAI ,WT CIT: 0.00
AUDITOR CONCENTRATION AND THE IMPACT OF INTERLOCKING DIRECTORATES
JAR SP 84 VOL: 22 PG:313 - 317 :: CORR. :PRIM. :OTH. :ORG.& ENVIR.

STEPHAN,J ; FIRS: DYCKMAN,TR ; SEC: PHILBRICK,D CIT: 0.60
A COMPARISON OF EVENT STUDY METHODOLOGIES USING DAILY STOCK RETURNS: A
  SIMULATION APPROACH
JAR ST 84 VOL: 22 PG:1 - 30 :: REGRESS. :SIM. :OTH.BEH. :METHOD.

STEPHENS,RG CIT: 0.00
AN INVESTIGATION OF THE DESCRIPTIVENESS OF THE GENERAL THEORY OF EVIDENCE AND
  AUDITING
AUD AU 83 VOL: 3 PG:55 - 74 :: NON-PAR. :LAB. :OTH.STAT. :JUDG.

STERLING,RR CIT: 0.08
ELEMENTS OF PURE ACCOUNTING THEORY
TAR JA 67 VOL: 42 PG:62 - 73 :: ANAL. :INT. LOG. :THEORY :FIN.METH.

STERLING,RR CIT: 0.08
THE GOING CONCERN: AN EXAMINATION
TAR JL 68 VOL: 43 PG:481 - 502 :: QUAL. :INT. LOG. :THEORY :OTH.FIN.ACC.

STERLING,RR ; SEC: RADOSEVICH,R CIT: 0.15
A VALUATION EXPERIMENT
JAR SP 69 VOL: 7 PG:90 - 95 :: DES.STAT. :LAB. :OTH. :AUD.

STERLING,RR CIT: 0.31
ON THEORY CONSTRUCTION AND VERIFICATION
TAR JL 70 VOL: 45 PG:444 - 457 :: QUAL. :INT. LOG. :THEORY :OTH.MANAG.

STERLING,RR ; SEC: FLAHERTY,RE CIT: 0.00
THE ROLE OF LIQUIDITY IN EXCHANGE VALUATION
TAR JL 71 VOL: 46 PG:441 - 456 :: ANAL. :INT. LOG. :THEORY :VALUAT.(INFL.)

STERLING,RR ; SEC: TOLLEFSON,SO ; THIR: FLAHERTY,RE CIT: 0.00
EXCHANGE VALUATION: AN EMPIRICAL TEST
TAR OC 72 VOL: 47 PG:709 - 721 :: DES.STAT. :LAB. :THEORY :VALUAT.(INFL.)

STERNER,JA CIT: 0.00
AN EMPIRICAL EVALUATION OF SFAS NO.55
JAR AU 83 VOL: 21 PG:623 - 628 :: OTH.QUANT. :PRIM. :OTH.STAT. :REV.REC.

STETTLER,HF CIT: 0.00
ACCREDITATION OF COLLEGIATE ACCOUNTING PROGRAMS
TAR OC 65 VOL: 40 PG:723 - 730 :: QUAL. :INT. LOG. :INSTIT. :OTH.MANAG.

STETTLER,HF ; FIRS: REILLY,FK CIT: 0.00
FACTORS INFLUENCING SUCCESS ON THE CPA EXAMINATION
JAR AU 72 VOL: 10 PG:308 - 321 :: REGRESS. :PRIM. :OTH.STAT. :EDUC.

STETTLER,HF ; FIRS: SMITH ,DB ; THIR: BEEDLES,W CIT: 0.00
AN INVESTIGATION OF THE INFORMATION CONTENT OF FOREIGN SENSITIVE PAYMENT
  DISCLOSURES
JAE AG 84 VOL: 6 PG:153 - 162 :: REGRESS. :PRIM. :EMH :N/A

STEUER,RE ; FIRS: BALACHANDRAN,KR CIT: 0.14
AN INTERACTIVE MODEL FOR THE CPA FIRM AUDIT STAFF PLANNING PROBLEM WITH
MULTIPLE OBJECTIVES
TAR JA 82 VOL: 57 PG:125 - 140 :: ANAL. :INT. LOG. :N/A :AUD.

STEVENSON,FL CIT: 0.50
NEW EVIDENCE ON LIFO ADOPTIONS: THE EFFECTS OF MORE PRECISE EVENT DATES
JAR AU 87 VOL: 25 PG:306 - 316 :: REGRESS. :PRIM. :EMH :INV.

STEVENSON,RA CIT: 0.00
CORPORATE STOCK REACQUISITIONS
TAR AP 66 VOL: 41 PG:312 - 317 :: QUAL. :CASE :N/A :INFO.STRUC.

STEVENSON,WC ; FIRS: WEBER ,RP CIT: 0.25
EVALUATIONS OF ACCOUNTING JOURNAL AND DEPARTMENT QUALITY
TAR JL 81 VOL: 56 PG:596 - 612 :: DES.STAT. :SIM. :OTH. :OTH.MANAG.

STICKEL,SE CIT: 0.00
THE EFFECT OF PREFERRED STOCK RATING CHANGES ON PREFERRED AND COMMON STOCK
PRICES
JAE OC 86 VOL: 8 PG:197 - 216 :: REGRESS. :PRIM. :EMH :LTD

STICKNEY,CP ; FIRS: ALIBER,RZ CIT: 0.15
ACCOUNTING MEASURES OF FOREIGN EXCHANGE EXPOSURE: THE LONG AND SHORT OF IT
TAR JA 75 VOL: 50 PG:44 - 57 :: QUAL. :INT. LOG. :INSTIT. :FOR.CUR.

STICKNEY,CP ; FIRS: CASEY JR,CJ ; SEC: MCGEE ,VE CIT: 0.33
DISCRIMINATING BETWEEN REORGANIZED AND LIQUIDATED FIRMS IN BANKRUPTCY
TAR AP 86 VOL: 61 PG:249 - 262 :: REGRESS. :PRIM. :OTH.STAT. :BUS.FAIL.

STOBER,TL CIT: 0.33
THE INCREMENTAL INFORMATION CONTENT OF FINANCIAL STATEMENT DISCLOSURES: THE
THE CASE OF LIFO INVENTORY LIQUIDATIONS
JAR ST 86 VOL: 24 PG:138 - 164 :: REGRESS. :PRIM. :EMH :INV.

STOCK ,D ; SEC: WATSON,CJ CIT: 0.40
HUMAN JUDGMENT ACCURACY, MULTIDIMENSIONAL GRAPHICS, AND HUMANS VERSUS MODEL
JAR SP 84 VOL: 22 PG:192 - 206 :: OTH.QUANT. :LAB. :HIPS :BUS.FAIL.

STOECKENIUS,J ; FIRS: NG   ,DS CIT: 0.60
AUDITING: INCENTIVES AND TRUTHFUL REPORTING
JAR ST 79 VOL: 17 PG:1 - 24 :: ANAL. :INT. LOG. :INF.ECO./AG. :AUD.

STOKES,DJ ; FIRS: FRANCIS,JR CIT: 0.67
AUDIT PRICES, PRODUCT DIFFERENTIATION, AND SCALE ECONOMIES: FURTHER
EVIDENCE FROM THE AUSTRALIAN MARKET
JAR AU 86 VOL: 24 PG:383 - 393 :: REGRESS. :PRIM. :OTH.STAT. :OPER.AUD.

STONE ,DE CIT: 0.00
THE OBJECTIVE OF FINANCIAL REPORTING IN THE ANNUAL REPORT
TAR AP 67 VOL: 42 PG:331 - 337 :: QUAL. :INT. LOG. :INSTIT. :FIN.METH.

STONE ,M ; SEC: BUBLITZ,B CIT: 0.20
AN ANALYSIS OF THE RELIABILITY OF THE FASB DATA BANK OF CHANGING PRICE AND
PENSION INFORMATION
TAR JL 84 VOL: 59 PG:469 - 473 :: DES.STAT. :PRIM. :OTH. :METHOD.

STONE ,M CIT: 0.00
A FINANCING EXPLANATION FOR OVERFUNDED PENSION PLAN TERMINATIONS
JAR AU 87 VOL: 25 PG:317 - 326 :: REGRESS. :PRIM. :OTH.STAT. :PENS.

STONE ,ML CIT: 0.00
PROBLEMS IN SEARCH OF SOLUTIONS THROUGH RESEARCH
JAR ST 68 VOL: 6 PG:59 - 66 :: QUAL. :INT. LOG. :INSTIT. :OTH.MANAG.

STONE ,WE CIT: 0.00
LEGAL IMPLICATIONS OF INTRACOMPANY PRICING
TAR JA 64 VOL: 39 PG:38 - 42 :: QUAL. :INT. LOG. :N/A :TRANS.PRIC.

STONE ,WE CIT: 0.08
ACCOUNTING DOCTORAL PROGRAMS IN AACSB COLLEGES OF BUSINESS ADMINISTRATION
TAR JA 65 VOL: 40 PG:190 - 195 :: DES.STAT. :PRIM. :INSTIT. :OTH.MANAG.

STONE ,WE CIT: 0.00
ANTECEDENTS OF THE ACCOUNTING PROFESSION
TAR AP 69 VOL: 44 PG:284 - 291 :: QUAL. :SEC. :HIST. :FIN.METH.

STONE ,WE CIT: 0.00
ABACISTS VERSUS ALGORISTS
JAR AU 72 VOL: 10 PG:345 - 350 :: QUAL. :INT. LOG. :HIST. :N/A

STOREY,J ; FIRS: HOPPER,T ; THIR: WILLMOTT,H CIT: 0.00
ACCOUNTING FOR ACCOUNTING: TOWARDS THE DEVELOPMENT OF A DIALECTICAL VIEW
AOS 05 87 VOL: 12 PG:437 - 456 :: DES.STAT. :INT. LOG. :THEORY :MANAG.

STOREY,R ; FIRS: ROSENFIELD,P CIT: 0.08
THE ACCOUNTING PRINCIPLES BOARD - A CORRECTION
TAR AP 66 VOL: 41 PG:327 - 330 :: QUAL. :INT. LOG. :INSTIT. :N/A

STRAND,KH ; FIRS: KROSS ,W ; SEC: CHAPMAN,G CIT: 0.00
FULLY DILUTED EARNINGS PER SHARE AND SECURITY RETURNS: SOME ADDITIONAL
    EVIDENCE
JAA AU 80 VOL: 4 PG:36 - 46 :: CORR. :SEC. :EMH :CASH DIV.

STRAWSER,JR ; FIRS: HARPER JR,RM ; SEC: MISTER,WG CIT: 0.00
THE IMPACT OF NEW PENSION DISCLOSURE RULES ON PERCEPTIONS OF DEBT
JAR AU 87 VOL: 25 PG:327 - 330 :: REGRESS. :LAB. :OTH.STAT. :PENS.

STRAWSER,RH ; FIRS: CARPENTER,CG CIT: 0.00
A STUDY OF THE JOB SATISFACTION OF ACADEMIC ACCOUNTANTS
TAR JL 71 VOL: 46 PG:509 - 518 :: NON-PAR. :SURV. :INSTIT. :OTH.MANAG.

STRAWSER,RH ; FIRS: COPELAND,RM ; SEC: FRANCIA,AJ CIT: 0.69
STUDENTS AS SUBJECTS IN BEHAVIOURAL BUSINESS RESEARCH
TAR AP 73 VOL: 48 PG:365 - 374 :: QUAL. :SURV. :OTH.BEH. :METHOD.

STRAWSER,RH ; FIRS: ROBBINS,WA ; SEC: APOSTOLOU,NG CIT: 0.00
MUNICIPAL ANNUAL REPORTS AND THE INFORMATION NEEDS OF INVESTORS
JAA SU 85 VOL: 8 PG:279 - 292 :: REGRESS. :PRIM. :THEORY :FIN.METH.

STRAWSER,RH ; FIRS: LICATA,MP ; THIR: WELKER,RB CIT: 0.00
A NOTE ON PARTICIPATION IN BUDGETING AND LOCUS OF CONTROL
TAR JA 86 VOL: 61 PG:112 - 117 :: REGRESS. :LAB. :OTH.BEH. :BUDG.& PLAN.

STREER,PJ CIT: 0.00
CONFORMING FINANCIAL AND TAX ACCOUNTING: WILL THE CONCEPTUAL FRAMEWORK HELP?
JAA SU 79 VOL: 2 PG:329 - 338 :: QUAL. :INT. LOG. :INSTIT. :FIN.METH.

STRINGER,KW CIT: 1.00
A STATISTICAL TECHNIQUE FOR ANALYTICAL REVIEW
JAR ST 75 VOL: 13 PG:1 - 9 :: QUAL. :INT. LOG. :OTH.STAT. :ANAL.REV.

STROCK,E ; FIRS: ELGERS,P ; SEC: CALLAHAN,C CIT: 0.00
THE EFFECT OF EARNINGS YIELDS UPON THE ASSOCIATION BETWEEN UNEXPECTED
EARNINGS AND SECURITY RETURNS; A RE-EXAMINATION
TAR OC 87 VOL: 62 PG:763 - 773 :: REGRESS. :PRIM. :EMH :METHOD.

STURROCK,T ; FIRS: THIES ,CF CIT: 0.00
WHAT DID INFLATION ACCOUNTING TELL US?
JAA AU 87 VOL: 2 PG:375 - 391 :: DES.STAT. :PRIM. :THEORY :VALUAT.(INFL.)

SUH   ,YS CIT: 0.50
COLLUSION AND NONCONTROLLABLE COST ALLOCATION
JAR ST 87 VOL: 25 PG:22 - 46 :: DES.STAT. :INT. LOG. :INF.ECO./AG. :COST.ALLOC.

SUH   ,YS CIT: 0.00
NONCONTROLLABLE COSTS AND OPTIMAL PERFORMANCE MEASUREMENTS
JAR SP 88 VOL: 26 PG:154 - 168 :: ANAL. :INT. LOG. :INF.ECO./AG. :REL.COSTS

SUMMERS,EL ; FIRS: CRUSE ,RB CIT: 0.00
ECONOMICS, ACCOUNTING PRACTICE AND ACCOUNTING RESEARCH STUDY NO.3
TAR JA 65 VOL: 40 PG:82 - 88 :: QUAL. :INT. LOG. :THEORY :FIN.METH.

SUMMERS,EL CIT: 0.00
OBSERVATION OF EFFECTS OF USING ALTERNATIVE REPORTING PRACTICES
TAR AP 68 VOL: 43 PG:257 - 265 :: ANOVA :PRIM. :N/A :FIN.METH.

SUMMERS,EL ; SEC: DESKINS,JW CIT: 0.00
A CLASSIFICATION SCHEMA OF METHODS FOR REPORTING EFFECTS OF RESOURCE PRICE
CHANGES
JAR SP 70 VOL: 8 PG:113 - 117 :: QUAL. :INT. LOG. :THEORY :VALUAT.(INFL.)

SUMMERS,EL CIT: 0.31
THE AUDIT STAFF ASSIGNMENT PROBLEM: A LINEAR PROGRAMMING ANALYSIS
TAR JL 72 VOL: 47 PG:443 - 453 :: ANAL. :INT. LOG. :MATH.PROG. :AUD.

SUMMERS,EL ; FIRS: CHEN ,K CIT: 0.25
A STUDY OF REPORTING PROBABILISTIC ACCOUNTING FIGURES
AOS 01 81 VOL: 6 PG:1 - 16 :: ANOVA :LAB. :HIPS :MANAG.

SUMNERS,GE ; SEC: WHITE ,RA ; THIR: CLAY JR,RJ CIT: 0.00
THE USE OF ENGAGEMENT LETTERS IN AUDIT, REVIEW, AND COMPILATION ENGAGEMENTS:
AN EMPIRICAL STUDY
AUD SP 87 VOL: 6 PG:116 - 122 :: REGRESS. :SURV. :OTH.BEH. :ORG.

SUNDEM,GL ; FIRS: MAY   ,RG CIT: 0.38
COST OF INFORMATION AND SECURITY PRICES: MARKET ASSOCIATION TESTS FOR
ACCOUNTING POLICY DECISIONS
TAR JA 73 VOL: 48 PG:80 - 94 :: ANAL. :INT. LOG. :EMH :INFO.STRUC.

SUNDEM,GL CIT: 0.38
EVALUATING SIMPLIFIED CAPITAL BUDGETING MODELS USING A TIME-STATE PREFERENCE
METRIC
TAR AP 74 VOL: 49 PG:306 - 320 :: ANAL. :INT. LOG. :N/A :CAP.BUDG.

SUNDEM,GL ; FIRS: MAY   ,RG CIT: 0.69
RESEARCH FOR ACCOUNTING POLICY: AN OVERVIEW
TAR OC 76 VOL: 51 PG:747 - 763 :: QUAL. :INT. LOG. :THEORY :FIN.METH.

SUNDEM,GL CIT: 0.50
A GAME THEORY MODEL OF THE INFORMATION EVALUATOR AND THE DECISION MAKER
JAR SP 79 VOL: 17 PG:243 - 261 :: ANAL. :INT. LOG. :INF.ECO./AG. :INFO.STRUC.

SUNDEM,GL ; FIRS: BOWEN ,RM CIT: 0.00
EDITORIAL AND PUBLICATION LAGS IN THE ACCOUNTING AND FINANCE LITERATURE
TAR OC 82 VOL: 57 PG:778 - 784 :: DES.STAT. :PRIM. :OTH. :N/A

SUNDER,S CIT: 2.23
RELATIONSHIP BETWEEN ACCOUNTING CHANGES AND STOCK PRICES: PROBLEMS OF
MEASUREMENT AND SOME EMPIRICAL EVIDENCE
JAR ST 73 VOL: 11 PG:1 - 45 :: REGRESS. :PRIM. :EMH :INV.

SUNDER,S CIT: 1.54
STOCK PRICE AND RISK RELATED TO ACCOUNTING CHANGES IN INVENTORY VALUATION
TAR AP 75 VOL: 50 PG:305 - 315 :: REGRESS. :PRIM. :EMH :INV.

SUNDER,S CIT: 0.54
A NOTE ON ESTIMATING THE ECONOMIC IMPACT OF THE LIFO METHOD OF INVENTORY
VALUATION
TAR AP 76 VOL: 51 PG:287 - 291 :: ANAL. :INT. LOG. :OTH.STAT. :INV.

SUNDER,S CIT: 0.54
OPTIMAL CHOICE BETWEEN FIFO AND LIFO
JAR AU 76 VOL: 14 PG:277 - 300 :: ANAL. :INT. LOG. :INF.ECO./AG. :INV.

SUNDER,S CIT: 0.77
PROPERTIES OF ACCOUNTING NUMBERS UNDER FULL COSTING AND SUCCESSFUL-EFFORTS
COSTING IN THE PETROLEUM INDUSTRY
TAR JA 76 VOL: 51 PG:1 - 18 :: ANAL. :INT. LOG. :OTH.STAT. :OIL & GAS

SUNDER,S CIT: 0.55
ACCURACY OF EXCHANGE VALUATION RULES
JAR AU 78 VOL: 16 PG:341 - 367 :: ANAL. :INT. LOG. :INSTIT. :VALUAT.(INFL.)

SUNDER,S ; FIRS: LEV   ,B CIT: 0.60
METHODOLOGICAL ISSUES IN THE USE OF FINANCIAL RATIOS
JAE DE 79 VOL: 1 PG:187 - 210 :: QUAL. :INT. LOG. :OTH.STAT. :METHOD.

SUNDER,S ; FIRS: PRAKASH,P CIT: 0.40
THE CASE AGAINST SEPARATION OF CURRENT OPERATING PROFIT AND HOLDING GAIN
TAR JA 79 VOL: 54 PG:1 - 22 :: QUAL. :INT. LOG. :THEORY :VALUAT.(INFL.)

SUNDER,S ; FIRS: DOPUCH,N CIT: 0.44
FASB'S STATEMENTS ON OBJECTIVES AND ELEMENTS OF FINANCIAL ACCOUNTING: A REVIEW
TAR JA 80 VOL: 55 PG:1 - 21 :: QUAL. :INT. LOG. :INSTIT. :FASB SUBM.

SUNDER,S ; FIRS: JOYCE ,EJ ; SEC: LIBBY ,R CIT: 0.00
USING THE FASB'S QUALITATIVE CHARACTERISTICS IN ACCOUNTING POLICY CHOICES
JAR AU 82 VOL: 20 PG:654 - 675 :: DES.STAT. :SURV. :INSTIT. :FASB SUBM.

SUNDER,S ; SEC: WAYMIRE,G CIT: 0.67
MARGINAL GAINS IN ACCURACY OF VALUATION FROM INCREASINGLY SPECIFIC PRICE
INDEXES: EMPIRICAL EVIDENCE FOR THE U.S. ECONOMY
JAR AU 83 VOL: 21 PG:565 - 580 :: MIXED :PRIM. :OTH.STAT. :VALUAT.(INFL.)

SUNDER,S CIT: 0.00
SIMPSON'S REVERSAL PARADOX AND COST ALLOCATION
JAR SP 83 VOL: 21 PG:222 - 233 :: ANAL. :INT. LOG. :OTH.STAT. :COST.ALLOC.

SUNDER,S ; SEC: WAYMIRE,G CIT: 0.60
ACCURACY OF EXCHANGE VALUATION RULES: ADDITIVITY AND UNBIASED ESTIMATION
JAR SP 84 VOL: 22 PG:396 - 405 :: ANAL. :INT. LOG. :THEORY :SPEC.ITEMS

SUNDER,S ; FIRS: AMERSHI,AH CIT: 0.00
FAILURE OF STOCK PRICES TO DISCIPLINE MANAGERS IN A RATIONAL EXPECTATIONS
    ECONOMY
JAR AU 87 VOL: 25 PG:177 - 195 :: DES.STAT. :INT. LOG. :INF.ECO./AG. :INV.

SURDICK,JJ ; FIRS: GAUMNITZ,BR ; SEC: NUNAMAKER,TR ; FOUR: THOMAS,MF CIT: 0.14
AUDITOR CONSENSUS IN INTERNAL CONTROL EVALUATION AND AUDIT PROGRAM PLANNING
JAR AU 82 VOL: 20 PG:745 - 755 :: CORR. :LAB. :HIPS :INT.CONT.

SUSSMAN,MR CIT: 0.00
PRESENT-VALUE SHORT CUTS
TAR AP 65 VOL: 40 PG:407 - 413 :: ANAL. :INT. LOG. :OTH.STAT. :OTH.MANAG.

SUTCLIFFE,P ; FIRS: LEWIS ,NR ; SEC: PARKER,LD CIT: 0.00
FINANCIAL REPORTING TO EMPLOYEES: THE PATTERN OF DEVELOPMENT 1919 TO 1979
AOS 34 84 VOL: 9 PG:275 - 289 :: DES.STAT. :SEC. :HIST. :HRA

SUTTON,TG CIT: 0.20
LOBBYING OF ACCOUNTING STANDARD-SETTING BODIES IN THE U.K. AND THE U.S.A.: A
    DOWNSIAN ANALYSIS
AOS 01 84 VOL: 9 PG:81 - 95 :: DES.STAT. :PRIM. :INSTIT. :FASB SUBM.

SUTTON,TG CIT: 0.00
THE PROPOSED INTRODUCTION OF CURRENT COST ACCOUNTING IN THE U.K.:
    DETERMINANTS OF CORPORATE PREFERENCE
JAE AP 88 VOL: 10 PG:127 - 149 :: REGRESS. :PRIM. :THEORY :VALUAT.(INFL.)

SVENSSON,G ; FIRS: JONSON,LC ; SEC: JONSSON,B CIT: 0.00
THE APPLICATION OF SOCIAL ACCOUNTING TO ABSENTEEISM AND PERSONNEL TURNOVER
AOS 34 78 VOL: 3 PG:261 - 268 :: DES.STAT. :CASE :OTH.BEH. :METHOD.

SWANSON,EB CIT: 0.18
THE TWO FACES OF ORGANIZATIONAL INFORMATION
AOS 34 78 VOL: 3 PG:237 - 248 :: QUAL. :INT. LOG. :OTH. :N/A

SWANSON,EP ; SEC: SHEARON,WT ; THIR: THOMAS,LR CIT: 0.00
PREDICTING CURRENT COST OPERATING PROFIT USING COMPONENT MODELS INCORPORATING
    ANALYSTS' FORECASTS
TAR OC 85 VOL: 60 PG:681 - 691 :: REGRESS. :PRIM. :TIME SER. :VALUAT.(INFL.)

SWANSON,EP ; FIRS: THOMAS,LR CIT: 0.00
ADDITIONAL CONSIDERATIONS WHEN USING THE FASB DATA BANK OF CHANGING PRICE
    INFORMATION
TAR AP 86 VOL: 61 PG:330 - 336 :: ANAL. :PRIM. :THEORY :VALUAT.(INFL.)

SWANSON,GA ; SEC: GARDNER,JC CIT: 0.00
NOT-FOR-PROFIT ACCOUNTING AND AUDITING IN THE EARLY EIGHTEENTH CENTURY: SOME
    ARCHIVAL EVIDENCE
TAR JL 88 VOL: 63 PG:436 - 447 :: REGRESS. :INT. LOG. :HIST. :AUD.

SWEENEY,JL ; FIRS: SWIERINGA,RJ ; SEC: GIBBINS,M ; THIR: LARSSON,L CIT: 1.85
EXPERIMENTS IN THE HEURISTICS OF HUMAN INFORMATION PROCESSING
JAR ST 76 VOL: 14 PG:159 - 187 :: MIXED :LAB. :HIPS :MANAG.

SWENSON,CW ; FIRS: MOORE ,ML ; SEC: STEECE,BM CIT: 0.00
SOME EMPIRICAL EVIDENCE ON TAXPAYER RATIONALITY
TAR JA 85 VOL: 60 PG:18 - 32 :: REGRESS. :PRIM. :TIME SER. :TAXES

SWENSON,CW CIT: 0.00
AN ANALYSIS OF ACRS DURING INFLATIONARY PERIODS
TAR JA 87 VOL: 62 PG:117 - 136 :: REGRESS. :SIM. :TIME SER. :VALUAT.(INFL.)

SWENSON,CW ; FIRS: MOORE ,ML ; SEC: STEECE,BM CIT: 0.00
AN ANALYSIS OF THE IMPACT OF STATE INCOME TAX RATES AND BASES ON FOREIGN
INVESTMENT
TAR OC 87 VOL: 62 PG:671 - 685 :: REGRESS. :PRIM. :TIME SER. :TAXES

SWIERINGA,RJ ; FIRS: CARMICHAEL,DR CIT: 0.00
THE COMPATIBILITY OF AUDITING INDEPENDENCE AND MANAGEMENT SERVICES: AN
IDENTIFICATION OF ISSUES
TAR OC 68 VOL: 43 PG:697 - 705 :: QUAL. :INT. LOG. :INSTIT. :INDEP.

SWIERINGA,RJ ; SEC: MONCUR,RH CIT: 0.46
THE RELATIONSHIP BETWEEN MANAGERS' BUDGET-ORIENTED BEHAVIOR AND SELECTED
ATTITUDE, POSITION, SIZE, AND PERFORMANCE MEASURES
JAR ST 72 VOL: 10 PG:194 - 209 :: OTH.QUANT. :FIELD :OTH.BEH. :BUDG.& PLAN.

SWIERINGA,RJ ; FIRS: DEMSKI,JS CIT: 0.62
A COOPERATIVE FORMULATION OF THE AUDIT CHOICE PROBLEM
TAR JL 74 VOL: 49 PG:506 - 513 :: ANAL. :INT. LOG. :OTH.STAT. :AUD.

SWIERINGA,RJ ; SEC: GIBBINS,M ; THIR: LARSSON,L ; FOUR: SWEENEY,JL CIT: 1.85
EXPERIMENTS IN THE HEURISTICS OF HUMAN INFORMATION PROCESSING
JAR ST 76 VOL: 14 PG:159 - 187 :: MIXED :LAB. :HIPS :MANAG.

SWIERINGA,RJ ; FIRS: HILTON,RW ; THIR: HOSKIN,RE CIT: 0.88
PERCEPTION OF ACCURACY AS A DETERMINANT OF INFORMATION VALUE
JAR SP 81 VOL: 19 PG:86 - 108 :: ANOVA :LAB. :OTH.BEH. :MANAG.

SWIERINGA,RJ ; FIRS: HILTON,RW CIT: 0.50
PERCEPTION OF INITIAL UNCERTAINTY AS A DETERMINANT OF INFORMATION VALUE
JAR SP 81 VOL: 19 PG:109 - 119 :: ANOVA :LAB. :HIPS :OTH.MANAG.

SWIERINGA,RJ ; SEC: WEICK ,KE CIT: 1.14
AN ASSESSMENT OF LABORATORY EXPERIMENTS IN ACCOUNTING
JAR ST 82 VOL: 20 PG:56 - 101 :: DES.STAT. :SEC. :OTH.BEH. :METHOD.

SWIERINGA,RJ ; FIRS: DYCKMAN,TR ; SEC: HOSKIN,RE CIT: 0.57
AN ACCOUNTING CHANGE AND INFORMATION PROCESSING CHANGES
AOS 01 82 VOL: 7 PG:1 - 12 :: REGRESS. :LAB. :HIPS :ACC.CHNG.

SWIERINGA,RJ ; SEC: WATERHOUSE,JH CIT: 0.29
ORGANIZATIONAL VIEWS OF TRANSFER PRICING
AOS 02 82 VOL: 7 PG:149 - 166 :: QUAL. :INT. LOG. :OTH. :TRANS.PRIC.

SWIERINGA,RJ ; SEC: WEICK ,KE CIT: 0.50
MANAGEMENT ACCOUNTING AND ACTION
AOS 03 87 VOL: 12 PG:293 - 308 :: DES.STAT. :INT. LOG. :HIST. :MANAG.

SWIERINGA,RJ ; FIRS: HILTON,RW ; THIR: TURNER,MJ CIT: 0.00
PRODUCT PRICING, ACCOUNTING COSTS AND USE OF PRODUCT-COSTING SYSTEMS
TAR AP 88 VOL: 63 PG:195 - 218 :: REGRESS. :LAB. :OTH.BEH. :REL.COSTS

TABOR ,RH CIT: 0.17
INTERNAL CONTROL EVALUATIONS AND AUDIT PROGRAM REVISIONS: SOME ADDITIONAL
EVIDENCE
JAR SP 83 VOL: 21 PG:348 - 354 :: MIXED :LAB. :OTH.BEH. :INT.CONT.

TABOR ,RH ; SEC: WILLIS,JT CIT: 0.00
EMPIRICAL EVIDENCE ON THE CHANGING ROLE OF ANALYTICAL REVIEW PROCEDURES
AUD SP 85 VOL: 4 PG:93 - 109 :: REGRESS. :PRIM. :OTH.STAT. :ANAL.REV.

TAMURA,H ; FIRS: FROST ,PA CIT: 0.57
JACKKNIFED RATIO ESTIMATION IN STATISTICAL AUDITING
JAR SP 82 VOL: 20 PG:103 - 120 :: DES.STAT. :SIM. :OTH.STAT. :SAMP.

TAMURA,H CIT: 0.00
ANALYSIS OF THE GARSTKA-OHLSON BOUNDS
AUD SP 85 VOL: 4 PG:133 - 142 :: DES.STAT. :INT. LOG. :OTH.STAT. :SAMP.

TAMURA,H ; SEC: FROST ,PA CIT: 0.33
TIGHTENING CAV (DUS) BOUNDS BY USING A PARAMETRIC MODEL
JAR AU 86 VOL: 24 PG:364 - 371 :: DES.STAT. :SIM. :OTH.STAT. :SAMP.

TAMURA,H ; FIRS: FROST ,PA CIT: 0.00
ACCURACY OF AUXILIARY INFORMATION INTERVAL ESTIMATION IN STATISTICAL
AUDITING
JAR SP 86 VOL: 24 PG:57 - 75 :: DES.STAT. :SIM. :OTH.STAT. :SAMP.

TAUSSIG,RA CIT: 0.00
GOVERNMENTAL ACCOUNTING: FUND FLOW OR SERVICE COST?
TAR JL 63 VOL: 38 PG:562 - 567 :: QUAL. :INT. LOG. :INSTIT. :FIN.METH.

TAUSSIG,RA CIT: 0.00
INFORMATION REQUIREMENTS OF REPLACEMENT MODELS
JAR SP 64 VOL: 2 PG:67 - 79 :: ANAL. :INT. LOG. :THEORY :VALUAT.(INFL.)

TAUSSIG,RA ; SEC: HAYES ,SC CIT: 0.00
CASH TAKE-OVERS AND ACCOUNTING VALUATIONS
TAR JA 68 VOL: 43 PG:68 - 74 :: ANOVA :PRIM. :N/A :INV.

TAUSSIG,RA CIT: 0.00
IMPACT OF SFAS NO.52 ON THE TRANSLATION OF FOREIGN FINANCIAL STATEMENTS OF
COMPANIES IN HIGHLY INFLATIONARY ECONOMIES
JAA WI 83 VOL: 6 PG:142 - 156 :: DES.STAT. :SIM. :THEORY :N/A

TAYLOR,KW ; FIRS: LEV ,B CIT: 0.00
ACCOUNTING RECOGNITION OF IMPUTED INTEREST ON EQUITY: AN EMPIRICAL
INVESTIGATION
JAA SP 79 VOL: 2 PG:232 - 243 :: REGRESS. :PRIM. :EMH :FIN.METH.

TAYLOR,M ; FIRS: HARRELL,AM ; SEC: CHEWNING,EG CIT: 0.00
ORGANIZATIONAL-PROFESSIONAL CONFLICT AND THE JOB SATISFACTION AND TURNOVER
INTENTIONS OF INTERNAL AUDITORS
AUD SP 86 VOL: 5 PG:111 - 121 :: REGRESS. :SURV. :OTH.BEH. :AUD.TRAIL

TAYLOR,ME ; FIRS: SMITH ,CH ; SEC: LANIER,RA CIT: 0.15
THE NEED FOR AND SCOPE OF THE AUDIT OF MANAGEMENT: A SURVEY OF ATTITUDES
TAR AP 72 VOL: 47 PG:270 - 283 :: DES.STAT. :SURV. :INSTIT. :AUD.

TAYLOR,ME ; FIRS: RECKERS,PMJ CIT: 0.30
CONSISTENCY IN AUDITORS' EVALUATIONS OF INTERNAL ACCOUNTING CONTROLS
JAA AU 79 VOL: 3 PG:42 - 55 :: ANOVA :LAB. :OTH.BEH. :INT.CONT.

TAYLOR,ME ; FIRS: SCHNEE,EJ CIT: 0.00
IRS ACCESS TO ACCOUNTANTS' WORK PAPERS - THE RULES MAY BE CHANGING
JAA AU 81 VOL: 5 PG:18 - 29 :: QUAL. :INT. LOG. :INSTIT. :PROF.RESP.

TAYLOR,RD ; FIRS: WRIGHT,GB CIT: 0.00
REPORTING MATERIALITY FOR INVESTORS
JAA SU 82 VOL: 5 PG:301 - 309 :: DES.STAT. :SURV. :OTH. :MAT.

TAYLOR,RG CIT: 0.00
A LOOK AT PUBLISHED INTERIM REPORTS
TAR JA 65 VOL: 40 PG:89 - 96 :: QUAL. :INT. LOG. :INSTIT. :INT.REP.

TAYLOR,RL ; FIRS: COPELAND,RM ; THIR: BROWN ,SH CIT: 0.13
OBSERVATION ERROR AND BIAS IN ACCOUNTING RESEARCH
JAR SP 81 VOL: 19 PG:197 - 207 :: ANOVA :LAB. :OTH.BEH. :METHOD.

TAYLOR,WM ; SEC: WEYGANDT,JJ CIT: 0.00
ACCOUNTING FOR STOCK-BASED AWARDS USING THE MINIMUM VALUE METHOD
JAR AU 82 VOL: 20 PG:497 - 502 :: ANAL. :INT. LOG. :THEORY :SPEC.ITEMS

TEARNEY,MG ; FIRS: WOLK ,HI CIT: 0.00
INCOME TAX ALLOCATION AND LOSS CARRYFORWARDS: EXPLORING UNCHARTED GROUND
TAR AP 73 VOL: 48 PG:292 - 299 :: ANAL. :INT. LOG. :THEORY :SPEC.ITEMS

TEHRANIAN,H ; SEC: WAEGELEIN,JF CIT: 0.25
MARKET REACTION TO SHORT-TERM EXECUTIVE COMPENSATION PLAN ADOPTION
JAE AP 85 VOL: 7 PG:131 - 144 :: REGRESS. :PRIM. :EMH :EXEC.COMP.

TEHRANIAN,H ; SEC: TRAVLOS,NG ; THIR: WAEGELEIN,JF CIT: 0.00
MANAGEMENT COMPENSATION CONTRACTS AND MERGER-INDUCED ABNORMAL RETURNS
JAR ST 87 VOL: 25 PG:51 - 76 :: ANOVA :PRIM. :OTH.STAT. :BUS.COMB.

TEITLEBAUM,AD ; SEC: ROBINSON,CF CIT: 0.15
THE REAL RISKS IN AUDIT SAMPLING
JAR ST 75 VOL: 13 PG:70 - 91 :: MIXED :INT. LOG. :OTH.STAT. :SAMP.

TENNANT,KL ; FIRS: FERRIS,KR CIT: 0.20
AN INVESTIGATION OF THE IMPACT OF THE QUALITATIVE NATURE OF COMPLIANCE ERRORS
ON INTERNAL CONTROL ASSESSMENTS
AUD SP 84 VOL: 3 PG:31 - 43 :: NON-PAR. :LAB. :OTH.STAT. :INT.CONT.

TENNYSON,BM ; FIRS: FRAZIER,KB ; SEC: INGRAM,RW CIT: 0.20
A METHODOLOGY FOR THE ANALYSIS OF NARRATIVE ACCOUNTING DISCLOSURES
JAR SP 84 VOL: 22 PG:318 - 331 :: OTH.QUANT. :PRIM. :OTH.STAT. :FOREC.

TEOH ,HY ; SEC: THONG ,G CIT: 0.00
ANOTHER LOOK AT CORPORATE SOCIAL RESPONSIBILITY AND REPORTING: AN EMPIRICAL
STUDY IN A DEVELOPING COUNTRY
AOS 02 84 VOL: 9 PG:189 - 206 :: MIXED :SURV. :THEORY :HRA

THEIL ,H CIT: 0.08
HOW TO WORRY ABOUT INCREASED EXPENDITURES
TAR JA 69 VOL: 44 PG:27 - 37 :: ANAL. :INT. LOG. :INF.ECO./AG. :LIAB.

THEIL ,H ; FIRS: LEV ,B CIT: 0.00
A MAXIMUM ENTROPY APPROACH TO THE CHOICE OF ASSET DEPRECIATION
JAR AU 78 VOL: 16 PG:286 - 293 :: ANAL. :INT. LOG. :THEORY :PP&E / DEPR

THIES ,CF ; SEC: STURROCK,T CIT: 0.00
WHAT DID INFLATION ACCOUNTING TELL US?
JAA AU 87 VOL: 2 PG:375 - 391 :: DES.STAT. :PRIM. :THEORY :VALUAT.(INFL.)

THIES ,JB ; FIRS: REVSINE,L CIT: 0.15
PRODUCTIVITY CHANGES AND ALTERNATIVE INCOME SERIES: A SIMULATION
TAR AP 76 VOL: 51 PG:255 - 268 :: ANAL. :SIM. :OTH.STAT. :DEC.AIDS

THIRKELL,JE ; FIRS: JACKSON-COX,J ; THIR: MCQUEENEY,J CIT: 0.00
THE DISCLOSURE OF COMPANY INFORMATION TO TRADE UNIONS: THE RELEVANCE OF THE
  ACAS CODE OF PRACTICE ON DISCLOSURE
AOS 34 84 VOL: 9 PG:253 - 273 :: QUAL. :SURV. :INSTIT. :N/A

THODE ,SF ; SEC: DRTINA,RE ; THIR: LARGAY III,JA CIT: 0.00
OPERATING CASH FLOWS: A GROWING NEED FOR SEPARATE REPORTING
JAA WI 86 VOL: 1 PG:46 - 61 :: REGRESS. :PRIM. :EMH :OTH.FIN.ACC.

THOMAS,AL CIT: 0.00
DISCOUNTED SERVICES AGAIN: THE HOMOGENEITY PROBLEM
TAR JA 64 VOL: 39 PG:1 - 11 :: ANAL. :INT. LOG. :THEORY :PP&E / DEPR

THOMAS,AL CIT: 0.00
"VALUE-ITIS" - AN IMPRACTICAL THEORIST'S REPLY
TAR JL 64 VOL: 39 PG:574 - 581 :: QUAL. :INT. LOG. :THEORY :VALUAT.(INFL.)

THOMAS,AL CIT: 0.00
THE AMORTIZATION PROBLEM: A SIMPLIFIED MODEL AND SOME UNANSWERED QUESTIONS
JAR SP 65 VOL: 3 PG:103 - 113 :: ANAL. :INT. LOG. :THEORY :PP&E / DEPR

THOMAS,AL CIT: 0.15
USEFUL ARBITRARY ALLOCATIONS (WITH A COMMENT ON THE NEUTRALITY OF FINANCIAL
  ACCOUNTING REPORTS)
TAR JL 71 VOL: 46 PG:472 - 479 :: ANAL. :INT. LOG. :THEORY :PP&E / DEPR

THOMAS,AP CIT: 0.00
THE CONTINGENCY THEORY OF CORPORATE REPORTING: SOME EMPIRICAL EVIDENCE
AOS 03 86 VOL: 11 PG:253 - 270 :: REGRESS. :PRIM. :THEORY :ORG.FORM

THOMAS,JK CIT: 0.00
CORPORATE TAXES AND DEFINED BENEFIT PENSION PLANS
JAE JL 88 VOL: 10 PG:199 - 237 :: REGRESS. :INT. LOG. :EMH :TAXES

THOMAS,LR ; FIRS: PUTNAM,K CIT: 0.00
DOES PREDICTABILITY CHANGE WHEN GAAP CHANGE?
JAA AU 84 VOL: 8 PG:15 - 23 :: MIXED :PRIM. :TIME SER. :FOREC.

THOMAS,LR ; FIRS: SWANSON,EP ; SEC: SHEARON,WT CIT: 0.00
PREDICTING CURRENT COST OPERATING PROFIT USING COMPONENT MODELS INCORPORATINC
  ANALYSTS' FORECASTS
TAR OC 85 VOL: 60 PG:681 - 691 :: REGRESS. :PRIM. :TIME SER. :VALUAT.(INFL.)

THOMAS,LR ; SEC: SWANSON,EP CIT: 0.00
ADDITIONAL CONSIDERATIONS WHEN USING THE FASB DATA BANK OF CHANGING PRICE
  INFORMATION
TAR AP 86 VOL: 61 PG:330 - 336 :: ANAL. :PRIM. :THEORY :VALUAT.(INFL.)

THOMAS,MF ; FIRS: GAUMNITZ,BR ; SEC: NUNAMAKER,TR ; THIR: SURDICK,JJ CIT: 0.14
AUDITOR CONSENSUS IN INTERNAL CONTROL EVALUATION AND AUDIT PROGRAM PLANNING
JAR AU 82 VOL: 20 PG:745 - 755 :: CORR. :LAB. :HIPS :INT.CONT.

THOMPSON II,RB ; SEC: OLSEN ,C ; THIR: DIETRICH,JR CIT: 0.00
ATTRIBUTES OF NEWS ABOUT FIRMS: AN ANALYSIS OF FIRM-SPECIFIC NEWS REPORTED IN
  THE WALL STREET JOURNAL INDEX
JAR AU 87 VOL: 25 PG:245 - 274 :: REGRESS. :PRIM. :INSTIT. :INFO.STRUC.

THOMPSON,G CIT: 0.50
INFLATION ACCOUNTING IN A THEORY OF CALCULATION
AOS 05 87 VOL: 12 PG:523 - 543 :: DES.STAT. :INT. LOG. :THEORY :VALUAT.(INFL.)

THOMPSON,GL ; FIRS: IJIRI ,Y CIT: 0.00
APPLICATIONS OF MATHEMATICAL CONTROL THEORY TO ACCOUNTING AND BUDGETING (THE
   CONTINUOUS WHEAT TRADING MODEL)
TAR AP 70 VOL: 45 PG:246 - 258 :: ANAL. :INT. LOG. :OTH.STAT. :BUDG.& PLAN.

THOMPSON,GL ; FIRS: KAPLAN,RS CIT: 0.38
OVERHEAD ALLOCATION VIA MATHEMATICAL PROGRAMMING MODELS
TAR AP 71 VOL: 46 PG:352 - 364 :: ANAL. :INT. LOG. :MATH.PROG. :OVER.ALLOC.

THOMPSON,R ; FIRS: SCHIPPER,K CIT: 2.67
THE IMPACT OF MERGER-RELATED REGULATIONS ON THE SHAREHOLDERS OF ACQUIRING
   FIRMS
JAR SP 83 VOL: 21 PG:184 - 221 :: REGRESS. :PRIM. :EMH :BUS.COMB.

THOMPSON,R ; FIRS: SCHIPPER,K CIT: 0.00
THE IMPACT OF MERGER-RELATED REGULATIONS USING EXACT DISTRIBUTIONS OF TEST
   STATISTICS
JAR SP 85 VOL: 23 PG:408 - 415 :: DES.STAT. :PRIM. :EMH :BUS.COMB.

THOMPSON,R ; FIRS: SEFCIK,SE CIT: 0.33
AN APPROACH TO STAT. INFERENCE IN CROSS-SECTIONAL MODELS WITH SECURITY
   ABNORMAL RETURNS AS DEPENDENT VARIABLE
JAR AU 86 VOL: 24 PG:316 - 334 :: DES.STAT. :INT. LOG. :OTH.STAT. :METHOD.

THOMPSON,RB ; SEC: OLSEN ,C ; THIR: DIETRICH,JR CIT: 0.00
THE INFLUENCE OF ESTIMATION PERIOD NEWS EVENTS ON STANDARDIZED MARKET MODEL
   PREDICTION ERRORS
TAR JL 88 VOL: 63 PG:448 - 471 :: REGRESS. :PRIM. :EMH :METHOD.

THOMPSON,WW ; SEC: KEMPER,EL CIT: 0.00
PROBABILITY MEASURES FOR ESTIMATED DATA
TAR JL 65 VOL: 40 PG:574 - 578 :: ANAL. :INT. LOG. :N/A :PROB.ELIC.

THOMSEN,CT ; FIRS: JENSEN,RE CIT: 0.00
STATISTICAL ANALYSIS IN COST MEASUREMENT AND CONTROL
TAR JA 68 VOL: 43 PG:83 - 93 :: ANAL. :INT. LOG. :OTH.STAT. :VAR.

THONG ,G ; FIRS: TEOH ,HY CIT: 0.00
ANOTHER LOOK AT CORPORATE SOCIAL RESPONSIBILITY AND REPORTING: AN EMPIRICAL
   STUDY IN A DEVELOPING COUNTRY
AOS 02 84 VOL: 9 PG:189 - 206 :: MIXED :SURV. :THEORY :HRA

THORNTON,DB CIT: 0.20
INFORMATION AND INSTITUTIONS IN THE CAPITAL MARKET
AOS 03 79 VOL: 4 PG:211 - 234 :: QUAL. :INT. LOG. :EMH :N/A

TIESSEN, P ; SEC: WATERHOUSE,JH CIT: 1.67
TOWARDS A DESCRIPTIVE THEORY OF MANAGEMENT ACCOUNTING
AOS 23 83 VOL: 8 PG:251 - 268 :: QUAL. :INT. LOG. :THEORY :MANAG.

TIESSEN,P ; FIRS: WATERHOUSE,JH CIT: 3.18
A CONTINGENCY FRAMEWORK FOR MANAGEMENT ACCOUNTING SYSTEMS RESEARCH
AOS 01 78 VOL: 3 PG:65 - 76 :: QUAL. :INT. LOG. :HIPS :METHOD.

TILLER,MG CIT: 0.17
THE DISSONANCE MODEL OF PARTICIPATIVE BUDGETING: AN EMPIRICAL EXPLORATION
JAR AU 83 VOL: 21 PG:581 - 595 :: ANOVA :LAB. :OTH.BEH. :BUDG.& PLAN.

TILLER,MG ; SEC: MAUTZ ,RD CIT: 0.00
THE IMPACT OF STATE-MANDATED ACCOUNTING AND AUDITING REQUIREMENTS ON
MUNICIPAL BOND RATINGS
JAA SU 85 VOL: 8 PG:293 - 304 :: REGRESS. :PRIM. :OTH.STAT. :LTD

TINKER,AM CIT: 1.56
TOWARDS A POLITICAL ECONOMY OF ACCOUNTING: AN EMPIRICAL ILLUSTRATION OF THE
CAMBRIDGE CONTROVERSIES
AOS 01 80 VOL: 5 PG:147 - 160 :: QUAL. :INT. LOG. :THEORY :N/A

TINKER,AM ; SEC: MERINO,BD ; THIR: NEIMARK,M CIT: 1.57
THE NORMATIVE ORIGINS OF POSITIVE THEORIES: IDEOLOGY AND ACCOUNTING THOUGHT
AOS 02 82 VOL: 7 PG:167 - 200 :: QUAL. :INT. LOG. :THEORY :N/A

TINKER,T ; FIRS: NEIMARK,M CIT: 0.67
THE SOCIAL CONSTRUCTION OF MANAGEMENT CONTROL SYSTEM
AOS 45 86 VOL: 11 PG:369 - 396 :: REGRESS. :INT. LOG. :THEORY :INT.CONT.

TINKER,T ; SEC: NEIMARK,M CIT: 0.00
THE ROLE OF ANNUAL REPORTS IN GENDER AND CLASS CONTRADICTIONS AT GENERAL
MOTORS: 1917-1976
AOS 01 87 VOL: 12 PG:71 - 88 :: DES.STAT. :INT. LOG. :INSTIT. :ORG.& ENVIR.

TINKER,T ; FIRS: LEHMAN,C CIT: 0.00
THE "REAL" CULTURAL SIGNIFICANCE OF ACCOUNTS
AOS 05 87 VOL: 12 PG:503 - 522 :: DES.STAT. :SEC. :HIST. :OTH.MANAG.

TINKER,T CIT: 0.00
PANGLOSSIAN ACCOUNTING THEORIES: THE SCIENCE OF APOLOGIZING IN STYLE
AOS 02 88 VOL: 13 PG:165 - 189 :: DES.STAT. :INT. LOG. :THEORY :OTH.MANAG.

TITMAN,S ; SEC: TRUEMAN,B CIT: 0.67
INFORMATION QUALITY AND THE VALUATION OF NEW ISSUES
JAE JN 86 VOL: 8 PG:159 - 172 :: DES.STAT. :INT. LOG. :INF.ECO./AG. :
VALUAT.(INFL.)

TOBA ,Y CIT: 0.23
A GENERAL THEORY OF EVIDENCE AS THE CONCEPTUAL FOUNDATION IN AUDITING THEORY
TAR JA 75 VOL: 50 PG:7 - 24 :: ANAL. :INT. LOG. :OTH.STAT. :AUD.

TOBA ,Y CIT: 0.00
A SEMANTIC MEANING ANALYSIS OF THE ULTIMATE PROPOSITION TO BE VERIFIED BY
INDEPENDENT AUDITORS
TAR OC 80 VOL: 55 PG:604 - 619 :: ANAL. :INT. LOG. :THEORY :OPIN.

TOLLEFSON,SO ; FIRS: STERLING,RR ; THIR: FLAHERTY,RE CIT: 0.00
EXCHANGE VALUATION: AN EMPIRICAL TEST
TAR OC 72 VOL: 47 PG:709 - 721 :: DES.STAT. :LAB. :THEORY :VALUAT.(INFL.)

TOMASSINI,LA CIT: 0.15
BEHAVIOURAL RESEARCH ON HUMAN RESOURCE ACCOUNTING: A CONTINGENCY FRAMEWORI
AOS 23 76 VOL: 1 PG:239 - 252 :: QUAL. :INT. LOG. :OTH.BEH. :HRA

TOMASSINI,LA CIT: 0.17
ASSESSING THE IMPACT OF HUMAN RESOURCE ACCOUNTING: AN EXPERIMENTAL STUDY OF
MANAGERIAL DECISION PREFERENCES
TAR OC 77 VOL: 52 PG:904 - 913 :: ANOVA :LAB. :OTH.BEH. :HRA

TOMASSINI,LA ; FIRS: SOLOMON,I ; SEC: KROGSTAD,JL ; THIR: ROMNEY,MB CIT: 0.57
AUDITORS' PRIOR PROBABILITY DISTRIBUTIONS FOR ACCOUNT BALANCES
AOS 01 82 VOL: 7 PG:27 - 42 :: DES.STAT. :LAB. :HIPS :PROB.ELIC.

TOMASSINI,LA ; FIRS: HARRISON JR,WT ; THIR: DIETRICH,JR CIT: 0.17
THE USE OF CONTROL GROUPS IN CAPITAL MARKET RESEARCH
JAR SP 83 VOL: 21 PG:65 - 77 :: NON-PAR. :PRIM. :EMH :METHOD.

TOMASSINI,LA ; FIRS: BECK ,PJ ; SEC: SOLOMON,I CIT: 0.25
SUBJECTIVE PRIOR PROBABILITY DISTRIBUTIONS AND AUDIT RISK
JAR SP 85 VOL: 23 PG:37 - 56 :: REGRESS. :INT. LOG. :OTH.BEH. :RISK

TOMKINS,C ; SEC: GROVES,R CIT: 2.50
THE EVERYDAY ACCOUNTANT AND RESEARCHING HIS REALITY
AOS 04 83 VOL: 8 PG:361 - 374 :: QUAL. :INT. LOG. :THEORY :METHOD.

TOMKINS,L ; FIRS: ROSENBERG,D ; THIR: DAY ,P CIT: 0.00
A WORK ROLE PERSPECTIVE OF ACCOUNTANTS IN LOCAL GOVERNMENT SERVICE DEPARTMENTS
AOS 02 82 VOL: 7 PG:123 - 138 :: QUAL. :SURV. :OTH.BEH. :N/A

TOOLE ,HR ; FIRS: LOY ,LD CIT: 0.11
ACCOUNTING FOR DISCOUNTED CONVERTIBLE BOND EXCHANGES: A SURVEY OF RESULTS
JAA SP 80 VOL: 3 PG:227 - 243 :: DES.STAT. :PRIM. :OTH. :METHOD.

TOOLE ,HR ; FIRS: LEMBKE,VC CIT: 0.00
DIFFERENCES IN DEPRECIATION METHODS AND THE ANALYSIS OF SUPPLEMENTAL
    CURRENT-COST AND REPLACEMENT COST DATA
JAA WI 81 VOL: 4 PG:128 - 135 :: ANAL. :INT. LOG. :THEORY :VALUAT.(INFL.)

TOPIOL,J CIT: 0.00
ACCOUNTING FOR PUBLIC HEALTH NURSING ASSOCIATIONS
TAR JA 66 VOL: 41 PG:83 - 91 :: QUAL. :INT. LOG. :N/A :FIN.METH.

TOWNSEND,LA CIT: 0.00
A CAREER IN BUSINESS ACCOUNTING
TAR JA 67 VOL: 42 PG:1 - 6 :: QUAL. :INT. LOG. :INSTIT. :OTH.MANAG.

TRACY ,JA ; FIRS: MONSON,NP CIT: 0.00
STOCK RIGHTS AND ACCOUNTING WRONGS
TAR OC 64 VOL: 39 PG:890 - 893 :: ANAL. :INT. LOG. :THEORY :STK.DIV.

TRACY ,JA CIT: 0.08
A DISSENT TO THE GENERAL PRICE-LEVEL ADJUSTMENT PROPOSAL
TAR JA 65 VOL: 40 PG:163 - 175 :: QUAL. :INT. LOG. :THEORY :VALUAT.(INFL.)

TRACY ,JA CIT: 0.54
BAYESIAN STATISTICAL METHODS IN AUDITING
TAR JA 69 VOL: 44 PG:90 - 98 :: ANAL. :INT. LOG. :OTH.STAT. :SAMP.

TRADER,RL ; FIRS: HUSS ,HF CIT: 0.00
A NOTE ON OPT. SAM. SIZE IN COMPLIANCE TESTS USING A FORMAL BAYESIAN
    DECISION-THEORETIC APPROACH FOR FINITE AND INFINITE POPULATIONS
JAR AU 86 VOL: 24 PG:394 - 399 :: DES.STAT. :SIM. :OTH.STAT. :SAMP.

TRAPNELL,JE ; FIRS: WELSH ,MJ CIT: 0.00
LABOR MARKET MODELS AND EMPLOYER ACCOUNTING FOR PENSIONS
JAA WI 85 VOL: 8 PG:100 - 111 :: DES.STAT. :INT. LOG. :THEORY :PENS.

TRAVLOS,NG ; FIRS: TEHRANIAN,H ; THIR: WAEGELEIN,JF CIT: 0.00
MANAGEMENT COMPENSATION CONTRACTS AND MERGER-INDUCED ABNORMAL RETURNS
JAR ST 87 VOL: 25 PG:51 - 76 :: ANOVA :PRIM. :OTH.STAT. :BUS.COMB.

TRITSCHLER,CA CIT: 0.54
STATISTICAL CRITERIA FOR ASSET VALUATION BY SPECIFIC PRICE INDEX
TAR JA 69 VOL: 44 PG:99 - 123 :: CORR. :PRIM. :N/A :VALUAT.(INFL.)

TROMPETER,GM ; FIRS: FARMER,TA ; SEC: RITTENBERG,LE CIT: 0.00
AN INVESTIGATION OF THE IMPACT OF ECONOMIC AND ORGANIZATIONAL FACTORS
ON AUDITOR INDEPENDENCE
AUD AU 87 VOL: 7 PG:1 - 14 :: REGRESS. :LAB. :OTH.BEH. :INDEP.

TROTMAN,KT ; SEC: BRADLEY,G CIT: 0.38
ASSOCIATIONS BETWEEN SOCIAL RESPONSIBILITY DISCLOSURE AND CHARACTERISTICS OF
COMPANIES
AOS 04 81 VOL: 6 PG:355 - 362 :: NON-PAR. :PRIM. :OTH. :HRA

TROTMAN,KT ; SEC: YETTON,PW ; THIR: ZIMMER,I CIT: 0.33
INDIVIDUAL AND GROUP JUDGMENTS OF INTERNAL CONTROL SYSTEMS
JAR SP 83 VOL: 21 PG:286 - 292 :: CORR. :LAB. :HIPS :MANAG.

TROTMAN,KT CIT: 0.25
THE REVIEW PROCESS AND THE ACCURACY OF AUDITOR JUDGMENTS
JAR AU 85 VOL: 23 PG:740 - 752 :: REGRESS. :LAB. :HIPS :JUDG.

TROTMAN,KT ; SEC: YETTON,PW CIT: 0.00
THE EFFECT OF THE REVIEW PROCESS ON AUDITOR JUDGMENTS
JAR SP 85 VOL: 23 PG:256 - 267 :: REGRESS. :LAB. :OTH.BEH. :JUDG.

TRUEBLOOD,RM CIT: 0.00
EDUCATION FOR A CHANGING PROFESSION
JAR SP 63 VOL: 1 PG:86 - 95 :: QUAL. :INT. LOG. :OTH. :AUD.TRAIN.

TRUEBLOOD,RM CIT: 0.00
ACCOUNTING PRINCIPLES: THE BOARD AND ITS PROBLEMS
JAR ST 66 VOL: 4 PG:183 - 191 :: QUAL. :INT. LOG. :INSTIT. :N/A

TRUEMAN,B ; FIRS: TITMAN,S CIT: 0.67
INFORMATION QUALITY AND THE VALUATION OF NEW ISSUES
JAE JN 86 VOL: 8 PG:159 - 172 :: DES.STAT. :INT. LOG. :INF.ECO./AG. :
VALUAT.(INFL.)

TRUEMAN,B CIT: 0.67
WHY DO MANAGERS VOLUNTARILY RELEASE EARNINGS FORECASTS?
JAE MR 86 VOL: 8 PG:53 - 72 :: DES.STAT. :INT. LOG. :THEORY :FOREC.

TRUMBULL,WP CIT: 0.00
WHEN IS A LIABILITY?
TAR JA 63 VOL: 38 PG:46 - 51 :: QUAL. :INT. LOG. :THEORY :SPEC.ITEMS

TRUMBULL,WP CIT: 0.00
DIFFERENCES BETWEEN FINANCIAL AND TAX DEPRECIATION
TAR JL 68 VOL: 43 PG:459 - 468 :: QUAL. :INT. LOG. :THEORY :TAXES

TSAY ,JJ ; FIRS: NICHOLS,DR ; THIR: LARKIN,PD CIT: 0.00
INVESTOR TRADING RESPONSES TO DIFFERING CHARACTERISTICS OF VOLUNTARILY
DISCLOSED EARNINGS FORECASTS
TAR AP 79 VOL: 54 PG:376 - 382 :: NON-PAR. :PRIM. :EMH :FOREC.

TSAY ,JJ ; FIRS: NICHOLS,DR CIT: 0.60
SECURITY PRICE REACTIONS TO LONG-RANGE EXECUTIVE EARNINGS FORECASTS
JAR SP 79 VOL: 17 PG:140 - 155 :: REGRESS. :PRIM. :EMH :FOREC.

TSCHIRHART,JT ; FIRS: HAMLEN,SS ; SEC: HAMLEN,WA CIT: 0.58
THE USE OF CORE THEORY IN EVALUATING JOINT COST ALLOCATION SCHEMES
TAR JL 77 VOL: 52 PG:616 - 627 :: ANAL. :INT. LOG. :MATH.PROG. :OVER.ALLOC.

TSCHIRHART,JT ; FIRS: HAMLEN,SS ; SEC: HAMLEN,WA CIT: 0.11
THE USE OF THE GENERALIZED SHAPLEY ALLOCATION IN JOINT COST ALLOCATION
TAR AP 80 VOL: 55 PG:269 - 287 :: ANAL. :INT. LOG. :OTH.STAT. :COST.ALLOC.

TSE ,S CIT: 0.00
INTRA-YEAR TRENDS IN THE DEGREE OF ASSOC. BETWEEN ACCOUNTING NUMBERS AND
   SECURITY PRICES
TAR JL 86 VOL: 61 PG:475 - 497 :: REGRESS. :PRIM. :EMH :FIN.METH.

TSUI ,AS ; FIRS: FLAMHOLTZ,EG ; SEC: DAS   ,TK CIT: 0.25
TOWARD AN INTEGRATIVE FRAMEWORK OF ORGANIZATIONAL CONTROL
AOS 01 85 VOL: 10 PG:35 - 50 :: DES.STAT. :INT. LOG. :OTH.BEH. :HRA

TSUI ,KL ; FIRS: TSUI ,KW ; SEC: MATSUMURA,EM CIT: 0.50
MULTINOMINAL-DIRICHLET BOUNDS FOR DOLLAR-UNIT SAMPLING IN AUDITING
TAR JA 85 VOL: 60 PG:76 - 96 :: DES.STAT. :SIM. :OTH.STAT. :SAMP.

TSUI ,KW ; FIRS: MATSUMURA,EM CIT: 0.14
STEIN-TYPE POISSON ESTIMATORS IN AUDIT SAMPLING
JAR SP 82 VOL: 20 PG:162 - 170 :: CORR. :INT. LOG. :N/A :SAMP.

TSUI ,KW ; SEC: MATSUMURA,EM ; THIR: TSUI ,KL CIT: 0.50
MULTINOMINAL-DIRICHLET BOUNDS FOR DOLLAR-UNIT SAMPLING IN AUDITING
TAR JA 85 VOL: 60 PG:76 - 96 :: DES.STAT. :SIM. :OTH.STAT. :SAMP.

TUCKERMAN,B CIT: 0.00
OBJECTIVE CONSOLIDATION STANDARDS FOR FOREIGN SUBSIDIARIES
TAR JA 64 VOL: 39 PG:32 - 37 :: QUAL. :INT. LOG. :THEORY :BUS.COMB.

TUGGLE,FD ; FIRS: GORDON,LA ; SEC: LARCKER,DF CIT: 0.82
STRATEGIC DECISION PROCESSES AND THE DESIGN OF ACCOUNTING INFORMATION
   SYSTEMS: CONCEPTUAL LINKAGES
AOS 34 78 VOL: 3 PG:203 - 214 :: QUAL. :INT. LOG. :OTH. :INFO.STRUC.

TURLEY,S ; FIRS: MOIZER,P CIT: 0.00
SURROGATES FOR AUDIT FEES IN CONCENTRATION STUDIES
AUD AU 87 VOL: 7 PG:118 - 123 :: REGRESS. :PRIM. :OTH.STAT. :ORG.

TURNER,MJ ; FIRS: HILTON,RW ; SEC: SWIERINGA,RJ CIT: 0.00
PRODUCT PRICING, ACCOUNTING COSTS AND USE OF PRODUCT-COSTING SYSTEMS
TAR AP 88 VOL: 63 PG:195 - 218 :: REGRESS. :LAB. :OTH.BEH. :REL.COSTS

TUROPOLEC,L ; FIRS: BIRNBERG,JG ; THIR: YOUNG ,SM CIT: 1.83
THE ORGANIZATIONAL CONTEXT OF ACCOUNTING
AOS 23 83 VOL: 8 PG:111 - 130 :: QUAL. :SEC. :OTH.BEH. :REL.COSTS

TWARK ,RD ; FIRS: KRATCHMAN,SH ; SEC: MALCOM,RE CIT: 0.08
AN INTRA-INDUSTRY COMPARISON OF ALTERNATIVE INCOME CONCEPTS AND RELATIVE
   PERFORMANCE EVALUATIONS
TAR OC 74 VOL: 49 PG:682 - 689 :: NON-PAR. :PRIM. :N/A :VALUAT.(INFL.)

TWARK ,RD ; FIRS: BASI ,BA ; SEC: CAREY ,KJ CIT: 1.00
A COMPARISON OF THE ACCURACY OF CORPORATE AND SECURITY ANALYSTS' FORECASTS
   OF EARNINGS
TAR AP 76 VOL: 51 PG:244 - 254 :: ANOVA :PRIM. :TIME SER. :FOREC.

TWOMBLY,JR ; FIRS: EGGLETON,IRC ; SEC: PENMAN,SH CIT: 0.92
ACCOUNTING CHANGES AND STOCK PRICES: AN EXAMINATION OF SELECTED UNCONTROLLEI
VARIABLES
JAR SP 76 VOL: 14 PG:66 - 88 :: NON-PAR. :PRIM :EMH :ACC.CHNG.

TZUR ,J ; FIRS: HALPERIN,R CIT: 0.00
MONETARY COMPENSATION AND NONTAXABLE EMPLOYEE BENEFITS: AN ANALYTICAL
PERSPECTIVE
TAR OC 85 VOL: 60 PG:670 - 680 :: REGRESS. :INT. LOG. :THEORY :EXEC.COMP.

UECKER,WC CIT: 0.08
AN INQUIRY INTO THE NEED FOR CURRENTLY FEASIBLE EXTENSIONS OF THE ATTEST
FUNCTION IN CORPORATE ANNUAL REPORTS
AOS 01 77 VOL: 2 PG:47 - 58 :: OTH.QUANT. :LAB. :OTH.BEH. :FIN.METH.

UECKER,WC ; SEC: KINNEY JR,WR CIT: 0.83
JUDGMENTAL EVALUATION OF SAMPLE RESULTS: A STUDY OF THE TYPE AND SEVERITY OF
ERRORS MADE BY PRACTICING CPAS
AOS 03 77 VOL: 2 PG:269 - 275 :: DES.STAT. :LAB. :OTH.STAT. :SAMP.

UECKER,WC CIT: 1.09
A BEHAVIOURAL STUDY OF INFORMATION SYSTEM CHOICE
JAR SP 78 VOL: 16 PG:169 - 189 :: ANOVA :LAB. :INF.ECO./AG. :INFO.STRUC.

UECKER,WC CIT: 0.56
THE EFFECTS OF KNOWLEDGE OF THE USER'S DECISION MODEL IN SIMPLIFIED
INFORMATION EVALUATION
JAR SP 80 VOL: 18 PG:191 - 213 :: ANOVA :LAB. :HIPS :INFO.STRUC.

UECKER,WC ; SEC: BRIEF ,AP ; THIR: KINNEY JR,WR CIT: 0.25
PERCEPTION OF THE INTERNAL AND EXTERNAL AUDITOR AS A DETERRENT TO CORPORATE
IRREGULARITIES
TAR JL 81 VOL: 56 PG:465 - 478 :: ANOVA :LAB. :OTH.BEH. :AUD.BEH.

UECKER,WC CIT: 0.14
THE QUALITY OF GROUP PERFORMANCE IN SIMPLIFIED INFORMATION EVALUATION
JAR AU 82 VOL: 20 PG:388 - 402 :: DES.STAT. :LAB. :OTH.BEH. :INFO.STRUC.

UECKER,WC ; FIRS: KINNEY JR,WR CIT: 0.57
MITIGATING THE CONSEQUENCES OF ANCHORING IN AUDITOR JUDGMENTS
TAR JA 82 VOL: 57 PG:55 - 69 :: DES.STAT. :LAB. :HIPS :ANAL.REV.

UECKER,WC ; FIRS: SCHEPANSKI,A CIT: 0.17
TOWARD A POSITIVE THEORY OF INFORMATION EVALUATION
TAR AP 83 VOL: 58 PG:259 - 283 :: ANAL. :INT. LOG. :INF.ECO./AG. :OTH.MANAG.

UECKER,WC ; FIRS: DEJONG,DV ; SEC: FORSYTHE,R CIT: 0.25
THE METHODOLOGY OF LABORATORY MARKETS AND ITS IMPLICATIONS FOR AGENCY
RESEARCH IN ACCOUNTING AND AUDITING
JAR AU 85 VOL: 23 PG:753 - 793 :: REGRESS. :LAB. :INF.ECO./AG. :METHOD.

UECKER,WC ; SEC: SCHEPANSKI,A ; THIR: SHIN ,J CIT: 0.00
TOWARD A POSITIVE THEORY OF INFORMATION EVALUATION: RELEVANT TESTS OF
COMPETING MODELS IN A PRINCIPAL-AGENCY SETTING
TAR JL 85 VOL: 60 PG:430 - 457 :: REGRESS. :LAB. :INF.ECO./AG. :MANAG.

UECKER,WC ; FIRS: DEJONG,DV ; SEC: FORSYTHE,R ; THIR: LUNDHOLM,RJ CIT: 0.00
A LABORATORY INVESTIGATION OF THE MORAL HAZARD PROBLEM IN AN AGENCY
RELATIONSHIP
JAR ST 85 VOL: 23 PG:81 - 120 :: REGRESS. :LAB. :INF.ECO./AG. :MAN.DEC.CHAR.

UECKER,WC ; FIRS: MADEO ,SA ; SEC: SCHEPANSKI,A CIT: 0.00
MODELING JUDGMENTS OF TAXPAYER COMPLIANCE
TAR AP 87 VOL: 62 PG:323 - 342 :: REGRESS. :LAB. :OTH.STAT. :TAXES

ULLMANN,AA CIT: 0.08
THE CORPORATE ENVIRONMENTAL ACCOUNTING SYSTEM: A MANAGEMENT TOOL FOR FIGHTING
  ENVIRONMENTAL DEGRADATION
AOS 01 76 VOL: 1 PG:71 - 80 :: QUAL. :INT. LOG. :THEORY :HRA

ULLMANN,AA CIT: 0.00
CORPORATE SOCIAL REPORTING: POLITICAL INTERESTS AND CONFLICTS IN GERMANY
AOS 12 79 VOL: 4 PG:123 - 134 :: QUAL. :INT. LOG. :INSTIT. :HRA

UNG   ,S ; FIRS: STANDISH,PEM CIT: 0.00
CORPORATE SIGNALING, ASSET REVALUATIONS, AND STOCK PRICES OF BRITISH COMPANIES
TAR OC 82 VOL: 57 PG:701 - 715 :: REGRESS. :PRIM. :EMH :VALUAT.(INFL.)

UPHOFF,HL ; FIRS: ELLIOTT,JW CIT: 0.15
PREDICTING THE NEAR TERM PROFIT AND LOSS STATEMENT WITH AN ECONOMETRIC MODEL:
  A FEASIBILITY STUDY
JAR AU 72 VOL: 10 PG:259 - 274 :: MIXED :PRIM. :TIME SER. :BUDG.& PLAN.

USHMAN,N ; FIRS: MORSE ,D CIT: 0.17
THE EFFECT OF INFORMATION ANNOUNCEMENTS ON THE MARKET MICROSTRUCTURE
TAR AP 83 VOL: 58 PG:247 - 258 :: ANOVA :PRIM. :OTH. :FIN.METH.

USRY ,MF CIT: 0.00
COST ACCOUNTING ON THE CPA EXAMINATION
TAR OC 66 VOL: 41 PG:754 - 762 :: DES.STAT. :PRIM. :N/A :N/A

VANCE ,LL CIT: 0.00
WHAT THE EDITOR OF AN ACADEMIC JOURNAL EXPECTS FROM AUTHORS
TAR JA 66 VOL: 41 PG:48 - 51 :: QUAL. :INT. LOG. :N/A :OTH.MANAG.

VANCE ,LL CIT: 0.00
THE ROAD TO REFORM OF ACCOUNTING PRINCIPLES
TAR OC 69 VOL: 44 PG:692 - 703 :: QUAL. :INT. LOG. :HIST. :FIN.METH.

VANDERWEIDE,JH ; FIRS: BROWN ,LD ; SEC: HUGHES,JS ; THIR: ROZEFF,MS CIT: 0.00
EXPECTATIONS DATA AND THE PREDICTIVE VALUE OF INTERIM REPORTING: A COMMENT
JAR SP 80 VOL: 18 PG:278 - 288 :: REGRESS. :PRIM. :TIME SER. :FOREC.

VANECEK,M ; FIRS: WHITE ,D CIT: 0.00
INTENDED USE: A UNIFORM TAX DEFINITION OF SOFTWARE
JAA SU 82 VOL: 5 PG:338 - 354 :: QUAL. :INT. LOG. :THEORY :TAXES

VASARHELYI,MA ; FIRS: MOCK ,TJ ; SEC: ESTRIN,TL CIT: 0.77
LEARNING PATTERNS, DECISION APPROACH, AND VALUE OF INFORMATION
JAR SP 72 VOL: 10 PG:129 - 153 :: ANOVA :LAB. :HIPS :INFO.STRUC.

VASARHELYI,MA CIT: 0.50
MAN-MACHINE PLANNING SYSTEMS: A COGNITIVE STYLE EXAMINATION OF INTERACTIVE
  DECISION MAKING
JAR SP 77 VOL: 15 PG:138 - 153 :: ANOVA :LAB. :HIPS :MAN.DEC.CHAR.

VASARHELYI,MA ; FIRS: MOCK ,TJ CIT: 0.00
A SYNTHESIS OF THE INFORMATION ECONOMICS AND LENS MODELS
JAR AU 78 VOL: 16 PG:414 - 423 :: ANAL. :INT. LOG. :HIPS :METHOD.

VASARHELYI,MA CIT: 0.00
AUTOMATION AND CHANGES IN THE AUDIT PROCESS
AUD AU 84 VOL: 4 PG:100 - 106 :: QUAL. :INT. LOG. :OTH. :AUD.

VASARHELYI,MA ; SEC: BAILEY JR,AD ; THIR: CAMARDESSE JR,JE ; FOUR: GROOMER, SM
; FIFT: LAMPE ,JC CIT: 0.00
THE USAGE OF COMPUTERS IN AUDITING TEACHING AND RESEARCH
AUD SP 84 VOL: 3 PG:98 - 103 :: QUAL. :SIM. :OTH. :EDP AUD.

VASARHELYI,MA ; FIRS: SRINIDHI,BN CIT: 0.00
AUDITOR JUDGMENT CONCERNING ESTABLISHMENT OF SUBSTANTIVE TESTS BASED ON
INTERNAL CONTROL RELIABILITY
AUD SP 86 VOL: 5 PG:64 - 76 :: REGRESS. :LAB. :OTH.STAT. :INT.CONT.

VASARHELYI,MA ; FIRS: BAO ,BH ; SEC: BAO ,DH CIT: 0.00
A STOCHASTIC MODEL OF PROFESSIONAL ACCOUNTANT TURNOVER
AOS 03 86 VOL: 11 PG:289 - 296 :: DES.STAT. :PRIM. :OTH.BEH. :ORG.

VASARHELYI,MA ; FIRS: KNAUF ,JB CIT: 0.00
EMPIRICAL CHARACTERISTICS OF DEBENTURE CONVERSIONS: THE ISSUE OF EQUIVALENCY
JAA WI 87 VOL: 2 PG:43 - 64 :: REGRESS. :PRIM. :THEORY :LTD

VASARHELYI,MA ; FIRS: BROWN ,LD ; SEC: GARDNER,JC CIT: 0.00
AN ANALYSIS OF THE RESEARCH CONTRIBUTIONS OF ACCOUNTING, ORGANIZATIONS AND
SOCIETY, 1976-1984
AOS 02 87 VOL: 12 PG:193 - 204 :: REGRESS. :SEC. :HIST. :METHOD.

VATTER,W CIT: 0.08
INCOME MODELS, BOOK YIELD, AND THE RATE OF RETURN
TAR OC 66 VOL: 41 PG:681 - 698 :: ANAL. :INT. LOG. :THEORY :PP&E / DEPR

VATTER,WJ CIT: 0.23
POSTULATES AND PRINCIPLES
JAR AU 63 VOL: 1 PG:179 - 197 :: QUAL. :INT. LOG. :THEORY :N/A

VATTER,WJ CIT: 0.08
E(M3)I - AN EVALUATION
TAR JL 63 VOL: 38 PG:470 - 477 :: QUAL. :INT. LOG. :THEORY :FIN.METH.

VATTER,WJ CIT: 0.15
ACCOUNTING FOR LEASES
JAR AU 66 VOL: 4 PG:133 - 148 :: QUAL. :INT. LOG. :THEORY :LEASES

VATTER,WJ CIT: 0.00
THE USE OF OPERATIONS RESEARCH IN AMERICAN COMPANIES
TAR OC 67 VOL: 42 PG:721 - 730 :: DES.STAT. :SURV. :N/A :OTH.MANAG.

VATTER,WJ CIT: 0.30
STATE OF THE ART - NON-BUSINESS ACCOUNTING
TAR JL 79 VOL: 54 PG:563 - 573 :: QUAL. :SEC. :THEORY :N/A

VERRECCHIA, RE CIT: 1.00
MANAGERIAL DISCRETION IN THE CHOICE AMONG FINANCIAL REPORTING ALTERNATIVES
JAE OC 86 VOL: 8 PG:175 - 196 :: DES.STAT. :INT. LOG. :INF.ECO./AG. :
INFO.STRUC.

VERRECCHIA,RE CIT: 0.09
ON THE CHOICE OF ACCOUNTING METHOD FOR PARTNERSHIPS
JAR SP 78 VOL: 16 PG:150 - 168 :: ANAL. :INT. LOG. :INF.ECO./AG. :FIN.METH.

VERRECCHIA,RE CIT: 0.60
ON THE THEORY OF MARKET INFORMATION EFFICIENCY
JAE MR 79 VOL: 1 PG:77 - 90 :: ANAL. :INT. LOG. :INF.ECO./AG. :METHOD.

VERRECCHIA,RE CIT: 0.56
THE RAPIDITY OF PRICE ADJUSTMENTS TO INFORMATION
JAE MR 80 VOL: 2 PG:63 - 92 :: ANAL. :INT. LOG. :INF.ECO./AG. :INFO.STRUC.

VERRECCHIA,RE ; FIRS: BILLERA,LJ ; SEC: HEATH ,DC CIT: 0.25
A UNIQUE PROCEDURE FOR ALLOCATING COMMON COSTS FROM A PRODUCTION PROCESS
JAR SP 81 VOL: 19 PG:185 - 196 :: ANAL. :INT. LOG. :INF.ECO./AG. :N/A

VERRECCHIA,RE CIT: 0.25
ON THE RELATIONSHIP BETWEEN VOLUME REACTION AND CONSENSUS OF INVESTORS:
   IMPLICATIONS FOR INTERPRETING TESTS OF INFORMATION CONTENT
JAR SP 81 VOL: 19 PG:271 - 283 :: ANAL. :INT. LOG. :OTH.STAT. :FIN.METH.

VERRECCHIA,RE CIT: 0.00
AN ANALYSIS OF TWO COST ALLOCATION CASES
TAR JL 82 VOL: 57 PG:579 - 593 :: ANAL. :INT. LOG. :OTH.STAT. :COST.ALLOC.

VERRECCHIA,RE CIT: 0.57
THE USE OF MATHEMATICAL MODELS IN FINANCIAL ACCOUNTING
JAR ST 82 VOL: 20 PG:1 - 42 :: ANAL. :SEC. :EMH :FIN.METH.

VERRECCHIA,RE CIT: 1.17
DISCRETIONARY DISCLOSURE
JAE DE 83 VOL: 5 PG:179 - 194 :: ANAL. :INT. LOG. :OTH. :INFO.STRUC.

VERRECCHIA,RE ; SEC: LANEN ,WN CIT: 0.00
OPERATING DECISIONS AND THE DISCLOSURE OF MANAGEMENT ACCOUNTING INFORMATION
JAR ST 87 VOL: 25 PG:165 - 189 :: ANAL. :INT. LOG. :THEORY :MANAG.

VERRECCHIA,RE ; FIRS: HOLTHAUSEN,RW CIT: 0.00
THE EFFECT OF SEQUENTIAL INFORMATION RELEASES ON THE VARIANCE OF PRICE
   CHANGES IN AN INTERTEMPORAL MULTI-ASSET MARKET
JAR SP 88 VOL: 26 PG:82 - 106 :: ANAL. :INT. LOG. :INF.ECO./AG. :INFO.STRUC.

VICKREY,DW CIT: 0.15
IS ACCOUNTING A MEASUREMENT DISCIPLINE?
TAR OC 70 VOL: 45 PG:731 - 742 :: ANAL. :INT. LOG. :THEORY :OTH.FIN.ACC.

VICKREY,DW CIT: 0.15
GENERAL-PRICE-LEVEL-ADJUSTED HISTORICAL-COST STATEMENTS AND THE RATIO-SCALE
   VIEW
TAR JA 76 VOL: 51 PG:31 - 40 :: QUAL. :INT. LOG. :THEORY :OTH.FIN.ACC.

VICKREY,DW ; FIRS: FOSTER III,TW CIT: 0.00
THE INFORMATION CONTENT OF STOCK DIVIDEND ANNOUNCEMENTS
TAR AP 78 VOL: 53 PG:360 - 370 :: REGRESS. :PRIM. :EMH :STK.DIV.

VICKREY,DW ; FIRS: FOSTER III,TW CIT: 0.36
THE INCREMENTAL INFORMATION CONTENT OF THE 10-K
TAR OC 78 VOL: 53 PG:921 - 934 :: ANOVA :PRIM. :EMH :FIN.METH.

VICKREY,DW ; FIRS: SCHROEDER,MS ; SEC: SOLOMON,I CIT: 0.00
AUDIT QUALITY: THE PERCEPTIONS OF AUDIT-COMMITTEE CHAIRPERSONS AND AUDIT
   PARTNERS
AUD SP 86 VOL: 5 PG:86 - 94 :: REGRESS. :SURV. :OTH.BEH. :OPER.AUD.

VIGELAND,RL CIT: 0.38
THE MARKET REACTION TO STATEMENT OF FINANCIAL ACCOUNTING STANDARDS NO.2
TAR AP 81 VOL: 56 PG:309 - 325 :: ANOVA :PRIM. :EMH :R & D

VIGELAND,RL CIT: 0.14
DILUTION OF EARNINGS PER SHARE IN AN OPTION PRICING FRAMEWORK
TAR AP 82 VOL: 57 PG:348 - 357 :: ANAL. :INT. LOG. :THEORY :AUD.TRAIN.

VIGELAND,RL ; FIRS: DALEY ,LA CIT: 0.83
THE EFFECTS OF DEBT COVENANTS AND POLITICAL COSTS ON THE CHOICE OF ACCOUNTING
METHODS: THE CASE OF ACCOUNTING FOR R & D COSTS
JAE DE 83 VOL: 5 PG:195 - 211 :: OTH.QUANT. :PRIM. :OTH.STAT. :R & D

VIGELAND,RL ; FIRS: DALEY ,LA ; SEC: SENKOW,DW CIT: 0.00
ANALYSTS' FORECASTS, EARNINGS VARIABILITY, AND OPTION PRICING: EMPIRICAL
EVIDENCE
TAR OC 88 VOL: 63 PG:563 - 585 :: REGRESS. :PRIM. :TIME SER. :FOREC.

VIRGIL JR,RL ; FIRS: PANKOFF,LD CIT: 0.15
ON THE USEFULNESS OF FINANCIAL STATEMENT INFORMATION: A SUGGESTED RESEARCH
APPROACH
TAR AP 70 VOL: 45 PG:269 - 279 :: DES.STAT. :LAB. :N/A :OTH.MANAG.

VIRGIL JR,RL ; FIRS: PANKOFF,LD CIT: 0.62
SOME PRELIMINARY FINDINGS FROM A LABORATORY EXPERIMENT ON THE USEFULNESS OF
FINANCIAL ACCOUNTING INFORMATION TO SECURITY ANALYSTS
JAR ST 70 VOL: 8 PG:1 - 48 :: MIXED :LAB. :OTH.BEH. :FIN.METH.

VIRGIL JR,RL ; FIRS: SPILLER JR,EA CIT: 0.08
EFFECTIVENESS OF APB OPINION NO.19 IN IMPROVING FUNDS REPORTING
JAR SP 74 VOL: 12 PG:112 - 142 :: DES.STAT. :LAB. :THEORY :INFO.STRUC.

VOGT ,RA CIT: 0.00
A CORPORATE STRATEGY FOR REALIZING EQUAL EMPLOYMENT OPPORTUNITY
AOS 01 77 VOL: 2 PG:59 - 80 :: QUAL. :INT. LOG. :HIPS :HRA

VOLKAN,AG ; FIRS: RUE ,JC CIT: 0.00
FINANCIAL AND ECONOMIC CONSEQUENCES OF THE NEW PENSION ACCOUNTING PROPOSALS:
IS THE GLOOM JUSTIFIED?
JAA SU 84 VOL: 7 PG:306 - 322 :: DES.STAT. :PRIM. :THEORY :PENS.

VOSS ,WM CIT: 0.00
ACCELERATED DEPRECIATION AND DEFERRED TAX ALLOCATION
JAR AU 68 VOL: 6 PG:262 - 269 :: DES.STAT. :PRIM. :N/A :TAXES

VOSS ,WM ; FIRS: BEAVER,WH ; SEC: KENNELLY,JW CIT: 0.92
PREDICTIVE ABILITY AS A CRITERION FOR THE EVALUATION OF ACCOUNTING DATA
TAR OC 68 VOL: 43 PG:675 - 683 :: QUAL. :INT. LOG. :THEORY :FIN.METH.

WADE ,HH CIT: 0.00
ACCOUNTING FOR THE INVESTMENT CREDIT
TAR OC 63 VOL: 38 PG:714 - 718 :: QUAL. :INT. LOG. :THEORY :N/A

WAEGELEIN,JF ; FIRS: TEHRANIAN,H CIT: 0.25
MARKET REACTION TO SHORT-TERM EXECUTIVE COMPENSATION PLAN ADOPTION
JAE AP 85 VOL: 7 PG:131 - 144 :: REGRESS. :PRIM. :EMH :EXEC.COMP.

WAEGELEIN,JF ; FIRS: TEHRANIAN,H ; SEC: TRAVLOS,NG CIT: 0.00
MANAGEMENT COMPENSATION CONTRACTS AND MERGER-INDUCED ABNORMAL RETURNS
JAR ST 87 VOL: 25 PG:51 - 76 :: ANOVA :PRIM. :OTH.STAT. :BUS.COMB.

WAGNER,JW CIT: 0.15
DEFINING OBJECTIVITY IN ACCOUNTING
TAR JL 65 VOL: 40 PG:599 - 605 :: QUAL. :INT. LOG. :THEORY :OTH.FIN.ACC.

WAGNER,JW CIT: 0.00
EDP AND THE AUDITOR OF THE 1970'S
TAR JL 69 VOL: 44 PG:600 - 604 :: QUAL. :INT. LOG. :N/A :EDP AUD.

WAI ,WT ; FIRS: DAVISON,AG ; SEC: STENING,BW CIT: 0.00
AUDITOR CONCENTRATION AND THE IMPACT OF INTERLOCKING DIRECTORATES
JAR SP 84 VOL: 22 PG:313 - 317 :: CORR. :PRIM. :OTH. :ORG.& ENVIR.

WAKEMAN,LM CIT: 0.00
OPTIMAL TAX DEPRECIATION
JAE DE 80 VOL: 2 PG:213 - 237 :: ANAL. :INT. LOG. :THEORY :AMOR./DEPL.

WALKER,M CIT: 0.00
RISK ATTITUDES, VALUE-RESTRICTED PREFERENCES AND PUBLIC CHOICE OVER LOTTERIES
    AND INFORMATION SYSTEMS
TAR AP 84 VOL: 59 PG:278 - 286 :: ANAL. :INT. LOG. :OTH.STAT. :N/A

WALKER,NR ; SEC: PIERCE,LT CIT: 0.00
THE PRICE WATERHOUSE AUDIT: A STATE OF THE ART APPROACH
AUD AU 88 VOL: 08 PG:1 - 22 :: DES.STAT. :INT. LOG. :THEORY :AUD.THEOR.

WALKER,RG ; FIRS: SHARPE,IG CIT: 0.08
ASSET REVALUATIONS AND STOCK MARKET PRICES
JAR AU 75 VOL: 13 PG:293 - 310 :: REGRESS. :PRIM. :EMH :VALUAT.(INFL.)

WALLACE,WA CIT: 0.50
THE ASSOCIATION BETWEEN MUNICIPAL MARKET MEASURES AND SELECTED FINANCIAL
    REPORTING PRACTICES
JAR AU 81 VOL: 19 PG:502 - 520 :: REGRESS. :PRIM. :EMH :FIN.METH.

WALLACE,WA CIT: 0.00
THE ACCEPTABILITY OF REGRESSION ANALYSIS AS EVIDENCE IN A COURTROOM -
    IMPLICATIONS FOR THE AUDITOR
AUD SP 83 VOL: 2 PG:66 - 90 :: REGRESS. :INT. LOG. :OTH.STAT. :LIAB.

WALLACE,WA ; FIRS: KREUTZFELDT,RW CIT: 0.00
ERROR CHARACTERISTICS IN AUDIT POPULATIONS: THEIR PROFILE AND RELATIONSHIP TO
    ENVIRONMENTAL FACTORS
AUD AU 86 VOL: 6 PG:20 - 43 :: DES.STAT. :SURV. :OTH.STAT. :ERRORS

WALLER,WS ; SEC: FELIX JR,WL CIT: 0.40
THE EFFECTS OF INCOMPLETE OUTCOME FEEDBACK ON AUDITORS' SELF-PERCEPTIONS OF
    JUDGEMENT ABILITY
TAR OC 84 VOL: 59 PG:637 - 646 :: ANOVA :LAB. :HIPS :JUDG.

WALLER,WS ; FIRS: JIAMBALVO,J CIT: 0.00
DECOMPOSITION AND ASSESSMENTS OF AUDIT RISK
AUD SP 84 VOL: 3 PG:80 - 88 :: NON-PAR. :LAB. :OTH.STAT. :RISK

WALLER,WS ; SEC: FELIX JR,WL CIT: 1.40
THE AUDITOR AND LEARNING FROM EXPERIENCE: SOME CONJECTURES
AOS 34 84 VOL: 9 PG:383 - 406 :: QUAL. :INT. LOG. :HIPS :N/A

WALLER,WS CIT: 0.25
SELF-SELECTION AND THE PROBABILITY OF QUITTING: A CONTRACTING APPROACH TO
EMPLOYEE TURNOVER IN PUBLIC ACCOUNTING
JAR AU 85 VOL: 23 PG:817 - 828 :: REGRESS. :LAB. :OTH.BEH. :ORG.

WALLER,WS ; SEC: CHOW ,CW CIT: 0.50
THE SELF-SELECTION AND EFFORT EFFECTS OF STANDARD-BASED EMPLOYEE CONTRACTS: A
FRAMEWORK AND SOME EMPIRICAL EVIDENCE
TAR JL 85 VOL: 60 PG:458 - 476 :: REGRESS. :LAB. :OTH.BEH. :EXEC.COMP.

WALLER,WS ; SEC: FELIX JR,WL CIT: 0.00
AUDITORS' COVARIATION JUDGMENTS
TAR AP 87 VOL: 62 PG:275 - 292 :: REGRESS. :LAB. :HIPS :JUDG.

WALLER,WS ; FIRS: SMITH ,VL ; SEC: SCHATZBERG,J CIT: 0.00
EXPERIMENTAL ECONOMICS AND AUDITING
AUD AU 87 VOL: 7 PG:71 - 93 :: DES.STAT. :INT. LOG. :OTH. :METHOD.

WALLER,WS ; FIRS: SHIELDS,MD ; SEC: SOLOMON,I CIT: 0.00
EFFECTS OF ALTERNATIVE SAMPLE SPACE REPRESENTATIONS ON THE ACCURACY OF
AUDITORS' UNCERTAINTY JUDGEMENTS
AOS 04 87 VOL: 12 PG:375 - 385 :: REGRESS. :LAB. :HIPS :MAN.DEC.CHAR.

WALLER,WS ; FIRS: CHOW ,CW ; SEC: COOPER,JC CIT: 0.00
PARTICIPATIVE BUDGETING: EFFECTS OF A TRUTH-INDUCING PAY SCHEME AND
INFORMATION ASYMMETRY ON SLACK AND PERFORMANCE
TAR JA 88 VOL: 63 PG:111 - 122 :: REGRESS. :LAB. :OTH.BEH. :BUDG.& PLAN.

WALLER,WS CIT: 0.00
SLACK IN PARTICIPATIVE BUDGETING: THE JOINT EFFECT OF A TRUTH-INDUCING PAY
SCHEME AND RISK PREFERENCES
AOS 01 88 VOL: 13 PG:87 - 98 :: REGRESS. :LAB. :OTH.BEH. :BUDG.& PLAN.

WALLER,WS ; FIRS: SHIELDS,MD CIT: 0.00
A BEHAVIORAL STUDY OF ACCOUNTING VARIABLES IN PERFORMANCE-INCENTIVE CONTRAC
AOS 06 88 VOL: 13 PG:581 - 594 :: REGRESS. :LAB. :INF.ECO./AG. :EXEC.COMP.

WALTHER,LM CIT: 0.29
A COMPARISON OF ESTIMATED AND REPORTED HISTORICAL COST/CONSTANT DOLLAR DATA
TAR AP 82 VOL: 57 PG:376 - 383 :: DES.STAT. :PRIM. :OTH.STAT. :VALUAT.(INFL.)

WARD ,BH CIT: 0.54
AN INVESTIGATION OF THE MATERIALITY CONSTRUCT IN AUDITING
JAR SP 76 VOL: 14 PG:138 - 152 :: NON-PAR. :LAB. :OTH.BEH. :MAT.

WARREN,CS CIT: 0.00
CONFIRMATION INFORMATIVENESS
JAR SP 74 VOL: 12 PG:158 - 177 :: ANOVA :FIELD :OTH.STAT. :OPER.AUD.

WARREN,CS CIT: 0.31
UNIFORMITY OF AUDITING STANDARDS
JAR SP 75 VOL: 13 PG:162 - 176 :: ANOVA :PRIM. :OTH.STAT. :OPIN.

WARREN,CS CIT: 0.17
CHARACTERISTICS OF FIRMS REPORTING CONSISTENCY EXCEPTIONS - A CROSS SECTIONAL
ANALYSIS
TAR JA 77 VOL: 52 PG:150 - 161 :: ANOVA :PRIM. :OTH.STAT. :ACC.CHNG.

WARREN,CS CIT: 0.00
UNIFORMITY OF AUDITING STANDARDS: A REPLICATION
JAR SP 80 VOL: 18 PG:312 - 324 :: ANOVA :PRIM. :INSTIT. :OPIN.

WASSERMAN,W ; FIRS: HANNUM,WH CIT: 0.00
GENERAL ADJUSTMENTS AND PRICE LEVEL MEASUREMENT
TAR AP 68 VOL: 43 PG:295 - 302 :: QUAL. :INT. LOG. :THEORY :VALUAT.(INFL.)

WATERHOUSE,JH ; FIRS: BRUNS JR,WJ CIT: 3.62
BUDGETARY CONTROL AND ORGANIZATION STRUCTURE
JAR AU 75 VOL: 13 PG:177 - 203 :: OTH.QUANT. :FIELD :OTH.BEH. :ORG.FORM

WATERHOUSE,JH ; SEC: TIESSEN,P CIT: 3.18
A CONTINGENCY FRAMEWORK FOR MANAGEMENT ACCOUNTING SYSTEMS RESEARCH
AOS 01 78 VOL: 3 PG:65 - 76 :: QUAL. :INT. LOG. :HIPS :METHOD.

WATERHOUSE,JH ; FIRS: SWIERINGA,RJ CIT: 0.29
ORGANIZATIONAL VIEWS OF TRANSFER PRICING
AOS 02 82 VOL: 7 PG:149 - 166 :: QUAL. :INT. LOG. :OTH. :TRANS.PRIC.

WATERHOUSE,JH ; FIRS: TIESSEN, P CIT: 1.67
TOWARDS A DESCRIPTIVE THEORY OF MANAGEMENT ACCOUNTING
AOS 23 83 VOL: 8 PG:251 - 268 :: QUAL. :INT. LOG. :THEORY :MANAG.

WATKINS,PR CIT: 0.00
MULTIDIMENSIONAL SCALING MEASUREMENT AND ACCOUNTING RESEARCH
JAR SP 84 VOL: 22 PG:406 - 411 :: OTH.QUANT. :INT. LOG. :OTH.STAT. :METHOD.

WATKINS,PR ; FIRS: BIGGS ,SF ; SEC: MOCK ,TJ CIT: 0.00
AUDITOR'S USE OF ANALYTICAL REVIEW IN AUDIT PROGRAM DESIGN
TAR JA 88 VOL: 63 PG:148 - 162 :: REGRESS. :LAB. :OTH.BEH. :ANAL.REV.

WATSON,CJ ; FIRS: STOCK ,D CIT: 0.40
HUMAN JUDGMENT ACCURACY, MULTIDIMENSIONAL GRAPHICS, AND HUMANS VERSUS MODELS
JAR SP 84 VOL: 22 PG:192 - 206 :: OTH.QUANT. :LAB. :HIPS :BUS.FAIL.

WATSON,DJ CIT: 0.38
THE STRUCTURE OF PROJECT TEAMS FACING DIFFERENTIATED ENVIRONMENTS: AN
    EXPLORATORY STUDY IN PUBLIC ACCOUNTING FIRMS
TAR AP 75 VOL: 50 PG:259 - 273 :: ANOVA :SURV. :OTH.BEH. :ORG.

WATSON,DJ CIT: 0.15
THE STRUCTURE OF PROJECT TEAMS FACING DIFFERENTIATED ENVIRONMENTS: AN
    EXPLORATORY STUDY IN PUBLIC ACCOUNTING FIRMS
TAR AP 75 VOL: 50 PG:259 - 273 :: ANOVA :SURV. :OTH.BEH. :ORG.

WATSON,DJ ; SEC: BAUMLER,JV CIT: 0.69
TRANSFER PRICING: A BEHAVIOURAL CONTEXT
TAR JL 75 VOL: 50 PG:466 - 474 :: QUAL. :INT. LOG. :OTH.BEH. :TRANS.PRIC.

WATSON,DJ ; FIRS: JIAMBALVO,J ; THIR: BAUMLER,JV CIT: 0.17
AN EXAMINATION OF PERFORMANCE EVALUATION DECISIONS IN CPA FIRM SUBUNITS
AOS 01 83 VOL: 8 PG:13 - 30 :: REGRESS. :LAB. :OTH.BEH. :ORG.

WATTS ,RL ; FIRS: DOPUCH,N CIT: 1.08
USING TIME-SERIES MODELS TO ASSESS THE SIGNIFICANCE OF ACCOUNTING CHANGES
JAR SP 72 VOL: 10 PG:180 - 194 :: MIXED :PRIM. :TIME SER. :ACC.CHNG.

WATTS ,RL ; FIRS: BALL ,R ; SEC: LEV ,B CIT: 0.23
INCOME VARIATION AND BALANCE SHEET COMPOSITIONS
JAR SP 76 VOL: 14 PG:1 - 9 :: REGRESS. :PRIM. :OTH.STAT. :REV.REC.

WATTS ,RL ; SEC: LEFTWICH,RW CIT: 2.58
THE TIME SERIES OF ANNUAL ACCOUNTING EARNINGS
JAR AU 77 VOL: 15 PG:253 - 271 :: MIXED :PRIM. :TIME SER. :FOREC.

WATTS ,RL ; SEC: ZIMMERMAN,JL CIT: 7.91
TOWARDS A POSITIVE THEORY OF THE DETERMINATION OF ACCOUNTING STANDARDS
TAR JA 78 VOL: 53 PG:112 - 134 :: OTH.QUANT. :PRIM. :OTH.STAT. :FASB SUBM.

WATTS ,RL ; SEC: ZIMMERMAN,JL CIT: 3.80
THE DEMAND FOR AND SUPPLY OF ACCOUNTING THEORIES: THE MARKET FOR EXCUSES
TAR AP 79 VOL: 54 PG:273 - 305 :: QUAL. :INT. LOG. :THEORY :FIN.METH.

WATTS ,RL ; SEC: ZIMMERMAN,JL CIT: 0.44
ON THE IRRELEVANCE OF REPLACEMENT COST DISCLOSURES FOR SECURITY PRICES
JAE AG 80 VOL: 2 PG:95 - 106 :: QUAL. :SEC. :OTH. :VALUAT.(INFL.)

WATTS ,RL ; FIRS: LEFTWICH,RW ; THIR: ZIMMERMAN,JL CIT: 0.75
VOLUNTARY CORPORATE DISCLOSURE: THE CASE OF INTERIM REPORTING
JAR ST 81 VOL: 19 PG:50 - 77 :: ANAL. :PRIM. :OTH.STAT. :FIN.METH.

WAUGH ,JB CIT: 0.00
THE INTERPERIOD ALLOCATION OF CORPORATE INCOME TAXES: A PROPOSAL
TAR JL 68 VOL: 43 PG:535 - 539 :: QUAL. :INT. LOG. :THEORY :TAXES

WAYMIRE,G ; FIRS: SUNDER,S CIT: 0.67
MARGINAL GAINS IN ACCURACY OF VALUATION FROM INCREASINGLY SPECIFIC PRICE
INDEXES: EMPIRICAL EVIDENCE FOR THE U.S. ECONOMY
JAR AU 83 VOL: 21 PG:565 - 580 :: MIXED :PRIM. :OTH.STAT. :VALUAT.(INFL.)

WAYMIRE,G ; SEC: POWNALL,G CIT: 0.00
SOME EVIDENCE ON POTENTIAL EFFECTS OF CONTEMPORANEOUS EARN. DISCLOSURES IN
TESTS OF CAPITAL MARKET EFFECTS ASSOC. WITH FASB EXPOSURE DRAFT NO.19
JAR AU 83 VOL: 21 PG:629 - 643 :: REGRESS. :PRIM. :EMH :OIL & GAS

WAYMIRE,G CIT: 1.00
ADDITIONAL EVIDENCE ON THE INFORMATION CONTENT OF MANAGEMENT EARNINGS
FORECASTS
JAR AU 84 VOL: 22 PG:703 - 718 :: REGRESS. :PRIM. :EMH :FOREC.

WAYMIRE,G ; FIRS: SUNDER,S CIT: 0.60
ACCURACY OF EXCHANGE VALUATION RULES: ADDITIVITY AND UNBIASED ESTIMATION
JAR SP 84 VOL: 22 PG:396 - 405 :: ANAL. :INT. LOG. :THEORY :SPEC.ITEMS

WAYMIRE,G CIT: 0.00
EARNINGS VOLATILITY AND VOLUNTARY MANAGEMENT FORECAST DISCLOSURE
JAR SP 85 VOL: 23 PG:268 - 295 :: REGRESS. :PRIM. :OTH.STAT. :FOREC.

WAYMIRE,G CIT: 0.00
ADDITIONAL EVIDENCE ON THE ACCURACY OF ANALYST FORECASTS BEFORE AND AFTER
VOLUNTARY MANAGEMENT EARNINGS FORECASTS
TAR JA 86 VOL: 61 PG:129 - 142 :: REGRESS. :PRIM. :TIME SER. :FOREC.

WEBB ,J ; FIRS: BARNES,P CIT: 0.67
MANAGEMENT INFORMATION CHANGES AND FUNCTIONAL FIXATION: SOME EXPERIMENTAL
EVIDENCE FROM THE PUBLIC SECTOR
AOS 01 86 VOL: 11 PG:1 - 18 :: REGRESS. :LAB. :HIPS :COST.ALLOC.

WEBER ,C CIT: 0.00
THE MATHEMATICS OF VARIANCE ANALYSIS
TAR JL 63 VOL: 38 PG:534 - 539 :: ANAL. :SEC. :OTH. :VAR.

WEBER ,R ; FIRS: EVEREST,GL CIT: 0.25
A RELATIONAL APPROACH TO ACCOUNTING MODELS
TAR AP 77 VOL: 52 PG:340 - 359 :: ANAL. :INT. LOG. :OTH.STAT. :N/A

WEBER ,R CIT: 0.18
AUDITOR DECISION MAKING ON OVERALL SYSTEM RELIABILITY: ACCURACY, CONSENSUS,
AND THE USEFULNESS OF A SIMULATION DECISION AID
JAR AU 78 VOL: 16 PG:368 - 388 :: REGRESS. :LAB. :HIPS :INT.CONT.

WEBER ,R CIT: 0.27
AUDITOR DECISION MAKING ON OVERALL SYSTEM RELIABILITY: ACCURACY, CONSENSUS,
AND THE USEFULNESS OF A SIMULATION DECISION AID
JAR FL 78 VOL: 16 PG:368 - 388 :: REGRESS. :LAB. :HIPS :INT.CONT.

WEBER ,R CIT: 0.44
SOME CHARACTERISTICS OF THE FREE RECALL OF COMPUTER CONTROLS BY EDP AUDITORS
JAR SP 80 VOL: 18 PG:214 - 241 :: NON-PAR. :LAB. :HIPS :AUD.BEH.

WEBER ,R CIT: 0.14
AUDIT TRAIL SYSTEM SUPPORT IN ADVANCED COMPUTER-BASED ACCOUNTING SYSTEMS
TAR AP 82 VOL: 57 PG:311 - 325 :: QUAL. :INT. LOG. :OTH. :AUD.TRAIL

WEBER ,R CIT: 0.00
DATA MODELS RESEARCH IN ACCOUNTING: AN EVALUATION OF WHOLESALE DISTRIBUTION
SOFTWARE
TAR JL 86 VOL: 61 PG:498 - 518 :: REGRESS. :SURV. :OTH.STAT. :INFO.STRUC.

WEBER ,R ; FIRS: DAVIS ,GB CIT: 0.00
THE IMPACT OF ADVANCED COMPUTER SYSTEMS ON CONTROLS AND AUDIT PROCEDURES: A
THEORY AND AN EMPIRICAL TEST
AUD SP 86 VOL: 5 PG:35 - 49 :: REGRESS. :LAB. :OTH.STAT. :EDP AUD.

WEBER ,RP CIT: 0.00
MISLEADING TAX FIGURES - A PROBLEM FOR ACCOUNTANTS
TAR JA 77 VOL: 52 PG:172 - 185 :: ANAL. :INT. LOG. :THEORY :TAXES

WEBER ,RP ; SEC: STEVENSON,WC CIT: 0.25
EVALUATIONS OF ACCOUNTING JOURNAL AND DEPARTMENT QUALITY
TAR JL 81 VOL: 56 PG:596 - 612 :: DES.STAT. :SIM. :OTH. :OTH.MANAG.

WEICK ,KE ; FIRS: SWIERINGA,RJ CIT: 1.14
AN ASSESSMENT OF LABORATORY EXPERIMENTS IN ACCOUNTING
JAR ST 82 VOL: 20 PG:56 - 101 :: DES.STAT. :SEC. :OTH.BEH. :METHOD.

WEICK ,KE ; FIRS: SWIERINGA,RJ CIT: 0.50
MANAGEMENT ACCOUNTING AND ACTION
AOS 03 87 VOL: 12 PG:293 - 308 :: DES.STAT. :INT. LOG. :HIST. :MANAG.

WEIGAND,RE CIT: 0.00
THE ACCOUNTANT AND MARKETING CHANNELS
TAR JL 63 VOL: 38 PG:584 - 590 :: QUAL. :INT. LOG. :INSTIT. :OTH.MANAG.

WEIL ,RL CIT: 0.00
RECIPROCAL OR MUTUAL HOLDINGS: ALLOCATING EARNINGS AND SELECTING THE
ACCOUNTING METHOD
TAR OC 73 VOL: 48 PG:749 - 758 :: QUAL. :INT. LOG. :THEORY :BUS.COMB.

WEIL ,RL ; FIRS: DAVIDSON,S CIT: 0.09
INCOME TAX IMPLICATIONS OF VARIOUS METHODS OF ACCOUNTING FOR CHANGING PRICE
JAR ST 78 VOL: 16 PG:154 - 233 :: DES.STAT. :PRIM. :OTH.STAT. :VALUAT.(INFL.)

WEINGARTER,HM CIT: 0.00
THE EXCESS PRESENT VALUE INDEX - A THEORETICAL BASIS AND CRITIQUE
JAR AU 63 VOL: 1 PG:213 - 224 :: ANAL. :INT. LOG. :MATH.PROG. :N/A

WEINSTEIN,MG ; FIRS: BRENNER,VC ; SEC: CARMACK,CW CIT: 0.00
AN EMPIRICAL TEST OF THE MOTIVATION-HYGIENE THEORY
JAR AU 71 VOL: 9 PG:359 - 366 :: CORR. :SURV. :OTH.BEH. :AUD.BEH.

WEIS ,WL ; FIRS: RAMANATHAN,KV CIT: 0.13
SUPPLEMENTING COLLEGIATE FINANCIAL STATEMENTS WITH ACROSS-FUND AGGREGATIONS:
    AN EXPERIMENTAL INQUIRY
AOS 02 81 VOL: 6 PG:143 - 152 :: ANOVA :LAB. :THEORY :INFO.STRUC.

WEISER,HJ CIT: 0.00
ACCOUNTING EDUCATION - PRESENT AND FUTURE
TAR JL 66 VOL: 41 PG:518 - 524 :: QUAL. :INT. LOG. :INSTIT. :OTH.MANAG.

WELAM ,VP ; FIRS: KAPLAN,RS CIT: 0.38
OVERHEAD ALLOCATION WITH IMPERFECT MARKETS AND NONLINEAR TECHNOLOGY
TAR JL 74 VOL: 49 PG:477 - 484 :: ANAL. :INT. LOG. :MATH.PROG. :OVER.ALLOC.

WELCH ,PR CIT: 0.00
A GENERALIZED DISTRIBUTED LAG MODEL FOR PREDICTING QUARTERLY EARNINGS
JAR AU 84 VOL: 22 PG:744 - 757 :: NON-PAR. :PRIM. :TIME SER. :FOREC.

WELKE ,WR CIT: 0.00
ACCOUNTING SYSTEMS IN THE CURRICULUM
TAR AP 66 VOL: 41 PG:253 - 256 :: QUAL. :INT. LOG. :N/A :OTH.MANAG.

WELKER,RB CIT: 0.15
DISCRIMINANT ANALYSIS AS AN AID TO EMPLOYEE SELECTION
TAR JL 74 VOL: 49 PG:514 - 523 :: OTH.QUANT. :INT. LOG. :OTH.STAT. :AUD.

WELKER,RB ; FIRS: GROSSMAN,SD ; SEC: KRATCHMAN,SH CIT: 0.00
COMMENT: THE EFFECT OF REPLACEMENT COST DISCLOSURES ON SECURITY PRICES
JAA WI 81 VOL: 4 PG:136 - 143 :: DES.STAT. :PRIM. :EMH :VALUAT.(INFL.)

WELKER,RB ; FIRS: APOSTOLOU,NG ; SEC: GIROUX,GA CIT: 0.00
THE INFORMATION CONTENT OF MUNICIPAL SPENDING RATE DATA
JAR AU 85 VOL: 23 PG:853 - 858 :: REGRESS. :PRIM. :INSTIT. :LTD

WELKER,RB ; FIRS: LICATA,MP ; SEC: STRAWSER,RH CIT: 0.00
A NOTE ON PARTICIPATION IN BUDGETING AND LOCUS OF CONTROL
TAR JA 86 VOL: 61 PG:112 - 117 :: REGRESS. :LAB. :OTH.BEH. :BUDG.& PLAN.

WELKER,RB ; FIRS: MEIXNER,WF CIT: 0.00
JUDGMENT CONSENSUS AND AUDITOR EXPERIENCE: AN EXAMINATION OF ORGANIZATIONAL
    RELATIONS
AUD JL 88 VOL: 63 PG:505 - 513 :: CORR. :LAB. :OTH.BEH. :JUDG.

WELLING,P CIT: 0.08
A GOAL PROGRAMMING MODEL FOR HUMAN RESOURCE ACCOUNTING IN A CPA FIRM
AOS 04 77 VOL: 2 PG:307 - 316 :: ANAL. :SIM. :MATH.PROG. :HRA

WELLS ,MC ; SEC: COTTON,W CIT: 0.00
HOLDING GAINS ON FIXED ASSETS
TAR OC 65 VOL: 40 PG:829 - 833 :: QUAL. :INT. LOG. :THEORY :VALUAT.(INFL.)

WELLS ,MC CIT: 0.00
A NOTE ON THE AMORTIZATION OF FIXED ASSETS
TAR AP 68 VOL: 43 PG:373 - 376 :: QUAL. :INT. LOG. :THEORY :PP&E / DEPR

WELLS ,MC CIT: 0.00
A REVOLUTION IN ACCOUNTING THOUGHT?
TAR JL 76 VOL: 51 PG:471 - 482 :: QUAL. :SEC. :HIST. :FIN.METH.

WELSCH,GA CIT: 0.00
SOME CHALLENGES FOR ACCOUNTING EDUCATION
TAR OC 64 VOL: 39 PG:008 - 013 :: QUAL. :INT. LOG. :INSTIT. :OTH.MANAG.

WELSH ,MJ ; SEC: TRAPNELL,JE CIT: 0.00
LABOR MARKET MODELS AND EMPLOYER ACCOUNTING FOR PENSIONS
JAA WI 85 VOL: 8 PG:100 - 111 :: DES.STAT. :INT. LOG. :THEORY :PENS.

WERNER,CA ; SEC: KOSTOLANSKY,JW CIT: 0.00
ACCOUNTING LIABILITIES UNDER ERISA
JAA AU 83 VOL: 7 PG:54 - 64 :: QUAL. :INT. LOG. :THEORY :PENS.

WERNER,CA ; SEC: KOSTOLANSKY,JW CIT: 0.00
ACCOUNTING LIABILITIES UNDER THE MULTIEMPLOYER PENSION PLAN AMENDMENTS ACT
JAA SP 84 VOL: 7 PG:212 - 224 :: QUAL. :INT. LOG. :THEORY :PENS.

WESCOTT,SH CIT: 0.20
ACCOUNTING NUMBERS AND SOCIOECONOMIC VARIABLES AS PREDICTORS OF MUNICIPAL
    GENERAL OBLIGATION BOND RATINGS
JAR SP 84 VOL: 22 PG:412 - 423 :: OTH.QUANT. :PRIM. :OTH.STAT. :ORG.& ENVIR.

WEST ,M ; FIRS: REILLY,FK ; SEC: MORGENSON,DL CIT: 0.23
THE PREDICTIVE ABILITY OF ALTERNATIVE PARTS OF INTERIM FINANCIAL STATEMENTS
JAR ST 72 VOL: 10 PG:105 - 124 :: REGRESS. :PRIM. :EMH :INT.REP.

WEST ,RR CIT: 0.31
AN ALTERNATIVE APPROACH TO PREDICTING CORPORATE BOND RATINGS
JAR SP 70 VOL: 8 PG:118 - 125 :: REGRESS. :PRIM. :OTH.STAT. :METHOD.

WEST ,RR ; FIRS: HOFSTEDT,TR CIT: 0.08
THE APB, YIELD INDICES, AND PREDICTIVE ABILITY
TAR AP 71 VOL: 46 PG:329 - 337 :: DES.STAT. :PRIM. :OTH.STAT. :PENS.

WEST ,SG ; FIRS: HARRISON,PD ; THIR: RENEAU,JH CIT: 0.00
INITIAL ATTRIBUTIONS AND INFORMATION-SEEKING BY SUPERIORS AND SUBORDINATES IN
    PRODUCTION VARIANCE INVESTIGATIONS
TAR AP 88 VOL: 63 PG:307 - 320 :: REGRESS. :LAB. :OTH.BEH. :VAR.

WEYGANDT,JJ ; FIRS: IMDIEKE,LF CIT: 0.00
CLASSIFICATION OF CONVERTIBLE DEBT
TAR OC 69 VOL: 44 PG:798 - 805 :: QUAL. :INT. LOG. :THEORY :LTD

WEYGANDT,JJ ; FIRS: FRANK ,WG CIT: 0.15
CONVERTIBLE DEBT AND EARNINGS PER SHARE: PRAGMATISM VS. GOOD THEORY
TAR AP 70 VOL: 45 PG:280 - 289 :: DES.STAT. :PRIM. :N/A :PENS.

WEYGANDT,JJ CIT: 0.00
THE CPA AND HIS DUTY TO SILENCE
TAR JA 70 VOL: 45 PG:69 - 75 :: QUAL. :SEC. :INSTIT. :INT.AUD.

WEYGANDT,JJ ; FIRS: LLOYD ,BM CIT: 0.00
MARKET VALUE INFORMATION FOR NONSUBSIDIARY INVESTMENTS
TAR OC 71 VOL: 46 PG:756 - 764 :: DES.STAT. :PRIM. :N/A :BUS.COMB.

WEYGANDT,JJ ; FIRS: FRANK ,WG CIT: 0.08
A PREDICTION MODEL FOR CONVERTIBLE DEBENTURES
JAR SP 71 VOL: 9 PG:116 - 126 :: OTH.QUANT. :PRIM. :OTH. :LTD

WEYGANDT,JJ ; FIRS: BOLLOM,WJ CIT: 0.08
AN EXAMINATION OF SOME INTERIM REPORTING THEORIES FOR A SEASONAL BUSINESS
TAR JA 72 VOL: 47 PG:75 - 84 :: QUAL. :SEC. :THEORY :INT.REP.

WEYGANDT,JJ CIT: 0.17
VALUATION OF STOCK OPTION CONTRACTS
TAR JA 77 VOL: 52 PG:40 - 51 :: ANAL. :INT. LOG. :OTH.STAT. :VALUAT.(INFL.)

WEYGANDT,JJ ; FIRS: TAYLOR,WM CIT: 0.00
ACCOUNTING FOR STOCK-BASED AWARDS USING THE MINIMUM VALUE METHOD
JAR AU 82 VOL: 20 PG:497 - 502 :: ANAL. :INT. LOG. :THEORY :SPEC.ITEMS

WEYGANDT,JJ ; FIRS: HIRSCHEY,M CIT: 0.00
AMORTIZATION POLICY FOR ADVERTISING AND RESEARCH AND DEVELOPMENT EXPENDITURES
JAR SP 85 VOL: 23 PG:326 - 335 :: REGRESS. :PRIM. :TIME SER. :R & D

WHALEY,RE ; SEC: CHEUNG,JK CIT: 0.14
ANTICIPATION OF QUARTERLY EARNINGS ANNOUNCEMENTS: A TEST OF OPTION MARKET
   EFFICIENCY
JAE OC 82 VOL: 4 PG:57 - 83 :: REGRESS. :SEC. :EMH :INT.REP.

WHEELER,JE ; FIRS: OUTSLAY,E CIT: 0.00
SEPARATING THE ANNUITY AND INCOME TRANSFER ELEMENTS OF SOCIAL SECURITY
TAR OC 82 VOL: 57 PG:716 - 733 :: DES.STAT. :PRIM. :OTH.STAT. :TAXES

WHEELER,JT CIT: 0.00
ACCOUNTING THEORY AND RESEARCH IN PERSPECTIVE
TAR JA 70 VOL: 45 PG:1 - 10 :: QUAL. :INT. LOG. :THEORY :OTH.MANAG.

WHINSTON,AB ; FIRS: COLANTONI,CS ; SEC: MANES ,RP CIT: 0.08
PROGRAMMING, PROFIT RATES AND PRICING DECISIONS
TAR JL 69 VOL: 44 PG:467 - 481 :: ANAL. :INT. LOG. :MATH.PROG. :REL.COSTS

WHINSTON,AB ; FIRS: COLANTONI,CS ; SEC: MANES ,RP CIT: 0.46
A UNIFIED APPROACH TO THE THEORY OF ACCOUNTING AND INFORMATION SYSTEMS
TAR JA 71 VOL: 46 PG:90 - 102 :: QUAL. :INT. LOG. :N/A :MANAG.

WHINSTON,AB ; FIRS: LIEBERMAN,AZ CIT: 0.46
A STRUCTURING OF AN EVENTS-ACCOUNTING INFORMATION SYSTEM
TAR AP 75 VOL: 50 PG:246 - 258 :: QUAL. :INT. LOG. :OTH.STAT. :N/A

WHINSTON,AB ; FIRS: HASEMAN,WD CIT: 0.46
DESIGN OF A MULTIDIMENSIONAL ACCOUNTING SYSTEM
TAR JA 76 VOL: 51 PG:65 - 79 :: ANAL. :INT. LOG. :N/A :MANAG.

WHINSTON,AB ; FIRS: CASH JR,JI ; SEC: BAILEY JR,AD CIT: 0.08
A SURVEY OF TECHNIQUES FOR AUDITING EDP-BASED ACCOUNTING INFORMATION SYSTEMS
TAR OC 77 VOL: 52 PG:813 - 832 :: QUAL. :SEC. :N/A :ANAL.REV.

WHINSTON,AB ; FIRS: BAILEY,AP ; SEC: MCAFEE,RP CIT: 0.13
AN APPLICATION OF COMPLEXITY THEORY TO THE ANALYSIS OF INTERNAL CONTROL
   SYSTEMS
AUD SU 81 VOL: 1 PG:38 - 52 :: ANAL. :INT. LOG. :OTH.STAT. :INT.CONT.

WHINSTON,AB ; FIRS: BAILEY JR,AD ; SEC: DUKE ,GL ; THIR: GERLACH,JH ; FOUR:
KO   ,CE FIFT: MESERVY,RD CIT: 0.00
TICOM AND THE ANALYSIS OF INTERNAL CONTROLS
TAR AP 85 VOL: 60 PG:186 - 201 :: CORR. :INT. LOG. :OTH. :INT.CONT.

WHITE ,D ; SEC: VANECEK,M CIT: 0.00
INTENDED USE: A UNIFORM TAX DEFINITION OF SOFTWARE
JAA SU 82 VOL: 5 PG:338 - 354 :: QUAL. :INT. LOG. :THEORY :TAXES

WHITE ,GE CIT: 0.38
DISCRETIONARY ACCOUNTING DECISIONS AND INCOME NORMALIZATION
JAR AU 70 VOL: 8 PG:260 - 273 :: ANOVA :PRIM. :TIME SER. :FIN.METH.

WHITE ,GT ; FIRS: WYER ,JC ; THIR: JANSON,EC CIT: 0.00
AUDITS OF PUBLIC COMPANIES BY SMALLER CPA FIRMS: CLIENTS, REPORTS, AND QUALITY
AUD SP 88 VOL: 07 PG:164 - 173 :: REGRESS. :PRIM. :INSTIT. :ORG.

WHITE ,L ; FIRS: NELSON,J ; SEC: RONEN ,J CIT: 0.00
LEGAL LIABILITIES AND THE MARKET FOR AUDITING SERVICES
JAA SU 88 VOL: 03 PG:255 - 296 :: DES.STAT. :INT. LOG. :INF.ECO./AG. :LIAB.

WHITE ,RA CIT: 0.17
EMPLOYEE PREFERENCES FOR NONTAXABLE COMPENSATION OFFERED IN A CAFETERIA
COMPENSATION PLAN: AN EMPIRICAL STUDY
TAR JL 83 VOL: 58 PG:539 - 561 :: ANOVA :SURV. :OTH.BEH. :TAXES

WHITE ,RA ; FIRS: JOHNSON,DA ; SEC: PANY ,K CIT: 0.00
AUDIT REPORTS AND THE LOAN DECISION: ACTIONS AND PERCEPTIONS
AUD SP 83 VOL: 2 PG:38 - 51 :: ANOVA :LAB. :OTH.BEH. :OPIN.

WHITE ,RA ; FIRS: SUMNERS,GE ; THIR: CLAY JR,RJ CIT: 0.00
THE USE OF ENGAGEMENT LETTERS IN AUDIT, REVIEW, AND COMPILATION ENGAGEMENTS:
AN EMPIRICAL STUDY
AUD SP 87 VOL: 6 PG:116 - 122 :: REGRESS. :SURV. :OTH.BEH. :ORG.

WHITE JR,CE CIT: 0.23
EFFECTS OF DISCRETIONARY ACCOUNTING POLICY ON VARIABLE AND DECLINING
PERFORMANCE TRENDS
JAR AU 72 VOL: 10 PG:351 - 358 :: DES.STAT. :PRIM. :TIME SER. :ACC.CHNG.

WHITE JR,CE ; FIRS: KUNITAKE,WK CIT: 0.00
ETHICS FOR INDEPENDENT AUDITORS
JAA SU 86 VOL: 1 PG:222 - 231 :: DES.STAT. :INT. LOG. :INSTIT. :PROF.RESP.

WHITEHURST,FD CIT: 0.00
THE PREDICTABILITY OF INVESTOR CASH RETURN FROM HISTORICAL INCOME TRENDS OF
COMMON STOCKS
TAR JL 70 VOL: 45 PG:553 - 564 :: CORR. :PRIM. :TIME SER. :CASH

WHITFORD,DT ; FIRS: GENTRY,JA ; SEC: NEWBOLD,P CIT: 0.50
CLASSIFYING BANKRUPT FIRMS WITH FUNDS FLOW COMPONENTS
JAR SP 85 VOL: 23 PG:146 - 160 :: REGRESS. :PRIM. :OTH.STAT. :BUS.FAIL.

WHITLEY,R CIT: 0.67
THE TRANSFORMATION OF BUSINESS FINANCE INTO FINANCIAL ECONOMICS: THE ROLES OF
ACADEMIC EXPANSION AND CHANGES IN U.S. CAPITAL MARKETS
AOS 02 86 VOL: 11 PG:171 - 192 :: DES.STAT. :INT. LOG. :OTH. :OTH.MANAG.

WHITSELL,GM ; FIRS: RHODE ,JG ; THIR: KELSEY,RL CIT: 0.31
AN ANALYSIS OF CLIENT-INDUSTRY CONCENTRATIONS FOR LARGE PUBLIC ACCOUNTING
FIRMS
TAR OC 74 VOL: 49 PG:772 - 787 :: DES.STAT. :PRIM. :INSTIT. :AUD.

WHITTENBURG,G ; FIRS: WHITTINGTON,OR CIT: 0.00
JUDICIAL CLASSIFICATION OF DEBT VERSUS EQUITY - AN EMPIRICAL STUDY
TAR JL 80 VOL: 55 PG:409 - 418 :: OTH.QUANT. :PRIM. :OTH.STAT. :N/A

WHITTINGTON,OR ; SEC: WHITTENBURG,G CIT: 0.00
JUDICIAL CLASSIFICATION OF DEBT VERSUS EQUITY - AN EMPIRICAL STUDY
TAR JL 80 VOL: 55 PG:409 - 418 :: OTH.QUANT. :PRIM. :OTH.STAT. :N/A

WHITTINGTON,OR ; SEC: ADAMS ,SJ CIT: 0.00
TEMPORARY BREAKDOWNS OF INTERNAL CONTROL: IMPLICATIONS FOR EXTERNAL AND
   INTERNAL AUDITORS
JAA SU 82 VOL: 5 PG:310 - 319 :: QUAL. :INT. LOG. :OTH. :N/A

WHITTINGTON,OR ; FIRS: CARMICHAEL,DR CIT: 0.00
THE AUDITOR'S CHANGING ROLE IN FINANCIAL REPORTING
JAA SU 84 VOL: 7 PG:347 - 361 :: QUAL. :INT. LOG. :OTH. :PROF.RESP.

WHITTRED,G CIT: 0.50
THE DERIVED DEMAND FOR CONSOLIDATED FINANCIAL REPORTING
JAE DE 87 VOL: 9 PG:259 - 285 :: REGRESS. :PRIM. :THEORY :BUS.COMB.

WHITTRED,GP CIT: 0.78
AUDIT QUALIFICATION AND THE TIMELINESS OF CORPORATE ANNUAL REPORTS
TAR OC 80 VOL: 55 PG:563 - 577 :: NON-PAR. :PRIM. :OTH. :OPIN.

WHITTRED,GP ; SEC: ZIMMER,I CIT: 0.00
TIMELINESS OF FINANCIAL REPORTING AND FINANCIAL DISTRESS
TAR AP 84 VOL: 59 PG:287 - 295 :: DES.STAT. :PRIM. :OTH.STAT. :FIN.ST.TIM.

WICHMANN JR,H ; FIRS: NIX ,HM CIT: 0.00
THE GOVERNMENTAL AUDIT REPORT
JAA SU 83 VOL: 6 PG:341 - 352 :: DES.STAT. :PRIM. :OTH. :OPIN.

WIESEN,JL ; FIRS: SCHIFF,M ; SEC: SORTER,GH CIT: 0.00
THE EVOLVING ROLE OF CORPORATE AUDIT COMMITTEES
JAA AU 77 VOL: 1 PG:19 - 44 :: QUAL. :INT. LOG. :INSTIT. :OTH.MANAG.

WIESEN,JL ; SEC: ENG ,R CIT: 0.00
CORPORATE PERKS: DISCLOSURE AND TAX CONSIDERATIONS
JAA WI 79 VOL: 2 PG:101 - 121 :: QUAL. :INT. LOG. :THEORY :TAXES

WIESEN,JL CIT: 0.00
REPORTING CONCEPTS FOR THE 1980S
JAA SU 81 VOL: 4 PG:309 - 324 :: QUAL. :INT. LOG. :INSTIT. :FASB SUBM.

WIGGIN,CE ; FIRS: BENJAMIN,JJ ; SEC: GROSSMAN,SD CIT: 0.00
THE IMPACT OF FOREIGN CURRENCY TRANSLATION ON REPORTING DURING THE PHASE-IN
   OF SFAS NO.52
JAA SU 86 VOL: 1 PG:177 - 184 :: REGRESS. :PRIM. :THEORY :FOR.CUR.

WILCOX,JA CIT: 0.31
A PREDICTION OF BUSINESS FAILURE USING ACCOUNTING DATA
JAR ST 73 VOL: 11 PG:163 - 179 :: DES.STAT. :PRIM. :OTH.STAT. :BUS.FAIL.

WILCOX,KA ; SEC: SMITH ,CH CIT: 0.00
ROLE DISCREPANCIES AND THE AUDITOR-CLIENT RELATIONSHIP
AOS 01 77 VOL: 2 PG:81 - 97 :: NON-PAR. :FIELD :OTH.STAT. :AUD.

WILD ,JJ ; FIRS: BIGGS ,SF CIT: 0.40
A NOTE ON THE PRACTICE OF ANALYTICAL REVIEW
AUD SP 84 VOL: 3 PG:68 - 79 :: CORR. :SURV. :OTH.STAT. :ANAL.REV.

WILD ,JJ ; FIRS: BIGGS ,SF CIT: 0.25
AN INVESTIGATION OF AUDITOR JUDGMENT IN ANALYTICAL REVIEW
TAR OC 85 VOL: 60 PG:607 - 633 :: REGRESS. :LAB. :HIPS :ANAL.REV.

WILD ,JJ CIT: 0.00
THE PREDICTION PERFORMANCE OF A STRUCTURAL MODEL OF ACCOUNTING NUMBERS
JAR SP 87 VOL: 25 PG:139 - 160 :: DES.STAT. :CASE :THEORY :FOREC.

WILDAVSKY,A CIT: 0.64
POLICY ANALYSIS IS WHAT INFORMATION SYSTEMS ARE NOT
AOS 01 78 VOL: 3 PG:77 - 88 :: QUAL. :INT. LOG. :OTH. :METHOD.

WILKERSON JR,JE CIT: 0.00
SELECTING EXPERIMENTAL AND COMPARISON SAMPLES FOR USE IN STUDIES OF AUDITOR
   REPORTING DECISIONS
JAR SP 87 VOL: 25 PG:161 - 167 :: DES.STAT. :PRIM. :OTH.STAT. :METHOD.

WILKINS,T ; SEC: ZIMMER,I CIT: 0.17
THE EFFECT OF LEASING AND DIFFERENT METHODS OF ACCOUNTING FOR LEASES ON
   CREDIT EVALUATIONS
TAR OC 83 VOL: 58 PG:749 - 764 :: ANOVA :LAB. :OTH.BEH. :LEASES

WILKINSON,JR ; SEC: DONEY ,LD CIT: 0.08
EXTENDING AUDIT AND REPORTING BOUNDARIES
TAR OC 65 VOL: 40 PG:753 - 756 :: QUAL. :INT. LOG. :INSTIT. :AUD.

WILKINSON,TL CIT: 0.00
CAN ACCOUNTING BE AN INTERNATIONAL LANGUAGE?
TAR JA 64 VOL: 39 PG:133 - 139 :: QUAL. :INT. LOG. :THEORY :INT.DIFF.

WILL ,HJ CIT: 0.23
AUDITING IN SYSTEMS PERSPECTIVE
TAR OC 74 VOL: 49 PG:690 - 706 :: QUAL. :INT. LOG. :N/A :AUD.

WILLIAMS,D CIT: 0.00
REPORTING LOSS CARRYOVERS IN FINANCIAL STATEMENTS
TAR AP 66 VOL: 41 PG:226 - 234 :: QUAL. :INT. LOG. :THEORY :TAXES

WILLIAMS,DD ; SEC: DIRSMITH,MW CIT: 0.00
THE EFFECTS OF AUDIT TECHNOLOGY ON AUDITOR EFFICIENCY: AUDITING AND THE
   TIMELINESS OF CLIENT EARNINGS ANNOUNCEMENTS
AOS 05 88 VOL: 13 PG:487 - 508 :: REGRESS. :PRIM. :INSTIT. :OPER.AUD.

WILLIAMS,DJ ; SEC: LILLIS,A CIT: 0.00
EDP AUDITS OF OPERATING SYSTEMS - AN EXPLORATORY STUDY OF THE DETERMINANTS OF
   THE PRIOR PROBABILITY RISK
AUD SP 85 VOL: 4 PG:110 - 117 :: REGRESS. :SURV. :OTH.STAT. :EDP AUD.

WILLIAMS,DJ CIT: 0.00
SHAREHOLDERS BONDING IN FINANCIAL MUTUALS: AN EXPLORATORY STUDY OF THE
   RELATIVE EFFECTS OF ALTRUISM AND AGENCY
AOS 03 86 VOL: 11 PG:271 - 288 :: REGRESS. :PRIM. :INF.ECO./AG. :ORG.FORM

WILLIAMS,JJ CIT: 0.00
ZERO-BASE BUDGETING: PROSPECTS FOR DEVELOPING A SEMI-CONFUSING BUDGETING
   INFORMATION SYSTEM
AOS 02 81 VOL: 6 PG:153 - 166 :: QUAL. :INT. LOG. :THEORY :BUDG.& PLAN.

WILLIAMS,JJ ; SEC: NEWTON,JD ; THIR: MORGAN,EA CIT: 0.00
THE INTEGRATION OF ZERO-BASE BUDGETING WITH MANAGEMENT-BY-OBJECTIVES: AN
EMPIRICAL INQUIRY
AOS 04 85 VOL: 10 PG:457 - 478 :: REGRESS. :FIELD :OTH.BEH. :BUDG.& PLAN.

WILLIAMS,JJ ; SEC: HININGS,CR CIT: 0.00
A NOTE ON MATCHING CONTROL SYSTEM IMPLICATIONS WITH ORGANIZATIONAL
CHARACTERISTICS: ZBB AND MBO REVISITED
AOS 02 88 VOL: 13 PG:191 - 198 :: REGRESS. :SURV. :OTH.BEH. :BUDG.& PLAN.

WILLIAMS,PF CIT: 0.11
THE EVALUATIVE RELEVANCE OF SOCIAL DATA
TAR JA 80 VOL: 55 PG:62 - 77 :: ANOVA :SURV. :OTH.STAT. :HRA

WILLIAMS,PF CIT: 0.00
THE PREDICTIVE ABILITY PARADOX IN BEHAVIOURAL ACCOUNTING RESEARCH
AOS 04 82 VOL: 7 PG:405 - 410 :: ANAL. :INT. LOG. :OTH.BEH. :METHOD.

WILLIAMS,PF CIT: 0.00
THE LEGITIMATE CONCERN WITH FAIRNESS
AOS 02 87 VOL: 12 PG:169 - 192 :: DES.STAT. :INT. LOG. :THEORY :FIN.METH.

WILLIAMS,PF ; FIRS: ROCKNESS,J CIT: 0.00
A DESCRIPTIVE STUDY OF SOCIAL RESPONSIBILITY MUTUAL FUNDS
AOS 04 88 VOL: 13 PG:397 - 411 :: REGRESS. :SURV. :INSTIT. :HRA

WILLIAMS,TH ; SEC: GRIFFIN,CH CIT: 0.08
MATRIX THEORY AND COST ALLOCATION
TAR JL 64 VOL: 39 PG:671 - 678 :: ANAL. :INT. LOG. :MATH.PROG. :COST.ALLOC.

WILLIAMS,TH ; FIRS: ROLLER,J CIT: 0.00
PROFESSIONAL SCHOOLS OF ACCOUNTING
TAR AP 67 VOL: 42 PG:349 - 355 :: QUAL. :INT. LOG. :INSTIT. :OTH.MANAG.

WILLIAMS,TH ; SEC: GRIFFIN,CH CIT: 0.00
INCOME DEFINITION AND MEASUREMENT: A STRUCTURAL APPROACH
TAR OC 67 VOL: 42 PG:642 - 649 :: QUAL. :INT. LOG. :THEORY :OTH.MANAG.

WILLIAMSON,JE CIT: 0.00
THE EFFECTS OF MEASUREMENT CONCEPTS ON THE INVESTMENT DECISIONS OF TRUSTEES
TAR JA 71 VOL: 46 PG:139 - 148 :: ANAL. :INT. LOG. :N/A :OTH.FIN.ACC.

WILLIAMSON,JP ; FIRS: BOWER ,RS ; SEC: HERRINGER,F CIT: 0.00
LEASE EVALUATION
TAR AP 66 VOL: 41 PG:257 - 265 :: ANAL. :INT. LOG. :OTH.STAT. :REL.COSTS

WILLINGER,GL CIT: 0.00
A CONTINGENT CLAIMS MODEL FOR PENSION COSTS
JAR SP 85 VOL: 23 PG:351 - 359 :: DES.STAT. :INT. LOG. :THEORY :PENS.

WILLINGHAM,JJ ; FIRS: GRAY J ; THIR: JOHNSTON,K CIT: 0.00
A BUSINESS GAME FOR THE INTRODUCTORY COURSE IN ACCOUNTING
TAR AP 63 VOL: 38 PG:336 - 346 :: QUAL. :INT. LOG. :OTH. :EDUC.

WILLINGHAM,JJ CIT: 0.00
THE ACCOUNTING ENTITY: A CONCEPTUAL MODEL
TAR JL 64 VOL: 39 PG:543 - 552 :: QUAL. :INT. LOG. :THEORY :FIN.METH.

WILLINGHAM,JJ ; FIRS: BLOCHER,E ; SEC: ESPOSITO,RS CIT: 0.17
AUDITOR'S ANALYTICAL REVIEW JUDGMENTS FOR PAYROLL EXPENSE
AUD AU 83 VOL: 3 PG:75 - 91 :: DES.STAT. :LAB. :OTH.BEH. :ANAL.REV.

WILLINGHAM,JJ ; FIRS: MOCK ,TJ CIT: 0.00
AN IMPROVED METHOD OF DOCUMENTING AND EVALUATING A SYSTEM OF INTERNAL
ACCOUNTING CONTROLS
AUD SP 83 VOL: 2 PG:91 - 99 :: QUAL. :INT. LOG. :OTH. :INT.CONT.

WILLINGHAM,JJ ; FIRS: LIBBY ,R ; SEC: ARTMAN,JT CIT: 0.50
PROCESS SUSCEPTIBILITY, CONTROL RISK, AND AUDIT PLANNING
TAR AP 85 VOL: 60 PG:212 - 230 :: REGRESS. :LAB. :HIPS :INT.CONT.

WILLINGHAM,JJ ; SEC: WRIGHT,WF CIT: 0.00
FINANCIAL STATEMENT ERRORS AND INTERNAL CONTROL JUDGMENTS
AUD AU 85 VOL: 5 PG:57 - 70 :: REGRESS. :PRIM. :OTH.STAT. :ERRORS

WILLINGHAM,JJ ; FIRS: ASHTON,RH ; THIR: ELLIOTT,RK CIT: 0.00
AN EMPIRICAL ANALYSIS OF AUDIT DELAY
JAR AU 87 VOL: 25 PG:275 - 292 :: REGRESS. :SURV. :INSTIT. :TIM.

WILLIS,JT ; FIRS: TABOR ,RH CIT: 0.00
EMPIRICAL EVIDENCE ON THE CHANGING ROLE OF ANALYTICAL REVIEW PROCEDURES
AUD SP 85 VOL: 4 PG:93 - 109 :: REGRESS. :PRIM. :OTH.STAT. :ANAL.REV.

WILLMOTT,H CIT: 0.67
ORGANIZING THE PROFESSION: A THEORETICAL AND HISTORICAL EXAMINATION OF THE
DEVELOPMENT OF THE MAJOR ACCOUNTING BODIES IN THE U.K.
AOS 06 86 VOL: 11 PG:555 - 582 :: REGRESS. :PRIM. :INSTIT. :ORG.& ENVIR.

WILLMOTT,H ; FIRS: HOPPER,T ; SEC: STOREY,J CIT: 0.00
ACCOUNTING FOR ACCOUNTING: TOWARDS THE DEVELOPMENT OF A DIALECTICAL VIEW
AOS 05 87 VOL: 12 PG:437 - 456 :: DES.STAT. :INT. LOG. :THEORY :MANAG.

WILLMOTT,HC ; FIRS: PUXTY ,AG ; THIR: COOPER,DJ ; FOUR: LOWE ,T CIT: 0.50
MODES OF REGULATION IN ADVANCED CAPITALISM: LOCATING ACCOUNTANCY IN
FOUR COUNTRIES
AOS 03 87 VOL: 12 PG:273 - 291 :: DES.STAT. :INT. LOG. :THEORY :ORG.& ENVIR.

WILNER,N CIT: 0.43
SFAS 8 AND INFORMATION INDUCTANCE: AN EXPERIMENT
AOS 01 82 VOL: 7 PG:43 - 52 :: NON-PAR. :LAB. :OTH.BEH. :N/A

WILNER,N ; FIRS: JIAMBALVO,J CIT: 0.00
AUDITOR EVALUATION OF CONTINGENT CLAIMS
AUD AU 85 VOL: 5 PG:1 - 11 :: REGRESS. :SURV. :OTH.STAT. :AUD.

WILNER,N ; SEC: BIRNBERG,JG CIT: 0.67
METHODOLOGICAL PROBLEMS IN FUNCTIONAL FIXATION RESEARCH: CRITICISM AND
SUGGESTIONS
AOS 01 86 VOL: 11 PG:71 - 82 :: REGRESS. :INT. LOG. :HIPS :METHOD.

WILSON GP CIT: 1.33
THE RELATIVE INFO. CONTENT OF ACCRUALS AND CASH FLOWS: COMBINED EVIDENCE AT
THE ANNOUNCEMENT & ANNUAL REPORT RELEASE DATE
JAR ST 86 VOL: 24 PG:165 - 203 :: REGRESS. :PRIM. :EMH :SPEC.ITEMS

WILSON,ER ; SEC: HOWARD,TP CIT: 0.00
THE ASSOCIATION BETWEEN MUNICIPAL MARKET MEASURES AND SELECTED FINANCIAL
REPORTING PRACTICES: ADDITIONAL EVIDENCE
JAR SP 84 VOL: 22 PG:207 - 224 :: REGRESS. :PRIM. :OTH.STAT. :N/A

WILSON,ER ; FIRS: FRANCIS,JR CIT: 0.00
AUDITOR CHANGES: A JOINT TEST OF THEORIES RELATING TO AGENCY COSTS AND
  AUDITOR DIFFERENTIATION
TAR OC 88 VOL: 63 PG:663 - 682 :: REGRESS. :PRIM. :OTH.STAT. :ORG.

WILSON,GP CIT: 3.00
THE INCREMENTAL INFORMATION CONTENT OF THE ACCRUAL AND FUNDS COMPONENTS OF
  EARNINGS AFTER CONTROLLING FOR EARNINGS
TAR AP 87 VOL: 62 PG:293 - 322 :: REGRESS. :PRIM. :EMH :FIN.METH.

WINBORNE,MG CIT: 0.00
THE OPERATING CYCLE CONCEPT - ACCEPTED?
TAR JL 64 VOL: 39 PG:622 - 626 :: DES.STAT. :SURV. :N/A :FIN.METH.

WINBORNE,MG ; SEC: KLEESPIE,DC CIT: 0.00
TAX ALLOCATION IN PERSPECTIVE
TAR OC 66 VOL: 41 PG:737 - 744 :: QUAL. :INT. LOG. :N/A :TAXES

WINDAL,FW CIT: 0.00
LEGAL BACKGROUND FOR THE ACCOUNTING CONCEPT OF REALIZATION
TAR JA 63 VOL: 38 PG:29 - 36 :: QUAL. :INT. LOG. :THEORY :REV.REC.

WINJUM,JO CIT: 0.00
ACCOUNTING IN ITS AGE OF STAGNATION
TAR OC 70 VOL: 45 PG:743 - 761 :: QUAL. :SEC. :HIST. :FIN.METH.

WINJUM,JO CIT: 0.00
ACCOUNTING AND THE RISE OF CAPITALISM: AN ACCOUNTANT'S VIEW
JAR AU 71 VOL: 9 PG:333 - 350 :: QUAL. :INT. LOG. :HIST. :OTH.MANAG.

WINJUM,JO CIT: 0.00
THE JOURNAL OF THOMAS GRESHAM
TAR JA 71 VOL: 46 PG:149 - 155 :: QUAL. :SEC. :HIST. :FIN.METH.

WISEMAN,J CIT: 0.14
AN EVALUATION OF ENVIRONMENTAL DISCLOSURES MADE IN CORPORATE ANNUAL REPORTS
AOS 01 82 VOL: 7 PG:53 - 64 :: CORR. :PRIM. :OTH.STAT. :HRA

WOJDAK,JF ; FIRS: COPELAND,RM CIT: 0.08
INCOME MANIPULATION AND THE PURCHASE-POOLING CHOICE
JAR AU 69 VOL: 7 PG:188 - 195 :: DES.STAT. :PRIM. :OTH. :BUS.COMB.

WOJDAK,JF CIT: 0.08
A THEORETICAL FOUNDATION FOR LEASES AND OTHER EXECUTORY CONTRACTS
TAR JL 69 VOL: 44 PG:562 - 570 :: QUAL. :INT. LOG. :THEORY :LEASES

WOJDAK,JF CIT: 0.08
LEVELS OF OBJECTIVITY IN THE ACCOUNTING PROCESS
TAR JA 70 VOL: 45 PG:88 - 97 :: QUAL. :INT. LOG. :THEORY :OTH.FIN.ACC.

WOLF ,FM CIT: 0.13
THE NATURE OF MANAGERIAL WORK: AN INVESTIGATION OF THE WORK OF THE AUDIT
  MANAGER
TAR OC 81 VOL: 56 PG:861 - 881 :: DES.STAT. :SURV. :OTH.BEH. :ORG.

WOLF ,FM ; FIRS: COOPER,DJ ; SEC: HAYES ,DC CIT: 0.75
ACCOUNTING IN ORGANIZED ANARCHIES: UNDERSTANDING AND DESIGNING ACCOUNTING
  SYSTEMS IN AMBIGUOUS SITUATIONS
AOS 03 81 VOL: 6 PG:175 - 192 :: QUAL. :INT. LOG. :THEORY :N/A

WOLF ,FM ; FIRS: GIBBINS,M CIT: 0.57
AUDITORS' SUBJECTIVE DECISION ENVIRONMENT - THE CASE OF A NORMAL EXTERNAL
  AUDIT
TAR JA 82 VOL: 57 PG:105 - 124 :: DES.STAT. :SURV. :OTH.BEH. :AUD.

WOLF ,G ; FIRS: YOUNG ,SM ; SEC: SHIELDS,MD CIT: 0.00
MANUFACTURING CONTROLS AND PERFORMANCE: AN EXPERIMENT
AOS 06 88 VOL: 13 PG:607 - 618 :: REGRESS. :LAB. :OTH.BEH. :EXEC.COMP.

WOLFSON,MA ; FIRS: PATELL,JM CIT: 1.30
ANTICIPATED INFORMATION RELEASES REFLECTED IN CALL OPTION PRICES
JAE AG 79 VOL: 1 PG:117 - 140 :: ANOVA :PRIM. :EMH :INFO.STRUC.

WOLFSON,MA ; FIRS: NOREEN,EW CIT: 0.38
EQUILIBRIUM WARRANT PRICING MODELS AND ACCOUNTING FOR EXECUTIVE STOCK OPTIONS
JAR AU 81 VOL: 19 PG:384 - 398 :: CORR. :PRIM. :EMH :N/A

WOLFSON,MA ; FIRS: PATELL,JM CIT: 1.50
THE EX ANTE AND EX POST PRICE EFFECTS OF QUARTERLY EARNINGS ANNOUNCEMENTS
REFLECTED IN OPTION AND STOCK PRICES
JAR AU 81 VOL: 19 PG:434 - 458 :: REGRESS. :PRIM. :EMH :FIN.METH.

WOLFSON,MA ; FIRS: BEAVER,WH CIT: 0.00
FOREIGN CURRENCY TRANSLATION AND CHANGING PRICES IN PERFECT AND COMPLETE
  MARKETS
JAR AU 82 VOL: 20 PG:528 - 550 :: ANAL. :INT. LOG. :OTH.STAT. :VALUAT.(INFL.)

WOLFSON,MA ; FIRS: PATELL,JM CIT: 1.71
GOOD NEWS, BAD NEWS, AND THE INTRADAY TIMING OF CORPORATE DISCLOSURES
TAR JL 82 VOL: 57 PG:509 - 527 :: REGRESS. :PRIM. :EMH :FIN.ST.TIM.

WOLFSON,MA ; FIRS: DEMSKI,JS ; SEC: PATELL,JM CIT: 1.60
DECENTRALIZED CHOICE OF MONITORING SYSTEMS
TAR JA 84 VOL: 59 PG:16 - 34 :: ANAL. :INT. LOG. :INF.ECO./AG. :MANAG.

WOLFSON,MA ; FIRS: MARAIS,ML ; SEC: PATELL,JM CIT: 0.20
THE EXPERIMENTAL DESIGN OF CLASSIFICATORY MODELS: AN APPLICATION OF RECURSIVE
  PARTITIONING AND BOOTSTRAPPING COMMERCIAL BANK LOAN CLASSIFICATION
JAR ST 84 VOL: 22 PG:87 - 114 :: OTH.QUANT. :PRIM. :OTH.STAT. :BUS.FAIL.

WOLFSON,MA ; FIRS: FELLINGHAM,JC CIT: 0.00
TAXES AND RISK SHARING
TAR JA 85 VOL: 60 PG:10 - 17 :: DES.STAT. :INT. LOG. :INF.ECO./AG. :TAXES

WOLK ,HI CIT: 0.00
CURRENT VALUE DEPRECIATION: A CONCEPTUAL CLARIFICATION
TAR JL 70 VOL: 45 PG:544 - 552 :: ANAL. :INT. LOG. :THEORY :VALUAT.(INFL.)

WOLK ,HI ; SEC: HILLMAN,AP CIT: 0.08
MATERIALS MIX AND YIELD VARIANCES: A SUGGESTED IMPROVEMENT
TAR JL 72 VOL: 47 PG:549 - 555 :: ANAL. :INT. LOG. :MATH.PROG. :VAR.

WOLK ,HI ; SEC: TEARNEY,MG CIT: 0.00
INCOME TAX ALLOCATION AND LOSS CARRYFORWARDS: EXPLORING UNCHARTED GROUND
TAR AP 73 VOL: 48 PG:292 - 299 :: ANAL. :INT. LOG. :THEORY :SPEC.ITEMS

WONG ,J CIT: 0.00
ECONOMIC INCENTIVES FOR THE VOLUNTARY DISCLOSURE OF CURRENT COST FINANCIAL
  STATEMENTS
JAE AP 88 VOL: 10 PG:151 - 167 :: REGRESS. :PRIM. :THEORY :VALUAT.(INFL.)

WONG ,J CIT: 0.00
POLITICAL COSTS AND AN INTRAPERIOD ACCOUNTING CHOICE FOR EXPORT TAX CREDITS
JAE JA 88 VOL: 10 PG:37 - 51 :: REGRESS. :PRIM. :THEORY :TAXES

WONG-BOREN,A ; FIRS: CHOW ,CW CIT: 0.00
VOLUNTARY FINANCIAL DISCLOSURE BY MEXICAN CORPORATIONS
TAR JL 87 VOL: 62 PG:533 - 541 :: REGRESS. :PRIM. :OTH.STAT. :FIN.METH.

WOODS ,RS CIT: 0.00
SOME DIMENSIONS OF INTEGRATED SYSTEMS
TAR JL 64 VOL: 39 PG:598 - 614 :: QUAL. :INT. LOG. :N/A :OTH.MANAG.

WOOLSEY,SM CIT: 0.00
ACCOUNTING FOR "INVESTMENT CREDIT"
TAR OC 63 VOL: 38 PG:709 - 713 :: QUAL. :INT. LOG. :THEORY :N/A

WRAGGE,JH ; FIRS: ABDEL-KHALIK,AR ; SEC: SNOWBALL,D CIT: 0.00
THE EFFECTS OF CERTAIN INTERNAL AUDIT VARIABLES ON THE PLANNING OF EXTERNAL
    AUDIT PROGRAMS
TAR AP 83 VOL: 58 PG:215 - 227 :: ANOVA :LAB. :OTH.BEH. :INT.AUD.

WRIGHT,A ; FIRS: MOCK ,TJ CIT: 0.00
EVALUATING THE EFFECTIVENESS OF AUDIT PROCEDURES
AUD AU 82 VOL: 2 PG:33 - 44 :: QUAL. :INT. LOG. :THEORY :OPER.AUD.

WRIGHT,A CIT: 0.00
AN INVESTIGATION OF THE ENGAGEMENT EVALUATION PROCESS FOR STAFF AUDITORS
JAR SP 82 VOL: 20 PG:227 - 239 :: ANOVA :LAB. :OTH.BEH. :AUD.

WRIGHT,A CIT: 0.00
THE IMPACT OF CPA-FIRM SIZE ON AUDITOR DISCLOSURE PREFERENCES
TAR JL 83 VOL: 58 PG:621 - 632 :: DES.STAT. :LAB. :OTH.BEH. :ORG.

WRIGHT,A ; FIRS: LIN ,WT ; SEC: MOCK ,TJ CIT: 0.00
THE USE OF ANALYTIC HIERARCHY PROCESS AS AN AID IN PLANNING THE NATURE AND
    EXTENT OF AUDIT PROCEDURES
AUD AU 84 VOL: 4 PG:89 - 99 :: ANAL. :INT. LOG. :OTH.STAT. :PLAN.

WRIGHT,A CIT: 0.00
PERFORMANCE EVALUATION OF STAFF AUDITORS: A BEHAVIOURALLY ANCHORED RATING SC/
AUD SP 86 VOL: 5 PG:86 - 94 :: REGRESS. :LAB. :OTH.BEH. :OPER.AUD.

WRIGHT,A ; FIRS: ABDOLMOHAMMADI,MJ CIT: 0.00
AN EXAMINATION OF THE EFFECTS OF EXPERIENCE AND TASK COMPLEXITY ON AUDIT
    JUDGEMENTS
TAR JA 87 VOL: 62 PG:1 - 13 :: REGRESS. :LAB. :OTH.BEH. :JUDG.

WRIGHT,A CIT: 0.00
THE IMPACT OF PRIOR WORKING PAPERS ON AUDITOR EVIDENTIAL PLANNING JUDGMENTS
AOS 06 88 VOL: 13 PG:595 - 605 :: REGRESS. :LAB. :OTH.BEH. :PLAN.

WRIGHT,CJ ; SEC: GROFF ,JE CIT: 0.33
USES OF INDEXES AND DATA BASES FOR INFORMATION RELEASE ANALYSIS
TAR JA 86 VOL: 61 PG:91 - 100 :: REGRESS. :PRIM. :EMH :METHOD.

WRIGHT,FK CIT: 0.00
DEPRECIATION THEORY AND THE COST OF FUNDS
TAR JA 63 VOL: 38 PG:87 - 90 :: ANAL. :INT. LOG. :THEORY :PP&E / DEPR

WRIGHT,FK   CIT: 0.00
TOWARDS A GENERAL THEORY OF DEPRECIATION
JAR SP 64 VOL: 2 PG:80 - 90 :: ANAL. :INT. LOG. :THEORY :PP&E / DEPR

WRIGHT,FK   CIT: 0.08
DEPRECIATION AND OBSOLESCENCE IN CURRENT VALUE ACCOUNTING
JAR AU 65 VOL: 3 PG:167 - 181 :: QUAL. :INT. LOG. :THEORY :PP&E / DEPR

WRIGHT,FK   CIT: 0.08
DEPRECIATION AND OBSOLESCENCE IN CURRENT VALUE ACCOUNTING
JAR FL 65 VOL: 3 PG:167 - 181 :: QUAL. :INT. LOG. :THEORY :PP&E / DEPR

WRIGHT,FK   CIT: 0.00
AN EVALUATION OF LADELLE'S THEORY OF DEPRECIATION
JAR AU 67 VOL: 5 PG:173 - 179 :: QUAL. :INT. LOG. :HIST. :PP&E / DEPR

WRIGHT,FK   CIT: 0.00
MEASURING ASSET SERVICES: A LINEAR PROGRAMMING APPROACH
JAR AU 68 VOL: 6 PG:222 - 236 :: ANAL. :INT. LOG. :MATH.PROG. :PP&E / DEPR

WRIGHT,FK   CIT: 0.08
DUAL VARIABLES IN INVENTORY MEASUREMENT
TAR JA 70 VOL: 45 PG:129 - 133 :: ANAL. :INT. LOG. :MATH.PROG. :INV.

WRIGHT,GB ; SEC: TAYLOR,RD   CIT: 0.00
REPORTING MATERIALITY FOR INVESTORS
JAA SU 82 VOL: 5 PG:301 - 309 :: DES.STAT. :SURV. :OTH. :MAT.

WRIGHT,HW   CIT: 0.00
ALLOCATION OF GENERAL AND ADMINISTRATIVE EXPENSES
TAR OC 66 VOL: 41 PG:626 - 633 :: QUAL. :INT. LOG. :THEORY :COST.ALLOC.

WRIGHT,RL ; FIRS: ROSHWALB,A ; THIR: GODFREY,JT   CIT: 0.00
A NEW APPROACH FOR STRATIFIED SAMPLING IN INVENTORY COST ESTIMATION
AUD AU 87 VOL: 7 PG:54 - 70 :: DES.STAT. :SIM. :OTH.STAT. :SAMP.

WRIGHT,WF   CIT: 0.83
FINANCIAL INFORMATION PROCESSING MODELS: AN EMPIRICAL STUDY
TAR JL 77 VOL: 52 PG:676 - 689 :: REGRESS. :LAB. :HIPS :N/A

WRIGHT,WF   CIT: 0.25
SELF-INSIGHT INTO THE COGNITIVE PROCESSING OF FINANCIAL INFORMATION
AOS 04 77 VOL: 2 PG:323 - 332 :: CORR. :LAB. :HIPS :INFO.STRUC.

WRIGHT,WF ; FIRS: BEAVER,WH ; SEC: CLARKE,R   CIT: 4.20
THE ASSOCIATION BETWEEN UNSYSTEMATIC SECURITY RETURNS AND THE MAGNITUDE OF
   EARNINGS FORECAST ERRORS
JAR AU 79 VOL: 17 PG:316 - 340 :: NON-PAR. :PRIM. :EMH :FOREC.

WRIGHT,WF ; FIRS: HAMILTON,RE   CIT: 0.43
INTERNAL CONTROL JUDGMENTS AND EFFECTS OF EXPERIENCE: REPLICATIONS AND
   EXTENSIONS
JAR AU 82 VOL: 20 PG:756 - 765 :: MIXED :LAB. :HIPS :INT.CONT.

WRIGHT,WF   CIT: 0.14
COMPARISON OF THE LENS AND SUBJECTIVE PROBABILITY PARADIGMS FOR FINANCIAL
   RESEARCH PURPOSES
AOS 01 82 VOL: 7 PG:65 - 78 :: QUAL. :INT. LOG. :HIPS :METHOD.

WRIGHT,WF ; FIRS: WILLINGHAM,JJ CIT: 0.00
FINANCIAL STATEMENT ERRORS AND INTERNAL CONTROL JUDGMENTS
AUD AU 85 VOL: 5 PG:57 - 70 :: REGRESS. :PRIM. :OTH.STAT. :ERRORS

WU   ,C ; FIRS: LEE   ,CF CIT: 0.00
EXPECTATION FORMATION AND FINANCIAL RATIO ADJUSTMENT PROCESSES
TAR AP 88 VOL: 63 PG:292 - 306 :: DES.STAT. :PRIM. :OTH.STAT. :METHOD.

WYATT ,AR CIT: 0.00
ACCOUNTING FOR BUSINESS COMBINATIONS: WHAT NEXT?
TAR JL 65 VOL: 40 PG:527 - 535 :: QUAL. :INT. LOG. :THEORY :BUS.COMB.

WYATT ,AR ; FIRS: KETZ ,JE CIT: 0.00
THE FASB IN A WORLD WITH PARTIALLY EFFICIENT MARKETS
JAA AU 83 VOL: 7 PG:29 - 43 :: QUAL. :INT. LOG. :EMH :OTH.MANAG.

WYER ,JC ; SEC: WHITE ,GT ; THIR: JANSON,EC CIT: 0.00
AUDITS OF PUBLIC COMPANIES BY SMALLER CPA FIRMS: CLIENTS, REPORTS, AND QUALITY
AUD SP 88 VOL: 07 PG:164 - 173 :: REGRESS. :PRIM. :INSTIT. :ORG.

WYMAN ,HE CIT: 0.15
FINANCIAL LEASE EVALUATION UNDER CONDITIONS OF UNCERTAINTY
TAR JL 73 VOL: 48 PG:489 - 493 :: ANAL. :SIM. :N/A :LEASES

WYMAN ,HE CIT: 0.00
ANALYSIS OF GAINS OR LOSSES FROM FOREIGN MONETARY ITEMS: AN APPLICATION OF
    PURCHASING POWER PARITY CONCEPTS
TAR JL 76 VOL: 51 PG:545 - 558 :: ANAL. :INT. LOG. :THEORY :FIN.ST.TIM.

WYNDELTS,RW ; FIRS: JENSEN,HL CIT: 0.00
THROUGH THE LOOKING GLASS: AN EMPIRICAL LOOK AT DISCRIMINATION IN THE FEDERAL
    INCOME TAX RATE STRUCTURE
TAR OC 76 VOL: 51 PG:846 - 853 :: ANAL. :SIM. :INSTIT. :OTH.MANAG.

YAMEY ,BS CIT: 0.23
ACCOUNTING AND THE RISE OF CAPITALISM: FURTHER NOTES ON A THEME BY SOMBART
JAR AU 64 VOL: 2 PG:117 - 136 :: QUAL. :INT. LOG. :HIST. :N/A

YAMEY ,BS CIT: 0.08
FIFTEENTH AND SIXTEENTH CENTURY MANUSCRIPTS ON THE ART OF BOOKKEEPING
JAR SP 67 VOL: 5 PG:51 - 76 :: QUAL. :SEC. :HIST. :N/A

YAMEY ,BS CIT: 0.10
COMPOUND JOURNAL ENTRIES IN EARLY TREATISES ON BOOKKEEPING
TAR AP 79 VOL: 54 PG:323 - 329 :: QUAL. :INT. LOG. :HIST. :OTH.MANAG.

YAMEY ,BS CIT: 0.00
THE INDEX TO THE LEDGER: SOME HISTORICAL NOTES
TAR JL 80 VOL: 55 PG:419 - 425 :: QUAL. :INT. LOG. :HIST. :N/A

YETTON,PW ; FIRS: TROTMAN,KT ; THIR: ZIMMER,I CIT: 0.33
INDIVIDUAL AND GROUP JUDGMENTS OF INTERNAL CONTROL SYSTEMS
JAR SP 83 VOL: 21 PG:286 - 292 :: CORR. :LAB. :HIPS :MANAG.

YETTON,PW ; FIRS: TROTMAN,KT CIT: 0.00
THE EFFECT OF THE REVIEW PROCESS ON AUDITOR JUDGMENTS
JAR SP 85 VOL: 23 PG:256 - 267 :: REGRESS. :LAB. :OTH.BEH. :JUDG.

YETTON,PY CIT: 0.15
THE INTERACTION BETWEEN A STANDARD TIME INCENTIVE PAYMENT SCHEME AND A SIMPLE
    ACCOUNTING INFORMATION SYSTEM
AOS 01 76 VOL: 1 PG:81 - 90 :: QUAL. :INT. LOG. :THEORY :REL.COSTS

YOUNG ,AE ; FIRS: CHOTTINER,S CIT: 0.08
A TEST OF THE AICPA DIFFERENTIATION BETWEEN STOCK DIVIDENDS AND STOCK SPLITS
JAR AU 71 VOL: 9 PG:367 - 374 :: DES.STAT. :PRIM. :OTH. :STK.DIV.

YOUNG ,AE ; FIRS: HORWITZ,BN CIT: 0.00
AN EMPIRICAL STUDY OF ACCOUNTING POLICY AND TENDER OFFERS
JAR SP 72 VOL: 10 PG:96 - 107 :: DES.STAT. :PRIM. :OTH.STAT. :BUS.COMB.

YOUNG ,AE CIT: 0.00
ACCOUNTING FOR TREASURY STOCKS
JAA SP 78 VOL: 1 PG:217 - 230 :: DES.STAT. :PRIM. :THEORY :FIN.METH.

YOUNG ,AE CIT: 0.00
COMMON STOCK REPURCHASING: ANOTHER MEANS OF REDUCING CORPORATE SIZE
JAA SP 80 VOL: 3 PG:244 - 250 :: QUAL. :INT. LOG. :THEORY :METHOD.

YOUNG ,AE ; FIRS: FRANKFURTER,GM CIT: 0.00
FINANCIAL THEORY: ITS MESSAGE TO THE ACCOUNTANT
JAA SU 83 VOL: 6 PG:314 - 324 :: QUAL. :INT. LOG. :OTH. :N/A

YOUNG ,DW CIT: 0.00
ACCOUNTING FOR THE COST OF INTEREST: IMPLICATIONS FOR THE TIMBER INDUSTRY
TAR OC 76 VOL: 51 PG:788 - 799 :: QUAL. :CASE :THEORY :FIN.METH.

YOUNG ,DW CIT: 0.20
ADMINISTRATIVE THEORY AND ADMINISTRATIVE SYSTEMS: A SYNTHESIS AMONG DIVERGING
    FIELDS OF INQUIRY
AOS 03 79 VOL: 4 PG:235 - 244 :: QUAL. :INT. LOG. :OTH. :N/A

YOUNG ,R CIT: 0.00
A NOTE ON "ECONOMICALLY OPTIMAL PERFORMANCE EVALUATION AND CONTROL SYSTEMS":
    THE OPTIMALITY OF TWO-TAILED INVESTIGATIONS
JAR SP 86 VOL: 24 PG:231 - 240 :: REGRESS. :INT. LOG. :OTH.STAT. :INT.CONT.

YOUNG ,RA ; FIRS: ANDERSON,U CIT: 0.00
INTERNAL AUDIT PLANNING IN AN INTERACTIVE ENVIRONMENT
AUD AU 88 VOL: 08 PG:23 - 42 :: DES.STAT. :INT. LOG. :OTH.BEH. :TIM.

YOUNG ,SD CIT: 0.00
INSIDER TRADING: WHY THE CONCERN?
JAA SP 85 VOL: 8 PG:178 - 183 :: DES.STAT. :INT. LOG. :INSTIT. :INS.TRAD.

YOUNG ,SD CIT: 0.00
THE ECONOMIC THEORY OF REGULATION: EVIDENCE FROM THE UNIFORM CPA EXAMINATION
TAR AP 88 VOL: 63 PG:283 - 291 :: REGRESS. :PRIM. :OTH.STAT. :AUD.TRAIN.

YOUNG ,SM ; FIRS: LEWIS ,BL ; SEC: SHIELDS,MD CIT: 1.17
EVALUATING HUMAN JUDGMENTS AND DECISION AIDS
JAR SP 83 VOL: 21 PG:271 - 285 :: DES.STAT. :LAB. :HIPS :ORG.& ENVIR.

YOUNG ,SM ; FIRS: BIRNBERG,JG ; SEC: TUROPOLEC,L CIT: 1.83
THE ORGANIZATIONAL CONTEXT OF ACCOUNTING
AOS 23 83 VOL: 8 PG:111 - 130 :: QUAL. :SEC. :OTH.BEH. :REL.COSTS

YOUNG ,SM CIT: 0.25
PARTICIPATIVE BUDGETING: THE EFFECTS OF RISK AVERSION AND ASYMMETRIC
INFORMATION ON BUDGETARY SLACK
JAR AU 85 VOL: 23 PG:829 - 842 :: REGRESS. :LAB. :INF.ECO./AG. :BUDG.& PLAN.

YOUNG ,SM ; SEC: SHIELDS,MD ; THIR: WOLF ,G CIT: 0.00
MANUFACTURING CONTROLS AND PERFORMANCE: AN EXPERIMENT
AOS 06 88 VOL: 13 PG:607 - 618 :: REGRESS. :LAB. :OTH.BEH. :EXEC.COMP.

YOUNG ,TN ; SEC: PEIRSON,CG CIT: 0.00
DEPRECIATION - FUTURE SERVICES BASIS
TAR AP 67 VOL: 42 PG:338 - 341 :: ANAL. :INT. LOG. :THEORY :PP&E / DEPR

YU ,S ; SEC: NETER ,J CIT: 0.62
A STOCHASTIC MODEL OF THE INTERNAL CONTROL SYSTEM
JAR AU 73 VOL: 11 PG:273 - 295 :: ANAL. :INT. LOG. :OTH.STAT. :INT.CONT.

YU ,SC CIT: 0.00
MICROACCOUNTING AND MACROACCOUNTING
TAR JA 66 VOL: 41 PG:8 - 20 :: QUAL. :INT. LOG. :THEORY :OTH.MANAG.

YU ,SC CIT: 0.00
A FLOW-OF-RESOURCES STATEMENT FOR BUSINESS ENTERPRISES
TAR JL 69 VOL: 44 PG:571 - 582 :: QUAL. :INT. LOG. :THEORY :FIN.METH.

ZALD ,MN CIT: 0.33
THE SOCIOLOGY OF ENTERPRISE, ACCOUNTING AND BUDGET RULES: IMPLICATIONS FOR
ORGANIZATIONAL THEORY
AOS 45 86 VOL: 11 PG:321 - 326 :: ANOVA :INT. LOG. :THEORY :BUDG.& PLAN.

ZANNETOS,ZS CIT: 0.00
MATHEMATICS AS A TOOL OF ACCOUNTING INSTRUCTION AND RESEARCH
TAR AP 63 VOL: 38 PG:326 - 335 :: QUAL. :INT. LOG. :OTH. :EDUC.

ZANNETOS,ZS CIT: 0.00
ON THE MATHEMATICS OF VARIANCE ANALYSIS
TAR JL 63 VOL: 38 PG:528 - 533 :: ANAL. :INT. LOG. :OTH. :VAR.

ZANNETOS,ZS CIT: 0.15
STANDARD COSTS AS A FIRST STEP TO PROBABILISTIC CONTROL: A THEORETICAL
JUSTIFICATION, AND EXTENSION AND IMPLICATIONS
TAR AP 64 VOL: 39 PG:296 - 304 :: ANAL. :INT. LOG. :OTH.STAT. :VAR.

ZANNETOS,ZS CIT: 0.00
SOME THOUGHTS ON INTERNAL CONTROL SYSTEMS OF THE FIRM
TAR OC 64 VOL: 39 PG:860 - 868 :: QUAL. :INT. LOG. :N/A :INT.CONT.

ZANNETOS,ZS CIT: 0.00
PROGRAMMED INSTRUCTION AND COMPUTER TECHNOLOGY
TAR JL 67 VOL: 42 PG:566 - 571 :: QUAL. :INT. LOG. :N/A :OTH.MANAG.

ZAROWIN,P CIT: 0.00
NON-LINEARITIES AND NOMINAL CONTRACTING EFFECTS: THE CASE OF THE DEPRECIATION
TAX SHIELD
JAE AP 88 VOL: 10 PG:89 - 110 :: REGRESS. :PRIM. :THEORY :PP&E / DEPR

ZEFF ,SA ; SEC: MAXWELL,WD CIT: 0.00
HOLDING GAINS ON FIXED ASSETS - A DEMURRER
TAR JA 65 VOL: 40 PG:65 - 75 :: QUAL. :INT. LOG. :THEORY :VALUAT.(INFL.)

ZEFF ,SA ; SEC: FOSSUM,RL CIT: 0.31
AN ANALYSIS OF LARGE AUDIT CLIENTS
TAR AP 67 VOL: 42 PG:298 - 320 :: DES.STAT. :PRIM. :INSTIT. :AUD.

ZEFF ,SA CIT: 0.00
TRUTH IN ACCOUNTING: THE ORDEAL OF KENNETH MACNEAL
TAR JL 82 VOL: 57 PG:528 - 553 :: QUAL. :INT. LOG. :HIST. :N/A

ZEFF ,SA CIT: 0.40
SOME JUNCTURES IN THE EVOLUTION OF THE PROCESS OF ESTABLISHING ACCOUNTING
   PRINCIPLES IN THE U.S.A.: 1917-1972
TAR JL 84 VOL: 59 PG:447 - 468 :: QUAL. :SEC. :HIST. :FIN.METH.

ZEFF ,SA ; FIRS: DYCKMAN,TR CIT: 1.20
TWO DECADES OF THE JOURNAL OF ACCOUNTING RESEARCH
JAR SP 84 VOL: 22 PG:225 - 297 :: DES.STAT. :SEC. :INSTIT. :METHOD.

ZEFF ,SA CIT: 0.00
BIG EIGHT FIRMS AND THE ACCOUNTING LITERATURE: THE FALLOFF IN ADVOCACY WRITING
JAA SP 86 VOL: 1 PG:131 - 154 :: REGRESS. :SEC. :HIST. :ORG.& ENVIR.

ZIEBART,DA CIT: 0.00
CONTROL OF BETA RELIABILITY IN STUDIES OF ABNORMAL RETURN MAGNITUDE
JAR AU 85 VOL: 23 PG:920 - 926 :: DES.STAT. :PRIM. :EMH :METHOD.

ZIEBART,DA ; SEC: KIM   ,DH CIT: 0.00
AN EXAMINATION OF THE MARKET REACTIONS ASSOCIATED WITH SFAS NO. 8 AND SFAS
   NO. 52
TAR AP 87 VOL: 62 PG:343 - 357 :: REGRESS. :PRIM. :EMH :FOR.CUR.

ZIEGLER,RE ; FIRS: BEDFORD,NM CIT: 0.08
THE CONTRIBUTIONS OF A.C. LITTLETON TO ACCOUNTING THOUGHT AND PRACTICE
TAR JL 75 VOL: 50 PG:435 - 443 :: QUAL. :SEC. :THEORY :FIN.METH.

ZIMMER,I ; FIRS: WILKINS,T CIT: 0.17
THE EFFECT OF LEASING AND DIFFERENT METHODS OF ACCOUNTING FOR LEASES ON
   CREDIT EVALUATIONS
TAR OC 83 VOL: 58 PG:749 - 764 :: ANOVA :LAB. :OTH.BEH. :LEASES

ZIMMER,I ; FIRS: TROTMAN,KT ; SEC: YETTON,PW CIT: 0.33
INDIVIDUAL AND GROUP JUDGMENTS OF INTERNAL CONTROL SYSTEMS
JAR SP 83 VOL: 21 PG:286 - 292 :: CORR. :LAB. :HIPS :MANAG.

ZIMMER,I ; FIRS: WHITTRED,GP CIT: 0.00
TIMELINESS OF FINANCIAL REPORTING AND FINANCIAL DISTRESS
TAR AP 84 VOL: 59 PG:287 - 295 :: DES.STAT. :PRIM. :OTH.STAT. :FIN.ST.TIM.

ZIMMER,I CIT: 1.00
ACCOUNTING FOR INTEREST BY REAL ESTATE DEVELOPERS
JAE MR 86 VOL: 8 PG:37 - 52 :: REGRESS. :PRIM. :THEORY :BUS.COMB.

ZIMMERMAN,JL CIT: 0.15
BUDGET UNCERTAINTY AND THE ALLOCATION DECISION IN A NONPROFIT ORGANIZATION
JAR AU 76 VOL: 14 PG:301 - 319 :: REGRESS. :CASE :OTH.STAT. :OVER.ALLOC.

ZIMMERMAN,JL CIT: 0.92
THE MUNICIPAL ACCOUNTING MAZE: AN ANALYSIS OF POLITICAL INCENTIVES
JAR ST 77 VOL: 15 PG:107 - 144 :: DES.STAT. :PRIM. :INF.ECO./AG. :OTH.MANAG.

ZIMMERMAN,JL ; FIRS: WATTS ,RL CIT: 7.91
TOWARDS A POSITIVE THEORY OF THE DETERMINATION OF ACCOUNTING STANDARDS
TAR JA 78 VOL: 53 PG:112 - 134 :: OTH.QUANT. :PRIM. :OTH.STAT. :FASB SUBM.

ZIMMERMAN,JL ; FIRS: WATTS ,RL CIT: 3.80
THE DEMAND FOR AND SUPPLY OF ACCOUNTING THEORIES: THE MARKET FOR EXCUSES
TAR AP 79 VOL: 54 PG:273 - 305 :: QUAL. :INT. LOG. :THEORY :FIN.METH.

ZIMMERMAN,JL CIT: 2.10
THE COST AND BENEFITS OF COST ALLOCATIONS
TAR JL 79 VOL: 54 PG:504 - 521 :: ANAL. :INT. LOG. :INF.ECO./AG. :COST.ALLOC.

ZIMMERMAN,JL ; FIRS: WATTS ,RL CIT: 0.44
ON THE IRRELEVANCE OF REPLACEMENT COST DISCLOSURES FOR SECURITY PRICES
JAE AG 80 VOL: 2 PG:95 - 106 :: QUAL. :SEC. :OTH. :VALUAT.(INFL.)

ZIMMERMAN,JL ; FIRS: LEFTWICH,RW ; SEC: WATTS ,RL CIT: 0.75
VOLUNTARY CORPORATE DISCLOSURE: THE CASE OF INTERIM REPORTING
JAR ST 81 VOL: 19 PG:50 - 77 :: ANAL. :PRIM. :OTH.STAT. :FIN.METH.

ZIMMERMAN,JL CIT: 1.33
TAXES AND FIRM SIZE
JAE AG 83 VOL: 5 PG:119 - 149 :: ANOVA :PRIM. :THEORY :TAXES

ZIMMERMAN,JL ; FIRS: JENSEN,MC CIT: 0.00
MANAGEMENT COMPENSATION AND THE MANAGERIAL LABOR MARKET
JAE AP 85 VOL: 7 PG:3 - 10 :: REGRESS. :INT. LOG. :THEORY :EXEC.COMP.

ZIMMERMAN,JL ; FIRS: LIBERTY, SE CIT: 1.00
LABOR UNION CONTRACT NEGOTIATIONS AND ACCOUNTING CHOICES
TAR OC 86 VOL: 61 PG:692 - 712 :: REGRESS. :PRIM. :OTH.STAT. :INFO.STRUC.

ZMIJEWSKI,ME ; FIRS: HAGERMAN,RL CIT: 3.80
SOME ECONOMIC DETERMINANTS OF ACCOUNTING POLICY CHOICE
JAE AG 79 VOL: 1 PG:141 - 161 :: OTH.QUANT. :PRIM. :OTH.STAT. :ACC.CHNG.

ZMIJEWSKI,ME ; SEC: HAGERMAN,RL CIT: 2.63
AN INCOME STRATEGY APPROACH TO THE POSITIVE THEORY OF ACCOUNTING STANDARD
SETTING/CHOICE
JAE AG 81 VOL: 3 PG:129 - 149 :: OTH.QUANT. :SEC. :OTH.STAT. :METHOD.

ZMIJEWSKI,ME ; FIRS: HAGERMAN,RL ; THIR: SHAH ,P CIT: 0.00
THE ASSOCIATION BETWEEN THE MAGNITUDE OF QUARTERLY EARNINGS FORECAST ERRORS
AND RISK-ADJUSTED STOCK RETURNS
JAR AU 84 VOL: 22 PG:526 - 540 :: REGRESS. :PRIM. :EMH :FOREC.

ZMIJEWSKI,ME CIT: 1.20
METHODOLOGICAL ISSUES RELATED TO THE ESTIMATION OF FINANCIAL DISTRESS
PREDICTION MODELS
JAR ST 84 VOL: 22 PG:59 - 82 :: OTH.QUANT. :PRIM. :OTH.STAT. :BUS.FAIL.

ZMIJEWSKI,ME ; FIRS: BROWN ,LD ; SEC: GRIFFIN,PA ; THIR: HAGERMAN,RL CIT: 2.50
SECURITY ANALYST SUPERIORITY RELATIVE TO UNIVARIATE TIME-SERIES MODELS IN
FORECASTING QUARTERLY EARNINGS
JAE AP 87 VOL: 9 PG:61 - 87 :: REGRESS. :PRIM. :TIME SER. :FOREC.

ZMIJEWSKI,ME ; FIRS: BROWN ,LD ; SEC: GRIFFIN,PA ; THIR: HAGERMAN,RL CIT: 2.00
AN EVALUATION OF ALTERNATIVE PROXIES FOR THE MARKET'S ASSESSMENT OF
UNEXPECTED EARNINGS
JAE JL 87 VOL: 9 PG:159 - 193 :: REGRESS. :PRIM. :TIME SER. :METHOD.

ZMUD ,RW ; FIRS: BLOCHER,E ; SEC: MOFFIE,RP CIT: 0.00
REPORT FORMAT AND TASK COMPLEXITY: INTERACTION IN RISK JUDGMENTS
AOS 06 86 VOL: 11 PG:457 - 470 :: REGRESS. :LAB. :HIPS :INFO.STRUC.

ZOLTNERS,AA ; FIRS: BALACHANDRAN,BV CIT: 0.00
AN INTERACTIVE AUDIT-STAFF SCHEDULING DECISION SUPPORT SYSTEM
TAR OC 81 VOL: 56 PG:801 - 812 :: ANAL. :INT. LOG. :OTH.STAT. :AUD.BEH.

Part2: Articles Classified Four Ways

PART 2

ARTICLES
CLASSIFIED IN FOUR WAYS-

- MODE OF REASONING
- RESEARCH METHOD
- SCHOOL OF THOUGHT
- TREATMENT- Subject Area

1.1 MODE OF REASONING(METHOD)=QUANTITATIVE: DESCRIPTIVE STATS

CITE IND-EX	FIRST AUTHOR	ISS-UE	YE-AR	JOUR-NAL	SECOND AUTHOR	THIRD AUTHOR	PAG BEG	PAG END
4.50	HOPWOOD,AG	03	87	AOS			207	234
3.75	BURCHELL,S	04	85	AOS	CLUBB,C	HOPWOOD,AG	381	414
3.63	BOWEN,RM	AG	81	JAE	NOREEN,EW	LACEY,JM	151	179
3.00	LOFT,A	02	86	AOS			137	170
2.50	MILLER,P	03	87	AOS	O'LEARY,T		235	265
2.17	LEFTWICH,RW	JA	83	TAR			23	42
2.00	ROBERTS,J	04	85	AOS	SCAPENS,RW		443	456
1.80	GOVINDARAJAN,V	02	84	AOS			125	135
1.75	JOHNSON,JR	AP	81	TAR	LEITCH,RA	NETER,J	270	293
1.50	DEMSKI,JS	SP	87	JAR	SAPPINGTON,DEM		68	89
1.46	DECOSTER,DT	AU	68	JAR	FERTAKIS,JP		237	246
1.38	BEAVER,WH	ST	66	JAR			71	111
1.33	HOSKIN,KW	02	86	AOS	MACVE,RH		105	136
1.33	HUGHES,PJ	JN	86	JAE			119	142
1.31	CORLESS,JC	JL	72	TAR			556	566
1.20	DYCKMAN,TR	SP	84	JAR	ZEFF,SA		225	297
1.20	KINNEY JR,WR	ST	79	JAR			148	165
1.17	LEWIS,BL	SP	83	JAR	SHIELDS,MD	YOUNG,SM	271	285
1.14	CHOW,CW	AP	82	TAR			272	291
1.14	SOLOMON,I	AU	82	JAR			689	710
1.14	SWIERINGA,RJ	ST	82	JAR	WEICK,KE		56	101
1.00	CHRISTIE,AA	DE	87	JAE			231	258
1.00	FELIX JR,WL	OC	76	TAR			800	807
1.00	GIVOLY,D	DE	79	JAE	LAKONISHOK,J		165	185
1.00	IMHOFF JR,EA	AU	82	JAR	PARE,PV		429	439
1.00	MORSE,D	SP	83	JAR	RICHARDSON,G		106	127
1.00	VERRECCHIA,RE	OC	86	JAE		175	196	
0.92	CUSHING,BE	AU	69	JAR			196	203
0.92	GOSMAN,ML	JA	73	TAR			1	11
0.92	MCDONALD,CL	JL	73	TAR			502	510
0.92	ZIMMERMAN,JL	ST	77	JAR			107	144
0.90	RAMAGE,JG	ST	79	JAR	KRIEGER,AM	SPERO,LL	72	102
0.89	ABDEL-KHALIK,AR	AU	80	JAR	EL-SHESHAI,KM		325	342
0.86	HYLAS,RE	OC	82	TAR	ASHTON,RH		751	765
0.86	LEITCH,RA	AP	82	TAR	NETER,J	PLANTE,R	384	400
0.85	HARIED,AA	SP	73	JAR			117	145
0.83	BIGGS,SF	SP	83	JAR	MOCK,TJ		234	255
0.83	UECKER,WC	03	77	AOS	KINNEY JR,WR		269	275
0.80	MARAIS,ML	ST	84	JAR			34	54
0.77	BUZBY,SL	JL	74	TAR			423	435
0.77	KENNEDY,HA	SP	75	JAR			97	116
0.77	ROSE,R	ST	70	JAR	BEAVER,WH	BECKER,S	138	148
0.75	BENSTON,GJ	AP	85	JAE			67	84
0.75	PARKER,JE	JA	77	TAR			69	96
0.71	CHOW,CW	AP	82	TAR	RICE,SJ		326	335
0.71	DEANGELO,LE	DE	82	JAE			171	203
0.70	GARSTKA,SJ	SP	79	JAR	OHLSON,PA		23	59
0.69	ARCHIBALD,TR	ST	67	JAR			164	186

MODE OF REASONING(METHOD)=QUANTITATIVE: DESCRIPTIVE STATS

CITE IND-EX	FIRST AUTHOR	ISS-UE	YE-AR	JOUR-NAL	SECOND AUTHOR	THIRD AUTHOR	PAG BEG	PAG END
0.69	GAGNON,JM	ST	67	JAR			187	204
0.67	CHUA,WF	OC	86	TAR			601	632
0.67	GAA,JC	JL	86	TAR			435	454
0.67	TITMAN,S	JN	86	JAE	TRUEMAN,B		159	172
0.67	TRUEMAN,B	MR	86	JAE			53	72
0.67	WHITLEY,R	02	86	AOS			171	192
0.63	CROSBY,MA	AP	81	TAR			355	365
0.62	BEAVER,WH	JA	68	TAR			113	122
0.62	GREEN,D	ST	66	JAR	SEGALL,J		21	36
0.62	SCHWAN,ES	23	76	AOS			219	238
0.60	MENZEFRICKE,U	AU	84	JAR	SMIELIAUSKAS,W		588	604
0.60	MORIARITY,S	SP	79	JAR			205	224
0.57	FROST,PA	SP	82	JAR	TAMURA,H		103	120
0.57	GIBBINS,M	JA	82	TAR	WOLF,FM		105	124
0.57	KINNEY JR,WR	JA	82	TAR	UECKER,WC		55	69
0.57	SILHAN,PA	SP	82	JAR			255	262
0.57	SOLOMON,I	01	82	AOS	KROGSTAD,JL	ROMNEY,MB	27	42
0.55	RULAND,W	AP	78	TAR			439	447
0.54	DICKHAUT,JW	SP	75	JAR	EGGLETON,IRC		38	72
0.54	DOPUCH,N	AU	73	JAR	RONEN,J		191	211
0.50	BEAVER,WH	JA	87	TAR			137	144
0.50	CONROY,RM	JA	87	TAR	HUGHES,JS	50	66	
0.50	HOWARD,TP	OC	83	TAR	NIKOLAI,LA		765	776
0.50	MELUMAD,ND	ST	87	JAR	REICHELSTEIN,S		1	18
0.50	PUXTY,AG	03	87	AOS	WILLMOTT,HC	COOPER,DJ	273	291
0.50	SHANE,PB	JL	83	TAR	SPICER,BH		521	538
0.50	SUH,YS	ST	87	JAR			22	46
0.50	SWIERINGA,RJ	03	87	AOS	WEICK,KE		293	308
0.50	THOMPSON,G	05	87	AOS			523	543
0.50	TSUI,KW	JA	85	TAR	MATSUMURA,EM	TSUI,KL	76	96
0.46	BEAVER,WH	AU	68	JAR			179	192
0.46	NEUMANN,FL	ST	68	JAR			1	17
0.46	SINGHVI,SS	JA	71	TAR	DESAI,HB		129	138
0.43	DANOS,P	WI	82	AUD	IMHOFF JR,EA		23	34
0.42	COOPER,DJ	03	77	AOS	ESSEX,S		201	218
0.40	BIGGS,SF	34	84	AOS			313	323
0.40	BUZBY,SL	JA	79	TAR	FALK,H		23	37
0.40	DITTMAN,DA	AP	79	TAR	PRAKASH,P		358	373
0.40	MAYER-SOMMER,AP	JA	79	TAR			88	106
0.40	ST.PIERRE,K	AP	84	TAR	ANDERSON,JA		242	263
0.38	BERNSTEIN,LA	JA	67	TAR			86	95
0.38	COPELAND,RM	ST	71	JAR	SHANK,JK		196	224
0.36	SHANK,JK	OC	78	TAR	MURDOCK,RJ		824	835
0.33	DWORIN,L	JA	86	TAR	GRIMLUND,RA		36	57
0.33	FRECKA,TJ	JA	83	TAR	HOPWOOD,WS		115	128
0.33	ROBERTS,DM	SP	86	JAR			111	126
0.33	SEFCIK,SE	AU	86	JAR	THOMPSON,R		316	334
0.33	SMITH,DB	AU	86	AUD			95	108
0.33	TAMURA,H	AU	86	JAR	FROST,PA		364	371
0.31	BARRETT,ME	SP	76	JAR			10	26

MODE OF REASONING(METHOD)=QUANTITATIVE: DESCRIPTIVE STATS

CITE IND-EX	FIRST AUTHOR	ISS-UE	YE-AR	JOUR-NAL	SECOND AUTHOR	THIRD AUTHOR	PAG BEG	PAG END
0.31	CHANDRA,G	OC	74	TAR			733	742
0.31	DASCHER,PE	AU	70	JAR	MALCOM,RE		253	259
0.31	HOFSTEDT,TR	01	76	AOS			43	58
0.31	LIVINGSTONE,JL	AP	67	TAR			233	240
0.31	MCRAE,TW	SP	74	JAR			80	92
0.31	RHODE,JG	OC	74	TAR	WHITSELL,GM	KELSEY,RL	772	787
0.31	WILCOX,JA	ST	73	JAR			163	179
0.31	ZEFF,SA	AP	67	TAR	FOSSUM,RL		298	320
0.30	BLOCHER,E	JL	79	TAR			563	573
0.30	NAIR,RD	SP	79	JAR			225	242
0.29	HOPWOOD,WS	AU	82	JAR	NEWBOLD,P	SILHAN,PA	724	732
0.29	WALTHER,LM	AP	82	TAR			376	383
0.27	BUZBY,SL	34	78	AOS	FALK,H		191	202
0.25	FLAMHOLTZ,EG	01	85	AOS	DAS,TK	TSUI,AS	35	50
0.25	GARSTKA,SJ	AU	77	JAR			179	192
0.25	KELLY,LK	JA	77	TAR			97	108
0.25	OGDEN,S	02	85	AOS	BOUGEN,P		211	226
0.25	STAUBUS,GJ	JA	85	TAR			53	75
0.25	WEBER,RP	JL	81	TAR	STEVENSON,WC		596	612
0.23	BOWMAN,EH	01	76	AOS	HAIRE,M		11	22
0.23	CAPLAN,EM	AP	68	TAR			342	362
0.23	FALK,H	SP	73	JAR	OPHIR,T		108	116
0.23	HEINTZ,JA	OC	73	TAR			679	689
0.23	ORTMAN,RF	AP	75	TAR			298	304
0.23	PROBST,FR	JA	71	TAR			113	118
0.23	WHITE JR,CE	AU	72	JAR			351	358
0.22	HUSSEIN,ME	SU	80	JAA	KETZ,JE		354	367
0.22	RONEN,J	SU	80	JAA	SADAN,S		339	353
0.20	BROCKHOFF,K	12	79	AOS			77	86
0.20	CUSHING,BE	ST	79	JAR	SEARFOSS,DG	RANDALL,RH	172	216
0.20	DIERKES,M	12	79	AOS			87	108
0.20	MOST,KS	AU	84	JAR			782	788
0.20	MUTCHLER,JF	SP	84	AUD			17	30
0.20	RICCHIUTE,DN	12	79	AOS			67	76
0.20	SMITH,G	AU	84	AUD	KROGSTAD,JL		107	117
0.20	STONE,M	JL	84	TAR	BUBLITZ,B		469	473
0.20	SUTTON,TG	01	84	AOS			81	95
0.17	BLOCHER,E	AU	83	AUD	ESPOSITO,RS	WILLINGHAM,JJ	75	91
0.17	HOLDER,WW	SP	83	AUD			100	108
0.17	MCLEAY,S	01	83	AOS			31	56
0.15	BRILOFF,AJ	JL	66	TAR			484	495
0.15	CHURCHILL,NC	OC	65	TAR	COOPER,WW		767	781
0.15	DOPUCH,N	ST	66	JAR	DRAKE,DF		192	219
0.15	FRANK,WG	AP	70	TAR	WEYGANDT,JJ		280	289
0.15	GREENBALL,MN	SP	68	JAR			114	129
0.15	KIGER,JE	JA	74	TAR			1	7
0.15	LINDHE,R	AU	63	JAR			139	148
0.15	LIVINGSTONE,JL	AU	70	JAR	SALAMON,GL		199	216
0.15	PANKOFF,LD	AP	70	TAR	VIRGIL JR,RL		269	279
0.15	RITTS,BA	SP	74	JAR			93	111

MODE OF REASONING(METHOD)=QUANTITATIVE: DESCRIPTIVE STATS

CITE IND- EX	FIRST AUTHOR	ISS- UE	YE- AR	JOUR -NAL	SECOND AUTHOR	THIRD AUTHOR	PAG BEG	PAG END
0.15	ROBERTSON,JC	JL	71	TAR	CLARKE,RW		562	571
0.15	SMITH,CH	AP	72	TAR	LANIER,RA	TAYLOR,ME	270	283
0.15	STERLING,RR	SP	69	JAR	RADOSEVICH,R		90	95
0.14	EGGLETON,IRC	SP	82	JAR			68	102
0.14	JIAMBALVO,J	SP	82	JAR			152	161
0.14	SCHWARTZ,KB	AU	82	JAA			32	43
0.14	SELTO,FH	AU	82	JAR	GROVE,HD		676	688
0.14	SKINNER,RC	SP	82	JAR			210	226
0.14	UECKER,WC	AU	82	JAR			388	402
0.13	ALFORD,MR	SP	81	JAA	EDMONDS,TP		255	264
0.13	MAHER,MW	OC	81	TAR			751	770
0.13	WOLF,FM	OC	81	TAR			861	881
0.11	FERRIS,KR	04	80	AOS	DILLARD,JF	NETHERCOTT,L	361	368
0.11	FLAHERTY,RE	AU	80	JAA	SCHWARTZ,BN		47	56
0.11	LOY,LD	SP	80	JAA	TOOLE,HR		227	243
0.10	CHAN,JL	04	79	AOS			273	282
0.09	DAVIDSON,S	ST	78	JAR	WEIL,RL		154	233
0.09	GRAY,SJ	AU	78	JAR			242	253
0.09	JACOBS,FH	SP	78	JAR			190	203
0.08	BRUNS JR,WJ	ST	66	JAR			1	14
0.08	CHOTTINER,S	AU	71	JAR	YOUNG,AE		367	374
0.08	COPELAND,RM	AU	69	JAR	WOJDAK,JF		188	195
0.08	DAVIDSON,S	AU	66	JAR	KOHLMEIER,JM		183	212
0.08	FOGELBERG,G	AU	71	JAR			215	235
0.08	FRANKFURTER,GM	AP	72	TAR	HORWITZ,BN		245	259
0.08	HOFSTEDT,TR	AP	71	TAR	WEST,RR		329	337
0.08	KELLY,LK	JA	77	TAR			97	108
0.08	LOEB,SE	JA	72	TAR			1	10
0.08	MAGEE,RP	JA	77	TAR			190	199
0.08	MCCOSH,AM	04	76	AOS	RAHMAN,M		339	356
0.08	NEUMANN,FL	JL	69	TAR			546	554
0.08	SAN MIGUEL,JG	04	77	AOS	SHANK,JK	GOVINDARAJAN,V	333	348
0.08	SAULS,EH	JA	72	TAR			109	115
0.08	SCHROEDER,RG	01	77	AOS	IMDIEKE,LF		39	46
0.08	SIMPSON,RH	OC	69	TAR			806	817
0.08	SOPER,FJ	AP	64	TAR	DOLPHIN,R		358	362
0.08	SPILLER JR,EA	SP	74	JAR	VIRGIL JR,RL		112	142
0.08	STONE,WE	JA	65	TAR			190	195
0.00	ALDERMAN,CW	WI	82	AUD	DEITRICK,JW		54	68
0.00	AMERSHI,AH	AU	87	JAR	SUNDER,S		177	195
0.00	ANDERSON,JC	JL	86	TAR	KRAUSHAAR,JM		379	399
0.00	ANDERSON,U	AU	88	AUD	YOUNG,RA		23	42
0.00	ARNETT,HE	JA	65	TAR			54	64
0.00	ASHTON,RH	SU	81	JAA	HYLAS,RE		325	332
0.00	ASKARI,H	AP	76	TAR	CAIN,P	SHAW,R	331	334
0.00	BABER,WR	JA	85	TAR			1	9
0.00	BAILEY JR,AD	SP	68	JAR	GRAY,J		98	105
0.00	BALACHANDRAN,BV	SP	87	JAR	RAMAKRISHNAN,RT		111	126
0.00	BALACHANDRAN,BV	WI	88	JAA	RAMANAN,R		1	13
0.00	BALACHANDRAN,KR	02	77	AOS	LIVINGSTONE,JL		153	164

MODE OF REASONING(METHOD)=QUANTITATIVE: DESCRIPTIVE STATS

CITE IND-EX	FIRST AUTHOR	ISS-UE	YE-AR	JOUR -NAL	SECOND AUTHOR	THIRD AUTHOR	PAG BEG	PAG END
0.00	BALACHANDRAN,KR	SP	87	JAA	SRINIDHI,BN		151	169
0.00	BANKER,RD	AU	87	JAA	DATAR,SM	RAJAN,MV	319	347
0.00	BANKER,RD	JL	88	JAE	DATAR,SM	KEKRE,S	171	197
0.00	BAO,BH	03	86	AOS	BAO,DH	VASARHELYI,MA	289	296
0.00	BARKMAN,A	JA	77	TAR			450	464
0.00	BARLEV,B	AU	79	JAR	LEVY,H		305	315
0.00	BARTON,RF	SP	69	JAR			116	122
0.00	BEAVER,WH	DE	81	JAE	LANDSMAN,WR		233	241
0.00	BECK,PJ	SP	85	AUD	SOLOMON,I		1	10
0.00	BENISHAY,H	SU	87	JAA			203	238
0.00	BERRY,LE	JA	87	TAR	HARWOOD,GB	KATZ,JL	14	28
0.00	BIERMAN JR,H	WI	86	JAA			62	70
0.00	BIERMAN,H	SP	85	JAA			184	194
0.00	BORITZ,JE	AU	86	AUD	BROCA,DS		1	19
0.00	BOWEN,RM	OC	82	TAR	SUNDEM,GL		778	784
0.00	BOWSHER,CA	WI	86	JAA			7	16
0.00	BRADBURY,ME	AP	88	TAR	CALDERWOOD,SC		330	347
0.00	BROWN,PR	SU	82	JAA			282	290
0.00	BURRELL,G	01	87	AOS			89	102
0.00	BURTON,JC	WI	82	AUD	FAIRFIELD,P		1	22
0.00	CALLEN,JL	SP	88	JAA			87	108
0.00	CAMPBELL,DR	SP	83	JAA			196	211
0.00	CAMPBELL,JE	34	84	AOS			329	342
0.00	CHAN,KH	OC	86	TAR	DODIN,B		726	734
0.00	CHOUDHURY,N	06	88	AOS			549	557
0.00	CHUA,WF	06	86	AOS			583	598
0.00	COE,TL	SP	79	JAA			244	253
0.00	COOPER,DJ	05	87	AOS	HOPPER,TM		407	414
0.00	DANOS,P	SP	87	AUD	HOLT,DL	BAILEY JR,AD	134	149
0.00	DERMER,JD	06	86	AOS	LUCAS,RG		471	482
0.00	DERMER,JD	01	88	AOS			25	36
0.00	DEVINE,CT	ST	66	JAR			160	176
0.00	DIERKES,M	01	85	AOS	ANTAL,AB		29	34
0.00	DOPUCH,N	SU	88	JAA			245	250
0.00	DUGAN,MT	SP	85	AUD	GENTRY,JA	SHRIVER,KA	11	22
0.00	DYE,RA	AU	88	JAR			195	235
0.00	ENGSTROM,JH	SP	84	JAA			197	211
0.00	EVANS III,JH	06	86	AOS	LEWIS,BL	PATTON,JM	483	498
0.00	FAIRCLOTH,AW	01	81	AOS	RICCHIUTE,DN		53	68
0.00	FEINSCHREIBER,R	SP	69	JAR			17	21
0.00	FELIX JR,WL	SP	88	AUD	NILES,MS		43	60
0.00	FELLINGHAM,JC	JA	85	TAR	WOLFSON,MA		10	17
0.00	FINLEY,DR	SP	87	AUD	BOOCKHOLDT,JL		22	39
0.00	FIRMIN,PA	ST	68	JAR	GOODMAN,SS	HENDRICKS,TE	122	155
0.00	FLAMHOLTZ,EG	04	87	AOS			309	318
0.00	FREDRIKSON,EB	AU	68	JAR			208	221
0.00	FRIEDLOB,GT	WI	83	JAA			100	107
0.00	FRISHKOFF,P	AU	84	JAA	FRISHKOFF,PA	BOUWMAN,MJ	44	53
0.00	FROST,PA	SP	86	JAR	TAMURA,H		57	75
0.00	GAMBLE,GO	SP	86	JAA			102	117

MODE OF REASO! ING(METHOD)=QUANTITATIVE: DESCRIPTIVE STATS

CITE IND-EX	FIRST AUTHOR	ISS-UE	YE-AR	JOUR-NAL	SECOND AUTHOR	THIRD AUTHOR	PAG BEG	PAG END
0.00	GAMBLING,T	04	85	AOS			415	426
0.00	GAMBLING,T	04	87	AOS			319	329
0.00	GERLACH,JH	SP	88	AUD			61	76
0.00	GOLDIN,HJ	SU	85	JAA			269	278
0.00	GOLDWASSER,DL	SU	88	JAA			217	232
0.00	GORDON,LA	JL	88	AUD	HAMER,MH		514	521
0.00	GOVINDARAJAN,V	SU	79	JAA			339	343
0.00	GOVINDARAJAN,V	04	80	AOS			383	392
0.00	GRANOF,MH	SU	84	JAA	SHORT,DG		323	333
0.00	GRAY,D	AU	84	JAR			760	764
0.00	GRAY,SJ	SP	84	JAR	RADEBAUGH,LH		351	360
0.00	GREENBALL,MN	ST	68	JAR			27	49
0.00	GRIMLUND,RA	AU	85	JAR			575	594
0.00	GRIMLUND,RA	JL	87	TAR	FELIX JR,WL		455	479
0.00	GRIMLUND,RA	SP	88	AUD			77	104
0.00	GROSSMAN,SD	WI	81	JAA	KRATCHMAN,SH	WELKER,RB	136	143
0.00	HARRISON,GL	03	86	AOS	MCKINNON,JL		233	252
0.00	HINES,RD	OC	88	TAR			642	656
0.00	HIRST,MK	OC	87	TAR			774	784
0.00	HOLDREN,GC	JA	64	TAR			70	85
0.00	HONIG,LE	SP	78	JAA			231	236
0.00	HOPPER,T	05	87	AOS	STOREY,J	WILLMOTT,H	437	456
0.00	HOPWOOD,AG	01	87	AOS			65	70
0.00	HORRIGAN,JO	JL	65	TAR			558	568
0.00	HORWITZ,BN	SP	72	JAR	YOUNG,AE		96	107
0.00	HOSKIN,KW	01	88	AOS	MACVE,RH		37	73
0.00	HOUGHTON,KA	AU	84	JAR	SENGUPTA,R		768	775
0.00	HOUGHTON,KA	SP	84	JAR			361	368
0.00	HUSS,HF	AU	85	JAA			60	66
0.00	HUSS,HF	AU	86	JAR	TRADER,RL		394	399
0.00	HUSSEIN,ME	AU	86	AUD	BAVISHI,VB	GANGOLLY,JS	124	133
0.00	IJIRI,Y	OC	86	TAR			745	760
0.00	IVES,M	SU	85	JAA			253	268
0.00	JACOBS,FH	JA	87	TAR	MARSHALL,RM		67	78
0.00	JOHNSON,O	OC	76	TAR			808	823
0.00	JONSON,LC	34	78	AOS	JONSSON,B	SVENSSON,G	261	268
0.00	JONSSON,S	05	88	AOS	GRONLUND,A		513	532
0.00	JOYCE,EJ	AU	82	JAR	LIBBY,R	SUNDER,S	654	675
0.00	JUNG,WO	SP	88	JAR	KWON,YK		146	153
0.00	KAHN,N	SU	82	JAA			327	337
0.00	KATZ,BG	SU	87	JAA	OWEN,J		266	298
0.00	KIM,HS	SP	87	AUD	NETER,J	GODFREY,JT	40	58
0.00	KING,RD	JL	84	TAR			419	431
0.00	KING,TE	JL	88	AUD	ORTEGREN,AK		522	535
0.00	KINNEY JR,WR	SP	87	AUD			59	73
0.00	KNECHEL,WR	JA	88	TAR			74	95
0.00	KNECHEL,WR	AU	88	AUD			87	107
0.00	KNIGHTS,D	05	87	AOS	COLLINSON,D		457	477
0.00	KNUTSON,PH	ST	71	JAR			99	112
0.00	KO,CE	SP	88	AUD	NACHTSHEIM,CJ	DUKE,GL	119	136

MODE OF REASONING(METHOD)=QUANTITATIVE: DESCRIPTIVE STATS

CITE IND-EX	FIRST AUTHOR	ISS-UE	YE-AR	JOUR-NAL	SECOND AUTHOR	THIRD AUTHOR	PAG BEG	PAG END
0.00	KREISER,L	AP	77	TAR			427	437
0.00	KREUTZFELDT,RW	AU	86	AUD	WALLACE,WA		20	43
0.00	KUBLIN,M	JL	65	TAR			626	635
0.00	KUNITAKE,WK	SU	86	JAA	WHITE JR,CE		222	231
0.00	LANDSMAN,WR	OC	88	TAR	MAGLIOLO,J		586	604
0.00	LAUGHLIN,RC	05	87	AOS			479	502
0.00	LAVOIE,D	06	87	AOS			579	604
0.00	LAWRENCE,EC	AU	83	JAR			606	610
0.00	LEE,CF	AP	88	TAR	WU,C		292	306
0.00	LEHMAN,C	05	87	AOS	TINKER,T		503	522
0.00	LEMBKE,VC	WI	80	JAA	SMITH,JH		147	162
0.00	LERE,JC	AP	86	TAR			318	324
0.00	LEV,B	ST	69	JAR			182	197
0.00	LEVY,H	AU	87	JAA	BYUN,YH		355	369
0.00	LEWIS,NR	34	84	AOS	PARKER,LD	SUTCLIFFE,P	275	289
0.00	LIGHTNER,SM	AU	82	AUD	ADAMS,SJ	LIGHTNER,KM	1	12
0.00	LIVINGSTONE,JL	SP	67	JAR			77	94
0.00	LLOYD,BM	OC	71	TAR	WEYGANDT,JJ		756	764
0.00	LOWE,RE	OC	65	TAR			839	846
0.00	LUDMAN,EA	SP	86	JAA			118	124
0.00	MAGEE,RP	JA	88	TAR			42	54
0.00	MARCH,JG	02	87	AOS			153	168
0.00	MCCONNELL,DK	SP	84	AUD			44	56
0.00	MCGAHRAN,KT	JA	88	TAR			23	41
0.00	MEHTA,DR	SP	68	JAR	ANDREWS,VL		50	57
0.00	MELLMAN,M	JA	63	TAR			118	123
0.00	MENZEFRICKE,U	AU	86	JAR			570	587
0.00	MESERVY,RD	AU	86	AUD	BAILEY JR,AD	JOHNSON,PE	44	74
0.00	MILLAR,JA	JA	77	TAR			52	55
0.00	MILLS,RH	JA	67	TAR			74	81
0.00	MORGAN,G	05	88	AOS			477	485
0.00	MUTCHLER,JF	AU	86	AUD			148	.
0.00	NAIR,RD	SP	83	JAA	RITTENBERG,LE		234	243
0.00	NELSON,J	SU	88	JAA	RONEN,J	WHITE,L	255	296
0.00	NIELSEN,CC	OC	65	TAR			795	804
0.00	NIX,HM	SU	83	JAA	WICHMANN JR,H		341	352
0.00	NOREEN,EW	04	88	AOS			359	369
0.00	NURNBERG,H	AU	85	JAA	CIANCIOLO,ST		50	59
0.00	O'DONNELL,JL	JA	65	TAR			135	143
0.00	O'DONNELL,JL	JL	68	TAR			549	553
0.00	OUTSLAY,E	OC	82	TAR	WHEELER,JE		716	733
0.00	OWEN,DL	03	85	AOS	LLOYD,AJ		329	352
0.00	PALMROSE,ZV	SP	87	AUD			90	103
0.00	PANY,K	SP	84	AUD	RECKERS,PMJ		89	97
0.00	PATTEN,RJ	OC	64	TAR			876	879
0.00	PELES,YC	AP	86	TAR			325	329
0.00	PLANTE,R	AU	85	AUD	NETER,J	LEITCH,RA	40	56
0.00	POWELL,RM	JL	66	TAR			525	534
0.00	PURDY,D	04	81	AOS			327	338
0.00	RICHARDSON,AJ	04	87	AOS			341	355

MODE OF REASONING(METHOD)=QUANTITATIVE: DESCRIPTIVE STATS

CITE IND- EX	FIRST AUTHOR	ISS- UE	YE- AR	JOUR -NAL	SECOND AUTHOR	THIRD AUTHOR	PAG BEG	PAG END
0.00	RODEN,PF	WI	87	JAA			79	89
0.00	ROHRBACH.KJ	SP	86	JAR			127	150
0.00	ROSHWALB,A	AU	87	AUD	WRIGHT,RL	GODFREY,JT	54	70
0.00	RUE,JC	SU	84	JAA	VOLKAN,AG		306	322
0.00	RUNDFELT,R	SP	86	JAA			125	130
0.00	SAMUELSON,LA	01	86	AOS			35	46
0.00	SAN MIGUEL,JG	JL	77	TAR			638	641
0.00	SCHACHTER,B	AU	85	JAR			907	910
0.00	SCHEINER,JH	AU	82	JAR	KIGER,JE		482	496
0.00	SCHEINER,JH	AU	84	JAR			789	797
0.00	SCHIFF,M	SP	79	JAA			224	231
0.00	SCHIPPER,K	SP	85	JAR	THOMPSON,R		408	415
0.00	SCHWARTZ,BN	SP	83	JAA			244	253
0.00	SINGER,FA	OC	65	TAR			847	853
0.00	SMIELIAUSKAS,W	JA	86	TAR			118	128
0.00	SMIELIAUSKAS,W	SP	86	JAR			217	230
0.00	SMITH,DB	OC	82	JAE	NICHOLS,DR		109	120
0.00	SMITH,VL	AU	87	AUD	SCHATZBERG,J	WALLER,WS	71	93
0.00	SOMEYA,K	OC	64	TAR			983	989
0.00	SORTER,GH	SP	87	JAA	INGBERMAN,M		99	116
0.00	SORTER,GH	SU	88	JAA	SIEGEL,S	SLAIN,J	233	244
0.00	SPENCER,CH	JA	65	TAR	BARNISEL,TS		144	153
0.00	SPICER,BH	03	88	AOS			303	322
0.00	SRIVASTAVA,RP	AU	86	JAR			422	427
0.00	ST.PIERRE,K	SP	82	JAA	ANDERSON,JA		229	247
0.00	STERLING,RR	OC	72	TAR	TOLLEFSON,SO	FLAHERTY,RE	709	721
0.00	TAMURA,H	SP	85	AUD			133	142
0.00	TAUSSIG,RA	WI	83	JAA			142	156
0.00	THIES,CF	AU	87	JAA	STURROCK,T		375	391
0.00	TINKER,T	01	87	AOS	NEIMARK,M		71	88
0.00	TINKER,T	02	88	AOS			165	189
0.00	USRY,MF	OC	66	TAR			754	762
0.00	VATTER,WJ	OC	67	TAR			721	730
0.00	VOSS,WM	AU	68	JAR			262	269
0.00	WALKER,NR	AU	88	AUD	PIERCE,LT		1	22
0.00	WELSH,MJ	WI	85	JAA	TRAPNELL,JE		100	111
0.00	WHITTRED,GP	AP	84	TAR	ZIMMER,I		287	295
0.00	WILD,JJ	SP	87	JAR			139	160
0.00	WILKERSON JR,JE	SP	87	JAR			161	167
0.00	WILLIAMS,PF	02	87	AOS			169	192
0.00	WILLINGER,GL	SP	85	JAR			351	359
0.00	WINBORNE,MG	JL	64	TAR			622	626
0.00	WRIGHT,A	JL	83	TAR			621	632
0.00	WRIGHT,GB	SU	82	JAA	TAYLOR,RD		301	309
0.00	YOUNG,AE	SP	78	JAA			217	230
0.00	YOUNG,SD	SP	85	JAA			178	183
0.00	ZIEBART,DA	AU	85	JAR			920	926

MODE OF REASONING(METHOD)=QUANTITATIVE: DESCRIPTIVE STATS

1.2 MODE OF REASONING(METHOD)=QUANTITATIVE: REGRESSION

CITE IND-EX	FIRST AUTHOR	ISS-UE	YE-AR	JOUR-NAL	SECOND AUTHOR	THIRD AUTHOR	PAG BEG	PAG END
4.85	BEAVER,WH	ST	68	JAR			67	92
4.54	PATELL,JM	AU	76	JAR			246	276
3.88	COLLINS,DW	MR	81	JAE	ROZEFF,MS	DHALIWAL,DS	37	71
3.50	BERRY,AJ	01	85	AOS	CAPPS,T	COOPER,D	3	28
3.50	HEALY,PM	AP	85	JAE			85	108
3.50	HOLTHAUSEN,RW	MR	81	JAE			73	109
3.00	WILSON,GP	AP	87	TAR			293	322
2.67	SCHIPPER,K	SP	83	JAR	THOMPSON,R		184	221
2.54	BALL,R	ST	72	JAR			1	38
2.50	ATIASE,RK	SP	85	JAR			21	36
2.50	BERNARD,VL	SP	87	JAR			1	48
2.50	BROWN,LD	AP	87	JAE	GRIFFIN,PA	HAGERMAN,RL	61	87
2.50	LARCKER,DF	AP	83	JAE			3	30
2.44	BEAVER,WH	MR	80	JAE	LAMBERT,RA	MORSE,D	3	28
2.40	CHAMBERS,AE	SP	84	JAR	PENMAN,SH		21	47
2.40	LEV,B	JL	79	TAR			485	503
2.29	RICKS,WE	AU	82	JAR			367	387
2.23	GONEDES,NJ	AU	75	JAR			220	256
2.23	SUNDER,S	ST	73	JAR			1	45
2.08	BEAVER,WH	OC	70	TAR	KETTLER,P	SCHOLES,M	654	682
2.00	ARMSTRONG,P	02	85	AOS			129	148
2.00	ARMSTRONG,P	05	87	AOS			415	436
2.00	BEAVER,WH	AG	80	JAE	CHRISTIE,AA	GRIFFIN,PA	127	157
2.00	BROWN,LD	JL	87	JAE	GRIFFIN,PA	HAGERMAN,RL	159	193
2.00	HUGHES,JS	JA	87	TAR	RICKS,WE		158	175
2.00	RAYBURN,J	ST	86	JAR			112	137
2.00	SIMUNIC,DA	SP	80	JAR			161	190
1.92	MAY,RG	ST	71	JAR			119	163
1.89	PENMAN,SH	SP	80	JAR			132	160
1.86	GIVOLY,D	JL	82	TAR	PALMON,D		486	508
1.75	MURPHY,KJ	AP	85	JAE			11	42
1.71	PATELL,JM	JL	82	TAR	WOLFSON,MA		509	527
1.62	BEAVER,WH	AP	72	TAR	DUKES,RE		320	332
1.60	DODD,P	AP	84	JAE	DOPUCH,N	HOLTHAUSEN,RW	3	38
1.57	BROWNELL,P	SP	82	JAR			12	27
1.56	RO,BT	AG	80	JAE			159	189
1.54	SUNDER,S	AP	75	TAR			305	315
1.50	BUBLITZ,B	ST	85	JAR	FRECKA,TJ	MCKEOWN,JC	1	23
1.50	COUGHLAN,AT	AP	85	JAE	SCHMIDT,RM		43	66
1.50	PATELL,JM	AU	81	JAR	WOLFSON,MA		434	458
1.44	GRANT,EB	SP	80	JAR			255	268
1.40	FOSTER,G	OC	84	TAR	OLSEN,C	SHEVLIN,T	574	603
1.38	BROWNELL,P	OC	81	TAR			844	860
1.33	BAMBER,LS	SP	86	JAR			40	56
1.33	HARRISON,T	SP	77	JAR			84	107
1.33	PALMROSE,ZV	SP	86	JAR			97	110
1.33	WILSON	GP	ST	86	JAR		165	203
1.31	FOSTER,G	SP	73	JAR			25	37

MODE OF REASONING(METHOD)=QUANTITATIVE: REGRESSION

CITE INDEX	FIRST AUTHOR	ISSUE	YEAR	JOURNAL	SECOND AUTHOR	THIRD AUTHOR	PAG BEG	PAG END
1.30	JIAMBALVO,J	AU	79	JAR			436	455
1.29	LILIEN,S	DE	82	JAE	PASTENA,V		145	170
1.25	FERRIS,KR	JL	77	TAR			605	615
1.25	GOVINDARAJAN,V	01	85	AOS	GUPTA,AK		51	66
1.25	HOPWOOD,AG	03	85	AOS			361	376
1.25	LIBBY,R	AU	85	JAR			648	667
1.15	ARCHIBALD,TR	JA	72	TAR			22	30
1.15	GONEDES,NJ	AU	73	JAR			212	237
1.13	MORSE,D	AU	81	JAR			374	383
1.11	BROWN,RM	SP	80	JAR			38	63
1.09	COLLINS,F	AP	78	TAR			324	335
1.00	ABDEL-KHALIK,AR	AU	85	JAR			427	447
1.00	BEAVER,WH	JL	87	JAE	LAMBERT,RA	RYAN,SG	139	157
1.00	BELL,TB	SP	83	JAR			1	17
1.00	BIDDLE,GC	AU	88	JAR	RICKS,WE		169	194
1.00	BROWN,LD	SP	87	JAR	RICHARDSON,GD	SCHWAGER,SJ	49	67
1.00	CHENHALL,RH	JA	86	TAR	MORRIS,D		16	35
1.00	COLLINS,DW	JL	87	JAE	KOTHARI,SP	RAYBURN,JD	111	138
1.00	DYE,RA	SP	85	JAR			123	145
1.00	ELLIOTT,JA	AU	82	JAR			617	638
1.00	FREEMAN,RN	JL	87	JAE			195	228
1.00	GONEDES,NJ	SP	74	JAR			26	62
1.00	HARRIS,TS	OC	87	TAR	OHLSON,JA		651	670
1.00	HEALY,PM	AP	87	JAE	KANG,SH	PALEPU,KG	7	34
1.00	HUGHES,JS	AG	84	JAE	RICKS,WE		101	132
1.00	JAIN,PC	DE	82	JAE			205	228
1.00	KAPLAN,RS	45	86	AOS			429	452
1.00	LIBERTY,SE	OC	86	TAR	ZIMMERMAN,JL	692	712	
1.00	LYS,T	AP	84	JAE			39	65
1.00	RUBIN,MA	AP	88	TAR			219	236
1.00	WAYMIRE,G	AU	84	JAR			703	718
1.00	ZIMMER,I	MR	86	JAE			37	52
0.91	KINNEY JR,WR	JA	78	TAR			48	60
0.90	LOREK,KS	SP	79	JAR			190	204
0.86	FREEMAN,RN	AU	82	JAR	OHLSON,JA	PENMAN,SH	639	653
0.83	FREEMAN,RN	SP	83	JAR			42	64
0.83	JOY,OM	AU	77	JAR	LITZENBERGER,RH	MCENALLY,RW	207	225
0.83	WRIGHT,WF	JL	77	TAR			676	689
0.80	KROSS,W	SP	84	JAR	SCHROEDER,DA		153	176
0.80	SCHAEFER,TF	AU	84	JAR			647	656
0.77	LOREK,KS	AP	76	TAR	MCDONALD,CL	PATZ,DH	321	330
0.75	ANTLE,R	SP	85	JAR	SMITH,A		296	325
0.75	BOWEN,RM	JA	81	TAR			1	22
0.75	BRICKLEY,JA	AP	85	JAE	BHAGAT,S	LEASE,RC	115	130
0.75	BROWN,LD	AP	85	TAR	GARDNER,JC		262	277
0.75	MERCHANT,KA	02	85	AOS			201	210
0.75	MUTCHLER,JF	AU	85	JAR			668	682
0.75	OLSEN,C	ST	85	JAR			28	53
0.71	HOPWOOD,WS	AU	82	JAR	MCKEOWN,JC	NEWBOLD,P	343	349
0.69	BEAVER,WH	JL	73	TAR	DUKES,RE		549	559

MODE OF REASONING(METHOD)=QUANTITATIVE: REGRESSION

CITE IND-EX	FIRST AUTHOR	ISS-UE	YE-AR	JOUR-NAL	SECOND AUTHOR	THIRD AUTHOR	PAG BEG	PAG END
0.67	ANTLE,R	SP	86	JAR	SMITH,A		1	39
0.67	AYRES,FL	JN	86	JAE			143	158
0.67	BARNES,P	01	86	AOS	WEBB,J		1	18
0.67	BOLAND,RJ	45	86	AOS	PONDY,LR		403	422
0.67	BOWEN,RM	OC	86	TAR	BURGSTAHLER,D	DALEY,LA	713	725
0.67	BROWNELL,P	OC	86	TAR	MCINNES,M	587	600	
0.67	DEANGELO,LE	JL	86	TAR			400	420
0.67	FRANCIS,JR	AU	86	JAR	STOKES,DJ		383	393
0.67	HOSKIN,RE	ST	86	JAR	HUGHES,JS	RICKS,WE	1	36
0.67	KINNEY JR,WR	MR	86	JAE			73	89
0.67	LARCKER,DF	OC	83	TAR	REVSINE,L		706	732
0.67	LIPE,RC	ST	86	JAR			37	68
0.67	MAGLIOLO,J	ST	86	JAR			69	111
0.67	NEIMARK,M	45	86	AOS	TINKER,T		369	396
0.67	PALEPU,KG	MR	86	JAE			3	36
0.67	RICKS,WE	SP	86	JAR			206	216
0.67	WILLMOTT,H	06	86	AOS			555	582
0.67	WILNER,N	01	86	AOS	BIRNBERG,JG		71	82
0.64	RO,BT	AU	78	JAR			315	340
0.63	ASHTON,RH	SP	81	JAR			42	61
0.62	BEIDLEMAN,CR	OC	73	TAR			653	667
0.60	DALEY,LA	AP	84	TAR			177	198
0.60	DYCKMAN,TR	ST	84	JAR	PHILBRICK,D	STEPHAN,J	1	30
0.60	FRANCIS,JR	AG	84	JAE			133	151
0.60	NICHOLS,DR	SP	79	JAR	TSAY,JJ		140	155
0.57	BANKS,DW	SP	82	JAR	KINNEY JR,WR		240	254
0.57	DYCKMAN,TR	01	82	AOS	HOSKIN,RE	SWIERINGA,RJ	1	12
0.50	ASHTON,AH	AP	85	TAR			173	185
0.50	BABER,WR	DE	83	JAE			213	227
0.50	BROWN,LD	AU	79	JAR	ROZEFF,MS		341	351
0.50	BROWN,LD	SP	85	JAR	GARDNER,JC		84	109
0.50	CASLER,DJ	SP	85	JAR	HALL,TW		110	122
0.50	DOPUCH,N	JL	87	TAR	HOLTHAUSEN,RW	LEFTWICH,RW	431	454
0.50	FRANCIS,JR	JA	87	TAR	SIMON,DT		145	157
0.50	FRANCIS,JR	AP	87	JAE	REITER,SA		35	59
0.50	GENTRY,JA	SP	85	JAR	NEWBOLD,P	WHITFORD,DT	146	160
0.50	HAKA,SF	OC	85	TAR	GORDON,LA	PINCHES,GE	651	669
0.50	HAM,J	JL	85	TAR	LOSELL,D	SMIELIAUSKAS,W	387	406
0.50	HUNT III,HG	AU	85	JAR		448	467	
0.50	JARRELL,GA	AG	79	JAE			93	116
0.50	LEE,CJ	AU	85	JAR	HSIEH,DA		468	485
0.50	LEWELLEN,W	AP	85	JAE	LODERER,C	ROSENFELD,A	209	232
0.50	LIBBY,R	AP	85	TAR	ARTMAN,JT	WILLINGHAM,JJ	212	230
0.50	MACINTOSH,NB	01	87	AOS	DAFT,RL		49	61
0.50	MERCHANT,KA	01	85	AOS			67	86
0.50	O'LEARY,T	01	85	AOS			87	104
0.50	OLSEN,C	ST	85	JAR	DIETRICH,JR		144	166
0.50	SAVICH,RS	JL	77	TAR			642	652
0.50	STEVENSON,FL	AU	87	JAR			306	316
0.50	WALLACE,WA	AU	81	JAR			502	520

MODE OF REASONING(METHOD)=QUANTITATIVE: REGRESSION

CITE IND-EX	FIRST AUTHOR	ISS-UE	YE-AR	JOUR-NAL	SECOND AUTHOR	THIRD AUTHOR	PAG BEG	PAG END
0.50	WALLER,WS	JL	85	TAR	CHOW,CW		458	476
0.50	WHITTRED,G	DE	87	JAE			259	285
0.46	DEAKIN,EB	OC	74	TAR	GRANOF,MH		764	771
0.46	LOOKABILL,LL	OC	76	TAR			724	738
0.45	BENSTON,GJ	ST	78	JAR	KRASNEY,MA		1	30
0.44	LEV,B	AU	80	JAR			524	550
0.43	DIETRICH,JR	JA	82	TAR	KAPLAN,RS		18	38
0.43	LUSTGARTEN,S	OC	82	JAE			121	141
0.40	IMHOFF JR,EA	AU	84	JAR	LOBO,GJ		541	554
0.40	KINNEY JR,WR	AU	79	JAR			456	475
0.40	MCDONALD,B	JL	84	TAR	MORRIS,MH		432	446
0.38	BENSTON,GJ	ST	67	JAR			1	54
0.38	BILDERSEE,JS	JA	75	TAR			81	98
0.38	CAMMANN,C	04	76	AOS			301	314
0.38	FOSTER,G	AU	75	JAR			283	292
0.36	ABDEL-KHALIK,AR	SP	78	JAR	ESPEJO,J		1	13
0.36	JAGGI,B	OC	78	TAR			961	967
0.36	RICE,SJ	AP	78	TAR			429	438
0.33	ANDERSON,JC	JL	80	TAR	FRANKLE,AW		467	479
0.33	BELKAOUI,A	AU	80	JAR			362	374
0.33	BROWNELL,P	AU	83	JAR			456	472
0.33	CASEY JR,CJ	AP	86	TAR	MCGEE,VE	STICKNEY,CP	249	262
0.33	CHOW,CW	JL	83	TAR			485	520
0.33	COVALESKI,MA	03	86	AOS	DIRSMITH,MW		193	214
0.33	DANOS,P	OC	86	TAR	EICHENSEHER,JW		633	650
0.33	DOPUCH,N	JN	86	JAE	HOLTHAUSEN,RW	LEFTWICH,RW	93	118
0.33	EL-GAZZAR,S	OC	86	JAE	LILIEN,S	PASTENA,V	217	238
0.33	FREDERICK,DM	AU	86	JAR	LIBBY,R		270	290
0.33	HASSELL,JM	JA	86	TAR	JENNINGS,RH		58	75
0.33	MURDOCH,B	AP	86	TAR			273	287
0.33	NICHOLS,DR	AU	83	JAR	SMITH,DB		534	544
0.33	OPPONG,A	AU	80	JAR			574	584
0.33	PALMROSE,ZV	AU	86	JAR			405	411
0.33	PASTENA,V	AP	86	TAR	RULAND,W		288	301
0.33	PRESTON,A	06	86	AOS			521	540
0.33	SENATRA,PT	OC	86	TAR			594	603
0.33	SHRIVER,KA	SP	86	JAR			151	165
0.33	STOBER,TL	ST	86	JAR			138	164
0.33	WRIGHT,CJ	JA	86	TAR	GROFF,JE		91	100
0.31	KLAMMER,T	AP	73	TAR			353	364
0.31	LEV,B	AU	69	JAR			290	299
0.31	WEST,RR	SP	70	JAR			118	125
0.29	DAVIS,RR	AU	82	AUD			13	32
0.27	WEBER,R	FL	78	JAR			368	388
0.25	ANDERSON,MJ	AU	85	JAR			843	852
0.25	ANELL,B	04	85	AOS			479	492
0.25	BECK,PJ	SP	85	JAR	SOLOMON,I	TOMASSINI,LA	37	56
0.25	BIDDLE,GC	SP	85	JAR	MARTIN,RK		57	83
0.25	BIGGS,SF	OC	85	TAR	WILD,JJ		607	633
0.25	BROWNELL,P	AU	85	JAR			502	512

MODE OF REASONING(METHOD)=QUANTITATIVE: REGRESSION

CITE IND-EX	FIRST AUTHOR	ISS-UE	YE-AR	JOUR-NAL	SECOND AUTHOR	THIRD AUTHOR	PAG BEG	PAG END
0.25	DEJONG,DV	AU	85	JAR	FORSYTHE,R	UECKER,WC	753	793
0.25	DYE,RA	AU	85	JAR			544	574
0.25	EASTON,PD	ST	85	JAR			54	77
0.25	INGRAM,RW	AU	85	JAR			595	618
0.25	JENNINGS,R	SP	85	JAR	STARKS,L		336	350
0.25	KELLY,R	AU	85	JAR			619	632
0.25	LAMBERT,RA	AP	85	JAE	LARCKER,DF		179	204
0.25	MADEO,SA	JL	85	TAR	PINCUS,M		407	429
0.25	MILLIRON,VC	AU	85	JAR			794	816
0.25	MULFORD,CW	AU	85	JAR			897	906
0.25	PENNO,M	SP	85	JAR			240	255
0.25	PLUMLEE,RD	AU	85	JAR			683	699
0.25	SCHWARTZ,KB	AP	85	TAR	MENON,K		248	261
0.25	TEHRANIAN,H	AP	85	JAE	WAEGELEIN,JF		131	144
0.25	TROTMAN,KT	AU	85	JAR			740	752
0.25	WALLER,WS	AU	85	JAR			817	828
0.25	YOUNG,SM	AU	85	JAR			829	842
0.23	BALL,R	SP	76	JAR	LEV,B	WATTS,RL	1	9
0.23	BALOFF,N	AU	67	JAR	KENNELLY,JW		131	143
0.23	BARNEA,A	JA	76	TAR	RONEN,J	SADAN,S	110	122
0.23	BENSTON,GJ	OC	66	TAR			657	672
0.23	DEAKIN,EB	JL	76	TAR			590	603
0.23	ESKEW,RK	AP	75	TAR			316	324
0.23	MOCK,TJ	JL	73	TAR			520	534
0.23	REILLY,FK	ST	72	JAR	MORGENSON,DL	WEST,M	105	124
0.23	SAMUELSON,RA	AU	72	JAR			322	344
0.22	BOWMAN,RG	AP	80	TAR			237	253
0.22	HARRELL,AM	04	80	AOS	KLICK,HD		393	400
0.20	KELLOGG,RL	DE	84	JAE			185	204
0.20	SIMUNIC,DA	AU	84	JAR			679	702
0.18	WEBER,R	AU	78	JAR			368	388
0.17	JIAMBALVO,J	01	83	AOS	WATSON,DJ	BAUMLER,JV	13	30
0.15	ABDEL-KHALIK,AR	OC	75	TAR			657	670
0.15	GRIFFIN,PA	JL	76	TAR			499	515
0.15	MEYERS,SL	AP	73	TAR			318	322
0.15	MLYNARCZYK,FA	ST	69	JAR			63	81
0.15	O'CONNOR,MC	AP	73	TAR			339	352
0.15	PELES,YC	SP	70	JAR			128	137
0.15	STAUBUS,GJ	JA	65	TAR			119	134
0.15	ZIMMERMAN,JL	AU	76	JAR			301	319
0.14	ABDEL-KHALIK,AR	OC	82	TAR	AJINKYA,BB		661	680
0.14	EGER,C	AU	82	JAR	DICKHAUT,JW		711	723
0.14	INGRAM,RW	AU	82	JAR	COPELAND,RM		766	772
0.14	KINNEY JR,WR	AU	82	JAR	SALAMON,GL		350	366
0.14	SEPE,J	JL	82	TAR			467	485
0.14	WHALEY,RE	OC	82	JAE	CHEUNG,JK		57	83
0.13	MANEGOLD,JG	AU	81	JAR			360	373
0.11	BARAN,A	JA	80	TAR	LAKONISHOK,J	OFER,AR	22	35
0.10	ENGLEBRECHT,TD	JL	79	TAR	JAMISON,RW		554	562
0.10	HILLISON,WA	SP	79	JAR			60	73

MODE OF REASONING(METHOD)=QUANTITATIVE: REGRESSION

CITE IND- EX	FIRST AUTHOR	ISS- UE	YE- AR	JOUR -NAL	SECOND AUTHOR	THIRD AUTHOR	PAG BEG	PAG END
0.08	COMISKEY,EE	AP	66	TAR			235	238
0.08	FALK,H	SP	77	JAR	MILLER,JC		12	22
0.08	JENSEN,RE	AP	67	TAR			265	273
0.08	LIVINGSTONE,JL	AU	69	JAR			245	256
0.08	MABERT,VA	JA	74	TAR	RADCLIFFE,RC		61	75
0.08	MCKEOWN,JC	SP	73	JAR			62	99
0.08	SHARPE,IG	AU	75	JAR	WALKER,RG		293	310
0.00	ABDEL-KHALIK,AR	AU	86	JAR	GRAUL,PR	NEWTON,JD	372	382
0.00	ABDOLMOHAMMADI,MJ		86	AUD			1	16
0.00	ABDOLMOHAMMADI,MJ		87	TAR	WRIGHT,A		1	13
0.00	AMIT,R	WI	88	JAA	LIVNAT,J		19	43
0.00	ANDERSON JR,KE	JL	85	TAR			357	371
0.00	ANDERSON,MJ	05	88	AOS			431	446
0.00	ANSARI,SL	06	87	AOS	EUSKE,KJ		549	570
0.00	APOSTOLOU,NG	AU	85	JAR	GIROUX,GA	WELKER,RB	853	858
0.00	ARRINGTON,CE	SP	85	JAR	BAILEY,CD	HOPWOOD,WS	1	20
0.00	ASHTON,AH	JL	84	TAR			361	375
0.00	ASHTON,AH	OC	88	TAR	ASHTON,RH		623	641
0.00	ASHTON,RH	AU	87	JAR	WILLINGHAM,JJ	ELLIOTT,RK	275	292
0.00	ATIASE,RK	SP	87	JAR			168	176
0.00	AYRES,FL	SP	86	JAR			166	169
0.00	BABER,WR	SP	85	JAR			360	369
0.00	BABER,WR	AU	87	JAR	BROOKS,EH	RICKS,WE	293	305
0.00	BAGINSKI,SP	AU	87	JAR			196	216
0.00	BAILEY,CD	SP	86	AUD	BALLARD,G		77	85
0.00	BALLEW,V	JA	82	TAR			88	104
0.00	BALVERS,RJ	OC	88	TAR	MCDONALD,B	MILLER,RE	605	622
0.00	BAMBER,EM	JL	88	AUD	SNOWBALL,D		490	504
0.00	BAMBER,EM	SP	88	AUD	BAMBER,LS	BYLINSKI,JH	137	149
0.00	BAMBER,LS	JL	87	TAR			510	532
0.00	BATHKE,AW	AP	84	TAR	LOREK,KS		163	176
0.00	BEATTY,RP	WI	85	JAA	JOHNSON,SB		112	124
0.00	BENJAMIN,JJ	SU	86	JAA	GROSSMAN,SD	WIGGIN,CE	177	184
0.00	BERNARD,VL	AU	84	JAR			445	466
0.00	BERNARD,VL	OC	87	TAR	RULAND,RG		707	722
0.00	BIDWELL III,CM	SP	81	JAA	RIDDLE JR,JR		198	214
0.00	BIGGS,SF	SP	87	AUD	MESSIER JR,WF	HANSEN,JV	1	21
0.00	BIGGS,SF	JA	88	TAR	MOCK,TJ	WATKINS,PR	148	162
0.00	BILDERSEE,JS	SU	87	JAA	KAHN,N		239	256
0.00	BINDER,JJ	SP	85	JAR			370	383
0.00	BIRNBERG,JG	05	88	AOS	SNODGRASS,C		447	464
0.00	BLANCHARD,GA	JA	86	TAR	CHOW,CW	NOREEN,EW	1	15
0.00	BLOCHER,E	AU	85	AUD	BYLINSKI,JH		79	90
0.00	BLOCHER,E	06	86	AOS	MOFFIE,RP	ZMUD,RW	457	470
0.00	BLOCHER,E	SP	88	AUD	COOPER,JC		1	28
0.00	BORITZ,JE	AU	86	JAR			335	348
0.00	BOUWMAN,MJ	01	87	AOS	FRISHKOFF,PA	FRISHKOFF,P	1	30
0.00	BOWEN,RM	OC	87	TAR	BURGSTAHLER,D	DALEY,LA	723	747
0.00	BRANCH,B	SP	81	JAA	BERKOWITZ,B		215	219
0.00	BRIEF,RP	JA	69	TAR			20	26

MODE OF REASONING(METHOD)=QUANTITATIVE: REGRESSION

CITE IND-EX	FIRST AUTHOR	ISS-UE	YE-AR	JOUR -NAL	SECOND AUTHOR	THIRD AUTHOR	PAG BEG	PAG END
0.00	BROWN,BC	SU	86	JAA	BRANDI,JT		185	205
0.00	BROWN,C	03	85	AOS			255	266
0.00	BROWN,C	JL	87	TAR	SOLOMON,I		564	577
0.00	BROWN,LD	SP	80	JAR	HUGHES,JS	ROZEFF,MS	278	288
0.00	BROWN,LD	02	87	AOS	GARDNER,JC	VASARHELYI,MA	193	204
0.00	BROWNELL,P	AU	86	JAR	HIRST,MK		241	249
0.00	BUCHMAN,TA	03	85	AOS			267	286
0.00	BULLEN,ML	03	85	AOS	FLAMHOLTZ,EG		287	302
0.00	BURGSTAHLER,D	AP	86	TAR	JIAMBALVO,J		233	248
0.00	BURGSTAHLER,D	SP	86	JAR	NOREEN,EW		170	186
0.00	BUTLER,SA	AU	85	JAR			513	526
0.00	BUTLER,SA	JA	86	TAR			101	111
0.00	BUTT,JL	AU	88	JAR			315	330
0.00	CARSLAW,C	AP	88	TAR			321	327
0.00	CASEY JR,CJ	SP	85	JAR	BARTCZAK,N		384	401
0.00	CASEY JR,CJ	AP	86	TAR	SELLING,T		302	317
0.00	CASSIDY,DB	AU	76	JAR			212	229
0.00	CHALOS,P	AU	85	JAR			527	543
0.00	CHENHALL,RH	AP	86	TAR			263	272
0.00	CHIU,JS	OC	66	TAR	DECOSTER,DT		673	680
0.00	CHOO,F	SP	86	AUD			17	34
0.00	CHOW,CW	SP	87	AUD	MCNAMEE,AH	PLUMLEE,RD	123	133
0.00	CHOW,CW	JL	87	TAR	WONG-BOREN,A		533	541
0.00	CHOW,CW	JA	88	TAR	COOPER,JC	WALLER,WS	111	122
0.00	CLARK,TN	ST	77	JAR			54	94
0.00	CLINCH,GJ	AP	87	JAE	SINCLAIR,NA		89	106
0.00	COGLITORE,F	SP	88	AUD	BERRYMAN,RG		150	163
0.00	COLBERT,JL	02	88	AOS			111	121
0.00	COLIGNON,R	06	88	AOS	COVALESKI,M		559	579
0.00	COLLINS,F	JA	87	TAR	MUNTER,P	FINN,DW	29	49
0.00	COOPER,WW	AU	85	JAA	HO,JL	HUNTER,JE	22	39
0.00	COTTELL JR,PG	WI	86	JAA			30	45
0.00	COVALESKI,MA	01	88	AOS	DIRSMITH,MW		1	24
0.00	COWEN,SS	02	87	AOS	FERRERI,LB	PARKER,LD	111	122
0.00	COX,CT	OC	85	TAR			692	701
0.00	CREADY,WM	JL	87	TAR	SHANK,JK		589	596
0.00	CREADY,WM	SP	88	JAR			1	27
0.00	CROSBY,MA	SP	85	AUD			118	132
0.00	CZARNIAWSKA-,B	04	88	AOS			415	430
0.00	DALEY,LA	OC	88	TAR	SENKOW,DW	VIGELAND,RL	563	585
0.00	DANIEL,SJ	SP	88	AUD			174	181
0.00	DAROCA,FP	SP	85	AUD	HOLDER,WW		80	92
0.00	DAS,H	03	88	AOS			215	232
0.00	DAVIS,GB	SP	86	AUD	WEBER,R		35	49
0.00	DAVIS,ML	AP	88	TAR	LARGAY III,JA		348	363
0.00	DEAN,RA	03	88	AOS	FERRIS,KR	KONSTANS,C	235	250
0.00	DEANGELO,LE	JA	88	JAE			3	36
0.00	DEJONG,DV	ST	85	JAR	FORSYTHE,R	LUNDHOLM,RJ	81	120
0.00	DEMSKI,JS	SP	69	JAR			96	115
0.00	DHALIWAL,DS	OC	86	TAR			651	661

MODE OF REASONING(METHOD)=QUANTITATIVE: REGRESSION

CITE INDEX	FIRST AUTHOR	ISSUE	YEAR	JOURNAL	SECOND AUTHOR	THIRD AUTHOR	PAG BEG	PAG END
0.00	DIETRICH,JR	AP	84	JAE			67	96
0.00	DIRSMITH,MW	AU	85	JAA	COVALESKI,MA		5	21
0.00	DIRSMITH,MW	02	85	AOS	COVALESKI,MA		149	170
0.00	DOPUCH,N	SP	88	JAR	PINCUS,M		28	59
0.00	DORAN,BM	JL	88	TAR	COLLINS,DW	DHALIWAL,DS	389	413
0.00	DORAN,DT	SP	88	JAA	NACHTMANN,R		113	132
0.00	DYL,EA	02	85	AOS	LILLY,MS		171	176
0.00	EICHENSEHER,JW	SP	85	JAA			195	209
0.00	ELGERS,P	OC	87	TAR	CALLAHAN,C	STROCK,E	763	773
0.00	ELGERS,PT	JL	80	TAR			389	408
0.00	ELGERS,PT	AP	82	TAR	MURRAY,D		358	375
0.00	ELNICKI,RA	ST	77	JAR			209	218
0.00	ENGSTROM,JH	SU	85	JAA			305	318
0.00	ENIS,CR	02	88	AOS			123	145
0.00	ETTREDGE,M	SP	88	AUD	SHANE,PB	SMITH,D	29	42
0.00	FARMER,TA	AU	87	AUD	RITTENBERG,LE	TROMPETER,GM	1	14
0.00	FARRELY,GE	AP	85	TAR	FERRIS,KR	REICHENSTEIN,WR	278	288
0.00	FELIX JR,WL	JA	72	TAR			52	63
0.00	FELLINGHAM,JC	OC	85	TAR	NEWMAN,DP		634	650
0.00	FERRIS,KR	03	82	AOS			225	230
0.00	FIRTH,MA	AU	81	JAR			521	529
0.00	FIRTH,MA	SP	85	AUD			23	37
0.00	FLESHER,DL	JL	86	TAR	FLESHER,TK		421	434
0.00	FOSTER III,TW	AP	78	TAR	VICKREY,DW		360	370
0.00	FRANCIS,JR	OC	88	TAR	WILSON,ER		663	682
0.00	FRECKA,TJ	SP	83	JAR	LEE,CF		308	316
0.00	FREEMAN,RN	ST	78	JAR			111	145
0.00	FRIED,D	WI	87	JAA	HOSLER,C		5	23
0.00	GIROUX,GA	06	86	AOS	MAYPER,AG	DAFT,RL	499	520
0.00	GIVOLY,D	JL	85	TAR			372	386
0.00	GIVOLY,D	SP	87	JAA	LAKONISHOK,J		117	137
0.00	GLEZEN,GW	AU	85	JAR	MILLAR,JA		859	870
0.00	GONEDES,NJ	ST	69	JAR			90	113
0.00	GONEDES,NJ	JL	71	TAR			535	551
0.00	GORMLEY,RJ	SU	88	JAA			185	212
0.00	GREENBERG,RR	AU	86	JAA	JOHNSON,GL	RAMESH,K	266	277
0.00	GRIMLUND,RA	AU	88	AUD	SCHROEDER,MS		53	62
0.00	HAGERMAN,RL	AU	84	JAR	ZMIJEWSKI,ME	SHAH,P	526	540
0.00	HAKA,S	JL	86	TAR	FRIEDMAN,L	JONES,V	455	474
0.00	HAKA,SF	01	87	AOS			31	48
0.00	HALL,TW	SU	83	JAA			299	313
0.00	HALL,TW	SP	85	JAA	CASLER,DJ		210	224
0.00	HALPERIN,R	OC	85	TAR	TZUR,J		670	680
0.00	HALPERIN,R	AP	87	TAR	LANEN,WN		378	384
0.00	HALPERIN,R	OC	87	TAR	SRINIDHI,BN		686	706
0.00	HARMON,WK	AU	84	JAA			24	34
0.00	HARPER JR,RM	AU	87	JAR	MISTER,WG	STRAWSER,JR	327	330
0.00	HARRELL,AM	SP	86	AUD	CHEWNING,EG	TAYLOR,M	111	121
0.00	HARRELL,AM	SP	88	AUD	EICKHOFF,R		105	118
0.00	HARRISON,PD	AP	88	TAR	WEST,SG	RENEAU,JH	307	320

MODE OF REASONING(METHOD)=QUANTITATIVE: REGRESSION

CITE IND-EX	FIRST AUTHOR	ISS-UE	YE-AR	JOUR-NAL	SECOND AUTHOR	THIRD AUTHOR	PAG BEG	PAG END
0.00	HARTE,GF	02	87	AOS	OWEN,DL		123	142
0.00	HASKINS,M	JL	87	TAR			542	563
0.00	HAW,IM	WI	87	JAA	PASTENA,V	LILIEN,S	24	42
0.00	HAW,IM	AU	88	JAR	LUSTGARTEN,S		331	352
0.00	HECK,JL	OC	86	TAR	BREMSER,WG		735	744
0.00	HILKE,JC	WI	86	JAA			17	29
0.00	HILTON,RW	AP	88	TAR	SWIERINGA,RJ	TURNER,MJ	195	218
0.00	HIRSCHEY,M	SP	85	JAR	WEYGANDT,JJ		326	335
0.00	HIRST,MK	AU	83	JAR			596	605
0.00	HOLT,DL	06	87	AOS			571	578
0.00	HOPWOOD,WS	SP	85	JAR	MCKEOWN,JC		161	174
0.00	HORVITZ,JS	WI	85	JAA	COLDWELL,S		86	99
0.00	HORWITZ,B	JL	88	TAR	NORMOLLE,D		414	435
0.00	HOUGHTON,KA	02	87	AOS			143	152
0.00	HOUGHTON,KA	03	88	AOS			263	280
0.00	IMHOFF JR,EA	SU	81	JAA			333	351
0.00	IMHOFF JR,EA	SP	88	AUD			182	191
0.00	INGRAM,RW	JL	83	TAR	CHEWNING,EG		562	580
0.00	ISELIN,ER	02	88	AOS			147	164
0.00	JAIN,PC	JL	83	TAR			633	638
0.00	JAIN,PC	SP	86	JAR			76	96
0.00	JAIN,PC	SP	86	JAR			187	193
0.00	JENNINGS,M	SP	87	AUD	KNEER,DC	RECKERS,PMJ	104	115
0.00	JENNINGS,R	SP	87	JAR			90	110
0.00	JENSEN,MC	AP	85	JAE	ZIMMERMAN,JL		3	10
0.00	JIAMBALVO,J	AU	85	AUD	WILNER,N		1	11
0.00	JOHNSON,WB	AP	85	JAE	MAGEE,RP	NAGARAJAN,NJ	151	174
0.00	JOHNSON,WB	AU	88	JAR	DHALIWAL,DS		236	272
0.00	JOHNSON,WB	JA	88	TAR	RAMANAN,R		96	110
0.00	JONES,CS	03	85	AOS			303	328
0.00	JONES,CS	02	85	AOS			177	200
0.00	KAHN,N	AU	85	JAA	SCHIFF,A		40	49
0.00	KAPLAN,RS	SP	83	AUD			52	65
0.00	KAPLAN,SE	AU	85	AUD			12	25
0.00	KAPLAN,SE	AU	85	JAR			871	877
0.00	KAPLAN,SE	04	88	AOS	RECKERS,PMJ	ROARK,SJ	371	379
0.00	KIM,KK	JL	88	TAR			472	489
0.00	KIM,M	AP	88	JAE	MOORE,G		111	125
0.00	KING,RD	JA	86	TAR	O'KEEFE,TB		76	90
0.00	KISSINGER,JN	SP	86	JAA			90	101
0.00	KNAPP,MC	AP	85	TAR			202	211
0.00	KNAPP,MC	JL	87	TAR			578	588
0.00	KNAUF,JB	WI	87	JAA	VASARHELYI,MA		43	64
0.00	KNECHEL,WR	SP	85	JAR			194	212
0.00	KNECHEL,WR	SP	85	AUD			38	62
0.00	KRAMER,SS	JA	82	TAR			70	87
0.00	LAMBERT,RA	AU	85	JAR			633	647
0.00	LAMBERT,RA	ST	87	JAR	LARCKER,DF		85	125
0.00	LANDSMAN,WR	OC	86	TAR			662	691
0.00	LAU,AH	SP	87	JAR			127	138

MODE OF REASONING(METHOD)=QUANTITATIVE: REGRESSION

CITE INDEX	FIRST AUTHOR	ISSUE	YEAR	JOUR-NAL	SECOND AUTHOR	THIRD AUTHOR	PAG BEG	PAG END
0.00	LEE,CJ	SP	85	JAR			213	227
0.00	LEV,B	SP	79	JAA	TAYLOR,KW		232	243
0.00	LEVITAN,AS	AU	85	AUD	KNOBLETT,JA		26	39
0.00	LEWELLEN,W	DE	87	JAE	LODERER,C	MARTIN,K	287	310
0.00	LEWIS,BL	SP	85	JAR	BELL,J		228	239
0.00	LEWIS,BL	AP	88	TAR	PATTON,JM	GREEN,SL	270	282
0.00	LICATA,MP	JA	86	TAR	STRAWSER,RH	WELKER,RB	112	117
0.00	LILIEN,S	OC	88	TAR	MELLMAN,M	PASTENA,V	642	656
0.00	LIVINGSTONE,JL	ST	67	JAR			93	123
0.00	LIVNAT,J	AU	81	JAR			350	359
0.00	LOEBBECKE,JK	SP	87	AUD	STEINBART,PJ		74	89
0.00	LOREK,KS	SP	83	JAR	ICERMAN,JD	ABDULKADER,AA	317	328
0.00	LOVATA,LM	AU	88	AUD			72	86
0.00	LUCAS,HC	OC	75	TAR			735	746
0.00	LUKKA,K	03	88	AOS			281	301
0.00	LYS,T	AU	88	JAR	SIVARAMAKRISHNAN,K		273	299
0.00	MADEO,SA	AP	87	TAR	SCHEPANSKI,A	UECKER,WC	323	342
0.00	MAHER,JJ	OC	87	TAR			785	798
0.00	MAKSY,MM	OC	88	TAR			683	699
0.00	MANEGOLD,JG	SU	86	JAA			206	221
0.00	MANES,RP	ST	67	JAR	SAMUELS,JM	SMYTH,DJ	139	156
0.00	MARGHEIM,LL	SP	86	AUD	PANY,K		50	63
0.00	MARGHEIM,LL	SP	86	JAR			194	205
0.00	MARKS,BR	AU	85	JAR	RAMAN,KK		878	886
0.00	MARKS,BR	AU	87	AUD	RAMAN,KK		106	117
0.00	MARSTON,F	SP	88	JAA	HARRIS,RS		147	164
0.00	MARTIN,A	ST	71	JAR			1	31
0.00	MARTIN,JD	WI	79	JAA	ANDERSON,PF	KEOWN,AJ	151	164
0.00	MCKINELY,S	AU	85	JAR	PANY,K	RECKERS,PMJ	887	896
0.00	MCNICHOLS,M	JL	88	JAE			239	273
0.00	MCROBERTS,HA	04	85	AOS	HUDSON,J		493	502
0.00	MEAR,R	JA	87	TAR	FIRTH,MA		176	182
0.00	MEAR,R	04	87	AOS	FIRTH,MA		331	340
0.00	MELLMAN,M	AU	86	JAA	SEILER,ME		305	318
0.00	MERINO,BD	OC	87	TAR	KOCH,BS	MACRITCHIE,KL	748	762
0.00	MESSIER JR,WF	AU	87	AUD	HANSEN,JV		94	105
0.00	MIA,L	05	88	AOS			465	475
0.00	MIELKE,DE	WI	87	JAA	SEIFERT,J		65	78
0.00	MOIZER,P	AU	87	AUD	TURLEY,S		118	123
0.00	MOODY,SM	AU	86	JAA	FLESHER,DL		319	330
0.00	MOORE,ML	JA	85	TAR	STEECE,BM	SWENSON,CW	18	32
0.00	MOORE,ML	OC	87	TAR	STEECE,BM	SWENSON,CW	671	685
0.00	MOORES,K	01	86	AOS	STEADMAN,GT		19	34
0.00	MORRIS,MH	AP	88	TAR	NICHOLS,WD		237	254
0.00	MOSES,OD	AP	87	TAR			358	377
0.00	MULFORD,CW	JL	86	TAR	COMISKEY,EE		519	525
0.00	MURRAY,D	WI	82	JAA			154	159
0.00	MURRAY,D	AU	86	JAR	FRAZIER,KB		400	404
0.00	NAHAPIET,JE	04	88	AOS			333	358
0.00	NAIR,RD	AU	87	AUD	RITTENBERG,LE		15	38

MODE OF REASONING(METHOD)=QUANTITATIVE: REGRESSION

CITE INDEX	FIRST AUTHOR	ISSUE	YEAR	JOUR NAL	SECOND AUTHOR	THIRD AUTHOR	PAG BEG	PAG END
0.00	NICHOLS,DR	JA	87	TAR			183	190
0.00	NOREEN,EW	SP	88	JAR			119	133
0.00	NURNBERG,H	AU	69	JAR			257	261
0.00	O'BRIEN,PC	JA	88	JAE			53	83
0.00	OHLSON,JA	ST	72	JAR			45	84
0.00	PALMROSE,ZV	JA	88	TAR			55	73
0.00	PALMROSE,ZV	AU	88	AUD			63	71
0.00	PANY,K	AU	87	AUD	RECKERS,PMJ		39	53
0.00	PEAVY,JW	WI	85	JAA	EDGAR,SM		125	135
0.00	PENMAN,SH	DE	84	JAE			165	183
0.00	PHILIPS,GE	ST	70	JAR	MAYNE,LS		178	188
0.00	PILLSBURY,CM	SP	85	AUD			63	79
0.00	PORCANO,TM	OC	84	TAR			619	636
0.00	POWNALL,G	AU	86	JAR			291	315
0.00	PRATT,J	04	85	AOS			427	442
0.00	PURO,M	SP	85	JAA			165	177
0.00	RANSOM,CR	ST	85	JAR			124	143
0.00	RAUN,DL	OC	64	TAR			927	945
0.00	RAVIV,A	AP	85	JAE			239	246
0.00	REBELE,JE	AU	88	AUD	HEINTZ,JA	BRIDEN,GE	43	52
0.00	REILLY,FK	AU	72	JAR	STETTLER,HF		308	321
0.00	RICHARDSON,AJ	04	88	AOS			381	396
0.00	ROBBINS,WA	SU	85	JAA	APOSTOLOU,NG	STRAWSER,RH	279	292
0.00	ROBBINS,WA	AU	86	JAR	AUSTIN,KR		412	421
0.00	ROCKNESS,J	04	88	AOS	WILLIAMS,PF		397	411
0.00	ROSE,PS	AU	82	JAA	ANDREWS,WT	GIROUX,GA	20	31
0.00	SANNELLA,AJ	AU	86	JAA			288	304
0.00	SCAPENS,RW	AP	85	TAR	SALE,JT		231	247
0.00	SCHACHTER,B	AU	88	JAR			353	372
0.00	SCHAEFER,T	AU	86	JAA	KENNELLEY,M		278	287
0.00	SCHNEIDER,A	AU	85	JAR			911	919
0.00	SCHROEDER,MS	SP	86	AUD	SOLOMON,I	VICKREY,DW	86	94
0.00	SCHWEIKART,JA	06	86	AOS			541	554
0.00	SELTO,FH	AU	85	JAR	CLOUSE,ML		700	717
0.00	SHAW,WH	AP	87	TAR			385	400
0.00	SHAW,WH	SP	88	JAR			60	81
0.00	SHEVLIN,T	JL	87	TAR			480	509
0.00	SHIELDS,MD	04	87	AOS	SOLOMON,I	WALLER,WS	375	385
0.00	SHIELDS,MD	06	88	AOS	WALLER,WS		581	594
0.00	SHRIVER,KA	JA	87	TAR			79	96
0.00	SILHAN,PA	SP	85	JAR	MCKEOWN,JC		416	426
0.00	SIMON,DT	AU	85	AUD			71	78
0.00	SIMON,DT	AP	88	TAR	FRANCIS,JR		255	269
0.00	SIMONS,R	04	87	AOS			357	374
0.00	SMIELIAUSKAS,W	AU	85	JAR			718	739
0.00	SMITH,DB	AG	84	JAE	STETTLER,HF	BEEDLES,W	153	162
0.00	SMITH,DB	SP	88	JAR			134	145
0.00	SMITH,G	AU	88	AUD			108	117
0.00	SNOWBALL,D	01	86	AOS			47	70
0.00	SOETERS,J	01	88	AOS	SCHREUDER,H		75	85

MODE OF REASONING(METHOD)=QUANTITATIVE: REGRESSION

CITE IND-EX	FIRST AUTHOR	ISS-UE	YE-AR	JOUR-NAL	SECOND AUTHOR	THIRD AUTHOR	PAG BEG	PAG END
0.00	SRINIDHI,BN	SP	86	AUD	VASARHELYI,MA		64	76
0.00	STANDISH,PEM	OC	82	TAR	UNG,S		701	715
0.00	STEINBART,PJ	JA	87	TAR			97	116
0.00	STICKEL,SE	OC	86	JAE			197	216
0.00	STONE,M	AU	87	JAR			317	326
0.00	SUMNERS,GE	SP	87	AUD	WHITE,RA	CLAY JR,RJ	116	122
0.00	SUTTON,TG	AP	88	JAE			127	149
0.00	SWANSON,EP	OC	85	TAR	SHEARON,WT	THOMAS,LR	681	691
0.00	SWANSON,GA	JL	88	TAR	GARDNER,JC		436	447
0.00	SWENSON,CW	JA	87	TAR			117	136
0.00	TABOR,RH	SP	85	AUD	WILLIS,JT		93	109
0.00	THODE,SF	WI	86	JAA	DRTINA,RE	LARGAY III,JA	46	61
0.00	THOMAS,AP	03	86	AOS			253	270
0.00	THOMAS,JK	JL	88	JAE			199	237
0.00	THOMPSON II,RB	AU	87	JAR	OLSEN,C	DIETRICH,JR	245	274
0.00	THOMPSON,RB	JL	88	TAR	OLSEN,C	DIETRICH,JR	448	471
0.00	TILLER,MG	SU	85	JAA	MAUTZ,RD		293	304
0.00	TROTMAN,KT	SP	85	JAR	YETTON,PW		256	267
0.00	TSE,S	JL	86	TAR			475	497
0.00	UECKER,WC	JL	85	TAR	SCHEPANSKI,A	SHIN,J	430	457
0.00	WALLACE,WA	SP	83	AUD			66	90
0.00	WALLER,WS	AP	87	TAR	FELIX JR,WL		275	292
0.00	WALLER,WS	01	88	AOS			87	98
0.00	WAYMIRE,G	AU	83	JAR	POWNALL,G		629	643
0.00	WAYMIRE,G	SP	85	JAR			268	295
0.00	WAYMIRE,G	JA	86	TAR			129	142
0.00	WEBER,R	JL	86	TAR			498	518
0.00	WILLIAMS,DD	05	88	AOS	DIRSMITH,MW		487	508
0.00	WILLIAMS,DJ	SP	85	AUD	LILLIS,A		110	117
0.00	WILLIAMS,DJ	03	86	AOS			271	288
0.00	WILLIAMS,JJ	04	85	AOS	NEWTON,JD	MORGAN,EA	457	478
0.00	WILLIAMS,JJ	02	88	AOS	HININGS,CR		191	198
0.00	WILLINGHAM,JJ	AU	85	AUD	WRIGHT,WF		57	70
0.00	WILSON,ER	SP	84	JAR	HOWARD,TP		207	224
0.00	WONG,J	JA	88	JAE			37	51
0.00	WONG,J	AP	88	JAE			151	167
0.00	WRIGHT,A	SP	86	AUD			86	94
0.00	WRIGHT,A	06	88	AOS			595	605
0.00	WYER,JC	SP	88	AUD	WHITE,GT	JANSON,EC	164	173
0.00	YOUNG,R	SP	86	JAR			231	240
0.00	YOUNG,SD	AP	88	TAR			283	291
0.00	YOUNG,SM	06	88	AOS	SHIELDS,MD	WOLF,G	607	618
0.00	ZAROWIN,P	AP	88	JAE			89	110
0.00	ZEFF,SA	SP	86	JAA			131	154
0.00	ZIEBART,DA	AP	87	TAR	KIM,DH		343	357

MODE OF REASONING(METHOD)=QUANTITATIVE: REGRESSION

1.3 MODE OF REASONING(METHOD)=QUANTITATIVE: ANOVA

CITE IND- EX	FIRST AUTHOR	ISS- UE	YE- AR	JOUR -NAL	SECOND AUTHOR	THIRD AUTHOR	PAG BEG	PAG END
2.38	JOYCE,EJ	ST	76	JAR			29	60
1.69	LIBBY,R	JL	75	TAR			475	489
1.63	JOYCE,EJ	SP	81	JAR	BIDDLE,GC		120	145
1.33	ZIMMERMAN,JL	AG	83	JAE			119	149
1.30	PATELL,JM	AG	79	JAE	WOLFSON,MA		117	140
1.22	COLLINS,WA	AU	80	JAR	HOPWOOD,WS		390	406
1.17	SHIELDS,MD	AP	83	TAR			284	303
1.13	JOYCE,EJ	AU	81	JAR	BIDDLE,GC		323	349
1.11	SHIELDS,MD	04	80	AOS			429	442
1.09	ABDEL-KHALIK,AR	OC	78	TAR	MCKEOWN,JC		851	868
1.09	CRICHFIELD,T	JL	78	TAR	DYCKMAN,TR	LAKONISHOK,J	651	668
1.09	UECKER,WC	SP	78	JAR			169	189
1.08	ELIAS,N	ST	72	JAR			215	233
1.00	BASI,BA	AP	76	TAR	CAREY,KJ	TWARK,RD	244	254
1.00	CASEY JR,CJ	JA	80	TAR			36	49
1.00	MCGHEE,W	JL	78	TAR	SHIELDS,MD	BIRNBERG,JG	681	697
0.92	DICKHAUT,JW	JA	73	TAR			61	79
0.92	KINNEY JR,WR	SP	71	JAR			127	136
0.90	BENBASAT,I	OC	79	TAR	DEXTER,AS		735	749
0.88	HILTON,RW	SP	81	JAR	SWIERINGA,RJ	HOSKIN,RE	86	108
0.85	ABDEL-KHALIK,AR	ST	73	JAR			104	138
0.85	BAREFIELD,RM	AU	72	JAR			229	242
0.85	CHERRINGTON,DJ	ST	73	JAR	CHERRINGTON,JO		225	253
0.85	FORAN,MF	OC	74	TAR	DECOSTER,DT		751	763
0.78	LEWIS,BL	AU	80	JAR			594	602
0.77	HOFSTEDT,TR	OC	72	TAR			679	692
0.77	MOCK,TJ	SP	72	JAR	ESTRIN,TL	VASARHELYI,MA	129	153
0.75	LARCKER,DF	JL	81	TAR			519	538
0.75	SCHULTZ JR,JJ	AU	81	JAR	RECKERS,PMJ		482	501
0.70	LIBBY,R	ST	79	JAR			35	57
0.69	SORENSEN,JE	JL	67	TAR			553	565
0.67	CHOW,CW	OC	83	TAR			667	685
0.67	MESSIER JR,WF	AU	83	JAR			611	618
0.67	ROCKNESS,HO	OC	77	TAR			893	903
0.64	SCHULTZ JR,JJ	JL	78	TAR	GUSTAVSON,SG		626	641
0.62	MAGEE,RP	AU	74	JAR			270	287
0.62	OLIVER,BL	AU	74	JAR			299	316
0.62	RONEN,J	AU	71	JAR			307	332
0.60	AJINKYA,BB	AU	84	JAR	GIFT,MJ		425	444
0.58	HARRELL,AM	OC	77	TAR			833	841
0.57	DANOS,P	JA	82	TAR	IMHOFF JR,EA		39	54
0.56	SNOWBALL,D	03	80	AOS			323	340
0.56	UECKER,WC	SP	80	JAR			191	213
0.55	FIRTH,MA	JL	78	TAR			642	650
0.55	MAGEE,RP	AU	78	JAR	DICKHAUT,JW		294	314
0.54	CHESLEY,GR	SP	76	JAR			27	48
0.50	HILTON,RW	SP	81	JAR	SWIERINGA,RJ		109	119
0.50	SHIELDS,MD	01	81	AOS	BIRNBERG,JG	FRIEZE,IH	69	96

MODE OF REASONING(METHOD)=QUANTITATIVE: ANOVA

CITE INDEX	FIRST AUTHOR	ISSUE	YEAR	JOURNAL	SECOND AUTHOR	THIRD AUTHOR	PAG BEG	PAG END
0.50	VASARHELYI,MA	SP	77	JAR			138	153
0.46	ANSARI,SL	AU	76	JAR			189	211
0.46	COOK,DM	ST	67	JAR			213	224
0.46	JENSEN,RE	AU	66	JAR			224	238
0.46	SORTER,GH	AU	64	JAR	BECKER,S	ARCHIBALD,TR	183	196
0.45	NEUMANN,BR	AU	78	JAR	FRIEDMAN,LA		400	410
0.44	BOWMAN,RG	SP	80	JAR			242	254
0.43	DANOS,P	AU	82	JAR	EICHENSEHER,JW		604	616
0.43	HALL,TW	SP	82	JAR			139	151
0.40	DANOS,P	OC	84	TAR	HOLT,DL	IMHOFF JR,EA	547	573
0.40	KROGSTAD,JL	AU	84	AUD	ETTENSON,RT	SHANTEAU,J	54	74
0.40	MAHER,MW	AU	79	JAR	RAMANATHAN,KV	PETERSON,RB	476	503
0.40	WALLER,WS	OC	84	TAR	FELIX JR,WL		637	646
0.38	BECKER,S	AU	74	JAR	RONEN,J	SORTER,GH	317	329
0.38	BROWN,C	SP	81	JAR			62	85
0.38	COMISKEY,EE	AP	71	TAR			279	285
0.38	EGGLETON,IRC	ST	76	JAR			68	131
0.38	KESSLER,L	SP	81	JAR	ASHTON,RH		146	162
0.38	LAVIN,D	JA	76	TAR			41	50
0.38	MCINTYRE,EV	JL	73	TAR			575	585
0.38	MOCK,TJ	ST	69	JAR			124	159
0.38	RO,BT	JA	81	TAR			70	84
0.38	SHOCKLEY,RA	OC	81	TAR			785	800
0.38	STALLMAN,JC	ST	69	JAR			29	43
0.38	VIGELAND,RL	AP	81	TAR			309	325
0.38	WATSON,DJ	AP	75	TAR			259	273
0.38	WHITE,GE	AU	70	JAR			260	273
0.36	ABDEL-KHALIK,AR	ST	78	JAR	MCKEOWN,JC		46	77
0.36	FOSTER III,TW	OC	78	TAR	VICKREY,DW		921	934
0.36	INGRAM,RW	AU	78	JAR			270	285
0.36	KEYS,DE	AU	78	JAR			389	399
0.33	BELKAOUI,A	03	80	AOS			263	284
0.33	COVALESKI,M	45	86	AOS	AIKEN,M		297	320
0.33	FRIEDMAN,LA	AU	80	JAR	NEUMANN,BR		407	419
0.33	KELLER,SB	AU	83	AUD	DAVIDSON,LF		1	22
0.33	MEYER,JW	45	86	AOS			345	356
0.33	ZALD,MN	45	86	AOS			321	326
0.31	DEAKIN,EB	JA	76	TAR			90	96
0.31	WARREN,CS	SP	75	JAR			162	176
0.30	ADELBERG,AH	AU	79	JAR			565	592
0.30	FIRTH,MA	04	79	AOS			283	296
0.30	RECKERS,PMJ	AU	79	JAA	TAYLOR,ME		42	55
0.29	ASHTON,AH	AU	82	JAR			415	428
0.29	BENBASAT,I	SP	82	JAR	DEXTER,AS		1	11
0.27	BASU,S	JL	78	TAR			599	625
0.27	CHESLEY,GR	AU	78	JAR			225	241
0.27	HICKS JR,JO	AP	78	TAR			371	388
0.27	HIRSCH JR,ML	AU	78	JAR			254	269
0.25	CHEN,K	01	81	AOS	SUMMERS,EL		1	16
0.25	GORDON,FE	04	77	AOS	RHODE,JG	MERCHANT,KA	295	306

MODE OF REASONING(METHOD)=QUANTITATIVE: ANOVA

CITE IND-EX	FIRST AUTHOR	ISS-UE	YE-AR	JOUR-NAL	SECOND AUTHOR	THIRD AUTHOR	PAG BEG	PAG END
0.25	UECKER,WC	JL	81	TAR	BRIEF,AP	KINNEY JR,WR	465	478
0.23	BREMSER,WG	JL	75	TAR			563	573
0.23	CHASTEEN,LG	JL	71	TAR			504	508
0.23	COPELAND,RM	JL	68	TAR	LICASTRO,RD		540	545
0.23	DASCHER,PE	SP	71	JAR	COPELAND,RM		32	39
0.23	HOLSTRUM,GL	AU	71	JAR			268	277
0.22	GRAY,SJ	SP	80	JAR			64	76
0.22	PANY,K	JA	80	TAR	RECKERS,PMJ		50	61
0.20	ARANYA,N	JA	84	TAR	FERRIS,KR		1	15
0.20	DAROCA,FP	01	84	AOS			13	32
0.20	ESKEW,RK	JA	79	TAR			107	118
0.20	GUL,FA	AP	84	TAR			264	277
0.20	HARVEY,DW	03	79	AOS	RHODE,JG	MERCHANT,KA	187	210
0.20	NANNI JR,AJ	02	84	AOS			149	163
0.18	KAMIN,JY	02	78	AOS	RONEN,J		141	160
0.18	LIN,WT	JA	78	TAR			61	76
0.18	PATTON,JM	AP	78	TAR			402	414
0.17	BROWN,C	AU	83	JAR			413	431
0.17	BROWNELL,P	04	83	AOS			307	322
0.17	DANOS,P	AU	83	JAR	IMHOFF JR,EA		473	494
0.17	HOSKIN,RE	SP	83	JAR			78	95
0.17	JOHNSON,WB	JA	83	TAR			78	97
0.17	MORSE,D	AP	83	TAR	USHMAN,N		247	258
0.17	SCHIPPER,K	ST	77	JAR			1	40
0.17	TILLER,MG	AU	83	JAR			581	595
0.17	TOMASSINI,LA	OC	77	TAR			904	913
0.17	WARREN,CS	JA	77	TAR			150	161
0.17	WHITE,RA	JL	83	TAR			539	561
0.17	WILKINS,T	OC	83	TAR	ZIMMER,I		749	764
0.15	CHURCHILL,NC	OC	75	TAR	SHANK,JK		643	656
0.15	DECOSTER,DT	OC	71	TAR	RHODE,JG		651	664
0.15	LENGERMANN,JJ	OC	71	TAR			665	675
0.15	PATZ,DH	AU	72	JAR	BOATSMAN,JR		392	403
0.15	SCHULTE JR,AA	JL	65	TAR			587	593
0.15	SORENSEN,JE	OC	72	TAR	FRANKS,DD		735	746
0.15	WATSON,DJ	AP	75	TAR			259	273
0.14	JIAMBALVO,J	OC	82	TAR	PRATT,J		734	750
0.14	OTLEY,DT	SP	82	JAR	DIAS,FJB		171	188
0.13	COPELAND,RM	SP	81	JAR	TAYLOR,RL	BROWN,SH	197	207
0.13	KOCH,BS	JL	81	TAR			574	586
0.13	RAMANATHAN,KV	02	81	AOS	WEIS,WL		143	152
0.13	RECKERS,PMJ	SU	81	AUD	STAGLIANO,AJ		23	37
0.11	FIRTH,MA	JL	80	TAR			451	466
0.11	WILLIAMS,PF	JA	80	TAR			62	77
0.09	GIVOLY,D	SU	78	JAA	RONEN,J	SCHIFF,A	361	372
0.08	ALY,HF	JA	71	TAR	DUBOFF,JI		119	128
0.08	BOLLOM,WJ	JA	73	TAR			12	22
0.08	CULPEPPER,RC	AP	70	TAR			322	332
0.08	DALTON,FE	JA	70	TAR	MINER,JB		134	139
0.08	PARKER,JE	JL	75	TAR			512	524

MODE OF REASONING(METHOD)=QUANTITATIVE: ANOVA

CITE IND- EX	FIRST AUTHOR	ISS- UE	YE- AR	JOUR -NAL	SECOND AUTHOR	THIRD AUTHOR	PAG BEG	PAG END
0.08	SAULS,EH	ST	70	JAR			157	171
0.00	ABDEL-KHALIK,AR	AP	83	TAR	SNOWBALL,D	WRAGGE,JH	215	227
0.00	AJINKYA,BB	AU	80	JAR			343	361
0.00	ASHTON,RH	SU	81	AUD	HYLAS,RE		12	22
0.00	BAMBER,EM	AU	83	JAR			396	412
0.00	BROWN,PR	AU	86	AUD	KARAN,V		134	147
0.00	CHENHALL,RH	03	88	AOS	BROWNELL,P		225	233
0.00	CHURCHILL,NC	WI	82	AUD	COOPER,WW	GOVINDARAJAN,V	69	91
0.00	DEFEO,VJ	AU	86	JAR			349	363
0.00	DYKXHOORN,HJ	04	82	AOS	SINNING,KE		337	348
0.00	FERRIS,KR	01	82	AOS			13	26
0.00	HASSELBACK,JR	AP	76	TAR			269	276
0.00	HINES,RD	03	88	AOS			251	261
0.00	JOHNSON,DA	SP	83	AUD	PANY,K	WHITE,RA	38	51
0.00	JOHNSON,DA	AU	84	JAR	PANY,K		731	743
0.00	JOHNSON,WB	04	82	AOS			349	368
0.00	KAPLAN,SE	AU	84	AUD	RECKERS,PMJ		1	19
0.00	KHEMAKHEM,A	JL	68	TAR			522	534
0.00	KIDA,TE	SP	84	JAR			145	152
0.00	KIDA,TE	SP	84	JAR			332	340
0.00	LIVINGSTONE,JL	JL	67	TAR			544	552
0.00	MEEK,GK	AP	83	TAR			394	402
0.00	PANY,K	AU	82	JAR	SMITH,CH		472	481
0.00	PURDY,CR	ST	69	JAR	SMITH JR,JM	GRAY,J	1	18
0.00	RECKERS,PMJ	AU	82	AUD	SCHULTZ JR,JJ		64	74
0.00	RICKS,WE	JA	85	TAR	HUGHES,JS		33	52
0.00	STAUBUS,GJ	JL	68	TAR			413	424
0.00	SUMMERS,EL	AP	68	TAR			257	265
0.00	TAUSSIG,RA	JA	68	TAR	HAYES,SC		68	74
0.00	TEHRANIAN,H	ST	87	JAR	TRAVLOS,NG	WAEGELEIN,JF	51	76
0.00	WARREN,CS	SP	74	JAR			158	177
0.00	WARREN,CS	SP	80	JAR			312	324
0.00	WRIGHT,A	SP	82	JAR			227	239

MODE OF REASONING(METHOD)=QUANTITATIVE: ANOVA

1.4 MODE OF REASONING(METHOD)=QUANTITATIVE: FACT.ANAL ,MDA ,PROBIT ,DISCR.

CITE IND- EX	FIRST AUTHOR	ISS- UE	YE- AR	JOUR -NAL	SECOND AUTHOR	THIRD AUTHOR	PAG BEG	PAG END
7.91	WATTS,RL	JA	78	TAR	ZIMMERMAN,JL		112	134
3.80	HAGERMAN,RL	AG	79	JAE	ZMIJEWSKI,ME		141	161
3.62	BRUNS JR,WJ	AU	75	JAR	WATERHOUSE,JH		177	203
2.75	HAYES,DC	JA	77	TAR			22	39
2.63	ZMIJEWSKI,ME	AG	81	JAE	HAGERMAN,RL		129	149
2.14	FRIED,D	OC	82	JAE	GIVOLY,D		85	107
1.20	ZMIJEWSKI,ME	ST	84	JAR			59	82
1.15	BOATSMAN,JR	AP	74	TAR	ROBERTSON,JC		342	352
1.15	DEAKIN,EB	SP	72	TAR			167	179
1.00	DEAKIN,EB	OC	79	TAR			722	734
1.00	EVANS III,JH	AG	83	JAE	PATTON,JM		151	175
1.00	ONSI,M	JL	73	TAR			535	548
0.88	BROWN,PR	SP	81	JAR			232	246
0.83	DALEY,LA	DE	83	JAE	VIGELAND,RL		195	211
0.80	LIBBY,R	SP	79	JAR			99	122
0.77	SAN MIGUEL,JG	04	76	AOS			357	374
0.70	MORIARITY,S	ST	79	JAR	BARRON,FH		114	135
0.62	FRISHKOFF,P	ST	70	JAR			116	129
0.60	MERCHANT,KA	34	84	AOS			291	309
0.55	FLAMHOLTZ,EG	02	78	AOS	COOK,E		115	140
0.50	DILLARD,JF	03	79	AOS	FERRIS,KR		179	186
0.50	RAMAN,KK	OC	81	TAR			910	926
0.50	SHOCKLEY,RA	AU	83	JAR	HOLT,RN		545	564
0.46	SWIERINGA,RJ	ST	72	JAR	MONCUR,RH		194	209
0.44	HOLT,RN	03	80	AOS	CARROLL,R		285	296
0.43	COPELAND,RM	AU	82	JAR	INGRAM,RW		275	289
0.40	BALDWIN,BA	JL	84	TAR			376	389
0.40	MCKEE,AJ	OC	84	TAR	BELL,TB	BOATSMAN,JR	647	659
0.40	STOCK,D	SP	84	JAR	WATSON,CJ		192	206
0.38	BLUM,M	SP	74	JAR			1	25
0.33	NAIR,RD	JL	80	TAR	FRANK,WG		426	450
0.30	CLANCY,DK	12	79	AOS	COLLINS,F		21	30
0.30	NORTON,CL	JA	79	TAR	SMITH,RE		72	87
0.25	INGRAM,RW	OC	81	TAR	COPELAND,RM		830	843
0.23	GUPTA,MC	SP	72	JAR	HUEFNER,RJ		77	95
0.23	SEARFOSS,DG	04	76	AOS			375	388
0.22	BENKE,RL	02	80	AOS	RHODE,JG		187	202
0.20	DILLARD,JF	12	79	AOS			31	38
0.20	FRANK,WG	AU	79	JAR			593	605
0.20	FRAZIER,KB	SP	84	JAR	INGRAM,RW	TENNYSON,BM	318	331
0.20	MARAIS,ML	ST	84	JAR	PATELL,JM	WOLFSON,MA	87	114
0.20	PURO,M	AU	84	JAR			624	646
0.20	WESCOTT,SH	SP	84	JAR			412	423
0.18	KETZ,JE	ST	78	JAR			273	284
0.18	SHORT,DG	ST	78	JAR			259	272
0.17	CASEY JR,CJ	SP	83	JAR			300	307
0.17	LARCKER,DF	JA	83	TAR	LESSIG,VP		58	77
0.15	WELKER,RB	JL	74	TAR			514	523

MODE OF REASONING(METHOD)=QUANTITATIVE: FACT.ANAL, MDA, PROBIT, DISCR.

CITE IND-EX	FIRST AUTHOR	ISS-UE	YE-AR	JOUR-NAL	SECOND AUTHOR	THIRD AUTHOR	PAG BEG	PAG END
0.14	ALTMAN,EI	AU	82	JAA			4	19
0.14	SEILER,RE	04	82	AOS	BARTLETT,RW		381	404
0.11	KELLY,LK	03	80	AOS			311	322
0.10	MADEO,SA	JL	79	TAR			538	553
0.10	PEARSON,MA	WI	79	JAA	LINDGREN,JH	MYERS,BL	122	134
0.08	FRANK,WG	SP	71	JAR	WEYGANDT,JJ		116	126
0.08	HARMELINK,PJ	SP	73	JAR			146	158
0.08	JENSEN,RE	JA	71	TAR			36	56
0.08	LUSK,EJ	JL	72	TAR			567	575
0.08	UECKER,WC	01	77	AOS			47	58
0.00	ARRINGTON,CE	SP	84	JAR	HILLISON,WA	JENSEN,RE	298	312
0.00	BAILEY,KE	AU	83	JAR	BYLINSKI,JH	SHIELDS,MD	355	370
0.00	BELKAOUI,A	04	81	AOS			281	290
0.00	FIRTH,MA	SP	73	JAR			16	24
0.00	GOMBOLA,MJ	JA	83	TAR	KETZ,JE		105	114
0.00	MENSAH,YM	WI	83	JAA			130	141
0.00	MENSAH,YM	AP	83	TAR			228	246
0.00	MENSAH,YM	SP	84	JAR			380	395
0.00	MONAHAN,TF	SU	83	JAA	BARENBAUM,L		325	340
0.00	NEUMANN,BR	SP	79	JAR			123	139
0.00	RAMAN,KK	WI	82	JAA			144	153
0.00	RAMAN,KK	AU	82	JAA			44	50
0.00	STERNER,JA	AU	83	JAR			623	628
0.00	WATKINS,PR	SP	84	JAR			406	411
0.00	WHITTINGTON,OR	JL	80	TAR	WHITTENBURG,G		409	418

MODE OF REASONING(METHOD)=QUANTITATIVE: FACT.ANAL, MDA, PROBIT, DISCR.

1.5 MODE OF REASONING(METHOD)=QUANTITATIVE: MARKOV

CITE IND-EX	FIRST AUTHOR	ISS-UE	YE-AR	JOUR-NAL	SECOND AUTHOR	THIRD AUTHOR	PAG BEG	PAG END
0.38	JAGGI,B	AP	74	TAR	LAU,HS		321	329
0.13	BALACHANDRAN,KR	JA	81	TAR	MASCHMEYER,R	LIVINGSTONE,JL	115	124
0.08	GONEDES,NJ	AU	71	JAR			236	252
0.08	SHANK,JK	JA	71	TAR			57	74

1.6 MODE OF REASONING(METHOD)=QUANTITATIVE: NON-PARAMETRIC

CITE IND-EX	FIRST AUTHOR	ISS-UE	YE-AR	JOUR -NAL	SECOND AUTHOR	THIRD AUTHOR	PAG BEG	PAG END
7.00	BALL,R	AU	68	JAR	BROWN,P		159	178
4.20	BEAVER,WH	AU	79	JAR	CLARKE,R	WRIGHT,WF	316	340
3.00	COLLINS,DW	MR	79	JAE	DENT,WT		3	44
3.00	GONEDES,NJ	SP	76	JAR	DOPUCH,N	PENMAN,SH	89	137
2.40	DYCKMAN,TR	MR	79	JAE	SMITH,AJ		45	75
1.92	MILANI,K	AP	75	TAR			274	284
1.86	DHALIWAL,DS	JL	82	JAE	SALAMON,GL	SMITH,ED	41	53
1.78	ASHTON,RH	SP	80	JAR	KRAMER,SS		1	15
1.56	BIDDLE,GC	ST	80	JAR			235	280
1.46	KAPLAN,RS	AU	73	JAR			238	258
1.44	DUKES,RE	ST	80	JAR	DYCKMAN,TR	ELLIOTT,JA	1	26
1.31	ABDEL-KHALIK,AR	OC	74	TAR			743	750
1.15	ASHTON,RH	ST	76	JAR			1	17
1.15	HOPWOOD,AG	JL	74	TAR			485	495
1.00	ELLIOTT,JA	SP	84	JAR	RICHARDSON,G	DYCKMAN,TR	85	102
0.92	EGGLETON,IRC	SP	76	JAR	PENMAN,SH	TWOMBLY,JR	66	88
0.83	PINCUS,M	SP	83	JAR			155	183
0.82	NETER,J	JA	78	TAR	LEITCH,RA	FIENBERG,SE	77	93
0.78	WHITTRED,GP	OC	80	TAR			563	577
0.77	COPELAND,RM	ST	68	JAR			101	116
0.77	SMITH,ED	OC	76	TAR			707	723
0.73	SPICER,BM	JA	78	TAR			94	111
0.67	HORWITZ,BN	ST	80	JAR	KOLODNY,R		38	74
0.67	RHODE,JG	02	77	AOS	SORENSEN,JE	LAWLER III,EE	165	176
0.62	LUSK,EJ	ST	73	JAR			191	202
0.62	MOORE,ML	SP	73	JAR			100	107
0.58	CHESLEY,GR	SP	77	JAR			1	11
0.55	IMHOFF JR,EA	OC	78	TAR			836	850
0.54	DERSTINE,RP	AU	74	JAR	HUEFNER,RJ		216	234
0.54	FLAMHOLTZ,EG	23	76	AOS			153	166
0.54	OLIVER,BL	SP	72	JAR			154	166
0.54	PETERSEN,RJ	JA	73	TAR			34	43
0.54	WARD,BH	SP	76	JAR			138	152
0.50	PASTENA,V	AU	79	JAR	RONEN,J		550	564
0.46	DYCKMAN,TR	SP	64	JAR			91	107
0.46	DYER,JC	AU	75	JAR	MCHUGH,AJ		204	219
0.46	ELAM,R	JA	75	TAR			25	43
0.44	WEBER,R	SP	80	JAR			214	241
0.43	WILNER,N	01	82	AOS			43	52
0.40	DHARAN,BG	AP	84	TAR			199	217
0.40	MCCONNELL,DK	WI	84	JAA			178	181
0.38	BARRETT,ME	ST	71	JAR			50	65
0.38	FRIED,D	AP	81	TAR	SCHIFF,A		326	341
0.38	KIGER,JE	SP	72	JAR			113	128
0.38	TROTMAN,KT	04	81	AOS	BRADLEY,G		355	362
0.33	EICHENSEHER,JW	SP	83	AUD	SHIELDS,D		23	37
0.33	KIDA,TE	AU	80	JAR			506	523
0.33	LARCKER,DF	JL	83	TAR	REDER,RE	SIMON,DT	606	620

MODE OF REASONING(METHOD)=QUANTITATIVE: NON-PARAMETRIC

CITE IND- EX	FIRST AUTHOR	ISS- UE	YE- AR	JOUR -NAL	SECOND AUTHOR	THIRD AUTHOR	PAG BEG	PAG END
0.31	BRENNER,VC	AU	70	JAR			159	166
0.31	FLAMHOLTZ,EG	ST	72	JAR			241	266
0.31	SHANK,JK	JL	73	TAR	COPELAND,RM		494	501
0.31	SMITH,JE	JL	71	TAR	SMITH,NP		552	561
0.23	BAREFIELD,RM	AU	71	JAR	COMISKEY,EE		351	358
0.23	BAREFIELD,RM	AP	72	TAR	COMISKEY,EE		291	298
0.23	BRUNS JR,WJ	AP	65	TAR			345	357
0.23	CHOI,FD	AU	73	JAR			159	175
0.23	DYCKMAN,TR	AP	64	TAR			285	295
0.23	FRANK,WG	SP	69	JAR			123	136
0.23	GAGNON,JM	SP	71	JAR			52	72
0.20	BROWN,LD	JL	79	TAR	ROZEFF,MS		585	591
0.20	COLLINS,WA	AU	84	JAR	HOPWOOD,WS	MCKEOWN,JC	467	479
0.20	FERRIS,KR	SP	84	AUD	TENNANT,KL		31	43
0.20	RICCHIUTE,DN	SP	84	JAR			341	350
0.20	SCHREUDER,H	JA	84	TAR	KLAASSEN,J		64	77
0.17	BROWN,LD	AU	83	JAR			432	443
0.17	HARRISON JR,WT	SP	83	JAR	TOMASSINI,LA	DIETRICH,JR	65	77
0.17	MURRAY,D	SP	83	JAR			128	140
0.15	ACLAND,D	23	76	AOS			133	142
0.15	COPELAND,RM	SP	68	JAR	FREDERICKS,W		106	113
0.15	FALK,H	AP	73	TAR	OPHIR,T		323	338
0.15	MCDONALD,DL	SP	68	JAR			38	49
0.15	MORTON,JR	AU	74	JAR			288	298
0.15	RONEN,J	OC	73	TAR	FALK,G		696	717
0.14	EMERY,DR	AU	82	JAR	BARRON,FH	MESSIER JR,WF	450	458
0.13	HORWITZ,BN	WI	81	JAA	KOLODNY,R		102	113
0.13	SCHREUDER,H	AP	81	TAR			294	308
0.11	ASHTON,RH	SP	80	JAR	BROWN,PR		269	277
0.11	HOPPER,TM	04	80	AOS			401	412
0.08	ARNOLD,DF	JA	73	TAR	HUMANN,TE		23	33
0.08	BUZBY,SL	SP	75	JAR			16	37
0.08	CARPER,WB	23	76	AOS	POSEY,JM		143	152
0.08	CUMMING,J	ST	73	JAR			60	95
0.08	ESTES,RW	AU	68	JAR			200	207
0.08	GREER JR,WR	JL	74	TAR			496	505
0.08	KRATCHMAN,SH	OC	74	TAR	MALCOM,RE	TWARK,RD	682	689
0.00	BROWN,PR	AU	83	JAR			444	455
0.00	BUCHMAN,TA	AU	83	AUD			92	103
0.00	CARPENTER,CG	JL	71	TAR	STRAWSER,RH		509	518
0.00	CHAN,JL	AP	78	TAR			309	323
0.00	DAVIS,HZ	AU	82	JAR	KAHN,N		738	744
0.00	DAVIS,HZ	AU	84	JAR	KAHN,N	ROZEN,E	480	490
0.00	DHARAN,BG	SP	83	JAR			256	270
0.00	DIRSMITH,MW	04	82	AOS	LEWIS,BL		319	336
0.00	DYKXHOORN,HJ	JA	81	TAR	SINNING,KE		97	107
0.00	FALK,H	OC	75	TAR	HEINTZ,JA		758	779
0.00	FULMER,JG	AU	84	JAA	MOON,JE		5	14
0.00	GARSOMBKE,HP	SU	83	JAA	ALLEN,G		285	298
0.00	GORDON,LA	02	84	AOS	HAKA,S	SCHICK,AG	111	123

MODE OF REASONING(METHOD)=QUANTITATIVE: NON-PARAMETRIC

CITE IND-EX	FIRST AUTHOR	ISS-UE	YE-AR	JOUR-NAL	SECOND AUTHOR	THIRD AUTHOR	PAG BEG	PAG END
0.00	GREENBERG,R	AU	84	JAR			719	730
0.00	GUL,FA	34	84	AOS			233	239
0.00	IMHOFF JR,EA	OC	78	TAR			869	881
0.00	JIAMBALVO,J	SP	84	AUD	WALLER,WS		80	88
0.00	KIDA,TE	02	84	AOS			137	147
0.00	KROSS,W	AU	82	JAR			459	471
0.00	MAYPER,AG	AU	82	JAR			773	783
0.00	MUNTER,P	WI	83	JAA	RATCLIFFE,TA		108	114
0.00	NICHOLS,DR	AP	79	TAR	TSAY,JJ	LARKIN,PD	376	382
0.00	PETERSEN,RJ	JL	75	TAR			525	532
0.00	PRATT,J	04	82	AOS	JIAMBALVO,J		369	380
0.00	SAN MIGUEL,JG	02	84	AOS	GOVINDARAJAN,V		179	188
0.00	SCHNEIDER,A	AU	84	JAR			657	678
0.00	SELTO,FH	AU	83	JAR	GROVE,HD		619	622
0.00	SILHAN,PA	SP	83	JAR			341	347
0.00	STEPHENS,RG	AU	83	AUD			55	74
0.00	WELCH,PR	AU	84	JAR			744	757
0.00	WILCOX,KA	01	77	AOS	SMITH,CH		81	97

MODE OF REASONING(METHOD)=QUANTITATIVE: NON-PARAMETRIC

1.7   MODE OF REASONING(METHOD)=QUANTITATIVE: CORRELATION

CITE IND- EX	FIRST AUTHOR	ISS- UE	YE- AR	JOUR -NAL	SECOND AUTHOR	THIRD AUTHOR	PAG BEG	PAG END
2.00	OTLEY,DT	SP	78	JAR			122	149
1.88	MERCHANT,KA	OC	81	TAR			813	829
1.75	FOSTER,G	DE	81	JAE			201	232
1.70	KENIS,I	OC	79	TAR			707	721
1.46	DERMER,JD	JL	73	TAR			511	519
1.25	NOREEN,EW	AP	81	TAR	SEPE,J		253	269
1.15	BROWN,P	ST	67	JAR	BALL,R		55	77
1.15	KHANDWALLA,PN	AU	72	JAR			275	285
1.00	COLLINS,DW	JA	82	TAR	ROZEFF,MS	SALATKA,WK	1	17
0.88	SMITH,AJ	ST	81	JAR			174	211
0.77	HARIED,AA	AU	72	JAR			376	391
0.69	HORRIGAN,JO	ST	66	JAR			44	62
0.62	DAILY,RA	OC	71	TAR			686	692
0.60	GORDON,LA	01	84	AOS	NARAYANAN,VK		33	47
0.60	ROCKNESS,HO	02	84	AOS	SHIELDS,MD		165	177
0.54	HENDRICKS,JA	AP	76	TAR			292	305
0.54	TRITSCHLER,CA	JA	69	TAR			99	123
0.50	COVALESKI,MA	04	83	AOS	DIRSMITH,MW		323	340
0.46	LEV,B	AP	74	TAR	KUNITZKY,S		259	270
0.40	BIGGS,SF	SP	84	AUD	WILD,JJ		68	79
0.40	SHIELDS,MD	34	84	AOS			355	363
0.38	HOPWOOD,WS	AU	81	JAR	MCKEOWN,JC		313	322
0.38	IJIRI,Y	SP	71	JAR	KAPLAN,RS		73	87
0.38	NOREEN,EW	AU	81	JAR	WOLFSON,MA		384	398
0.38	PRATT,J	02	81	AOS	JIAMBALVO,J		133	142
0.33	PEASNELL,KV	SP	77	JAR	SKERRATT,CL		108	119
0.33	SCHEPANSKI,A	JL	83	TAR			581	599
0.33	TROTMAN,KT	SP	83	JAR	YETTON,PW	ZIMMER,I	286	292
0.31	ABDEL-KHALIK,AR	AP	74	TAR			271	283
0.25	WRIGHT,WF	04	77	AOS			323	332
0.23	HORWITZ,BN	AP	71	TAR	SHABAHANG,R		243	252
0.23	RONEN,J	SP	75	JAR	SADAN,S		133	149
0.17	FERRIS,KR	01	83	AOS	LARCKER,DF		1	12
0.15	DERMER,JD	JA	74	TAR	SIEGEL,JP		88	97
0.15	JOHNSON,O	AU	67	JAR			164	172
0.14	GAUMNITZ,BR	AU	82	JAR	NUNAMAKER,TR	SURDICK,JJ	745	755
0.14	MATSUMURA,EM	SP	82	JAR	TSUI,KW		162	170
0.14	PRATT,J	SP	82	JAR			189	209
0.14	WISEMAN,J	01	82	AOS			53	64
0.13	FERRIS,KR	04	81	AOS			317	326
0.13	ROSENZWEIG,K	04	81	AOS			339	354
0.08	FERRIS,KR	01	77	AOS			23	28
0.08	KINNEY JR,WR	AP	72	TAR			339	345
0.08	NYSTROM,PC	04	77	AOS			317	322
0.00	ANDERSON JR,TN	AU	82	JAR	KIDA,TE		403	414
0.00	ARANYA,N	03	82	AOS	LACHMAN,R	AMERNIC,J	201	216
0.00	BAILEY JR,AD	AP	85	TAR	DUKE,GL	GERLACH,JH	186	201
0.00	BRENNER,VC	AU	71	JAR	CARMACK,CW	WEINSTEIN,MG	359	366

MODE OF REASONING(METHOD)=QUANTITATIVE: CORRELATION

CITE IND-EX	FIRST AUTHOR	ISS-UE	YE-AR	JOUR -NAL	SECOND AUTHOR	THIRD AUTHOR	PAG BEG	PAG END
0.00	CLARK,JJ	OC	73	TAR	ELGERS,PT		668	678
0.00	COGGER,KO	AU	82	JAR	RULAND,W		733	737
0.00	DAVISON,AG	SP	84	JAR	STENING,BW	WAI,WT	313	317
0.00	GIVOLY,D	AU	81	JAR	PALMON,D		530	543
0.00	HARRELL,AM	34	84	AOS	STAHL,MJ		241	252
0.00	KROSS,W	AU	80	JAA	CHAPMAN,G	STRAND,KH	36	46
0.00	LEV,B	AP	83	JAE			31	48
0.00	LOREK,KS	SP	84	JAR	BATHKE,AW		369	379
0.00	MCCLENON,PR	JL	63	TAR			540	547
0.00	MCKENNA,EF	03	80	AOS			297	310
0.00	MEIXNER,WF	JL	88	AUD	WELKER,RB		505	513
0.00	NORRIS,DR	01	84	AOS	NIEBUHR,RE		49	59
0.00	SALAMON,GL	AP	82	TAR			292	302
0.00	SHIELDS,D	01	84	AOS			61	80
0.00	WHITEHURST,FD	JL	70	TAR			553	564

MODE OF REASONING(METHOD)=QUANTITATIVE: CORRELATION

1.8 MODE OF REASONING(METHOD)=QUANTITATIVE: ANALYTICAL

CITE IND-EX	FIRST AUTHOR	ISS-UE	YE-AR	JOUR-NAL	SECOND AUTHOR	THIRD AUTHOR	PAG BEG	PAG END
5.15	GONEDES,NJ	ST	74	JAR	DOPUCH,N		48	129
3.67	FOSTER,G	MR	80	JAE			29	62
3.18	DEMSKI,JS	AP	78	TAR	FELTHAM,GA		336	359
2.10	ZIMMERMAN,JL	JL	79	TAR			504	521
1.67	BAIMAN,S	AU	83	JAR	EVANS III,JH		371	395
1.60	DEMSKI,JS	JA	84	TAR	PATELL,JM	WOLFSON,MA	16	34
1.50	DYE,RA	AU	83	JAR			514	533
1.44	BAIMAN,S	ST	80	JAR	DEMSKI,JS		184	220
1.38	BEAVER,WH	SP	81	JAR			163	184
1.33	DEMSKI,JS	AU	86	JAR	SAPPINGTON,DEM		250	269
1.25	DEANGELO,LE	AG	81	JAE			113	127
1.25	GJESDAL,F	SP	81	JAR			208	231
1.20	CHRISTIE,AA	DE	84	JAE	KENNELLEY,MD	KING,JW	205	217
1.20	PENNO,M	SP	84	JAR			177	191
1.17	FELIX JR,WL	SP	77	JAR	GRIMLUND,RA		23	41
1.17	VERRECCHIA,RE	DE	83	JAE			179	194
1.14	ANTLE,R	AU	82	JAR			504	527
1.08	SCOTT,WR	AU	73	JAR			304	330
1.00	CHRISTENSEN,J	AU	82	JAR			589	603
1.00	DEMSKI,JS	AP	74	TAR			221	232
1.00	FELTHAM,GA	OC	70	TAR	DEMSKI,JS		623	640
1.00	HILTON,RW	AU	80	JAR			477	505
1.00	KINNEY JR,WR	ST	75	JAR			14	29
0.92	KINNEY JR,WR	SP	75	JAR			117	132
0.85	BEAVER,WH	ST	74	JAR	DEMSKI,JS		170	187
0.85	KAPLAN,RS	SP	73	JAR			38	46
0.85	LEV,B	JA	71	TAR	SCHWARTZ,A		103	112
0.85	MAGEE,RP	JL	76	TAR			529	544
0.83	HAKANSSON,NH	AP	77	TAR			396	416
0.77	DEMSKI,JS	AU	76	JAR			230	245
0.77	IJIRI,Y	JL	66	TAR	JAEDICKE,RK		474	483
0.77	ITAMI,H	SP	75	JAR			73	96
0.77	KAPLAN,RS	SP	69	JAR			32	43
0.77	SUNDER,S	JA	76	TAR			1	18
0.75	LEFTWICH,RW	ST	81	JAR	WATTS,RL	ZIMMERMAN,JL	50	77
0.71	GRIMLUND,RA	AU	82	JAR			316	342
0.69	DEMSKI,JS	AU	72	JAR			243	258
0.69	DYCKMAN,TR	AU	69	JAR			215	244
0.69	SCOTT,WR	ST	75	JAR			98	117
0.67	CUSHING,BE	AU	83	AUD	LOEBBECKE,JK		23	41
0.67	KINNEY JR,WR	SP	83	AUD			13	22
0.64	NG,DS	OC	78	TAR			910	920
0.63	HAKANSSON,NH	ST	81	JAR			1	35
0.62	BAIMAN,S	SP	75	JAR			1	15
0.62	BENSTON,GJ	JL	69	TAR			515	532
0.62	CUSHING,BE	JA	74	TAR			24	41
0.62	DEMSKI,JS	JL	74	TAR	SWIERINGA,RJ		506	513
0.62	YU,S	AU	73	JAR	NETER,J		273	295

MODE OF REASONING(METHOD)=QUANTITATIVE: ANALYTICAL

CITE IND-EX	FIRST AUTHOR	ISS-UE	YE-AR	JOUR-NAL	SECOND AUTHOR	THIRD AUTHOR	PAG BEG	PAG END
0.60	ATKINSON,AA	SP	79	JAR			1	22
0.60	LAMBERT,RA	OC	84	TAR			604	618
0.60	MATOLCSY,ZP	AU	84	JAR			555	569
0.60	NG,DS	ST	79	JAR	STOECKENIUS,J		1	24
0.60	OHLSON,JA	DE	79	JAE			211	232
0.60	PATELL,JM	AU	79	JAR			528	549
0.60	SUNDER,S	SP	84	JAR	WAYMIRE,G		396	405
0.60	VERRECCHIA,RE	MR	79	JAE			77	90
0.58	HAMLEN,SS	JL	77	TAR	HAMLEN,WA	TSCHIRHART,JT	616	627
0.58	JENSEN,DL	OC	77	TAR			842	856
0.57	VERRECCHIA,RE	ST	82	JAR			1	42
0.56	MAGEE,RP	AU	80	JAR			551	573
0.56	VERRECCHIA,RE	MR	80	JAE			63	92
0.55	RENEAU,JH	JL	78	TAR			669	680
0.55	SUNDER,S	AU	78	JAR			341	367
0.54	FELTHAM,GA	OC	68	TAR			684	696
0.54	JAEDICKE,RK	OC	64	TAR	ROBICHEK,AA		917	926
0.54	SORENSEN,JE	JL	69	TAR			555	561
0.54	SUNDER,S	AP	76	TAR			287	291
0.54	SUNDER,S	AU	76	JAR			277	300
0.54	TRACY,JA	JA	69	TAR			90	98
0.50	BAIMAN,S	AU	85	JAR	NOEL,J		486	501
0.50	CUSHING,BE	AP	77	TAR			308	321
0.50	OHLSON,JA	SP	83	JAR			141	154
0.50	SUNDEM,GL	SP	79	JAR			243	261
0.46	BUTTERWORTH,JE	SP	72	JAR			1	27
0.46	DEMSKI,JS	SP	72	JAR			58	76
0.46	GONEDES,NJ	AU	74	JAR	IJIRI,Y		251	269
0.46	HASEMAN,WD	JA	76	TAR	WHINSTON,AB		65	79
0.46	MARSHALL,RM	AU	72	JAR			286	307
0.46	REVSINE,L	JL	70	TAR			513	523
0.46	SIMMONS,JK	OC	69	TAR	GRAY,J		757	776
0.44	GARMAN,MB	AU	80	JAR	OHLSON,JA		420	440
0.44	GONEDES,NJ	AU	80	JAR			441	476
0.40	ANTLE,R	SP	84	JAR			1	20
0.40	GODFREY,JT	AU	84	JAR	NETER,J		497	525
0.38	BODNAR,G	OC	75	TAR			747	757
0.38	BUZBY,SL	JA	74	TAR			42	49
0.38	DEMSKI,JS	OC	67	TAR			701	712
0.38	DITTMAN,DA	SP	76	JAR	JURIS,HA	REVSINE,L	49	65
0.38	HILLIARD,JE	JA	75	TAR	LEITCH,RA		69	80
0.38	KAPLAN,RS	AP	71	TAR	THOMPSON,GL		352	364
0.38	KAPLAN,RS	JL	74	TAR	WELAM,VP		477	484
0.38	KAPLAN,RS	ST	75	JAR			126	133
0.38	LEV,B	AU	68	JAR			247	261
0.38	LIAO,M	OC	75	TAR			780	790
0.38	MAY,RG	JA	73	TAR	SUNDEM,GL		80	94
0.38	MORIARITY,S	OC	75	TAR			791	795
0.38	OHLSON,JA	AU	81	JAR	BUCKMAN,AG		399	433
0.38	RONEN,J	SP	70	JAR	MCKINNEY,G		99	112

MODE OF REASONING(METHOD)=QUANTITATIVE: ANALYTICAL

CITE IND- EX	FIRST AUTHOR	ISS- UE	YE- AR	JOUR -NAL	SECOND AUTHOR	THIRD AUTHOR	PAG BEG	PAG END
0.38	SUNDEM,GL	AP	74	TAR			306	320
0.36	DITTMAN,DA	SP	78	JAR	PRAKASH,P		14	25
0.36	KETZ,JE	OC	78	TAR			952	960
0.33	COHEN,MA	AU	80	JAR	HALPERIN,R		375	389
0.33	CROSBY,MA	AU	80	JAR			585	593
0.33	DHARAN,BG	SP	83	JAR			18	41
0.33	EVANS III,JH	ST	80	JAR			108	128
0.33	EVANS III,JH	ST	80	JAR			108	128
0.33	KAPLAN,RS	AP	77	TAR			369	378
0.33	MENZEFRICKE,U	SP	83	JAR			96	105
0.33	NEWMAN,DP	02	80	AOS			217	230
0.31	ABDEL-KHALIK,AR	JL	71	TAR			457	471
0.31	BARNEA,A	JA	75	TAR	RONEN,J	SADAN,S	58	68
0.31	FERRARA,WL	AP	72	TAR	HAYYA,JC	NACHMAN,DA	299	307
0.31	FRIEDMAN,A	AU	74	JAR	LEV,B		235	250
0.31	IJIRI,Y	OC	69	TAR	KAPLAN,RS		743	756
0.31	KILLOUGH,LN	AP	73	TAR	SOUDERS,TL		268	279
0.31	OZAN,T	SP	71	JAR	DYCKMAN,TR		88	115
0.31	SUMMERS,EL	JL	72	TAR			443	453
0.30	HALPERIN,R	JA	79	TAR			58	71
0.30	HILTON,RW	AU	79	JAR			411	435
0.30	KANODIA,CS	SP	79	JAR			74	98
0.29	GODFREY,JT	AU	82	JAR	ANDREWS,RW		304	315
0.27	CALLEN,JL	AP	78	TAR			303	308
0.27	KOTTAS,JF	AP	78	TAR	LAU,AH	LAU,HS	389	401
0.27	LOEB,M	SP	78	JAR	MAGAT,WA		103	121
0.25	BEAVER,WH	JA	81	TAR			23	37
0.25	BILLERA,LJ	SP	81	JAR	HEATH,DC	VERRECCHIA,RE	185	196
0.25	COGGER,KO	AU	81	JAR			285	298
0.25	EVEREST,GL	AP	77	TAR	WEBER,R		340	359
0.25	RONEN,J	AU	81	JAR	LIVNAT,J		459	481
0.25	SCOTT,WR	SP	77	JAR			120	137
0.25	VERRECCHIA,RE	SP	81	JAR			271	283
0.23	DEMSKI,JS	JA	70	TAR			76	87
0.23	DEMSKI,JS	AU	70	JAR			178	198
0.23	FRIBERG,RA	JA	73	TAR			50	60
0.23	IJIRI,Y	OC	73	TAR	ITAMI,H		724	737
0.23	MARSHALL,RM	JA	75	TAR			99	111
0.23	MCKEOWN,JC	JA	71	TAR			12	29
0.23	MOCK,TJ	OC	71	TAR			765	777
0.23	OHLSON,JA	AU	75	JAR			267	282
0.23	RONEN,J	JA	74	TAR			50	60
0.23	TOBA,Y	JA	75	TAR			7	24
0.22	BALACHANDRAN,BV	ST	80	JAR	RAMAKRISHNAN,RT		140	171
0.22	BROMWICH,M	AP	80	TAR			288	300
0.22	HAMLEN,SS	OC	80	TAR			578	593
0.20	MORSE,D	AU	84	JAR			605	623
0.20	NETER,J	AU	84	AUD	KIM,HS	GRAHAM,LE	75	88
0.18	HUGHES,JS	OC	78	TAR			882	894
0.18	MERVILLE,LJ	OC	78	TAR	PETTY,JW		935	951

MODE OF REASONING(METHOD)=QUANTITATIVE: ANALYTICAL

CITE IND-EX	FIRST AUTHOR	ISS-UE	YE-AR	JOUR -NAL	SECOND AUTHOR	THIRD AUTHOR	PAG BEG	PAG END
0.17	DICKHAUT,JW	AU	83	JAR	LERE,JC		495	513
0.17	HEIMANN,SR	AU	77	JAR	CHESLEY,GR		193	206
0.17	HUGHES,JS	JA	77	TAR			56	68
0.17	MAGEE,RP	OC	77	TAR			869	880
0.17	SCHEPANSKI,A	AP	83	TAR	UECKER,WC		259	283
0.17	WEYGANDT,JJ	JA	77	TAR			40	51
0.15	BENISHAY,H	SP	65	JAR			114	132
0.15	BRIEF,RP	AU	70	JAR	OWEN,J		167	177
0.15	CHAMBERS,RJ	AU	65	JAR			242	252
0.15	DAVIDSON,HJ	AU	67	JAR	NETER,J	PETRAN,AS	186	207
0.15	DEMSKI,JS	OC	69	TAR			669	679
0.15	DEMSKI,JS	AP	71	TAR			268	278
0.15	DEMSKI,JS	AU	73	JAR			176	190
0.15	DOPUCH,N	JL	67	TAR	BIRNBERG,JG	DEMSKI,JS	526	536
0.15	EAVES,BC	JL	66	TAR			426	442
0.15	GORDON,MJ	JL	70	TAR			427	443
0.15	GREER JR,WR	JA	70	TAR			103	114
0.15	HARTLEY,RV	OC	71	TAR			746	755
0.15	HINOMOTO,H	AU	71	JAR			253	267
0.15	IJIRI,Y	AU	63	JAR	LEVY,FK	LYON,RC	198	212
0.15	IJIRI,Y	AP	76	TAR			227	243
0.15	JEN,FC	AP	70	TAR	HUEFNER,RJ		290	298
0.15	JOHNSON,GL	AU	71	JAR	SIMIK,SS		278	286
0.15	JOHNSON,GL	SP	74	JAR	SIMIK,SS		67	79
0.15	JOHNSON,O	OC	70	TAR			641	653
0.15	KAPLAN,RS	OC	73	TAR			738	748
0.15	KORNBLUTH,JS	AP	74	TAR			284	295
0.15	LEV,B	SP	70	JAR			78	94
0.15	LIM,R	OC	66	TAR			642	651
0.15	LUH,FS	JA	68	TAR			123	132
0.15	PETRI,E	AP	74	TAR	MINCH,RA		330	341
0.15	REVSINE,L	AP	76	TAR	THIES,JB		255	268
0.15	SALAMON,GL	AU	73	JAR			296	303
0.15	SAMUELS,JM	AU	65	JAR			182	191
0.15	SMITH,KA	AP	72	TAR			260	269
0.15	THOMAS,AL	JL	71	TAR			472	479
0.15	VICKREY,DW	OC	70	TAR			731	742
0.15	WYMAN,HE	JL	73	TAR			489	493
0.15	ZANNETOS,ZS	AP	64	TAR			296	304
0.14	BALACHANDRAN,KR	JA	82	TAR	STEUER,RE		125	140
0.14	EMERY,GW	AU	82	JAR	COGGER,KO		290	303
0.14	GIBBINS,M	SP	82	JAR			121	138
0.14	VIGELAND,RL	AP	82	TAR			348	357
0.13	BAILEY,AP	SU	81	AUD	MCAFEE,RP	WHINSTON,AB	38	52
0.13	BOATSMAN,JR	JA	81	TAR	BASKIN,EF		38	53
0.13	FRIED,D	JL	81	TAR	LIVNAT,J		493	509
0.13	GANGOLLY,JS	AU	81	JAR			299	312
0.13	NEWMAN,DP	ST	81	JAR			134	156
0.11	HAMLEN,SS	AP	80	TAR	HAMLEN,WA	TSCHIRHART,JT	269	287
0.10	OHLSON,JA	AU	79	JAR			506	527

MODE OF REASONING(METHOD)=QUANTITATIVE: ANALYTICAL

CITE IND-EX	FIRST AUTHOR	ISS-UE	YE-AR	JOUR-NAL	SECOND AUTHOR	THIRD AUTHOR	PAG BEG	PAG END
0.10	SHIH,W	OC	79	TAR			687	706
0.09	SCAPENS,RW	AP	78	TAR			448	469
0.09	SCAPENS,RW	AP	78	TAR			448	469
0.09	VERRECCHIA,RE	SP	78	JAR			150	168
0.08	AIKEN,ME	JL	75	TAR	BLACKETT,LA	ISAACS,G	544	562
0.08	AMATO,HN	OC	76	TAR	ANDERSON,EE	HARVEY,DW	854	862
0.08	BAILEY JR,AD	JL	73	TAR			560	574
0.08	BAREFIELD,RM	JL	70	TAR			490	501
0.08	BAXTER,WT	AU	71	JAR	CARRIER,NH		189	214
0.08	BEAVER,WH	AU	74	JAR	DUKES,RE		205	215
0.08	BIERMAN JR,H	AP	66	TAR			271	274
0.08	BIERMAN JR,H	JL	74	TAR			448	454
0.08	BRADFORD,WD	AP	74	TAR			296	305
0.08	BRIEF,RP	SP	73	JAR	OWEN,J		1	15
0.08	BULLOCK,CL	JA	74	TAR			98	103
0.08	BUTTERWORTH,JE	OC	71	TAR	SIGLOCH,BA		701	716
0.08	CHARNES,A	SP	63	JAR	COOPER,WW	IJIRI,Y	16	43
0.08	CHARNES,A	JA	67	TAR	COOPER,WW		24	52
0.08	CHARNES,A	JA	72	TAR	COLANTONI,CS	COOPER,WW	85	108
0.08	CHURCHILL,NC	OC	64	TAR			894	904
0.08	COLANTONI,CS	JL	69	TAR	MANES,RP	WHINSTON,AB	467	481
0.08	COOK,JS	OC	76	TAR	HOLZMANN,OJ		778	787
0.08	CORCORAN,AW	JA	73	TAR	LEININGER,WE		105	114
0.08	DICKENS,RL	AP	64	TAR	BLACKBURN,JO		312	329
0.08	DOPUCH,N	SP	64	JAR	DRAKE,DF		10	24
0.08	DREBIN,AR	JA	65	TAR			154	162
0.08	FELTHAM,GA	JA	70	TAR			11	26
0.08	FRANK,WG	JL	67	TAR	MANES,RP		516	525
0.08	GONEDES,NJ	SP	70	JAR			1	20
0.08	GREENBALL,MN	AU	69	JAR			262	289
0.08	GROVES,R	JL	70	TAR	MANES,RP	SORENSEN,R	481	489
0.08	HARTLEY,RV	AP	70	TAR			223	234
0.08	HARVEY,DW	OC	76	TAR			838	845
0.08	HASSELDINE,CR	JL	67	TAR			497	515
0.08	HEIMANN,SR	JA	76	TAR	LUSK,EJ		51	64
0.08	HUEFNER,RJ	OC	71	TAR			717	732
0.08	IJIRI,Y	SP	65	JAR	JAEDICKE,RK	LIVINGSTONE,JL	63	74
0.08	IJIRI,Y	SP	70	JAR	KAPLAN,RS		34	46
0.08	JENSEN,DL	JL	74	TAR			465	476
0.08	JOHNSON,O	SP	68	JAR			29	37
0.08	KINNEY JR,WR	SP	69	JAR			44	52
0.08	KISSINGER,JN	AP	77	TAR			322	339
0.08	LEMKE,KW	SP	70	JAR			47	77
0.08	LIVINGSTONE,JL	JL	68	TAR			503	508
0.08	MAGEE,RP	AU	75	JAR			257	266
0.08	MCDONALD,DL	OC	67	TAR			662	679
0.08	MCINTYRE,EV	JA	77	TAR			162	171
0.08	MORRISON,TA	AP	69	TAR	KACZKA,E		330	343
0.08	MORSE,WJ	OC	72	TAR			761	773
0.08	ONSI,M	JL	70	TAR			535	543

MODE OF REASONING(METHOD)=QUANTITATIVE: ANALYTICAL

CITE INDEX	FIRST AUTHOR	ISSUE	YEAR	JOURNAL	SECOND AUTHOR	THIRD AUTHOR	PAG BEG	PAG END
0.08	RAPPAPORT,A	JL	67	TAR			441	456
0.08	RICKS,RB	JL	64	TAR			685	688
0.08	SCHRODERHEIM,G	JL	64	TAR			679	684
0.08	SCHWAB,B	AP	69	TAR	NICOL,RE		292	296
0.08	SHWAYDER,KR	AP	69	TAR			304	316
0.08	SHWAYDER,KR	AP	71	TAR			306	319
0.08	SHWAYDER,KR	AU	73	JAR			259	272
0.08	SORENSEN,JE	JL	77	TAR	GROVE,HD		658	675
0.08	STALLMAN,JC	OC	72	TAR			774	790
0.08	STERLING,RR	JA	67	TAR			62	73
0.08	THEIL,H	JA	69	TAR			27	37
0.08	VATTER,W	OC	66	TAR			681	698
0.08	WELLING,P	04	77	AOS			307	316
0.08	WILLIAMS,TH	JL	64	TAR	GRIFFIN,CH		671	678
0.08	WOLK,HI	JL	72	TAR	HILLMAN,AP		549	555
0.08	WRIGHT,FK	JA	70	TAR			129	133
0.00	ABRANOVIC,WA	OC	76	TAR			863	874
0.00	AGRAWAL,SP	OC	77	TAR			789	809
0.00	AGRAWAL,SP	WI	80	JAA	HALLBAUER,RC	PERRITT,GW	163	173
0.00	ALVEY,KL	JA	63	TAR			124	125
0.00	ANDERSON,JA	JL	75	TAR			509	511
0.00	BAIMAN,S	AU	87	JAR	EVANS III,JH	NOEL,J	217	244
0.00	BAINBRIDGE,DR	SU	84	JAA			334	346
0.00	BALACHANDRAN,BV	JA	81	TAR	RAMAKRISHNAN,RT		85	96
0.00	BALACHANDRAN,BV	OC	81	TAR	ZOLTNERS,AA		801	812
0.00	BARLEV,B	AP	83	TAR			385	393
0.00	BASTABLE,CW	SP	81	JAA	BEAMS,FA		248	254
0.00	BEAVER,WH	AU	82	JAR	WOLFSON,MA		528	550
0.00	BEJA,A	AU	77	JAR	AHARONI,Y		169	178
0.00	BERANEK,W	OC	64	TAR			914	916
0.00	BIERMAN JR,H	OC	67	TAR			731	737
0.00	BIERMAN JR,H	AU	67	JAR	SMIDT,S		144	153
0.00	BIERMAN JR,H	OC	68	TAR			657	661
0.00	BIERMAN JR,H	OC	70	TAR			690	697
0.00	BIERMAN JR,H	OC	71	TAR			693	700
0.00	BOATSMAN,JR	AU	84	JAA	DOWELL,CD	KIMBRELL,JI	35	43
0.00	BODNAR,G	OC	77	TAR	LUSK,EJ		857	868
0.00	BOWER,RS	AP	66	TAR	HERRINGER,F	WILLIAMSON,JP	257	265
0.00	BRIEF,RP	AU	68	JAR	OWEN,J		193	199
0.00	BRIEF,RP	AP	68	TAR	OWEN,J		367	372
0.00	BRIEF,RP	SP	69	JAR	OWEN,J		12	16
0.00	BRIGHAM,EF	JA	68	TAR			46	61
0.00	BRIGHAM,EF	JL	74	TAR	NANTELL,TJ		436	447
0.00	BROCKETT,P	JL	84	TAR	CHARNES,A	COOPER,WW	474	487
0.00	BRUNDAGE,MV	JL	69	TAR	LIVINGSTONE,JL		539	545
0.00	BUCKMAN,AG	SP	82	JAR	MILLER,BL		28	41
0.00	BURGHER,PH	JA	64	TAR			103	120
0.00	BURT,OR	SP	72	JAR			28	57
0.00	BYRNE,R	JA	68	TAR	CHARNES,A	COOPER,WW	18	37
0.00	CALL,DV	OC	69	TAR			711	719

MODE OF REASONING(METHOD)=QUANTITATIVE: ANALYTICAL

CITE IND-EX	FIRST AUTHOR	ISS-UE	YE-AR	JOUR-NAL	SECOND AUTHOR	THIRD AUTHOR	PAG BEG	PAG END
0.00	CARLSON,ML	JL	81	TAR	LAMB,JW		554	573
0.00	CARSBERG,BV	AU	69	JAR			165	182
0.00	CASPARI,JA	OC	76	TAR			739	746
0.00	CERF,AR	JL	75	TAR			451	465
0.00	CHAMBERS,RJ	JL	72	TAR			488	509
0.00	CHARNES,A	AP	64	TAR	DAVIDSON,HJ	KORTANEK,KO	241	250
0.00	CHARNES,A	04	76	AOS	COLANTONI,CS	COOPER,WW	315	338
0.00	CHASTEEN,LG	OC	73	TAR			764	767
0.00	CHEN,JT	JL	83	TAR			600	605
0.00	CHUMACHENKO,NG	OC	68	TAR			753	762
0.00	COHEN,SI	AP	82	TAR	LOEB,M		336	347
0.00	COMISKEY,EE	AP	68	TAR	MLYNARCZYK,FA		248	256
0.00	CORCORAN,AW	AU	65	JAR	KWANG,CW		206	217
0.00	CORCORAN,AW	AP	69	TAR			359	374
0.00	CURLEY,AJ	JL	71	TAR			519	528
0.00	DAVIS,GB	SP	63	JAR			96	101
0.00	DAVIS,PM	JA	66	TAR			121	126
0.00	DEMING,WE	SP	79	JAA			197	208
0.00	DESKINS,JW	JA	65	TAR			76	81
0.00	DOPUCH,N	OC	63	TAR			745	753
0.00	DREBIN,AR	JL	66	TAR			413	425
0.00	DREBIN,AR	SP	66	JAR			68	86
0.00	DREBIN,AR	AU	69	JAR			204	214
0.00	DUVALL,RM	JL	65	TAR	BULLOCH,J		569	573
0.00	FARAG,SM	AP	68	TAR			312	320
0.00	FERRARA,WL	JA	66	TAR			106	114
0.00	FERRARA,WL	JL	77	TAR			597	604
0.00	FOGLER,HR	JA	72	TAR			134	143
0.00	FRIED,D	SU	81	JAA			295	308
0.00	GAMBLING,TE	JA	70	TAR	NOUR,A		98	102
0.00	GLOVER,F	AP	69	TAR			300	303
0.00	GODFREY,JT	AP	71	TAR			286	297
0.00	GONEDES,NJ	AP	71	TAR			320	328
0.00	GYNTHER,MM	OC	68	TAR			706	718
0.00	HAKANSSON,NH	JL	69	TAR			495	514
0.00	HAKANSSON,NH	SP	69	JAR			11	31
0.00	HANSEN,DR	JA	77	TAR	SHAFTEL,TL		109	123
0.00	HANSEN,JV	AU	86	AUD	MESSIER JR,WF		109	123
0.00	HEEBINK,DV	JA	64	TAR			90	93
0.00	HOBBS,JB	OC	64	TAR			905	913
0.00	HOLTHAUSEN,RW	SP	88	JAR	VERRECCHIA,RE		82	106
0.00	IJIRI,Y	JA	65	TAR			36	53
0.00	IJIRI,Y	AP	70	TAR	THOMPSON,GL		246	258
0.00	IJIRI,Y	JA	84	TAR	NOEL,J		52	63
0.00	JARRETT,JE	SP	72	JAR			108	112
0.00	JARRETT,JE	SP	74	JAR			63	66
0.00	JENSEN,HL	OC	76	TAR	WYNDELTS,RW		846	853
0.00	JENSEN,RE	JA	68	TAR	THOMSEN,CT		83	93
0.00	JENSEN,RE	JL	68	TAR			425	446
0.00	JOHNSON,GL	JL	66	TAR			510	517

MODE OF REASONING(METHOD)=QUANTITATIVE: ANALYTICAL

CITE IND-EX	FIRST AUTHOR	ISS-UE	YE-AR	JOUR-NAL	SECOND AUTHOR	THIRD AUTHOR	PAG BEG	PAG END
0.00	JOHNSON,GL	OC	67	TAR	NEWTON,SW		738	746
0.00	KANODIA,CS	SP	85	JAR			175	193
0.00	KISTNER,KP	SP	80	JAR	SALMI,T		297	311
0.00	LANGHOLM,O	AU	65	JAR			218	227
0.00	LARSON,KD	OC	69	TAR	GONEDES,NJ		720	728
0.00	LAU,AH	SP	78	JAR	LAU,HS		80	102
0.00	LAVALLE,IH	AP	68	TAR	RAPPAPORT,A		225	230
0.00	LEA,RB	AP	72	TAR			346	350
0.00	LEE,CJ	AU	84	JAR			776	781
0.00	LEE,LC	AP	69	TAR	BEDFORD,NM		256	275
0.00	LEMBKE,VC	WI	81	JAA	TOOLE,HR		128	135
0.00	LEV,B	OC	69	TAR			704	710
0.00	LEV,B	JL	70	TAR			532	534
0.00	LEV,B	AU	78	JAR	THEIL,H		286	293
0.00	LEV,B	JA	88	TAR			1	22
0.00	LILLESTOL,J	SP	81	JAR			263	267
0.00	LIN,WT	AU	84	AUD	MOCK,TJ	WRIGHT,A	89	99
0.00	LIVINGSTONE,JL	JA	69	TAR			48	64
0.00	LOWE,HD	AP	63	TAR			293	301
0.00	LUNDHOLM,RJ	SP	88	JAR			107	118
0.00	LUNESKI,C	OC	67	TAR			767	771
0.00	MAHER,MW	SP	83	JAR	NANTELL,TJ		329	340
0.00	MAITRE,P	34	78	AOS			227	236
0.00	MANES,RP	JA	65	TAR	SMITH,VL		31	35
0.00	MANES,RP	SP	66	JAR			87	100
0.00	MANES,RP	JL	82	TAR	PARK,SH	JENSEN,RE	594	606
0.00	MARCINKO,D	JL	84	TAR	PETRI,E		488	495
0.00	MAXIM,LD	JA	76	TAR	CULLEN,PE	COOK,FX	97	109
0.00	MCBRIDE,HJ	AP	63	TAR			363	370
0.00	MCCOSH,AM	OC	67	TAR			693	700
0.00	MCINTYRE,EV	JL	82	TAR			607	618
0.00	MCKEOWN,JC	JL	72	TAR			527	532
0.00	MELBERG,WF	JA	72	TAR			116	133
0.00	MENSAH,YM	OC	82	TAR			681	700
0.00	MITCHELL,GB	AP	70	TAR			308	314
0.00	MOBLEY,SC	JA	67	TAR			114	123
0.00	MOCK,TJ	AU	78	JAR	VASARHELYI,MA		414	423
0.00	MONSON,NP	OC	64	TAR	TRACY,JA		890	893
0.00	MOORE,CL	JA	64	TAR			94	102
0.00	MORRISON,TA	JL	68	TAR	BUZBY,SL		517	521
0.00	NAKANO,I	OC	72	TAR			693	708
0.00	NIKOLAI,LA	JA	79	TAR	ELAM,R		119	131
0.00	NORDHAUSER,SL	JA	81	TAR	KRAMER,JL		54	69
0.00	NURNBERG,H	AU	70	JAR			217	231
0.00	ONSI,M	AP	67	TAR			321	330
0.00	OVADIA,A	WI	80	JAA	RONEN,J		113	137
0.00	OVADIA,A	WI	83	JAA	RONEN,J		115	129
0.00	PAINE,NR	AP	64	TAR			330	332
0.00	PESANDO,JE	OC	83	TAR	CLARKE,CK		733	748
0.00	PETRI,E	JL	73	TAR			483	488

MODE OF REASONING(METHOD)=QUANTITATIVE: ANALYTICAL

CITE IND-EX	FIRST AUTHOR	ISS-UE	YE-AR	JOUR -NAL	SECOND AUTHOR	THIRD AUTHOR	PAG BEG	PAG END
0.00	PETRI,E	JL	74	TAR	MINCH,RA		455	464
0.00	PETRI,E	AP	78	TAR	MINCH,RA		415	428
0.00	PETRI,E	AP	79	TAR	GELFAND,J		330	345
0.00	PURDY,CR	AU	65	JAR			228	241
0.00	RAMANATHAN,KV	OC	71	TAR	RAPPAPORT,A		733	745
0.00	RAPPAPORT,A	AP	69	TAR			297	299
0.00	RAUN,DL	OC	63	TAR			754	758
0.00	ROBBINS,SM	AU	77	JAA			5	18
0.00	ROBERTS,DM	AU	80	JAA			57	69
0.00	RONEN,J	AU	70	JAR			232	252
0.00	RONEN,J	AU	88	JAR	BALACHANDRAN,KR		300	314
0.00	ROSS,WR	JL	66	TAR			464	473
0.00	SAMUELSON,RA	AP	80	TAR			254	268
0.00	SCOTT,WR	SP	79	JAR			156	178
0.00	SEAGLE,JP	JA	77	TAR	PETRI,E		124	136
0.00	SHERMAN,HD	AU	84	AUD			35	53
0.00	SHWAYDER,KR	AP	70	TAR			299	307
0.00	SHWAYDER,KR	OC	72	TAR			747	760
0.00	SKERRATT,LC	SU	84	JAA			362	368
0.00	SOLOMONS,D	JL	68	TAR			447	452
0.00	STERLING,RR	JL	71	TAR	FLAHERTY,RE		441	456
0.00	SUH,YS	SP	88	JAR			154	168
0.00	SUNDER,S	SP	83	JAR			222	233
0.00	SUSSMAN,MR	AP	65	TAR			407	413
0.00	TAUSSIG,RA	SP	64	JAR			67	79
0.00	TAYLOR,WM	AU	82	JAR	WEYGANDT,JJ		497	502
0.00	THOMAS,AL	JA	64	TAR			1	11
0.00	THOMAS,AL	SP	65	JAR			103	113
0.00	THOMAS,LR	AP	86	TAR	SWANSON,EP		330	336
0.00	THOMPSON,WW	JL	65	TAR	KEMPER,EL		574	578
0.00	TOBA,Y	OC	80	TAR			604	619
0.00	VERRECCHIA,RE	JL	82	TAR			579	593
0.00	VERRECCHIA,RE	ST	87	JAR	LANEN,WN		165	189
0.00	WAKEMAN,LM	DE	80	JAE			213	237
0.00	WALKER,M	AP	84	TAR			278	286
0.00	WEBER,C	JL	63	TAR			534	539
0.00	WEBER,RP	JA	77	TAR			172	185
0.00	WEINGARTER,HM	AU	63	JAR			213	224
0.00	WILLIAMS,PF	04	82	AOS			405	410
0.00	WILLIAMSON,JE	JA	71	TAR			139	148
0.00	WOLK,HI	JL	70	TAR			544	552
0.00	WOLK,HI	AP	73	TAR	TEARNEY,MG		292	299
0.00	WRIGHT,FK	JA	63	TAR			87	90
0.00	WRIGHT,FK	SP	64	JAR			80	90
0.00	WRIGHT,FK	AU	68	JAR			222	236
0.00	WYMAN,HE	JL	76	TAR			545	558
0.00	YOUNG,TN	AP	67	TAR	PEIRSON,CG		338	341
0.00	ZANNETOS,ZS	JL	63	TAR			528	533

MODE OF REASONING(METHOD)=QUANTITATIVE: ANALYTICAL

1.9 MODE OF REASONING(METHOD)=MIXED

CITE IND-EX	FIRST AUTHOR	ISS-UE	YE-AR	JOUR-NAL	SECOND AUTHOR	THIRD AUTHOR	PAG BEG	PAG END
4.25	FOSTER,G	JA	77	TAR			1	21
3.63	LEFTWICH,RW	MR	81	JAE			3	36
2.62	ASHTON,RH	SP	74	JAR			143	157
2.58	WATTS,RL	AU	77	JAR	LEFTWICH,RW		253	271
2.43	BALL,R	ST	82	JAR	FOSTER,G		161	234
2.43	BEAVER,WH	JL	82	JAE	GRIFFIN,PA	LANDSMAN,WR	15	39
2.43	BIDDLE,GC	AU	82	JAR	LINDAHL,FW		551	588
2.25	GRIFFIN,PA	SP	77	JAR			71	83
2.20	BROWN,LD	SP	79	JAR	ROZEFF,MS		179	189
2.08	HOPWOOD,AG	ST	72	JAR			156	182
2.00	ALBRECHT,WS	AU	77	JAR	LOOKABILL,LL	MCKEOWN,JC	226	244
2.00	DRIVER,MJ	JL	75	TAR	MOCK,TJ		490	508
1.85	SWIERINGA,RJ	ST	76	JAR	GIBBINS,M	LARSSON,L	159	187
1.82	GONEDES,NJ	SP	78	JAR			26	79
1.67	GHEYARA,K	AG	80	JAE	BOATSMAN,JR		107	125
1.44	OHLSON,JA	SP	80	JAR			109	131
1.40	COLLINS,DW	SP	84	JAR	DENT,WT		48	84
1.38	BEAVER,WH	ST	70	JAR			62	99
1.23	LIBBY,R	SP	75	JAR			150	161
1.18	HONG,H	JA	78	TAR	KAPLAN,RS	MANDELKER,G	31	47
1.14	DUKE,GL	SP	82	JAR	NETER,J	LEITCH,RA	42	67
1.08	DOPUCH,N	SP	72	JAR	WATTS,RL		180	194
0.92	HOFSTEDT,TR	AP	77	TAR	HUGHES,GD		379	395
0.92	MORIARITY,S	AU	76	JAR	BARRON,FH		320	341
0.88	EICHENSEHER,JW	JL	81	TAR	DANOS,P		479	492
0.67	SUNDER,S	AU	83	JAR	WAYMIRE,G		565	580
0.62	PANKOFF,LD	ST	70	JAR	VIRGIL JR,RL		1	48
0.60	BOUWMAN,MJ	34	84	AOS			325	327
0.60	DWORIN,L	AP	84	TAR	GRIMLUND,RA		218	241
0.60	INGRAM,RW	SP	84	JAR			126	144
0.60	MCCRAY,JH	JA	84	TAR			35	51
0.54	BASKIN,EF	JA	72	TAR			38	51
0.54	DEMSKI,JS	JL	72	TAR	FELTHAM,GA		533	548
0.54	FOSTER,G	OC	75	TAR			686	698
0.50	MCNICHOLS,M	AP	83	JAE	MANEGOLD,JG		49	74
0.50	NEWMAN,DP	SP	81	JAR			247	262
0.43	CHOW,CW	WI	82	AUD	RICE,SJ		35	53
0.43	HAMILTON,RE	AU	82	JAR	WRIGHT,WF		756	765
0.42	FELTHAM,GA	SP	77	JAR			42	70
0.38	COATES,R	ST	72	JAR			132	144
0.38	DOWNES,D	AP	73	TAR	DYCKMAN,TR		300	317
0.33	HOPWOOD,WS	SP	80	JAR			77	90
0.31	HAGERMAN,RL	OC	75	TAR			699	709
0.25	HUSSEIN,ME	01	81	AOS			27	38
0.23	KOCHANEK,RF	AP	74	TAR			245	258
0.22	BECK,PJ	SP	80	JAR			16	37
0.22	IJIRI,Y	SP	80	JAR	LEITCH,RA		91	108
0.20	BLOOM,R	01	84	AOS	ELGERS,PT	MURRAY,D	1	11

MODE OF REASONING(METHOD)=MIXED

CITE IND- EX	FIRST AUTHOR	ISS- UE	YE- AR	JOUR -NAL	SECOND AUTHOR	THIRD AUTHOR	PAG BEG	PAG END
0.20	COLLINS,DW	AU	79	JAR	SIMONDS,RR		352	383
0.17	TABOR,RH	SP	83	JAR			348	354
0.15	ELLIOTT,JW	AU	72	JAR	UPHOFF,HL		259	274
0.15	GREENBALL,MN	ST	71	JAR			172	190
0.15	LOEB,SE	AU	71	JAR			287	306
0.15	TEITLEBAUM,AD	ST	75	JAR	ROBINSON,CF		70	91
0.13	DILLARD,JF	01	81	AOS			17	26
0.09	DAVIS,DW	JA	78	TAR	BOATSMAN,JR	BASKIN,EF	1	10
0.08	ALBRECHT,WS	OC	76	TAR			824	837
0.00	ABDEL-KHALIK,AR	SP	83	JAR			293	296
0.00	AGGARWAL,R	SP	78	JAA			197	216
0.00	ARANYA,N	04	81	AOS	POLLOCK,J	AMERNIC,J	271	280
0.00	BAILEY,WT	OC	81	TAR			882	896
0.00	BIERMAN JR,H	AU	64	JAR			229	235
0.00	BROWNELL,P	OC	82	TAR			766	777
0.00	CHARNES,A	01	80	AOS	COOPER,WW		87	107
0.00	COOPER,T	WI	80	JAA			138	146
0.00	EVANS III,JH	ST	87	JAR	PATTON,JM		130	164
0.00	EVERETT,JO	SP	84	JAA	PORTER,GA		241	256
0.00	FALK,H	AU	72	JAR			359	375
0.00	FINLEY,DR	AU	83	AUD			104	116
0.00	HAWKINS,CA	SP	84	JAA	GIRARD,D		225	240
0.00	HOPWOOD,WS	SP	80	JAR			289	296
0.00	KINNEY JR,WR	AU	81	JAA			5	17
0.00	KISSINGER,JN	AU	83	AUD			42	54
0.00	MORRIS,MH	SU	84	JAA	NICHOLS,WD		293	305
0.00	NEWMAN,DP	OC	81	TAR			897	909
0.00	PUTNAM,K	AU	84	JAA	THOMAS,LR		15	23
0.00	TEOH,HY	02	84	AOS	THONG,G		189	206

MODE OF REASONING(METHOD)=MIXED

1.10 MODE OF REASONING(METHOD)=QUALITATIVE

CITE IND-EX	FIRST AUTHOR	ISS-UE	YE-AR	JOUR-NAL	SECOND AUTHOR	THIRD AUTHOR	PAG BEG	PAG END
4.83	HOLTHAUSEN,RW	AG	83	JAE	LEFTWICH,RW		77	117
3.89	BURCHELL,S	01	80	AOS	CLUBB,C	HOPWOOD,AG	5	27
3.80	WATTS,RL	AP	79	TAR	ZIMMERMAN,JL		273	305
3.40	KAPLAN,RS	JL	84	TAR			390	418
3.18	WATERHOUSE,JH	01	78	AOS	TIESSEN,P		65	76
2.92	LIBBY,R	03	77	AOS	LEWIS,BL		245	268
2.71	LIBBY,R	03	82	AOS	LEWIS,BL		231	286
2.67	HOPWOOD,AG	23	83	AOS			287	305
2.67	OTLEY,DT	04	80	AOS			413	428
2.60	COOPER,DJ	34	84	AOS	SHERER,MJ		207	232
2.50	TOMKINS,C	04	83	AOS	GROVES,R		361	374
2.43	LEV,B	ST	82	JAR	OHLSON,JA		249	322
2.33	BOLAND,RJ	23	83	AOS	PONDY,LR		223	234
2.18	HEDBERG,B	01	78	AOS	JONSSON,S		47	64
2.18	HOPWOOD,AG	01	78	AOS			3	14
2.00	HAYES,DC	23	83	AOS			241	250
1.83	BIRNBERG,JG	23	83	AOS	TUROPOLEC,L	YOUNG,SM	111	130
1.83	COOPER,DJ	23	83	AOS			269	286
1.83	KAPLAN,RS	OC	83	TAR			686	705
1.77	RONEN,J	OC	75	TAR	LIVINGSTONE,JL		671	685
1.75	PRAKASH,P	01	77	AOS	RAPPAPORT,A		29	38
1.69	GORDON,LA	01	76	AOS	MILLER,D		59	70
1.67	TIESSEN,P	23	83	AOS	WATERHOUSE,JH	251	268	
1.60	GIBBINS,M	SP	84	JAR			103	125
1.57	TINKER,AM	02	82	AOS	MERINO,BD	NEIMARK,M	167	200
1.56	TINKER,AM	01	80	AOS			147	160
1.50	CHRISTENSON,C	JA	83	TAR			1	22
1.40	WALLER,WS	34	84	AOS	FELIX JR,WL		383	406
1.38	COLVILLE,I	02	81	AOS			119	132
1.38	DEANGELO,LE	DE	81	JAE			183	199
1.38	EINHORN,HJ	SP	81	JAR	HOGARTH,RM		1	31
1.33	JOHNSON,HT	23	83	AOS			139	146
1.30	BEAVER,WH	JA	79	TAR	DEMSKI,JS		38	46
1.23	DEMSKI,JS	OC	73	TAR			718	723
1.23	SCHIFF,M	AP	70	TAR	LEWIN,AY		259	268
1.22	OTLEY,DT	02	80	AOS	BERRY,AJ		231	246
1.20	BOLAND,RJ	04	79	AOS			259	272
1.15	ASHTON,RH	OC	74	TAR			719	732
1.00	ANSARI,SL	02	77	AOS			101	112
1.00	BANBURY,J	03	79	AOS	NAHAPIET,JE		163	178
1.00	CHESLEY,GR	AP	75	TAR			325	337
1.00	DEMSKI,JS	ST	82	JAR	KREPS,DM		117	148
1.00	EINHORN,HJ	ST	76	JAR			196	206
1.00	FLAMHOLTZ,EG	23	83	AOS			153	170
1.00	GAMBLING,TE	02	77	AOS			141	152
1.00	SORTER,GH	JA	69	TAR			12	19
1.00	SPICER,BH	01	83	AOS	BALLEW,V		73	98
1.00	STRINGER,KW	ST	75	JAR			1	9

MODE OF REASONING(METHOD)=QUALITATIVE

CITE IND-EX	FIRST AUTHOR	ISS-UE	YE-AR	JOUR-NAL	SECOND AUTHOR	THIRD AUTHOR	PAG BEG	PAG END
0.92	BEAVER,WH	OC	68	TAR	KENNELLY,JW	VOSS,WM	675	683
0.86	FELIX JR,WL	AP	82	TAR	KINNEY JR,WR		245	271
0.85	CAPLAN,EM	JL	66	TAR			496	509
0.85	GORDON,MJ	AP	64	TAR			251	263
0.83	ARGYRIS,C	02	77	AOS			113	124
0.83	LIBBY,R	AU	77	JAR	FISHBURN,PC		272	292
0.82	GORDON,LA	34	78	AOS	LARCKER,DF	TUGGLE,FD	203	214
0.77	ABDEL-KHALIK,AR	JA	74	TAR	LUSK,EJ		8	23
0.77	FLAMHOLTZ,EG	AP	71	TAR			253	267
0.75	COOPER,DJ	03	81	AOS	HAYES,DC	WOLF,FM	175	192
0.75	HIRST,MK	OC	81	TAR			771	784
0.75	JOHNSON,HT	JL	81	TAR			510	518
0.73	BARIFF,ML	01	78	AOS	GALBRAITH,JR		15	28
0.71	HITE,GL	JL	82	JAE	LONG,MS		3	14
0.70	ANSARI,SL	03	79	AOS			149	162
0.70	CHANDLER,AD	12	79	AOS	DAEMS,H		3	20
0.70	GONEDES,NJ	AU	79	JAR	DOPUCH,N		384	410
0.69	COPELAND,RM	AP	73	TAR	FRANCIA,AJ	STRAWSER,RH	365	374
0.69	MAY,RG	OC	76	TAR	SUNDEM,GL		747	763
0.69	REVSINE,L	OC	70	TAR			704	711
0.69	WATSON,DJ	JL	75	TAR	BAUMLER,JV		466	474
0.64	WILDAVSKY,A	01	78	AOS			77	88
0.63	HOFSTEDE,G	03	81	AOS			193	216
0.62	ASHTON,RH	OC	75	TAR			710	722
0.62	DRAKE,DF	AU	65	JAR	DOPUCH,N		192	205
0.60	LEV,B	DE	79	JAE	SUNDER,S		187	210
0.57	COLLINS,F	02	82	AOS			107	122
0.56	GINZBERG,MJ	04	80	AOS			369	382
0.56	LEFTWICH,RW	DE	80	JAE			193	211
0.55	BELKAOUI,A	02	78	AOS			97	104
0.54	BENSTON,GJ	AP	63	TAR			347	354
0.54	BIRNBERG,JG	JA	68	TAR	NATH,R		38	45
0.54	BRUMMET,RL	AP	68	TAR	FLAMHOLTZ,EG	PYLE,WC	217	224
0.54	EPSTEIN,MJ	01	76	AOS	FLAMHOLTZ,EG	MCDONOUGH,JJ	23	42
0.54	ESTES,RW	AP	72	TAR			284	290
0.50	HAGG,J	12	79	AOS	HEDLUND,G		135	143
0.50	JOYCE,EJ	AU	81	JAR	LIBBY,R		544	550
0.50	MACINTOSH,NB	01	81	AOS			39	52
0.50	MARKUS,ML	23	83	AOS	PFEFFER,J		205	218
0.46	COLANTONI,CS	JA	71	TAR	MANES,RP	WHINSTON,AB	90	102
0.46	FLAMHOLTZ,EG	OC	72	TAR			666	678
0.46	GONEDES,NJ	JA	72	TAR			11	21
0.46	HOFSTEDT,TR	JA	70	TAR	KINARD,JC		38	54
0.46	LIEBERMAN,AZ	AP	75	TAR	WHINSTON,AB		246	258
0.46	MILLER,H	JA	72	TAR			31	37
0.45	HERTOG,JF	01	78	AOS			29	46
0.44	DOPUCH,N	JA	80	TAR	SUNDER,S		1	21
0.44	WATTS,RL	AG	80	JAE	ZIMMERMAN,JL		95	106
0.43	DAVIS,SW	04	82	AOS	MENON,K	MORGAN,G	307	318
0.43	JONSSON,S	03	82	AOS			287	304

MODE OF REASONING(METHOD)=QUALITATIVE

CITE IND-EX	FIRST AUTHOR	ISS-UE	YE-AR	JOUR-NAL	SECOND AUTHOR	THIRD AUTHOR	PAG BEG	PAG END
0.42	BAKER,CR	JL	77	TAR			576	586
0.42	DIERKES,M	01	77	AOS	PRESTON,LE		3	22
0.40	DIRSMITH,MW	12	79	AOS	JABLONSKY,SF		39	52
0.40	MCCARTHY,WE	OC	79	TAR			667	686
0.40	PRAKASH,P	JA	79	TAR	SUNDER,S		1	22
0.40	ZEFF,SA	JL	84	TAR			447	468
0.38	ASHTON,RH	04	76	AOS			289	300
0.38	BRUNS JR,WJ	JL	68	TAR			469	480
0.38	CARMICHAEL,DR	AP	70	TAR			235	245
0.38	EWUSI-MENSAH,K	04	81	AOS			301	316
0.38	GOLEMBIEWSKI,RT	AP	64	TAR			333	341
0.38	IJIRI,Y	SP	68	JAR	KINARD,JC	PUTNEY,FB	1	28
0.38	JAIN,TN	JA	73	TAR			95	104
0.38	RAMANATHAN,KV	JL	76	TAR			516	528
0.36	CHERNS,AB	02	78	AOS			105	114
0.36	DIRSMITH,MW	34	78	AOS	JABLONSKY,SF		215	226
0.33	ASHTON,RH	JL	77	TAR			567	575
0.33	BIRNBERG,JG	03	77	AOS	FRIEZE,IH	SHIELDS,MD	189	200
0.33	ELLIOTT,RK	SP	83	AUD			1	12
0.33	GROJER,JE	04	77	AOS	STARK,A		349	385
0.33	MIRVIS,PH	23	83	AOS	LAWLER III,EE		175	190
0.33	MITROFF,II	23	83	AOS	MASON,RO		195	204
0.31	BARTON,AD	OC	74	TAR			664	681
0.31	CHEN,RS	JL	75	TAR			533	543
0.31	CRUMBLEY,DL	OC	73	TAR			759	763
0.31	GYNTHER,RS	AP	67	TAR			274	290
0.31	JOHNSON,HT	JL	75	TAR			444	450
0.31	STERLING,RR	JL	70	TAR			444	457
0.30	REVSINE,L	AP	79	TAR			306	322
0.30	SCHREUDER,H	12	79	AOS			109	122
0.30	VATTER,WJ	JL	79	TAR			563	573
0.29	SWIERINGA,RJ	02	82	AOS	WATERHOUSE,JH		149	166
0.25	BOLAND,RJ	02	81	AOS			109	118
0.25	DYCKMAN,TR	04	81	AOS			291	300
0.25	PERAGALLO,E	OC	77	TAR			881	892
0.23	ANTON,HR	SP	64	JAR			1	9
0.23	BIRNBERG,JG	JL	67	TAR	NATH,R		468	479
0.23	CHAMBERS,RJ	AP	64	TAR			264	274
0.23	CHAMBERS,RJ	OC	65	TAR			731	741
0.23	FERTAKIS,JP	OC	69	TAR			680	691
0.23	GERBOTH,DL	JL	73	TAR			475	482
0.23	GOLDMAN,A	OC	74	TAR	BARLEV,B		707	718
0.23	MACY,BA	23	76	AOS	MIRVIS,PH		179	194
0.23	MOBLEY,SC	OC	70	TAR			762	768
0.23	NICHOLS,DR	AP	76	TAR	PRICE,KH		335	346
0.23	OGAN,P	AP	76	TAR			306	320
0.23	PRAKASH,P	OC	75	TAR	RAPPAPORT,A		723	734
0.23	VATTER,WJ	AU	63	JAR			179	197
0.23	WILL,HJ	OC	74	TAR			690	706
0.23	YAMEY,BS	AU	64	JAR			117	136

MODE OF REASONING(METHOD)=QUALITATIVE

CITE IND-EX	FIRST AUTHOR	ISS-UE	YE-AR	JOUR -NAL	SECOND AUTHOR	THIRD AUTHOR	PAG BEG	PAG END
0.20	BIRNBERG,JG	34	84	AOS	SHIELDS,MD		365	382
0.20	GROVE,HD	JL	79	TAR	SAVICH,RS		522	537
0.20	OHLSON,JA	AU	79	JAR	PATELL,JM		504	505
0.20	THORNTON,DB	03	79	AOS			211	234
0.20	YOUNG,DW	03	79	AOS			235	244
0.18	DILLON,RD	JA	78	TAR	NASH,JF		11	17
0.18	IJIRI,Y	SU	78	JAA			331	348
0.18	SWANSON,EB	34	78	AOS			237	248
0.17	ANDERSON,JA	AP	77	TAR			417	426
0.17	BROMWICH,M	JL	77	TAR			587	596
0.17	COPPOCK,R	02	77	AOS			125	130
0.17	KILMANN,RH	04	83	AOS			341	360
0.17	LAVIN,D	03	77	AOS			237	244
0.17	LESSEM,R	04	77	AOS			279	294
0.17	RONEN,J	AP	77	TAR			438	449
0.15	ALIBER,RZ	JA	75	TAR	STICKNEY,CP		44	57
0.15	ANDERSON,HM	JL	70	TAR	GIESE,J	BOOKER,J	524	531
0.15	BAILEY JR,AD	JL	76	TAR	BOE,WJ		559	573
0.15	BALL,R	SP	71	JAR			1	31
0.15	BERNHARDT,I	SP	70	JAR	COPELAND,RM		95	98
0.15	BIERMAN JR,H	JL	63	TAR			501	507
0.15	BIRD,FA	AP	74	TAR	DAVIDSON,LF	SMITH,CH	233	244
0.15	BRIEF,RP	SP	65	JAR			12	31
0.15	BRIEF,RP	AP	75	TAR			285	297
0.15	CAUSEY JR,DY	JA	76	TAR			19	30
0.15	CHAMBERS,RJ	SP	63	JAR			3	15
0.15	CHAMBERS,RJ	SP	65	JAR			32	62
0.15	CHAMBERS,RJ	JL	66	TAR			443	457
0.15	CHAMBERS,RJ	OC	67	TAR			751	757
0.15	CYERT,RM	ST	74	JAR	IJIRI,Y		29	42
0.15	DOCKWEILER,RC	OC	69	TAR			729	742
0.15	EDWARDS,EO	AP	75	TAR			235	245
0.15	GODFREY,JT	JA	71	TAR	PRINCE,TR		75	89
0.15	GOETZ,BE	JA	67	TAR			53	61
0.15	GREEN,D	JA	66	TAR			52	64
0.15	GYNTHER,RS	OC	70	TAR			712	730
0.15	HANSON,EI	AP	66	TAR			239	243
0.15	KNUTSON,PH	JA	70	TAR			55	68
0.15	LARSON,KD	JA	69	TAR			38	47
0.15	LEMKE,KW	JA	66	TAR			32	41
0.15	LORIG,AN	JL	64	TAR			563	573
0.15	MATTESSICH,R	JL	72	TAR			469	487
0.15	MAUTZ,RK	AP	63	TAR			317	325
0.15	MOONITZ,M	JL	70	TAR			465	475
0.15	SCHIFF,M	SP	66	JAR			62	67
0.15	SEIDLER,LJ	OC	67	TAR			775	781
0.15	SNAVELY,HJ	AP	67	TAR			223	232
0.15	TOMASSINI,LA	23	76	AOS			239	252
0.15	VATTER,WJ	AU	66	JAR			133	148
0.15	VICKREY,DW	JA	76	TAR			31	40

MODE OF REASONING(METHOD)=QUALITATIVE

CITE IND-EX	FIRST AUTHOR	ISS-UE	YE-AR	JOUR-NAL	SECOND AUTHOR	THIRD AUTHOR	PAG BEG	PAG END
0.15	WAGNER,JW	JL	65	TAR			599	605
0.15	YETTON,PY	01	76	AOS			81	90
0.14	BENSTON,GJ	02	82	AOS			87	106
0.14	MCCARTHY,WE	JL	82	TAR			554	578
0.14	SELTO,FH	02	82	AOS			139	148
0.14	SHOCKLEY,RA	WI	82	JAA			126	143
0.14	WEBER,R	AP	82	TAR			311	325
0.14	WRIGHT,WF	01	82	AOS			65	78
0.13	PERAGALLO,E	JL	81	TAR			587	595
0.11	ANSARI,SL	01	80	AOS	MCDONOUGH,JJ		129	142
0.11	BAKER,CR	SP	80	JAA			197	206
0.11	FLAMHOLTZ,EG	01	80	AOS			31	42
0.11	PALMON,D	SP	80	JAA	KWATINETZ,M		207	226
0.10	AMEY,LR	04	79	AOS			247	258
0.10	RAMAN,KK	AU	79	JAA			31	41
0.10	YAMEY,BS	AP	79	TAR			323	329
0.09	CARLSSON,J	34	78	AOS	EHN,P	ERLANDER,B	249	260
0.09	KOTTAS,JF	JL	78	TAR	LAU,HS		698	707
0.08	ABEL,R	SP	69	JAR			1	11
0.08	ADAR,Z	JA	77	TAR	BARNEA,A	LEV,B	137	149
0.08	ARNETT,HE	AP	67	TAR			291	297
0.08	ARNOLD,DF	AU	77	JAR	HUEFNER,RJ		245	252
0.08	BALADOUNI,V	AP	66	TAR			215	225
0.08	BEDFORD,NM	JL	68	TAR	IINO,T		453	458
0.08	BEDFORD,NM	JL	75	TAR	ZIEGLER,RE		435	443
0.08	BIRNBERG,JG	OC	65	TAR			814	820
0.08	BIRNBERG,JG	01	76	AOS	GANDHI,NM		5	10
0.08	BOLLOM,WJ	JA	72	TAR	WEYGANDT,JJ		75	84
0.08	BRADISH,RD	OC	65	TAR			757	766
0.08	BRIEF,RP	SP	67	JAR			27	38
0.08	BRIEF,RP	OC	73	TAR	OWEN,J		690	695
0.08	BUCKLEY,JW	AP	68	TAR	KIRCHER,P	MATHEWS,RL	274	283
0.08	BURKE,EJ	OC	64	TAR			837	849
0.08	CARSBERG,BV	SP	66	JAR			1	15
0.08	CHURCHILL,NC	ST	66	JAR			128	156
0.08	CLARKE,RW	OC	68	TAR			769	776
0.08	COOPER,WW	OC	68	TAR	DOPUCH,N	KELLER,TF	640	648
0.08	COWAN,TK	OC	65	TAR			788	794
0.08	CURRY,DW	JL	71	TAR			490	503
0.08	DAVIDSON,S	AU	63	JAR			117	126
0.08	DEVINE,CT	AU	63	JAR			127	138
0.08	ECKEL,LG	OC	76	TAR			764	777
0.08	FEKRAT,MA	AP	72	TAR			351	355
0.08	FIELD,JE	JL	69	TAR			593	599
0.08	FIRMIN,PA	JA	68	TAR	LINN,JJ		75	82
0.08	FLOWER,JF	SP	66	JAR			16	36
0.08	FRANCIS,ME	AP	73	TAR			245	257
0.08	FREMGEN,JM	OC	68	TAR			649	656
0.08	GAMBLING,TE	23	76	AOS			167	174
0.08	GREEN,D	SP	64	JAR			35	49

MODE OF REASONING(METHOD)=QUALITATIVE

CITE IND-EX	FIRST AUTHOR	ISS-UE	YE-AR	JOUR-NAL	SECOND AUTHOR	THIRD AUTHOR	PAG BEG	PAG END
0.08	GREENE,ED	AP	63	TAR			355	362
0.08	GROVE,HD	03	77	AOS	MOCK,TJ	EHRENREICH,K	219	236
0.08	HEATH,LC	JL	72	TAR			458	468
0.08	HECK,WR	JL	63	TAR			577	578
0.08	HICKS,EL	AU	64	JAR			158	171
0.08	HORNGREN,CT	AP	65	TAR			323	333
0.08	HORNGREN,CT	JA	71	TAR			1	11
0.08	HUME,LJ	SP	70	JAR			21	33
0.08	ISELIN,ER	AP	68	TAR			231	238
0.08	JAENICKE,HR	JA	70	TAR			115	128
0.08	JOHNSON,O	JA	72	TAR			64	74
0.08	KEMP,PS	OC	65	TAR			782	787
0.08	LANGENDERFER,HQ	OC	69	TAR	ROBERTSON,JC		777	787
0.08	LARSON,KD	JL	67	TAR			480	488
0.08	LOEBBECKE,JK	ST	75	JAR	NETER,J		38	52
0.08	MARQUES,E	23	76	AOS			175	178
0.08	MATHEWS,RL	JL	68	TAR			509	516
0.08	MAUTZ,RK	AP	66	TAR	MINI,DL		283	291
0.08	MCDONOUGH,JJ	OC	71	TAR			676	685
0.08	MCRAE,TW	AP	70	TAR			315	321
0.08	MEYERS,SL	JA	73	TAR			44	49
0.08	MOONITZ,M	AU	66	JAR	RUSS,A		155	168
0.08	MURPHY,GJ	AP	76	TAR			277	286
0.08	NURNBERG,H	OC	68	TAR			719	729
0.08	OGAN,P	23	76	AOS			195	218
0.08	PARKER,RH	SP	68	JAR			58	71
0.08	PENMAN,SH	AP	70	TAR			333	346
0.08	RAPPAPORT,A	AP	65	TAR			373	376
0.08	ROSENFIELD,P	AP	66	TAR	STOREY,R		327	330
0.08	SNAVELY,HJ	AP	69	TAR			344	353
0.08	STAUBUS,GJ	OC	67	TAR			650	661
0.08	STAUBUS,GJ	JL	76	TAR			574	589
0.08	STERLING,RR	JL	68	TAR			481	502
0.08	TRACY,JA	JA	65	TAR			163	175
0.08	ULLMANN,AA	01	76	AOS			71	80
0.08	VATTER,WJ	JL	63	TAR			470	477
0.08	WILKINSON,JR	OC	65	TAR	DONEY,LD		753	756
0.08	WOJDAK,JF	JL	69	TAR			562	570
0.08	WOJDAK,JF	JA	70	TAR			88	97
0.08	WRIGHT,FK	AU	65	JAR			167	181
0.08	WRIGHT,FK	FL	65	JAR			167	181
0.08	YAMEY,BS	SP	67	JAR			51	76
0.00	ABDEL-KHALIK,AR	SP	66	JAR			37	46
0.00	ABDEL-MAGID,MF	AP	79	TAR			346	357
0.00	ADAMS,KD	WI	84	JAA			151	163
0.00	AHARONI,Y	SP	67	JAR	OPHIR,T		1	26
0.00	ALFRED,AM	AU	64	JAR			172	182
0.00	ALLYN,RG	JA	64	TAR			121	127
0.00	ALLYN,RG	AP	66	TAR			303	311
0.00	ANDERSON,HM	OC	63	TAR	GRIFFIN,FB		813	818

MODE OF REASONING(METHOD)=QUALITATIVE

CITE IND- EX	FIRST AUTHOR	ISS- UE	YE- AR	JOUR -NAL	SECOND AUTHOR	THIRD AUTHOR	PAG BEG	PAG END
0.00	ANDERSON,JJ	JL	67	TAR			583	588
0.00	ANDERSON,JM	AU	64	JAR			236	238
0.00	ARNETT,HE	OC	63	TAR			733	741
0.00	ARNETT,HE	JL	69	TAR			482	494
0.00	BACKER,M	JL	69	TAR			533	538
0.00	BAGGETT,WD	SP	83	JAA			227	233
0.00	BAKER,RE	JA	64	TAR			52	61
0.00	BAKER,RE	JA	66	TAR			98	105
0.00	BARRETT,WB	JA	68	TAR			105	112
0.00	BEAMS,FA	AP	69	TAR			382	388
0.00	BEAVER,WH	DE	84	JAE	GRIFFIN,PA	LANDSMAN,WR	219	223
0.00	BEDFORD,NM	JA	67	TAR			82	85
0.00	BEDFORD,NM	AP	72	TAR	MCKEOWN,JC		333	338
0.00	BEECHY,TH	AP	69	TAR			375	381
0.00	BENNINGER,LJ	JL	65	TAR			547	557
0.00	BENSTON,GJ	JL	76	TAR			483	498
0.00	BERG,KB	JL	63	TAR	MUELLER,FJ		554	561
0.00	BERKOW,WF	AP	64	TAR			377	386
0.00	BIERMAN JR,H	JA	63	TAR			61	63
0.00	BIERMAN JR,H	JL	65	TAR			541	546
0.00	BIERMAN JR,H	JA	68	TAR	LIU,E		62	67
0.00	BIERMAN JR,H	JA	69	TAR			65	78
0.00	BIERMAN JR,H	AP	69	TAR	DAVIDSON,S		239	246
0.00	BIRD,PA	SP	65	JAR			1	11
0.00	BIRNBERG,JG	OC	64	TAR			963	971
0.00	BIRNBERG,JG	01	80	AOS			71	80
0.00	BJORN-ANDERSEN,N	02	80	AOS	PEDERSEN,PH		203	216
0.00	BLAKELY,EJ	JA	63	TAR	KNUTSON,PH		75	86
0.00	BOER,G	JA	66	TAR			92	97
0.00	BOGART,FO	OC	65	TAR			834	838
0.00	BOTTS,RR	OC	63	TAR			789	795
0.00	BOURN,AM	AU	66	JAR			213	223
0.00	BOUTELL,WS	AP	64	TAR			305	311
0.00	BOWEN,EK	OC	67	TAR			782	787
0.00	BOWER,JB	AP	65	TAR	SCHLOSSER,RE		338	344
0.00	BRAVENEC,LL	02	77	AOS	EPSTEIN,MJ	CRUMBLEY,DL	131	140
0.00	BRIEF,RP	OC	77	TAR			810	812
0.00	BRIGHTON,GD	JA	69	TAR			137	144
0.00	BRILOFF,AJ	JA	64	TAR			12	15
0.00	BRILOFF,AJ	JL	67	TAR			489	496
0.00	BRUGEMAN,DC	OC	63	TAR	BRIGHTON,GD		764	770
0.00	BRUGGE,WG	JL	63	TAR			596	600
0.00	BUBLITZ,B	WI	84	JAA	KEE,R		123	137
0.00	BUCKLEY,JW	JA	66	TAR			75	82
0.00	BUCKLEY,JW	JL	67	TAR			572	582
0.00	BUCKLEY,JW	01	80	AOS			49	64
0.00	BURKE,WL	OC	63	TAR			802	812
0.00	BURNS,JS	JA	63	TAR	JAEDICKE,RK	SANGSTER,JM	1	13
0.00	CAMPFIELD,WL	JL	63	TAR			521	527
0.00	CAMPFIELD,WL	JL	65	TAR			594	598

MODE OF REASONING(METHOD)=QUALITATIVE

CITE IND-EX	FIRST AUTHOR	ISS-UE	YE-AR	JOUR-NAL	SECOND AUTHOR	THIRD AUTHOR	PAG BEG	PAG END
0.00	CAMPFIELD,WL	OC	70	TAR			683	689
0.00	CAREY,JL	JA	68	TAR			1	9
0.00	CAREY,JL	JA	69	TAR			79	85
0.00	CARLISLE,HM	JA	66	TAR			115	120
0.00	CARMICHAEL,DR	OC	68	TAR	SWIERINGA,RJ		697	705
0.00	CARMICHAEL,DR	SU	79	JAA			294	306
0.00	CARMICHAEL,DR	SU	84	JAA	WHITTINGTON,OR		347	361
0.00	CARSON,AB	AP	65	TAR			334	337
0.00	CARTER,WK	JA	81	TAR			108	114
0.00	CAUSEY JR,DY	AP	73	TAR			258	267
0.00	CHAMBERS,RJ	AP	67	TAR			241	253
0.00	CHAMBERS,RJ	AP	68	TAR			239	247
0.00	CHAMBERS,RJ	OC	79	TAR			764	775
0.00	CHAMBERS,RJ	01	80	AOS			167	180
0.00	CHAN,KH	WI	84	JAA	CHENG,TT		164	177
0.00	CHATFIELD,M	JA	75	TAR			1	6
0.00	CHURCHMAN,CW	JA	71	TAR			30	35
0.00	COHEN,MF	JA	65	TAR			1	8
0.00	COPELAND,TE	AU	78	JAA			33	48
0.00	CORBIN,DA	OC	63	TAR			742	744
0.00	CORBIN,DA	OC	67	TAR			635	641
0.00	COWAN,TK	JA	65	TAR			9	20
0.00	COWAN,TK	JA	68	TAR			94	100
0.00	COWIE,JB	JA	70	TAR	FREMGEN,JM		27	37
0.00	CRAMER JR,JJ	OC	64	TAR			869	875
0.00	CRAMER JR,JJ	JL	65	TAR			606	616
0.00	CRAMER JR,JJ	OC	70	TAR	SCHRADER,WJ		698	703
0.00	CRAMER JR,JJ	WI	79	JAA	NEYHART,CA		135	150
0.00	CRANDALL,RH	JL	69	TAR			457	466
0.00	CRUMBLEY,DL	JL	68	TAR			554	564
0.00	CRUMBLEY,DL	JA	75	TAR	SAVICH,RS		112	117
0.00	CRUSE,RB	JA	65	TAR	SUMMERS,EL		82	88
0.00	CUSHING,BE	OC	68	TAR			668	671
0.00	DAVIDSON,S	AP	63	TAR			278	284
0.00	DEAN,J	AP	63	TAR	HARRISS,CL		229	242
0.00	DECOSTER,DT	AP	66	TAR			297	302
0.00	DEFLIESE,PL	JL	65	TAR			517	521
0.00	DEINZER,HT	JA	66	TAR			21	31
0.00	DEITRICK,JW	SU	79	JAA	ALDERMAN,CW		316	328
0.00	DEJONG,DV	AU	84	AUD	SMITH,JH		20	34
0.00	DEMARIS,EJ	JA	63	TAR			37	45
0.00	DERY,D	03	82	AOS			217	224
0.00	DEWHIRST,JF	AP	71	TAR			365	373
0.00	DILLARD,JF	34	84	AOS			343	354
0.00	DIRSMITH,MW	SP	82	JAA	MCALLISTER,JP		214	228
0.00	DIRSMITH,MW	AU	82	JAA	MCALLISTER,JP		60	74
0.00	DOWELL,CD	AU	81	JAA	HALL,JA		30	40
0.00	DREBIN,AR	JL	63	TAR			579	583
0.00	DREBIN,AR	SP	64	JAR			25	34
0.00	DRINKWATER,D	JL	65	TAR	EDWARDS,JD		579	582

MODE OF REASONING(METHOD)=QUALITATIVE

CITE IND-EX	FIRST AUTHOR	ISS-UE	YE-AR	JOUR -NAL	SECOND AUTHOR	THIRD AUTHOR	PAG BEG	PAG END
0.00	EDEY,HC	AP	63	TAR			262	265
0.00	EIGEN,MM	JL	65	TAR			536	540
0.00	ELLIOTT,EL	OC	68	TAR	LARREA,J	RIVERA,JM	763	768
0.00	FAGERBERG,P	JL	72	TAR			454	457
0.00	FARMAN,WL	JA	63	TAR	HOU,C		133	141
0.00	FARMAN,WL	AP	64	TAR			392	404
0.00	FERRARA,WL	OC	63	TAR			719	722
0.00	FERTAKIS,JP	JL	70	TAR			509	512
0.00	FESS,PE	OC	63	TAR			723	732
0.00	FESS,PE	AP	66	TAR			266	270
0.00	FIRMIN,PA	AP	63	TAR			270	277
0.00	FISHER,M	SU	78	JAA			349	360
0.00	FITZGERALD,RD	AU	79	JAA	KELLEY,EM		5	20
0.00	FLESHER,DL	04	79	AOS	FLESHER,TK		297	304
0.00	FORD,A	OC	69	TAR			818	822
0.00	FORD,A	AP	75	TAR			338	344
0.00	FRANK,WG	OC	65	TAR			854	862
0.00	FRANKFURTER,GM	SU	83	JAA	YOUNG,AE		314	324
0.00	FREMGEN,JM	JA	64	TAR			43	51
0.00	FREMGEN,JM	JL	67	TAR			457	467
0.00	FRIEDMAN,LA	JA	78	TAR			18	30
0.00	FRIEDMAN,LA	OC	78	TAR			895	909
0.00	FU,P	SP	71	JAR			40	51
0.00	FURLONG,WL	AP	66	TAR			244	252
0.00	GAMBLE,GO	SP	81	JAA			220	237
0.00	GAMBLE,GO	SU	82	JAA			320	326
0.00	GIBBS,G	OC	64	TAR			4	7
0.00	GIBSON,JL	JL	63	TAR			492	500
0.00	GIBSON,RW	JA	65	TAR			196	203
0.00	GILLES JR,LH	OC	63	TAR			776	784
0.00	GIVENS,HR	JL	66	TAR			458	463
0.00	GLATZER,W	03	81	AOS			219	234
0.00	GOETZ,BE	JL	67	TAR			435	440
0.00	GOGGANS,TP	JL	64	TAR			627	630
0.00	GOLDBERG,L	JL	63	TAR			457	469
0.00	GOLDSCHMIDT,Y	AP	69	TAR	SMIDT,S		317	329
0.00	GOLDSCHMIDT,Y	AU	84	JAA	SHASHUA,L		54	67
0.00	GOMBERG,M	JL	64	TAR	FARBER,A		615	617
0.00	GORMLEY,RJ	SU	80	JAA			293	312
0.00	GORMLEY,RJ	AU	82	JAA			51	59
0.00	GRADY,P	JA	65	TAR			21	30
0.00	GRAESE,CE	AP	64	TAR			387	391
0.00	GRAY,J	AP	63	TAR	WILLINGHAM,JJ	JOHNSTON,K	336	346
0.00	GREER,HC	JA	64	TAR			22	31
0.00	GREER JR,WR	AU	78	JAA	MORRISSEY,LE		49	57
0.00	GROBSTEIN,M	SP	84	AUD	CRAIG,PW		1	16
0.00	GROSS,H	OC	66	TAR			745	753
0.00	GUTBERLET,LG	SU	80	JAA			313	338
0.00	GUTBERLET,LG	AU	83	JAA			16	28
0.00	GYNTHER,RS	AP	69	TAR			247	255

MODE OF REASONING(METHOD)=QUALITATIVE

CITE IND-EX	FIRST AUTHOR	ISS-UE	YE-AR	JOUR -NAL	SECOND AUTHOR	THIRD AUTHOR	PAG BEG	PAG END
0.00	HAFNER,GF	OC	64	TAR			979	982
0.00	HAIN,HP	OC	66	TAR			699	703
0.00	HAIN,HP	AU	67	JAR			154	163
0.00	HAKANSSON,NH	JL	78	TAR			717	725
0.00	HANNUM,WH	AP	68	TAR	WASSERMAN,W		295	302
0.00	HANSEN,ES	ST	77	JAR			156	201
0.00	HARTLEY,RV	AP	68	TAR			321	332
0.00	HASEMAN,WC	OC	68	TAR			738	752
0.00	HATFIELD,HR	AU	66	JAR			169	182
0.00	HEARD,JE	03	81	AOS	BOLCE,WJ		247	254
0.00	HEIN,LW	JL	63	TAR			508	520
0.00	HEIN,LW	AP	63	TAR			252	261
0.00	HEINS,EB	AP	66	TAR			323	326
0.00	HELMKAMP,JG	JL	69	TAR			605	610
0.00	HENDRICKSON,HS	AP	68	TAR			363	366
0.00	HENDRIKSEN,ES	JL	63	TAR			483	491
0.00	HENNESSY,VC	SU	78	JAA			317	330
0.00	HERBERT,L	JL	71	TAR			433	440
0.00	HICKS,SA	JL	78	TAR			708	716
0.00	HILL,HP	WI	82	JAA			99	109
0.00	HIRSCH,AJ	OC	64	TAR			972	978
0.00	HIRSCHMAN,RW	JA	65	TAR			176	183
0.00	HOLDER,WW	WI	82	JAA	EUDY,KH		110	125
0.00	HOLMES,W	JA	79	TAR			47	57
0.00	HOLSTRUM,GL	AU	82	AUD	MESSIER JR,WF		45	63
0.00	HOLZER,HP	AP	63	TAR	SCHONFELD,HM		377	381
0.00	HOLZER,HP	AP	63	TAR	SCHONFELD,HM		382	388
0.00	HOLZER,HP	AP	64	TAR	SCHONFELD,HM		405	413
0.00	HOLZMANN,OJ	WI	84	JAA	MEANS,KM		138	150
0.00	HORNE,JC	JA	63	TAR			56	60
0.00	HORNGREN,CT	AP	64	TAR	SORTER,GH		417	420
0.00	HORNGREN,CT	AP	67	TAR			254	264
0.00	HORNGREN,CT	JA	69	TAR			86	89
0.00	HORRIGAN,JO	AP	68	TAR			284	294
0.00	HORVITZ,JS	WI	81	JAA	HAINKEL,M		114	127
0.00	HORWITZ,BN	OC	63	TAR			819	826
0.00	HORWITZ,BN	AU	80	JAA	KOLODNY,R		20	35
0.00	HORWITZ,RM	JL	64	TAR			618	621
0.00	HUDSON,RR	OC	63	TAR			796	801
0.00	HYLTON,DP	JL	64	TAR			667	670
0.00	HYLTON,DP	OC	65	TAR			824	828
0.00	IJIRI,Y	OC	68	TAR			662	667
0.00	IJIRI,Y	JL	72	TAR			510	526
0.00	IJIRI,Y	01	80	AOS	KELLY,EC		115	123
0.00	IMDIEKE,LF	OC	69	TAR	WEYGANDT,JJ		798	805
0.00	IMKE,FJ	AP	66	TAR			318	322
0.00	INGBERMAN,M	AU	78	JAA	SORTER,GH		58	62
0.00	INGBERMAN,M	WI	80	JAA			101	112
0.00	JACKSON-COX,J	34	84	AOS	THIRKELL,JE	MCQUEENEY,J	253	273
0.00	JACOBSEN,LE	AP	63	TAR			285	292

MODE OF REASONING(METHOD)=QUALITATIVE

CITE IND- EX	FIRST AUTHOR	ISS- UE	YE- AR	JOUR -NAL	SECOND AUTHOR	THIRD AUTHOR	PAG BEG	PAG END
0.00	JACOBSEN,LE	AU	64	JAR			221	228
0.00	JENKINS,DO	JL	64	TAR			648	653
0.00	JENSEN,RE	JL	70	TAR			502	508
0.00	JENTZ,GA	JL	66	TAR			535	541
0.00	JENTZ,GA	AP	67	TAR			362	365
0.00	JERSTON,JE	OC	65	TAR			812	813
0.00	JEYNES,PH	JA	65	TAR			105	118
0.00	JOHNSON,GL	OC	65	TAR			821	823
0.00	JOHNSON,O	SP	65	JAR			75	85
0.00	JOHNSON,O	JL	68	TAR			546	548
0.00	JOHNSON,O	OC	74	TAR	GUNN,S		649	663
0.00	JOHNSON,O	ST	81	JAR			89	119
0.00	JOHNSON,SB	SP	82	JAA	MESSIER JR,WF		195	213
0.00	JOHNSTON,DJ	SP	80	JAA	LEMON,WM	NEUMANN,FL	251	263
0.00	JOLIVET,V	JL	64	TAR			689	692
0.00	KABBES,SM	AP	65	TAR			395	400
0.00	KALINSKI,BD	JL	63	TAR			591	595
0.00	KAPLAN,HG	JA	64	TAR	SOLOMON,KI		145	149
0.00	KARLINSKY,SS	WI	83	JAA			157	167
0.00	KARLINSKY,SS	AU	83	JAA			65	76
0.00	KAUFMAN,F	OC	67	TAR			713	720
0.00	KAY,RS	SU	79	JAA			307	315
0.00	KEISTER JR,OR	AP	63	TAR			371	376
0.00	KEISTER JR,OR	AP	64	TAR			414	416
0.00	KELL,WG	AP	68	TAR			266	273
0.00	KELLER,TF	JA	65	TAR			184	189
0.00	KEMP,PS	JA	63	TAR			126	132
0.00	KETZ,JE	AU	83	JAA	WYATT,AR		29	43
0.00	KING,RR	JA	74	TAR	BARON,CD		76	87
0.00	KING,TE	SP	79	JAA			209	223
0.00	KIRCHER,P	OC	65	TAR			742	752
0.00	KIRCHER,P	JL	67	TAR			537	543
0.00	KISTLER,LH	OC	67	TAR			758	766
0.00	KOHLER,EL	AP	63	TAR			266	269
0.00	KOLLARITSCH,FP	AP	65	TAR			382	385
0.00	KRIPKE,H	AU	78	JAA			4	32
0.00	LAIBSTAIN,S	AP	71	TAR			342	351
0.00	LAMDEN,CW	JA	64	TAR			128	132
0.00	LANDSITTEL,DL	SU	82	JAA	SERLIN,JE		291	300
0.00	LARGAY III,JA	JA	73	TAR			115	119
0.00	LARGAY III,JA	AU	83	JAA			44	53
0.00	LARSON,KD	OC	66	TAR	SCHATTKE,RW		634	641
0.00	LAUVER,RC	JA	66	TAR			65	74
0.00	LAWLER,J	ST	67	JAR			86	92
0.00	LEA,RB	SU	81	AUD			53	94
0.00	LEE,GA	SP	73	JAR			47	61
0.00	LEE,GA	JL	81	TAR			539	553
0.00	LEE,SS	JL	65	TAR			622	625
0.00	LEMBKE,VC	JL	70	TAR			458	464
0.00	LENTILHON,RW	OC	64	TAR			880	883

MODE OF REASONING(METHOD)=QUALITATIVE

CITE IND-EX	FIRST AUTHOR	ISS-UE	YE-AR	JOUR-NAL	SECOND AUTHOR	THIRD AUTHOR	PAG BEG	PAG END
0.00	LESSARD,DR	JL	77	TAR	LORANGE,P		628	637
0.00	LEWIS,CD	JA	67	TAR			96	105
0.00	LI,DH	OC	63	TAR			771	775
0.00	LI,DH	JA	63	TAR			52	55
0.00	LI,DH	SP	63	JAR			102	107
0.00	LI,DH	OC	64	TAR			946	950
0.00	LINOWES,DF	JA	65	TAR			97	104
0.00	LITTLETON,AC	JL	70	TAR			476	480
0.00	LIVOCK,DM	SP	65	JAR			86	102
0.00	LONGSTRETH,B	WI	84	JAA			110	122
0.00	LORIG,AN	OC	63	TAR			759	763
0.00	LOUDERBACK,JG	AP	71	TAR			298	305
0.00	LOWE,HD	AP	67	TAR			356	360
0.00	LUNESKI,C	JL	64	TAR			591	597
0.00	LYNN,ES	AP	64	TAR			371	376
0.00	MACKENZIE,O	AP	64	TAR			363	370
0.00	MANES,RP	JL	64	TAR			631	638
0.00	MARPLE,RM	JL	63	TAR			478	482
0.00	MATEER,WH	JL	65	TAR			583	586
0.00	MATTINGLY,LA	OC	64	TAR			996	3
0.00	MAURIELLO,JA	JA	63	TAR			26	28
0.00	MAURIELLO,JA	AP	64	TAR			347	357
0.00	MAUTZ,RK	AP	65	TAR			299	311
0.00	MAUTZ,RK	JL	69	TAR	SKOUSEN,KF		447	456
0.00	MAUTZ,RK	AP	77	TAR	PREVITS,GJ		301	307
0.00	MAY,PT	JL	69	TAR			583	592
0.00	MCDONALD,DL	12	79	AOS	PUXTY,AG		53	66
0.00	MCRAE,TW	AU	65	JAR			255	260
0.00	MEPHAM,MJ	JA	83	TAR			43	57
0.00	METCALF,RW	JA	64	TAR			16	21
0.00	MEYER,PE	JA	76	TAR			80	89
0.00	MILLER,EM	AU	80	JAA			6	19
0.00	MILLER,HE	JA	66	TAR			1	7
0.00	MILLER,MC	AP	73	TAR			280	291
0.00	MOBLEY,SC	AP	66	TAR			292	296
0.00	MOBLEY,SC	AP	68	TAR			333	341
0.00	MOCK,TJ	AU	82	AUD	WRIGHT,A		33	44
0.00	MOCK,TJ	SP	83	AUD	WILLINGHAM,JJ		91	99
0.00	MOONITZ,M	SP	66	JAR			47	61
0.00	MORENO,RG	OC	64	TAR			990	995
0.00	MOREY,L	JA	63	TAR			102	108
0.00	MORRISON,TA	OC	66	TAR			704	713
0.00	MOST,KS	SP	67	JAR			39	50
0.00	MOST,KS	JA	69	TAR			145	152
0.00	MOST,KS	OC	72	TAR			722	734
0.00	MUELLER,GG	JA	63	TAR			142	147
0.00	MUELLER,GG	AU	64	JAR			148	157
0.00	MUELLER,GG	AP	65	TAR			386	394
0.00	MURRAY,D	AU	83	JAA	JOHNSON,R		4	15
0.00	NELSON,GK	JA	66	TAR			42	47

MODE OF REASONING(METHOD)=QUALITATIVE

CITE IND-EX	FIRST AUTHOR	ISS-UE	YE-AR	JOUR-NAL	SECOND AUTHOR	THIRD AUTHOR	PAG BEG	PAG END
0.00	NEUBIG,RD	JA	64	TAR			86	89
0.00	NICHOLS,AC	OC	68	TAR	GRAWOIG,DE		631	639
0.00	NOBES,CW	AP	82	TAR			303	310
0.00	NORGAARD,CT	JL	72	TAR			433	442
0.00	NURNBERG,H	OC	72	TAR			655	665
0.00	O'CONNOR,MC	AP	72	TAR	HAMRE,JC		308	319
0.00	OLIPHANT,WJ	ST	71	JAR			93	98
0.00	PARKE,R	03	81	AOS	PETERSON,JL		235	246
0.00	PARKER,WM	OC	63	TAR			785	788
0.00	PARKER,WM	AU	66	JAR			149	154
0.00	PATON,WA	AP	63	TAR			243	251
0.00	PATON,WA	SP	63	JAR			44	72
0.00	PATON,WA	JA	67	TAR			7	23
0.00	PATON,WA	SP	68	JAR			72	85
0.00	PATON,WA	AP	69	TAR			276	283
0.00	PATRICK,AW	JA	63	TAR	QUITTMEYER,CL		109	117
0.00	PATTERSON,RG	OC	67	TAR			772	774
0.00	PEASNELL,KV	JA	77	TAR			186	189
0.00	PEIRSON,G	OC	66	TAR			729	736
0.00	PERAGALLO,E	JL	71	TAR			529	534
0.00	PERAGALLO,E	JA	83	TAR			98	104
0.00	PETERSON,WA	AP	66	TAR			275	282
0.00	PHILIPS,GE	OC	63	TAR			696	708
0.00	PHILIPS,GE	JA	63	TAR			14	25
0.00	PHILIPS,GE	JA	68	TAR			10	17
0.00	PHILLIPS,LC	AP	65	TAR			377	381
0.00	POMERANZ,F	AU	77	JAA			45	52
0.00	PRATER,GI	OC	66	TAR			619	625
0.00	PRESTON,LE	03	81	AOS			255	262
0.00	PRINCE,TR	JL	64	TAR			553	562
0.00	RABY,WL	JL	63	TAR	NEUBIG,RD		568	576
0.00	RABY,WL	OC	66	TAR			714	720
0.00	RABY,WL	JA	69	TAR			1	11
0.00	RAMAN,KK	SU	81	JAA			352	359
0.00	RAPPAPORT,A	OC	64	TAR			951	962
0.00	RATSCH,H	JA	64	TAR			140	144
0.00	RAYMAN,RA	SP	69	JAR			53	89
0.00	REVSINE,L	AP	69	TAR			354	358
0.00	REVSINE,L	JL	71	TAR			480	489
0.00	REVSINE,L	AP	81	TAR			342	354
0.00	REYNOLDS,IN	AP	64	TAR			342	346
0.00	RICHARD,DL	OC	68	TAR			730	737
0.00	ROBERTSON,JC	WI	81	JAA	ALDERMAN,CW		144	161
0.00	ROBERTSON,JC	SP	84	AUD			57	67
0.00	ROBINSON,LA	JA	64	TAR	HALL,TP		62	69
0.00	ROLLER,J	AP	67	TAR	WILLIAMS,TH		349	355
0.00	RORKE,CH	03	82	AOS			305	306
0.00	ROSE,H	AU	64	JAR			137	147
0.00	ROSEN,LS	JA	67	TAR			106	113
0.00	ROSEN,LS	JA	69	TAR	DECOSTER,DT		124	136

MODE OF REASONING(METHOD)=QUALITATIVE

CITE INDEX	FIRST AUTHOR	ISSUE	YEAR	JOURNAL	SECOND AUTHOR	THIRD AUTHOR	PAG BEG	PAG END
0.00	ROSENBERG,D	02	82	AOS	TOMKINS,L	DAY,P	123	138
0.00	ROSENFIELD,P	OC	69	TAR			788	797
0.00	ROSS,H	ST	70	JAR			108	115
0.00	SALGADO,AP	AP	63	TAR			389	397
0.00	SAN MIGUEL,JG	02	77	AOS			177	186
0.00	SAPIENZA,SR	JA	63	TAR			91	101
0.00	SAPIENZA,SR	JL	64	TAR			582	590
0.00	SAPIENZA,SR	SP	64	JAR			50	66
0.00	SAVOIE,LM	ST	69	JAR			55	62
0.00	SCHACHNER,L	AP	68	TAR			303	311
0.00	SCHATTKE,RW	OC	65	TAR			805	811
0.00	SCHATTKE,RW	AP	72	TAR			233	244
0.00	SCHIENEMAN,GS	AU	79	JAA			21	30
0.00	SCHIENEMAN,GS	SP	83	JAA			212	226
0.00	SCHIFF,M	AU	77	JAA	SORTER,GH	WIESEN,JL	19	44
0.00	SCHNEE,EJ	AU	81	JAA	TAYLOR,ME		18	29
0.00	SCHNEIDER,AJ	AP	67	TAR			342	348
0.00	SCHNEPPER,JA	JL	77	TAR			653	657
0.00	SCHULTE JR,AA	OC	66	TAR			721	728
0.00	SCHWARTZ,BN	SP	81	JAA			238	247
0.00	SCOTT,RA	OC	79	TAR			750	763
0.00	SEAMAN,JL	JL	65	TAR			617	621
0.00	SEELYE,AL	AP	63	TAR			302	309
0.00	SEIDLER,LJ	SU	79	JAA			285	293
0.00	SEILER,RE	OC	66	TAR			652	656
0.00	SHILLINGLAW,G	SP	63	JAR			73	85
0.00	SHPILBERG,D	AU	86	AUD	GRAHAM,LE		75	94
0.00	SHWAYDER,KR	JA	68	TAR			101	104
0.00	SHWAYDER,KR	SP	68	JAR			86	97
0.00	SIMMONS,JK	OC	67	TAR			680	692
0.00	SIMON,SI	OC	64	TAR			884	889
0.00	SIMON,SI	AP	65	TAR			401	406
0.00	SLAVIN,NS	AP	77	TAR			360	368
0.00	SMOLINSKI,EJ	AU	63	JAR			149	178
0.00	SOMMERFELD,RM	OC	67	TAR			747	750
0.00	SORTER,GH	ST	74	JAR	GANS,MS		1	12
0.00	SORTER,GH	SP	82	JAA			188	194
0.00	SOTTO,R	01	83	AOS			57	72
0.00	SPACEK,L	AP	64	TAR			275	284
0.00	SPENCER,MH	AP	63	TAR			310	316
0.00	SPILLER JR,EA	OC	64	TAR			850	859
0.00	SPROUSE,RT	OC	63	TAR			687	695
0.00	SPROUSE,RT	JL	65	TAR			522	526
0.00	ST.PIERRE,K	SP	84	JAA			257	263
0.00	STAATS,EB	SU	81	AUD			1	11
0.00	STANDISH,PEM	JL	64	TAR			654	666
0.00	STANLEY,CH	JL	64	TAR			639	647
0.00	STAUBUS,GJ	JA	63	TAR			64	74
0.00	STAUBUS,GJ	JL	66	TAR			397	412
0.00	STETTLER,HF	OC	65	TAR			723	730

MODE OF REASONING(METHOD)=QUALITATIVE

CITE IND-EX	FIRST AUTHOR	ISS-UE	YE-AR	JOUR-NAL	SECOND AUTHOR	THIRD AUTHOR	PAG BEG	PAG END
0.00	STEVENSON,RA	AP	66	TAR			312	317
0.00	STONE,DE	AP	67	TAR			331	337
0.00	STONE,ML	ST	68	JAR			59	66
0.00	STONE,WE	JA	64	TAR			38	42
0.00	STONE,WE	AP	69	TAR			284	291
0.00	STONE,WE	AU	72	JAR			345	350
0.00	STREER,PJ	SU	79	JAA			329	338
0.00	SUMMERS,EL	SP	70	JAR	DESKINS,JW		113	117
0.00	TAUSSIG,RA	JL	63	TAR			562	567
0.00	TAYLOR,RG	JA	65	TAR			89	96
0.00	THOMAS,AL	JL	64	TAR			574	581
0.00	TOPIOL,J	JA	66	TAR			83	91
0.00	TOWNSEND,LA	JA	67	TAR			1	6
0.00	TRUEBLOOD,RM	SP	63	JAR			86	95
0.00	TRUEBLOOD,RM	ST	66	JAR			183	191
0.00	TRUMBULL,WP	JA	63	TAR			46	51
0.00	TRUMBULL,WP	JL	68	TAR			459	468
0.00	TUCKERMAN,B	JA	64	TAR			32	37
0.00	ULLMANN,AA	12	79	AOS			123	134
0.00	VANCE,LL	JA	66	TAR			48	51
0.00	VANCE,LL	OC	69	TAR			692	703
0.00	VASARHELYI,MA	AU	84	AUD			100	106
0.00	VASARHELYI,MA	SP	84	AUD	BAILEY JR,AD	CAMARDESSE JR,J	88	103
0.00	VOGT,RA	01	77	AOS			59	80
0.00	WADE,HH	OC	63	TAR			714	718
0.00	WAGNER,JW	JL	69	TAR			600	604
0.00	WAUGH,JB	JL	68	TAR			535	539
0.00	WEIGAND,RE	JL	63	TAR			584	590
0.00	WEIL,RL	OC	73	TAR			749	758
0.00	WEISER,HJ	JL	66	TAR			518	524
0.00	WELKE,WR	AP	66	TAR			253	256
0.00	WELLS,MC	OC	65	TAR	COTTON,W		829	833
0.00	WELLS,MC	AP	68	TAR			373	376
0.00	WELLS,MC	JL	76	TAR			471	482
0.00	WELSCH,GA	OC	64	TAR			8	13
0.00	WERNER,CA	AU	83	JAA	KOSTOLANSKY,JW		54	64
0.00	WERNER,CA	SP	84	JAA	KOSTOLANSKY,JW		212	224
0.00	WEYGANDT,JJ	JA	70	TAR			69	75
0.00	WHEELER,JT	JA	70	TAR			1	10
0.00	WHITE,D	SU	82	JAA	VANECEK,M		338	354
0.00	WHITTINGTON,OR	SU	82	JAA	ADAMS,SJ		310	319
0.00	WIESEN,JL	WI	79	JAA	ENG,R		101	121
0.00	WIESEN,JL	SU	81	JAA			309	324
0.00	WILKINSON,TL	JA	64	TAR			133	139
0.00	WILLIAMS,D	AP	66	TAR			226	234
0.00	WILLIAMS,JJ	02	81	AOS			153	166
0.00	WILLIAMS,TH	OC	67	TAR	GRIFFIN,CH		642	649
0.00	WILLINGHAM,JJ	JL	64	TAR			543	552
0.00	WINBORNE,MG	OC	66	TAR	KLEESPIE,DC		737	744
0.00	WINDAL,FW	JA	63	TAR			29	36

MODE OF REASONING(METHOD)=QUALITATIVE

CITE IND-EX	FIRST AUTHOR	ISS-UE	YE-AR	JOUR -NAL	SECOND AUTHOR	THIRD AUTHOR	PAG BEG	PAG END
0.00	WINJUM,JO	OC	70	TAR			743	761
0.00	WINJUM,JO	AU	71	JAR			333	350
0.00	WINJUM,JO	JA	71	TAR			149	155
0.00	WOODS,RS	JL	64	TAR			598	614
0.00	WOOLSEY,SM	OC	63	TAR			709	713
0.00	WRIGHT,FK	AU	67	JAR			173	179
0.00	WRIGHT,HW	OC	66	TAR			626	633
0.00	WYATT,AR	JL	65	TAR			527	535
0.00	YAMEY,BS	JL	80	TAR			419	425
0.00	YOUNG,AE	SP	80	JAA			244	250
0.00	YOUNG,DW	OC	76	TAR			788	799
0.00	YU,SC	JA	66	TAR			8	20
0.00	YU,SC	JL	69	TAR			571	582
0.00	ZANNETOS,ZS	AP	63	TAR			326	335
0.00	ZANNETOS,ZS	OC	64	TAR			860	868
0.00	ZANNETOS,ZS	JL	67	TAR			566	571
0.00	ZEFF,SA	JA	65	TAR	MAXWELL,WD		65	75
0.00	ZEFF,SA	JL	82	TAR			528	553

MODE OF REASONING(METHOD)=QUALITATIVE

2.1 RESEARCH METHOD=ANALYTICAL - INTERNAL LOGIC

CITE IND- EX	FIRST AUTHOR	ISS- UE	YE- AR	JOUR -NAL	SECOND AUTHOR	THIRD AUTHOR	PAG BEG	PAG END
4.50	HOPWOOD,AG	03	87	AOS			207	234
3.89	BURCHELL,S	01	80	AOS	CLUBB,C	HOPWOOD,AG	5	27
3.80	WATTS,RL	AP	79	TAR	ZIMMERMAN,JL		273	305
3.75	BURCHELL,S	04	85	AOS	CLUBB,C	HOPWOOD,AG	381	414
3.63	BOWEN,RM	AG	81	JAE	NOREEN,EW	LACEY,JM	151	179
3.40	KAPLAN,RS	JL	84	TAR			390	418
3.18	DEMSKI,JS	AP	78	TAR	FELTHAM,GA		336	359
3.18	WATERHOUSE,JH	01	78	AOS	TIESSEN,P		65	76
3.00	LOFT,A	02	86	AOS			137	170
2.67	HOPWOOD,AG	23	83	AOS			287	305
2.67	OTLEY,DT	04	80	AOS			413	428
2.50	MILLER,P	03	87	AOS	O'LEARY,T		235	265
2.50	TOMKINS,C	04	83	AOS	GROVES,R		361	374
2.18	HEDBERG,B	01	78	AOS	JONSSON,S		47	64
2.10	ZIMMERMAN,JL	JL	79	TAR			504	521
2.00	ARMSTRONG,P	02	85	AOS			129	148
2.00	ARMSTRONG,P	05	87	AOS			415	436
2.00	HAYES,DC	23	83	AOS			241	250
2.00	ROBERTS,J	04	85	AOS	SCAPENS,RW		443	456
1.83	KAPLAN,RS	OC	83	TAR			686	705
1.77	RONEN,J	OC	75	TAR	LIVINGSTONE,JL		671	685
1.75	PRAKASH,P	01	77	AOS	RAPPAPORT,A		29	38
1.69	GORDON,LA	01	76	AOS	MILLER,D		59	70
1.67	BAIMAN,S	AU	83	JAR	EVANS III,JH		371	395
1.67	TIESSEN,P	23	83	AOS	WATERHOUSE,JH	251	268	
1.60	DEMSKI,JS	JA	84	TAR	PATELL,JM	WOLFSON,MA	16	34
1.60	GIBBINS,M	SP	84	JAR			103	125
1.57	TINKER,AM	02	82	AOS	MERINO,BD	NEIMARK,M	167	200
1.56	TINKER,AM	01	80	AOS			147	160
1.50	DEMSKI,JS	SP	87	JAR	SAPPINGTON,DEM		68	89
1.50	DYE,RA	AU	83	JAR			514	533
1.44	BAIMAN,S	ST	80	JAR	DEMSKI,JS		184	220
1.40	WALLER,WS	34	84	AOS	FELIX JR,WL		383	406
1.38	BEAVER,WH	SP	81	JAR			163	184
1.38	COLVILLE,I	02	81	AOS			119	132
1.38	DEANGELO,LE	DE	81	JAE			183	199
1.33	DEMSKI,JS	AU	86	JAR	SAPPINGTON,DEM		250	269
1.33	HOSKIN,KW	02	86	AOS	MACVE,RH		105	136
1.33	HUGHES,PJ	JN	86	JAE			119	142
1.33	JOHNSON,HT	23	83	AOS			139	146
1.30	BEAVER,WH	JA	79	TAR	DEMSKI,JS		38	46
1.25	DEANGELO,LE	AG	81	JAE			113	127
1.25	GJESDAL,F	SP	81	JAR			208	231
1.25	HOPWOOD,AG	03	85	AOS			361	376
1.23	DEMSKI,JS	OC	73	TAR			718	723
1.23	SCHIFF,M	AP	70	TAR	LEWIN,AY		259	268
1.22	OTLEY,DT	02	80	AOS	BERRY,AJ		231	246
1.20	BOLAND,RJ	04	79	AOS			259	272

CITE IND- EX	FIRST AUTHOR	ISS- UE	YE- AR	JOUR -NAL	SECOND AUTHOR	THIRD AUTHOR	PAG BEG	PAG END
1.20	CHRISTIE,AA	DE	84	JAE	KENNELLEY,MD	KING,JW	205	217
1.20	PENNO,M	SP	84	JAR			177	191
1.17	FELIX JR,WL	SP	77	JAR	GRIMLUND,RA		23	41
1.17	VERRECCHIA,RE	DE	83	JAE			179	194
1.15	ASHTON,RH	OC	74	TAR			719	732
1.14	ANTLE,R	AU	82	JAR			504	527
1.08	SCOTT,WR	AU	73	JAR			304	330
1.00	ANSARI,SL	02	77	AOS			101	112
1.00	BANBURY,J	03	79	AOS	NAHAPIET,JE		163	178
1.00	CHRISTENSEN,J	AU	82	JAR			589	603
1.00	CHRISTIE,AA	DE	87	JAE			231	258
1.00	DEMSKI,JS	AP	74	TAR			221	232
1.00	DYE,RA	SP	85	JAR			123	145
1.00	EINHORN,HJ	ST	76	JAR			196	206
1.00	FELTHAM,GA	OC	70	TAR	DEMSKI,JS		623	640
1.00	GAMBLING,TE	02	77	AOS			141	152
1.00	HILTON,RW	AU	80	JAR			477	505
1.00	KAPLAN,RS	45	86	AOS			429	452
1.00	KINNEY JR,WR	ST	75	JAR			14	29
1.00	SORTER,GH	JA	69	TAR			12	19
1.00	SPICER,BH	01	83	AOS	BALLEW,V		73	98
1.00	STRINGER,KW	ST	75	JAR			1	9
1.00	VERRECCHIA,	RE	OC	86	JAE		175	196
0.92	BEAVER,WH	OC	68	TAR	KENNELLY,JW	VOSS,WM	675	683
0.92	KINNEY JR,WR	SP	75	JAR			117	132
0.85	CAPLAN,EM	JL	66	TAR			496	509
0.85	GORDON,MJ	AP	64	TAR			251	263
0.85	KAPLAN,RS	SP	73	JAR			38	46
0.85	LEV,B	JA	71	TAR	SCHWARTZ,A		103	112
0.83	ARGYRIS,C	02	77	AOS			113	124
0.83	HAKANSSON,NH	AP	77	TAR			396	416
0.82	GORDON,LA	34	78	AOS	LARCKER,DF	TUGGLE,FD	203	214
0.77	DEMSKI,JS	AU	76	JAR			230	245
0.77	FLAMHOLTZ,EG	AP	71	TAR			253	267
0.77	IJIRI,Y	JL	66	TAR	JAEDICKE,RK		474	483
0.77	ITAMI,H	SP	75	JAR			73	96
0.77	KAPLAN,RS	SP	69	JAR			32	43
0.77	SUNDER,S	JA	76	TAR			1	18
0.75	COOPER,DJ	03	81	AOS	HAYES,DC	WOLF,FM	175	192
0.75	HIRST,MK	OC	81	TAR			771	784
0.75	JOHNSON,HT	JL	81	TAR			510	518
0.73	BARIFF,ML	01	78	AOS	GALBRAITH,JR		15	28
0.71	GRIMLUND,RA	AU	82	JAR			316	342
0.71	HITE,GL	JL	82	JAE	LONG,MS		3	14
0.70	ANSARI,SL	03	79	AOS			149	162
0.70	CHANDLER,AD	12	79	AOS	DAEMS,H		3	20
0.70	GONEDES,NJ	AU	79	JAR	DOPUCH,N		384	410
0.69	DEMSKI,JS	AU	72	JAR			243	258
0.69	DYCKMAN,TR	AU	69	JAR			215	244
0.69	MAY,RG	OC	76	TAR	SUNDEM,GL		747	763

RESEARCH METHOD=ANALYTICAL - INTERNAL LOGIC

CITE IND-EX	FIRST AUTHOR	ISS-UE	YE-AR	JOUR-NAL	SECOND AUTHOR	THIRD AUTHOR	PAG BEG	PAG END
0.69	REVSINE,L	OC	70	TAR			704	711
0.69	WATSON,DJ	JL	75	TAR	BAUMLER,JV		466	474
0.67	CHUA,WF	OC	86	TAR			601	632
0.67	GAA,JC	JL	86	TAR			435	454
0.67	KINNEY JR,WR	SP	83	AUD			13	22
0.67	NEIMARK,M	45	86	AOS	TINKER,T		369	396
0.67	TITMAN,S	JN	86	JAE	TRUEMAN,B		159	172
0.67	TRUEMAN,B	MR	86	JAE			53	72
0.67	WHITLEY,R	02	86	AOS			171	192
0.67	WILNER,N	01	86	AOS	BIRNBERG,JG		71	82
0.64	NG,DS	OC	78	TAR			910	920
0.64	WILDAVSKY,A	01	78	AOS			77	88
0.63	HAKANSSON,NH	ST	81	JAR			1	35
0.63	HOFSTEDE,G	03	81	AOS			193	216
0.62	BAIMAN,S	SP	75	JAR			1	15
0.62	CUSHING,BE	JA	74	TAR			24	41
0.62	DEMSKI,JS	JL	74	TAR	SWIERINGA,RJ		506	513
0.62	DRAKE,DF	AU	65	JAR	DOPUCH,N		192	205
0.62	YU,S	AU	73	JAR	NETER,J		273	295
0.60	ATKINSON,AA	SP	79	JAR			1	22
0.60	LAMBERT,RA	OC	84	TAR			604	618
0.60	LEV,B	DE	79	JAE	SUNDER,S		187	210
0.60	MATOLCSY,ZP	AU	84	JAR			555	569
0.60	NG,DS	ST	79	JAR	STOECKENIUS,J		1	24
0.60	OHLSON,JA	DE	79	JAE			211	232
0.60	PATELL,JM	AU	79	JAR			528	549
0.60	SUNDER,S	SP	84	JAR	WAYMIRE,G		396	405
0.60	VERRECCHIA,RE	MR	79	JAE			77	90
0.58	HAMLEN,SS	JL	77	TAR	HAMLEN,WA	TSCHIRHART,JT	616	627
0.58	JENSEN,DL	OC	77	TAR			842	856
0.56	GINZBERG,MJ	04	80	AOS			369	382
0.56	LEFTWICH,RW	DE	80	JAE			193	211
0.56	MAGEE,RP	AU	80	JAR			551	573
0.56	VERRECCHIA,RE	MR	80	JAE			63	92
0.55	BELKAOUI,A	02	78	AOS			97	104
0.55	SUNDER,S	AU	78	JAR			341	367
0.54	BENSTON,GJ	AP	63	TAR			347	354
0.54	BIRNBERG,JG	JA	68	TAR	NATH,R		38	45
0.54	BRUMMET,RL	AP	68	TAR	FLAMHOLTZ,EG	PYLE,WC	217	224
0.54	ESTES,RW	AP	72	TAR			284	290
0.54	FELTHAM,GA	OC	68	TAR			684	696
0.54	JAEDICKE,RK	OC	64	TAR	ROBICHEK,AA		917	926
0.54	SORENSEN,JE	JL	69	TAR			555	561
0.54	SUNDER,S	AP	76	TAR			287	291
0.54	SUNDER,S	AU	76	JAR			277	300
0.54	TRACY,JA	JA	69	TAR			90	98
0.50	BABER,WR	DE	83	JAE			213	227
0.50	BAIMAN,S	AU	85	JAR	NOEL,J		486	501
0.50	BEAVER,WH	JA	87	TAR			137	144
0.50	CONROY,	RM	JA	87	TAR		HUGHES,JS	50	66

RESEARCH METHOD=ANALYTICAL - INTERNAL LOGIC

CITE IND-EX	FIRST AUTHOR	ISS-UE	YE-AR	JOUR-NAL	SECOND AUTHOR	THIRD AUTHOR	PAG BEG	PAG END
0.50	CUSHING,BE	AP	77	TAR			308	321
0.50	HAGG,J	12	79	AOS	HEDLUND,G		135	143
0.50	JOYCE,EJ	AU	81	JAR	LIBBY,R		544	550
0.50	MACINTOSH,NB	01	81	AOS			39	52
0.50	MELUMAD,ND	ST	87	JAR	REICHELSTEIN,S		1	18
0.50	O'LEARY,T	01	85	AOS			87	104
0.50	OHLSON,JA	SP	83	JAR			141	154
0.50	PUXTY,AG	03	87	AOS	WILLMOTT,HC	COOPER,DJ	273	291
0.50	SUH,YS	ST	87	JAR			22	46
0.50	SUNDEM,GL	SP	79	JAR			243	261
0.50	SWIERINGA,RJ	03	87	AOS	WEICK,KE		293	308
0.50	THOMPSON,G	05	87	AOS			523	543
0.46	BUTTERWORTH,JE	SP	72	JAR			1	27
0.46	COLANTONI,CS	JA	71	TAR	MANES,RP	WHINSTON,AB	90	102
0.46	DEAKIN,EB	OC	74	TAR	GRANOF,MH		764	771
0.46	DEMSKI,JS	SP	72	JAR			58	76
0.46	FLAMHOLTZ,EG	OC	72	TAR			666	678
0.46	GONEDES,NJ	JA	72	TAR			11	21
0.46	GONEDES,NJ	AU	74	JAR	IJIRI,Y		251	269
0.46	HASEMAN,WD	JA	76	TAR	WHINSTON,AB		65	79
0.46	HOFSTEDT,TR	JA	70	TAR	KINARD,JC		38	54
0.46	LIEBERMAN,AZ	AP	75	TAR	WHINSTON,AB		246	258
0.46	MARSHALL,RM	AU	72	JAR			286	307
0.46	MILLER,H	JA	72	TAR			31	37
0.46	REVSINE,L	JL	70	TAR			513	523
0.45	HERTOG,JF	01	78	AOS			29	46
0.44	DOPUCH,N	JA	80	TAR	SUNDER,S		1	21
0.44	GARMAN,MB	AU	80	JAR	OHLSON,JA		420	440
0.44	GONEDES,NJ	AU	80	JAR			441	476
0.43	DAVIS,SW	04	82	AOS	MENON,K	MORGAN,G	307	318
0.42	DIERKES,M	01	77	AOS	PRESTON,LE		3	22
0.40	ANTLE,R	SP	84	JAR			1	20
0.40	DIRSMITH,MW	12	79	AOS	JABLONSKY,SF		39	52
0.40	MCCARTHY,WE	OC	79	TAR			667	686
0.40	PRAKASH,P	JA	79	TAR	SUNDER,S		1	22
0.38	ASHTON,RH	04	76	AOS			289	300
0.38	BERNSTEIN,LA	JA	67	TAR			86	95
0.38	BODNAR,G	OC	75	TAR			747	757
0.38	BRUNS JR,WJ	JL	68	TAR			469	480
0.38	BUZBY,SL	JA	74	TAR			42	49
0.38	CARMICHAEL,DR	AP	70	TAR			235	245
0.38	DEMSKI,JS	OC	67	TAR			701	712
0.38	DITTMAN,DA	SP	76	JAR	JURIS,HA	REVSINE,L	49	65
0.38	EWUSI-MENSAH,K	04	81	AOS			301	316
0.38	GOLEMBIEWSKI,RT	AP	64	TAR			333	341
0.38	HILLIARD,JE	JA	75	TAR	LEITCH,RA		69	80
0.38	IJIRI,Y	SP	71	JAR	KAPLAN,RS		73	87
0.38	JAGGI,B	AP	74	TAR	LAU,HS		321	329
0.38	JAIN,TN	JA	73	TAR			95	104
0.38	KAPLAN,RS	AP	71	TAR	THOMPSON,GL		352	364

RESEARCH METHOD=ANALYTICAL - INTERNAL LOGIC

CITE IND- EX	FIRST AUTHOR	ISS- UE	YE- AR	JOUR -NAL	SECOND AUTHOR	THIRD AUTHOR	PAG BEG	PAG END
0.38	KAPLAN,RS	JL	74	TAR	WELAM,VP		477	484
0.38	KAPLAN,RS	ST	75	JAR			126	133
0.38	LEV,B	AU	68	JAR			247	261
0.38	LIAO,M	OC	75	TAR			780	790
0.38	MAY,RG	JA	73	TAR	SUNDEM,GL		80	94
0.38	MORIARITY,S	OC	75	TAR			791	795
0.38	OHLSON,JA	AU	81	JAR	BUCKMAN,AG		399	433
0.38	RAMANATHAN,KV	JL	76	TAR			516	528
0.38	RONEN,J	SP	70	JAR	MCKINNEY,G		99	112
0.38	SUNDEM,GL	AP	74	TAR			306	320
0.36	CHERNS,AB	02	78	AOS			105	114
0.36	DIRSMITH,MW	34	78	AOS	JABLONSKY,SF		215	226
0.36	DITTMAN,DA	SP	78	JAR	PRAKASH,P		14	25
0.33	ASHTON,RH	JL	77	TAR			567	575
0.33	BIRNBERG,JG	03	77	AOS	FRIEZE,IH	SHIELDS,MD	189	200
0.33	COVALESKI,M	45	86	AOS	AIKEN,M		297	320
0.33	CROSBY,MA	AU	80	JAR			585	593
0.33	ELLIOTT,RK	SP	83	AUD			1	12
0.33	EVANS III,JH	ST	80	JAR			108	128
0.33	EVANS III,JH	ST	80	JAR			108	128
0.33	KAPLAN,RS	AP	77	TAR			369	378
0.33	LARCKER,DF	JL	83	TAR	REDER,RE	SIMON,DT	606	620
0.33	MENZEFRICKE,U	SP	83	JAR			96	105
0.33	MEYER,JW	45	86	AOS			345	356
0.33	MITROFF,II	23	83	AOS	MASON,RO		195	204
0.33	NEWMAN,DP	02	80	AOS			217	230
0.33	SEFCIK,SE	AU	86	JAR	THOMPSON,R		316	334
0.33	ZALD,MN	45	86	AOS			321	326
0.31	ABDEL-KHALIK,AR	JL	71	TAR			457	471
0.31	BARNEA,A	JA	75	TAR	RONEN,J	SADAN,S	58	68
0.31	BARTON,AD	OC	74	TAR			664	681
0.31	CHEN,RS	JL	75	TAR			533	543
0.31	CRUMBLEY,DL	OC	73	TAR			759	763
0.31	FRIEDMAN,A	AU	74	JAR	LEV,B		235	250
0.31	GYNTHER,RS	AP	67	TAR			274	290
0.31	IJIRI,Y	OC	69	TAR	KAPLAN,RS		743	756
0.31	JOHNSON,HT	JL	75	TAR			444	450
0.31	KILLOUGH,LN	AP	73	TAR	SOUDERS,TL		268	279
0.31	OZAN,T	SP	71	JAR	DYCKMAN,TR		88	115
0.31	STERLING,RR	JL	70	TAR			444	457
0.31	SUMMERS,EL	JL	72	TAR			443	453
0.30	HALPERIN,R	JA	79	TAR			58	71
0.30	HILTON,RW	AU	79	JAR			411	435
0.30	KANODIA,CS	SP	79	JAR			74	98
0.30	REVSINE,L	AP	79	TAR			306	322
0.30	SCHREUDER,H	12	79	AOS			109	122
0.29	GODFREY,JT	AU	82	JAR	ANDREWS,RW		304	315
0.29	SWIERINGA,RJ	02	82	AOS	WATERHOUSE,JH		149	166
0.27	CALLEN,JL	AP	78	TAR			303	308
0.27	KOTTAS,JF	AP	78	TAR	LAU,AH	LAU,HS	389	401

RESEARCH METHOD=ANALYTICAL - INTERNAL LOGIC

CITE IND- EX	FIRST AUTHOR	ISS- UE	YE- AR	JOUR -NAL	SECOND AUTHOR	THIRD AUTHOR	PAG BEG	PAG END
0.27	LOEB,M	SP	78	JAR	MAGAT,WA		103	121
0.25	BEAVER,WH	JA	81	TAR			23	37
0.25	BECK,PJ	SP	85	JAR	SOLOMON,I	TOMASSINI,LA	37	56
0.25	BILLERA,LJ	SP	81	JAR	HEATH,DC	VERRECCHIA,RE	185	196
0.25	BOLAND,RJ	02	81	AOS			109	118
0.25	COGGER,KO	AU	81	JAR			285	298
0.25	DYCKMAN,TR	04	81	AOS			291	300
0.25	DYE,RA	AU	85	JAR			544	574
0.25	EVEREST,GL	AP	77	TAR	WEBER,R		340	359
0.25	FLAMHOLTZ,EG	01	85	AOS	DAS,TK	TSUI,AS	35	50
0.25	OGDEN,S	02	85	AOS	BOUGEN,P		211	226
0.25	PENNO,M	SP	85	JAR			240	255
0.25	RONEN,J	AU	81	JAR	LIVNAT,J		459	481
0.25	SCOTT,WR	SP	77	JAR			120	137
0.25	STAUBUS,GJ	JA	85	TAR			53	75
0.25	VERRECCHIA,RE	SP	81	JAR			271	283
0.23	ANTON,HR	SP	64	JAR			1	9
0.23	BENSTON,GJ	OC	66	TAR			657	672
0.23	CHAMBERS,RJ	AP	64	TAR			264	274
0.23	CHAMBERS,RJ	OC	65	TAR			731	741
0.23	DEMSKI,JS	AU	70	JAR			178	198
0.23	FERTAKIS,JP	OC	69	TAR			680	691
0.23	FRIBERG,RA	JA	73	TAR			50	60
0.23	GERBOTH,DL	JL	73	TAR			475	482
0.23	GOLDMAN,A	OC	74	TAR	BARLEV,B		707	718
0.23	IJIRI,Y	OC	73	TAR	ITAMI,H		724	737
0.23	MARSHALL,RM	JA	75	TAR			99	111
0.23	MOBLEY,SC	OC	70	TAR			762	768
0.23	MOCK,TJ	OC	71	TAR			765	777
0.23	NICHOLS,DR	AP	76	TAR	PRICE,KH		335	346
0.23	OGAN,P	AP	76	TAR			306	320
0.23	OHLSON,JA	AU	75	JAR			267	282
0.23	PRAKASH,P	OC	75	TAR	RAPPAPORT,A		723	734
0.23	RONEN,J	JA	74	TAR			50	60
0.23	TOBA,Y	JA	75	TAR			7	24
0.23	VATTER,WJ	AU	63	JAR			179	197
0.23	WILL,HJ	OC	74	TAR			690	706
0.23	YAMEY,BS	AU	64	JAR			117	136
0.22	BALACHANDRAN,B	VST	80	JAR	RAMAKRISHNAN,RT		140	171
0.22	BROMWICH,M	AP	80	TAR			288	300
0.22	HAMLEN,SS	OC	80	TAR			578	593
0.22	IJIRI,Y	SP	80	JAR	LEITCH,RA		91	108
0.20	BIRNBERG,JG	34	84	AOS	SHIELDS,MD		365	382
0.20	BROWN,LD	JL	79	TAR	ROZEFF,MS		585	591
0.20	NETER,J	AU	84	AUD	KIM,HS	GRAHAM,LE	75	88
0.20	OHLSON,JA	AU	79	JAR	PATELL,JM		504	505
0.20	THORNTON,DB	03	79	AOS			211	234
0.20	YOUNG,DW	03	79	AOS			235	244
0.18	DILLON,RD	JA	78	TAR	NASH,JF		11	17
0.18	HUGHES,JS	OC	78	TAR			882	894

RESEARCH METHOD=ANALYTICAL - INTERNAL LOGIC

CITE IND- EX	FIRST AUTHOR	ISS- UE	YE- AR	JOUR -NAL	SECOND AUTHOR	THIRD AUTHOR	PAG BEG	PAG END
0.18	IJIRI,Y	SU	78	JAA			331	348
0.18	MERVILLE,LJ	OC	78	TAR	PETTY,JW		935	951
0.18	SWANSON,EB	34	78	AOS			237	248
0.17	ANDERSON,JA	AP	77	TAR			417	426
0.17	BROMWICH,M	JL	77	TAR			587	596
0.17	COPPOCK,R	02	77	AOS			125	130
0.17	DICKHAUT,JW	AU	83	JAR	LERE,JC		495	513
0.17	HEIMANN,SR	AU	77	JAR	CHESLEY,GR		193	206
0.17	HUGHES,JS	JA	77	TAR			56	68
0.17	KILMANN,RH	04	83	AOS			341	360
0.17	RONEN,J	AP	77	TAR			438	449
0.17	SCHEPANSKI,A	AP	83	TAR	UECKER,WC		259	283
0.17	WEYGANDT,JJ	JA	77	TAR			40	51
0.15	ALIBER,RZ	JA	75	TAR	STICKNEY,CP		44	57
0.15	ANDERSON,HM	JL	70	TAR	GIESE,J	BOOKER,J	524	531
0.15	BAILEY JR,AD	JL	76	TAR	BOE,WJ		559	573
0.15	BENISHAY,H	SP	65	JAR			114	132
0.15	BERNHARDT,I	SP	70	JAR	COPELAND,RM		95	98
0.15	BIERMAN JR,H	JL	63	TAR			501	507
0.15	BIRD,FA	AP	74	TAR	DAVIDSON,LF	SMITH,CH	233	244
0.15	BRIEF,RP	SP	65	JAR			12	31
0.15	BRIEF,RP	AU	70	JAR	OWEN,J		167	177
0.15	BRIEF,RP	AP	75	TAR			285	297
0.15	CHAMBERS,RJ	SP	63	JAR			3	15
0.15	CHAMBERS,RJ	SP	65	JAR			32	62
0.15	CHAMBERS,RJ	AU	65	JAR			242	252
0.15	CHAMBERS,RJ	JL	66	TAR			443	457
0.15	CHAMBERS,RJ	OC	67	TAR			751	757
0.15	CYERT,RM	ST	74	JAR	IJIRI,Y		29	42
0.15	DAVIDSON,HJ	AU	67	JAR	NETER,J	PETRAN,AS	186	207
0.15	DEMSKI,JS	OC	69	TAR			669	679
0.15	DEMSKI,JS	AU	73	JAR			176	190
0.15	DOPUCH,N	JL	67	TAR	BIRNBERG,JG	DEMSKI,JS	526	536
0.15	EAVES,BC	JL	66	TAR			426	442
0.15	EDWARDS,EO	AP	75	TAR			235	245
0.15	GODFREY,JT	JA	71	TAR	PRINCE,TR		75	89
0.15	GOETZ,BE	JA	67	TAR			53	61
0.15	GORDON,MJ	JL	70	TAR			427	443
0.15	GREEN,D	JA	66	TAR			52	64
0.15	GREER JR,WR	JA	70	TAR			103	114
0.15	GYNTHER,RS	OC	70	TAR			712	730
0.15	HANSON,EI	AP	66	TAR			239	243
0.15	HARTLEY,RV	OC	71	TAR			746	755
0.15	HINOMOTO,H	AU	71	JAR			253	267
0.15	IJIRI,Y	AU	63	JAR	LEVY,FK	LYON,RC	198	212
0.15	IJIRI,Y	AP	76	TAR			227	243
0.15	JEN,FC	AP	70	TAR	HUEFNER,RJ		290	298
0.15	JOHNSON,GL	AU	71	JAR	SIMIK,SS		278	286
0.15	JOHNSON,GL	SP	74	JAR	SIMIK,SS		67	79
0.15	JOHNSON,O	OC	70	TAR			641	653

RESEARCH METHOD=ANALYTICAL - INTERNAL LOGIC

CITE INDEX	FIRST AUTHOR	ISSUE	YEAR	JOURNAL	SECOND AUTHOR	THIRD AUTHOR	PAG BEG	PAG END
0.15	KAPLAN,RS	OC	73	TAR			738	748
0.15	KNUTSON,PH	JA	70	TAR			55	68
0.15	KORNBLUTH,JS	AP	74	TAR			284	295
0.15	LARSON,KD	JA	69	TAR			38	47
0.15	LEMKE,KW	JA	66	TAR			32	41
0.15	LEV,B	SP	70	JAR			78	94
0.15	LIM,R	OC	66	TAR			642	651
0.15	LORIG,AN	JL	64	TAR			563	573
0.15	LUH,FS	JA	68	TAR			123	132
0.15	MATTESSICH,R	JL	72	TAR			469	487
0.15	MAUTZ,RK	AP	63	TAR			317	325
0.15	MOONITZ,M	JL	70	TAR			465	475
0.15	PETRI,E	AP	74	TAR	MINCH,RA		330	341
0.15	SALAMON,GL	AU	73	JAR			296	303
0.15	SAMUELS,JM	AU	65	JAR			182	191
0.15	SEIDLER,LJ	OC	67	TAR			775	781
0.15	SMITH,KA	AP	72	TAR			260	269
0.15	SNAVELY,HJ	AP	67	TAR			223	232
0.15	TEITLEBAUM,AD	ST	75	JAR	ROBINSON,CF		70	91
0.15	THOMAS,AL	JL	71	TAR			472	479
0.15	TOMASSINI,LA	23	76	AOS			239	252
0.15	VATTER,WJ	AU	66	JAR			133	148
0.15	VICKREY,DW	OC	70	TAR			731	742
0.15	VICKREY,DW	JA	76	TAR			31	40
0.15	WAGNER,JW	JL	65	TAR			599	605
0.15	WELKER,RB	JL	74	TAR			514	523
0.15	YETTON,PY	01	76	AOS			81	90
0.15	ZANNETOS,ZS	AP	64	TAR			296	304
0.14	BALACHANDRAN,KR	A	82	TAR	STEUER,RE		125	140
0.14	GIBBINS,M	SP	82	JAR			121	138
0.14	MATSUMURA,EM	SP	82	JAR	TSUI,KW		162	170
0.14	MCCARTHY,WE	JL	82	TAR			554	578
0.14	SELTO,FH	02	82	AOS			139	148
0.14	SHOCKLEY,RA	WI	82	JAA			126	143
0.14	VIGELAND,RL	AP	82	TAR			348	357
0.14	WEBER,R	AP	82	TAR			311	325
0.14	WRIGHT,WF	01	82	AOS			65	78
0.13	BAILEY,AP	SU	81	AUD	MCAFEE,RP	WHINSTON,AB	38	52
0.13	BALACHANDRAN,KR	A	81	TAR	MASCHMEYER,R	LIVINGSTONE,JL	115	124
0.13	BOATSMAN,JR	JA	81	TAR	BASKIN,EF		38	53
0.13	FRIED,D	JL	81	TAR	LIVNAT,J		493	509
0.13	GANGOLLY,JS	AU	81	JAR			299	312
0.13	NEWMAN,DP	ST	81	JAR			134	156
0.13	PERAGALLO,E	JL	81	TAR			587	595
0.11	ANSARI,SL	01	80	AOS	MCDONOUGH,JJ		129	142
0.11	BAKER,CR	SP	80	JAA			197	206
0.11	FLAMHOLTZ,EG	01	80	AOS			31	42
0.11	HAMLEN,SS	AP	80	TAR	HAMLEN,WA	TSCHIRHART,JT	269	287
0.11	PALMON,D	SP	80	JAA	KWATINETZ,M		207	226
0.10	AMEY,LR	04	79	AOS			247	258

RESEARCH METHOD=ANALYTICAL - INTERNAL LOGIC

CITE IND-EX	FIRST AUTHOR	ISS-UE	YE-AR	JOUR-NAL	SECOND AUTHOR	THIRD AUTHOR	PAG BEG	PAG END
0.10	OHLSON,JA	AU	79	JAR			506	527
0.10	RAMAN,KK	AU	79	JAA			31	41
0.10	SHIH,W	OC	79	TAR			687	706
0.10	YAMEY,BS	AP	79	TAR			323	329
0.09	KOTTAS,JF	JL	78	TAR	LAU,HS		698	707
0.09	SCAPENS,RW	AP	78	TAR			448	469
0.09	SCAPENS,RW	AP	78	TAR			448	469
0.09	VERRECCHIA,RE	SP	78	JAR			150	168
0.08	ADAR,Z	JA	77	TAR	BARNEA,A	LEV,B	137	149
0.08	AIKEN,ME	JL	75	TAR	BLACKETT,LA	ISAACS,G	544	562
0.08	AMATO,HN	OC	76	TAR	ANDERSON,EE	HARVEY,DW	854	862
0.08	ARNETT,HE	AP	67	TAR			291	297
0.08	BAILEY JR,AD	JL	73	TAR			560	574
0.08	BALADOUNI,V	AP	66	TAR			215	225
0.08	BAREFIELD,RM	JL	70	TAR			490	501
0.08	BAXTER,WT	AU	71	JAR	CARRIER,NH		189	214
0.08	BEAVER,WH	AU	74	JAR	DUKES,RE		205	215
0.08	BEDFORD,NM	JL	68	TAR	IINO,T		453	458
0.08	BIERMAN JR,H	AP	66	TAR			271	274
0.08	BIERMAN JR,H	JL	74	TAR			448	454
0.08	BIRNBERG,JG	OC	65	TAR			814	820
0.08	BIRNBERG,JG	01	76	AOS	GANDHI,NM		5	10
0.08	BRADFORD,WD	AP	74	TAR			296	305
0.08	BRIEF,RP	OC	73	TAR	OWEN,J		690	695
0.08	BRIEF,RP	SP	73	JAR	OWEN,J		1	15
0.08	BUCKLEY,JW	AP	68	TAR	KIRCHER,P	MATHEWS,RL	274	283
0.08	BULLOCK,CL	JA	74	TAR			98	103
0.08	BURKE,EJ	OC	64	TAR			837	849
0.08	BUTTERWORTH,JE	OC	71	TAR	SIGLOCH,BA		701	716
0.08	CARSBERG,BV	SP	66	JAR			1	15
0.08	CHARNES,A	SP	63	JAR	COOPER,WW	IJIRI,Y	16	43
0.08	CHARNES,A	JA	67	TAR	COOPER,WW		24	52
0.08	CHARNES,A	JA	72	TAR	COLANTONI,CS	COOPER,WW	85	108
0.08	CHURCHILL,NC	OC	64	TAR			894	904
0.08	CLARKE,RW	OC	68	TAR			769	776
0.08	COLANTONI,CS	JL	69	TAR	MANES,RP	WHINSTON,AB	467	481
0.08	COMISKEY,EE	AP	66	TAR			235	238
0.08	COOK,JS	OC	76	TAR	HOLZMANN,OJ		778	787
0.08	COOPER,WW	OC	68	TAR	DOPUCH,N	KELLER,TF	640	648
0.08	CORCORAN,AW	JA	73	TAR	LEININGER,WE		105	114
0.08	COWAN,TK	OC	65	TAR			788	794
0.08	CURRY,DW	JL	71	TAR			490	503
0.08	DAVIDSON,S	AU	63	JAR			117	126
0.08	DEVINE,CT	AU	63	JAR			127	138
0.08	DICKENS,RL	AP	64	TAR	BLACKBURN,JO		312	329
0.08	DOPUCH,N	SP	64	JAR	DRAKE,DF		10	24
0.08	DREBIN,AR	JA	65	TAR			154	162
0.08	ECKEL,LG	OC	76	TAR			764	777
0.08	FEKRAT,MA	AP	72	TAR			351	355
0.08	FELTHAM,GA	JA	70	TAR			11	26

RESEARCH METHOD=ANALYTICAL - INTERNAL LOGIC

CITE IND-EX	FIRST AUTHOR	ISS-UE	YE-AR	JOUR-NAL	SECOND AUTHOR	THIRD AUTHOR	PAG BEG	PAG END
0.08	FIELD,JE	JL	69	TAR			593	599
0.08	FIRMIN,PA	JA	68	TAR	LINN,JJ		75	82
0.08	FRANCIS,ME	AP	73	TAR			245	257
0.08	FRANK,WG	JL	67	TAR	MANES,RP		516	525
0.08	FREMGEN,JM	OC	68	TAR			649	656
0.08	GAMBLING,TE	23	76	AOS			167	174
0.08	GONEDES,NJ	SP	70	JAR			1	20
0.08	GONEDES,NJ	AU	71	JAR			236	252
0.08	GREEN,D	SP	64	JAR			35	49
0.08	GREENBALL,MN	AU	69	JAR			262	289
0.08	GREENE,ED	AP	63	TAR			355	362
0.08	GROVES,R	JL	70	TAR	MANES,RP	SORENSEN,R	481	489
0.08	HARTLEY,RV	AP	70	TAR			223	234
0.08	HARVEY,DW	OC	76	TAR			838	845
0.08	HASSELDINE,CR	JL	67	TAR			497	515
0.08	HEATH,LC	JL	72	TAR			458	468
0.08	HECK,WR	JL	63	TAR			577	578
0.08	HEIMANN,SR	JA	76	TAR	LUSK,EJ		51	64
0.08	HICKS,EL	AU	64	JAR			158	171
0.08	HORNGREN,CT	AP	65	TAR			323	333
0.08	HORNGREN,CT	JA	71	TAR			1	11
0.08	HUEFNER,RJ	OC	71	TAR			717	732
0.08	IJIRI,Y	SP	65	JAR	JAEDICKE,RK	LIVINGSTONE,JL	63	74
0.08	IJIRI,Y	SP	70	JAR	KAPLAN,RS		34	46
0.08	ISELIN,ER	AP	68	TAR			231	238
0.08	JAENICKE,HR	JA	70	TAR			115	128
0.08	JENSEN,DL	JL	74	TAR			465	476
0.08	JENSEN,RE	AP	67	TAR			265	273
0.08	JOHNSON,O	SP	68	JAR			29	37
0.08	JOHNSON,O	JA	72	TAR			64	74
0.08	KEMP,PS	OC	65	TAR			782	787
0.08	KINNEY JR,WR	SP	69	JAR			44	52
0.08	KISSINGER,JN	AP	77	TAR			322	339
0.08	LANGENDERFER,HQ	OC	69	TAR	ROBERTSON,JC		777	787
0.08	LARSON,KD	JL	67	TAR			480	488
0.08	LEMKE,KW	SP	70	JAR			47	77
0.08	LIVINGSTONE,JL	JL	68	TAR			503	508
0.08	LOEBBECKE,JK	ST	75	JAR	NETER,J		38	52
0.08	LUSK,EJ	JL	72	TAR			567	575
0.08	MABERT,VA	JA	74	TAR	RADCLIFFE,RC		61	75
0.08	MAGEE,RP	AU	75	JAR			257	266
0.08	MATHEWS,RL	JL	68	TAR			509	516
0.08	MAUTZ,RK	AP	66	TAR	MINI,DL		283	291
0.08	MCDONALD,DL	OC	67	TAR			662	679
0.08	MCDONOUGH,JJ	OC	71	TAR			676	685
0.08	MCINTYRE,EV	JA	77	TAR			162	171
0.08	MEYERS,SL	JA	73	TAR			44	49
0.08	MOONITZ,M	AU	66	JAR	RUSS,A		155	168
0.08	MORRISON,TA	AP	69	TAR	KACZKA,E		330	343
0.08	MORSE,WJ	OC	72	TAR			761	773

RESEARCH METHOD=ANALYTICAL - INTERNAL LOGIC

CITE IND-EX	FIRST AUTHOR	ISS-UE	YE-AR	JOUR-NAL	SECOND AUTHOR	THIRD AUTHOR	PAG BEG	PAG END
0.08	MURPHY,GJ	AP	76	TAR			277	286
0.08	NURNBERG,H	OC	68	TAR			719	729
0.08	ONSI,M	JL	70	TAR			535	543
0.08	PENMAN,SH	AP	70	TAR			333	346
0.08	RAPPAPORT,A	AP	65	TAR			373	376
0.08	RAPPAPORT,A	JL	67	TAR			441	456
0.08	RICKS,RB	JL	64	TAR			685	688
0.08	ROSENFIELD,P	AP	66	TAR	STOREY,R		327	330
0.08	SCHRODERHEIM,G	JL	64	TAR			679	684
0.08	SCHROEDER,RG	01	77	AOS	IMDIEKE,LF		39	46
0.08	SHWAYDER,KR	AP	69	TAR			304	316
0.08	SHWAYDER,KR	AP	71	TAR			306	319
0.08	SNAVELY,HJ	AP	69	TAR			344	353
0.08	STALLMAN,JC	OC	72	TAR			774	790
0.08	STAUBUS,GJ	OC	67	TAR			650	661
0.08	STAUBUS,GJ	JL	76	TAR			574	589
0.08	STERLING,RR	JA	67	TAR			62	73
0.08	STERLING,RR	JL	68	TAR			481	502
0.08	THEIL,H	JA	69	TAR			27	37
0.08	TRACY,JA	JA	65	TAR			163	175
0.08	ULLMANN,AA	01	76	AOS			71	80
0.08	VATTER,W	OC	66	TAR			681	698
0.08	VATTER,WJ	JL	63	TAR			470	477
0.08	WILKINSON,JR	OC	65	TAR	DONEY,LD		753	756
0.08	WILLIAMS,TH	JL	64	TAR	GRIFFIN,CH		671	678
0.08	WOJDAK,JF	JL	69	TAR			562	570
0.08	WOJDAK,JF	JA	70	TAR			88	97
0.08	WOLK,HI	JL	72	TAR	HILLMAN,AP		549	555
0.08	WRIGHT,FK	AU	65	JAR			167	181
0.08	WRIGHT,FK	FL	65	JAR			167	181
0.08	WRIGHT,FK	JA	70	TAR			129	133
0.00	ABDEL-KHALIK,AR	SP	66	JAR			37	46
0.00	ABDEL-MAGID,MF	AP	79	TAR			346	357
0.00	ABRANOVIC,WA	OC	76	TAR			863	874
0.00	ADAMS,KD	WI	84	JAA			151	163
0.00	AGGARWAL,R	SP	78	JAA			197	216
0.00	AGRAWAL,SP	OC	77	TAR			789	809
0.00	AGRAWAL,SP	WI	80	JAA	HALLBAUER,RC	PERRITT,GW	163	173
0.00	AHARONI,Y	SP	67	JAR	OPHIR,T		1	26
0.00	ALFRED,AM	AU	64	JAR			172	182
0.00	ALLYN,RG	JA	64	TAR			121	127
0.00	ALLYN,RG	AP	66	TAR			303	311
0.00	ALVEY,KL	JA	63	TAR			124	125
0.00	AMERSHI,AH	AU	87	JAR	SUNDER,S		177	195
0.00	ANDERSON,HM	OC	63	TAR	GRIFFIN,FB		813	818
0.00	ANDERSON,JA	JL	75	TAR			509	511
0.00	ANDERSON,JJ	JL	67	TAR			583	588
0.00	ANDERSON,JM	AU	64	JAR			236	238
0.00	ANDERSON,U	AU	88	AUD	YOUNG,RA		23	42
0.00	ARNETT,HE	OC	63	TAR			733	741

RESEARCH METHOD=ANALYTICAL - INTERNAL LOGIC

CITE INDEX	FIRST AUTHOR	ISSUE	YEAR	JOURNAL	SECOND AUTHOR	THIRD AUTHOR	PAG BEG	PAG END
0.00	ARNETT,HE	JL	69	TAR			482	494
0.00	BABER,WR	JA	85	TAR			1	9
0.00	BABER,WR	SP	85	JAR			360	369
0.00	BACKER,M	JL	69	TAR			533	538
0.00	BAGGETT,WD	SP	83	JAA			227	233
0.00	BAILEY JR,AD	AP	85	TAR	DUKE,GL	GERLACH,JH	186	201
0.00	BAIMAN,S	AU	87	JAR	EVANS III,JH	NOEL,J	217	244
0.00	BAINBRIDGE,DR	SU	84	JAA			334	346
0.00	BAKER,RE	JA	64	TAR			52	61
0.00	BAKER,RE	JA	66	TAR			98	105
0.00	BALACHANDRAN,BV	JA	81	TAR	RAMAKRISHNAN,RT		85	96
0.00	BALACHANDRAN,BV	OC	81	TAR	ZOLTNERS,AA		801	812
0.00	BALACHANDRAN,BV	SP	87	JAR	RAMAKRISHNAN,RT		111	126
0.00	BALACHANDRAN,BV	WI	88	JAA	RAMANAN,R		1	13
0.00	BALACHANDRAN,KR	SP	87	JAA	SRINIDHI,BN		151	169
0.00	BANKER,RD	JL	88	JAE	DATAR,SM	KEKRE,S	171	197
0.00	BARLEV,B	AP	83	TAR			385	393
0.00	BARRETT,WB	JA	68	TAR			105	112
0.00	BASTABLE,CW	SP	81	JAA	BEAMS,FA		248	254
0.00	BEAMS,FA	AP	69	TAR			382	388
0.00	BEAVER,WH	AU	82	JAR	WOLFSON,MA		528	550
0.00	BEAVER,WH	DE	84	JAE	GRIFFIN,PA	LANDSMAN,WR	219	223
0.00	BECK,PJ	SP	85	AUD	SOLOMON,I		1	10
0.00	BEDFORD,NM	JA	67	TAR			82	85
0.00	BEDFORD,NM	AP	72	TAR	MCKEOWN,JC		333	338
0.00	BEECHY,TH	AP	69	TAR			375	381
0.00	BEJA,A	AU	77	JAR	AHARONI,Y		169	178
0.00	BENISHAY,H	SU	87	JAA			203	238
0.00	BENNINGER,LJ	JL	65	TAR			547	557
0.00	BENSTON,GJ	JL	76	TAR			483	498
0.00	BERANEK,W	OC	64	TAR			914	916
0.00	BERG,KB	JL	63	TAR	MUELLER,FJ		554	561
0.00	BERKOW,WF	AP	64	TAR			377	386
0.00	BIERMAN JR,H	JA	63	TAR			61	63
0.00	BIERMAN JR,H	AU	64	JAR			229	235
0.00	BIERMAN JR,H	JL	65	TAR			541	546
0.00	BIERMAN JR,H	OC	67	TAR			731	737
0.00	BIERMAN JR,H	AU	67	JAR	SMIDT,S		144	153
0.00	BIERMAN JR,H	OC	68	TAR			657	661
0.00	BIERMAN JR,H	JA	68	TAR	LIU,E		62	67
0.00	BIERMAN JR,H	JA	69	TAR			65	78
0.00	BIERMAN JR,H	AP	69	TAR	DAVIDSON,S		239	246
0.00	BIERMAN JR,H	OC	70	TAR			690	697
0.00	BIERMAN JR,H	OC	71	TAR			693	700
0.00	BIERMAN JR,H	WI	86	JAA			62	70
0.00	BIERMAN,H	SP	85	JAA			184	194
0.00	BIRD,PA	SP	65	JAR			1	11
0.00	BIRNBERG,JG	OC	64	TAR			963	971
0.00	BIRNBERG,JG	01	80	AOS			71	80
0.00	BLAKELY,EJ	JA	63	TAR	KNUTSON,PH		75	86

RESEARCH METHOD=ANALYTICAL - INTERNAL LOGIC

CITE INDEX	FIRST AUTHOR	ISSUE	YEAR	JOURNAL	SECOND AUTHOR	THIRD AUTHOR	PAG BEG	PAG END
0.00	BOATSMAN,JR	AU	84	JAA	DOWELL,CD	KIMBRELL,JI	35	43
0.00	BODNAR,G	OC	77	TAR	LUSK,EJ		857	868
0.00	BOER,G	JA	66	TAR			92	97
0.00	BOGART,FO	OC	65	TAR			834	838
0.00	BOTTS,RR	OC	63	TAR			789	795
0.00	BOURN,AM	AU	66	JAR			213	223
0.00	BOUTELL,WS	AP	64	TAR			305	311
0.00	BOWEN,EK	OC	67	TAR			782	787
0.00	BOWER,JB	AP	65	TAR	SCHLOSSER,RE		338	344
0.00	BOWER,RS	AP	66	TAR	HERRINGER,F	WILLIAMSON,JP	257	265
0.00	BOWSHER,CA	WI	86	JAA			7	16
0.00	BRADBURY,ME	AP	88	TAR	CALDERWOOD,SC		330	347
0.00	BRAVENEC,LL	02	77	AOS	EPSTEIN,MJ	CRUMBLEY,DL	131	140
0.00	BRIEF,RP	AU	68	JAR	OWEN,J		193	199
0.00	BRIEF,RP	AP	68	TAR	OWEN,J		367	372
0.00	BRIEF,RP	SP	69	JAR	OWEN,J		12	16
0.00	BRILOFF,AJ	JA	64	TAR			12	15
0.00	BRILOFF,AJ	JL	67	TAR			489	496
0.00	BROCKETT,P	JL	84	TAR	CHARNES,A	COOPER,WW	474	487
0.00	BRUGEMAN,DC	OC	63	TAR	BRIGHTON,GD		764	770
0.00	BRUGGE,WG	JL	63	TAR			596	600
0.00	BUBLITZ,B	WI	84	JAA	KEE,R		123	137
0.00	BUCKLEY,JW	JL	67	TAR			572	582
0.00	BUCKMAN,AG	SP	82	JAR	MILLER,BL		28	41
0.00	BURGHER,PH	JA	64	TAR			103	120
0.00	BURKE,WL	OC	63	TAR			802	812
0.00	BURNS,JS	JA	63	TAR	JAEDICKE,RK	SANGSTER,JM	1	13
0.00	BURRELL,G	01	87	AOS			89	102
0.00	BURT,OR	SP	72	JAR			28	57
0.00	BURTON,JC	WI	82	AUD	FAIRFIELD,P		1	22
0.00	BYRNE,R	JA	68	TAR	CHARNES,A	COOPER,WW	18	37
0.00	CALL,DV	OC	69	TAR			711	719
0.00	CALLEN,JL	SP	88	JAA			87	108
0.00	CAMPFIELD,WL	JL	63	TAR			521	527
0.00	CAMPFIELD,WL	JL	65	TAR			594	598
0.00	CAMPFIELD,WL	OC	70	TAR			683	689
0.00	CAREY,JL	JA	68	TAR			1	9
0.00	CAREY,JL	JA	69	TAR			79	85
0.00	CARLISLE,HM	JA	66	TAR			115	120
0.00	CARLSON,ML	JL	81	TAR	LAMB,JW		554	573
0.00	CARMICHAEL,DR	OC	68	TAR	SWIERINGA,RJ		697	705
0.00	CARMICHAEL,DR	SU	79	JAA			294	306
0.00	CARMICHAEL,DR	SU	84	JAA	WHITTINGTON,OR		347	361
0.00	CARSBERG,BV	AU	69	JAR			165	182
0.00	CARSON,AB	AP	65	TAR			334	337
0.00	CARTER,WK	JA	81	TAR			108	114
0.00	CASPARI,JA	OC	76	TAR			739	746
0.00	CAUSEY JR,DY	AP	73	TAR			258	267
0.00	CERF,AR	JL	75	TAR			451	465
0.00	CHAMBERS,RJ	AP	67	TAR			241	253

RESEARCH METHOD=ANALYTICAL - INTERNAL LOGIC

CITE INDEX	FIRST AUTHOR	ISSUE	YEAR	JOURNAL	SECOND AUTHOR	THIRD AUTHOR	PAG BEG	PAG END
0.00	CHAMBERS,RJ	AP	68	TAR			239	247
0.00	CHAMBERS,RJ	JL	72	TAR			488	509
0.00	CHAMBERS,RJ	OC	79	TAR			764	775
0.00	CHAMBERS,RJ	01	80	AOS			167	180
0.00	CHAN,KH	WI	84	JAA	CHENG,TT		164	177
0.00	CHAN,KH	OC	86	TAR	DODIN,B		726	734
0.00	CHARNES,A	AP	64	TAR	DAVIDSON,HJ	KORTANEK,KO	241	250
0.00	CHARNES,A	04	76	AOS	COLANTONI,CS	COOPER,WW	315	338
0.00	CHASTEEN,LG	OC	73	TAR			764	767
0.00	CHEN,JT	JL	83	TAR			600	605
0.00	CHIU,JS	OC	66	TAR	DECOSTER,DT		673	680
0.00	CHOUDHURY,N	06	88	AOS			549	557
0.00	CHUA,WF	06	86	AOS			583	598
0.00	CHUMACHENKO,NG	OC	68	TAR			753	762
0.00	CHURCHMAN,CW	JA	71	TAR			30	35
0.00	COHEN,SI	AP	82	TAR	LOEB,M		336	347
0.00	COOPER,DJ	05	87	AOS	HOPPER,TM		407	414
0.00	CORBIN,DA	OC	63	TAR			742	744
0.00	CORBIN,DA	OC	67	TAR			635	641
0.00	CORCORAN,AW	AU	65	JAR	KWANG,CW		206	217
0.00	CORCORAN,AW	AP	69	TAR			359	374
0.00	COWAN,TK	JA	65	TAR			9	20
0.00	COWAN,TK	JA	68	TAR			94	100
0.00	COWIE,JB	JA	70	TAR	FREMGEN,JM		27	37
0.00	CRAMER JR,JJ	OC	64	TAR			869	875
0.00	CRAMER JR,JJ	JL	65	TAR			606	616
0.00	CRAMER JR,JJ	OC	70	TAR	SCHRADER,WJ		698	703
0.00	CRAMER JR,JJ	WI	79	JAA	NEYHART,CA		135	150
0.00	CRANDALL,RH	JL	69	TAR			457	466
0.00	CRUMBLEY,DL	JL	68	TAR			554	564
0.00	CRUMBLEY,DL	JA	75	TAR	SAVICH,RS		112	117
0.00	CRUSE,RB	JA	65	TAR	SUMMERS,EL		82	88
0.00	CURLEY,AJ	JL	71	TAR			519	528
0.00	CUSHING,BE	OC	68	TAR			668	671
0.00	DANOS,P	SP	87	AUD	HOLT,DL	BAILEY JR,AD	134	149
0.00	DAVIS,GB	SP	63	JAR			96	101
0.00	DAVIS,PM	JA	66	TAR			121	126
0.00	DEAN,J	AP	63	TAR	HARRISS,CL		229	242
0.00	DECOSTER,DT	AP	66	TAR			297	302
0.00	DEFLIESE,PL	JL	65	TAR			517	521
0.00	DEINZER,HT	JA	66	TAR			21	31
0.00	DEITRICK,JW	SU	79	JAA	ALDERMAN,CW		316	328
0.00	DEJONG,DV	AU	84	AUD	SMITH,JH		20	34
0.00	DEMARIS,EJ	JA	63	TAR			37	45
0.00	DEMING,WE	SP	79	JAA			197	208
0.00	DERMER,JD	06	86	AOS	LUCAS,RG		471	482
0.00	DERMER,JD	01	88	AOS			25	36
0.00	DERY,D	03	82	AOS			217	224
0.00	DESKINS,JW	JA	65	TAR			76	81
0.00	DEWHIRST,JF	AP	71	TAR			365	373

RESEARCH METHOD=ANALYTICAL - INTERNAL LOGIC

CITE IND-EX	FIRST AUTHOR	ISS-UE	YE-AR	JOUR-NAL	SECOND AUTHOR	THIRD AUTHOR	PAG BEG	PAG END
0.00	DIERKES,M	01	85	AOS	ANTAL,AB		29	34
0.00	DILLARD,JF	34	84	AOS			343	354
0.00	DIRSMITH,MW	SP	82	JAA	MCALLISTER,JP		214	228
0.00	DIRSMITH,MW	AU	82	JAA	MCALLISTER,JP		60	74
0.00	DIRSMITH,MW	02	85	AOS	COVALESKI,MA		149	170
0.00	DOPUCH,N	OC	63	TAR			745	753
0.00	DOPUCH,N	SU	88	JAA			245	250
0.00	DREBIN,AR	JL	63	TAR			579	583
0.00	DREBIN,AR	SP	64	JAR			25	34
0.00	DREBIN,AR	JL	66	TAR			413	425
0.00	DREBIN,AR	SP	66	JAR			68	86
0.00	DREBIN,AR	AU	69	JAR			204	214
0.00	DRINKWATER,D	JL	65	TAR	EDWARDS,JD		579	582
0.00	DUGAN,MT	SP	85	AUD	GENTRY,JA	SHRIVER,KA	11	22
0.00	DUVALL,RM	JL	65	TAR	BULLOCH,J		569	573
0.00	DYE,RA	AU	88	JAR			195	235
0.00	EDEY,HC	AP	63	TAR			262	265
0.00	EIGEN,MM	JL	65	TAR			536	540
0.00	ELLIOTT,EL	OC	68	TAR	LARREA,J	RIVERA,JM	763	768
0.00	ENGSTROM,JH	SP	84	JAA			197	211
0.00	EVANS III,JH	06	86	AOS	LEWIS,BL	PATTON,JM	483	498
0.00	EVERETT,JO	SP	84	JAA	PORTER,GA		241	256
0.00	FAGERBERG,P	JL	72	TAR			454	457
0.00	FARAG,SM	AP	68	TAR			312	320
0.00	FARMAN,WL	JA	63	TAR	HOU,C		133	141
0.00	FARMAN,WL	AP	64	TAR			392	404
0.00	FELLINGHAM,JC	JA	85	TAR	WOLFSON,MA		10	17
0.00	FELLINGHAM,JC	OC	85	TAR	NEWMAN,DP		634	650
0.00	FERRARA,WL	OC	63	TAR			719	722
0.00	FERRARA,WL	JA	66	TAR			106	114
0.00	FERTAKIS,JP	JL	70	TAR			509	512
0.00	FESS,PE	OC	63	TAR			723	732
0.00	FESS,PE	AP	66	TAR			266	270
0.00	FINLEY,DR	AU	83	AUD			104	116
0.00	FIRMIN,PA	AP	63	TAR			270	277
0.00	FISHER,M	SU	78	JAA			349	360
0.00	FITZGERALD,RD	AU	79	JAA	KELLEY,EM		5	20
0.00	FLESHER,DL	04	79	AOS	FLESHER,TK		297	304
0.00	FOGLER,HR	JA	72	TAR			134	143
0.00	FORD,A	OC	69	TAR			818	822
0.00	FORD,A	AP	75	TAR			338	344
0.00	FRANK,WG	OC	65	TAR			854	862
0.00	FRANKFURTER,GM	SU	83	JAA	YOUNG,AE		314	324
0.00	FREMGEN,JM	JA	64	TAR			43	51
0.00	FREMGEN,JM	JL	67	TAR			457	467
0.00	FRIED,D	SU	81	JAA			295	308
0.00	FRIEDMAN,LA	JA	78	TAR			18	30
0.00	FRIEDMAN,LA	OC	78	TAR			895	909
0.00	FURLONG,WL	AP	66	TAR			244	252
0.00	GAMBLE,GO	SP	81	JAA			220	237

RESEARCH METHOD=ANALYTICAL - INTERNAL LOGIC

CITE IND- EX	FIRST AUTHOR	ISS- UE	YE- AR	JOUR -NAL	SECOND AUTHOR	THIRD AUTHOR	PAG BEG	PAG END
0.00	GAMBLE,GO	SU	82	JAA			320	326
0.00	GAMBLE,GO	SP	86	JAA			102	117
0.00	GAMBLING,T	04	85	AOS			415	426
0.00	GAMBLING,T	04	87	AOS			319	329
0.00	GAMBLING,TE	JA	70	TAR	NOUR,A		98	102
0.00	GIBSON,RW	JA	65	TAR			196	203
0.00	GILLES JR,LH	OC	63	TAR			776	784
0.00	GIVENS,HR	JL	66	TAR			458	463
0.00	GLATZER,W	03	81	AOS			219	234
0.00	GLOVER,F	AP	69	TAR			300	303
0.00	GODFREY,JT	AP	71	TAR			286	297
0.00	GOETZ,BE	JL	67	TAR			435	440
0.00	GOGGANS,TP	JL	64	TAR			627	630
0.00	GOLDBERG,L	JL	63	TAR			457	469
0.00	GOLDIN,HJ	SU	85	JAA			269	278
0.00	GOLDSCHMIDT,Y	AP	69	TAR	SMIDT,S		317	329
0.00	GOLDSCHMIDT,Y	AU	84	JAA	SHASHUA,L		54	67
0.00	GOLDWASSER,DL	SU	88	JAA			217	232
0.00	GOMBERG,M	JL	64	TAR	FARBER,A		615	617
0.00	GONEDES,NJ	AP	71	TAR			320	328
0.00	GORDON,LA	JL	88	AUD	HAMER,MH		514	521
0.00	GORMLEY,RJ	SU	80	JAA			293	312
0.00	GORMLEY,RJ	AU	82	JAA			51	59
0.00	GRAESE,CE	AP	64	TAR			387	391
0.00	GRAY,J	AP	63	TAR	WILLINGHAM,JJ	JOHNSTON,K	336	346
0.00	GREER,HC	JA	64	TAR			22	31
0.00	GREER JR,WR	AU	78	JAA	MORRISSEY,LE		49	57
0.00	GROBSTEIN,M	SP	84	AUD	CRAIG,PW		1	16
0.00	GROSS,H	OC	66	TAR			745	753
0.00	GUTBERLET,LG	SU	80	JAA			313	338
0.00	GUTBERLET,LG	AU	83	JAA			16	28
0.00	GYNTHER,RS	AP	69	TAR			247	255
0.00	HAFNER,GF	OC	64	TAR			979	982
0.00	HAKANSSON,NH	JL	69	TAR			495	514
0.00	HAKANSSON,NH	SP	69	JAR			11	31
0.00	HAKANSSON,NH	JL	78	TAR			717	725
0.00	HALPERIN,R	OC	85	TAR	TZUR,J		670	680
0.00	HALPERIN,R	OC	87	TAR	SRINIDHI,BN		686	706
0.00	HANNUM,WH	AP	68	TAR	WASSERMAN,W		295	302
0.00	HANSEN,DR	JA	77	TAR	SHAFTEL,TL		109	123
0.00	HARRISON,GL	03	86	AOS	MCKINNON,JL		233	252
0.00	HARTE,GF	02	87	AOS	OWEN,DL		123	142
0.00	HARTLEY,RV	AP	68	TAR			321	332
0.00	HASEMAN,WC	OC	68	TAR			738	752
0.00	HASSELBACK,JR	AP	76	TAR			269	276
0.00	HATFIELD,HR	AU	66	JAR			169	182
0.00	HAWKINS,CA	SP	84	JAA	GIRARD,D		225	240
0.00	HEARD,JE	03	81	AOS	BOLCE,WJ		247	254
0.00	HEEBINK,DV	JA	64	TAR			90	93
0.00	HEIN,LW	JL	63	TAR			508	520

RESEARCH METHOD=ANALYTICAL - INTERNAL LOGIC

CITE INDEX	FIRST AUTHOR	ISSUE	YEAR	JOURNAL	SECOND AUTHOR	THIRD AUTHOR	PAG BEG	PAG END
0.00	HEIN,LW	AP	63	TAR			252	261
0.00	HELMKAMP,JG	JL	69	TAR			605	610
0.00	HENDRICKSON,HS	AP	68	TAR			363	366
0.00	HENDRIKSEN,ES	JL	63	TAR			483	491
0.00	HENNESSY,VC	SU	78	JAA			317	330
0.00	HERBERT,L	JL	71	TAR			433	440
0.00	HICKS,SA	JL	78	TAR			708	716
0.00	HILL,HP	WI	82	JAA			99	109
0.00	HINES,RD	03	88	AOS			251	261
0.00	HINES,RD	OC	88	TAR			642	656
0.00	HIRSCH,AJ	OC	64	TAR			972	978
0.00	HIRSCHMAN,RW	JA	65	TAR			176	183
0.00	HIRST,MK	OC	87	TAR			774	784
0.00	HOBBS,JB	OC	64	TAR			905	913
0.00	HOLDER,WW	WI	82	JAA	EUDY,KH		110	125
0.00	HOLTHAUSEN,RW	SP	88	JAR	VERRECCHIA,RE		82	106
0.00	HOLZER,HP	AP	63	TAR	SCHONFELD,HM		377	381
0.00	HOLZER,HP	AP	63	TAR	SCHONFELD,HM		382	388
0.00	HOLZER,HP	AP	64	TAR	SCHONFELD,HM		405	413
0.00	HOLZMANN,OJ	WI	84	JAA	MEANS,KM		138	150
0.00	HOPPER,T	05	87	AOS	STOREY,J	WILLMOTT,H	437	456
0.00	HOPWOOD,AG	01	87	AOS			65	70
0.00	HORNE,JC	JA	63	TAR			56	60
0.00	HORNGREN,CT	AP	64	TAR	SORTER,GH		417	420
0.00	HORNGREN,CT	AP	67	TAR			254	264
0.00	HORNGREN,CT	JA	69	TAR			86	89
0.00	HORWITZ,BN	OC	63	TAR			819	826
0.00	HORWITZ,BN	AU	80	JAA	KOLODNY,R		20	35
0.00	HORWITZ,RM	JL	64	TAR			618	621
0.00	HOSKIN,KW	01	88	AOS	MACVE,RH		37	73
0.00	HUDSON,RR	OC	63	TAR			796	801
0.00	HUSS,HF	AU	85	JAA			60	66
0.00	HYLTON,DP	JL	64	TAR			667	670
0.00	HYLTON,DP	OC	65	TAR			824	828
0.00	IJIRI,Y	JA	65	TAR			36	53
0.00	IJIRI,Y	OC	68	TAR			662	667
0.00	IJIRI,Y	AP	70	TAR	THOMPSON,GL		246	258
0.00	IJIRI,Y	JL	72	TAR			510	526
0.00	IJIRI,Y	01	80	AOS	KELLY,EC		115	123
0.00	IJIRI,Y	JA	84	TAR	NOEL,J		52	63
0.00	IJIRI,Y	OC	86	TAR			745	760
0.00	IMDIEKE,LF	OC	69	TAR	WEYGANDT,JJ		798	805
0.00	IMKE,FJ	AP	66	TAR			318	322
0.00	INGBERMAN,M	AU	78	JAA	SORTER,GH		58	62
0.00	INGBERMAN,M	WI	80	JAA			101	112
0.00	IVES,M	SU	85	JAA			253	268
0.00	JACOBS,FH	JA	87	TAR	MARSHALL,RM		67	78
0.00	JACOBSEN,LE	AP	63	TAR			285	292
0.00	JACOBSEN,LE	AU	64	JAR			221	228
0.00	JAIN,PC	SP	86	JAR			187	193

RESEARCH METHOD=ANALYTICAL - INTERNAL LOGIC

CITE INDEX	FIRST AUTHOR	ISSUE	YEAR	JOURNAL	SECOND AUTHOR	THIRD AUTHOR	PAG BEG	PAG END
0.00	JARRETT,JE	SP	72	JAR			108	112
0.00	JARRETT,JE	SP	74	JAR			63	66
0.00	JENKINS,DO	JL	64	TAR			648	653
0.00	JENSEN,MC	AP	85	JAE	ZIMMERMAN,JL		3	10
0.00	JENSEN,RE	JA	68	TAR	THOMSEN,CT		83	93
0.00	JENSEN,RE	JL	68	TAR			425	446
0.00	JENSEN,RE	JL	70	TAR			502	508
0.00	JENTZ,GA	JL	66	TAR			535	541
0.00	JERSTON,JE	OC	65	TAR			812	813
0.00	JEYNES,PH	JA	65	TAR			105	118
0.00	JOHNSON,GL	OC	65	TAR			821	823
0.00	JOHNSON,GL	JL	66	TAR			510	517
0.00	JOHNSON,GL	OC	67	TAR	NEWTON,SW		738	746
0.00	JOHNSON,O	SP	65	JAR			75	85
0.00	JOHNSON,O	JL	68	TAR			546	548
0.00	JOHNSON,O	OC	74	TAR	GUNN,S		649	663
0.00	JOHNSON,O	ST	81	JAR			89	119
0.00	JOHNSON,SB	SP	82	JAA	MESSIER JR,WF		195	213
0.00	JOHNSTON,DJ	SP	80	JAA	LEMON,WM	NEUMANN,FL	251	263
0.00	JOLIVET,V	JL	64	TAR			689	692
0.00	JUNG,WO	SP	88	JAR	KWON,YK		146	153
0.00	KABBES,SM	AP	65	TAR			395	400
0.00	KAHN,N	AU	85	JAA	SCHIFF,A		40	49
0.00	KALINSKI,BD	JL	63	TAR			591	595
0.00	KANODIA,CS	SP	85	JAR			175	193
0.00	KAPLAN,HG	JA	64	TAR	SOLOMON,KI		145	149
0.00	KARLINSKY,SS	WI	83	JAA			157	167
0.00	KARLINSKY,SS	AU	83	JAA			65	76
0.00	KATZ,BG	SU	87	JAA	OWEN,J		266	298
0.00	KAUFMAN,F	OC	67	TAR			713	720
0.00	KAY,RS	SU	79	JAA			307	315
0.00	KEISTER JR,OR	AP	63	TAR			371	376
0.00	KEISTER JR,OR	AP	64	TAR			414	416
0.00	KELL,WG	AP	68	TAR			266	273
0.00	KELLER,TF	JA	65	TAR			184	189
0.00	KEMP,PS	JA	63	TAR			126	132
0.00	KETZ,JE	AU	83	JAA	WYATT,AR		29	43
0.00	KING,RR	JA	74	TAR	BARON,CD		76	87
0.00	KING,TE	SP	79	JAA			209	223
0.00	KING,TE	JL	88	AUD	ORTEGREN,AK		522	535
0.00	KIRCHER,P	OC	65	TAR			742	752
0.00	KIRCHER,P	JL	67	TAR			537	543
0.00	KISSINGER,JN	SP	86	JAA			90	101
0.00	KISTNER,KP	SP	80	JAR	SALMI,T		297	311
0.00	KNIGHTS,D	05	87	AOS	COLLINSON,D		457	477
0.00	KOHLER,EL	AP	63	TAR			266	269
0.00	KOLLARITSCH,FP	AP	65	TAR			382	385
0.00	KRIPKE,H	AU	78	JAA			4	32
0.00	KUNITAKE,WK	SU	86	JAA	WHITE JR,CE		222	231
0.00	LAIBSTAIN,S	AP	71	TAR			342	351

CITE IND-EX	FIRST AUTHOR	ISS-UE	YE-AR	JOUR-NAL	SECOND AUTHOR	THIRD AUTHOR	PAG BEG	PAG END
0.00	LAMBERT,RA	AU	85	JAR			633	647
0.00	LAMDEN,CW	JA	64	TAR			128	132
0.00	LANDSITTEL,DL	SU	82	JAA	SERLIN,JE		291	300
0.00	LANDSMAN,WR	OC	88	TAR	MAGLIOLO,J		586	604
0.00	LANGHOLM,O	AU	65	JAR			218	227
0.00	LARGAY III,JA	JA	73	TAR			115	119
0.00	LARGAY III,JA	AU	83	JAA			44	53
0.00	LARSON,KD	OC	66	TAR	SCHATTKE,RW		634	641
0.00	LARSON,KD	OC	69	TAR	GONEDES,NJ		720	728
0.00	LAU,AH	SP	78	JAR	LAU,HS		80	102
0.00	LAUGHLIN,RC	05	87	AOS			479	502
0.00	LAUVER,RC	JA	66	TAR			65	74
0.00	LAVALLE,IH	AP	68	TAR	RAPPAPORT,A		225	230
0.00	LAVOIE,D	06	87	AOS			579	604
0.00	LEA,RB	AP	72	TAR			346	350
0.00	LEA,RB	SU	81	AUD			53	94
0.00	LEE,CJ	AU	84	JAR			776	781
0.00	LEE,GA	SP	73	JAR			47	61
0.00	LEE,GA	JL	81	TAR			539	553
0.00	LEE,LC	AP	69	TAR	BEDFORD,NM		256	275
0.00	LEE,SS	JL	65	TAR			622	625
0.00	LEMBKE,VC	JL	70	TAR			458	464
0.00	LEMBKE,VC	WI	81	JAA	TOOLE,HR		128	135
0.00	LENTILHON,RW	OC	64	TAR			880	883
0.00	LERE,JC	AP	86	TAR			318	324
0.00	LESSARD,DR	JL	77	TAR	LORANGE,P		628	637
0.00	LEV,B	OC	69	TAR			704	710
0.00	LEV,B	JL	70	TAR			532	534
0.00	LEV,B	AU	78	JAR	THEIL,H		286	293
0.00	LEV,B	JA	88	TAR			1	22
0.00	LI,DH	OC	63	TAR			771	775
0.00	LI,DH	JA	63	TAR			52	55
0.00	LI,DH	SP	63	JAR			102	107
0.00	LI,DH	OC	64	TAR			946	950
0.00	LIN,WT	AU	84	AUD	MOCK,TJ	WRIGHT,A	89	99
0.00	LINOWES,DF	JA	65	TAR			97	104
0.00	LITTLETON,AC	JL	70	TAR			476	480
0.00	LIVINGSTONE,JL	JA	69	TAR			48	64
0.00	LIVOCK,DM	SP	65	JAR			86	102
0.00	LONGSTRETH,B	WI	84	JAA			110	122
0.00	LORIG,AN	OC	63	TAR			759	763
0.00	LOUDERBACK,JG	AP	71	TAR			298	305
0.00	LOWE,HD	AP	63	TAR			293	301
0.00	LOWE,HD	AP	67	TAR			356	360
0.00	LUDMAN,EA	SP	86	JAA			118	124
0.00	LUNDHOLM,RJ	SP	88	JAR			107	118
0.00	LUNESKI,C	JL	64	TAR			591	597
0.00	LUNESKI,C	OC	67	TAR			767	771
0.00	LYNN,ES	AP	64	TAR			371	376
0.00	MACKENZIE,O	AP	64	TAR			363	370

RESEARCH METHOD=ANALYTICAL - INTERNAL LOGIC

CITE IND-EX	FIRST AUTHOR	ISS-UE	YE-AR	JOUR-NAL	SECOND AUTHOR	THIRD AUTHOR	PAG BEG	PAG END
0.00	MAGEE,RP	JA	88	TAR			42	54
0.00	MAHER,MW	SP	83	JAR	NANTELL,TJ		329	340
0.00	MAITRE,P	34	78	AOS			227	236
0.00	MAKSY,MM	OC	88	TAR			683	699
0.00	MANES,RP	JA	65	TAR	SMITH,VL		31	35
0.00	MANES,RP	SP	66	JAR			87	100
0.00	MANES,RP	JL	82	TAR	PARK,SH	JENSEN,RE	594	606
0.00	MARCH,JG	02	87	AOS			153	168
0.00	MARCINKO,D	JL	84	TAR	PETRI,E		488	495
0.00	MARPLE,RM	JL	63	TAR			478	482
0.00	MATEER,WH	JL	65	TAR			583	586
0.00	MATTINGLY,LA	OC	64	TAR			996	3
0.00	MAURIELLO,JA	JA	63	TAR			26	28
0.00	MAURIELLO,JA	AP	64	TAR			347	357
0.00	MAUTZ,RK	AP	65	TAR			299	311
0.00	MAUTZ,RK	JL	69	TAR	SKOUSEN,KF		447	456
0.00	MAUTZ,RK	AP	77	TAR	PREVITS,GJ		301	307
0.00	MAXIM,LD	JA	76	TAR	CULLEN,PE	COOK,FX	97	109
0.00	MAY,PT	JL	69	TAR			583	592
0.00	MCBRIDE,HJ	AP	63	TAR			363	370
0.00	MCCLENON,PR	JL	63	TAR			540	547
0.00	MCDONALD,DL	12	79	AOS	PUXTY,AG		53	66
0.00	MCINTYRE,EV	JL	82	TAR			607	618
0.00	MCKEOWN,JC	JL	72	TAR			527	532
0.00	MCRAE,TW	AU	65	JAR			255	260
0.00	MELBERG,WF	JA	72	TAR			116	133
0.00	MENSAH,YM	OC	82	TAR			681	700
0.00	MEPHAM,MJ	JA	83	TAR			43	57
0.00	MERINO,BD	OC	87	TAR	KOCH,BS	MACRITCHIE,KL	748	762
0.00	METCALF,RW	JA	64	TAR			16	21
0.00	MILLER,EM	AU	80	JAA			6	19
0.00	MILLER,HE	JA	66	TAR			1	7
0.00	MILLER,MC	AP	73	TAR			280	291
0.00	MITCHELL,GB	AP	70	TAR			308	314
0.00	MOBLEY,SC	AP	66	TAR			292	296
0.00	MOBLEY,SC	JA	67	TAR			114	123
0.00	MOBLEY,SC	AP	68	TAR			333	341
0.00	MOCK,TJ	AU	78	JAR	VASARHELYI,MA		414	423
0.00	MOCK,TJ	AU	82	AUD	WRIGHT,A		33	44
0.00	MOCK,TJ	SP	83	AUD	WILLINGHAM,JJ		91	99
0.00	MONSON,NP	OC	64	TAR	TRACY,JA		890	893
0.00	MOONITZ,M	SP	66	JAR			47	61
0.00	MOORE,CL	JA	64	TAR			94	102
0.00	MORENO,RG	OC	64	TAR			990	995
0.00	MOREY,L	JA	63	TAR			102	108
0.00	MORGAN,G	05	88	AOS			477	485
0.00	MORRISON,TA	OC	66	TAR			704	713
0.00	MORRISON,TA	JL	68	TAR	BUZBY,SL		517	521
0.00	MOST,KS	JA	69	TAR			145	152
0.00	MUELLER,GG	JA	63	TAR			142	147

RESEARCH METHOD=ANALYTICAL - INTERNAL LOGIC

CITE IND-EX	FIRST AUTHOR	ISS-UE	YE-AR	JOUR-NAL	SECOND AUTHOR	THIRD AUTHOR	PAG BEG	PAG END
0.00	MUELLER,GG	AU	64	JAR			148	157
0.00	MUELLER,GG	AP	65	TAR			386	394
0.00	MURRAY,D	AU	83	JAA	JOHNSON,R		4	15
0.00	NAKANO,I	OC	72	TAR			693	708
0.00	NELSON,GK	JA	66	TAR			42	47
0.00	NELSON,J	SU	88	JAA	RONEN,J	WHITE,L	255	296
0.00	NEUBIG,RD	JA	64	TAR			86	89
0.00	NICHOLS,AC	OC	68	TAR	GRAWOIG,DE		631	639
0.00	NOBES,CW	AP	82	TAR			303	310
0.00	NORDHAUSER,SL	JA	81	TAR	KRAMER,JL		54	69
0.00	NOREEN,EW	04	88	AOS			359	369
0.00	NURNBERG,H	AU	70	JAR			217	231
0.00	NURNBERG,H	OC	72	TAR			655	665
0.00	NURNBERG,H	AU	85	JAA	CIANCIOLO,ST		50	59
0.00	O'CONNOR,MC	AP	72	TAR	HAMRE,JC		308	319
0.00	OLIPHANT,WJ	ST	71	JAR			93	98
0.00	ONSI,M	AP	67	TAR			321	330
0.00	OVADIA,A	WI	83	JAA	RONEN,J		115	129
0.00	OWEN,DL	03	85	AOS	LLOYD,AJ		329	352
0.00	PAINE,NR	AP	64	TAR			330	332
0.00	PARKE,R	03	81	AOS	PETERSON,JL		235	246
0.00	PARKER,WM	OC	63	TAR			785	788
0.00	PARKER,WM	AU	66	JAR			149	154
0.00	PATON,WA	AP	63	TAR			243	251
0.00	PATON,WA	SP	63	JAR			44	72
0.00	PATON,WA	JA	67	TAR			7	23
0.00	PATON,WA	SP	68	JAR			72	85
0.00	PATON,WA	AP	69	TAR			276	283
0.00	PATRICK,AW	JA	63	TAR	QUITTMEYER,CL		109	117
0.00	PATTERSON,RG	OC	67	TAR			772	774
0.00	PEASNELL,KV	JA	77	TAR			186	189
0.00	PEIRSON,G	OC	66	TAR			729	736
0.00	PELES,YC	AP	86	TAR			325	329
0.00	PERAGALLO,E	JA	83	TAR			98	104
0.00	PESANDO,JE	OC	83	TAR	CLARKE,CK		733	748
0.00	PETERSON,WA	AP	66	TAR			275	282
0.00	PETRI,E	JL	73	TAR			483	488
0.00	PETRI,E	JL	74	TAR	MINCH,RA		455	464
0.00	PETRI,E	AP	78	TAR	MINCH,RA		415	428
0.00	PETRI,E	AP	79	TAR	GELFAND,J		330	345
0.00	PHILIPS,GE	OC	63	TAR			696	708
0.00	PHILIPS,GE	JA	63	TAR			14	25
0.00	PHILIPS,GE	JA	68	TAR			10	17
0.00	PHILLIPS,LC	AP	65	TAR			377	381
0.00	POMERANZ,F	AU	77	JAA			45	52
0.00	PRATER,GI	OC	66	TAR			619	625
0.00	PRESTON,LE	03	81	AOS			255	262
0.00	PRINCE,TR	JL	64	TAR			553	562
0.00	PURDY,CR	AU	65	JAR			228	241
0.00	RABY,WL	JL	63	TAR	NEUBIG,RD		568	576

RESEARCH METHOD=ANALYTICAL - INTERNAL LOGIC

CITE INDEX	FIRST AUTHOR	ISSUE	YEAR	JOURNAL	SECOND AUTHOR	THIRD AUTHOR	PAG BEG	PAG END
0.00	RABY,WL	OC	66	TAR			714	720
0.00	RABY,WL	JA	69	TAR			1	11
0.00	RAMAN,KK	SU	81	JAA			352	359
0.00	RAPPAPORT,A	OC	64	TAR			951	962
0.00	RAPPAPORT,A	AP	69	TAR			297	299
0.00	RATSCH,H	JA	64	TAR			140	144
0.00	RAUN,DL	OC	63	TAR			754	758
0.00	RAUN,DL	OC	64	TAR			927	945
0.00	RAVIV,A	AP	85	JAE			239	246
0.00	RAYMAN,RA	SP	69	JAR			53	89
0.00	REVSINE,L	AP	69	TAR			354	358
0.00	REVSINE,L	JL	71	TAR			480	489
0.00	REYNOLDS,IN	AP	64	TAR			342	346
0.00	RICHARD,DL	OC	68	TAR			730	737
0.00	RICHARDSON,AJ	04	87	AOS			341	355
0.00	ROBBINS,SM	AU	77	JAA			5	18
0.00	ROBERTS,DM	AU	80	JAA			57	69
0.00	ROBERTSON,JC	WI	81	JAA	ALDERMAN,CW		144	161
0.00	ROBERTSON,JC	SP	84	AUD			57	67
0.00	ROBINSON,LA	JA	64	TAR	HALL,TP		62	69
0.00	RODEN,PF	WI	87	JAA			79	89
0.00	ROLLER,J	AP	67	TAR	WILLIAMS,TH		349	355
0.00	RONEN,J	AU	70	JAR			232	252
0.00	RONEN,J	AU	88	JAR	BALACHANDRAN,KR		300	314
0.00	RORKE,CH	03	82	AOS			305	306
0.00	ROSE,H	AU	64	JAR			137	147
0.00	ROSEN,LS	JA	67	TAR			106	113
0.00	ROSENFIELD,P	OC	69	TAR			788	797
0.00	ROSS,H	ST	70	JAR			108	115
0.00	ROSS,WR	JL	66	TAR			464	473
0.00	RUNDFELT,R	SP	86	JAA			125	130
0.00	SALAMON,GL	AP	82	TAR			292	302
0.00	SALGADO,AP	AP	63	TAR			389	397
0.00	SAMUELSON,LA	01	86	AOS			35	46
0.00	SAMUELSON,RA	AP	80	TAR			254	268
0.00	SAN MIGUEL,JG	02	77	AOS			177	186
0.00	SAPIENZA,SR	JL	64	TAR			582	590
0.00	SAPIENZA,SR	SP	64	JAR			50	66
0.00	SAVOIE,LM	ST	69	JAR			55	62
0.00	SCHACHNER,L	AP	68	TAR			303	311
0.00	SCHACHTER,B	AU	85	JAR			907	910
0.00	SCHATTKE,RW	AP	72	TAR			233	244
0.00	SCHIENEMAN,GS	AU	79	JAA			21	30
0.00	SCHIENEMAN,GS	SP	83	JAA			212	226
0.00	SCHIFF,M	AU	77	JAA	SORTER,GH	WIESEN,JL	19	44
0.00	SCHNEE,EJ	AU	81	JAA	TAYLOR,ME		18	29
0.00	SCHNEIDER,AJ	AP	67	TAR			342	348
0.00	SCHULTE JR,AA	OC	66	TAR			721	728
0.00	SCHWARTZ,BN	SP	81	JAA			238	247
0.00	SCOTT,RA	OC	79	TAR			750	763

RESEARCH METHOD=ANALYTICAL - INTERNAL LOGIC

CITE INDEX	FIRST AUTHOR	ISSUE	YEAR	JOURNAL	SECOND AUTHOR	THIRD AUTHOR	PAG BEG	PAG END
0.00	SCOTT,WR	SP	79	JAR			156	178
0.00	SEAGLE,JP	JA	77	TAR	PETRI,E		124	136
0.00	SEAMAN,JL	JL	65	TAR			617	621
0.00	SEELYE,AL	AP	63	TAR			302	309
0.00	SEIDLER,LJ	SU	79	JAA			285	293
0.00	SEILER,RE	OC	66	TAR			652	656
0.00	SHERMAN,HD	AU	84	AUD			35	53
0.00	SHILLINGLAW,G	SP	63	JAR			73	85
0.00	SHWAYDER,KR	JA	68	TAR			101	104
0.00	SHWAYDER,KR	SP	68	JAR			86	97
0.00	SHWAYDER,KR	AP	70	TAR			299	307
0.00	SHWAYDER,KR	OC	72	TAR			747	760
0.00	SIMMONS,JK	OC	67	TAR			680	692
0.00	SKERRATT,LC	SU	84	JAA			362	368
0.00	SMIELIAUSKAS,W	JA	86	TAR			118	128
0.00	SMITH,VL	AU	87	AUD	SCHATZBERG,J	WALLER,WS	71	93
0.00	SMOLINSKI,EJ	AU	63	JAR			149	178
0.00	SOLOMONS,D	JL	68	TAR			447	452
0.00	SOMMERFELD,RM	OC	67	TAR			747	750
0.00	SORTER,GH	ST	74	JAR	GANS,MS		1	12
0.00	SORTER,GH	SP	82	JAA			188	194
0.00	SORTER,GH	SP	87	JAA	INGBERMAN,M		99	116
0.00	SORTER,GH	SU	88	JAA	SIEGEL,S	SLAIN,J	233	244
0.00	SOTTO,R	01	83	AOS			57	72
0.00	SPACEK,L	AP	64	TAR			275	284
0.00	SPENCER,MH	AP	63	TAR			310	316
0.00	SPICER,BH	03	88	AOS			303	322
0.00	SPILLER JR,EA	OC	64	TAR			850	859
0.00	SPROUSE,RT	OC	63	TAR			687	695
0.00	SPROUSE,RT	JL	65	TAR			522	526
0.00	SRIVASTAVA,RP	AU	86	JAR			422	427
0.00	ST.PIERRE,K	SP	84	JAA			257	263
0.00	STAATS,EB	SU	81	AUD			1	11
0.00	STANDISH,PEM	JL	64	TAR			654	666
0.00	STANLEY,CH	JL	64	TAR			639	647
0.00	STAUBUS,GJ	JA	63	TAR			64	74
0.00	STAUBUS,GJ	JL	66	TAR			397	412
0.00	STEINBART,PJ	JA	87	TAR			97	116
0.00	STERLING,RR	JL	71	TAR	FLAHERTY,RE		441	456
0.00	STETTLER,HF	OC	65	TAR			723	730
0.00	STONE,DE	AP	67	TAR			331	337
0.00	STONE,ML	ST	68	JAR			59	66
0.00	STONE,WE	JA	64	TAR			38	42
0.00	STONE,WE	AU	72	JAR			345	350
0.00	STREER,PJ	SU	79	JAA			329	338
0.00	SUH,YS	SP	88	JAR			154	168
0.00	SUMMERS,EL	SP	70	JAR	DESKINS,JW		113	117
0.00	SUNDER,S	SP	83	JAR			222	233
0.00	SUSSMAN,MR	AP	65	TAR			407	413
0.00	SWANSON,GA	JL	88	TAR	GARDNER,JC		436	447

RESEARCH METHOD=ANALYTICAL - INTERNAL LOGIC

CITE IND-EX	FIRST AUTHOR	ISS-UE	YE-AR	JOUR -NAL	SECOND AUTHOR	THIRD AUTHOR	PAG BEG	PAG END
0.00	TAMURA,H	SP	85	AUD			133	142
0.00	TAUSSIG,RA	JL	63	TAR			562	567
0.00	TAUSSIG,RA	SP	64	JAR			67	79
0.00	TAYLOR,RG	JA	65	TAR			89	96
0.00	TAYLOR,WM	AU	82	JAR	WEYGANDT,JJ		497	502
0.00	THOMAS,AL	JL	64	TAR			574	581
0.00	THOMAS,AL	JA	64	TAR			1	11
0.00	THOMAS,AL	SP	65	JAR			103	113
0.00	THOMAS,JK	JL	88	JAE			199	237
0.00	THOMPSON,WW	JL	65	TAR	KEMPER,EL		574	578
0.00	TINKER,T	01	87	AOS	NEIMARK,M		71	88
0.00	TINKER,T	02	88	AOS			165	189
0.00	TOBA,Y	OC	80	TAR			604	619
0.00	TOPIOL,J	JA	66	TAR			83	91
0.00	TOWNSEND,LA	JA	67	TAR			1	6
0.00	TRUEBLOOD,RM	SP	63	JAR			86	95
0.00	TRUEBLOOD,RM	ST	66	JAR			183	191
0.00	TRUMBULL,WP	JA	63	TAR			46	51
0.00	TRUMBULL,WP	JL	68	TAR			459	468
0.00	TUCKERMAN,B	JA	64	TAR			32	37
0.00	ULLMANN,AA	12	79	AOS			123	134
0.00	VANCE,LL	JA	66	TAR			48	51
0.00	VANCE,LL	OC	69	TAR			692	703
0.00	VASARHELYI,MA	AU	84	AUD			100	106
0.00	VERRECCHIA,RE	JL	82	TAR			579	593
0.00	VERRECCHIA,RE	ST	87	JAR	LANEN,WN		165	189
0.00	VOGT,RA	01	77	AOS			59	80
0.00	WADE,HH	OC	63	TAR			714	718
0.00	WAGNER,JW	JL	69	TAR			600	604
0.00	WAKEMAN,LM	DE	80	JAE			213	237
0.00	WALKER,M	AP	84	TAR			278	286
0.00	WALKER,NR	AU	88	AUD	PIERCE,LT		1	22
0.00	WALLACE,WA	SP	83	AUD			66	90
0.00	WATKINS,PR	SP	84	JAR			406	411
0.00	WAUGH,JB	JL	68	TAR			535	539
0.00	WEBER,RP	JA	77	TAR			172	185
0.00	WEIGAND,RE	JL	63	TAR			584	590
0.00	WEIL,RL	OC	73	TAR			749	758
0.00	WEINGARTER,HM	AU	63	JAR			213	224
0.00	WEISER,HJ	JL	66	TAR			518	524
0.00	WELKE,WR	AP	66	TAR			253	256
0.00	WELLS,MC	OC	65	TAR	COTTON,W		829	833
0.00	WELLS,MC	AP	68	TAR			373	376
0.00	WELSCH,GA	OC	64	TAR			8	13
0.00	WELSH,MJ	WI	85	JAA	TRAPNELL,JE		100	111
0.00	WERNER,CA	AU	83	JAA	KOSTOLANSKY,JW		54	64
0.00	WERNER,CA	SP	84	JAA	KOSTOLANSKY,JW		212	224
0.00	WHEELER,JT	JA	70	TAR			1	10
0.00	WHITE,D	SU	82	JAA	VANECEK,M		338	354
0.00	WHITTINGTON,OR	SU	82	JAA	ADAMS,SJ		310	319

RESEARCH METHOD=ANALYTICAL - INTERNAL LOGIC

CITE IND-EX	FIRST AUTHOR	ISS-UE	YE-AR	JOUR-NAL	SECOND AUTHOR	THIRD AUTHOR	PAG BEG	PAG END
0.00	WIESEN,JL	WI	79	JAA	ENG,R		101	121
0.00	WIESEN,JL	SU	81	JAA			309	324
0.00	WILKINSON,TL	JA	64	TAR			133	139
0.00	WILLIAMS,D	AP	66	TAR			226	234
0.00	WILLIAMS,JJ	02	81	AOS			153	166
0.00	WILLIAMS,PF	04	82	AOS			405	410
0.00	WILLIAMS,PF	02	87	AOS			169	192
0.00	WILLIAMS,TH	OC	67	TAR	GRIFFIN,CH		642	649
0.00	WILLIAMSON,JE	JA	71	TAR			139	148
0.00	WILLINGER,GL	SP	85	JAR			351	359
0.00	WILLINGHAM,JJ	JL	64	TAR			543	552
0.00	WINBORNE,MG	OC	66	TAR	KLEESPIE,DC		737	744
0.00	WINDAL,FW	JA	63	TAR			29	36
0.00	WINJUM,JO	AU	71	JAR			333	350
0.00	WOLK,HI	JL	70	TAR			544	552
0.00	WOLK,HI	AP	73	TAR	TEARNEY,MG		292	299
0.00	WOODS,RS	JL	64	TAR			598	614
0.00	WOOLSEY,SM	OC	63	TAR			709	713
0.00	WRIGHT,FK	JA	63	TAR			87	90
0.00	WRIGHT,FK	SP	64	JAR			80	90
0.00	WRIGHT,FK	AU	67	JAR			173	179
0.00	WRIGHT,FK	AU	68	JAR			222	236
0.00	WRIGHT,HW	OC	66	TAR			626	633
0.00	WYATT,AR	JL	65	TAR			527	535
0.00	WYMAN,HE	JL	76	TAR			545	558
0.00	YAMEY,BS	JL	80	TAR			419	425
0.00	YOUNG,AE	SP	80	JAA			244	250
0.00	YOUNG,R	SP	86	JAR			231	240
0.00	YOUNG,SD	SP	85	JAA			178	183
0.00	YOUNG,TN	AP	67	TAR	PEIRSON,CG		338	341
0.00	YU,SC	JA	66	TAR			8	20
0.00	YU,SC	JL	69	TAR			571	582
0.00	ZANNETOS,ZS	JL	63	TAR			528	533
0.00	ZANNETOS,ZS	AP	63	TAR			326	335
0.00	ZANNETOS,ZS	OC	64	TAR			860	868
0.00	ZANNETOS,ZS	JL	67	TAR			566	571
0.00	ZEFF,SA	JA	65	TAR	MAXWELL,WD		65	75
0.00	ZEFF,SA	JL	82	TAR			528	553

RESEARCH METHOD=ANALYTICAL - INTERNAL LOGIC

2.2 RESEARCH METHOD=ANALYTICAL - SIMULATION

CITE IND-EX	FIRST AUTHOR	ISS-UE	YE-AR	JOUR-NAL	SECOND AUTHOR	THIRD AUTHOR	PAG BEG	PAG END
1.46	KAPLAN,RS	AU	73	JAR			238	258
1.40	COLLINS,DW	SP	84	JAR	DENT,WT		48	84
0.86	LEITCH,RA	AP	82	TAR	NETER,J	PLANTE,R	384	400
0.85	MAGEE,RP	JL	76	TAR			529	544
0.82	NETER,J	JA	78	TAR	LEITCH,RA	FIENBERG,SE	77	93
0.70	GARSTKA,SJ	SP	79	JAR	OHLSON,PA		23	59
0.69	SCOTT,WR	ST	75	JAR			98	117
0.67	MESSIER JR,WF	AU	83	JAR			611	618
0.60	DWORIN,L	AP	84	TAR	GRIMLUND,RA		218	241
0.60	DYCKMAN,TR	ST	84	JAR	PHILBRICK,D	STEPHAN,J	1	30
0.60	MCCRAY,JH	JA	84	TAR			35	51
0.60	MENZEFRICKE,U	AU	84	JAR	SMIELIAUSKAS,W		588	604
0.57	FROST,PA	SP	82	JAR	TAMURA,H		103	120
0.57	SILHAN,PA	SP	82	JAR			255	262
0.55	RENEAU,JH	JL	78	TAR			669	680
0.54	DEMSKI,JS	JL	72	TAR	FELTHAM,GA		533	548
0.50	CASLER,DJ	SP	85	JAR	HALL,TW		110	122
0.50	TSUI,KW	JA	85	TAR	MATSUMURA,EM	TSUI,KL	76	96
0.46	SIMMONS,JK	OC	69	TAR	GRAY,J		757	776
0.42	FELTHAM,GA	SP	77	JAR			42	70
0.40	DITTMAN,DA	AP	79	TAR	PRAKASH,P		358	373
0.40	GODFREY,JT	AU	84	JAR	NETER,J		497	525
0.40	KINNEY JR,WR	AU	79	JAR			456	475
0.33	COHEN,MA	AU	80	JAR	HALPERIN,R		375	389
0.33	DHARAN,BG	SP	83	JAR			18	41
0.33	DWORIN,L	JA	86	TAR	GRIMLUND,RA		36	57
0.33	ROBERTS,DM	SP	86	JAR			111	126
0.33	TAMURA,H	AU	86	JAR	FROST,PA		364	371
0.31	FERRARA,WL	AP	72	TAR	HAYYA,JC	NACHMAN,DA	299	307
0.25	BIDDLE,GC	SP	85	JAR	MARTIN,RK		57	83
0.25	GARSTKA,SJ	AU	77	JAR			179	192
0.25	WEBER,RP	JL	81	TAR	STEVENSON,WC		596	612
0.23	DEMSKI,JS	JA	70	TAR			76	87
0.22	BECK,PJ	SP	80	JAR			16	37
0.18	LIN,WT	JA	78	TAR			61	76
0.17	MAGEE,RP	OC	77	TAR			869	880
0.15	DEMSKI,JS	AP	71	TAR			268	278
0.15	GREENBALL,MN	SP	68	JAR			114	129
0.15	LIVINGSTONE,JL	AU	70	JAR	SALAMON,GL		199	216
0.15	REVSINE,L	AP	76	TAR	THIES,JB		255	268
0.15	WYMAN,HE	JL	73	TAR			489	493
0.14	EMERY,DR	AU	82	JAR	BARRON,FH	MESSIER JR,WF	450	458
0.14	KINNEY JR,WR	AU	82	JAR	SALAMON,GL		350	366
0.08	ABEL,R	SP	69	JAR			1	11
0.08	DAVIDSON,S	AU	66	JAR	KOHLMEIER,JM		183	212
0.08	FRANKFURTER,GM	AP	72	TAR	HORWITZ,BN		245	259
0.08	LIVINGSTONE,JL	AU	69	JAR			245	256
0.08	MAGEE,RP	JA	77	TAR			190	199

RESEARCH METHOD=ANALYTICAL - SIMULATION

CITE INDEX	FIRST AUTHOR	ISSUE	YEAR	JOURNAL	SECOND AUTHOR	THIRD AUTHOR	PAG BEG	PAG END
0.08	SCHWAB,B	AP	69	TAR	NICOL,RE		292	296
0.08	SHWAYDER,KR	AU	73	JAR			259	272
0.08	WELLING,P	04	77	AOS			307	316
0.00	ANDERSON,JC	JL	86	TAR	KRAUSHAAR,JM		379	399
0.00	BAILEY JR,AD	SP	68	JAR	GRAY,J		98	105
0.00	BARKMAN,A	JA	77	TAR			450	464
0.00	BORITZ,JE	AU	86	AUD	BROCA,DS		1	19
0.00	BRIGHAM,EF	JA	86	TAR			46	61
0.00	BRIGHAM,EF	JL	74	TAR	NANTELL,TJ		436	447
0.00	BRUNDAGE,MV	JL	69	TAR	LIVINGSTONE,JL		539	545
0.00	COGLITORE,F	SP	88	AUD	BERRYMAN,RG		150	163
0.00	COMISKEY,EE	AP	68	TAR	MLYNARCZYK,FA		248	256
0.00	DEMSKI,JS	SP	69	JAR			96	115
0.00	FEINSCHREIBER,R	SP	69	JAR			17	21
0.00	FERRARA,WL	JL	77	TAR			597	604
0.00	FINLEY,DR	SP	87	AUD	BOOCKHOLDT,JL		22	39
0.00	FIRMIN,PA	ST	68	JAR	GOODMAN,SS	HENDRICKS,TE	122	155
0.00	FREDRIKSON,EB	AU	68	JAR			208	221
0.00	FROST,PA	SP	86	JAR	TAMURA,H		57	75
0.00	GERLACH,JH	SP	88	AUD			61	76
0.00	GREENBALL,MN	ST	68	JAR			27	49
0.00	GRIMLUND,RA	AU	85	JAR			575	594
0.00	GRIMLUND,RA	JL	87	TAR	FELIX JR,WL		455	479
0.00	GRIMLUND,RA	SP	88	AUD			77	104
0.00	GRIMLUND,RA	AU	88	AUD	SCHROEDER,MS		53	62
0.00	GYNTHER,MM	OC	68	TAR			706	718
0.00	HUSS,HF	AU	86	JAR	TRADER,RL		394	399
0.00	JENSEN,HL	OC	76	TAR	WYNDELTS,RW		846	853
0.00	KIM,HS	SP	87	AUD	NETER,J	GODFREY,JT	40	58
0.00	KNECHEL,WR	SP	85	JAR			194	212
0.00	KNECHEL,WR	SP	85	AUD			38	62
0.00	KNECHEL,WR	JA	88	TAR			74	95
0.00	KNECHEL,WR	AU	88	AUD			87	107
0.00	KO,CE	SP	88	AUD	NACHTSHEIM,CJ	DUKE,GL	119	136
0.00	LILLESTOL,J	SP	81	JAR			263	267
0.00	LOEBBECKE,JK	SP	87	AUD	STEINBART,PJ		74	89
0.00	MCCOSH,AM	OC	67	TAR			693	700
0.00	MCNICHOLS,M	JL	88	JAE			239	273
0.00	MEHTA,DR	SP	68	JAR	ANDREWS,VL		50	57
0.00	MENZEFRICKE,U	AU	84	JAR			570	587
0.00	NIKOLAI,LA	JA	79	TAR	ELAM,R		119	131
0.00	NURNBERG,H	AU	69	JAR			257	261
0.00	PLANTE,R	AU	85	AUD	NETER,J	LEITCH,RA	40	56
0.00	RAMANATHAN,KV	OC	71	TAR	RAPPAPORT,A		733	745
0.00	ROHRBACH.KJ	SP	86	JAR			127	150
0.00	ROSHWALB,A	AU	87	AUD	WRIGHT,RL	GODFREY,JT	54	70
0.00	SMIELIAUSKAS,W	AU	85	JAR			718	739
0.00	SMIELIAUSKAS,W	SP	86	JAR			217	230
0.00	SWENSON,CW	JA	87	TAR			117	136
0.00	TAUSSIG,RA	WI	83	JAA			142	156

RESEARCH METHOD=ANALYTICAL - SIMULATION

CITE IND- EX	FIRST AUTHOR	ISS- UE	YE- AR	JOUR -NAL	SECOND AUTHOR	THIRD AUTHOR	PAG BEG	PAG END
0.00	VASARHELYI,MA	SP	84	AUD	BAILEY JR,AD	CAMARDESSE JR,JE	98	103

RESEARCH METHOD=ANALYTICAL - SIMULATION

2.3 RESEARCH METHOD=ARCHIVAL - PRIMARY

CITE IND-EX	FIRST AUTHOR	ISS-UE	YE-AR	JOUR-NAL	SECOND AUTHOR	THIRD AUTHOR	PAG BEG	PAG END
7.91	WATTS,RL	JA	78	TAR	ZIMMERMAN,JL		112	134
7.00	BALL,R	AU	68	JAR	BROWN,P		159	178
4.85	BEAVER,WH	ST	68	JAR			67	92
4.54	PATELL,JM	AU	76	JAR			246	276
4.25	FOSTER,G	JA	77	TAR			1	21
4.20	BEAVER,WH	AU	79	JAR	CLARKE,R	WRIGHT,WF	316	340
3.88	COLLINS,DW	MR	81	JAE	ROZEFF,MS	DHALIWAL,DS	37	71
3.80	HAGERMAN,RL	AG	79	JAE	ZMIJEWSKI,ME		141	161
3.63	LEFTWICH,RW	MR	81	JAE			3	36
3.50	HEALY,PM	AP	85	JAE			85	108
3.50	HOLTHAUSEN,RW	MR	81	JAE			73	109
3.00	COLLINS,DW	MR	79	JAE	DENT,WT		3	44
3.00	GONEDES,NJ	SP	76	JAR	DOPUCH,N	PENMAN,SH	89	137
3.00	WILSON,GP	AP	87	TAR			293	322
2.67	SCHIPPER,K	SP	83	JAR	THOMPSON,R		184	221
2.58	WATTS,RL	AU	77	JAR	LEFTWICH,RW		253	271
2.54	BALL,R	ST	72	JAR			1	38
2.50	ATIASE,RK	SP	85	JAR			21	36
2.50	BERNARD,VL	SP	87	JAR			1	48
2.50	BROWN,LD	AP	87	JAE	GRIFFIN,PA	HAGERMAN,RL	61	87
2.50	LARCKER,DF	AP	83	JAE			3	30
2.44	BEAVER,WH	MR	80	JAE	LAMBERT,RA	MORSE,D	3	28
2.43	BEAVER,WH	JL	82	JAE	GRIFFIN,PA	LANDSMAN,WR	15	39
2.43	BIDDLE,GC	AU	82	JAR	LINDAHL,FW		551	588
2.40	CHAMBERS,AE	SP	84	JAR	PENMAN,SH		21	47
2.40	DYCKMAN,TR	MR	79	JAE	SMITH,AJ		45	75
2.40	LEV,B	JL	79	TAR			485	503
2.29	RICKS,WE	AU	82	JAR			367	387
2.25	GRIFFIN,PA	SP	77	JAR			71	83
2.23	GONEDES,NJ	AU	75	JAR			220	256
2.23	SUNDER,S	ST	73	JAR			1	45
2.20	BROWN,LD	SP	79	JAR	ROZEFF,MS		179	189
2.17	LEFTWICH,RW	JA	83	TAR			23	42
2.08	BEAVER,WH	OC	70	TAR	KETTLER,P	SCHOLES,M	654	682
2.00	ALBRECHT,WS	AU	77	JAR	LOOKABILL,LL	MCKEOWN,JC	226	244
2.00	BEAVER,WH	AG	80	JAE	CHRISTIE,AA	GRIFFIN,PA	127	157
2.00	BROWN,LD	JL	87	JAE	GRIFFIN,PA	HAGERMAN,RL	159	193
2.00	HUGHES,JS	JA	87	TAR	RICKS,WE		158	175
2.00	RAYBURN,J	ST	86	JAR			112	137
1.92	MAY,RG	ST	71	JAR			119	163
1.89	PENMAN,SH	SP	80	JAR			132	160
1.86	GIVOLY,D	JL	82	TAR	PALMON,D		486	508
1.82	GONEDES,NJ	SP	78	JAR			26	79
1.75	FOSTER,G	DE	81	JAE			201	232
1.75	JOHNSON,JR	AP	81	TAR	LEITCH,RA	NETER,J	270	293
1.75	MURPHY,KJ	AP	85	JAE			11	42
1.71	PATELL,JM	JL	82	TAR	WOLFSON,MA		509	527
1.67	GHEYARA,K	AG	80	JAE	BOATSMAN,JR		107	125

RESEARCH METHOD=ARCHIVAL - PRIMARY

CITE IND-EX	FIRST AUTHOR	ISS-UE	YE-AR	JOUR-NAL	SECOND AUTHOR	THIRD AUTHOR	PAG BEG	PAG END
1.62	BEAVER,WH	AP	72	TAR	DUKES,RE		320	332
1.60	DODD,P	AP	84	JAE	DOPUCH,N	HOLTHAUSEN,RW	3	38
1.56	BIDDLE,GC	ST	80	JAR			235	280
1.56	RO,BT	AG	80	JAE			159	189
1.54	SUNDER,S	AP	75	TAR			305	315
1.50	BUBLITZ,B	ST	85	JAR	FRECKA,TJ	MCKEOWN,JC	1	23
1.50	COUGHLAN,AT	AP	85	JAE	SCHMIDT,RM		43	66
1.50	PATELL,JM	AU	81	JAR	WOLFSON,MA		434	458
1.44	DUKES,RE	ST	80	JAR	DYCKMAN,TR	ELLIOTT,JA	1	26
1.44	GRANT,EB	SP	80	JAR			255	268
1.44	OHLSON,JA	SP	80	JAR			109	131
1.40	FOSTER,G	OC	84	TAR	OLSEN,C	SHEVLIN,T	574	603
1.38	BEAVER,WH	ST	66	JAR			71	111
1.38	BEAVER,WH	ST	70	JAR			62	99
1.33	BAMBER,LS	SP	86	JAR			40	56
1.33	HARRISON,T	SP	77	JAR			84	107
1.33	PALMROSE,ZV	SP	86	JAR			97	110
1.33	WILSON,GP	ST	86	JAR		165	203	
1.33	ZIMMERMAN,JL	AG	83	JAE			119	149
1.31	FOSTER,G	SP	73	JAR			25	37
1.30	PATELL,JM	AG	79	JAE	WOLFSON,MA		117	140
1.29	LILIEN,S	DE	82	JAE	PASTENA,V		145	170
1.25	NOREEN,EW	AP	81	TAR	SEPE,J		253	269
1.22	COLLINS,WA	AU	80	JAR	HOPWOOD,WS		390	406
1.20	KINNEY JR,WR	ST	79	JAR			148	165
1.20	ZMIJEWSKI,ME	ST	84	JAR			59	82
1.18	HONG,H	JA	78	TAR	KAPLAN,RS	MANDELKER,G	31	47
1.15	ARCHIBALD,TR	JA	72	TAR			22	30
1.15	BROWN,P	ST	67	JAR	BALL,R		55	77
1.15	DEAKIN,EB	SP	72	JAR			167	179
1.15	GONEDES,NJ	AU	73	JAR			212	237
1.14	CHOW,CW	AP	82	TAR			272	291
1.14	DUKE,GL	SP	82	JAR	NETER,J	LEITCH,RA	42	67
1.13	MORSE,D	AU	81	JAR			374	383
1.11	BROWN,RM	SP	80	JAR			38	63
1.09	ABDEL-KHALIK,AR	OC	78	TAR	MCKEOWN,JC		851	868
1.09	CRICHFIELD,T	JL	78	TAR	DYCKMAN,TR	LAKONISHOK,J	651	668
1.08	DOPUCH,N	SP	72	JAR	WATTS,RL		180	194
1.00	ABDEL-KHALIK,AR	AU	85	JAR			427	447
1.00	BASI,BA	AP	76	TAR	CAREY,KJ	TWARK,RD	244	254
1.00	BEAVER,WH	JL	87	JAE	LAMBERT,RA	RYAN,SG	139	157
1.00	BELL,TB	SP	83	JAR			1	17
1.00	BIDDLE,GC	AU	88	JAR	RICKS,WE		169	194
1.00	BROWN,LD	SP	87	JAR	RICHARDSON,GD	SCHWAGER,SJ	49	67
1.00	COLLINS,DW	JA	82	TAR	ROZEFF,MS	SALATKA,WK	1	17
1.00	COLLINS,DW	JL	87	JAE	KOTHARI,SP	RAYBURN,JD	111	138
1.00	DEAKIN,EB	OC	79	TAR			722	734
1.00	ELLIOTT,JA	AU	82	JAR			617	638
1.00	ELLIOTT,JA	SP	84	JAR	RICHARDSON,G	DYCKMAN,TR	85	102
1.00	EVANS III,JH	AG	83	JAE	PATTON,JM		151	175

RESEARCH METHOD=ARCHIVAL   - PRIMARY

CITE IND- EX	FIRST AUTHOR	ISS- UE	YE- AR	JOUR -NAL	SECOND AUTHOR	THIRD AUTHOR	PAG BEG	PAG END
1.00	FREEMAN,RN	JL	87	JAE			195	228
1.00	GIVOLY,D	DE	79	JAE	LAKONISHOK,J		165	185
1.00	GONEDES,NJ	SP	74	JAR			26	62
1.00	HARRIS,TS	OC	87	TAR	OHLSON,JA		651	670
1.00	HEALY,PM	AP	87	JAE	KANG,SH	PALEPU,KG	7	34
1.00	HUGHES,JS	AG	84	JAE	RICKS,WE		101	132
1.00	IMHOFF JR,EA	AU	82	JAR	PARE,PV		429	439
1.00	JAIN,PC	DE	82	JAE			205	228
1.00	LIBERTY,SE	OC	86	TAR	ZIMMERMAN,JL	692	712	
1.00	LYS,T	AP	84	JAE			39	65
1.00	MORSE,D	SP	83	JAR	RICHARDSON,G		106	127
1.00	RUBIN,MA	AP	88	TAR			219	236
1.00	WAYMIRE,G	AU	84	JAR			703	718
1.00	ZIMMER,I	MR	86	JAE			37	52
0.92	CUSHING,BE	AU	69	JAR			196	203
0.92	EGGLETON,IRC	SP	76	JAR	PENMAN,SH	TWOMBLY,JR	66	88
0.92	GOSMAN,ML	JA	73	TAR			1	11
0.92	KINNEY JR,WR	SP	71	JAR			127	136
0.92	MCDONALD,CL	JL	73	TAR			502	510
0.92	ZIMMERMAN,JL	ST	77	JAR			107	144
0.91	KINNEY JR,WR	JA	78	TAR			48	60
0.90	LOREK,KS	SP	79	JAR			190	204
0.90	RAMAGE,JG	ST	79	JAR	KRIEGER,AM	SPERO,LL	72	102
0.88	BROWN,PR	SP	81	JAR			232	246
0.88	EICHENSEHER,JW	JL	81	TAR	DANOS,P		479	492
0.88	SMITH,AJ	ST	81	JAR			174	211
0.86	FREEMAN,RN	AU	82	JAR	OHLSON,JA	PENMAN,SH	639	653
0.83	DALEY,LA	DE	83	JAE	VIGELAND,RL		195	211
0.83	FREEMAN,RN	SP	83	JAR			42	64
0.83	JOY,OM	AU	77	JAR	LITZENBERGER,RH	MCENALLY,RW	207	225
0.83	PINCUS,M	SP	83	JAR			155	183
0.80	KROSS,W	SP	84	JAR	SCHROEDER,DA		153	176
0.80	MARAIS,ML	ST	84	JAR			34	54
0.80	SCHAEFER,TF	AU	84	JAR			647	656
0.78	WHITTRED,GP	OC	80	TAR			563	577
0.77	COPELAND,RM	ST	68	JAR			101	116
0.77	LOREK,KS	AP	76	TAR	MCDONALD,CL	PATZ,DH	321	330
0.77	SMITH,ED	OC	76	TAR			707	723
0.75	ANTLE,R	SP	85	JAR	SMITH,A		296	325
0.75	BENSTON,GJ	AP	85	JAE			67	84
0.75	BOWEN,RM	JA	81	TAR			1	22
0.75	BRICKLEY,JA	AP	85	JAE	BHAGAT,S	LEASE,RC	115	130
0.75	LEFTWICH,RW	ST	81	JAR	WATTS,RL	ZIMMERMAN,JL	50	77
0.75	MUTCHLER,JF	AU	85	JAR			668	682
0.75	PARKER,JE	JA	77	TAR			69	96
0.75	SCHULTZ JR,JJ	AU	81	JAR	RECKERS,PMJ		482	501
0.73	SPICER,BM	JA	78	TAR			94	111
0.71	CHOW,CW	AP	82	TAR	RICE,SJ		326	335
0.71	HOPWOOD,WS	AU	82	JAR	MCKEOWN,JC	NEWBOLD,P	343	349
0.69	ARCHIBALD,TR	ST	67	JAR			164	186

RESEARCH METHOD=ARCHIVAL - PRIMARY

CITE IND-EX	FIRST AUTHOR	ISS-UE	YE-AR	JOUR-NAL	SECOND AUTHOR	THIRD AUTHOR	PAG BEG	PAG END
0.69	BEAVER,WH	JL	73	TAR	DUKES,RE		549	559
0.69	GAGNON,JM	ST	67	JAR			187	204
0.69	HORRIGAN,JO	ST	66	JAR			44	62
0.67	ANTLE,R	SP	86	JAR	SMITH,A		1	39
0.67	AYRES,FL	JN	86	JAE			143	158
0.67	BOWEN,RM	OC	86	TAR	BURGSTAHLER,D	DALEY,LA	713	725
0.67	DEANGELO,LE	JL	86	TAR			400	420
0.67	FRANCIS,JR	AU	86	JAR	STOKES,DJ		383	393
0.67	HORWITZ,BN	ST	80	JAR	KOLODNY,R		38	74
0.67	HOSKIN,RE	ST	86	JAR	HUGHES,JS	RICKS,WE	1	36
0.67	KINNEY JR,WR	MR	86	JAE			73	89
0.67	LARCKER,DF	OC	83	TAR	REVSINE,L		706	732
0.67	LIPE,RC	ST	86	JAR			37	68
0.67	MAGLIOLO,J	ST	86	JAR			69	111
0.67	PALEPU,KG	MR	86	JAE			3	36
0.67	RICKS,WE	SP	86	JAR			206	216
0.67	SUNDER,S	AU	83	JAR	WAYMIRE,G		565	580
0.67	WILLMOTT,H	06	86	AOS			555	582
0.64	RO,BT	AU	78	JAR			315	340
0.62	BEAVER,WH	JA	68	TAR			113	122
0.62	BEIDLEMAN,CR	OC	73	TAR			653	667
0.62	BENSTON,GJ	JL	69	TAR			515	532
0.62	DAILY,RA	OC	71	TAR			686	692
0.62	FRISHKOFF,P	ST	70	JAR			116	129
0.62	GREEN,D	ST	66	JAR	SEGALL,J		21	36
0.62	MAGEE,RP	AU	74	JAR			270	287
0.62	MOORE,ML	SP	73	JAR			100	107
0.60	AJINKYA,BB	AU	84	JAR	GIFT,MJ		425	444
0.60	DALEY,LA	AP	84	TAR			177	198
0.60	FRANCIS,JR	AG	84	JAE			133	151
0.60	INGRAM,RW	SP	84	JAR			126	144
0.60	NICHOLS,DR	SP	79	JAR	TSAY,JJ		140	155
0.57	BANKS,DW	SP	82	JAR	KINNEY JR,WR		240	254
0.55	FIRTH,MA	JL	78	TAR			642	650
0.55	IMHOFF JR,EA	OC	78	TAR			836	850
0.55	RULAND,W	AP	78	TAR			439	447
0.54	BASKIN,EF	JA	72	TAR			38	51
0.54	DERSTINE,RP	AU	74	JAR	HUEFNER,RJ		216	234
0.54	FOSTER,G	OC	75	TAR			686	698
0.54	PETERSEN,RJ	JA	73	TAR			34	43
0.54	TRITSCHLER,CA	JA	69	TAR			99	123
0.50	BROWN,LD	AU	79	JAR	ROZEFF,MS		341	351
0.50	DOPUCH,N	JL	87	TAR	HOLTHAUSEN,RW	LEFTWICH,RW	431	454
0.50	FRANCIS,JR	AP	87	JAE	REITER,SA		35	59
0.50	GENTRY,JA	SP	85	JAR	NEWBOLD,P	WHITFORD,DT	146	160
0.50	HAKA,SF	OC	85	TAR	GORDON,LA	PINCHES,GE	651	669
0.50	HAM,J	JL	85	TAR	LOSELL,D	SMIELIAUSKAS,W	387	406
0.50	HUNT III,HG	AU	85	JAR		448	467	
0.50	LEE,CJ	AU	85	JAR	HSIEH,DA		468	485
0.50	LEWELLEN,W	AP	85	JAE	LODERER,C	ROSENFELD,A	209	232

RESEARCH METHOD=ARCHIVAL - PRIMARY

CITE IND-EX	FIRST AUTHOR	ISS-UE	YE-AR	JOUR-NAL	SECOND AUTHOR	THIRD AUTHOR	PAG BEG	PAG END
0.50	MCNICHOLS,M	AP	83	JAE	MANEGOLD,JG		49	74
0.50	OLSEN,C	ST	85	JAR	DIETRICH,JR		144	166
0.50	PASTENA,V	AU	79	JAR	RONEN,J		550	564
0.50	RAMAN,KK	OC	81	TAR			910	926
0.50	SHANE,PB	JL	83	TAR	SPICER,BH		521	538
0.50	STEVENSON,FL	AU	87	JAR			306	316
0.50	WALLACE,WA	AU	81	JAR			502	520
0.50	WHITTRED,G	DE	87	JAE			259	285
0.46	BEAVER,WH	AU	68	JAR			179	192
0.46	DYER,JC	AU	75	JAR	MCHUGH,AJ		204	219
0.46	ELAM,R	JA	75	TAR			25	43
0.46	LEV,B	AP	74	TAR	KUNITZKY,S		259	270
0.46	LOOKABILL,LL	OC	76	TAR			724	738
0.46	NEUMANN,FL	ST	68	JAR			1	17
0.46	SINGHVI,SS	JA	71	TAR	DESAI,HB		129	138
0.44	BOWMAN,RG	SP	80	JAR			242	254
0.44	LEV,B	AU	80	JAR			524	550
0.43	CHOW,CW	WI	82	AUD	RICE,SJ		35	53
0.43	COPELAND,RM	AU	82	JAR	INGRAM,RW		275	289
0.43	DANOS,P	AU	82	JAR	EICHENSEHER,JW		604	616
0.43	DIETRICH,JR	JA	82	TAR	KAPLAN,RS		18	38
0.43	HALL,TW	SP	82	JAR			139	151
0.43	LUSTGARTEN,S	OC	82	JAE			121	141
0.40	BALDWIN,BA	JL	84	TAR			376	389
0.40	DHARAN,BG	AP	84	TAR			199	217
0.40	IMHOFF JR,EA	AU	84	JAR	LOBO,GJ		541	554
0.40	MCCONNELL,DK	WI	84	JAA			178	181
0.40	MCDONALD,B	JL	84	TAR	MORRIS,MH		432	446
0.40	MCKEE,AJ	OC	84	TAR	BELL,TB	BOATSMAN,JR	647	659
0.40	ST.PIERRE,K	AP	84	TAR	ANDERSON,JA		242	263
0.38	BENSTON,GJ	ST	67	JAR			1	54
0.38	BILDERSEE,JS	JA	75	TAR			81	98
0.38	BLUM,M	SP	74	JAR			1	25
0.38	COATES,R	ST	72	JAR			132	144
0.38	COMISKEY,EE	AP	71	TAR			279	285
0.38	COPELAND,RM	ST	71	JAR	SHANK,JK		196	224
0.38	FOSTER,G	AU	75	JAR			283	292
0.38	FRIED,D	AP	81	TAR	SCHIFF,A		326	341
0.38	HOPWOOD,WS	AU	81	JAR	MCKEOWN,JC		313	322
0.38	KIGER,JE	SP	72	JAR			113	128
0.38	NOREEN,EW	AU	81	JAR	WOLFSON,MA		384	398
0.38	RO,BT	JA	81	TAR			70	84
0.38	TROTMAN,KT	04	81	AOS	BRADLEY,G		355	362
0.38	VIGELAND,RL	AP	81	TAR			309	325
0.38	WHITE,GE	AU	70	JAR			260	273
0.36	ABDEL-KHALIK,AR	ST	78	JAR	MCKEOWN,JC		46	77
0.36	FOSTER III,TW	OC	78	TAR	VICKREY,DW		921	934
0.36	INGRAM,RW	AU	78	JAR			270	285
0.36	JAGGI,B	OC	78	TAR			961	967
0.36	RICE,SJ	AP	78	TAR			429	438

RESEARCH METHOD=ARCHIVAL   - PRIMARY

CITE IND-EX	FIRST AUTHOR	ISS-UE	YE-AR	JOUR-NAL	SECOND AUTHOR	THIRD AUTHOR	PAG BEG	PAG END
0.36	SHANK,JK	OC	78	TAR	MURDOCK,RJ		824	835
0.33	ANDERSON,JC	JL	80	TAR	FRANKLE,AW		467	479
0.33	CASEY JR,CJ	AP	86	TAR	MCGEE,VE	STICKNEY,CP	249	262
0.33	CHOW,CW	JL	83	TAR			485	520
0.33	DANOS,P	OC	86	TAR	EICHENSEHER,JW		633	650
0.33	DOPUCH,N	JN	86	JAE	HOLTHAUSEN,RW	LEFTWICH,RW	93	118
0.33	EL-GAZZAR,S	OC	86	JAE	LILIEN,S	PASTENA,V	217	238
0.33	HASSELL,JM	JA	86	TAR	JENNINGS,RH		58	75
0.33	HOPWOOD,WS	SP	80	JAR			77	90
0.33	KELLER,SB	AU	83	AUD	DAVIDSON,LF		1	22
0.33	MURDOCH,B	AP	86	TAR			273	287
0.33	NAIR,RD	JL	80	TAR	FRANK,WG		426	450
0.33	NICHOLS,DR	AU	83	JAR	SMITH,DB		534	544
0.33	OPPONG,A	AU	80	JAR			574	584
0.33	PALMROSE,ZV	AU	86	JAR			405	411
0.33	PASTENA,V	AP	86	TAR	RULAND,W		288	301
0.33	PEASNELL,KV	SP	77	JAR	SKERRATT,CL		108	119
0.33	SHRIVER,KA	SP	86	JAR			151	165
0.33	SMITH,DB	AU	86	AUD			95	108
0.33	STOBER,TL	ST	86	JAR			138	164
0.33	WRIGHT,CJ	JA	86	TAR	GROFF,JE		91	100
0.31	BARRETT,ME	SP	76	JAR			10	26
0.31	DASCHER,PE	AU	70	JAR	MALCOM,RE		253	259
0.31	DEAKIN,EB	JA	76	TAR			90	96
0.31	HAGERMAN,RL	OC	75	TAR			699	709
0.31	LEV,B	AU	69	JAR			290	299
0.31	LIVINGSTONE,JL	AP	67	TAR			233	240
0.31	RHODE,JG	OC	74	TAR	WHITSELL,GM	KELSEY,RL	772	787
0.31	SHANK,JK	JL	73	TAR	COPELAND,RM		494	501
0.31	SMITH,JE	JL	71	TAR	SMITH,NP		552	561
0.31	WARREN,CS	SP	75	JAR			162	176
0.31	WEST,RR	SP	70	JAR			118	125
0.31	WILCOX,JA	ST	73	JAR			163	179
0.31	ZEFF,SA	AP	67	TAR	FOSSUM,RL		298	320
0.30	ADELBERG,AH	AU	79	JAR			565	592
0.30	NAIR,RD	SP	79	JAR			225	242
0.30	NORTON,CL	JA	79	TAR	SMITH,RE		72	87
0.29	DAVIS,RR	AU	82	AUD			13	32
0.29	HOPWOOD,WS	AU	82	JAR	NEWBOLD,P	SILHAN,PA	724	732
0.29	WALTHER,LM	AP	82	TAR			376	383
0.27	BASU,S	JL	78	TAR			599	625
0.25	ANELL,B	04	85	AOS			479	492
0.25	EASTON,PD	ST	85	JAR			54	77
0.25	INGRAM,RW	OC	81	TAR	COPELAND,RM		830	843
0.25	INGRAM,RW	AU	85	JAR			595	618
0.25	JENNINGS,R	SP	85	JAR	STARKS,L		336	350
0.25	KELLY,R	AU	85	JAR			619	632
0.25	LAMBERT,RA	AP	85	JAE	LARCKER,DF		179	204
0.25	MULFORD,CW	AU	85	JAR			897	906
0.25	PERAGALLO,E	OC	77	TAR			881	892

RESEARCH METHOD=ARCHIVAL   - PRIMARY

CITE IND- EX	FIRST AUTHOR	ISS- UE	YE- AR	JOUR -NAL	SECOND AUTHOR	THIRD AUTHOR	PAG BEG	PAG END
0.25	SCHWARTZ,KB	AP	85	TAR	MENON,K		248	261
0.25	TEHRANIAN,H	AP	85	JAE	WAEGELEIN,JF		131	144
0.23	BALL,R	SP	76	JAR	LEV,B	WATTS,RL	1	9
0.23	BAREFIELD,RM	AU	71	JAR	COMISKEY,EE		351	358
0.23	BAREFIELD,RM	AP	72	TAR	COMISKEY,EE		291	298
0.23	BARNEA,A	JA	76	TAR	RONEN,J	SADAN,S	110	122
0.23	BOWMAN,EH	01	76	AOS	HAIRE,M		11	22
0.23	BREMSER,WG	JL	75	TAR			563	573
0.23	CHASTEEN,LG	JL	71	TAR			504	508
0.23	CHOI,FD	AU	73	JAR			159	175
0.23	COPELAND,RM	JL	68	TAR	LICASTRO,RD		540	545
0.23	DEAKIN,EB	JL	76	TAR			590	603
0.23	ESKEW,RK	AP	75	TAR			316	324
0.23	FRANK,WG	SP	69	JAR			123	136
0.23	GAGNON,JM	SP	71	JAR			52	72
0.23	GUPTA,MC	SP	72	JAR	HUEFNER,RJ		77	95
0.23	HORWITZ,BN	AP	71	TAR	SHABAHANG,R		243	252
0.23	KOCHANEK,RF	AP	74	TAR			245	258
0.23	REILLY,FK	ST	72	JAR	MORGENSON,DL	WEST,M	105	124
0.23	RONEN,J	SP	75	JAR	SADAN,S		133	149
0.23	SAMUELSON,RA	AU	72	JAR			322	344
0.23	WHITE JR,CE	AU	72	JAR			351	358
0.22	BOWMAN,RG	AP	80	TAR			237	253
0.22	GRAY,SJ	SP	80	JAR			64	76
0.20	BROCKHOFF,K	12	79	AOS			77	86
0.20	COLLINS,DW	AU	79	JAR	SIMONDS,RR		352	383
0.20	COLLINS,WA	AU	84	JAR	HOPWOOD,WS	MCKEOWN,JC	467	479
0.20	DIERKES,M	12	79	AOS			87	108
0.20	ESKEW,RK	JA	79	TAR			107	118
0.20	FRANK,WG	AU	79	JAR			593	605
0.20	FRAZIER,KB	SP	84	JAR	INGRAM,RW	TENNYSON,BM	318	331
0.20	KELLOGG,RL	DE	84	JAE			185	204
0.20	MARAIS,ML	ST	84	JAR	PATELL,JM	WOLFSON,MA	87	114
0.20	PURO,M	AU	84	JAR			624	646
0.20	SCHREUDER,H	JA	84	TAR	KLAASSEN,J		64	77
0.20	SIMUNIC,DA	AU	84	JAR			679	702
0.20	STONE,M	JL	84	TAR	BUBLITZ,B		469	473
0.20	SUTTON,TG	01	84	AOS			81	95
0.20	WESCOTT,SH	SP	84	JAR			412	423
0.18	KAMIN,JY	02	78	AOS	RONEN,J		141	160
0.18	KETZ,JE	ST	78	JAR			273	284
0.18	SHORT,DG	ST	78	JAR			259	272
0.17	BROWN,LD	AU	83	JAR			432	443
0.17	CASEY JR,CJ	SP	83	JAR			300	307
0.17	HARRISON JR,WT	SP	83	JAR	TOMASSINI,LA	DIETRICH,JR	65	77
0.17	LESSEM,R	04	77	AOS			279	294
0.17	MCLEAY,S	01	83	AOS			31	56
0.17	MORSE,D	AP	83	TAR	USHMAN,N		247	258
0.17	MURRAY,D	SP	83	JAR			128	140
0.17	SCHIPPER,K	ST	77	JAR			1	40

RESEARCH METHOD=ARCHIVAL   - PRIMARY

CITE IND-EX	FIRST AUTHOR	ISS-UE	YE-AR	JOUR-NAL	SECOND AUTHOR	THIRD AUTHOR	PAG BEG	PAG END
0.17	WARREN,CS	JA	77	TAR			150	161
0.15	ABDEL-KHALIK,AR	OC	75	TAR			657	670
0.15	COPELAND,RM	SP	68	JAR	FREDERICKS,W		106	113
0.15	DOPUCH,N	ST	66	JAR	DRAKE,DF		192	219
0.15	ELLIOTT,JW	AU	72	JAR	UPHOFF,HL		259	274
0.15	FRANK,WG	AP	70	TAR	WEYGANDT,JJ		280	289
0.15	GREENBALL,MN	ST	71	JAR			172	190
0.15	GRIFFIN,PA	JL	76	TAR			499	515
0.15	JOHNSON,O	AU	67	JAR			164	172
0.15	KIGER,JE	JA	74	TAR			1	7
0.15	LINDHE,R	AU	63	JAR			139	148
0.15	MEYERS,SL	AP	73	TAR			318	322
0.15	MLYNARCZYK,FA	ST	69	JAR			63	81
0.15	O'CONNOR,MC	AP	73	TAR			339	352
0.15	PATZ,DH	AU	72	JAR	BOATSMAN,JR		392	403
0.15	ROBERTSON,JC	JL	71	TAR	CLARKE,RW		562	571
0.15	STAUBUS,GJ	JA	65	TAR			119	134
0.14	ABDEL-KHALIK,AR	OC	82	TAR	AJINKYA,BB		661	680
0.14	ALTMAN,EI	AU	82	JAA			4	19
0.14	EMERY,GW	AU	82	JAR	COGGER,KO		290	303
0.14	INGRAM,RW	AU	82	JAR	COPELAND,RM		766	772
0.14	SCHWARTZ,KB	AU	82	JAA			32	43
0.14	SELTO,FH	AU	82	JAR	GROVE,HD		676	688
0.14	SEPE,J	JL	82	TAR			467	485
0.14	SKINNER,RC	SP	82	JAR			210	226
0.14	WISEMAN,J	01	82	AOS			53	64
0.13	MAHER,MW	OC	81	TAR			751	770
0.13	MANEGOLD,JG	AU	81	JAR			360	373
0.11	BARAN,A	JA	80	TAR	LAKONISHOK,J	OFER,AR	22	35
0.11	KELLY,LK	03	80	AOS			311	322
0.11	LOY,LD	SP	80	JAA	TOOLE,HR		227	243
0.10	CHAN,JL	04	79	AOS			273	282
0.10	ENGLEBRECHT,TD	JL	79	TAR	JAMISON,RW		554	562
0.10	HILLISON,WA	SP	79	JAR			60	73
0.10	MADEO,SA	JL	79	TAR			538	553
0.10	PEARSON,MA	WI	79	JAA	LINDGREN,JH	MYERS,BL	122	134
0.09	DAVIDSON,S	ST	78	JAR	WEIL,RL		154	233
0.09	DAVIS,DW	JA	78	TAR	BOATSMAN,JR	BASKIN,EF	1	10
0.09	GIVOLY,D	SU	78	JAA	RONEN,J	SCHIFF,A	361	372
0.09	GRAY,SJ	AU	78	JAR			242	253
0.08	ARNOLD,DF	JA	73	TAR	HUMANN,TE		23	33
0.08	CHOTTINER,S	AU	71	JAR	YOUNG,AE		367	374
0.08	COPELAND,RM	AU	69	JAR	WOJDAK,JF		188	195
0.08	CULPEPPER,RC	AP	70	TAR			322	332
0.08	FALK,H	SP	77	JAR	MILLER,JC		12	22
0.08	FRANK,WG	SP	71	JAR	WEYGANDT,JJ		116	126
0.08	HARMELINK,PJ	SP	73	JAR			146	158
0.08	HOFSTEDT,TR	AP	71	TAR	WEST,RR		329	337
0.08	HUME,LJ	SP	70	JAR			21	33
0.08	JENSEN,RE	JA	71	TAR			36	56

RESEARCH METHOD=ARCHIVAL   - PRIMARY

CITE INDEX	FIRST AUTHOR	ISSUE	YEAR	JOURNAL	SECOND AUTHOR	THIRD AUTHOR	PAG BEG	PAG END
0.08	KINNEY JR,WR	AP	72	TAR			339	345
0.08	KRATCHMAN,SH	OC	74	TAR	MALCOM,RE	TWARK,RD	682	689
0.08	LOEB,SE	JA	72	TAR			1	10
0.08	NEUMANN,FL	JL	69	TAR			546	554
0.08	SAN MIGUEL,JG	04	77	AOS	SHANK,JK	GOVINDARAJAN,V	333	348
0.08	SHARPE,IG	AU	75	JAR	WALKER,RG		293	310
0.08	SIMPSON,RH	OC	69	TAR			806	817
0.08	SOPER,FJ	AP	64	TAR	DOLPHIN,R		358	362
0.08	STONE,WE	JA	65	TAR			190	195
0.00	ABDEL-KHALIK,AR	SP	83	JAR			293	296
0.00	AJINKYA,BB	AU	80	JAR			343	361
0.00	AMIT,R	WI	88	JAA	LIVNAT,J		19	43
0.00	ANDERSON JR,KE	JL	85	TAR			357	371
0.00	APOSTOLOU,NG	AU	85	JAR	GIROUX,GA	WELKER,RB	853	858
0.00	ARNETT,HE	JA	65	TAR			54	64
0.00	ASKARI,H	AP	76	TAR	CAIN,P	SHAW,R	331	334
0.00	ATIASE,RK	SP	87	JAR			168	176
0.00	AYRES,FL	SP	86	JAR			166	169
0.00	BABER,WR	AU	87	JAR	BROOKS,EH	RICKS,WE	293	305
0.00	BAGINSKI,SP	AU	87	JAR			196	216
0.00	BALACHANDRAN,KR	02	77	AOS	LIVINGSTONE,JL		153	164
0.00	BALVERS,RJ	OC	88	TAR	MCDONALD,B	MILLER,RE	605	622
0.00	BAMBER,LS	JL	87	TAR			510	532
0.00	BAO,BH	03	86	AOS	BAO,DH	VASARHELYI,MA	289	296
0.00	BARLEV,B	AU	79	JAR	LEVY,H		305	315
0.00	BATHKE,AW	AP	84	TAR	LOREK,KS		163	176
0.00	BEATTY,RP	WI	85	JAA	JOHNSON,SB		112	124
0.00	BEAVER,WH	DE	81	JAE	LANDSMAN,WR		233	241
0.00	BENJAMIN,JJ	SU	86	JAA	GROSSMAN,SD	WIGGIN,CE	177	184
0.00	BERNARD,VL	AU	84	JAR			445	466
0.00	BERNARD,VL	OC	87	TAR	RULAND,RG		707	722
0.00	BIDWELL III,CM	SP	81	JAA	RIDDLE JR,JR		198	214
0.00	BILDERSEE,JS	SU	87	JAA	KAHN,N		239	256
0.00	BINDER,JJ	SP	85	JAR			370	383
0.00	BLANCHARD,GA	JA	86	TAR	CHOW,CW	NOREEN,EW	1	15
0.00	BOWEN,RM	OC	82	TAR	SUNDEM,GL		778	784
0.00	BOWEN,RM	OC	87	TAR	BURGSTAHLER,D	DALEY,LA	723	747
0.00	BRIEF,RP	JA	69	TAR			20	26
0.00	BROWN,BC	SU	86	JAA	BRANDI,JT		185	205
0.00	BROWN,LD	SP	80	JAR	HUGHES,JS	ROZEFF,MS	278	288
0.00	BROWN,PR	SU	82	JAA			282	290
0.00	BURGSTAHLER,D	SP	86	JAR	NOREEN,EW		170	186
0.00	CAMPBELL,DR	SP	83	JAA			196	211
0.00	CARSLAW,C	AP	88	TAR			321	327
0.00	CASEY JR,CJ	SP	85	JAR	BARTCZAK,N		384	401
0.00	CASSIDY,DB	AU	76	JAR			212	229
0.00	CHARNES,A	01	80	AOS			87	107
0.00	CHOW,CW	JL	87	TAR	WONG-BOREN,A		533	541
0.00	CHURCHILL,NC	WI	82	AUD	COOPER,WW	GOVINDARAJAN,V	69	91
0.00	CLARK,TN	ST	77	JAR			54	94

RESEARCH METHOD=ARCHIVAL   - PRIMARY

CITE INDEX	FIRST AUTHOR	ISS-UE	YE-AR	JOUR-NAL	SECOND AUTHOR	THIRD AUTHOR	PAG BEG	PAG END
0.00	CLINCH,GJ	AP	87	JAE	SINCLAIR,NA		89	106
0.00	COE,TL	SP	79	JAA			244	253
0.00	COGGER,KO	AU	82	JAR	RULAND,W		733	737
0.00	COWEN,SS	02	87	AOS	FERRERI,LB	PARKER,LD	111	122
0.00	COX,CT	OC	85	TAR			692	701
0.00	CREADY,WM	JL	87	TAR	SHANK,JK		589	596
0.00	CREADY,WM	SP	88	JAR			1	27
0.00	DALEY,LA	OC	88	TAR	SENKOW,DW	VIGELAND,RL	563	585
0.00	DAVIS,HZ	AU	82	JAR	KAHN,N		738	744
0.00	DAVIS,HZ	AU	84	JAR	KAHN,N	ROZEN,E	480	490
0.00	DAVIS,ML	AP	88	TAR	LARGAY III,JA		348	363
0.00	DAVISON,AG	SP	84	JAR	STENING,BW	WAI,WT	313	317
0.00	DEANGELO,LE	JA	88	JAE			3	36
0.00	DEFEO,VJ	AU	86	JAR			349	363
0.00	DHALIWAL,DS	OC	86	TAR			651	661
0.00	DHARAN,BG	SP	83	JAR			256	270
0.00	DIETRICH,JR	AP	84	JAE			67	96
0.00	DOPUCH,N	SP	88	JAR	PINCUS,M		28	59
0.00	DORAN,BM	JL	88	TAR	COLLINS,DW	DHALIWAL,DS	389	413
0.00	DORAN,DT	SP	88	JAA	NACHTMANN,R		113	132
0.00	EICHENSEHER,JW	SP	85	JAA			195	209
0.00	ELGERS,P	OC	87	TAR	CALLAHAN,C	STROCK,E	763	773
0.00	ELGERS,PT	JL	80	TAR			389	408
0.00	ELGERS,PT	AP	82	TAR	MURRAY,D		358	375
0.00	ELNICKI,RA	ST	77	JAR			209	218
0.00	ETTREDGE,M	SP	88	AUD	SHANE,PB	SMITH,D	29	42
0.00	FALK,H	OC	75	TAR	HEINTZ,JA		758	779
0.00	FELIX JR,WL	JA	72	TAR			52	63
0.00	FIRTH,MA	SP	73	JAR			16	24
0.00	FIRTH,MA	AU	81	JAR			521	529
0.00	FIRTH,MA	SP	85	AUD			23	37
0.00	FOSTER III,TW	AP	78	TAR	VICKREY,DW		360	370
0.00	FRANCIS,JR	OC	88	TAR	WILSON,ER		663	682
0.00	FRECKA,TJ	SP	83	JAR	LEE,CF		308	316
0.00	FREEMAN,RN	ST	78	JAR			111	145
0.00	FRIED,D	WI	87	JAA	HOSLER,C		5	23
0.00	FRIEDLOB,GT	WI	83	JAA			100	107
0.00	FU,P	SP	71	JAR			40	51
0.00	FULMER,JG	AU	84	JAA	MOON,JE		5	14
0.00	GARSOMBKE,HP	SU	83	JAA	ALLEN,G		285	298
0.00	GIVOLY,D	AU	81	JAR	PALMON,D		530	543
0.00	GIVOLY,D	JL	85	TAR			372	386
0.00	GIVOLY,D	SP	87	JAA	LAKONISHOK,J		117	137
0.00	GLEZEN,GW	AU	85	JAR	MILLAR,JA		859	870
0.00	GONEDES,NJ	ST	69	JAR			90	113
0.00	GONEDES,NJ	JL	71	TAR			535	551
0.00	GORDON,LA	02	84	AOS	HAKA,S	SCHICK,AG	111	123
0.00	GORMLEY,RJ	SU	88	JAA			185	212
0.00	GOVINDARAJAN,V	SU	79	JAA			339	343
0.00	GOVINDARAJAN,V	04	80	AOS			383	392

RESEARCH METHOD=ARCHIVAL   - PRIMARY

CITE IND- EX	FIRST AUTHOR	ISS- UE	YE- AR	JOUR -NAL	SECOND AUTHOR	THIRD AUTHOR	PAG BEG	PAG END
0.00	GRAY,D	AU	84	JAR			760	764
0.00	GRAY,SJ	SP	84	JAR	RADEBAUGH,LH		351	360
0.00	GREENBERG,R	AU	84	JAR			719	730
0.00	GREENBERG,RR	AU	86	JAA	JOHNSON,GL	RAMESH,K	266	277
0.00	GROSSMAN,SD	WI	81	JAA	KRATCHMAN,SH	WELKER,RB	136	143
0.00	HAGERMAN,RL	AU	84	JAR	ZMIJEWSKI,ME	SHAH,P	526	540
0.00	HAIN,HP	OC	66	TAR			699	703
0.00	HALL,TW	SU	83	JAA			299	313
0.00	HALL,TW	SP	85	JAA	CASLER,DJ		210	224
0.00	HALPERIN,R	AP	87	TAR	LANEN,WN		378	384
0.00	HANSEN,ES	ST	77	JAR			156	201
0.00	HARMON,WK	AU	84	JAA			24	34
0.00	HAW,IM	WI	87	JAA	PASTENA,V	LILIEN,S	24	42
0.00	HAW,IM	AU	88	JAR	LUSTGARTEN,S		331	352
0.00	HIRSCHEY,M	SP	85	JAR	WEYGANDT,JJ		326	335
0.00	HOLDREN,GC	JA	64	TAR			70	85
0.00	HOPWOOD,WS	SP	80	JAR			289	296
0.00	HOPWOOD,WS	SP	85	JAR	MCKEOWN,JC		161	174
0.00	HORRIGAN,JO	JL	65	TAR			558	568
0.00	HORWITZ,B	JL	88	TAR	NORMOLLE,D		414	435
0.00	HORWITZ,BN	SP	72	JAR	YOUNG,AE		96	107
0.00	HOUGHTON,KA	SP	84	JAR			361	368
0.00	HUSSEIN,ME	AU	86	AUD	BAVISHI,VB	GANGOLLY,JS	124	133
0.00	IMHOFF JR,EA	SU	81	JAA			333	351
0.00	INGRAM,RW	JL	83	TAR	CHEWNING,EG		562	580
0.00	JAIN,PC	JL	83	TAR			633	638
0.00	JAIN,PC	SP	86	JAR			76	96
0.00	JENNINGS,R	SP	87	JAR			90	110
0.00	JOHNSON,O	OC	76	TAR			808	823
0.00	JOHNSON,WB	AP	85	JAE	MAGEE,RP	NAGARAJAN,NJ	151	174
0.00	JOHNSON,WB	AU	88	JAR	DHALIWAL,DS		236	272
0.00	JOHNSON,WB	JA	88	TAR	RAMANAN,R		96	110
0.00	KAHN,N	SU	82	JAA			327	337
0.00	KIM,M	AP	88	JAE	MOORE,G		111	125
0.00	KING,RD	JL	84	TAR			419	431
0.00	KING,RD	JA	86	TAR	O'KEEFE,TB		76	90
0.00	KISSINGER,JN	AU	83	AUD			42	54
0.00	KNAUF,JB	WI	87	JAA	VASARHELYI,MA		43	64
0.00	KNUTSON,PH	ST	71	JAR			99	112
0.00	KRAMER,SS	JA	82	TAR			70	87
0.00	KROSS,W	AU	82	JAR			459	471
0.00	LAMBERT,RA	ST	87	JAR	LARCKER,DF		85	125
0.00	LANDSMAN,WR	OC	86	TAR			662	691
0.00	LAU,AH	SP	87	JAR			127	138
0.00	LAWRENCE,EC	AU	83	JAR			606	610
0.00	LEE,CF	AP	88	TAR	WU,C		292	306
0.00	LEE,CJ	SP	85	JAR			213	227
0.00	LEMBKE,VC	WI	80	JAA	SMITH,JH		147	162
0.00	LEV,B	ST	69	JAR			182	197
0.00	LEV,B	SP	79	JAA	TAYLOR,KW		232	243

RESEARCH METHOD=ARCHIVAL   - PRIMARY

CITE IND-EX	FIRST AUTHOR	ISS-UE	YE-AR	JOUR -NAL	SECOND AUTHOR	THIRD AUTHOR	PAG BEG	PAG END
0.00	LEV,B	AP	83	JAE			31	48
0.00	LEVITAN,AS	AU	85	AUD	KNOBLETT,JA		26	39
0.00	LEVY,H	AU	87	JAA	BYUN,YH		355	369
0.00	LEWELLEN,W	DE	87	JAE	LODERER,C	MARTIN,K	287	310
0.00	LILIEN,S	OC	88	TAR	MELLMAN,M	PASTENA,V	642	656
0.00	LIVINGSTONE,JL	JL	67	TAR			544	552
0.00	LIVINGSTONE,JL	ST	67	JAR			93	123
0.00	LIVINGSTONE,JL	SP	67	JAR			77	94
0.00	LIVNAT,J	AU	81	JAR			350	359
0.00	LLOYD,BM	OC	71	TAR	WEYGANDT,JJ		756	764
0.00	LOREK,KS	SP	83	JAR	ICERMAN,JD	ABDULKADER,AA	317	328
0.00	LOREK,KS	SP	84	JAR	BATHKE,AW		369	379
0.00	LYS,T	AU	88	JAR	SIVARAMAKRISHNAN,K		273	299
0.00	MAHER,JJ	OC	87	TAR			785	798
0.00	MANEGOLD,JG	SU	86	JAA			206	221
0.00	MANES,RP	ST	67	JAR	SAMUELS,JM	SMYTH,DJ	139	156
0.00	MARKS,BR	AU	85	JAR	RAMAN,KK		878	886
0.00	MARKS,BR	AU	87	AUD	RAMAN,KK		106	117
0.00	MARSTON,F	SP	88	JAA	HARRIS,RS		147	164
0.00	MARTIN,A	ST	71	JAR			1	31
0.00	MARTIN,JD	WI	79	JAA	ANDERSON,PF	KEOWN,AJ	151	164
0.00	MCCONNELL,DK	SP	84	AUD			44	56
0.00	MCGAHRAN,KT	JA	88	TAR			23	41
0.00	MEAR,R	04	87	AOS	FIRTH,MA		331	340
0.00	MEEK,GK	AP	83	TAR			394	402
0.00	MELLMAN,M	AU	86	JAA	SEILER,ME		305	318
0.00	MENSAH,YM	WI	83	JAA			130	141
0.00	MENSAH,YM	AP	83	TAR			228	246
0.00	MENSAH,YM	SP	84	JAR			380	395
0.00	MIELKE,DE	WI	87	JAA	SEIFERT,J		65	78
0.00	MILLAR,JA	JA	77	TAR			52	55
0.00	MILLS,RH	JA	67	TAR			74	81
0.00	MOIZER,P	AU	87	AUD	TURLEY,S		118	123
0.00	MONAHAN,TF	SU	83	JAA	BARENBAUM,L		325	340
0.00	MOODY,SM	AU	86	JAA	FLESHER,DL		319	330
0.00	MOORE,ML	JA	85	TAR	STEECE,BM	SWENSON,CW	18	32
0.00	MOORE,ML	OC	87	TAR	STEECE,BM	SWENSON,CW	671	685
0.00	MORRIS,MH	SU	84	JAA	NICHOLS,WD		293	305
0.00	MORRIS,MH	AP	88	TAR	NICHOLS,WD		237	254
0.00	MOSES,OD	AP	87	TAR			358	377
0.00	MULFORD,CW	JL	86	TAR	COMISKEY,EE		519	525
0.00	MURRAY,D	WI	82	JAA			154	159
0.00	MUTCHLER,JF	AU	86	AUD			148	
0.00	NEUMANN,BR	SP	79	JAR			123	139
0.00	NEWMAN,DP	OC	81	TAR			897	909
0.00	NICHOLS,DR	AP	79	TAR	TSAY,JJ	LARKIN,PD	376	382
0.00	NICHOLS,DR	JA	87	TAR			183	190
0.00	NIELSEN,CC	OC	65	TAR			795	804
0.00	NIX,HM	SU	83	JAA	WICHMANN JR,H		341	352
0.00	NOREEN,EW	SP	88	JAR			119	133

RESEARCH METHOD=ARCHIVAL   - PRIMARY

CITE INDEX	FIRST AUTHOR	ISSUE	YEAR	JOUR-NAL	SECOND AUTHOR	THIRD AUTHOR	PAG BEG	PAG END
0.00	O'BRIEN,PC	JA	88	JAE			53	83
0.00	O'DONNELL,JL	JA	65	TAR			135	143
0.00	O'DONNELL,JL	JL	68	TAR			549	553
0.00	OHLSON,JA	ST	72	JAR			45	84
0.00	OUTSLAY,E	OC	82	TAR	WHEELER,JE		716	733
0.00	PALMROSE,ZV	JA	88	TAR			55	73
0.00	PATTEN,RJ	OC	64	TAR			876	879
0.00	PEAVY,JW	WI	85	JAA	EDGAR,SM		125	135
0.00	PENMAN,SH	DE	84	JAE			165	183
0.00	PETERSEN,RJ	JL	75	TAR			525	532
0.00	PHILIPS,GE	ST	70	JAR	MAYNE,LS		178	188
0.00	POWNALL,G	AU	86	JAR			291	315
0.00	PURO,M	SP	85	JAA			165	177
0.00	PUTNAM,K	AU	84	JAA	THOMAS,LR		15	23
0.00	RAMAN,KK	WI	82	JAA			144	153
0.00	RAMAN,KK	AU	82	JAA			44	50
0.00	RANSOM,CR	ST	85	JAR			124	143
0.00	REILLY,FK	AU	72	JAR	STETTLER,HF		308	321
0.00	RICHARDSON,AJ	04	88	AOS			381	396
0.00	RICKS,WE	JA	85	TAR	HUGHES,JS		33	52
0.00	ROBBINS,WA	SU	85	JAA	APOSTOLOU,NG	STRAWSER,RH	279	292
0.00	ROSE,PS	AU	82	JAA	ANDREWS,WT	GIROUX,GA	20	31
0.00	RUE,JC	SU	84	JAA	VOLKAN,AG		306	322
0.00	SAN MIGUEL,JG	JL	77	TAR			638	641
0.00	SCHACHTER,B	AU	88	JAR			353	372
0.00	SCHAEFER,T	AU	86	JAA	KENNELLEY,M		278	287
0.00	SCHEINER,JH	AU	82	JAR	KIGER,JE		482	496
0.00	SCHEINER,JH	AU	84	JAR			789	797
0.00	SCHIFF,M	SP	79	JAA			224	231
0.00	SCHIPPER,K	SP	85	JAR	THOMPSON,R		408	415
0.00	SCHWARTZ,BN	SP	83	JAA			244	253
0.00	SELTO,FH	AU	83	JAR	GROVE,HD		619	622
0.00	SELTO,FH	AU	85	JAR	CLOUSE,ML		700	717
0.00	SHAW,WH	AP	87	TAR			385	400
0.00	SHAW,WH	SP	88	JAR			60	81
0.00	SHEVLIN,T	JL	87	TAR			480	509
0.00	SILHAN,PA	SP	83	JAR			341	347
0.00	SILHAN,PA	SP	85	JAR	MCKEOWN,JC		416	426
0.00	SIMON,DT	AU	85	AUD			71	78
0.00	SIMON,DT	AP	88	TAR	FRANCIS,JR		255	269
0.00	SMITH,DB	AG	84	JAE	STETTLER,HF	BEEDLES,W	153	162
0.00	SMITH,DB	SP	88	JAR			134	145
0.00	ST.PIERRE,K	SP	82	JAA	ANDERSON,JA		229	247
0.00	STANDISH,PEM	OC	82	TAR	UNG,S		701	715
0.00	STAUBUS,GJ	JL	68	TAR			413	424
0.00	STERNER,JA	AU	83	JAR			623	628
0.00	STICKEL,SE	OC	86	JAE			197	216
0.00	STONE,M	AU	87	JAR			317	326
0.00	SUMMERS,EL	AP	68	TAR			257	265
0.00	SUTTON,TG	AP	88	JAE			127	149

RESEARCH METHOD=ARCHIVAL   - PRIMARY

CITE IND-EX	FIRST AUTHOR	ISS-UE	YE-AR	JOUR-NAL	SECOND AUTHOR	THIRD AUTHOR	PAG BEG	PAG END
0.00	SWANSON,EP	OC	85	TAR	SHEARON,WT	THOMAS,LR	681	691
0.00	TABOR,RH	SP	85	AUD	WILLIS,JT		93	109
0.00	TAUSSIG,RA	JA	68	TAR	HAYES,SC		68	74
0.00	TEHRANIAN,H	ST	87	JAR	TRAVLOS,NG	WAEGELEIN,JF	51	76
0.00	THIES,CF	AU	87	JAA	STURROCK,T		375	391
0.00	THODE,SF	WI	86	JAA	DRTINA,RE	LARGAY III,JA	46	61
0.00	THOMAS,AP	03	86	AOS			253	270
0.00	THOMAS,LR	AP	86	TAR	SWANSON,EP		330	336
0.00	THOMPSON II,RB	AU	87	JAR	OLSEN,C	DIETRICH,JR	245	274
0.00	THOMPSON,RB	JL	88	JAR	OLSEN,C	DIETRICH,JR	448	471
0.00	TILLER,MG	SU	85	JAA	MAUTZ,RD		293	304
0.00	TSE,S	JL	86	TAR			475	497
0.00	USRY,MF	OC	66	TAR			754	762
0.00	VOSS,WM	AU	68	JAR			262	269
0.00	WARREN,CS	SP	80	JAR			312	324
0.00	WAYMIRE,G	AU	83	JAR	POWNALL,G		629	643
0.00	WAYMIRE,G	SP	85	JAR			268	295
0.00	WAYMIRE,G	JA	86	TAR			129	142
0.00	WELCH,PR	AU	84	JAR			744	757
0.00	WHITEHURST,FD	JL	70	TAR			553	564
0.00	WHITTINGTON,OR	JL	80	TAR	WHITTENBURG,G		409	418
0.00	WHITTRED,GP	AP	84	TAR	ZIMMER,I		287	295
0.00	WILKERSON JR,JE	SP	87	JAR			161	167
0.00	WILLIAMS,DD	05	88	AOS	DIRSMITH,MW		487	508
0.00	WILLIAMS,DJ	03	86	AOS			271	288
0.00	WILLINGHAM,JJ	AU	85	AUD	WRIGHT,WF		57	70
0.00	WILSON,ER	SP	84	JAR	HOWARD,TP		207	224
0.00	WONG,J	JA	88	JAE			37	51
0.00	WONG,J	AP	88	JAE			151	167
0.00	WYER,JC	SP	88	AUD	WHITE,GT	JANSON,EC	164	173
0.00	YOUNG,AE	SP	78	JAA			217	230
0.00	YOUNG,SD	AP	88	TAR			283	291
0.00	ZAROWIN,P	AP	88	JAE			89	110
0.00	ZIEBART,DA	AU	85	JAR			920	926
0.00	ZIEBART,DA	AP	87	TAR	KIM,DH		343	357

2.4 RESEARCH METHOD=ARCHIVAL - SECONDARY

CITE IND-EX	FIRST AUTHOR	ISS-UE	YE-AR	JOUR-NAL	SECOND AUTHOR	THIRD AUTHOR	PAG BEG	PAG END
5.15	GONEDES,NJ	ST	74	JAR	DOPUCH,N		48	129
4.83	HOLTHAUSEN,RW	AG	83	JAE	LEFTWICH,RW		77	117
3.67	FOSTER,G	MR	80	JAE			29	62
2.92	LIBBY,R	03	77	AOS	LEWIS,BL		245	268
2.71	LIBBY,R	03	82	AOS	LEWIS,BL		231	286
2.63	ZMIJEWSKI,ME	AG	81	JAE	HAGERMAN,RL		129	149
2.43	BALL,R	ST	82	JAR	FOSTER,G		161	234
2.43	LEV,B	ST	82	JAR	OHLSON,JA		249	322
2.18	HOPWOOD,AG	01	78	AOS			3	14
2.14	FRIED,D	OC	82	JAE	GIVOLY,D		85	107
1.86	DHALIWAL,DS	JL	82	JAE	SALAMON,GL	SMITH,ED	41	53
1.83	BIRNBERG,JG	23	83	AOS	TUROPOLEC,L	YOUNG,SM	111	130
1.83	COOPER,DJ	23	83	AOS			269	286
1.50	CHRISTENSON,C	JA	83	TAR			1	22
1.38	EINHORN,HJ	SP	81	JAR	HOGARTH,RM		1	31
1.20	DYCKMAN,TR	SP	84	JAR	ZEFF,SA		225	297
1.14	SWIERINGA,RJ	ST	82	JAR	WEICK,KE		56	101
1.00	CHESLEY,GR	AP	75	TAR			325	337
1.00	DEMSKI,JS	ST	82	JAR	KREPS,DM		117	148
0.86	FELIX JR,WL	AP	82	TAR	KINNEY JR,WR		245	271
0.85	BEAVER,WH	ST	74	JAR	DEMSKI,JS		170	187
0.83	LIBBY,R	AU	77	JAR	FISHBURN,PC		272	292
0.77	ABDEL-KHALIK,AR	JA	74	TAR	LUSK,EJ		8	23
0.75	BROWN,LD	AP	85	TAR	GARDNER,JC		262	277
0.71	DEANGELO,LE	DE	82	JAE			171	203
0.67	CUSHING,BE	AU	83	AUD	LOEBBECKE,JK		23	41
0.62	ASHTON,RH	OC	75	TAR			710	722
0.57	VERRECCHIA,RE	ST	82	JAR			1	42
0.54	EPSTEIN,MJ	01	76	AOS	FLAMHOLTZ,EG	MCDONOUGH,JJ	23	42
0.50	BROWN,LD	SP	85	JAR	GARDNER,JC		84	109
0.50	JARRELL,GA	AG	79	JAE			93	116
0.44	WATTS,RL	AG	80	JAE	ZIMMERMAN,JL		95	106
0.40	ZEFF,SA	JL	84	TAR			447	468
0.38	DOWNES,D	AP	73	TAR	DYCKMAN,TR		300	317
0.38	IJIRI,Y	SP	68	JAR	KINARD,JC	PUTNEY,FB	1	28
0.36	KETZ,JE	OC	78	TAR			952	960
0.31	HOFSTEDT,TR	01	76	AOS			43	58
0.31	MCRAE,TW	SP	74	JAR			80	92
0.30	VATTER,WJ	JL	79	TAR			563	573
0.23	BIRNBERG,JG	JL	67	TAR	NATH,R		468	479
0.22	HUSSEIN,ME	SU	80	JAA	KETZ,JE		354	367
0.22	RONEN,J	SU	80	JAA	SADAN,S		339	353
0.20	GROVE,HD	JL	79	TAR	SAVICH,RS		522	537
0.20	MORSE,D	AU	84	JAR			605	623
0.20	SMITH,G	AU	84	AUD	KROGSTAD,JL		107	117
0.17	LAVIN,D	03	77	AOS			237	244
0.15	BALL,R	SP	71	JAR			1	31
0.15	CAUSEY JR,DY	JA	76	TAR			19	30

CITE IND-EX	FIRST AUTHOR	ISS-UE	YE-AR	JOUR-NAL	SECOND AUTHOR	THIRD AUTHOR	PAG BEG	PAG END
0.14	WHALEY,RE	OC	82	JAE	CHEUNG,JK		57	83
0.13	ALFORD,MR	SP	81	JAA	EDMONDS,TP		255	264
0.11	FLAHERTY,RE	AU	80	JAA	SCHWARTZ,BN		47	56
0.08	BEDFORD,NM	JL	75	TAR	ZIEGLER,RE		435	443
0.08	BOLLOM,WJ	JA	72	TAR	WEYGANDT,JJ		75	84
0.08	BRIEF,RP	SP	67	JAR			27	38
0.08	GROVE,HD	03	77	AOS	MOCK,TJ	EHRENREICH,K	219	236
0.08	MCRAE,TW	AP	70	TAR			315	321
0.08	PARKER,RH	SP	68	JAR			58	71
0.08	SORENSEN,JE	JL	77	TAR	GROVE,HD		658	675
0.08	YAMEY,BS	SP	67	JAR			51	76
0.00	BRANCH,B	SP	81	JAA	BERKOWITZ,B		215	219
0.00	BRIEF,RP	OC	77	TAR			810	812
0.00	BRIGHTON,GD	JA	69	TAR			137	144
0.00	BROWN,LD	02	87	AOS	GARDNER,JC	VASARHELYI,MA	193	204
0.00	BUCKLEY,JW	JA	66	TAR			75	82
0.00	BUCKLEY,JW	01	80	AOS			49	64
0.00	CHATFIELD,M	JA	75	TAR			1	6
0.00	COHEN,MF	JA	65	TAR			1	8
0.00	COOPER,T	WI	80	JAA			138	146
0.00	COOPER,WW	AU	85	JAA	HO,JL	HUNTER,JE	22	39
0.00	COPELAND,TE	AU	78	JAA			33	48
0.00	CROSBY,MA	SP	85	AUD			118	132
0.00	DAVIDSON,S	AP	63	TAR			278	284
0.00	DYL,EA	02	85	AOS	LILLY,MS		171	176
0.00	FELIX JR,WL	SP	88	AUD	NILES,MS		43	60
0.00	FLESHER,DL	JL	86	TAR	FLESHER,TK		421	434
0.00	GIBBS,G	OC	64	TAR			4	7
0.00	GRADY,P	JA	65	TAR			21	30
0.00	HAIN,HP	AU	67	JAR			154	163
0.00	HECK,JL	OC	86	TAR	BREMSER,WG		735	744
0.00	HOLMES,W	JA	79	TAR			47	57
0.00	HOLSTRUM,GL	AU	82	AUD	MESSIER JR,WF		45	63
0.00	HORRIGAN,JO	AP	68	TAR			284	294
0.00	JENTZ,GA	AP	67	TAR			362	365
0.00	KINNEY JR,WR	AU	81	JAA			5	17
0.00	KROSS,W	AU	80	JAA	CHAPMAN,G	STRAND,KH	36	46
0.00	LEHMAN,C	05	87	AOS	TINKER,T		503	522
0.00	LEWIS,CD	JA	67	TAR			96	105
0.00	LEWIS,NR	34	84	AOS	PARKER,LD	SUTCLIFFE,P	275	289
0.00	MANES,RP	JL	64	TAR			631	638
0.00	MEYER,PE	JA	76	TAR			80	89
0.00	MOST,KS	SP	67	JAR			39	50
0.00	MOST,KS	OC	72	TAR			722	734
0.00	NORGAARD,CT	JL	72	TAR			433	442
0.00	OVADIA,A	WI	80	JAA	RONEN,J		113	137
0.00	PERAGALLO,E	JL	71	TAR			529	534
0.00	REVSINE,L	AP	81	TAR			342	354
0.00	ROSEN,LS	JA	69	TAR	DECOSTER,DT		124	136
0.00	SCHNEPPER,JA	JL	77	TAR			653	657

RESEARCH METHOD=ARCHIVAL   - SECONDARY

CITE IND- EX	FIRST AUTHOR	ISS- UE	YE- AR	JOUR -NAL	SECOND AUTHOR	THIRD AUTHOR	PAG BEG	PAG END
0.00	SIMON,SI	OC	64	TAR			884	889
0.00	SIMON,SI	AP	65	TAR			401	406
0.00	SLAVIN,NS	AP	77	TAR			360	368
0.00	SMITH,DB	OC	82	JAE	NICHOLS,DR		109	120
0.00	SMITH,G	AU	88	AUD			108	117
0.00	SNOWBALL,D	01	86	AOS			47	70
0.00	STONE,WE	AP	69	TAR			284	291
0.00	WEBER,C	JL	63	TAR			534	539
0.00	WELLS,MC	JL	76	TAR			471	482
0.00	WEYGANDT,JJ	JA	70	TAR			69	75
0.00	WINJUM,JO	OC	70	TAR			743	761
0.00	WINJUM,JO	JA	71	TAR			149	155
0.00	ZEFF,SA	SP	86	JAA			131	154

RESEARCH METHOD=ARCHIVAL - SECONDARY

2.5 RESEARCH METHOD=EMPIRICAL - CASE

CITE IND-EX	FIRST AUTHOR	ISS-UE	YE-AR	JOUR -NAL	SECOND AUTHOR	THIRD AUTHOR	PAG BEG	PAG END
2.33	BOLAND,RJ	23	83	AOS	PONDY,LR		223	234
0.50	MARKUS,ML	23	83	AOS	PFEFFER,J		205	218
0.50	NEWMAN,DP	SP	81	JAR			247	262
0.43	JONSSON,S	03	82	AOS			287	304
0.42	BAKER,CR	JL	77	TAR			576	586
0.38	CAMMANN,C	04	76	AOS			301	314
0.33	GROJER,JE	04	77	AOS	STARK,A		349	385
0.33	PRESTON,A	06	86	AOS			521	540
0.30	BLOCHER,E	JL	79	TAR			563	573
0.23	BALOFF,N	AU	67	JAR	KENNELLY,JW		131	143
0.23	MACY,BA	23	76	AOS	MIRVIS,PH		179	194
0.23	MCKEOWN,JC	JA	71	TAR			12	29
0.15	DOCKWEILER,RC	OC	69	TAR			729	742
0.15	FALK,H	AP	73	TAR	OPHIR,T		323	338
0.15	PELES,YC	SP	70	JAR			128	137
0.15	SCHIFF,M	SP	66	JAR			62	67
0.15	ZIMMERMAN,JL	AU	76	JAR			301	319
0.08	ALBRECHT,WS	OC	76	TAR			824	837
0.08	ALY,HF	JA	71	TAR	DUBOFF,JI		119	128
0.08	CHURCHILL,NC	ST	66	JAR			128	156
0.08	FLOWER,JF	SP	66	JAR			16	36
0.08	FOGELBERG,G	AU	71	JAR			215	235
0.08	MCKEOWN,JC	SP	73	JAR			62	99
0.08	SHANK,JK	JA	71	TAR			57	74
0.00	BJORN-ANDERSEN,N	02	80	AOS	PEDERSEN,PH		203	216
0.00	CHAN,JL	AP	78	TAR			309	323
0.00	CLARK,JJ	OC	73	TAR	ELGERS,PT		668	678
0.00	COLIGNON,R	06	88	AOS	COVALESKI,M		559	579
0.00	COVALESKI,MA	01	88	AOS	DIRSMITH,MW		1	24
0.00	CZARNIAWSKA-,B	04	88	AOS			415	430
0.00	GIBSON,JL	JL	63	TAR			492	500
0.00	HORVITZ,JS	WI	81	JAA	HAINKEL,M		114	127
0.00	HORVITZ,JS	WI	85	JAA	COLDWELL,S		86	99
0.00	JONSON,LC	34	78	AOS	JONSSON,B	SVENSSON,G	261	268
0.00	JONSSON,S	05	88	AOS	GRONLUND,A		513	532
0.00	KAPLAN,RS	SP	83	AUD			52	65
0.00	KINNEY JR,WR	SP	87	AUD			59	73
0.00	KISTLER,LH	OC	67	TAR			758	766
0.00	LUKKA,K	03	88	AOS			281	301
0.00	SAPIENZA,SR	JA	63	TAR			91	101
0.00	SCHATTKE,RW	OC	65	TAR			805	811
0.00	SPENCER,CH	JA	65	TAR	BARNISEL,TS		144	153
0.00	STEVENSON,RA	AP	66	TAR			312	317
0.00	WILD,JJ	SP	87	JAR			139	160
0.00	YOUNG,DW	OC	76	TAR			788	799

2.6 RESEARCH METHOD=EMPIRICAL - FIELD

CITE IND-EX	FIRST AUTHOR	ISS-UE	YE-AR	JOUR -NAL	SECOND AUTHOR	THIRD AUTHOR	PAG BEG	PAG END
3.62	BRUNS JR,WJ	AU	75	JAR	WATERHOUSE,JH		177	203
3.50	BERRY,AJ	01	85	AOS	CAPPS,T	COOPER,D	3	28
2.75	HAYES,DC	JA	77	TAR			22	39
2.08	HOPWOOD,AG	ST	72	JAR			156	182
2.00	OTLEY,DT	SP	78	JAR			122	149
2.00	SIMUNIC,DA	SP	80	JAR			161	190
1.92	MILANI,K	AP	75	TAR			274	284
1.25	FERRIS,KR	JL	77	TAR			605	615
1.15	HOPWOOD,AG	JL	74	TAR			485	495
1.09	COLLINS,F	AP	78	TAR			324	335
1.00	FLAMHOLTZ,EG	23	83	AOS			153	170
0.86	HYLAS,RE	OC	82	TAR	ASHTON,RH		751	765
0.75	MERCHANT,KA	02	85	AOS			201	210
0.67	BOLAND,RJ	45	86	AOS	PONDY,LR		403	422
0.55	FLAMHOLTZ,EG	02	78	AOS	COOK,E		115	140
0.50	MERCHANT,KA	01	85	AOS			67	86
0.46	SWIERINGA,RJ	ST	72	JAR	MONCUR,RH		194	209
0.40	MAHER,MW	AU	79	JAR	RAMANATHAN,KV	PETERSON,RB	476	503
0.38	PRATT,J	02	81	AOS	JIAMBALVO,J		133	142
0.33	MIRVIS,PH	23	83	AOS	LAWLER III,EE		175	190
0.31	ABDEL-KHALIK,AR	AP	74	TAR			271	283
0.31	FLAMHOLTZ,EG	ST	72	JAR			241	266
0.23	ORTMAN,RF	AP	75	TAR			298	304
0.23	PROBST,FR	JA	71	TAR			113	118
0.23	SEARFOSS,DG	04	76	AOS			375	388
0.20	CUSHING,BE	ST	79	JAR	SEARFOSS,DG	RANDALL,RH	172	216
0.15	CHURCHILL,NC	OC	65	TAR	COOPER,WW		767	781
0.15	CHURCHILL,NC	OC	75	TAR	SHANK,JK		643	656
0.15	SORENSEN,JE	OC	72	TAR	FRANKS,DD		735	746
0.11	HOPPER,TM	04	80	AOS			401	412
0.09	CARLSSON,J	34	78	AOS	EHN,P	ERLANDER,B	249	260
0.09	JACOBS,FH	SP	78	JAR			190	203
0.08	ARNOLD,DF	AU	77	JAR	HUEFNER,RJ		245	252
0.08	OGAN,P	23	76	AOS			195	218
0.08	SAULS,EH	JA	72	TAR			109	115
0.00	ASHTON,AH	JL	84	TAR			361	375
0.00	ASHTON,RH	SU	81	JAA	HYLAS,RE		325	332
0.00	ASHTON,RH	SU	81	AUD	HYLAS,RE		12	22
0.00	BANKER,RD	AU	87	JAA	DATAR,SM	RAJAN,MV	319	347
0.00	BROWNELL,P	OC	82	TAR			766	777
0.00	FALK,H	AU	72	JAR			359	375
0.00	FLAMHOLTZ,EG	04	87	AOS			309	318
0.00	LUCAS,HC	OC	75	TAR			735	746
0.00	MCROBERTS,HA	04	85	AOS	HUDSON,J		493	502
0.00	SHRIVER,KA	JA	87	TAR			79	96
0.00	WARREN,CS	SP	74	JAR			158	177
0.00	WILCOX,KA	01	77	AOS	SMITH,CH		81	97
0.00	WILLIAMS,JJ	04	85	AOS	NEWTON,JD	MORGAN,EA	457	478

RESEARCH METHOD=EMPIRICAL - FIELD

CITE IND- EX	FIRST AUTHOR	ISS- UE	YE- AR	JOUR -NAL	SECOND AUTHOR	THIRD AUTHOR	PAG BEG	PAG END

RESEARCH METHOD=EMPIRICAL - FIELD

2.7 RESEARCH METHOD=EMPIRICAL - LAB

CITE IND- EX	FIRST AUTHOR	ISS- UE	YE- AR	JOUR -NAL	SECOND AUTHOR	THIRD AUTHOR	PAG BEG	PAG END
2.62	ASHTON,RH	SP	74	JAR			143	157
2.38	JOYCE,EJ	ST	76	JAR			29	60
2.00	DRIVER,MJ	JL	75	TAR	MOCK,TJ		490	508
1.85	SWIERINGA,RJ	ST	76	JAR	GIBBINS,M	LARSSON,L	159	187
1.78	ASHTON,RH	SP	80	JAR	KRAMER,SS		1	15
1.69	LIBBY,R	JL	75	TAR			475	489
1.63	JOYCE,EJ	SP	81	JAR	BIDDLE,GC		120	145
1.57	BROWNELL,P	SP	82	JAR			12	27
1.46	DERMER,JD	JL	73	TAR			511	519
1.38	BROWNELL,P	OC	81	TAR			844	860
1.31	ABDEL-KHALIK,AR	OC	74	TAR			743	750
1.31	CORLESS,JC	JL	72	TAR			556	566
1.30	JIAMBALVO,J	AU	79	JAR			436	455
1.25	LIBBY,R	AU	85	JAR			648	667
1.23	LIBBY,R	SP	75	JAR			150	161
1.17	LEWIS,BL	SP	83	JAR	SHIELDS,MD	YOUNG,SM	271	285
1.17	SHIELDS,MD	AP	83	TAR			284	303
1.15	ASHTON,RH	ST	76	JAR			1	17
1.15	BOATSMAN,JR	AP	74	TAR	ROBERTSON,JC		342	352
1.14	SOLOMON,I	AU	82	JAR			689	710
1.13	JOYCE,EJ	AU	81	JAR	BIDDLE,GC		323	349
1.11	SHIELDS,MD	04	80	AOS			429	442
1.09	UECKER,WC	SP	78	JAR			169	189
1.08	ELIAS,N	ST	72	JAR			215	233
1.00	CASEY JR,CJ	JA	80	TAR			36	49
1.00	FELIX JR,WL	OC	76	TAR			800	807
1.00	MCGHEE,W	JL	78	TAR	SHIELDS,MD	BIRNBERG,JG	681	697
0.92	DICKHAUT,JW	JA	73	TAR			61	79
0.92	HOFSTEDT,TR	AP	77	TAR	HUGHES,GD		379	395
0.92	MORIARITY,S	AU	76	JAR	BARRON,FH		320	341
0.90	BENBASAT,I	OC	79	TAR	DEXTER,AS		735	749
0.89	ABDEL-KHALIK,AR	AU	80	JAR	EL-SHESHAI,KM		325	342
0.88	HILTON,RW	SP	81	JAR	SWIERINGA,RJ	HOSKIN,RE	86	108
0.85	ABDEL-KHALIK,AR	ST	73	JAR			104	138
0.85	BAREFIELD,RM	AU	72	JAR			229	242
0.85	CHERRINGTON,DJ	ST	73	JAR	CHERRINGTON,JO		225	253
0.85	FORAN,MF	OC	74	TAR	DECOSTER,DT		751	763
0.83	BIGGS,SF	SP	83	JAR	MOCK,TJ		234	255
0.83	UECKER,WC	03	77	AOS	KINNEY JR,WR		269	275
0.83	WRIGHT,WF	JL	77	TAR			676	689
0.80	LIBBY,R	SP	79	JAR			99	122
0.78	LEWIS,BL	AU	80	JAR			594	602
0.77	HARIED,AA	AU	72	JAR			376	391
0.77	HOFSTEDT,TR	OC	72	TAR			679	692
0.77	KENNEDY,HA	SP	75	JAR			97	116
0.77	MOCK,TJ	SP	72	JAR	ESTRIN,TL	VASARHELYI,MA	129	153
0.77	ROSE,R	ST	70	JAR	BEAVER,WH	BECKER,S	138	148
0.77	SAN MIGUEL,JG	04	76	AOS			357	374

RESEARCH METHOD=EMPIRICAL - LAB

CITE INDEX	FIRST AUTHOR	ISSUE	YEAR	JOURNAL	SECOND AUTHOR	THIRD AUTHOR	PAG BEG	PAG END
0.75	LARCKER,DF	JL	81	TAR			519	538
0.70	LIBBY,R	ST	79	JAR			35	57
0.70	MORIARITY,S	ST	79	JAR	BARRON,FH		114	135
0.67	BARNES,P	01	86	AOS	WEBB,J		1	18
0.67	CHOW,CW	OC	83	TAR			667	685
0.67	ROCKNESS,HO	OC	77	TAR			893	903
0.64	SCHULTZ JR,JJ	JL	78	TAR	GUSTAVSON,SG		626	641
0.63	ASHTON,RH	SP	81	JAR			42	61
0.63	CROSBY,MA	AP	81	TAR			355	365
0.62	LUSK,EJ	ST	73	JAR			191	202
0.62	PANKOFF,LD	ST	70	JAR	VIRGIL JR,RL		1	48
0.62	RONEN,J	AU	71	JAR			307	332
0.62	SCHWAN,ES	23	76	AOS			219	238
0.60	BOUWMAN,MJ	34	84	AOS			325	327
0.60	MORIARITY,S	SP	79	JAR			205	224
0.58	CHESLEY,GR	SP	77	JAR			1	11
0.58	HARRELL,AM	OC	77	TAR			833	841
0.57	DANOS,P	JA	82	TAR	IMHOFF JR,EA		39	54
0.57	DYCKMAN,TR	01	82	AOS	HOSKIN,RE	SWIERINGA,RJ	1	12
0.57	KINNEY JR,WR	JA	82	TAR	UECKER,WC		55	69
0.57	SOLOMON,I	01	82	AOS	KROGSTAD,JL	ROMNEY,MB	27	42
0.56	SNOWBALL,D	03	80	AOS			323	340
0.56	UECKER,WC	SP	80	JAR			191	213
0.55	MAGEE,RP	AU	78	JAR	DICKHAUT,JW		294	314
0.54	CHESLEY,GR	SP	76	JAR			27	48
0.54	DICKHAUT,JW	SP	75	JAR	EGGLETON,IRC		38	72
0.54	DOPUCH,N	AU	73	JAR	RONEN,J		191	211
0.54	FLAMHOLTZ,EG	23	76	AOS			153	166
0.54	HENDRICKS,JA	AP	76	TAR			292	305
0.54	OLIVER,BL	SP	72	JAR			154	166
0.54	WARD,BH	SP	76	JAR			138	152
0.50	ASHTON,AH	AP	85	TAR			173	185
0.50	HILTON,RW	SP	81	JAR	SWIERINGA,RJ		109	119
0.50	LIBBY,R	AP	85	TAR	ARTMAN,JT	WILLINGHAM,JJ	212	230
0.50	SAVICH,RS	JL	77	TAR			642	652
0.50	SHIELDS,MD	01	81	AOS	BIRNBERG,JG	FRIEZE,IH	69	96
0.50	SHOCKLEY,RA	AU	83	JAR	HOLT,RN		545	564
0.50	VASARHELYI,MA	SP	77	JAR			138	153
0.50	WALLER,WS	JL	85	TAR	CHOW,CW		458	476
0.46	ANSARI,SL	AU	76	JAR			189	211
0.46	COOK,DM	ST	67	JAR			213	224
0.46	DYCKMAN,TR	SP	64	JAR			91	107
0.46	JENSEN,RE	AU	66	JAR			224	238
0.45	NEUMANN,BR	AU	78	JAR	FRIEDMAN,LA		400	410
0.44	HOLT,RN	03	80	AOS	CARROLL,R		285	296
0.44	WEBER,R	SP	80	JAR			214	241
0.43	DANOS,P	WI	82	AUD	IMHOFF JR,EA		23	34
0.43	HAMILTON,RE	AU	82	JAR	WRIGHT,WF		756	765
0.43	WILNER,N	01	82	AOS			43	52
0.40	BIGGS,SF	34	84	AOS			313	323

RESEARCH METHOD=EMPIRICAL - LAB

CITE IND-EX	FIRST AUTHOR	ISS-UE	YE-AR	JOUR-NAL	SECOND AUTHOR	THIRD AUTHOR	PAG BEG	PAG END
0.40	DANOS,P	OC	84	TAR	HOLT,DL	IMHOFF JR,EA	547	573
0.40	KROGSTAD,JL	AU	84	AUD	ETTENSON,RT	SHANTEAU,J	54	74
0.40	SHIELDS,MD	34	84	AOS			355	363
0.40	STOCK,D	SP	84	JAR	WATSON,CJ		192	206
0.40	WALLER,WS	OC	84	TAR	FELIX JR,WL		637	646
0.38	BARRETT,ME	ST	71	JAR			50	65
0.38	BECKER,S	AU	74	JAR	RONEN,J	SORTER,GH	317	329
0.38	BROWN,C	SP	81	JAR			62	85
0.38	EGGLETON,IRC	ST	76	JAR			68	131
0.38	KESSLER,L	SP	81	JAR	ASHTON,RH		146	162
0.38	MCINTYRE,EV	JL	73	TAR			575	585
0.38	MOCK,TJ	ST	69	JAR			124	159
0.38	STALLMAN,JC	ST	69	JAR			29	43
0.36	ABDEL-KHALIK,AR	SP	78	JAR	ESPEJO,J		1	13
0.36	KEYS,DE	AU	78	JAR			389	399
0.33	BELKAOUI,A	03	80	AOS			263	284
0.33	FRECKA,TJ	JA	83	TAR	HOPWOOD,WS		115	128
0.33	FREDERICK,DM	AU	86	JAR	LIBBY,R		270	290
0.33	FRIEDMAN,LA	AU	80	JAR	NEUMANN,BR		407	419
0.33	KIDA,TE	AU	80	JAR			506	523
0.33	SCHEPANSKI,A	JL	83	TAR			581	599
0.33	TROTMAN,KT	SP	83	JAR	YETTON,PW	ZIMMER,I	286	292
0.31	CHANDRA,G	OC	74	TAR			733	742
0.30	FIRTH,MA	04	79	AOS			283	296
0.30	RECKERS,PMJ	AU	79	JAA	TAYLOR,ME		42	55
0.29	ASHTON,AH	AU	82	JAR			415	428
0.29	BENBASAT,I	SP	82	JAR	DEXTER,AS		1	11
0.27	CHESLEY,GR	AU	78	JAR			225	241
0.27	HIRSCH JR,ML	AU	78	JAR			254	269
0.27	WEBER,R	FL	78	JAR			368	388
0.25	ANDERSON,MJ	AU	85	JAR			843	852
0.25	BIGGS,SF	OC	85	TAR	WILD,JJ		607	633
0.25	CHEN,K	01	81	AOS	SUMMERS,EL		1	16
0.25	DEJONG,DV	AU	85	JAR	FORSYTHE,R	UECKER,WC	753	793
0.25	GORDON,FE	04	77	AOS	RHODE,JG	MERCHANT,KA	295	306
0.25	KELLY,LK	JA	77	TAR			97	108
0.25	MADEO,SA	JL	85	TAR	PINCUS,M		407	429
0.25	MILLIRON,VC	AU	85	JAR			794	816
0.25	PLUMLEE,RD	AU	85	JAR			683	699
0.25	TROTMAN,KT	AU	85	JAR			740	752
0.25	UECKER,WC	JL	81	TAR	BRIEF,AP	KINNEY JR,WR	465	478
0.25	WALLER,WS	AU	85	JAR			817	828
0.25	WRIGHT,WF	04	77	AOS			323	332
0.25	YOUNG,SM	AU	85	JAR			829	842
0.23	BRUNS JR,WJ	AP	65	TAR			345	357
0.23	DASCHER,PE	SP	71	JAR	COPELAND,RM		32	39
0.23	DYCKMAN,TR	AP	64	TAR			285	295
0.23	FALK,H	SP	73	JAR	OPHIR,T		108	116
0.23	HEINTZ,JA	OC	73	TAR			679	689
0.23	HOLSTRUM,GL	AU	71	JAR			268	277

RESEARCH METHOD=EMPIRICAL - LAB

CITE IND-EX	FIRST AUTHOR	ISS-UE	YE-AR	JOUR-NAL	SECOND AUTHOR	THIRD AUTHOR	PAG BEG	PAG END
0.23	MOCK,TJ	JL	73	TAR			520	534
0.22	HARRELL,AM	04	80	AOS	KLICK,HD		393	400
0.22	PANY,K	JA	80	TAR	RECKERS,PMJ		50	61
0.20	BLOOM,R	01	84	AOS	ELGERS,PT	MURRAY,D	1	11
0.20	DAROCA,FP	01	84	AOS			13	32
0.20	FERRIS,KR	SP	84	AUD	TENNANT,KL		31	43
0.20	GUL,FA	AP	84	TAR			264	277
0.20	HARVEY,DW	03	79	AOS	RHODE,JG	MERCHANT,KA	187	210
0.20	NANNI JR,AJ	02	84	AOS			149	163
0.20	RICCHIUTE,DN	12	79	AOS			67	76
0.20	RICCHIUTE,DN	SP	84	JAR			341	350
0.18	PATTON,JM	AP	78	TAR			402	414
0.18	WEBER,R	AU	78	JAR			368	388
0.17	BLOCHER,E	AU	83	AUD	ESPOSITO,RS	WILLINGHAM,JJ	75	91
0.17	BROWN,C	AU	83	JAR			413	431
0.17	DANOS,P	AU	83	JAR	IMHOFF JR,EA		473	494
0.17	HOLDER,WW	SP	83	AUD			100	108
0.17	HOSKIN,RE	SP	83	JAR			78	95
0.17	JIAMBALVO,J	01	83	AOS	WATSON,DJ	BAUMLER,JV	13	30
0.17	JOHNSON,WB	JA	83	TAR			78	97
0.17	LARCKER,DF	JA	83	TAR	LESSIG,VP		58	77
0.17	TABOR,RH	SP	83	JAR			348	354
0.17	TILLER,MG	AU	83	JAR			581	595
0.17	TOMASSINI,LA	OC	77	TAR			904	913
0.17	WILKINS,T	OC	83	TAR	ZIMMER,I		749	764
0.15	ACLAND,D	23	76	AOS			133	142
0.15	DERMER,JD	JA	74	TAR	SIEGEL,JP		88	97
0.15	MCDONALD,DL	SP	68	JAR			38	49
0.15	PANKOFF,LD	AP	70	TAR	VIRGIL JR,RL		269	279
0.15	RONEN,J	OC	73	TAR	FALK,G		696	717
0.15	STERLING,RR	SP	69	JAR	RADOSEVICH,R		90	95
0.14	EGER,C	AU	82	JAR	DICKHAUT,JW		711	723
0.14	EGGLETON,IRC	SP	82	JAR			68	102
0.14	GAUMNITZ,BR	AU	82	JAR	NUNAMAKER,TR	SURDICK,JJ	745	755
0.14	JIAMBALVO,J	SP	82	JAR			152	161
0.14	JIAMBALVO,J	OC	82	TAR	PRATT,J		734	750
0.14	OTLEY,DT	SP	82	JAR	DIAS,FJB		171	188
0.14	PRATT,J	SP	82	JAR			189	209
0.14	UECKER,WC	AU	82	JAR			388	402
0.13	COPELAND,RM	SP	81	JAR	TAYLOR,RL	BROWN,SH	197	207
0.13	KOCH,BS	JL	81	TAR			574	586
0.13	RAMANATHAN,KV	02	81	AOS	WEIS,WL		143	152
0.13	RECKERS,PMJ	SU	81	AUD	STAGLIANO,AJ		23	37
0.11	ASHTON,RH	SP	80	JAR	BROWN,PR		269	277
0.11	FERRIS,KR	04	80	AOS	DILLARD,JF	NETHERCOTT,L	361	368
0.08	BOLLOM,WJ	JA	73	TAR			12	22
0.08	BRUNS JR,WJ	ST	66	JAR			1	14
0.08	DALTON,FE	JA	70	TAR	MINER,JB		134	139
0.08	GREER JR,WR	JL	74	TAR			496	505
0.08	KELLY,LK	JA	77	TAR			97	108

RESEARCH METHOD=EMPIRICAL - LAB

CITE IND-EX	FIRST AUTHOR	ISS-UE	YE-AR	JOUR -NAL	SECOND AUTHOR	THIRD AUTHOR	PAG BEG	PAG END
0.08	MCCOSH,AM	04	76	AOS	RAHMAN,M		339	356
0.08	SAULS,EH	ST	70	JAR			157	171
0.08	SPILLER JR,EA	SP	74	JAR	VIRGIL JR,RL		112	142
0.08	UECKER,WC	01	77	AOS			47	58
0.00	ABDEL-KHALIK,AR	AP	83	TAR	SNOWBALL,D	WRAGGE,JH	215	227
0.00	ABDEL-KHALIK,AR	AU	86	JAR	GRAUL,PR	NEWTON,JD	372	382
0.00	ABDOLMOHAM.,MJ	SP	86	AUD			1	16
0.00	ABDOLMOHAM.,MJ	JA	87	TAR	WRIGHT,A		1	13
0.00	ANDERSON JR,TN	AU	82	JAR	KIDA,TE		403	414
0.00	ANDERSON,MJ	05	88	AOS			431	446
0.00	ARANYA,N	04	81	AOS	POLLOCK,J	AMERNIC,J	271	280
0.00	ARRINGTON,CE	SP	84	JAR	HILLISON,WA	JENSEN,RE	298	312
0.00	ARRINGTON,CE	SP	85	JAR	BAILEY,CD	HOPWOOD,WS	1	20
0.00	ASHTON,AH	OC	88	TAR	ASHTON,RH		623	641
0.00	BAILEY,CD	SP	86	AUD	BALLARD,G		77	85
0.00	BAILEY,KE	AU	83	JAR	BYLINSKI,JH	SHIELDS,MD	355	370
0.00	BAILEY,WT	OC	81	TAR			882	896
0.00	BALLEW,V	JA	82	TAR			88	104
0.00	BAMBER,EM	AU	83	JAR			396	412
0.00	BAMBER,EM	JL	88	AUD	SNOWBALL,D		490	504
0.00	BAMBER,EM	SP	88	AUD	BAMBER,LS	BYLINSKI,JH	137	149
0.00	BARTON,RF	SP	69	JAR			116	122
0.00	BIGGS,SF	SP	87	AUD	MESSIER JR,WF	HANSEN,JV	1	21
0.00	BIGGS,SF	JA	88	TAR	MOCK,TJ	WATKINS,PR	148	162
0.00	BLOCHER,E	AU	85	AUD	BYLINSKI,JH		79	90
0.00	BLOCHER,E	06	86	AOS	MOFFIE,RP	ZMUD,RW	457	470
0.00	BLOCHER,E	SP	88	AUD	COOPER,JC		1	28
0.00	BORITZ,JE	AU	86	JAR			335	348
0.00	BOUWMAN,MJ	01	87	AOS	FRISHKOFF,PA	FRISHKOFF,P	1	30
0.00	BROWN,C	03	85	AOS			255	266
0.00	BROWN,C	JL	87	TAR	SOLOMON,I		564	577
0.00	BROWN,PR	AU	83	JAR			444	455
0.00	BROWN,PR	AU	86	AUD	KARAN,V		134	147
0.00	BUCHMAN,TA	03	85	AOS			267	286
0.00	BURGSTAHLER,D	AP	86	TAR	JIAMBALVO,J		233	248
0.00	BUTLER,SA	AU	85	JAR			513	526
0.00	BUTLER,SA	JA	86	TAR			101	111
0.00	BUTT,JL	AU	88	JAR			315	330
0.00	CAMPBELL,JE	34	84	AOS			329	342
0.00	CASEY JR,CJ	AP	86	TAR	SELLING,T		302	317
0.00	CHALOS,P	AU	85	JAR			527	543
0.00	CHOW,CW	JA	88	TAR	COOPER,JC	WALLER,WS	111	122
0.00	COLBERT,JL	02	88	AOS			111	121
0.00	DANIEL,SJ	SP	88	AUD			174	181
0.00	DAS,H	03	86	AOS			215	232
0.00	DAVIS,GB	SP	86	AUD	WEBER,R		35	49
0.00	DEJONG,DV	ST	85	JAR	FORSYTHE,R	LUNDHOLM,RJ	81	120
0.00	DYKXHOORN,HJ	04	82	AOS	SINNING,KE		337	348
0.00	ENIS,CR	02	88	AOS			123	145
0.00	FARMER,TA	AU	87	AUD	RITTENBERG,LE	TROMPETER,GM	1	14

RESEARCH METHOD=EMPIRICAL - LAB

CITE IND-EX	FIRST AUTHOR	ISS-UE	YE-AR	JOUR-NAL	SECOND AUTHOR	THIRD AUTHOR	PAG BEG	PAG END
0.00	FRISHKOFF,P	AU	84	JAA	FRISHKOFF,PA	BOUWMAN,MJ	44	53
0.00	GOMBOLA,MJ	JA	83	TAR	KETZ,JE		105	114
0.00	GUL,FA	34	84	AOS			233	239
0.00	HAKA,S	JL	86	TAR	FRIEDMAN,L	JONES,V	455	474
0.00	HANSEN,JV	AU	86	AUD	MESSIER JR,WF		109	123
0.00	HARPER JR,RM	AU	87	JAR	MISTER,WG	STRAWSER,JR	327	330
0.00	HARRELL,AM	34	84	AOS	STAHL,MJ		241	252
0.00	HARRISON,PD	AP	88	TAR	WEST,SG	RENEAU,JH	307	320
0.00	HILTON,RW	AP	88	TAR	SWIERINGA,RJ	TURNER,MJ	195	218
0.00	HOLT,DL	06	87	AOS			571	578
0.00	HOUGHTON,KA	AU	84	JAR	SENGUPTA,R		768	775
0.00	HOUGHTON,KA	02	87	AOS			143	152
0.00	HOUGHTON,KA	03	88	AOS			263	280
0.00	ISELIN,ER	02	88	AOS			147	164
0.00	JENNINGS,M	SP	87	AUD	KNEER,DC	RECKERS,PMJ	104	115
0.00	JIAMBALVO,J	SP	84	AUD	WALLER,WS		80	88
0.00	JOHNSON,DA	SP	83	AUD	PANY,K	WHITE,RA	38	51
0.00	JOHNSON,DA	AU	84	JAR	PANY,K		731	743
0.00	JOHNSON,WB	04	82	AOS			349	368
0.00	KAPLAN,SE	AU	84	AUD	RECKERS,PMJ		1	19
0.00	KAPLAN,SE	AU	85	AUD			12	25
0.00	KAPLAN,SE	AU	85	JAR			871	877
0.00	KAPLAN,SE	04	88	AOS	RECKERS,PMJ	ROARK,SJ	371	379
0.00	KHEMAKHEM,A	JL	68	TAR			522	534
0.00	KIDA,TE	SP	84	JAR			145	152
0.00	KIDA,TE	SP	84	JAR			332	340
0.00	KNAPP,MC	AP	85	TAR			202	211
0.00	KNAPP,MC	JL	87	TAR			578	588
0.00	LEWIS,BL	SP	85	JAR	BELL,J		228	239
0.00	LEWIS,BL	AP	88	TAR	PATTON,JM	GREEN,SL	270	282
0.00	LICATA,MP	JA	86	TAR	STRAWSER,RH	WELKER,RB	112	117
0.00	MADEO,SA	AP	87	TAR	SCHEPANSKI,A	UECKER,WC	323	342
0.00	MARGHEIM,LL	SP	86	AUD	PANY,K		50	63
0.00	MARGHEIM,LL	SP	86	JAR			194	205
0.00	MAYPER,AG	AU	82	JAR			773	783
0.00	MCKENNA,EF	03	80	AOS			297	310
0.00	MCKINELY,S	AU	85	JAR	PANY,K	RECKERS,PMJ	887	896
0.00	MEAR,R	JA	87	TAR	FIRTH,MA		176	182
0.00	MEIXNER,WF	JL	88	AUD	WELKER,RB		505	513
0.00	MESERVY,RD	AU	86	AUD	BAILEY JR,AD	JOHNSON,PE	44	74
0.00	MIA,L	05	88	AOS			465	475
0.00	MUNTER,P	WI	83	JAA	RATCLIFFE,TA		108	114
0.00	MURRAY,D	AU	86	JAR	FRAZIER,KB		400	404
0.00	NAIR,RD	AU	87	AUD	RITTENBERG,LE		15	38
0.00	PANY,K	AU	82	JAR	SMITH,CH		472	481
0.00	PANY,K	AU	87	AUD	RECKERS,PMJ		39	53
0.00	PILLSBURY,CM	SP	85	AUD			63	79
0.00	PORCANO,TM	OC	84	TAR			619	636
0.00	PURDY,CR	ST	69	JAR	SMITH JR,JM	GRAY,J	1	18
0.00	REBELE,JE	AU	88	AUD	HEINTZ,JA	BRIDEN,GE	43	52

RESEARCH METHOD=EMPIRICAL - LAB

CITE IND-EX	FIRST AUTHOR	ISS-UE	YE-AR	JOUR-NAL	SECOND AUTHOR	THIRD AUTHOR	PAG BEG	PAG END
0.00	RECKERS,PMJ	AU	82	AUD	SCHULTZ JR,JJ		64	74
0.00	SCHNEIDER,A	AU	84	JAR			657	678
0.00	SCHNEIDER,A	AU	85	JAR			911	919
0.00	SHIELDS,MD	04	87	AOS	SOLOMON,I	WALLER,WS	375	385
0.00	SHIELDS,MD	06	88	AOS	WALLER,WS		581	594
0.00	SHPILBERG,D	AU	86	AUD	GRAHAM,LE		75	94
0.00	SINGER,FA	OC	65	TAR			847	853
0.00	SRINIDHI,BN	SP	86	AUD	VASARHELYI,MA		64	76
0.00	STEPHENS,RG	AU	83	AUD			55	74
0.00	STERLING,RR	OC	72	TAR	TOLLEFSON,SO	FLAHERTY,RE	709	721
0.00	TROTMAN,KT	SP	85	JAR	YETTON,PW		256	267
0.00	UECKER,WC	JL	85	TAR	SCHEPANSKI,A	SHIN,J	430	457
0.00	WALLER,WS	AP	87	TAR	FELIX JR,WL		275	292
0.00	WALLER,WS	01	88	AOS			87	98
0.00	WRIGHT,A	SP	82	JAR			227	239
0.00	WRIGHT,A	JL	83	TAR			621	632
0.00	WRIGHT,A	SP	86	AUD			86	94
0.00	WRIGHT,A	06	88	AOS			595	605
0.00	YOUNG,SM	06	88	AOS	SHIELDS,MD	WOLF,G	607	618

RESEARCH METHOD=EMPIRICAL - LAB

2.8 RESEARCH METHOD=OPINION - SURVEY

CITE INDEX	FIRST AUTHOR	ISSUE	YEAR	JOURNAL	SECOND AUTHOR	THIRD AUTHOR	PAG BEG	PAG END
2.60	COOPER,DJ	34	84	AOS	SHERER,MJ		207	232
1.88	MERCHANT,KA	OC	81	TAR			813	829
1.80	GOVINDARAJAN,V	02	84	AOS			125	135
1.70	KENIS,I	OC	79	TAR			707	721
1.46	DECOSTER,DT	AU	68	JAR	FERTAKIS,JP		237	246
1.25	GOVINDARAJAN,V	01	85	AOS	GUPTA,AK		51	66
1.15	KHANDWALLA,PN	AU	72	JAR			275	285
1.00	CHENHALL,RH	JA	86	TAR	MORRIS,D		16	35
1.00	ONSI,M	JL	73	TAR			535	548
0.85	HARIED,AA	SP	73	JAR			117	145
0.77	BUZBY,SL	JL	74	TAR			423	435
0.75	OLSEN,C	ST	85	JAR			28	53
0.69	COPELAND,RM	AP	73	TAR	FRANCIA,AJ	STRAWSER,RH	365	374
0.69	SORENSEN,JE	JL	67	TAR			553	565
0.67	BROWNELL,P	OC	86	TAR	MCINNES,	M	587	600
0.67	RHODE,JG	02	77	AOS	SORENSEN,JE	LAWLER III,EE	165	176
0.62	OLIVER,BL	AU	74	JAR			299	316
0.60	GORDON,LA	01	84	AOS	NARAYANAN,VK		33	47
0.60	MERCHANT,KA	34	84	AOS			291	309
0.60	ROCKNESS,HO	02	84	AOS	SHIELDS,MD		165	177
0.57	COLLINS,F	02	82	AOS			107	122
0.57	GIBBINS,M	JA	82	TAR	WOLF,FM		105	124
0.50	COVALESKI,MA	04	83	AOS	DIRSMITH,MW		323	340
0.50	DILLARD,JF	03	79	AOS	FERRIS,KR		179	186
0.50	FRANCIS,JR	JA	87	TAR	SIMON,DT		145	157
0.50	HOWARD,TP	OC	83	TAR	NIKOLAI,LA		765	776
0.50	MACINTOSH,NB	01	87	AOS	DAFT,RL		49	61
0.46	SORTER,GH	AU	64	JAR	BECKER,S	ARCHIBALD,TR	183	196
0.45	BENSTON,GJ	ST	78	JAR	KRASNEY,MA		1	30
0.42	COOPER,DJ	03	77	AOS	ESSEX,S		201	218
0.40	BIGGS,SF	SP	84	AUD	WILD,JJ		68	79
0.40	BUZBY,SL	JA	79	TAR	FALK,H		23	37
0.40	MAYER-SOMMER,AP	JA	79	TAR			88	106
0.38	LAVIN,D	JA	76	TAR			41	50
0.38	SHOCKLEY,RA	OC	81	TAR			785	800
0.38	WATSON,DJ	AP	75	TAR			259	273
0.33	BELKAOUI,A	AU	80	JAR			362	374
0.33	BROWNELL,P	AU	83	JAR			456	472
0.33	COVALESKI,MA	03	86	AOS	DIRSMITH,MW		193	214
0.33	EICHENSEHER,JW	SP	83	AUD	SHIELDS,D		23	37
0.33	SENATRA,PT	OC	80	TAR			594	603
0.31	BRENNER,VC	AU	70	JAR			159	166
0.31	KLAMMER,T	AP	73	TAR			353	364
0.30	CLANCY,DK	12	79	AOS	COLLINS,F		21	30
0.27	BUZBY,SL	34	78	AOS	FALK,H		191	202
0.27	HICKS JR,JO	AP	78	TAR			371	388
0.25	BROWNELL,P	AU	85	JAR			502	512
0.25	HUSSEIN,ME	01	81	AOS			27	38

RESEARCH METHOD=OPINION - SURVEY

CITE IND-EX	FIRST AUTHOR	ISS-UE	YE-AR	JOUR-NAL	SECOND AUTHOR	THIRD AUTHOR	PAG BEG	PAG END
0.23	CAPLAN,EM	AP	68	TAR			342	362
0.22	BENKE,RL	02	80	AOS	RHODE,JG		187	202
0.20	ARANYA,N	JA	84	TAR	FERRIS,KR		1	15
0.20	DILLARD,JF	12	79	AOS			31	38
0.20	MOST,KS	AU	84	JAR			782	788
0.20	MUTCHLER,JF	SP	84	AUD			17	30
0.17	BROWNELL,P	04	83	AOS			307	322
0.17	FERRIS,KR	01	83	AOS	LARCKER,DF		1	12
0.17	WHITE,RA	JL	83	TAR			539	561
0.15	BRILOFF,AJ	JL	66	TAR			484	495
0.15	DECOSTER,DT	OC	71	TAR	RHODE,JG		651	664
0.15	LENGERMANN,JJ	OC	71	TAR			665	675
0.15	LOEB,SE	AU	71	JAR			287	306
0.15	MORTON,JR	AU	74	JAR			288	298
0.15	RITTS,BA	SP	74	JAR			93	111
0.15	SCHULTE JR,AA	JL	65	TAR			587	593
0.15	SMITH,CH	AP	72	TAR	LANIER,RA	TAYLOR,ME	270	283
0.15	WATSON,DJ	AP	75	TAR			259	273
0.14	BENSTON,GJ	02	82	AOS			87	106
0.14	SEILER,RE	04	82	AOS	BARTLETT,RW		381	404
0.13	DILLARD,JF	01	81	AOS			17	26
0.13	FERRIS,KR	04	81	AOS			317	326
0.13	HORWITZ,BN	WI	81	JAA	KOLODNY,R		102	113
0.13	ROSENZWEIG,K	04	81	AOS			339	354
0.13	SCHREUDER,H	AP	81	TAR			294	308
0.13	WOLF,FM	OC	81	TAR			861	881
0.11	FIRTH,MA	JL	80	TAR			451	466
0.11	WILLIAMS,PF	JA	80	TAR			62	77
0.08	BRADISH,RD	OC	65	TAR			757	766
0.08	BUZBY,SL	SP	75	JAR			16	37
0.08	CARPER,WB	23	76	AOS	POSEY,JM		143	152
0.08	CUMMING,J	ST	73	JAR			60	95
0.08	ESTES,RW	AU	68	JAR			200	207
0.08	FERRIS,KR	01	77	AOS			23	28
0.08	MARQUES,E	23	76	AOS			175	178
0.08	NYSTROM,PC	04	77	AOS			317	322
0.08	PARKER,JE	JL	75	TAR			512	524
0.00	ALDERMAN,CW	WI	82	AUD	DEITRICK,JW		54	68
0.00	ANSARI,SL	06	87	AOS	EUSKE,KJ		549	570
0.00	ARANYA,N	03	82	AOS	LACHMAN,R	AMERNIC,J	201	216
0.00	ASHTON,RH	AU	87	JAR	WILLINGHAM,JJ	ELLIOTT,RK	275	292
0.00	BELKAOUI,A	04	81	AOS			281	290
0.00	BERRY,LE	JA	87	TAR	HARWOOD,GB	KATZ,JL	14	28
0.00	BIRNBERG,JG	05	88	AOS	SNODGRASS,C		447	464
0.00	BRENNER,VC	AU	71	JAR	CARMACK,CW	WEINSTEIN,MG	359	366
0.00	BROWNELL,P	AU	86	JAR	HIRST,MK		241	249
0.00	BUCHMAN,TA	AU	83	AUD			92	103
0.00	BULLEN,ML	03	85	AOS	FLAMHOLTZ,EG		287	302
0.00	CARPENTER,CG	JL	71	TAR	STRAWSER,RH		509	518
0.00	CHENHALL,RH	AP	86	TAR			263	272

CITE IND- EX	FIRST AUTHOR	ISS- UE	YE- AR	JOUR -NAL	SECOND AUTHOR	THIRD AUTHOR	PAG BEG	PAG END
0.00	CHENHALL,RH	03	88	AOS	BROWNELL,P		225	233
0.00	CHOO,F	SP	86	AUD			17	34
0.00	CHOW,CW	SP	87	AUD	MCNAMEE,AH	PLUMLEE,RD	123	133
0.00	COLLINS,F	JA	87	TAR	MUNTER,P	FINN,DW	29	49
0.00	COTTELL JR,PG	WI	86	JAA			30	45
0.00	DAROCA,FP	SP	85	AUD	HOLDER,WW		80	92
0.00	DEAN,RA	03	88	AOS	FERRIS,KR	KONSTANS,C	235	250
0.00	DEVINE,CT	ST	66	JAR			160	176
0.00	DIRSMITH,MW	04	82	AOS	LEWIS,BL		319	336
0.00	DIRSMITH,MW	AU	85	JAA	COVALESKI,MA		5	21
0.00	DOWELL,CD	AU	81	JAA	HALL,JA		30	40
0.00	DYKXHOORN,HJ	JA	81	TAR	SINNING,KE		97	107
0.00	ENGSTROM,JH	SU	85	JAA			305	318
0.00	EVANS III,JH	ST	87	JAR	PATTON,JM		130	164
0.00	FAIRCLOTH,AW	01	81	AOS	RICCHIUTE,DN		53	68
0.00	FARRELY,GE	AP	85	TAR	FERRIS,KR	REICHENSTEIN,WR	278	288
0.00	FERRIS,KR	01	82	AOS			13	26
0.00	FERRIS,KR	03	82	AOS			225	230
0.00	GIROUX,GA	06	86	AOS	MAYPER,AG	DAFT,RL	499	520
0.00	GRANOF,MH	SU	84	JAA	SHORT,DG		323	333
0.00	HAKA,SF	01	87	AOS			31	48
0.00	HARRELL,AM	SP	86	AUD	CHEWNING,EG	TAYLOR,M	111	121
0.00	HARRELL,AM	SP	88	AUD	EICKHOFF,R		105	118
0.00	HASKINS,M	JL	87	TAR			542	563
0.00	HEINS,EB	AP	66	TAR			323	326
0.00	HILKE,JC	WI	86	JAA			17	29
0.00	HIRST,MK	AU	83	JAR			596	605
0.00	HONIG,LE	SP	78	JAA			231	236
0.00	IMHOFF JR,EA	OC	78	TAR			869	881
0.00	IMHOFF JR,EA	SP	88	AUD			182	191
0.00	JACKSON-COX,J	34	84	AOS	THIRKELL,JE	MCQUEENEY,J	253	273
0.00	JIAMBALVO,J	AU	85	AUD	WILNER,N		1	11
0.00	JONES,CS	03	85	AOS			303	328
0.00	JONES,CS	02	85	AOS			177	200
0.00	JOYCE,EJ	AU	82	JAR	LIBBY,R	SUNDER,S	654	675
0.00	KIDA,TE	02	84	AOS			137	147
0.00	KIM,KK	JL	88	TAR			472	489
0.00	KREISER,L	AP	77	TAR			427	437
0.00	KREUTZFELDT,RW	AU	86	AUD	WALLACE,WA		20	43
0.00	KUBLIN,M	JL	65	TAR			626	635
0.00	LAWLER,J	ST	67	JAR			86	92
0.00	LIGHTNER,SM	AU	82	AUD	ADAMS,SJ	LIGHTNER,KM	1	12
0.00	LOVATA,LM	AU	88	AUD			72	86
0.00	LOWE,RE	OC	65	TAR			839	846
0.00	MELLMAN,M	JA	63	TAR			118	123
0.00	MESSIER JR,WF	AU	87	AUD	HANSEN,JV		94	105
0.00	MOORES,K	01	86	AOS	STEADMAN,GT		19	34
0.00	NAHAPIET,JE	04	88	AOS			333	358
0.00	NAIR,RD	SP	83	JAA	RITTENBERG,LE		234	243
0.00	NORRIS,DR	01	84	AOS	NIEBUHR,RE		49	59

RESEARCH METHOD=OPINION   - SURVEY

CITE IND-EX	FIRST AUTHOR	ISS-UE	YE-AR	JOUR -NAL	SECOND AUTHOR	THIRD AUTHOR	PAG BEG	PAG END
0.00	PALMROSE,ZV	SP	87	AUD			90	103
0.00	PALMROSE,ZV	AU	88	AUD			63	71
0.00	PANY,K	SP	84	AUD	RECKERS,PMJ		89	97
0.00	POWELL,RM	JL	66	TAR			525	534
0.00	PRATT,J	04	82	AOS	JIAMBALVO,J		369	380
0.00	PRATT,J	04	85	AOS			427	442
0.00	PURDY,D	04	81	AOS			327	338
0.00	ROBBINS,WA	AU	86	JAR	AUSTIN,KR		412	421
0.00	ROCKNESS,J	04	88	AOS	WILLIAMS,PF		397	411
0.00	ROSENBERG,D	02	82	AOS	TOMKINS,L	DAY,P	123	138
0.00	SAN MIGUEL,JG	02	84	AOS	GOVINDARAJAN,V		179	188
0.00	SANNELLA,AJ	AU	86	JAA			288	304
0.00	SCAPENS,RW	AP	85	TAR	SALE,JT		231	247
0.00	SCHROEDER,MS	SP	86	AUD	SOLOMON,I	VICKREY,DW	86	94
0.00	SCHWEIKART,JA	06	86	AOS			541	554
0.00	SHIELDS,D	01	84	AOS			61	80
0.00	SIMONS,R	04	87	AOS			357	374
0.00	SOETERS,J	01	88	AOS	SCHREUDER,H		75	85
0.00	SOMEYA,K	OC	64	TAR			983	989
0.00	SUMNERS,GE	SP	87	AUD	`WHITE,RA	CLAY JR,RJ	116	122
0.00	TEOH,HY	02	84	AOS	THONG,G		189	206
0.00	VATTER,WJ	OC	67	TAR			721	730
0.00	WEBER,R	JL	86	TAR			498	518
0.00	WILLIAMS,DJ	SP	85	AUD	LILLIS,A		110	117
0.00	WILLIAMS,JJ	02	88	AOS	HININGS,CR		191	198
0.00	WINBORNE,MG	JL	64	TAR			622	626
0.00	WRIGHT,GB	SU	82	JAA	TAYLOR,RD		301	309

RESEARCH METHOD=OPINION   - SURVEY

3.1 SCHOOL OF THOUGHT=BEHAVIORAL - HIPS

CITE IND-EX	FIRST AUTHOR	ISS-UE	YE-AR	JOUR-NAL	SECOND AUTHOR	THIRD AUTHOR	PAG BEG	PAG END
3.18	WATERHOUSE,JH	01	78	AOS	TIESSEN,P		65	76
2.92	LIBBY,R	03	77	AOS	LEWIS,BL		245	268
2.71	LIBBY,R	03	82	AOS	LEWIS,BL		231	286
2.62	ASHTON,RH	SP	74	JAR			143	157
2.38	JOYCE,EJ	ST	76	JAR			29	60
2.00	DRIVER,MJ	JL	75	TAR	MOCK,TJ		490	508
1.85	SWIERINGA,RJ	ST	76	JAR	GIBBINS,M	LARSSON,L	159	187
1.78	ASHTON,RH	SP	80	JAR	KRAMER,SS		1	15
1.75	PRAKASH,P	01	77	AOS	RAPPAPORT,A		29	38
1.69	LIBBY,R	JL	75	TAR			475	489
1.60	GIBBINS,M	SP	84	JAR			103	125
1.40	WALLER,WS	34	84	AOS	FELIX JR,WL		383	406
1.38	EINHORN,HJ	SP	81	JAR	HOGARTH,RM		1	31
1.25	LIBBY,R	AU	85	JAR			648	667
1.23	LIBBY,R	SP	75	JAR			150	161
1.17	LEWIS,BL	SP	83	JAR	SHIELDS,MD	YOUNG,SM	271	285
1.17	SHIELDS,MD	AP	83	TAR			284	303
1.15	ASHTON,RH	OC	74	TAR			719	732
1.15	ASHTON,RH	ST	76	JAR			1	17
1.14	SOLOMON,I	AU	82	JAR			689	710
1.13	JOYCE,EJ	AU	81	JAR	BIDDLE,GC		323	349
1.11	SHIELDS,MD	04	80	AOS			429	442
1.00	CASEY JR,CJ	JA	80	TAR			36	49
1.00	EINHORN,HJ	ST·	76	JAR			196	206
1.00	HILTON,RW	AU	80	JAR			477	505
1.00	MCGHEE,W	JL	78	TAR	SHIELDS,MD	BIRNBERG,JG	681	697
0.92	DICKHAUT,JW	JA	73	TAR			61	79
0.92	HOFSTEDT,TR	AP	77	TAR	HUGHES,GD		379	395
0.90	BENBASAT,I	OC	79	TAR	DEXTER,AS		735	749
0.89	ABDEL-KHALIK,AR	AU	80	JAR	EL-SHESHAI,KM		325	342
0.85	BAREFIELD,RM	AU	72	JAR			229	242
0.83	BIGGS,SF	SP	83	JAR	MOCK,TJ		234	255
0.83	WRIGHT,WF	JL	77	TAR			676	689
0.80	LIBBY,R	SP	79	JAR			99	122
0.78	LEWIS,BL	AU	80	JAR			594	602
0.77	KENNEDY,HA	SP	75	JAR			97	116
0.77	MOCK,TJ	SP	72	JAR	ESTRIN,TL	VASARHELYI,MA	129	153
0.70	LIBBY,R	ST	79	JAR			35	57
0.67	BARNES,P	01	86	AOS	WEBB,J		1	18
0.67	BOLAND,RJ	45	86	AOS	PONDY,LR		403	422
0.67	MESSIER JR,WF	AU	83	JAR			611	618
0.67	WILNER,N	01	86	AOS	BIRNBERG,JG		71	82
0.64	SCHULTZ JR,JJ	JL	78	TAR	GUSTAVSON,SG		626	641
0.63	ASHTON,RH	SP	81	JAR			42	61
0.62	ASHTON,RH	OC	75	TAR			710	722
0.62	LUSK,EJ	ST	73	JAR			191	202
0.60	BOUWMAN,MJ	34	84	AOS			325	327
0.58	CHESLEY,GR	SP	77	JAR			1	11

CITE INDEX	FIRST AUTHOR	ISSUE	YEAR	JOURNAL	SECOND AUTHOR	THIRD AUTHOR	PAG BEG	PAG END
0.58	HARRELL,AM	OC	77	TAR			833	841
0.57	DYCKMAN,TR	01	82	AOS	HOSKIN,RE	SWIERINGA,RJ	1	12
0.57	KINNEY JR,WR	JA	82	TAR	UECKER,WC		55	69
0.57	SOLOMON,I	01	82	AOS	KROGSTAD,JL	ROMNEY,MB	27	42
0.56	SNOWBALL,D	03	80	AOS			323	340
0.56	UECKER,WC	SP	80	JAR			191	213
0.55	MAGEE,RP	AU	78	JAR	DICKHAUT,JW		294	314
0.54	CHESLEY,GR	SP	76	JAR			27	48
0.54	DICKHAUT,JW	SP	75	JAR	EGGLETON,IRC		38	72
0.50	ASHTON,AH	AP	85	TAR			173	185
0.50	HILTON,RW	SP	81	JAR	SWIERINGA,RJ		109	119
0.50	JOYCE,EJ	AU	81	JAR	LIBBY,R		544	550
0.50	LIBBY,R	AP	85	TAR	ARTMAN,JT	WILLINGHAM,JJ	212	230
0.50	SAVICH,RS	JL	77	TAR			642	652
0.50	VASARHELYI,MA	SP	77	JAR			138	153
0.46	JENSEN,RE	AU	66	JAR			224	238
0.46	MILLER,H	JA	72	TAR			31	37
0.44	HOLT,RN	03	80	AOS	CARROLL,R		285	296
0.44	WEBER,R	SP	80	JAR			214	241
0.43	HAMILTON,RE	AU	82	JAR	WRIGHT,WF		756	765
0.40	BIGGS,SF	34	84	AOS			313	323
0.40	SHIELDS,MD	34	84	AOS			355	363
0.40	STOCK,D	SP	84	JAR	WATSON,CJ		192	206
0.40	WALLER,WS	OC	84	TAR	FELIX JR,WL		637	646
0.38	BROWN,C	SP	81	JAR			62	85
0.38	EGGLETON,IRC	ST	76	JAR			68	131
0.38	JAIN,TN	JA	73	TAR			95	104
0.38	KESSLER,L	SP	81	JAR	ASHTON,RH		146	162
0.33	ASHTON,RH	JL	77	TAR			567	575
0.33	FREDERICK,DM	AU	86	JAR	LIBBY,R		270	290
0.33	NEWMAN,DP	02	80	AOS			217	230
0.33	SCHEPANSKI,A	JL	83	TAR			581	599
0.33	TROTMAN,KT	SP	83	JAR	YETTON,PW	ZIMMER,I	286	292
0.30	FIRTH,MA	04	79	AOS			283	296
0.29	BENBASAT,I	SP	82	JAR	DEXTER,AS		1	11
0.27	CHESLEY,GR	AU	78	JAR			225	241
0.27	WEBER,R	FL	78	JAR			368	388
0.25	ANDERSON,MJ	AU	85	JAR			843	852
0.25	BIGGS,SF	OC	85	TAR	WILD,JJ		607	633
0.25	CHEN,K	01	81	AOS	SUMMERS,EL		1	16
0.25	MILLIRON,VC	AU	85	JAR			794	816
0.25	PLUMLEE,RD	AU	85	JAR			683	699
0.25	TROTMAN,KT	AU	85	JAR			740	752
0.25	WRIGHT,WF	04	77	AOS			323	332
0.20	BIRNBERG,JG	34	84	AOS	SHIELDS,MD		365	382
0.20	BLOOM,R	01	84	AOS	ELGERS,PT	MURRAY,D	1	11
0.20	GUL,FA	AP	84	TAR			264	277
0.20	RICCHIUTE,DN	SP	84	JAR			341	350
0.18	PATTON,JM	AP	78	TAR			402	414
0.18	WEBER,R	AU	78	JAR			368	388

SCHOOL OF THOUGHT=BEHAVIORAL - HIPS

CITE IND-EX	FIRST AUTHOR	ISS-UE	YE-AR	JOUR-NAL	SECOND AUTHOR	THIRD AUTHOR	PAG BEG	PAG END
0.17	BROWN,C	AU	83	JAR			413	431
0.17	JOHNSON,WB	JA	83	TAR			78	97
0.17	LARCKER,DF	JA	83	TAR	LESSIG,VP		58	77
0.15	HANSON,EI	AP	66	TAR			239	243
0.14	EGER,C	AU	82	JAR	DICKHAUT,JW		711	723
0.14	EGGLETON,IRC	SP	82	JAR			68	102
0.14	EMERY,DR	AU	82	JAR	BARRON,FH	MESSIER JR,WF	450	458
0.14	GAUMNITZ,BR	AU	82	JAR	NUNAMAKER,TR	SURDICK,JJ	745	755
0.14	GIBBINS,M	SP	82	JAR			121	138
0.14	OTLEY,DT	SP	82	JAR	DIAS,FJB		171	188
0.14	PRATT,J	SP	82	JAR			189	209
0.14	WRIGHT,WF	01	82	AOS			65	78
0.11	ASHTON,RH	SP	80	JAR	BROWN,PR		269	277
0.11	BARAN,A	JA	80	TAR	LAKONISHOK,J	OFER,AR	22	35
0.08	MCCOSH,AM	04	76	AOS	RAHMAN,M		339	356
0.00	ABDEL-KHALIK,AR	AU	86	JAR	GRAUL,PR	NEWTON,JD	372	382
0.00	ANDERSON,MJ	05	88	AOS			431	446
0.00	ARRINGTON,CE	SP	84	JAR	HILLISON,WA	JENSEN,RE	298	312
0.00	ASHTON,AH	JL	84	TAR			361	375
0.00	ASHTON,AH	OC	88	TAR	ASHTON,RH		623	641
0.00	BAMBER,EM	AU	83	JAR			396	412
0.00	BAMBER,EM	SP	88	AUD	BAMBER,LS	BYLINSKI,JH	137	149
0.00	BERNARD,VL	AU	84	JAR			445	466
0.00	BIGGS,SF	SP	87	AUD	MESSIER JR,WF	HANSEN,JV	1	21
0.00	BIRNBERG,JG	01	80	AOS			71	80
0.00	BLOCHER,E	06	86	AOS	MOFFIE,RP	ZMUD,RW	457	470
0.00	BORITZ,JE	AU	86	JAR			335	348
0.00	BOUWMAN,MJ	01	87	AOS	FRISHKOFF,PA	FRISHKOFF,P	1	30
0.00	BROWN,PR	AU	83	JAR			444	455
0.00	BURGSTAHLER,D	AP	86	TAR	JIAMBALVO,J		233	248
0.00	BUTLER,SA	AU	85	JAR			513	526
0.00	BUTLER,SA	JA	86	TAR			101	111
0.00	CAMPBELL,JE	34	84	AOS			329	342
0.00	CASEY JR,CJ	AP	86	TAR	SELLING,T		302	317
0.00	CHAN,JL	AP	78	TAR			309	323
0.00	CHOO,F	SP	86	AUD			17	34
0.00	COLBERT,JL	02	88	AOS			111	121
0.00	DILLARD,JF	34	84	AOS			343	354
0.00	DIRSMITH,MW	04	82	AOS	LEWIS,BL		319	336
0.00	DYKXHOORN,HJ	04	82	AOS	SINNING,KE		337	348
0.00	ENIS,CR	02	88	AOS			123	145
0.00	FAIRCLOTH,AW	01	81	AOS	RICCHIUTE,DN		53	68
0.00	FRISHKOFF,P	AU	84	JAA	FRISHKOFF,PA	BOUWMAN,MJ	44	53
0.00	HAKA,S	JL	86	TAR	FRIEDMAN,L	JONES,V	455	474
0.00	HOLT,DL	06	87	AOS			571	578
0.00	HOUGHTON,KA	AU	84	JAR	SENGUPTA,R		768	775
0.00	ISELIN,ER	02	88	AOS			147	164
0.00	KAPLAN,SE	AU	85	JAR			871	877
0.00	KIDA,TE	SP	84	JAR			145	152
0.00	KIDA,TE	SP	84	JAR			332	340

SCHOOL OF THOUGHT=BEHAVIORAL - HIPS

CITE IND-EX	FIRST AUTHOR	ISS-UE	YE-AR	JOUR-NAL	SECOND AUTHOR	THIRD AUTHOR	PAG BEG	PAG END
0.00	KIDA,TE	02	84	AOS			137	147
0.00	LEWIS,BL	SP	85	JAR	BELL,J		228	239
0.00	MARTIN,A	ST	71	JAR			1	31
0.00	MAYPER,AG	AU	82	JAR			773	783
0.00	MEAR,R	JA	87	TAR	FIRTH,MA		176	182
0.00	MEAR,R	04	87	AOS	FIRTH,MA		331	340
0.00	MOCK,TJ	AU	78	JAR	VASARHELYI,MA		414	423
0.00	NAIR,RD	AU	87	AUD	RITTENBERG,LE		15	38
0.00	PRATT,J	04	82	AOS	JIAMBALVO,J		369	380
0.00	SCHEINER,JH	AU	82	JAR	KIGER,JE		482	496
0.00	SCHNEIDER,A	AU	84	JAR			657	678
0.00	SHIELDS,D	01	84	AOS			61	80
0.00	SHIELDS,MD	04	87	AOS	SOLOMON,I	WALLER,WS	375	385
0.00	SNOWBALL,D	01	86	AOS			47	70
0.00	VOGT,RA	01	77	AOS			59	80
0.00	WALLER,WS	AP	87	TAR	FELIX JR,WL		275	292

SCHOOL OF THOUGHT=BEHAVIORAL - HIPS

3.2 SCHOOL OF THOUGHT=BEHAVIORAL - OTHER

CITE IND-EX	FIRST AUTHOR	ISS-UE	YE-AR	JOUR-NAL	SECOND AUTHOR	THIRD AUTHOR	PAG BEG	PAG END
3.62	BRUNS JR,WJ	AU	75	JAR	WATERHOUSE,JH		177	203
3.50	BERRY,AJ	01	85	AOS	CAPPS,T	COOPER,D	3	28
2.08	HOPWOOD,AG	ST	72	JAR			156	182
2.00	OTLEY,DT	SP	78	JAR			122	149
1.92	MILANI,K	AP	75	TAR			274	284
1.88	MERCHANT,KA	OC	81	TAR			813	829
1.83	BIRNBERG,JG	23	83	AOS	TUROPOLEC,L	YOUNG,SM	111	130
1.80	GOVINDARAJAN,V	02	84	AOS			125	135
1.77	RONEN,J	OC	75	TAR	LIVINGSTONE,JL		671	685
1.70	KENIS,I	OC	79	TAR			707	721
1.69	GORDON,LA	01	76	AOS	MILLER,D		59	70
1.63	JOYCE,EJ	SP	81	JAR	BIDDLE,GC		120	145
1.57	BROWNELL,P	SP	82	JAR			12	27
1.46	DECOSTER,DT	AU	68	JAR	FERTAKIS,JP		237	246
1.46	DERMER,JD	JL	73	TAR			511	519
1.38	BROWNELL,P	OC	81	TAR			844	860
1.38	COLVILLE,I	02	81	AOS			119	132
1.30	JIAMBALVO,J	AU	79	JAR			436	455
1.25	FERRIS,KR	JL	77	TAR			605	615
1.25	GOVINDARAJAN,V	01	85	AOS	GUPTA,AK		51	66
1.23	SCHIFF,M	AP	70	TAR	LEWIN,AY		259	268
1.22	OTLEY,DT	02	80	AOS	BERRY,AJ		231	246
1.15	HOPWOOD,AG	JL	74	TAR			485	495
1.14	SWIERINGA,RJ	ST	82	JAR	WEICK,KE		56	101
1.09	COLLINS,F	AP	78	TAR			324	335
1.08	ELIAS,N	ST	72	JAR			215	233
1.00	CHESLEY,GR	AP	75	TAR			325	337
1.00	FLAMHOLTZ,EG	23	83	AOS			153	170
1.00	ONSI,M	JL	73	TAR			535	548
0.92	GOSMAN,ML	JA	73	TAR			1	11
0.92	MORIARITY,S	AU	76	JAR	BARRON,FH		320	341
0.88	HILTON,RW	SP	81	JAR	SWIERINGA,RJ	HOSKIN,RE	86	108
0.85	CAPLAN,EM	JL	66	TAR			496	509
0.85	CHERRINGTON,DJ	ST	73	JAR	CHERRINGTON,JO		225	253
0.85	FORAN,MF	OC	74	TAR	DECOSTER,DT		751	763
0.85	HARIED,AA	SP	73	JAR			117	145
0.83	ARGYRIS,C	02	77	AOS			113	124
0.83	LIBBY,R	AU	77	JAR	FISHBURN,PC		272	292
0.77	FLAMHOLTZ,EG	AP	71	TAR			253	267
0.77	HOFSTEDT,TR	OC	72	TAR			679	692
0.77	ROSE,R	ST	70	JAR	BEAVER,WH	BECKER,S	138	148
0.75	HIRST,MK	OC	81	TAR			771	784
0.75	LARCKER,DF	JL	81	TAR			519	538
0.75	MERCHANT,KA	02	85	AOS			201	210
0.75	SCHULTZ JR,JJ	AU	81	JAR	RECKERS,PMJ		482	501
0.73	BARIFF,ML	01	78	AOS	GALBRAITH,JR		15	28
0.70	ANSARI,SL	03	79	AOS			149	162
0.69	COPELAND,RM	AP	73	TAR	FRANCIA,AJ	STRAWSER,RH	365	374

CITE IND-EX	FIRST AUTHOR	ISS-UE	YE-AR	JOUR-NAL	SECOND AUTHOR	THIRD AUTHOR	PAG BEG	PAG END
0.69	REVSINE,L	OC	70	TAR			704	711
0.69	SORENSEN,JE	JL	67	TAR			553	565
0.69	WATSON,DJ	JL	75	TAR	BAUMLER,JV		466	474
0.67	BROWNELL,P	OC	86	TAR	MCINNES,M	587	600	
0.67	ROCKNESS,HO	OC	77	TAR			893	903
0.63	CROSBY,MA	AP	81	TAR			355	365
0.62	OLIVER,BL	AU	74	JAR			299	316
0.62	PANKOFF,LD	ST	70	JAR	VIRGIL JR,RL		1	48
0.62	RONEN,J	AU	71	JAR			307	332
0.62	SCHWAN,ES	23	76	AOS			219	238
0.60	DYCKMAN,TR	ST	84	JAR	PHILBRICK,D	STEPHAN,J	1	30
0.60	MERCHANT,KA	34	84	AOS			291	309
0.60	MORIARITY,S	SP	79	JAR			205	224
0.60	ROCKNESS,HO	02	84	AOS	SHIELDS,MD		165	177
0.57	COLLINS,F	02	82	AOS			107	122
0.57	DANOS,P	JA	82	TAR	IMHOFF JR,EA		39	54
0.57	GIBBINS,M	JA	82	TAR	WOLF,FM		105	124
0.55	FLAMHOLTZ,EG	02	78	AOS	COOK,E		115	140
0.54	BENSTON,GJ	AP	63	TAR			347	354
0.54	BRUMMET,RL	AP	68	TAR	FLAMHOLTZ,EG	PYLE,WC	217	224
0.54	FLAMHOLTZ,EG	23	76	AOS			153	166
0.54	OLIVER,BL	SP	72	JAR			154	166
0.54	WARD,BH	SP	76	JAR			138	152
0.50	COVALESKI,MA	04	83	AOS	DIRSMITH,MW		323	340
0.50	DILLARD,JF	03	79	AOS	FERRIS,KR		179	186
0.50	MACINTOSH,NB	01	87	AOS	DAFT,RL		49	61
0.50	MERCHANT,KA	01	85	AOS			67	86
0.50	SHIELDS,MD	01	81	AOS	BIRNBERG,JG	FRIEZE,IH	69	96
0.50	WALLER,WS	JL	85	TAR	CHOW,CW		458	476
0.46	ANSARI,SL	AU	76	JAR			189	211
0.46	COOK,DM	ST	67	JAR			213	224
0.46	DYCKMAN,TR	SP	64	JAR			91	107
0.46	FLAMHOLTZ,EG	OC	72	TAR			666	678
0.46	HOFSTEDT,TR	JA	70	TAR	KINARD,JC		38	54
0.46	SWIERINGA,RJ	ST	72	JAR	MONCUR,RH		194	209
0.45	HERTOG,JF	01	78	AOS			29	46
0.45	NEUMANN,BR	AU	78	JAR	FRIEDMAN,LA		400	410
0.43	DANOS,P	WI	82	AUD	IMHOFF JR,EA		23	34
0.43	WILNER,N	01	82	AOS			43	52
0.42	BAKER,CR	JL	77	TAR			576	586
0.42	COOPER,DJ	03	77	AOS	ESSEX,S		201	218
0.40	DANOS,P	OC	84	TAR	HOLT,DL	IMHOFF JR,EA	547	573
0.40	KROGSTAD,JL	AU	84	AUD	ETTENSON,RT	SHANTEAU,J	54	74
0.40	MAHER,MW	AU	79	JAR	RAMANATHAN,KV	PETERSON,RB	476	503
0.38	ASHTON,RH	04	76	AOS			289	300
0.38	BARRETT,ME	ST	71	JAR			50	65
0.38	BECKER,S	AU	74	JAR	RONEN,J	SORTER,GH	317	329
0.38	BRUNS JR,WJ	JL	68	TAR			469	480
0.38	CAMMANN,C	04	76	AOS			301	314
0.38	CARMICHAEL,DR	AP	70	TAR			235	245

SCHOOL OF THOUGHT=BEHAVIORAL - OTHER

CITE IND- EX	FIRST AUTHOR	ISS- UE	YE- AR	JOUR -NAL	SECOND AUTHOR	THIRD AUTHOR	PAG BEG	PAG END
0.38	DITTMAN,DA	SP	76	JAR	JURIS,HA	REVSINE,L	49	65
0.38	GOLEMBIEWSKI,RT	AP	64	TAR			333	341
0.38	IJIRI,Y	SP	68	JAR	KINARD,JC	PUTNEY,FB	1	28
0.38	MOCK,TJ	ST	69	JAR			124	159
0.38	PRATT,J	02	81	AOS	JIAMBALVO,J		133	142
0.38	SHOCKLEY,RA	OC	81	TAR			785	800
0.38	WATSON,DJ	AP	75	TAR			259	273
0.33	BELKAOUI,A	AU	80	JAR			362	374
0.33	BELKAOUI,A	03	80	AOS			263	284
0.33	BIRNBERG,JG	03	77	AOS	FRIEZE,IH	SHIELDS,MD	189	200
0.33	BROWNELL,P	AU	83	JAR			456	472
0.33	COVALESKI,MA	03	86	AOS	DIRSMITH,MW		193	214
0.33	CROSBY,MA	AU	80	JAR			585	593
0.33	EICHENSEHER,JW	SP	83	AUD	SHIELDS,D		23	37
0.33	FRIEDMAN,LA	AU	80	JAR	NEUMANN,BR		407	419
0.33	KIDA,TE	AU	80	JAR			506	523
0.33	MIRVIS,PH	23	83	AOS	LAWLER III,EE		175	190
0.33	PRESTON,A	06	86	AOS			521	540
0.33	SENATRA,PT	OC	80	TAR			594	603
0.31	FLAMHOLTZ,EG	ST	72	JAR			241	266
0.31	FRIEDMAN,A	AU	74	JAR	LEV,B		235	250
0.31	GYNTHER,RS	AP	67	TAR			274	290
0.31	HOFSTEDT,TR	01	76	AOS			43	58
0.30	ADELBERG,AH	AU	79	JAR			565	592
0.30	BLOCHER,E	JL	79	TAR			563	573
0.30	RECKERS,PMJ	AU	79	JAA	TAYLOR,ME		42	55
0.29	ASHTON,AH	AU	82	JAR			415	428
0.27	BUZBY,SL	34	78	AOS	FALK,H		191	202
0.25	BECK,PJ	SP	85	JAR	SOLOMON,I	TOMASSINI,LA	37	56
0.25	BROWNELL,P	AU	85	JAR			502	512
0.25	FLAMHOLTZ,EG	01	85	AOS	DAS,TK	TSUI,AS	35	50
0.25	GORDON,FE	04	77	AOS	RHODE,JG	MERCHANT,KA	295	306
0.25	UECKER,WC	JL	81	TAR	BRIEF,AP	KINNEY JR,WR	465	478
0.25	WALLER,WS	AU	85	JAR			817	828
0.23	BIRNBERG,JG	JL	67	TAR	NATH,R		468	479
0.23	CAPLAN,EM	AP	68	TAR			342	362
0.23	DASCHER,PE	SP	71	JAR	COPELAND,RM		32	39
0.23	FALK,H	SP	73	JAR	OPHIR,T		108	116
0.23	FERTAKIS,JP	OC	69	TAR			680	691
0.23	HOLSTRUM,GL	AU	71	JAR			268	277
0.23	MACY,BA	23	76	AOS	MIRVIS,PH		179	194
0.23	MOCK,TJ	JL	73	TAR			520	534
0.23	NICHOLS,DR	AP	76	TAR	PRICE,KH		335	346
0.23	SEARFOSS,DG	04	76	AOS			375	388
0.22	BENKE,RL	02	80	AOS	RHODE,JG		187	202
0.22	HARRELL,AM	04	80	AOS	KLICK,HD		393	400
0.22	PANY,K	JA	80	TAR	RECKERS,PMJ		50	61
0.20	ARANYA,N	JA	84	TAR	FERRIS,KR		1	15
0.20	DAROCA,FP	01	84	AOS			13	32
0.20	DILLARD,JF	12	79	AOS			31	38

SCHOOL OF THOUGHT=BEHAVIORAL - OTHER

CITE IND-EX	FIRST AUTHOR	ISS-UE	YE-AR	JOUR-NAL	SECOND AUTHOR	THIRD AUTHOR	PAG BEG	PAG END
0.20	GROVE,HD	JL	79	TAR	SAVICH,RS		522	537
0.20	HARVEY,DW	03	79	AOS	RHODE,JG	MERCHANT,KA	187	210
0.20	NANNI JR,AJ	02	84	AOS			149	163
0.17	BLOCHER,E	AU	83	AUD	ESPOSITO,RS	WILLINGHAM,JJ	75	91
0.17	BROWNELL,P	04	83	AOS			307	322
0.17	CASEY JR,CJ	SP	83	JAR			300	307
0.17	DANOS,P	AU	83	JAR	IMHOFF JR,EA		473	494
0.17	FERRIS,KR	01	83	AOS	LARCKER,DF		1	12
0.17	HOSKIN,RE	SP	83	JAR			78	95
0.17	JIAMBALVO,J	01	83	AOS	WATSON,DJ	BAUMLER,JV	13	30
0.17	LAVIN,D	03	77	AOS			237	244
0.17	TABOR,RH	SP	83	JAR			348	354
0.17	TILLER,MG	AU	83	JAR			581	595
0.17	TOMASSINI,LA	OC	77	TAR			904	913
0.17	WHITE,RA	JL	83	TAR			539	561
0.17	WILKINS,T	OC	83	TAR	ZIMMER,I		749	764
0.15	ACLAND,D	23	76	AOS			133	142
0.15	CHURCHILL,NC	OC	65	TAR	COOPER,WW		767	781
0.15	DECOSTER,DT	OC	71	TAR	RHODE,JG		651	664
0.15	DERMER,JD	JA	74	TAR	SIEGEL,JP		88	97
0.15	LENGERMANN,JJ	OC	71	TAR			665	675
0.15	LOEB,SE	AU	71	JAR			287	306
0.15	MORTON,JR	AU	74	JAR			288	298
0.15	SORENSEN,JE	OC	72	TAR	FRANKS,DD		735	746
0.15	TOMASSINI,LA	23	76	AOS			239	252
0.15	WATSON,DJ	AP	75	TAR			259	273
0.14	JIAMBALVO,J	SP	82	JAR			152	161
0.14	JIAMBALVO,J	OC	82	TAR	PRATT,J		734	750
0.14	SEILER,RE	04	82	AOS	BARTLETT,RW		381	404
0.14	UECKER,WC	AU	82	JAR			388	402
0.13	COPELAND,RM	SP	81	JAR	TAYLOR,RL	BROWN,SH	197	207
0.13	DILLARD,JF	01	81	AOS			17	26
0.13	FERRIS,KR	04	81	AOS			317	326
0.13	RECKERS,PMJ	SU	81	AUD	STAGLIANO,AJ		23	37
0.13	ROSENZWEIG,K	04	81	AOS			339	354
0.13	WOLF,FM	OC	81	TAR			861	881
0.11	FERRIS,KR	04	80	AOS	DILLARD,JF	NETHERCOTT,L	361	368
0.11	HOPPER,TM	04	80	AOS			401	412
0.08	BRUNS JR,WJ	ST	66	JAR			1	14
0.08	CARPER,WB	23	76	AOS	POSEY,JM		143	152
0.08	CUMMING,J	ST	73	JAR			60	95
0.08	FERRIS,KR	01	77	AOS			23	28
0.08	FIELD,JE	JL	69	TAR			593	599
0.08	GAMBLING,TE	23	76	AOS			167	174
0.08	GROVE,HD	03	77	AOS	MOCK,TJ	EHRENREICH,K	219	236
0.08	MCDONOUGH,JJ	OC	71	TAR			676	685
0.08	NYSTROM,PC	04	77	AOS			317	322
0.08	OGAN,P	23	76	AOS			195	218
0.08	SAULS,EH	ST	70	JAR			157	171
0.08	UECKER,WC	01	77	AOS			47	58

SCHOOL OF THOUGHT=BEHAVIORAL - OTHER

CITE IND- EX	FIRST AUTHOR	ISS- UE	YE- AR	JOUR -NAL	SECOND AUTHOR	THIRD AUTHOR	PAG BEG	PAG END
0.00	ABDEL-KHALIK,AR	AP	83	TAR	SNOWBALL,D	WRAGGE,JH	215	227
0.00	ABDOLMOHAM.,MJ	SP	86	AUD			1	16
0.00	ABDOLMOHAM.,MJ	JA	87	TAR	WRIGHT,A		1	13
0.00	ALDERMAN,CW	WI	82	AUD	DEITRICK,JW		54	68
0.00	ANDERSON JR,TN	AU	82	JAR	KIDA,TE		403	414
0.00	ANDERSON,U	AU	88	AUD	YOUNG,RA		23	42
0.00	ANSARI,SL	06	87	AOS	EUSKE,KJ		549	570
0.00	ARANYA,N	04	81	AOS	POLLOCK,J	AMERNIC,J	271	280
0.00	ARANYA,N	03	82	AOS	LACHMAN,R	AMERNIC,J	201	216
0.00	ARRINGTON,CE	SP	85	JAR	BAILEY,CD	HOPWOOD,WS	1	20
0.00	BAILEY,CD	SP	86	AUD	BALLARD,G		77	85
0.00	BAILEY,KE	AU	83	JAR	BYLINSKI,JH	SHIELDS,MD	355	370
0.00	BAILEY,WT	OC	81	TAR			882	896
0.00	BAMBER,EM	JL	88	AUD	SNOWBALL,D		490	504
0.00	BAO,BH	03	86	AOS	BAO,DH	VASARHELYI,MA	289	296
0.00	BARTON,RF	SP	69	JAR			116	122
0.00	BELKAOUI,A	04	81	AOS			281	290
0.00	BIGGS,SF	JA	88	TAR	MOCK,TJ	WATKINS,PR	148	162
0.00	BIRNBERG,JG	05	88	AOS	SNODGRASS,C		447	464
0.00	BJORN-ANDERSEN,N	02	80	AOS	PEDERSEN,PH		203	216
0.00	BLOCHER,E	AU	85	AUD	BYLINSKI,JH		79	90
0.00	BLOCHER,E	SP	88	AUD	COOPER,JC		1	28
0.00	BODNAR,G	OC	77	TAR	LUSK,EJ		857	868
0.00	BRENNER,VC	AU	71	JAR	CARMACK,CW	WEINSTEIN,MG	359	366
0.00	BROWN,C	03	85	AOS			255	266
0.00	BROWN,C	JL	87	TAR	SOLOMON,I		564	577
0.00	BROWNELL,P	OC	82	TAR			766	777
0.00	BROWNELL,P	AU	86	JAR	HIRST,MK		241	249
0.00	BUCHMAN,TA	AU	83	AUD			92	103
0.00	BUCHMAN,TA	03	85	AOS			267	286
0.00	BULLEN,ML	03	85	AOS	FLAMHOLTZ,EG		287	302
0.00	BUTT,JL	AU	88	JAR			315	330
0.00	CHALOS,P	AU	85	JAR			527	543
0.00	CHENHALL,RH	AP	86	TAR			263	272
0.00	CHOW,CW	JA	88	TAR	COOPER,JC	WALLER,WS	111	122
0.00	COLLINS,F	JA	87	TAR	MUNTER,P	FINN,DW	29	49
0.00	DAS,H	03	86	AOS			215	232
0.00	DEAN,RA	03	88	AOS	FERRIS,KR	KONSTANS,C	235	250
0.00	DIERKES,M	01	85	AOS	ANTAL,AB		29	34
0.00	DYKXHOORN,HJ	JA	81	TAR	SINNING,KE		97	107
0.00	FARMER,TA	AU	87	AUD	RITTENBERG,LE	TROMPETER,GM	1	14
0.00	FERRIS,KR	01	82	AOS			13	26
0.00	FERRIS,KR	03	82	AOS			225	230
0.00	FERTAKIS,JP	JL	70	TAR			509	512
0.00	FLAMHOLTZ,EG	04	87	AOS			309	318
0.00	GUL,FA	34	84	AOS			233	239
0.00	HAKA,SF	01	87	AOS			31	48
0.00	HARRELL,AM	34	84	AOS	STAHL,MJ		241	252
0.00	HARRELL,AM	SP	86	AUD	CHEWNING,EG	TAYLOR,M	111	121
0.00	HARRELL,AM	SP	88	AUD	EICKHOFF,R		105	118

SCHOOL OF THOUGHT=BEHAVIORAL - OTHER

CITE IND-EX	FIRST AUTHOR	ISS-UE	YE-AR	JOUR-NAL	SECOND AUTHOR	THIRD AUTHOR	PAG BEG	PAG END
0.00	HARRISON,PD	AP	88	TAR	WEST,SG	RENEAU,JH	307	320
0.00	HASKINS,M	JL	87	TAR			542	563
0.00	HILTON,RW	AP	88	TAR	SWIERINGA,RJ	TURNER,MJ	195	218
0.00	HIRST,MK	AU	83	JAR			596	605
0.00	HIRST,MK	OC	87	TAR			774	784
0.00	HOUGHTON,KA	SP	84	JAR			361	368
0.00	HOUGHTON,KA	02	87	AOS			143	152
0.00	HOUGHTON,KA	03	88	AOS			263	280
0.00	JENNINGS,M	SP	87	AUD	KNEER,DC	RECKERS,PMJ	104	115
0.00	JENSEN,RE	JL	70	TAR			502	508
0.00	JOHNSON,DA	SP	83	AUD	PANY,K	WHITE,RA	38	51
0.00	JOHNSON,DA	AU	84	JAR	PANY,K		731	743
0.00	JOHNSON,WB	04	82	AOS			349	368
0.00	JONSON,LC	34	78	AOS	JONSSON,B	SVENSSON,G	261	268
0.00	KAPLAN,SE	AU	84	AUD	RECKERS,PMJ		1	19
0.00	KAPLAN,SE	04	88	AOS	RECKERS,PMJ	ROARK,SJ	371	379
0.00	KIM,KK	JL	88	TAR			472	489
0.00	KNAPP,MC	AP	85	TAR			202	211
0.00	KNAPP,MC	JL	87	TAR			578	588
0.00	LAU,AH	SP	78	JAR	LAU,HS		80	102
0.00	LICATA,MP	JA	86	TAR	STRAWSER,RH	WELKER,RB	112	117
0.00	LUCAS,HC	OC	75	TAR			735	746
0.00	LUKKA,K	03	88	AOS			281	301
0.00	MARGHEIM,LL	SP	86	AUD	PANY,K		50	63
0.00	MCKINELY,S	AU	85	JAR	PANY,K	RECKERS,PMJ	887	896
0.00	MEIXNER,WF	JL	88	AUD	WELKER,RB		505	513
0.00	MIA,L	05	88	AOS			465	475
0.00	MURRAY,D	AU	86	JAR	FRAZIER,KB		400	404
0.00	NAIR,RD	SP	83	JAA	RITTENBERG,LE		234	243
0.00	NORRIS,DR	01	84	AOS	NIEBUHR,RE		49	59
0.00	PANY,K	AU	82	JAR	SMITH,CH		472	481
0.00	PANY,K	AU	87	AUD	RECKERS,PMJ		39	53
0.00	PORCANO,TM	OC	84	TAR			619	636
0.00	PRATT,J	04	85	AOS			427	442
0.00	PURDY,CR	ST	69	JAR	SMITH JR,JM	GRAY,J	1	18
0.00	REBELE,JE	AU	88	AUD	HEINTZ,JA	BRIDEN,GE	43	52
0.00	RECKERS,PMJ	AU	82	AUD	SCHULTZ JR,JJ		64	74
0.00	ROSENBERG,D	02	82	AOS	TOMKINS,L	DAY,P	123	138
0.00	SAMUELSON,LA	01	86	AOS			35	46
0.00	SAN MIGUEL,JG	02	77	AOS			177	186
0.00	SAN MIGUEL,JG	02	84	AOS	GOVINDARAJAN,V		179	188
0.00	SCHNEIDER,A	AU	85	JAR			911	919
0.00	SCHROEDER,MS	SP	86	AUD	SOLOMON,I	VICKREY,DW	86	94
0.00	SIMONS,R	04	87	AOS			357	374
0.00	SOETERS,J	01	88	AOS	SCHREUDER,H		75	85
0.00	SUMNERS,GE	SP	87	AUD	WHITE,RA	CLAY JR,RJ	116	122
0.00	TROTMAN,KT	SP	85	JAR	YETTON,PW		256	267
0.00	WALLER,WS	01	88	AOS			87	98
0.00	WILLIAMS,JJ	04	85	AOS	NEWTON,JD	MORGAN,EA	457	478
0.00	WILLIAMS,JJ	02	88	AOS	HININGS,CR		191	198

SCHOOL OF THOUGHT=BEHAVIORAL - OTHER

CITE IND-EX	FIRST AUTHOR	ISS-UE	YE-AR	JOUR-NAL	SECOND AUTHOR	THIRD AUTHOR	PAG BEG	PAG END
0.00	WILLIAMS,PF	04	82	AOS			405	410
0.00	WRIGHT,A	SP	82	JAR			227	239
0.00	WRIGHT,A	JL	83	TAR			621	632
0.00	WRIGHT,A	SP	86	AUD			86	94
0.00	WRIGHT,A	06	88	AOS			595	605
0.00	YOUNG,SM	06	88	AOS	SHIELDS,MD	WOLF,G	607	618

SCHOOL OF THOUGHT=BEHAVIORAL - OTHER

3.3 SCHOOL OF THOUGHT=STAT.MODEL. - EMH

CITE IND- EX	FIRST AUTHOR	ISS- UE	YE- AR	JOUR -NAL	SECOND AUTHOR	THIRD AUTHOR	PAG BEG	PAG END
7.00	BALL,R	AU	68	JAR	BROWN,P		159	178
5.15	GONEDES,NJ	ST	74	JAR	DOPUCH,N		48	129
4.85	BEAVER,WH	ST	68	JAR			67	92
4.83	HOLTHAUSEN,RW	AG	83	JAE	LEFTWICH,RW		77	117
4.54	PATELL,JM	AU	76	JAR			246	276
4.20	BEAVER,WH	AU	79	JAR	CLARKE,R	WRIGHT,WF	316	340
3.88	COLLINS,DW	MR	81	JAE	ROZEFF,MS	DHALIWAL,DS	37	71
3.67	FOSTER,G	MR	80	JAE			29	62
3.63	LEFTWICH,RW	MR	81	JAE			3	36
3.50	HOLTHAUSEN,RW	MR	81	JAE			73	109
3.00	COLLINS,DW	MR	79	JAE	DENT,WT		3	44
3.00	GONEDES,NJ	SP	76	JAR	DOPUCH,N	PENMAN,SH	89	137
3.00	WILSON,GP	AP	87	TAR			293	322
2.67	SCHIPPER,K	SP	83	JAR	THOMPSON,R		184	221
2.54	BALL,R	ST	72	JAR			1	38
2.50	ATIASE,RK	SP	85	JAR			21	36
2.50	BERNARD,VL	SP	87	JAR			1	48
2.50	LARCKER,DF	AP	83	JAE			3	30
2.44	BEAVER,WH	MR	80	JAE	LAMBERT,RA	MORSE,D	3	28
2.43	BEAVER,WH	JL	82	JAE	GRIFFIN,PA	LANDSMAN,WR	15	39
2.43	BIDDLE,GC	AU	82	JAR	LINDAHL,FW		551	588
2.43	LEV,B	ST	82	JAR	OHLSON,JA		249	322
2.40	CHAMBERS,AE	SP	84	JAR	PENMAN,SH		21	47
2.40	DYCKMAN,TR	MR	79	JAE	SMITH,AJ		45	75
2.40	LEV,B	JL	79	TAR			485	503
2.29	RICKS,WE	AU	82	JAR			367	387
2.23	GONEDES,NJ	AU	75	JAR			220	256
2.23	SUNDER,S	ST	73	JAR			1	45
2.00	BEAVER,WH	AG	80	JAE	CHRISTIE,AA	GRIFFIN,PA	127	157
2.00	HUGHES,JS	JA	87	TAR	RICKS,WE		158	175
2.00	RAYBURN,J	ST	86	JAR			112	137
1.92	MAY,RG	ST	71	JAR			119	163
1.89	PENMAN,SH	SP	80	JAR			132	160
1.86	GIVOLY,D	JL	82	TAR	PALMON,D		486	508
1.82	GONEDES,NJ	SP	78	JAR			26	79
1.75	FOSTER,G	DE	81	JAE			201	232
1.71	PATELL,JM	JL	82	TAR	WOLFSON,MA		509	527
1.67	GHEYARA,K	AG	80	JAE	BOATSMAN,JR		107	125
1.62	BEAVER,WH	AP	72	TAR	DUKES,RE		320	332
1.60	DODD,P	AP	84	JAE	DOPUCH,N	HOLTHAUSEN,RW	3	38
1.56	RO,BT	AG	80	JAE			159	189
1.54	SUNDER,S	AP	75	TAR			305	315
1.50	BUBLITZ,B	ST	85	JAR	FRECKA,TJ	MCKEOWN,JC	1	23
1.50	PATELL,JM	AU	81	JAR	WOLFSON,MA		434	458
1.44	GRANT,EB	SP	80	JAR			255	268
1.40	COLLINS,DW	SP	84	JAR	DENT,WT		48	84
1.40	FOSTER,G	OC	84	TAR	OLSEN,C	SHEVLIN,T	574	603
1.38	BEAVER,WH	SP	81	JAR			163	184

CITE IND- EX	FIRST AUTHOR	ISS- UE	YE- AR	JOUR -NAL	SECOND AUTHOR	THIRD AUTHOR	PAG BEG	PAG END
1.33	BAMBER,LS	SP	86	JAR			40	56
1.33	HARRISON,T	SP	77	JAR			84	107
1.33	WILSON,GP	ST	86	JAR		165	203	
1.31	FOSTER,G	SP	73	JAR			25	37
1.30	PATELL,JM	AG	79	JAE	WOLFSON,MA		117	140
1.25	NOREEN,EW	AP	81	TAR	SEPE,J		253	269
1.18	HONG,H	JA	78	TAR	KAPLAN,RS	MANDELKER,G	31	47
1.15	ARCHIBALD,TR	JA	72	TAR			22	30
1.15	BROWN,P	ST	67	JAR	BALL,R		55	77
1.15	DEAKIN,EB	SP	72	JAR			167	179
1.13	MORSE,D	AU	81	JAR			374	383
1.11	BROWN,RM	SP	80	JAR			38	63
1.09	ABDEL-KHALIK,AR	OC	78	TAR	MCKEOWN,JC		851	868
1.00	BEAVER,WH	JL	87	JAE	LAMBERT,RA	RYAN,SG	139	157
1.00	BELL,TB	SP	83	JAR			1	17
1.00	BIDDLE,GC	AU	88	JAR	RICKS,WE		169	194
1.00	CHRISTIE,AA	DE	87	JAE			231	258
1.00	COLLINS,DW	JA	82	TAR	ROZEFF,MS	SALATKA,WK	1	17
1.00	COLLINS,DW	JL	87	JAE	KOTHARI,SP	RAYBURN,JD	111	138
1.00	ELLIOTT,JA	AU	82	JAR			617	638
1.00	ELLIOTT,JA	SP	84	JAR	RICHARDSON,G	DYCKMAN,TR	85	102
1.00	FREEMAN,RN	JL	87	JAE			195	228
1.00	GIVOLY,D	DE	79	JAE	LAKONISHOK,J		165	185
1.00	GONEDES,NJ	SP	74	JAR			26	62
1.00	HARRIS,TS	OC	87	TAR	OHLSON,JA		651	670
1.00	HUGHES,JS	AG	84	JAE	RICKS,WE		101	132
1.00	JAIN,PC	DE	82	JAE			205	228
1.00	LYS,T	AP	84	JAE			39	65
1.00	WAYMIRE,G	AU	84	JAR			703	718
0.92	EGGLETON,IRC	SP	76	JAR	PENMAN,SH	TWOMBLY,JR	66	88
0.88	SMITH,AJ	ST	81	JAR			174	211
0.86	FREEMAN,RN	AU	82	JAR	OHLSON,JA	PENMAN,SH	639	653
0.83	FREEMAN,RN	SP	83	JAR			42	64
0.83	JOY,OM	AU	77	JAR	LITZENBERGER,RH	MCENALLY,RW	207	225
0.83	PINCUS,M	SP	83	JAR			155	183
0.80	KROSS,W	SP	84	JAR	SCHROEDER,DA		153	176
0.80	MARAIS,ML	ST	84	JAR			34	54
0.80	SCHAEFER,TF	AU	84	JAR			647	656
0.75	BOWEN,RM	JA	81	TAR			1	22
0.75	BRICKLEY,JA	AP	85	JAE	BHAGAT,S	LEASE,RC	115	130
0.75	OLSEN,C	ST	85	JAR			28	53
0.69	BEAVER,WH	JL	73	TAR	DUKES,RE		549	559
0.67	HOSKIN,RE	ST	86	JAR	HUGHES,JS	RICKS,WE	1	36
0.67	LARCKER,DF	OC	83	TAR	REVSINE,L		706	732
0.67	LIPE,RC	ST	86	JAR			37	68
0.67	MAGLIOLO,J	ST	86	JAR			69	111
0.67	RICKS,WE	SP	86	JAR			206	216
0.64	RO,BT	AU	78	JAR			315	340
0.62	MAGEE,RP	AU	74	JAR			270	287
0.60	AJINKYA,BB	AU	84	JAR	GIFT,MJ		425	444

SCHOOL OF THOUGHT=STAT.MODEL. - EMH

CITE IND-EX	FIRST AUTHOR	ISS-UE	YE-AR	JOUR-NAL	SECOND AUTHOR	THIRD AUTHOR	PAG BEG	PAG END
0.60	LAMBERT,RA	OC	84	TAR			604	618
0.60	NICHOLS,DR	SP	79	JAR	TSAY,JJ		140	155
0.60	OHLSON,JA	DE	79	JAE			211	232
0.60	PATELL,JM	AU	79	JAR			528	549
0.57	BANKS,DW	SP	82	JAR	KINNEY JR,WR		240	254
0.57	VERRECCHIA,RE	ST	82	JAR			1	42
0.55	FIRTH,MA	JL	78	TAR			642	650
0.54	BASKIN,EF	JA	72	TAR			38	51
0.54	FOSTER,G	OC	75	TAR			686	698
0.50	BEAVER,WH	JA	87	TAR			137	144
0.50	DOPUCH,N	JL	87	TAR	HOLTHAUSEN,RW	LEFTWICH,RW	431	454
0.50	HAKA,SF	OC	85	TAR	GORDON,LA	PINCHES,GE	651	669
0.50	HUNT III,HG	AU	85	JAR		448	467	
0.50	MCNICHOLS,M	AP	83	JAE	MANEGOLD,JG		49	74
0.50	OHLSON,JA	SP	83	JAR			141	154
0.50	OLSEN,C	ST	85	JAR	DIETRICH,JR		144	166
0.50	SHANE,PB	JL	83	TAR	SPICER,BH		521	538
0.50	STEVENSON,FL	AU	87	JAR			306	316
0.50	WALLACE,WA	AU	81	JAR			502	520
0.46	GONEDES,NJ	JA	72	TAR			11	21
0.44	BOWMAN,RG	SP	80	JAR			242	254
0.43	CHOW,CW	WI	82	AUD	RICE,SJ		35	53
0.43	LUSTGARTEN,S	OC	82	JAE			121	141
0.40	IMHOFF JR,EA	AU	84	JAR	LOBO,GJ		541	554
0.40	MAYER-SOMMER,AP	JA	79	TAR			88	106
0.40	MCDONALD,B	JL	84	TAR	MORRIS,MH		432	446
0.38	BENSTON,GJ	ST	67	JAR			1	54
0.38	BILDERSEE,JS	JA	75	TAR			81	98
0.38	DOWNES,D	AP	73	TAR	DYCKMAN,TR		300	317
0.38	FOSTER,G	AU	75	JAR			283	292
0.38	FRIED,D	AP	81	TAR	SCHIFF,A		326	341
0.38	KIGER,JE	SP	72	JAR			113	128
0.38	MAY,RG	JA	73	TAR	SUNDEM,GL		80	94
0.38	NOREEN,EW	AU	81	JAR	WOLFSON,MA		384	398
0.38	RO,BT	JA	81	TAR			70	84
0.38	VIGELAND,RL	AP	81	TAR			309	325
0.36	ABDEL-KHALIK,AR	ST	78	JAR	MCKEOWN,JC		46	77
0.36	FOSTER III,TW	OC	78	TAR	VICKREY,DW		921	934
0.36	JAGGI,B	OC	78	TAR			961	967
0.36	RICE,SJ	AP	78	TAR			429	438
0.36	SHANK,JK	OC	78	TAR	MURDOCK,RJ		824	835
0.33	ANDERSON,JC	JL	80	TAR	FRANKLE,AW		467	479
0.33	CHOW,CW	JL	83	TAR			485	520
0.33	DOPUCH,N	JN	86	JAE	HOLTHAUSEN,RW	LEFTWICH,RW	93	118
0.33	KELLER,SB	AU	83	AUD	DAVIDSON,LF		1	22
0.33	LARCKER,DF	JL	83	TAR	REDER,RE	SIMON,DT	606	620
0.33	MURDOCH,B	AP	86	TAR			273	287
0.33	NICHOLS,DR	AU	83	JAR	SMITH,DB		534	544
0.33	OPPONG,A	AU	80	JAR			574	584
0.33	STOBER,TL	ST	86	JAR			138	164

SCHOOL OF THOUGHT=STAT.MODEL. - EMH

CITE IND- EX	FIRST AUTHOR	ISS- UE	YE- AR	JOUR -NAL	SECOND AUTHOR	THIRD AUTHOR	PAG BEG	PAG END
0.33	WRIGHT,CJ	JA	86	TAR	GROFF,JE		91	100
0.31	HAGERMAN,RL	OC	75	TAR			699	709
0.31	KLAMMER,T	AP	73	TAR			353	364
0.29	DAVIS,RR	AU	82	AUD			13	32
0.27	BASU,S	JL	78	TAR			599	625
0.25	BEAVER,WH	JA	81	TAR			23	37
0.25	EASTON,PD	ST	85	JAR			54	77
0.25	INGRAM,RW	AU	85	JAR			595	618
0.25	JENNINGS,R	SP	85	JAR	STARKS,L		336	350
0.25	LAMBERT,RA	AP	85	JAE	LARCKER,DF		179	204
0.25	MADEO,SA	JL	85	TAR	PINCUS,M		407	429
0.25	MULFORD,CW	AU	85	JAR			897	906
0.25	RONEN,J	AU	81	JAR	LIVNAT,J		459	481
0.25	TEHRANIAN,H	AP	85	JAE	WAEGELEIN,JF		131	144
0.23	DEAKIN,EB	JL	76	TAR			590	603
0.23	ESKEW,RK	AP	75	TAR			316	324
0.23	MARSHALL,RM	JA	75	TAR			99	111
0.23	OHLSON,JA	AU	75	JAR			267	282
0.23	REILLY,FK	ST	72	JAR	MORGENSON,DL	WEST,M	105	124
0.22	BOWMAN,RG	AP	80	TAR			237	253
0.20	COLLINS,DW	AU	79	JAR	SIMONDS,RR		352	383
0.20	KELLOGG,RL	DE	84	JAE			185	204
0.20	MORSE,D	AU	84	JAR			605	623
0.20	OHLSON,JA	AU	79	JAR	PATELL,JM		504	505
0.20	THORNTON,DB	03	79	AOS			211	234
0.18	KETZ,JE	ST	78	JAR			273	284
0.18	SHORT,DG	ST	78	JAR			259	272
0.17	ANDERSON,JA	AP	77	TAR			417	426
0.17	HARRISON JR,WT	SP	83	JAR	TOMASSINI,LA	DIETRICH,JR	65	77
0.17	MURRAY,D	SP	83	JAR			128	140
0.15	GRIFFIN,PA	JL	76	TAR			499	515
0.15	MEYERS,SL	AP	73	TAR			318	322
0.15	MLYNARCZYK,FA	ST	69	JAR			63	81
0.15	O'CONNOR,MC	AP	73	TAR			339	352
0.15	PATZ,DH	AU	72	JAR	BOATSMAN,JR		392	403
0.14	ABDEL-KHALIK,AR	OC	82	TAR	AJINKYA,BB		661	680
0.14	SEPE,J	JL	82	TAR			467	485
0.14	WHALEY,RE	OC	82	JAE	CHEUNG,JK		57	83
0.13	BOATSMAN,JR	JA	81	TAR	BASKIN,EF		38	53
0.10	HILLISON,WA	SP	79	JAR			60	73
0.10	OHLSON,JA	AU	79	JAR			506	527
0.09	DAVIS,DW	JA	78	TAR	BOATSMAN,JR	BASKIN,EF	1	10
0.08	KINNEY JR,WR	AP	72	TAR			339	345
0.08	MAGEE,RP	AU	75	JAR			257	266
0.08	SHARPE,IG	AU	75	JAR	WALKER,RG		293	310
0.00	AJINKYA,BB	AU	80	JAR			343	361
0.00	AMIT,R	WI	88	JAA	LIVNAT,J		19	43
0.00	ATIASE,RK	SP	87	JAR			168	176
0.00	BAMBER,LS	JL	87	TAR			510	532
0.00	BEATTY,RP	WI	85	JAA	JOHNSON,SB		112	124

SCHOOL OF THOUGHT=STAT.MODEL. - EMH

CITE IND- EX	FIRST AUTHOR	ISS- UE	YE- AR	JOUR -NAL	SECOND AUTHOR	THIRD AUTHOR	PAG BEG	PAG END
0.00	BEAVER,WH	DE	81	JAE	LANDSMAN,WR		233	241
0.00	BERNARD,VL	OC	87	TAR	RULAND,RG		707	722
0.00	BIDWELL III,CM	SP	81	JAA	RIDDLE JR,JR		198	214
0.00	BINDER,JJ	SP	85	JAR			370	383
0.00	BOWEN,RM	OC	87	TAR	BURGSTAHLER,D	DALEY,LA	723	747
0.00	BROWN,BC	SU	86	JAA	BRANDI,JT		185	205
0.00	BURGSTAHLER,D	SP	86	JAR	NOREEN,EW		170	186
0.00	CASSIDY,DB	AU	76	JAR			212	229
0.00	CHENHALL,RH	03	88	AOS	BROWNELL,P		225	233
0.00	CLINCH,GJ	AP	87	JAE	SINCLAIR,NA		89	106
0.00	COOPER,T	WI	80	JAA			138	146
0.00	COPELAND,TE	AU	78	JAA			33	48
0.00	COX,CT	OC	85	TAR			692	701
0.00	CREADY,WM	JL	87	TAR	SHANK,JK		589	596
0.00	CREADY,WM	SP	88	JAR			1	27
0.00	DEANGELO,LE	JA	88	JAE			3	36
0.00	DEFEO,VJ	AU	86	JAR			349	363
0.00	DHALIWAL,DS	OC	86	TAR			651	661
0.00	DIETRICH,JR	AP	84	JAE			67	96
0.00	DORAN,BM	JL	88	TAR	COLLINS,DW	DHALIWAL,DS	389	413
0.00	DORAN,DT	SP	88	JAA	NACHTMANN,R		113	132
0.00	ELGERS,P	OC	87	TAR	CALLAHAN,C	STROCK,E	763	773
0.00	ELGERS,PT	JL	80	TAR			389	408
0.00	ELGERS,PT	AP	82	TAR	MURRAY,D		358	375
0.00	ETTREDGE,M	SP	88	AUD	SHANE,PB	SMITH,D	29	42
0.00	FIRTH,MA	AU	81	JAR			521	529
0.00	FOSTER III,TW	AP	78	TAR	VICKREY,DW		360	370
0.00	FRECKA,TJ	SP	83	JAR	LEE,CF		308	316
0.00	FREEMAN,RN	ST	78	JAR			111	145
0.00	GIVOLY,D	AU	81	JAR	PALMON,D		530	543
0.00	GIVOLY,D	SP	87	JAA	LAKONISHOK,J		117	137
0.00	GONEDES,NJ	ST	69	JAR			90	113
0.00	GONEDES,NJ	JL	71	TAR			535	551
0.00	GROSSMAN,SD	WI	81	JAA	KRATCHMAN,SH	WELKER,RB	136	143
0.00	HAGERMAN,RL	AU	84	JAR	ZMIJEWSKI,ME	SHAH,P	526	540
0.00	HALPERIN,R	AP	87	TAR	LANEN,WN		378	384
0.00	HARMON,WK	AU	84	JAA			24	34
0.00	HAW,IM	WI	87	JAA	PASTENA,V	LILIEN,S	24	42
0.00	HAW,IM	AU	88	JAR	LUSTGARTEN,S		331	352
0.00	HOPWOOD,WS	SP	85	JAR	MCKEOWN,JC		161	174
0.00	INGRAM,RW	JL	83	TAR	CHEWNING,EG		562	580
0.00	JAIN,PC	JL	83	TAR			633	638
0.00	JAIN,PC	SP	86	JAR			76	96
0.00	JAIN,PC	SP	86	JAR			187	193
0.00	JENNINGS,R	SP	87	JAR			90	110
0.00	JOHNSON,WB	AP	85	JAE	MAGEE,RP	NAGARAJAN,NJ	151	174
0.00	JOHNSON,WB	AU	88	JAR	DHALIWAL,DS		236	272
0.00	KETZ,JE	AU	83	JAA	WYATT,AR		29	43
0.00	KRAMER,SS	JA	82	TAR			70	87
0.00	KROSS,W	AU	80	JAA	CHAPMAN,G	STRAND,KH	36	46

SCHOOL OF THOUGHT=STAT.MODEL. - EMH

CITE IND-EX	FIRST AUTHOR	ISS-UE	YE-AR	JOUR-NAL	SECOND AUTHOR	THIRD AUTHOR	PAG BEG	PAG END
0.00	KROSS,W	AU	82	JAR			459	471
0.00	LAMBERT,RA	ST	87	JAR	LARCKER,DF		85	125
0.00	LANDSMAN,WR	OC	86	TAR			662	691
0.00	LANDSMAN,WR	OC	88	TAR	MAGLIOLO,J		586	604
0.00	LAWRENCE,EC	AU	83	JAR			606	610
0.00	LEE,CJ	SP	85	JAR			213	227
0.00	LEV,B	SP	79	JAA	TAYLOR,KW		232	243
0.00	LEV,B	AP	83	JAE			31	48
0.00	LIVNAT,J	AU	81	JAR			350	359
0.00	LYS,T	AU	88	JAR	SIVARAMAKRISHNAN,K		273	299
0.00	MARSTON,F	SP	88	JAA	HARRIS,RS		147	164
0.00	MARTIN,JD	WI	79	JAA	ANDERSON,PF	KEOWN,AJ	151	164
0.00	MCGAHRAN,KT	JA	88	TAR			23	41
0.00	MCNICHOLS,M	JL	88	JAE			239	273
0.00	MEEK,GK	AP	83	TAR			394	402
0.00	MILLAR,JA	JA	77	TAR			52	55
0.00	MILLER,EM	AU	80	JAA			6	19
0.00	MORRIS,MH	AP	88	TAR	NICHOLS,WD		237	254
0.00	MOSES,OD	AP	87	TAR			358	377
0.00	MURRAY,D	WI	82	JAA			154	159
0.00	NICHOLS,DR	AP	79	TAR	TSAY,JJ	LARKIN,PD	376	382
0.00	OHLSON,JA	ST	72	JAR			45	84
0.00	PENMAN,SH	DE	84	JAE			165	183
0.00	PETERSEN,RJ	JL	75	TAR			525	532
0.00	RANSOM,CR	ST	85	JAR			124	143
0.00	RICKS,WE	JA	85	TAR	HUGHES,JS		33	52
0.00	SCHACHTER,B	AU	88	JAR			353	372
0.00	SCHAEFER,T	AU	86	JAA	KENNELLEY,M		278	287
0.00	SCHIPPER,K	SP	85	JAR	THOMPSON,R		408	415
0.00	SELTO,FH	AU	85	JAR	CLOUSE,ML		700	717
0.00	SHAW,WH	SP	88	JAR			60	81
0.00	SILHAN,PA	SP	83	JAR			341	347
0.00	SMITH,DB	OC	82	JAE	NICHOLS,DR		109	120
0.00	SMITH,DB	AG	84	JAE	STETTLER,HF	BEEDLES,W	153	162
0.00	SMITH,DB	SP	88	JAR			134	145
0.00	STANDISH,PEM	OC	82	TAR	UNG,S		701	715
0.00	STICKEL,SE	OC	86	JAE			197	216
0.00	THODE,SF	WI	86	JAA	DRTINA,RE	LARGAY III,JA	46	61
0.00	THOMAS,JK	JL	88	JAE			199	237
0.00	THOMPSON,RB	JL	88	TAR	OLSEN,C	DIETRICH,JR	448	471
0.00	TSE,S	JL	86	TAR			475	497
0.00	WAYMIRE,G	AU	83	JAR	POWNALL,G		629	643
0.00	ZIEBART,DA	AU	85	JAR			920	926
0.00	ZIEBART,DA	AP	87	TAR	KIM,DH		343	357

SCHOOL OF THOUGHT=STAT.MODEL. - EMH

3.4 SCHOOL OF THOUGHT=STAT.MODEL. - TIME SERIES

CITE IND-EX	FIRST AUTHOR	ISS-UE	YE-AR	JOUR-NAL	SECOND AUTHOR	THIRD AUTHOR	PAG BEG	PAG END
4.25	FOSTER,G	JA	77	TAR			1	21
2.58	WATTS,RL	AU	77	JAR	LEFTWICH,RW		253	271
2.50	BROWN,LD	AP	87	JAE	GRIFFIN,PA	HAGERMAN,RL	61	87
2.25	GRIFFIN,PA	SP	77	JAR			71	83
2.20	BROWN,LD	SP	79	JAR	ROZEFF,MS		179	189
2.14	FRIED,D	OC	82	JAE	GIVOLY,D		85	107
2.08	BEAVER,WH	OC	70	TAR	KETTLER,P	SCHOLES,M	654	682
2.00	ALBRECHT,WS	AU	77	JAR	LOOKABILL,LL	MCKEOWN,JC	226	244
2.00	BROWN,LD	JL	87	JAE	GRIFFIN,PA	HAGERMAN,RL	159	193
1.86	DHALIWAL,DS	JL	82	JAE	SALAMON,GL	SMITH,ED	41	53
1.38	BEAVER,WH	ST	70	JAR			62	99
1.25	DEANGELO,LE	AG	81	JAE			113	127
1.22	COLLINS,WA	AU	80	JAR	HOPWOOD,WS		390	406
1.15	GONEDES,NJ	AU	73	JAR			212	237
1.09	CRICHFIELD,T	JL	78	TAR	DYCKMAN,TR	LAKONISHOK,J	651	668
1.08	DOPUCH,N	SP	72	JAR	WATTS,RL		180	194
1.00	BASI,BA	AP	76	TAR	CAREY,KJ	TWARK,RD	244	254
1.00	BROWN,LD	SP	87	JAR	RICHARDSON,GD	SCHWAGER,SJ	49	67
1.00	IMHOFF JR,EA	AU	82	JAR	PARE,PV		429	439
0.92	KINNEY JR,WR	SP	71	JAR			127	136
0.91	KINNEY JR,WR	JA	78	TAR			48	60
0.90	LOREK,KS	SP	79	JAR			190	204
0.77	LOREK,KS	AP	76	TAR	MCDONALD,CL	PATZ,DH	321	330
0.71	HOPWOOD,WS	AU	82	JAR	MCKEOWN,JC	NEWBOLD,P	343	349
0.62	BEIDLEMAN,CR	OC	73	TAR			653	667
0.55	RULAND,W	AP	78	TAR			439	447
0.50	BROWN,LD	AU	79	JAR	ROZEFF,MS		341	351
0.46	BEAVER,WH	AU	68	JAR			179	192
0.46	LEV,B	AP	74	TAR	KUNITZKY,S		259	270
0.46	LOOKABILL,LL	OC	76	TAR			724	738
0.44	LEV,B	AU	80	JAR			524	550
0.38	COATES,R	ST	72	JAR			132	144
0.38	HOPWOOD,WS	AU	81	JAR	MCKEOWN,JC		313	322
0.38	WHITE,GE	AU	70	JAR			260	273
0.36	ABDEL-KHALIK,AR	SP	78	JAR	ESPEJO,J		1	13
0.33	DHARAN,BG	SP	83	JAR			18	41
0.33	HASSELL,JM	JA	86	TAR	JENNINGS,RH		58	75
0.33	HOPWOOD,WS	SP	80	JAR			77	90
0.31	DASCHER,PE	AU	70	JAR	MALCOM,RE		253	259
0.31	LEV,B	AU	69	JAR			290	299
0.29	HOPWOOD,WS	AU	82	JAR	NEWBOLD,P	SILHAN,PA	724	732
0.25	COGGER,KO	AU	81	JAR			285	298
0.23	BALOFF,N	AU	67	JAR	KENNELLY,JW		131	143
0.23	BAREFIELD,RM	AU	71	JAR	COMISKEY,EE		351	358
0.23	BAREFIELD,RM	AP	72	TAR	COMISKEY,EE		291	298
0.23	BARNEA,A	JA	76	TAR	RONEN,J	SADAN,S	110	122
0.23	BENSTON,GJ	OC	66	TAR			657	672
0.23	COPELAND,RM	JL	68	TAR	LICASTRO,RD		540	545

SCHOOL OF THOUGHT=STAT.MODEL. - TIME SERIES

CITE IND- EX	FIRST AUTHOR	ISS- UE	YE- AR	JOUR -NAL	SECOND AUTHOR	THIRD AUTHOR	PAG BEG	PAG END
0.23	SAMUELSON,RA	AU	72	JAR			322	344
0.23	WHITE JR,CE	AU	72	JAR			351	358
0.22	RONEN,J	SU	80	JAA	SADAN,S		339	353
0.20	BROWN,LD	JL	79	TAR	ROZEFF,MS		585	591
0.20	COLLINS,WA	AU	84	JAR	HOPWOOD,WS	MCKEOWN,JC	467	479
0.15	ABDEL-KHALIK,AR	OC	75	TAR			657	670
0.15	ELLIOTT,JW	AU	72	JAR	UPHOFF,HL		259	274
0.15	GREENBALL,MN	ST	71	JAR			172	190
0.15	JOHNSON,O	AU	67	JAR			164	172
0.15	KIGER,JE	JA	74	TAR			1	7
0.15	STAUBUS,GJ	JA	65	TAR			119	134
0.13	FRIED,D	JL	81	TAR	LIVNAT,J		493	509
0.13	MANEGOLD,JG	AU	81	JAR			360	373
0.08	JENSEN,RE	AP	67	TAR			265	273
0.08	KINNEY JR,WR	SP	69	JAR			44	52
0.08	MABERT,VA	JA	74	TAR	RADCLIFFE,RC		61	75
0.00	ABDEL-KHALIK,AR	SP	83	JAR			293	296
0.00	BARLEV,B	AU	79	JAR	LEVY,H		305	315
0.00	BATHKE,AW	AP	84	TAR	LOREK,KS		163	176
0.00	BRIEF,RP	JA	69	TAR			20	26
0.00	BROWN,LD	SP	80	JAR	HUGHES,JS	ROZEFF,MS	278	288
0.00	CHIU,JS	OC	66	TAR	DECOSTER,DT		673	680
0.00	COGGER,KO	AU	82	JAR	RULAND,W		733	737
0.00	DALEY,LA	OC	88	TAR	SENKOW,DW	VIGELAND,RL	563	585
0.00	DHARAN,BG	SP	83	JAR			256	270
0.00	DUGAN,MT	SP	85	AUD	GENTRY,JA	SHRIVER,KA	11	22
0.00	ELNICKI,RA	ST	77	JAR			209	218
0.00	FELIX JR,WL	JA	72	TAR			52	63
0.00	GONEDES,NJ	AP	71	TAR			320	328
0.00	GREENBERG,R	AU	84	JAR			719	730
0.00	HIRSCHEY,M	SP	85	JAR	WEYGANDT,JJ		326	335
0.00	HOPWOOD,WS	SP	80	JAR			289	296
0.00	LIVINGSTONE,JL	SP	67	JAR			77	94
0.00	LOREK,KS	SP	83	JAR	ICERMAN,JD	ABDULKADER,AA	317	328
0.00	LOREK,KS	SP	84	JAR	BATHKE,AW		369	379
0.00	MELBERG,WF	JA	72	TAR			116	133
0.00	MOORE,ML	JA	85	TAR	STEECE,BM	SWENSON,CW	18	32
0.00	MOORE,ML	OC	87	TAR	STEECE,BM	SWENSON,CW	671	685
0.00	O'BRIEN,PC	JA	88	JAE			53	83
0.00	O'DONNELL,JL	JA	65	TAR			135	143
0.00	OVADIA,A	WI	80	JAA	RONEN,J		113	137
0.00	PHILIPS,GE	ST	70	JAR	MAYNE,LS		178	188
0.00	PUTNAM,K	AU	84	JAA	THOMAS,LR		15	23
0.00	RAUN,DL	OC	64	TAR			927	945
0.00	ROSE,PS	AU	82	JAA	ANDREWS,WT	GIROUX,GA	20	31
0.00	SILHAN,PA	SP	85	JAR	MCKEOWN,JC		416	426
0.00	SWANSON,EP	OC	85	TAR	SHEARON,WT	THOMAS,LR	681	691
0.00	SWENSON,CW	JA	87	TAR			117	136
0.00	WAYMIRE,G	JA	86	TAR			129	142
0.00	WELCH,PR	AU	84	JAR			744	757

SCHOOL OF THOUGHT=STAT.MODEL. - TIME SERIES

CITE IND- EX	FIRST AUTHOR	ISS- UE	YE- AR	JOUR -NAL	SECOND AUTHOR	THIRD AUTHOR	PAG BEG	PAG END
0.00	WHITEHURST,FD	JL	70	TAR			553	564

SCHOOL OF THOUGHT=STAT.MODEL. - TIME SERIES

3.5 SCHOOL OF THOUGHT=STAT.MODEL. - INFO ECON./AGENCY

CITE IND-EX	FIRST AUTHOR	ISS-UE	YE-AR	JOUR -NAL	SECOND AUTHOR	THIRD AUTHOR	PAG BEG	PAG END
3.63	BOWEN,RM	AG	81	JAE	NOREEN,EW	LACEY,JM	151	179
3.18	DEMSKI,JS	AP	78	TAR	FELTHAM,GA		336	359
2.10	ZIMMERMAN,JL	JL	79	TAR			504	521
2.00	HAYES,DC	23	83	AOS			241	250
1.67	BAIMAN,S	AU	83	JAR	EVANS III,JH		371	395
1.60	DEMSKI,JS	JA	84	TAR	PATELL,JM	WOLFSON,MA	16	34
1.50	DEMSKI,JS	SP	87	JAR	SAPPINGTON,DEM		68	89
1.50	DYE,RA	AU	83	JAR			514	533
1.33	DEMSKI,JS	AU	86	JAR	SAPPINGTON,DEM		250	269
1.33	HUGHES,PJ	JN	86	JAE			119	142
1.30	BEAVER,WH	JA	79	TAR	DEMSKI,JS		38	46
1.25	GJESDAL,F	SP	81	JAR			208	231
1.20	PENNO,M	SP	84	JAR			177	191
1.14	ANTLE,R	AU	82	JAR			504	527
1.14	CHOW,CW	AP	82	TAR			272	291
1.09	UECKER,WC	SP	78	JAR			169	189
1.00	CHRISTENSEN,J	AU	82	JAR			589	603
1.00	DEMSKI,JS	AP	74	TAR			221	232
1.00	DYE,RA	SP	85	JAR			123	145
1.00	FELTHAM,GA	OC	70	TAR	DEMSKI,JS		623	640
1.00	VERRECCHIA,RE	OC	86	JAE		175	196	
0.92	KINNEY JR,WR	SP	75	JAR			117	132
0.92	ZIMMERMAN,JL	ST	77	JAR			107	144
0.85	MAGEE,RP	JL	76	TAR			529	544
0.77	DEMSKI,JS	AU	76	JAR			230	245
0.77	ITAMI,H	SP	75	JAR			73	96
0.69	DEMSKI,JS	AU	72	JAR			243	258
0.67	TITMAN,S	JN	86	JAE	TRUEMAN,B		159	172
0.64	NG,DS	OC	78	TAR			910	920
0.62	BAIMAN,S	SP	75	JAR			1	15
0.60	ATKINSON,AA	SP	79	JAR			1	22
0.60	NG,DS	ST	79	JAR	STOECKENIUS,J		1	24
0.60	VERRECCHIA,RE	MR	79	JAE			77	90
0.56	LEFTWICH,RW	DE	80	JAE			193	211
0.56	MAGEE,RP	AU	80	JAR			551	573
0.56	VERRECCHIA,RE	MR	80	JAE			63	92
0.54	DEMSKI,JS	JL	72	TAR	FELTHAM,GA		533	548
0.54	SUNDER,S	AU	76	JAR			277	300
0.50	BAIMAN,S	AU	85	JAR	NOEL,J		486	501
0.50	CONROY,RM	JA	87	TAR	HUGHES,JS	50	66	
0.50	JARRELL,GA	AG	79	JAE			93	116
0.50	MELUMAD,ND	ST	87	JAR	REICHELSTEIN,S		1	18
0.50	SUH,YS	ST	87	JAR			22	46
0.50	SUNDEM,GL	SP	79	JAR			243	261
0.46	BUTTERWORTH,JE	SP	72	JAR			1	27
0.46	DEMSKI,JS	SP	72	JAR			58	76
0.46	GONEDES,NJ	AU	74	JAR	IJIRI,Y		251	269
0.46	MARSHALL,RM	AU	72	JAR			286	307

CITE IND- EX	FIRST AUTHOR	ISS- UE	YE- AR	JOUR -NAL	SECOND AUTHOR	THIRD AUTHOR	PAG BEG	PAG END
0.44	GONEDES,NJ	AU	80	JAR			441	476
0.42	FELTHAM,GA	SP	77	JAR			42	70
0.40	ANTLE,R	SP	84	JAR			1	20
0.38	DEMSKI,JS	OC	67	TAR			701	712
0.38	LEV,B	AU	68	JAR			247	261
0.33	EVANS III,JH	ST	80	JAR			108	128
0.33	EVANS III,JH	ST	80	JAR			108	128
0.31	ABDEL-KHALIK,AR	AP	74	TAR			271	283
0.30	HILTON,RW	AU	79	JAR			411	435
0.27	LOEB,M	SP	78	JAR	MAGAT,WA		103	121
0.25	BILLERA,LJ	SP	81	JAR	HEATH,DC	VERRECCHIA,RE	185	196
0.25	DEJONG,DV	AU	85	JAR	FORSYTHE,R	UECKER,WC	753	793
0.25	PENNO,M	SP	85	JAR			240	255
0.25	YOUNG,SM	AU	85	JAR			829	842
0.23	DEMSKI,JS	AU	70	JAR			178	198
0.23	MOCK,TJ	OC	71	TAR			765	777
0.22	BALACHANDRAN,BV	ST	80	JAR	RAMAKRISHNAN,RT		140	171
0.17	DICKHAUT,JW	AU	83	JAR	LERE,JC		495	513
0.17	MAGEE,RP	OC	77	TAR			869	880
0.17	SCHEPANSKI,A	AP	83	TAR	UECKER,WC		259	283
0.15	BERNHARDT,I	SP	70	JAR	COPELAND,RM		95	98
0.15	DEMSKI,JS	OC	69	TAR			669	679
0.15	DEMSKI,JS	AP	71	TAR			268	278
0.15	GODFREY,JT	JA	71	TAR	PRINCE,TR		75	89
0.15	LEV,B	SP	70	JAR			78	94
0.15	RONEN,J	OC	73	TAR	FALK,G		696	717
0.09	VERRECCHIA,RE	SP	78	JAR			150	168
0.08	THEIL,H	JA	69	TAR			27	37
0.00	AMERSHI,AH	AU	87	JAR	SUNDER,S		177	195
0.00	BABER,WR	JA	85	TAR			1	9
0.00	BAIMAN,S	AU	87	JAR	EVANS III,JH	NOEL,J	217	244
0.00	BALACHANDRAN,BV	SP	87	JAR	RAMAKRISHNAN,RT		111	126
0.00	BALACHANDRAN,BV	WI	88	JAA	RAMANAN,R		1	13
0.00	BENISHAY,H	SU	87	JAA			203	238
0.00	CRANDALL,RH	JL	69	TAR			457	466
0.00	CUSHING,BE	OC	68	TAR			668	671
0.00	DEJONG,DV	AU	84	AUD	SMITH,JH		20	34
0.00	DEJONG,DV	ST	85	JAR	FORSYTHE,R	LUNDHOLM,RJ	81	120
0.00	DYE,RA	AU	88	JAR			195	235
0.00	EVANS III,JH	06	86	AOS	LEWIS,BL	PATTON,JM	483	498
0.00	EVANS III,JH	ST	87	JAR	PATTON,JM		130	164
0.00	FELLINGHAM,JC	JA	85	TAR	WOLFSON,MA		10	17
0.00	HAKANSSON,NH	JL	69	TAR			495	514
0.00	HOLTHAUSEN,RW	SP	88	JAR	VERRECCHIA,RE		82	106
0.00	JUNG,WO	SP	88	JAR	KWON,YK		146	153
0.00	KANODIA,CS	SP	85	JAR			175	193
0.00	LAMBERT,RA	AU	85	JAR			633	647
0.00	LAVALLE,IH	AP	68	TAR	RAPPAPORT,A		225	230
0.00	LEE,LC	AP	69	TAR	BEDFORD,NM		256	275
0.00	LEV,B	OC	69	TAR			704	710

SCHOOL OF THOUGHT=STAT.MODEL. - INFO ECON./AGENCY

CITE IND-EX	FIRST AUTHOR	ISS-UE	YE-AR	JOUR-NAL	SECOND AUTHOR	THIRD AUTHOR	PAG BEG	PAG END
0.00	LUNDHOLM,RJ	SP	88	JAR			107	118
0.00	MAGEE,RP	JA	88	TAR			42	54
0.00	NAKANO,I	OC	72	TAR			693	708
0.00	NELSON,J	SU	88	JAA	RONEN,J	WHITE,L	255	296
0.00	NOREEN,EW	04	88	AOS			359	369
0.00	RONEN,J	AU	88	JAR	BALACHANDRAN,KR		300	314
0.00	SCOTT,WR	SP	79	JAR			156	178
0.00	SHIELDS,MD	06	88	AOS	WALLER,WS		581	594
0.00	SUH,YS	SP	88	JAR			154	168
0.00	UECKER,WC	JL	85	TAR	SCHEPANSKI,A	SHIN,J	430	457
0.00	WILLIAMS,DJ	03	86	AOS			271	288

SCHOOL OF THOUGHT=STAT.MODEL. - INFO ECON./AGENCY

3.6   SCHOOL OF THOUGHT=STAT.MODEL. - MATH. PROGRAMMING

CITE IND-EX	FIRST AUTHOR	ISS-UE	YE-AR	JOUR-NAL	SECOND AUTHOR	THIRD AUTHOR	PAG BEG	PAG END
0.82	NETER,J	JA	78	TAR	LEITCH,RA	FIENBERG,SE	77	93
0.77	KAPLAN,RS	SP	69	JAR			32	43
0.77	SAN MIGUEL,JG	04	76	AOS			357	374
0.69	DYCKMAN,TR	AU	69	JAR			215	244
0.58	HAMLEN,SS	JL	77	TAR	HAMLEN,WA	TSCHIRHART,JT	616	627
0.58	JENSEN,DL	OC	77	TAR			842	856
0.38	KAPLAN,RS	AP	71	TAR	THOMPSON,GL		352	364
0.38	KAPLAN,RS	JL	74	TAR	WELAM,VP		477	484
0.33	COHEN,MA	AU	80	JAR	HALPERIN,R		375	389
0.31	KILLOUGH,LN	AP	73	TAR	SOUDERS,TL		268	279
0.31	OZAN,T	SP	71	JAR	DYCKMAN,TR		88	115
0.31	SUMMERS,EL	JL	72	TAR			443	453
0.30	KANODIA,CS	SP	79	JAR			74	98
0.27	KOTTAS,JF	AP	78	TAR	LAU,AH	LAU,HS	389	401
0.22	HAMLEN,SS	OC	80	TAR			578	593
0.18	LIN,WT	JA	78	TAR			61	76
0.18	MERVILLE,LJ	OC	78	TAR	PETTY,JW		935	951
0.17	HEIMANN,SR	AU	77	JAR	CHESLEY,GR		193	206
0.15	BAILEY JR,AD	JL	76	TAR	BOE,WJ		559	573
0.15	HARTLEY,RV	OC	71	TAR			746	755
0.15	HINOMOTO,H	AU	71	JAR			253	267
0.15	IJIRI,Y	AU	63	JAR	LEVY,FK	LYON,RC	198	212
0.15	KAPLAN,RS	OC	73	TAR			738	748
0.15	KORNBLUTH,JS	AP	74	TAR			284	295
0.15	SAMUELS,JM	AU	65	JAR			182	191
0.08	BAILEY JR,AD	JL	73	TAR			560	574
0.08	BAREFIELD,RM	JL	70	TAR			490	501
0.08	BUTTERWORTH,JE	OC	71	TAR	SIGLOCH,BA		701	716
0.08	CHARNES,A	SP	63	JAR	COOPER,WW	IJIRI,Y	16	43
0.08	CHARNES,A	JA	67	TAR	COOPER,WW		24	52
0.08	CHARNES,A	JA	72	TAR	COLANTONI,CS	COOPER,WW	85	108
0.08	CHURCHILL,NC	OC	64	TAR			894	904
0.08	COLANTONI,CS	JL	69	TAR	MANES,RP	WHINSTON,AB	467	481
0.08	CORCORAN,AW	JA	73	TAR	LEININGER,WE		105	114
0.08	DOPUCH,N	SP	64	JAR	DRAKE,DF		10	24
0.08	FELTHAM,GA	JA	70	TAR			11	26
0.08	FRANK,WG	JL	67	TAR	MANES,RP		516	525
0.08	GONEDES,NJ	SP	70	JAR			1	20
0.08	GROVES,R	JL	70	TAR	MANES,RP	SORENSEN,R	481	489
0.08	HARTLEY,RV	AP	70	TAR			223	234
0.08	LIVINGSTONE,JL	JL	68	TAR			503	508
0.08	MAGEE,RP	JA	77	TAR			190	199
0.08	ONSI,M	JL	70	TAR			535	543
0.08	RAPPAPORT,A	JL	67	TAR			441	456
0.08	WELLING,P	04	77	AOS			307	316
0.08	WILLIAMS,TH	JL	64	TAR	GRIFFIN,CH		671	678
0.08	WOLK,HI	JL	72	TAR	HILLMAN,AP		549	555
0.08	WRIGHT,FK	JA	70	TAR			129	133

CITE IND-EX	FIRST AUTHOR	ISS-UE	YE-AR	JOUR-NAL	SECOND AUTHOR	THIRD AUTHOR	PAG BEG	PAG END
0.00	BALACHANDRAN,BV	JA	81	TAR	RAMAKRISHNAN,RT		85	96
0.00	BALACHANDRAN,KR	SP	87	JAA	SRINIDHI,BN		151	169
0.00	BALVERS,RJ	OC	88	TAR	MCDONALD,B	MILLER,RE	605	622
0.00	BRIEF,RP	AU	68	JAR	OWEN,J		193	199
0.00	BROCKETT,P	JL	84	TAR	CHARNES,A	COOPER,WW	474	487
0.00	BYRNE,R	JA	68	TAR	CHARNES,A	COOPER,WW	18	37
0.00	CARSBERG,BV	AU	69	JAR			165	182
0.00	CASEY JR,CJ	SP	85	JAR	BARTCZAK,N		384	401
0.00	CHAN,KH	OC	86	TAR	DODIN,B		726	734
0.00	CHARNES,A	04	76	AOS	COLANTONI,CS	COOPER,WW	315	338
0.00	DAVIS,GB	SP	63	JAR			96	101
0.00	DOPUCH,N	OC	63	TAR			745	753
0.00	FARAG,SM	AP	68	TAR			312	320
0.00	FOGLER,HR	JA	72	TAR			134	143
0.00	GLOVER,F	AP	69	TAR			300	303
0.00	GODFREY,JT	AP	71	TAR			286	297
0.00	HANSEN,DR	JA	77	TAR	SHAFTEL,TL		109	123
0.00	HARTLEY,RV	AP	68	TAR			321	332
0.00	JENSEN,RE	JL	68	TAR			425	446
0.00	LEA,RB	AP	72	TAR			346	350
0.00	LIVINGSTONE,JL	JA	69	TAR			48	64
0.00	MANES,RP	JL	82	TAR	PARK,SH	JENSEN,RE	594	606
0.00	RAPPAPORT,A	AP	69	TAR			297	299
0.00	SHERMAN,HD	AU	84	AUD			35	53
0.00	WEINGARTER,HM	AU	63	JAR			213	224
0.00	WRIGHT,FK	AU	68	JAR			222	236

SCHOOL OF THOUGHT=STAT.MODEL. - MATH. PROGRAMMING

3.7   SCHOOL OF THOUGHT=STAT.MODEL. - OTHER

CITE IND-EX	FIRST AUTHOR	ISSUE	YEAR	JOURNAL	SECOND AUTHOR	THIRD AUTHOR	PAG BEG	PAG END
7.91	WATTS,RL	JA	78	TAR	ZIMMERMAN,JL		112	134
3.80	HAGERMAN,RL	AG	79	JAE	ZMIJEWSKI,ME		141	161
3.50	HEALY,PM	AP	85	JAE			85	108
2.75	HAYES,DC	JA	77	TAR			22	39
2.63	ZMIJEWSKI,ME	AG	81	JAE	HAGERMAN,RL		129	149
2.00	SIMUNIC,DA	SP	80	JAR			161	190
1.75	MURPHY,KJ	AP	85	JAE			11	42
1.50	COUGHLAN,AT	AP	85	JAE	SCHMIDT,RM		43	66
1.46	KAPLAN,RS	AU	73	JAR			238	258
1.44	OHLSON,JA	SP	80	JAR			109	131
1.38	BEAVER,WH	ST	66	JAR			71	111
1.33	PALMROSE,ZV	SP	86	JAR			97	110
1.31	CORLESS,JC	JL	72	TAR			556	566
1.29	LILIEN,S	DE	82	JAE	PASTENA,V		145	170
1.20	CHRISTIE,AA	DE	84	JAE	KENNELLEY,MD	KING,JW	205	217
1.20	KINNEY JR,WR	ST	79	JAR			148	165
1.20	ZMIJEWSKI,ME	ST	84	JAR			59	82
1.17	FELIX JR,WL	SP	77	JAR	GRIMLUND,RA		23	41
1.15	BOATSMAN,JR	AP	74	TAR	ROBERTSON,JC		342	352
1.14	DUKE,GL	SP	82	JAR	NETER,J	LEITCH,RA	42	67
1.08	SCOTT,WR	AU	73	JAR			304	330
1.00	ABDEL-KHALIK,AR	AU	85	JAR			427	447
1.00	CHENHALL,RH	JA	86	TAR	MORRIS,D		16	35
1.00	DEAKIN,EB	OC	79	TAR			722	734
1.00	DEMSKI,JS	ST	82	JAR	KREPS,DM		117	148
1.00	FELIX JR,WL	OC	76	TAR			800	807
1.00	HEALY,PM	AP	87	JAE	KANG,SH	PALEPU,KG	7	34
1.00	KINNEY JR,WR	ST	75	JAR			14	29
1.00	LIBERTY,SE	OC	86	TAR	ZIMMERMAN,JL	692	712	
1.00	MORSE,D	SP	83	JAR	RICHARDSON,G		106	127
1.00	STRINGER,KW	ST	75	JAR			1	9
0.92	MCDONALD,CL	JL	73	TAR			502	510
0.90	RAMAGE,JG	ST	79	JAR	KRIEGER,AM	SPERO,LL	72	102
0.88	EICHENSEHER,JW	JL	81	TAR	DANOS,P		479	492
0.86	LEITCH,RA	AP	82	TAR	NETER,J	PLANTE,R	384	400
0.85	KAPLAN,RS	SP	73	JAR			38	46
0.83	DALEY,LA	DE	83	JAE	VIGELAND,RL		195	211
0.83	UECKER,WC	03	77	AOS	KINNEY JR,WR		269	275
0.77	HARIED,AA	AU	72	JAR			376	391
0.77	IJIRI,Y	JL	66	TAR	JAEDICKE,RK		474	483
0.77	SUNDER,S	JA	76	TAR			1	18
0.75	ANTLE,R	SP	85	JAR	SMITH,A		296	325
0.75	BROWN,LD	AP	85	TAR	GARDNER,JC		262	277
0.75	LEFTWICH,RW	ST	81	JAR	WATTS,RL	ZIMMERMAN,JL	50	77
0.75	MUTCHLER,JF	AU	85	JAR			668	682
0.73	SPICER,BM	JA	78	TAR			94	111
0.71	GRIMLUND,RA	AU	82	JAR			316	342
0.70	GARSTKA,SJ	SP	79	JAR	OHLSON,PA		23	59

SCHOOL OF THOUGHT=STAT.MODEL. - OTHER

CITE IND- EX	FIRST AUTHOR	ISS- UE	YE- AR	JOUR -NAL	SECOND AUTHOR	THIRD AUTHOR	PAG BEG	PAG END
0.70	MORIARITY,S	ST	79	JAR	BARRON,FH		114	135
0.69	HORRIGAN,JO	ST	66	JAR			44	62
0.69	SCOTT,WR	ST	75	JAR			98	117
0.67	ANTLE,R	SP	86	JAR	SMITH,A		1	39
0.67	AYRES,FL	JN	86	JAE			143	158
0.67	BOWEN,RM	OC	86	TAR	BURGSTAHLER,D	DALEY,LA	713	725
0.67	CHOW,CW	OC	83	TAR			667	685
0.67	CUSHING,BE	AU	83	AUD	LOEBBECKE,JK		23	41
0.67	FRANCIS,JR	AU	86	JAR	STOKES,DJ		383	393
0.67	KINNEY JR,WR	SP	83	AUD			13	22
0.67	PALEPU,KG	MR	86	JAE			3	36
0.67	SUNDER,S	AU	83	JAR	WAYMIRE,G		565	580
0.62	CUSHING,BE	JA	74	TAR			24	41
0.62	DEMSKI,JS	JL	74	TAR	SWIERINGA,RJ		506	513
0.62	GREEN,D	ST	66	JAR	SEGALL,J		21	36
0.62	YU,S	AU	73	JAR	NETER,J		273	295
0.60	DALEY,LA	AP	84	TAR			177	198
0.60	DWORIN,L	AP	84	TAR	GRIMLUND,RA		218	241
0.60	FRANCIS,JR	AG	84	JAE			133	151
0.60	LEV,B	DE	79	JAE	SUNDER,S		187	210
0.60	MATOLCSY,ZP	AU	84	JAR			555	569
0.60	MCCRAY,JH	JA	84	TAR			35	51
0.60	MENZEFRICKE,U	AU	84	JAR	SMIELIAUSKAS,W		588	604
0.57	FROST,PA	SP	82	JAR	TAMURA,H		103	120
0.57	SILHAN,PA	SP	82	JAR			255	262
0.55	RENEAU,JH	JL	78	TAR			669	680
0.54	JAEDICKE,RK	OC	64	TAR	ROBICHEK,AA		917	926
0.54	SORENSEN,JE	JL	69	TAR			555	561
0.54	SUNDER,S	AP	76	TAR			287	291
0.54	TRACY,JA	JA	69	TAR			90	98
0.50	BABER,WR	DE	83	JAE			213	227
0.50	CASLER,DJ	SP	85	JAR	HALL,TW		110	122
0.50	FRANCIS,JR	JA	87	TAR	SIMON,DT		145	157
0.50	FRANCIS,JR	AP	87	JAE	REITER,SA		35	59
0.50	GENTRY,JA	SP	85	JAR	NEWBOLD,P	WHITFORD,DT	146	160
0.50	HAM,J	JL	85	TAR	LOSELL,D	SMIELIAUSKAS,W	387	406
0.50	LEWELLEN,W	AP	85	JAE	LODERER,C	ROSENFELD,A	209	232
0.50	RAMAN,KK	OC	81	TAR			910	926
0.50	TSUI,KW	JA	85	TAR	MATSUMURA,EM	TSUI,KL	76	96
0.46	DEAKIN,EB	OC	74	TAR	GRANOF,MH		764	771
0.46	DYER,JC	AU	75	JAR	MCHUGH,AJ		204	219
0.46	LIEBERMAN,AZ	AP	75	TAR	WHINSTON,AB		246	258
0.45	BENSTON,GJ	ST	78	JAR	KRASNEY,MA		1	30
0.43	COPELAND,RM	AU	82	JAR	INGRAM,RW		275	289
0.43	DANOS,P	AU	82	JAR	EICHENSEHER,JW		604	616
0.43	DIETRICH,JR	JA	82	TAR	KAPLAN,RS		18	38
0.43	HALL,TW	SP	82	JAR			139	151
0.40	BALDWIN,BA	JL	84	TAR			376	389
0.40	BIGGS,SF	SP	84	AUD	WILD,JJ		68	79
0.40	DHARAN,BG	AP	84	TAR			199	217

SCHOOL OF THOUGHT=STAT.MODEL. - OTHER

CITE IND- EX	FIRST AUTHOR	ISS- UE	YE- AR	JOUR -NAL	SECOND AUTHOR	THIRD AUTHOR	PAG BEG	PAG END
0.40	DITTMAN,DA	AP	79	TAR	PRAKASH,P		358	373
0.40	GODFREY,JT	AU	84	JAR	NETER,J		497	525
0.40	KINNEY JR,WR	AU	79	JAR			456	475
0.38	BLUM,M	SP	74	JAR			1	25
0.38	BODNAR,G	OC	75	TAR			747	757
0.38	BUZBY,SL	JA	74	TAR			42	49
0.38	HILLIARD,JE	JA	75	TAR	LEITCH,RA		69	80
0.38	JAGGI,B	AP	74	TAR	LAU,HS		321	329
0.38	KAPLAN,RS	ST	75	JAR			126	133
0.38	LIAO,M	OC	75	TAR			780	790
0.38	STALLMAN,JC	ST	69	JAR			29	43
0.36	DITTMAN,DA	SP	78	JAR	PRAKASH,P		14	25
0.36	INGRAM,RW	AU	78	JAR			270	285
0.36	KETZ,JE	OC	78	TAR			952	960
0.36	KEYS,DE	AU	78	JAR			389	399
0.33	CASEY JR,CJ	AP	86	TAR	MCGEE,VE	STICKNEY,CP	249	262
0.33	DANOS,P	OC	86	TAR	EICHENSEHER,JW		633	650
0.33	DWORIN,L	JA	86	TAR	GRIMLUND,RA		36	57
0.33	EL-GAZZAR,S	OC	86	JAE	LILIEN,S	PASTENA,V	217	238
0.33	FRECKA,TJ	JA	83	TAR	HOPWOOD,WS		115	128
0.33	MENZEFRICKE,U	SP	83	JAR			96	105
0.33	NAIR,RD	JL	80	TAR	FRANK,WG		426	450
0.33	PALMROSE,ZV	AU	86	JAR			405	411
0.33	ROBERTS,DM	SP	86	JAR			111	126
0.33	SEFCIK,SE	AU	86	JAR	THOMPSON,R		316	334
0.33	SMITH,DB	AU	86	AUD			95	108
0.33	TAMURA,H	AU	86	JAR	FROST,PA		364	371
0.31	DEAKIN,EB	JA	76	TAR			90	96
0.31	FERRARA,WL	AP	72	TAR	HAYYA,JC	NACHMAN,DA	299	307
0.31	IJIRI,Y	OC	69	TAR	KAPLAN,RS		743	756
0.31	SHANK,JK	JL	73	TAR	COPELAND,RM		494	501
0.31	WARREN,CS	SP	75	JAR			162	176
0.31	WEST,RR	SP	70	JAR			118	125
0.31	WILCOX,JA	ST	73	JAR			163	179
0.30	NAIR,RD	SP	79	JAR			225	242
0.30	NORTON,CL	JA	79	TAR	SMITH,RE		72	87
0.29	GODFREY,JT	AU	82	JAR	ANDREWS,RW		304	315
0.29	WALTHER,LM	AP	82	TAR			376	383
0.27	CALLEN,JL	AP	78	TAR			303	308
0.27	HIRSCH JR,ML	AU	78	JAR			254	269
0.25	BIDDLE,GC	SP	85	JAR	MARTIN,RK		57	83
0.25	EVEREST,GL	AP	77	TAR	WEBER,R		340	359
0.25	GARSTKA,SJ	AU	77	JAR			179	192
0.25	SCOTT,WR	SP	77	JAR			120	137
0.25	VERRECCHIA,RE	SP	81	JAR			271	283
0.23	BALL,R	SP	76	JAR	LEV,B	WATTS,RL	1	9
0.23	DEMSKI,JS	JA	70	TAR			76	87
0.23	FRIBERG,RA	JA	73	TAR			50	60
0.23	GUPTA,MC	SP	72	JAR	HUEFNER,RJ		77	95
0.23	IJIRI,Y	OC	73	TAR	ITAMI,H		724	737

SCHOOL OF THOUGHT=STAT.MODEL. - OTHER

CITE IND-EX	FIRST AUTHOR	ISS-UE	YE-AR	JOUR -NAL	SECOND AUTHOR	THIRD AUTHOR	PAG BEG	PAG END
0.23	KOCHANEK,RF	AP	74	TAR			245	258
0.23	PROBST,FR	JA	71	TAR			113	118
0.23	RONEN,J	JA	74	TAR			50	60
0.23	TOBA,Y	JA	75	TAR			7	24
0.22	BECK,PJ	SP	80	JAR			16	37
0.22	HUSSEIN,ME	SU	80	JAA	KETZ,JE		354	367
0.22	IJIRI,Y	SP	80	JAR	LEITCH,RA		91	108
0.20	CUSHING,BE	ST	79	JAR	SEARFOSS,DG	RANDALL,RH	172	216
0.20	ESKEW,RK	JA	79	TAR			107	118
0.20	FERRIS,KR	SP	84	AUD	TENNANT,KL		31	43
0.20	FRAZIER,KB	SP	84	JAR	INGRAM,RW	TENNYSON,BM	318	331
0.20	MARAIS,ML	ST	84	JAR	PATELL,JM	WOLFSON,MA	87	114
0.20	NETER,J	AU	84	AUD	KIM,HS	GRAHAM,LE	75	88
0.20	SCHREUDER,H	JA	84	TAR	KLAASSEN,J		64	77
0.20	SIMUNIC,DA	AU	84	JAR			679	702
0.20	SMITH,G	AU	84	AUD	KROGSTAD,JL		107	117
0.20	WESCOTT,SH	SP	84	JAR			412	423
0.18	KAMIN,JY	02	78	AOS	RONEN,J		141	160
0.17	BROWN,LD	AU	83	JAR			432	443
0.17	HUGHES,JS	JA	77	TAR			56	68
0.17	MCLEAY,S	01	83	AOS			31	56
0.17	SCHIPPER,K	ST	77	JAR			1	40
0.17	WARREN,CS	JA	77	TAR			150	161
0.17	WEYGANDT,JJ	JA	77	TAR			40	51
0.15	BRIEF,RP	AU	70	JAR	OWEN,J		167	177
0.15	CHURCHILL,NC	OC	75	TAR	SHANK,JK		643	656
0.15	DAVIDSON,HJ	AU	67	JAR	NETER,J	PETRAN,AS	186	207
0.15	DEMSKI,JS	AU	73	JAR			176	190
0.15	DOPUCH,N	JL	67	TAR	BIRNBERG,JG	DEMSKI,JS	526	536
0.15	GREENBALL,MN	SP	68	JAR			114	129
0.15	GREER JR,WR	JA	70	TAR			103	114
0.15	JEN,FC	AP	70	TAR	HUEFNER,RJ		290	298
0.15	JOHNSON,GL	AU	71	JAR	SIMIK,SS		278	286
0.15	JOHNSON,GL	SP	74	JAR	SIMIK,SS		67	79
0.15	LIM,R	OC	66	TAR			642	651
0.15	LIVINGSTONE,JL	AU	70	JAR	SALAMON,GL		199	216
0.15	LUH,FS	JA	68	TAR			123	132
0.15	REVSINE,L	AP	76	TAR	THIES,JB		255	268
0.15	SALAMON,GL	AU	73	JAR			296	303
0.15	SMITH,KA	AP	72	TAR			260	269
0.15	TEITLEBAUM,AD	ST	75	JAR	ROBINSON,CF		70	91
0.15	WELKER,RB	JL	74	TAR			514	523
0.15	ZANNETOS,ZS	AP	64	TAR			296	304
0.15	ZIMMERMAN,JL	AU	76	JAR			301	319
0.14	ALTMAN,EI	AU	82	JAA			4	19
0.14	EMERY,GW	AU	82	JAR	COGGER,KO		290	303
0.14	INGRAM,RW	AU	82	JAR	COPELAND,RM		766	772
0.14	KINNEY JR,WR	AU	82	JAR	SALAMON,GL		350	366
0.14	SCHWARTZ,KB	AU	82	JAA			32	43
0.14	WISEMAN,J	01	82	AOS			53	64

SCHOOL OF THOUGHT=STAT.MODEL. - OTHER

CITE IND-EX	FIRST AUTHOR	ISS-UE	YE-AR	JOUR-NAL	SECOND AUTHOR	THIRD AUTHOR	PAG BEG	PAG END
0.13	BAILEY,AP	SU	81	AUD	MCAFEE,RP	WHINSTON,AB	38	52
0.13	BALACHANDRAN,KR	JA	81	TAR	MASCHMEYER,R	LIVINGSTONE,JL	115	124
0.13	GANGOLLY,JS	AU	81	JAR			299	312
0.11	HAMLEN,SS	AP	80	TAR	HAMLEN,WA	TSCHIRHART,JT	269	287
0.11	KELLY,LK	03	80	AOS			311	322
0.11	WILLIAMS,PF	JA	80	TAR			62	77
0.10	ENGLEBRECHT,TD	JL	79	TAR	JAMISON,RW		554	562
0.10	MADEO,SA	JL	79	TAR			538	553
0.10	SHIH,W	OC	79	TAR			687	706
0.09	DAVIDSON,S	ST	78	JAR	WEIL,RL		154	233
0.09	JACOBS,FH	SP	78	JAR			190	203
0.09	KOTTAS,JF	JL	78	TAR	LAU,HS		698	707
0.08	ALBRECHT,WS	OC	76	TAR			824	837
0.08	ALY,HF	JA	71	TAR	DUBOFF,JI		119	128
0.08	ARNOLD,DF	JA	73	TAR	HUMANN,TE		23	33
0.08	BEAVER,WH	AU	74	JAR	DUKES,RE		205	215
0.08	BRIEF,RP	SP	73	JAR	OWEN,J		1	15
0.08	COMISKEY,EE	AP	66	TAR			235	238
0.08	DAVIDSON,S	AU	66	JAR	KOHLMEIER,JM		183	212
0.08	FALK,H	SP	77	JAR	MILLER,JC		12	22
0.08	GONEDES,NJ	AU	71	JAR			236	252
0.08	GREENBALL,MN	AU	69	JAR			262	289
0.08	HARVEY,DW	OC	76	TAR			838	845
0.08	HASSELDINE,CR	JL	67	TAR			497	515
0.08	HEIMANN,SR	JA	76	TAR	LUSK,EJ		51	64
0.08	HOFSTEDT,TR	AP	71	TAR	WEST,RR		329	337
0.08	HUEFNER,RJ	OC	71	TAR			717	732
0.08	IJIRI,Y	SP	70	JAR	KAPLAN,RS		34	46
0.08	JENSEN,RE	JA	71	TAR			36	56
0.08	LEMKE,KW	SP	70	JAR			47	77
0.08	LIVINGSTONE,JL	AU	69	JAR			245	256
0.08	LOEBBECKE,JK	ST	75	JAR	NETER,J		38	52
0.08	LUSK,EJ	JL	72	TAR			567	575
0.08	MORRISON,TA	AP	69	TAR	KACZKA,E		330	343
0.08	MORSE,WJ	OC	72	TAR			761	773
0.08	MURPHY,GJ	AP	76	TAR			277	286
0.08	SCHRODERHEIM,G	JL	64	TAR			679	684
0.08	SCHROEDER,RG	01	77	AOS	IMDIEKE,LF		39	46
0.08	SCHWAB,B	AP	69	TAR	NICOL,RE		292	296
0.08	SHANK,JK	JA	71	TAR			57	74
0.08	SORENSEN,JE	JL	77	TAR	GROVE,HD		658	675
0.08	STALLMAN,JC	OC	72	TAR			774	790
0.00	ABDEL-MAGID,MF	AP	79	TAR			346	357
0.00	ABRANOVIC,WA	OC	76	TAR			863	874
0.00	AGRAWAL,SP	WI	80	JAA	HALLBAUER,RC	PERRITT,GW	163	173
0.00	ANDERSON,JC	JL	86	TAR	KRAUSHAAR,JM		379	399
0.00	BABER,WR	SP	85	JAR			360	369
0.00	BABER,WR	AU	87	JAR	BROOKS,EH	RICKS,WE	293	305
0.00	BAGINSKI,SP	AU	87	JAR			196	216
0.00	BALACHANDRAN,BV	OC	81	TAR	ZOLTNERS,AA		801	812

SCHOOL OF THOUGHT=STAT.MODEL. - OTHER

CITE INDEX	FIRST AUTHOR	ISSUE	YEAR	JOURNAL	SECOND AUTHOR	THIRD AUTHOR	PAG BEG	PAG END
0.00	BALACHANDRAN,KR	02	77	AOS	LIVINGSTONE,JL		153	164
0.00	BALLEW,V	JA	82	TAR			88	104
0.00	BANKER,RD	AU	87	JAA	DATAR,SM	RAJAN,MV	319	347
0.00	BANKER,RD	JL	88	JAE	DATAR,SM	KEKRE,S	171	197
0.00	BARKMAN,A	JA	77	TAR			450	464
0.00	BEAVER,WH	AU	82	JAR	WOLFSON,MA		528	550
0.00	BEAVER,WH	DE	84	JAE	GRIFFIN,PA	LANDSMAN,WR	219	223
0.00	BECK,PJ	SP	85	AUD	SOLOMON,I		1	10
0.00	BERRY,LE	JA	87	TAR	HARWOOD,GB	KATZ,JL	14	28
0.00	BILDERSEE,JS	SU	87	JAA	KAHN,N		239	256
0.00	BOATSMAN,JR	AU	84	JAA	DOWELL,CD	KIMBRELL,JI	35	43
0.00	BORITZ,JE	AU	86	AUD	BROCA,DS		1	19
0.00	BOWER,RS	AP	66	TAR	HERRINGER,F	WILLIAMSON,JP	257	265
0.00	BRANCH,B	SP	81	JAA	BERKOWITZ,B		215	219
0.00	BRIEF,RP	SP	69	JAR	OWEN,J		12	16
0.00	BRIGHAM,EF	JA	68	TAR			46	61
0.00	BRIGHAM,EF	JL	74	TAR	NANTELL,TJ		436	447
0.00	BUCKMAN,AG	SP	82	JAR	MILLER,BL		28	41
0.00	BURGHER,PH	JA	64	TAR			103	120
0.00	CALLEN,JL	SP	88	JAA			87	108
0.00	CHARNES,A	AP	64	TAR	DAVIDSON,HJ	KORTANEK,KO	241	250
0.00	CHARNES,A	01	80	AOS	COOPER,WW		87	107
0.00	CHEN,JT	JL	83	TAR			600	605
0.00	CHOW,CW	SP	87	AUD	MCNAMEE,AH	PLUMLEE,RD	123	133
0.00	CHOW,CW	JL	87	TAR	WONG-BOREN,A		533	541
0.00	CHURCHILL,NC	WI	82	AUD	COOPER,WW	GOVINDARAJAN,V	69	91
0.00	CLARK,JJ	OC	73	TAR	ELGERS,PT		668	678
0.00	CLARK,TN	ST	77	JAR			54	94
0.00	COHEN,SI	AP	82	TAR	LOEB,M		336	347
0.00	CROSBY,MA	SP	85	AUD			118	132
0.00	DAVIS,GB	SP	86	AUD	WEBER,R		35	49
0.00	DAVIS,HZ	AU	82	JAR	KAHN,N		738	744
0.00	DAVIS,HZ	AU	84	JAR	KAHN,N	ROZEN,E	480	490
0.00	DEMING,WE	SP	79	JAA			197	208
0.00	DEMSKI,JS	SP	69	JAR			96	115
0.00	DOPUCH,N	SP	88	JAR	PINCUS,M		28	59
0.00	DREBIN,AR	SP	66	JAR			68	86
0.00	DUVALL,RM	JL	65	TAR	BULLOCH,J		569	573
0.00	FALK,H	AU	72	JAR			359	375
0.00	FARRELY,GE	AP	85	TAR	FERRIS,KR	REICHENSTEIN,WR	278	288
0.00	FELLINGHAM,JC	OC	85	TAR	NEWMAN,DP		634	650
0.00	FERRARA,WL	JL	77	TAR			597	604
0.00	FINLEY,DR	AU	83	AUD			104	116
0.00	FINLEY,DR	SP	87	AUD	BOOCKHOLDT,JL		22	39
0.00	FIRMIN,PA	ST	68	JAR	GOODMAN,SS	HENDRICKS,TE	122	155
0.00	FIRTH,MA	SP	85	AUD			23	37
0.00	FRANCIS,JR	OC	88	TAR	WILSON,ER		663	682
0.00	FRIED,D	SU	81	JAA			295	308
0.00	FROST,PA	SP	86	JAR	TAMURA,H		57	75
0.00	FULMER,JG	AU	84	JAA	MOON,JE		5	14

SCHOOL OF THOUGHT=STAT.MODEL. - OTHER

CITE INDEX	FIRST AUTHOR	ISSUE	YEAR	JOURNAL	SECOND AUTHOR	THIRD AUTHOR	PAG BEG	PAG END
0.00	GAMBLING,TE	JA	70	TAR	NOUR,A		98	102
0.00	GERLACH,JH	SP	88	AUD			61	76
0.00	GIROUX,GA	06	86	AOS	MAYPER,AG	DAFT,RL	499	520
0.00	GOMBOLA,MJ	JA	83	TAR	KETZ,JE		105	114
0.00	GRIMLUND,RA	AU	85	JAR			575	594
0.00	GRIMLUND,RA	JL	87	TAR	FELIX JR,WL		455	479
0.00	GRIMLUND,RA	SP	88	AUD			77	104
0.00	GRIMLUND,RA	AU	88	AUD	SCHROEDER,MS		53	62
0.00	GYNTHER,MM	OC	68	TAR			706	718
0.00	HAKANSSON,NH	SP	69	JAR			11	31
0.00	HARPER JR,RM	AU	87	JAR	MISTER,WG	STRAWSER,JR	327	330
0.00	HOBBS,JB	OC	64	TAR			905	913
0.00	HORWITZ,B	JL	88	TAR	NORMOLLE,D		414	435
0.00	HORWITZ,BN	SP	72	JAR	YOUNG,AE		96	107
0.00	HUSS,HF	AU	86	JAR	TRADER,RL		394	399
0.00	IJIRI,Y	AP	70	TAR	THOMPSON,GL		246	258
0.00	IMHOFF JR,EA	SU	81	JAA			333	351
0.00	JARRETT,JE	SP	72	JAR			108	112
0.00	JENSEN,RE	JA	68	TAR	THOMSEN,CT		83	93
0.00	JIAMBALVO,J	SP	84	AUD	WALLER,WS		80	88
0.00	JIAMBALVO,J	AU	85	AUD	WILNER,N		1	11
0.00	JOHNSON,GL	JL	66	TAR			510	517
0.00	JOHNSON,WB	JA	88	TAR	RAMANAN,R		96	110
0.00	KAHN,N	SU	82	JAA			327	337
0.00	KAPLAN,RS	SP	83	AUD			52	65
0.00	KAPLAN,SE	AU	85	AUD			12	25
0.00	KIM,HS	SP	87	AUD	NETER,J	GODFREY,JT	40	58
0.00	KING,RD	JL	84	TAR			419	431
0.00	KING,RD	JA	86	TAR	O'KEEFE,TB		76	90
0.00	KINNEY JR,WR	AU	81	JAA			5	17
0.00	KINNEY JR,WR	SP	87	AUD			59	73
0.00	KNECHEL,WR	SP	85	JAR			194	212
0.00	KNECHEL,WR	SP	85	AUD			38	62
0.00	KNECHEL,WR	JA	88	TAR			74	95
0.00	KNECHEL,WR	AU	88	AUD			87	107
0.00	KO,CE	SP	88	AUD	NACHTSHEIM,CJ	DUKE,GL	119	136
0.00	KREUTZFELDT,RW	AU	86	AUD	WALLACE,WA		20	43
0.00	LAU,AH	SP	87	JAR			127	138
0.00	LEE,CF	AP	88	TAR	WU,C		292	306
0.00	LEV,B	ST	69	JAR			182	197
0.00	LEVITAN,AS	AU	85	AUD	KNOBLETT,JA		26	39
0.00	LEWELLEN,W	DE	87	JAE	LODERER,C	MARTIN,K	287	310
0.00	LEWIS,BL	AP	88	TAR	PATTON,JM	GREEN,SL	270	282
0.00	LIGHTNER,SM	AU	82	AUD	ADAMS,SJ	LIGHTNER,KM	1	12
0.00	LILLESTOL,J	SP	81	JAR			263	267
0.00	LIN,WT	AU	84	AUD	MOCK,TJ	WRIGHT,A	89	99
0.00	LIVINGSTONE,JL	ST	67	JAR			93	123
0.00	LOEBBECKE,JK	SP	87	AUD	STEINBART,PJ		74	89
0.00	MADEO,SA	AP	87	TAR	SCHEPANSKI,A	UECKER,WC	323	342
0.00	MAHER,JJ	OC	87	TAR			785	798

SCHOOL OF THOUGHT=STAT.MODEL. - OTHER

CITE INDEX	FIRST AUTHOR	ISSUE	YEAR	JOURNAL	SECOND AUTHOR	THIRD AUTHOR	PAG BEG	PAG END
0.00	MANES,RP	SP	66	JAR			87	100
0.00	MARKS,BR	AU	85	JAR	RAMAN,KK		878	886
0.00	MAXIM,LD	JA	76	TAR	CULLEN,PE	COOK,FX	97	109
0.00	MCCLENON,PR	JL	63	TAR			540	547
0.00	MCCONNELL,DK	SP	84	AUD			44	56
0.00	MCKENNA,EF	03	80	AOS			297	310
0.00	MEHTA,DR	SP	68	JAR	ANDREWS,VL		50	57
0.00	MELLMAN,M	JA	63	TAR			118	123
0.00	MENSAH,YM	AP	83	TAR			228	246
0.00	MENSAH,YM	SP	84	JAR			380	395
0.00	MENZEFRICKE,U	AU	84	JAR			570	587
0.00	MOIZER,P	AU	87	AUD	TURLEY,S		118	123
0.00	MONAHAN,TF	SU	83	JAA	BARENBAUM,L		325	340
0.00	MORRIS,MH	SU	84	JAA	NICHOLS,WD		293	305
0.00	MULFORD,CW	JL	86	TAR	COMISKEY,EE		519	525
0.00	MUTCHLER,JF	AU	86	AUD			148	
0.00	NEUMANN,BR	SP	79	JAR			123	139
0.00	NICHOLS,DR	JA	87	TAR			183	190
0.00	NIKOLAI,LA	JA	79	TAR	ELAM,R		119	131
0.00	NORDHAUSER,SL	JA	81	TAR	KRAMER,JL		54	69
0.00	NOREEN,EW	SP	88	JAR			119	133
0.00	ONSI,M	AP	67	TAR			321	330
0.00	OUTSLAY,E	OC	82	TAR	WHEELER,JE		716	733
0.00	PANY,K	SP	84	AUD	RECKERS,PMJ		89	97
0.00	PEAVY,JW	WI	85	JAA	EDGAR,SM		125	135
0.00	PESANDO,JE	OC	83	TAR	CLARKE,CK		733	748
0.00	PETRI,E	AP	78	TAR	MINCH,RA		415	428
0.00	PILLSBURY,CM	SP	85	AUD			63	79
0.00	PLANTE,R	AU	85	AUD	NETER,J	LEITCH,RA	40	56
0.00	RAMANATHAN,KV	OC	71	TAR	RAPPAPORT,A		733	745
0.00	RAUN,DL	OC	63	TAR			754	758
0.00	REILLY,FK	AU	72	JAR	STETTLER,HF		308	321
0.00	ROHRBACH.KJ	SP	86	JAR			127	150
0.00	RONEN,J	AU	70	JAR			232	252
0.00	ROSHWALB,A	AU	87	AUD	WRIGHT,RL	GODFREY,JT	54	70
0.00	ROSS,WR	JL	66	TAR			464	473
0.00	SALAMON,GL	AP	82	TAR			292	302
0.00	SCAPENS,RW	AP	85	TAR	SALE,JT		231	247
0.00	SCHACHTER,B	AU	85	JAR			907	910
0.00	SHEVLIN,T	JL	87	TAR			480	509
0.00	SIMON,DT	AU	85	AUD			71	78
0.00	SIMON,DT	AP	88	TAR	FRANCIS,JR		255	269
0.00	SMIELIAUSKAS,W	AU	85	JAR			718	739
0.00	SMIELIAUSKAS,W	JA	86	TAR			118	128
0.00	SMIELIAUSKAS,W	SP	86	JAR			217	230
0.00	SRINIDHI,BN	SP	86	AUD	VASARHELYI,MA		64	76
0.00	SRIVASTAVA,RP	AU	86	JAR			422	427
0.00	STEPHENS,RG	AU	83	AUD			55	74
0.00	STERNER,JA	AU	83	JAR			623	628
0.00	STONE,M	AU	87	JAR			317	326

SCHOOL OF THOUGHT=STAT.MODEL. - OTHER

CITE IND-EX	FIRST AUTHOR	ISS-UE	YE-AR	JOUR-NAL	SECOND AUTHOR	THIRD AUTHOR	PAG BEG	PAG END
0.00	SUNDER,S	SP	83	JAR			222	233
0.00	SUSSMAN,MR	AP	65	TAR			407	413
0.00	TABOR,RH	SP	85	AUD	WILLIS,JT		93	109
0.00	TAMURA,H	SP	85	AUD			133	142
0.00	TEHRANIAN,H	ST	87	JAR	TRAVLOS,NG	WAEGELEIN,JF	51	76
0.00	TILLER,MG	SU	85	JAA	MAUTZ,RD		293	304
0.00	VERRECCHIA,RE	JL	82	TAR			579	593
0.00	WALKER,M	AP	84	TAR			278	286
0.00	WALLACE,WA	SP	83	AUD			66	90
0.00	WARREN,CS	SP	74	JAR			158	177
0.00	WATKINS,PR	SP	84	JAR			406	411
0.00	WAYMIRE,G	SP	85	JAR			268	295
0.00	WEBER,R	JL	86	TAR			498	518
0.00	WHITTINGTON,OR	JL	80	TAR	WHITTENBURG,G		409	418
0.00	WHITTRED,GP	AP	84	TAR	ZIMMER,I		287	295
0.00	WILCOX,KA	01	77	AOS	SMITH,CH		81	97
0.00	WILKERSON JR,JE	SP	87	JAR			161	167
0.00	WILLIAMS,DJ	SP	85	AUD	LILLIS,A		110	117
0.00	WILLINGHAM,JJ	AU	85	AUD	WRIGHT,WF		57	70
0.00	WILSON,ER	SP	84	JAR	HOWARD,TP		207	224
0.00	YOUNG,R	SP	86	JAR			231	240
0.00	YOUNG,SD	AP	88	TAR			283	291

SCHOOL OF THOUGHT=STAT.MODEL. - OTHER

3.8 SCHOOL OF THOUGHT=ACCOUNTING THEORY

CITE IND-EX	FIRST AUTHOR	ISS-UE	YE-AR	JOUR-NAL	SECOND AUTHOR	THIRD AUTHOR	PAG BEG	PAG END
3.89	BURCHELL,S	01	80	AOS	CLUBB,C	HOPWOOD,AG	5	27
3.80	WATTS,RL	AP	79	TAR	ZIMMERMAN,JL		273	305
3.75	BURCHELL,S	04	85	AOS	CLUBB,C	HOPWOOD,AG	381	414
3.40	KAPLAN,RS	JL	84	TAR			390	418
2.67	HOPWOOD,AG	23	83	AOS			287	305
2.60	COOPER,DJ	34	84	AOS	SHERER,MJ		207	232
2.50	TOMKINS,C	04	83	AOS	GROVES,R		361	374
2.17	LEFTWICH,RW	JA	83	TAR			23	42
2.00	ROBERTS,J	04	85	AOS	SCAPENS,RW		443	456
1.83	KAPLAN,RS	OC	83	TAR			686	705
1.67	TIESSEN,P	23	83	AOS	WATERHOUSE,JH	251	268	
1.57	TINKER,AM	02	82	AOS	MERINO,BD	NEIMARK,M	167	200
1.56	TINKER,AM	01	80	AOS			147	160
1.44	DUKES,RE	ST	80	JAR	DYCKMAN,TR	ELLIOTT,JA	1	26
1.38	DEANGELO,LE	DE	81	JAE			183	199
1.33	ZIMMERMAN,JL	AG	83	JAE			119	149
1.23	DEMSKI,JS	OC	73	TAR			718	723
1.00	GAMBLING,TE	02	77	AOS			141	152
1.00	KAPLAN,RS	45	86	AOS			429	452
1.00	SORTER,GH	JA	69	TAR			12	19
1.00	SPICER,BH	01	83	AOS	BALLEW,V		73	98
1.00	ZIMMER,I	MR	86	JAE			37	52
0.92	BEAVER,WH	OC	68	TAR	KENNELLY,JW	VOSS,WM	675	683
0.85	BEAVER,WH	ST	74	JAR	DEMSKI,JS		170	187
0.85	GORDON,MJ	AP	64	TAR			251	263
0.85	LEV,B	JA	71	TAR	SCHWARTZ,A		103	112
0.83	HAKANSSON,NH	AP	77	TAR			396	416
0.75	BENSTON,GJ	AP	85	JAE			67	84
0.75	COOPER,DJ	03	81	AOS	HAYES,DC	WOLF,FM	175	192
0.75	PARKER,JE	JA	77	TAR			69	96
0.71	DEANGELO,LE	DE	82	JAE			171	203
0.71	HITE,GL	JL	82	JAE	LONG,MS		3	14
0.70	GONEDES,NJ	AU	79	JAR	DOPUCH,N		384	410
0.69	ARCHIBALD,TR	ST	67	JAR			164	186
0.69	GAGNON,JM	ST	67	JAR			187	204
0.69	MAY,RG	OC	76	TAR	SUNDEM,GL		747	763
0.67	CHUA,WF	OC	86	TAR			601	632
0.67	DEANGELO,LE	JL	86	TAR			400	420
0.67	GAA,JC	JL	86	TAR			435	454
0.67	NEIMARK,M	45	86	AOS	TINKER,T		369	396
0.67	TRUEMAN,B	MR	86	JAE			53	72
0.62	DRAKE,DF	AU	65	JAR	DOPUCH,N		192	205
0.62	FRISHKOFF,P	ST	70	JAR			116	129
0.60	SUNDER,S	SP	84	JAR	WAYMIRE,G		396	405
0.54	DOPUCH,N	AU	73	JAR	RONEN,J		191	211
0.54	EPSTEIN,MJ	01	76	AOS	FLAMHOLTZ,EG	MCDONOUGH,JJ	23	42
0.54	FELTHAM,GA	OC	68	TAR			684	696
0.54	HENDRICKS,JA	AP	76	TAR			292	305

CITE IND- EX	FIRST AUTHOR	ISS- UE	YE- AR	JOUR -NAL	SECOND AUTHOR	THIRD AUTHOR	PAG BEG	PAG END
0.54	PETERSEN,RJ	JA	73	TAR			34	43
0.50	PUXTY,AG	03	87	AOS	WILLMOTT,HC	COOPER,DJ	273	291
0.50	THOMPSON,G	05	87	AOS			523	543
0.50	WHITTRED,G	DE	87	JAE			259	285
0.46	NEUMANN,FL	ST	68	JAR			1	17
0.46	REVSINE,L	JL	70	TAR			513	523
0.46	SIMMONS,JK	OC	69	TAR	GRAY,J		757	776
0.46	SORTER,GH	AU	64	JAR	BECKER,S	ARCHIBALD,TR	183	196
0.43	DAVIS,SW	04	82	AOS	MENON,K	MORGAN,G	307	318
0.42	DIERKES,M	01	77	AOS	PRESTON,LE		3	22
0.40	PRAKASH,P	JA	79	TAR	SUNDER,S		1	22
0.38	BERNSTEIN,LA	JA	67	TAR			86	95
0.38	COPELAND,RM	ST	71	JAR	SHANK,JK		196	224
0.38	MCINTYRE,EV	JL	73	TAR			575	585
0.38	MORIARITY,S	OC	75	TAR			791	795
0.38	OHLSON,JA	AU	81	JAR	BUCKMAN,AG		399	433
0.36	DIRSMITH,MW	34	78	AOS	JABLONSKY,SF		215	226
0.33	COVALESKI,M	45	86	AOS	AIKEN,M		297	320
0.33	GROJER,JE	04	77	AOS	STARK,A		349	385
0.33	KAPLAN,RS	AP	77	TAR			369	378
0.33	MEYER,JW	45	86	AOS			345	356
0.33	PASTENA,V	AP	86	TAR	RULAND,W		288	301
0.33	PEASNELL,KV	SP	77	JAR	SKERRATT,CL		108	119
0.33	SHRIVER,KA	SP	86	JAR			151	165
0.33	ZALD,MN	45	86	AOS			321	326
0.31	BARNEA,A	JA	75	TAR	RONEN,J	SADAN,S	58	68
0.31	BARRETT,ME	SP	76	JAR			10	26
0.31	BARTON,AD	OC	74	TAR			664	681
0.31	CHEN,RS	JL	75	TAR			533	543
0.31	LIVINGSTONE,JL	AP	67	TAR			233	240
0.31	STERLING,RR	JL	70	TAR			444	457
0.30	CLANCY,DK	12	79	AOS	COLLINS,F		21	30
0.30	REVSINE,L	AP	79	TAR			306	322
0.30	SCHREUDER,H	12	79	AOS			109	122
0.30	VATTER,WJ	JL	79	TAR			563	573
0.25	ANELL,B	04	85	AOS			479	492
0.25	DYCKMAN,TR	04	81	AOS			291	300
0.25	DYE,RA	AU	85	JAR			544	574
0.25	KELLY,LK	JA	77	TAR			97	108
0.25	KELLY,R	AU	85	JAR			619	632
0.25	STAUBUS,GJ	JA	85	TAR			53	75
0.23	ANTON,HR	SP	64	JAR			1	9
0.23	BOWMAN,EH	01	76	AOS	HAIRE,M		11	22
0.23	CHAMBERS,RJ	AP	64	TAR			264	274
0.23	CHAMBERS,RJ	OC	65	TAR			731	741
0.23	HEINTZ,JA	OC	73	TAR			679	689
0.23	MCKEOWN,JC	JA	71	TAR			12	29
0.23	MOBLEY,SC	OC	70	TAR			762	768
0.23	ORTMAN,RF	AP	75	TAR			298	304
0.23	RONEN,J	SP	75	JAR	SADAN,S		133	149

SCHOOL OF THOUGHT=ACCOUNTING THEORY

CITE IND-EX	FIRST AUTHOR	ISS-UE	YE-AR	JOUR-NAL	SECOND AUTHOR	THIRD AUTHOR	PAG BEG	PAG END
0.23	VATTER,WJ	AU	63	JAR			179	197
0.20	BROCKHOFF,K	12	79	AOS			77	86
0.20	DIERKES,M	12	79	AOS			87	108
0.20	MOST,KS	AU	84	JAR			782	788
0.18	DILLON,RD	JA	78	TAR	NASH,JF		11	17
0.18	HUGHES,JS	OC	78	TAR			882	894
0.18	IJIRI,Y	SU	78	JAA			331	348
0.17	BROMWICH,M	JL	77	TAR			587	596
0.17	KILMANN,RH	04	83	AOS			341	360
0.17	LESSEM,R	04	77	AOS			279	294
0.17	RONEN,J	AP	77	TAR			438	449
0.15	BENISHAY,H	SP	65	JAR			114	132
0.15	BIERMAN JR,H	JL	63	TAR			501	507
0.15	BIRD,FA	AP	74	TAR	DAVIDSON,LF	SMITH,CH	233	244
0.15	BRIEF,RP	AP	75	TAR			285	297
0.15	CHAMBERS,RJ	SP	63	JAR			3	15
0.15	CHAMBERS,RJ	SP	65	JAR			32	62
0.15	CHAMBERS,RJ	AU	65	JAR			242	252
0.15	CHAMBERS,RJ	JL	66	TAR			443	457
0.15	CHAMBERS,RJ	OC	67	TAR			751	757
0.15	COPELAND,RM	SP	68	JAR	FREDERICKS,W		106	113
0.15	CYERT,RM	ST	74	JAR	IJIRI,Y		29	42
0.15	DOCKWEILER,RC	OC	69	TAR			729	742
0.15	DOPUCH,N	ST	66	JAR	DRAKE,DF		192	219
0.15	EAVES,BC	JL	66	TAR			426	442
0.15	EDWARDS,EO	AP	75	TAR			235	245
0.15	FALK,H	AP	73	TAR	OPHIR,T		323	338
0.15	GYNTHER,RS	OC	70	TAR			712	730
0.15	IJIRI,Y	AP	76	TAR			227	243
0.15	JOHNSON,O	OC	70	TAR			641	653
0.15	KNUTSON,PH	JA	70	TAR			55	68
0.15	LARSON,KD	JA	69	TAR			38	47
0.15	LEMKE,KW	JA	66	TAR			32	41
0.15	LINDHE,R	AU	63	JAR			139	148
0.15	LORIG,AN	JL	64	TAR			563	573
0.15	MATTESSICH,R	JL	72	TAR			469	487
0.15	MAUTZ,RK	AP	63	TAR			317	325
0.15	MOONITZ,M	JL	70	TAR			465	475
0.15	PELES,YC	SP	70	JAR			128	137
0.15	RITTS,BA	SP	74	JAR			93	111
0.15	SCHIFF,M	SP	66	JAR			62	67
0.15	SNAVELY,HJ	AP	67	TAR			223	232
0.15	THOMAS,AL	JL	71	TAR			472	479
0.15	VATTER,WJ	AU	66	JAR			133	148
0.15	VICKREY,DW	OC	70	TAR			731	742
0.15	VICKREY,DW	JA	76	TAR			31	40
0.15	WAGNER,JW	JL	65	TAR			599	605
0.15	YETTON,PY	01	76	AOS			81	90
0.14	BENSTON,GJ	02	82	AOS			87	106
0.14	MCCARTHY,WE	JL	82	TAR			554	578

SCHOOL OF THOUGHT=ACCOUNTING THEORY

CITE IND-EX	FIRST AUTHOR	ISS-UE	YE-AR	JOUR-NAL	SECOND AUTHOR	THIRD AUTHOR	PAG BEG	PAG END
0.14	SKINNER,RC	SP	82	JAR			210	226
0.14	VIGELAND,RL	AP	82	TAR			348	357
0.13	ALFORD,MR	SP	81	JAA	EDMONDS,TP		255	264
0.13	HORWITZ,BN	WI	81	JAA	KOLODNY,R		102	113
0.13	KOCH,BS	JL	81	TAR			574	586
0.13	RAMANATHAN,KV	02	81	AOS	WEIS,WL		143	152
0.11	ANSARI,SL	01	80	AOS	MCDONOUGH,JJ		129	142
0.11	FLAHERTY,RE	AU	80	JAA	SCHWARTZ,BN		47	56
0.11	FLAMHOLTZ,EG	01	80	AOS			31	42
0.11	PALMON,D	SP	80	JAA	KWATINETZ,M		207	226
0.10	CHAN,JL	04	79	AOS			273	282
0.09	GRAY,SJ	AU	78	JAR			242	253
0.09	SCAPENS,RW	AP	78	TAR			448	469
0.09	SCAPENS,RW	AP	78	TAR			448	469
0.08	ADAR,Z	JA	77	TAR	BARNEA,A	LEV,B	137	149
0.08	AIKEN,ME	JL	75	TAR	BLACKETT,LA	ISAACS,G	544	562
0.08	ARNETT,HE	AP	67	TAR			291	297
0.08	ARNOLD,DF	AU	77	JAR	HUEFNER,RJ		245	252
0.08	BAXTER,WT	AU	71	JAR	CARRIER,NH		189	214
0.08	BEDFORD,NM	JL	68	TAR	IINO,T		453	458
0.08	BEDFORD,NM	JL	75	TAR	ZIEGLER,RE		435	443
0.08	BIERMAN JR,H	AP	66	TAR			271	274
0.08	BIRNBERG,JG	OC	65	TAR			814	820
0.08	BIRNBERG,JG	01	76	AOS	GANDHI,NM		5	10
0.08	BOLLOM,WJ	JA	72	TAR	WEYGANDT,JJ		75	84
0.08	BOLLOM,WJ	JA	73	TAR			12	22
0.08	BRADFORD,WD	AP	74	TAR			296	305
0.08	BRIEF,RP	OC	73	TAR	OWEN,J		690	695
0.08	BUCKLEY,JW	AP	68	TAR	KIRCHER,P	MATHEWS,RL	274	283
0.08	BULLOCK,CL	JA	74	TAR			98	103
0.08	BURKE,EJ	OC	64	TAR			837	849
0.08	BUZBY,SL	SP	75	JAR			16	37
0.08	CHURCHILL,NC	ST	66	JAR			128	156
0.08	COOK,JS	OC	76	TAR	HOLZMANN,OJ		778	787
0.08	COOPER,WW	OC	68	TAR	DOPUCH,N	KELLER,TF	640	648
0.08	CURRY,DW	JL	71	TAR			490	503
0.08	DAVIDSON,S	AU	63	JAR			117	126
0.08	DEVINE,CT	AU	63	JAR			127	138
0.08	DICKENS,RL	AP	64	TAR	BLACKBURN,JO		312	329
0.08	DREBIN,AR	JA	65	TAR			154	162
0.08	ECKEL,LG	OC	76	TAR			764	777
0.08	FEKRAT,MA	AP	72	TAR			351	355
0.08	FOGELBERG,G	AU	71	JAR			215	235
0.08	FRANCIS,ME	AP	73	TAR			245	257
0.08	FRANKFURTER,GM	AP	72	TAR	HORWITZ,BN		245	259
0.08	FREMGEN,JM	OC	68	TAR			649	656
0.08	GREEN,D	SP	64	JAR			35	49
0.08	HEATH,LC	JL	72	TAR			458	468
0.08	HECK,WR	JL	63	TAR			577	578
0.08	HICKS,EL	AU	64	JAR			158	171

SCHOOL OF THOUGHT=ACCOUNTING THEORY

CITE INDEX	FIRST AUTHOR	ISS-UE	YE-AR	JOUR-NAL	SECOND AUTHOR	THIRD AUTHOR	PAG BEG	PAG END
0.08	HORNGREN,CT	AP	65	TAR			323	333
0.08	IJIRI,Y	SP	65	JAR	JAEDICKE,RK	LIVINGSTONE,JL	63	74
0.08	ISELIN,ER	AP	68	TAR			231	238
0.08	JOHNSON,O	SP	68	JAR			29	37
0.08	KELLY,LK	JA	77	TAR			97	108
0.08	KISSINGER,JN	AP	77	TAR			322	339
0.08	LARSON,KD	JL	67	TAR			480	488
0.08	MARQUES,E	23	76	AOS			175	178
0.08	MATHEWS,RL	JL	68	TAR			509	516
0.08	MCDONALD,DL	OC	67	TAR			662	679
0.08	MCINTYRE,EV	JA	77	TAR			162	171
0.08	MEYERS,SL	JA	73	TAR			44	49
0.08	MOONITZ,M	AU	66	JAR	RUSS,A		155	168
0.08	NEUMANN,FL	JL	69	TAR			546	554
0.08	NURNBERG,H	OC	68	TAR			719	729
0.08	PARKER,JE	JL	75	TAR			512	524
0.08	PENMAN,SH	AP	70	TAR			333	346
0.08	RAPPAPORT,A	AP	65	TAR			373	376
0.08	SHWAYDER,KR	AP	69	TAR			304	316
0.08	SHWAYDER,KR	AP	71	TAR			306	319
0.08	SHWAYDER,KR	AU	73	JAR			259	272
0.08	SNAVELY,HJ	AP	69	TAR			344	353
0.08	SPILLER JR,EA	SP	74	JAR	VIRGIL JR,RL		112	142
0.08	STAUBUS,GJ	OC	67	TAR			650	661
0.08	STAUBUS,GJ	JL	76	TAR			574	589
0.08	STERLING,RR	JA	67	TAR			62	73
0.08	STERLING,RR	JL	68	TAR			481	502
0.08	TRACY,JA	JA	65	TAR			163	175
0.08	ULLMANN,AA	01	76	AOS			71	80
0.08	VATTER,W	OC	66	TAR			681	698
0.08	VATTER,WJ	JL	63	TAR			470	477
0.08	WOJDAK,JF	JL	69	TAR			562	570
0.08	WOJDAK,JF	JA	70	TAR			88	97
0.08	WRIGHT,FK	AU	65	JAR			167	181
0.08	WRIGHT,FK	FL	65	JAR			167	181
0.00	ADAMS,KD	WI	84	JAA			151	163
0.00	AGGARWAL,R	SP	78	JAA			197	216
0.00	AGRAWAL,SP	OC	77	TAR			789	809
0.00	AHARONI,Y	SP	67	JAR	OPHIR,T		1	26
0.00	ALFRED,AM	AU	64	JAR			172	182
0.00	ALVEY,KL	JA	63	TAR			124	125
0.00	ANDERSON JR,KE	JL	85	TAR			357	371
0.00	ANDERSON,HM	OC	63	TAR	GRIFFIN,FB		813	818
0.00	ANDERSON,JM	AU	64	JAR			236	238
0.00	ARNETT,HE	OC	63	TAR			733	741
0.00	ARNETT,HE	JA	65	TAR			54	64
0.00	AYRES,FL	SP	86	JAR			166	169
0.00	BAINBRIDGE,DR	SU	84	JAA			334	346
0.00	BAKER,RE	JA	64	TAR			52	61
0.00	BARRETT,WB	JA	68	TAR			105	112

SCHOOL OF THOUGHT=ACCOUNTING THEORY

CITE IND-EX	FIRST AUTHOR	ISS-UE	YE-AR	JOUR-NAL	SECOND AUTHOR	THIRD AUTHOR	PAG BEG	PAG END
0.00	BEAMS,FA	AP	69	TAR			382	388
0.00	BEDFORD,NM	JA	67	TAR			82	85
0.00	BEDFORD,NM	AP	72	TAR	MCKEOWN,JC		333	338
0.00	BEJA,A	AU	77	JAR	AHARONI,Y		169	178
0.00	BENJAMIN,JJ	SU	86	JAA	GROSSMAN,SD	WIGGIN,CE	177	184
0.00	BENNINGER,LJ	JL	65	TAR			547	557
0.00	BERG,KB	JL	63	TAR	MUELLER,FJ		554	561
0.00	BIERMAN JR,H	JA	63	TAR			61	63
0.00	BIERMAN JR,H	AU	64	JAR			229	235
0.00	BIERMAN JR,H	JL	65	TAR			541	546
0.00	BIERMAN JR,H	OC	67	TAR			731	737
0.00	BIERMAN JR,H	AU	67	JAR	SMIDT,S		144	153
0.00	BIERMAN JR,H	OC	68	TAR			657	661
0.00	BIERMAN JR,H	JA	68	TAR	LIU,E		62	67
0.00	BIERMAN JR,H	AP	69	TAR	DAVIDSON,S		239	246
0.00	BIERMAN JR,H	OC	71	TAR			693	700
0.00	BIERMAN JR,H	WI	86	JAA			62	70
0.00	BIERMAN,H	SP	85	JAA			184	194
0.00	BIRD,PA	SP	65	JAR			1	11
0.00	BLAKELY,EJ	JA	63	TAR	KNUTSON,PH		75	86
0.00	BOTTS,RR	OC	63	TAR			789	795
0.00	BRADBURY,ME	AP	88	TAR	CALDERWOOD,SC		330	347
0.00	BRAVENEC,LL	02	77	AOS	EPSTEIN,MJ	CRUMBLEY,DL	131	140
0.00	BRIEF,RP	AP	68	TAR	OWEN,J		367	372
0.00	BRILOFF,AJ	JA	64	TAR			12	15
0.00	BRILOFF,AJ	JL	67	TAR			489	496
0.00	BRUGEMAN,DC	OC	63	TAR	BRIGHTON,GD		764	770
0.00	BRUGGE,WG	JL	63	TAR			596	600
0.00	BUCKLEY,JW	01	80	AOS			49	64
0.00	BURKE,WL	OC	63	TAR			802	812
0.00	BURNS,JS	JA	63	TAR	JAEDICKE,RK	SANGSTER,JM	1	13
0.00	BURT,OR	SP	72	JAR			28	57
0.00	CARLSON,ML	JL	81	TAR	LAMB,JW		554	573
0.00	CARSON,AB	AP	65	TAR			334	337
0.00	CARTER,WK	JA	81	TAR			108	114
0.00	CASPARI,JA	OC	76	TAR			739	746
0.00	CERF,AR	JL	75	TAR			451	465
0.00	CHAMBERS,RJ	AP	67	TAR			241	253
0.00	CHAMBERS,RJ	AP	68	TAR			239	247
0.00	CHAMBERS,RJ	JL	72	TAR			488	509
0.00	CHAMBERS,RJ	01	80	AOS			167	180
0.00	CHAN,KH	WI	84	JAA	CHENG,TT		164	177
0.00	CHOUDHURY,N	06	88	AOS			549	557
0.00	CHUA,WF	06	86	AOS			583	598
0.00	COGLITORE,F	SP	88	AUD	BERRYMAN,RG		150	163
0.00	COLIGNON,R	06	88	AOS	COVALESKI,M		559	579
0.00	COMISKEY,EE	AP	68	TAR	MLYNARCZYK,FA		248	256
0.00	COOPER,DJ	05	87	AOS	HOPPER,TM		407	414
0.00	COOPER,WW	AU	85	JAA	HO,JL	HUNTER,JE	22	39
0.00	CORBIN,DA	OC	63	TAR			742	744

SCHOOL OF THOUGHT=ACCOUNTING THEORY

CITE IND-EX	FIRST AUTHOR	ISS-UE	YE-AR	JOUR-NAL	SECOND AUTHOR	THIRD AUTHOR	PAG BEG	PAG END
0.00	CORBIN,DA	OC	67	TAR			635	641
0.00	CORCORAN,AW	AU	65	JAR	KWANG,CW		206	217
0.00	COTTELL JR,PG	WI	86	JAA			30	45
0.00	COVALESKI,MA	01	88	AOS	DIRSMITH,MW		1	24
0.00	COWAN,TK	JA	65	TAR			9	20
0.00	COWAN,TK	JA	68	TAR			94	100
0.00	COWEN,SS	02	87	AOS	FERRERI,LB	PARKER,LD	111	122
0.00	CRAMER JR,JJ	OC	70	TAR	SCHRADER,WJ		698	703
0.00	CRAMER JR,JJ	WI	79	JAA	NEYHART,CA		135	150
0.00	CRUMBLEY,DL	JA	75	TAR	SAVICH,RS		112	117
0.00	CRUSE,RB	JA	65	TAR	SUMMERS,EL		82	88
0.00	DANOS,P	SP	87	AUD	HOLT,DL	BAILEY JR,AD	134	149
0.00	DAVIS,ML	AP	88	TAR	LARGAY III,JA		348	363
0.00	DEAN,J	AP	63	TAR	HARRISS,CL		229	242
0.00	DEFLIESE,PL	JL	65	TAR			517	521
0.00	DEINZER,HT	JA	66	TAR			21	31
0.00	DEMARIS,EJ	JA	63	TAR			37	45
0.00	DERMER,JD	06	86	AOS	LUCAS,RG		471	482
0.00	DEWHIRST,JF	AP	71	TAR			365	373
0.00	DOWELL,CD	AU	81	JAA	HALL,JA		30	40
0.00	DREBIN,AR	JL	63	TAR			579	583
0.00	DREBIN,AR	SP	64	JAR			25	34
0.00	DREBIN,AR	JL	66	TAR			413	425
0.00	DRINKWATER,D	JL	65	TAR	EDWARDS,JD		579	582
0.00	EIGEN,MM	JL	65	TAR			536	540
0.00	ENGSTROM,JH	SP	84	JAA			197	211
0.00	ENGSTROM,JH	SU	85	JAA			305	318
0.00	EVERETT,JO	SP	84	JAA	PORTER,GA		241	256
0.00	FARMAN,WL	JA	63	TAR	HOU,C		133	141
0.00	FELIX JR,WL	SP	88	AUD	NILES,MS		43	60
0.00	FERRARA,WL	OC	63	TAR			719	722
0.00	FESS,PE	OC	63	TAR			723	732
0.00	FESS,PE	AP	66	TAR			266	270
0.00	FIRMIN,PA	AP	63	TAR			270	277
0.00	FORD,A	OC	69	TAR			818	822
0.00	FREDRIKSON,EB	AU	68	JAR			208	221
0.00	FREMGEN,JM	JA	64	TAR			43	51
0.00	FREMGEN,JM	JL	67	TAR			457	467
0.00	FRIED,D	WI	87	JAA	HOSLER,C		5	23
0.00	FRIEDLOB,GT	WI	83	JAA			100	107
0.00	FRIEDMAN,LA	JA	78	TAR			18	30
0.00	FRIEDMAN,LA	OC	78	TAR			895	909
0.00	GAMBLE,GO	SP	81	JAA			220	237
0.00	GAMBLE,GO	SU	82	JAA			320	326
0.00	GAMBLING,T	04	85	AOS			415	426
0.00	GAMBLING,T	04	87	AOS			319	329
0.00	GARSOMBKE,HP	SU	83	JAA	ALLEN,G		285	298
0.00	GIBSON,JL	JL	63	TAR			492	500
0.00	GILLES JR,LH	OC	63	TAR			776	784
0.00	GIVENS,HR	JL	66	TAR			458	463

SCHOOL OF THOUGHT=ACCOUNTING THEORY

CITE IND- EX	FIRST AUTHOR	ISS- UE	YE- AR	JOUR -NAL	SECOND AUTHOR	THIRD AUTHOR	PAG BEG	PAG END
0.00	GOLDBERG,L	JL	63	TAR			457	469
0.00	GOLDIN,HJ	SU	85	JAA			269	278
0.00	GOLDSCHMIDT,Y	AP	69	TAR	SMIDT,S		317	329
0.00	GOLDSCHMIDT,Y	AU	84	JAA	SHASHUA,L		54	67
0.00	GOMBERG,M	JL	64	TAR	FARBER,A		615	617
0.00	GORDON,LA	JL	88	AUD	HAMER,MH		514	521
0.00	GORMLEY,RJ	SU	80	JAA			293	312
0.00	GOVINDARAJAN,V	SU	79	JAA			339	343
0.00	GOVINDARAJAN,V	04	80	AOS			383	392
0.00	GRADY,P	JA	65	TAR			21	30
0.00	GRANOF,MH	SU	84	JAA	SHORT,DG		323	333
0.00	GRAY,D	AU	84	JAR			760	764
0.00	GRAY,SJ	SP	84	JAR	RADEBAUGH,LH		351	360
0.00	GREENBALL,MN	ST	68	JAR			27	49
0.00	GREENBERG,RR	AU	86	JAA	JOHNSON,GL	RAMESH,K	266	277
0.00	GREER,HC	JA	64	TAR			22	31
0.00	GUTBERLET,LG	SU	80	JAA			313	338
0.00	GUTBERLET,LG	AU	83	JAA			16	28
0.00	GYNTHER,RS	AP	69	TAR			247	255
0.00	HAKANSSON,NH	JL	78	TAR			717	725
0.00	HALL,TW	SU	83	JAA			299	313
0.00	HALL,TW	SP	85	JAA	CASLER,DJ		210	224
0.00	HALPERIN,R	OC	85	TAR	TZUR,J		670	680
0.00	HALPERIN,R	OC	87	TAR	SRINIDHI,BN		686	706
0.00	HANNUM,WH	AP	68	TAR	WASSERMAN,W		295	302
0.00	HARTE,GF	02	87	AOS	OWEN,DL		123	142
0.00	HASEMAN,WC	OC	68	TAR			738	752
0.00	HATFIELD,HR	AU	66	JAR			169	182
0.00	HAWKINS,CA	SP	84	JAA	GIRARD,D		225	240
0.00	HENDRICKSON,HS	AP	68	TAR			363	366
0.00	HENDRIKSEN,ES	JL	63	TAR			483	491
0.00	HENNESSY,VC	SU	78	JAA			317	330
0.00	HILKE,JC	WI	86	JAA			17	29
0.00	HILL,HP	WI	82	JAA			99	109
0.00	HINES,RD	03	88	AOS			251	261
0.00	HINES,RD	OC	88	TAR			642	656
0.00	HIRSCH,AJ	OC	64	TAR			972	978
0.00	HIRSCHMAN,RW	JA	65	TAR			176	183
0.00	HOLDER,WW	WI	82	JAA	EUDY,KH		110	125
0.00	HOLZER,HP	AP	64	TAR	SCHONFELD,HM		405	413
0.00	HOLZMANN,OJ	WI	84	JAA	MEANS,KM		138	150
0.00	HOPPER,T	05	87	AOS	STOREY,J	WILLMOTT,H	437	456
0.00	HORNE,JC	JA	63	TAR			56	60
0.00	HORVITZ,JS	WI	85	JAA	COLDWELL,S		86	99
0.00	HORWITZ,BN	OC	63	TAR			819	826
0.00	HORWITZ,BN	AU	80	JAA	KOLODNY,R		20	35
0.00	HORWITZ,RM	JL	64	TAR			618	621
0.00	HOSKIN,KW	01	88	AOS	MACVE,RH		37	73
0.00	HUDSON,RR	OC	63	TAR			796	801
0.00	HUSS,HF	AU	85	JAA			60	66

SCHOOL OF THOUGHT=ACCOUNTING THEORY

CITE IND-EX	FIRST AUTHOR	ISS-UE	YE-AR	JOUR-NAL	SECOND AUTHOR	THIRD AUTHOR	PAG BEG	PAG END
0.00	HYLTON,DP	OC	65	TAR			824	828
0.00	IJIRI,Y	JA	65	TAR			36	53
0.00	IJIRI,Y	OC	68	TAR			662	667
0.00	IJIRI,Y	JL	72	TAR			510	526
0.00	IJIRI,Y	01	80	AOS	KELLY,EC		115	123
0.00	IJIRI,Y	JA	84	TAR	NOEL,J		52	63
0.00	IJIRI,Y	OC	86	TAR			745	760
0.00	IMDIEKE,LF	OC	69	TAR	WEYGANDT,JJ		798	805
0.00	IMKE,FJ	AP	66	TAR			318	322
0.00	IVES,M	SU	85	JAA			253	268
0.00	JACOBS,FH	JA	87	TAR	MARSHALL,RM		67	78
0.00	JACOBSEN,LE	AP	63	TAR			285	292
0.00	JARRETT,JE	SP	74	JAR			63	66
0.00	JENKINS,DO	JL	64	TAR			648	653
0.00	JENSEN,MC	AP	85	JAE	ZIMMERMAN,JL		3	10
0.00	JERSTON,JE	OC	65	TAR			812	813
0.00	JOHNSON,GL	OC	65	TAR			821	823
0.00	JOHNSON,O	SP	65	JAR			75	85
0.00	JOHNSON,O	JL	68	TAR			546	548
0.00	JOHNSON,O	OC	76	TAR			808	823
0.00	JOHNSTON,DJ	SP	80	JAA	LEMON,WM	NEUMANN,FL	251	263
0.00	JOLIVET,V	JL	64	TAR			689	692
0.00	JONES,CS	03	85	AOS			303	328
0.00	JONES,CS	02	85	AOS			177	200
0.00	JONSSON,S	05	88	AOS	GRONLUND,A		513	532
0.00	KAHN,N	AU	85	JAA	SCHIFF,A		40	49
0.00	KARLINSKY,SS	WI	83	JAA			157	167
0.00	KARLINSKY,SS	AU	83	JAA			65	76
0.00	KATZ,BG	SU	87	JAA	OWEN,J		266	298
0.00	KELLER,TF	JA	65	TAR			184	189
0.00	KEMP,PS	JA	63	TAR			126	132
0.00	KIM,M	AP	88	JAE	MOORE,G		111	125
0.00	KING,RR	JA	74	TAR	BARON,CD		76	87
0.00	KING,TE	SP	79	JAA			209	223
0.00	KING,TE	JL	88	AUD	ORTEGREN,AK		522	535
0.00	KIRCHER,P	OC	65	TAR			742	752
0.00	KIRCHER,P	JL	67	TAR			537	543
0.00	KISSINGER,JN	SP	86	JAA			90	101
0.00	KISTNER,KP	SP	80	JAR	SALMI,T		297	311
0.00	KNAUF,JB	WI	87	JAA	VASARHELYI,MA		43	64
0.00	KNIGHTS,D	05	87	AOS	COLLINSON,D		457	477
0.00	KNUTSON,PH	ST	71	JAR			99	112
0.00	LAIBSTAIN,S	AP	71	TAR			342	351
0.00	LANGHOLM,O	AU	65	JAR			218	227
0.00	LARGAY III,JA	AU	83	JAA			44	53
0.00	LARSON,KD	OC	66	TAR	SCHATTKE,RW		634	641
0.00	LAUGHLIN,RC	05	87	AOS			479	502
0.00	LAUVER,RC	JA	66	TAR			65	74
0.00	LAVOIE,D	06	87	AOS			579	604
0.00	LAWLER,J	ST	67	JAR			86	92

SCHOOL OF THOUGHT=ACCOUNTING THEORY

CITE IND- EX	FIRST AUTHOR	ISS- UE	YE- AR	JOUR -NAL	SECOND AUTHOR	THIRD AUTHOR	PAG BEG	PAG END
0.00	LEE,SS	JL	65	TAR			622	625
0.00	LEMBKE,VC	JL	70	TAR			458	464
0.00	LEMBKE,VC	WI	80	JAA	SMITH,JH		147	162
0.00	LEMBKE,VC	WI	81	JAA	TOOLE,HR		128	135
0.00	LENTILHON,RW	OC	64	TAR			880	883
0.00	LERE,JC	AP	86	TAR			318	324
0.00	LESSARD,DR	JL	77	TAR	LORANGE,P		628	637
0.00	LEV,B	AU	78	JAR	THEIL,H		286	293
0.00	LEV,B	JA	88	TAR			1	22
0.00	LI,DH	OC	63	TAR			771	775
0.00	LI,DH	JA	63	TAR			52	55
0.00	LI,DH	SP	63	JAR			102	107
0.00	LI,DH	OC	64	TAR			946	950
0.00	LILIEN,S	OC	88	TAR	MELLMAN,M	PASTENA,V	642	656
0.00	LITTLETON,AC	JL	70	TAR			476	480
0.00	LORIG,AN	OC	63	TAR			759	763
0.00	LOUDERBACK,JG	AP	71	TAR			298	305
0.00	LOWE,HD	AP	63	TAR			293	301
0.00	LUDMAN,EA	SP	86	JAA			118	124
0.00	MAHER,MW	SP	83	JAR	NANTELL,TJ		329	340
0.00	MAITRE,P	34	78	AOS			227	236
0.00	MAKSY,MM	OC	88	TAR			683	699
0.00	MANEGOLD,JG	SU	86	JAA			206	221
0.00	MANES,RP	ST	67	JAR	SAMUELS,JM	SMYTH,DJ	139	156
0.00	MARCH,JG	02	87	AOS			153	168
0.00	MARKS,BR	AU	87	AUD	RAMAN,KK		106	117
0.00	MARPLE,RM	JL	63	TAR			478	482
0.00	MATEER,WH	JL	65	TAR			583	586
0.00	MAURIELLO,JA	JA	63	TAR			26	28
0.00	MAURIELLO,JA	AP	64	TAR			347	357
0.00	MCCOSH,AM	OC	67	TAR			693	700
0.00	MCDONALD,DL	12	79	AOS	PUXTY,AG		53	66
0.00	MCINTYRE,EV	JL	82	TAR			607	618
0.00	MCKEOWN,JC	JL	72	TAR			527	532
0.00	MENSAH,YM	WI	83	JAA			130	141
0.00	METCALF,RW	JA	64	TAR			16	21
0.00	MEYER,PE	JA	76	TAR			80	89
0.00	MIELKE,DE	WI	87	JAA	SEIFERT,J		65	78
0.00	MILLER,MC	AP	73	TAR			280	291
0.00	MOBLEY,SC	AP	66	TAR			292	296
0.00	MOBLEY,SC	JA	67	TAR			114	123
0.00	MOBLEY,SC	AP	68	TAR			333	341
0.00	MOCK,TJ	AU	82	AUD	WRIGHT,A		33	44
0.00	MONSON,NP	OC	64	TAR	TRACY,JA		890	893
0.00	MORGAN,G	05	88	AOS			477	485
0.00	MOST,KS	JA	69	TAR			145	152
0.00	MUELLER,GG	JA	63	TAR			142	147
0.00	MUELLER,GG	AU	64	JAR			148	157
0.00	MUNTER,P	WI	83	JAA	RATCLIFFE,TA		108	114
0.00	MURRAY,D	AU	83	JAA	JOHNSON,R		4	15

SCHOOL OF THOUGHT=ACCOUNTING THEORY

CITE INDEX	FIRST AUTHOR	ISSUE	YEAR	JOURNAL	SECOND AUTHOR	THIRD AUTHOR	PAG BEG	PAG END
0.00	NELSON,GK	JA	66	TAR			42	47
0.00	NICHOLS,AC	OC	68	TAR	GRAWOIG,DE		631	639
0.00	NIELSEN,CC	OC	65	TAR			795	804
0.00	NURNBERG,H	OC	72	TAR			655	665
0.00	NURNBERG,H	AU	85	JAA	CIANCIOLO,ST		50	59
0.00	O'CONNOR,MC	AP	72	TAR	HAMRE,JC		308	319
0.00	OLIPHANT,WJ	ST	71	JAR			93	98
0.00	OVADIA,A	WI	83	JAA	RONEN,J		115	129
0.00	OWEN,DL	03	85	AOS	LLOYD,AJ		329	352
0.00	PALMROSE,ZV	SP	87	AUD			90	103
0.00	PALMROSE,ZV	JA	88	TAR			55	73
0.00	PARKER,WM	OC	63	TAR			785	788
0.00	PARKER,WM	AU	66	JAR			149	154
0.00	PATON,WA	AP	63	TAR			243	251
0.00	PATON,WA	SP	63	JAR			44	72
0.00	PATON,WA	SP	68	JAR			72	85
0.00	PATON,WA	AP	69	TAR			276	283
0.00	PATTEN,RJ	OC	64	TAR			876	879
0.00	PATTERSON,RG	OC	67	TAR			772	774
0.00	PEASNELL,KV	JA	77	TAR			186	189
0.00	PELES,YC	AP	86	TAR			325	329
0.00	PETERSON,WA	AP	66	TAR			275	282
0.00	PETRI,E	JL	73	TAR			483	488
0.00	PHILIPS,GE	OC	63	TAR			696	708
0.00	PHILIPS,GE	JA	63	TAR			14	25
0.00	PHILIPS,GE	JA	68	TAR			10	17
0.00	PHILLIPS,LC	AP	65	TAR			377	381
0.00	PRINCE,TR	JL	64	TAR			553	562
0.00	RABY,WL	JL	63	TAR	NEUBIG,RD		568	576
0.00	RABY,WL	JA	69	TAR			1	11
0.00	RAMAN,KK	SU	81	JAA			352	359
0.00	RAMAN,KK	WI	82	JAA			144	153
0.00	RAMAN,KK	AU	82	JAA			44	50
0.00	RAVIV,A	AP	85	JAE			239	246
0.00	RAYMAN,RA	SP	69	JAR			53	89
0.00	REVSINE,L	AP	69	TAR			354	358
0.00	REVSINE,L	AP	81	TAR			342	354
0.00	REYNOLDS,IN	AP	64	TAR			342	346
0.00	RICHARD,DL	OC	68	TAR			730	737
0.00	RICHARDSON,AJ	04	87	AOS			341	355
0.00	ROBBINS,WA	SU	85	JAA	APOSTOLOU,NG	STRAWSER,RH	279	292
0.00	ROBBINS,WA	AU	86	JAR	AUSTIN,KR		412	421
0.00	ROBERTS,DM	AU	80	JAA			57	69
0.00	ROBERTSON,JC	WI	81	JAA	ALDERMAN,CW		144	161
0.00	ROBERTSON,JC	SP	84	AUD			57	67
0.00	RODEN,PF	WI	87	JAA			79	89
0.00	RORKE,CH	03	82	AOS			305	306
0.00	ROSE,H	AU	64	JAR			137	147
0.00	ROSEN,LS	JA	67	TAR			106	113
0.00	ROSENFIELD,P	OC	69	TAR			788	797

SCHOOL OF THOUGHT=ACCOUNTING THEORY

CITE IND-EX	FIRST AUTHOR	ISS-UE	YE-AR	JOUR -NAL	SECOND AUTHOR	THIRD AUTHOR	PAG BEG	PAG END
0.00	RUE,JC	SU	84	JAA	VOLKAN,AG		306	322
0.00	RUNDFELT,R	SP	86	JAA			125	130
0.00	SAMUELSON,RA	AP	80	TAR			254	268
0.00	SANNELLA,AJ	AU	86	JAA			288	304
0.00	SAPIENZA,SR	JA	63	TAR			91	101
0.00	SAPIENZA,SR	JL	64	TAR			582	590
0.00	SAPIENZA,SR	SP	64	JAR			50	66
0.00	SAVOIE,LM	ST	69	JAR			55	62
0.00	SCHACHNER,L	AP	68	TAR			303	311
0.00	SCHATTKE,RW	OC	65	TAR			805	811
0.00	SCHATTKE,RW	AP	72	TAR			233	244
0.00	SCHWARTZ,BN	SP	81	JAA			238	247
0.00	SCHWARTZ,BN	SP	83	JAA			244	253
0.00	SCHWEIKART,JA	06	86	AOS			541	554
0.00	SCOTT,RA	OC	79	TAR			750	763
0.00	SEAGLE,JP	JA	77	TAR	PETRI,E		124	136
0.00	SHAW,WH	AP	87	TAR			385	400
0.00	SHILLINGLAW,G	SP	63	JAR			73	85
0.00	SHRIVER,KA	JA	87	TAR			79	96
0.00	SHWAYDER,KR	SP	68	JAR			86	97
0.00	SHWAYDER,KR	OC	72	TAR			747	760
0.00	SIMMONS,JK	OC	67	TAR			680	692
0.00	SKERRATT,LC	SU	84	JAA			362	368
0.00	SLAVIN,NS	AP	77	TAR			360	368
0.00	SMITH,G	AU	88	AUD			108	117
0.00	SMOLINSKI,EJ	AU	63	JAR			149	178
0.00	SORTER,GH	ST	74	JAR	GANS,MS		1	12
0.00	SORTER,GH	SP	82	JAA			188	194
0.00	SORTER,GH	SP	87	JAA	INGBERMAN,M		99	116
0.00	SORTER,GH	SU	88	JAA	SIEGEL,S	SLAIN,J	233	244
0.00	SOTTO,R	01	83	AOS			57	72
0.00	SPACEK,L	AP	64	TAR			275	284
0.00	SPENCER,CH	JA	65	TAR	BARNISEL,TS		144	153
0.00	SPENCER,MH	AP	63	TAR			310	316
0.00	SPICER,BH	03	88	AOS			303	322
0.00	SPILLER JR,EA	OC	64	TAR			850	859
0.00	SPROUSE,RT	OC	63	TAR			687	695
0.00	SPROUSE,RT	JL	65	TAR			522	526
0.00	STANLEY,CH	JL	64	TAR			639	647
0.00	STAUBUS,GJ	JA	63	TAR			64	74
0.00	STERLING,RR	JL	71	TAR	FLAHERTY,RE		441	456
0.00	STERLING,RR	OC	72	TAR	TOLLEFSON,SO	FLAHERTY,RE	709	721
0.00	SUMMERS,EL	SP	70	JAR	DESKINS,JW		113	117
0.00	SUTTON,TG	AP	88	JAE			127	149
0.00	TAUSSIG,RA	SP	64	JAR			67	79
0.00	TAUSSIG,RA	WI	83	JAA			142	156
0.00	TAYLOR,WM	AU	82	JAR	WEYGANDT,JJ		497	502
0.00	TEOH,HY	02	84	AOS	THONG,G		189	206
0.00	THIES,CF	AU	87	JAA	STURROCK,T		375	391
0.00	THOMAS,AL	JL	64	TAR			574	581

SCHOOL OF THOUGHT=ACCOUNTING THEORY

CITE IND-EX	FIRST AUTHOR	ISS-UE	YE-AR	JOUR-NAL	SECOND AUTHOR	THIRD AUTHOR	PAG BEG	PAG END
0.00	THOMAS,AL	JA	64	TAR			1	11
0.00	THOMAS,AL	SP	65	JAR			103	113
0.00	THOMAS,AP	03	86	AOS			253	270
0.00	THOMAS,LR	AP	86	TAR	SWANSON,EP		330	336
0.00	TINKER,T	02	88	AOS			165	189
0.00	TOBA,Y	OC	80	TAR			604	619
0.00	TRUMBULL,WP	JA	63	TAR			46	51
0.00	TRUMBULL,WP	JL	68	TAR			459	468
0.00	TUCKERMAN,B	JA	64	TAR			32	37
0.00	VERRECCHIA,RE	ST	87	JAR	LANEN,WN		165	189
0.00	WADE,HH	OC	63	TAR			714	718
0.00	WAKEMAN,LM	DE	80	JAE			213	237
0.00	WALKER,NR	AU	88	AUD	PIERCE,LT		1	22
0.00	WAUGH,JB	JL	68	TAR			535	539
0.00	WEBER,RP	JA	77	TAR			172	185
0.00	WEIL,RL	OC	73	TAR			749	758
0.00	WELLS,MC	OC	65	TAR	COTTON,W		829	833
0.00	WELLS,MC	AP	68	TAR			373	376
0.00	WELSH,MJ	WI	85	JAA	TRAPNELL,JE		100	111
0.00	WERNER,CA	AU	83	JAA	KOSTOLANSKY,JW		54	64
0.00	WERNER,CA	SP	84	JAA	KOSTOLANSKY,JW		212	224
0.00	WHEELER,JT	JA	70	TAR			1	10
0.00	WHITE,D	SU	82	JAA	VANECEK,M		338	354
0.00	WIESEN,JL	WI	79	JAA	ENG,R		101	121
0.00	WILD,JJ	SP	87	JAR			139	160
0.00	WILKINSON,TL	JA	64	TAR			133	139
0.00	WILLIAMS,D	AP	66	TAR			226	234
0.00	WILLIAMS,JJ	02	81	AOS			153	166
0.00	WILLIAMS,PF	02	87	AOS			169	192
0.00	WILLIAMS,TH	OC	67	TAR	GRIFFIN,CH		642	649
0.00	WILLINGER,GL	SP	85	JAR			351	359
0.00	WILLINGHAM,JJ	JL	64	TAR			543	552
0.00	WINDAL,FW	JA	63	TAR			29	36
0.00	WOLK,HI	JL	70	TAR			544	552
0.00	WOLK,HI	AP	73	TAR	TEARNEY,MG		292	299
0.00	WONG,J	JA	88	JAE			37	51
0.00	WONG,J	AP	88	JAE			151	167
0.00	WOOLSEY,SM	OC	63	TAR			709	713
0.00	WRIGHT,FK	JA	63	TAR			87	90
0.00	WRIGHT,FK	SP	64	JAR			80	90
0.00	WRIGHT,HW	OC	66	TAR			626	633
0.00	WYATT,AR	JL	65	TAR			527	535
0.00	WYMAN,HE	JL	76	TAR			545	558
0.00	YOUNG,AE	SP	78	JAA			217	230
0.00	YOUNG,AE	SP	80	JAA			244	250
0.00	YOUNG,DW	OC	76	TAR			788	799
0.00	YOUNG,TN	AP	67	TAR	PEIRSON,CG		338	341
0.00	YU,SC	JA	66	TAR			8	20
0.00	YU,SC	JL	69	TAR			571	582
0.00	ZAROWIN,P	AP	88	JAE			89	110

SCHOOL OF THOUGHT=ACCOUNTING THEORY

CITE IND-EX	FIRST AUTHOR	ISS-UE	YE-AR	JOUR-NAL	SECOND AUTHOR	THIRD AUTHOR	PAG BEG	PAG END
0.00	ZEFF,SA		JA	65	TAR	MAXWELL,WD		65	75

SCHOOL OF THOUGHT=ACCOUNTING THEORY

3.9 SCHOOL OF THOUGHT=ACCOUNTING HISTORY

CITE IND-EX	FIRST AUTHOR	ISS-UE	YE-AR	JOUR-NAL	SECOND AUTHOR	THIRD AUTHOR	PAG BEG	PAG END
4.50	HOPWOOD,AG	03	87	AOS			207	234
3.00	LOFT,A	02	86	AOS			137	170
2.50	MILLER,P	03	87	AOS	O'LEARY,T		235	265
2.00	ARMSTRONG,P	05	87	AOS			415	436
1.33	HOSKIN,KW	02	86	AOS	MACVE,RH		105	136
1.33	JOHNSON,HT	23	83	AOS			139	146
0.75	JOHNSON,HT	JL	81	TAR			510	518
0.70	CHANDLER,AD	12	79	AOS	DAEMS,H		3	20
0.50	BROWN,LD	SP	85	JAR	GARDNER,JC		84	109
0.50	SWIERINGA,RJ	03	87	AOS	WEICK,KE		293	308
0.40	ZEFF,SA	JL	84	TAR			447	468
0.31	JOHNSON,HT	JL	75	TAR			444	450
0.25	PERAGALLO,E	OC	77	TAR			881	892
0.23	YAMEY,BS	AU	64	JAR			117	136
0.15	BRIEF,RP	SP	65	JAR			12	31
0.13	PERAGALLO,E	JL	81	TAR			587	595
0.10	YAMEY,BS	AP	79	TAR			323	329
0.08	BRIEF,RP	SP	67	JAR			27	38
0.08	CARSBERG,BV	SP	66	JAR			1	15
0.08	HUME,LJ	SP	70	JAR			21	33
0.08	PARKER,RH	SP	68	JAR			58	71
0.08	YAMEY,BS	SP	67	JAR			51	76
0.00	BOER,G	JA	66	TAR			92	97
0.00	BRIEF,RP	OC	77	TAR			810	812
0.00	BRIGHTON,GD	JA	69	TAR			137	144
0.00	BROWN,LD	02	87	AOS	GARDNER,JC	VASARHELYI,MA	193	204
0.00	CHAMBERS,RJ	OC	79	TAR			764	775
0.00	CHATFIELD,M	JA	75	TAR			1	6
0.00	CZARNIAWSKA-,B	04	88	AOS			415	430
0.00	DAVIDSON,S	AP	63	TAR			278	284
0.00	FLESHER,DL	04	79	AOS	FLESHER,TK		297	304
0.00	FLESHER,DL	JL	86	TAR	FLESHER,TK		421	434
0.00	FU,P	SP	71	JAR			40	51
0.00	HAIN,HP	OC	66	TAR			699	703
0.00	HAIN,HP	AU	67	JAR			154	163
0.00	HECK,JL	OC	86	TAR	BREMSER,WG		735	744
0.00	HEIN,LW	JL	63	TAR			508	520
0.00	HERBERT,L	JL	71	TAR			433	440
0.00	HOLMES,W	JA	79	TAR			47	57
0.00	HOLZER,HP	AP	63	TAR	SCHONFELD,HM		377	381
0.00	HOLZER,HP	AP	63	TAR	SCHONFELD,HM		382	388
0.00	HORRIGAN,JO	AP	68	TAR			284	294
0.00	INGBERMAN,M	WI	80	JAA			101	112
0.00	JACOBSEN,LE	AU	64	JAR			221	228
0.00	KEISTER JR,OR	AP	63	TAR			371	376
0.00	KEISTER JR,OR	AP	64	TAR			414	416
0.00	LEE,GA	SP	73	JAR			47	61
0.00	LEE,GA	JL	81	TAR			539	553

SCHOOL OF THOUGHT=ACCOUNTING HISTORY

CITE IND-EX	FIRST AUTHOR	ISS-UE	YE-AR	JOUR-NAL	SECOND AUTHOR	THIRD AUTHOR	PAG BEG	PAG END
0.00	LEHMAN,C	05	87	AOS	TINKER,T		503	522
0.00	LEWIS,NR	34	84	AOS	PARKER,LD	SUTCLIFFE,P	275	289
0.00	LIVOCK,DM	SP	65	JAR			86	102
0.00	MAUTZ,RK	AP	77	TAR	PREVITS,GJ		301	307
0.00	MEPHAM,MJ	JA	83	TAR			43	57
0.00	MERINO,BD	OC	87	TAR	KOCH,BS	MACRITCHIE,KL	748	762
0.00	MOST,KS	SP	67	JAR			39	50
0.00	MOST,KS	OC	72	TAR			722	734
0.00	NOBES,CW	AP	82	TAR			303	310
0.00	NURNBERG,H	AU	70	JAR			217	231
0.00	PERAGALLO,E	JL	71	TAR			529	534
0.00	PERAGALLO,E	JA	83	TAR			98	104
0.00	ROSEN,LS	JA	69	TAR	DECOSTER,DT		124	136
0.00	SALGADO,AP	AP	63	TAR			389	397
0.00	STONE,WE	AP	69	TAR			284	291
0.00	STONE,WE	AU	72	JAR			345	350
0.00	SWANSON,GA	JL	88	TAR	GARDNER,JC		436	447
0.00	VANCE,LL	OC	69	TAR			692	703
0.00	WELLS,MC	JL	76	TAR			471	482
0.00	WINJUM,JO	OC	70	TAR			743	761
0.00	WINJUM,JO	AU	71	JAR			333	350
0.00	WINJUM,JO	JA	71	TAR			149	155
0.00	WRIGHT,FK	AU	67	JAR			173	179
0.00	YAMEY,BS	JL	80	TAR			419	425
0.00	ZEFF,SA	JL	82	TAR			528	553
0.00	ZEFF,SA	SP	86	JAA			131	154

SCHOOL OF THOUGHT=ACCOUNTING HISTORY

3.10 SCHOOL OF THOUGHT=INSTITUTIONAL

CITE IND-EX	FIRST AUTHOR	ISS-UE	YE-AR	JOUR-NAL	SECOND AUTHOR	THIRD AUTHOR	PAG BEG	PAG END
2.00	ARMSTRONG,P	02	85	AOS			129	148
1.25	HOPWOOD,AG	03	85	AOS			361	376
1.20	DYCKMAN,TR	SP	84	JAR	ZEFF,SA		225	297
1.00	EVANS III,JH	AG	83	JAE	PATTON,JM		151	175
1.00	RUBIN,MA	AP	88	TAR			219	236
0.88	BROWN,PR	SP	81	JAR			232	246
0.67	KINNEY JR,WR	MR	86	JAE			73	89
0.67	WILLMOTT,H	06	86	AOS			555	582
0.63	HAKANSSON,NH	ST	81	JAR			1	35
0.62	BENSTON,GJ	JL	69	TAR			515	532
0.60	INGRAM,RW	SP	84	JAR			126	144
0.55	SUNDER,S	AU	78	JAR			341	367
0.54	ESTES,RW	AP	72	TAR			284	290
0.50	CUSHING,BE	AP	77	TAR			308	321
0.50	NEWMAN,DP	SP	81	JAR			247	262
0.50	O'LEARY,T	01	85	AOS			87	104
0.50	SHOCKLEY,RA	AU	83	JAR	HOLT,RN		545	564
0.44	DOPUCH,N	JA	80	TAR	SUNDER,S		1	21
0.40	BUZBY,SL	JA	79	TAR	FALK,H		23	37
0.40	MCCONNELL,DK	WI	84	JAA			178	181
0.40	MCKEE,AJ	OC	84	TAR	BELL,TB	BOATSMAN,JR	647	659
0.40	ST.PIERRE,K	AP	84	TAR	ANDERSON,JA		242	263
0.38	LAVIN,D	JA	76	TAR			41	50
0.38	RAMANATHAN,KV	JL	76	TAR			516	528
0.31	CRUMBLEY,DL	OC	73	TAR			759	763
0.31	RHODE,JG	OC	74	TAR	WHITSELL,GM	KELSEY,RL	772	787
0.31	ZEFF,SA	AP	67	TAR	FOSSUM,RL		298	320
0.27	HICKS JR,JO	AP	78	TAR			371	388
0.25	HUSSEIN,ME	01	81	AOS			27	38
0.25	INGRAM,RW	OC	81	TAR	COPELAND,RM		830	843
0.25	OGDEN,S	02	85	AOS	BOUGEN,P		211	226
0.23	CHOI,FD	AU	73	JAR			159	175
0.23	GERBOTH,DL	JL	73	TAR			475	482
0.23	GOLDMAN,A	OC	74	TAR	BARLEV,B		707	718
0.23	PRAKASH,P	OC	75	TAR	RAPPAPORT,A		723	734
0.22	BROMWICH,M	AP	80	TAR			288	300
0.20	FRANK,WG	AU	79	JAR			593	605
0.20	PURO,M	AU	84	JAR			624	646
0.20	RICCHIUTE,DN	12	79	AOS			67	76
0.20	SUTTON,TG	01	84	AOS			81	95
0.15	ALIBER,RZ	JA	75	TAR	STICKNEY,CP		44	57
0.15	ANDERSON,HM	JL	70	TAR	GIESE,J	BOOKER,J	524	531
0.15	BRILOFF,AJ	JL	66	TAR			484	495
0.15	CAUSEY JR,DY	JA	76	TAR			19	30
0.15	GOETZ,BE	JA	67	TAR			53	61
0.15	SCHULTE JR,AA	JL	65	TAR			587	593
0.15	SMITH,CH	AP	72	TAR	LANIER,RA	TAYLOR,ME	270	283
0.14	SELTO,FH	02	82	AOS			139	148

SCHOOL OF THOUGHT=INSTITUTIONAL

CITE IND- EX	FIRST AUTHOR	ISS- UE	YE- AR	JOUR -NAL	SECOND AUTHOR	THIRD AUTHOR	PAG BEG	PAG END
0.14	SELTO,FH	AU	82	JAR	GROVE,HD		676	688
0.13	MAHER,MW	OC	81	TAR			751	770
0.13	NEWMAN,DP	ST	81	JAR			134	156
0.13	SCHREUDER,H	AP	81	TAR			294	308
0.11	BAKER,CR	SP	80	JAA			197	206
0.10	PEARSON,MA	WI	79	JAA	LINDGREN,JH	MYERS,BL	122	134
0.10	RAMAN,KK	AU	79	JAA			31	41
0.09	GIVOLY,D	SU	78	JAA	RONEN,J	SCHIFF,A	361	372
0.08	BALADOUNI,V	AP	66	TAR			215	225
0.08	BRADISH,RD	OC	65	TAR			757	766
0.08	CLARKE,RW	OC	68	TAR			769	776
0.08	COWAN,TK	OC	65	TAR			788	794
0.08	CULPEPPER,RC	AP	70	TAR			322	332
0.08	FLOWER,JF	SP	66	JAR			16	36
0.08	GREENE,ED	AP	63	TAR			355	362
0.08	HORNGREN,CT	JA	71	TAR			1	11
0.08	KEMP,PS	OC	65	TAR			782	787
0.08	LANGENDERFER,HQ	OC	69	TAR	ROBERTSON,JC		777	787
0.08	LOEB,SE	JA	72	TAR			1	10
0.08	ROSENFIELD,P	AP	66	TAR	STOREY,R		327	330
0.08	STONE,WE	JA	65	TAR			190	195
0.08	WILKINSON,JR	OC	65	TAR	DONEY,LD		753	756
0.00	ABDEL-KHALIK,AR	SP	66	JAR			37	46
0.00	ALLYN,RG	JA	64	TAR			121	127
0.00	ALLYN,RG	AP	66	TAR			303	311
0.00	APOSTOLOU,NG	AU	85	JAR	GIROUX,GA	WELKER,RB	853	858
0.00	ARNETT,HE	JL	69	TAR			482	494
0.00	ASHTON,RH	AU	87	JAR	WILLINGHAM,JJ	ELLIOTT,RK	275	292
0.00	BACKER,M	JL	69	TAR			533	538
0.00	BENSTON,GJ	JL	76	TAR			483	498
0.00	BOWER,JB	AP	65	TAR	SCHLOSSER,RE		338	344
0.00	BROWN,PR	SU	82	JAA			282	290
0.00	BROWN,PR	AU	86	AUD	KARAN,V		134	147
0.00	BUBLITZ,B	WI	84	JAA	KEE,R		123	137
0.00	BURRELL,G	01	87	AOS			89	102
0.00	BURTON,JC	WI	82	AUD	FAIRFIELD,P		1	22
0.00	CAMPFIELD,WL	JL	63	TAR			521	527
0.00	CAMPFIELD,WL	JL	65	TAR			594	598
0.00	CAREY,JL	JA	68	TAR			1	9
0.00	CAREY,JL	JA	69	TAR			79	85
0.00	CARMICHAEL,DR	OC	68	TAR	SWIERINGA,RJ		697	705
0.00	CARMICHAEL,DR	SU	79	JAA			294	306
0.00	CARPENTER,CG	JL	71	TAR	STRAWSER,RH		509	518
0.00	CHURCHMAN,CW	JA	71	TAR			30	35
0.00	COE,TL	SP	79	JAA			244	253
0.00	COHEN,MF	JA	65	TAR			1	8
0.00	CRAMER JR,JJ	JL	65	TAR			606	616
0.00	DAROCA,FP	SP	85	AUD	HOLDER,WW		80	92
0.00	DEITRICK,JW	SU	79	JAA	ALDERMAN,CW		316	328
0.00	DERMER,JD	01	88	AOS			25	36

SCHOOL OF THOUGHT=INSTITUTIONAL

CITE IND- EX	FIRST AUTHOR	ISS- UE	YE- AR	JOUR -NAL	SECOND AUTHOR	THIRD AUTHOR	PAG BEG	PAG END
0.00	DESKINS,JW	JA	65	TAR			76	81
0.00	DIRSMITH,MW	02	85	AOS	COVALESKI,MA		149	170
0.00	DOPUCH,N	SU	88	JAA			245	250
0.00	DYL,EA	02	85	AOS	LILLY,MS		171	176
0.00	EDEY,HC	AP	63	TAR			262	265
0.00	ELLIOTT,EL	OC	68	TAR	LARREA,J	RIVERA,JM	763	768
0.00	FARMAN,WL	AP	64	TAR			392	404
0.00	FEINSCHREIBER,R	SP	69	JAR			17	21
0.00	FISHER,M	SU	78	JAA			349	360
0.00	FITZGERALD,RD	AU	79	JAA	KELLEY,EM		5	20
0.00	GAMBLE,GO	SP	86	JAA			102	117
0.00	GIBSON,RW	JA	65	TAR			196	203
0.00	GLEZEN,GW	AU	85	JAR	MILLAR,JA		859	870
0.00	GOGGANS,TP	JL	64	TAR			627	630
0.00	GOLDWASSER,DL	SU	88	JAA			217	232
0.00	GORMLEY,RJ	SU	88	JAA			185	212
0.00	GREER JR,WR	AU	78	JAA	MORRISSEY,LE		49	57
0.00	HANSEN,ES	ST	77	JAR			156	201
0.00	HARRISON,GL	03	86	AOS	MCKINNON,JL		233	252
0.00	HASSELBACK,JR	AP	76	TAR			269	276
0.00	HEIN,LW	AP	63	TAR			252	261
0.00	HOPWOOD,AG	01	87	AOS			65	70
0.00	HORVITZ,JS	WI	81	JAA	HAINKEL,M		114	127
0.00	HUSSEIN,ME	AU	86	AUD	BAVISHI,VB	GANGOLLY,JS	124	133
0.00	IMHOFF JR,EA	OC	78	TAR			869	881
0.00	IMHOFF JR,EA	SP	88	AUD			182	191
0.00	INGBERMAN,M	AU	78	JAA	SORTER,GH		58	62
0.00	JACKSON-COX,J	34	84	AOS	THIRKELL,JE	MCQUEENEY,J	253	273
0.00	JENSEN,HL	OC	76	TAR	WYNDELTS,RW		846	853
0.00	JENTZ,GA	JL	66	TAR			535	541
0.00	JOHNSON,O	OC	74	TAR	GUNN,S		649	663
0.00	JOHNSON,O	ST	81	JAR			89	119
0.00	JOHNSON,SB	SP	82	JAA	MESSIER JR,WF		195	213
0.00	JOYCE,EJ	AU	82	JAR	LIBBY,R	SUNDER,S	654	675
0.00	KABBES,SM	AP	65	TAR			395	400
0.00	KALINSKI,BD	JL	63	TAR			591	595
0.00	KAPLAN,HG	JA	64	TAR	SOLOMON,KI		145	149
0.00	KAUFMAN,F	OC	67	TAR			713	720
0.00	KAY,RS	SU	79	JAA			307	315
0.00	KELL,WG	AP	68	TAR			266	273
0.00	KOHLER,EL	AP	63	TAR			266	269
0.00	KOLLARITSCH,FP	AP	65	TAR			382	385
0.00	KRIPKE,H	AU	78	JAA			4	32
0.00	KUBLIN,M	JL	65	TAR			626	635
0.00	KUNITAKE,WK	SU	86	JAA	WHITE JR,CE		222	231
0.00	LAMDEN,CW	JA	64	TAR			128	132
0.00	LEA,RB	SU	81	AUD			53	94
0.00	LINOWES,DF	JA	65	TAR			97	104
0.00	LONGSTRETH,B	WI	84	JAA			110	122
0.00	LOWE,HD	AP	67	TAR			356	360

SCHOOL OF THOUGHT=INSTITUTIONAL

CITE IND-EX	FIRST AUTHOR	ISS-UE	YE-AR	JOUR-NAL	SECOND AUTHOR	THIRD AUTHOR	PAG BEG	PAG END
1.00	LOWE,RE	OC	65	TAR			839	846
1.00	LYNN,ES	AP	64	TAR			371	376
1.00	MACKENZIE,O	AP	64	TAR			363	370
1.00	MATTINGLY,LA	OC	64	TAR			996	3
1.00	MAUTZ,RK	AP	65	TAR			299	311
1.00	MCROBERTS,HA	04	85	AOS	HUDSON,J		493	502
1.00	MELLMAN,M	AU	86	JAA	SEILER,ME		305	318
1.00	MILLER,HE	JA	66	TAR			1	7
1.00	MOODY,SM	AU	86	JAA	FLESHER,DL		319	330
1.00	MOONITZ,M	SP	66	JAR			47	61
1.00	MOORES,K	01	86	AOS	STEADMAN,GT		19	34
1.00	MORENO,RG	OC	64	TAR			990	995
1.00	MUELLER,GG	AP	65	TAR			386	394
1.00	NAHAPIET,JE	04	88	AOS			333	358
1.00	NEWMAN,DP	OC	81	TAR			897	909
1.00	NORGAARD,CT	JL	72	TAR			433	442
1.00	PALMROSE,ZV	AU	88	AUD			63	71
1.00	PATON,WA	JA	67	TAR			7	23
1.00	POMERANZ,F	AU	77	JAA			45	52
1.00	POWELL,RM	JL	66	TAR			525	534
1.00	POWNALL,G	AU	86	JAR			291	315
1.00	PURO,M	SP	85	JAA			165	177
1.00	RAPPAPORT,A	OC	64	TAR			951	962
1.00	RATSCH,H	JA	64	TAR			140	144
1.00	RICHARDSON,AJ	04	88	AOS			381	396
1.00	ROCKNESS,J	04	88	AOS	WILLIAMS,PF		397	411
1.00	ROLLER,J	AP	67	TAR	WILLIAMS,TH		349	355
1.00	ROSS,H	ST	70	JAR			108	115
1.00	SCHEINER,JH	AU	84	JAR			789	797
1.00	SCHIENEMAN,GS	AU	79	JAA			21	30
1.00	SCHIFF,M	AU	77	JAA	SORTER,GH	WIESEN,JL	19	44
1.00	SCHNEE,EJ	AU	81	JAA	TAYLOR,ME		18	29
1.00	SEAMAN,JL	JL	65	TAR			617	621
1.00	SEELYE,AL	AP	63	TAR			302	309
1.00	SEIDLER,LJ	SU	79	JAA			285	293
1.00	SEILER,RE	OC	66	TAR			652	656
1.00	SELTO,FH	AU	83	JAR	GROVE,HD		619	622
1.00	SIMON,SI	OC	64	TAR			884	889
1.00	SIMON,SI	AP	65	TAR			401	406
1.00	SOMEYA,K	OC	64	TAR			983	989
1.00	STAATS,EB	SU	81	AUD			1	11
1.00	STANDISH,PEM	JL	64	TAR			654	666
1.00	STETTLER,HF	OC	65	TAR			723	730
1.00	STONE,DE	AP	67	TAR			331	337
1.00	STONE,ML	ST	68	JAR			59	66
1.00	STREER,PJ	SU	79	JAA			329	338
1.00	TAUSSIG,RA	JL	63	TAR			562	567
1.00	TAYLOR,RG	JA	65	TAR			89	96
1.00	THOMPSON II,RB	AU	87	JAR	OLSEN,C	DIETRICH,JR	245	274
1.00	TINKER,T	01	87	AOS	NEIMARK,M		71	88

SCHOOL OF THOUGHT=INSTITUTIONAL

CITE IND-EX	FIRST AUTHOR	ISS-UE	YE-AR	JOUR-NAL	SECOND AUTHOR	THIRD AUTHOR	PAG BEG	PAG END
0.00	TOWNSEND,LA	JA	67	TAR			1	6
0.00	TRUEBLOOD,RM	ST	66	JAR			183	191
0.00	ULLMANN,AA	12	79	AOS			123	134
0.00	WARREN,CS	SP	80	JAR			312	324
0.00	WEIGAND,RE	JL	63	TAR			584	590
0.00	WEISER,HJ	JL	66	TAR			518	524
0.00	WELSCH,GA	OC	64	TAR			8	13
0.00	WEYGANDT,JJ	JA	70	TAR			69	75
0.00	WIESEN,JL	SU	81	JAA			309	324
0.00	WILLIAMS,DD	05	88	AOS	DIRSMITH,MW		487	508
0.00	WYER,JC	SP	88	AUD	WHITE,GT	JANSON,EC	164	173
0.00	YOUNG,SD	SP	85	JAA			178	183

SCHOOL OF THOUGHT=INSTITUTIONAL

3.11 SCHOOL OF THOUGHT=OTHER

CITE INDEX	FIRST AUTHOR	ISSUE	YEAR	JOURNAL	SECOND AUTHOR	THIRD AUTHOR	PAG BEG	PAG END
2.67	OTLEY,DT	04	80	AOS			413	428
2.43	BALL,R	ST	82	JAR	FOSTER,G		161	234
2.33	BOLAND,RJ	23	83	AOS	PONDY,LR		223	234
2.18	HEDBERG,B	01	78	AOS	JONSSON,S		47	64
2.18	HOPWOOD,AG	01	78	AOS			3	14
1.83	COOPER,DJ	23	83	AOS			269	286
1.75	JOHNSON,JR	AP	81	TAR	LEITCH,RA	NETER,J	270	293
1.56	BIDDLE,GC	ST	80	JAR			235	280
1.50	CHRISTENSON,C	JA	83	TAR			1	22
1.44	BAIMAN,S	ST	80	JAR	DEMSKI,JS		184	220
1.20	BOLAND,RJ	04	79	AOS			259	272
1.17	VERRECCHIA,RE	DE	83	JAE			179	194
1.15	KHANDWALLA,PN	AU	72	JAR			275	285
1.00	ANSARI,SL	02	77	AOS			101	112
1.00	BANBURY,J	03	79	AOS	NAHAPIET,JE		163	178
0.92	CUSHING,BE	AU	69	JAR			196	203
0.86	FELIX JR,WL	AP	82	TAR	KINNEY JR,WR		245	271
0.85	ABDEL-KHALIK,AR	ST	73	JAR			104	138
0.82	GORDON,LA	34	78	AOS	LARCKER,DF	TUGGLE,FD	203	214
0.78	WHITTRED,GP	OC	80	TAR			563	577
0.77	SMITH,ED	OC	76	TAR			707	723
0.71	CHOW,CW	AP	82	TAR	RICE,SJ		326	335
0.67	HORWITZ,BN	ST	80	JAR	KOLODNY,R		38	74
0.67	RHODE,JG	02	77	AOS	SORENSEN,JE	LAWLER III,EE	165	176
0.67	WHITLEY,R	02	86	AOS			171	192
0.64	WILDAVSKY,A	01	78	AOS			77	88
0.63	HOFSTEDE,G	03	81	AOS			193	216
0.62	MOORE,ML	SP	73	JAR			100	107
0.60	GORDON,LA	01	84	AOS	NARAYANAN,VK		33	47
0.56	GINZBERG,MJ	04	80	AOS			369	382
0.55	BELKAOUI,A	02	78	AOS			97	104
0.55	IMHOFF JR,EA	OC	78	TAR			836	850
0.54	DERSTINE,RP	AU	74	JAR	HUEFNER,RJ		216	234
0.50	HAGG,J	12	79	AOS	HEDLUND,G		135	143
0.50	HOWARD,TP	OC	83	TAR	NIKOLAI,LA		765	776
0.50	LEE,CJ	AU	85	JAR	HSIEH,DA		468	485
0.50	MACINTOSH,NB	01	81	AOS			39	52
0.50	MARKUS,ML	23	83	AOS	PFEFFER,J		205	218
0.50	PASTENA,V	AU	79	JAR	RONEN,J		550	564
0.46	ELAM,R	JA	75	TAR			25	43
0.44	GARMAN,MB	AU	80	JAR	OHLSON,JA		420	440
0.44	WATTS,RL	AG	80	JAE	ZIMMERMAN,JL		95	106
0.43	JONSSON,S	03	82	AOS			287	304
0.40	DIRSMITH,MW	12	79	AOS	JABLONSKY,SF		39	52
0.40	MCCARTHY,WE	OC	79	TAR			667	686
0.38	EWUSI-MENSAH,K	04	81	AOS			301	316
0.38	IJIRI,Y	SP	71	JAR	KAPLAN,RS		73	87
0.38	RONEN,J	SP	70	JAR	MCKINNEY,G		99	112

SCHOOL OF THOUGHT=OTHER

CITE IND-EX	FIRST AUTHOR	ISS-UE	YE-AR	JOUR-NAL	SECOND AUTHOR	THIRD AUTHOR	PAG BEG	PAG END
0.38	TROTMAN,KT	04	81	AOS	BRADLEY,G		355	362
0.36	CHERNS,AB	02	78	AOS			105	114
0.33	ELLIOTT,RK	SP	83	AUD			1	12
0.33	MITROFF,II	23	83	AOS	MASON,RO		195	204
0.31	BRENNER,VC	AU	70	JAR			159	166
0.31	MCRAE,TW	SP	74	JAR			80	92
0.29	SWIERINGA,RJ	02	82	AOS	WATERHOUSE,JH		149	166
0.25	BOLAND,RJ	02	81	AOS			109	118
0.25	WEBER,RP	JL	81	TAR	STEVENSON,WC		596	612
0.23	FRANK,WG	SP	69	JAR			123	136
0.23	GAGNON,JM	SP	71	JAR			52	72
0.22	GRAY,SJ	SP	80	JAR			64	76
0.20	MUTCHLER,JF	SP	84	AUD			17	30
0.20	STONE,M	JL	84	TAR	BUBLITZ,B		469	473
0.20	YOUNG,DW	03	79	AOS			235	244
0.18	SWANSON,EB	34	78	AOS			237	248
0.17	COPPOCK,R	02	77	AOS			125	130
0.17	HOLDER,WW	SP	83	AUD			100	108
0.17	MORSE,D	AP	83	TAR	USHMAN,N		247	258
0.15	BALL,R	SP	71	JAR			1	31
0.15	STERLING,RR	SP	69	JAR	RADOSEVICH,R		90	95
0.14	SHOCKLEY,RA	WI	82	JAA			126	143
0.14	WEBER,R	AP	82	TAR			311	325
0.11	FIRTH,MA	JL	80	TAR			451	466
0.11	LOY,LD	SP	80	JAA	TOOLE,HR		227	243
0.10	AMEY,LR	04	79	AOS			247	258
0.09	CARLSSON,J	34	78	AOS	EHN,P	ERLANDER,B	249	260
0.08	ABEL,R	SP	69	JAR			1	11
0.08	AMATO,HN	OC	76	TAR	ANDERSON,EE	HARVEY,DW	854	862
0.08	CHOTTINER,S	AU	71	JAR	YOUNG,AE		367	374
0.08	COPELAND,RM	AU	69	JAR	WOJDAK,JF		188	195
0.08	FRANK,WG	SP	71	JAR	WEYGANDT,JJ		116	126
0.08	HARMELINK,PJ	SP	73	JAR			146	158
0.08	MCKEOWN,JC	SP	73	JAR			62	99
0.08	SAN MIGUEL,JG	04	77	AOS	SHANK,JK	GOVINDARAJAN,V	333	348
0.00	ASHTON,RH	SU	81	JAA	HYLAS,RE		325	332
0.00	ASHTON,RH	SU	81	AUD	HYLAS,RE		12	22
0.00	BAGGETT,WD	SP	83	JAA			227	233
0.00	BAILEY JR,AD	AP	85	TAR	DUKE,GL	GERLACH,JH	186	201
0.00	BARLEV,B	AP	83	TAR			385	393
0.00	BASTABLE,CW	SP	81	JAA	BEAMS,FA		248	254
0.00	BOURN,AM	AU	66	JAR			213	223
0.00	BOWEN,RM	OC	82	TAR	SUNDEM,GL		778	784
0.00	BOWSHER,CA	WI	86	JAA			7	16
0.00	CAMPBELL,DR	SP	83	JAA			196	211
0.00	CARMICHAEL,DR	SU	84	JAA	WHITTINGTON,OR		347	361
0.00	CARSLAW,C	AP	88	TAR			321	327
0.00	CAUSEY JR,DY	AP	73	TAR			258	267
0.00	DANIEL,SJ	SP	88	AUD			174	181
0.00	DAVISON,AG	SP	84	JAR	STENING,BW	WAI,WT	313	317

SCHOOL OF THOUGHT=OTHER

CITE IND-EX	FIRST AUTHOR	ISS-UE	YE-AR	JOUR-NAL	SECOND AUTHOR	THIRD AUTHOR	PAG BEG	PAG END
0.00	DERY,D	03	82	AOS			217	224
0.00	DEVINE,CT	ST	66	JAR			160	176
0.00	DIRSMITH,MW	SP	82	JAA	MCALLISTER,JP		214	228
0.00	DIRSMITH,MW	AU	82	JAA	MCALLISTER,JP		60	74
0.00	DIRSMITH,MW	AU	85	JAA	COVALESKI,MA		5	21
0.00	DREBIN,AR	AU	69	JAR			204	214
0.00	EICHENSEHER,JW	SP	85	JAA			195	209
0.00	FIRTH,MA	SP	73	JAR			16	24
0.00	FORD,A	AP	75	TAR			338	344
0.00	FRANKFURTER,GM	SU	83	JAA	YOUNG,AE		314	324
0.00	GLATZER,W	03	81	AOS			219	234
0.00	GORDON,LA	02	84	AOS	HAKA,S	SCHICK,AG	111	123
0.00	GORMLEY,RJ	AU	82	JAA			51	59
0.00	GRAY,J	AP	63	TAR	WILLINGHAM,JJ	JOHNSTON,K	336	346
0.00	GROBSTEIN,M	SP	84	AUD	CRAIG,PW		1	16
0.00	HEARD,JE	03	81	AOS	BOLCE,WJ		247	254
0.00	HOLSTRUM,GL	AU	82	AUD	MESSIER JR,WF		45	63
0.00	HONIG,LE	SP	78	JAA			231	236
0.00	KISSINGER,JN	AU	83	AUD			42	54
0.00	LANDSITTEL,DL	SU	82	JAA	SERLIN,JE		291	300
0.00	LEE,CJ	AU	84	JAR			776	781
0.00	LEVY,H	AU	87	JAA	BYUN,YH		355	369
0.00	LOVATA,LM	AU	88	AUD			72	86
0.00	MARCINKO,D	JL	84	TAR	PETRI,E		488	495
0.00	MARGHEIM,LL	SP	86	JAR			194	205
0.00	MCBRIDE,HJ	AP	63	TAR			363	370
0.00	MCRAE,TW	AU	65	JAR			255	260
0.00	MOCK,TJ	SP	83	AUD	WILLINGHAM,JJ		91	99
0.00	NIX,HM	SU	83	JAA	WICHMANN JR,H		341	352
0.00	NURNBERG,H	AU	69	JAR			257	261
0.00	PARKE,R	03	81	AOS	PETERSON,JL		235	246
0.00	PETRI,E	AP	79	TAR	GELFAND,J		330	345
0.00	PRESTON,LE	03	81	AOS			255	262
0.00	PURDY,CR	AU	65	JAR			228	241
0.00	PURDY,D	04	81	AOS			327	338
0.00	ROBBINS,SM	AU	77	JAA			5	18
0.00	SCHIENEMAN,GS	SP	83	JAA			212	226
0.00	SCHIFF,M	SP	79	JAA			224	231
0.00	SMITH,VL	AU	87	AUD	SCHATZBERG,J	WALLER,WS	71	93
0.00	ST.PIERRE,K	SP	82	JAA	ANDERSON,JA		229	247
0.00	ST.PIERRE,K	SP	84	JAA			257	263
0.00	TRUEBLOOD,RM	SP	63	JAR			86	95
0.00	VASARHELYI,MA	AU	84	AUD			100	106
0.00	VASARHELYI,MA	SP	84	AUD	BAILEY JR,AD	CAMARDESSE JR,JE	98	103
0.00	WEBER,C	JL	63	TAR			534	539
0.00	WHITTINGTON,OR	SU	82	JAA	ADAMS,SJ		310	319
0.00	WRIGHT,GB	SU	82	JAA	TAYLOR,RD		301	309
0.00	ZANNETOS,ZS	JL	63	TAR			528	533
0.00	ZANNETOS,ZS	AP	63	TAR			326	335

SCHOOL OF THOUGHT=OTHER

3.12 SCHOOL OF THOUGHT=EXPERT SYSTEMS

CITE IND- EX	FIRST AUTHOR	ISS- UE	YE- AR	JOUR -NAL	SECOND AUTHOR	THIRD AUTHOR	PAG BEG	PAG END
0.00	HANSEN,JV	AU	86	AUD	MESSIER JR,WF		109	123
0.00	MESERVY,RD	AU	86	AUD	BAILEY JR,AD	JOHNSON,PE	44	74
0.00	MESSIER JR,WF	AU	87	AUD	HANSEN,JV		94	105
0.00	SHPILBERG,D	AU	86	AUD	GRAHAM,LE		75	94
0.00	STEINBART,PJ	JA	87	TAR			97	116

4.1 TREATMENTS= FINANCIAL ACCOUNTING METHODS

CITE IND-EX	FIRST AUTHOR	ISS-UE	YE-AR	JOUR -NAL	SECOND AUTHOR	THIRD AUTHOR	PAG BEG	PAG END
7.00	BALL,R	AU	68	JAR	BROWN,P		159	178
5.15	GONEDES,NJ	ST	74	JAR	DOPUCH,N		48	129
4.85	BEAVER,WH	ST	68	JAR			67	92
3.80	WATTS,RL	AP	79	TAR	ZIMMERMAN,JL		273	305
3.00	WILSON,GP	AP	87	TAR			293	322
2.50	ATIASE,RK	SP	85	JAR			21	36
2.44	BEAVER,WH	MR	80	JAE	LAMBERT,RA	MORSE,D	3	28
2.43	BALL,R	ST	82	JAR	FOSTER,G		161	234
2.08	BEAVER,WH	OC	70	TAR	KETTLER,P	SCHOLES,M	654	682
2.00	ARMSTRONG,P	05	87	AOS			415	436
2.00	ROBERTS,J	04	85	AOS	SCAPENS,RW		443	456
1.75	FOSTER,G	DE	81	JAE			201	232
1.50	PATELL,JM	AU	81	JAR	WOLFSON,MA		434	458
1.38	BEAVER,WH	ST	70	JAR			62	99
1.33	BAMBER,LS	SP	86	JAR			40	56
1.23	DEMSKI,JS	OC	73	TAR			718	723
1.15	ASHTON,RH	OC	74	TAR			719	732
1.15	GONEDES,NJ	AU	73	JAR			212	237
1.00	BEAVER,WH	JL	87	JAE	LAMBERT,RA	RYAN,SG	139	157
1.00	DEMSKI,JS	AP	74	TAR			221	232
1.00	DYE,RA	SP	85	JAR			123	145
1.00	EVANS III,JH	AG	83	JAE	PATTON,JM		151	175
1.00	FREEMAN,RN	JL	87	JAE			195	228
1.00	GONEDES,NJ	SP	74	JAR			26	62
0.92	BEAVER,WH	OC	68	TAR	KENNELLY,JW	VOSS,WM	675	683
0.85	BEAVER,WH	ST	74	JAR	DEMSKI,JS		170	187
0.85	HARIED,AA	SP	73	JAR			117	145
0.77	SMITH,ED	OC	76	TAR			707	723
0.75	BOWEN,RM	JA	81	TAR			1	22
0.75	LEFTWICH,RW	ST	81	JAR	WATTS,RL	ZIMMERMAN,JL	50	77
0.69	MAY,RG	OC	76	TAR	SUNDEM,GL		747	763
0.67	LIPE,RC	ST	86	JAR			37	68
0.62	BEIDLEMAN,CR	OC	73	TAR			653	667
0.62	MAGEE,RP	AU	74	JAR			270	287
0.62	OLIVER,BL	AU	74	JAR			299	316
0.62	PANKOFF,LD	ST	70	JAR	VIRGIL JR,RL		1	48
0.57	VERRECCHIA,RE	ST	82	JAR			1	42
0.54	FOSTER,G	OC	75	TAR			686	698
0.54	OLIVER,BL	SP	72	JAR			154	166
0.50	CUSHING,BE	AP	77	TAR			308	321
0.50	OLSEN,C	ST	85	JAR	DIETRICH,JR		144	166
0.50	RAMAN,KK	OC	81	TAR			910	926
0.50	WALLACE,WA	AU	81	JAR			502	520
0.46	GONEDES,NJ	JA	72	TAR			11	21
0.46	LEV,B	AP	74	TAR	KUNITZKY,S		259	270
0.43	COPELAND,RM	AU	82	JAR	INGRAM,RW		275	289
0.40	ZEFF,SA	JL	84	TAR			447	468
0.38	BENSTON,GJ	ST	67	JAR			1	54

TREATMENTS= FINANCIAL ACCOUNTING METHODS

CITE IND-EX	FIRST AUTHOR	ISS-UE	YE-AR	JOUR-NAL	SECOND AUTHOR	THIRD AUTHOR	PAG BEG	PAG END
0.38	BILDERSEE,JS	JA	75	TAR			81	98
0.38	DOWNES,D	AP	73	TAR	DYCKMAN,TR		300	317
0.38	JAIN,TN	JA	73	TAR			95	104
0.38	WHITE,GE	AU	70	JAR			260	273
0.36	FOSTER III,TW	OC	78	TAR	VICKREY,DW		921	934
0.36	RICE,SJ	AP	78	TAR			429	438
0.33	BELKAOUI,A	AU	80	JAR			362	374
0.33	CHOW,CW	JL	83	TAR			485	520
0.31	ABDEL-KHALIK,AR	JL	71	TAR			457	471
0.31	DASCHER,PE	AU	70	JAR	MALCOM,RE		253	259
0.31	DEAKIN,EB	JA	76	TAR			90	96
0.31	GYNTHER,RS	AP	67	TAR			274	290
0.31	HAGERMAN,RL	OC	75	TAR			699	709
0.30	ADELBERG,AH	AU	79	JAR			565	592
0.27	BASU,S	JL	78	TAR			599	625
0.25	BEAVER,WH	JA	81	TAR			23	37
0.25	PERAGALLO,E	OC	77	TAR			881	892
0.25	VERRECCHIA,RE	SP	81	JAR			271	283
0.23	BAREFIELD,RM	AU	71	JAR	COMISKEY,EE		351	358
0.23	BAREFIELD,RM	AP	72	TAR	COMISKEY,EE		291	298
0.23	DEAKIN,EB	JL	76	TAR			590	603
0.23	ESKEW,RK	AP	75	TAR			316	324
0.23	FALK,H	SP	73	JAR	OPHIR,T		108	116
0.23	HORWITZ,BN	AP	71	TAR	SHABAHANG,R		243	252
0.20	ESKEW,RK	JA	79	TAR			107	118
0.20	FRANK,WG	AU	79	JAR			593	605
0.18	IJIRI,Y	SU	78	JAA			331	348
0.17	MORSE,D	AP	83	TAR	USHMAN,N		247	258
0.15	BIERMAN JR,H	JL	63	TAR			501	507
0.15	BIRD,FA	AP	74	TAR	DAVIDSON,LF	SMITH,CH	233	244
0.15	CHAMBERS,RJ	JL	66	TAR			443	457
0.15	CYERT,RM	ST	74	JAR	IJIRI,Y		29	42
0.15	DEMSKI,JS	AU	73	JAR			176	190
0.15	DOPUCH,N	ST	66	JAR	DRAKE,DF		192	219
0.15	EAVES,BC	JL	66	TAR			426	442
0.15	JOHNSON,O	OC	70	TAR			641	653
0.15	LIVINGSTONE,JL	AU	70	JAR	SALAMON,GL		199	216
0.15	LORIG,AN	JL	64	TAR			563	573
0.15	MATTESSICH,R	JL	72	TAR			469	487
0.15	MLYNARCZYK,FA	ST	69	JAR			63	81
0.15	MORTON,JR	AU	74	JAR			288	298
0.15	SALAMON,GL	AU	73	JAR			296	303
0.15	SNAVELY,HJ	AP	67	TAR			223	232
0.14	ALTMAN,EI	AU	82	JAA			4	19
0.14	INGRAM,RW	AU	82	JAR	COPELAND,RM		766	772
0.13	BOATSMAN,JR	JA	81	TAR	BASKIN,EF		38	53
0.10	RAMAN,KK	AU	79	JAA			31	41
0.09	DAVIS,DW	JA	78	TAR	BOATSMAN,JR	BASKIN,EF	1	10
0.09	VERRECCHIA,RE	SP	78	JAR			150	168
0.08	BEDFORD,NM	JL	75	TAR	ZIEGLER,RE		435	443

TREATMENTS= FINANCIAL ACCOUNTING METHODS

CITE IND-EX	FIRST AUTHOR	ISS-UE	YE-AR	JOUR -NAL	SECOND AUTHOR	THIRD AUTHOR	PAG BEG	PAG END
0.08	BRADISH,RD	OC	65	TAR			757	766
0.08	BUCKLEY,JW	AP	68	TAR	KIRCHER,P	MATHEWS,RL	274	283
0.08	CHARNES,A	JA	72	TAR	COLANTONI,CS	COOPER,WW	85	108
0.08	COOPER,WW	OC	68	TAR	DOPUCH,N	KELLER,TF	640	648
0.08	COWAN,TK	OC	65	TAR			788	794
0.08	CULPEPPER,RC	AP	70	TAR			322	332
0.08	FRANKFURTER,GM	AP	72	TAR	HORWITZ,BN		245	259
0.08	KEMP,PS	OC	65	TAR			782	787
0.08	LEMKE,KW	SP	70	JAR			47	77
0.08	SIMPSON,RH	OC	69	TAR			806	817
0.08	STERLING,RR	JA	67	TAR			62	73
0.08	UECKER,WC	01	77	AOS			47	58
0.08	VATTER,WJ	JL	63	TAR			470	477
0.00	ABDEL-MAGID,MF	AP	79	TAR			346	357
0.00	ADAMS,KD	WI	84	JAA			151	163
0.00	AHARONI,Y	SP	67	JAR	OPHIR,T		1	26
0.00	ANDERSON,JA	JL	75	TAR			509	511
0.00	ARNETT,HE	JL	69	TAR			482	494
0.00	BAMBER,LS	JL	87	TAR			510	532
0.00	BARLEV,B	AU	79	JAR	LEVY,H		305	315
0.00	BARLEV,B	AP	83	TAR			385	393
0.00	BARRETT,WB	JA	68	TAR			105	112
0.00	BEAMS,FA	AP	69	TAR			382	388
0.00	BEDFORD,NM	JA	67	TAR			82	85
0.00	BIERMAN JR,H	JL	65	TAR			541	546
0.00	BIERMAN JR,H	AP	69	TAR	DAVIDSON,S		239	246
0.00	BRILOFF,AJ	JA	64	TAR			12	15
0.00	BRUGGE,WG	JL	63	TAR			596	600
0.00	BUCKLEY,JW	JA	66	TAR			75	82
0.00	CARSON,AB	AP	65	TAR			334	337
0.00	CARTER,WK	JA	81	TAR			108	114
0.00	CHAMBERS,RJ	AP	67	TAR			241	253
0.00	CHOW,CW	JL	87	TAR	WONG-BOREN,A		533	541
0.00	CLINCH,GJ	AP	87	JAE	SINCLAIR,NA		89	106
0.00	COOPER,DJ	05	87	AOS	HOPPER,TM		407	414
0.00	COPELAND,TE	AU	78	JAA			33	48
0.00	COWAN,TK	JA	65	TAR			9	20
0.00	COWAN,TK	JA	68	TAR			94	100
0.00	CRAMER JR,JJ	OC	64	TAR			869	875
0.00	CRAMER JR,JJ	JL	65	TAR			606	616
0.00	CRUSE,RB	JA	65	TAR	SUMMERS,EL		82	88
0.00	DIRSMITH,MW	04	82	AOS	LEWIS,BL		319	336
0.00	EDEY,HC	AP	63	TAR			262	265
0.00	ENGSTROM,JH	SU	85	JAA			305	318
0.00	EVANS III,JH	ST	87	JAR	PATTON,JM		130	164
0.00	FAGERBERG,P	JL	72	TAR			454	457
0.00	FAIRCLOTH,AW	01	81	AOS	RICCHIUTE,DN		53	68
0.00	FALK,H	OC	75	TAR	HEINTZ,JA		758	779
0.00	FREMGEN,JM	JL	67	TAR			457	467
0.00	FULMER,JG	AU	84	JAA	MOON,JE		5	14

TREATMENTS= FINANCIAL ACCOUNTING METHODS

CITE INDEX	FIRST AUTHOR	ISSUE	YEAR	JOURNAL	SECOND AUTHOR	THIRD AUTHOR	PAG BEG	PAG END
0.00	GIVENS,HR	JL	66	TAR			458	463
0.00	GOLDIN,HJ	SU	85	JAA			269	278
0.00	GOMBERG,M	JL	64	TAR	FARBER,A		615	617
0.00	GONEDES,NJ	ST	69	JAR			90	113
0.00	GONEDES,NJ	JL	71	TAR			535	551
0.00	GONEDES,NJ	AP	71	TAR			320	328
0.00	GORDON,LA	JL	88	AUD	HAMER,MH		514	521
0.00	GOVINDARAJAN,V	SU	79	JAA			339	343
0.00	GRADY,P	JA	65	TAR			21	30
0.00	GREENBALL,MN	ST	68	JAR			27	49
0.00	GREER,HC	JA	64	TAR			22	31
0.00	GREER JR,WR	AU	78	JAA	MORRISSEY,LE		49	57
0.00	HAIN,HP	OC	66	TAR			699	703
0.00	HAKANSSON,NH	JL	78	TAR			717	725
0.00	HARMON,WK	AU	84	JAA			24	34
0.00	HEIN,LW	AP	63	TAR			252	261
0.00	HINES,RD	03	88	AOS			251	261
0.00	HOLMES,W	JA	79	TAR			47	57
0.00	HOLZER,HP	AP	63	TAR	SCHONFELD,HM		377	381
0.00	HOLZER,HP	AP	63	TAR	SCHONFELD,HM		382	388
0.00	HOLZER,HP	AP	64	TAR	SCHONFELD,HM		405	413
0.00	HORRIGAN,JO	AP	68	TAR			284	294
0.00	IJIRI,Y	JA	65	TAR			36	53
0.00	INGBERMAN,M	AU	78	JAA	SORTER,GH		58	62
0.00	INGRAM,RW	JL	83	TAR	CHEWNING,EG		562	580
0.00	IVES,M	SU	85	JAA			253	268
0.00	JOHNSON,GL	OC	65	TAR			821	823
0.00	JOHNSON,GL	JL	66	TAR			510	517
0.00	JOHNSON,O	OC	74	TAR	GUNN,S		649	663
0.00	KABBES,SM	AP	65	TAR			395	400
0.00	KEISTER JR,OR	AP	64	TAR			414	416
0.00	KHEMAKHEM,A	JL	68	TAR			522	534
0.00	KING,RR	JA	74	TAR	BARON,CD		76	87
0.00	KOHLER,EL	AP	63	TAR			266	269
0.00	KOLLARITSCH,FP	AP	65	TAR			382	385
0.00	KROSS,W	AU	82	JAR			459	471
0.00	LAVOIE,D	06	87	AOS			579	604
0.00	LEMBKE,VC	JL	70	TAR			458	464
0.00	LEV,B	SP	79	JAA	TAYLOR,KW		232	243
0.00	LEV,B	JA	88	TAR			1	22
0.00	LONGSTRETH,B	WI	84	JAA			110	122
0.00	LOUDERBACK,JG	AP	71	TAR			298	305
0.00	MAITRE,P	34	78	AOS			227	236
0.00	MAKSY,MM	OC	88	TAR			683	699
0.00	MANES,RP	JL	64	TAR			631	638
0.00	MARCH,JG	02	87	AOS			153	168
0.00	MARPLE,RM	JL	63	TAR			478	482
0.00	MARTIN,A	ST	71	JAR			1	31
0.00	MCCOSH,AM	OC	67	TAR			693	700
0.00	MEEK,GK	AP	83	TAR			394	402

TREATMENTS= FINANCIAL ACCOUNTING METHODS

CITE IND-EX	FIRST AUTHOR	ISS-UE	YE-AR	JOUR -NAL	SECOND AUTHOR	THIRD AUTHOR	PAG BEG	PAG END
0.00	MERINO,BD	OC	87	TAR	KOCH,BS	MACRITCHIE,KL	748	762
0.00	MEYER,PE	JA	76	TAR			80	89
0.00	MUELLER,GG	AP	65	TAR			386	394
0.00	MURRAY,D	WI	82	JAA			154	159
0.00	NEUBIG,RD	JA	64	TAR			86	89
0.00	OHLSON,JA	ST	72	JAR			45	84
0.00	PATON,WA	AP	63	TAR			243	251
0.00	PERAGALLO,E	JL	71	TAR			529	534
0.00	PRINCE,TR	JL	64	TAR			553	562
0.00	RAMAN,KK	WI	82	JAA			144	153
0.00	RANSOM,CR	ST	85	JAR			124	143
0.00	RAYMAN,RA	SP	69	JAR			53	89
0.00	REVSINE,L	JL	71	TAR			480	489
0.00	RICHARDSON,AJ	04	87	AOS			341	355
0.00	ROBBINS,WA	SU	85	JAA	APOSTOLOU,NG	STRAWSER,RH	279	292
0.00	ROSEN,LS	JA	69	TAR	DECOSTER,DT		124	136
0.00	ROSS,H	ST	70	JAR			108	115
0.00	SALGADO,AP	AP	63	TAR			389	397
0.00	SCHATTKE,RW	OC	65	TAR			805	811
0.00	SCHATTKE,RW	AP	72	TAR			233	244
0.00	SHWAYDER,KR	SP	68	JAR			86	97
0.00	SIMMONS,JK	OC	67	TAR			680	692
0.00	SIMON,SI	AP	65	TAR			401	406
0.00	SORTER,GH	ST	74	JAR	GANS,MS		1	12
0.00	SPILLER JR,EA	OC	64	TAR			850	859
0.00	STONE,DE	AP	67	TAR			331	337
0.00	STONE,WE	AP	69	TAR			284	291
0.00	STREER,PJ	SU	79	JAA			329	338
0.00	SUMMERS,EL	AP	68	TAR			257	265
0.00	TAUSSIG,RA	JL	63	TAR			562	567
0.00	TOPIOL,J	JA	66	TAR			83	91
0.00	TSE,S	JL	86	TAR			475	497
0.00	VANCE,LL	OC	69	TAR			692	703
0.00	WELLS,MC	JL	76	TAR			471	482
0.00	WILLIAMS,PF	02	87	AOS			169	192
0.00	WILLINGHAM,JJ	JL	64	TAR			543	552
0.00	WINBORNE,MG	JL	64	TAR			622	626
0.00	WINJUM,JO	OC	70	TAR			743	761
0.00	WINJUM,JO	JA	71	TAR			149	155
0.00	YOUNG,AE	SP	78	JAA			217	230
0.00	YOUNG,DW	OC	76	TAR			788	799
0.00	YU,SC	JL	69	TAR			571	582

TREATMENTS= FINANCIAL ACCOUNTING METHODS

4.2 TREATMENTS= CASH

CITE IND-EX	FIRST AUTHOR	ISS-UE	YE-AR	JOUR-NAL	SECOND AUTHOR	THIRD AUTHOR	PAG BEG	PAG END
0.00	FREDRIKSON,EB	AU	68	JAR			208	221
0.00	FREEMAN,RN	ST	78	JAR			111	145
0.00	GOVINDARAJAN,V	04	80	AOS			383	392
0.00	SORTER,GH	SP	82	JAA			188	194
0.00	WHITEHURST,FD	JL	70	TAR			553	564

TREATMENTS= CASH

4.3 TREATMENTS= INVENTORY

CITE IND-EX	FIRST AUTHOR	ISS-UE	YE-AR	JOUR-NAL	SECOND AUTHOR	THIRD AUTHOR	PAG BEG	PAG END
2.43	BIDDLE,GC	AU	82	JAR	LINDAHL,FW		551	588
2.29	RICKS,WE	AU	82	JAR			367	387
2.23	SUNDER,S	ST	73	JAR			1	45
1.56	BIDDLE,GC	ST	80	JAR			235	280
1.54	SUNDER,S	AP	75	TAR			305	315
1.11	BROWN,RM	SP	80	JAR			38	63
1.09	ABDEL-KHALIK,AR	OC	78	TAR	MCKEOWN,JC		851	868
1.00	ABDEL-KHALIK,AR	AU	85	JAR			427	447
1.00	BIDDLE,GC	AU	88	JAR	RICKS,WE		169	194
1.00	HEALY,PM	AP	87	JAE	KANG,SH	PALEPU,KG	7	34
1.00	MORSE,D	SP	83	JAR	RICHARDSON,G		106	127
0.67	RICKS,WE	SP	86	JAR			206	216
0.54	DERSTINE,RP	AU	74	JAR	HUEFNER,RJ		216	234
0.54	DOPUCH,N	AU	73	JAR	RONEN,J		191	211
0.54	SUNDER,S	AP	76	TAR			287	291
0.54	SUNDER,S	AU	76	JAR			277	300
0.50	HUNT III,HG	AU	85	JAR		448	467	
0.50	LEE,CJ	AU	85	JAR	HSIEH,DA		468	485
0.50	STEVENSON,FL	AU	87	JAR			306	316
0.46	DYCKMAN,TR	SP	64	JAR			91	107
0.38	COPELAND,RM	ST	71	JAR	SHANK,JK		196	224
0.33	COHEN,MA	AU	80	JAR	HALPERIN,R		375	389
0.33	STOBER,TL	ST	86	JAR			138	164
0.30	HALPERIN,R	JA	79	TAR			58	71
0.25	BIDDLE,GC	SP	85	JAR	MARTIN,RK		57	83
0.23	BRUNS JR,WJ	AP	65	TAR			345	357
0.23	CHASTEEN,LG	JL	71	TAR			504	508
0.23	DYCKMAN,TR	AP	64	TAR			285	295
0.17	MURRAY,D	SP	83	JAR			128	140
0.08	BAILEY JR,AD	JL	73	TAR			560	574
0.08	DREBIN,AR	JA	65	TAR			154	162
0.08	WRIGHT,FK	JA	70	TAR			129	133
0.00	AMERSHI,AH	AU	87	JAR	SUNDER,S		177	195
0.00	BAGINSKI,SP	AU	87	JAR			196	216
0.00	BAINBRIDGE,DR	SU	84	JAA			334	346
0.00	BIERMAN JR,H	OC	67	TAR			731	737
0.00	COTTELL JR,PG	WI	86	JAA			30	45
0.00	DAVIS,HZ	AU	82	JAR	KAHN,N		738	744
0.00	DAVIS,HZ	AU	84	JAR	KAHN,N	ROZEN,E	480	490
0.00	DOPUCH,N	SP	88	JAR	PINCUS,M		28	59
0.00	DREBIN,AR	SP	66	JAR			68	86
0.00	FIRMIN,PA	AP	63	TAR			270	277
0.00	GRANOF,MH	SU	84	JAA	SHORT,DG		323	333
0.00	HALPERIN,R	AP	87	TAR	LANEN,WN		378	384
0.00	HILKE,JC	WI	86	JAA			17	29
0.00	HIRSCHMAN,RW	JA	65	TAR			176	183
0.00	HOLDREN,GC	JA	64	TAR			70	85
0.00	JOHNSON,WB	AU	88	JAR	DHALIWAL,DS		236	272

TREATMENTS= INVENTORY

CITE IND- EX	FIRST AUTHOR	ISS- UE	YE- AR	JOUR -NAL	SECOND AUTHOR	THIRD AUTHOR	PAG BEG	PAG END
0.00	LARGAY III,JA	JA	73	TAR			115	119
0.00	MANES,RP	ST	67	JAR	SAMUELS,JM	SMYTH,DJ	139	156
0.00	MOST,KS	SP	67	JAR			39	50
0.00	PETRI,E	JL	73	TAR			483	488
0.00	PETRI,E	JL	74	TAR	MINCH,RA		455	464
0.00	RAUN,DL	OC	63	TAR			754	758
0.00	STAUBUS,GJ	JL	68	TAR			413	424
0.00	TAUSSIG,RA	JA	68	TAR	HAYES,SC		68	74

TREATMENTS= INVENTORY

4.4 TREATMENTS= OTHER CURRENT ASSETS

CITE IND-EX	FIRST AUTHOR	ISS-UE	YE-AR	JOUR-NAL	SECOND AUTHOR	THIRD AUTHOR	PAG BEG	PAG END
0.15	BENISHAY,H	SP	65	JAR			114	132
0.08	HARMELINK,PJ	SP	73	JAR			146	158
0.08	SCHRODERHEIM,G	JL	64	TAR			679	684
0.00	ABRANOVIC,WA	OC	76	TAR			863	874
1.62	BEAVER,WH	AP	72	TAR	DUKES,RE		320	332
0.69	BEAVER,WH	JL	73	TAR	DUKES,RE		549	559
0.50	JARRELL,GA	AG	79	JAE			93	116
0.43	HALL,TW	SP	82	JAR			139	151
0.38	COMISKEY,EE	AP	71	TAR			279	285
0.31	IJIRI,Y	OC	69	TAR	KAPLAN,RS		743	756
0.23	FRIBERG,RA	JA	73	TAR			50	60
0.20	BLOOM,R	01	84	AOS	ELGERS,PT	MURRAY,D	1	11
0.20	MOST,KS	AU	84	JAR			782	788
0.15	BRIEF,RP	AU	70	JAR	OWEN,J		167	177
0.15	JEN,FC	AP	70	TAR	HUEFNER,RJ		290	298
0.15	LINDHE,R	AU	63	JAR			139	148
0.15	THOMAS,AL	JL	71	TAR			472	479
0.14	SKINNER,RC	SP	82	JAR			210	226
0.08	BEAVER,WH	AU	74	JAR	DUKES,RE		205	215
0.08	BIERMAN JR,H	AP	66	TAR			271	274
0.08	BIERMAN JR,H	JL	74	TAR			448	454
0.08	BRIEF,RP	SP	67	JAR			27	38
0.08	BRIEF,RP	OC	73	TAR	OWEN,J		690	695
0.08	BRIEF,RP	SP	73	JAR	OWEN,J		1	15
0.08	BULLOCK,CL	JA	74	TAR			98	103
0.08	GREENE,ED	AP	63	TAR			355	362
0.08	IJIRI,Y	SP	70	JAR	KAPLAN,RS		34	46
0.08	JOHNSON,O	SP	68	JAR			29	37
0.08	MCINTYRE,EV	JA	77	TAR			162	171
0.08	NURNBERG,H	OC	68	TAR			719	729
0.08	RICKS,RB	JL	64	TAR			685	688
0.08	SCHWAB,B	AP	69	TAR	NICOL,RE		292	296
0.08	SHWAYDER,KR	AU	73	JAR			259	272
0.08	VATTER,W	OC	66	TAR			681	698
0.08	WRIGHT,FK	AU	65	JAR			167	181
0.08	WRIGHT,FK	FL	65	JAR			167	181
0.00	BIERMAN JR,H	JA	69	TAR			65	78
0.00	BRIEF,RP	AP	68	TAR	OWEN,J		367	372
0.00	BRIEF,RP	OC	77	TAR			810	812
0.00	BRIGHAM,EF	JA	68	TAR			46	61
0.00	BURT,OR	SP	72	JAR			28	57
0.00	CARSBERG,BV	AU	69	JAR			165	182
0.00	CORCORAN,AW	AU	65	JAR	KWANG,CW		206	217
0.00	FEINSCHREIBER,R	SP	69	JAR			17	21
0.00	FRIED,D	SU	81	JAA			295	308
0.00	GYNTHER,MM	OC	68	TAR			706	718
0.00	HAWKINS,CA	SP	84	JAA	GIRARD,D		225	240
0.00	HIRSCH,AJ	OC	64	TAR			972	978

TREATMENTS= OTHER CURRENT ASSETS

CITE IND-EX	FIRST AUTHOR	ISS-UE	YE-AR	JOUR-NAL	SECOND AUTHOR	THIRD AUTHOR	PAG BEG	PAG END
0.00	HORWITZ,BN	OC	63	TAR			819	826
0.00	JOHNSON,O	JL	68	TAR			546	548
0.00	KIM,M	AP	88	JAE	MOORE,G		111	125

TREATMENTS= OTHER CURRENT ASSETS

4.5   TREATMENTS= PROP,PLANT & EQUIP / DEPR

CITE IND-EX	FIRST AUTHOR	ISS-UE	YE-AR	JOUR-NAL	SECOND AUTHOR	THIRD AUTHOR	PAG BEG	PAG END
0.00	LEV,B	AU	78	JAR	THEIL,H		286	293
0.00	LIVINGSTONE,JL	ST	67	JAR			93	123
0.00	LIVINGSTONE,JL	SP	67	JAR			77	94
0.00	LOWE,HD	AP	63	TAR			293	301
0.00	MOBLEY,SC	JA	67	TAR			114	123
0.00	O'DONNELL,JL	JA	65	TAR			135	143
0.00	REYNOLDS,IN	AP	64	TAR			342	346
0.00	THOMAS,AL	JA	64	TAR			1	11
0.00	THOMAS,AL	SP	65	JAR			103	113
0.00	WELLS,MC	AP	68	TAR			373	376
0.00	WRIGHT,FK	JA	63	TAR			87	90
0.00	WRIGHT,FK	SP	64	JAR			80	90
0.00	WRIGHT,FK	AU	67	JAR			173	179
0.00	WRIGHT,FK	AU	68	JAR			222	236
0.00	YOUNG,TN	AP	67	TAR	PEIRSON,CG		338	341
0.00	ZAROWIN,P	AP	88	JAE			89	110

TREATMENTS= PROP,PLANT & EQUIP / DEPR

4.6 TREATMENTS= OTHER NON-CURRENT ASSETS

CITE IND- EX	FIRST AUTHOR	ISS- UE	YE- AR	JOUR -NAL	SECOND AUTHOR	THIRD AUTHOR	PAG BEG	PAG END
0.15	ABDEL-KHALIK,AR	OC	75	TAR			657	670
0.15	PELES,YC	SP	70	JAR			128	137
0.15	SCHIFF,M	SP	66	JAR			62	67
0.09	SCAPENS,RW	AP	78	TAR			448	469
0.09	SCAPENS,RW	AP	78	TAR			448	469
0.08	CARSBERG,BV	SP	66	JAR			1	15
0.00	BRIEF,RP	JA	69	TAR			20	26
0.00	DREBIN,AR	JL	66	TAR			413	425
0.00	GYNTHER,RS	AP	69	TAR			247	255
0.00	JOHNSON,O	OC	76	TAR			808	823
0.00	MILLER,MC	AP	73	TAR			280	291
0.00	MILLS,RH	JA	67	TAR			74	81

.7 TREATMENTS= LEASES

CITE IND-X	FIRST AUTHOR	ISS-UE	YE-AR	JOUR -NAL	SECOND AUTHOR	THIRD AUTHOR	PAG BEG	PAG END
.64	RO,BT	AU	78	JAR			315	340
.33	EL-GAZZAR,S	OC	86	JAE	LILIEN,S	PASTENA,V	217	238
.31	LEV,B	AU	69	JAR			290	299
.22	BOWMAN,RG	AP	80	TAR			237	253
.17	WILKINS,T	OC	83	TAR	ZIMMER,I		749	764
.15	VATTER,WJ	AU	66	JAR			133	148
.15	WYMAN,HE	JL	73	TAR			489	493
.11	BAKER,CR	SP	80	JAA			197	206
.11	PALMON,D	SP	80	JAA	KWATINETZ,M		207	226
.08	RAPPAPORT,A	AP	65	TAR			373	376
.08	WOJDAK,JF	JL	69	TAR			562	570
.00	BEECHY,TH	AP	69	TAR			375	381
.00	CHASTEEN,LG	OC	73	TAR			764	767
.00	EVERETT,JO	SP	84	JAA	PORTER,GA		241	256
.00	MARSTON,F	SP	88	JAA	HARRIS,RS		147	164
.00	MARTIN,JD	WI	79	JAA	ANDERSON,PF	KEOWN,AJ	151	164
.00	MUNTER,P	WI	83	JAA	RATCLIFFE,TA		108	114
.00	SHAW,WH	AP	87	TAR			385	400

TREATMENTS= LEASES

4.8   TREATMENTS= LONG TERM DEBT

CITE IND-EX	FIRST AUTHOR	ISS-UE	YE-AR	JOUR-NAL	SECOND AUTHOR	THIRD AUTHOR	PAG BEG	PAG END
0.69	HORRIGAN,JO	ST	66	JAR			44	62
0.44	BOWMAN,RG	SP	80	JAR			242	254
0.25	INGRAM,RW	AU	85	JAR			595	618
0.25	MULFORD,CW	AU	85	JAR			897	906
0.08	ARNOLD,DF	JA	73	TAR	HUMANN,TE		23	33
0.08	CURRY,DW	JL	71	TAR			490	503
0.08	FRANK,WG	SP	71	JAR	WEYGANDT,JJ		116	126
0.00	APOSTOLOU,NG	AU	85	JAR	GIROUX,GA	WELKER,RB	853	858
0.00	BEATTY,RP	WI	85	JAA	JOHNSON,SB		112	124
0.00	BIERMAN JR,H	AU	67	JAR	SMIDT,S		144	153
0.00	BIERMAN JR,H	OC	68	TAR			657	661
0.00	BIERMAN JR,H	WI	86	JAA			62	70
0.00	DIETRICH,JR	AP	84	JAE			67	96
0.00	FORD,A	OC	69	TAR			818	822
0.00	FRIED,D	WI	87	JAA	HOSLER,C		5	23
0.00	GIVOLY,D	AU	81	JAR	PALMON,D		530	543
0.00	GLOVER,F	AP	69	TAR			300	303
0.00	IMDIEKE,LF	OC	69	TAR	WEYGANDT,JJ		798	805
0.00	KAHN,N	SU	82	JAA			327	337
0.00	KING,RD	JL	84	TAR			419	431
0.00	KNAUF,JB	WI	87	JAA	VASARHELYI,MA		43	64
0.00	KNUTSON,PH	ST	71	JAR			99	112
0.00	LYS,T	AU	88	JAR	SIVARAMAKRISHNAN,K		273	299
0.00	MIELKE,DE	WI	87	JAA	SEIFERT,J		65	78
0.00	PAINE,NR	AP	64	TAR			330	332
0.00	PEAVY,JW	WI	85	JAA	EDGAR,SM		125	135
0.00	RAPPAPORT,A	AP	69	TAR			297	299
0.00	RODEN,PF	WI	87	JAA			79	89
0.00	STICKEL,SE	OC	86	JAE			197	216
0.00	TILLER,MG	SU	85	JAA	MAUTZ,RD		293	304

.9 TREATMENTS= TAXES

CITE IND- EX	FIRST AUTHOR	ISS- UE	YE- AR	JOUR -NAL	SECOND AUTHOR	THIRD AUTHOR	PAG BEG	PAG END
.33	ZIMMERMAN,JL	AG	83	JAE			119	149
.71	HITE,GL	JL	82	JAE	LONG,MS		3	14
.31	CRUMBLEY,DL	OC	73	TAR			759	763
.25	MADEO,SA	JL	85	TAR	PINCUS,M		407	429
.25	MILLIRON,VC	AU	85	JAR			794	816
.17	WHITE,RA	JL	83	TAR			539	561
.15	GRIFFIN,PA	JL	76	TAR			499	515
.10	ENGLEBRECHT,TD	JL	79	TAR	JAMISON,RW		554	562
.10	MADEO,SA	JL	79	TAR			538	553
.08	ADAR,Z	JA	77	TAR	BARNEA,A	LEV,B	137	149
.08	GREENBALL,MN	AU	69	JAR			262	289
.08	LIVINGSTONE,JL	AU	69	JAR			245	256
.08	MEYERS,SL	JA	73	TAR			44	49
.00	ALFRED,AM	AU	64	JAR			172	182
.00	ALVEY,KL	JA	63	TAR			124	125
.00	ANDERSON JR,KE	JL	85	TAR			357	371
.00	BERG,KB	JL	63	TAR	MUELLER,FJ		554	561
.00	BIERMAN,H	SP	85	JAA			184	194
.00	BOGART,FO	OC	65	TAR			834	838
.00	BRIGHAM,EF	JL	74	TAR	NANTELL,TJ		436	447
.00	DEAN,J	AP	63	TAR	HARRISS,CL		229	242
.00	DRINKWATER,D	JL	65	TAR	EDWARDS,JD		579	582
.00	FELLINGHAM,JC	JA	85	TAR	WOLFSON,MA		10	17
.00	HASSELBACK,JR	AP	76	TAR			269	276
.00	HICKS,SA	JL	78	TAR			708	716
.00	HOPWOOD,WS	SP	85	JAR	MCKEOWN,JC		161	174
.00	HORNE,JC	JA	63	TAR			56	60
.00	HORWITZ,RM	JL	64	TAR			618	621
.00	HUSS,HF	AU	85	JAA			60	66
.00	JERSTON,JE	OC	65	TAR			812	813
.00	KAPLAN,SE	04	88	AOS	RECKERS,PMJ	ROARK,SJ	371	379
.00	KARLINSKY,SS	WI	83	JAA			157	167
.00	KARLINSKY,SS	AU	83	JAA			65	76
.00	KELLER,TF	JA	65	TAR			184	189
.00	KRAMER,SS	JA	82	TAR			70	87
.00	LAIBSTAIN,S	AP	71	TAR			342	351
.00	LEWIS,CD	JA	67	TAR			96	105
.00	LIVINGSTONE,JL	JL	67	TAR			544	552
.00	MADEO,SA	AP	87	TAR	SCHEPANSKI,A	UECKER,WC	323	342
.00	MEHTA,DR	SP	68	JAR	ANDREWS,VL		50	57
.00	MOONITZ,M	SP	66	JAR			47	61
.00	MOORE,ML	JA	85	TAR	STEECE,BM	SWENSON,CW	18	32
.00	MOORE,ML	OC	87	TAR	STEECE,BM	SWENSON,CW	671	685
.00	NIKOLAI,LA	JA	79	TAR	ELAM,R		119	131
.00	NURNBERG,H	AU	69	JAR			257	261
.00	NURNBERG,H	AU	70	JAR			217	231
.00	NURNBERG,H	OC	72	TAR			655	665
.00	NURNBERG,H	AU	85	JAA	CIANCIOLO,ST		50	59

TREATMENTS= TAXES

CITE IND-EX	FIRST AUTHOR	ISS-UE	YE-AR	JOUR-NAL	SECOND AUTHOR	THIRD AUTHOR	PAG BEG	PAG END
0.00	O'DONNELL,JL	JL	68	TAR			549	553
0.00	OUTSLAY,E	OC	82	TAR	WHEELER,JE		716	733
0.00	PATTEN,RJ	OC	64	TAR			876	879
0.00	PORCANO,TM	OC	84	TAR			619	636
0.00	RABY,WL	JL	63	TAR	NEUBIG,RD		568	576
0.00	REVSINE,L	AP	69	TAR			354	358
0.00	RICHARD,DL	OC	68	TAR			730	737
0.00	SCHWARTZ,BN	SP	81	JAA			238	247
0.00	SCHWARTZ,BN	SP	83	JAA			244	253
0.00	SEAMAN,JL	JL	65	TAR			617	621
0.00	SHAW,WH	SP	88	JAR			60	81
0.00	SHPILBERG,D	AU	86	AUD	GRAHAM,LE		75	94
0.00	SOMMERFELD,RM	OC	67	TAR			747	750
0.00	THOMAS,JK	JL	88	JAE			199	237
0.00	TRUMBULL,WP	JL	68	TAR			459	468
0.00	VOSS,WM	AU	68	JAR			262	269
0.00	WAUGH,JB	JL	68	TAR			535	539
0.00	WEBER,RP	JA	77	TAR			172	185
0.00	WHITE,D	SU	82	JAA	VANECEK,M		338	354
0.00	WIESEN,JL	WI	79	JAA	ENG,R		101	121
0.00	WILLIAMS,D	AP	66	TAR			226	234
0.00	WINBORNE,MG	OC	66	TAR	KLEESPIE,DC		737	744
0.00	WONG,J	JA	88	JAE			37	51

TREATMENTS= TAXES

.10   TREATMENTS= OTHER LIABILITIES

CITE IND-EX	FIRST AUTHOR	ISS-UE	YE-AR	JOUR -NAL	SECOND AUTHOR	THIRD AUTHOR	PAG BEG	PAG END
.57	BANKS,DW	SP	82	JAR	KINNEY JR,WR		240	254
).18	HUGHES,JS	OC	78	TAR			882	894
).15	DAVIDSON,HJ	AU	67	JAR	NETER,J	PETRAN,AS	186	207
).13	BALACHANDRAN,KR	JA	81	TAR	MASCHMEYER,R	LIVINGSTONE,JL	115	124
0.08	AMATO,HN	OC	76	TAR	ANDERSON,EE	HARVEY,DW	854	862
0.08	HECK,WR	JL	63	TAR			577	578
0.00	BRIGHTON,GD	JA	69	TAR			137	144
0.00	CRAMER JR,JJ	OC	70	TAR	SCHRADER,WJ		698	703
0.00	DEWHIRST,JF	AP	71	TAR			365	373
0.00	DREBIN,AR	JL	63	TAR			579	583
0.00	HENNESSY,VC	SU	78	JAA			317	330
0.00	KING,TE	JL	88	AUD	ORTEGREN,AK		522	535
0.00	TRUMBULL,WP	JA	63	TAR			46	51
0.00	WOLK,HI	AP	73	TAR	TEARNEY,MG		292	299

TREATMENTS= OTHER LIABILITIES

4.11 TREATMENTS= VALUATION (INFLATION)

CITE IND-EX	FIRST AUTHOR	ISS-UE	YE-AR	JOUR-NAL	SECOND AUTHOR	THIRD AUTHOR	PAG BEG	PAG END
2.43	BEAVER,WH	JL	82	JAE	GRIFFIN,PA	LANDSMAN,WR	15	39
2.00	BEAVER,WH	AG	80	JAE	CHRISTIE,AA	GRIFFIN,PA	127	157
1.67	GHEYARA,K	AG	80	JAE	BOATSMAN,JR		107	125
1.56	RO,BT	AG	80	JAE			159	189
1.50	BUBLITZ,B	ST	85	JAR	FRECKA,TJ	MCKEOWN,JC	1	23
1.25	NOREEN,EW	AP	81	TAR	SEPE,J		253	269
0.83	FREEMAN,RN	SP	83	JAR			42	64
0.80	SCHAEFER,TF	AU	84	JAR			647	656
0.75	OLSEN,C	ST	85	JAR			28	53
0.75	PARKER,JE	JA	77	TAR			69	96
0.67	SUNDER,S	AU	83	JAR	WAYMIRE,G		565	580
0.67	TITMAN,S	JN	86	JAE	TRUEMAN,B		159	172
0.55	SUNDER,S	AU	78	JAR			341	367
0.54	PETERSEN,RJ	JA	73	TAR			34	43
0.54	TRITSCHLER,CA	JA	69	TAR			99	123
0.50	CASLER,DJ	SP	85	JAR	HALL,TW		110	122
0.50	THOMPSON,G	05	87	AOS			523	543
0.46	REVSINE,L	JL	70	TAR			513	523
0.46	SIMMONS,JK	OC	69	TAR	GRAY,J		757	776
0.45	BENSTON,GJ	ST	78	JAR	KRASNEY,MA		1	30
0.44	WATTS,RL	AG	80	JAE	ZIMMERMAN,JL		95	106
0.43	LUSTGARTEN,S	OC	82	JAE			121	141
0.40	MCDONALD,B	JL	84	TAR	MORRIS,MH		432	446
0.40	PRAKASH,P	JA	79	TAR	SUNDER,S		1	22
0.38	MCINTYRE,EV	JL	73	TAR			575	585
0.38	RO,BT	JA	81	TAR			70	84
0.36	ABDEL-KHALIK,AR	ST	78	JAR	MCKEOWN,JC		46	77
0.36	KETZ,JE	OC	78	TAR			952	960
0.33	KAPLAN,RS	AP	77	TAR			369	378
0.33	MURDOCH,B	AP	86	TAR			273	287
0.33	PEASNELL,KV	SP	77	JAR	SKERRATT,CL		108	119
0.33	SHRIVER,KA	SP	86	JAR			151	165
0.31	BARTON,AD	OC	74	TAR			664	681
0.31	BRENNER,VC	AU	70	JAR			159	166
0.31	LIVINGSTONE,JL	AP	67	TAR			233	240
0.30	NORTON,CL	JA	79	TAR	SMITH,RE		72	87
0.30	REVSINE,L	AP	79	TAR			306	322
0.29	WALTHER,LM	AP	82	TAR			376	383
0.23	CHAMBERS,RJ	OC	65	TAR			731	741
0.23	FRANK,WG	SP	69	JAR			123	136
0.23	HEINTZ,JA	OC	73	TAR			679	689
0.23	MCKEOWN,JC	JA	71	TAR			12	29
0.23	SAMUELSON,RA	AU	72	JAR			322	344
0.18	KETZ,JE	ST	78	JAR			273	284
0.18	SHORT,DG	ST	78	JAR			259	272
0.17	BROMWICH,M	JL	77	TAR			587	596
0.17	WEYGANDT,JJ	JA	77	TAR			40	51
0.15	CHAMBERS,RJ	SP	65	JAR			32	62

TREATMENTS= VALUATION (INFLATION)

TE ID- X	FIRST AUTHOR	ISS- UE	YE- AR	JOUR -NAL	SECOND AUTHOR	THIRD AUTHOR	PAG BEG	PAG END
15	CHAMBERS,RJ	AU	65	JAR			242	252
15	CHAMBERS,RJ	OC	67	TAR			751	757
15	DOCKWEILER,RC	OC	69	TAR			729	742
15	EDWARDS,EO	AP	75	TAR			235	245
15	GREENBALL,MN	SP	68	JAR			114	129
15	GYNTHER,RS	OC	70	TAR			712	730
15	IJIRI,Y	AP	76	TAR			227	243
15	LEMKE,KW	JA	66	TAR			32	41
15	MCDONALD,DL	SP	68	JAR			38	49
15	MOONITZ,M	JL	70	TAR			465	475
15	STAUBUS,GJ	JA	65	TAR			119	134
14	SEPE,J	JL	82	TAR			467	485
11	BARAN,A	JA	80	TAR	LAKONISHOK,J	OFER,AR	22	35
11	KELLY,LK	03	80	AOS			311	322
10	HILLISON,WA	SP	79	JAR			60	73
09	DAVIDSON,S	ST	78	JAR	WEIL,RL		154	233
08	ARNOLD,DF	AU	77	JAR	HUEFNER,RJ		245	252
08	BAXTER,WT	AU	71	JAR	CARRIER,NH		189	214
08	BRADFORD,WD	AP	74	TAR			296	305
08	COOK,JS	OC	76	TAR	HOLZMANN,OJ		778	787
08	DICKENS,RL	AP	64	TAR	BLACKBURN,JO		312	329
08	ESTES,RW	AU	68	JAR			200	207
08	HEATH,LC	JL	72	TAR			458	468
08	HORNGREN,CT	AP	65	TAR			323	333
08	ISELIN,ER	AP	68	TAR			231	238
08	KRATCHMAN,SH	OC	74	TAR	MALCOM,RE	TWARK,RD	682	689
08	MATHEWS,RL	JL	68	TAR			509	516
08	MCKEOWN,JC	SP	73	JAR			62	99
08	PENMAN,SH	AP	70	TAR			333	346
08	SHARPE,IG	AU	75	JAR	WALKER,RG		293	310
08	SHWAYDER,KR	AP	69	TAR			304	316
08	SHWAYDER,KR	AP	71	TAR			306	319
08	SNAVELY,HJ	AP	69	TAR			344	353
08	STAUBUS,GJ	OC	67	TAR			650	661
08	STAUBUS,GJ	JL	76	TAR			574	589
08	TRACY,JA	JA	65	TAR			163	175
00	AGRAWAL,SP	OC	77	TAR			789	809
00	AGRAWAL,SP	WI	80	JAA	HALLBAUER,RC	PERRITT,GW	163	173
00	ARNETT,HE	OC	63	TAR			733	741
00	BEAVER,WH	AU	82	JAR	WOLFSON,MA		528	550
00	BEDFORD,NM	AP	72	TAR	MCKEOWN,JC		333	338
00	BEJA,A	AU	77	JAR	AHARONI,Y		169	178
00	BERNARD,VL	AU	84	JAR			445	466
00	BERNARD,VL	OC	87	TAR	RULAND,RG		707	722
00	BIERMAN JR,H	OC	71	TAR			693	700
00	BOER,G	JA	66	TAR			92	97
00	CHAMBERS,RJ	AP	68	TAR			239	247
00	COOPER,T	WI	80	JAA			138	146
00	CORBIN,DA	OC	63	TAR			742	744
00	CORBIN,DA	OC	67	TAR			635	641

TREATMENTS= VALUATION (INFLATION)

CITE IND-EX	FIRST AUTHOR	ISS-UE	YE-AR	JOUR-NAL	SECOND AUTHOR	THIRD AUTHOR	PAG BEG	PAG END
0.00	DEFLIESE,PL	JL	65	TAR			517	521
0.00	DREBIN,AR	AU	69	JAR			204	214
0.00	ENIS,CR	02	88	AOS			123	145
0.00	FRIEDMAN,LA	JA	78	TAR			18	30
0.00	FRIEDMAN,LA	OC	78	TAR			895	909
0.00	GAMBLE,GO	SU	82	JAA			320	326
0.00	GOLDSCHMIDT,Y	AP	69	TAR	SMIDT,S		317	329
0.00	GOLDSCHMIDT,Y	AU	84	JAA	SHASHUA,L		54	67
0.00	GROSSMAN,SD	WI	81	JAA	KRATCHMAN,SH	WELKER,RB	136	143
0.00	HAKANSSON,NH	SP	69	JAR			11	31
0.00	HALL,TW	SP	85	JAA	CASLER,DJ		210	224
0.00	HANNUM,WH	AP	68	TAR	WASSERMAN,W		295	302
0.00	HAW,IM	AU	88	JAR	LUSTGARTEN,S		331	352
0.00	HENDRIKSEN,ES	JL	63	TAR			483	491
0.00	INGBERMAN,M	WI	80	JAA			101	112
0.00	JARRETT,JE	SP	74	JAR			63	66
0.00	JOLIVET,V	JL	64	TAR			689	692
0.00	KISTNER,KP	SP	80	JAR	SALMI,T		297	311
0.00	LARSON,KD	OC	66	TAR	SCHATTKE,RW		634	641
0.00	LEE,SS	JL	65	TAR			622	625
0.00	LEMBKE,VC	WI	80	JAA	SMITH,JH		147	162
0.00	LEMBKE,VC	WI	81	JAA	TOOLE,HR		128	135
0.00	MAHER,MW	SP	83	JAR	NANTELL,TJ		329	340
0.00	MCINTYRE,EV	JL	82	TAR			607	618
0.00	MCKEOWN,JC	JL	72	TAR			527	532
0.00	MONAHAN,TF	SU	83	JAA	BARENBAUM,L		325	340
0.00	NAKANO,I	OC	72	TAR			693	708
0.00	NELSON,GK	JA	66	TAR			42	47
0.00	OVADIA,A	WI	80	JAA	RONEN,J		113	137
0.00	OVADIA,A	WI	83	JAA	RONEN,J		115	129
0.00	PATON,WA	SP	68	JAR			72	85
0.00	PEASNELL,KV	JA	77	TAR			186	189
0.00	PEIRSON,G	OC	66	TAR			729	736
0.00	PETERSEN,RJ	JL	75	TAR			525	532
0.00	PETERSON,WA	AP	66	TAR			275	282
0.00	PHILIPS,GE	ST	70	JAR	MAYNE,LS		178	188
0.00	RABY,WL	JA	69	TAR			1	11
0.00	REVSINE,L	AP	81	TAR			342	354
0.00	RORKE,CH	03	82	AOS			305	306
0.00	ROSEN,LS	JA	67	TAR			106	113
0.00	ROSENFIELD,P	OC	69	TAR			788	797
0.00	SHRIVER,KA	JA	87	TAR			79	96
0.00	SKERRATT,LC	SU	84	JAA			362	368
0.00	SPENCER,CH	JA	65	TAR	BARNISEL,TS		144	153
0.00	SPROUSE,RT	OC	63	TAR			687	695
0.00	SPROUSE,RT	JL	65	TAR			522	526
0.00	STANDISH,PEM	OC	82	TAR	UNG,S		701	715
0.00	STANLEY,CH	JL	64	TAR			639	647
0.00	STERLING,RR	JL	71	TAR	FLAHERTY,RE		441	456
0.00	STERLING,RR	OC	72	TAR	TOLLEFSON,SO	FLAHERTY,RE	709	721

TREATMENTS= VALUATION (INFLATION)

CITE IND- EX	FIRST AUTHOR	ISS- UE	YE- AR	JOUR -NAL	SECOND AUTHOR	THIRD AUTHOR	PAG BEG	PAG END
0.00	SUMMERS,EL	SP	70	JAR	DESKINS,JW		113	117
0.00	SUTTON,TG	AP	88	JAE			127	149
0.00	SWANSON,EP	OC	85	TAR	SHEARON,WT	THOMAS,LR	681	691
0.00	SWENSON,CW	JA	87	TAR			117	136
0.00	TAUSSIG,RA	SP	64	JAR			67	79
0.00	THIES,CF	AU	87	JAA	STURROCK,T		375	391
0.00	THOMAS,AL	JL	64	TAR			574	581
0.00	THOMAS,LR	AP	86	TAR	SWANSON,EP		330	336
0.00	WELLS,MC	OC	65	TAR	COTTON,W		829	833
0.00	WOLK,HI	JL	70	TAR			544	552
0.00	WONG,J	AP	88	JAE			151	167
0.00	ZEFF,SA	JA	65	TAR	MAXWELL,WD		65	75

TREATMENTS= VALUATION (INFLATION)

4.12 TREATMENTS= SPECIAL ITEMS

CITE IND-EX	FIRST AUTHOR	ISS-UE	YE-AR	JOUR -NAL	SECOND AUTHOR	THIRD AUTHOR	PAG BEG	PAG END
3.63	BOWEN,RM	AG	81	JAE	NOREEN,EW	LACEY,JM	151	179
2.23	GONEDES,NJ	AU	75	JAR			220	256
2.00	RAYBURN,J	ST	86	JAR			112	137
1.33	WILSON	GP	ST	86	JAR		165	203
1.00	JAIN,PC	DE	82	JAE			205	228
0.67	HOSKIN,RE	ST	86	JAR	HUGHES,JS	RICKS,WE	1	36
0.60	SUNDER,S	SP	84	JAR	WAYMIRE,G		396	405
0.31	BARNEA,A	JA	75	TAR	RONEN,J	SADAN,S	58	68
0.15	PETRI,E	AP	74	TAR	MINCH,RA		330	341
0.08	CUMMING,J	ST	73	JAR			60	95
0.00	BOWEN,RM	OC	87	TAR	BURGSTAHLER,D	DALEY,LA	723	747
0.00	BURNS,JS	JA	63	TAR	JAEDICKE,RK	SANGSTER,JM	1	13
0.00	FURLONG,WL	AP	66	TAR			244	252
0.00	GOMBOLA,MJ	JA	83	TAR	KETZ,JE		105	114
0.00	GREENBERG,RR	AU	86	JAA	JOHNSON,GL	RAMESH,K	266	277
0.00	GRIMLUND,RA	AU	85	JAR			575	594
0.00	KATZ,BG	SU	87	JAA	OWEN,J		266	298
0.00	MANEGOLD,JG	SU	86	JAA			206	221
0.00	PATON,WA	AP	69	TAR			276	283
0.00	SCHAEFER,T	AU	86	JAA	KENNELLEY,M		278	287
0.00	SHWAYDER,KR	OC	72	TAR			747	760
0.00	TAYLOR,WM	AU	82	JAR	WEYGANDT,JJ		497	502

4.13 TREATMENTS= REVENUE RECOGNITION

CITE INDEX	FIRST AUTHOR	ISS-UE	YE-AR	JOUR-NAL	SECOND AUTHOR	THIRD AUTHOR	PAG BEG	PAG END
1.15	BROWN,P	ST	67	JAR	BALL,R		55	77
0.86	FREEMAN,RN	AU	82	JAR	OHLSON,JA	PENMAN,SH	639	653
0.67	BOWEN,RM	OC	86	TAR	BURGSTAHLER,D	DALEY,LA	713	725
0.62	DRAKE,DF	AU	65	JAR	DOPUCH,N		192	205
0.60	LAMBERT,RA	OC	84	TAR			604	618
0.23	BALL,R	SP	76	JAR	LEV,B	WATTS,RL	1	9
0.23	RONEN,J	SP	75	JAR	SADAN,S		133	149
0.13	KOCH,BS	JL	81	TAR			574	586
0.08	SHANK,JK	JA	71	TAR			57	74
0.00	BAKER,RE	JA	66	TAR			98	105
0.00	CERF,AR	JL	75	TAR			451	465
0.00	COMISKEY,EE	AP	68	TAR	MLYNARCZYK,FA		248	256
0.00	DEFEO,VJ	AU	86	JAR			349	363
0.00	DEMARIS,EJ	JA	63	TAR			37	45
0.00	DYE,RA	AU	88	JAR			195	235
0.00	FRIEDLOB,GT	WI	83	JAA			100	107
0.00	HENDRICKSON,HS	AP	68	TAR			363	366
0.00	HUDSON,RR	OC	63	TAR			796	801
0.00	HYLTON,DP	OC	65	TAR			824	828
0.00	IJIRI,Y	JA	84	TAR	NOEL,J		52	63
0.00	JACOBSEN,LE	AP	63	TAR			285	292
0.00	KAHN,N	AU	85	JAA	SCHIFF,A		40	49
0.00	LITTLETON,AC	JL	70	TAR			476	480
0.00	MAURIELLO,JA	JA	63	TAR			26	28
0.00	MENSAH,YM	WI	83	JAA			130	141
0.00	MOBLEY,SC	AP	66	TAR			292	296
0.00	MOBLEY,SC	AP	68	TAR			333	341
0.00	PHILIPS,GE	JA	63	TAR			14	25
0.00	SAMUELSON,RA	AP	80	TAR			254	268
0.00	SORTER,GH	SP	87	JAA	INGBERMAN,M		99	116
0.00	STERNER,JA	AU	83	JAR			623	628
0.00	WINDAL,FW	JA	63	TAR			29	36

TREATMENTS= REVENUE RECOGNITION

4.14 TREATMENTS= ACCTG CHANGES

CITE IND- EX	FIRST AUTHOR	ISS- UE	YE- AR	JOUR -NAL	SECOND AUTHOR	THIRD AUTHOR	PAG BEG	PAG END
3.80	HAGERMAN,RL	AG	79	JAE	ZMIJEWSKI,ME		141	161
3.63	LEFTWICH,RW	MR	81	JAE			3	36
2.54	BALL,R	ST	72	JAR			1	38
1.33	HARRISON,T	SP	77	JAR			84	107
1.15	ARCHIBALD,TR	JA	72	TAR			22	30
1.08	DOPUCH,N	SP	72	JAR	WATTS,RL		180	194
1.00	HUGHES,JS	AG	84	JAE	RICKS,WE		101	132
0.92	CUSHING,BE	AU	69	JAR			196	203
0.92	EGGLETON,IRC	SP	76	JAR	PENMAN,SH	TWOMBLY,JR	66	88
0.71	DEANGELO,LE	DE	82	JAE			171	203
0.69	ARCHIBALD,TR	ST	67	JAR			164	186
0.62	MOORE,ML	SP	73	JAR			100	107
0.57	DYCKMAN,TR	01	82	AOS	HOSKIN,RE	SWIERINGA,RJ	1	12
0.54	BASKIN,EF	JA	72	TAR			38	51
0.23	BREMSER,WG	JL	75	TAR			563	573
0.23	WHITE JR,CE	AU	72	JAR			351	358
0.17	BROWN,LD	AU	83	JAR			432	443
0.17	WARREN,CS	JA	77	TAR			150	161
0.14	SCHWARTZ,KB	AU	82	JAA			32	43
0.13	HORWITZ,BN	WI	81	JAA	KOLODNY,R		102	113
0.08	NEUMANN,FL	JL	69	TAR			546	554
0.00	CREADY,WM	JL	87	TAR	SHANK,JK		589	596
0.00	LILIEN,S	OC	88	TAR	MELLMAN,M	PASTENA,V	642	656
0.00	MOSES,OD	AP	87	TAR			358	377
0.00	RICKS,WE	JA	85	TAR	HUGHES,JS		33	52

4.15   TREATMENTS= BUSINESS COMBINATIONS

CITE IND-EX	FIRST AUTHOR	ISS-UE	YE-AR	JOUR -NAL	SECOND AUTHOR	THIRD AUTHOR	PAG BEG	PAG END
2.67	SCHIPPER,K	SP	83	JAR	THOMPSON,R		184	221
1.18	HONG,H	JA	78	TAR	KAPLAN,RS	MANDELKER,G	31	47
1.00	ZIMMER,I	MR	86	JAE			37	52
0.69	GAGNON,JM	ST	67	JAR			187	204
0.67	PALEPU,KG	MR	86	JAE			3	36
0.57	SILHAN,PA	SP	82	JAR			255	262
0.50	LEWELLEN,W	AP	85	JAE	LODERER,C	ROSENFELD,A	209	232
0.50	WHITTRED,G	DE	87	JAE			259	285
0.38	BLUM,M	SP	74	JAR			1	25
0.33	PASTENA,V	AP	86	TAR	RULAND,W		288	301
0.23	GAGNON,JM	SP	71	JAR			52	72
0.18	PATTON,JM	AP	78	TAR			402	414
0.08	COPELAND,RM	AU	69	JAR	WOJDAK,JF		188	195
0.00	BOATSMAN,JR	AU	84	JAA	DOWELL,CD	KIMBRELL,JI	35	43
0.00	BRADBURY,ME	AP	88	TAR	CALDERWOOD,SC		330	347
0.00	BRILOFF,AJ	JL	67	TAR			489	496
0.00	CRUMBLEY,DL	JL	68	TAR			554	564
0.00	CURLEY,AJ	JL	71	TAR			519	528
0.00	DAVIS,ML	AP	88	TAR	LARGAY III,JA		348	363
0.00	DEANGELO,LE	JA	88	JAE			3	36
0.00	EIGEN,MM	JL	65	TAR			536	540
0.00	HAW,IM	WI	87	JAA	PASTENA,V	LILIEN,S	24	42
0.00	HOLZMANN,OJ	WI	84	JAA	MEANS,KM		138	150
0.00	HORWITZ,BN	SP	72	JAR	YOUNG,AE		96	107
0.00	JONES,CS	03	85	AOS			303	328
0.00	JONES,CS	02	85	AOS			177	200
0.00	KING,TE	SP	79	JAA			209	223
0.00	LAUVER,RC	JA	66	TAR			65	74
0.00	LEV,B	JL	70	TAR			532	534
0.00	LLOYD,BM	OC	71	TAR	WEYGANDT,JJ		756	764
0.00	MULFORD,CW	JL	86	TAR	COMISKEY,EE		519	525
0.00	NIELSEN,CC	OC	65	TAR			795	804
0.00	NORDHAUSER,SL	JA	81	TAR	KRAMER,JL		54	69
0.00	O'CONNOR,MC	AP	72	TAR	HAMRE,JC		308	319
0.00	PARKER,WM	AU	66	JAR			149	154
0.00	PHILLIPS,LC	AP	65	TAR			377	381
0.00	RAMANATHAN,KV	OC	71	TAR	RAPPAPORT,A		733	745
0.00	SAPIENZA,SR	JA	63	TAR			91	101
0.00	SAPIENZA,SR	JL	64	TAR			582	590
0.00	SAPIENZA,SR	SP	64	JAR			50	66
0.00	SCHIPPER,K	SP	85	JAR	THOMPSON,R		408	415
0.00	SILHAN,PA	SP	85	JAR	MCKEOWN,JC		416	426
0.00	SMOLINSKI,EJ	AU	63	JAR			149	178
0.00	TEHRANIAN,H	ST	87	JAR	TRAVLOS,NG	WAEGELEIN,JF	51	76
0.00	TUCKERMAN,B	JA	64	TAR			32	37
0.00	WEIL,RL	OC	73	TAR			749	758
0.00	WYATT,AR	JL	65	TAR			527	535

TREATMENTS= BUSINESS COMBINATIONS

4.16 TREATMENTS= INTERIM REPORTING

CITE IND- EX	FIRST AUTHOR	ISS- UE	YE- AR	JOUR -NAL	SECOND AUTHOR	THIRD AUTHOR	PAG BEG	PAG END
1.92	MAY,RG	ST	71	JAR			119	163
1.44	GRANT,EB	SP	80	JAR			255	268
0.83	HAKANSSON,NH	AP	77	TAR			396	416
0.83	JOY,OM	AU	77	JAR	LITZENBERGER,RH	MCENALLY,RW	207	225
0.71	HOPWOOD,WS	AU	82	JAR	MCKEOWN,JC	NEWBOLD,P	343	349
0.62	GREEN,D	ST	66	JAR	SEGALL,J		21	36
0.50	MCNICHOLS,M	AP	83	JAE	MANEGOLD,JG		49	74
0.38	COATES,R	ST	72	JAR			132	144
0.38	KIGER,JE	SP	72	JAR			113	128
0.23	REILLY,FK	ST	72	JAR	MORGENSON,DL	WEST,M	105	124
0.20	COLLINS,WA	AU	84	JAR	HOPWOOD,WS	MCKEOWN,JC	467	479
0.15	KIGER,JE	JA	74	TAR			1	7
0.14	WHALEY,RE	OC	82	JAE	CHEUNG,JK		57	83
0.13	ALFORD,MR	SP	81	JAA	EDMONDS,TP		255	264
0.08	BOLLOM,WJ	JA	72	TAR	WEYGANDT,JJ		75	84
0.08	BOLLOM,WJ	JA	73	TAR			12	22
0.08	BRUNS JR,WJ	ST	66	JAR			1	14
0.08	FOGELBERG,G	AU	71	JAR			215	235
0.00	CREADY,WM	SP	88	JAR			1	27
0.00	LOREK,KS	SP	83	JAR	ICERMAN,JD	ABDULKADER,AA	317	328
0.00	LOREK,KS	SP	84	JAR	BATHKE,AW		369	379
0.00	SCHACHTER,B	AU	88	JAR			353	372
0.00	TAYLOR,RG	JA	65	TAR			89	96

4.17   TREATMENTS= AMORTIZATION/DEPLETION

CITE IND-EX	FIRST AUTHOR	ISS-UE	YE-AR	JOUR -NAL	SECOND AUTHOR	THIRD AUTHOR	PAG BEG	PAG END
3.50	HOLTHAUSEN,RW	MR	81	JAE			73	109
1.86	DHALIWAL,DS	JL	82	JAE	SALAMON,GL	SMITH,ED	41	53
0.08	FALK,H	SP	77	JAR	MILLER,JC		12	22
0.00	BIERMAN JR,H	AU	64	JAR			229	235
0.00	GILLES JR,LH	OC	63	TAR			776	784
0.00	SCHACHNER,L	AP	68	TAR			303	311
0.00	WAKEMAN,LM	DE	80	JAE			213	237

TREATMENTS= AMORTIZATION/DEPLETION

4.18 TREATMENTS= SEGMENT REPORTS

CITE IND-EX	FIRST AUTHOR	ISS-UE	YE-AR	JOUR -NAL	SECOND AUTHOR	THIRD AUTHOR	PAG BEG	PAG END
0.92	KINNEY JR,WR	SP	71	JAR			127	136
0.40	BALDWIN,BA	JL	84	TAR			376	389
0.38	FOSTER,G	AU	75	JAR			283	292
0.29	HOPWOOD,WS	AU	82	JAR	NEWBOLD,P	SILHAN,PA	724	732
0.25	RONEN,J	AU	81	JAR	LIVNAT,J		459	481
0.23	DASCHER,PE	SP	71	JAR	COPELAND,RM		32	39
0.23	KOCHANEK,RF	AP	74	TAR			245	258
0.23	ORTMAN,RF	AP	75	TAR			298	304
0.20	COLLINS,DW	AU	79	JAR	SIMONDS,RR		352	383
0.08	KINNEY JR,WR	AP	72	TAR			339	345
0.00	AJINKYA,BB	AU	80	JAR			343	361
0.00	EICHENSEHER,JW	SP	85	JAA			195	209
0.00	HORWITZ,BN	AU	80	JAA	KOLODNY,R		20	35
0.00	SANNELLA,AJ	AU	86	JAA			288	304

4.19   TREATMENTS= FOREIGN CURRENCY

CITE IND-EX	FIRST AUTHOR	ISS-UE	YE-AR	JOUR-NAL	SECOND AUTHOR	THIRD AUTHOR	PAG BEG	PAG END
0.67	AYRES,FL	JN	86	JAE			143	158
0.15	ALIBER,RZ	JA	75	TAR	STICKNEY,CP		44	57
0.00	AGGARWAL,R	SP	78	JAA			197	216
0.00	AYRES,FL	SP	86	JAR			166	169
0.00	BENJAMIN,JJ	SU	86	JAA	GROSSMAN,SD	WIGGIN,CE	177	184
0.00	BROWN,BC	SU	86	JAA	BRANDI,JT		185	205
0.00	GRAY,D	AU	84	JAR			760	764
0.00	HALL,TW	SU	83	JAA			299	313
0.00	LARGAY III,JA	AU	83	JAA			44	53
0.00	ZIEBART,DA	AP	87	TAR	KIM,DH		343	357

TREATMENTS= FOREIGN CURRENCY

4.20 TREATMENTS= DIVIDENDS-CASH

CITE IND-EX	FIRST AUTHOR	ISS-UE	YE-AR	JOUR-NAL	SECOND AUTHOR	THIRD AUTHOR	PAG BEG	PAG END
1.82	GONEDES,NJ	SP	78	JAR			26	79
0.25	EASTON,PD	ST	85	JAR			54	77
0.23	COPELAND,RM	JL	68	TAR	LICASTRO,RD		540	545
0.00	KROSS,W	AU	80	JAA	CHAPMAN,G	STRAND,KH	36	46

TREATMENTS= DIVIDENDS-CASH

4.21 TREATMENTS= DIVIDENDS-STOCK

CITE IND-EX	FIRST AUTHOR	ISS-UE	YE-AR	JOUR-NAL	SECOND AUTHOR	THIRD AUTHOR	PAG BEG	PAG END
0.08	CHOTTINER,S	AU	71	JAR	YOUNG,AE		367	374
0.08	JAENICKE,HR	JA	70	TAR			115	128
0.00	DORAN,DT	SP	88	JAA	NACHTMANN,R		113	132
0.00	FIRTH,MA	SP	73	JAR			16	24
0.00	FOSTER III,TW	AP	78	TAR	VICKREY,DW		360	370
0.00	KISTLER,LH	OC	67	TAR			758	766
0.00	MILLAR,JA	JA	77	TAR			52	55
0.00	MONSON,NP	OC	64	TAR	TRACY,JA		890	893

TREATMENTS= DIVIDENDS-STOCK

4.22 TREATMENTS= PENSION (FUNDS)

CITE IND-EX	FIRST AUTHOR	ISS-UE	YE-AR	JOUR-NAL	SECOND AUTHOR	THIRD AUTHOR	PAG BEG	PAG END
0.60	DALEY,LA	AP	84	TAR			177	198
0.50	FRANCIS,JR	AP	87	JAE	REITER,SA		35	59
0.15	FRANK,WG	AP	70	TAR	WEYGANDT,JJ		280	289
0.15	O'CONNOR,MC	AP	73	TAR			339	352
0.08	HOFSTEDT,TR	AP	71	TAR	WEST,RR		329	337
0.08	MOONITZ,M	AU	66	JAR	RUSS,A		155	168
0.00	BAKER,RE	JA	64	TAR			52	61
0.00	BIERMAN JR,H	JA	68	TAR	LIU,E		62	67
0.00	DHALIWAL,DS	OC	86	TAR			651	661
0.00	ENGSTROM,JH	SP	84	JAA			197	211
0.00	HARPER JR,RM	AU	87	JAR	MISTER,WG	STRAWSER,JR	327	330
0.00	JENKINS,DO	JL	64	TAR			648	653
0.00	LANDSMAN,WR	OC	86	TAR			662	691
0.00	MAHER,JJ	OC	87	TAR			785	798
0.00	MARKS,BR	AU	85	JAR	RAMAN,KK		878	886
0.00	MORRIS,MH	SU	84	JAA	NICHOLS,WD		293	305
0.00	PESANDO,JE	OC	83	TAR	CLARKE,CK		733	748
0.00	PHILIPS,GE	JA	68	TAR			10	17
0.00	RUE,JC	SU	84	JAA	VOLKAN,AG		306	322
0.00	STONE,M	AU	87	JAR			317	326
0.00	WELSH,MJ	WI	85	JAA	TRAPNELL,JE		100	111
0.00	WERNER,CA	AU	83	JAA	KOSTOLANSKY,JW		54	64
0.00	WERNER,CA	SP	84	JAA	KOSTOLANSKY,JW		212	224
0.00	WILLINGER,GL	SP	85	JAR			351	359

4.23   TREATMENTS= OTHER -FIN.ACCGT

CITE IND-EX	FIRST AUTHOR	ISS-UE	YE-AR	JOUR-NAL	SECOND AUTHOR	THIRD AUTHOR	PAG BEG	PAG END
1.30	BEAVER,WH	JA	79	TAR	DEMSKI,JS		38	46
1.15	BOATSMAN,JR	AP	74	TAR	ROBERTSON,JC		342	352
0.85	GORDON,MJ	AP	64	TAR			251	263
0.77	IJIRI,Y	JL	66	TAR	JAEDICKE,RK		474	483
0.33	ASHTON,RH	JL	77	TAR			567	575
0.23	CHAMBERS,RJ	AP	64	TAR			264	274
0.15	LARSON,KD	JA	69	TAR			38	47
0.15	LIM,R	OC	66	TAR			642	651
0.15	VICKREY,DW	OC	70	TAR			731	742
0.15	VICKREY,DW	JA	76	TAR			31	40
0.15	WAGNER,JW	JL	65	TAR			599	605
0.08	ARNETT,HE	AP	67	TAR			291	297
0.08	BEDFORD,NM	JL	68	TAR	IINO,T		453	458
0.08	BURKE,EJ	OC	64	TAR			837	849
0.08	FREMGEN,JM	OC	68	TAR			649	656
0.08	LARSON,KD	JL	67	TAR			480	488
0.08	MCDONALD,DL	OC	67	TAR			662	679
0.08	MURPHY,GJ	AP	76	TAR			277	286
0.08	PARKER,JE	JL	75	TAR			512	524
0.08	STERLING,RR	JL	68	TAR			481	502
0.08	WOJDAK,JF	JA	70	TAR			88	97
0.00	AMIT,R	WI	88	JAA	LIVNAT,J		19	43
0.00	BIRNBERG,JG	OC	64	TAR			963	971
0.00	BOUWMAN,MJ	01	87	AOS	FRISHKOFF,PA	FRISHKOFF,P	1	30
0.00	CHAMBERS,RJ	JL	72	TAR			488	509
0.00	IJIRI,Y	JL	72	TAR			510	526
0.00	METCALF,RW	JA	64	TAR			16	21
0.00	PATTERSON,RG	OC	67	TAR			772	774
0.00	SCOTT,RA	OC	79	TAR			750	763
0.00	SPACEK,L	AP	64	TAR			275	284
0.00	THODE,SF	WI	86	JAA	DRTINA,RE	LARGAY III,JA	46	61
0.00	WILLIAMSON,JE	JA	71	TAR			139	148

4.24 TREATMENTS= FIN. STATEMENT TIMING

CITE IND- EX	FIRST AUTHOR	ISS- UE	YE- AR	JOUR -NAL	SECOND AUTHOR	THIRD AUTHOR	PAG BEG	PAG END
2.40	CHAMBERS,AE	SP	84	JAR	PENMAN,SH		21	47
1.86	GIVOLY,D	JL	82	TAR	PALMON,D		486	508
1.71	PATELL,JM	JL	82	TAR	WOLFSON,MA		509	527
0.80	KROSS,W	SP	84	JAR	SCHROEDER,DA		153	176
0.77	COPELAND,RM	ST	68	JAR			101	116
0.33	OPPONG,A	AU	80	JAR			574	584
0.31	ABDEL-KHALIK,AR	AP	74	TAR			271	283
0.00	LAWRENCE,EC	AU	83	JAR			606	610
0.00	PENMAN,SH	DE	84	JAE			165	183
0.00	WHITTRED,GP	AP	84	TAR	ZIMMER,I		287	295
0.00	WYMAN,HE	JL	76	TAR			545	558

4.25 TREATMENTS= R&D

CITE IND-EX	FIRST AUTHOR	ISS-UE	YE-AR	JOUR-NAL	SECOND AUTHOR	THIRD AUTHOR	PAG BEG	PAG END
1.44	DUKES,RE	ST	80	JAR	DYCKMAN,TR	ELLIOTT,JA	1	26
1.00	ELLIOTT,JA	SP	84	JAR	RICHARDSON,G	DYCKMAN,TR	85	102
0.83	DALEY,LA	DE	83	JAE	VIGELAND,RL		195	211
0.67	HORWITZ,BN	ST	80	JAR	KOLODNY,R		38	74
0.60	ROCKNESS,HO	02	84	AOS	SHIELDS,MD		165	177
0.38	VIGELAND,RL	AP	81	TAR			309	325
0.15	JOHNSON,O	AU	67	JAR			164	172
0.00	HIRSCHEY,M	SP	85	JAR	WEYGANDT,JJ		326	335
0.00	HORWITZ,B	JL	88	TAR	NORMOLLE,D		414	435
0.00	PRATT,J	04	85	AOS			427	442
0.00	SELTO,FH	AU	85	JAR	CLOUSE,ML		700	717

4.26 TREATMENTS= OIL & GAS

CITE IND- EX	FIRST AUTHOR	ISS- UE	YE- AR	JOUR -NAL	SECOND AUTHOR	THIRD AUTHOR	PAG BEG	PAG END
3.88	COLLINS,DW	MR	81	JAE	ROZEFF,MS	DHALIWAL,DS	37	71
3.67	FOSTER,G	MR	80	JAE			29	62
3.00	COLLINS,DW	MR	79	JAE	DENT,WT		3	44
2.40	DYCKMAN,TR	MR	79	JAE	SMITH,AJ		45	75
2.40	LEV,B	JL	79	TAR			485	503
1.29	LILIEN,S	DE	82	JAE	PASTENA,V		145	170
1.00	BELL,TB	SP	83	JAR			1	17
1.00	COLLINS,DW	JA	82	TAR	ROZEFF,MS	SALATKA,WK	1	17
1.00	DEAKIN,EB	OC	79	TAR			722	734
1.00	HARRIS,TS	OC	87	TAR	OHLSON,JA		651	670
1.00	LYS,T	AP	84	JAE			39	65
0.88	SMITH,AJ	ST	81	JAR			174	211
0.77	SUNDER,S	JA	76	TAR			1	18
0.67	LARCKER,DF	OC	83	TAR	REVSINE,L		706	732
0.67	MAGLIOLO,J	ST	86	JAR			69	111
0.40	DHARAN,BG	AP	84	TAR			199	217
0.33	LARCKER,DF	JL	83	TAR	REDER,RE	SIMON,DT	606	620
0.15	PATZ,DH	AU	72	JAR	BOATSMAN,JR		392	403
0.00	DORAN,BM	JL	88	TAR	COLLINS,DW	DHALIWAL,DS	389	413
0.00	GARSOMBKE,HP	SU	83	JAA	ALLEN,G		285	298
0.00	JAIN,PC	JL	83	TAR			633	638
0.00	JOHNSON,WB	JA	88	TAR	RAMANAN,R		96	110
0.00	KING,RD	JA	86	TAR	O'KEEFE,TB		76	90
0.00	WAYMIRE,G	AU	83	JAR	POWNALL,G		629	643

4.27 TREATMENTS= AUDITING

CITE IND-EX	FIRST AUTHOR	ISS-UE	YE-AR	JOUR -NAL	SECOND AUTHOR	THIRD AUTHOR	PAG BEG	PAG END
1.14	CHOW,CW	AP	82	TAR			272	291
0.64	NG,DS	OC	78	TAR			910	920
0.62	DEMSKI,JS	JL	74	TAR	SWIERINGA,RJ		506	513
0.60	NG,DS	ST	79	JAR	STOECKENIUS,J		1	24
0.57	DANOS,P	JA	82	TAR	IMHOFF JR,EA		39	54
0.57	GIBBINS,M	JA	82	TAR	WOLF,FM		105	124
0.50	BABER,WR	DE	83	JAE			213	227
0.40	MCCONNELL,DK	WI	84	JAA			178	181
0.33	EVANS III,JH	ST	80	JAR			108	128
0.33	EVANS III,JH	ST	80	JAR			108	128
0.33	NICHOLS,DR	AU	83	JAR	SMITH,DB		534	544
0.31	RHODE,JG	OC	74	TAR	WHITSELL,GM	KELSEY,RL	772	787
0.31	SUMMERS,EL	JL	72	TAR			443	453
0.31	ZEFF,SA	AP	67	TAR	FOSSUM,RL		298	320
0.25	SCOTT,WR	SP	77	JAR			120	137
0.23	NICHOLS,DR	AP	76	TAR	PRICE,KH		335	346
0.23	TOBA,Y	JA	75	TAR			7	24
0.23	WILL,HJ	OC	74	TAR			690	706
0.22	BALACHANDRAN,BV	ST	80	JAR	RAMAKRISHNAN,RT		140	171
0.15	ANDERSON,HM	JL	70	TAR	GIESE,J	BOOKER,J	524	531
0.15	BRILOFF,AJ	JL	66	TAR			484	495
0.15	CHURCHILL,NC	OC	65	TAR	COOPER,WW		767	781
0.15	DECOSTER,DT	OC	71	TAR	RHODE,JG		651	664
0.15	LENGERMANN,JJ	OC	71	TAR			665	675
0.15	ROBERTSON,JC	JL	71	TAR	CLARKE,RW		562	571
0.15	SMITH,CH	AP	72	TAR	LANIER,RA	TAYLOR,ME	270	283
0.15	STERLING,RR	SP	69	JAR	RADOSEVICH,R		90	95
0.15	WELKER,RB	JL	74	TAR			514	523
0.14	BALACHANDRAN,KR	JA	82	TAR	STEUER,RE		125	140
0.09	GIVOLY,D	SU	78	JAA	RONEN,J	SCHIFF,A	361	372
0.08	CHURCHILL,NC	ST	66	JAR			128	156
0.08	SAN MIGUEL,JG	04	77	AOS	SHANK,JK	GOVINDARAJAN,V	333	348
0.08	WILKINSON,JR	OC	65	TAR	DONEY,LD		753	756
0.00	ARRINGTON,CE	SP	85	JAR	BAILEY,CD	HOPWOOD,WS	1	20
0.00	BERRY,LE	JA	87	TAR	HARWOOD,GB	KATZ,JL	14	28
0.00	CAREY,JL	JA	68	TAR			1	9
0.00	CARMICHAEL,DR	SU	79	JAA			294	306
0.00	CHARNES,A	01	80	AOS	COOPER,WW		87	107
0.00	COHEN,MF	JA	65	TAR			1	8
0.00	DAVIS,GB	SP	63	JAR			96	101
0.00	DEITRICK,JW	SU	79	JAA	ALDERMAN,CW		316	328
0.00	DIRSMITH,MW	SP	82	JAA	MCALLISTER,JP		214	228
0.00	DIRSMITH,MW	AU	82	JAA	MCALLISTER,JP		60	74
0.00	GIBSON,RW	JA	65	TAR			196	203
0.00	HAFNER,GF	OC	64	TAR			979	982
0.00	IJIRI,Y	OC	68	TAR			662	667
0.00	JIAMBALVO,J	AU	85	AUD	WILNER,N		1	11
0.00	KAY,RS	SU	79	JAA			307	315

TREATMENTS= AUDITING

CITE IND- EX	FIRST AUTHOR	ISS- UE	YE- AR	JOUR -NAL	SECOND AUTHOR	THIRD AUTHOR	PAG BEG	PAG END
0.00	KNAPP,MC	JL	87	TAR			578	588
0.00	MARKS,BR	AU	87	AUD	RAMAN,KK		106	117
0.00	MCCONNELL,DK	SP	84	AUD			44	56
0.00	MOREY,L	JA	63	TAR			102	108
0.00	RAMAN,KK	SU	81	JAA			352	359
0.00	SEIDLER,LJ	SU	79	JAA			285	293
0.00	STAATS,EB	SU	81	AUD			1	11
0.00	SWANSON,GA	JL	88	TAR	GARDNER,JC		436	447
0.00	VASARHELYI,MA	AU	84	AUD			100	106
0.00	WILCOX,KA	01	77	AOS	SMITH,CH		81	97
0.00	WRIGHT,A	SP	82	JAR			227	239

TREATMENTS= AUDITING

4.28 TREATMENTS= OPINION

CITE INDEX	FIRST AUTHOR	ISSUE	YEAR	JOURNAL	SECOND AUTHOR	THIRD AUTHOR	PAG BEG	PAG END
1.60	DODD,P	AP	84	JAE	DOPUCH,N	HOLTHAUSEN,RW	3	38
1.00	ELLIOTT,JA	AU	82	JAR			617	638
0.80	LIBBY,R	SP	79	JAR			99	122
0.78	WHITTRED,GP	OC	80	TAR			563	577
0.75	MUTCHLER,JF	AU	85	JAR			668	682
0.71	CHOW,CW	AP	82	TAR	RICE,SJ		326	335
0.70	LIBBY,R	ST	79	JAR			35	57
0.55	FIRTH,MA	JL	78	TAR			642	650
0.50	DOPUCH,N	JL	87	TAR	HOLTHAUSEN,RW	LEFTWICH,RW	431	454
0.43	CHOW,CW	WI	82	AUD	RICE,SJ		35	53
0.36	SHANK,JK	OC	78	TAR	MURDOCK,RJ		824	835
0.33	DOPUCH,N	JN	86	JAE	HOLTHAUSEN,RW	LEFTWICH,RW	93	118
0.33	KELLER,SB	AU	83	AUD	DAVIDSON,LF		1	22
0.33	KIDA,TE	AU	80	JAR			506	523
0.33	SMITH,DB	AU	86	AUD			95	108
0.31	WARREN,CS	SP	75	JAR			162	176
0.29	DAVIS,RR	AU	82	AUD			13	32
0.20	MUTCHLER,JF	SP	84	AUD			17	30
0.08	CLARKE,RW	OC	68	TAR			769	776
0.08	KINNEY JR,WR	SP	69	JAR			44	52
0.08	KISSINGER,JN	AP	77	TAR			322	339
0.00	ABDEL-KHALIK,AR	AU	86	JAR	GRAUL,PR	NEWTON,JD	372	382
0.00	BAILEY,KE	AU	83	JAR	BYLINSKI,JH	SHIELDS,MD	355	370
0.00	BAILEY,WT	OC	81	TAR			882	896
0.00	DANOS,P	SP	87	AUD	HOLT,DL	BAILEY JR,AD	134	149
0.00	JOHNSON,DA	SP	83	AUD	PANY,K	WHITE,RA	38	51
0.00	KNAPP,MC	AP	85	TAR			202	211
0.00	LEVITAN,AS	AU	85	AUD	KNOBLETT,JA		26	39
0.00	MUTCHLER,JF	AU	86	AUD			148	
0.00	NIX,HM	SU	83	JAA	WICHMANN JR,H		341	352
0.00	NORGAARD,CT	JL	72	TAR			433	442
0.00	PANY,K	AU	82	JAR	SMITH,CH		472	481
0.00	PILLSBURY,CM	SP	85	AUD			63	79
0.00	TOBA,Y	OC	80	TAR			604	619
0.00	WARREN,CS	SP	80	JAR			312	324

TREATMENTS= OPINION

4.29 TREATMENTS= SAMPLING

CITE IND-EX	FIRST AUTHOR	ISS-UE	YE-AR	JOUR-NAL	SECOND AUTHOR	THIRD AUTHOR	PAG BEG	PAG END
1.46	KAPLAN,RS	AU	73	JAR			238	258
1.31	CORLESS,JC	JL	72	TAR			556	566
1.17	FELIX JR,WL	SP	77	JAR	GRIMLUND,RA		23	41
1.08	SCOTT,WR	AU	73	JAR			304	330
1.00	KINNEY JR,WR	ST	75	JAR			14	29
0.92	KINNEY JR,WR	SP	75	JAR			117	132
0.86	LEITCH,RA	AP	82	TAR	NETER,J	PLANTE,R	384	400
0.85	KAPLAN,RS	SP	73	JAR			38	46
0.83	UECKER,WC	03	77	AOS	KINNEY JR,WR		269	275
0.82	NETER,J	JA	78	TAR	LEITCH,RA	FIENBERG,SE	77	93
0.71	GRIMLUND,RA	AU	82	JAR			316	342
0.70	GARSTKA,SJ	SP	79	JAR	OHLSON,PA		23	59
0.69	SCOTT,WR	ST	75	JAR			98	117
0.60	DWORIN,L	AP	84	TAR	GRIMLUND,RA		218	241
0.60	MCCRAY,JH	JA	84	TAR			35	51
0.57	FROST,PA	SP	82	JAR	TAMURA,H		103	120
0.55	RENEAU,JH	JL	78	TAR			669	680
0.54	SORENSEN,JE	JL	69	TAR			555	561
0.54	TRACY,JA	JA	69	TAR			90	98
0.50	TSUI,KW	JA	85	TAR	MATSUMURA,EM	TSUI,KL	76	96
0.46	DEAKIN,EB	OC	74	TAR	GRANOF,MH		764	771
0.40	GODFREY,JT	AU	84	JAR	NETER,J		497	525
0.40	KINNEY JR,WR	AU	79	JAR			456	475
0.38	IJIRI,Y	SP	71	JAR	KAPLAN,RS		73	87
0.38	KAPLAN,RS	ST	75	JAR			126	133
0.33	DWORIN,L	JA	86	TAR	GRIMLUND,RA		36	57
0.33	MENZEFRICKE,U	SP	83	JAR			96	105
0.33	ROBERTS,DM	SP	86	JAR			111	126
0.33	TAMURA,H	AU	86	JAR	FROST,PA		364	371
0.29	GODFREY,JT	AU	82	JAR	ANDREWS,RW		304	315
0.25	GARSTKA,SJ	AU	77	JAR			179	192
0.20	NETER,J	AU	84	AUD	KIM,HS	GRAHAM,LE	75	88
0.17	HEIMANN,SR	AU	77	JAR	CHESLEY,GR		193	206
0.15	SMITH,KA	AP	72	TAR			260	269
0.15	TEITLEBAUM,AD	ST	75	JAR	ROBINSON,CF		70	91
0.14	MATSUMURA,EM	SP	82	JAR	TSUI,KW		162	170
0.08	ALY,HF	JA	71	TAR	DUBOFF,JI		119	128
0.08	LOEBBECKE,JK	ST	75	JAR	NETER,J		38	52
0.08	SAULS,EH	ST	70	JAR			157	171
0.08	SAULS,EH	JA	72	TAR			109	115
0.00	ABDOLMOHAM.,MJ	SP	86	AUD			1	16
0.00	ANDERSON,JC	JL	86	TAR	KRAUSHAAR,JM		379	399
0.00	BECK,PJ	SP	85	AUD	SOLOMON,I		1	10
0.00	BLOCHER,E	AU	85	AUD	BYLINSKI,JH		79	90
0.00	CHARNES,A	AP	64	TAR	DAVIDSON,HJ	KORTANEK,KO	241	250
0.00	CROSBY,MA	SP	85	AUD			118	132
0.00	DEMING,WE	SP	79	JAA			197	208
0.00	FINLEY,DR	AU	83	AUD			104	116

CITE IND-EX	FIRST AUTHOR	ISS-UE	YE-AR	JOUR-NAL	SECOND AUTHOR	THIRD AUTHOR	PAG BEG	PAG END
0.00	FINLEY,DR	SP	87	AUD	BOOCKHOLDT,JL		22	39
0.00	FROST,PA	SP	86	JAR	TAMURA,H		57	75
0.00	GRIMLUND,RA	JL	87	TAR	FELIX JR,WL		455	479
0.00	GRIMLUND,RA	SP	88	AUD			77	104
0.00	GRIMLUND,RA	AU	88	AUD	SCHROEDER,MS		53	62
0.00	HANSEN,DR	JA	77	TAR	SHAFTEL,TL		109	123
0.00	HUSS,HF	AU	86	JAR	TRADER,RL		394	399
0.00	KIM,HS	SP	87	AUD	NETER,J	GODFREY,JT	40	58
0.00	KO,CE	SP	88	AUD	NACHTSHEIM,CJ	DUKE,GL	119	136
0.00	MAXIM,LD	JA	76	TAR	CULLEN,PE	COOK,FX	97	109
0.00	PLANTE,R	AU	85	AUD	NETER,J	LEITCH,RA	40	56
0.00	ROBERTS,DM	AU	80	JAA			57	69
0.00	ROHRBACH.KJ	SP	86	JAR			127	150
0.00	ROSHWALB,A	AU	87	AUD	WRIGHT,RL	GODFREY,JT	54	70
0.00	SMIELIAUSKAS,W	JA	86	TAR			118	128
0.00	SMIELIAUSKAS,W	SP	86	JAR			217	230
0.00	TAMURA,H	SP	85	AUD			133	142

TREATMENTS= SAMPLING

4.30 TREATMENTS= LIABILITY

CITE IND-EX	FIRST AUTHOR	ISS-UE	YE-AR	JOUR -NAL	SECOND AUTHOR	THIRD AUTHOR	PAG BEG	PAG END
0.64	SCHULTZ JR,JJ	JL	78	TAR	GUSTAVSON,SG		626	641
0.60	MATOLCSY,ZP	AU	84	JAR			555	569
0.60	MENZEFRICKE,U	AU	84	JAR	SMIELIAUSKAS,W		588	604
0.40	ST.PIERRE,K	AP	84	TAR	ANDERSON,JA		242	263
0.17	ANDERSON,JA	AP	77	TAR			417	426
0.15	CAUSEY JR,DY	JA	76	TAR			19	30
0.08	THEIL,H	JA	69	TAR			27	37
0.00	DEJONG,DV	AU	84	AUD	SMITH,JH		20	34
0.00	DOPUCH,N	SU	88	JAA			245	250
0.00	GOLDWASSER,DL	SU	88	JAA			217	232
0.00	GORMLEY,RJ	SU	88	JAA			185	212
0.00	LILLESTOL,J	SP	81	JAR			263	267
0.00	MENZEFRICKE,U	AU	84	JAR			570	587
0.00	NELSON,J	SU	88	JAA	RONEN,J	WHITE,L	255	296
0.00	SCHNEPPER,JA	JL	77	TAR			653	657
0.00	SLAVIN,NS	AP	77	TAR			360	368
0.00	SORTER,GH	SU	88	JAA	SIEGEL,S	SLAIN,J	233	244
0.00	WALLACE,WA	SP	83	AUD			66	90

4.31 TREATMENTS= RISK

CITE IND-EX	FIRST AUTHOR	ISS-UE	YE-AR	JOUR -NAL	SECOND AUTHOR	THIRD AUTHOR	PAG BEG	PAG END
0.67	CUSHING,BE	AU	83	AUD	LOEBBECKE,JK		23	41
0.67	KINNEY JR,WR	SP	83	AUD			13	22
0.25	BECK,PJ	SP	85	JAR	SOLOMON,I	TOMASSINI,LA	37	56
0.00	BARKMAN,A	JA	77	TAR			450	464
0.00	BUTLER,SA	JA	86	TAR			101	111
0.00	DANIEL,SJ	SP	88	AUD			174	181
0.00	GORMLEY,RJ	SU	80	JAA			293	312
0.00	GROBSTEIN,M	SP	84	AUD	CRAIG,PW		1	16
0.00	JIAMBALVO,J	SP	84	AUD	WALLER,WS		80	88
0.00	SMIELIAUSKAS,W	AU	85	JAR			718	739

TREATMENTS= RISK

4.32   TREATMENTS= INDEPENDENCE

CITE IND-EX	FIRST AUTHOR	ISS-UE	YE-AR	JOUR-NAL	SECOND AUTHOR	THIRD AUTHOR	PAG BEG	PAG END
1.25	DEANGELO,LE	AG	81	JAE			113	127
0.40	ANTLE,R	SP	84	JAR			1	20
0.38	LAVIN,D	JA	76	TAR			41	50
0.38	SHOCKLEY,RA	OC	81	TAR			785	800
0.23	GOLDMAN,A	OC	74	TAR	BARLEV,B		707	718
0.22	PANY,K	JA	80	TAR	RECKERS,PMJ		50	61
0.20	SIMUNIC,DA	AU	84	JAR			679	702
0.17	LAVIN,D	03	77	AOS			237	244
0.15	SCHULTE JR,AA	JL	65	TAR			587	593
0.14	SHOCKLEY,RA	WI	82	JAA			126	143
0.13	RECKERS,PMJ	SU	81	AUD	STAGLIANO,AJ		23	37
0.11	FIRTH,MA	JL	80	TAR			451	466
0.00	CARMICHAEL,DR	OC	68	TAR	SWIERINGA,RJ		697	705
0.00	DYKXHOORN,HJ	JA	81	TAR	SINNING,KE		97	107
0.00	DYKXHOORN,HJ	04	82	AOS	SINNING,KE		337	348
0.00	FARMER,TA	AU	87	AUD	RITTENBERG,LE	TROMPETER,GM	1	14
0.00	IMHOFF JR,EA	OC	78	TAR			869	881
0.00	KELL,WG	AP	68	TAR			266	273
0.00	PANY,K	SP	84	AUD	RECKERS,PMJ		89	97
0.00	PANY,K	AU	87	AUD	RECKERS,PMJ		39	53
0.00	SCHULTE JR,AA	OC	66	TAR			721	728
0.00	ST.PIERRE,K	SP	84	JAA			257	263

4.33   TREATMENTS= ANALYTICAL REVIEW

CITE IND-EX	FIRST AUTHOR	ISS-UE	YE-AR	JOUR-NAL	SECOND AUTHOR	THIRD AUTHOR	PAG BEG	PAG END
1.25	LIBBY,R	AU	85	JAR			648	667
1.20	KINNEY JR,WR	ST	79	JAR			148	165
1.00	STRINGER,KW	ST	75	JAR			1	9
0.91	KINNEY JR,WR	JA	78	TAR			48	60
0.57	KINNEY JR,WR	JA	82	TAR	UECKER,WC		55	69
0.44	LEV,B	AU	80	JAR			524	550
0.40	BIGGS,SF	SP	84	AUD	WILD,JJ		68	79
0.25	BIGGS,SF	OC	85	TAR	WILD,JJ		607	633
0.17	BLOCHER,E	AU	83	AUD	ESPOSITO,RS	WILLINGHAM,JJ	75	91
0.17	HOLDER,WW	SP	83	AUD			100	108
0.14	KINNEY JR,WR	AU	82	JAR	SALAMON,GL		350	366
0.00	ARRINGTON,CE	SP	84	JAR	HILLISON,WA	JENSEN,RE	298	312
0.00	BIGGS,SF	JA	88	TAR	MOCK,TJ	WATKINS,PR	148	162
0.00	BLOCHER,E	SP	88	AUD	COOPER,JC		1	28
0.00	COGLITORE,F	SP	88	AUD	BERRYMAN,RG		150	163
0.00	DAROCA,FP	SP	85	AUD	HOLDER,WW		80	92
0.00	DUGAN,MT	SP	85	AUD	GENTRY,JA	SHRIVER,KA	11	22
0.00	IMHOFF JR,EA	SU	81	JAA			333	351
0.00	KAPLAN,RS	SP	83	AUD			52	65
0.00	KINNEY JR,WR	AU	81	JAA			5	17
0.00	KINNEY JR,WR	SP	87	AUD			59	73
0.00	KNECHEL,WR	JA	88	TAR			74	95
0.00	KNECHEL,WR	AU	88	AUD			87	107
0.00	LOEBBECKE,JK	SP	87	AUD	STEINBART,PJ		74	89
0.00	TABOR,RH	SP	85	AUD	WILLIS,JT		93	109

TREATMENTS= ANALYTICAL REVIEW

4.34　TREATMENTS= INTERNAL CONTROL

CITE INDEX	FIRST AUTHOR	ISS-UE	YE-AR	JOUR-NAL	SECOND AUTHOR	THIRD AUTHOR	PAG BEG	PAG END
2.62	ASHTON,RH	SP	74	JAR			143	157
0.83	BIGGS,SF	SP	83	JAR	MOCK,TJ		234	255
0.67	NEIMARK,M	45	86	AOS	TINKER,T		369	396
0.62	CUSHING,BE	JA	74	TAR			24	41
0.62	YU,S	AU	73	JAR	NETER,J		273	295
0.50	LIBBY,R	AP	85	TAR	ARTMAN,JT	WILLINGHAM,JJ	212	230
0.43	HAMILTON,RE	AU	82	JAR	WRIGHT,WF		756	765
0.38	BODNAR,G	OC	75	TAR			747	757
0.38	CARMICHAEL,DR	AP	70	TAR			235	245
0.30	RECKERS,PMJ	AU	79	JAA	TAYLOR,ME		42	55
0.27	WEBER,R	FL	78	JAR			368	388
0.20	FERRIS,KR	SP	84	AUD	TENNANT,KL		31	43
0.20	NANNI JR,AJ	02	84	AOS			149	163
0.18	WEBER,R	AU	78	JAR			368	388
0.17	TABOR,RH	SP	83	JAR			348	354
0.14	GAUMNITZ,BR	AU	82	JAR	NUNAMAKER,TR	SURDICK,JJ	745	755
0.13	BAILEY,AP	SU	81	AUD	MCAFEE,RP	WHINSTON,AB	38	52
0.11	ASHTON,RH	SP	80	JAR	BROWN,PR		269	277
0.08	MAUTZ,RK	AP	66	TAR	MINI,DL		283	291
0.00	BABER,WR	SP	85	JAR			360	369
0.00	BAILEY JR,AD	AP	85	TAR	DUKE,GL	GERLACH,JH	186	201
0.00	BALACHANDRAN,BV	WI	88	JAA	RAMANAN,R		1	13
0.00	BOWER,JB	AP	65	TAR	SCHLOSSER,RE		338	344
0.00	DAS,H	03	86	AOS			215	232
0.00	DERMER,JD	06	86	AOS	LUCAS,RG		471	482
0.00	EVANS III,JH	06	86	AOS	LEWIS,BL	PATTON,JM	483	498
0.00	FELIX JR,WL	SP	88	AUD	NILES,MS		43	60
0.00	FISHER,M	SU	78	JAA			349	360
0.00	GERLACH,JH	SP	88	AUD			61	76
0.00	HASKINS,M	JL	87	TAR			542	563
0.00	KAPLAN,SE	AU	85	JAR			871	877
0.00	KNECHEL,WR	SP	85	AUD			38	62
0.00	MCBRIDE,HJ	AP	63	TAR			363	370
0.00	MESERVY,RD	AU	86	AUD	BAILEY JR,AD	JOHNSON,PE	44	74
0.00	MOCK,TJ	SP	83	AUD	WILLINGHAM,JJ		91	99
0.00	NICHOLS,DR	JA	87	TAR			183	190
0.00	SRINIDHI,BN	SP	86	AUD	VASARHELYI,MA		64	76
0.00	SRIVASTAVA,RP	AU	86	JAR			422	427
0.00	YOUNG,R	SP	86	JAR			231	240
0.00	ZANNETOS,ZS	OC	64	TAR			860	868

4.35 TREATMENTS= TIMING

CITE IND- EX	FIRST AUTHOR	ISS- UE	YE- AR	JOUR -NAL	SECOND AUTHOR	THIRD AUTHOR	PAG BEG	PAG END
0.46	DYER,JC	AU	75	JAR	MCHUGH,AJ		204	219
0.17	HUGHES,JS	JA	77	TAR			56	68
0.00	ANDERSON,U	AU	88	AUD	YOUNG,RA		23	42
0.00	ASHTON,RH	AU	87	JAR	WILLINGHAM,JJ	ELLIOTT,RK	275	292
0.00	KISSINGER,JN	AU	83	AUD			42	54

TREATMENTS= TIMING

4.36 TREATMENTS= MATERIALITY

CITE IND-EX	FIRST AUTHOR	ISS-UE	YE-AR	JOUR-NAL	SECOND AUTHOR	THIRD AUTHOR	PAG BEG	PAG END
0.92	MORIARITY,S	AU	76	JAR	BARRON,FH		320	341
0.77	ROSE,R	ST	70	JAR	BEAVER,WH	BECKER,S	138	148
0.70	MORIARITY,S	ST	79	JAR	BARRON,FH		114	135
0.67	MESSIER JR,WF	AU	83	JAR			611	618
0.62	FRISHKOFF,P	ST	70	JAR			116	129
0.54	WARD,BH	SP	76	JAR			138	152
0.46	NEUMANN,FL	ST	68	JAR			1	17
0.40	KROGSTAD,JL	AU	84	AUD	ETTENSON,RT	SHANTEAU,J	54	74
0.38	BERNSTEIN,LA	JA	67	TAR			86	95
0.30	FIRTH,MA	04	79	AOS			283	296
0.25	KELLY,LK	JA	77	TAR			97	108
0.08	HICKS,EL	AU	64	JAR			158	171
0.08	KELLY,LK	JA	77	TAR			97	108
0.00	HOLSTRUM,GL	AU	82	AUD	MESSIER JR,WF		45	63
0.00	JENNINGS,M	SP	87	AUD	KNEER,DC	RECKERS,PMJ	104	115
0.00	LANDSITTEL,DL	SU	82	JAA	SERLIN,JE		291	300
0.00	MAYPER,AG	AU	82	JAR			773	783
0.00	MORRIS,MH	AP	88	TAR	NICHOLS,WD		237	254
0.00	STEINBART,PJ	JA	87	TAR			97	116
0.00	WRIGHT,GB	SU	82	JAA	TAYLOR,RD		301	309

4.37 TREATMENTS= EDP AUDIT

CITE IND-EX	FIRST AUTHOR	ISS-UE	YE-AR	JOUR-NAL	SECOND AUTHOR	THIRD AUTHOR	PAG BEG	PAG END
0.00	BIGGS,SF	SP	87	AUD	MESSIER JR,WF	HANSEN,JV	1	21
0.00	DAVIS,GB	SP	86	AUD	WEBER,R		35	49
0.00	DOWELL,CD	AU	81	JAA	HALL,JA		30	40
0.00	HANSEN,JV	AU	86	AUD	MESSIER JR,WF		109	123
0.00	LOVATA,LM	AU	88	AUD			72	86
0.00	VASARHELYI,MA	SP	84	AUD	BAILEY JR,AD	CAMARDESSE JR,JE	98	103
0.00	WAGNER,JW	JL	69	TAR			600	604
0.00	WILLIAMS,DJ	SP	85	AUD	LILLIS,A		110	117

TREATMENTS= EDP AUDIT

4.38 TREATMENTS= ORGANIZATON

CITE IND- EX	FIRST AUTHOR	ISS- UE	YE- AR	JOUR -NAL	SECOND AUTHOR	THIRD AUTHOR	PAG BEG	PAG END
1.00	RUBIN,MA	AP	88	TAR			219	236
0.88	EICHENSEHER,JW	JL	81	TAR	DANOS,P		479	492
0.67	RHODE,JG	02	77	AOS	SORENSEN,JE	LAWLER III,EE	165	176
0.60	FRANCIS,JR	AG	84	JAE			133	151
0.50	FRANCIS,JR	JA	87	TAR	SIMON,DT		145	157
0.50	SHOCKLEY,RA	AU	83	JAR	HOLT,RN		545	564
0.43	DANOS,P	AU	82	JAR	EICHENSEHER,JW		604	616
0.38	WATSON,DJ	AP	75	TAR			259	273
0.33	EICHENSEHER,JW	SP	83	AUD	SHIELDS,D		23	37
0.33	SENATRA,PT	OC	80	TAR			594	603
0.31	KILLOUGH,LN	AP	73	TAR	SOUDERS,TL		268	279
0.30	BLOCHER,E	JL	79	TAR			563	573
0.25	WALLER,WS	AU	85	JAR			817	828
0.22	BENKE,RL	02	80	AOS	RHODE,JG		187	202
0.17	FERRIS,KR	01	83	AOS	LARCKER,DF		1	12
0.17	JIAMBALVO,J	01	83	AOS	WATSON,DJ	BAUMLER,JV	13	30
0.15	WATSON,DJ	AP	75	TAR			259	273
0.14	JIAMBALVO,J	OC	82	TAR	PRATT,J		734	750
0.13	DILLARD,JF	01	81	AOS			17	26
0.13	WOLF,FM	OC	81	TAR			861	881
0.08	SCHROEDER,RG	01	77	AOS	IMDIEKE,LF		39	46
0.00	BABER,WR	AU	87	JAR	BROOKS,EH	RICKS,WE	293	305
0.00	BALACHANDRAN,BV	SP	87	JAR	RAMAKRISHNAN,RT		111	126
0.00	BALLEW,V	JA	82	TAR			88	104
0.00	BAO,BH	03	86	AOS	BAO,DH	VASARHELYI,MA	289	296
0.00	BULLEN,ML	03	85	AOS	FLAMHOLTZ,EG		287	302
0.00	BURTON,JC	WI	82	AUD	FAIRFIELD,P		1	22
0.00	CHAN,KH	OC	86	TAR	DODIN,B		726	734
0.00	DIRSMITH,MW	AU	85	JAA	COVALESKI,MA		5	21
0.00	DIRSMITH,MW	02	85	AOS	COVALESKI,MA		149	170
0.00	FERRIS,KR	01	82	AOS			13	26
0.00	FIRTH,MA	SP	85	AUD			23	37
0.00	FRANCIS,JR	OC	88	TAR	WILSON,PR		663	682
0.00	GLEZEN,GW	AU	85	JAR	MILLAR,JA		859	870
0.00	IMHOFF JR,EA	SP	88	AUD			182	191
0.00	LEA,RB	SU	81	AUD			53	94
0.00	LIGHTNER,SM	AU	82	AUD	ADAMS,SJ	LIGHTNER,KM	1	12
0.00	MARGHEIM,LL	SP	86	AUD	PANY,K		50	63
0.00	MARGHEIM,LL	SP	86	JAR			194	205
0.00	MCKINELY,S	AU	85	JAR	PANY,K	RECKERS,PMJ	887	896
0.00	MOIZER,P	AU	87	AUD	TURLEY,S		118	123
0.00	PALMROSE,ZV	AU	88	AUD			63	71
0.00	RABY,WL	OC	66	TAR			714	720
0.00	ROBERTSON,JC	WI	81	JAA	ALDERMAN,CW		144	161
0.00	SIMON,DT	AU	85	AUD			71	78
0.00	SIMON,DT	AP	88	TAR	FRANCIS,JR		255	269
0.00	SUMNERS,GE	SP	87	AUD	WHITE,RA	CLAY JR,RJ	116	122
0.00	WRIGHT,A	JL	83	TAR			621	632

TREATMENTS= ORGANIZATON

CITE IND-EX	FIRST AUTHOR	ISS-UE	YE-AR	JOUR-NAL	SECOND AUTHOR	THIRD AUTHOR	PAG BEG	PAG END
0.00	WYER,JC	SP	88	AUD	WHITE,GT	JANSON,EC	164	173

TREATMENTS= ORGANIZATON

4.39 TREATMENTS= INTERNAL AUDIT

CITE IND-EX	FIRST AUTHOR	ISS-UE	YE-AR	JOUR -NAL	SECOND AUTHOR	THIRD AUTHOR	PAG BEG	PAG END
0.25	PLUMLEE,RD	AU	85	JAR			683	699
0.00	ABDEL-KHALIK,AR	AP	83	TAR	SNOWBALL,D	WRAGGE,JH	215	227
0.00	BORITZ,JE	AU	86	AUD	BROCA,DS		1	19
0.00	BROWN,PR	AU	83	JAR			444	455
0.00	BROWN,PR	AU	86	AUD	KARAN,V		134	147
0.00	BUCHMAN,TA	AU	83	AUD			92	103
0.00	BURGHER,PH	JA	64	TAR			103	120
0.00	SAN MIGUEL,JG	02	84	AOS	GOVINDARAJAN,V		179	188
0.00	SCHNEIDER,A	AU	84	JAR			657	678
0.00	SCHNEIDER,A	AU	85	JAR			911	919
0.00	WEYGANDT,JJ	JA	70	TAR			69	75

4.40   TREATMENTS= ERRORS

CITE IND- EX	FIRST AUTHOR	ISS- UE	YE- AR	JOUR -NAL	SECOND AUTHOR	THIRD AUTHOR	PAG BEG	PAG END
1.75	JOHNSON,JR	AP	81	TAR	LEITCH,RA	NETER,J	270	293
1.14	DUKE,GL	SP	82	JAR	NETER,J	LEITCH,RA	42	67
0.90	RAMAGE,JG	ST	79	JAR	KRIEGER,AM	SPERO,LL	72	102
0.86	HYLAS,RE	OC	82	TAR	ASHTON,RH		751	765
0.50	HAM,J	JL	85	TAR	LOSELL,D	SMIELIAUSKAS,W	387	406
0.14	JIAMBALVO,J	SP	82	JAR			152	161
0.00	ALDERMAN,CW	WI	82	AUD	DEITRICK,JW		54	68
0.00	BURGSTAHLER,D	AP	86	TAR	JIAMBALVO,J		233	248
0.00	KNECHEL,WR	SP	85	JAR			194	212
0.00	KREUTZFELDT,RW	AU	86	AUD	WALLACE,WA		20	43
0.00	ST.PIERRE,K	SP	82	JAA	ANDERSON,JA		229	247
0.00	WILLINGHAM,JJ	AU	85	AUD	WRIGHT,WF		57	70

TREATMENTS= ERRORS

4.41 TREATMENTS= TRAIL

CITE IND-EX	FIRST AUTHOR	ISS-UE	YE-AR	JOUR-NAL	SECOND AUTHOR	THIRD AUTHOR	PAG BEG	PAG END
0.14	WEBER,R	AP	82	TAR			311	325
0.00	HARRELL,AM	SP	86	AUD	CHEWNING,EG	TAYLOR,M	111	121

4.42   TREATMENTS= JUDGMENT

CITE IND-EX	FIRST AUTHOR	ISS-UE	YE-AR	JOUR-NAL	SECOND AUTHOR	THIRD AUTHOR	PAG BEG	PAG END
1.60	GIBBINS,M	SP	84	JAR			103	125
1.38	DEANGELO,LE	DE	81	JAE			183	199
0.78	LEWIS,BL	AU	80	JAR			594	602
0.40	WALLER,WS	OC	84	TAR	FELIX JR,WL		637	646
0.33	FREDERICK,DM	AU	86	JAR	LIBBY,R		270	290
0.25	TROTMAN,KT	AU	85	JAR			740	752
0.17	DANOS,P	AU	83	JAR	IMHOFF JR,EA		473	494
0.00	ABDOLMOHAM.,MJ	JA	87	TAR	WRIGHT,A		1	13
0.00	ASHTON,AH	OC	88	TAR	ASHTON,RH		623	641
0.00	BAMBER,EM	AU	83	JAR			396	412
0.00	BAMBER,EM	JL	88	AUD	SNOWBALL,D		490	504
0.00	BUTT,JL	AU	88	JAR			315	330
0.00	COLBERT,JL	02	88	AOS			111	121
0.00	HOLT,DL	06	87	AOS			571	578
0.00	KIDA,TE	SP	84	JAR			332	340
0.00	MEIXNER,WF	JL	88	AUD	WELKER,RB		505	513
0.00	MESSIER JR,WF	AU	87	AUD	HANSEN,JV		94	105
0.00	REBELE,JE	AU	88	AUD	HEINTZ,JA	BRIDEN,GE	43	52
0.00	RECKERS,PMJ	AU	82	AUD	SCHULTZ JR,JJ		64	74
0.00	STEPHENS,RG	AU	83	AUD			55	74
0.00	TROTMAN,KT	SP	85	JAR	YETTON,PW		256	267
0.00	WALLER,WS	AP	87	TAR	FELIX JR,WL		275	292

4.43 TREATMENTS= PLANNING

CITE IND- EX	FIRST AUTHOR	ISS- UE	YE- AR	JOUR -NAL	SECOND AUTHOR	THIRD AUTHOR	PAG BEG	PAG END
2.38	JOYCE,EJ	ST	76	JAR			29	60
1.13	JOYCE,EJ	AU	81	JAR	BIDDLE,GC		323	349
0.20	CUSHING,BE	ST	79	JAR	SEARFOSS,DG	RANDALL,RH	172	216
0.00	BORITZ,JE	AU	86	JAR			335	348
0.00	FELLINGHAM,JC	OC	85	TAR	NEWMAN,DP		634	650
0.00	KAPLAN,SE	AU	84	AUD	RECKERS,PMJ		1	19
0.00	KAPLAN,SE	AU	85	AUD			12	25
0.00	LIN,WT	AU	84	AUD	MOCK,TJ	WRIGHT,A	89	99
0.00	WRIGHT,A	06	88	AOS			595	605

4.44 TREATMENTS= EFFICIENCY - OPERATIONAL

CITE IND- EX	FIRST AUTHOR	ISS- UE	YE- AR	JOUR -NAL	SECOND AUTHOR	THIRD AUTHOR	PAG BEG	PAG END
1.33	PALMROSE,ZV	SP	86	JAR			97	110
0.67	FRANCIS,JR	AU	86	JAR	STOKES,DJ		383	393
0.33	PALMROSE,ZV	AU	86	JAR			405	411
0.00	ASHTON,RH	SU	81	JAA	HYLAS,RE		325	332
0.00	CHURCHILL,NC	WI	82	AUD	COOPER,WW	GOVINDARAJAN,V	69	91
0.00	MCROBERTS,HA	04	85	AOS	HUDSON,J		493	502
0.00	MOCK,TJ	AU	82	AUD	WRIGHT,A		33	44
0.00	SCHROEDER,MS	SP	86	AUD	SOLOMON,I	VICKREY,DW	86	94
0.00	SHERMAN,HD	AU	84	AUD			35	53
0.00	WARREN,CS	SP	74	JAR			158	177
0.00	WILLIAMS,DD	05	88	AOS	DIRSMITH,MW		487	508
0.00	WRIGHT,A	SP	86	AUD			86	94

4.45 TREATMENTS= AUDIT THEORY

CITE IND- EX	FIRST AUTHOR	ISS- UE	YE- AR	JOUR -NAL	SECOND AUTHOR	THIRD AUTHOR	PAG BEG	PAG END
0.33	ELLIOTT,RK	SP	83	AUD			1	12
0.00	BALVERS,RJ	OC	88	TAR	MCDONALD,B	MILLER,RE	605	622
0.00	CHOW,CW	SP	87	AUD	MCNAMEE,AH	PLUMLEE,RD	123	133
0.00	ETTREDGE,M	SP	88	AUD	SHANE,PB	SMITH,D	29	42
0.00	NAIR,RD	AU	87	AUD	RITTENBERG,LE		15	38
0.00	ROBERTSON,JC	SP	84	AUD			57	67
0.00	SMITH,DB	SP	88	JAR			134	145
0.00	WALKER,NR	AU	88	AUD	PIERCE,LT		1	22

4.46   TREATMENTS= CONFIRMATIONS

CITE IND- EX	FIRST AUTHOR	ISS- UE	YE- AR	JOUR -NAL	SECOND AUTHOR	THIRD AUTHOR	PAG BEG	PAG END
0.00	ASHTON,RH	SU	81	AUD	HYLAS,RE		12	22
0.00	BAILEY,CD	SP	86	AUD	BALLARD,G		77	85

TREATMENTS= CONFIRMATIONS

4.47 TREATMENTS= MANAGERIAL

CITE IND-EX	FIRST AUTHOR	ISS-UE	YE-AR	JOUR-NAL	SECOND AUTHOR	THIRD AUTHOR	PAG BEG	PAG END
3.50	BERRY,AJ	01	85	AOS	CAPPS,T	COOPER,D	3	28
3.40	KAPLAN,RS	JL	84	TAR			390	418
2.92	LIBBY,R	03	77	AOS	LEWIS,BL		245	268
2.71	LIBBY,R	03	82	AOS	LEWIS,BL		231	286
2.67	OTLEY,DT	04	80	AOS			413	428
2.50	MILLER,P	03	87	AOS	O'LEARY,T		235	265
2.00	HAYES,DC	23	83	AOS			241	250
1.85	SWIERINGA,RJ	ST	76	JAR	GIBBINS,M	LARSSON,L	159	187
1.83	COOPER,DJ	23	83	AOS			269	286
1.67	BAIMAN,S	AU	83	JAR	EVANS III,JH		371	395
1.67	TIESSEN,P	23	83	AOS	WATERHOUSE,JH	251	268	
1.60	DEMSKI,JS	JA	84	TAR	PATELL,JM	WOLFSON,MA	16	34
1.50	DEMSKI,JS	SP	87	JAR	SAPPINGTON,DEM		68	89
1.44	BAIMAN,S	ST	80	JAR	DEMSKI,JS		184	220
1.33	JOHNSON,HT	23	83	AOS			139	146
1.25	GOVINDARAJAN,V	01	85	AOS	GUPTA,AK		51	66
1.20	BOLAND,RJ	04	79	AOS			259	272
1.20	PENNO,M	SP	84	JAR			177	191
1.15	ASHTON,RH	ST	76	JAR			1	17
1.15	KHANDWALLA,PN	AU	72	JAR			275	285
1.00	FELTHAM,GA	OC	70	TAR	DEMSKI,JS		623	640
1.00	SPICER,BH	01	83	AOS	BALLEW,V		73	98
0.88	HILTON,RW	SP	81	JAR	SWIERINGA,RJ	HOSKIN,RE	86	108
0.85	CAPLAN,EM	JL	66	TAR			496	509
0.77	DEMSKI,JS	AU	76	JAR			230	245
0.77	ITAMI,H	SP	75	JAR			73	96
0.69	DEMSKI,JS	AU	72	JAR			243	258
0.63	ASHTON,RH	SP	81	JAR			42	61
0.60	ATKINSON,AA	SP	79	JAR			1	22
0.50	CONROY,RM	JA	87	TAR	HUGHES,JS	50	66	
0.50	JOYCE,EJ	AU	81	JAR	LIBBY,R		544	550
0.50	MARKUS,ML	23	83	AOS	PFEFFER,J		205	218
0.50	MERCHANT,KA	01	85	AOS			67	86
0.50	SWIERINGA,RJ	03	87	AOS	WEICK,KE		293	308
0.46	COLANTONI,CS	JA	71	TAR	MANES,RP	WHINSTON,AB	90	102
0.46	HASEMAN,WD	JA	76	TAR	WHINSTON,AB		65	79
0.40	SHIELDS,MD	34	84	AOS			355	363
0.38	BRUNS JR,WJ	JL	68	TAR			469	480
0.38	DEMSKI,JS	OC	67	TAR			701	712
0.33	BIRNBERG,JG	03	77	AOS	FRIEZE,IH	SHIELDS,MD	189	200
0.33	FRIEDMAN,LA	AU	80	JAR	NEUMANN,BR		407	419
0.33	PRESTON,A	06	86	AOS			521	540
0.33	TROTMAN,KT	SP	83	JAR	YETTON,PW	ZIMMER,I	286	292
0.31	HOFSTEDT,TR	01	76	AOS			43	58
0.25	CHEN,K	01	81	AOS	SUMMERS,EL		1	16
0.23	BIRNBERG,JG	JL	67	TAR	NATH,R		468	479
0.23	CAPLAN,EM	AP	68	TAR			342	362
0.23	DEMSKI,JS	AU	70	JAR			178	198

TREATMENTS= MANAGERIAL

CITE IND-EX	FIRST AUTHOR	ISS-UE	YE-AR	JOUR-NAL	SECOND AUTHOR	THIRD AUTHOR	PAG BEG	PAG END
0.22	HAMLEN,SS	OC	80	TAR			578	593
0.15	DEMSKI,JS	OC	69	TAR			669	679
0.15	GODFREY,JT	JA	71	TAR	PRINCE,TR		75	89
0.15	HINOMOTO,H	AU	71	JAR			253	267
0.15	KORNBLUTH,JS	AP	74	TAR			284	295
0.13	ROSENZWEIG,K	04	81	AOS			339	354
0.11	FLAMHOLTZ,EG	01	80	AOS			31	42
0.10	AMEY,LR	04	79	AOS			247	258
0.08	BUTTERWORTH,JE	OC	71	TAR	SIGLOCH,BA		701	716
0.08	CHARNES,A	JA	67	TAR	COOPER,WW		24	52
0.08	FIELD,JE	JL	69	TAR			593	599
0.08	FLOWER,JF	SP	66	JAR			16	36
0.08	GONEDES,NJ	SP	70	JAR			1	20
0.08	GONEDES,NJ	AU	71	JAR			236	252
0.08	HARVEY,DW	OC	76	TAR			838	845
0.08	HEIMANN,SR	JA	76	TAR	LUSK,EJ		51	64
0.08	IJIRI,Y	SP	65	JAR	JAEDICKE,RK	LIVINGSTONE,JL	63	74
0.08	MCDONOUGH,JJ	OC	71	TAR			676	685
0.08	STALLMAN,JC	OC	72	TAR			774	790
0.00	BALACHANDRAN,KR	02	77	AOS	LIVINGSTONE,JL		153	164
0.00	BANKER,RD	AU	87	JAA	DATAR,SM	RAJAN,MV	319	347
0.00	BENNINGER,LJ	JL	65	TAR			547	557
0.00	CARLISLE,HM	JA	66	TAR			115	120
0.00	CHAN,JL	AP	78	TAR			309	323
0.00	CZARNIAWSKA-,B	04	88	AOS			415	430
0.00	DAVIS,PM	JA	66	TAR			121	126
0.00	FIRMIN,PA	ST	68	JAR	GOODMAN,SS	HENDRICKS,TE	122	155
0.00	GIBSON,JL	JL	63	TAR			492	500
0.00	HARTLEY,RV	AP	68	TAR			321	332
0.00	HASEMAN,WC	OC	68	TAR			738	752
0.00	HELMKAMP,JG	JL	69	TAR			605	610
0.00	HOPPER,T	05	87	AOS	STOREY,J	WILLMOTT,H	437	456
0.00	JONSSON,S	05	88	AOS	GRONLUND,A		513	532
0.00	KANODIA,CS	SP	85	JAR			175	193
0.00	LEA,RB	AP	72	TAR			346	350
0.00	LUNESKI,C	JL	64	TAR			591	597
0.00	MCKENNA,EF	03	80	AOS			297	310
0.00	NEUMANN,BR	SP	79	JAR			123	139
0.00	PURDY,D	04	81	AOS			327	338
0.00	SIMON,SI	OC	64	TAR			884	889
0.00	SOMEYA,K	OC	64	TAR			983	989
0.00	UECKER,WC	JL	85	TAR	SCHEPANSKI,A	SHIN,J	430	457
0.00	VERRECCHIA,RE	ST	87	JAR	LANEN,WN		165	189

TREATMENTS= MANAGERIAL

4.48 TREATMENTS= TRANSFER PRICING

CITE IND- EX	FIRST AUTHOR	ISS- UE	YE- AR	JOUR -NAL	SECOND AUTHOR	THIRD AUTHOR	PAG BEG	PAG END
0.77	ABDEL-KHALIK,AR	JA	74	TAR	LUSK,EJ		8	23
0.69	WATSON,DJ	JL	75	TAR	BAUMLER,JV		466	474
0.38	RONEN,J	SP	70	JAR	MCKINNEY,G		99	112
0.29	SWIERINGA,RJ	02	82	AOS	WATERHOUSE,JH		149	166
0.18	MERVILLE,LJ	OC	78	TAR	PETTY,JW		935	951
0.15	BAILEY JR,AD	JL	76	TAR	BOE,WJ		559	573
0.15	GORDON,MJ	JL	70	TAR			427	443
0.08	DOPUCH,N	SP	64	JAR	DRAKE,DF		10	24
0.08	ONSI,M	JL	70	TAR			535	543
0.00	GOETZ,BE	JL	67	TAR			435	440
0.00	HALPERIN,R	OC	87	TAR	SRINIDHI,BN		686	706
0.00	LESSARD,DR	JL	77	TAR	LORANGE,P		628	637
0.00	RONEN,J	AU	88	JAR	BALACHANDRAN,KR		300	314
0.00	SCHIFF,M	SP	79	JAA			224	231
0.00	SPICER,BH	03	88	AOS			303	322
0.00	STONE,WE	JA	64	TAR			38	42

4.49 TREATMENTS= BREAKEVEN, CVPA

CITE IND-EX	FIRST AUTHOR	ISS-UE	YE-AR	JOUR-NAL	SECOND AUTHOR	THIRD AUTHOR	PAG BEG	PAG END
0.54	JAEDICKE,RK	OC	64	TAR	ROBICHEK,AA		917	926
0.38	BUZBY,SL	JA	74	TAR			42	49
0.38	HILLIARD,JE	JA	75	TAR	LEITCH,RA		69	80
0.38	LIAO,M	OC	75	TAR			780	790
0.31	FERRARA,WL	AP	72	TAR	HAYYA,JC	NACHMAN,DA	299	307
0.30	HILTON,RW	AU	79	JAR			411	435
0.27	KOTTAS,JF	AP	78	TAR	LAU,AH	LAU,HS	389	401
0.23	IJIRI,Y	OC	73	TAR	ITAMI,H		724	737
0.15	JOHNSON,GL	AU	71	JAR	SIMIK,SS		278	286
0.15	JOHNSON,GL	SP	74	JAR	SIMIK,SS		67	79
0.10	SHIH,W	OC	79	TAR			687	706
0.09	KOTTAS,JF	JL	78	TAR	LAU,HS		698	707
0.08	CHARNES,A	SP	63	JAR	COOPER,WW	IJIRI,Y	16	43
0.08	MAGEE,RP	AU	75	JAR			257	266
0.08	MORRISON,TA	AP	69	TAR	KACZKA,E		330	343
0.00	BROCKETT,P	JL	84	TAR	CHARNES,A	COOPER,WW	474	487
0.00	MANES,RP	SP	66	JAR			87	100
0.00	RAUN,DL	OC	64	TAR			927	945
0.00	SOLOMONS,D	JL	68	TAR			447	452

4.50   TREATMENTS= BUDGETING & PLANNING

CITE IND-EX	FIRST AUTHOR	ISS-UE	YE-AR	JOUR-NAL	SECOND AUTHOR	THIRD AUTHOR	PAG BEG	PAG END
3.18	DEMSKI,JS	AP	78	TAR	FELTHAM,GA		336	359
2.00	OTLEY,DT	SP	78	JAR			122	149
1.92	MILANI,K	AP	75	TAR			274	284
1.88	MERCHANT,KA	OC	81	TAR			813	829
1.77	RONEN,J	OC	75	TAR	LIVINGSTONE,JL		671	685
1.70	KENIS,I	OC	79	TAR			707	721
1.57	BROWNELL,P	SP	82	JAR			12	27
1.46	DECOSTER,DT	AU	68	JAR	FERTAKIS,JP		237	246
1.38	BROWNELL,P	OC	81	TAR			844	860
1.23	SCHIFF,M	AP	70	TAR	LEWIN,AY		259	268
1.15	HOPWOOD,AG	JL	74	TAR			485	495
1.09	COLLINS,F	AP	78	TAR			324	335
1.00	CHRISTENSEN,J	AU	82	JAR			589	603
1.00	FLAMHOLTZ,EG	23	83	AOS			153	170
0.85	CHERRINGTON,DJ	ST	73	JAR	CHERRINGTON,JO		225	253
0.85	FORAN,MF	OC	74	TAR	DECOSTER,DT		751	763
0.75	MERCHANT,KA	02	85	AOS			201	210
0.70	ANSARI,SL	03	79	AOS			149	162
0.67	BOLAND,RJ	45	86	AOS	PONDY,LR		403	422
0.67	BROWNELL,P	OC	86	TAR	MCINNES,M	587	600	
0.67	CHOW,CW	OC	83	TAR			667	685
0.67	ROCKNESS,HO	OC	77	TAR			893	903
0.63	HOFSTEDE,G	03	81	AOS			193	216
0.62	ASHTON,RH	OC	75	TAR			710	722
0.56	MAGEE,RP	AU	80	JAR			551	573
0.54	BENSTON,GJ	AP	63	TAR			347	354
0.54	DEMSKI,JS	JL	72	TAR	FELTHAM,GA		533	548
0.50	COVALESKI,MA	04	83	AOS	DIRSMITH,MW		323	340
0.50	SHIELDS,MD	01	81	AOS	BIRNBERG,JG	FRIEZE,IH	69	96
0.46	COOK,DM	ST	67	JAR			213	224
0.46	SWIERINGA,RJ	ST	72	JAR	MONCUR,RH		194	209
0.43	JONSSON,S	03	82	AOS			287	304
0.38	CAMMANN,C	04	76	AOS			301	314
0.38	IJIRI,Y	SP	68	JAR	KINARD,JC	PUTNEY,FB	1	28
0.38	KESSLER,L	SP	81	JAR	ASHTON,RH		146	162
0.36	DIRSMITH,MW	34	78	AOS	JABLONSKY,SF		215	226
0.33	BROWNELL,P	AU	83	JAR			456	472
0.33	COVALESKI,MA	03	86	AOS	DIRSMITH,MW		193	214
0.33	ZALD,MN	45	86	AOS			321	326
0.30	KANODIA,CS	SP	79	JAR			74	98
0.25	BROWNELL,P	AU	85	JAR			502	512
0.25	YOUNG,SM	AU	85	JAR			829	842
0.23	BENSTON,GJ	OC	66	TAR			657	672
0.23	HOLSTRUM,GL	AU	71	JAR			268	277
0.23	SEARFOSS,DG	04	76	AOS			375	388
0.20	DAROCA,FP	01	84	AOS			13	32
0.18	LIN,WT	JA	78	TAR			61	76
0.17	BROWNELL,P	04	83	AOS			307	322

CITE IND- EX	FIRST AUTHOR	ISS- UE	YE- AR	JOUR -NAL	SECOND AUTHOR	THIRD AUTHOR	PAG BEG	PAG END
0.17	TILLER,MG	AU	83	JAR			581	595
0.15	DEMSKI,JS	AP	71	TAR			268	278
0.15	ELLIOTT,JW	AU	72	JAR	UPHOFF,HL		259	274
0.15	HANSON,EI	AP	66	TAR			239	243
0.15	HARTLEY,RV	OC	71	TAR			746	755
0.15	IJIRI,Y	AU	63	JAR	LEVY,FK	LYON,RC	198	212
0.14	EGGLETON,IRC	SP	82	JAR			68	102
0.14	SEILER,RE	04	82	AOS	BARTLETT,RW		381	404
0.11	HOPPER,TM	04	80	AOS			401	412
0.09	CARLSSON,J	34	78	AOS	EHN,P	ERLANDER,B	249	260
0.08	FELTHAM,GA	JA	70	TAR			11	26
0.08	GROVES,R	JL	70	TAR	MANES,RP	SORENSEN,R	481	489
0.08	HARTLEY,RV	AP	70	TAR			223	234
0.08	JENSEN,RE	AP	67	TAR			265	273
0.08	MABERT,VA	JA	74	TAR	RADCLIFFE,RC		61	75
0.08	RAPPAPORT,A	JL	67	TAR			441	456
0.00	ASHTON,AH	JL	84	TAR			361	375
0.00	BABER,WR	JA	85	TAR			1	9
0.00	BLANCHARD,GA	JA	86	TAR	CHOW,CW	NOREEN,EW	1	15
0.00	BROWN,C	JL	87	TAR	SOLOMON,I		564	577
0.00	BROWNELL,P	OC	82	TAR			766	777
0.00	BROWNELL,P	AU	86	JAR	HIRST,MK		241	249
0.00	BYRNE,R	JA	68	TAR	CHARNES,A	COOPER,WW	18	37
0.00	CHENHALL,RH	AP	86	TAR			263	272
0.00	CHENHALL,RH	03	88	AOS	BROWNELL,P		225	233
0.00	CHOW,CW	JA	88	TAR	COOPER,JC	WALLER,WS	111	122
0.00	CLARK,JJ	OC	73	TAR	ELGERS,PT		668	678
0.00	COLIGNON,R	06	88	AOS	COVALESKI,M		559	579
0.00	COLLINS,F	JA	87	TAR	MUNTER,P	FINN,DW	29	49
0.00	COVALESKI,MA	01	88	AOS	DIRSMITH,MW		1	24
0.00	FARAG,SM	AP	68	TAR			312	320
0.00	FERRARA,WL	JA	66	TAR			106	114
0.00	GAMBLING,TE	JA	70	TAR	NOUR,A		98	102
0.00	GIROUX,GA	06	86	AOS	MAYPER,AG	DAFT,RL	499	520
0.00	GODFREY,JT	AP	71	TAR			286	297
0.00	GORDON,LA	02	84	AOS	HAKA,S	SCHICK,AG	111	123
0.00	HAKA,SF	01	87	AOS			31	48
0.00	HIRST,MK	OC	87	TAR			774	784
0.00	IJIRI,Y	AP	70	TAR	THOMPSON,GL		246	258
0.00	JENSEN,RE	JL	68	TAR			425	446
0.00	LEV,B	ST	69	JAR			182	197
0.00	LICATA,MP	JA	86	TAR	STRAWSER,RH	WELKER,RB	112	117
0.00	LUKKA,K	03	88	AOS			281	301
0.00	MIA,L	05	88	AOS			465	475
0.00	ROSS,WR	JL	66	TAR			464	473
0.00	SAMUELSON,LA	01	86	AOS			35	46
0.00	SIMONS,R	04	87	AOS			357	374
0.00	WALLER,WS	01	88	AOS			87	98
0.00	WILLIAMS,JJ	02	81	AOS			153	166
0.00	WILLIAMS,JJ	04	85	AOS	NEWTON,JD	MORGAN,EA	457	478

TREATMENTS= BUDGETING & PLANNING

CITE IND- EX	FIRST AUTHOR	ISS- UE	YE- AR	JOUR -NAL	SECOND AUTHOR	THIRD AUTHOR	PAG BEG	PAG END
0.00	WILLIAMS,JJ	02	88	AOS	HININGS,CR		191	198

TREATMENTS= BUDGETING & PLANNING

4.51 TREATMENTS= RELEVANT COSTS

CITE IND-EX	FIRST AUTHOR	ISS-UE	YE-AR	JOUR-NAL	SECOND AUTHOR	THIRD AUTHOR	PAG BEG	PAG END
1.83	BIRNBERG,JG	23	83	AOS	TUROPOLEC,L	YOUNG,SM	111	130
0.45	NEUMANN,BR	AU	78	JAR	FRIEDMAN,LA		400	410
0.38	BECKER,S	AU	74	JAR	RONEN,J	SORTER,GH	317	329
0.18	DILLON,RD	JA	78	TAR	NASH,JF		11	17
0.17	HOSKIN,RE	SP	83	JAR			78	95
0.15	SAMUELS,JM	AU	65	JAR			182	191
0.15	YETTON,PY	01	76	AOS			81	90
0.08	COLANTONI,CS	JL	69	TAR	MANES,RP	WHINSTON,AB	467	481
0.08	JENSEN,DL	JL	74	TAR			465	476
0.08	MCRAE,TW	AP	70	TAR			315	321
0.08	SORENSEN,JE	JL	77	TAR	GROVE,HD		658	675
0.00	BANKER,RD	JL	88	JAE	DATAR,SM	KEKRE,S	171	197
0.00	BERKOW,WF	AP	64	TAR			377	386
0.00	BOWER,RS	AP	66	TAR	HERRINGER,F	WILLIAMSON,JP	257	265
0.00	FERRARA,WL	OC	63	TAR			719	722
0.00	FESS,PE	OC	63	TAR			723	732
0.00	GROSS,H	OC	66	TAR			745	753
0.00	HAKA,S	JL	86	TAR	FRIEDMAN,L	JONES,V	455	474
0.00	HILTON,RW	AP	88	TAR	SWIERINGA,RJ	TURNER,MJ	195	218
0.00	LAVALLE,IH	AP	68	TAR	RAPPAPORT,A		225	230
0.00	MITCHELL,GB	AP	70	TAR			308	314
0.00	SUH,YS	SP	88	JAR			154	168

TREATMENTS= RELEVANT COSTS

4.52 TREATMENTS= RESPONSIBTY ACCTG

CITE IND-EX	FIRST AUTHOR	ISS-UE	YE-AR	JOUR-NAL	SECOND AUTHOR	THIRD AUTHOR	PAG BEG	PAG END
2.75	HAYES,DC	JA	77	TAR			22	39
0.58	HARRELL,AM	OC	77	TAR			833	841
0.50	BAIMAN,S	AU	85	JAR	NOEL,J		486	501
0.23	PROBST,FR	JA	71	TAR			113	118
0.00	BELKAOUI,A	04	81	AOS			281	290
0.00	FERRARA,WL	JL	77	TAR			597	604
0.00	GRAESE,CE	AP	64	TAR			387	391

TREATMENTS= RESPONSIBTY ACCTG

4.53 TREATMENTS= COST ALLOCS

CITE IND-EX	FIRST AUTHOR	ISS-UE	YE-AR	JOUR -NAL	SECOND AUTHOR	THIRD AUTHOR	PAG BEG	PAG END
3.00	LOFT,A	02	86	AOS			137	170
2.10	ZIMMERMAN,JL	JL	79	TAR			504	521
0.67	BARNES,P	01	86	AOS	WEBB,J		1	18
0.50	SUH,YS	ST	87	JAR			22	46
0.38	MORIARITY,S	OC	75	TAR			791	795
0.27	CALLEN,JL	AP	78	TAR			303	308
0.23	BALOFF,N	AU	67	JAR	KENNELLY,JW		131	143
0.17	MAGEE,RP	OC	77	TAR			869	880
0.15	KAPLAN,RS	OC	73	TAR			738	748
0.13	GANGOLLY,JS	AU	81	JAR			299	312
0.11	HAMLEN,SS	AP	80	TAR	HAMLEN,WA	TSCHIRHART,JT	269	287
0.08	CHURCHILL,NC	OC	64	TAR			894	904
0.08	CORCORAN,AW	JA	73	TAR	LEININGER,WE		105	114
0.08	ECKEL,LG	OC	76	TAR			764	777
0.08	LIVINGSTONE,JL	JL	68	TAR			503	508
0.08	MAGEE,RP	JA	77	TAR			190	199
0.08	MORSE,WJ	OC	72	TAR			761	773
0.08	WILLIAMS,TH	JL	64	TAR	GRIFFIN,CH		671	678
0.00	ANSARI,SL	06	87	AOS	EUSKE,KJ		549	570
0.00	BALACHANDRAN,BV	JA	81	TAR	RAMAKRISHNAN,RT		85	96
0.00	BALACHANDRAN,KR	SP	87	JAA	SRINIDHI,BN		151	169
0.00	BRIEF,RP	AU	68	JAR	OWEN,J		193	199
0.00	BRIEF,RP	SP	69	JAR	OWEN,J		12	16
0.00	CHAN,KH	WI	84	JAA	CHENG,TT		164	177
0.00	CHEN,JT	JL	83	TAR			600	605
0.00	CHIU,JS	OC	66	TAR	DECOSTER,DT		673	680
0.00	COHEN,SI	AP	82	TAR	LOEB,M		336	347
0.00	FREMGEN,JM	JA	64	TAR			43	51
0.00	HORNGREN,CT	AP	64	TAR	SORTER,GH		417	420
0.00	JACOBS,FH	JA	87	TAR	MARSHALL,RM		67	78
0.00	LERE,JC	AP	86	TAR			318	324
0.00	LIVINGSTONE,JL	JA	69	TAR			48	64
0.00	MAGEE,RP	JA	88	TAR			42	54
0.00	MANES,RP	JA	65	TAR	SMITH,VL		31	35
0.00	MCCLENON,PR	JL	63	TAR			540	547
0.00	MELLMAN,M	JA	63	TAR			118	123
0.00	NAHAPIET,JE	04	88	AOS			333	358
0.00	SHWAYDER,KR	AP	70	TAR			299	307
0.00	STAUBUS,GJ	JA	63	TAR			64	74
0.00	SUNDER,S	SP	83	JAR			222	233
0.00	VERRECCHIA,RE	JL	82	TAR			579	593
0.00	WRIGHT,HW	OC	66	TAR			626	633

4.54 TREATMENTS= CAPITAL BUDGETING

CITE IND- EX	FIRST AUTHOR	ISS- UE	YE- AR	JOUR -NAL	SECOND AUTHOR	THIRD AUTHOR	PAG BEG	PAG END
0.75	LARCKER,DF	JL	81	TAR			519	538
0.50	HAKA,SF	OC	85	TAR	GORDON,LA	PINCHES,GE	651	669
0.38	SUNDEM,GL	AP	74	TAR			306	320
0.31	KLAMMER,T	AP	73	TAR			353	364
0.15	GREER JR,WR	JA	70	TAR			103	114
0.08	GREER JR,WR	JL	74	TAR			496	505
0.08	LUSK,EJ	JL	72	TAR			567	575
0.08	PARKER,RH	SP	68	JAR			58	71
0.00	BAILEY JR,AD	SP	68	JAR	GRAY,J		98	105
0.00	BERANEK,W	OC	64	TAR			914	916
0.00	COOPER,WW	AU	85	JAA	HO,JL	HUNTER,JE	22	39
0.00	FOGLER,HR	JA	72	TAR			134	143
0.00	HEEBINK,DV	JA	64	TAR			90	93
0.00	JEYNES,PH	JA	65	TAR			105	118
0.00	JOHNSON,GL	OC	67	TAR	NEWTON,SW		738	746
0.00	MOORE,CL	JA	64	TAR			94	102
0.00	ROBBINS,SM	AU	77	JAA			5	18

4.55 TREATMENTS= TAX (TAX PLANNING)

CITE IND- EX	FIRST AUTHOR	ISS- UE	YE- AR	JOUR -NAL	SECOND AUTHOR	THIRD AUTHOR	PAG BEG	PAG END
0.00	ASKARI,H	AP	76	TAR	CAIN,P	SHAW,R	331	334
0.00	BIERMAN JR,H	OC	70	TAR			690	697
0.00	KISSINGER,JN	SP	86	JAA			90	101
0.00	MORRISON,TA	OC	66	TAR			704	713
0.00	MORRISON,TA	JL	68	TAR	BUZBY,SL		517	521

TREATMENTS= TAX (TAX PLANNING)

4.56 TREATMENTS= OVERHEAD ALLOCS.

CITE INDEX	FIRST AUTHOR	ISSUE	YEAR	JOURNAL	SECOND AUTHOR	THIRD AUTHOR	PAG BEG	PAG END
0.58	HAMLEN,SS	JL	77	TAR	HAMLEN,WA	TSCHIRHART,JT	616	627
0.58	JENSEN,DL	OC	77	TAR			842	856
0.38	KAPLAN,RS	AP	71	TAR	THOMPSON,GL		352	364
0.38	KAPLAN,RS	JL	74	TAR	WELAM,VP		477	484
0.15	ZIMMERMAN,JL	AU	76	JAR			301	319
0.08	FEKRAT,MA	AP	72	TAR			351	355
0.00	BARTON,RF	SP	69	JAR			116	122
0.00	BODNAR,G	OC	77	TAR	LUSK,EJ		857	868
0.00	DAVIDSON,S	AP	63	TAR			278	284
0.00	LENTILHON,RW	OC	64	TAR			880	883

TREATMENTS= OVERHEAD ALLOCS.

4.57 TREATMENTS= HRA-SOCIAL ACCTG

CITE IND- EX	FIRST AUTHOR	ISS- UE	YE- AR	JOUR -NAL	SECOND AUTHOR	THIRD AUTHOR	PAG BEG	PAG END
3.75	BURCHELL,S	04	85	AOS	CLUBB,C	HOPWOOD,AG	381	414
1.08	ELIAS,N	ST	72	JAR			215	233
0.85	LEV,B	JA	71	TAR	SCHWARTZ,A		103	112
0.77	FLAMHOLTZ,EG	AP	71	TAR			253	267
0.73	SPICER,BM	JA	78	TAR			94	111
0.62	SCHWAN,ES	23	76	AOS			219	238
0.54	BRUMMET,RL	AP	68	TAR	FLAMHOLTZ,EG	PYLE,WC	217	224
0.54	EPSTEIN,MJ	01	76	AOS	FLAMHOLTZ,EG	MCDONOUGH,JJ	23	42
0.54	ESTES,RW	AP	72	TAR			284	290
0.54	FLAMHOLTZ,EG	23	76	AOS			153	166
0.54	HENDRICKS,JA	AP	76	TAR			292	305
0.46	FLAMHOLTZ,EG	OC	72	TAR			666	678
0.42	COOPER,DJ	03	77	AOS	ESSEX,S		201	218
0.42	DIERKES,M	01	77	AOS	PRESTON,LE		3	22
0.40	BUZBY,SL	JA	79	TAR	FALK,H		23	37
0.38	DITTMAN,DA	SP	76	JAR	JURIS,HA	REVSINE,L	49	65
0.38	JAGGI,B	AP	74	TAR	LAU,HS		321	329
0.38	RAMANATHAN,KV	JL	76	TAR			516	528
0.38	TROTMAN,KT	04	81	AOS	BRADLEY,G		355	362
0.36	INGRAM,RW	AU	78	JAR			270	285
0.33	ANDERSON,JC	JL	80	TAR	FRANKLE,AW		467	479
0.33	BELKAOUI,A	03	80	AOS			263	284
0.33	GROJER,JE	04	77	AOS	STARK,A		349	385
0.31	FLAMHOLTZ,EG	ST	72	JAR			241	266
0.31	FRIEDMAN,A	AU	74	JAR	LEV,B		235	250
0.30	SCHREUDER,H	12	79	AOS			109	122
0.25	FLAMHOLTZ,EG	01	85	AOS	DAS,TK	TSUI,AS	35	50
0.25	GORDON,FE	04	77	AOS	RHODE,JG	MERCHANT,KA	295	306
0.23	BOWMAN,EH	01	76	AOS	HAIRE,M		11	22
0.23	MACY,BA	23	76	AOS	MIRVIS,PH		179	194
0.23	MOBLEY,SC	OC	70	TAR			762	768
0.23	OGAN,P	AP	76	TAR			306	320
0.22	HARRELL,AM	04	80	AOS	KLICK,HD		393	400
0.20	BROCKHOFF,K	12	79	AOS			77	86
0.20	DIERKES,M	12	79	AOS			87	108
0.17	LESSEM,R	04	77	AOS			279	294
0.17	TOMASSINI,LA	OC	77	TAR			904	913
0.15	ACLAND,D	23	76	AOS			133	142
0.15	CHURCHILL,NC	OC	75	TAR	SHANK,JK		643	656
0.15	DERMER,JD	JA	74	TAR	SIEGEL,JP		88	97
0.15	TOMASSINI,LA	23	76	AOS			239	252
0.14	BENSTON,GJ	02	82	AOS			87	106
0.14	WISEMAN,J	01	82	AOS			53	64
0.13	SCHREUDER,H	AP	81	TAR			294	308
0.11	WILLIAMS,PF	JA	80	TAR			62	77
0.10	CHAN,JL	04	79	AOS			273	282
0.08	BIRNBERG,JG	01	76	AOS	GANDHI,NM		5	10
0.08	CARPER,WB	23	76	AOS	POSEY,JM		143	152

TREATMENTS= HRA-SOCIAL ACCTG

CITE IND-EX	FIRST AUTHOR	ISS-UE	YE-AR	JOUR-NAL	SECOND AUTHOR	THIRD AUTHOR	PAG BEG	PAG END
0.08	FRANCIS,ME	AP	73	TAR			245	257
0.08	GAMBLING,TE	23	76	AOS			167	174
0.08	GROVE,HD	03	77	AOS	MOCK,TJ	EHRENREICH,K	219	236
0.08	MARQUES,E	23	76	AOS			175	178
0.08	OGAN,P	23	76	AOS			195	218
0.08	ULLMANN,AA	01	76	AOS			71	80
0.08	WELLING,P	04	77	AOS			307	316
0.00	BRAVENEC,LL	02	77	AOS	EPSTEIN,MJ	CRUMBLEY,DL	131	140
0.00	CHARNES,A	04	76	AOS	COLANTONI,CS	COOPER,WW	315	338
0.00	CHURCHMAN,CW	JA	71	TAR			30	35
0.00	COWEN,SS	02	87	AOS	FERRERI,LB	PARKER,LD	111	122
0.00	CRUMBLEY,DL	JA	75	TAR	SAVICH,RS		112	117
0.00	DIERKES,M	01	85	AOS	ANTAL,AB		29	34
0.00	FARMAN,WL	AP	64	TAR			392	404
0.00	FLAMHOLTZ,EG	04	87	AOS			309	318
0.00	GAMBLING,T	04	85	AOS			415	426
0.00	GLATZER,W	03	81	AOS			219	234
0.00	GUL,FA	34	84	AOS			233	239
0.00	HEARD,JE	03	81	AOS	BOLCE,WJ		247	254
0.00	KNIGHTS,D	05	87	AOS	COLLINSON,D		457	477
0.00	LAU,AH	SP	78	JAR	LAU,HS		80	102
0.00	LEWIS,NR	34	84	AOS	PARKER,LD	SUTCLIFFE,P	275	289
0.00	PARKE,R	03	81	AOS	PETERSON,JL		235	246
0.00	PRESTON,LE	03	81	AOS			255	262
0.00	ROCKNESS,J	04	88	AOS	WILLIAMS,PF		397	411
0.00	TEOH,HY	02	84	AOS	THONG,G		189	206
0.00	ULLMANN,AA	12	79	AOS			123	134
0.00	VOGT,RA	01	77	AOS			59	80

TREATMENTS= HRA-SOCIAL ACCTG

4.58 TREATMENTS= VARIANCES

CITE IND-EX	FIRST AUTHOR	ISS-UE	YE-AR	JOUR-NAL	SECOND AUTHOR	THIRD AUTHOR	PAG BEG	PAG END
0.85	MAGEE,RP	JL	76	TAR			529	544
0.77	KAPLAN,RS	SP	69	JAR			32	43
0.69	DYCKMAN,TR	AU	69	JAR			215	244
0.55	MAGEE,RP	AU	78	JAR	DICKHAUT,JW		294	314
0.46	ANSARI,SL	AU	76	JAR			189	211
0.40	DITTMAN,DA	AP	79	TAR	PRAKASH,P		358	373
0.38	BROWN,C	SP	81	JAR			62	85
0.36	DITTMAN,DA	SP	78	JAR	PRAKASH,P		14	25
0.31	OZAN,T	SP	71	JAR	DYCKMAN,TR		88	115
0.23	DEMSKI,JS	JA	70	TAR			76	87
0.23	RONEN,J	JA	74	TAR			50	60
0.15	DOPUCH,N	JL	67	TAR	BIRNBERG,JG	DEMSKI,JS	526	536
0.15	LUH,FS	JA	68	TAR			123	132
0.15	ZANNETOS,ZS	AP	64	TAR			296	304
0.09	JACOBS,FH	SP	78	JAR			190	203
0.08	COMISKEY,EE	AP	66	TAR			235	238
0.08	FRANK,WG	JL	67	TAR	MANES,RP		516	525
0.08	HASSELDINE,CR	JL	67	TAR			497	515
0.08	WOLK,HI	JL	72	TAR	HILLMAN,AP		549	555
0.00	BROWN,C	03	85	AOS			255	266
0.00	CALLEN,JL	SP	88	JAA			87	108
0.00	CHUMACHENKO,NG	OC	68	TAR			753	762
0.00	CUSHING,BE	OC	68	TAR			668	671
0.00	DECOSTER,DT	AP	66	TAR			297	302
0.00	DEMSKI,JS	SP	69	JAR			96	115
0.00	HARRISON,PD	AP	88	TAR	WEST,SG	RENEAU,JH	307	320
0.00	HOBBS,JB	OC	64	TAR			905	913
0.00	HORNGREN,CT	AP	67	TAR			254	264
0.00	HORNGREN,CT	JA	69	TAR			86	89
0.00	JENSEN,RE	JA	68	TAR	THOMSEN,CT		83	93
0.00	LAMBERT,RA	AU	85	JAR			633	647
0.00	LEV,B	OC	69	TAR			704	710
0.00	MARCINKO,D	JL	84	TAR	PETRI,E		488	495
0.00	ONSI,M	AP	67	TAR			321	330
0.00	PELES,YC	AP	86	TAR			325	329
0.00	RONEN,J	AU	70	JAR			232	252
0.00	SHWAYDER,KR	JA	68	TAR			101	104
0.00	WEBER,C	JL	63	TAR			534	539
0.00	ZANNETOS,ZS	JL	63	TAR			528	533

TREATMENTS= VARIANCES

4.59 TREATMENTS= EXEC.COMPENSATION

CITE IND-EX	FIRST AUTHOR	ISS-UE	YE-AR	JOUR-NAL	SECOND AUTHOR	THIRD AUTHOR	PAG BEG	PAG END
3.50	HEALY,PM	AP	85	JAE			85	108
2.50	LARCKER,DF	AP	83	JAE			3	30
1.75	MURPHY,KJ	AP	85	JAE			11	42
1.50	COUGHLAN,AT	AP	85	JAE	SCHMIDT,RM		43	66
0.75	ANTLE,R	SP	85	JAR	SMITH,A		296	325
0.75	BENSTON,GJ	AP	85	JAE			67	84
0.75	BRICKLEY,JA	AP	85	JAE	BHAGAT,S	LEASE,RC	115	130
0.67	ANTLE,R	SP	86	JAR	SMITH,A		1	39
0.50	WALLER,WS	JL	85	TAR	CHOW,CW		458	476
0.25	LAMBERT,RA	AP	85	JAE	LARCKER,DF		179	204
0.25	TEHRANIAN,H	AP	85	JAE	WAEGELEIN,JF		131	144
0.00	HALPERIN,R	OC	85	TAR	TZUR,J		670	680
0.00	JENSEN,MC	AP	85	JAE	ZIMMERMAN,JL		3	10
0.00	LAMBERT,RA	ST	87	JAR	LARCKER,DF		85	125
0.00	LEWELLEN,W	DE	87	JAE	LODERER,C	MARTIN,K	287	310
0.00	MCGAHRAN,KT	JA	88	TAR			23	41
0.00	RAVIV,A	AP	85	JAE			239	246
0.00	SHIELDS,MD	06	88	AOS	WALLER,WS		581	594
0.00	YOUNG,SM	06	88	AOS	SHIELDS,MD	WOLF,G	607	618

4.60 TREATMENTS= OTHER

CITE IND-EX	FIRST AUTHOR	ISS-UE	YE-AR	JOUR-NAL	SECOND AUTHOR	THIRD AUTHOR	PAG BEG	PAG END
2.33	BOLAND,RJ	23	83	AOS	PONDY,LR		223	234
1.69	LIBBY,R	JL	75	TAR			475	489
1.00	HILTON,RW	AU	80	JAR			477	505
1.00	MCGHEE,W	JL	78	TAR	SHIELDS,MD	BIRNBERG,JG	681	697
0.92	ZIMMERMAN,JL	ST	77	JAR			107	144
0.83	LIBBY,R	AU	77	JAR	FISHBURN,PC		272	292
0.67	WHITLEY,R	02	86	AOS			171	192
0.50	HILTON,RW	SP	81	JAR	SWIERINGA,RJ		109	119
0.50	PASTENA,V	AU	79	JAR	RONEN,J		550	564
0.46	HOFSTEDT,TR	JA	70	TAR	KINARD,JC		38	54
0.46	LOOKABILL,LL	OC	76	TAR			724	738
0.44	GARMAN,MB	AU	80	JAR	OHLSON,JA		420	440
0.40	MAYER-SOMMER,AP	JA	79	TAR			88	106
0.38	FRIED,D	AP	81	TAR	SCHIFF,A		326	341
0.38	GOLEMBIEWSKI,RT	AP	64	TAR			333	341
0.33	MEYER,JW	45	86	AOS			345	356
0.31	CHEN,RS	JL	75	TAR			533	543
0.31	JOHNSON,HT	JL	75	TAR			444	450
0.31	SMITH,JE	JL	71	TAR	SMITH,NP		552	561
0.31	STERLING,RR	JL	70	TAR			444	457
0.25	WEBER,RP	JL	81	TAR	STEVENSON,WC		596	612
0.23	PRAKASH,P	OC	75	TAR	RAPPAPORT,A		723	734
0.17	SCHEPANSKI,A	AP	83	TAR	UECKER,WC		259	283
0.15	GOETZ,BE	JA	67	TAR			53	61
0.15	GREEN,D	JA	66	TAR			52	64
0.15	MAUTZ,RK	AP	63	TAR			317	325
0.15	PANKOFF,LD	AP	70	TAR	VIRGIL JR,RL		269	279
0.15	SEIDLER,LJ	OC	67	TAR			775	781
0.15	SORENSEN,JE	OC	72	TAR	FRANKS,DD		735	746
0.10	YAMEY,BS	AP	79	TAR			323	329
0.08	AIKEN,ME	JL	75	TAR	BLACKETT,LA	ISAACS,G	544	562
0.08	BALADOUNI,V	AP	66	TAR			215	225
0.08	FERRIS,KR	01	77	AOS			23	28
0.08	FIRMIN,PA	JA	68	TAR	LINN,JJ		75	82
0.08	HORNGREN,CT	JA	71	TAR			1	11
0.08	HUEFNER,RJ	OC	71	TAR			717	732
0.08	HUME,LJ	SP	70	JAR			21	33
0.08	LANGENDERFER,HQ	OC	69	TAR	ROBERTSON,JC		777	787
0.08	LOEB,SE	JA	72	TAR			1	10
0.08	SOPER,FJ	AP	64	TAR	DOLPHIN,R		358	362
0.08	STONE,WE	JA	65	TAR			190	195
0.00	ALLYN,RG	JA	64	TAR			121	127
0.00	ALLYN,RG	AP	66	TAR			303	311
0.00	ANDERSON,JJ	JL	67	TAR			583	588
0.00	BOUTELL,WS	AP	64	TAR			305	311
0.00	BOWEN,EK	OC	67	TAR			782	787
0.00	BRUNDAGE,MV	JL	69	TAR	LIVINGSTONE,JL		539	545
0.00	BUCKLEY,JW	JL	67	TAR			572	582

TREATMENTS= OTHER

CITE IND-EX	FIRST AUTHOR	ISS-UE	YE-AR	JOUR-NAL	SECOND AUTHOR	THIRD AUTHOR	PAG BEG	PAG END
0.00	CALL,DV	OC	69	TAR			711	719
0.00	CAMPFIELD,WL	JL	65	TAR			594	598
0.00	CAMPFIELD,WL	OC	70	TAR			683	689
0.00	CAREY,JL	JA	69	TAR			79	85
0.00	CARPENTER,CG	JL	71	TAR	STRAWSER,RH		509	518
0.00	CASPARI,JA	OC	76	TAR			739	746
0.00	CLARK,TN	ST	77	JAR			54	94
0.00	COE,TL	SP	79	JAA			244	253
0.00	CORCORAN,AW	AP	69	TAR			359	374
0.00	COWIE,JB	JA	70	TAR	FREMGEN,JM		27	37
0.00	CRANDALL,RH	JL	69	TAR			457	466
0.00	DEINZER,HT	JA	66	TAR			21	31
0.00	DUVALL,RM	JL	65	TAR	BULLOCH,J		569	573
0.00	ELLIOTT,EL	OC	68	TAR	LARREA,J	RIVERA,JM	763	768
0.00	ELNICKI,RA	ST	77	JAR			209	218
0.00	FRANK,WG	OC	65	TAR			854	862
0.00	FU,P	SP	71	JAR			40	51
0.00	GIBBS,G	OC	64	TAR			4	7
0.00	GOGGANS,TP	JL	64	TAR			627	630
0.00	GOLDBERG,L	JL	63	TAR			457	469
0.00	HANSEN,ES	ST	77	JAR			156	201
0.00	HEIN,LW	JL	63	TAR			508	520
0.00	HEINS,EB	AP	66	TAR			323	326
0.00	HERBERT,L	JL	71	TAR			433	440
0.00	HORRIGAN,JO	JL	65	TAR			558	568
0.00	HOSKIN,KW	01	88	AOS	MACVE,RH		37	73
0.00	HYLTON,DP	JL	64	TAR			667	670
0.00	IMKE,FJ	AP	66	TAR			318	322
0.00	JENSEN,HL	OC	76	TAR	WYNDELTS,RW		846	853
0.00	JENTZ,GA	JL	66	TAR			535	541
0.00	JENTZ,GA	AP	67	TAR			362	365
0.00	JOHNSON,WB	AP	85	JAE	MAGEE,RP	NAGARAJAN,NJ	151	174
0.00	KALINSKI,BD	JL	63	TAR			591	595
0.00	KAPLAN,HG	JA	64	TAR	SOLOMON,KI		145	149
0.00	KAUFMAN,F	OC	67	TAR			713	720
0.00	KEISTER JR,OR	AP	63	TAR			371	376
0.00	KETZ,JE	AU	83	JAA	WYATT,AR		29	43
0.00	KIRCHER,P	OC	65	TAR			742	752
0.00	KIRCHER,P	JL	67	TAR			537	543
0.00	KRIPKE,H	AU	78	JAA			4	32
0.00	KUBLIN,M	JL	65	TAR			626	635
0.00	LAMDEN,CW	JA	64	TAR			128	132
0.00	LARSON,KD	OC	69	TAR	GONEDES,NJ		720	728
0.00	LAUGHLIN,RC	05	87	AOS			479	502
0.00	LEE,GA	SP	73	JAR			47	61
0.00	LEE,LC	AP	69	TAR	BEDFORD,NM		256	275
0.00	LEHMAN,C	05	87	AOS	TINKER,T		503	522
0.00	LEVY,H	AU	87	JAA	BYUN,YH		355	369
0.00	LI,DH	OC	64	TAR			946	950
0.00	LINOWES,DF	JA	65	TAR			97	104

TREATMENTS= OTHER

CITE IND- EX	FIRST AUTHOR	ISS- UE	YE- AR	JOUR -NAL	SECOND AUTHOR	THIRD AUTHOR	PAG BEG	PAG END
0.00	LOWE,HD	AP	67	TAR			356	360
0.00	LOWE,RE	OC	65	TAR			839	846
0.00	LUCAS,HC	OC	75	TAR			735	746
0.00	LUNESKI,C	OC	67	TAR			767	771
0.00	LYNN,ES	AP	64	TAR			371	376
0.00	MACKENZIE,O	AP	64	TAR			363	370
0.00	MATTINGLY,LA	OC	64	TAR			996	3
0.00	MAUTZ,RK	AP	65	TAR			299	311
0.00	MAUTZ,RK	JL	69	TAR	SKOUSEN,KF		447	456
0.00	MAY,PT	JL	69	TAR			583	592
0.00	MELBERG,WF	JA	72	TAR			116	133
0.00	MILLER,HE	JA	66	TAR			1	7
0.00	MORENO,RG	OC	64	TAR			990	995
0.00	MORGAN,G	05	88	AOS			477	485
0.00	MOST,KS	OC	72	TAR			722	734
0.00	NICHOLS,AC	OC	68	TAR	GRAWOIG,DE		631	639
0.00	PATON,WA	JA	67	TAR			7	23
0.00	PETRI,E	AP	78	TAR	MINCH,RA		415	428
0.00	PETRI,E	AP	79	TAR	GELFAND,J		330	345
0.00	POMERANZ,F	AU	77	JAA			45	52
0.00	POWELL,RM	JL	66	TAR			525	534
0.00	PRATER,GI	OC	66	TAR			619	625
0.00	RAPPAPORT,A	OC	64	TAR			951	962
0.00	RATSCH,H	JA	64	TAR			140	144
0.00	ROBINSON,LA	JA	64	TAR	HALL,TP		62	69
0.00	ROLLER,J	AP	67	TAR	WILLIAMS,TH		349	355
0.00	SCHIFF,M	AU	77	JAA	SORTER,GH	WIESEN,JL	19	44
0.00	SCHNEIDER,AJ	AP	67	TAR			342	348
0.00	SEILER,RE	OC	66	TAR			652	656
0.00	SINGER,FA	OC	65	TAR			847	853
0.00	SPENCER,MH	AP	63	TAR			310	316
0.00	STANDISH,PEM	JL	64	TAR			654	666
0.00	STETTLER,HF	OC	65	TAR			723	730
0.00	STONE,ML	ST	68	JAR			59	66
0.00	SUSSMAN,MR	AP	65	TAR			407	413
0.00	TINKER,T	02	88	AOS			165	189
0.00	TOWNSEND,LA	JA	67	TAR			1	6
0.00	VANCE,LL	JA	66	TAR			48	51
0.00	VATTER,WJ	OC	67	TAR			721	730
0.00	WEIGAND,RE	JL	63	TAR			584	590
0.00	WEISER,HJ	JL	66	TAR			518	524
0.00	WELKE,WR	AP	66	TAR			253	256
0.00	WELSCH,GA	OC	64	TAR			8	13
0.00	WHEELER,JT	JA	70	TAR			1	10
0.00	WILLIAMS,TH	OC	67	TAR	GRIFFIN,CH		642	649
0.00	WINJUM,JO	AU	71	JAR			333	350
0.00	WOODS,RS	JL	64	TAR			598	614
0.00	YU,SC	JA	66	TAR			8	20
0.00	ZANNETOS,ZS	JL	67	TAR			566	571

TREATMENTS= OTHER

4.61   TREATMENTS= SUBMISSN TO THE FASB ETC.

CITE IND-EX	FIRST AUTHOR	ISS-UE	YE-AR	JOUR-NAL	SECOND AUTHOR	THIRD AUTHOR	PAG BEG	PAG END
7.91	WATTS,RL	JA	78	TAR	ZIMMERMAN,JL		112	134
2.17	LEFTWICH,RW	JA	83	TAR			23	42
1.33	HOSKIN,KW	02	86	AOS	MACVE,RH		105	136
1.25	HOPWOOD,AG	03	85	AOS			361	376
0.88	BROWN,PR	SP	81	JAR			232	246
0.67	KINNEY JR,WR	MR	86	JAE			73	89
0.50	NEWMAN,DP	SP	81	JAR			247	262
0.50	O'LEARY,T	01	85	AOS			87	104
0.44	DOPUCH,N	JA	80	TAR	SUNDER,S		1	21
0.40	MCKEE,AJ	OC	84	TAR	BELL,TB	BOATSMAN,JR	647	659
0.25	HUSSEIN,ME	01	81	AOS			27	38
0.25	KELLY,R	AU	85	JAR			619	632
0.22	BROMWICH,M	AP	80	TAR			288	300
0.22	HUSSEIN,ME	SU	80	JAA	KETZ,JE		354	367
0.20	PURO,M	AU	84	JAR			624	646
0.20	SUTTON,TG	01	84	AOS			81	95
0.15	RITTS,BA	SP	74	JAR			93	111
0.14	SELTO,FH	AU	82	JAR	GROVE,HD		676	688
0.13	NEWMAN,DP	ST	81	JAR			134	156
0.10	PEARSON,MA	WI	79	JAA	LINDGREN,JH	MYERS,BL	122	134
0.00	BROWN,PR	SU	82	JAA			282	290
0.00	BUBLITZ,B	WI	84	JAA	KEE,R		123	137
0.00	CHUA,WF	06	86	AOS			583	598
0.00	GAMBLE,GO	SP	86	JAA			102	117
0.00	GUTBERLET,LG	AU	83	JAA			16	28
0.00	HARRISON,GL	03	86	AOS	MCKINNON,JL		233	252
0.00	HILL,HP	WI	82	JAA			99	109
0.00	HOLDER,WW	WI	82	JAA	EUDY,KH		110	125
0.00	JOHNSON,SB	SP	82	JAA	MESSIER JR,WF		195	213
0.00	JOYCE,EJ	AU	82	JAR	LIBBY,R	SUNDER,S	654	675
0.00	MELLMAN,M	AU	86	JAA	SEILER,ME		305	318
0.00	MOODY,SM	AU	86	JAA	FLESHER,DL		319	330
0.00	MOORES,K	01	86	AOS	STEADMAN,GT		19	34
0.00	MURRAY,D	AU	83	JAA	JOHNSON,R		4	15
0.00	NEWMAN,DP	OC	81	TAR			897	909
0.00	POWNALL,G	AU	86	JAR			291	315
0.00	PURO,M	SP	85	JAA			165	177
0.00	SAVOIE,LM	ST	69	JAR			55	62
0.00	SCHEINER,JH	AU	84	JAR			789	797
0.00	SELTO,FH	AU	83	JAR	GROVE,HD		619	622
0.00	WIESEN,JL	SU	81	JAA			309	324

TREATMENTS= SUBMISSN TO THE FASB ETC.

4.62　TREATMENTS= MANAGER DECISION CHARS.

CITE IND- EX	FIRST AUTHOR	ISS- UE	YE- AR	JOUR -NAL	SECOND AUTHOR	THIRD AUTHOR	PAG BEG	PAG END
2.08	HOPWOOD,AG	ST	72	JAR			156	182
1.50	DYE,RA	AU	83	JAR			514	533
1.46	DERMER,JD	JL	73	TAR			511	519
1.00	ONSI,M	JL	73	TAR			535	548
0.77	SAN MIGUEL,JG	04	76	AOS			357	374
0.50	SAVICH,RS	JL	77	TAR			642	652
0.50	VASARHELYI,MA	SP	77	JAR			138	153
0.33	MITROFF,II	23	83	AOS	MASON,RO		195	204
0.14	EGER,C	AU	82	JAR	DICKHAUT,JW		711	723
0.08	MCCOSH,AM	04	76	AOS	RAHMAN,M		339	356
0.00	ANDERSON JR,TN	AU	82	JAR	KIDA,TE		403	414
0.00	ANDERSON,MJ	05	88	AOS			431	446
0.00	CAMPBELL,JE	34	84	AOS			329	342
0.00	DEJONG,DV	ST	85	JAR	FORSYTHE,R	LUNDHOLM,RJ	81	120
0.00	HAIN,HP	AU	67	JAR			154	163
0.00	HOUGHTON,KA	02	87	AOS			143	152
0.00	MEAR,R	JA	87	TAR	FIRTH,MA		176	182
0.00	SHIELDS,MD	04	87	AOS	SOLOMON,I	WALLER,WS	375	385
0.00	SMITH,DB	OC	82	JAE	NICHOLS,DR		109	120

4.63 TREATMENTS= INFO STRCTRS (DISCL)

CITE IND-EX	FIRST AUTHOR	ISS-UE	YE-AR	JOUR-NAL	SECOND AUTHOR	THIRD AUTHOR	PAG BEG	PAG END
2.00	DRIVER,MJ	JL	75	TAR	MOCK,TJ		490	508
1.69	GORDON,LA	01	76	AOS	MILLER,D		59	70
1.33	DEMSKI,JS	AU	86	JAR	SAPPINGTON,DEM		250	269
1.33	HUGHES,PJ	JN	86	JAE			119	142
1.30	PATELL,JM	AG	79	JAE	WOLFSON,MA		117	140
1.25	GJESDAL,F	SP	81	JAR			208	231
1.17	VERRECCHIA,RE	DE	83	JAE			179	194
1.11	SHIELDS,MD	04	80	AOS			429	442
1.09	UECKER,WC	SP	78	JAR			169	189
1.00	LIBERTY,SE	OC	86	TAR	ZIMMERMAN,JL	692	712	
1.00	SORTER,GH	JA	69	TAR			12	19
1.00	VERRECCHIA,RE	OC	86	JAE		175	196	
0.92	DICKHAUT,JW	JA	73	TAR			61	79
0.92	HOFSTEDT,TR	AP	77	TAR	HUGHES,GD		379	395
0.90	BENBASAT,I	OC	79	TAR	DEXTER,AS		735	749
0.85	BAREFIELD,RM	AU	72	JAR			229	242
0.82	GORDON,LA	34	78	AOS	LARCKER,DF	TUGGLE,FD	203	214
0.77	BUZBY,SL	JL	74	TAR			423	435
0.77	HOFSTEDT,TR	OC	72	TAR			679	692
0.77	MOCK,TJ	SP	72	JAR	ESTRIN,TL	VASARHELYI,MA	129	153
0.69	REVSINE,L	OC	70	TAR			704	711
0.67	DEANGELO,LE	JL	86	TAR			400	420
0.63	HAKANSSON,NH	ST	81	JAR			1	35
0.62	BAIMAN,S	SP	75	JAR			1	15
0.62	BENSTON,GJ	JL	69	TAR			515	532
0.62	LUSK,EJ	ST	73	JAR			191	202
0.62	RONEN,J	AU	71	JAR			307	332
0.60	MORIARITY,S	SP	79	JAR			205	224
0.60	OHLSON,JA	DE	79	JAE			211	232
0.56	UECKER,WC	SP	80	JAR			191	213
0.56	VERRECCHIA,RE	MR	80	JAE			63	92
0.54	FELTHAM,GA	OC	68	TAR			684	696
0.50	SUNDEM,GL	SP	79	JAR			243	261
0.46	BUTTERWORTH,JE	SP	72	JAR			1	27
0.46	DEMSKI,JS	SP	72	JAR			58	76
0.46	JENSEN,RE	AU	66	JAR			224	238
0.46	MARSHALL,RM	AU	72	JAR			286	307
0.46	MILLER,H	JA	72	TAR			31	37
0.46	SINGHVI,SS	JA	71	TAR	DESAI,HB		129	138
0.44	GONEDES,NJ	AU	80	JAR			441	476
0.42	FELTHAM,GA	SP	77	JAR			42	70
0.38	LEV,B	AU	68	JAR			247	261
0.38	MAY,RG	JA	73	TAR	SUNDEM,GL		80	94
0.38	MOCK,TJ	ST	69	JAR			124	159
0.38	STALLMAN,JC	ST	69	JAR			29	43
0.31	CHANDRA,G	OC	74	TAR			733	742
0.27	HIRSCH JR,ML	AU	78	JAR			254	269
0.25	COGGER,KO	AU	81	JAR			285	298

TREATMENTS= INFO STRCTRS (DISCL)

CITE IND-EX	FIRST AUTHOR	ISS-UE	YE-AR	JOUR-NAL	SECOND AUTHOR	THIRD AUTHOR	PAG BEG	PAG END
0.25	DYE,RA	AU	85	JAR			544	574
0.25	STAUBUS,GJ	JA	85	TAR			53	75
0.25	WRIGHT,WF	04	77	AOS			323	332
0.23	BARNEA,A	JA	76	TAR	RONEN,J	SADAN,S	110	122
0.23	CHOI,FD	AU	73	JAR			159	175
0.23	FERTAKIS,JP	OC	69	TAR			680	691
0.23	MOCK,TJ	OC	71	TAR			765	777
0.23	MOCK,TJ	JL	73	TAR			520	534
0.23	OHLSON,JA	AU	75	JAR			267	282
0.17	DICKHAUT,JW	AU	83	JAR	LERE,JC		495	513
0.15	BERNHARDT,I	SP	70	JAR	COPELAND,RM		95	98
0.15	COPELAND,RM	SP	68	JAR	FREDERICKS,W		106	113
0.15	KNUTSON,PH	JA	70	TAR			55	68
0.15	LEV,B	SP	70	JAR			78	94
0.15	RONEN,J	OC	73	TAR	FALK,G		696	717
0.14	OTLEY,DT	SP	82	JAR	DIAS,FJB		171	188
0.14	PRATT,J	SP	82	JAR			189	209
0.14	UECKER,WC	AU	82	JAR			388	402
0.13	RAMANATHAN,KV	02	81	AOS	WEIS,WL		143	152
0.11	FLAHERTY,RE	AU	80	JAA	SCHWARTZ,BN		47	56
0.08	BIRNBERG,JG	OC	65	TAR			814	820
0.08	SPILLER JR,EA	SP	74	JAR	VIRGIL JR,RL		112	142
0.00	ARNETT,HE	JA	65	TAR			54	64
0.00	ATIASE,RK	SP	87	JAR			168	176
0.00	BACKER,M	JL	69	TAR			533	538
0.00	BIDWELL III,CM	SP	81	JAA	RIDDLE JR,JR		198	214
0.00	BILDERSEE,JS	SU	87	JAA	KAHN,N		239	256
0.00	BLOCHER,E	06	86	AOS	MOFFIE,RP	ZMUD,RW	457	470
0.00	FERTAKIS,JP	JL	70	TAR			509	512
0.00	FESS,PE	AP	66	TAR			266	270
0.00	FRISHKOFF,P	AU	84	JAA	FRISHKOFF,PA	BOUWMAN,MJ	44	53
0.00	HAKANSSON,NH	JL	69	TAR			495	514
0.00	HOLTHAUSEN,RW	SP	88	JAR	VERRECCHIA,RE		82	106
0.00	IJIRI,Y	01	80	AOS	KELLY,EC		115	123
0.00	IJIRI,Y	OC	86	TAR			745	760
0.00	ISELIN,ER	02	88	AOS			147	164
0.00	JENSEN,RE	JL	70	TAR			502	508
0.00	JUNG,WO	SP	88	JAR	KWON,YK		146	153
0.00	KIM,KK	JL	88	TAR			472	489
0.00	LEWIS,BL	SP	85	JAR	BELL,J		228	239
0.00	LUNDHOLM,RJ	SP	88	JAR			107	118
0.00	MAURIELLO,JA	AP	64	TAR			347	357
0.00	MILLER,EM	AU	80	JAA			6	19
0.00	MOST,KS	JA	69	TAR			145	152
0.00	MURRAY,D	AU	86	JAR	FRAZIER,KB		400	404
0.00	PURDY,CR	ST	69	JAR	SMITH JR,JM	GRAY,J	1	18
0.00	STAUBUS,GJ	JL	66	TAR			397	412
0.00	STEVENSON,RA	AP	66	TAR			312	317
0.00	THOMPSON II,RB	AU	87	JAR	OLSEN,C	DIETRICH,JR	245	274
0.00	WEBER,R	JL	86	TAR			498	518

TREATMENTS= INFO STRCTRS (DISCL)

CITE IND-EX	FIRST AUTHOR	ISS-UE	YE-AR	JOUR-NAL	SECOND AUTHOR	THIRD AUTHOR	PAG BEG	PAG END

TREATMENTS= INFO STRCTRS (DISCL)

4.64   TREATMENTS= AUDITOR TRAINING

CITE IND- EX	FIRST AUTHOR	ISS- UE	YE- AR	JOUR -NAL	SECOND AUTHOR	THIRD AUTHOR	PAG BEG	PAG END
2.20	BROWN,LD	SP	79	JAR	ROZEFF,MS		179	189
0.14	VIGELAND,RL	AP	82	TAR			348	357
0.08	DALTON,FE	JA	70	TAR	MINER,JB		134	139
0.00	KREISER,L	AP	77	TAR			427	437
0.00	MCRAE,TW	AU	65	JAR			255	260
0.00	TRUEBLOOD,RM	SP	63	JAR			86	95
0.00	YOUNG,SD	AP	88	TAR			283	291

TREATMENTS= AUDITOR TRAINING

4.65 TREATMENTS= INSIDER TRADING RULES

CITE IND-EX	FIRST AUTHOR	ISS-UE	YE-AR	JOUR-NAL	SECOND AUTHOR	THIRD AUTHOR	PAG BEG	PAG END
0.17	RONEN,J	AP	77	TAR			438	449
0.00	YOUNG,SD	SP	85	JAA			178	183

4.66   TREATMENTS= PROBABLTY ELICITATION

CITE IND-EX	FIRST AUTHOR	ISS-UE	YE-AR	JOUR-NAL	SECOND AUTHOR	THIRD AUTHOR	PAG BEG	PAG END
1.00	CHESLEY,GR	AP	75	TAR			325	337
1.00	FELIX JR,WL	OC	76	TAR			800	807
0.63	CROSBY,MA	AP	81	TAR			355	365
0.58	CHESLEY,GR	SP	77	JAR			1	11
0.57	SOLOMON,I	01	82	AOS	KROGSTAD,JL	ROMNEY,MB	27	42
0.54	CHESLEY,GR	SP	76	JAR			27	48
0.46	GONEDES,NJ	AU	74	JAR	IJIRI,Y		251	269
0.36	KEYS,DE	AU	78	JAR			389	399
0.33	CROSBY,MA	AU	80	JAR			585	593
0.27	CHESLEY,GR	AU	78	JAR			225	241
0.08	ALBRECHT,WS	OC	76	TAR			824	837
0.00	JOHNSON,WB	04	82	AOS			349	368
0.00	SCOTT,WR	SP	79	JAR			156	178
0.00	THOMPSON,WW	JL	65	TAR	KEMPER,EL		574	578

4.67 TREATMENTS= INTL DIFFERENCES

CITE IND-EX	FIRST AUTHOR	ISS-UE	YE-AR	JOUR-NAL	SECOND AUTHOR	THIRD AUTHOR	PAG BEG	PAG END
0.33	NAIR,RD	JL	80	TAR	FRANK,WG		426	450
0.31	BARRETT,ME	SP	76	JAR			10	26
0.27	LOEB,M	SP	78	JAR	MAGAT,WA		103	121
0.22	GRAY,SJ	SP	80	JAR			64	76
0.17	MCLEAY,S	01	83	AOS			31	56
0.11	FERRIS,KR	04	80	AOS	DILLARD,JF	NETHERCOTT,L	361	368
0.09	GRAY,SJ	AU	78	JAR			242	253
0.08	ABEL,R	SP	69	JAR			1	11
0.08	DAVIDSON,S	AU	66	JAR	KOHLMEIER,JM		183	212
0.00	BIRD,PA	SP	65	JAR			1	11
0.00	BIRNBERG,JG	05	88	AOS	SNODGRASS,C		447	464
0.00	FARMAN,WL	JA	63	TAR	HOU,C		133	141
0.00	FITZGERALD,RD	AU	79	JAA	KELLEY,EM		5	20
0.00	GRAY,SJ	SP	84	JAR	RADEBAUGH,LH		351	360
0.00	HATFIELD,HR	AU	66	JAR			169	182
0.00	HUSSEIN,ME	AU	86	AUD	BAVISHI,VB	GANGOLLY,JS	124	133
0.00	MUELLER,GG	JA	63	TAR			142	147
0.00	MUELLER,GG	AU	64	JAR			148	157
0.00	RICHARDSON,AJ	04	88	AOS			381	396
0.00	ROSE,H	AU	64	JAR			137	147
0.00	SCHIENEMAN,GS	AU	79	JAA			21	30
0.00	SCHWEIKART,JA	06	86	AOS			541	554
0.00	WILKINSON,TL	JA	64	TAR			133	139

4.68   TREATMENTS= FORM OF ORG. (PARTNER.)

CITE IND- EX	FIRST AUTHOR	ISS- UE	YE- AR	JOUR -NAL	SECOND AUTHOR	THIRD AUTHOR	PAG BEG	PAG END
3.62	BRUNS JR,WJ	AU	75	JAR	WATERHOUSE,JH		177	203
0.73	BARIFF,ML	01	78	AOS	GALBRAITH,JR		15	28
0.60	GORDON,LA	01	84	AOS	NARAYANAN,VK		33	47
0.46	SORTER,GH	AU	64	JAR	BECKER,S	ARCHIBALD,TR	183	196
0.45	HERTOG,JF	01	78	AOS			29	46
0.31	SHANK,JK	JL	73	TAR	COPELAND,RM		494	501
0.17	KILMANN,RH	04	83	AOS			341	360
0.00	DERMER,JD	01	88	AOS			25	36
0.00	SHEVLIN,T	JL	87	TAR			480	509
0.00	SHIELDS,D	01	84	AOS			61	80
0.00	THOMAS,AP	03	86	AOS			253	270
0.00	WILLIAMS,DJ	03	86	AOS			271	288

4.69 TREATMENTS= AUDITOR BEHAVIOR

CITE IND-EX	FIRST AUTHOR	ISS-UE	YE-AR	JOUR-NAL	SECOND AUTHOR	THIRD AUTHOR	PAG BEG	PAG END
2.18	HOPWOOD,AG	01	78	AOS			3	14
2.00	SIMUNIC,DA	SP	80	JAR			161	190
1.30	JIAMBALVO,J	AU	79	JAR			436	455
1.25	FERRIS,KR	JL	77	TAR			605	615
1.14	ANTLE,R	AU	82	JAR			504	527
1.14	SOLOMON,I	AU	82	JAR			689	710
0.92	GOSMAN,ML	JA	73	TAR			1	11
0.75	SCHULTZ JR,JJ	AU	81	JAR	RECKERS,PMJ		482	501
0.69	SORENSEN,JE	JL	67	TAR			553	565
0.56	GINZBERG,MJ	04	80	AOS			369	382
0.56	SNOWBALL,D	03	80	AOS			323	340
0.50	DILLARD,JF	03	79	AOS	FERRIS,KR		179	186
0.44	WEBER,R	SP	80	JAR			214	241
0.42	BAKER,CR	JL	77	TAR			576	586
0.40	MAHER,MW	AU	79	JAR	RAMANATHAN,KV	PETERSON,RB	476	503
0.38	PRATT,J	02	81	AOS	JIAMBALVO,J		133	142
0.25	UECKER,WC	JL	81	TAR	BRIEF,AP	KINNEY JR,WR	465	478
0.20	DILLARD,JF	12	79	AOS			31	38
0.20	RICCHIUTE,DN	12	79	AOS			67	76
0.15	LOEB,SE	AU	71	JAR			287	306
0.13	FERRIS,KR	04	81	AOS			317	326
0.08	JENSEN,RE	JA	71	TAR			36	56
0.00	BAIMAN,S	AU	87	JAR	EVANS III,JH	NOEL,J	217	244
0.00	BALACHANDRAN,BV	OC	81	TAR	ZOLTNERS,AA		801	812
0.00	BAMBER,EM	SP	88	AUD	BAMBER,LS	BYLINSKI,JH	137	149
0.00	BRENNER,VC	AU	71	JAR	CARMACK,CW	WEINSTEIN,MG	359	366
0.00	CHOO,F	SP	86	AUD			17	34
0.00	DEAN,RA	03	88	AOS	FERRIS,KR	KONSTANS,C	235	250
0.00	FELIX JR,WL	JA	72	TAR			52	63
0.00	HARRELL,AM	34	84	AOS	STAHL,MJ		241	252
0.00	HARRELL,AM	SP	88	AUD	EICKHOFF,R		105	118
0.00	KIDA,TE	02	84	AOS			137	147
0.00	PRATT,J	04	82	AOS	JIAMBALVO,J		369	380
0.00	SOETERS,J	01	88	AOS	SCHREUDER,H		75	85

4.70 TREATMENTS= METHODOLOGY

CITE IND-EX	FIRST AUTHOR	ISS-UE	YE-AR	JOUR-NAL	SECOND AUTHOR	THIRD AUTHOR	PAG BEG	PAG END
4.83	HOLTHAUSEN,RW	AG	83	JAE	LEFTWICH,RW		77	117
3.18	WATERHOUSE,JH	01	78	AOS	TIESSEN,P		65	76
2.63	ZMIJEWSKI,ME	AG	81	JAE	HAGERMAN,RL		129	149
2.50	BERNARD,VL	SP	87	JAR			1	48
2.50	TOMKINS,C	04	83	AOS	GROVES,R		361	374
2.43	LEV,B	ST	82	JAR	OHLSON,JA		249	322
2.00	BROWN,LD	JL	87	JAE	GRIFFIN,PA	HAGERMAN,RL	159	193
1.83	KAPLAN,RS	OC	83	TAR			686	705
1.78	ASHTON,RH	SP	80	JAR	KRAMER,SS		1	15
1.50	CHRISTENSON,C	JA	83	TAR			1	22
1.40	COLLINS,DW	SP	84	JAR	DENT,WT		48	84
1.38	BEAVER,WH	SP	81	JAR			163	184
1.31	ABDEL-KHALIK,AR	OC	74	TAR			743	750
1.20	CHRISTIE,AA	DE	84	JAE	KENNELLEY,MD	KING,JW	205	217
1.20	DYCKMAN,TR	SP	84	JAR	ZEFF,SA		225	297
1.14	SWIERINGA,RJ	ST	82	JAR	WEICK,KE		56	101
1.00	CHRISTIE,AA	DE	87	JAE			231	258
1.00	DEMSKI,JS	ST	82	JAR	KREPS,DM		117	148
1.00	EINHORN,HJ	ST	76	JAR			196	206
1.00	IMHOFF JR,EA	AU	82	JAR	PARE,PV		429	439
1.00	KAPLAN,RS	45	86	AOS			429	452
0.80	MARAIS,ML	ST	84	JAR			34	54
0.77	HARIED,AA	AU	72	JAR			376	391
0.77	LOREK,KS	AP	76	TAR	MCDONALD,CL	PATZ,DH	321	330
0.75	BROWN,LD	AP	85	TAR	GARDNER,JC		262	277
0.70	GONEDES,NJ	AU	79	JAR	DOPUCH,N		384	410
0.69	COPELAND,RM	AP	73	TAR	FRANCIA,AJ	STRAWSER,RH	365	374
0.67	CHUA,WF	OC	86	TAR			601	632
0.67	WILNER,N	01	86	AOS	BIRNBERG,JG		71	82
0.64	WILDAVSKY,A	01	78	AOS			77	88
0.60	DYCKMAN,TR	ST	84	JAR	PHILBRICK,D	STEPHAN,J	1	30
0.60	LEV,B	DE	79	JAE	SUNDER,S		187	210
0.60	PATELL,JM	AU	79	JAR			528	549
0.60	VERRECCHIA,RE	MR	79	JAE			77	90
0.56	LEFTWICH,RW	DE	80	JAE			193	211
0.55	FLAMHOLTZ,EG	02	78	AOS	COOK,E		115	140
0.54	BIRNBERG,JG	JA	68	TAR	NATH,R		38	45
0.50	BEAVER,WH	JA	87	TAR			137	144
0.50	BROWN,LD	SP	85	JAR	GARDNER,JC		84	109
0.50	HAGG,J	12	79	AOS	HEDLUND,G		135	143
0.50	HOWARD,TP	OC	83	TAR	NIKOLAI,LA		765	776
0.33	FRECKA,TJ	JA	83	TAR	HOPWOOD,WS		115	128
0.33	HOPWOOD,WS	SP	80	JAR			77	90
0.33	NEWMAN,DP	02	80	AOS			217	230
0.33	SEFCIK,SE	AU	86	JAR	THOMPSON,R		316	334
0.33	WRIGHT,CJ	JA	86	TAR	GROFF,JE		91	100
0.31	MCRAE,TW	SP	74	JAR			80	92
0.31	WEST,RR	SP	70	JAR			118	125

CITE IND-EX	FIRST AUTHOR	ISS-UE	YE-AR	JOUR-NAL	SECOND AUTHOR	THIRD AUTHOR	PAG BEG	PAG END
0.30	NAIR,RD	SP	79	JAR			225	242
0.29	ASHTON,AH	AU	82	JAR			415	428
0.27	BUZBY,SL	34	78	AOS	FALK,H		191	202
0.25	ANDERSON,MJ	AU	85	JAR			843	852
0.25	DEJONG,DV	AU	85	JAR	FORSYTHE,R	UECKER,WC	753	793
0.25	OGDEN,S	02	85	AOS	BOUGEN,P		211	226
0.23	GERBOTH,DL	JL	73	TAR			475	482
0.23	MARSHALL,RM	JA	75	TAR			99	111
0.22	BECK,PJ	SP	80	JAR			16	37
0.20	GROVE,HD	JL	79	TAR	SAVICH,RS		522	537
0.20	MORSE,D	AU	84	JAR			605	623
0.20	OHLSON,JA	AU	79	JAR	PATELL,JM		504	505
0.20	RICCHIUTE,DN	SP	84	JAR			341	350
0.20	SMITH,G	AU	84	AUD	KROGSTAD,JL		107	117
0.20	STONE,M	JL	84	TAR	BUBLITZ,B		469	473
0.17	HARRISON JR,WT	SP	83	JAR	TOMASSINI,LA	DIETRICH,JR	65	77
0.17	LARCKER,DF	JA	83	TAR	LESSIG,VP		58	77
0.15	BALL,R	SP	71	JAR			1	31
0.15	MEYERS,SL	AP	73	TAR			318	322
0.14	EMERY,DR	AU	82	JAR	BARRON,FH	MESSIER JR,WF	450	458
0.14	GIBBINS,M	SP	82	JAR			121	138
0.14	WRIGHT,WF	01	82	AOS			65	78
0.13	COPELAND,RM	SP	81	JAR	TAYLOR,RL	BROWN,SH	197	207
0.11	LOY,LD	SP	80	JAA	TOOLE,HR		227	243
0.10	OHLSON,JA	AU	79	JAR			506	527
0.08	JOHNSON,O	JA	72	TAR			64	74
0.00	ABDEL-KHALIK,AR	SP	83	JAR			293	296
0.00	BEAVER,WH	DE	84	JAE	GRIFFIN,PA	LANDSMAN,WR	219	223
0.00	BENISHAY,H	SU	87	JAA			203	238
0.00	BINDER,JJ	SP	85	JAR			370	383
0.00	BROWN,LD	02	87	AOS	GARDNER,JC	VASARHELYI,MA	193	204
0.00	BURGSTAHLER,D	SP	86	JAR	NOREEN,EW		170	186
0.00	CARSLAW,C	AP	88	TAR			321	327
0.00	COGGER,KO	AU	82	JAR	RULAND,W		733	737
0.00	DHARAN,BG	SP	83	JAR			256	270
0.00	DYL,EA	02	85	AOS	LILLY,MS		171	176
0.00	ELGERS,P	OC	87	TAR	CALLAHAN,C	STROCK,E	763	773
0.00	GAMBLE,GO	SP	81	JAA			220	237
0.00	HECK,JL	OC	86	TAR	BREMSER,WG		735	744
0.00	HINES,RD	OC	88	TAR			642	656
0.00	HONIG,LE	SP	78	JAA			231	236
0.00	HOUGHTON,KA	03	88	AOS			263	280
0.00	JAIN,PC	SP	86	JAR			76	96
0.00	JAIN,PC	SP	86	JAR			187	193
0.00	JONSON,LC	34	78	AOS	JONSSON,B	SVENSSON,G	261	268
0.00	LANDSMAN,WR	OC	88	TAR	MAGLIOLO,J		586	604
0.00	LEE,CF	AP	88	TAR	WU,C		292	306
0.00	LEE,CJ	AU	84	JAR			776	781
0.00	LEE,CJ	SP	85	JAR			213	227
0.00	LEV,B	AP	83	JAE			31	48

TREATMENTS= METHODOLOGY

CITE IND-EX	FIRST AUTHOR	ISS-UE	YE-AR	JOUR -NAL	SECOND AUTHOR	THIRD AUTHOR	PAG BEG	PAG END
0.00	LIVNAT,J	AU	81	JAR			350	359
0.00	MCNICHOLS,M	JL	88	JAE			239	273
0.00	MOCK,TJ	AU	78	JAR	VASARHELYI,MA		414	423
0.00	NOREEN,EW	SP	88	JAR			119	133
0.00	ROBBINS,WA	AU	86	JAR	AUSTIN,KR		412	421
0.00	SMITH,G	AU	88	AUD			108	117
0.00	SMITH,VL	AU	87	AUD	SCHATZBERG,J	WALLER,WS	71	93
0.00	SNOWBALL,D	01	86	AOS			47	70
0.00	THOMPSON,RB	JL	88	TAR	OLSEN,C	DIETRICH,JR	448	471
0.00	WATKINS,PR	SP	84	JAR			406	411
0.00	WILKERSON JR,JE	SP	87	JAR			161	167
0.00	WILLIAMS,PF	04	82	AOS			405	410
0.00	YOUNG,AE	SP	80	JAA			244	250
0.00	ZIEBART,DA	AU	85	JAR			920	926

TREATMENTS= METHODOLOGY

4.71 TREATMENTS= BUSINESS FAILURE

CITE IND-EX	FIRST AUTHOR	ISS-UE	YE-AR	JOUR-NAL	SECOND AUTHOR	THIRD AUTHOR	PAG BEG	PAG END
1.44	OHLSON,JA	SP	80	JAR			109	131
1.38	BEAVER,WH	ST	66	JAR			71	111
1.23	LIBBY,R	SP	75	JAR			150	161
1.20	ZMIJEWSKI,ME	ST	84	JAR			59	82
1.15	DEAKIN,EB	SP	72	JAR			167	179
1.00	CASEY JR,CJ	JA	80	TAR			36	49
0.89	ABDEL-KHALIK,AR	AU	80	JAR	EL-SHESHAI,KM		325	342
0.77	KENNEDY,HA	SP	75	JAR			97	116
0.62	BEAVER,WH	JA	68	TAR			113	122
0.50	GENTRY,JA	SP	85	JAR	NEWBOLD,P	WHITFORD,DT	146	160
0.46	BEAVER,WH	AU	68	JAR			179	192
0.46	ELAM,R	JA	75	TAR			25	43
0.44	HOLT,RN	03	80	AOS	CARROLL,R		285	296
0.40	STOCK,D	SP	84	JAR	WATSON,CJ		192	206
0.33	CASEY JR,CJ	AP	86	TAR	MCGEE,VE	STICKNEY,CP	249	262
0.31	WILCOX,JA	ST	73	JAR			163	179
0.25	ANELL,B	04	85	AOS			479	492
0.25	PENNO,M	SP	85	JAR			240	255
0.25	SCHWARTZ,KB	AP	85	TAR	MENON,K		248	261
0.20	MARAIS,ML	ST	84	JAR	PATELL,JM	WOLFSON,MA	87	114
0.17	JOHNSON,WB	JA	83	TAR			78	97
0.17	SCHIPPER,K	ST	77	JAR			1	40
0.14	EMERY,GW	AU	82	JAR	COGGER,KO		290	303
0.00	BUCHMAN,TA	03	85	AOS			267	286
0.00	CASEY JR,CJ	SP	85	JAR	BARTCZAK,N		384	401
0.00	CASEY JR,CJ	AP	86	TAR	SELLING,T		302	317
0.00	CHALOS,P	AU	85	JAR			527	543
0.00	FLESHER,DL	JL	86	TAR	FLESHER,TK		421	434
0.00	HOUGHTON,KA	AU	84	JAR	SENGUPTA,R		768	775
0.00	HOUGHTON,KA	SP	84	JAR			361	368
0.00	KIDA,TE	SP	84	JAR			145	152
0.00	LAU,AH	SP	87	JAR			127	138
0.00	MENSAH,YM	AP	83	TAR			228	246
0.00	MENSAH,YM	SP	84	JAR			380	395
0.00	RAMAN,KK	AU	82	JAA			44	50
0.00	ROSE,PS	AU	82	JAA	ANDREWS,WT	GIROUX,GA	20	31

TREATMENTS= BUSINESS FAILURE

4.72 TREATMENTS= EDUCATION

CITE IND-EX	FIRST AUTHOR	ISS-UE	YE-AR	JOUR-NAL	SECOND AUTHOR	THIRD AUTHOR	PAG BEG	PAG END
0.00	ANDERSON,HM	OC	63	TAR	GRIFFIN,FB		813	818
0.00	BOURN,AM	AU	66	JAR			213	223
0.00	FALK,H	AU	72	JAR			359	375
0.00	FERRIS,KR	03	82	AOS			225	230
0.00	GRAY,J	AP	63	TAR	WILLINGHAM,JJ	JOHNSTON,K	336	346
0.00	REILLY,FK	AU	72	JAR	STETTLER,HF		308	321
0.00	SEELYE,AL	AP	63	TAR			302	309
0.00	ZANNETOS,ZS	AP	63	TAR			326	335

4.73 TREATMENTS= PROF. RESPONSIBLTS

CITE IND-EX	FIRST AUTHOR	ISS-UE	YE-AR	JOUR-NAL	SECOND AUTHOR	THIRD AUTHOR	PAG BEG	PAG END
0.85	ABDEL-KHALIK,AR	ST	73	JAR			104	138
0.20	ARANYA,N	JA	84	TAR	FERRIS,KR		1	15
0.00	ABDEL-KHALIK,AR	SP	66	JAR			37	46
0.00	ARANYA,N	04	81	AOS	POLLOCK,J	AMERNIC,J	271	280
0.00	CAMPBELL,DR	SP	83	JAA			196	211
0.00	CAMPFIELD,WL	JL	63	TAR			521	527
0.00	CARMICHAEL,DR	SU	84	JAA	WHITTINGTON,OR		347	361
0.00	DEVINE,CT	ST	66	JAR			160	176
0.00	GORMLEY,RJ	AU	82	JAA			51	59
0.00	GUTBERLET,LG	SU	80	JAA			313	338
0.00	HORVITZ,JS	WI	81	JAA	HAINKEL,M		114	127
0.00	JOHNSTON,DJ	SP	80	JAA	LEMON,WM	NEUMANN,FL	251	263
0.00	KUNITAKE,WK	SU	86	JAA	WHITE JR,CE		222	231
0.00	NORRIS,DR	01	84	AOS	NIEBUHR,RE		49	59
0.00	SCHEINER,JH	AU	82	JAR	KIGER,JE		482	496
0.00	SCHIENEMAN,GS	SP	83	JAA			212	226
0.00	SCHNEE,EJ	AU	81	JAA	TAYLOR,ME		18	29

4.74 TREATMENTS= FORECASTS

CITE IND- EX	FIRST AUTHOR	ISS- UE	YE- AR	JOUR -NAL	SECOND AUTHOR	THIRD AUTHOR	PAG BEG	PAG END
4.54	PATELL,JM	AU	76	JAR			246	276
4.25	FOSTER,G	JA	77	TAR			1	21
4.20	BEAVER,WH	AU	79	JAR	CLARKE,R	WRIGHT,WF	316	340
3.00	GONEDES,NJ	SP	76	JAR	DOPUCH,N	PENMAN,SH	89	137
2.58	WATTS,RL	AU	77	JAR	LEFTWICH,RW		253	271
2.50	BROWN,LD	AP	87	JAE	GRIFFIN,PA	HAGERMAN,RL	61	87
2.25	GRIFFIN,PA	SP	77	JAR			71	83
2.14	FRIED,D	OC	82	JAE	GIVOLY,D		85	107
2.00	ALBRECHT,WS	AU	77	JAR	LOOKABILL,LL	MCKEOWN,JC	226	244
2.00	HUGHES,JS	JA	87	TAR	RICKS,WE		158	175
1.89	PENMAN,SH	SP	80	JAR			132	160
1.31	FOSTER,G	SP	73	JAR			25	37
1.22	COLLINS,WA	AU	80	JAR	HOPWOOD,WS		390	406
1.09	CRICHFIELD,T	JL	78	TAR	DYCKMAN,TR	LAKONISHOK,J	651	668
1.00	BASI,BA	AP	76	TAR	CAREY,KJ	TWARK,RD	244	254
1.00	BROWN,LD	SP	87	JAR	RICHARDSON,GD	SCHWAGER,SJ	49	67
1.00	GIVOLY,D	DE	79	JAE	LAKONISHOK,J		165	185
1.00	WAYMIRE,G	AU	84	JAR			703	718
0.92	MCDONALD,CL	JL	73	TAR			502	510
0.90	LOREK,KS	SP	79	JAR			190	204
0.83	PINCUS,M	SP	83	JAR			155	183
0.67	TRUEMAN,B	MR	86	JAE			53	72
0.62	DAILY,RA	OC	71	TAR			686	692
0.60	AJINKYA,BB	AU	84	JAR	GIFT,MJ		425	444
0.60	NICHOLS,DR	SP	79	JAR	TSAY,JJ		140	155
0.55	IMHOFF JR,EA	OC	78	TAR			836	850
0.55	RULAND,W	AP	78	TAR			439	447
0.50	ASHTON,AH	AP	85	TAR			173	185
0.50	BROWN,LD	AU	79	JAR	ROZEFF,MS		341	351
0.43	DANOS,P	WI	82	AUD	IMHOFF JR,EA		23	34
0.40	DANOS,P	OC	84	TAR	HOLT,DL	IMHOFF JR,EA	547	573
0.40	IMHOFF JR,EA	AU	84	JAR	LOBO,GJ		541	554
0.38	HOPWOOD,WS	AU	81	JAR	MCKEOWN,JC		313	322
0.36	ABDEL-KHALIK,AR	SP	78	JAR	ESPEJO,J		1	13
0.36	JAGGI,B	OC	78	TAR			961	967
0.33	HASSELL,JM	JA	86	TAR	JENNINGS,RH		58	75
0.22	RONEN,J	SU	80	JAA	SADAN,S		339	353
0.20	BROWN,LD	JL	79	TAR	ROZEFF,MS		585	591
0.20	FRAZIER,KB	SP	84	JAR	INGRAM,RW	TENNYSON,BM	318	331
0.20	SCHREUDER,H	JA	84	TAR	KLAASSEN,J		64	77
0.14	ABDEL-KHALIK,AR	OC	82	TAR	AJINKYA,BB		661	680
0.13	MANEGOLD,JG	AU	81	JAR			360	373
0.08	BAREFIELD,RM	JL	70	TAR			490	501
0.00	BATHKE,AW	AP	84	TAR	LOREK,KS		163	176
0.00	BRANCH,B	SP	81	JAA	BERKOWITZ,B		215	219
0.00	BROWN,LD	SP	80	JAR	HUGHES,JS	ROZEFF,MS	278	288
0.00	COX,CT	OC	85	TAR			692	701
0.00	DALEY,LA	OC	88	TAR	SENKOW,DW	VIGELAND,RL	563	585

CITE IND- EX	FIRST AUTHOR	ISS- UE	YE- AR	JOUR -NAL	SECOND AUTHOR	THIRD AUTHOR	PAG BEG	PAG END
0.00	FARRELY,GE	AP	85	TAR	FERRIS,KR	REICHENSTEIN,WR	278	288
0.00	GIVOLY,D	JL	85	TAR			372	386
0.00	GIVOLY,D	SP	87	JAA	LAKONISHOK,J		117	137
0.00	GREENBERG,R	AU	84	JAR			719	730
0.00	HAGERMAN,RL	AU	84	JAR	ZMIJEWSKI,ME	SHAH,P	526	540
0.00	HOPWOOD,WS	SP	80	JAR			289	296
0.00	JENNINGS,R	SP	87	JAR			90	110
0.00	JOHNSON,DA	AU	84	JAR	PANY,K		731	743
0.00	LEWIS,BL	AP	88	TAR	PATTON,JM	GREEN,SL	270	282
0.00	MEAR,R	04	87	AOS	FIRTH,MA		331	340
0.00	NICHOLS,DR	AP	79	TAR	TSAY,JJ	LARKIN,PD	376	382
0.00	O'BRIEN,PC	JA	88	JAE			53	83
0.00	PUTNAM,K	AU	84	JAA	THOMAS,LR		15	23
0.00	SILHAN,PA	SP	83	JAR			341	347
0.00	WAYMIRE,G	SP	85	JAR			268	295
0.00	WAYMIRE,G	JA	86	TAR			129	142
0.00	WELCH,PR	AU	84	JAR			744	757
0.00	WILD,JJ	SP	87	JAR			139	160

TREATMENTS= FORECASTS

4.75   TREATMENTS= DECISION AIDS

CITE IND-EX	FIRST AUTHOR	ISS-UE	YE-AR	JOUR-NAL	SECOND AUTHOR	THIRD AUTHOR	PAG BEG	PAG END
1.63	JOYCE,EJ	SP	81	JAR	BIDDLE,GC		120	145
1.17	SHIELDS,MD	AP	83	TAR			284	303
0.29	BENBASAT,I	SP	82	JAR	DEXTER,AS		1	11
0.15	REVSINE,L	AP	76	TAR	THIES,JB		255	268
0.00	BASTABLE,CW	SP	81	JAA	BEAMS,FA		248	254
0.00	BENSTON,GJ	JL	76	TAR			483	498
0.00	BUTLER,SA	AU	85	JAR			513	526

TREATMENTS= DECISION AIDS

4.76 TREATMENTS= ORGANIZATION * ENVIRONMENT

CITE IND-EX	FIRST AUTHOR	ISS-UE	YE-AR	JOUR-NAL	SECOND AUTHOR	THIRD AUTHOR	PAG BEG	PAG END
4.50	HOPWOOD,AG	03	87	AOS			207	234
2.67	HOPWOOD,AG	23	83	AOS			287	305
2.00	ARMSTRONG,P	02	85	AOS			129	148
1.80	GOVINDARAJAN,V	02	84	AOS			125	135
1.17	LEWIS,BL	SP	83	JAR	SHIELDS,MD	YOUNG,SM	271	285
1.00	CHENHALL,RH	JA	86	TAR	MORRIS,D		16	35
1.00	COLLINS,DW	JL	87	JAE	KOTHARI,SP	RAYBURN,JD	111	138
0.67	GAA,JC	JL	86	TAR			435	454
0.67	WILLMOTT,H	06	86	AOS			555	582
0.60	INGRAM,RW	SP	84	JAR			126	144
0.50	MACINTOSH,NB	01	87	AOS	DAFT,RL		49	61
0.50	MELUMAD,ND	ST	87	JAR	REICHELSTEIN,S		1	18
0.50	PUXTY,AG	03	87	AOS	WILLMOTT,HC	COOPER,DJ	273	291
0.50	SHANE,PB	JL	83	TAR	SPICER,BH		521	538
0.33	COVALESKI,M	45	86	AOS	AIKEN,M		297	320
0.33	DANOS,P	OC	86	TAR	EICHENSEHER,JW		633	650
0.33	MIRVIS,PH	23	83	AOS	LAWLER III,EE		175	190
0.20	WESCOTT,SH	SP	84	JAR			412	423
0.17	BROWN,C	AU	83	JAR			413	431
0.00	BOWSHER,CA	WI	86	JAA			7	16
0.00	BURRELL,G	01	87	AOS			89	102
0.00	CHOUDHURY,N	06	88	AOS			549	557
0.00	DAVISON,AG	SP	84	JAR	STENING,BW	WAI,WT	313	317
0.00	GAMBLING,T	04	87	AOS			319	329
0.00	HARTE,GF	02	87	AOS	OWEN,DL		123	142
0.00	HIRST,MK	AU	83	JAR			596	605
0.00	HOPWOOD,AG	01	87	AOS			65	70
0.00	NOREEN,EW	04	88	AOS			359	369
0.00	OWEN,DL	03	85	AOS	LLOYD,AJ		329	352
0.00	SCAPENS,RW	AP	85	TAR	SALE,JT		231	247
0.00	TINKER,T	01	87	AOS	NEIMARK,M		71	88
0.00	ZEFF,SA	SP	86	JAA			131	154

4.77 TREATMENTS= LITIGATION

CITE IND- EX	FIRST AUTHOR	ISS- UE	YE- AR	JOUR -NAL	SECOND AUTHOR	THIRD AUTHOR	PAG BEG	PAG END
0.2	KELLOGG,RL	DE	84	JAE			185	204
0.0	HORVITZ,JS	WI	85	JAA	COLDWELL,S		86	99
0.0	LUDMAN,EA	SP	86	JAA			118	124
0.0	PALMROSE,ZV	SP	87	AUD			90	103
0.0	PALMROSE,ZV	JA	88	TAR			55	73
0.0	RUNDFELT,R	SP	86	JAA			125	130

TREATMENTS= LITIGATION

5. ABBREVIATIONS AND GLOSSARY

5.1 ABBREVIATIONS

5.1.1 Classifications

1. Mode of Reasoning
   - 1. 1. Quantitative: Descriptive Statistics (Des. Stat.)
   - 1. 2. Quantitative: Regression (Regress.)
   - 1. 3. Quantitative: ANOVA (ANOVA)
   - 1. 4. Quantitative: Factor Analysis, Multiple Discriminant Analysis, Probit (Oth. Quant.)
   - 1. 5. Quantitative: Markov (MARKOV)
   - 1. 6. Quantitative: Non-Parametric (Non-Par.)
   - 1. 7. Quantitative: Correlation (Corr.)
   - 1. 8. Quantitative: Analytical (Anal.)
   - 1. 9. Mixed Quantitative/Qualitative (Mixed)
   - 1. 10. Qualitative (Qual.)

2. Research Method
   - 2. 1. Analytical-Internal Logic (Int. Log.)
   - 2. 2. Analytical-Simulation (Sim.)
   - 2. 3. Analytical-Primary (Prim.)
   - 2. 4. Analytical-Secondary (Sec.)
   - 2. 5. Empirical-Case (Case)
   - 2. 6. Empirical-Field (Field)
   - 2. 7. Empirical-Laboratory (Lab)
   - 2. 8. Opinion-Survey (Surv.)

3. School of Thought
   - 3. 1. Behavioral-Human Information Processing (HIPS)
   - 3. 2. Behavioral-Other (Oth. Beh.)
   - 3. 3. Statistical Modelling-Efficient Markets Hypothesis (EMH)
   - 3. 4. Statistical Modelling-Time Series (Time Ser.)
   - 3. 5. Statistical Modelling-Information Economics/Agency (Inf. Eco./Ag.)
   - 3. 6. Statistical Modelling-Math Programming (Math Prog.)
   - 3. 7. Statistical Modelling-Other (Oth. Stat.)
   - 3. 8. Accounting Theory (Theory)
   - 3. 9. Accounting History (Hist.)
   - 3. 10. Institutional (Instit.)
   - 3. 11. Other (Oth.)

4. Treatment
   - 4. 1. Financial Accounting Methods (Fin. Meth.)
   - 4. 2. Cash (Cash)
   - 4. 3. Inventory (Inv.)
   - 4. 4. Other Current Assets (Oth. C/A)
   - 4. 5. Property, Plant and Equipment/Depreciation (P/P/A)
   - 4. 6. Other Non-Current Assets (Oth. Non-C/A)
   - 4. 7. Leases (Leases)
   - 4. 8. Long Term Debt (LTD)

4. 9. Taxes (Taxes)
4. 10. Other Liabilities (Oth. L)
4. 11. Valuation [Inflation] (Val.)
4. 12. Special Items (Spec. Items)
4. 13. Revenue Recognition (Rev. Rec.)
4. 14. Accounting Changes (Acc. Chng.)
4. 15. Business Combinations (Bus. Comb.)
4. 16. Interim Reporting (Int. Rep.)
4. 17. Amortization/Depletion (Amor./Depl.)
4. 18. Segment Reports (Seg. Rep.)
4. 19. Foreign Currency (For. Cur.)
4. 20. Cash Dividends (Cash Div.)
4. 21. Stock Dividends (Stk. Div.)
4. 22. Pension (Pens.)
4. 23. Other Financial Accounting (Oth. Fin. Acc.)
4. 24. Financial Statement Timing (Fin. St. Tim.)
4. 25. Research and Development (R & D)
4. 26. Oil and Gas (Oil & Gas)
4. 27. Auditing (Aud.)
4. 28. Opinion (Opin.)
4. 29. Sampling (Samp.)
4. 30. Liability (Liab.)
4. 31. Risk (Risk)
4. 32. Independence (Indep.)
4. 33. Analytical Review (Anal. Rev.)
4. 34. Internal Control (Int. Cont.)
4. 35. Timing (Tim.)
4. 36. Materiality (Mat.)
4. 37. EDP Audit (EDP Aud.)
4. 38. Organization (Org.)
4. 39. Internal Audit (Int. Aud.)
4. 40. Errors (Errors)
4. 41. Audit Trail (Trail)
4. 42. Judgement (Judg.)
4. 43. Planning (Plan.)
4. 44. Efficiency - Operational (Oper.)
4. 45. Audit Theory (Aud. Theor.)
4. 46. Confirmations (Confirms.)
4. 47. Managerial (Manag.)
4. 48. Transfer Pricing (Trans. Pric.)
4. 49. Cost-Volume-Profit-Analysis (C-V-P-A)
4. 50. Budgeting and Planning (Budg. & Plan.)
4. 51. Relevant Costs (Rel. Costs)
4. 52. Responsibility Accounting (Resp. Acc.)
4. 53. Cost Allocation (Cost Alloc.)
4. 54. Capital Budgeting (Cap. Budg.)
4. 55. Tax [Tax Planning] (Tax)
4. 56. Overhead Allocation (Over. Alloc.)
4. 57. Human Resource Accounting-Social Accounting (HRA)
4. 58. Variances (Var.)
4. 59. Executive Compensation (Exec.Comp.)
4. 60. Managerial (Oth. Manag.)
4. 61. Submissions to the FASB (FASB Subm.)
4. 62. Manager Decision Characteristics (Man. Dec. Char.)

4. 63. Information Structures [Disclosures] (Info. Struc.)
4. 64. Auditor Training (Aud. Train.)
4. 65. Insider Trading Rules (Ins. Trad.)
4. 66. Probability Elicitation (Prob. Elic.)
4. 67. International Differences (Int. Diff.)
4. 68. Form of Organization [Partnerships, etc.] (Org. Form)
4. 69. Auditor Behavior (Aud. Beh.)
4. 70. Methodology (Method.)
4. 71. Business Failure (Bus. Fail.)
4. 72. Education (Educ.)
4. 73. Professional Responsibilities (Prof. Resp.)
4. 74. Forecasts (Forec.)
4. 75. Decision Aids (Dec. Aids)
4. 76. Organization and Environment (Org. & Envir.)
4. 77. Litigation (Litig.)

5.1.2 *Journals*

AOS   Accounting, Organizations and Society
TAR   The Accounting Review
AUD   Auditing: A Journal of Theory and Practice
JAA   Journal of Accounting and Finance
JAE   Journal of Accounting and Economics
JAR   Journal of Accounting Research

5.1.3 *Issues*

AU   Fall/Autumn
AG   August
AP   April
DE   December
JA   January
JL   July
MR   March
OC   October
SP   Spring
ST   Supplement
SU   Summer
WI   Winter

5.2 GLOSSARY

5.2.1 *MODE OF REASONING-(Key method of analysis)*

Quantitative -Descriptive Statistics

Relies primarily on the characteristics of the populations through frequencies, means and variances.

Quantitative -Regression

Uses regression as the primary statistical method of analysis or inference.

Quantitative   -ANOVA

Uses analysis of variance (covariance) as the primary statistical method of analysis or inference.

Quantitative   - Multivariate Clustering Methods

Uses multivariate clustering methods as: factor analysis, MDA, discriminant analysis, logit, probit, principal factor, etc.

Quantitative   -Markov

Uses Markov chains as the primary statistical method of analysis or inference.

Quantitative   -Non-parametric

Uses non-parametric analysis as the primary statistical method. This may be descriptive, correlation, ANOVA, etc.

Quantitative   -Correlation

Uses correlations as the primary statistical method of analysis or inference.

Quantitative   -Analytical

Uses analytical methods for argument support.

Mixed   -Quantitative/Qualitative

A combination of modes of reasoning.

Qualitative

Relies primarily on qualitative and "a-priori" arguments to advance arguments.

5.2.2 RESEARCH METHOD

Analytical   -Internal logic

Involves all analytical papers plus individual opinion type of research such as the early "a-priori" papers.

Analytical   -Simulation

Computer-based simulation papers with random numbers, etc.

Archival   -Primary

Use of data compiled by others in magnetic or non-magnetic form such as COMPUSTAT, VALUE LINE or (for example) looking up 10K's on paper.

Archival   -Secondary

Primarily literature reviews. Looks at an issue primarily through the comparison of other studies.

Empirical   -Case

Abbreviations and Glossary

Examines a particular issue through the careful examination of a particular field situation which is only being observed but not interfered with.

Empirical   -Field

Examines a particular issue through a field situation where there is interference and a control group.

Empirical   -Laboratory

Uses the experimental methodology on a simulated environment with manipulation of variables. A questionnaire containing a hypothetical case is a laboratory study.

Opinion   -Survey

Questionnaires and/or interviews asking for opinions or facts about certain issues.

5.2.3 SCHOOL OF THOUGHT **Behavioral   -HIPS**

Human Information Processing Studies including judgment, inference, bayesian revision, lens, cognitive style, etc.

Behavioral   -Other

Includes behavioral issues as budget-related issues, decision-maker attitudes, etc.

Statistical Modelling -Efficient Market Hypothesis (EMH)

Security price and volume studies

Statistical Modelling -Time series, Econometrics

Time series studies, forecasting, valuation models, etc.

Statistical Modelling -Information economics/ agency theory

Typically analytical papers Modelling management processes.

Statistical Modelling -Mathematical programming

Mathematical programming techniques such as linear programming, dynamic programming, etc.

Statistical Modelling -Other

Studies using other types of statistical modelling or a mix of modelling approaches.

Accounting Theory

Typically the development of accounting thought through "a priori" reasoning or other type of support.

Accounting History

Studies dealing with the evolution of accounting thought.

Institutional

Abbreviations and Glossary

Studies of accounting institutions such as the FASB, APB, and other accounting-related and standard-setting institutions.

Other

Studies that do not easily fall into the above paradigms or belong to lesser-divulged paradigms.

Abbreviations and Glossary